FORM AND FORCES

FORM AND FORCES

DESIGNING EFFICIENT, EXPRESSIVE STRUCTURES

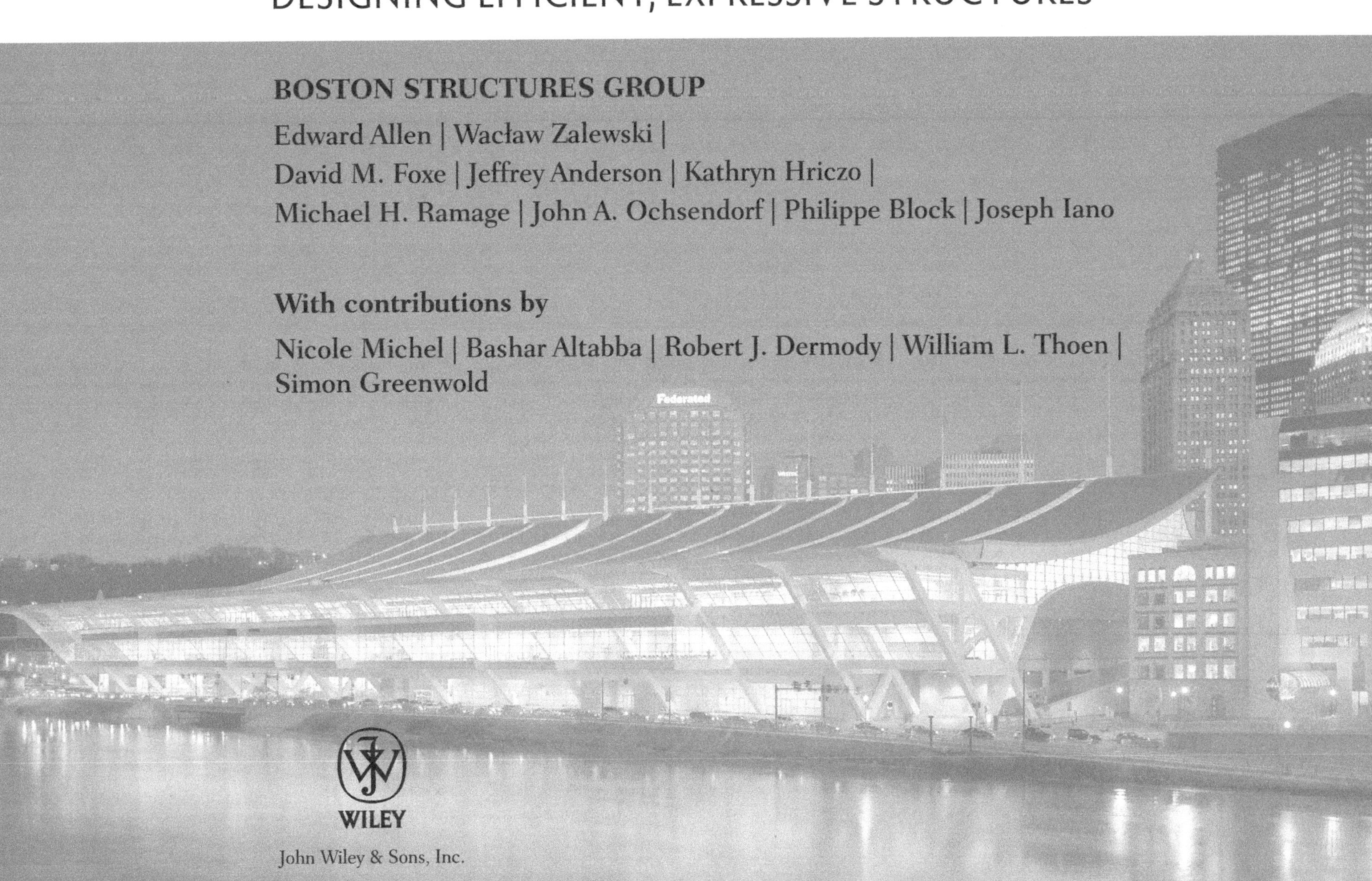

BOSTON STRUCTURES GROUP

Edward Allen | Wacław Zalewski |
David M. Foxe | Jeffrey Anderson | Kathryn Hriczo |
Michael H. Ramage | John A. Ochsendorf | Philippe Block | Joseph Iano

With contributions by

Nicole Michel | Bashar Altabba | Robert J. Dermody | William L. Thoen |
Simon Greenwold

WILEY

John Wiley & Sons, Inc.

Text and equations were edited in WordPerfect 12 and Word 2003. The typeface for drawings is Tekton, and the typeface for the text is Garamond.

Hand-drawn illustrations are primarily by Edward Allen, with additional sketches by David M. Foxe, Robert Dermody, Wacław Zalewski, and others, as noted. Computer-based drawings were created and edited by Jeffrey Anderson and Kathryn Hriczo in Autodesk AutoCAD, Rhinoceros, Formfinder, and Capri; images were further edited in Adobe Creative Suite. ANSYS output images are courtesy Bashar Altabba and the HNTB Corporation.

This book is printed on acid-free paper.

Published by John Wiley & Sons, Inc., Hoboken, New Jersey
Published simultaneously in Canada

For general information about our other products and services, please contact our Customer Care Department within the United States at (800) 762-2974, outside the United States at (317) 572-3993, or fax (317) 572-4002.

Wiley also publishes its books in a variety of electronic formats. Some content that appears in print may not be available in electronic books. For more information about Wiley products, visit our Web site at www.wiley.com.

Library of Congress Cataloging-in-Publication Data:

Allen, Edward, 1938–
Form and forces: designing efficient, expressive structures/ Edward Allen and Wacław Zalewski; with contributions by Iano . . . [et al.]
p. cm
Includes index.
ISBN 978-0-470-17465-4 (cloth)
1. Structural design. 2. Form (Aesthetics) 3. Structural dynamics. I. Zalewski, Wacław. II. Iano, Joseph. III. Title.
TA658. A44 2010
624.1'771—dc22

2009001793

Printed in the United States of America

SKY10059251_112923

Table of Contents

Project Team and Contributors

BOSTON STRUCTURES GROUP

The Boston Structures Group is an informal association of structures teachers, engineers, and architects who share the belief that structures is a design discipline and should be taught as such.

Core Project Team

Edward Allen, FAIA,
Primary Author

Ed is a Fellow of the American Institute of Architects and a recipient of the Topaz Medallion for Excellence in Architectural Education. He has taught at the University of Oregon, Yale University, University of California–San Diego, Montana State University, Liverpool University, University of Washington, and at the Massachusetts Institute of Technology. He is the designer of more than 50 constructed buildings. His books are read and used in universities and professional offices throughout the world.

Wacław Zalewski, PhD, Dipl.Ing.,
Coauthor, Philosophy and Concepts

Wacław is a structural engineer, constructor, and Professor Emeritus of Structural Design at MIT. He is a beloved mentor to legions of former students and associates. His design work ranges from lightweight concrete shells to deployable trusses, and has been constructed across Poland, Venezuela, Spain, and South Korea. He is the author with Edward Allen of *Shaping Structures: Statics* (John Wiley & Sons, Inc., 1998).

David M. Foxe, M.Arch, M.Phil, SB,
Editorial Director

David is an architectural designer, author, teacher, and musician educated at MIT; he was a Marshall Scholar to Clare College, Cambridge University (United Kingdom). He practices at EYP/Architecture and Engineering in Boston.

Jeffrey Anderson, M.Arch, B.Des,
Art Director and Chief Illustrator

Jeff is an architectural designer educated at the University of Florida and MIT. He practices at TriPyramid Structures in Westford, Massachusetts.

Kathryn Hriczo, B.Arch,
Illustrator

Kate is an architectural designer educated at the University of Massachusetts and the Boston Architectural College. She practices at Miller Dyer Spears Architects in Boston.

Contributing Authors

John A. Ochsendorf, PhD, M.Sc.,
Contributing Author

John is a structural engineer and Associate Professor of Building Technology at the MIT Department of Architecture. He studied at Cornell, Princeton, and the University of Cambridge (United Kingdom). He is a recipient of a 2008 MacArthur Grant for his research in structural engineering, and was a Fellow of the American Academy in Rome 2007–2008.

Michael H. Ramage, M.Arch, BSc,
Contributing Author and Illustrator

Michael is University Lecturer in the Department of Architecture at Cambridge University (United Kingdom). Educated in architecture at MIT, he specializes in the design and construction of structural masonry spans that have been built in the United States, England, and South Africa. He held a fellowship in the engineering firm of Conzett Bronzini Gartmann AG in Chur, Switzerland (2006).

Philippe Block, PhD, SMArchS,
Contributing Author and Illustrator

Philippe is a member of the structures faculty at the ETH (Swiss National Institute) in Zürich. He is an architectural engineer trained at the Vrije Universiteit in Brussels (Belgium). He recently completed a PhD in Building Technology at the MIT Department of Architecture in Cambridge, Massachusetts; his dissertation concerned the application of advanced graphical techniques to the design of masonry structures. He has been a researcher at the Institute for Lightweight Structures and Conceptual Design (ILEK) in Stuttgart (2008); and he has won the Hangai Prize from the International Association of Shell and Spatial Structures (2007).

Joseph Iano, RA,
Contributing Illustrator

Joseph is a practicing architect in Seattle, Washington, and a technical consultant to Olsen Sundberg Kundig Allen, Architects. He is coauthor of a number of books with Edward Allen, including *Shaping Structures, Statics,* from which many of his illustrations and DVD tutorial have been brought to this volume.

Contributors

Nicole Michel, RA, LEED AP, M.Arch,
Contributor

Nicole is a registered architect originally from Buenos Aires who studied at MIT and practiced architecture in New York City at Cannon Design and at Perkins + Will. Since 2006, she practices in Buenos Aires on projects both locally and abroad, and she is deeply involved with the creation of the Argentina Green Building Council.

Bashar Altabba, PE, M.Eng,
Contributor

Bashar Altabba is a bridge engineer with Parsons Corporation in New York City and a visiting faculty member of the Department of Civil and Environmental Engineering at MIT. He has appeared in several television documentaries on structures of historic importance.

Robert J. Dermody, RA, M.Arch, B.S.C.E.,
Contributor

Bob has degrees in both architecture and engineering, and is currently teaching structures as an Assistant Professor at the Roger Williams University School of Architecture, Art, and Historic Preservation, located in Bristol, Rhode Island. He has previously taught at the University of Illinois, first in Versailles and then in Champaign/Urbana.

William L. Thoen, PE, M.Eng,
Contributor

Bill is a structural engineer who was a principal for many years in LeMessurier Consultants, where he was involved in the design of many of their landmark projects.

Simon Greenwold, SM,
Contributor

Simon is a software developer who did graduate work at the MIT Media Lab. He has a special interest in interactive graphics, architecture, and engineering. His Active Statics program has won worldwide acclaim and has been translated into several foreign languages.

Acknowledgments

For their review of early versions of several chapters, we thank Prof. Richard Farley of the University of Pennsylvania, Prof. Martin Gehner of Yale University, and Prof. Kirk Martini of the University of Virginia. Our thanks also go to the many teachers and students who have tested tools and techniques as we have developed them, and who have often developed and sent to us innovations of their own. The influence of all these individuals is evident in many aspects of this work.

At John Wiley & Sons, Inc., Vice President and Publisher Amanda Miller has nurtured and encouraged this project since its inception. It could not have been brought to completion without the patience, understanding, skill, and astute guidance of Acquiring Editor Paul Drougas. Senior Production Editor Donna Conte overcame every obstacle, of which there were many, in managing the editing, composing, and printing of the book; she is unsurpassed at her difficult craft and remains a valued colleague after many projects together. We would also like to thank Janice Borzendowski for copyediting and Figaro for creating the graphic design.

Edward Allen and Wacław Zalewski are grateful for the extraordinary talents, tireless efforts, and buoyant enthusiasm of David M. Foxe, Jeffrey Anderson, and Kathryn Hriczo. Edward Allen thanks Donna Harris, who reintroduced him to graphic statics; Don Livingstone, whose student design project first revealed the potential of graphic statics to create efficient forms for structures; and Dr. William Abend, for his healing powers.

The members of the project team thank their colleagues, family, friends, and loved ones who have encouraged and assisted us during this long-running enterprise.

We dedicate this book to those students, teachers, and professionals who believe in the power of thoughtfully designed structures to support great loads, span vast distances, and nourish the human spirit.

Boston Structures Group
July 2009

Introduction

"Education is not the filling of a pail, but the lighting of a fire."
—William Butler Yeats (Poet, 1865–1939)

"There is some evidence that traditional engineering courses reduce the creativity of students . . ."
—Alan Holgate (Engineer/Author, b.1937)

Form and Forces is a project-based introduction to the design of structures for buildings and bridges. It is intended as the text for a first year of study of structures for students of engineering or architecture. Practicing architects and structural engineers will also find it useful.

Each chapter follows the entire design process for a whole structure: It begins with the formation of structural ideas. It continues with development of the ideas into workable solutions, preliminary design of details, and preliminary determination of member sizes. It concludes with planning of the construction process. The projects, which are generally large in scale, long in span, and elegant in form, are carefully chosen to bring out specific lessons that constitute a complete course in statics and strength of materials.

Students are assumed to have had no prior course in structures, yet this book engages them from the beginning in designing grand, imaginative structures. The fundamentals of statics and strength of materials emerge naturally in the context of the structural design process. Each principle or equation is introduced where it is first needed, so that the student understands its role. There is no need to teach "the basics" of statics and strength of materials in advance. In fact, to do so would risk diminishing the students' interest in structural design: Numerical methods detached from their context and role in design tend to be dry at best.

Graphical methods for designing and analyzing structures are a key ingredient of this approach. They contribute to intuitive understanding and visualization of behavior. They greatly facilitate all statical operations. In early stages of design, they have significant advantages over numerical methods in their simplicity, speed, transparency, and ability to generate efficient forms for cables, arches, trusses, and other structural devices. They are also the source of most of the mathematical expressions used in structural analysis, and give the same answers.

Numerical methods are introduced where needed in the design process, so that students do not merely learn them, but also understand their relevance and the contexts in which they are useful. This makes them easier to remember and utilize in later projects.

Master lessons, which are fictitious but realistic design dialogues between an architect and an engineer, are a unique feature of *Form and Forces*. These are scattered throughout the book. They were inspired by Galileo's dialogues concerning structures; the format was adopted here to help exemplify issues such as the nature of the design process and the interactions between engineer and architect. They also provide a refreshing change of pace from the chapters that are more conventional in their presentation.

Many teachers will feel a natural reluctance to abandon a way of teaching structures that they have perfected over a number of years. Many will doubt their ability to learn graphic statics well enough to teach it. I am one of the many who did not learn graphical techniques in school, but picked them up later through self-study. This learning process was not merely easy and pleasant: It was like discovering hidden treasure. Graphical techniques are almost magical in their uncanny power to generate good form while finding forces simultaneously. Suddenly they made clear structural concepts that had not been previously understood. They have made it possible for me to teach successful architectural design studios for the design of long-span structures, including in one instance a studio in traditional unreinforced masonry vaulted structures. They are also the basis for classroom courses in structures that are exciting and empowering for students and teacher alike.

The web site accompanying this book contains three supplemental features that facilitate the teacher's learning of the tools, as well as the students': Joseph Iano's step-by-step "Form and Forces Graphical Techniques" is a set of tested, perfected lessons that relate directly to the designs undertaken in the book. Simon Greenwold's "Active Statics" contains vivid, interactive learning tools that encourage experimentation and exploration. Simon Greenwold also developed the special-purpose graphic statics solver program, "Statics Pad," which makes it possible for teachers and students to do the graphical solutions in a neat, legible, precise manner, even if they are unskilled at drawing.

This book contains material from the earlier book by Wacław Zalewski and Edward Allen, *Shaping Structures: Statics* (John Wiley & Sons, Inc., 1998), to which it is a successor. Those who have used *Shaping Structures* will find the present volume to be substantially more comprehensive and more consistent in its approach.

All the great masters of structural design have reminded us repeatedly that structural design is not a science; it is a **craft** that relies on judgment rather than absolute certainty. This judgment must be based on a broad knowledge of structural principles, materials, details of construction, fabrication and erection processes, and analytical techniques both numerical and graphical. It is in this spirit that we offer *Form and Forces,* encouraging readers to develop this judgment by becoming active participants in the exciting process of designing efficient, expressive structures.

South Natick, Massachusetts
Edward Allen,
for the
Boston Structures Group

Visit www.wiley.com/go/formandforces

For the set of learning resources that accompany this book

Use the registration code on the card attached to this book's inside cover to access the resources.

If you receive an error message that the registration code is already in use, or already used and there is no card, please click on the "buy" button on the Login/Register page in order to purchase access.

CHAPTER 1

Designing a Series of Suspension Footbridges

- *Basic definitions of statics: loads, forces, tension, compression, stress*
- *Free-body diagrams; vectors and scalars; static equilibrium of concurrent forces*
- *The force polygon and funicular polygon for funicular structures; Bow's notation*
- *Detailing steel rod elements in tension, and anchoring to rock*
- *Lateral stability; stiffening a tensile structure*
- *Construction detailing and planning*

We have been commissioned to design a series of footbridges for a new scenic trail that will wind through a deep, narrow canyon in a national park in the southwestern United States. The walls of the canyon are often vertical and sometimes overhang, so that the trail must move from one side of the canyon to the other at a number of locations to follow a route that will avoid the steepest walls and minimize excavation of the rock. The lengths (*spans*) of the bridges will vary between 40 and 100 ft. The *decks* of all the bridges (the walking surfaces) will be 4 ft wide.

DESIGN CONCEPT

We have already developed, in cooperation with the Park Service, a basic design concept and a simple system of components for making these bridges (Figures 1.1, 1.2). Because of the remoteness of the bridge sites and the difficulty of working in the narrow canyon while standing on

Figure 1.1 This suspension span of 40 ft is the first bridge we will consider in this chapter.

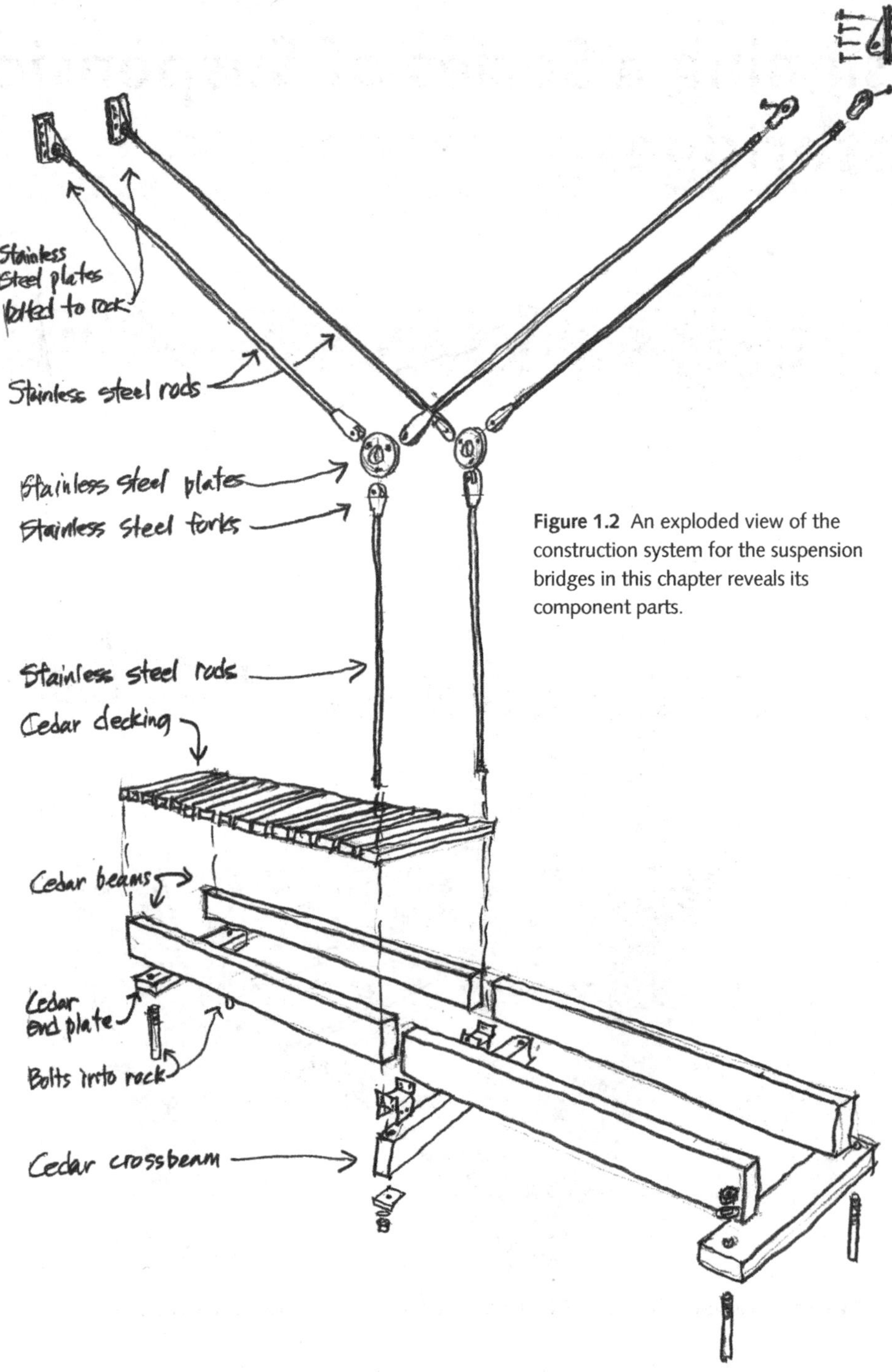

Figure 1.2 An exploded view of the construction system for the suspension bridges in this chapter reveals its component parts.

narrow rock ledges, as much of the work as possible will be done on components in a contractor's workshop. They will then be trucked to the site, where a construction crew will assemble them.

The beams of each bridge are made of wood and will be brought to the site in 20-ft lengths. Shorter lengths can be cut as needed to adjust bridge lengths to particular sites. We will support the ends of the beams that occur over the empty space of the canyon on short wood crossbeams that hang from steel rods. The rods will transmit their forces to steel plates anchored into the rock of the canyon walls. The beams, crossbeams, and rods will be used as a modular system to build *suspension bridges* of any necessary length for this trail (Figure 1.3). Suspension bridges tend to be lighter in weight than any other kind of bridge, which makes them particularly appropriate for the remote, difficult sites where they must be built in this park.

We have selected rods rather than cables because these bridges are small and the loads to be supported are correspondingly low. Cables, if we were to use them, would be very small in diameter, which would make them vulnerable to vandalism. Because the steel from which the rods are made is not as strong as that used in cables, the rods that we will use will be somewhat larger in diameter than cables of the same capacity. Rods are also easier and less costly to connect than cables. We will learn about cables and their connections in Chapter 2, in the context of a structure with much longer spans, where cables are appropriate and economical.

The beams and deck boards for the bridges are sawn from red cedar logs. We will use them in their rough, unplaned state, in keeping with the rustic nature of the canyon. Furthermore, rough beams are enough larger in dimension than planed ones that they have substantially larger structural capacities. Red cedar contains natural substances that are toxic to decay fungi, making the wood resistant to rot. However, cedar is a very soft, low-density wood that erodes gradually when exposed to severe winter weather, losing a few hundredths of an inch from each

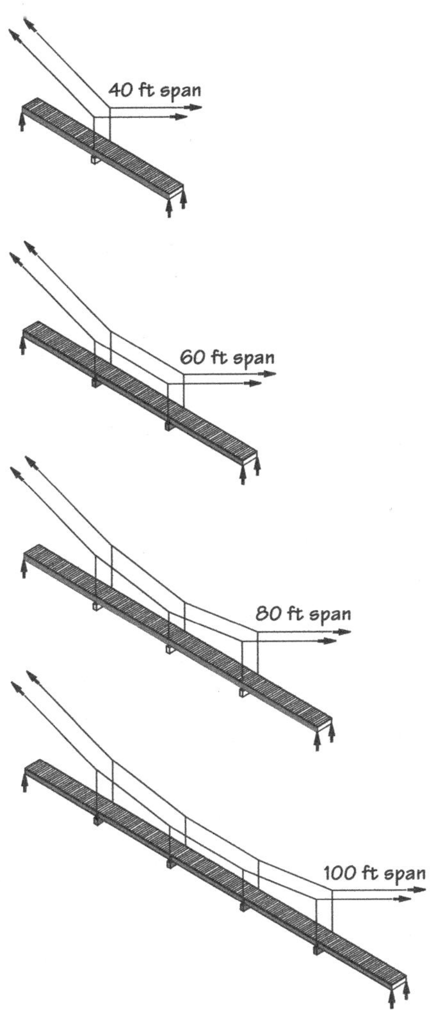

Figure 1.3 The construction system is modular, enabling it to be used for bridges of various spans.

surface every year. We have specified larger beams than are structurally necessary in order to provide for a few decades of erosion before they will have to be replaced.

With *stainless steel* rods and fittings, which do not rust, and cedar beams, which do not decay, the bridges will need no paint or chemical preservatives and should last for decades with little maintenance.

THE CHALLENGE

Our challenge is to design the bridges for this trail individually, taking into account for each of them the length of its span and the places above it where the rock is sufficiently solid to support the steel anchor plates. All the bridge sites have been surveyed to provide us with this information. As part of our design work, we need to determine the shapes that the rods will take in each situation, and the forces that they must transmit. This will enable us to specify the required lengths and diameters of the rods.

CONSTRUCTION DETAILS

We have given considerable thought to how the bridges will be put together. Figure 1.4 shows details of the major features. The rods are connected to the rock walls of the canyon with stainless steel anchor plates. Each anchor plate is secured with stainless steel bolts that are inserted into holes drilled in the rock and embedded there with *grout,* a fine-grained, high-strength mixture of sand, portland cement, and chemical admixtures that increase its strength and limit its shrinkage. The grout is poured into the holes in the form of a paste that hardens to unite the bolts securely with the rock. The rods, anchor plate assemblies, and other metallic components are all custom-fabricated for each bridge. We will determine the diameters of the rods in accordance with the amount of force each must carry when the bridge is fully loaded.

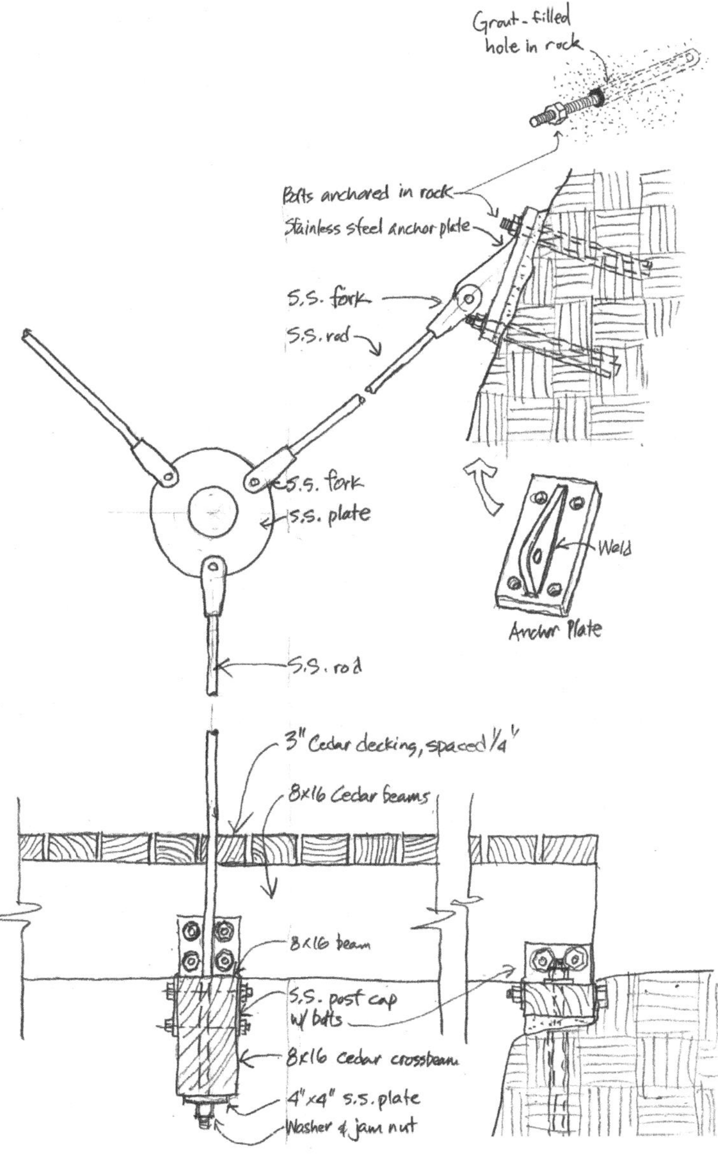

Figure 1.4 Typical details of the suspension bridge construction system.

The *fabricator* of the steel rods will prepare them to the exact lengths needed for each bridge. A *jaw* fitting (also called a *fork* or *clevis*) will be used wherever a rod joins a plate. Where a rod supports a wood beam, it will pass vertically through a hole drilled in the beam and a matching hole in a stainless steel plate 3/8 in. thick on the bottom of the beam (Figure 1.4). A circular *washer* and stainless steel *jam nut* transmit the force in the rod securely to the plate. The plate spreads this force over a large enough area of wood that the wood is not crushed. The jam nut is designed to develop a high degree of friction against the threaded rod so that it will not unscrew accidentally. The screw threads and nuts allow for easy assembly and fine-scale adjustment of the vertical positions of the beams, as well as easy disassembly when needed.

Where a vertical rod from a beam meets the sloping rods from the rock anchors, we will attach the rods with forks to a circular steel *plate* connector, as shown in Figure 1.4. A jaw fitting at the bottom of the plate will transfer force from the vertical rod to the plate, and the plate will pass this same force to the sloping rods and thence to the *anchor plates* and the rock walls of the canyon.

The details of the crossbeam, beams, and decking are straightforward. The deck boards will be nailed to the beams and spaced about 1/2 in. apart so that they will not retain water by capillary action after a rain or snow melt. The ends of each bridge deck will be held down by bolts anchored with grout into holes drilled in the rock.

A handrail must be provided on one side to give hikers something to hold as they cross the bridge. Because the trails that lead to the bridge are precarious and have steep drop-offs unprotected by railings, full railings and balusters are not required here as they are in buildings. Nevertheless, the handrail must be sturdy and reliable. We propose a steel pipe railing supported by tapered wood posts. The posts are fastened securely to the outside face of the deck beam with stainless steel angles and bolts (Figure 1.5).

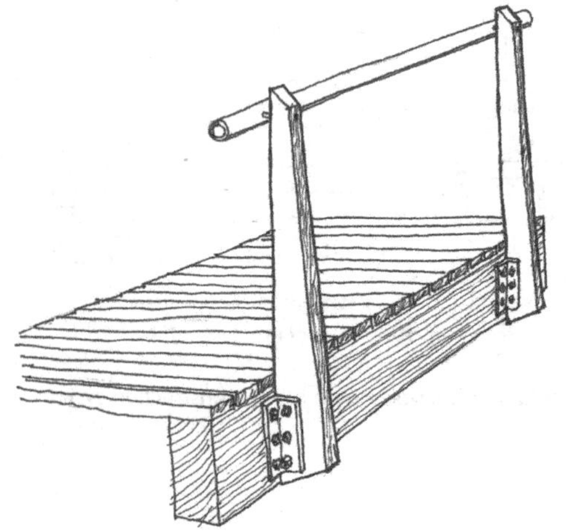

Figure 1.5 A sketch design for the handrail.

FINDING FORCES IN BRIDGE #1

Figure 1.6 is a section through the canyon at a place where a bridge of 40-ft span is required. The bridge is drawn accurately to scale. The center of the bridge, where the beams join one another, is supported by a system of rods on each side that connects with the crossbeam, as shown. We need to determine the maximum forces that are likely to occur in these rods in order to assign sizes.

To accomplish this, we will estimate the total maximum weight that each set of rods must support then determine how much force this weight creates in each of the rods. Once we know the forces, a table in the rod manufacturer's catalog will tell us how large a rod is needed for each member.

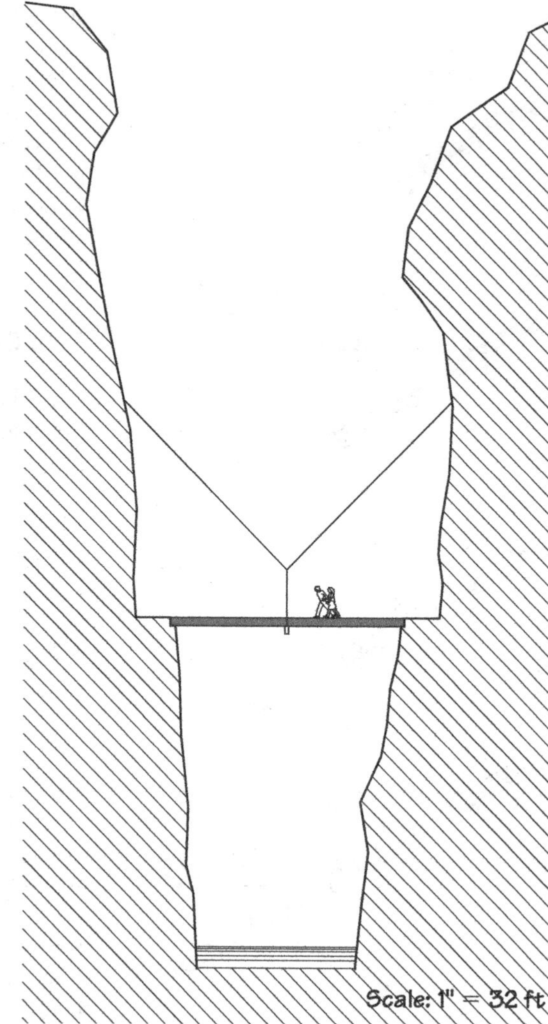

Figure 1.6 Bridge #1 utilizes two 20-ft lengths of deck beams to span 40 ft.

Estimating the Load Borne by the Rods

A *load* is a weight or other force that must be supported or resisted by a structure. How much load does each system of rods in this bridge have to carry? We estimate this load by adding together the *dead load,* which is the weight of the bridge itself, and the *live load,* which is the maximum probable total weight of hikers that might be on the bridge at one time. The dead load is unchanging and can be predicted fairly accurately. The live load varies from zero, when the bridge is unoccupied, to the weight of a large band of hikers all squeezing together on the bridge for a photograph, so it is much more difficult to predict with certainty than the dead load.

Dead Load

In this bridge, the dead load consists mainly of the weights of the cedar beams and crossbeam and the deck boards. Each beam is 16 in. deep and 8 in. wide. The density of red cedar is about 30 lb per cubic foot. Thus the weight of a one-foot length of beam is figured as follows:

$$\text{Weight of beam per foot of length} =$$
$$\frac{(8\text{ in.})(16\text{ in.})}{144\text{ in}^2/\text{ft}^2}(30\text{ lb}/\text{ft}^3) = 27\text{ lb}/\text{ft}$$

The weight of the beams for the entire bridge is calculated by multiplying this weight per foot by the total length of the beams in the bridge. There are two beams, each 40 ft long and made up of two 20-ft lengths:

$$\text{Total weight of beams} = 2(40\text{ ft})(27\text{ lb/ft}) = 2{,}160\text{ lb}$$

The crossbeam on which the beams rest is only 5 ft long. Because its span is so short, it, too, can be made of the same 8 in. by 16 in. cedar stock, even though it carries more weight than a longitudinal beam. Its weight is 5 ft times 27 lb per foot, which is 135 lb.

The decking will be made of 3-in.-thick cedar boards that are fastened to the beams with stainless steel nails. Three inches is one-quarter of a foot, so a square foot of decking will weigh about one-quarter of 30 lb per cubic foot, the density of the cedar, which comes to 7.5 lb. The total weight of the bridge decking is equal to this weight per square foot times the surface area of the bridge:

$$\text{Total weight of decking} =$$
$$(4\text{ ft})(40\text{ ft})(7.5\text{ lb/ft}^2) = 1{,}200\text{ lb}$$

We will assume for the moment that the weight of the steel rods and fasteners is negligible in comparison to these weights, an assumption that we will check later when we know the diameters and lengths of the rods. The dead load for the entire bridge is figured as follows:

Decking	1,200 lb
Beams	2,160 lb
Crossbeam	135 lb
Total dead load	3,495 lb, which we round to 3,500 lb

The average dead load per square foot of surface is 3,500 lb divided by the surface area of the bridge, 160 square ft, which is about 22 lb per square ft.

Live Load

As noted, the *live load,* the maximum possible total weight of hikers on the bridge, is more difficult to estimate with certainty than the dead load. An average hiker—taking into account males and females, adults and children—weighs about 160 lb and carries a pack weighing 30 lb, for a total of 190 lb. With backpack, a hiker occupies an area about 2 ft by 2 ft, which is 4 sq ft. Assuming that a group of hikers has crowded closely together on the bridge for a photograph, the maximum live load per square foot of bridge deck is 190 lb per hiker divided by 4 sq ft per hiker, which is 47.5 lb per sq ft. The total load per square foot, including both dead and live loads, is 22 lb dead load plus 47.5 lb live load, which is 69.5 lb, which we round up to 70. The total expected load on the bridge is thus estimated as:

$$\text{Total load on bridge} = (160\text{ ft}^2)(70\text{ lb/ft}^2) = 11{,}200\text{ lb}$$

How much of this load will be borne by each of the two vertical rods? In any symmetrically loaded beam, half of the load is conducted to each end. Referring to the top view of the bridge in Figure 1.7, each piece of decking will transmit half its load to one beam and half to the other, so that each line of beams carries half of the total load. Each beam is symmetrically loaded and made up of two pieces, each 20 ft long. For each of these pieces, half the load will be transmitted to the foundation at the end of the bridge and half to the crossbeam and the vertical rod. This means that each rod supports a *tributary area* that is 20 ft long (half the

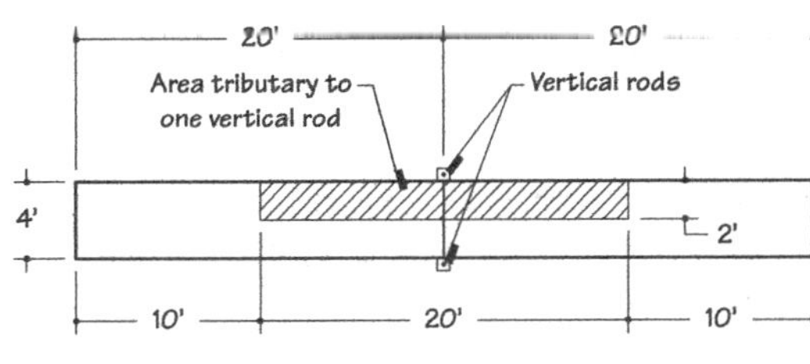

Figure 1.7 The tributary area for one vertical rod of Bridge #1 is shaded in this top view.

length of the bridge) and 2 ft wide (half the width), a total of 40 sq ft. The load per vertical rod is 40 sq ft times 70 lb per sq ft, or 2,800 lb.

FUNDAMENTAL CONCEPTS

Having estimated the force borne by each of the vertical rods, we need to develop a set of tools that we can use to determine the forces in all the rods, both vertical and sloping, that support the bridge. These tools are built on some basic concepts:

- *Force*: A force is a push or pull. Force tends to cause motion. Because we do not want our buildings and bridges to move, we design them in such a way that every force is balanced against an equal and opposite force that prevents motion. However, a force, even when it is balanced against another force, will cause *stresses* and *deformations* within the object, phenomena that we will begin to explore in Chapter 13.
- *Characteristics of a force*: A force has three primary characteristics (Figure 1.8):
  1. Its *magnitude,* in units of pounds or kips (A kip is a "kilopound," or 1,000 lb)
  2. The *direction* in which it acts
  3. The location of its *line of action,* a line along the centerline of the force that extends indefinitely in both directions

  Every force is exerted at a *point of application* somewhere on its line of action.

Magnitude of force

Line of action of force

60 KN

Direction of force

Point of application of force

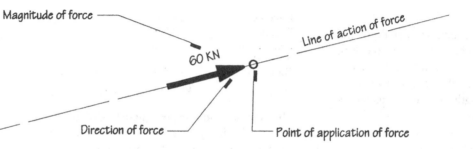

Figure 1.8 The characteristics of a force vector. On this diagram, the magnitude of the force is given by a number alongside the vector.

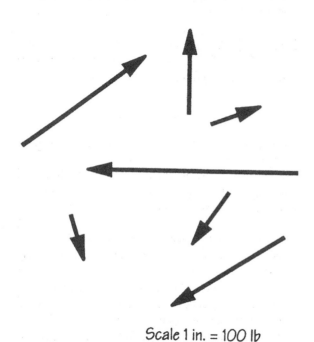

Scale 1 in. = 100 lb

Figure 1.9 Force vectors. The magnitudes of the forces on this diagram are represented by the lengths of the arrows.

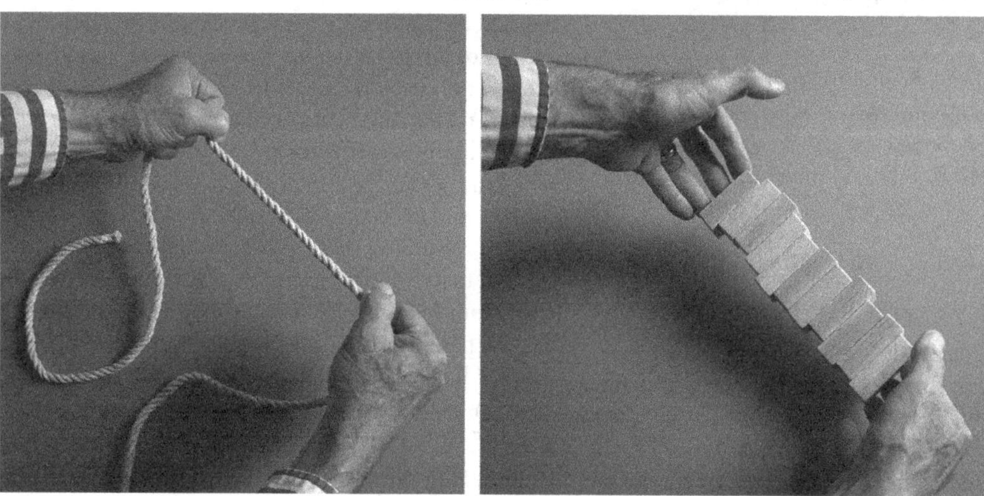

Figure 1.10 Tension is pulling; compression is pushing. The rope at the left can resist only tension. The stack of small wooden blocks to the right cannot resist tension but can resist compression, even though the blocks are not connected to one another except by friction.

- *Vectors*: A force is a vector quantity, which means that it has both magnitude and direction. (A quantity that has only magnitude and not direction is a *scalar* quantity. A sum of money is an example of a scalar quantity. So is a volume of water or a person's age.)

  We represent force vectors with arrows (Figure 1.9). The direction of an arrow indicates the direction of the force that it represents. The length of the arrow, including its head, is often used to indicate the magnitude of the force. Alternatively, magnitude may be indicated by a number alongside the arrow that gives the quantity and units of the force.
- *Tension and compression*: There are only two fundamental types of forces: pulls and pushes. Pulling is called tension, and pushing is compression (Figure 1.10). For purposes of analysis, every structural action, no matter how complex, can be reduced to pushes and pulls. Figure 1.11 shows how tension and compression are indicated symbolically with vectors.

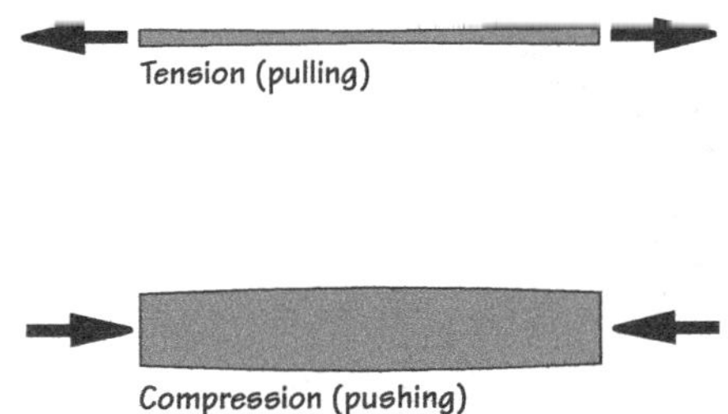

Figure 1.11 Tension and compression represented as bodies acted on by vectors.

> *"The remarkable, inherent simplicity of nature allows the structure to perform its task through two elementary actions only: pulling and pushing."*
>
> —MARIO SALVADORI

- *Transmissibility*: The effect of a force on a body as a whole is independent of where the force is applied along its line of action (Figure 1.12). This is called the *principle of transmissibility.*
- *Concurrent forces*: Forces whose lines of action pass through a common point are said to be concurrent (Figure 1.13). Forces that do not pass through a common point are *nonconcurrent.*
- *Free-body diagram*: The examination of any system of forces is easier and less subject to errors if it is done with reference to a simple, unambiguous sketch called a free-body diagram (FBD). An FBD is a simple picture of a portion of a structure that we want to study (the *free body*), completely detached as if it were floating in space. Vector arrows are added to indicate the external forces that **act upon** the free body. The free body may be a whole structure or a piece that is hypothetically unfastened, cut, or torn from the structure, whichever suits our purposes.

When using graphical methods of solution, as we will do throughout this book, we draw the free body and vector arrows with drafting instruments or CAD software to depict the directions and magnitudes of the forces as accurately as possible. Often, however, it is sufficient to draw the FBD freehand as reference for thought or discussion, or as the basis for a numerical calculation. Figure 1.14b is a free-body diagram of a *node* where three rods join one another in the bridge that we are about to examine. It is isolated from the rest of the structure by imaginary cutting of the three steel rods. Notice that it includes only forces that act **on** the free body, not forces exerted **by** the free body.

- *Static equilibrium*: A body at rest is said to be in a state of static equilibrium. "Static" means that the body is at rest; "equilibrium" means that the forces that act on the body balance one another exactly, leaving no net force remaining to set it in motion. We want buildings and bridges to remain at rest, so we design them to be in static equilibrium.

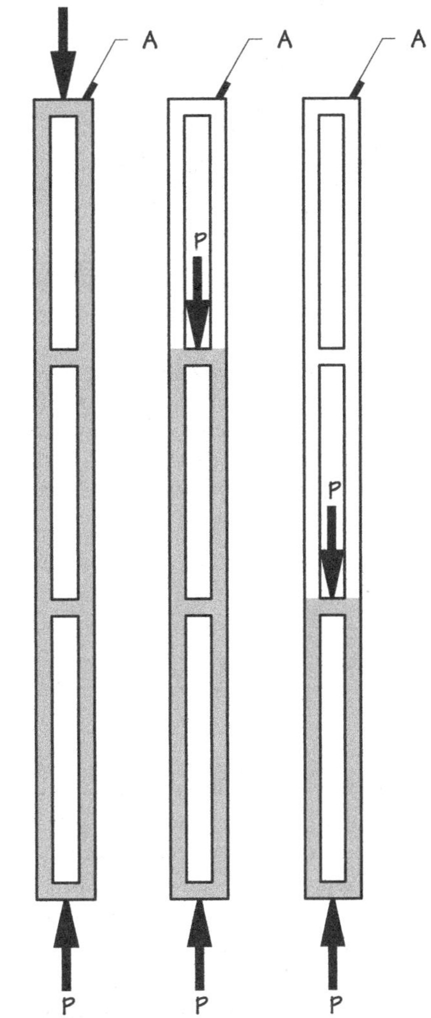

Figure 1.12 The principle of transmissibility: With respect to the external effects of a force on a body, the force *P* can be considered to act anywhere on its line of action. The internal effect of force *P* on body A, however, is dependent on the point of application of *P*. In the case of a force applied within the body, this effect is confined to the shaded area.

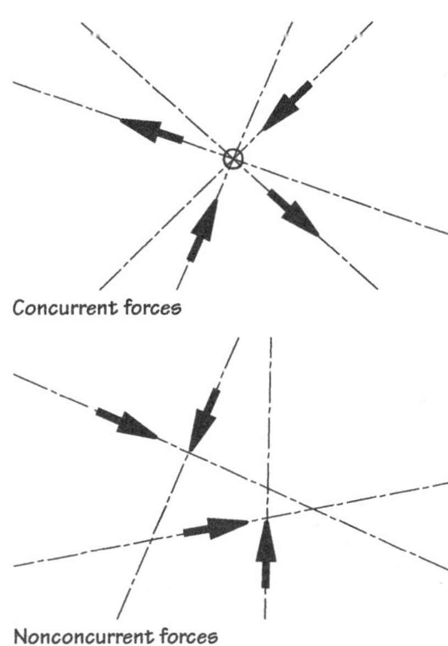

Figure 1.13 Concurrent and nonconcurrent forces. There are pairs of concurrent forces in the lower diagram, but there is no concurrence of more than two forces.

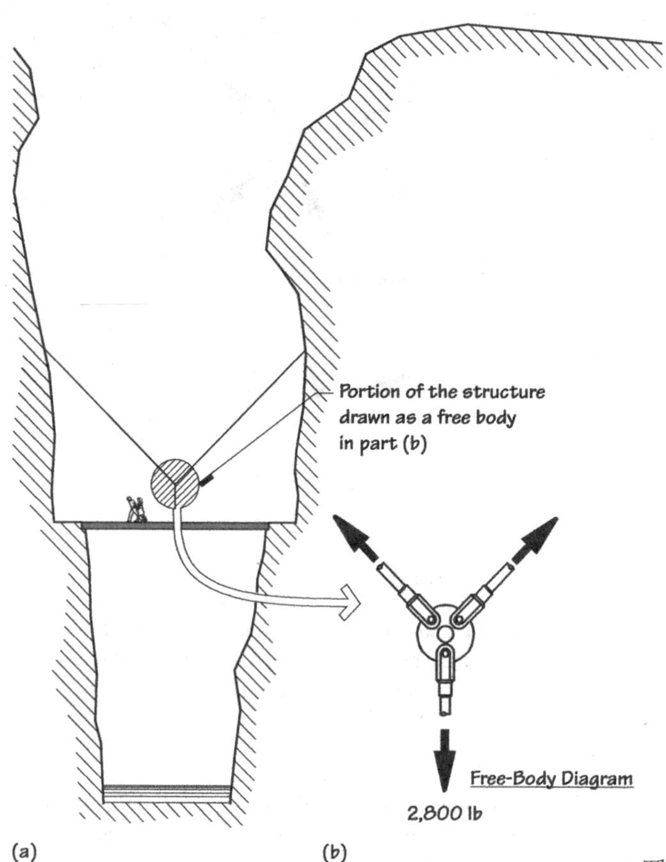

Figure 1.14 In part (a), a free-body diagram has been constructed of the rod intersection or node in Bridge #1. The intersection is cut imaginarily from the larger structure (a) and represented as a free body, isolated from the rest of the structure. Vectors are added to indicate all the external forces that act upon the free body. We know the magnitude and direction of the downward force on the free body (2,800 lb) but we know only the directions of the other two forces.

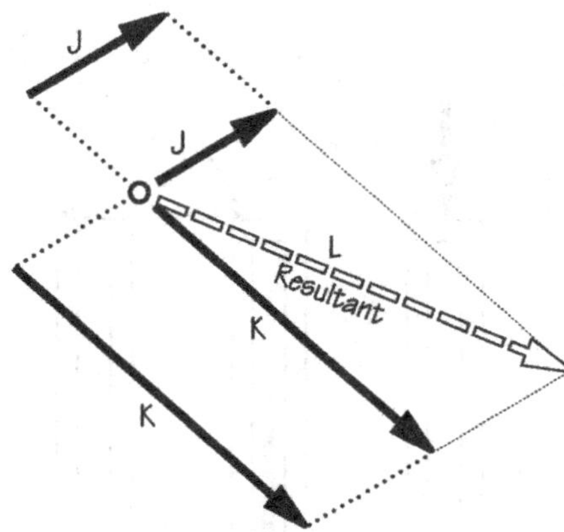

Figure 1.15 The parallelogram law. The resultant of vectors J and K is found by bringing them together as the adjacent sides of a parallelogram. The diagonal of the parallelogram, L, is their resultant, a single force that has the same effect as J and K acting together.

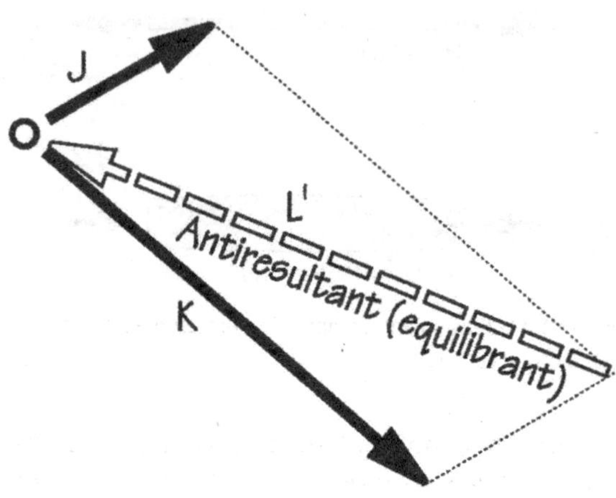

Figure 1.16 If the direction of the resultant in Figure 1.15 is reversed, it becomes an antiresultant or equilibrant, and the three forces are in static equilibrium.

- *The parallelogram law*: Often we need to add force vectors to find a single vector that will have the same effect as two other vectors acting together. This single vector is called the *resultant*. The parallelogram law states that the resultant of any two forces is a vector that is the diagonal of a parallelogram formed on their vectors (Figure 1.15). The parallelogram law is an axiom, which is another way of saying that it is always true but that it can't be proven mathematically.

  If the direction of the resultant of any system of forces is reversed, it becomes the *equilibrant*, also sometimes called the *antiresultant*, a single force that will balance the other forces in the system in a state of static equilibrium (Figure 1.16).

- *Tip-to-tail addition of vectors*: It follows from the parallelogram law that we can find the resultant of any two forces by connecting their vectors tip to tail and drawing a single vector, the resultant, from the tail of the first vector to the tip of the second one (Figure 1.17).

  If we wish to find the magnitude and direction of the resultant of more than two forces, we can connect their vectors tip to tail in a chain. The resultant is a vector whose tail lies at the tail of the first vector and whose tip lies at the tip of the last vector in the chain. The order in which the vectors are connected doesn't matter—the resultant will always be the same in both direction and magnitude (Figure 1.18). Any number of vectors may be added by this

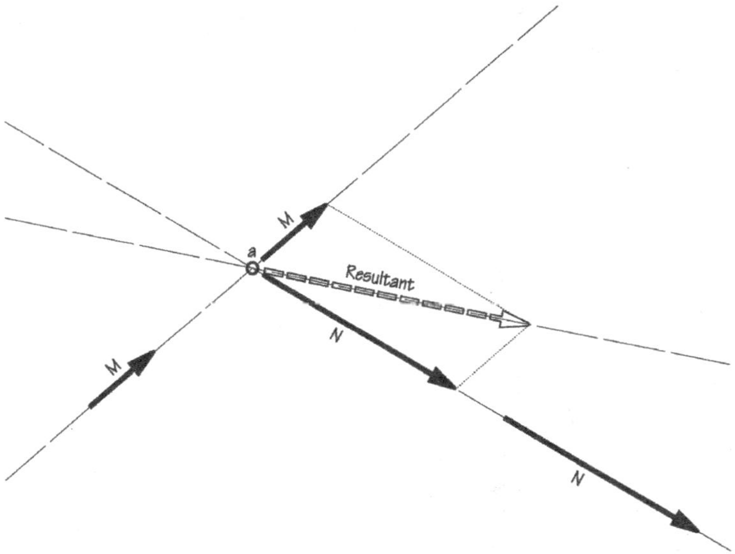

Figure 1.17 The resultant of two forces may also be found by connecting their vectors tip to tail and drawing a vector from the tail of the first force vector to the tip of the second. The line of action of the resultant passes through the intersection of the lines of action of the two original forces.

method. The diagram of tip-to-tail vectors and their resultant is called a *force polygon*. The resultant may be reversed in direction to serve as an equilibrant.

- *Equilibrium of concurrent forces*: If the chain of tip-to-tail vectors for a group of concurrent forces closes exactly upon itself, with the last tip at the same point as the first tail, the resultant has a value of zero (Figure 1.19). This means that the group of vectors exerts no net force and that, therefore, the group of forces is in static equilibrium. (Nonconcurrent forces may be in static equilibrium as well as concurrent forces, but their formation of a closed chain of vectors is insufficient by itself to prove equilibrium. We will take up the determination of equilibrium of groups of nonconcurrent forces in Chapter 5).

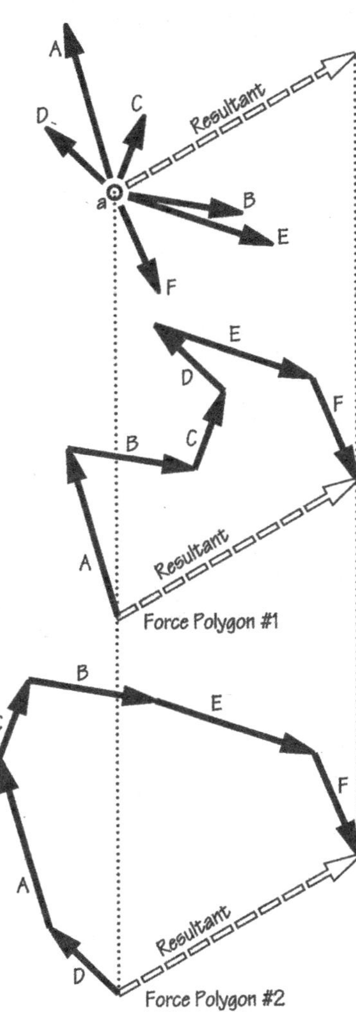

Figure 1.18 Tip-to-tail addition can be applied to any number of forces. The forces in this example have been connected in two different orders to show that the resultant is the same regardless of the order of connection. The line of action of the resultant passes through the point of concurrence of the vectors in their original locations.

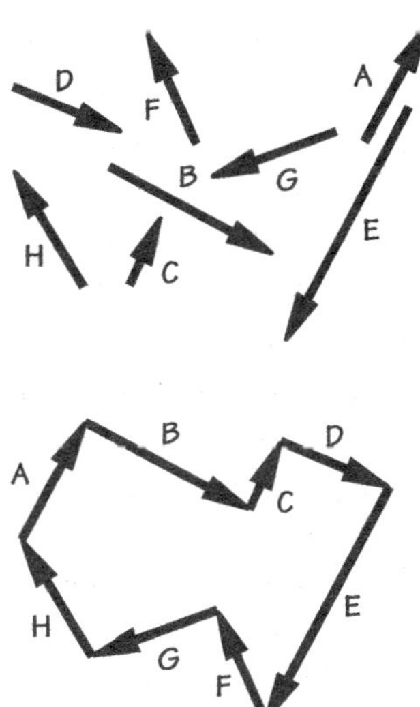

Figure 1.19 If the tip-to-tail polygon of forces closes upon itself, the resultant is zero. If all the forces are concurrent, the closure of the force polygon means that they are in static equilibrium.

GRAPHICAL SOLUTIONS

We will use a *graphical solution* to find the forces in the rods that support the bridge we are designing. In a graphical solution, we work with accurately drawn diagrams of vectors whose lengths we can measure to determine the magnitudes of the forces that they represent. The alternative to a graphical solution is a *numerical solution,* which employs numbers rather than scaled diagrams.

Each solution method has its advantages and disadvantages. A numerical solution is usually more compact that a graphical one and can be carried out to as many decimal places as the designer wishes. It is easily programmed for solution by a calculator or computer.

Drawing Parallel Lines*

Graphical analysis techniques require the drawing of many lines that are accurately parallel to other lines. What are some efficient, precise ways of drawing parallel lines on a drawing?

The traditional method is to use two drafting triangles, placing the hypotenuse of one tightly against the hypotenuse of the other (Fig. A). A leg of the upper triangle is aligned with the original line. Then the lower triangle is held firmly against the paper while the upper triangle is slid along its hypotenuse to a new location that allows a parallel line to be constructed through the desired point. It often takes a bit of experimentation to find the best way of arranging the triangles for a particular pair of lines. If the operation must occur over a long distance, it sometimes works better to substitute a long straightedge for the lower triangle (Fig. B).

An adjustable triangle (Fig. C), used in conjunction with a T-square or parallel rule, offers a means of drawing parallel lines that many designers find more convenient and secure than two triangles.

A drafting machine is an ideal instrument for graphical constructions, because it facilitates rapid, very accurate construction of parallel lines at any location on a sheet (Fig. D).

A rolling ruler offers a simple, easy way of ruling parallel lines, even if the paper is not fastened to a drawing board (Fig. E).

Computer-assisted drafting (CAD) offers graphical constructions that give results identical to those of numerical computations that are carried to the same number of decimal places. Every CAD program has a simple routine for drawing

Fig. A

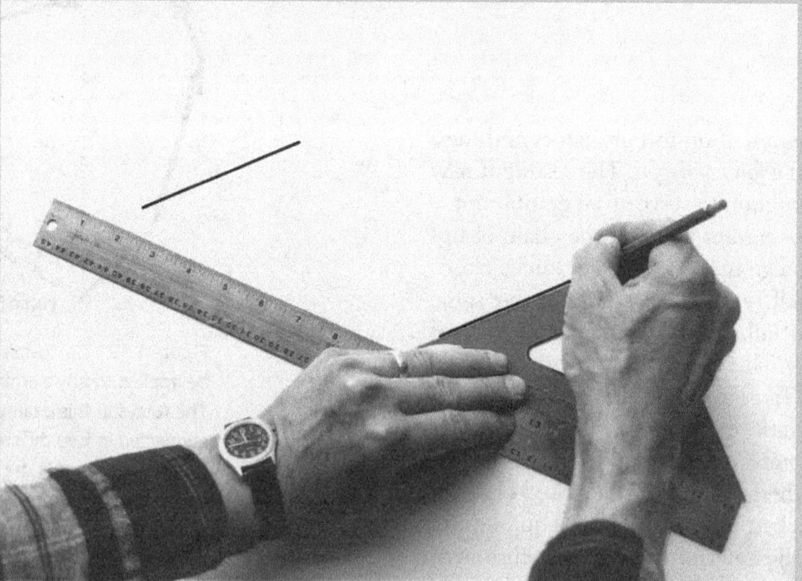

Fig. B

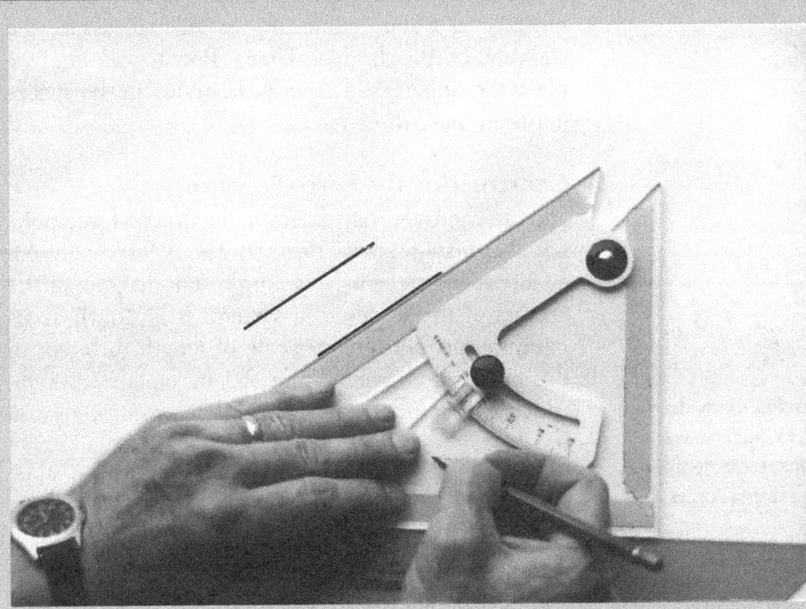

Fig. C

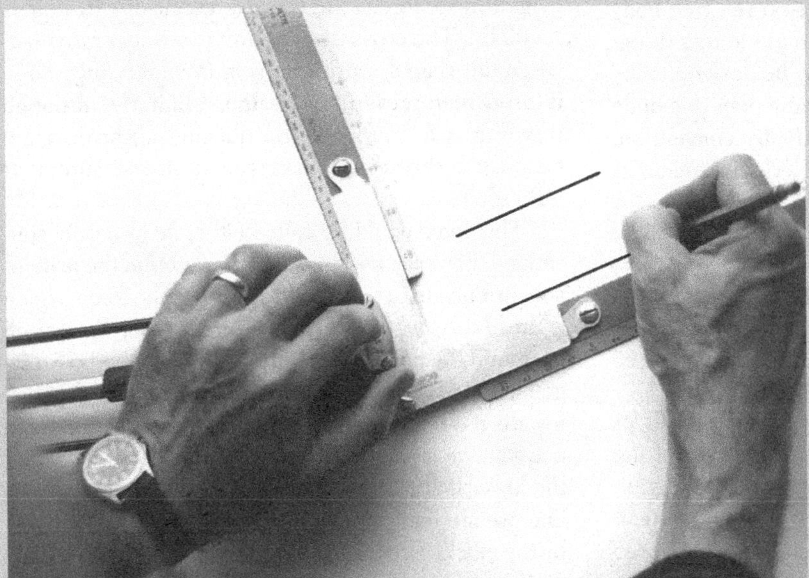

Fig. D

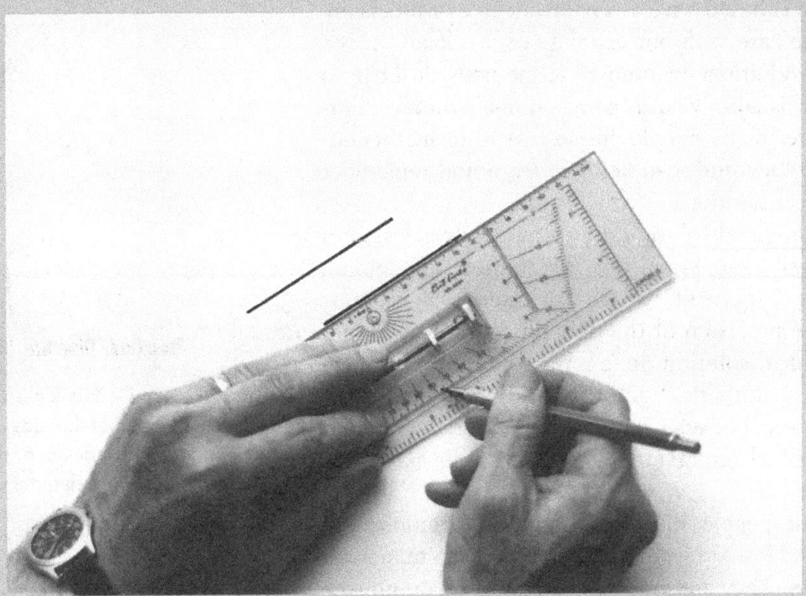

Fig. E

parallel lines, as well as another routine for scaling the lengths of line segments with extreme precision. As we noted earlier, however, extreme numerical accuracy is not usually required, and CAD construction of a force polygon is generally appropriate only when the entire process is being carried out by computer. If the structure is being designed on paper, it is easiest and more natural to analyze it on the same sheet of paper.

*Photos by Gregory D. Thomson from *Shaping Structures: Statics* by Wacław Zalewski and Edward Allen (New York: John Wiley & Sons, Inc.), 1998. Reprinted with permission.

However, the apparent accuracy of numerical methods often masks the fact that the data on which a solution is based have a very low degree of precision, as is the case with our estimate of live loads on the bridge. Additionally, numerical methods do little to help us visualize what is going on in a structure. Furthermore, many people are so fearful of mathematics that they find it difficult to learn and remember numerical solutions.

A graphical solution drawn manually is less precise than a numerical one. Its imprecision seldom exceeds 1 percent, which is generally far better than the precision of the data on which it is based. A graphical solution done on a computer is as precise as a numerical solution and gives an identical answer, because numerical methods are based on graphical understandings such as the parallelogram law.

Most people find that graphical solutions are faster and less subject to human error than numerical solutions. They are much more helpful than numerical methods in visualizing how a structure works and how its form may be improved. Graphical solutions may be used to find efficient forms for structures. For these reasons, we will use graphical solutions for most of the projects in this book.

Bow's Notation

We are about to begin an analysis of the forces that act on the node where a vertical rod intersects two sloping rods in the bridge structure. To keep track of the forces that act on the node, we will add to our free-body diagram a labeling system called *Bow's notation,* after Robert Bow, whose invention of it was published in 1873. Starting at any arbitrarily chosen location, we place uppercase letters **in the spaces between the lines of action** of the forces (Figure 1.20). Each force is named by the letters that lie on either side of it. The force to the upper right lies between spaces *A* and *B* on the free-body diagram. It may be called either force *ab* or force *ba.* The downward force is

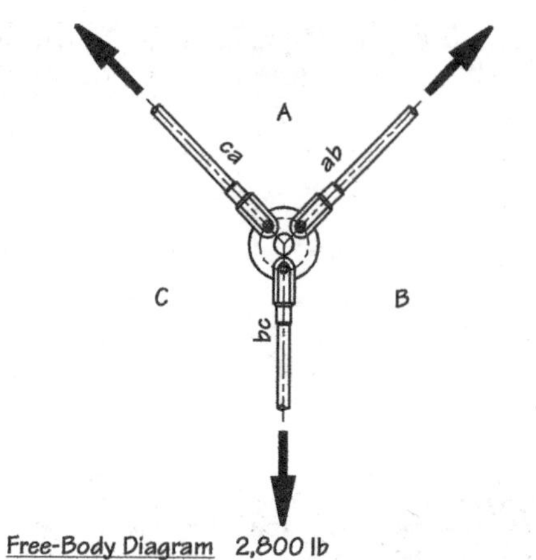

Figure 1.20 Bow's notation is applied to the free-body diagram of the intersection of the rods in Bridge #1. In practice, we would not draw the details of the intersection, because they have no effect on the determination of the exterior forces.

either *bc* or *cb,* and the force to the upper left either *ca* or *ac.* Notice that uppercase letters are used to label the spaces between the forces on the free-body diagram, while corresponding lowercase letters designate the forces. Points or nodes may be designated by the letters that surround them in sequence: this node may be called *ABC* or *BCA* or *CAB.* By convention, we name nodes using consistent clockwise readings of letters.

FINDING THE FORCES IN THE BRIDGE STRUCTURE

Constructing the Free-Body Diagram

We begin our graphical solution at the upper left of a sheet of paper by drawing accurately with drafting tools or a computer-aided drafting (CAD) program the free-body diagram of the node where the vertical rod joins the two inclined rods (Figure 1.21). Three forces act on this node: the 2,800-lb vertical load that we have estimated, and two inclined forces of known direction but unknown magnitude. These three forces must be in static equilibrium in order to assure the stability of the bridge. Using Bow's notation, we place the uppercase letters *A, B,* and *C* in the spaces between these three forces.

Constructing the Force Polygon

Next to the free-body diagram, we draw a force polygon for this system of three forces. A force polygon, as discussed previously, is a tip-to-tail diagram of the vectors of the forces in a system. It is drawn accurately to any convenient scale of length to force. In this case, we choose a scale of 1 in. equals 1,000 lb, which will produce a diagram that fits comfortably on the page.

We start construction of the force polygon by drawing a vertical line called the *load line* to represent the vertical direction of the external load, which is force *bc* (Figure 1.21). To this line we add two horizontal cross ticks exactly 2.8 in. apart. This distance between the ticks represents 2,800 lb, the magnitude of force *bc* at the given scale of 1 in. equals 1,000 lb. (The cross ticks permit more accurate measurement than a representation in which only a line is used to represent the value. Similarly, although this line is a vector, we do not add an arrowhead, because the head often makes accurate measurement difficult.)

This force could be called either *bc* or *cb.* By convention, however, we read clockwise around the point of concurrence to determine the name of the force, which is thus *bc.* As we read clockwise from space *B* to space *C* around the point of concurrence in the free-body diagram, force *bc* acts downward, from the top of the page toward the bottom. Turning our attention to the force polygon, we label the upper tick on the load line *b* and the lower tick *c,* so that as we read from *b* to *c* on this line, we are reading downward, the direction indicated by the clockwise reading of the letters on the free-body diagram.

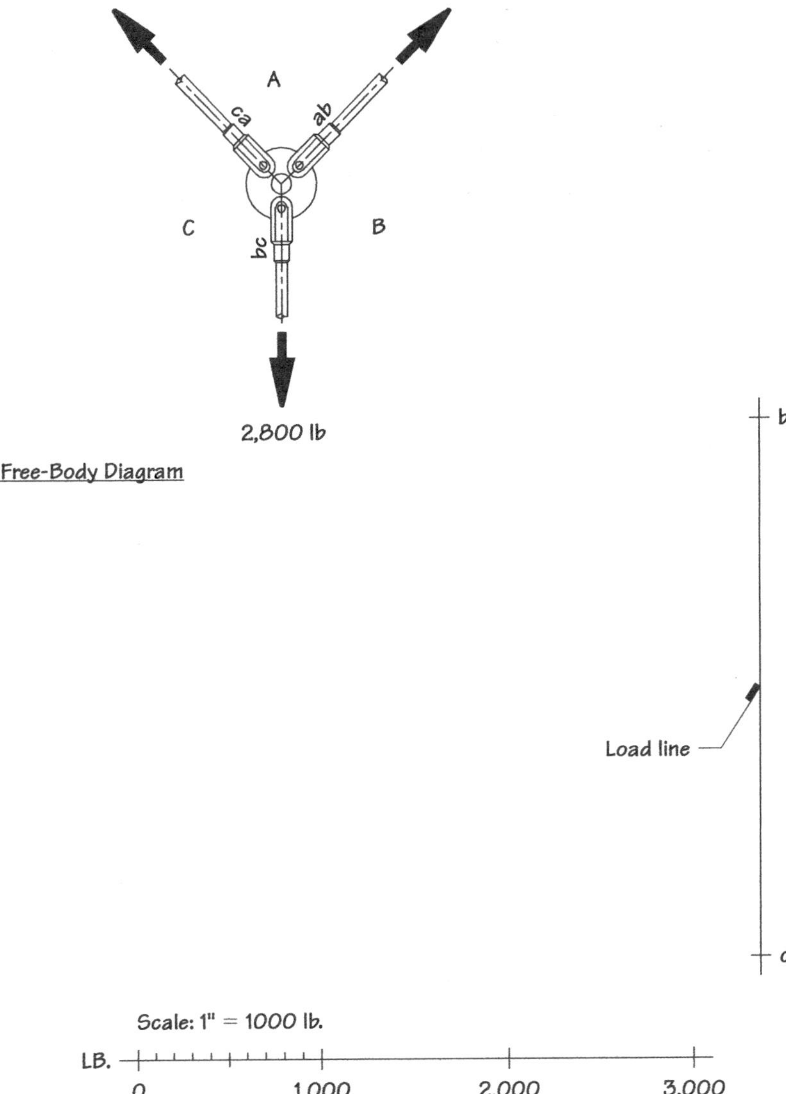

Figure 1.21 The first step in finding the magnitudes of the unknown rod forces is to represent the known force, *bc*, as a line segment whose length is equal to the magnitude of the force and whose direction is parallel to the force. Line *bc* is a force vector, but is generally drawn without an arrowhead. Any convenient scale of length to force may be used in this construction. There is no relationship between the scale of the free-body diagram and the scale of the force polygon.

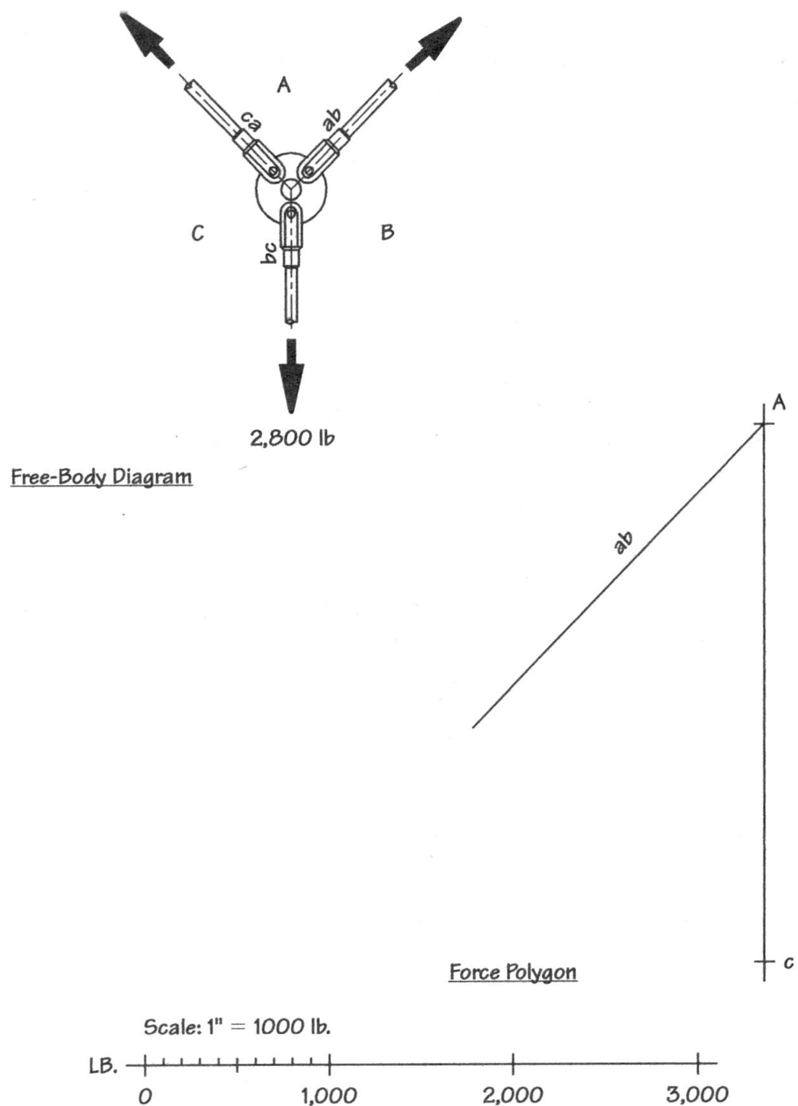

Figure 1.22 The second step in finding the magnitudes of the unknown rod forces is to draw a line on the force polygon to represent the direction of one of the forces. Bow's notation helps us to know where to connect this line to the line that represents the known force: The unknown force is *ab* and there is no letter *a* on the force polygon at the moment; therefore the new line must connect at *b*.

You will have noticed that uppercase letters that designate **spaces** on the free-body diagram become lowercase letters that designate **points** on the force polygon. This will seem strange at first, but as you will see, this system of notation is a powerful tool for making sure that each vector ends up in its proper place.

So far, we have represented on the force polygon only one force of the three that act on the node where the three rods come together. Now we will add the other two. Reading clockwise, the force that pulls to the upper right lies between letters *A* and *B* on the free-body diagram. Thus its name is *ab*. Of these two letters, only *b* appears on the load line at this stage. The *b* in the name of this force tells us that its vector will pass through point *b* on the load line. It must also pass through a point *a* that is not on the load line, but we don't yet know where *a* is. We draw line *ab* of indefinite length through *b* on the force polygon, accurately parallel to vector *AB* on the free-body diagram (Figure 1.22). We do not yet know the length of line *ab*, but we do know that *a*, which will mark its other end, will lie somewhere on it.

Lastly, we draw the vector for the remaining force, *ca* (Figure 1.23). Of these two letters, only *c* appears on the force polygon at this stage. The *c* in its name tells us that its vector must pass through point *c* on the force polygon and be parallel to the corresponding vector *CA* on the free-body diagram. The *a* in its name tells us that point *a* will lie somewhere on it. Line *ca* intersects line *ab*. Because the names of both lines contain the letter *a*, we name this intersection *a*.

The force polygon is now complete. We can measure its sides to determine that the force in member *AB* has a magnitude of 1,980 lb and the force in member *CA* is also 1,980 lb. If this solution is drawn by hand, the accuracy of these figures is plus or minus 1 percent at the small scale of our drawing, which is far better than the degree of certainty of our live load estimates. If greater accuracy is required, the force

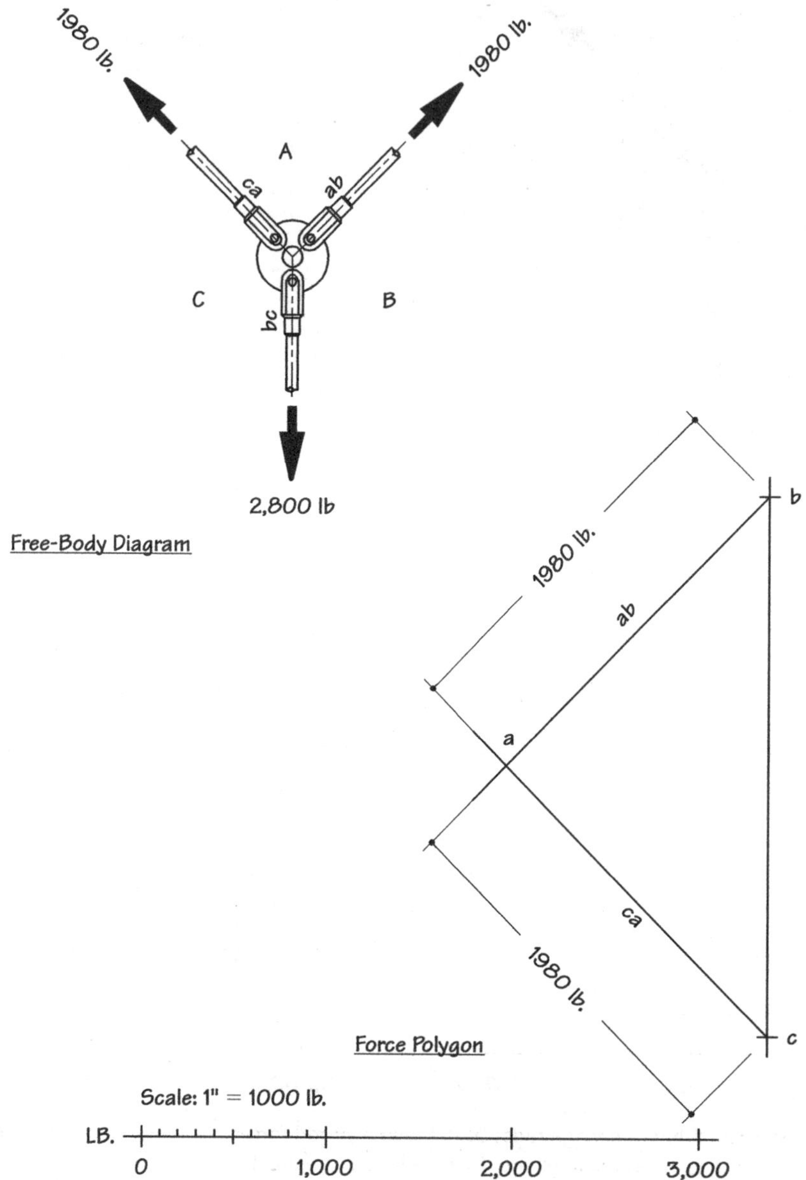

Figure 1.23 The force polygon is completed by repeating the previous step for the remaining unknown force. *a* is the intersection of the two lines that represent the unknown forces. Lines *ab* and *ca* are vectors that may be measured at the given scale to determine the magnitudes of the unknown forces.

polygon can be constructed at a larger scale, or in a CAD program.

Determining Directions of Forces

Slender rods are effective only in resisting tension, because if they are subjected to compression, they *buckle* sideways and have no resistance. How can we be certain that forces *ab* and *ca* are tensile? Bow's notation helps us find the answer. On the free-body diagram, the upper portion of Figure 1.23, we read the sequence of letters around the point of concurrence in clockwise order: The force to the upper left lies between spaces C and A, in that order, as we make that reading. We now direct our attention to the force polygon below: On the force polygon, as we move from point *c* to point *a,* we move from lower right to upper left. Returning to the FBD above, a force that moves along line *ca* from lower right to upper left is pulling away from the point of concurrence, which indicates that *ca* is a tensile force. We can follow the same procedure to find that *ab* is also in tension. We now know the directions and magnitudes of the three forces at this node. This completes our analysis of the forces in the three rods.

Sizing the Rods

Now that we know the forces in the rods under the estimated maximum load on the bridge, we are able to determine how large the rods must be in order to sustain these forces safely.

We work from a table of allowable strengths that is based on data furnished by a manufacturer of stainless steel rods (Figure 1.24). The *yield strength* of each diameter of rod, which is the tensile force at which the rod would begin to stretch irreversibly, has been divided by a *factor of safety* of 1.67 to arrive at the values in this table. If there were a full load on the bridge, each rod would be loaded to 1/1.67, or 0.6 of its yield strength. The remaining 0.4 is reserve strength, a portion of which may come into play under unexpected events such as floods and tornadoes.

Tensile Strengths of Medium-Strength Stainless Steel Rods

Rod Diameter		Yield Strength (F_y)		Allowable Strength ($0.6F_y$)	
Inches	mm	Pounds	kN	Pounds	kN
0.125	3.2	1,350	6.0	810	3.6
0.188	4.8	3,000	13.3	1,800	8.0
0.225	5.7	4,400	19.6	2,640	11.8
0.250	6.4	5,400	24.0	3,240	14.4
0.330	8.4	9,400	41.8	5,640	25.1
0.375	9.5	12,100	53.8	7,260	32.3
0.437	11.1	16,500	73.3	9,900	44.0
0.500	12.7	21,600	96.0	12,560	57.6
0.625	15.9	33,000	147	19,800	88.2

Figure 1.24 This table gives dimensions and allowable loads for stainless steel rods of the type that we will use in our bridge.

The bottom end of the vertical rod is *threaded,* which means that it has been given a helical ridge that will engage a nut or a fitting with a similar ridge. Threads are usually produced by removing material from a rod, but this reduces the diameter and strength of the rod. The manufacturer of these particular rods places the end of the rod in a machine that squeezes and re-forms it to produce an end region with a larger diameter. When threads are formed in this *upset end* detail, the minimum diameter at the roots of the threads exceeds slightly the diameter of the rod, and maintains the full strength of the rod even where it is threaded (Figure 1.25).

For our bridge we need rods to sustain safely tensile forces of 2,800 lb and 1,980 lb in the vertical and inclined rods, respectively. Starting from the top of the table in Figure 1.24, a 0.125-in. (1/8-in.) diameter rod can safely sustain a force of 810 lb. This is not enough for either of the rods in this bridge. A 0.188-in. diameter rod can carry 1,800 lb; again, not enough. A 0.225-in. rod can carry 2,640 lb, which is larger than the 1,980 lb carried by the sloping rods, so it is suitable for these members, but is not strong enough for the vertical members. The next larger rod is 0.250 in. (1/4 in.) in diameter and can carry 3,240 lb, which is larger than the forces in the vertical rods of our bridge. For ruggedness, better appearance, and simplicity of fabrication and maintenance, we decide to use quarter-inch rods throughout the structure. The use of quarter-inch fittings and rods for all the members of the bridge will increase the cost slightly, but it eliminates a potential source of construction error and reduces the number of parts that must be brought to the site.

We need to review our earlier assumption that the weight of the rods themselves is negligible in comparison to the overall dead and live loads on the bridge. The catalog data for the rods tell us that quarter-inch rods weigh 0.167 lb per foot of length. The two vertical rods total about 22 ft in length, taking into account their 8-ft exposed length and the additional length needed to pass through the crossbeam.

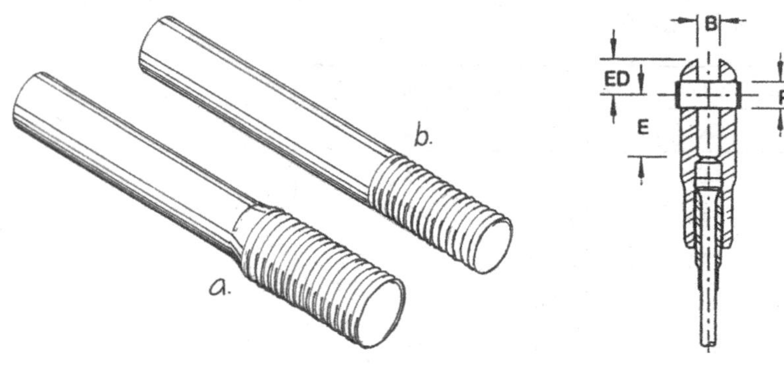

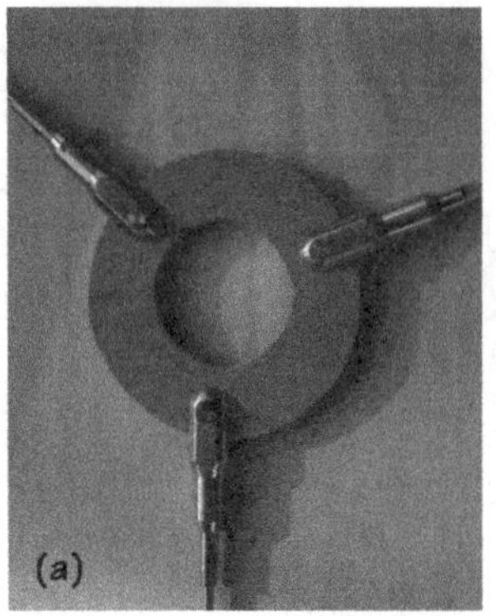

Rod Diameter Inch (mm)	Pin Diameter (P) Inch (mm)	Jaw Gap (B) Inch (mm)	Throat Depth (E) Inch (mm)	Edge Distance (ED) Inch (mm)	Take-up Inch (mm)
0.188 (4.8)	0.31 (8.0)	0.28 (7.1)	0.58 (14.7)	0.44 (11.2)	0.75 (19.1)
0.225 (5.7)	0.38 (9.5)	0.28 (7.1)	0.69 (17.5)	0.50 (12.7)	1.00 (25.4)
0.250 (6.4)	0.50 (12.7)	0.40 (10.2)	0.92 (23.4)	0.63 (15.9)	1.00 (25.4)
0.330 (8.4)	0.56 (14.3)	0.40 (10.2)	1.04 (26.4)	0.65 (16.5)	1.00 (25.4)
0.375 (9.5)	0.63 (15.9)	0.53 (13.5)	1.16 (29.5)	0.75 (19.1)	1.25 (31.8)
0.437 (11.1)	0.75 (19.1)	0.53 (13.5)	1.39 (35.3)	0.88 (22.4)	1.25 (31.8)
0.500 (12.7)	0.88 (22.2)	0.65 (16.5)	1.62 (41.1)	1.10 (27.9)	1.25 (31.8)
0.625 (15.9)	1.13 (28.6)	0.78 (19.8)	2.08 (52.8)	1.50 (38.1)	1.75 (44.5)

Figure 1.25 Dimensions of the jaw fitting for 1/2-in. rods. At the upper left, upset end (a) and plain threaded end rods.

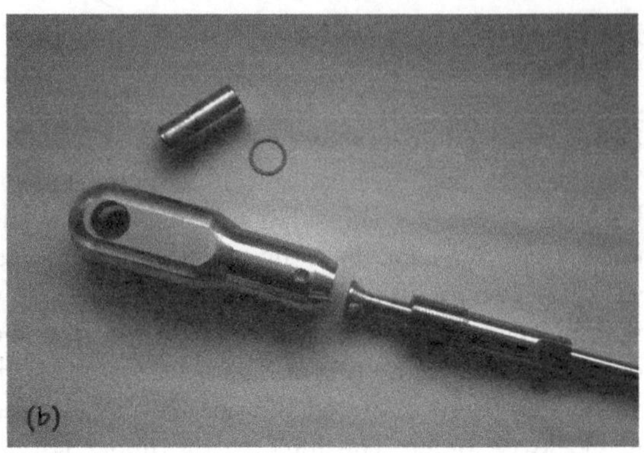

Figure 1.26 (a) A mockup of the main rod connection for the disk. For the sake of speed and ease of fabrication, the circular plate is modeled with medium-density fiberboard rather than stainless steel. (b) How the rod connection works: The stainless steel rod is cut to length. The end of the rod is cold-headed into a flared shape that seats snugly into a matching cavity in the end of the threaded bushing (right). The bushing, which rotates freely around the rod, is inserted into the fork fitting (left) and rotated clockwise to engage the threads. The pin (top) is inserted into one side of the fork, through the connecting plate, and out the other side. It is held in position by a small, flat stainless steel ring that snaps into a matching groove near the small end of the pin. Using a wrench on the flat end of the bushing, the assembly is tightened as needed to adjust the length of the rod and provide tension if necessary. A recessed screw in the side of the fork fitting is tightened to maintain the bushing in the desired position. This ingenious assembly avoids the need for a turnbuckle by building adjustability into the end fittings.

Photo: Edward Allen, The stainless steel components are manufactured by TriPyramid Structures, Westford, MA.

Multiplying 22 ft by 0.167 lb/ft, we find that the vertical rods weigh less than 4 lb. The four inclined rods are each about 34 ft long, for a total length of 136 ft. Their total weight is about 23 lb. The total weight of all the rods is 23 plus 4, or 27 lb. This is less than 1 percent of the weight of the beams and decking. We have chosen to use quarter-inch rods, which have an allowable tensile strength of 3,240 lb, to resist total forces that are unlikely to exceed 2,800 lb. This oversizing of the rods gives them an excess capacity of 440 lb, which is 16 times the weight of the rods themselves. Our design is sufficiently strong—and much more.

Selecting Fittings

The rod manufacturer furnishes detailed information on a wide variety of fittings for stainless steel rod structures. We select fittings that are attached to the tension rods by cold-heading the end of the rod. (*Cold-heading* is a room-temperature process of squeezing the end of the rod into a flared shape.) Adjustment is provided by a threaded bushing (nose) that is captured by the head on the rod. This bushing is free to rotate about the rod, threading into or out of the fitting to provide length adjustment. Threads are completely concealed when the fitting is properly adjusted (see Figure 1.26b).

Detailing the Rods

Figure 1.25 shows dimensions for a quarter-inch jaw fitting that we will use to attach the quarter-inch rods to the stainless steel plates. The opening of the jaws is 0.40 in. This suggests that we use 0.375 in. (3/8 in.)

plates for the connections, which will leave a *clearance* of 0.025 in., which will make it easy for workers to install the plates and fittings. These fittings are designed to be stronger than the quarter-inch rod with which they are used. In Figure 1.26a, we have mocked up the typical rod components at full scale.

BRIDGE #2

Bridge #2 is identical to #1 in every particular except that areas of weak, fractured rock in the canyon walls require that the cable anchorages be placed lower with respect to the deck of the bridge. Whereas the rods in Bridge #1 are inclined at about 45° to the horizontal, those in Bridge #2 are inclined at only 30°. What is the effect of the lower angle?

We find the answer to this question with the diagram in Figure 1.27. The force polygon for Bridge #1 is drawn with gray lines and that for Bridge #2 with solid black lines. The forces in the inclined rods are 2,800 lb in #2, as compared with 1,980 lb in #1.

We consult Figure 1.24 to find that the required rod size for the sloping members is still only 1/4 in. This is also the size we need for the vertical members.

BRIDGE #3

In Bridge #3, the span remains the same, except that the anchorages must be located higher on the cliffs, which increases the steepness of the inclined rods (Figure 1.28). The result is that while the inclined rods are substantially longer, the forces in the rods are only 1,530 lb, compared to 1,980 lb in #1, and 2,800 lb in #2.

From these first three bridges we can conclude that, in general, the steeper the inclination of the rods, the lower their forces will be. As the rods grow steeper, the overall structure of the bridge grows deeper. In all structures—beams, trusses, hanging cables, and arches—other factors being equal, a deeper structure (that is, one with a greater ratio of depth to span) will have lower internal forces.

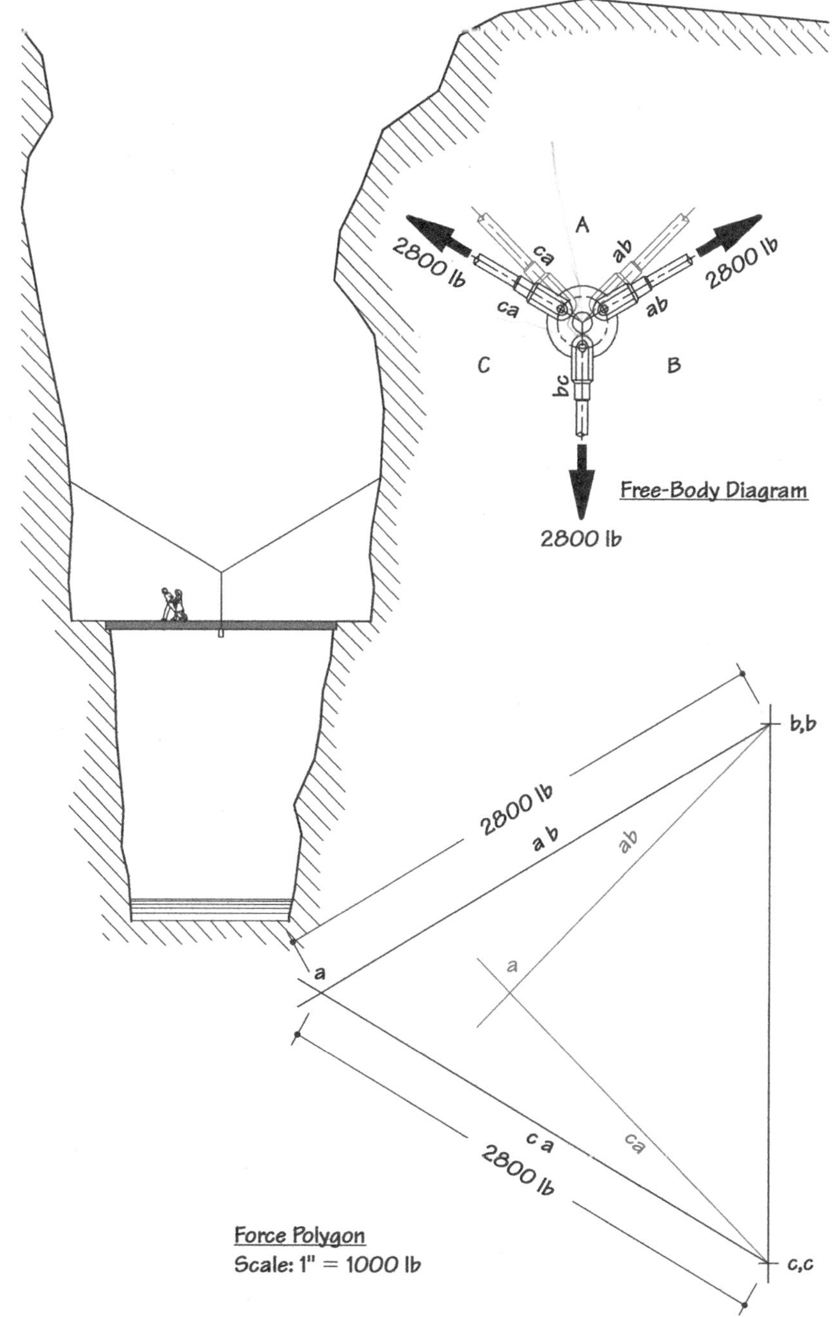

Figure 1.27 In Bridge #2, the slopes of the inclined rods are decreased, which causes the forces in the rods to rise. The lighter lines are the vectors for the original slopes; the solid lines represent the new slopes.

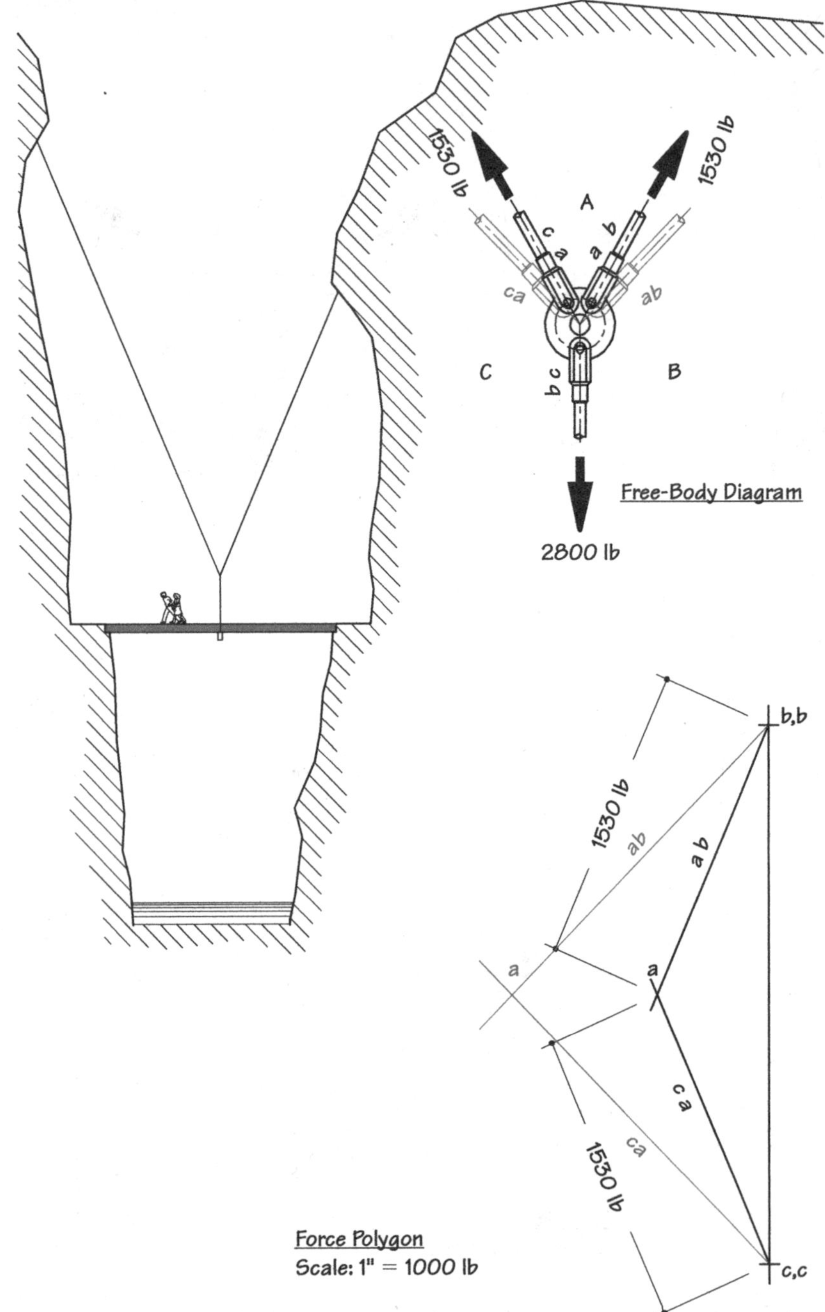

Figure 1.28 If the rods are sloped more steeply, as they are in Bridge #3, the forces in them decrease.

BRIDGE #4

Two areas of fractured rock on the site of Bridge #4 require us to relocate one of the anchorages. We test two alternative designs (Figures 1.29, 1.30). One has the anchorage higher than the top of the vertical rod and one has it lower. Both designs increase the force in the rod whose angle is unchanged from that of Bridge #1. Either design will work, but the higher of the two anchorage locations produces lower rod forces.

BRIDGE #5

Bridge #5 must span 60 ft instead of the 40 ft of the previous four bridges. We will do this by using three beams end-to-end, each supported at interior points by crossbeams and vertical rods (Figure 1.31). The tributary area of each vertical rod remains the same as before, but there are now four vertical rods, so the total load that must be supported by the inclined rods is doubled. We isolate as a free body the two nodes of the rod system and the horizontal rod between them. In Figure 1.31, we construct a force polygon for the node *abc*. In Figure 1.32, we construct a force polygon for the node *acd*. In doing this, we recognize that line *ac* occurs in both force polygons. Rather than draw this line twice, we simply attach the second force polygon to the first along line *ac*. This works out well: The two loads, *bc* and *cd*, form a single load line with point *c* common to both. We find that the accuracy of our construction of the force polygon is checked automatically—when we draw the last vector, *da*, on the force polygon, it must intersect both point *d* and point *a* with reasonable precision. If it does not, we must start the diagram over again. The forces in the two inclined rods measure as 3,960 lb, and the force in the horizontal segment is 2,800 lb. Reference to Figure 1.24 tells us that we must use rods with a diameter of 0.330 in. for the inclined tension members in this bridge.

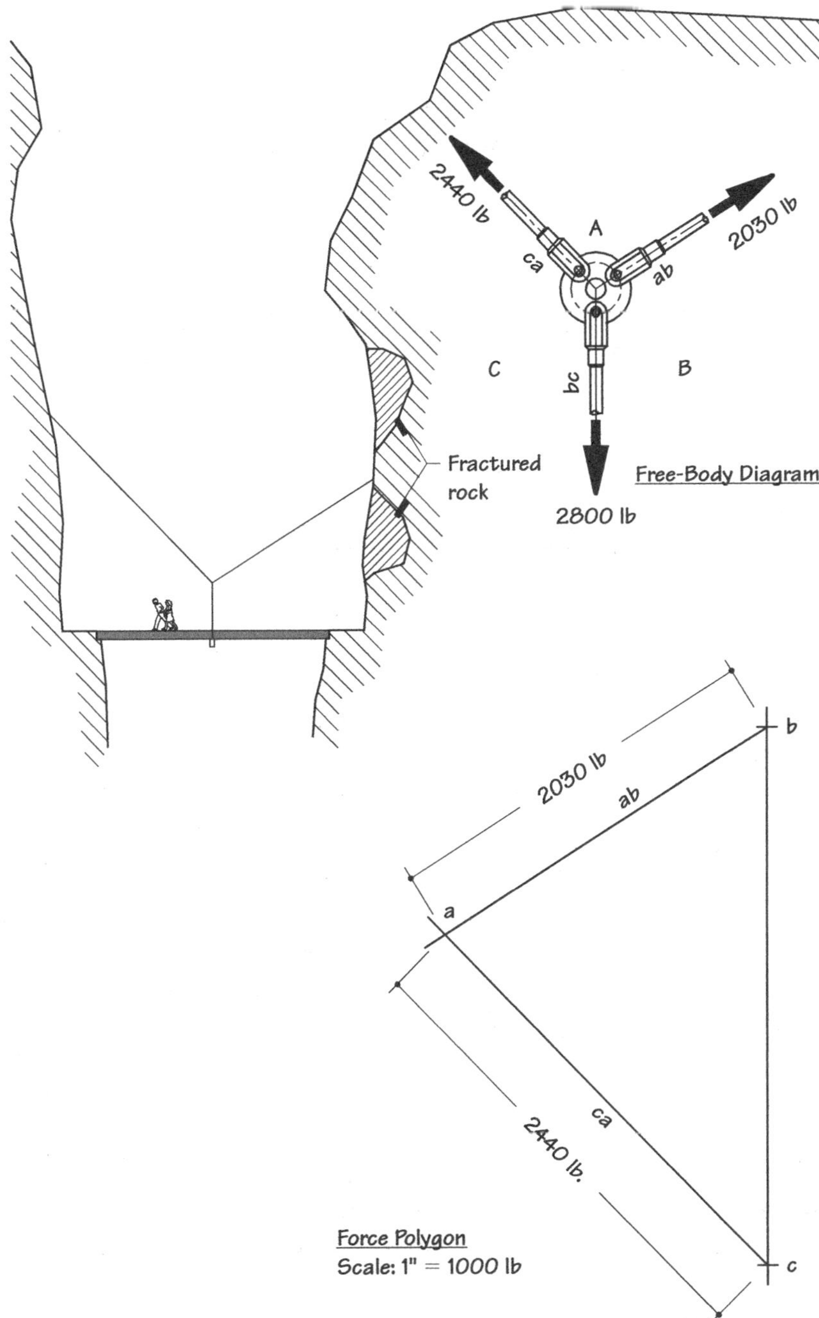

Figure 1.29 The outer end of one of the inclined rods in Bridge #4 is lowered to avoid areas of fractured rock. The magnitudes of the forces in the rods rise, but the bridge remains in static equilibrium.

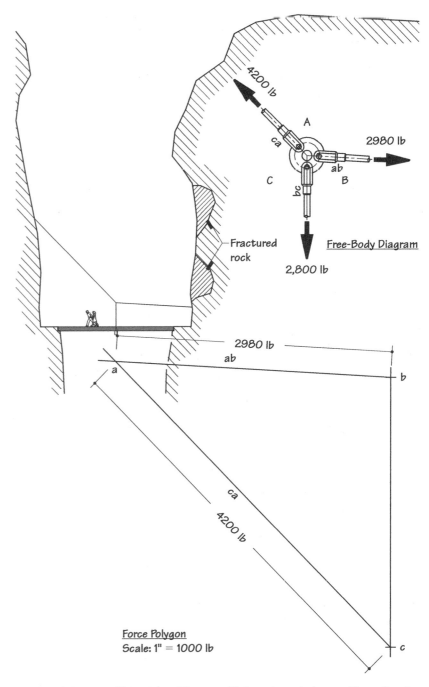

Figure 1.30 Static equilibrium is possible even with the outer end of one rod lower than its inner end.

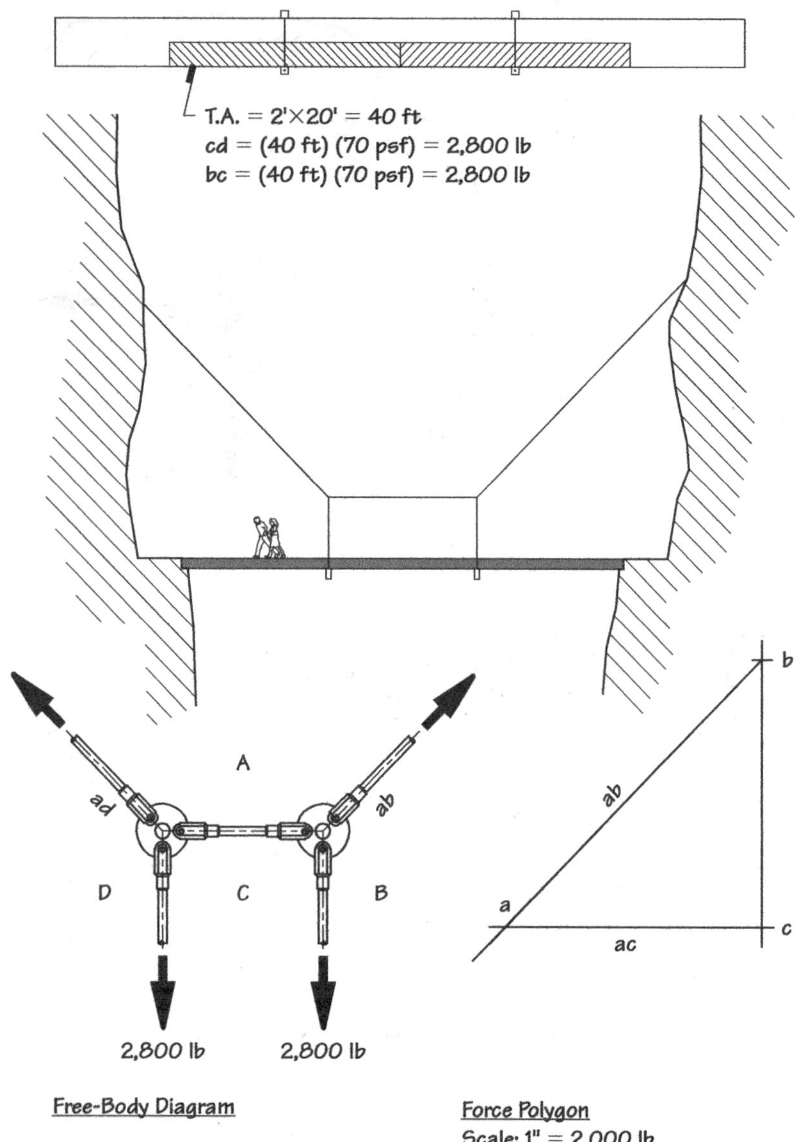

Figure 1.31 Finding forces in Bridge #5, which has a span of 60 ft. Step 1: A force polygon is constructed for the right node, *abc*.

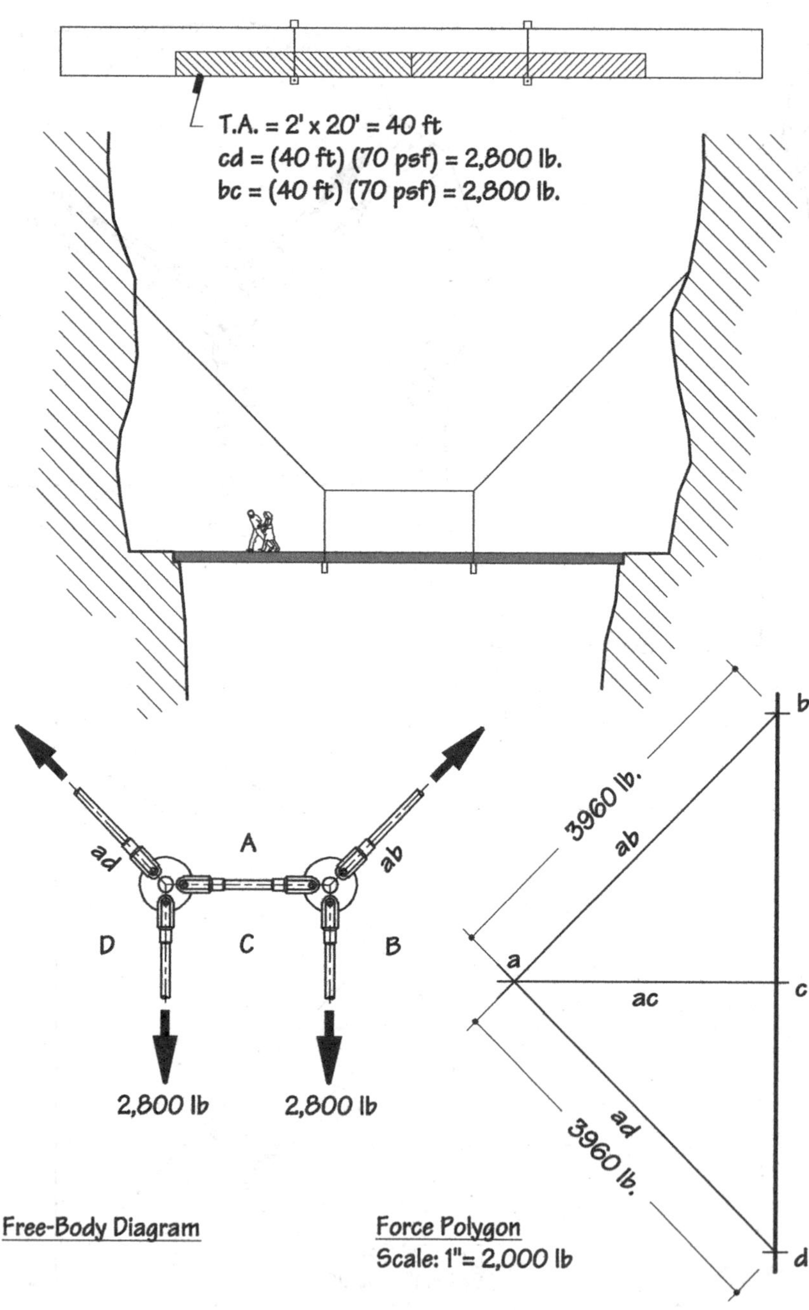

Figure 1.32 Step 2: The analysis is completed by constructing a force polygon for the left node as an extension of the force polygon for the right node.

Deformation by Nonuniform Loads

When the deck is supported at two points along each beam rather than one, a heavy load such as a group of hikers applied at one of the points can cause that point to sag and the other point to rise (Figure 1.33). This is a problem that occurs in any hanging structure that supports two or more loads. (You may find it helpful to your understanding to model this situation with a piece of string that supports two weights a short distance apart.) If nothing is done to accommodate this behavior, the bridge will feel unstable and the connections between beams and crossbeams may flex excessively, leading to eventual failure.

There are a number of ways of counteracting this problem, two of which are illustrated in Figure 1.34. In sketch (a), inclined *stay rods* have been installed below the deck at each crossbeam, anchored to the rock, and tightened. These hold the crossbeams down so that they cannot rise. They cannot sag, either, because in order for one of them to sag, the other would have to rise, and its stay rod will not allow it to do that. Sketch (b) in Figure 1.34 shows another way of dealing with this problem. It indicates symbolically that the joints have been eliminated from the wood deck beams, making the deck stiff throughout its length. The stiff deck allows only very slight rises and sags in the cables.

Figure 1.35 shows that a stiff deck could be created in this bridge by building up each beam from thinner beams placed side by side and nailed together.

Figure 1.33 A heavy live load concentrated at one of the vertical rods can cause serious disruption of the shape of the bridge.

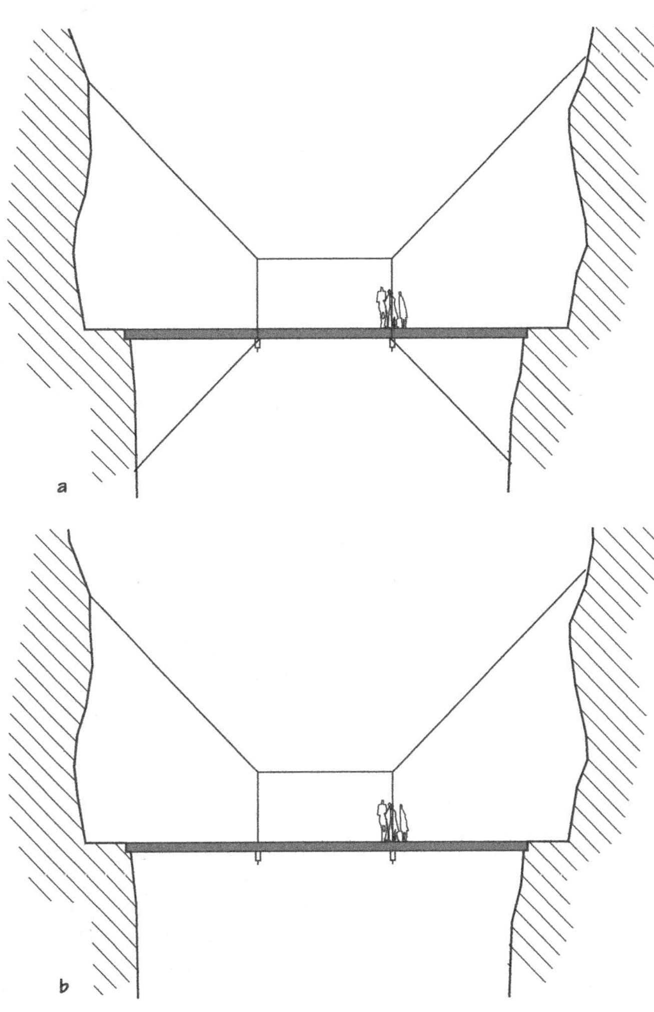

Figure 1.34 Two ways of avoiding or minimizing the problem illustrated in Figure 1.33: (a) Rods below the deck restrain the bridge against upward movement. (b) The deck is stiffened so that it is resistant to abrupt changes in shape at the supporting cables.

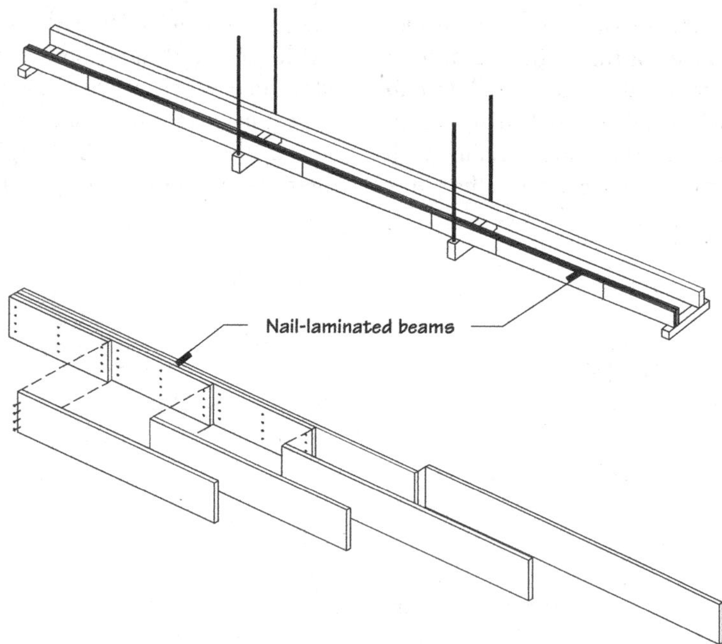

Figure 1.35 A stiff deck could be created for this bridge by nail-laminating thin planks together to form each of the beams, staggering the joints in the various layers so there are no points of major weakness.

The joints in the thinner beams would be staggered to avoid creating weak spots. The result would be a thick beam that is stiff all along its length and thus suitable for the strategy outlined in the previous paragraph. We could, of course, simply order very long beams direct from the sawmill but they would be so unwieldy that they would be almost impossible to install in the cramped space of the canyon. The nail-laminated beams would be much easier to put in place.

BRIDGE #6

The sixth bridge in the series also spans 60 ft, the same as #5, but the right anchorage must be lower to avoid an area of fractured rock in the cliff. We will attempt to do this while retaining the remainder of the bridge's geometry as it was in #5 (Figure 1.36).

We discover that this strategy doesn't work. The force polygon does not close, which indicates that this design is not in static equilibrium. Thus we discover that we can't give an arbitrary shape to a hanging rod or cable. When designing a hanging structure, we must learn what shape the structure itself wants to take. We can find this by using the force polygon to determine the geometry of the rods. We can start by establishing arbitrarily the inclination of any two rods of the three, but the inclination of the third rod must then be found by constructing its parallel ray on the force polygon in such a way that the force polygon closes. In Figure 1.37, we have chosen to incline rod *ad* at an angle of 45°and *ab* at 30°. Their corresponding vectors on the force polygon intersect to establish the location of *a*. Thus the inclination of vector *ac* is fixed because it must pass through points *a* and *c* on the force polygon. We draw rod segment *ac* parallel to these vectors and connect the ends of the rod segments to complete the picture of the bridge. We can scale the lines in the force polygon to find the forces in all the rods. You may wish to find the shape the rods must take if the center rod is horizontal and the inclination of one of the sloping rods is given.

The form that we have found for the upper rods of this bridge is a *funicular* form, one that would be taken by a rope, cable, chain, or string under a similar set of loads similarly placed. The word comes from the Latin *funiculus*, which means "string." Funicular forms experience only *axial* forces, pushes or pulls that act along the longitudinal axis of the element, when loaded in the pattern for which they are shaped. Axial forces can be resisted with the absolute minimum amount of structural material. If the form of a structure is not funicular for its loading, it will experience *bending* forces. Later in this book we will work with bending actions in structures, and we will find that a structure that acts in bending uses many times as much material to resist a force as a structure that acts axially.

Slender structural elements such as rods, cables, ropes, wires, and strings take funicular forms because they are very flexible, with no significant capability to resist bending forces. In a very real way, they are intelligent: In response to any new loading condition they always reshape themselves in such a way that they experience only axial tension. Because of this capability, funicular forms can span much farther than any other elements in the designer's repertoire.

BRIDGE #7

The seventh bridge has a span of 80 ft. This requires four 20-ft beams laid end-to-end on each side of the bridge, their ends supported at three points by

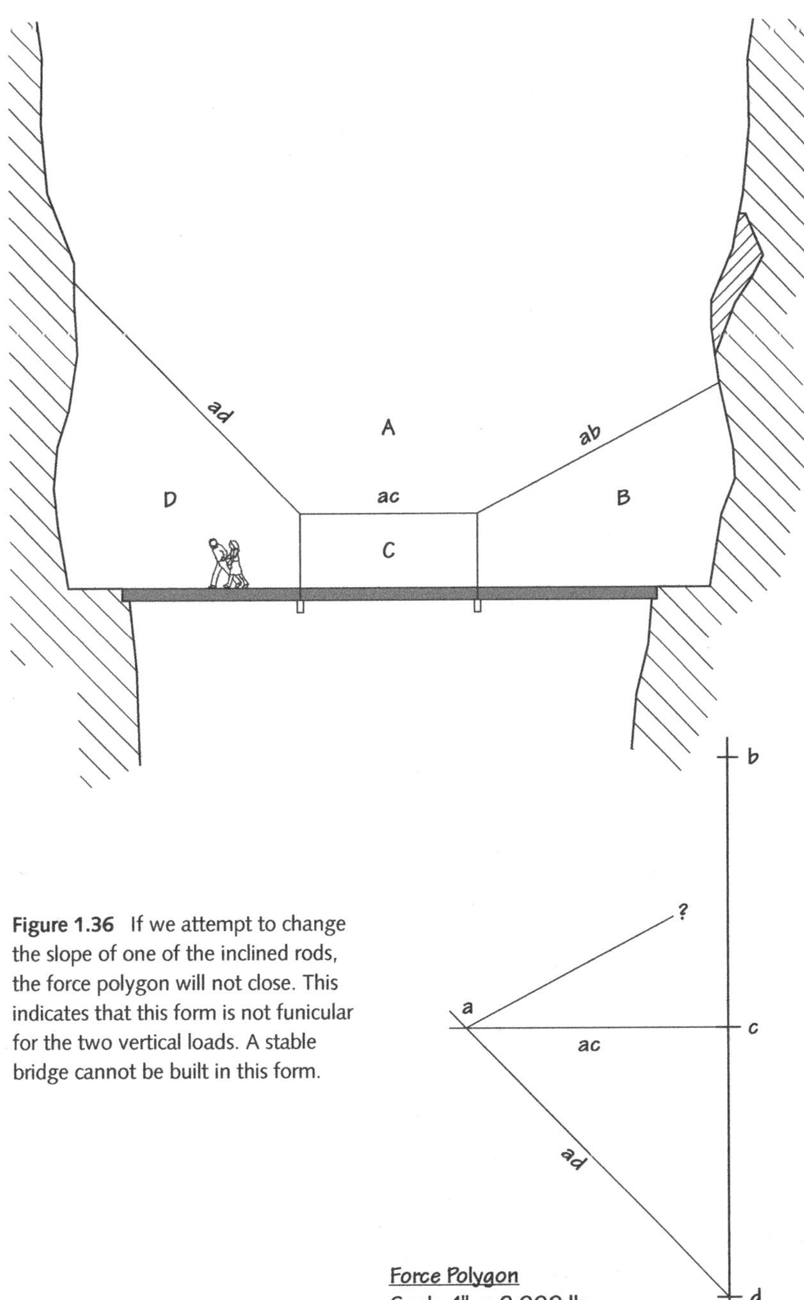

Figure 1.36 If we attempt to change the slope of one of the inclined rods, the force polygon will not close. This indicates that this form is not funicular for the two vertical loads. A stable bridge cannot be built in this form.

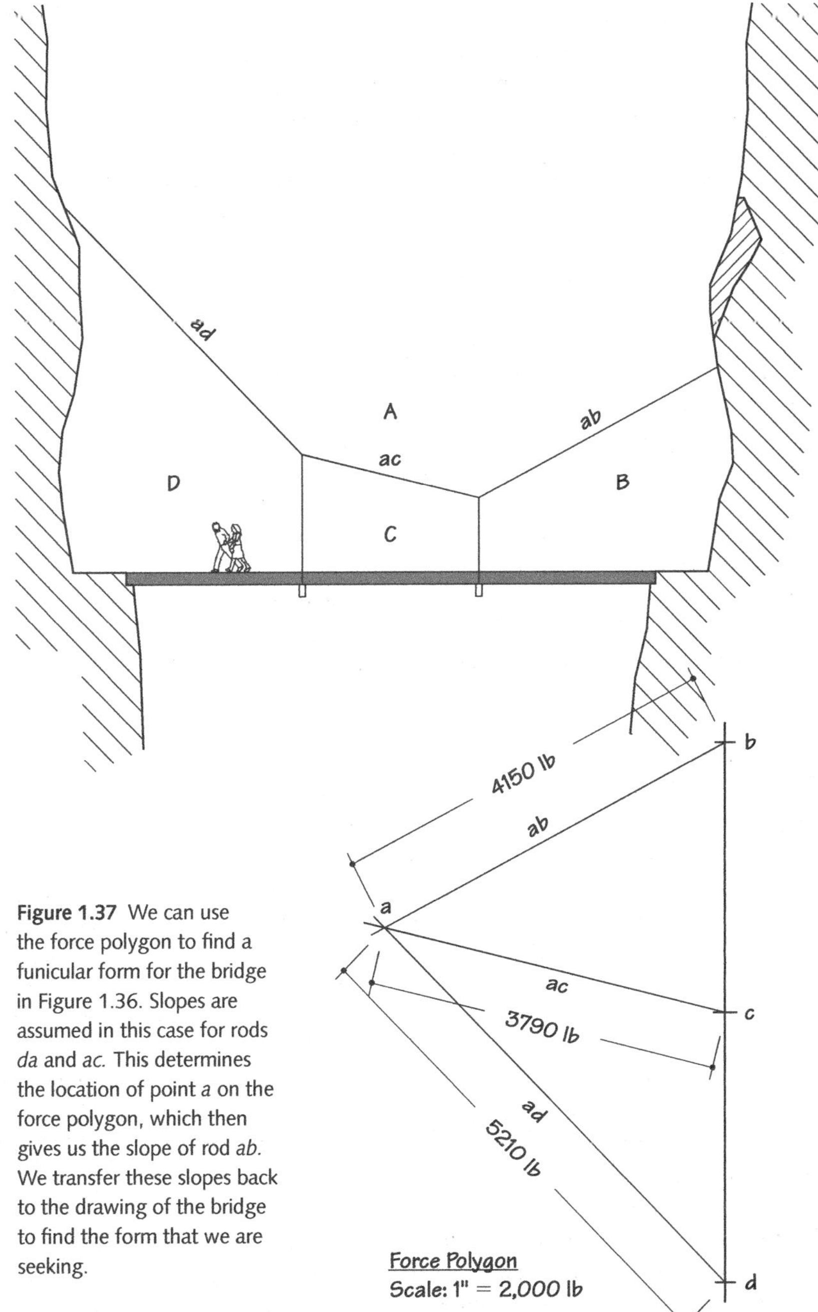

Figure 1.37 We can use the force polygon to find a funicular form for the bridge in Figure 1.36. Slopes are assumed in this case for rods *da* and *ac*. This determines the location of point *a* on the force polygon, which then gives us the slope of rod *ab*. We transfer these slopes back to the drawing of the bridge to find the form that we are seeking.

crossbeams and vertical rods (Figure 1.38). We have decided to make the arrangement of inclined rods symmetrical, with its low point 8 ft above the bridge deck. The Park Service has rods left over from an earlier project that can safely sustain a tensile force of 5,940 lb, and would like to use them in this bridge. We will use the force polygon to generate the shape of the inclined rods to meet these given conditions.

The load line is made up of three vertical segments, each of them 2,800 lb, that represent the forces in the three vertical rods on each side of the bridge. Because the arrangement of rods is symmetrical, the vectors that represent their forces on the force polygon will come together at a point that lies on a horizontal line through the center of the load line. We construct this line, but we do not yet know the location of the point on it where the vectors will converge.

To utilize the rods that the Park Service is offering from stock, the longest vector on the force polygon must have a length of 5,940 lb. Inspection of the force polygon tells us that either the topmost inclined vector or the bottommost will be the longest—each will be 5,940 lb long. Using a scale ruler and/or compass, we find the inclination of a line 5,940 lb long that has one end at point *b* and the other end on the horizontal line that we have just drawn. The point where it intersects the horizontal line is *a*.

Because all four segments of the rod have *a* in their names, all their vectors will pass through point *a* on the force polygon. We decided at the outset that the low point of the rods will be 8 ft above the bridge deck; this will occur at the middle of the span.

On the force polygon, we construct inclined vector *ac* first, because we know that the corresponding rod segment must pass through point *ACD,* which is 8 ft above the center of the span. We draw this segment parallel to vector *AC* on the picture of the bridge.

Vector *ab* is already drawn on the force polygon. We draw rod segment *ab* parallel to it through node *abc* on the picture of the bridge. To complete this construction, we draw vector *ad* on the force polygon, and rod segment *ad* parallel to it on the picture of the bridge.

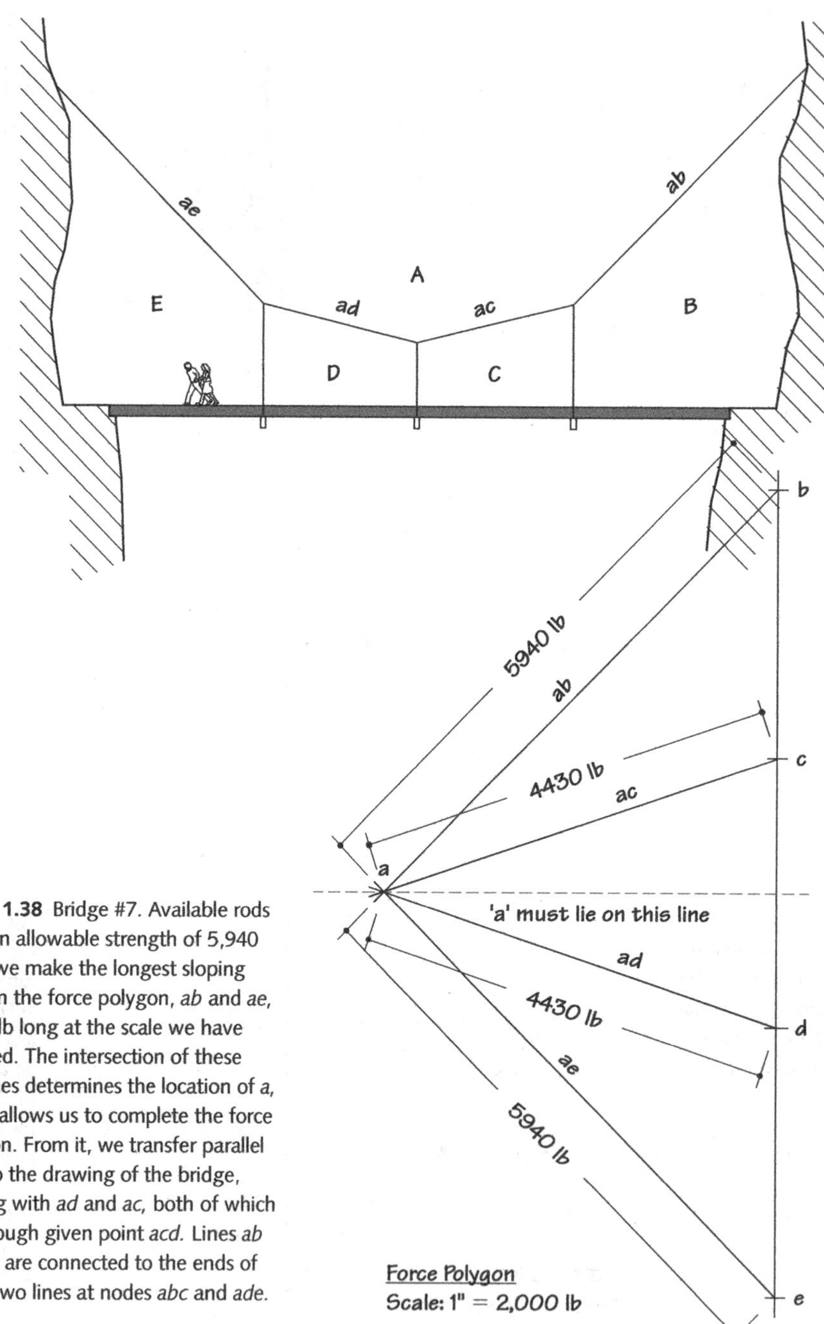

Figure 1.38 Bridge #7. Available rods have an allowable strength of 5,940 lb, so we make the longest sloping lines on the force polygon, *ab* and *ae,* 5,940 lb long at the scale we have adopted. The intersection of these two lines determines the location of *a,* which allows us to complete the force polygon. From it, we transfer parallel lines to the drawing of the bridge, starting with *ad* and *ac,* both of which go through given point *acd.* Lines *ab* and *ae* are connected to the ends of these two lines at nodes *abc* and *ade.*

Then, through node *ade,* we draw rod segment *ae* parallel to vector *ae* on the force polygon.

We scale the vectors on the force polygon to learn that *ab* and *ae* represent forces of 5,940 lb in their corresponding rod segments, and rods *ac* and *ad* carry 4,500 lb each. In theory, we could use smaller rods for these two segments than for the more heavily loaded segments. In practice, it is much simpler and will save labor to use the same diameter rod throughout.

This bridge, like its three-beam-span predecessor, will tend to distort in response to asymmetrical loading patterns, and we will have to provide a stiff deck or inclined stay cables from below to restrain such distortions.

BRIDGE #8

Bridge #8, with its 100-ft span is the longest of the group (Worksheet 1A, shown in Figure 1.39). It requires five lengths of beams, as well as vertical rod supports (often called *hangers*) at four locations. You have been assigned to find the form of this bridge

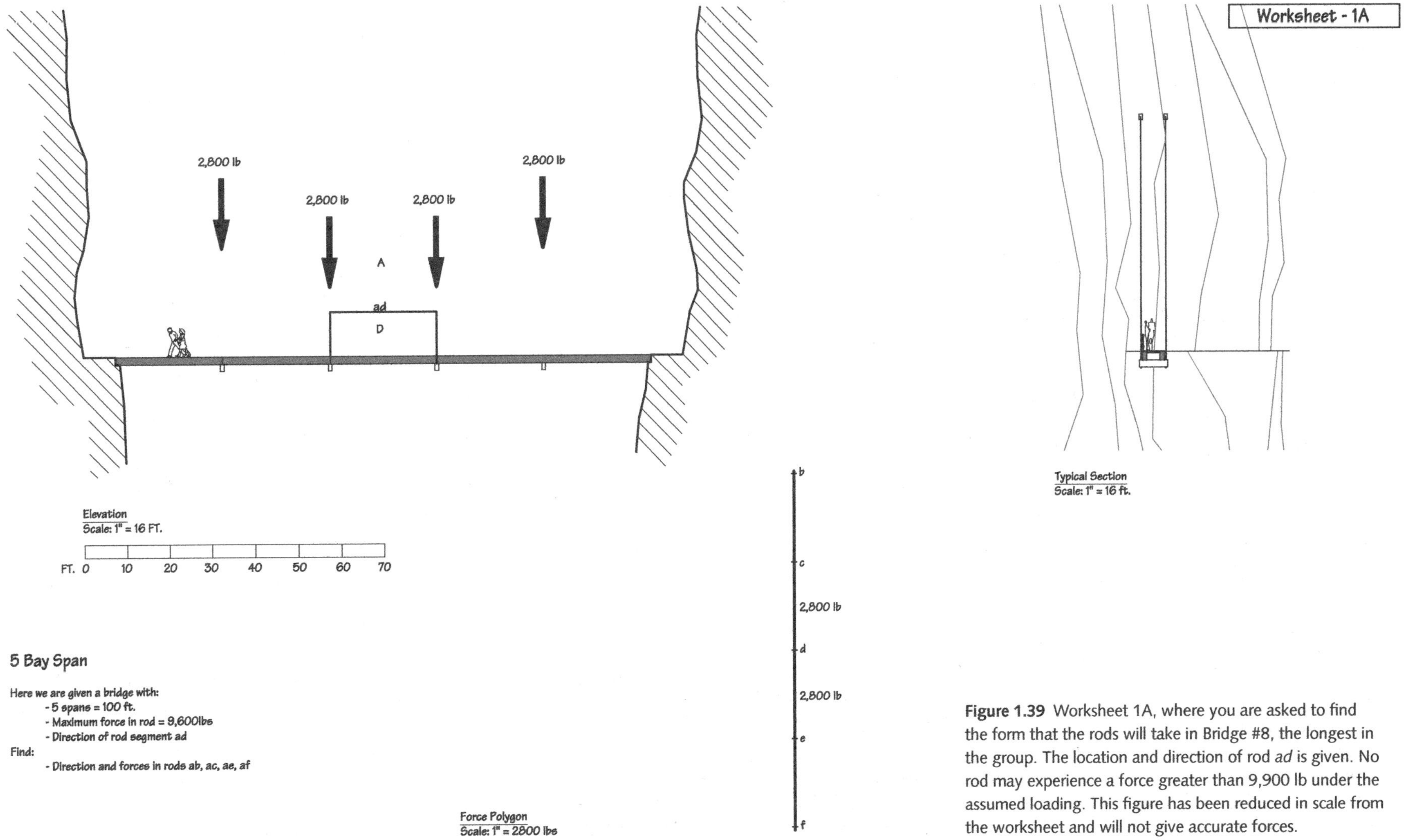

2,800 lb
2,800 lb
2,800 lb
2,800 lb
A
ad
D

Elevation
Scale: 1" = 16 FT.
FT. 0 10 20 30 40 50 60 70

5 Bay Span

Here we are given a bridge with:
- 5 spans = 100 ft.
- Maximum force in rod = 9,600lbs
- Direction of rod segment ad

Find:
- Direction and forces in rods ab, ac, ae, af

b
c
2,800 lb
d
2,800 lb
e
f

Force Polygon
Scale: 1" = 2800 lbs

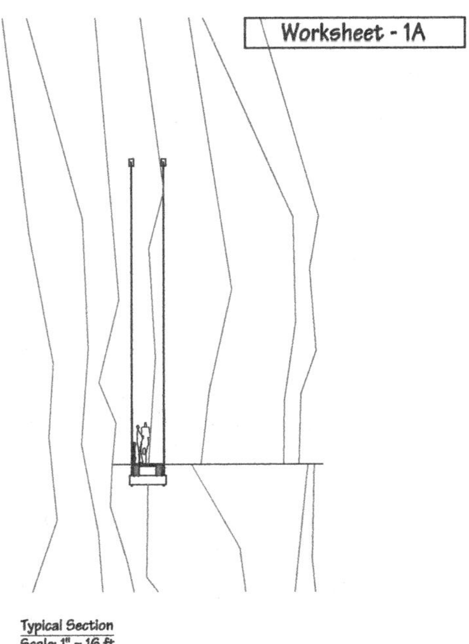

Figure 1.39 Worksheet 1A, where you are asked to find the form that the rods will take in Bridge #8, the longest in the group. The location and direction of rod *ad* is given. No rod may experience a force greater than 9,900 lb under the assumed loading. This figure has been reduced in scale from the worksheet and will not give accurate forces.

and the forces in all its rods. The group of designers working on the bridges has agreed that junctions of rods should never be less than 8 ft above the deck, so as to minimize vandalism, and the maximum force in the rods cannot exceed 9,900 lb (the allowable strength of a 0.437-in. rod). Given this information and the site as shown on Worksheet 1A, find the form of this bridge and the forces in all its rod segments. This bridge is the last of the series of suspension bridges for which we have been asked to prepare preliminary designs.

"Geometry is the mathematics of structural imagination."

—WACŁAW ZALEWSKI

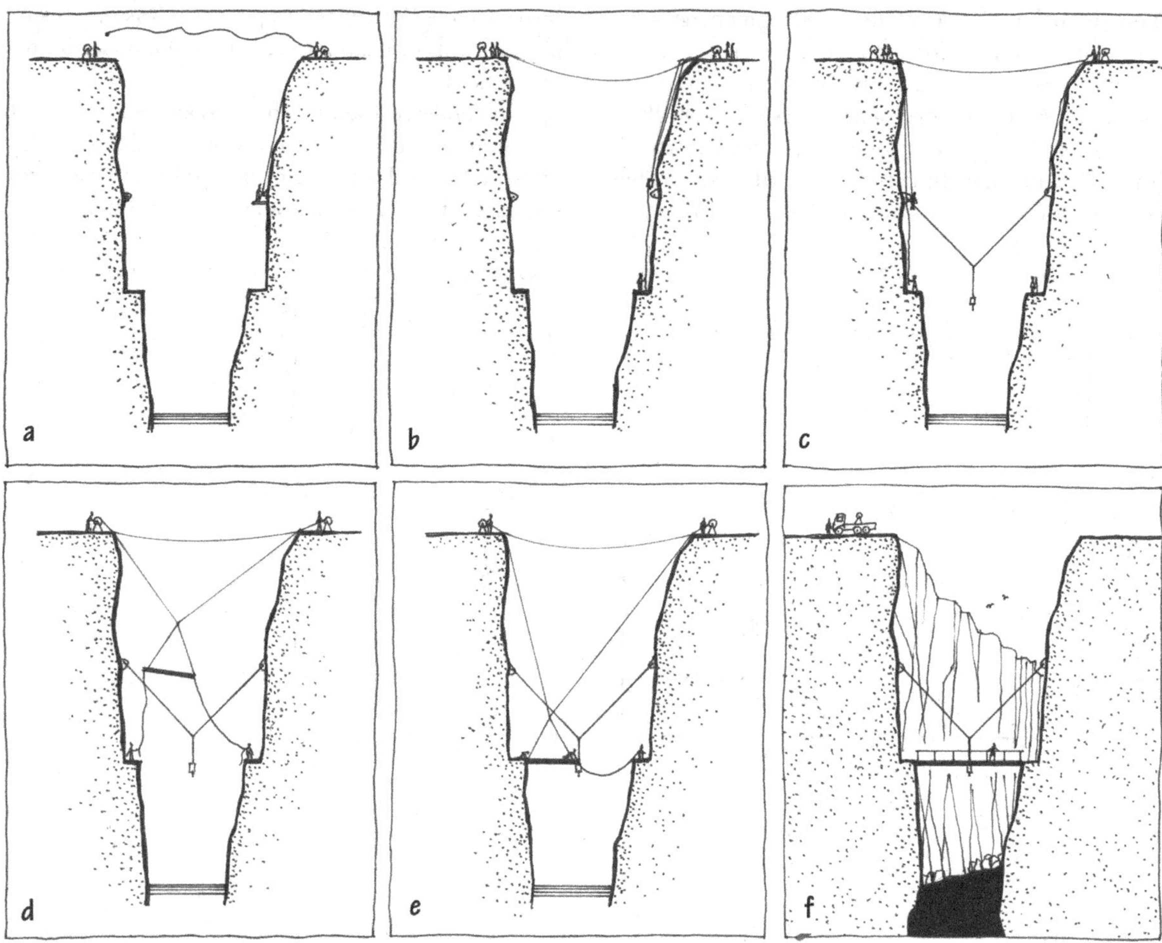

Figure 1.40 A proposed erection sequence for Bridge #1.

ERECTING THE BRIDGES

An important aspect of the design of any structure is to design the way in which it will be built. If we can't figure out at least one practical, economical way to build our bridges, it is unlikely that they will get built.

Figure 1.40 is a sequence of six sketches that we have prepared to suggest a construction method. In sketch *a,* workers in safety harnesses have been let down the canyon wall on ropes to drill bolt holes and install anchor plates on both sides. They stand on a small wooden platform called a *float* that hangs on ropes from the top of the cliff.

While this work is going on, a soft weight such as a small sack filled with sand is tied to the end of a long, sturdy cord and propelled across the top of the canyon with a slingshot, archery bow, or other throwing device. This cord is used to pull successively heavier cords and ropes across the top of the canyon until a rope sufficiently strong for the next step of construction has been installed. In sketch *b,* each of the rod assemblies is lowered down the cliff by a small *winch* on the canyon rim. The rope from the other rim is tied to the left top end of each assembly to act as a *tag line* that is used to pull it into place at the left anchorage. Workers attach the jaw fittings at the ends of the rod assemblies to the anchorages (sketch *c*).

The first beam is lowered by winches on both sides of the canyon working in coordination. Workers positioned below guide both ends of the beam with tag lines (*d*). In sketch *e,* the beam is bolted into its final position. This entire process is repeated for all the other components. The decking and railing are installed, and in sketch *f,* the last of the construction equipment is cleared away, leaving the bridge ready for service.

The bridge may not be erected in exactly this way. The workers and supervisors who do the actual work

High-Tech Architecture

During the late 1960s and 1970s, a group of architects and engineers centered in London developed a particular approach to structural expressionism that led to what is known generically as "high-tech architecture." This broad category, characterized by elaborately exposed, exquisitely finished structural members, mechanical equipment and services, and other typically hidden features, found resonance among designers such as Norman Foster, Renzo Piano, Richard Rogers, Nicholas Grimshaw, Anthony Hunt, and Meinhard von Gerkan. Peter Rice and Ted Happold, who both worked at the seminal interdisciplinary office founded by Danish-British engineer Ove Arup (1895–1988) in London, left to found independent engineering consulting practices (RFR and Buro Happold, respectively), which further expanded related design approaches. Buildings such as the Centre Pompidou (1972–1977) by Piano, Rogers, and Rice, with its cantilevered external tubular escalators and ducts, demonstrated how the "high-tech" look made possible some of the machine-oriented visions for futuristic architecture drawn by members of Archigram in London only a decade earlier. Many of these firms have grown as international practices even after changes in leadership or the death of their founders (e.g., Arup, Happold, Rice). Generally speaking, the Hi-Tech designers are structurally knowledgeable and have produced buildings whose structures are logically formed.

may have better ideas and methods. We will consult with them as soon as possible to seek agreement on how the work will be done, using this sequence of sketches as a starting point. It is likely that the method will be further modified during the construction process in response to problems and ideas that occur on the site.

RESISTING LATERAL AND UPLIFT FORCES

In addition to the downward *gravity forces* that we have been considering, the bridges also must resist wind forces from the side and from below, which are classified as *lateral forces* and *uplift forces,* respectively. *Lateral force resistance* is provided in most bridges by making the deck act as a beam lying on its side. A common way of doing this is to add *diagonal members* in a horizontal plane within the deck structure to create a *truss.* In our wooden bridges, the diagonals would be easy to install and highly effective in resisting lateral forces (Figure 1.41).

Uplift resistance is created automatically in many bridges: the dead weight of the bridge is substantially larger than the expected uplift forces. In our bridges, with their relatively lightweight wood decks, the dead weight is insufficient for this purpose. An appropriate solution would be to add steel rods under the bridge to pull it down. If these rods lie in two planes that are sufficiently tilted from the vertical, they can serve several purposes simultaneously: to resist both lateral and uplift forces created by wind, and to restrain the main supporting rods from changing shape in response to variable loading conditions (Figures 1.42, 1.43).

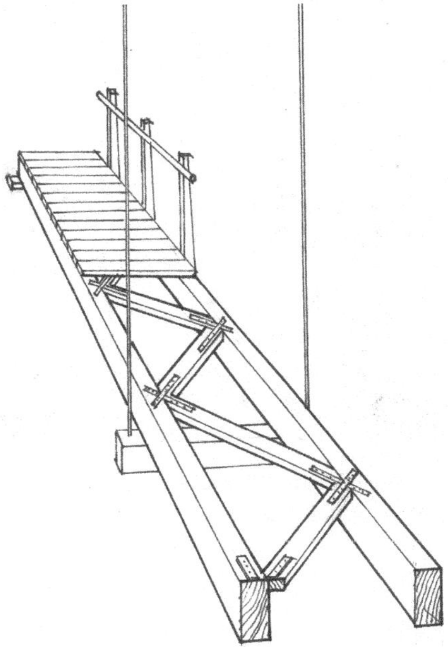

Figure 1.41 Diagonal bracing in a horizontal plane just below the deck creates a truss that prevents lateral distortion of the deck by wind loads.

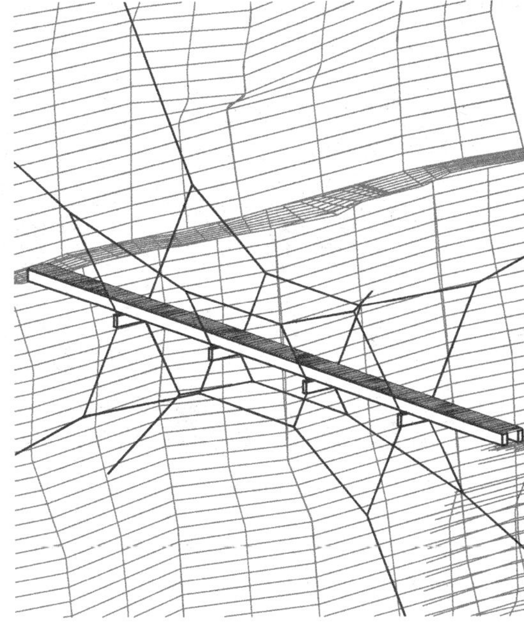

Figure 1.42 Funicular arrangements of rods could be used to resist both lateral forces and uplift forces on all the bridges. They would also help to restrain the bridge against changes of shape from concentrated loads.

Figure 1.43 The Royal Gorge Suspension Bridge, designed by George Cole and constructed in 1929, spans 268.2 m (880 ft) over the Arkansas River in Colorado. The river lies 321 m (1,053 ft) below. Two dramatic funicular cables pull both down and out on the deck to stabilize the narrow bridge. One is visible as a white arc to the lower left.

U.S. Air Force photo by Staff Sgt. Donald Branum.

ALTERNATIVE POSITIONS FOR THE RODS

There are many possible variations on our bridge design that involve changing the relationship of the rods to the deck. Figure 1.44 shows a configuration that simplifies the design by omitting the vertical rods. The bridge in Figure 1.45 relocates the rods below the deck, where they support the middle of the span by means of a central compression strut. The deck beams in this design must act in compression to resist the inward pull of the inclined rods. This bridge has no need for tensile anchors to the cliffs; it needs only simple anchor bolts at each end to keep the ends of the beams from moving sideways.

All these variations have advantages with respect to saving steel, lowering the overall profile of the bridges, and simplifying their appearance.

The building in Figure 1.46 makes ingenious use of steel rods to support the roof of a warehouse and showroom building. Figure 1.47 makes clear how the rods are deployed, and in Figure 1.48 we adapt this configuration to our 80-ft-long suspension bridge.

LOOKING AHEAD

In this lesson we have developed the rudiments of a graphical technique that can be used to design suspension bridges and suspension roofs, ones that are supported by rods or cables that take funicular forms. It is also applicable to the design of inverted forms of these structures that work in compression. In the next chapter, we will develop this technique further as we apply it to the design of a suspended roof. In the third chapter, we will explore the inverted, compressive application. Before we move on to these chapters, however, you are invited to apply what you have learned to the task of designing an aerial walkway for an ecological park.

Scale: 1" = 32 ft

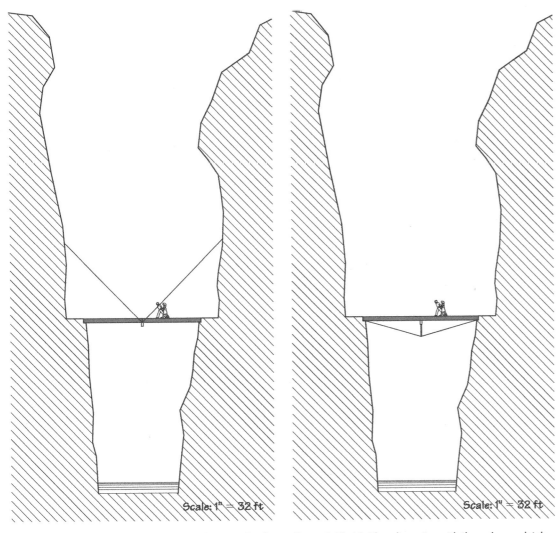

Figure 1.44 A bridge alternative that omits the vertical rods.

Scale: 1" = 32 ft

Figure 1.45 A bridge alternative with the rods completely below the deck.

Figure 1.46 The roof of the Renault Centre at Swindon, England, is supported by an ingenious arrangement of steel rods and beams. (Architect: Norman Foster. Structural engineer: Arup Associates.)

Photo courtesy of Richard Davies.

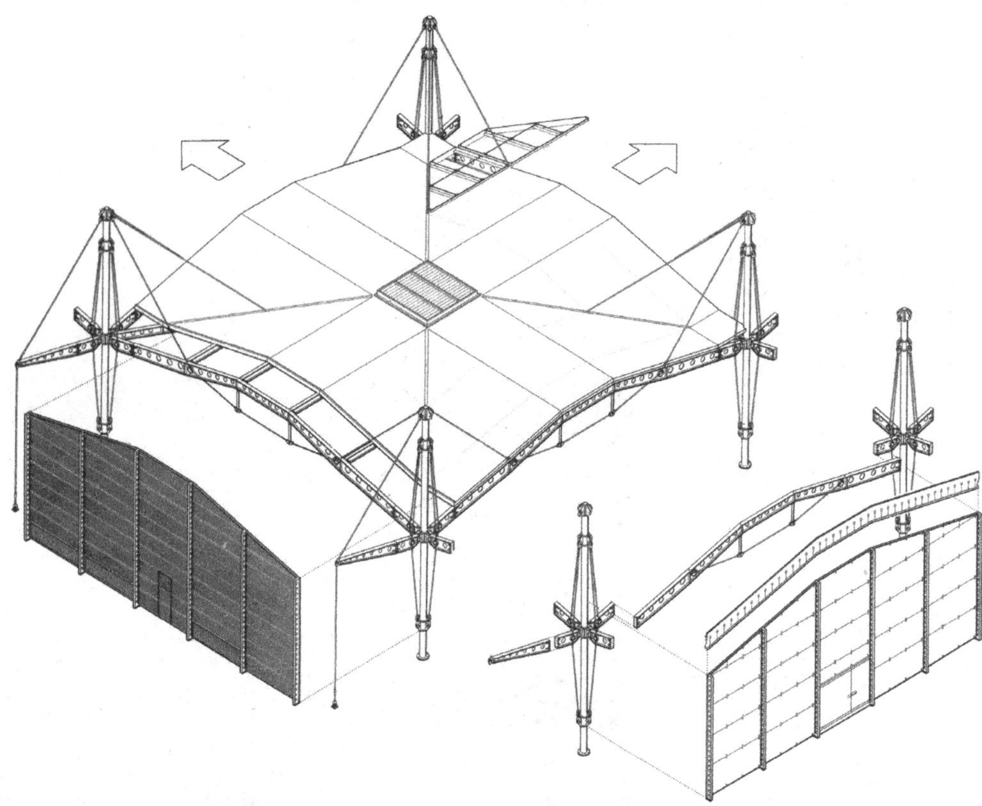

Figure 1.47 Given a measured drawing of the roof structure of the Renault Centre, how would you go about finding the forces in its members?

Image courtesy of Foster Associates, as shown in Chris Abel, *Renault Centre, Norman Foster.*

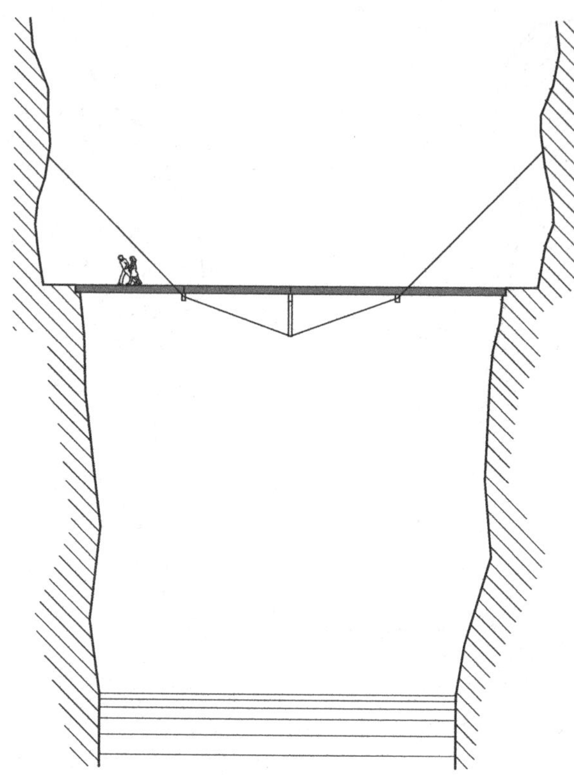

Figure 1.48 This configuration of rods and struts from the Renault Centre could be envisioned in modified form as a solution for the footbridge as well.

ANOTHER CHALLENGE: DESIGNING AN AERIAL WALKWAY

A new eco-park on the Pacific Coast of Oregon will feature an elevated walkway 8 ft wide that makes it possible for visitors to stroll through the treetops of mammoth Douglas firs and red cedars, where they can observe the birds, mammals, insects, fungi, lichens, and other life forms that make up the unique ecosystem of a forest canopy. Worksheet 1B (available on the supplemental website) is set up to make it easy for you to design this walkway (Figure 1.49). The structural concept that has been suggested by the client's structural engineer is to erect a series of 100-ft-high cedar log frames 72 ft apart, using these to support the walkway at a height of approximately 60 ft above the ground. The available wooden beams can span no farther than 24 ft between the stainless steel rod supports that you will provide. The gravity load includes a live load estimate of 100 lb per square foot (psf) and a dead load of 24 psf. You must propose ways of resisting gravity loads, lateral forces, and uplift forces from wind. A large construction crane is available to help erect the walkway.

To present your structural concept, you are to complete an elevation drawing (side view) of the bridge and a section, both of which are shown partially completed on the worksheet. Notice that in the elevation, because of the zigzagging path of the walkway, only Span II appears in its true size and shape, so you should find the form and forces on this span before transferring the shapes to the other spans. You are to determine the forces in the rods that support the walkway and to show your means of finding these forces on your drawing. A load line location is shown as the starting point for a force polygon. The force

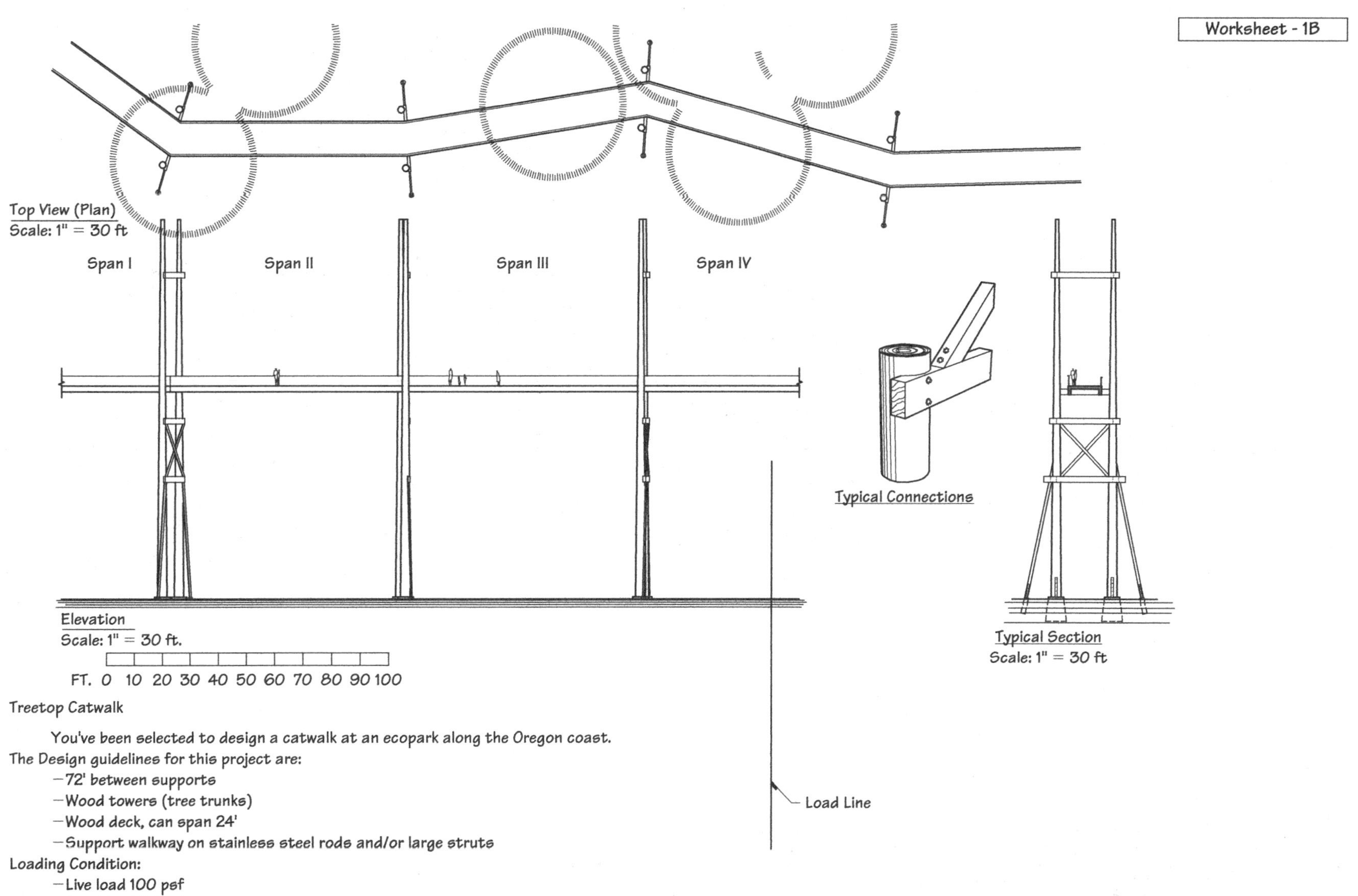

Worksheet - 1B
Top View (Plan)
Scale: 1" = 30 ft
Span I
Span II
Span III
Span IV
Typical Connections
Elevation
Scale: 1" = 30 ft.
FT. 0 10 20 30 40 50 60 70 80 90 100
Typical Section
Scale: 1" = 30 ft
Load Line
Treetop Catwalk
You've been selected to design a catwalk at an ecopark along the Oregon coast.
The Design guidelines for this project are:
—72' between supports
—Wood towers (tree trunks)
—Wood deck, can span 24'
—Support walkway on stainless steel rods and/or large struts
Loading Condition:
—Live load 100 psf
—Dead load 24 psf

Figure 1.49 Worksheet 1B shows the project of designing an aerial walkway in an eco-park. As with all the worksheets, the full-scale worksheet is available on the supplemental site.

polygon will overlap the elevation of the walkway, as is often done to save space on a sheet of drawings. Find and indicate the required diameters of the rods.

The meandering plan of the walkway presents a problem: At most towers, the suspension rods for the two adjoining spans do not lie in the same plane. If they did, their horizontal pulls would balance one another. In this nonorthogonal walkway layout, however, components of these forces will tend to pull the towers over sideways. Work out a simple way of resisting this tendency and show it on your drawings.

▸**Figure 1.50** The Menai Bridge (1818–1826) was designed and built by Thomas Telford to provide a crossing of the Menai Strait for the road connecting London and Holyhead. The eyebar links that make up the chains were made of wrought iron, which is much less brittle than cast iron, in the era before plentiful, economical steel was available. The span of the bridge, approximately 580 ft, was by far the longest in the world at the time of its construction. The bridge still carries vehicular traffic nearly two centuries later. For more information on Thomas Telford, see his biography on the overleaf.

Photo courtesy of Kyle Gann.

◂**Figure 1.51** Schlaich Bergermann collaborated in 1988 with architect Eberhard Schunck to use funicular rods to support a pedestrian bridge over the railroad tracks at Bad Windsheim in Germany.

Photo courtesy of Schlaich Bergermann and Partners.

◀**Figure 1.52** The engineers at Schlaich Bergermann used a similar arrangement of rods to suspend this large-span factory roof at Dachwig, Germany, providing an efficient solution and eye-catching profile to satisfy the client's desire for corporate identity. It is shown here during construction in 1993.

Photo courtesy of Schlaich Bergermann and Partners.

▶**Figure 1.53** The Lowry Bridge, a lifting footbridge over the Manchester (England) Ship Canal at Salford Quays, was designed by engineers at the Parkman (now Mouchel) Group and built in 2000. Its 92-m (301-ft) span has rod and cable elements that suspend the deck from inclined arches, in an arrangement designed to resist racking and vibration.

Photo: David M. Foxe.

THOMAS TELFORD

Thomas Telford was born in Scotland in 1757. He began his career as a mason and builder, but gradually transitioned to work as a surveyor and then to design and construction of several dozen road bridges in Shropshire. He became involved in the creation of the Ellesmere Canal, including, in 1797, the dramatic Pontcysyllte Aqueduct, which carries a navigable cast iron trough of water 126 ft above the River Dee. Between 1811 and 1826, he designed and constructed the 580-ft span Menai suspension bridge to enable travel between London and the port at Holyhead. This early suspension bridge was a major influence on the succeeding generation of British engineers. Among its notable features were its rock anchor design, its efficient depth of curvature, and its parallel bar wrought-iron chain and hangers. Nearly two centuries later it continues to carry traffic. Although Poet Laureate Robert Southey referred to Telford, in jest, as the "colossus of roads," in fact, Telford's professional output included docks, railway construction, buildings, travel writing, and even published poetry, in addition to his roadway, canal, and bridge projects. He became the first president of the Institute of Civil Engineers and served from 1820 until his death in 1834. He is buried in Westminster Abbey.

Key Terms and Concepts

span
deck
suspension bridge
stainless steel
grout
jaw
fork
clevis
steel fabricator
washer
jam nut
plate
anchor plate
load
dead load
live load
total load
pound
tributary area
force
push, pull
stress
deformation
magnitude of force
direction of force
line of action of force
point of application of force
scalar quantity
vector quantity
tension
compression
principle of transmissibility
concurrent forces
nonconcurrent forces
free-body diagram (FBD)
free body
graphical methods
numerical methods
node
static equilibrium
parallelogram law
resultant
equilibrant
antiresultant
tip-to-tail addition of vectors
force polygon
graphical solution
numerical solution
Bow's notation
load line
clockwise reading of member names
buckling
deformation
yield strength
factor of safety
threads
upset end
right-hand and left-hand threads
cold heading
clearance
ultimate load
stay rods
funicular
funicular form
axial force
bending force
restraining funicular structures
character of a force
gravity forces
lateral forces
diagonals
truss
uplift forces
hanger
winch
tag line

Further Resources

Abel, Chris. *Renault Centre, Norman Foster.* London, UK: Architecture Design and Technology Press, 1994.

www.clevelandcityforge.com: A manufacturer of rod and cable hardware. See especially "upset forged threaded rods."

www.ronstan.com: Another useful manufacturer's site; see the section on "Architectural rigging systems."

www.tripyramid.com: TriPyramid Structures is a firm that acts as a specialized consultant for designing and fabricating precision components, including architectural tension connections, cables, and rods. See the product and technical sections, in particular, for information about rod materials.

CHAPTER 2

Designing a Suspended Roof

- Designing and detailing a suspended roof
- Designing funicular curves with specified properties
- Families of funicular curves
- Static equilibrium
- Components of forces
- Steel cable fastenings and details
- Lateral bracing
- Regulating forces on masts and backstays

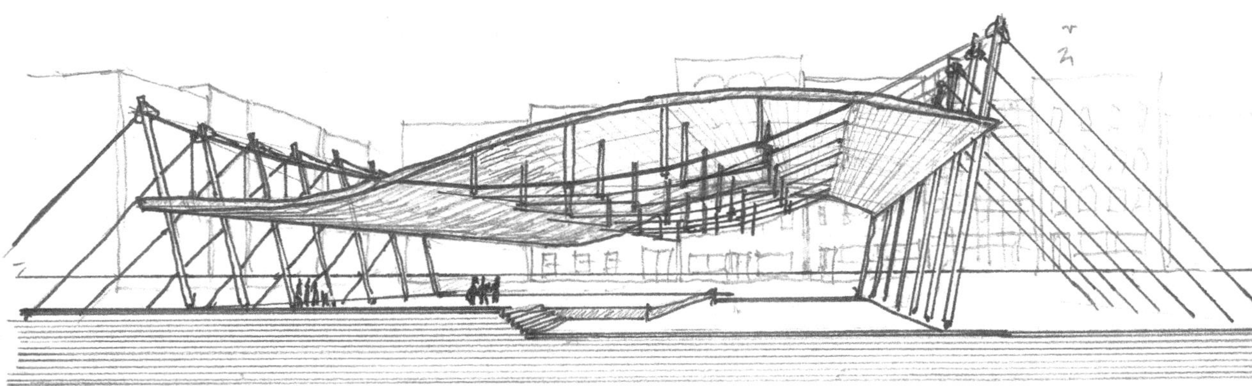

Figure 2.1 A very early perspective sketch of the roof for the high-speed bus terminal.

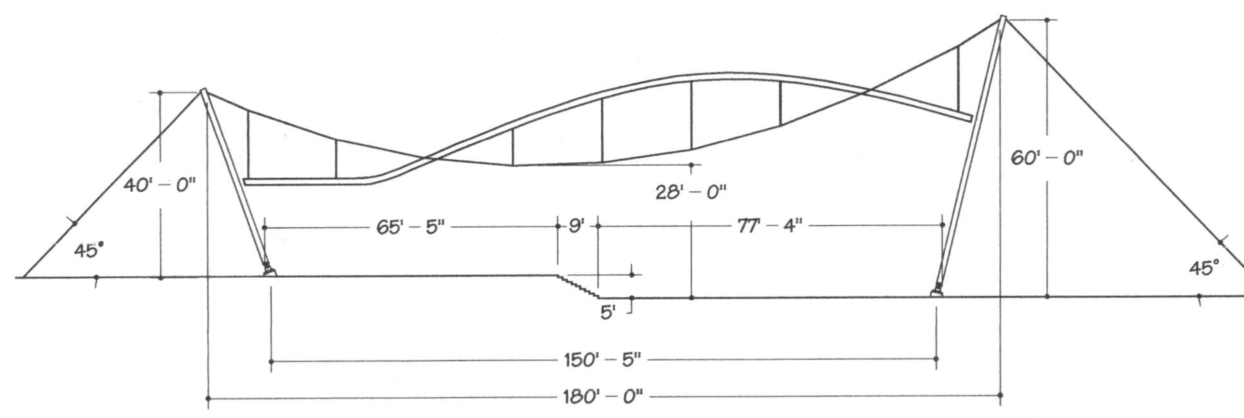

Figure 2.2 A cross section of the bus terminal roof, showing key dimensions.

The sketches on these pages show a preliminary design that we have prepared for the roof of a terminal building for a new high-speed intercity bus service (Figures 2.1, 2.2). The buses are low, sleek, and capable of speeds of over 200 miles per hour. They will run by automatic control on dedicated busways in shallow tunnels, rather than on the highways. This will allow them to operate safely and reliably in any weather and avoid having to cross roadways and railroad lines. Because of their all-weather operation and city-center terminal locations, travel on this system will be faster door-to-door than flying for most passengers.

The design of the terminal building is intended to enhance the excitement of this new mode of travel. Hanging steel *cables* support a structural roof surface made of corrugated steel decking. However, the roof surface does not follow the line of these main cables; it takes its own, arbitrary shape, which was chosen to create a soaring space as a welcome contrast to the confinement of the busway tunnels. Near the long edges of the building, the roof surface is below the cables and transmits its loads to them via steel rod *hangers* (vertical tensile members). In the middle portion of the building, this surface rises above the cables, and its load is transmitted to them by vertical steel tube *struts* (short compression members). Each cable is supported at each end by tall steel *masts,* which may also be called *columns* or *pylons*. The masts on one side of the building are 20 ft taller than those on the other side. Sloping cable *backstays* prevent the masts from being toppled inward by the pulls of the cables. The span of the cables between the tops of the masts is 180 ft. We judge that the low points of the main cables must be at least 28 ft above the lower floor level of the terminal to maintain the feeling of a soaring roof. These and other critical dimensions are shown in Figure 2.2.

We have estimated that the total maximum load on the roof is 60 lb per sq ft (psf). This includes a live-load estimate for snow of 20 psf and a dead-load estimate for the weight of the roof structure itself of 40 psf. The cables will be spaced 20 ft apart. We have assumed for the moment that the backstays will be inclined at 45°. We will experiment later with the mast and backstay inclinations to maximize the efficiency of the structure.

The fabricator of the cable has in stock a quantity of 2–1/8-in. diameter strand that is sufficient for the entire structure. This was left in his warehouse when another project was canceled and can be purchased for this project at a very favorable price. We would like to use this cable if possible.

Graphic Statics

All structural analysis is based on the science of *statics*, the study of the effects and distribution of forces on bodies that remain at rest. Statical analyses may be carried out either numerically or graphically. The body of graphical methods that we are studying is called *graphic statics*. The roots of graphic statics go back to early studies of the composition of forces by the Italians Leonardo da Vinci and Galileo Galilei. Dutch mathematician Simon Stevin (1548–1620) was the first person to represent force as a vector. In a 1608 publication, Stevin also presented a correct interpretation of the parallelogram of forces. The Englishman Isaac Newton (1642–1727) formulated the laws of force and motion upon which statics and its sister science of moving bodies, *dynamics*, are based. The Frenchman Varignon (1654–1722) presented the force polygon and the funicular polygon in a work published in 1725. In 1748, Giovanni Poleni published a graphical analysis of the structural action of the masonry dome of St. Peter's Basilica in Rome. Early nineteenth-century French and German texts presented many of the rudiments of graphic statics at about the same time as Louis Navier (see his biography on page 371) published in Paris the first comprehensive text on numerical methods of structural analysis (1826). In 1864, Britons James Clerk Maxwell and W. P. Taylor published a graphical method for analyzing forces in trusses, but this method was not widely known or accepted until Robert H. Bow explained and elaborated it in a book of 1873. Bow also introduced the system of interval notation that we use today. In Milan, in 1872, Luigi Cremona published a volume in which, independently of the Britons, he demonstrated the graphical analysis of trusses. The German engineer Karl Culmann (1821–1881) is generally acknowledged as the father of graphic statics (see his biography on page 113). In *Die graphische Statik*, first published in Zurich in 1866, Culmann presented the first consistent, comprehensive body of graphical techniques. He introduced many of the fundamental graphical methods that we use today and demonstrated how they could be used to solve a wide variety of structural problems. Culmann's work was further developed by his pupil and the successor to his teaching post at the Swiss Federal Technical Institute (ETH) in Zurich, Wilhelm Ritter (1847–1906). The German Otto Mohr (1835–1918) introduced many additional innovations and improvements.

The influence of the pioneers of graphic statics on the shape of modern structures is enormous. Maurice Koechlin, the co-designer of the Eiffel Tower, was Culmann's student. Robert Maillart studied under Ritter. Christian Menn became acquainted with Maillart's structures while still a child, and studied structures in Zurich with Ritter's pupil, Pierre Lardy. Pier Luigi Nervi and Riccardo Morandi were heirs to the legacy of Cremona. In Spain, Antoni Gaudí, Gaudí's structural engineer Mariano Rubió y Bellvé, vault builder Rafael Guastavino, and engineers Eduardo Torroja and Felix Candela were schooled in graphic statics. Santiago Calatrava journeyed from Spain in the 1970s to study engineering at the ETH in Zurich, where he learned graphic statics and studied bridge design under Christian Menn.

THE CHALLENGE

Our immediate challenge is to find the form that a main cable in this roof will take under the estimated loading, when the maximum force in the cable is equal to the allowable strength of the cable that is being offered from stock. We will meet this challenge by using the technique that we evolved in Chapter 1, which involves drawing a *funicular polygon* and its associated force polygon to find both form and forces for the cable simultaneously. But first we must learn more about this technique.

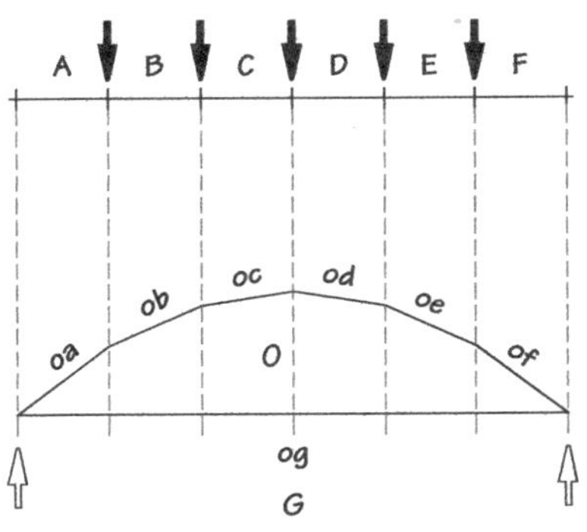

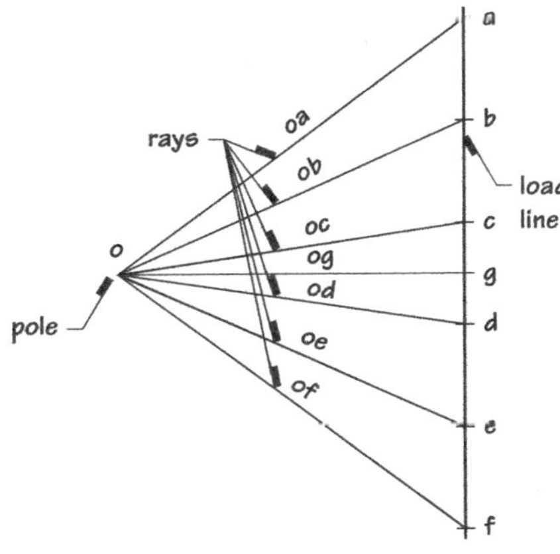

◀ **Figure 2.3** A typical force polygon for a funicular structure takes the shape of a traditional handheld fan.

▼ **Figure 2.4** With loads applied from above, a pole location to the left of the load line produces an arch, and a location to the right produces a cable.

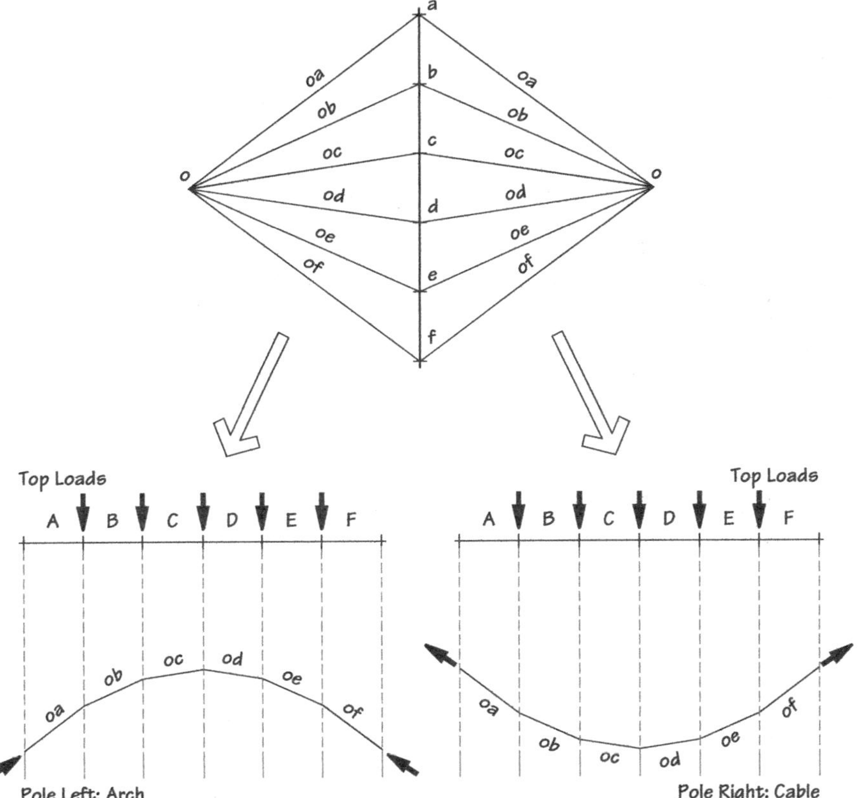

Properties of a Force Polygon for a Funicular Structure

In the previous chapter, we constructed force polygons to represent the forces in the systems of rods that supported several bridges. As the number of support points in the bridges increased, the force polygons grew more and more to resemble a traditional handheld Chinese fan. A fanlike shape is characteristic of all force polygons that relate to hanging structures, as well as to their inverted forms, funicular arched structures (Figure 2.3). A *load line*, vertical if it represents gravity loads, represents the external forces that act on the structure. The directions of the segments of the cable and the forces in those segments are represented by *rays*, vectors that radiate out to the load line from a point known as the *pole*.

The pole may lie on either side of the load line, depending on whether the structure to which it relates is an arch or a cable, and whether the external forces are shown as pushing down on the structure from above or pulling down on it from below. A common convention is to take advantage of the principle of transmissibility by showing all gravity loads as pushing down on the structure from above, regardless of their points of application in the actual structure. When this is done, the pole of a force polygon for an arch will always lie to the left of the load line, and the pole for a cable will always lie to the right (Figure 2.4).

To this point, we have worked with structures that support a series of equal loads at regular spacings, but the method is valid for unequal loads and irregular spacings as well. If the loads on a structure vary in intensity from one to the next, this variation is expressed in variable spaces between tick marks on the load line (Figure 2.5). Irregular spacings of loads on the structure are represented by varying distances between the loads on the funicular polygon.

If all the live and dead loads are gravity loads, the load line will be vertical, to reflect the vertical pull of earth's gravity. A load line for wind loads will contain horizontal and/or sloping segments, depending on the assumed directions of aerodynamic forces on the structure. The force polygon for an arch or cable that supports inclined loads will have a load line in which some or all of the segments are inclined (Figure 2.6).

A force polygon for a cable or arch is made up of a number of smaller, triangular force polygons, one for each node in the structure (Figure 2.7). When these triangles are separated from one another, it becomes apparent that each interior ray in the fanlike force polygon represents two equal forces that act in opposite directions, and therefore represents zero net force (Figure 2.8a). This phenomenon is explained by the fact that each segment of a cable pulls to the left on one of its nodes and exerts an equal pull to the right on the other node. If these zero-net-force interior rays are removed from the force polygon, only three forces remain: the load line, the first ray, and the last ray. These must be in static equilibrium. They represent, respectively, the directions and magnitudes of the external loads and the two *reactions*, the forces that must be exerted on the ends of the arch or cable to maintain it in static equilibrium (Figure 2.8b).

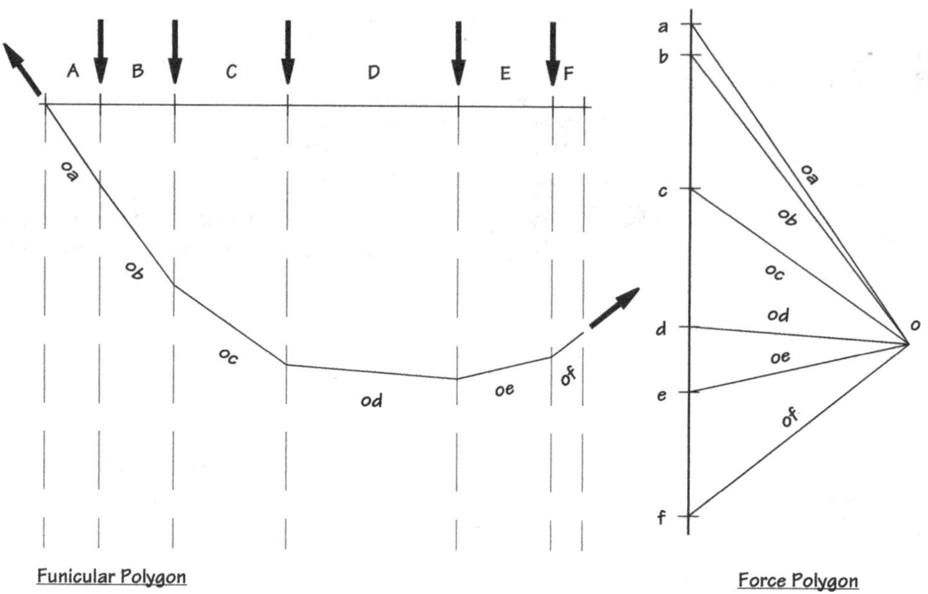

Figure 2.5 A force polygon and funicular polygon for a cable with unequal loads at unequal spacings.

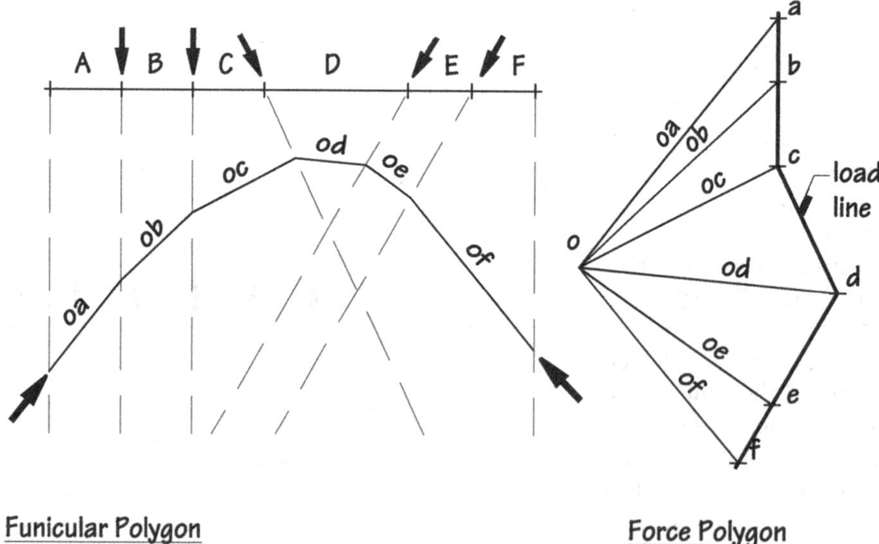

Figure 2.6 A force polygon and funicular polygon for a loading that includes inclined loads.

Pole Locations

There is an infinite number of possible pole locations with respect to a load line. These represent an infinite number of forms that are funicular for the loading that

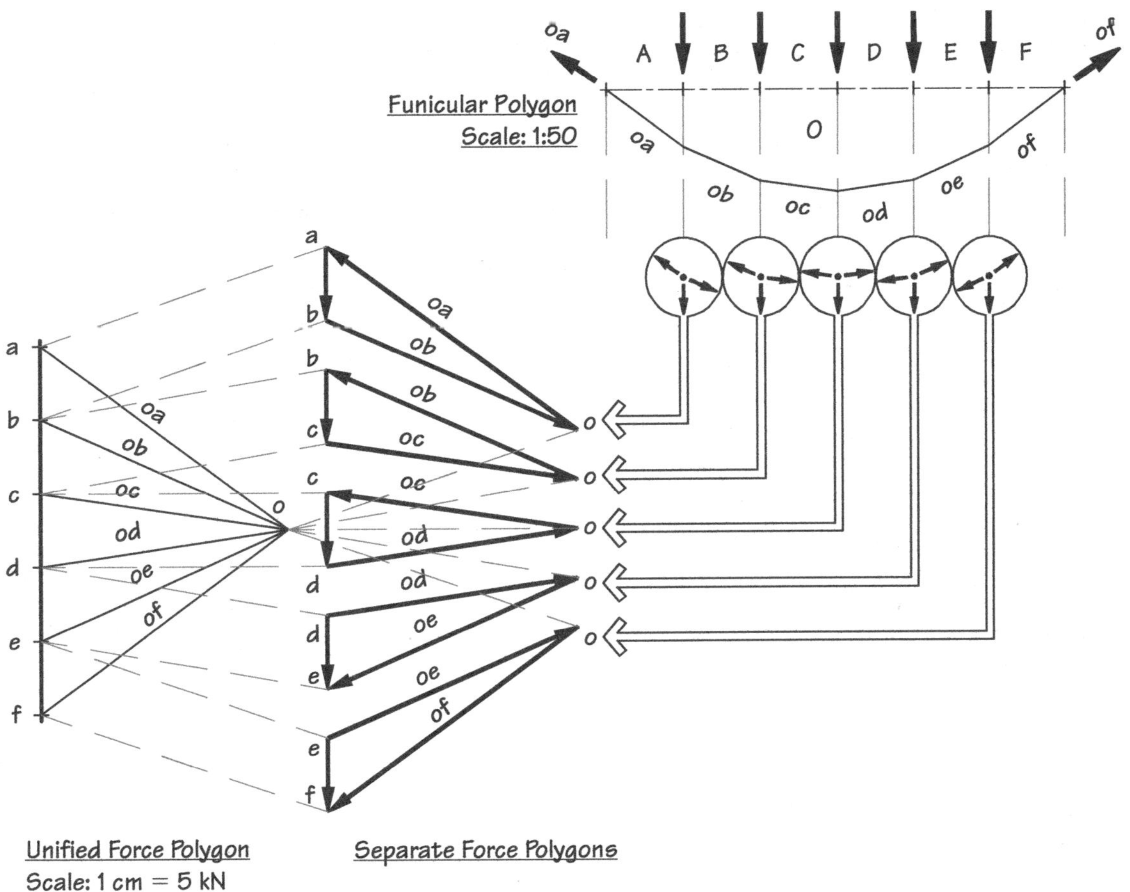

Figure 2.7 A force polygon for funicular shapes is composed of a number of smaller, triangular-force polygons, one for each node in the funicular polygon.

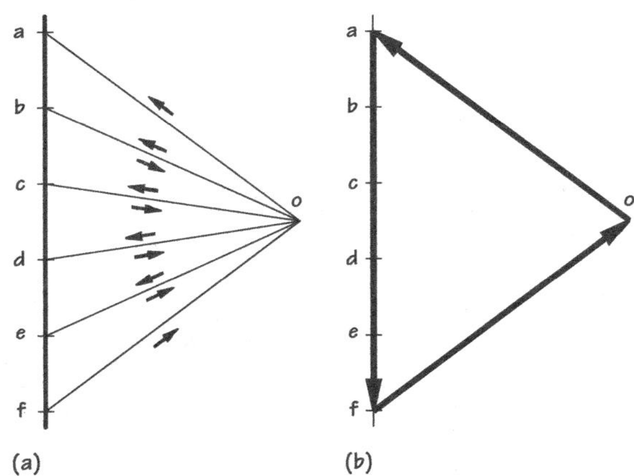

Figure 2.8 (a) Each interior ray represents two equal forces in opposing directions and is, therefore, in static equilibrium with a net value of zero force. (b) The load line and the first and last rays represent the external forces on the structure: the loads and the end reactions. These three vectors are in equilibrium.

the load line represents. Assuming for the moment that the loads on the structure are all vertical, all the same, and equally spaced, if the pole is on a line perpendicular to the center of the load line, the ends of the associated funicular polygon will lie on the same horizontal line (Figure 2.9). If the pole is raised above the center of the load line or lowered below the center, one end of the funicular polygon will be higher than the other (Figure 2.10). If the pole is moved toward the load line, the funicular polygon becomes deeper and the forces in its segments grow smaller. If the pole is moved away from the load line, the funicular polygon becomes shallower, and forces rise (Figure 2.11).

We can conclude from the preceding paragraphs that the force polygon/funicular polygon pair is a tool that is both versatile and powerful. It is versatile because it can represent any combination of loads in any orientations. Its power stems from its capability to generate good structural forms and find the forces in them with one simple graphical construction.

For the structural designer, the key to harnessing this power and versatility for a particular project is to develop ways of finding, among the infinite number of possible pole locations, the one location that will generate a funicular polygon with the desired properties. Such properties might be geometric: a funicular polygon of the desired span and vertical rise, or one that comes to earth at particular elevations. They might be structural: a funicular polygon whose maximum force is a predetermined value. Or they might be a combination of structural and geometric properties. We will develop several ways of finding appropriate pole locations in these early chapters.

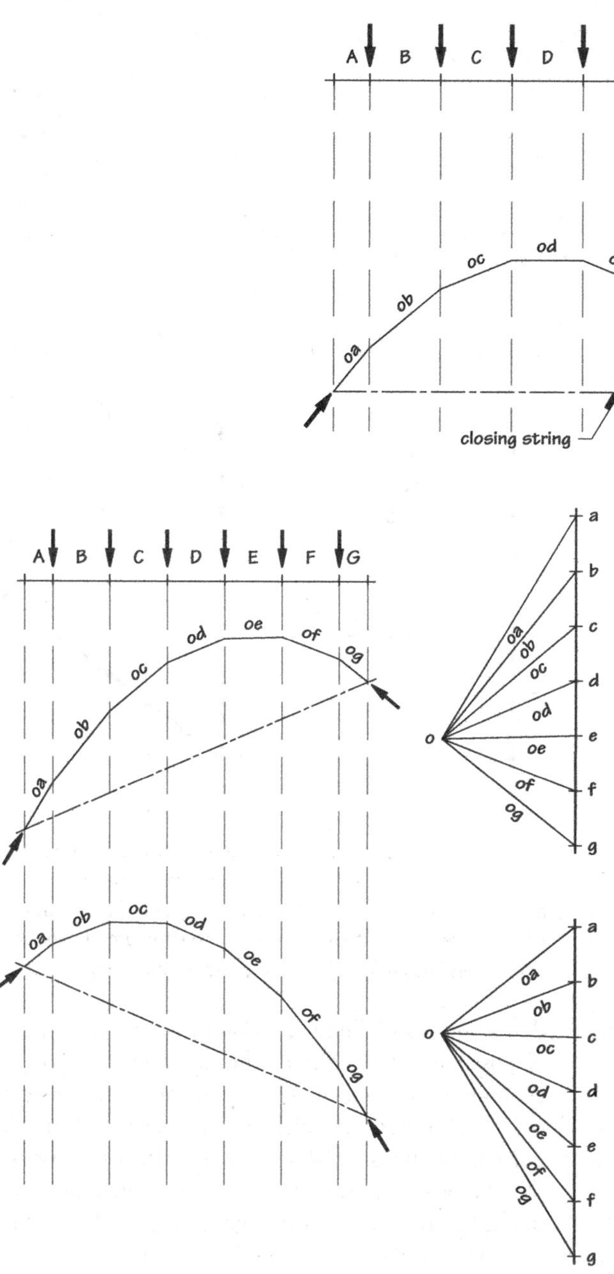

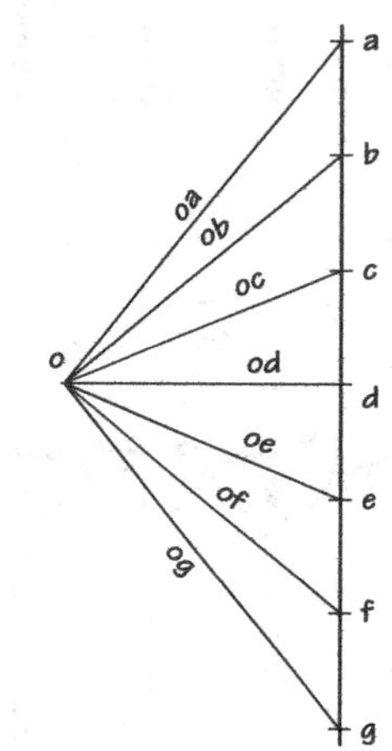

▲**Figure 2.9** If the pole lies on a line perpendicular to the center of the load line, the funicular polygon for a structure with equal loads at equal spacing will have a horizontal closing string.

◀**Figure 2.10** Raising and lowering the pole has the effect of changing the relative elevations of the ends of the funicular polygon.

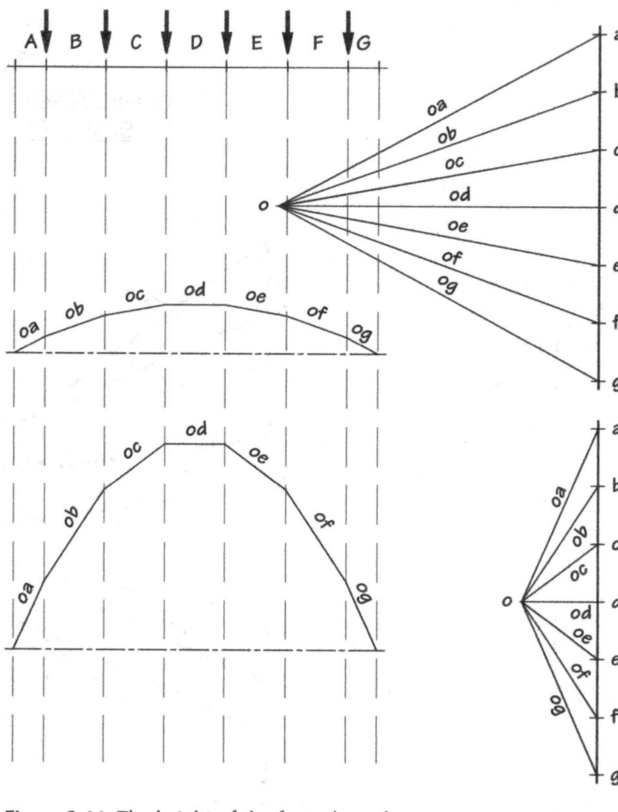

Figure 2.11 The height of the funicular polygon varies inversely with the distance of the pole from the load line.

Family of Funicular Forms

Because of its flexibility, when a cable is strung across a span and loads are applied to it, it can resist the loads only by means of internal tensile forces. To do this, as we learned in the previous chapter, it immediately shapes itself in such a way that it is in axial tension at every point along its length. In other words, it is funicular for that particular combination of loads and support conditions.

If we keep the span and loads constant but change the length of the cable or the heights of its supports with relation to one another, the cable will find funicular forms for these changed conditions, all of them members of a *family of funicular forms* (Figure 2.12). With the aid of a force polygon and a funicular polygon, we can find as many of the forms in this family as we wish.

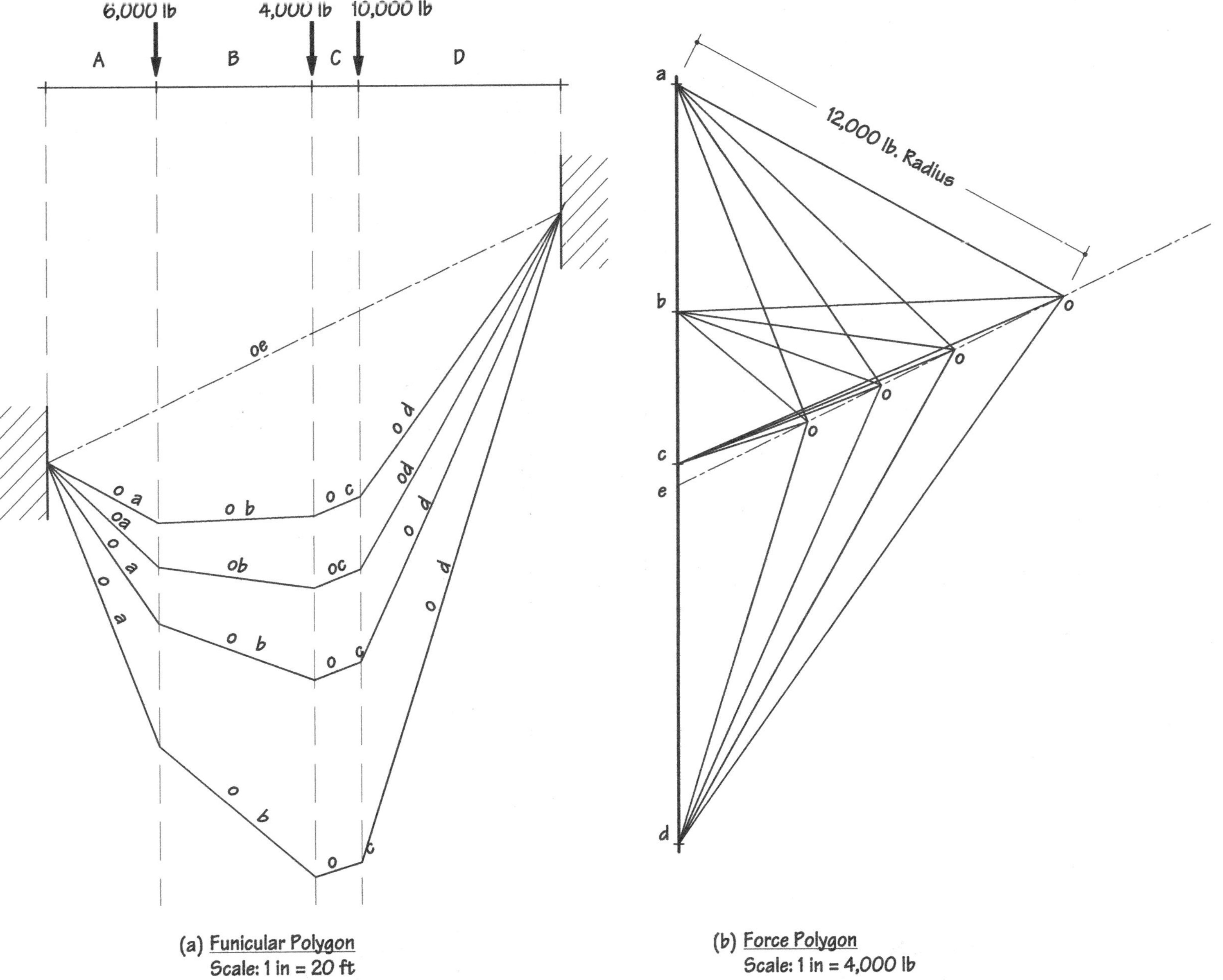

Figure 2.12 A family of funicular forms and their associated force polygons superimposed upon one another. Those on this page all have the same closing string. Those on the following page, part (b), have different closing strings but are still part of the same family.

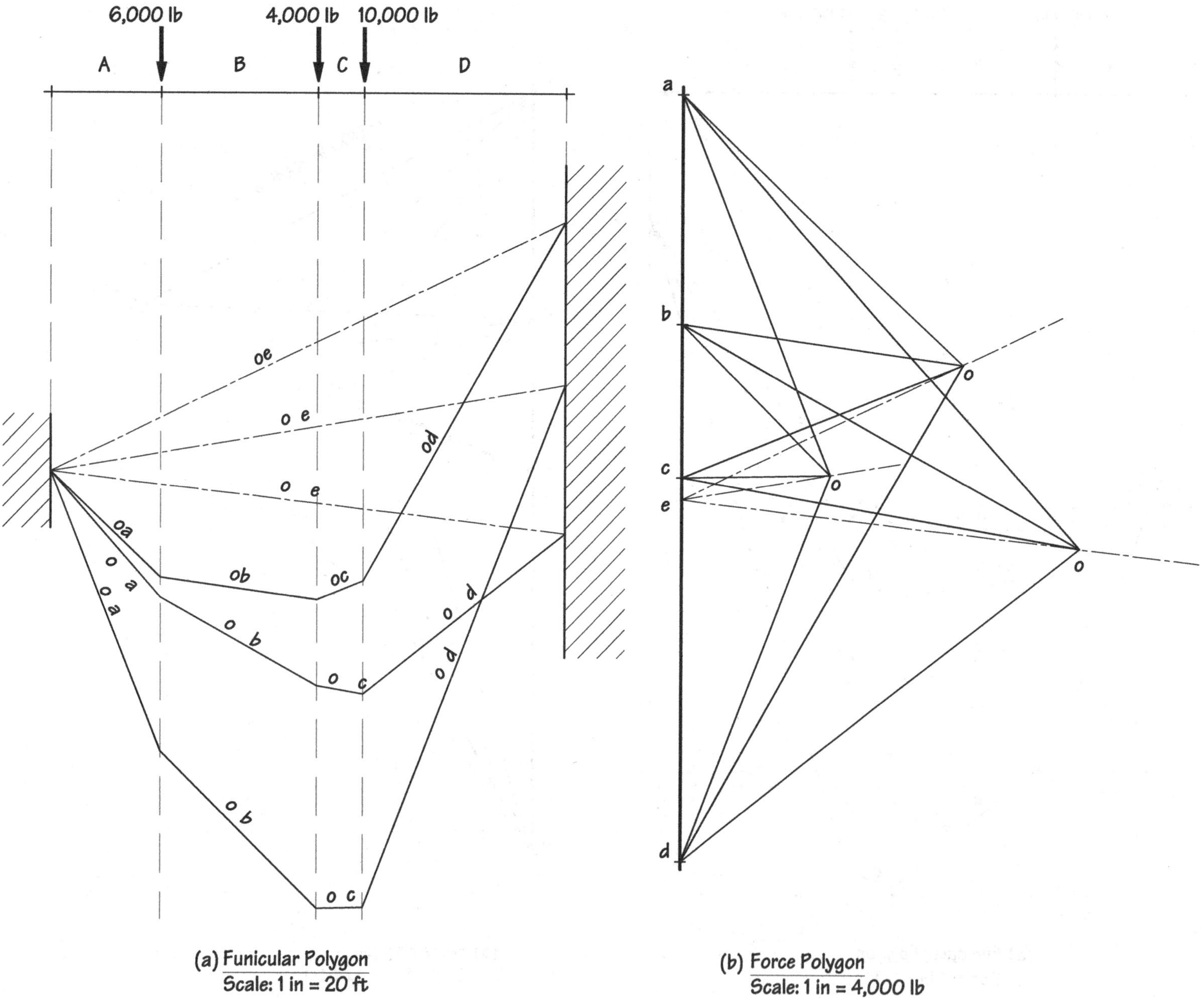

(a) Funicular Polygon
Scale: 1 in = 20 ft

(b) Force Polygon
Scale: 1 in = 4,000 lb

Figure 2.12 *(Continued)*

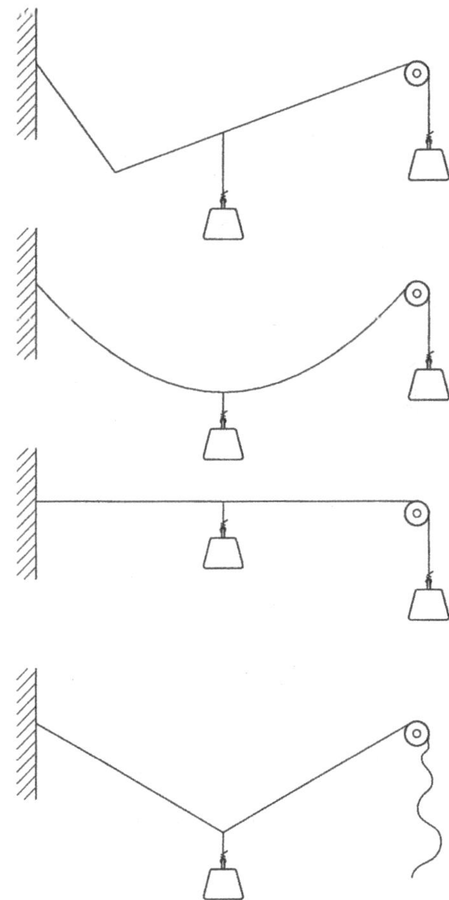

Figure 2.13 Shapes that cables cannot take.

We cannot force a cable to take a *nonfunicular* shape (Figure 2.13). We recognize immediately when a shape is grossly nonfunicular, because we learned in childhood through everyday experience what sort of shape a rope, string, or cable will take when loaded. If a nonfunicular shape were to be adopted for our structure, it would have to be made of a much thicker element that could resist bending, such as a beam made of steel, reinforced concrete, or laminated wood. **Thus, when we design a cable structure, our task is not to invent a form for the cable, but by means of the force polygon/funicular polygon pair to discover what shapes the cable will take under the assumed conditions of support and loading, and to find among these shapes the one that best suits our needs.**

Components of Forces

In Chapter 1, we learned to add two or more force vectors to find a single force that will have the same effect as the two vectors acting together. We can also work backward to convert a single force into two or more forces that will have the same effect. This technique is generally used for *resolving* an inclined force into two forces that lie in horizontal and vertical planes (Figure 2.14). These two forces are called the *horizontal component* and *vertical component* of the original force. Resolution enables us to convert a complex system of forces at various angles to an orderly system of horizontal and vertical forces that can easily be added together.

As a way of understanding how components of forces work, imagine for a moment that we are in the center of a city like New York or Chicago whose streets define a grid of rectangular blocks (Figure 2.15) and that we want to walk from point *A* to point *B*. There are many possible paths we can take. The net result of our walk, regardless of the path we choose, is the diagonal dimension *d*. Furthermore, if we add up for any path the north-south blocks that we walk, and all the east-west blocks, counting northward and eastward walks as positive blocks (because they get us nearer to our goal) and southward and westward as negative, we will find that these sums always come to three blocks east and four blocks north, which are the orthogonal (right-angle) components of the diagonal distance from *A* to *B*. Component forces act in much the same way.

If we draw a rectangular box over a fanlike force polygon that has a vertical load line, its horizontal dimension is the horizontal component of all of its rays (Figure 2.16). This tells us that in a cable or funicular arch that supports only vertical loads, the horizontal component of force is constant throughout the span. The vertical components, however, vary considerably.

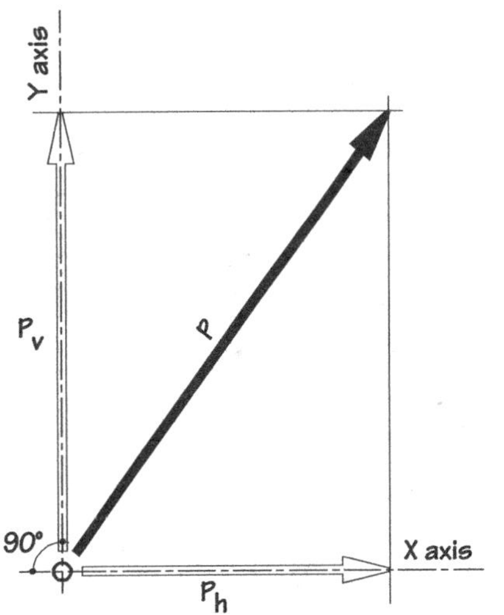

Figure 2.14 Horizontal and vertical components of a force.

Static Equilibrium

When we design a structure, we want it to be *static*, which means that we want it to stand still. (The word comes from the Latin *staticos*, which means "causing to stand.") When all the forces that act on a body are concurrent, there are two conditions that must both be satisfied in order for the body not to move, that is, for the body to be in *static equilibrium*:

1. The sum of the force components in the horizontal direction must be zero.
2. The sum of the force components in the vertical direction must be zero.

These conditions are expressed symbolically as:

$$\sum F_h = 0 \qquad [2\text{-}1]$$

$$\sum F_v = 0 \qquad [2\text{-}2]$$

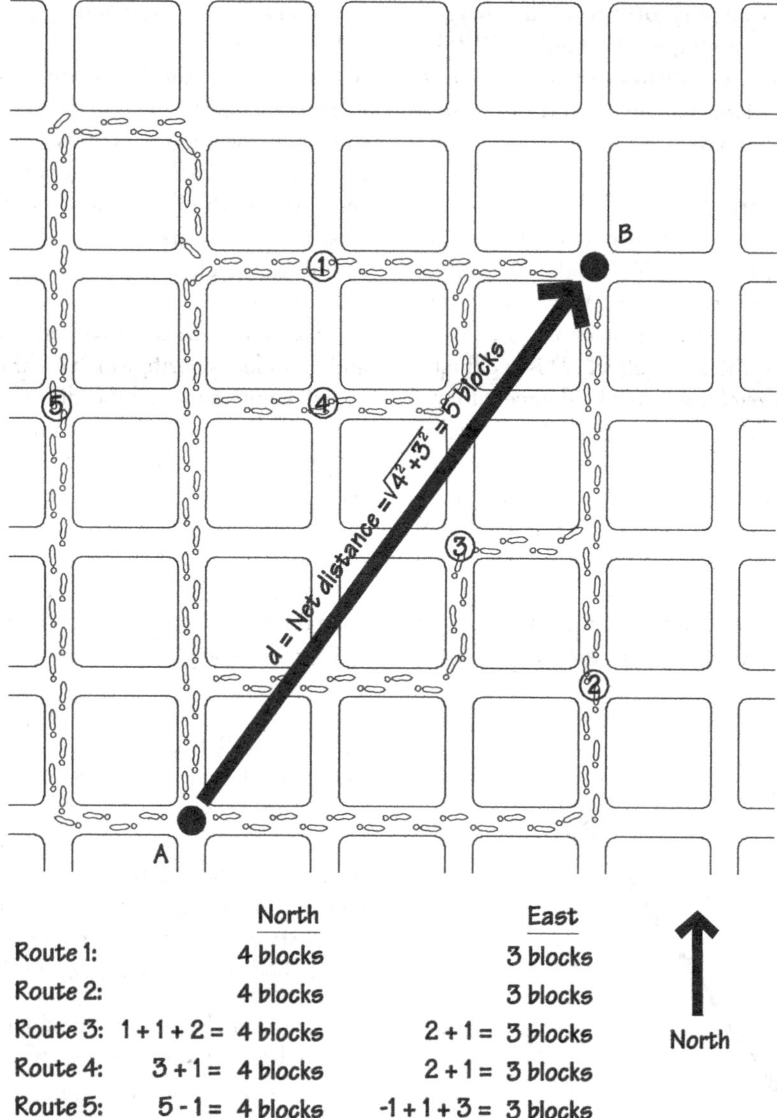

Figure 2.15 Components and resultants of forces can be compared to a set of alternative paths between two points in a city. All the paths have the same resultant, *R*, which is five blocks in length. All the paths have the same net distance walked, which is seven blocks.

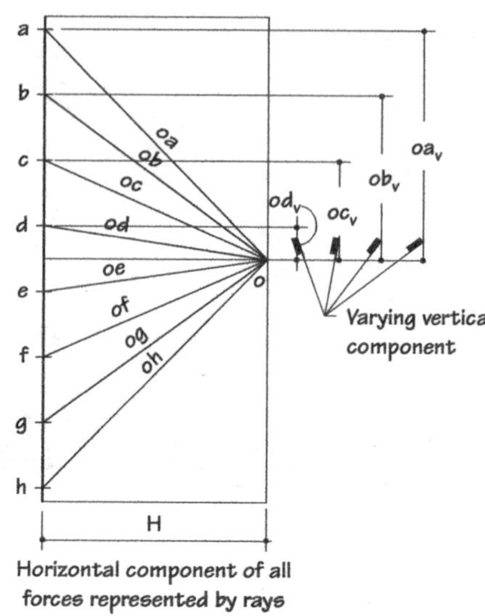

Figure 2.16 Components of forces in a force polygon for a funicular shape. All rays have the same horizontal component, but their vertical components vary.

These are read as: "The sum of the horizontal components of force equals zero" and "The sum of the vertical components of force equals zero." These expressions assume that all the forces in the system lie in the same plane and that they have been resolved into horizontal and vertical components. (It is also true, though seldom utilized, that static equilibrium is proven if the sums of the components of forces in **any** two directions are both zero. The directions do not need to be mutually perpendicular.)

DESIGNING THE CABLE ROOF

We are now ready to use the force polygon and funicular polygon as tools to meet the design challenge given at the beginning of this chapter, which is to find the form and forces for a typical cable in the roof of the high-speed bus terminal that we are designing, and to determine whether we can use the 2–1/8-in. diameter cable that has been offered at an advantageous price.

We estimated the total load at 60 lb per sq ft of roof surface. For simplicity, this is measured in *horizontal projection* rather than along the actual contours of the roof (Figure 2.17). The main cables are spaced 20 ft apart. The struts and hangers that transfer load from the roof to the cable are also spaced at 20 ft in both directions. Thus, the tributary area of each strut or hanger is (20 ft)(20 ft) = 400 ft². The total load at each point on the cable is this tributary area times the unit load of 60 psf, which is 24,000 lb. We will call this 24 kips (kilopounds) for convenience. Bow's notation

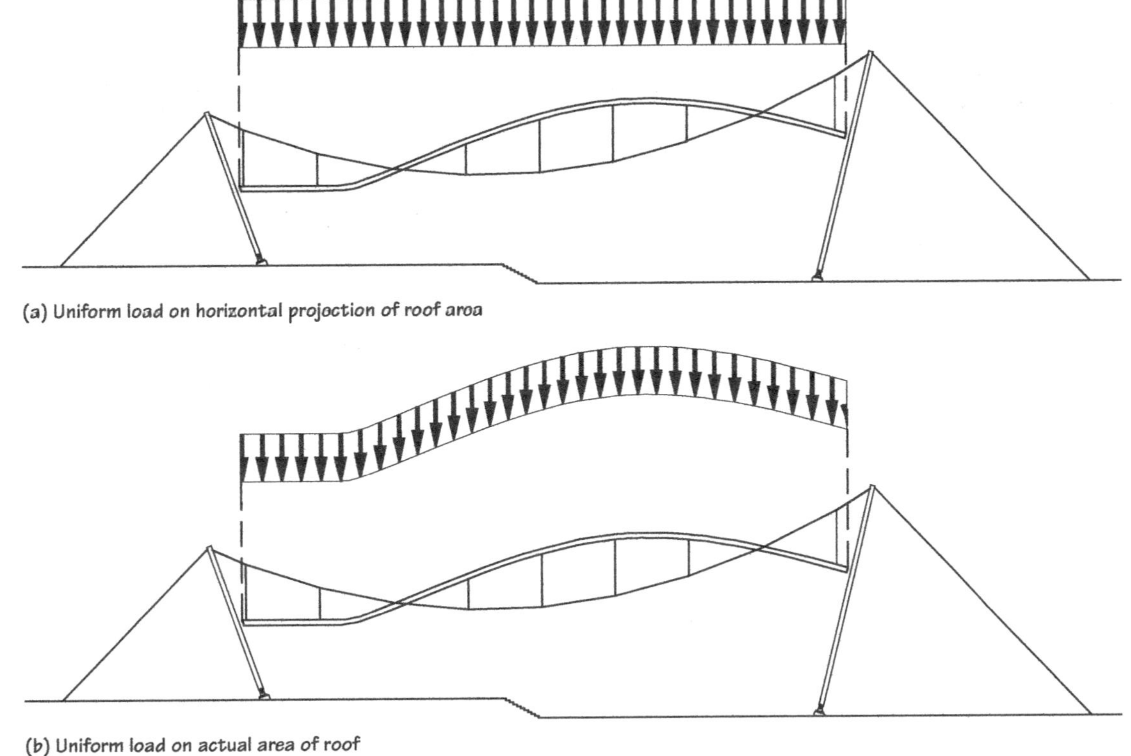

(a) Uniform load on horizontal projection of roof area
(b) Uniform load on actual area of roof

Figure 2.17 Two possible assumptions about load distribution on the hanging roof.

has already been applied to the diagram of the roof by placing uppercase letters in the spaces between the external forces on the cable, reserving the letter *O* for the space below the main cable. (See Worksheet 2A, Figure 2.18.)

Based on the loading information given, we draw a load line for the cable. It consists of nine vertical segments that represent the loads brought to the cable by the nine struts and hangers. Bow's notation has been applied to these segments by labeling the tick marks with lowercase letters that correspond to the uppercase letters on the section drawing. For example, the 24-kip load that lies between *A* and *B* on the section drawing becomes segment *ab* of the load line.

Pole-finding

We seek a pole location that will satisfy the given conditions:

- The ends of the cable must meet the connection points at the tops of the masts, 180 ft apart and 20 ft different in height.
- The cable must not descend lower than 28 ft above the lower floor level of the terminal.
- The maximum force in the cable must be equal to or less than its allowable strength.

STEEL CABLES

A *cable* is any flexible tension member that is made up of steel wires. The wires for structural cables are produced by rolling hot steel into thin rods, then pulling (*drawing*) the cooled rods at room temperature through a succession of smaller and smaller circular holes in hardened steel plates (*dies*) to reduce their diameters by 65 to 75 percent. This process strengthens the steel by *cold-working* its crystalline microstructure. The wires that it produces have allowable tensile stresses that are six to seven times higher than those of ordinary structural steel. There are three types of cables, two of which are produced in factories (Figure 2.19):

- *Strand* (a) is a cable made up of steel wires formed helically in concentric layers around a center wire.
- *Wire rope* (b) is composed of a number of strands laid helically around a stranded core. Wire rope is more flexible than strand, which is an advantage in applications where it must run around pulleys, such as construction cranes and elevators. A strand has higher tensile strength than a wire rope of the same diameter and is more suitable for structures in general, including the roof we are designing.
- A third type, *parallel wire cable* (c), is used only for very large suspension bridges. It is manufactured in place on the bridge by a traveling wheel that moves back and forth along the path of the cable, laying two or more parallel wires at each pass. When all the wires have been placed, they are clamped into a compact circular bundle and wrapped tightly with a winding of small-diameter wire.

Wires for cables are coated with zinc to make them resistant to corrosion. The heaviest zinc coating, Class C, gives maximum protection for bridges that cross saltwater, but the heavy coating means that fewer wires will fit into a cable of a given diameter. Thus, a cable made entirely of wires with the thinnest coating, Class A, is the strongest for its size.

To produce strand, the coated wires are twisted together by heavy machines. The cable is finished by drawing it through a circular die that squeezes

Worksheet - 2A

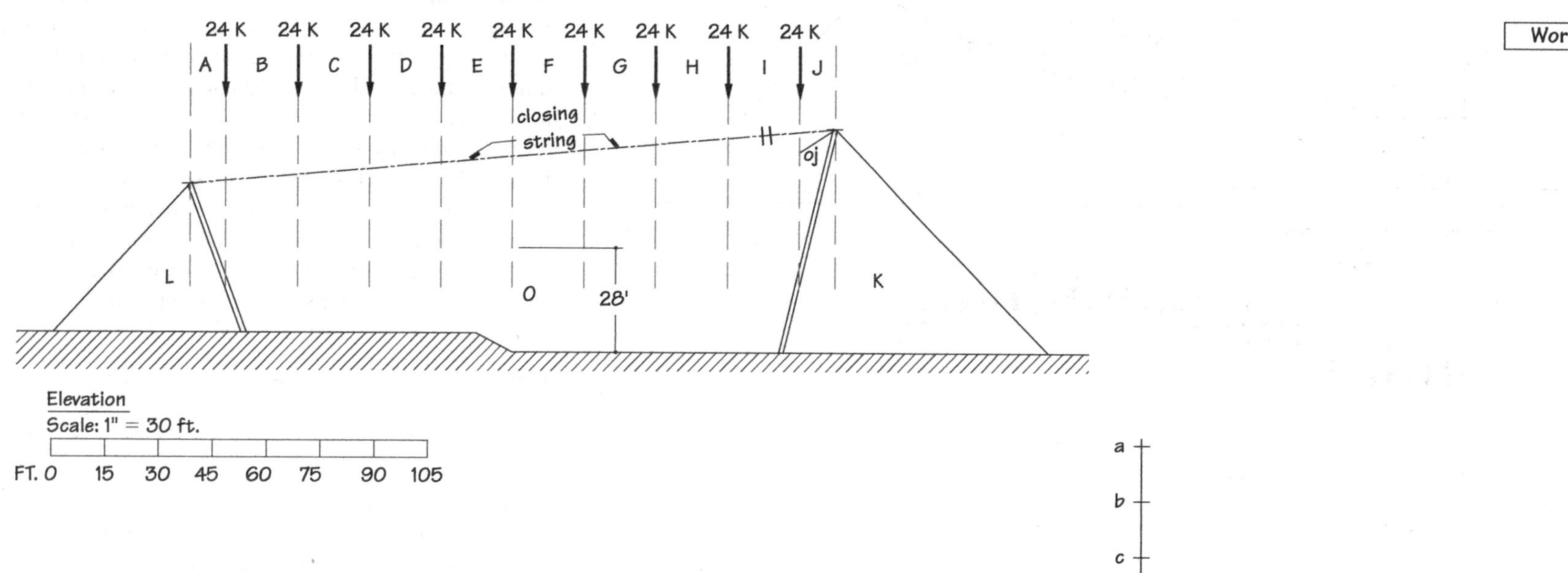

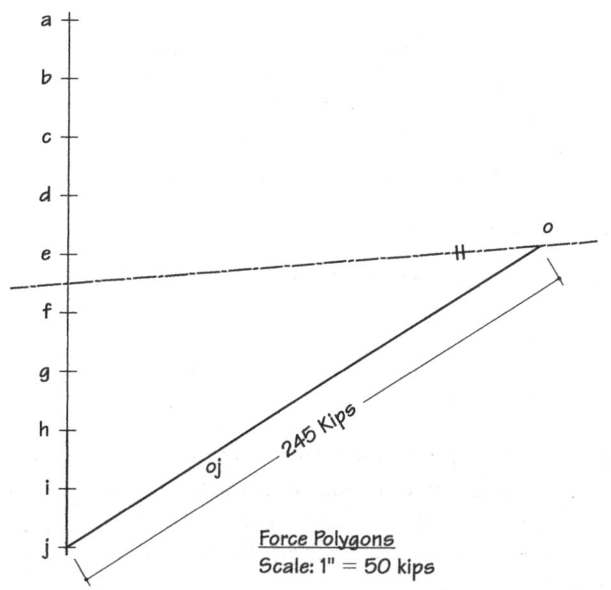

Hanging Roof

This worksheet allows you to develop the force polygon and funicular polygon for the cable-supported roof of the high-speed bus terminal described in this chapter. Remember from the text the following information:

- We estimated the total load at 60 pounds per square foot of roof surface, measured in horizontal projection.
- The main cables are spaced 20 ft. apart. The struts and hangers that transfer load from the roof to the cable are also spaced at 20 feet in both directions.
- The tributary area of each strut or hanger is (20 ft)(20 ft)=400 ft^2.
- Therefore, the total load at each point on the cable is this tributary area times the unit load of 60 psf, which is 24,000 lb. We will call this 24 kips (kilopounds) for convenience.
- This worksheet incorporates Bows notation, using capital letters in the spaces between the external forces on the cable, and reserving the letter O for the space below the main cable.

Based on these loads, we will use these diagrams to find the form of the cable.

Figure 2.18 A reduced copy of Worksheet 2A, finding form and forces for the bus terminal roof. You may download a full-sized copy of this worksheet from the supplemental site. This reproduction is not to scale.

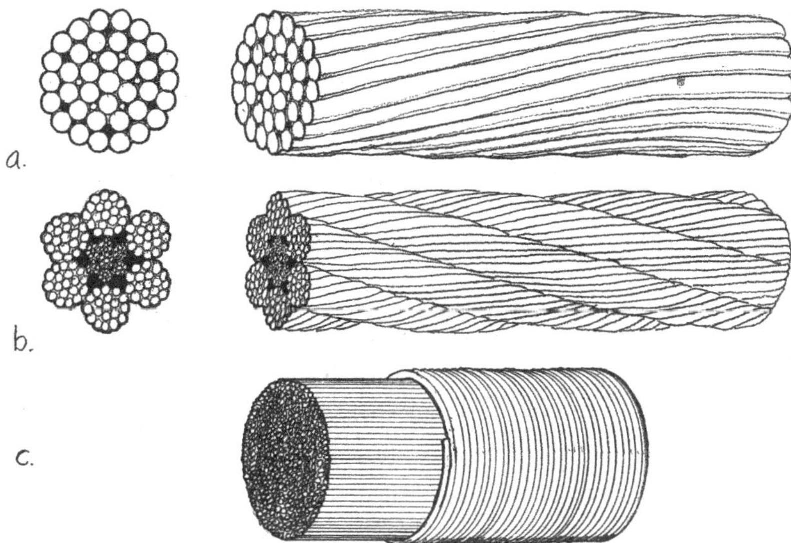

▲ **Figure 2.19** Three types of steel cables: (a) strand, (b) wire rope, and (c) parallel wire cable. Parallel wire cables are used only for large bridges.

▶ **Figure 2.20** Properties of zinc-coated strand.

Nominal Diameter in Inches	Approximate Minimum Breaking Strength in Tons of 2000 lbs. — Class "A" Coating Throughout	Class "A" Coating Inner Wires Class "B" Coating Outer Wires	Class "A" Coating Inner Wires Class "C" Coating Outer Wires	Approx. Metallic Area in Sq. In.	Approx. Weight Per Ft. in Lbs.
1/2	15.0	14.5	14.2	0.150	0.52
9/16	19.0	18.4	18.0	.190	.66
5/8	24.0	23.3	22.8	.234	.82
11/16	29.0	28.1	27.5	.284	.99
3/4	34.0	33.0	32.3	.338	1.18
13/16	40.0	38.8	38.0	.396	1.39
7/8	46.0	44.6	43.7	.459	1.61
15/16	54.0	52.4	51.3	.527	1.85
1	61.0	59.2	57.9	.600	2.10
1 1/16	69.0	66.9	65.5	.677	2.37
1 1/8	78.0	75.7	74.1	.759	2.66
1 3/16	86.0	83.4	81.7	.846	2.96
1 1/4	96.0	94.1	92.2	.938	3.28
1 5/16	106.0	104.0	102.0	1.03	3.62
1 3/8	116.0	114.0	111.0	1.13	3.97
1 7/16	126.0	123.0	121.0	1.24	4.34
1 1/2	138.0	135.0	132.0	1.35	4.73
1 9/16	150.0	147.0	144.0	1.47	5.13
1 5/8	162.0	159.0	155.0	1.59	5.55
1 11/16	176.0	172.0	169.0	1.71	5.98
1 3/4	188.0	184.0	180.0	1.84	6.43
1 13/16	202.0	198.0	194.0	1.97	6.90
1 7/8	216.0	212.0	207.0	2.11	7.39
1 15/16	230.0	226.0	221.0	2.25	7.89
2	245.0	241.0	238.0	2.40	8.40
2 1/16	261.0	257.0	253.0	2.55	8.94
2 1/8	277.0	273.0	269.0	2.71	9.49
2 3/16	293.0	289.0	284.0	2.87	10.05
2 1/4	310.0	305.0	301.0	3.04	10.64
2 5/16	327.0	322.0	317.0	3.21	11.24
2 3/8	344.0	339.0	334.0	3.38	11.85
2 7/16	360.0	355.0	349.0	3.57	12.48
2 1/2	376.0	370.0	365.0	3.75	13.13
2 9/16	392.0	386.0	380.0	3.94	13.80
2 5/8	417.0	411.0	404.0	4.13	14.47
2 11/16	432.0	425.0	419.0	4.33	15.16
2 3/4	452.0	445.0	438.0	4.54	15.88
2 7/8	494.0	486.0	479.0	4.96	17.36
3	538.0	530.0	522.0	5.40	18.90
3 1/8	584.0	575.0	566.0	5.86	20.51
3 1/4	625.0	616.0	606.0	6.34	22.18
3 3/8	673.0	663.0	653.0	6.83	23.92
3 1/2	724.0	714.0	702.0	7.35	25.73
3 5/8	768.0	757.0	745.0	7.88	27.60
3 3/4	822.0	810.0	797.0	8.44	29.53
3 7/8	878.0	865.0	852.0	9.01	31.53
4	925.0	911.0	897.0	9.60	33.60

the wires tightly together and gives the cable its final diameter. It is then coiled on reels for transportation.

Structural strands are manufactured in a number of standard diameters to make available a wide array of strengths, as shown in Figure 2.20. The figures given in this table are *breaking strengths*, which must be reduced by a *factor of safety* before using them to design a structure. A typical factor of safety for cable roofs is 2.2, which keeps the stresses in the cables low enough that even a fairly large overload on the roof, such as a very heavy snowstorm, will not break the cables or stretch them permanently.

We consult this table to find the breaking strength for the 2–1/8-in. cable that we hope to use in the bus terminal roof. In an earlier telephone call to the warehouse where the cable is stored, we determined that it has the most durable zinc coatings on its wires, Class A inner and Class C outer. The table tells us that this cable has a breaking strength of 269 tons, which is 538 kips. The allowable tension (f_{allow}) is 538 kips divided by the factor of safety, 2.2, which is 245 kips.

Cable materials other than steel are coming into use in experimental structures and will become more common as we gain experience with them. *Glass fiber* cables are stronger than ones of comparable diameter made of steel, but stretch considerably more under load than steel does. *Carbon fiber* and *aramid fiber* cables are both stronger and less stretchy than steel or glass. They are, however, much more costly at the time of this writing.

JOHN AUGUSTUS ROEBLING

The German-born John Augustus Roebling (1806–1869) made previously unimaginable bridge designs feasible and affordable. Educated as a civil engineer and completing a thesis on suspension bridge design, Roebling also studied with the philosopher Georg Wilhelm Hegel before immigrating to the United States in 1831. In contrast to his native Germany, ravaged by war, the American landscape in which he settled was fertile ground for new railways, canals, and bridges. Seeking ways to improve ropes for canal transportation, Roebling created steel-wire ropes at his own workshop and factory in Saxonburg, Pennsylvania in 1841. By 1844 he won a commission to use his rope in a suspended aqueduct, and then in a series of rail bridges in and beyond Pittsburgh. In 1867, he completed the 1057-ft span of the Cincinnati–Covington bridge, now known as the John A. Roebling Bridge. It was the world's longest suspension bridge until the Brooklyn Bridge, which Roebling began designing in New York City in 1867. Construction was underway by 1869, but Roebling did not live to see it completed. While he was overseeing an early stage of construction, his toes were crushed by a ferry and required amputation. He refused further medical treatment and soon died of tetanus. Roebling's sons Washington and Charles, along with Washington's wife Emily, completed the bridge and continued his work with bridges and wire rope innovations.

MEETING THE CHALLENGE: FINDING FORM AND FORCES FOR THE CABLE

The Closing String

We are going to base our form-finding method in part on the properties of the *closing string*, which is a straight line drawn from one end of a funicular polygon to the other. In our structure, the closing string is a line that passes through the points of attachment of the cable to the two masts. We draw this line on the section drawing in Figure 2.21. The closing string may be thought of as a baseline for the curve of the funicular polygon.

On any force polygon/funicular polygon system subjected to vertical loads only, a ray drawn from the pole parallel to the closing string will divide the load line into the vertical components of the reactions at the ends of the funicular polygon. In our structure, the load on the cable is uniform from one end to the other. This means that the vertical components of the reactions are the same, each being half of the total load on the cable. Accordingly, we measure the load line to find its center point, which is halfway between *e* and *f*, and draw a line parallel to the closing string through this point. The pole for the funicular polygon that we seek must lie somewhere on this line (Figure 2.21).

To find where on this line this pole is situated, we use another piece of information that we have already developed: The force in the cable cannot exceed 245 kips. This maximum allowable force will be represented by the length of the longest ray on the force polygon. By inspection of the force polygon, we see that ray *oj* will be the longest, due to the inclination of the ray that we have just drawn parallel to the closing string. We draw ray *oj* as a line that starts at *j*, ends on the ray parallel to the closing string, and is 245 kips in length at the given scale. Ideally, we would do this by setting a compass to a scaled radius of 245 kips, placing its point at *j* on the load line, and drawing an arc that intersects the ray that is parallel to the closing string; but it is sufficient to measure carefully with a scale instead. The intersection of these two rays is *o*, the pole location we are seeking.

From this pole, we construct the remainder of the rays, working from bottom to top on the force polygon (Figure 2.22). As we draw each ray, we draw a segment of the cable parallel to it on the funicular polygon, connecting each segment accurately to the one previously drawn. We use Bow's notation to be sure that each cable segment is properly drawn: The cable segment *oa* must be parallel to ray *oa*, and must lie within vertical space *A* on the funicular polygon. If we draw with a normal degree of precision, the last segment of the funicular polygon that we draw will arrive at the connector plate atop the left-hand mast as if by magic.

We measure each ray to find the value of the force that it represents and enter these forces on the segments of the cable on the section drawing of the building. We note that the cable does not descend quite as far as the 28-ft limit that was established as a condition of the design. If it had sagged too low, we would have to reduce the span a bit, increase the height of the masts, or specify a stronger cable.

The maximum vertical distance between a cable and its closing string is called its *sag*, *s*. The sag divided by the span of the cable in horizontal projection is the *sag ratio, n*:

$$\text{sag ratio} = \text{sag/span}$$
$$n = s/L \qquad [2\text{-}3]$$

For the structure we are designing, the sag scales at about 23.5 ft and the span is 180 ft Thus:

$$n = 23.5\ \text{ft}/180\ \text{ft} = 0.13$$

Sag ratios for cable roofs can go as low as 0.05. Our roof has more than twice the minimum sag. The practical consequence of this is that it has lower-than-average forces in its cables and could be flattened considerably and still remain feasible, provided that a sufficiently strong cable is available. For suspension bridges, sag ratios generally fall in the range of 0.8 to 0.125.

This completes the finding of the form of the cable and the forces in it. Because the cable is loaded with discrete vertical forces 20 ft apart, its funicular polygon will be made up of straight-line segments whose horizontal projections are each 20 ft long.

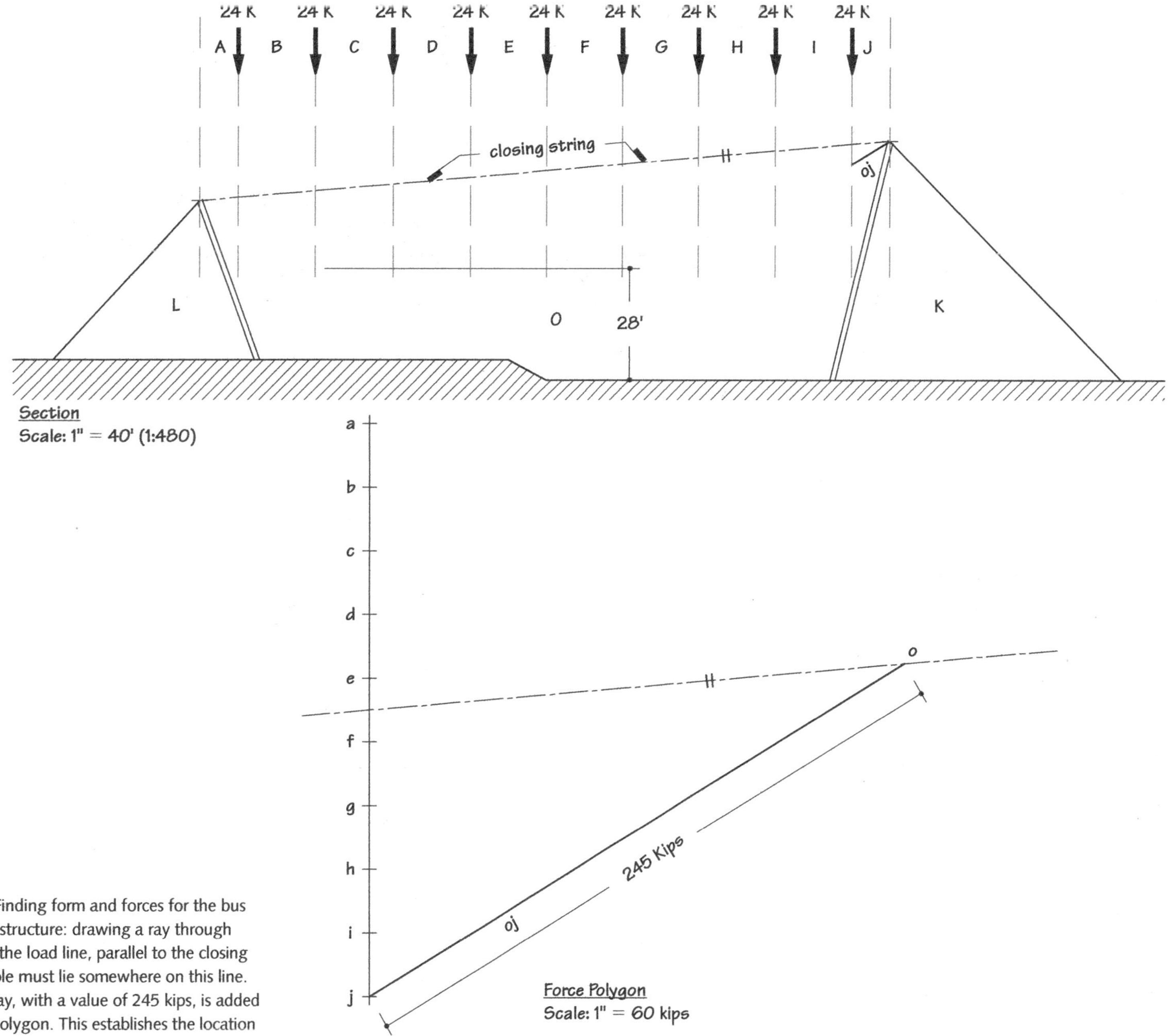

Figure 2.21 Finding form and forces for the bus terminal roof structure: drawing a ray through the center of the load line, parallel to the closing string. The pole must lie somewhere on this line. The longest ray, with a value of 245 kips, is added to the force polygon. This establishes the location of the pole, *o*.

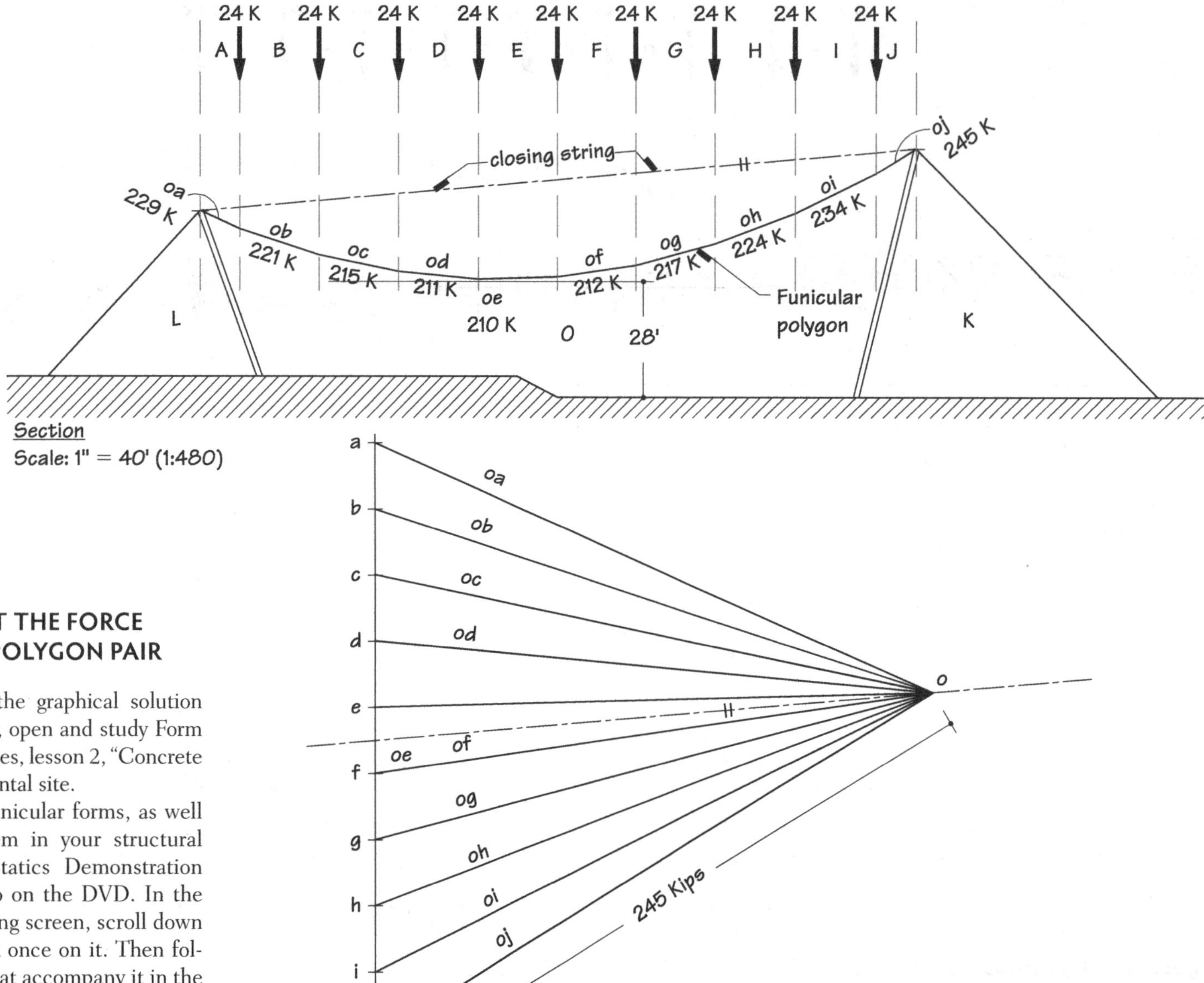

Figure 2.22 Completing the finding of form and forces for the main cables.

LEARNING MORE ABOUT THE FORCE POLYGON/FUNICULAR POLYGON PAIR

For an easy introduction to the graphical solution technique used in this chapter, open and study Form and Forces Graphical Techniques, lesson 2, "Concrete Arch Bridge," on the supplemental site.

To gain familiarity with funicular forms, as well as a facility in handling them in your structural design work, open Active Statics Demonstration 2 for Cables and Arches, also on the DVD. In the left-hand column of the opening screen, scroll down to "Hanging Cable," and click once on it. Then follow the written instructions that accompany it in the right-hand column.

Finding Forces in the Masts and Backstays

To complete the design of the roof structure, we need to know the magnitudes of the forces in the masts and backstays.

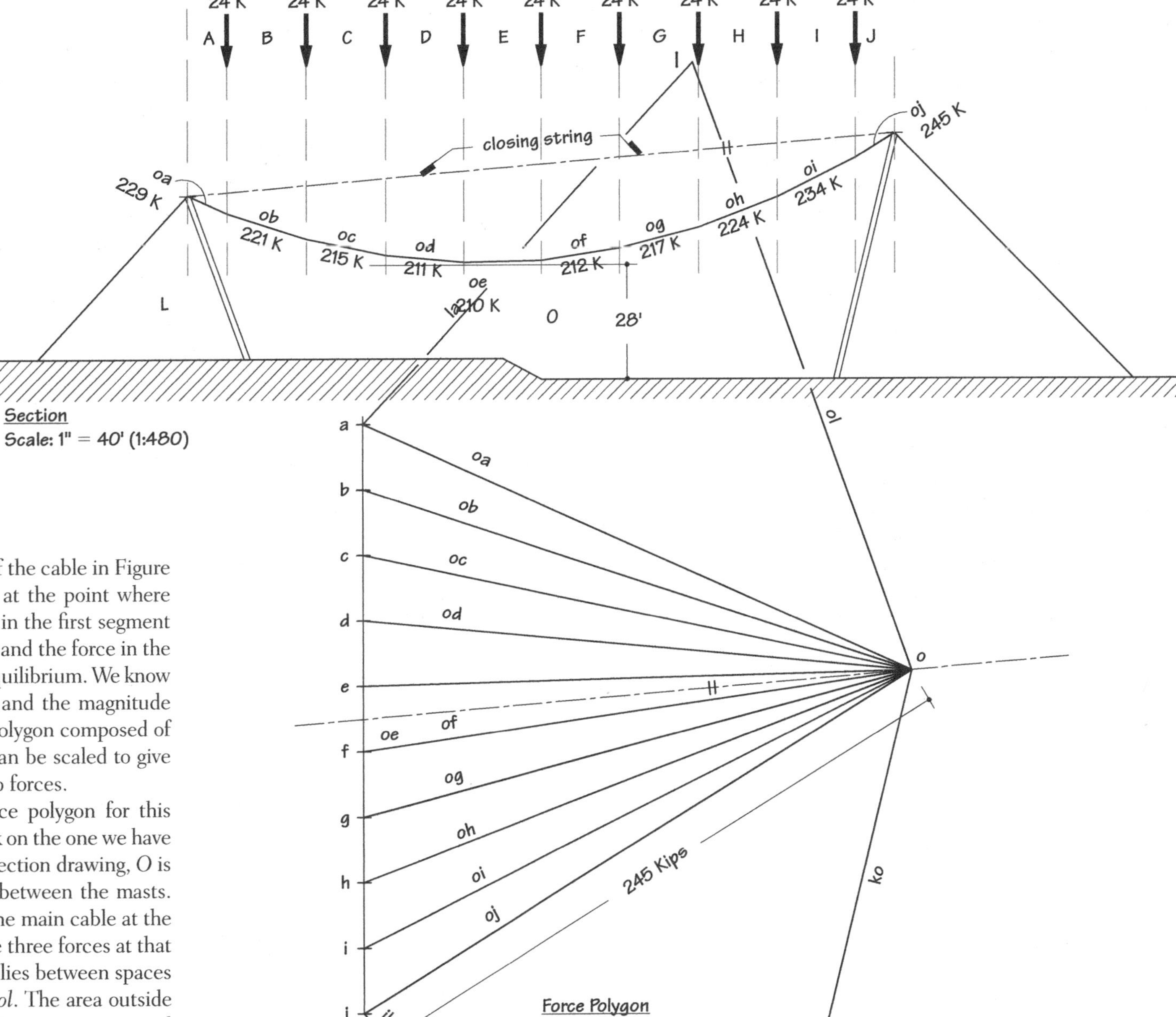

Figure 2.23 Finding forces in the masts and backstays.

Looking at the left-hand end of the cable in Figure 2.22, three forces are concurrent at the point where the cable joins the mast: the force in the first segment of the cable, the force in the mast, and the force in the backstay. These must be in static equilibrium. We know the directions of all three forces, and the magnitude of the force in the cable. A force polygon composed of the vectors of these three forces can be scaled to give us the magnitudes of the other two forces.

Rather than begin a new force polygon for this purpose, we will continue our work on the one we have just drawn (Figure 2.23). On the section drawing, *O* is the space beneath the cable and between the masts. Vector *oa* represents the force in the main cable at the left-hand mast, which is one of the three forces at that point. Because the left-hand mast lies between spaces *O* and *L*, the force in the mast is *ol*. The area outside the left backstay is *A*, because there is no external force acting on the system between the label *A* to the left of the first load arrow and the backstay. This means that the force in the backstay is named *la*.

We turn our attention to the force polygon, where the letters *a* and *o* already appear. The force in the mast, *ol*, is represented by a vector drawn through *o* on the force polygon parallel to the axis of the mast. The force in the backstay, *la*, is represented by a vector through *a* on the force polygon parallel to the backstay. The point of intersection of these two vectors is labeled *l*, the letter common to both their names. We scale *ol* and *la* to find that the backstay force is about 175 kips and the force in the mast is about 230 kips. We repeat this process for the other mast, *ok*, and backstay, *jk*.

Now we examine the force polygon to discover ways to reduce the forces in these four members, the masts and the backstays. Looking at vectors *la* and *ol*, it is apparent that if the bottom end of the backstay is moved leftward, so as to decrease the angle between the backstay and the ground, the parallel vector *la* on the force polygon rotates clockwise around point *a*, decreasing the forces in both backstay and mast. Also, if the left-hand mast, *la*, leans back more, away from the roof, the forces in it decrease. The limiting cases are reached when the centerline of the mast coincides with segment *oa* of the cable and has the same value as the force in *oa;* and when the backstay is horizontal, with its force equal to the horizontal component of the force polygon. Notice that some orientations may require masts that are substantially longer and more costly than others.

BUILDING THE SUSPENDED ROOF

We have found both form and forces for the suspended roof. Now we will consider how to build it.

Attaching the Cables

A cable is attached to a foundation, mast, or other structural element with standard steel fittings that are designed to be as strong as the cable itself. These come in two basic types, *swaged* and *socketed.*

Swaged fittings are used for strands up to 1–3/8 in. diameter and wire ropes to 2 in. (Figure 2.24).

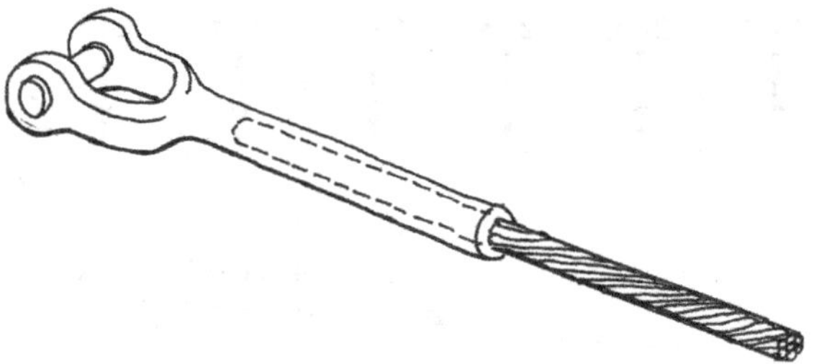

Figure 2.24 A swaged clevis fitting. The cable is inserted into the long sleeve, which is then squeezed in a hydraulic press to make the connection.

The end of the cable is inserted into a sleeve in the steel fitting. Then the fitting is placed in a shaped die in a hydraulic press and squeezed (swaged) so tightly that the steel of the fitting flows around the wires and attaches to them by friction.

Socketed fittings are used for strands of any size. The end of the cable is *broomed out* into individual wires and inserted into the conical steel basket of the fitting (Figure 2.25a). Molten zinc is poured into the basket to embed the wires and make the attachment (Figure 2.25b).

We will use *open socket* fittings to connect the cables in our roof to the masts and foundations. An open socket transfers the force from a cable to a steel plate by means of a cylindrical pin that passes through matching holes in the plate and the fitting. Figure 2.26 gives dimensions for open sockets for strand up to 4 in. in diameter.

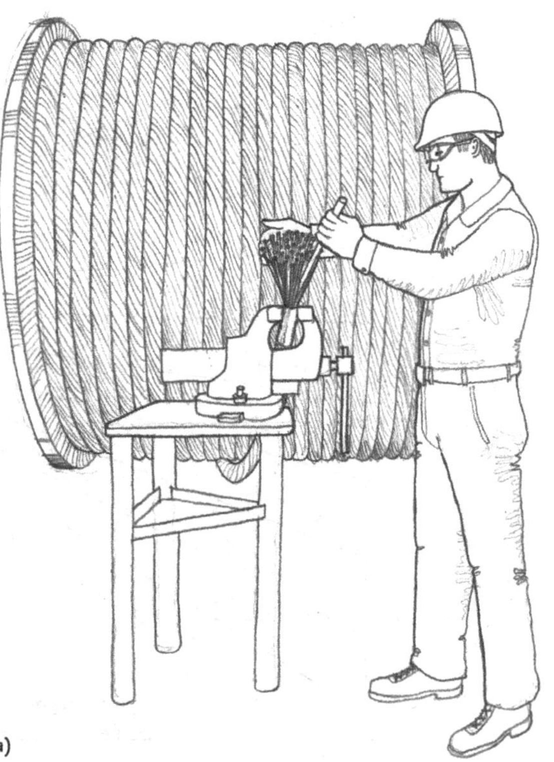

(a)

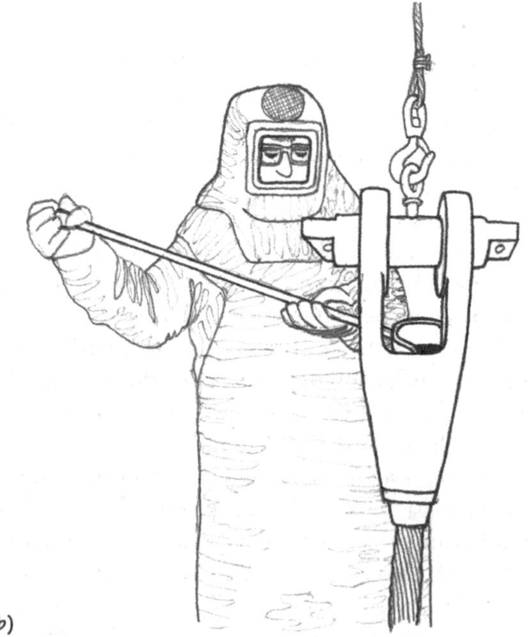

(b)

Figure 2.25 (a) Brooming out the end of a cable. The broomed wires are inserted into the basket of the socket, which is then filled with molten zinc (b)

We are working with a cable of 2–1/8 in. diameter. Looking down the table in Figure 2.26, we find that the socket for this diameter of cable is 25.5 in. long and weighs 252 lb. The aperture in the socket that receives the steel connecting plate is 5.0 in. wide. This suggests that the connecting plate at the tops of the masts should be 4 in. thick in order to slide easily into the 5-in. aperture during construction. The pin that joins the socket to the plate is 4–3/4 in. in diameter and will require a 5 in. hole in the plate.

The cost of cable construction is governed more by the cost of the fittings than by the cost of the cable. A roof cable that spans 500 ft is not much more costly than one that spans 100 ft because it has the same number of fittings. It is wise to plan a cable structure to span as far as possible so as to spread the cost of the fittings over as much enclosed floor area as possible, and to consider the design of such fittings early in the design process (Figure 2.27).

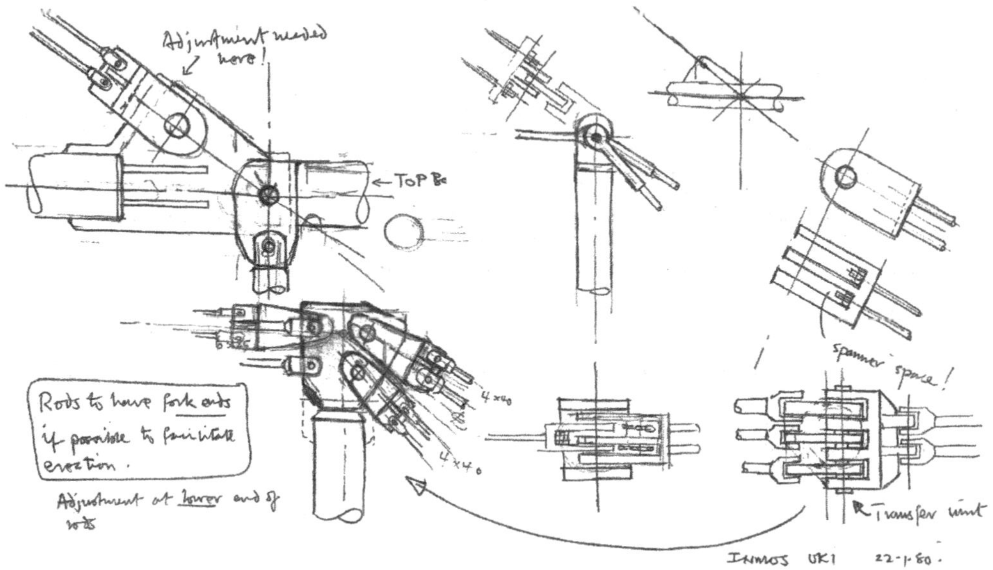

▲ **Figure 2.27** Structural engineer Anthony Hunt made these sketches as he began the process of detailing the Inmos microprocesser factory in Wales. High-quality details are a feature of Hunt's buildings, and they are considered from the very earliest stages of design.

Sketch courtesy of Anthony Hunt, as reproduced in *Tony Hunt's Second Sketchbook.* Oxford, UK: Architectural Press, an imprint of Elsevier Science, 2003, pp. 48, 49. Reprinted with permission.

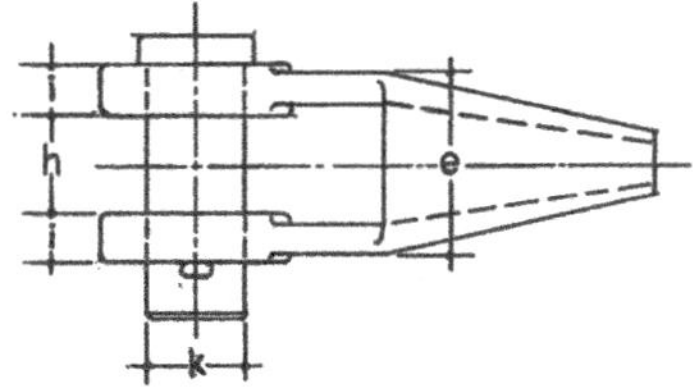

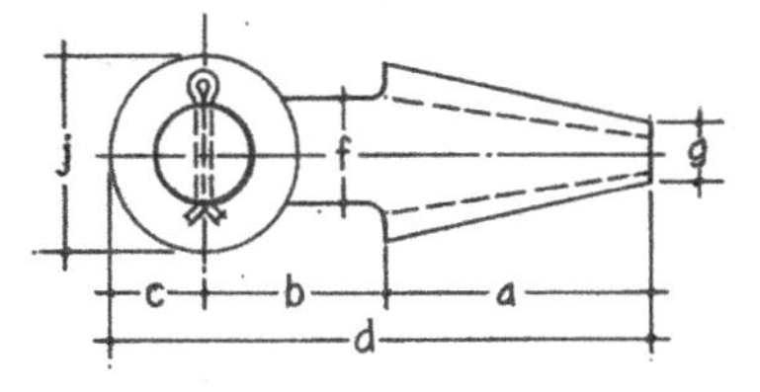

▼ **Figure 2.26** Dimensions and weights for open strand sockets.

TYPICAL DIMENSIONS OF OPEN STRAND SOCKETS, IN.

Strand Size	a	b	c	d	e	f	g	h	i	j	k	Weight, lb
1/2	3	2.5	1.25	6.75	2.25	1.25	1.125	1.25	0.563	2.25	1.188	4
9/16 & 5/8	5.5	3	1.438	9.938	2.625	1.5	1.25	1.5	0.675	2.625	1.375	8
11/16 & 3/4	6	3.5	1.75	11.25	3.125	1.75	1.5	1.75	0.75	3.125	1.625	13
13/16 & 7/8	6	4	2.063	12.063	3.625	2	1.75	2	0.875	3.75	2	19
15/16 & 1 1/8	6	5	2.688	13.688	4.625	2.75	2.25	2.5	1.125	4.75	2.5	35
1 3/16 & 1 1/4	6	6	3.125	15.125	5.25	3	2.75	3	1.188	5.375	2.75	47
1 5/16 & 1 3/8	6.5	6.5	3.25	16.25	5.5	3.25	3	3	1.313	5.75	3	55
1 7/16 & 1 5/8	7.5	7	3.75	18.25	6.375	3.875	3.125	3.5	1.563	6.5	3.5	85
1 11/16 & 1 3/4	8.5	9	4	21.5	7.375	4.25	3.75	4	1.813	7	3.75	125
1 13/16 & 1 7/8	9	10	4.5	23.5	8.25	4.375	4	4.5	2.125	7.75	4.25	165
1 15/16 & 2 1/8	9.75	10.75	5	25.5	9.25	4.625	4.5	5	2.375	8.5	4.75	252
2 3/16 & 2 7/16	11	11	5.25	27.25	10.75	4.875	4.875	5.25	2.875	9	5	315
2 1/2 & 2 5/8	12	11.25	5.75	29	11.5	5.25	5.25	5.75	3	9.5	5.25	380
2 3/4 & 2 7/8	13	11.75	6.125	30.875	12.25	5.75	5.75	6.25	3.125	10	5.5	434
3 & 3 1/8	14	12.5	6.75	33.25	13	6.25	6.5	6.75	3.25	10.75	6	563
3 1/4 & 3 3/8	15	13.5	7.75	36.25	14.25	7	7.25	7.5	3.5	12.5	7	783
3 3/4 & 4	16	15	7.75	38.75	15.25	8.5	7.75	8	3.75	14	7.25	1018

The Masts

The load on each mast is made up of components not merely of the main cable force but also of the backstay force. These add up to very heavy loads, as we have discovered by measuring vectors *ol* and *ok* on the force polygon. We will find in the second half of this book that the best shape for a steel mast is a hollow cylinder, a form that is highly resistant to buckling. Our structural engineer estimates that the masts for the bus terminal will need to be about 16 in. in diameter.

A preliminary sketch of the mast and backstay details is shown in Figure 2.28. The details are laid out on the centerlines of the two cables and the mast. The centerlines are made to intersect at a point of concurrency, called the *working point*, in each detail so as to avoid bending forces in the mast.

The masts are manufactured in a steel fabricator's shop. Steel pipes of the required diameter and wall thickness are ordered from a steel mill and delivered to the shop. They are cut to exact length and squareness with a diamond-bladed saw. A thick, circular steel plate is welded to each end to distribute the force from the connection into the walls of the pipe.

Both the main cable and the backstay are connected by means of open sockets to a single plate 4 in. thick. To prevent the plate from buckling under the large forces that it must transmit, triangular *stiffener plates* are welded to each side of it.

At the bottom of the mast, a single plate on the end of the tube transfers its force to the foundation through a large steel pin and plates on each side that are welded to a thick steel *base plate*. The base plate distributes the force from the mast over a large enough area of the concrete surface of the foundation that the allowable stress in the concrete, which is much lower than the allowable stress in steel, is not exceeded. The plate is bolted firmly into the concrete foundation pedestal with long threaded rods, washers, and nuts. We will not know what the foundation itself will be until our geotechnical engineer has examined soil samples from the site and designed an appropriate device—a concrete spread footing, a cluster of driven piles, or a drilled caisson—to transfer the load from the mast into the soil. The backstay foundations will be designed to resist being pulled from the soil.

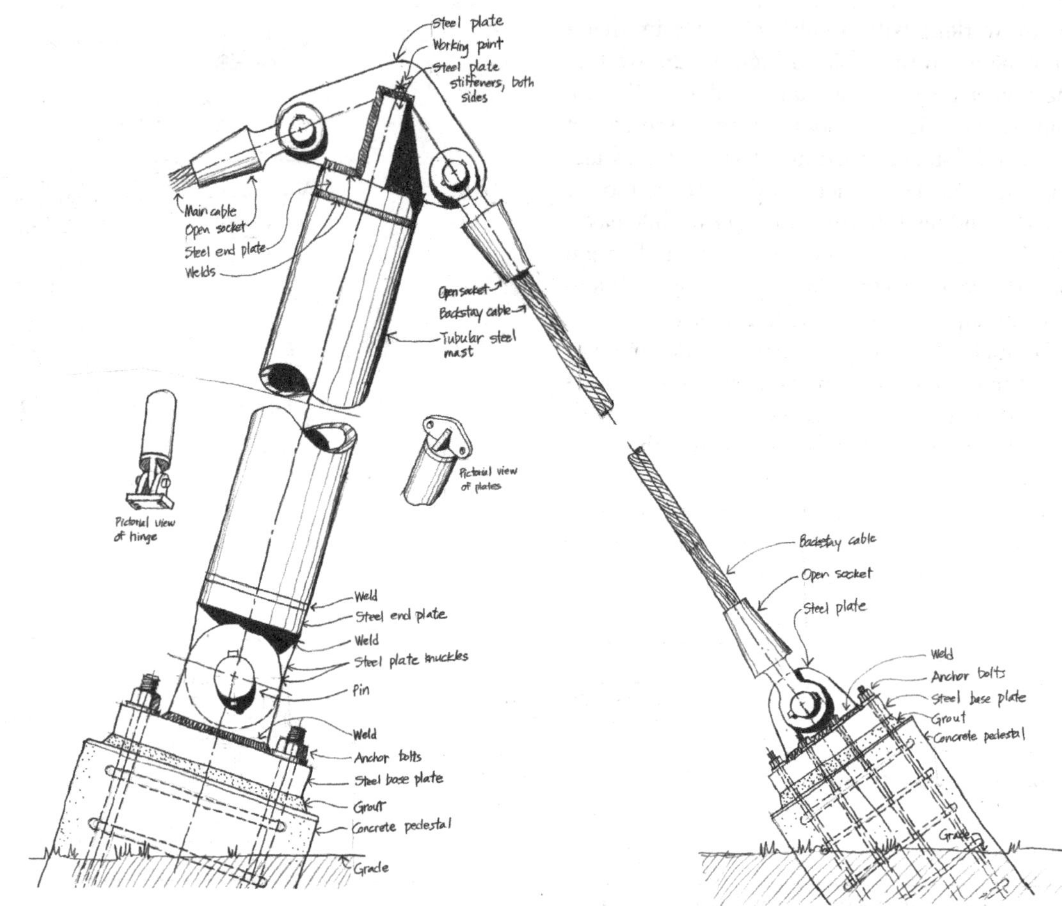

Figure 2.28 A preliminary sketch of details of the cable, mast, and foundations.

The pin and plates at the base of the mast form a *hinge* that allows the mast to move freely back and forth in the plane of the cable. This avoids the introduction of bending forces into the mast when the cable distorts from wind pressures, unequal snow loads, or thermal expansion and contraction in any part of the structure.

The Deck

Figure 2.29 shows a first pass at the details of the cables and roof deck. These, like the mast and backstay details, were done freehand for the sake of speed (Figures 2.27 to 2.29). Later, following further development, they will be drawn and dimensioned precisely and in complete detail so that they can guide the actual construction. The roof is structured around a grid of steel *wide-flange* beams that support a deck made of heavy-gauge corrugated sheet steel. (Wide-flange beams are commonly, and imprecisely, called "I-beams." The term "I-beam" belongs to an earlier steel beam shape, now obsolete, that does not utilize steel as efficiently as a wide-flange shape.)

We check the building code to determine whether the roof must have a fireproofing material applied to it. A transportation terminal is assigned to Occupancy Group A-3, Assembly, Miscellaneous, in the *International Building Code*. For a building of this size in this occupancy, we find that the steel structure of the roof may be left without protection if an automatic sprinkler system for fire protection is installed in the building, which we were going to do anyway.

The beams that run parallel to the cables must be bent to varying radii to achieve the roof shape that we have designed. This is done by specialist shops equipped with heavy-duty machines that pass the steel member through three large rollers to bend it by brute force (Figure 2.30).

The decking is welded or screwed to the beams. Rigid thermal insulation boards and a waterproof roofing membrane are applied over it. For greater energy efficiency, glass fiber batt insulation is added between the beams before the ceiling finish layer is applied. The ceiling is made of long aluminum planks that are snapped into special attachment strips at each line of beams. Acoustic absorbing material can be added just above the ceiling strips to reduce noise in the area below.

Figure 2.30 Bending a wide-flange beam between rollers. This beam is being bent the "easy way," the direction in which the beam is less resistant to bending. Beams are also routinely bent the "hard way," as must be done for our structure's shape. Photograph from RECO Nelson Co., Newark, New Jersey.

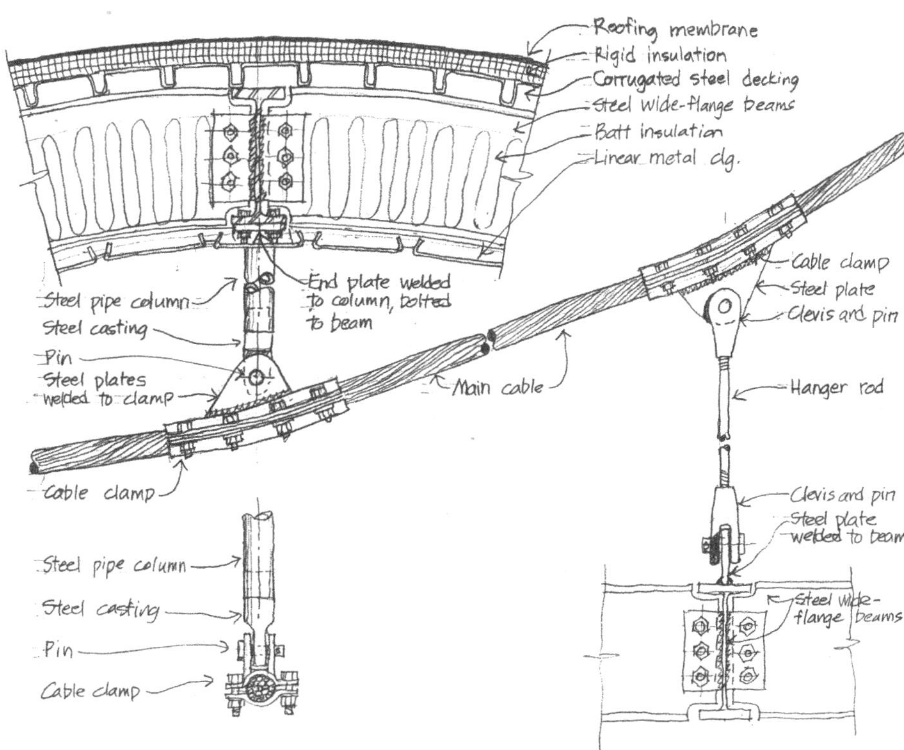

Figure 2.29 A preliminary sketch of details for the cable and roof deck.

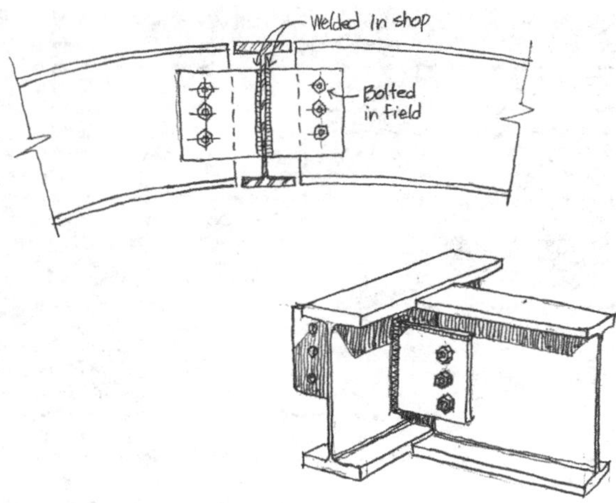

Figure 2.31 A single-plate beam connection.

The grid of beams is supported by the cables via either steel pipe struts or steel rod hangers, depending on whether the cable is above or below the roof. Special steel clamp fittings are manufactured to join the struts and rods to the cable.

The sketch details show the beams in the grid as being joined to one another by a *coped* connection, in which the flanges of one member are cut away at the ends to allow the beam to be inserted between the flanges of the other member. Because of the amount of cutting of the members that is involved, this is a relatively expensive detail. Given the large number of such connections in the roof, we will work with the fabricator to explore less expensive ways of forming these joints. It may be possible, for example, to weld *single-plate connectors* to the members in one direction that can be bolted directly to the members in the other direction (Figure 2.31).

Lateral Stability

We must brace the structure against horizontal forces that come from wind or earthquakes. For stability in three dimensions, the building needs to be braced in both its long and short directions. In the short direction of the building, the backstays, cables, and masts form a triangulated system that is stable against lateral loads except for a small amount of movement that its components can tolerate without damage. In the long direction of the building, we have made no provision so far for lateral forces. Figure 2.32 shows a couple of ideas for making such provisions. In further design projects in this book we will continue exploring these and other ways of resisting lateral forces.

Erection of the Roof

The length of any parabolic hanging cable can be approximated closely using the expression:

$$l = L(1 + 2.6n^2) \qquad [2\text{-}4]$$

where:

l is the length of the cable,

L is the span in horizontal projection, and

n is the sag ratio, which we determined earlier to be 0.13.

Thus:

$$l = (180 \text{ ft})(1 + 2.6(0.130)^2) = 187.98 \text{ ft}$$

Working from the tables in Figures 2.20 and 2.26, the weight of the cable alone is 188 ft of length times 9.49 lb per ft, which comes to 1785 lb. The two sockets add 252 lb each. The total weight of a cable and its two sockets is 2,290 lb.

Our structural engineer has estimated that the masts will weigh about 100 lb per foot of length, which means that the longer masts will weigh about 6,000 lb each. Even the pins that connect the sockets and hinges will weigh 80 to 90 lb each. It is apparent from these figures that the masts, cables, and fittings will not be lifted and installed by human muscle power alone. This is a very large structure; it is light for its size as compared to most other types of structures, but its components are nevertheless very heavy.

Many hours of careful planning will be devoted to deciding how to erect the structure safely and accurately. The sketches in Figure 2.33 are a first step in this process. In part (a), the masts have been installed and supported by temporary shoring at the proper angles. The backstays are installed next. Then the main cable, with its clamps already in place, is strung between the two masts with the aid of a construction crane. Workers standing on temporary platforms at the mastheads insert the pins to complete the connections.

Parts (b) and (c) show the steel framing components being added. Temporary walkways are installed over the cables to give workers access to the connections. The cable will change shape as each piece of the steel roof structure is added to it, and will assume its final form only when the entire structure is in place. This requires advance thought about the order in which components are added to the cable and how the changes of cable shape will be accommodated by the components that are already in place.

Sidewalls

The tall glass walls of the terminal need to be supported against gravity and wind loads. Heat-tempered glass will be used because it is very strong, does not break easily, and even if it does break, shatters into small granules rather than sharp spears. The gravity load on the glass will be only its self-weight, but the wind loads can be considerable on such large sheets of glass. We will adopt a proprietary system of suspended glazing, in which the glass sheets are hung from a horizontal beam at the top. The beam will be supported by slender columns that act also as the vertical *mullions*, the posts in which the glass is mounted (Figure 2.34). To support the glass against wind pressure, the vertical joints will be braced with stainless steel rods inside and out. These rods will follow funicular lines like those of the roof cables above, but turned 90° so as to resist the horizontal forces of wind. By having rods both inside and outside the glass, this system can resist both pressures and suctions. Small-diameter

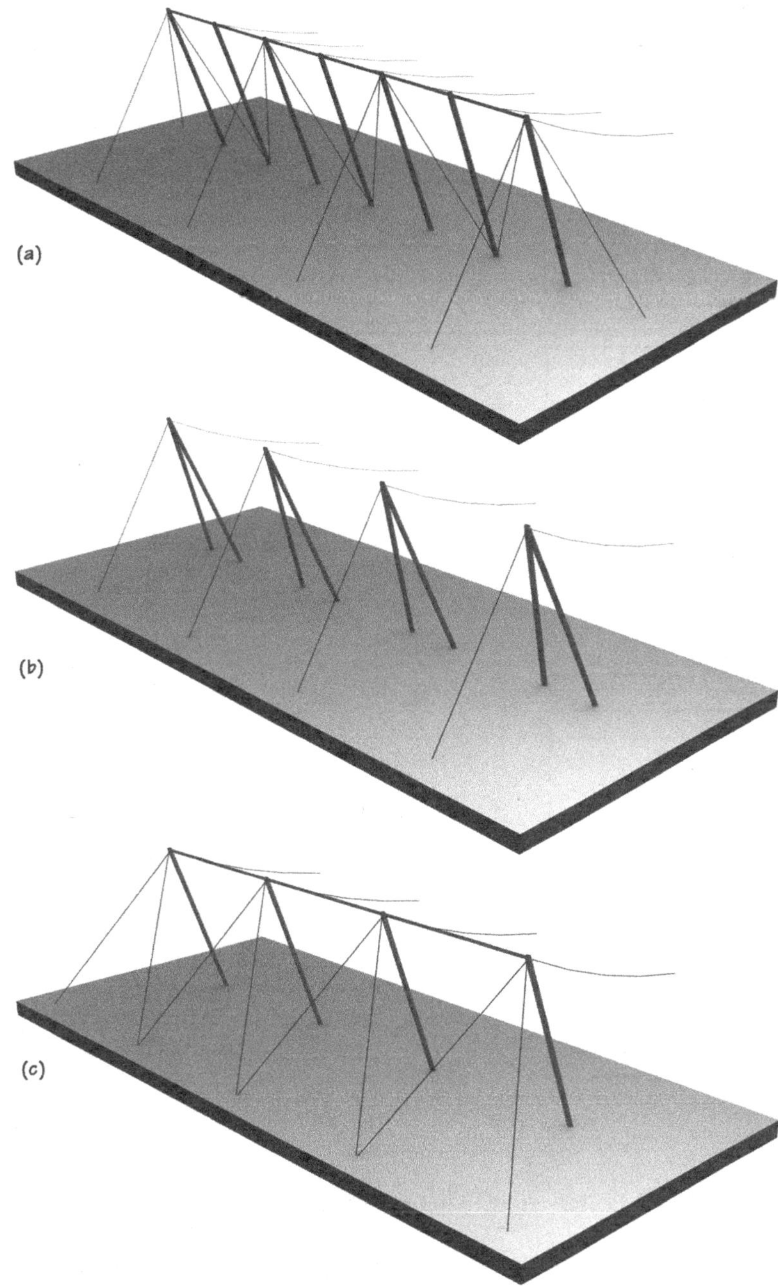

Figure 2.32 Ideas for a lateral bracing scheme for the terminal roof: (a) Diagonal bracing with rods or cables between masts, (b) using double mast A-frames, and (c) doubling the number of backstays so that the top of each mast is pulled in three directions.

diagonal rods allow the system to support the glass against nonuniform pressures.

The junction of the glass wall and the hanging roof presents an interesting detailing problem. The roof, being made of cables and supported on hinged masts, will move slightly with changing wind and snow conditions. If the glass walls were rigidly attached to the roof, large forces could develop at the junction and cause damage to the glass. We will use a connection detail that allows for comparatively large amounts of movement in this joint. The glass wall assembly is self-supporting from the bottom against gravity loads. Wind loads are transmitted to the floor slab through hinges at the bottom of the wall. The top connection transfers wind loads into the roof structure through a link at the top of each mullion. The link is hinged at both ends, which allows the wall and roof to move independently of one another. A large gap between the roof and wall allows for this movement. It is sealed against air leakage by a flexible rubber bellows.

NEXT STEPS

This completes our preliminary exploration of the design, detailing, and erection of the suspended roof for the high-speed bus terminal building. We have developed a tentative but complete picture of what the structure will look like (Figure 2.35), how it will be put together, and how it will be erected.

This is as far as we will take this project. If it were to be built, a more detailed analysis of the structure would be undertaken. This would confirm and fine-tune the results of our graphical calculations. It would go farther to explore the effects of various patterns of wind and snow on the roof, especially weights of drifting snow, aerodynamic pressure variations, and possible vibration problems, as well as lateral loads of wind and earthquake.

If the building were to be built, the soils that underlie the site would be tested and analyzed, and suitable foundations designed. Additionally, all the construction details would be reviewed for feasibility

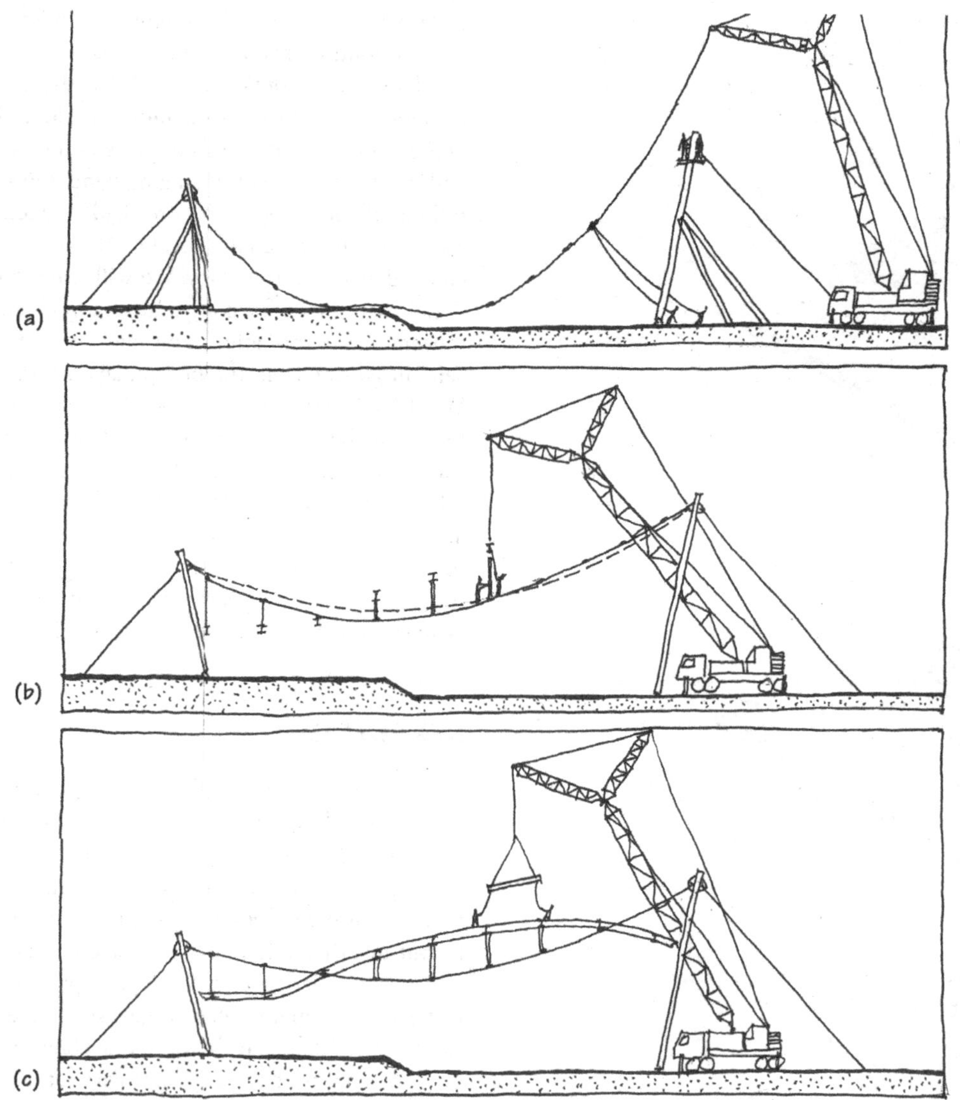

Figure 2.33 A construction sequence for the terminal roof.

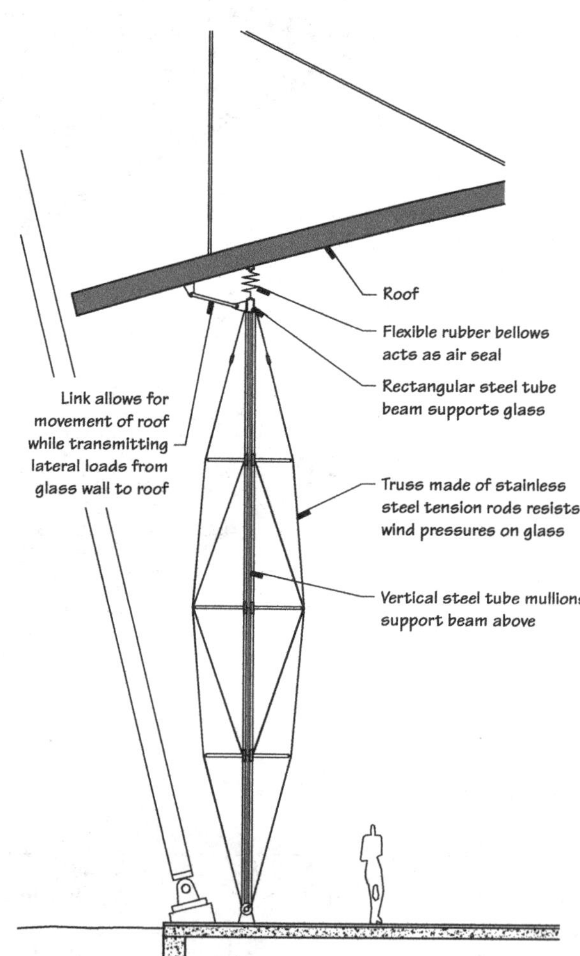

Figure 2.34 Details of the glass wall and how it joins the roof.

and economy, as well as for physical strength. Considerable time would be expended in working out the interactions between the structural system that we have designed and the walls, doors, floors, windows, heating and cooling devices, lighting systems, fire suppression system, informational signage, and public address system.

The photographs in Figures 2.36 to 2.41 illustrate some of the forms taken by suspension roofs and bridges that have actually been built. How does the design we have developed compare with these for practicality and excitement? How would you go about finding form and forces for each of them with the methods we have developed? What aspects of their structures would be challenging to analyze or construct?

Figure 2.35 A perspective view of the completed roof.
Design and image by Boston Structures Group.

▶ **Figure 2.36** The roof of an exhibition hall in Hanover, Germany, hangs on cables that are supported by A-frames made of steel wide-flange shapes. The A-frames create space for large clerestory windows that light the hall. Engineer: Schlaich Bergermann and Partners, Stuttgart, Germany.

Photo courtesy of Dieter Leistner.

◀ **Figure 2.37** In this stadium in Portugal, designed by Eduardo Souto de Moura, cables span from the back of one grandstand to the back of the other, but only the portions over the seats are decked, leaving the playing field with only bare cables overhead. What would the force polygon for this roof look like?

Photo courtesy of Christian Richters.

▲ **Figure 2.38** This suspension bridge at Obere Argen in Germany was designed to minimize the height of the tower in a scenic area. This was accomplished by placing the suspension cables below the deck for the major part of the span. Engineer: Schlaich Bergermann und Partner, Stuttgart, Germany.

Photo: Roland Halbe.

▶ **Figure 2.39** The David Lawrence Convention Center designed by Rafael Vinoly was completed in downtown Pittsburgh in 2003. Its suspended roof provides column-free exhibition spaces. This project has been recognized for its sustainability and efficiency, including the vast material reduction in steel usage due to use of a suspended roof rather than trusses or beams.

Photo courtesy of Brad Feinknopf.

Figure 2.40 The Fingal County Council in Dublin, Ireland, has a generous curving atrium facing a large park; its glass façade transfers wind loads back to the primary structure using a lateral application of design elements similar to those used in this chapter's design project. Architects: Bucholz McEvoy; Engineers: ARUP; Atrium Façade Consultant: RFR. To find out more about RFR, see the accompanying biography of Peter Rice.

Photo copyright 2002, Michael Moran.

PETER RICE

Peter Rice (1935–1992) was an inventive Irish engineer whose fruitful collaborations with internationally acclaimed architects led to some of the most recognizable landmarks constructed from the 1960s to the present. After graduating as an engineer and working at Arup Engineering in London, he was assigned as a junior team member doing computations for the challenging double-curved geometry of the Sydney Opera House in Australia. Since the roof forms of the competition-winning proposal by the Danish architect Jorn Utzon were not funicular, it took years to devise a geometric strategy that would be constructible, and Rice emerged as a key strategist in this endeavor.

After a year as a visiting scholar at Cornell, Rice rose to fame through his collaboration with Renzo Piano and Richard Rogers on the Beaubourg building (now known as the Centre Pompidou) in Paris. He was also instrumental in most of the national building projects in the City of Lights during the 1980s and 1990s, known as Les Grands Projets. Many visitors to the Centre Pompidou (by Piano and Rogers), the expanded pyramid-focused Grand Louvre (by Pei), Parc de la Villette (by Tschumi and Fainsilber), La Grande Arche (by Spreckelsen), and other projects in the French capital recognize the architects, but few know that these projects were all realized through the work of Peter Rice. His unique solutions with vertical lenticular trusses made of stainless steel tensile members and glass in both tension and compression produced extremely light, transparent structures.

After progressive promotions at Arup from engineer to director, Rice joined with Ian Ritchie and Martin Francis to form the interdisciplinary firm RFR. Later, Rice collaborated on projects that ranged from entire airport structures at Stansted, Roissy, and Kansai to engineering the internal supports for a sculpture by Frank Stella. Throughout his career Rice emphasized that he was not an architect but rather a creator who worked within engineering specialties to contribute to much larger international teams. Richard Rogers noted that "like his great predecessors, whether [I.K.] Brunel or [Fillippo] Brunelleschi, Peter Rice is able to step outside the confines of his professional training, transferring technical problems into poetical solutions." The firm RFR continues his collaborative approach from offices in Paris and Dublin, designing works such as the luminous glazed truss roofs at the Charles de Gaulle Airport, the double lenticular passerelle pedestrian bridge in southeastern Paris, and dynamic curtain wall façades, buildings, and works of infrastructure across Europe.

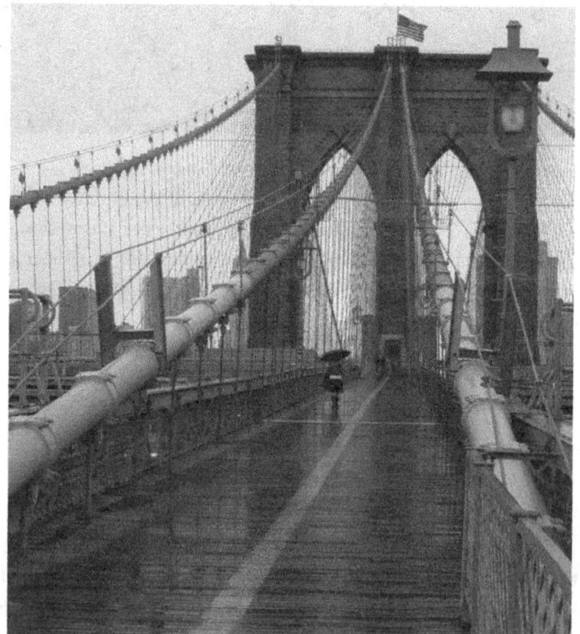

Figure 2.41 The Brooklyn Bridge, designed and constructed by the Roeblings (see the biography of the Roeblings on page 48).

Photo: David M. Foxe.

Exercises

1. Using the same load line and overall layout as that of the bus terminal roof, construct from the same pair of end points 3 to 5 funicular curves that are generated from poles that lie at various arbitrary locations along the ray that is parallel to the closing string of the original curve. All these curves are members of a family of funicular curves.

Next, extend the first and last segments of each curve until they intersect. What generalization(s) can you make about the locations of these intersections? Look for a pattern in the lateral position of these intersections and in their height above or below the closing string. Write down the conclusions you have reached.

2. A 1.75-in. diameter cable is anchored to the vertical face of a steel tube column 10 in. square. The cable approaches the column at a vertical angle of 45°. Design this connection and draw it accurately to a large scale, such as 1 – 1/2 in. = 1 ft, which is a proportion of 1: 8, or else 1:10. Obtain the measurements of the cable socket from Figure 2.26. Give the thickness of the connector plate, and indicate where welding is required.

3. Design a suspension footbridge to span between two Douglas fir trees, each 3 ft in diameter. The bridge should start and end about 30 ft above the ground. The trees are 110 ft apart center to center. Assume a uniformly distributed load of 60 lb/ft. How large a cable is needed? Draw details of the end of the bridge.

Key Terms and Concepts

strut
hanger
mast
column
pylon
backstay
funicular polygon
load line
ray
pole
reaction
family of funicular forms
nonfunicular
resolution of a force
horizontal component
vertical component
static
static equilibrium
$\Sigma F_h = 0$ [2-1]
$\Sigma F_v = 0$ [2-2]
horizontal projection
cable
drawing of wire
die
cold-working
strand
wire rope
parallel wire cable
breaking strength
allowable strength (f_{allow})
factor of safety
glass fiber, carbon fiber, aramid fiber
closing string
sag, *s*
sag ratio, *n*
$n = s/L$ [2-3]
swaged
socketed
broomed out
open socket
working point
stiffener plate
base plate
hinge
wide-flange beam
coped connection
single plate connection
lateral stability
$l = L(1 + 2.6n^2)$ [2-4]
mullion
$F = P/A$ [2-5]
$F_{allow} = P_{max}/A$ [2-6]
psi
ksi
graphic statics

Further Resources

Rice, Peter, and Hugh Dutton. *Structural Glass*. London, UK: E. and F. N. Spon, 1995. This book goes deeply into glass walls of the general type that we have projected for the bus terminal, in which funicular rods work together with the glass to make vertical trusses to resist wind loads. As noted in his biography on page 62, Peter Rice was the structural engineer chiefly responsible for the rapid development and implementation of contemporary glass walls, whose lightness makes them as close to miraculous as structures can be.

Scheuermann, Rudi, and Keith Boxer. *Tensile Architecture in the Urban Context*. Oxford, UK: Butterworth Architecture, 1996. Cable-supported roofs are presented in text and color photos, together with numerous details.

Vandenberg, Maritz. *Cable Nets*. Chichester, UK: Academy Editions, 1998. This book will be helpful in extending the simple structural concept of this chapter into vastly more complex cable net roofs.

www.wire-rope.org: A list of manufacturers of steel cable and their Web addresses.

http://muncy-upson.com: The Web site of a manufacturer of many kinds of sockets for cable connections.

CHAPTER 3

Designing a Cylindrical Shell Roof

- *Shaping funicular arches and vaults in compression*
- *Form-finding: catenary, parabola, circle*
- *Stiffening compressive structures against buckling and unbalanced loadings*
- *Detailing and constructing a thin single-curvature shell*

A small city in the American Southwest has decided to build a new arena for high school basketball, gymnastics, volleyball, wrestling, and other indoor sports. The proposed site on the edge of the city (Figure 3.1) has a natural profile of rock that, with minimal reshaping, will provide a slope for bleacher seating on one side of the court (Figure 3.2). Portable bleachers will be used on the other three sides.

After consideration of material costs and contractor capabilities in the area, a decision has been made to roof the arena with a concrete cylindrical *shell*. As the designers of this facility, our first task is to find the form and forces for the roof.

The major load on the roof will be its self-weight, which will be distributed uniformly over the surface of the vault. We estimate the self-weight of the vault, insulation, and roof membrane at about 75 lb/ft^2 (psf) of surface area. Because snow rarely falls in the area where this building is located, the estimated live load is light, only 10 psf.

The ideal shape for resisting loads distributed uniformly along a surface is a *catenary,* the curve taken under its own weight by a hanging chain or cable. An exact catenary is generally described mathematically by an equation of the form:

$$y = \cosh(x)$$

Since hyperbolic functions are relatively difficult to work with, we will base our preliminary shaping on a *parabola,* which is much simpler mathematically than a catenary yet is very close to the catenary in form, especially if its rise is less than 0.25 of the span (Figure 3.3). A parabola is the ideal curve for a load that is uniformly distributed on the horizontal projection of the vault, which is a flat, level rectangle whose span and width are the same as those of the vault.

When we have generated the parabola, we will perform a second step: redistribute the load over its curved surface, rather than its horizontal projection, then generate from this loading pattern a second curve that is very close to a catenary. We will compare this curve with the parabola that we generated first, in order to discover the degree of approximation that is represented by using a parabola rather than a catenary.

In early design sketches, we have drawn freehand an approximate form for the vault. We would like it to pass through points *X, Y,* and *Z,* with *Y* located at the midpoint of the span (Figure 3.4). We draw *XZ,* the closing string, and measure the rise of the vault above the closing string at *Y.* This vertical dimension is 42 ft;

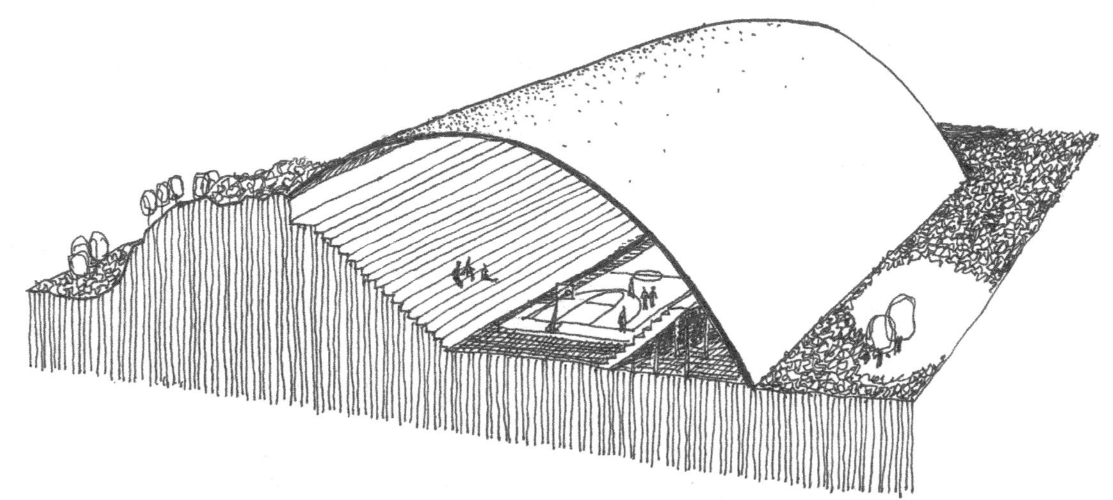

Figure 3.1 A sketch of the proposed site shows the vault over the sport venues.

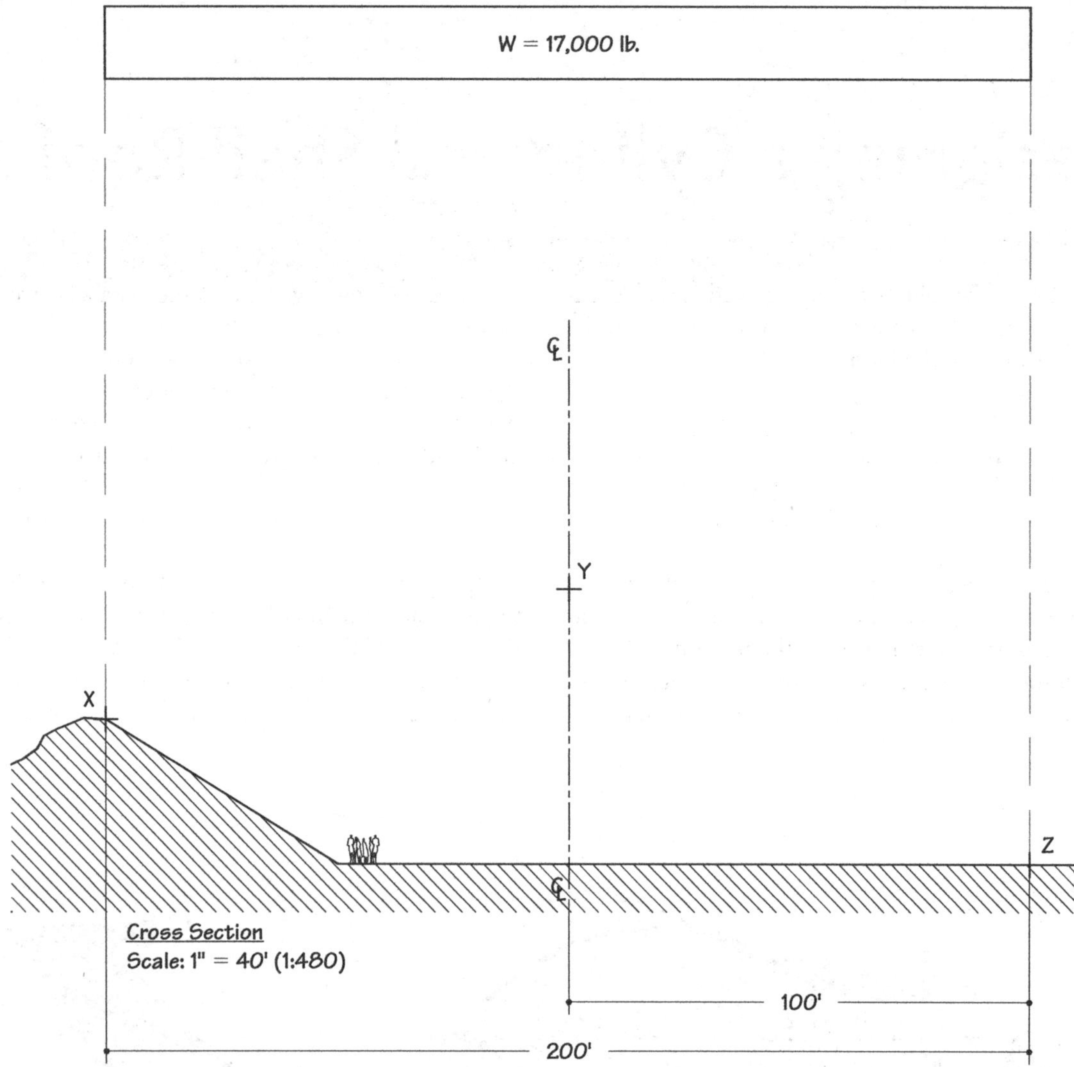

Figure 3.2 A diagram showing the proposed site in section with the regraded sloping portion.

the horizontal span is 200 ft. The ratio of rise to span is thus 42:200, or 0.21, which is less than the 0.25 limit above which a parabola begins to be a less satisfactory approximation of a catenary. Notice that we use the closing string rather than the floor of the arena as a starting point for measurements; the floor level is established arbitrarily and has no direct geometric relationship to the curve of the vault.

For convenience, we will base our graphical calculations on a strip of vault that is 1 ft wide. The total gravity load on this strip is 17,000 lb, which is the horizontal projection of its area, 200 ft^2, times the load per square foot, 85 lb. We divide the span arbitrarily into 10 portions, enough to give a relatively smooth curve but not so many as would create unnecessary work. The horizontal dimension of each of these portions is 20 ft. For the purpose of our simplified analysis, which is based on a parabola, the weight of each portion is 1,700 lb, one-tenth of the overall weight of the 1-ft strip.

To facilitate a graphical solution, we replace each portion with a concentrated load of 1,700 lb at its center. We extend the lines of action of these forces downward vertically over the section drawing of the site, where we will construct the curve of the vault and apply Bow's notation to the loads.

Next we construct a load line for these forces as a first step in drawing the force polygon. It is made up of 10 loads of 1,700 lb each. Because these are gravity loads, the load line is vertical.

FINDING THE POLE

We must find the unique pole location that will generate a funicular polygon that passes through the three designated points.

We will do this with a method that is based on a singular geometric property of a parabola. We begin by drawing a vertical line through point *Y*, at the center of the span of the funicular polygon (Figure 3.4). Next we draw *XZ*, the closing string.

Concerning Approximations

A high degree of precision is seldom required in structural design. There are many reasons for this; among the most important is our inability to predict with any but the most approximate numbers how heavily loaded a structure will be or the pattern in which the load will be distributed. We can calculate to as many decimal places as we wish the stresses and deformations in a structure, but their quantities in an actual structure are likely to vary by as much as plus or minus 50 percent with shifting winds, drifting snow, and changing human occupancies. Further uncertainties are created by such factors as variations in structural materials, variable workmanship, partial rigidities of joints that we assume to be hinges, and continuities of members such as truss chords, which were assumed for purposes of design as having no continuity.

Throughout this book, like all designers of structures, we use various approximations. In this chapter, we choose for simplicity to assume for the purpose of finding its form that the total load on the vault is uniformly distributed in horizontal projection, whereas its dead load is distributed uniformly over the curve of the vault and the distribution of its live load varies considerably with changing wind directions and intensities. There is no one shape for the vault that will be ideal for all contingencies.

If we were determining the orbits of objects moving through space, a high degree of accuracy would be justifiable, given an almost total lack of complicating factors. Celestial objects, like angels, are remarkably well-behaved. But structures, like human beings, are earthbound and behave in complex ways that are not fully predictable or quantifiable. As the greatest structural designers have all reminded us, structural calculations are merely approximations that serve to verify the judgment of the designer, and should not be taken as exact solutions that can be carried to as many decimal places as desired.

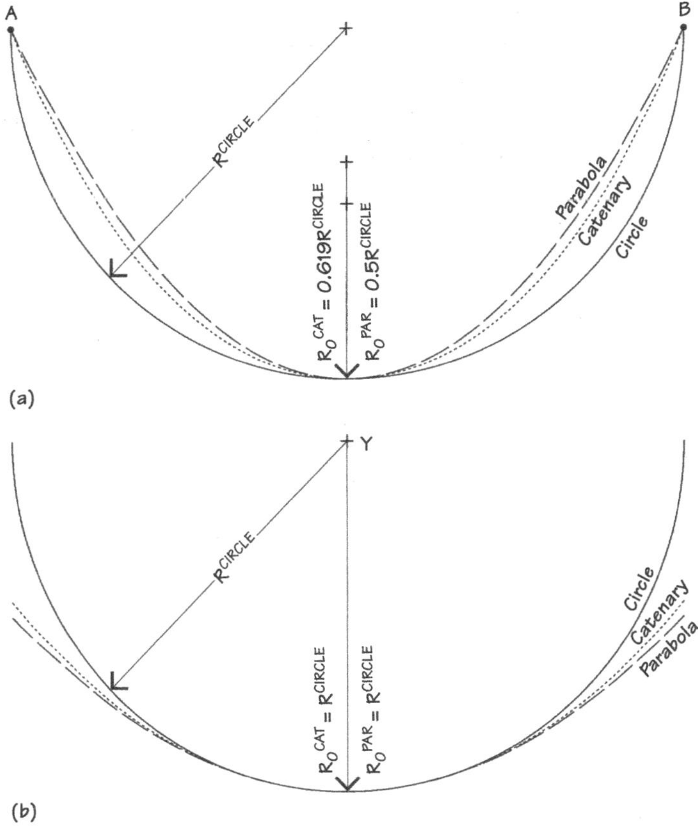

Figure 3.3 These diagrams show how parabolas are similar to catenary curves where the rise of the curve is less than one-quarter of the span. The first diagram (a) shows curves with matching endpoints with considerable variation in steeper portions, while the second (b) shows equal radii of curvature for a circle, a parabola, and a catenary.

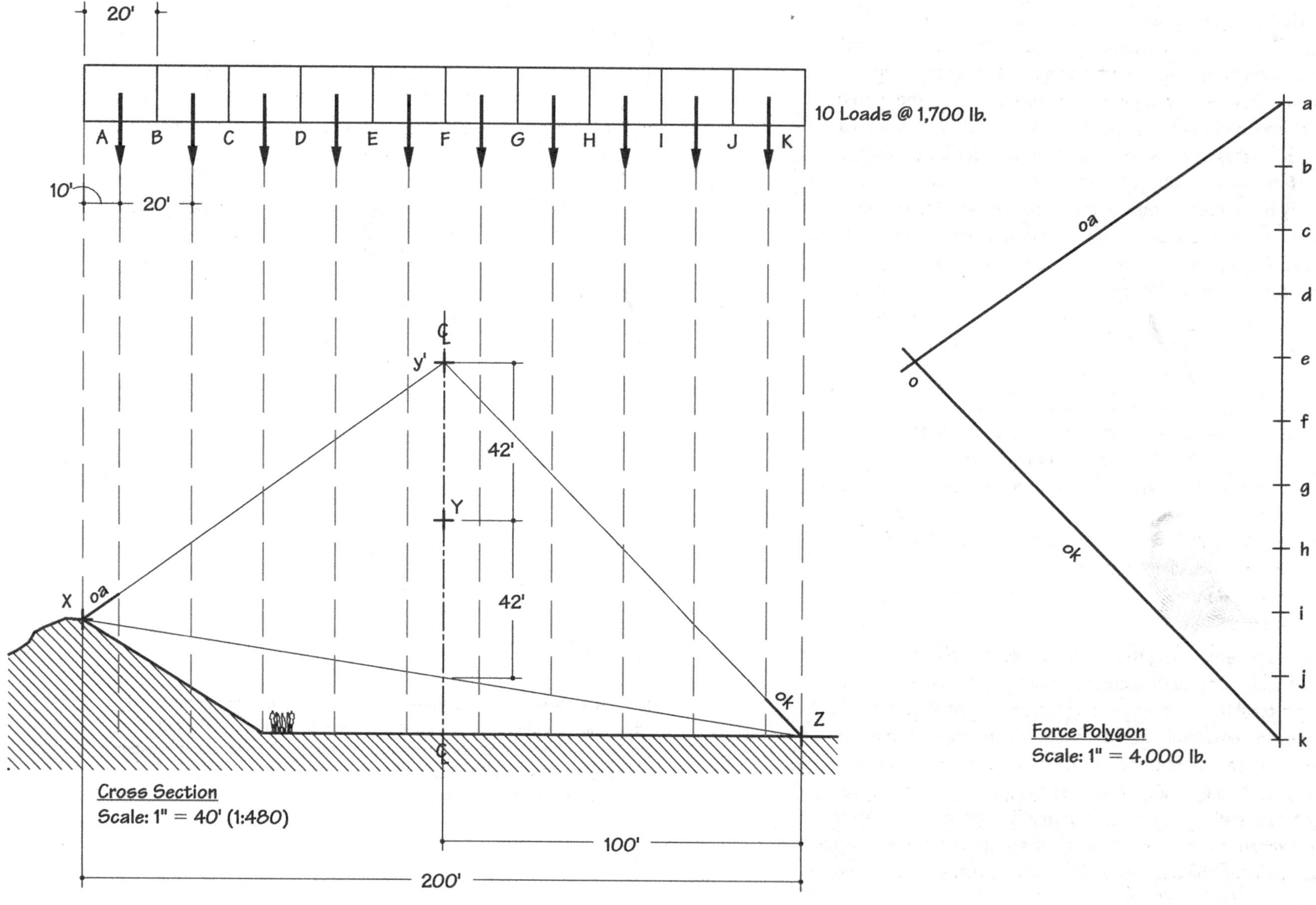

Figure 3.4 The vault will pass through X, Y, and Z, and the span is divided into 10 increments.

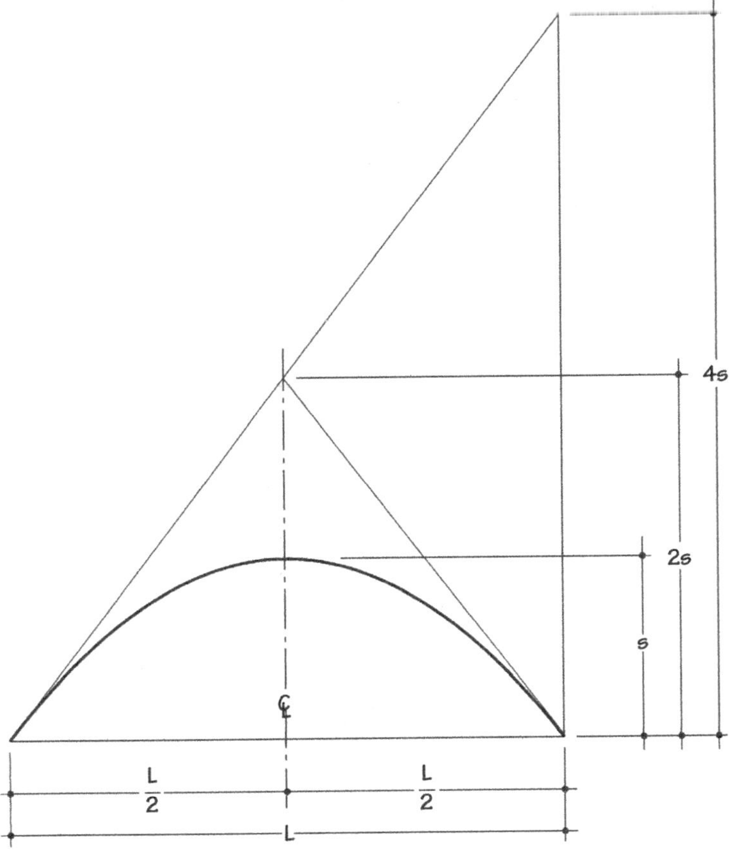

Figure 3.5 Geometric construction of a parabola.

Every parabola that is cut through by a closing string, regardless of whether the string is horizontal or sloping, has the property that lines tangent to the parabola at the points at which it intersects the closing string will intersect each other on the vertical centerline of the parabola. Furthermore, their point of intersection will occur at exactly twice the height of the parabola above the closing string, as measured on the vertical centerline (Figure 3.5). This means that we can find the pole for the curve of the arena roof by carrying out the following steps on Figures 3.4 and 3.6. (Also refer to Form and Forces Graphical Techniques 3 on the supplemental site, as an alternative way of learning this construction.)

1. On the funicular polygon, measure the height on the vertical centerline from the closing string to point *Y*.
2. Lay out an identical distance from *Y* to locate point *Y′* above it on the vertical centerline. The tangents to the ends of the parabolic vault must intersect at *Y′*.
3. Draw a line from *X* to *Y′*. This line is tangent to the parabola at *X*. The portion of it that runs through space *A* is also segment *oa* of the funicular polygon for this vault.
4. Draw a line from *Z* to *Y′*. This line is tangent to the parabola at *Z*. The portion of it that runs through space *K* is also segment *ok* of the funicular polygon.
5. On the force polygon, draw ray *oa* of indefinite length through point *a* on the load line and parallel to line *oa* on the funicular polygon.
6. On the force polygon, draw ray *ok* of indefinite length through point *k* on the load line and parallel to line *ok* on the funicular polygon.
7. The intersection of rays *oa* and *ok* on the force polygon is the pole that we seek, *o*.
8. On the force polygon, draw ray *ob*. In space *B* of the funicular polygon, parallel to this ray, draw segment *ob* of the funicular polygon so that its left end just touches the right end of *oa*.
9. Repeat step 8 for rays *oc* through *ok* to complete the funicular polygon. The funicular polygon should pass through point *Y* and arrive accurately at point *Z*. If it does not, we must review our work for mistakes or for an accumulation of small errors in plotting line segments.

The parabolic centerline of the concrete vault is a smooth curve that is tangent to the centers of the line segments of the funicular polygon that we have just drawn. Because the concentrated loads are located at the centers of the 10 equal portions of span, the first and last spaces between loads, *A* and *K*, are half as long as spaces *B* through *J*. The smooth curve therefore passes through the two endpoints of the funicular polygon.

We measure the longest ray, *ok*, to find the maximum force in the 1-ft strip of vault. It is approximately 13,800 lb.

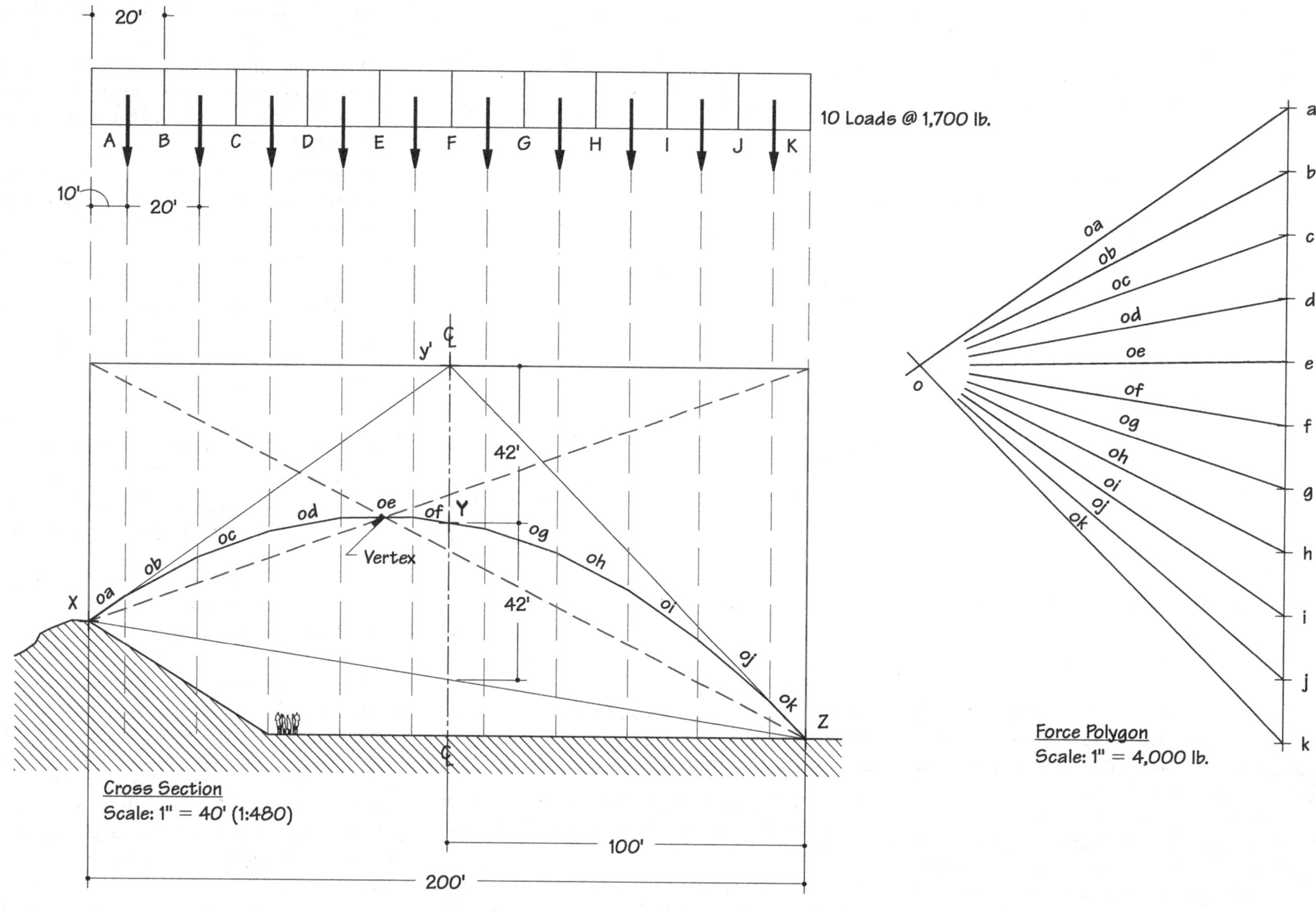

Figure 3.6 Finding the curve of the parabola and drawing the force polygon. Finding the vertex.

Although we established a vertical centerline for the parabolic vault, the vertex of the parabola (its highest point) does not necessarily lie on that line. In fact, as we look at the parabola we have constructed, it looks like the vertex is to the left of the centerline. Figure 3.6 shows us the geometric construction for locating the vertex of a parabola. Applying it to our parabolic vault, we find that the vertex is indeed about 18 ft to the left of the centerline.

Finding the Required Thickness of the Vault

We need to refine our estimate of the dead load of the vault before we proceed. To do this, we will find the required thickness of concrete for the parabolic vault whose curve we have just found.

The allowable stress in the concrete of a thin vault or shell is usually established at a rather low level so as to minimize the danger of buckling. A typical value might be only 600 psi. How thick must our vault be at this allowable stress?

Stress is equal to force divided by area:

$$F = P/A$$

where:

F is the stress,

P is the force, and

A is the cross-sectional area.

On the force polygon, we scale the maximum force in the vault, P, which is 13,800 lb. F in this case is F_{allow}, the allowable stress of 600 psi. We have based our analysis on a strip of vault 1 ft (12 in.) wide, so A in square inches will be equal to 12 in. times the thickness of the vault, t. Thus:

$$F_{allow} = \frac{P}{A}$$

$$600 \text{ psi} = \frac{13{,}800 \text{ lb}}{12t}$$

$$t = \frac{13{,}800 \text{ lb}}{(12 \text{ in.})(600 \text{ lb/in.}^2)}$$

$$t = 1.92 \text{ in.}$$

Caution

The parabolic construction that we have just followed is one of the easiest ways of finding a pole. But it is not mistake-proof, and it may not give the expected results depending on the three points chosen (Figure 3.7). Some common errors in employing it are:

1. Applying it to a structure whose loads are not all the same.
2. Applying it to a structure whose loads are not uniformly spaced across the span.
3. Applying it to a structure whose loads are uniformly spaced but start at a full interval from each end of the span rather than a half interval.

These errors are easier to avoid if you remember that the funicular polygon is a parabola only if the load is distributed uniformly over the horizontal projection of the span. Then this load must be divided into an arbitrary number of equal parts, and each part must be represented by a concentrated force vector through its center. This leads to the spacing pattern of load vectors that has a half space at each end of the span and full spaces between. As you explore various aspects of these vaults, you may also wish to consult the cable example in the Active Statics program on the supplemental site, and move the pole to the left of the load line; you will find yourself in the domain of arches and vaults that relate to our explorations in this chapter.

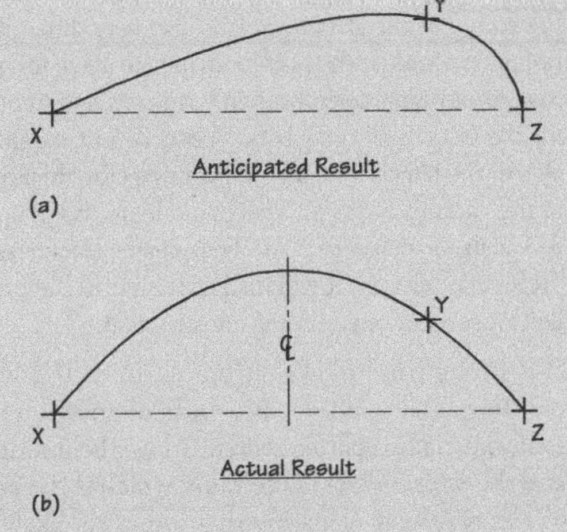

Figure 3.7 As an example of a possible surprise using three points to determine a parabola, the shape intended by the choice of three points (a) may not be the actual parabola that fits those points (b).

This would indicate that this concrete vault, which spans 200 ft, only needs to be 2 in. thick. Is this possible?

In theory, it is. The shape of the vault is funicular for its assumed loading. This produces only axial compression within the vault, which is a very efficient way of using structural material.

The reality is that there are several reasons why the vault cannot be this thin:

1. The vault will need to be reinforced with a grid of steel bars running both longitudinally and circumferentially. We can assume that these will be #4 reinforcing bars, which are nominally 1/2 in. in diameter. Their actual outside diameter, because of the ridges on their surfaces, is about 9/16 in. They must overlap one another where they cross, so they need 1–1/8 in. of thickness within the vault.
2. The bars must be embedded in a *cover* of concrete, both above and below, to protect them from fire and corrosion, and to assure that they act as a unit with the concrete to resist loads. For shells like ours, which will be covered with a waterproof roof membrane, the

concrete is not exposed to the weather, and only 1/2 in. of cover is required on each surface of the vault, adding 1 in. to the total thickness. It is not realistic, however, to expect the degree of precision in the shapes of the reinforcing bars that a mere half inch of cover would allow. If any bar is slightly crooked, or if it springs up off its supports in the formwork a bit, it is likely to poke through the surface of the wet concrete during pouring, making finishing of the outer surface of the shell difficult and compromising the fire safety of the structure. It is also very difficult to build formwork to the perfect shape. To allow for normal dimensional tolerances in formwork and in placing the steel reinforcing bars, a cover of 2 in. on either side of the bars is advisable. This brings the thickness of the vault to 5–1/8 in. This could be rounded up to 5–1/2 in. or down to 5 in. The greater thickness is preferable because it will further minimize the problems just mentioned during construction.

3. If a strong wind blows on the vault, or if a winter storm and wind deposit drifts of snow on the roof, the loading pattern will no longer be uniform, and the *pressure line* in the vault, which is the path of the resultant of its internal forces, is likely to stray outside its parabolic axis. This creates *bending stresses* for which the vault is not designed, making collapse possible. This danger will be reduced by adopting a 5–1/2 in. thickness.

APPROXIMATING MORE CLOSELY THE IDEAL CURVE FOR THE VAULT

The parabolic curve that we have just found for the vault is close to being the ideal shape for it, but is it close enough that we should go ahead and build it? We have developed enough information to enable us to find a curve for the roof that is theoretically closer to the ideal curve. This will tell us whether the parabola is a good enough approximation for most projects.

Our starting point for finding this closer approximation is to measure as closely as we can the actual length of each segment of the parabolic curve rather than its horizontal projection. From these lengths we will tabulate an approximate dead load for each segment, add this to the live load for the same segment, and find a funicular curve for this loading that passes through the same points X, Y, and Z. Finally, we will compare this new curve for the vault with the one that we found previously.

Estimating the Loads

A 5.5-in.-thick slab of concrete weighs about 69 lb per sq ft (psf). The weight of the thermal insulation and roof membrane will bring the total dead weight to about 75 psf. This is distributed uniformly over the surface of the roof, not its horizontal projection. The building-code-mandated live load estimate, however, is based on the horizontal projection of the roof, not its actual surface area. (We are, of course, ignoring lateral and unbalanced loads at this early stage of designing the structure.)

In Figure 3.8, we measure the actual lengths of the centerlines of the segments of the parabolic vault. These vary from a minimum of 20 ft–1 in. at the crown, to 27 ft at the right-hand support. We set up a table with a line for each vault segment. The columns contain the length of each segment, its dead load as based on this length, the live load for each segment of 20 ft times 10 psf, and the total load for that segment, which is the sum of the dead load and live load figures in the two previous columns. This gives us total gravity loads that vary from 1,705 to 2,225 lb, a range of about 30 percent.

Finding the Curve

Now all that is left to find is a funicular curve for this irregular loading that passes through the same three points as the previous curve, and to compare the two curves. But we can't use the same method for finding the pole location, because the loads are not uniform. We need a general method that will start with any loading pattern and then find a curve that will pass through any three designated points.

There is such a method. It is contained in lesson 4 of "Form and Forces Graphical Techniques" on the supplemental site. Here is how it works:

1. We construct a new load line that is made up of the total loads that we have just calculated. Its segments vary in length over a range of about 30 percent.
2. We set up to construct a funicular polygon by drawing the vectors of the loads at their proper spacings, with the vertical line of action of each vector extending to the bottom of the page.
3. We adopt any convenient pole, o'. From it, we construct a force polygon and a *trial funicular polygon*, $X'Y'Z'$, on the lines of action of the load vectors (Figure 3.9). This is not the funicular polygon that we are seeking; it is a necessary intermediate step to finding that polygon.
4. We draw partial closing string $x'y'$ on the trial funicular polygon that we have just constructed (Figure 3.10).
5. Through trial pole o', we draw a ray parallel to partial closing string $x'y'$. This intersects the load line at a point that we label m.
6. On the cross-section diagram of the roof that we wish to build, we draw chord *xy*, which is the segment with endpoints that are located on vertical lines through x' and y' on the trial funicular polygon; *xy* is the partial closing string of the curve that we seek.
7. Through point m on the load line, we construct a ray parallel to *xy*. The final pole must lie on this line.
8. We repeat steps 4 through 6 for partial closing string $y'z'$ (Figure 3.10). The intersection of rays *xy* and *yz* on the force polygon is the final pole, *o*, the one that will produce a funicular polygon that passes through points X, Y, and Z.
9. From final pole *o* we draw a new set of rays, *oa* through *ok* (Figure 3.11). As we draw each ray, we draw parallel to it the corresponding segment of the final funicular polygon, *XZ*. *XZ* passes through the three designated points.

Though more laborious than the method we pursued earlier for plotting the curve of a vault loaded uniformly over its horizontal projection, this method

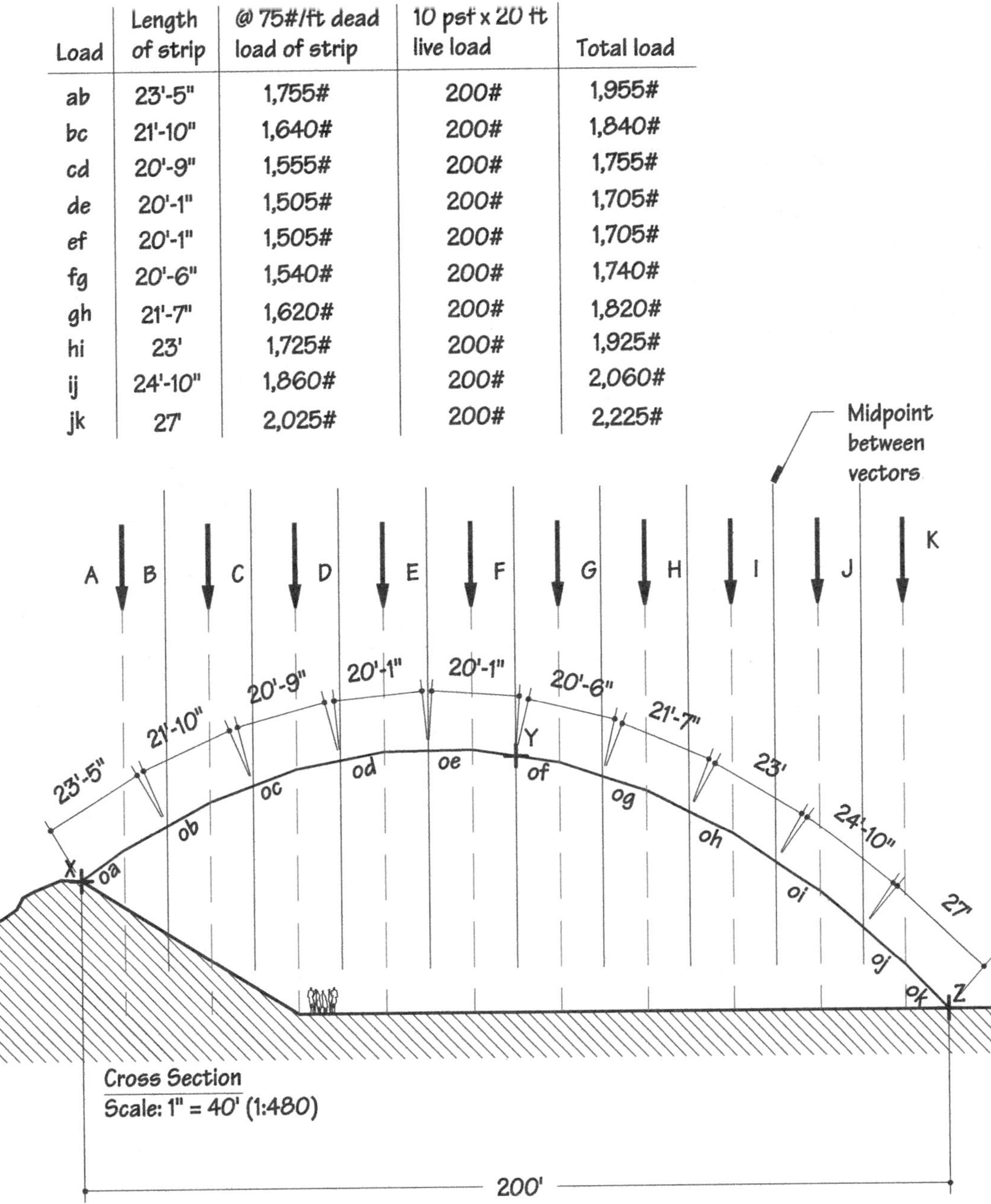

Load	Length of strip	@ 75#/ft dead load of strip	10 psf x 20 ft live load	Total load
ab	23'-5"	1,755#	200#	1,955#
bc	21'-10"	1,640#	200#	1,840#
cd	20'-9"	1,555#	200#	1,755#
de	20'-1"	1,505#	200#	1,705#
ef	20'-1"	1,505#	200#	1,705#
fg	20'-6"	1,540#	200#	1,740#
gh	21'-7"	1,620#	200#	1,820#
hi	23'	1,725#	200#	1,925#
ij	24'-10"	1,860#	200#	2,060#
jk	27'	2,025#	200#	2,225#

Figure 3.8 Measuring segment lengths along the parabola.

works for any load distribution, which makes it a valuable item in our growing box of structural design tools. The method works because a ray parallel to **any** partial or complete closing string for **any** member of a family of funicular polygons splits the portion of the load line to which it pertains into the vertical components of the end reactions on an arch or cable that takes the shape of the corresponding funicular polygon. Because all the members of a family have the same vertical components to their reactions, all closing strings for a family pass through the same point on the load line.

In drawing the partial closing strings, we divide the construction into that of two funicular polygons that share a common point, in this case *xy* and *yz*, which share the point *y*. For the family of each of these polygons, we found the point, *m* or *n*, where rays parallel to all its closing strings cross the load line. From that point for each funicular polygon, we drew a ray parallel to the closing string of the force polygon that we seek. The two rays crossed at the unique pole location that produced the larger force polygon with the desired geometry.

Comparing the Curves

In Figure 3.12, we show the curve that we just constructed (which is very close to the ideal curve for this loading) superimposed on the curve that we found first for this vault (which is based on the simplified parabolic construction). They differ only slightly; if constructed by hand, the two curves would be indistinguishable. Because we constructed them on a computer, we can enlarge them and discern these small differences. For most preliminary design purposes, the parabolic construction is indeed satisfactory. If the altitude of the curve is less than 25 percent of its span, even a segment of a circle would serve. We must keep in mind, too, that wind loads and unbalanced snow loads will create nonaxial loads in any shape vault that we make. There is little utility in searching for the precisely perfect curve. Instead, we should find a curve that is a close approximation, then turn our attention to stiffening the vault by giving it resistance to bending, so that it will be able to resist snow and wind loads.

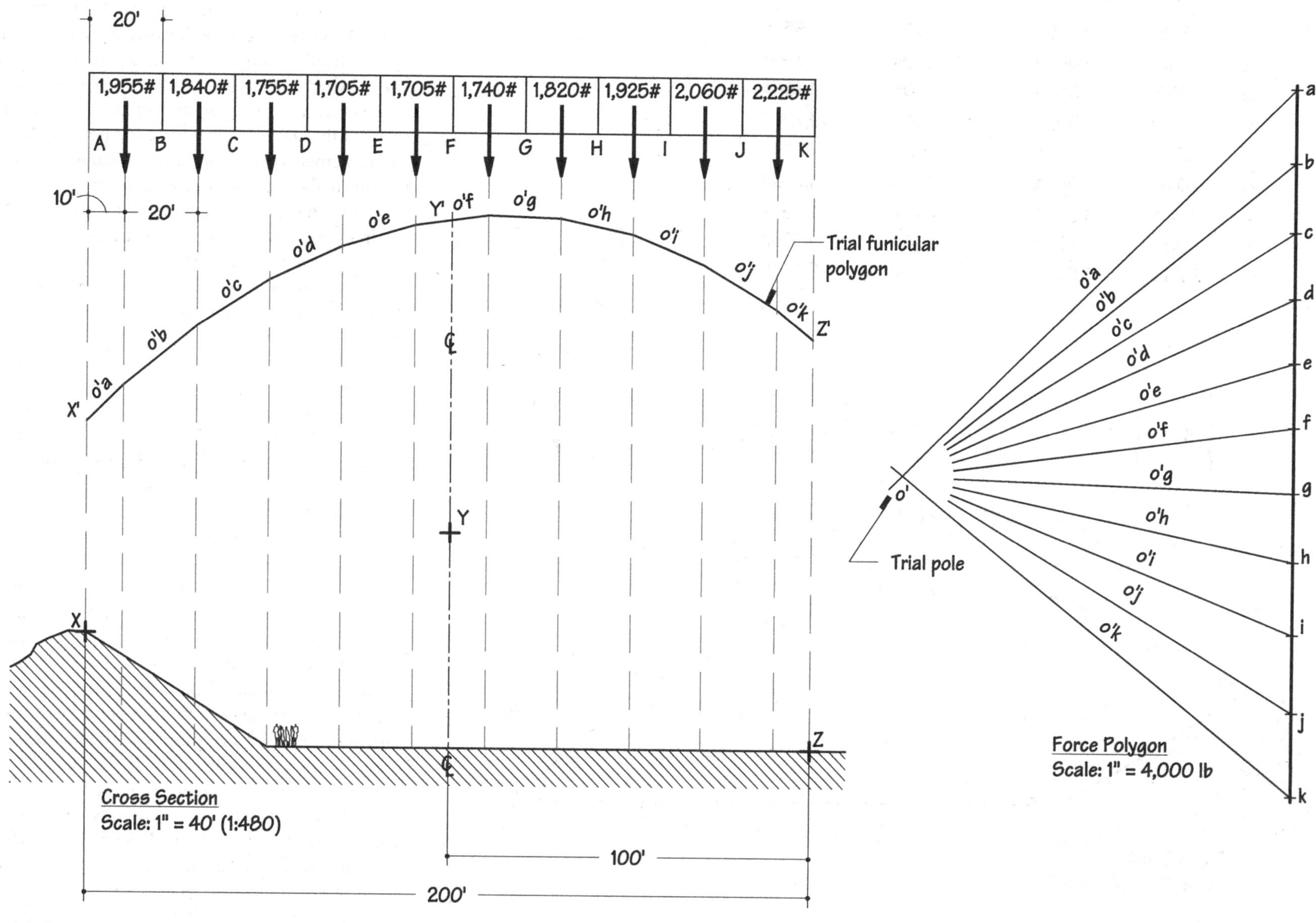

Figure 3.9 Constructing a trial pole and trial funicular polygon.

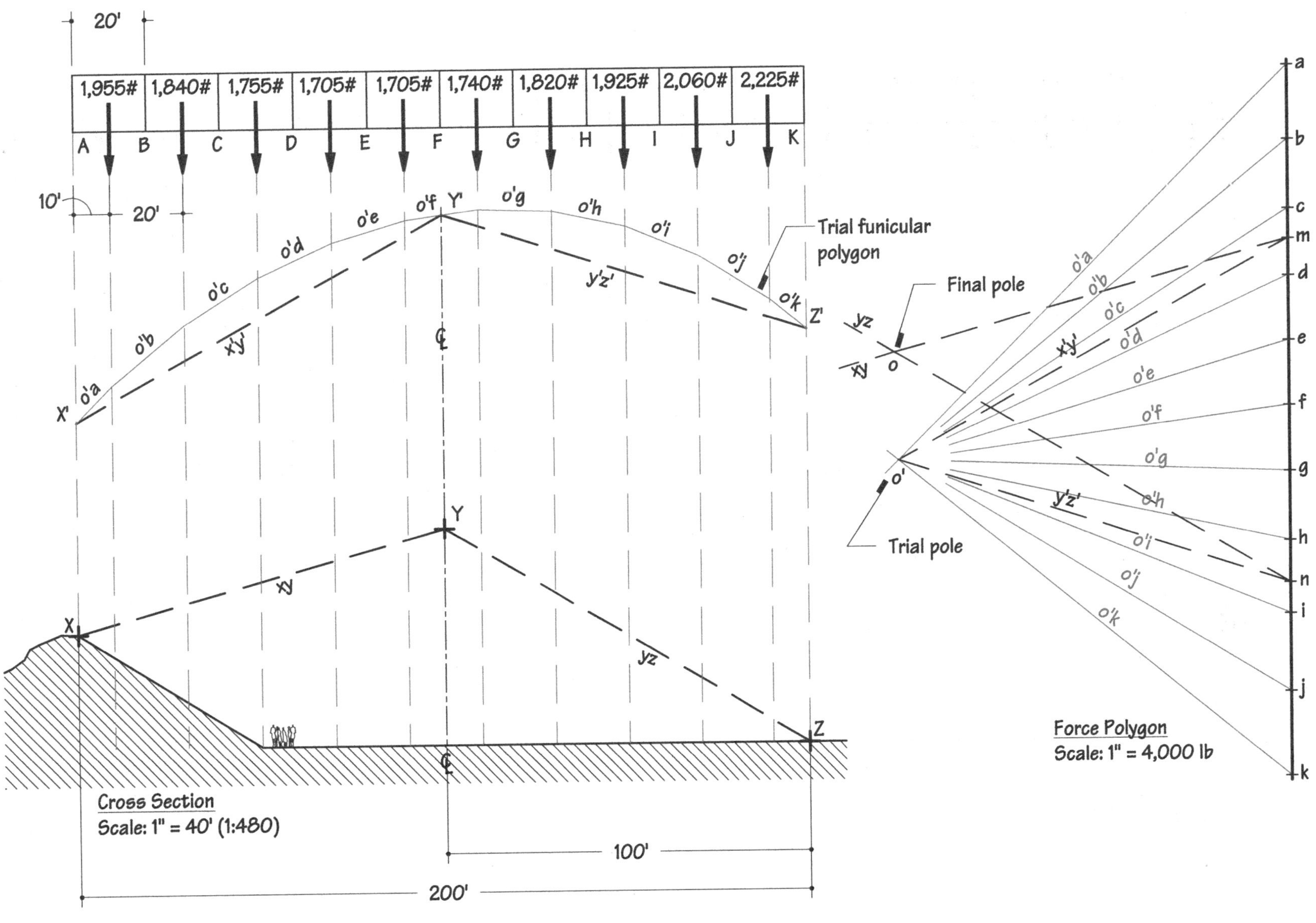

Figure 3.10 Locating a final pole.

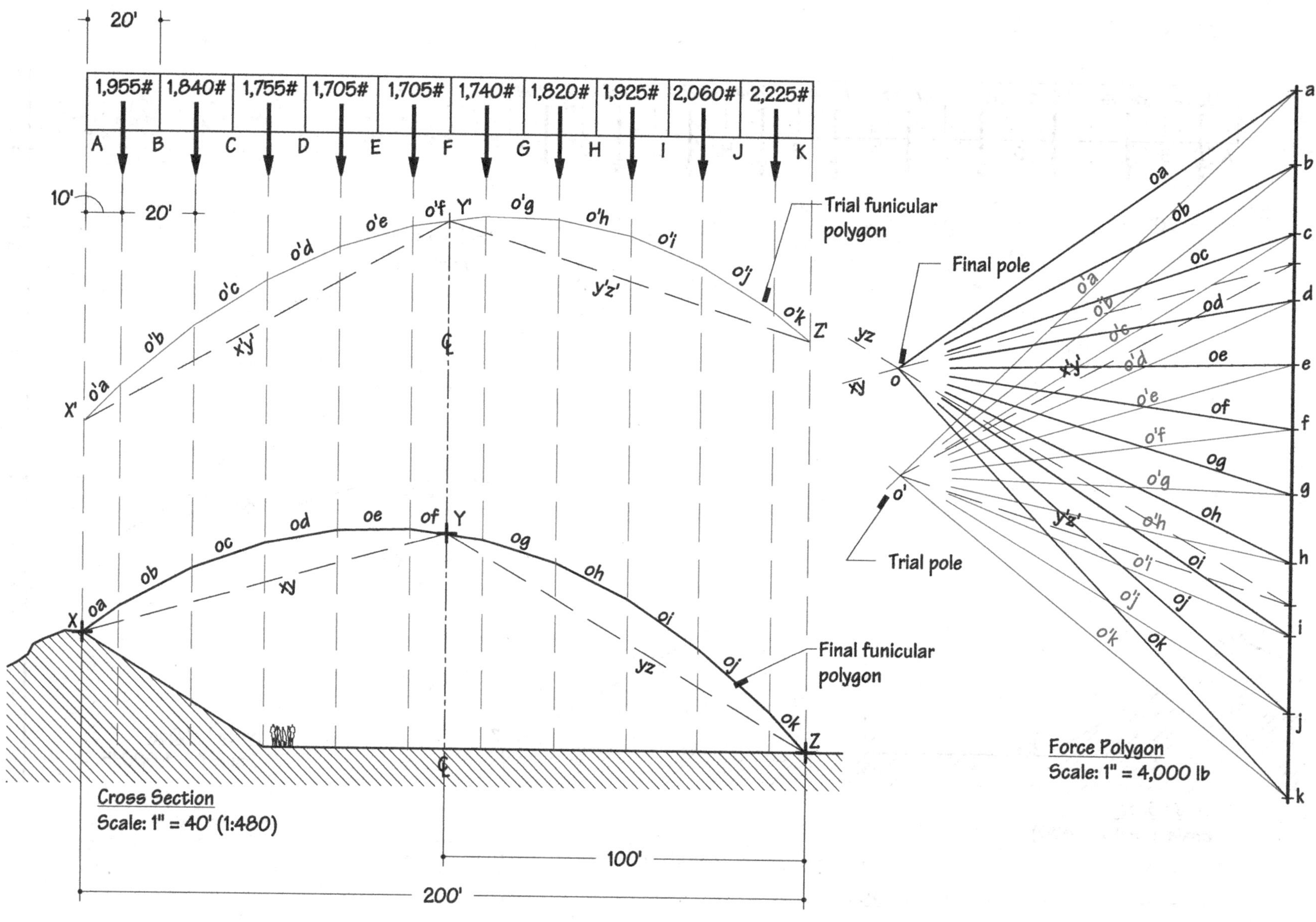

Figure 3.11 Completing the final funicular polygon.

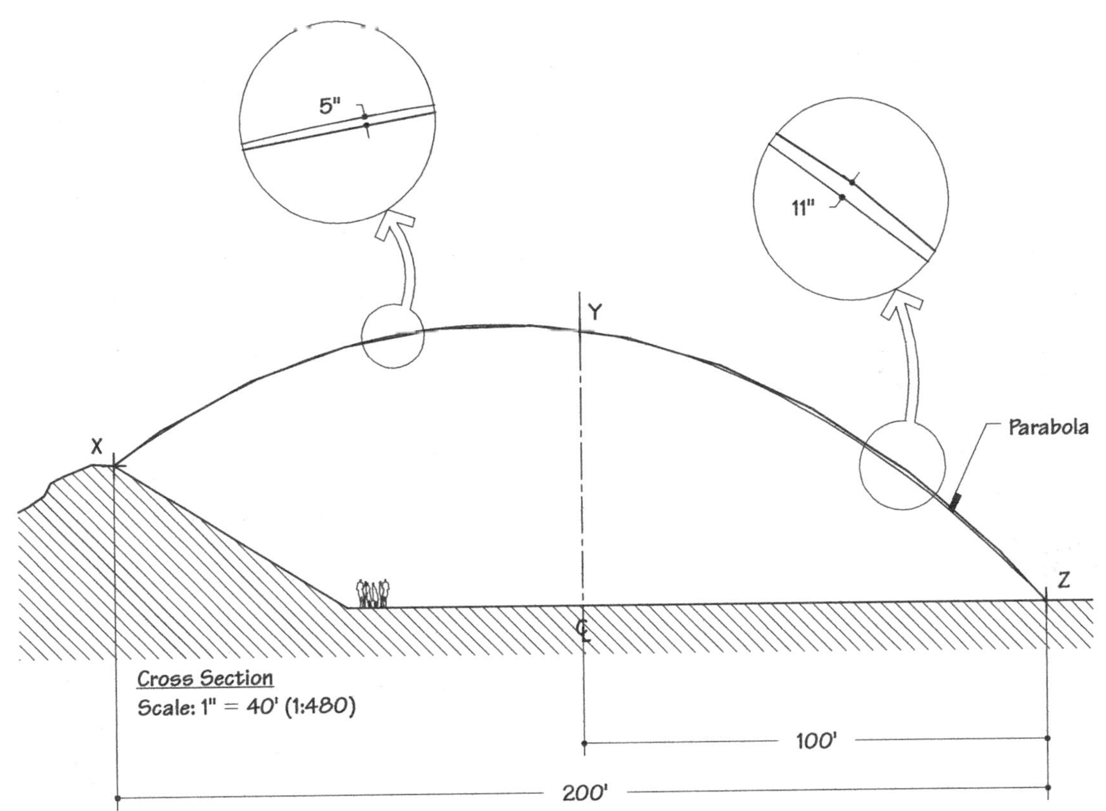

Figure 3.12 The difference between the parabolic curve and the near-catenary curve is insignificant when the rise-to-span ratio is 0.25 or less.

ADDING STIFFNESS TO THE VAULT

The funicular curve of the vault is more than 200 ft long, and even after we have nearly tripled the theoretically adequate depth of the vault, it is less than half a foot thick. It is more than 400 times as long as it is thick. A compression member this long and slender is likely to *buckle*—that is, to change shape and collapse—at a load that is far below its theoretical capacity.

We could deal with both nonuniform loads and buckling by increasing the thickness of the vault and the amount of reinforcing steel so as to create the necessary bending resistance. This would require that the vault be several feet thick. A more intelligent response would be to add deep stiffening ribs to the vault. These could be either outside or inside and would run in the cross-sectional direction, following the curve of the vault (Figure 3.13). They would be spaced perhaps 25 to 35 ft apart and reinforced fairly heavily so that they could act as beams. With a bit of imagination, such ribs could be patterned as attractive features of the architecture of the building (Figure 3.14).

Another good response to buckling and nonuniform loads would be to fold or corrugate the shell (Figure 3.15). The effect of this can be experienced by folding a piece of paper and comparing its stiffness to that of an unfolded sheet (Figure 3.16). Folding or corrugating increases greatly the depth of the vault without using very much more than the minimum amount of concrete and reinforcing steel. If the folds are 20 ft wide and slope at an angle of 30° to the curving plane of the vault, they would be about 5 ft deep. Thus, the overall depth of the folded vault slab would be about 1/40th of the span of the shell, compared to 1/400th for the flat vault slab. This 1000 percent increase in depth would use only about 12 percent more concrete.

Figure 3.17 shows a number of ways of shaping the surface of the shell to increase its stiffness. Notice that some of them allow daylight to enter. We have chosen to use cylindrical corrugations to stiffen the shell. They look graceful and display gradations of shadows in sunlight that highlight the exterior form in a pleasant way. We will not admit light through the vault because it could easily cause glare in the eyes of the athletes on the court below.

The arched corrugations primarily serve the purpose of stiffening the shell. But they also exert a secondary structural action, acting as arches in the direction parallel to the axis of the main shell. This causes them to thrust outward all along their length. The thrust is small enough that it can be resisted by an *edge beam* at each end of the roof. The edge beam can be created by turning up the edge of the vault for a distance of about a quarter of the span of the secondary arch, thickening it, and reinforcing it with steel bars as necessary (Figure 3.18).

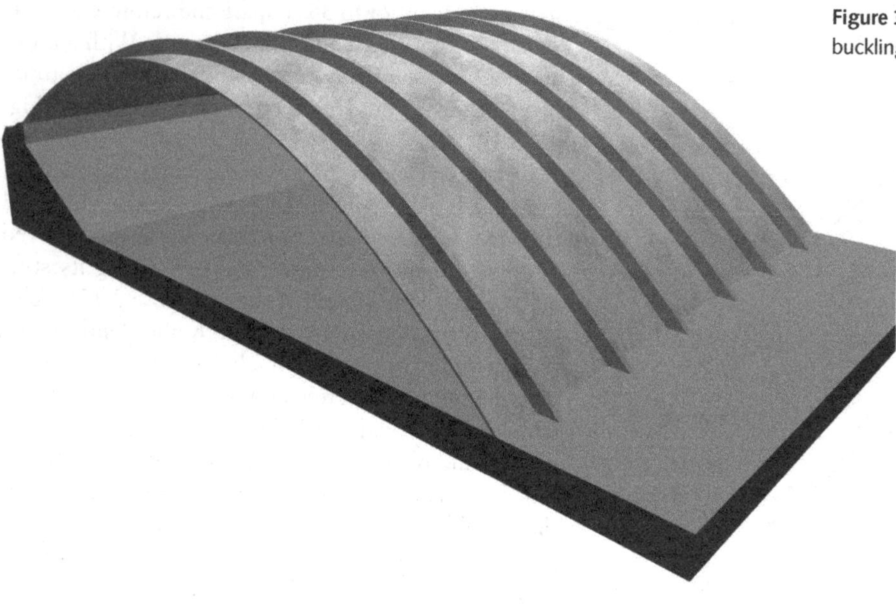

Figure 3.13 Adding ribs to resist buckling.

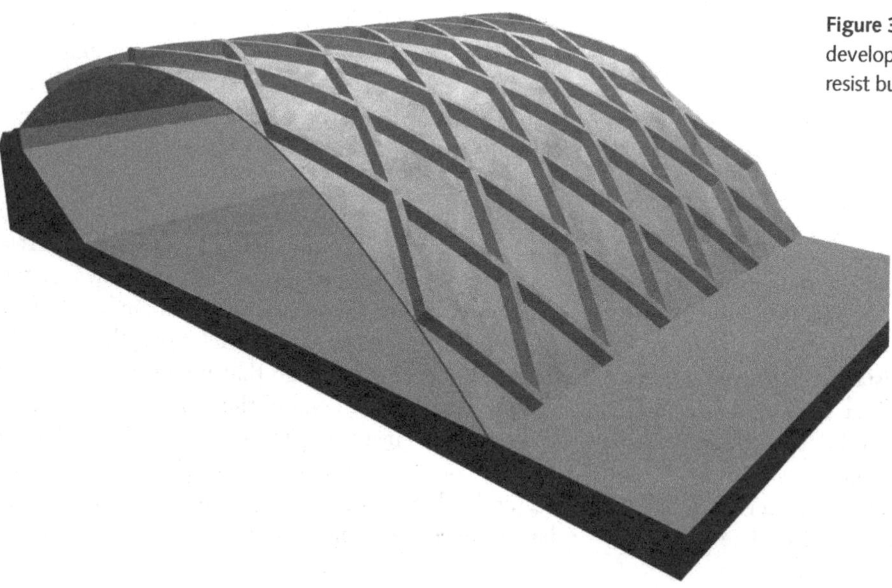

Figure 3.14 Further architectural development, using diagonal ribs to resist buckling.

ELADIO DIESTE

Eladio Dieste (1917–2000) was a Uruguayan engineer and builder who spent his long career designing arched and vaulted structures made of steel-reinforced brick masonry. Among his particularly creative works were the Church of Christ the Worker (Atlantida, 1960), which is made up of ruled surfaces with undulating curves, and the Church of San Pedro (Durazno, 1971), which is composed of folded plates. Both churches are made entirely of reinforced brickwork.

Most of Dieste's structures were low-cost roofs for factories and storage facilities in Uruguay that are based on parabolic or catenary sections. The dramatic and often surprising thinness of his designs is a Dieste hallmark. He wrote: "In many cases structures have the ability to move us and attract us because they are mysteriously expressive . . . . We perceive these structures not only with our eyes but with our spirit, and they display a more exact adaptation to the laws that control matter in equilibrium . . . . Giving form to a work . . . is like leaping into a void, and we want that jump to be more of a flight than a fall, [. . .] but we must remember that there is no art without science, and that it will take much rational effort to acquire the ability to take that jump." (Eladio Dieste, *La Estructura Ceramica.* Bogota: Escala, 1987, p. 152.)

Figure 3.15 This gymnasium roof in Montevideo, Uruguay, designed by Eladio Dieste, is made up of long, narrow shells in reinforced brick masonry. Each strip has an S-curved profile that stiffens it against buckling and allows for generous clerestory daylighting. To keep the interior space clear of tie rods, Dieste extended the columns above the high point of the roof and ran external tie rods horizontally at the tops of the columns.

Figure 3.16 An unfolded piece of paper has little rigidity compared to a corrugated sheet.

Figure 3.17 Variations on ribs and corrugations for the vault, including options with lateral skylights.

Edge beam

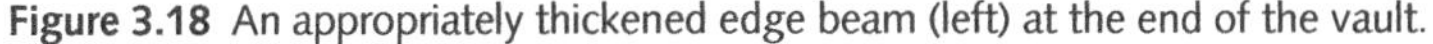

Figure 3.18 An appropriately thickened edge beam (left) at the end of the vault.

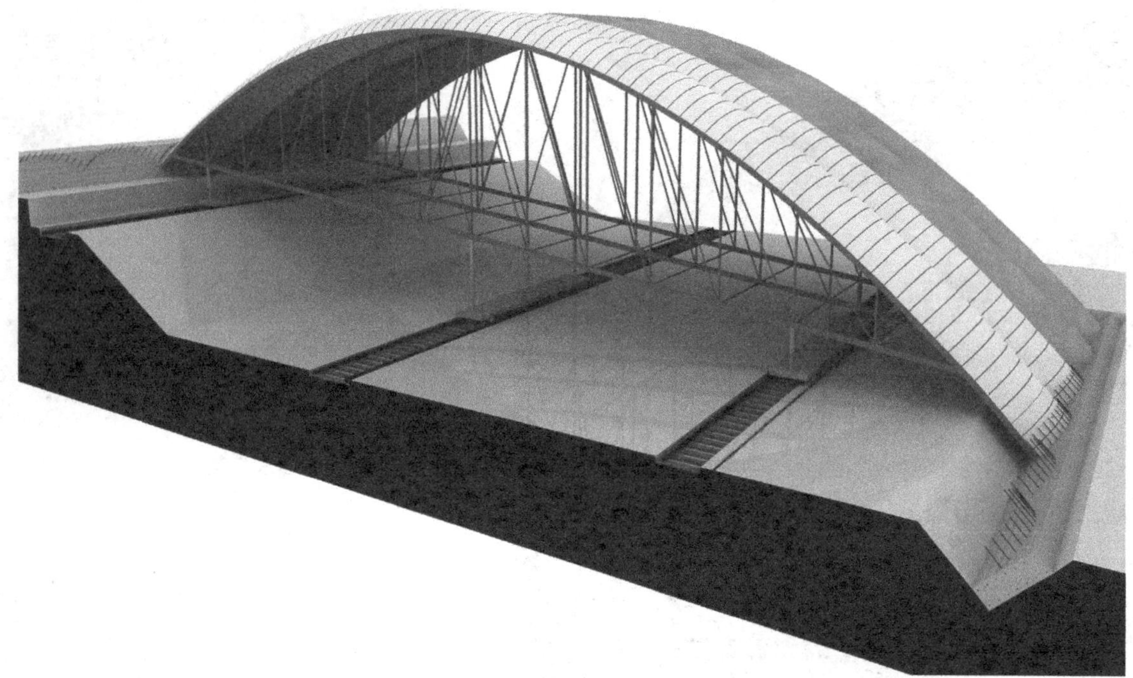

Figure 3.19 Construction diagram with single-sided formwork.

CONSTRUCTING THE VAULT

A concrete vault is usually constructed in increments on a broad strip of formwork that is used a number of times. The formwork is constructed as a unit that can be raised, lowered, and moved laterally on rails (Figure 3.19). It is jacked into position for the first strip and its surface is coated with a *form release compound* that prevents the wet concrete from sticking to the formwork. The reinforcing bars are placed over the formwork on *chairs,* small devices made of plastic or heavy wire. These support the bars at a specified distance above the surface of the form in order to produce the required concrete cover. The bars are wired together where they intersect one another to help keep them in place during pouring. Concrete is then cast over the formwork, embedding the bars and their supports. Small *test cylinders* are poured simultaneously from each batch of concrete and set alongside the vault to *cure* (harden) under the same conditions as the vault. The upper surface of the vault is finished smoothly with floats and trowels.

Curing of the concrete vault is facilitated by covering it with an impervious sheet of plastic or by spraying its surface with a *curing compound* that forms a water-retentive film. Either of these procedures acts to retain the water in the concrete for as long as possible in order to hydrate fully the complex mineral crystals that give concrete its strength. It is critical that the concrete not be allowed to dry out or to freeze for at least a month after casting.

The strip of vault must cure for some days before it is strong enough to support itself safely. Several of the cylinders that were made at the time of the pouring of the vault are transported from the site every few days and tested for strength in a materials laboratory. When these tests show that the required strength has been achieved, the formwork is lowered on its jacks and the strip of vault becomes self-supporting. The formwork is then moved parallel to the axis of the vault on its rails, and jacked up into position to cast the next strip (Figure 3.19). There it is cleaned and coated again with form release compound; then the cycle begins again, to be repeated as many times as needed to produce a structure of the required length.

"The resistant virtues of the structures that we seek depend on their form; it is through their form that they are stable, not because of an awkward accumulation of material. There is nothing more noble and elegant from an intellectual viewpoint than this: to resist through form."

—Eladio Dieste

As the curve of a vault approaches the ground, it becomes steeper and steeper. It is important that it not be so steep that gravity will pull the wet concrete off of it. This requires careful coordination of the geometry of the vault and the consistency of the concrete. The wet concrete may be made stiffer by lowering its water content, adding short fibers of polypropylene to the mix, or using chemical admixtures. If the vault surface becomes so steep that all these strategies taken together cannot keep the concrete in place, then an outer surface must be added to the formwork, which adds considerably to its cost and complexity (Figure 3.20). An example of a steep shell that used this double-surface formwork is shown in Figure 3.21.

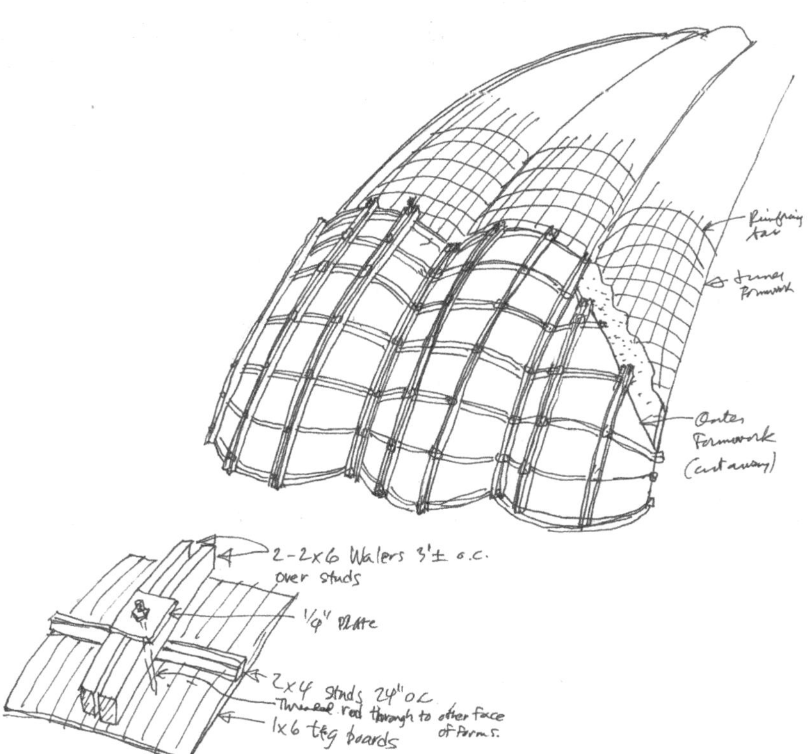

◀**Figure 3.20** A cutaway sketch showing the use of outer formwork.

(a)

(b)

Figure 3.21 Views of a dirigible hangar (a) built in 1916–1923 at Orly, France, by Eugene Freyssinet. A construction view (b) shows the outer formwork on the steeper portions. Note the door at the bottom for scale; each hangar was formed of shells less than 100 mm (4 in.) thick, yet formed a structure with a span of approximately 75 m (246 ft). At the top of the corrugations are longitudinal tie rods to resist spreading of the corrugations.

Source: As reproduced in Jose Fernandez-Ordonez, Eugene Freyssinet. 2c Editions, 1979.

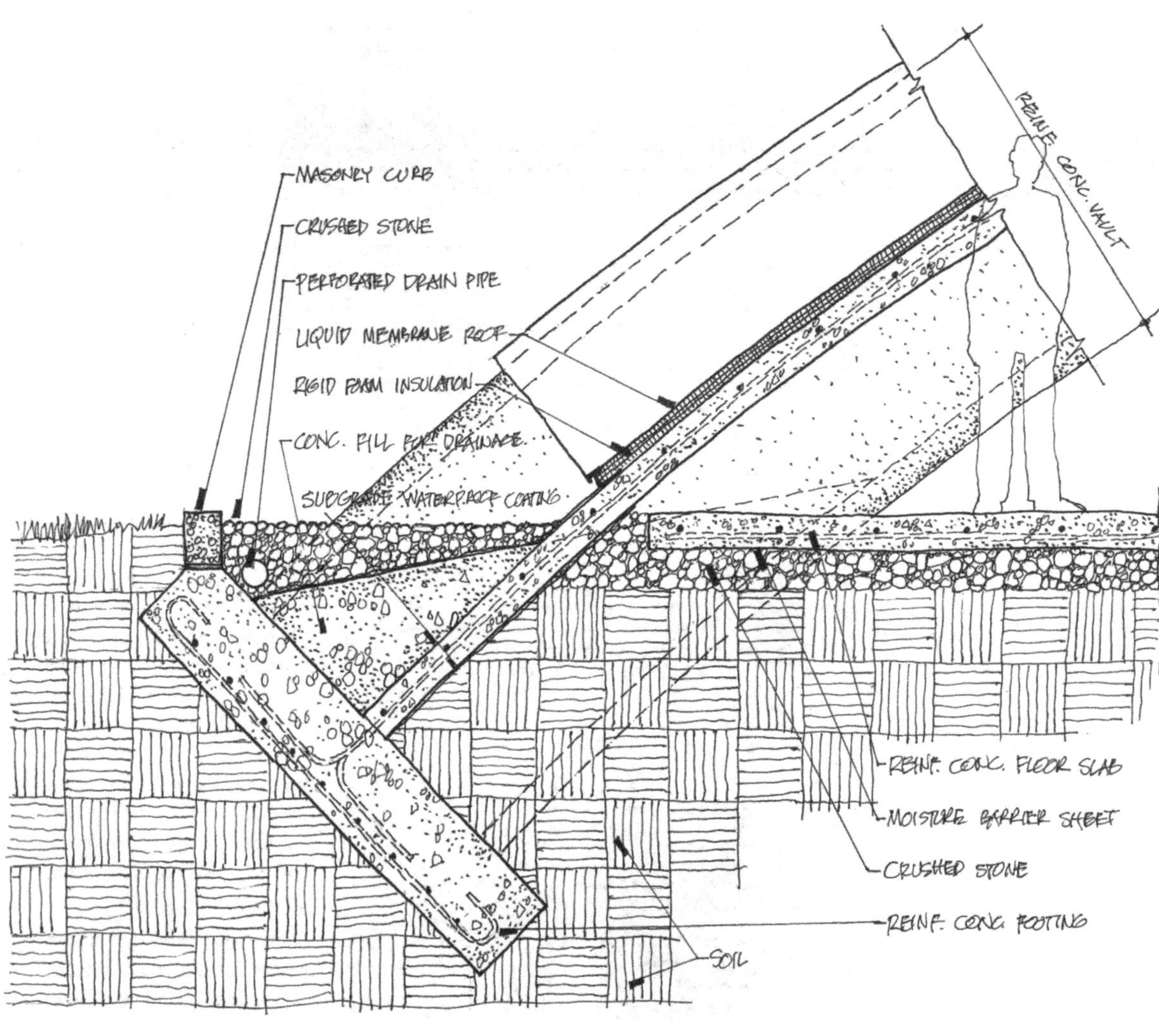

Figure 3.22 Early sketch detail of base of vault.

DETAILING THE VAULT

The details of the vault are comparatively simple (Figure 3.22). The reinforcing bars project out of the edge of each strip of vault in the direction of movement of the formwork. When the bars are placed for the next strip, they overlap these projecting bars to join the strips securely together.

The vault as a whole exerts a substantial lateral thrust, pushing outward against its foundations. If the vault is on flat ground, this thrust is usually resisted by placing steel rods inside the floor slab from the foundations at one long edge of the vault to the foundations at the other (Figure 3.23). These rods act in tension to balance the two thrusts against one another. In the case of the arena that we are designing, one side of the vault is considerably higher than the other. If we placed steel rods across the level floor and then up the steep incline of the bleachers, the thrust of the vault would tend to pull them up into a straight line, destroying the floor slab and allowing the vault to spread. Tensile foundations could be installed at the bends in the rods to prevent this problem by pulling down on the rods.

Another way of resisting the lateral thrust is to anchor each edge of the vault to the soil. If the soil is very hard and stable, like the rock on our site, this can be achieved with spread footings whose undersurface is perpendicular to the thrust line of the vault, or by level footings that have a substantial vertical surface that bears against the soil (Figure 3.24).

Finishing the Roof

There are various ways to insulate and waterproof a concrete shell roof. We decide to specify a system that insulates the roof with a thick, sprayed-on layer of plastic foam. A specially extruded molding makes a sharp, closed, water-resistant edge for the lower edge of the foam and membrane. The foam adheres tightly to the concrete, and its rough surface is trimmed flat before a liquid elastomeric (rubber-like) compound is sprayed on over the foam to make the roof watertight.

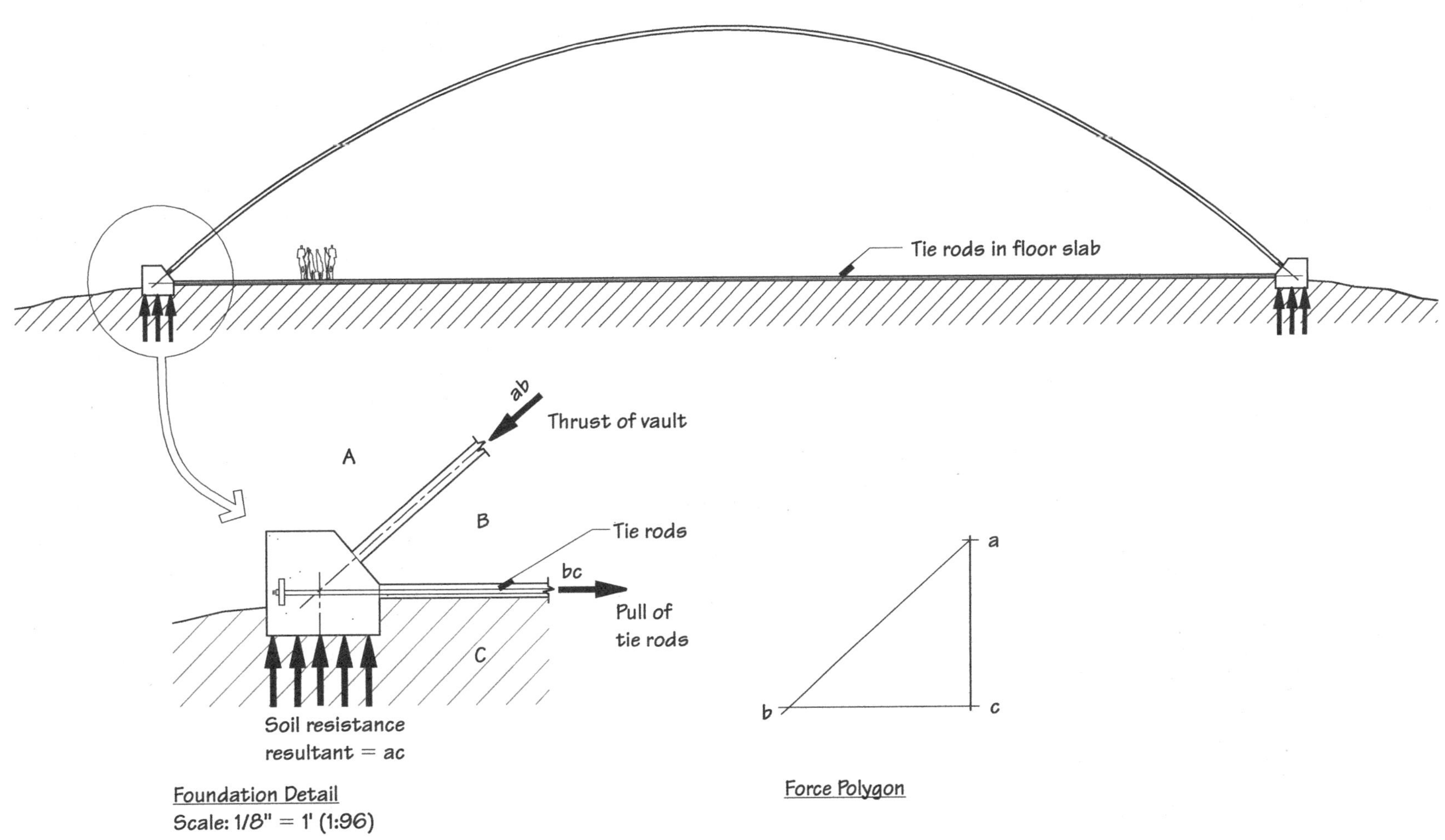

Figure 3.23 An alternate foundation configuration that incorporates tie rods on a flat site.

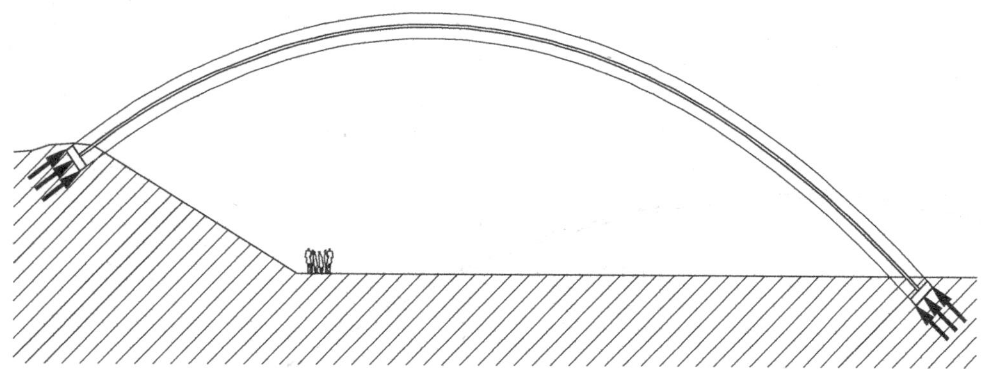

Figure 3.24 A section drawing showing inclined spread footing foundations.

Figure 3.25 A cutaway view of the material assembly for the end walls.

DESIGNING THE END WALLS

Many elegant roof shells have been defaced with inelegant end walls, a fate that we would like to avoid. We propose to echo the arched corrugations of the roof surface in end walls that are similar in form to the vaults. These will be built of reinforced masonry about 10 in. thick (Figure 3.25). A typical method of construction is for masons to lay an outer, nonstructural surface of brick masonry that is backed up by a 2-in. cavity and a structural, inner layer of concrete blocks. The blocks are reinforced with vertical and horizontal steel bars inserted into their hollow cores. The block cores are then filled with a cementitious *grout* to embed the bars. The 2-in. cavity is left empty to drain away any water that penetrates through the outer layer.

The interior surfaces of the concrete block walls will be insulated. This is usually done by installing light-gauge metal framing adjacent to the inner surface of the wall but not touching it, inserting glass fiber batts into the spaces between the framing, and finishing the wall with either gypsum wallboard or lath and plaster.

At the ends of the building, sloping glass skylights at the tops of the end walls will bring natural light into the finished building (Figure 3.26). These will be separate assemblies of glass in aluminum frames, fabricated off-site, lifted and lowered into place by cranes, and bolted down to the tops of the exterior walls (Figure 3.27). We will need to do studies to be sure that these skylights will not create glare.

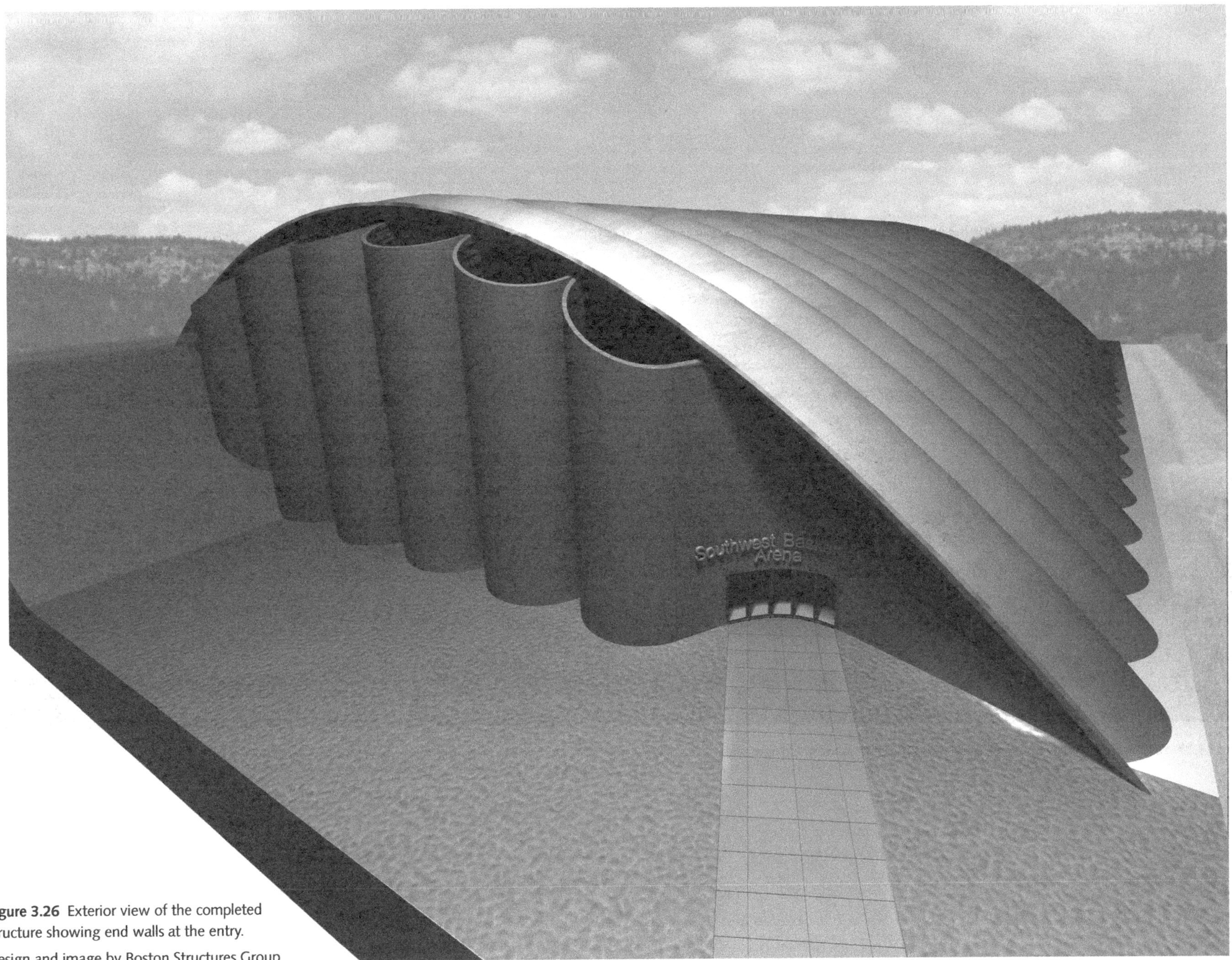

Figure 3.26 Exterior view of the completed structure showing end walls at the entry.

Design and image by Boston Structures Group.

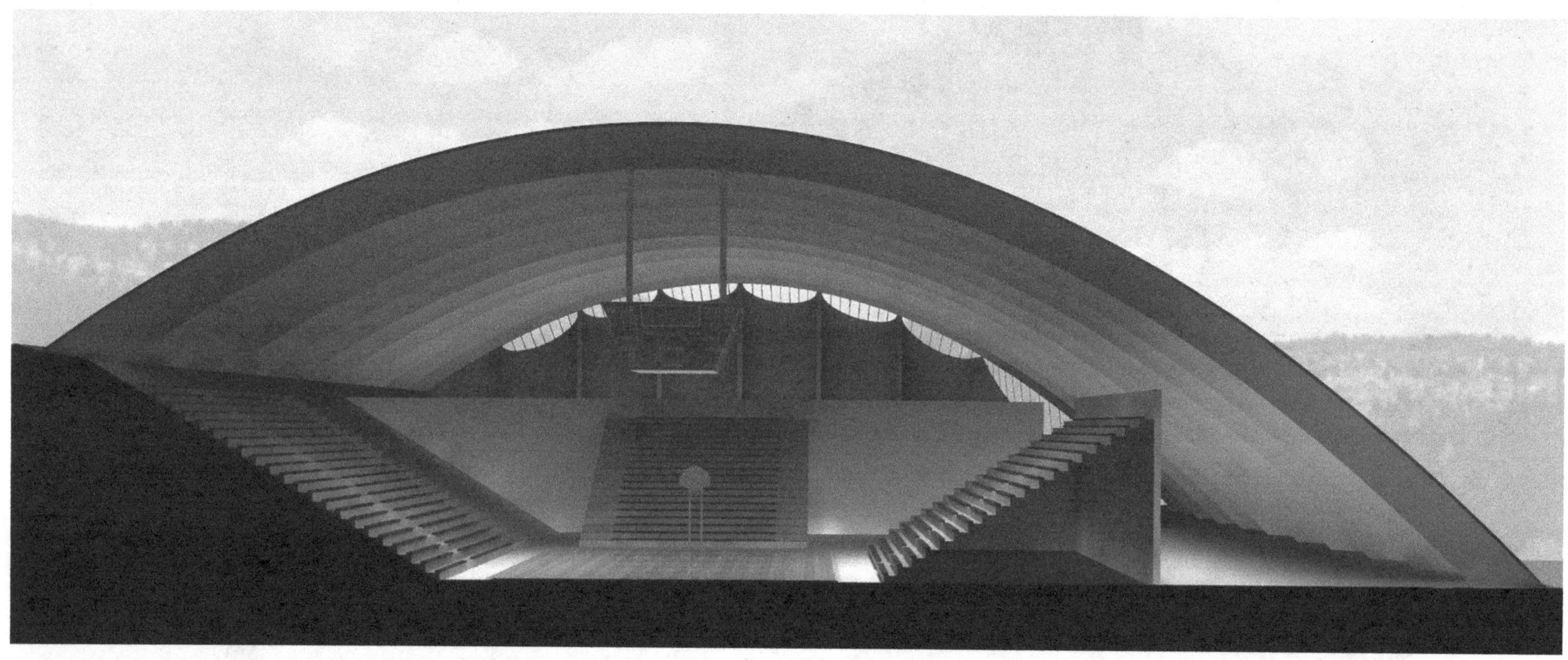

Figure 3.27 Sectional perspective view of the basketball courts and the skylights beyond.

APPLICATIONS IN OTHER MATERIALS

While we have completed this preliminary design of a vaulted form based on site-cast reinforced concrete, the form and many of the strategies we have developed could be adapted to other construction materials and systems. Figure 3.28 depicts assemblies of four such applications in other materials: (a) steel truss-joist arches with corrugated steel decking; (b) steel wide-flange arches and purlins with corrugated steel decking; (c) glue-laminated wood arches and purlins covered with tongue-and-groove wood decking; and (d) precast concrete arches with precast purlins and precast hollow-core decking.

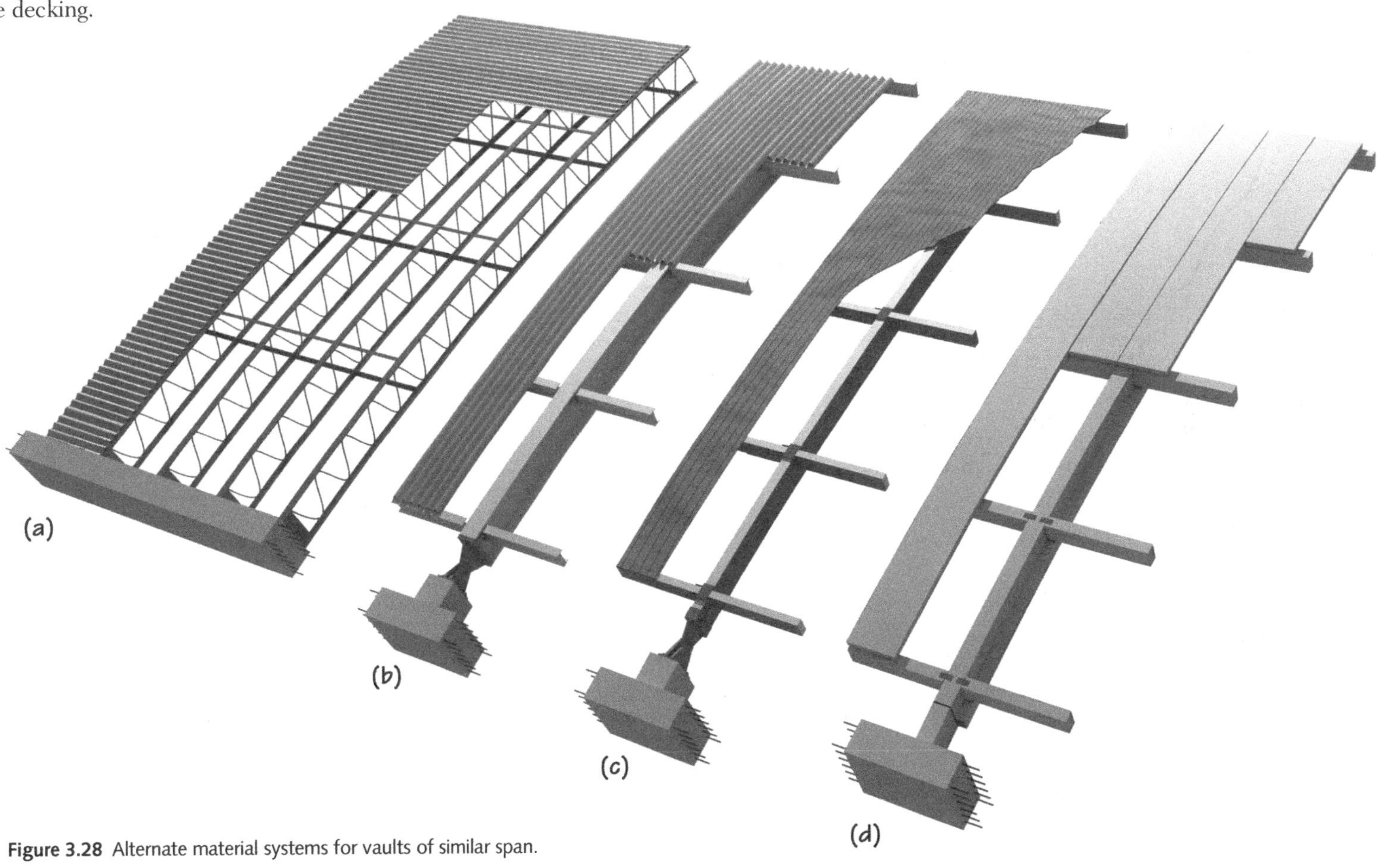

Figure 3.28 Alternate material systems for vaults of similar span.

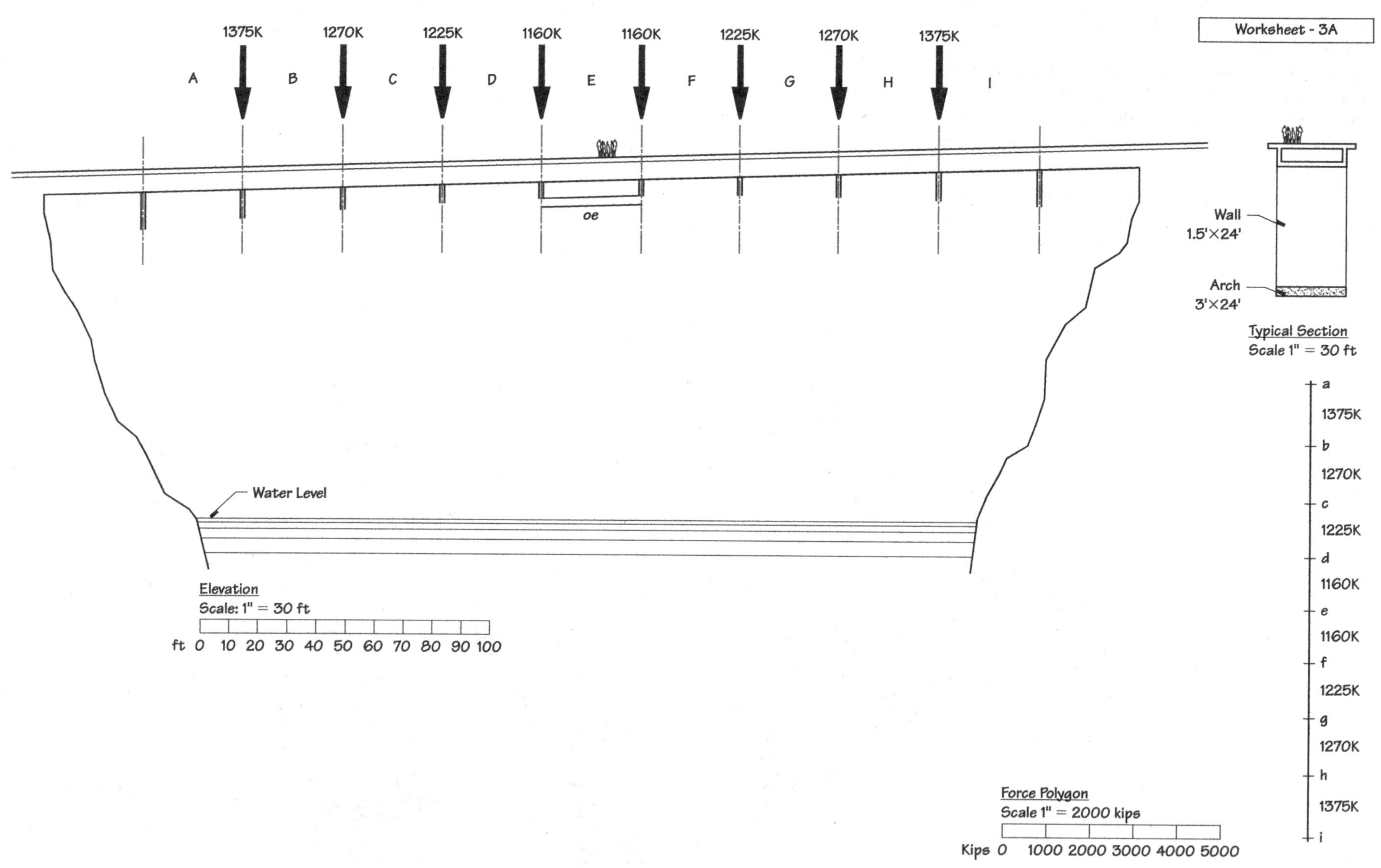

Figure 3.29 Worksheet #3A. A design challenge for a concrete arch bridge. This reproduction has been reduced to fit the page and cannot be scaled.

ANOTHER CHALLENGE

Figure 3.29 is a reduced version of Worksheet #3A, which may be downloaded and printed from the supplemental site provided with this book. It depicts a bridge deck that carries two lanes of automobile traffic over a river gorge. The clear span is 324 ft. The deck slopes at an inclination of 3 percent (3 ft in 100 ft).

The deck is supported at eight equally spaced locations by vertical concrete walls that transmit the loads to a concrete arch. Because of the rise and fall of the arch, the heights of these walls, and therefore their self-weights, vary considerably. The height of each wall has been estimated, its approximate self-weight has been determined, and the total load conducted to the arch by each wall, including the weights of the vehicles and the deck, has been recorded next to a vertical vector on the form diagram of the bridge. These loads have also been plotted on a load line on the worksheet.

The arch is a concrete slab of constant dimension, 3 ft thick by 24 ft wide. It will be made of concrete that has an allowable stress for this application of 800 psi. For a simple, natural appearance, we have decided that the center segment of the arch, *oe*, should be parallel to the bridge deck. Your challenge is to find the shape of the arch and to determine the force in each segment of it under the given loading.

How to Proceed

This would seem to be a very complicated problem. The deck isn't level, the loads vary, and the arch is not level. But a graphical solution is surprisingly easy and rewarding. As with any construction of a funicular shape, the problem is one of finding the right pole location for the force polygon. The loads are not identical, so we can't use the properties of a parabola to find the pole. We could use the method we just developed for finding a funicular curve through any three points, but this is laborious and it will not necessarily produce an arch whose center segment is parallel to the deck. Instead, we will use the information given to locate the pole:

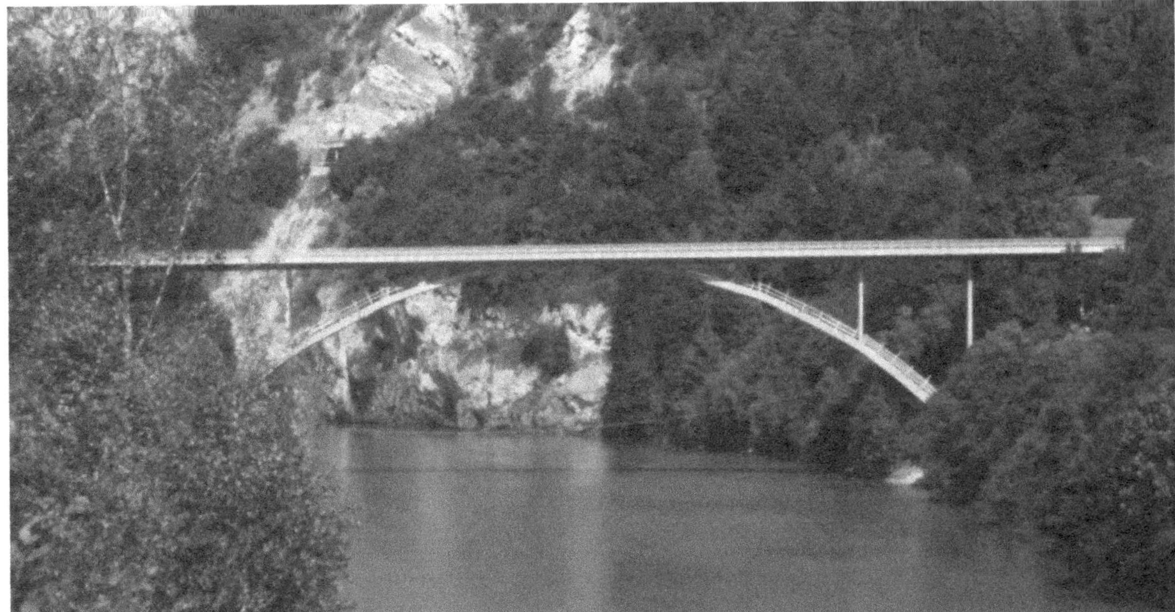

Figure 3.30 The Reichenau Bridge in Switzerland, designed by engineer Christian Menn, is similar to the bridge you are challenged with designing. Notice that the arch has a slight curvature between nodes so as to be funicular for its self-weight. The number of walls needed to bring the loads from the deck to the arch was reduced substantially by posttensioning the arch and deck to give them additional stiffness against unbalanced loads.

Photos: Edward Allen.

1. We know the inclination of the center segment of the arch, *oe*. Ray *oe* of the force polygon must have the same inclination.
2. We know the cross-sectional dimensions of the arch, 3 ft by 24 ft, and we know the allowable stress in the concrete, 800 lb per square inch. The maximum total force that can be exerted by the arch is determined by multiplying its cross-sectional area by the allowable stress. This maximum force will be represented by the longest ray on the force polygon.

With these two pieces of information, you should be able to locate the pole, generate the shape of the arch, and find the forces in its segments. When you have completed the centerline of the arch, draw the upper and lower edges of each segment of the arch 3 ft apart to show its thickness, and complete the vertical lines that represent the edges of the walls that bring the loads to the arch from the deck. This will complete the picture of the bridge. You may also consult the tutorial labeled "Designing a Concrete Arch Bridge" on the supplemental site.

◀ **Figure 3.31** The Winter Garden in Sheffield, United Kingdom, was designed by Pringle Richards Sharratt Architects as an urban greenhouse. One of the largest structures in the country to use glue-laminated wood, its arches reach a maximum of 21 m (69 ft) in height while remaining a consistent 22 m (72 ft) wide over the 70-m (230-ft) length of the structure. The design includes ventilation and temperature sensors that predict changes in internal temperature and act to prevent excessive variations while minimizing energy consumption.

Photo: David M. Foxe.

▲ **Figure 3.32** The Migöelou Dam, Lake Migöelou, France, 1958, expresses very poetically the way in which it holds back the waters of the reservoir behind. Designed and built by Electricite de France and the firm Coyne et Bellier, its nine shells are 147 ft high and span 82 ft each. They are 3 ft–3 in. thick, which is remarkably thin, given water pressures that reach more than 9,000 psf at the bottom of the dam. Notice that the axes of the shells are inclined to assist the buttresses in directing their thrust into the ground. What would be the ideal curve for these shells?

Photo courtesy of Photo Alix, as featured in the 1964 MoMA publication *Twentieth Century Engineering*.

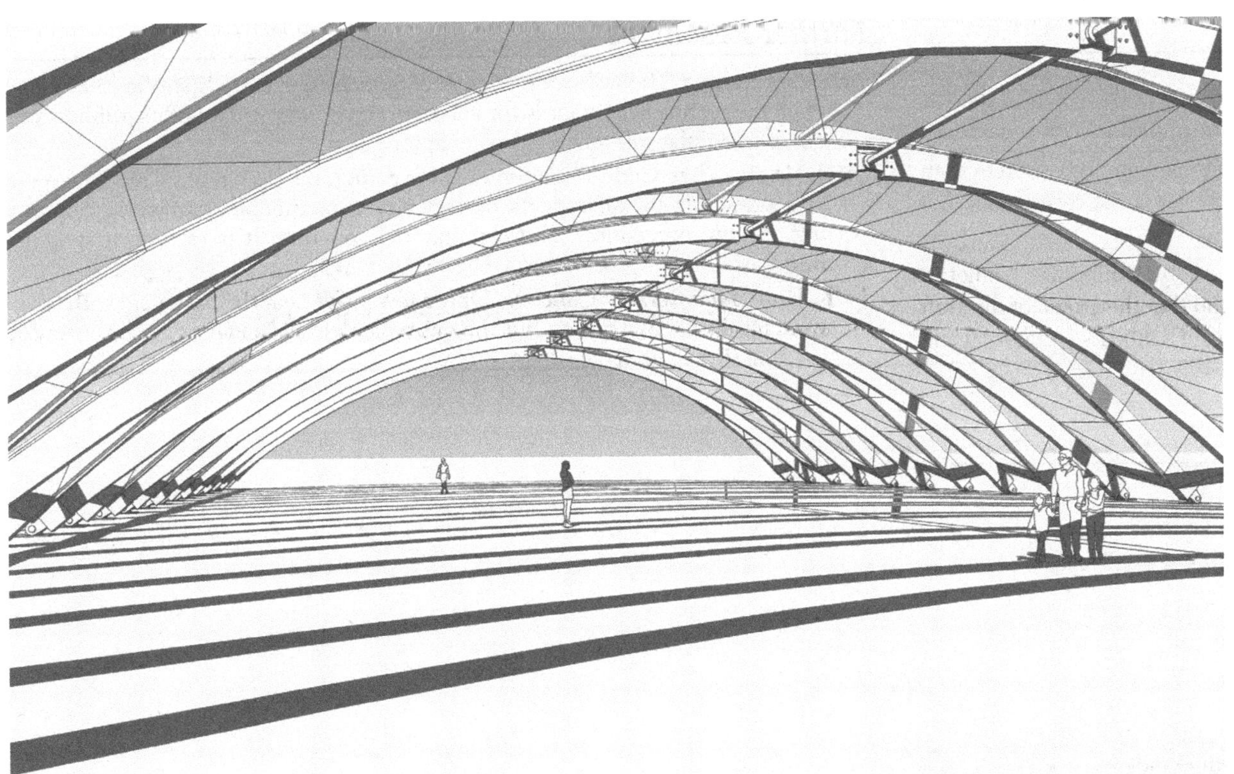

Figure 3.33 While a student at the Boston Architectural College, Karri Harlan designed this arched market roof as a project for her first structures course.

Photo courtesy of Karri Harlan.

Figure 3.34 The Olympic Oval in Calgary shelters a speed-skating rink with crossing arches made of precast concrete. The ends of the arch elements were cast as hollow troughs with protruding reinforcing bars inside the hollows. Bars from adjacent elements cross within each hollow. This produced a moment connection when the hollows were filled with grout.

Photo courtesy of GEC Architecture.

Exercises

1. Vary the thickness of the arch in the previous exercise so that each of its segments is fully stressed to 800 psi. Does this improve the appearance of the bridge?

2. Construct the curves of two more arches for the bridge, one for concrete with an allowable stress of 600 psi and one for 1,000 psi. What is the relationship between concrete strength and the depth of the arch?

3. The U.S. Coast Guard has just advised us that the actual shipping channel in the river lies 80 ft to the left of the center of the river and that the crown of the arch will have to occur in this location so that the tall masts of sailboats will not hit the arch. Develop a new form for the arch that will satisfy this requirement.

Key Terms

shell
catenary
parabola
vault
stress
allowable stress
pressure line
bending stress
pole
trial funicular polygon
buckle
edge beam
formwork
chairs
curing compound
grout

Further Resources

www.concrete.org: The web address of the American Concrete Institute, the source of all the technical standards for concrete construction. Two of its publications are of particular relevance to this chapter:

"ACI 318–Building Code Requirements for Structural Concrete." This document sets standards for all aspects of concrete construction: formwork, reinforcing, job-site procedures, and the material concrete. It is revised at frequent intervals.

M. K. Hurd. *Formwork for Concrete.* Only a few pages near the back deal with formwork for domes and vaults, but the entire book is a fascinating, well-illustrated introduction to its topic.

CHAPTER 4

Master Lesson: Designing a Trussed Roof

- *Structural idea generation in three dimensions: the creative process*
- *Graphical truss analysis: influence of truss form and depth on member forces*
- *Creative latitude in structural design and interactions between architects and engineers*

"This is a rough drawing of the truss that I want you to engineer," said the architect, pointing to a sheet he had laid on the conference table (4.1). "It's for the roof of a seafarers' chapel on the Rhode Island coast, overlooking Narragansett Bay. The original, nineteenth-century chapel was made of wood, and it burned to the ground a couple of years ago. Now the charitable trust that looks after the chapel is ready to rebuild, and they've asked for a contemporary design rather than a replica of the original."

The structural engineer looked at the sketch.

"A scissors truss? In wood?"

"Yes, wood, supported by rubble-stone load-bearing walls. I like the way the lifted bottom chord of the truss shapes the space of the chapel. It's not much of a span, only 22 ft, but I want the roof structure to be an important aspect of the architecture, and trusses seem to me to be a good way to do that."

"Trusses **are** *a good way to do that. Yours is a very slender truss. The top and bottom members meet at very acute angles."*

"Yes, I want it to be very slim and elegant."

"At what points are loads being applied to this truss?"

"I'm thinking that the roof will be framed with wood rafters 2 ft on center. The lower ends will rest on the tops of the walls. I would ordinarily want to have horizontal ties or ceiling joists at the bottom to keep the lower ends of the rafters from spreading, but that would spoil the grand space of the chapel. So my idea is to have the roof's ridge board be not just a board, but rather a ridge beam that supports the upper ends of the rafters. And the ridge beam is supported every 8 ft by scissors trusses."

"Okay, that makes sense. The trusses are loaded only at the top node, the apex."

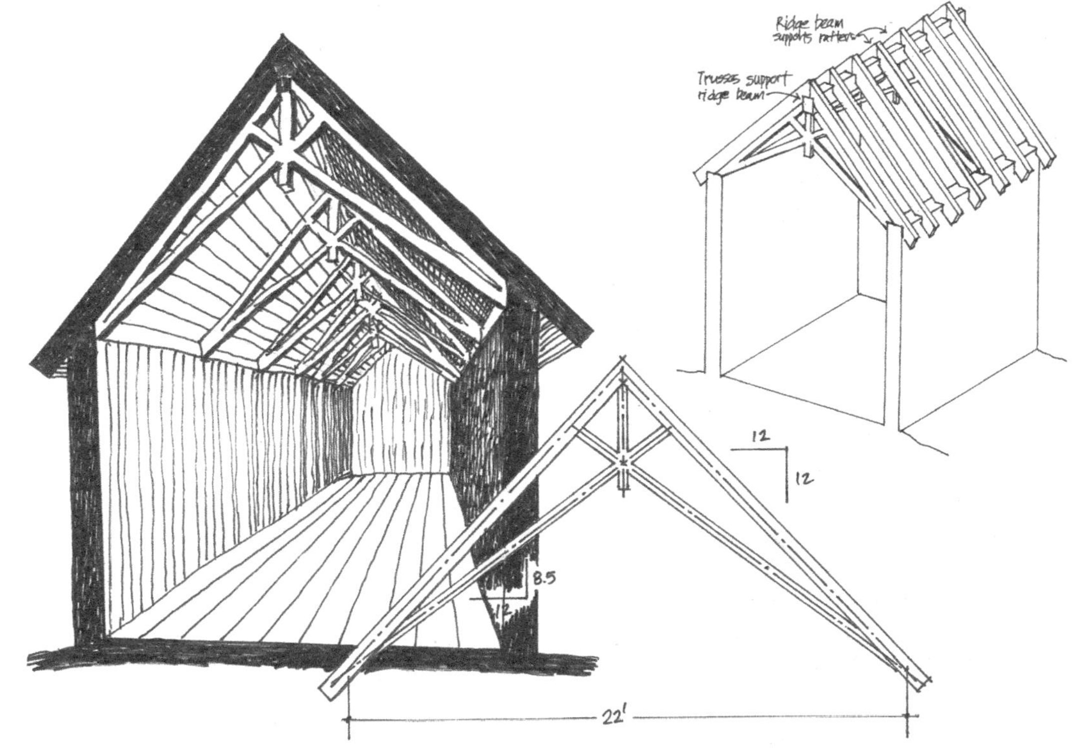

Figure 4.1

"That was my assumption."

The engineer studied the drawings for a few moments, then spoke.

"There's something about the geometric patterns of trusses that people seem to find fascinating. I think it's partly the way the truss members appear to overlap in changing ways as you walk beneath them, and partly that the shapes of trusses demonstrate how they work to support loads. These trusses that you've drawn form wonderful patterns and they give a good shape to the interior space. But before we go further, let me show you a few things about trusses that will be helpful in understanding this project. Suppose for a few minutes that we're designing a roof truss that's just a simple triangle."

A diagram emerged from the engineer's pencil (4.2).

"Not nearly as interesting as my scissors truss."

"I agree, it's not visually interesting at all; but in order to talk intelligently about your scissors trusses, I want to go through a few aspects of truss design with you, and a simple triangular truss is a good place to start. Let's look at the forces in its members."

Using a rolling ruler, the engineer drew the form of the truss, along with arrows to indicate a load on its apex and reactions at its lower corners.

"I'm going to do this graphically, which is a lot quicker than a numerical solution. I'll put the letters A, B, *and* C *between the external forces and the numeral* 1 *on the interior space of the truss, like this:"*(4.3) (A note to the reader: On the supplemental site, under "Form and Forces Graphical Techniques," the first interactive demonstration concerns a truss similar to the one being considered here.)

"Okay, but I fail to see the point of going into all this."

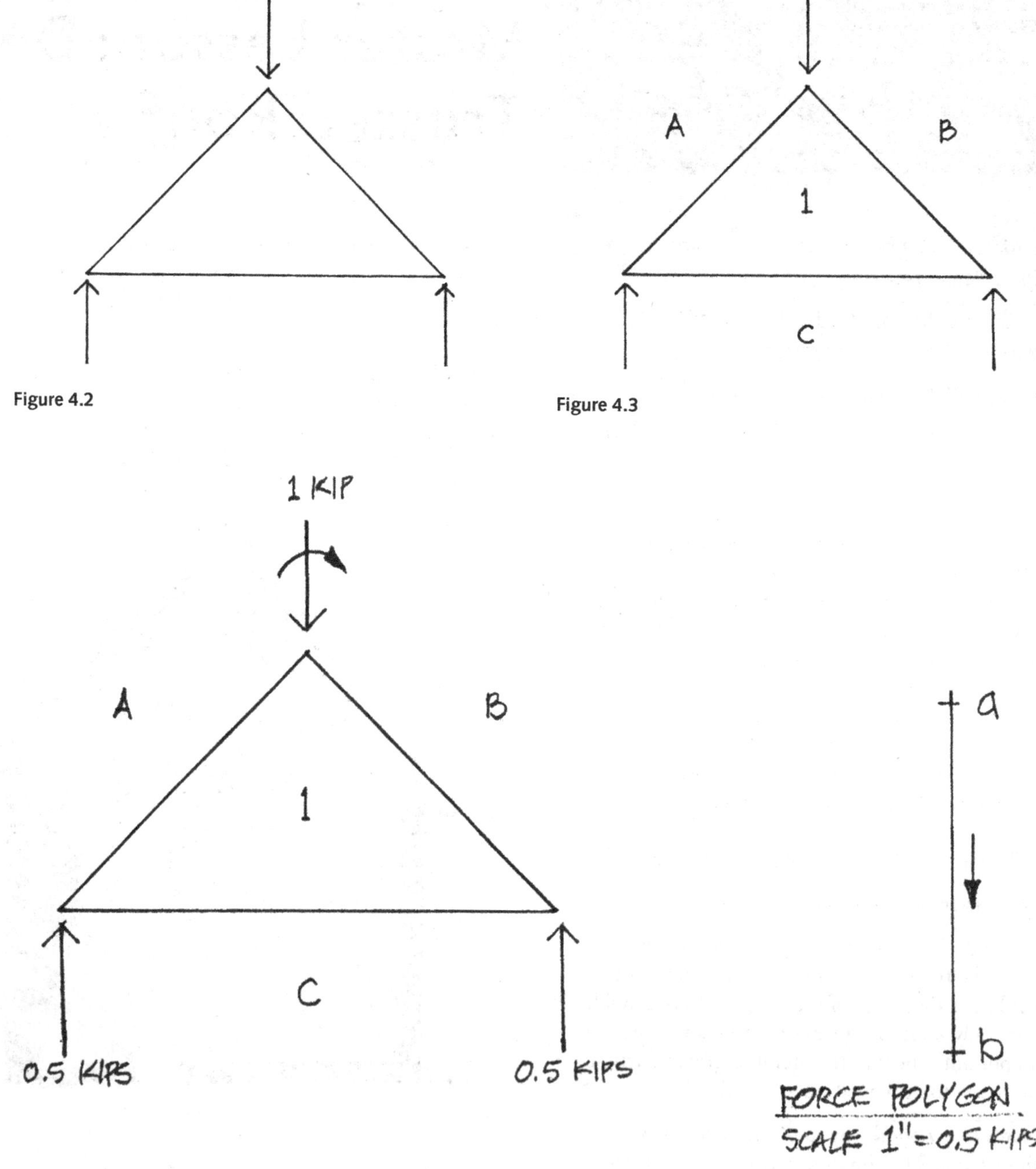

Figure 4.2

Figure 4.3

Figure 4.4

"Just bear with me for a few minutes. I assure you that this will be worth the little time that it will take. So far, I've drawn an accurate picture of the truss. It's called a form diagram. Now I'll draw a force polygon, which is a diagram of all the forces in this truss. It's drawn to a scale of inches to pounds or kips. In this case, I'm going to use a scale of 1 in. equals 0.5 kips. A kip is 1,000 lb, a kilopound, which has been shortened to kips. For simplicity, I'll assume that the load, P, *on the apex of the truss is one kip.*

"To start construction of the force polygon, I draw the load line, which is a diagram of the external forces on the truss (4.4). *I start the load line with* ab, *which is a vector that represents the load on the top joint. It's a vertical line whose length is equal to the load,* P, *which is one kip, or 2 in. at the scale we are using. Looking at the drawing of the form of the truss, when I go clockwise around the apex of the truss, where this load is applied, I go from* A *to* B. *This means that the load is named* AB, *not* BA. *When I go clockwise from* A *to* B, *the load is pushing down, so I put an* a *at the top of the vertical line and a* b *at the bottom, to indicate this downward direction of the force. Okay so far?"*

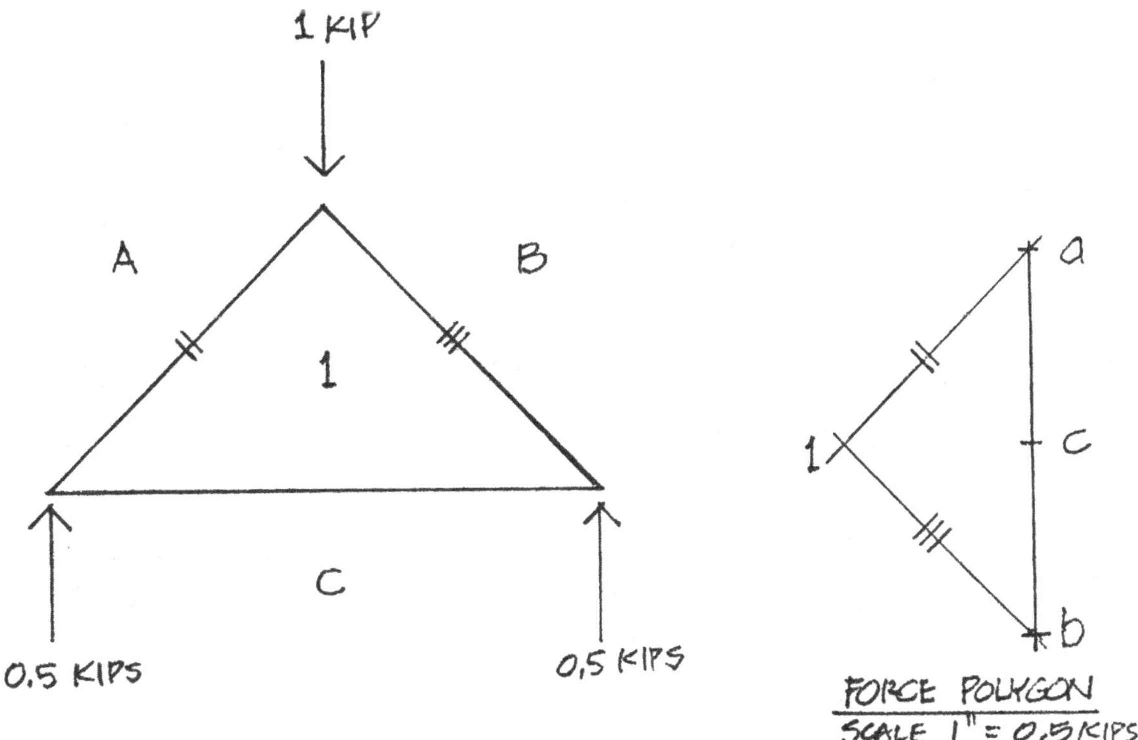

Figure 4.5

"Yes, I'm with you. But why do you put lowercase letters on the load line when you've used uppercase on the form diagram of the truss?"

"That's the conventional way of doing it. It helps to remind us that anything with lowercase letters is a vector representing the loads and forces, whereas anything with uppercase letters is only a picture of the form and not a vector representation. Now, continuing to read force names in clockwise order, the right-hand reaction is BC. *Its direction is up. That means that when I move from* b *to* c *on the load line, I am moving upward. Therefore, when I draw* bc *on the load line,* c *is above* b (4.5). *Because the truss is symmetrical, the two reactions are equal;* bc *is half of* ab, *which puts* c *in the center of the load line. Finally,* ca *is the other reaction, also in an upward direction. When I move from* c *to* a *on the load line, I am moving upward. This means that* a *must be above* c, *which brings us back to* a *on the load line. The load line closes, by which I mean that when we draw* bc *and* ca *we arrive back at* a, *the point from which we began."*

"Yes, I understand. But . . . "

"Now we'll plot lines representing the member forces on the force polygon. We do this by drawing lines parallel to the truss members on the form diagram. Each of these lines begins from the appropriate letter on the load line. We'll start at the top node, where members A1 *and* B1 *intersect* (4.6). *From* a *on the load line, I draw a line parallel to member* A1, *and from* b, *I draw a line parallel to* B1. *I'll put two hatches on both* A1 *and* a1 *to remind us that they're parallel, and three hatches on* B1 *and* b1. *The intersection on the force polygon of these two sloping lines,* a1 *and* b1, *is* 1. *Are you still following me?"*

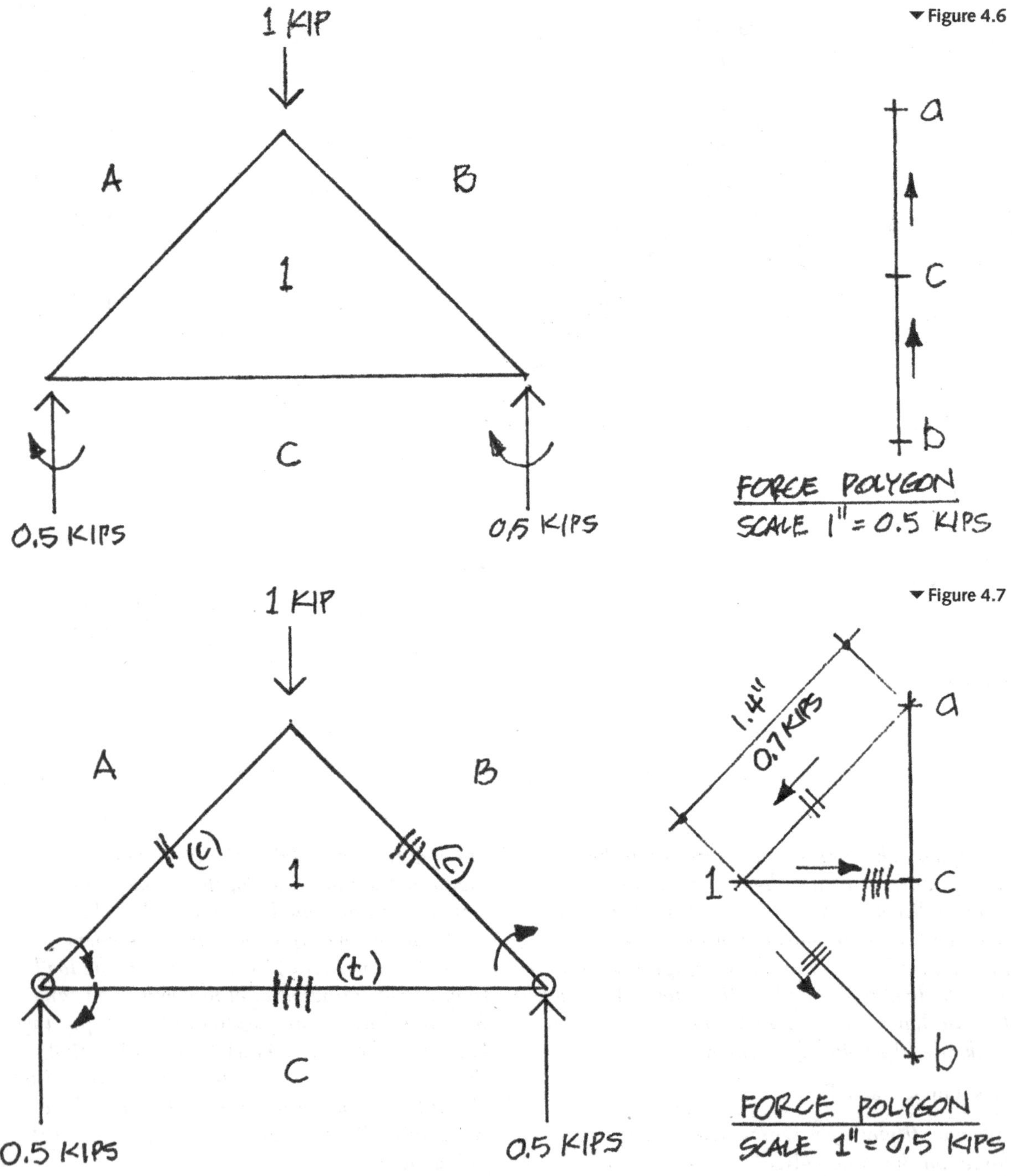

▾ Figure 4.6

▾ Figure 4.7

"Well, I'm a little confused. Tell me again how you know which point on the load line to connect to when you draw a line parallel to A1 on the force polygon, for example."

"Well, a1 *is the force in member* A1. *Because it has the letter* a *in its name, it connects with the letter* a *on the load line. And* b1, *because its name contains the letter* b, *connects to the load line at* b."

"Okay; it couldn't be simpler than that. Please go on."

"Let's see, we've plotted vectors for the forces in the two sloping members. That leaves just one more member force to plot, and that's c1. *This is represented by a line parallel to member* C1, *which is horizontal, so I draw a horizontal line through* c *on the force polygon. When I draw this line, it goes through point* 1 *that we just plotted. This means that the force polygon closes, which indicates that we've probably done everything right* (4.7)."

"It closes? What does that mean?"

"As I explained with the load line, it means that the last segment I draw on the force polygon connects perfectly to both of the points that should be on it. In this case, the last line has to be horizontal and has to go through c *and also* 1, *and that's what it does."*

"What if the force polygon doesn't close?"

"Then you have to figure out why not. Sometimes when you're analyzing a big truss, the last line will miss one of its points by a small amount. This is probably accumulated drafting error. If it's off by only 1 or 2 percent of the forces that come to that node, then you can just go ahead and use the values you measure from the force polygon, because accuracy to within 1 or 2 percent is a lot better than the accuracy of your live load estimates. If it misses by more than 5 percent, however, you'd better go back and redraw the diagram carefully from the beginning."

"All right, so what exactly is this force polygon showing us?"

"It shows the forces in all the members of the simple truss that I've drawn. I can measure the lines on the force polygon to find out what the forces are in the members of the truss. For example, line a1 is 1.4 in. long, meaning that it has about 700 lb of force in it. But I'm not interested so much in the numbers as I am in comparing relative forces in trusses of different shapes. I'll just use this example as a base case with which to compare other trusses that I'm about to draw. But before we do that, we should look at the character of the forces in the truss members: Which are in tension and which are in compression? We answer this question with a simple procedure. We start by selecting any node on the form diagram of the truss. Let's pick the lower left node. I will put my finger on this node to mark it temporarily. Now we read member names in clockwise order around this node. The sloping member, reading in clockwise order around my finger, is named A1. *As I read from* a *to* 1 *on the force polygon, I am reading downward and to the left. A force acting in this direction is pushing against my finger. This means that member* A1 *is in compression. I put a letter* c *in parentheses on the member in the form diagram as a shorthand indication of compression.*

"The bottom member, reading in clockwise order around my finger on the form diagram, is 1C. *As I read from* 1 *to* c *on the force polygon, I am reading rightward. A force acting in this direction is pulling away from my finger. Member* 1C *is in tension. To finish finding the characters of the forces, I'll move my finger to the lower right node on the form diagram. The sloping member, in clockwise order, is* 1B. *As I read from* 1 *to* b *on the force polygon, I'm moving down and to the right, which pushes against my finger;* 1B *is in compression. And just as a check, let's use this node to find again the direction of the force in the bottom member. Reading clockwise around the lower right-hand node, the bottom member is named* C1. *As I read from* C *to* 1 *on the force polygon, I'm moving from right to left. This pulls away from the lower right node.* C1 *is in tension."*

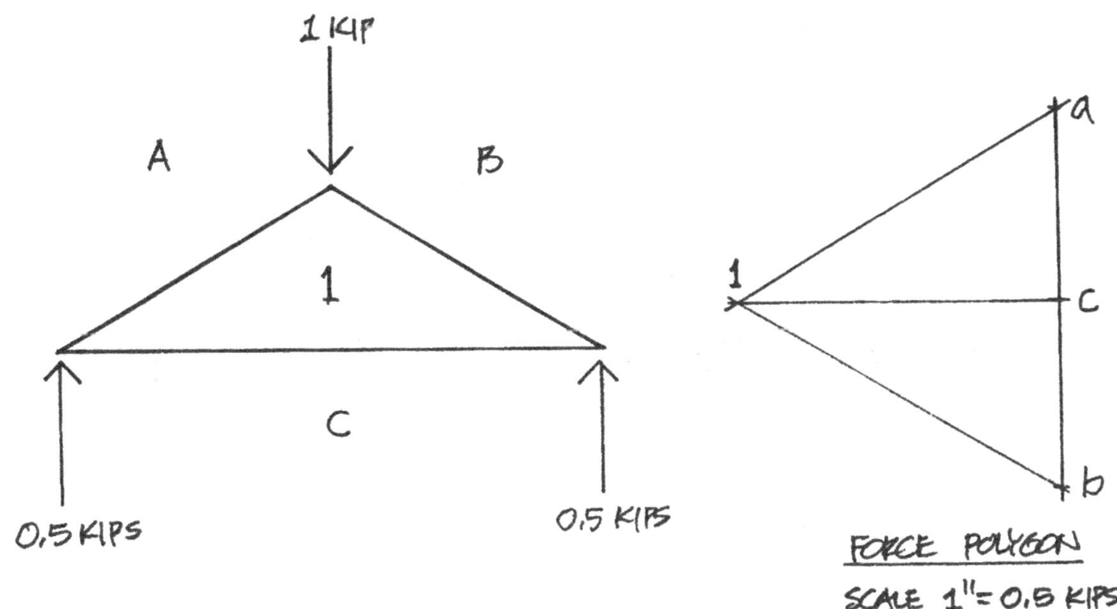

Figure 4.8

"Very clever! But what has this told us?"

"It hasn't told us anything yet; it just establishes a base case, to which I can compare the performances of some other simple trusses. For example, what happens if we reduce the height of the truss?"

The engineer drew a form diagram of another simple triangular truss, this one much flatter than the first one (4.8). As the rolling ruler skimmed back and forth, a new force polygon took shape on the whiteness of the paper.

"Okay, I've drawn the force polygons for both trusses to the same scale. When we compare the two, we can see at a glance that the member forces are much larger in the shallower truss."

"Engineering is not a science. Science studies particular events to find general laws. Engineering design makes use of these laws to solve particular problems. In this it is more closely related to art or craft; as in art, its problems are under-defined, there are many solutions, good, bad, or indifferent. The art is, by a synthesis of ends and means, to arrive at a good solution. This is a creative activity, involving imagination, intuition, and deliberate choice."

—Ove Arup

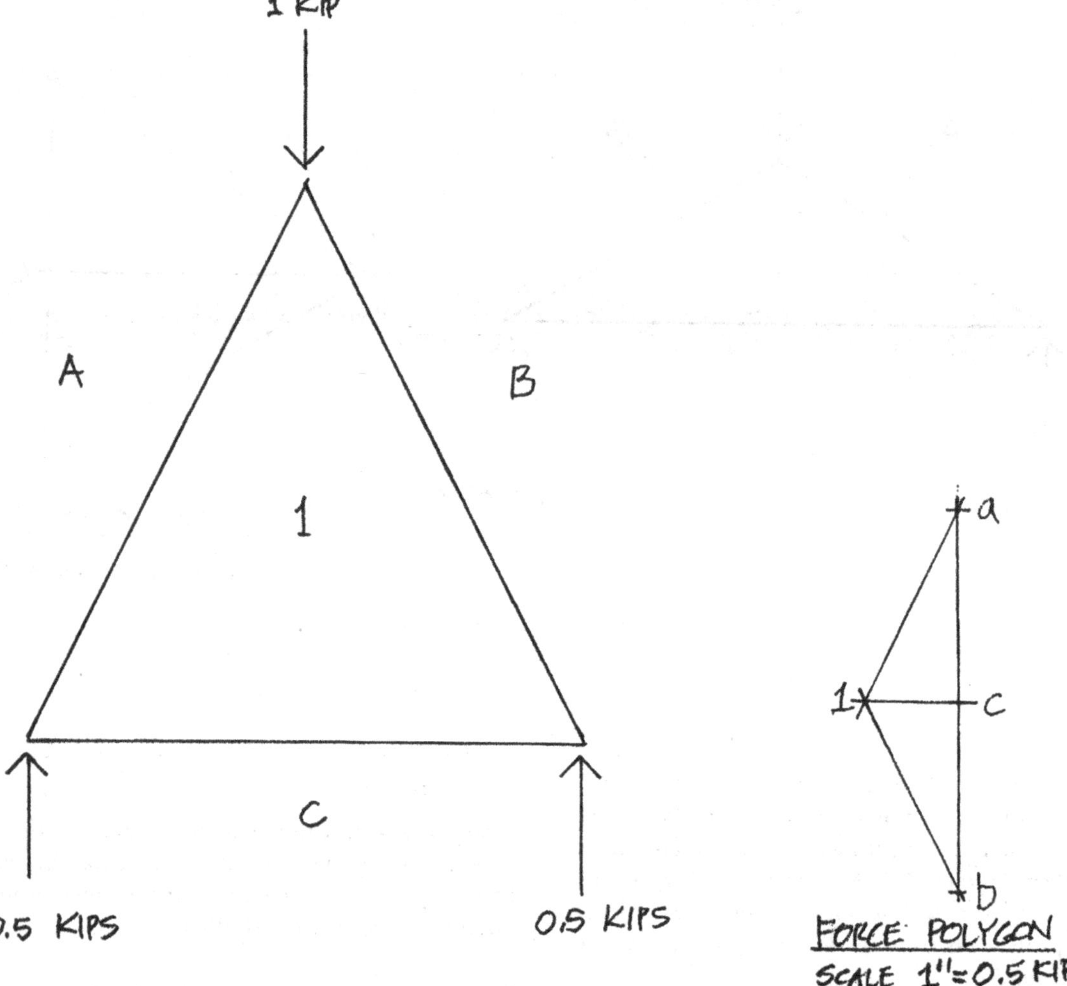

Figure 4.9

"Yes, that's obvious. But . . . ."

The engineer was already drawing a third example.

"Now I've drawn a truss that's deeper than the original one, and you can see from its force polygon that the member forces are much less than in either of the other two trusses (4.9). *So the first thing we've learned is that member forces vary inversely with the depth of the truss.*

"While we're at it, look at what happens if I invert the original truss, turning it upside down while keeping the directions of the external forces as they were."

A quick drawing showed the form diagram of a new truss and its force polygon (4.10).

"The force polygon looks the same; but let's check the directions of the forces. I'll read clockwise around point ab1 *on the form diagram. The left-hand sloping member, reading in clockwise order, is* b1. *As we move from* b *to* 1 *on the force polygon, we're moving up and to the left, pulling away from point* ab1 *on the form diagram of the truss.* B1 *is in tension. Similarly,* 1A *is in tension, and* C1 *is in compression. All the member forces reversed character when I inverted the truss. Tension members became compression members, and vice versa. This always happens when a truss, or any structure for that matter, is inverted and the directions of the external forces stay the same."*

"Okay, that's interesting, but I just want you to engineer my scissors truss. Why are you showing all this to me?"

"Because I want us to have a solid basis for talking about the form of your scissors truss."

The architect was visibly perplexed.

"What's to talk about? The form is already shown on the drawings I've brought for you."

"I want to explore some ideas with you. I think that we can improve the form. Just give me a few more minutes of your time to get you up to speed and you'll see what I mean. You'll be glad that we did it."

"Okay, just a few more minutes."

"Now, what do you think happens when we add a kingpost to the original truss? (4.11)*"*

"Hmm, I imagine that with another member to share the load, the member forces must go down."

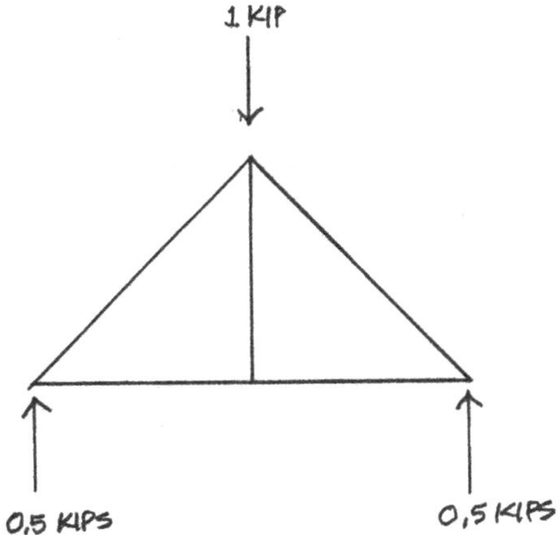

Figure 4.11

▼ Figure 4.10

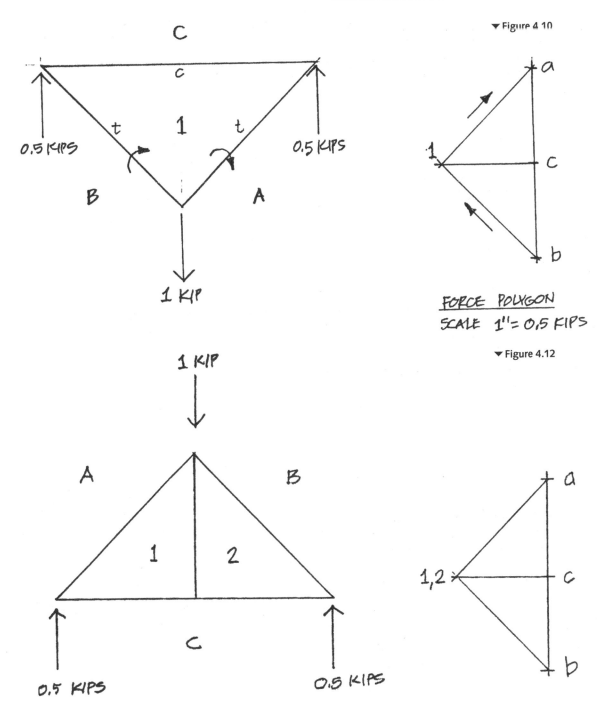

FORCE POLYGON
SCALE 1'' = 0.5 KIPS

▼ Figure 4.12

"Let's diagram the forces in the kingpost truss and find out (4.12)*. There are now two interior spaces in the truss, so we have numbers* 1 *and* 2 *to deal with. The intersection of* a1 *and* c1 *establishes point* 1 *on the force polygon. And from drawing* b2 *and* c2*, we find point* 2*. But points* 1 *and* 2 *turn out to be the same. What does this mean?"*

The architect thought for a moment.

"If *1* and 2 are in the same place on the force polygon, then line *1–2* on the force polygon has no length, so member *1–2* has zero force in it. That's the kingpost!"

"Right, the kingpost isn't doing anything. We might put a kingpost in a truss nevertheless, either to keep the bottom chord from sagging or just for looks. But let's not get distracted; you'll notice that the forces in the other members are exactly the same as they were without the kingpost."

"So they are."

"However, look what happens if we move the external load along its line of action and apply it to the bottom of the kingpost instead of the top."

The structural engineer drew a new force polygon (4.13).

"Now the kingpost is working. But the forces in the other members remain the same."

"Right! All that the kingpost is doing in this case is transmitting the load from the bottom of the truss up to the apex.

"Let's go a little farther with this. Let's put the load back up at the top, but make the bottom chord into two members that slope down from the two supports to the kingpost."

The engineer drew another form diagram and force polygon (4.14).

"Aha! That creates a force in the kingpost, too, and it's compressive. But this time the forces in the top chords are less than they were in the original triangular truss."

"Yes. Effectively we've increased the depth of the truss, which is why the forces are less. Now let's push the inside ends of the two bottom chord members upward along the kingpost instead of downward and see what that does (4.15)*."*

"Wow, the forces in the top chords have gone way up. In fact, they've almost doubled."

"They've gone up because the truss is shallower. And this brings us, at last, back to your scissors truss. I'll draw a force polygon for it. I can trace the form of it right from your drawing (4.16)*."*

Figure 4.13

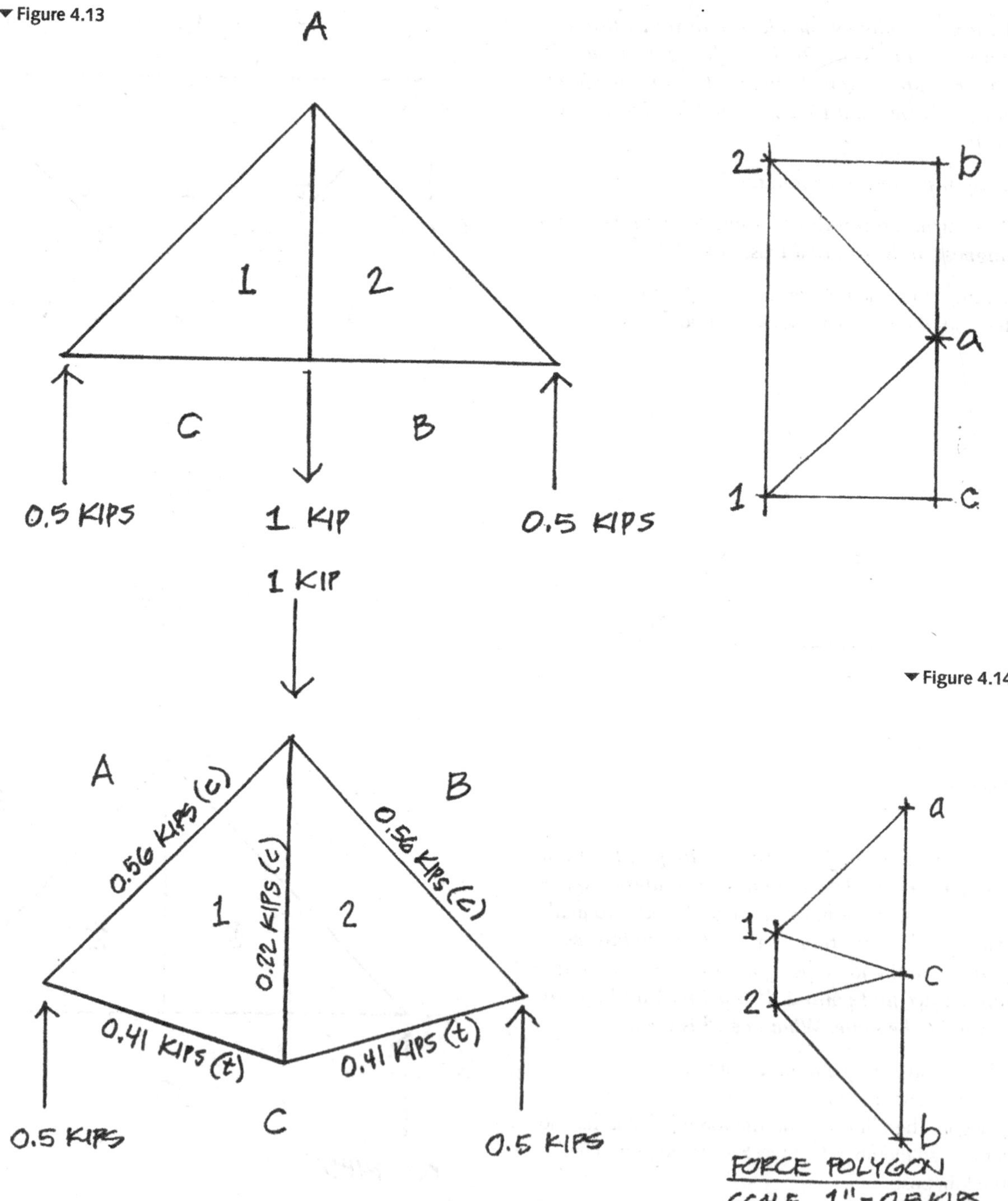

Figure 4.14

"I think I see where this is taking us . . ."

"Look at the forces in your truss. Two of the members, 1–2 and 3–4, have zero force. But you don't need to measure to see that the forces in all the other members have gone sky-high, so high that I'll have difficulty getting enough bolts into the two end joints to transfer forces between members. Your trusses need more depth at midspan, **lots** *more. You wanted your trusses to be slender and elegant, but you're trying to do this by reducing the depth, and you must pay a heavy price for this. Depth is your friend. A worthwhile goal when you're designing a structure is to maintain sufficient depth to keep forces low."*

Figure 4.16

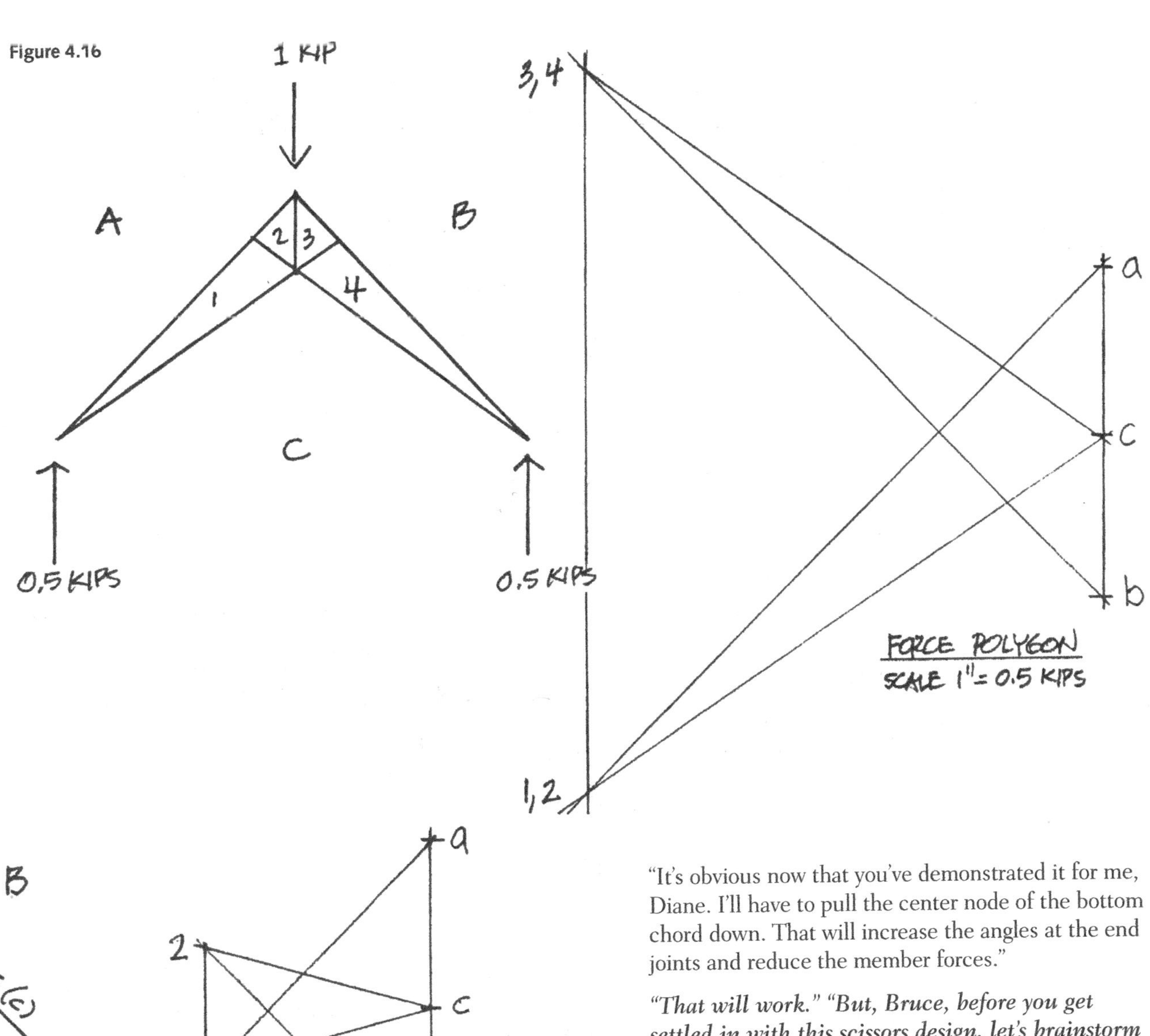

▼ Figure 4.15

"It's obvious now that you've demonstrated it for me, Diane. I'll have to pull the center node of the bottom chord down. That will increase the angles at the end joints and reduce the member forces."

"That will work." "But, Bruce, before you get settled in with this scissors design, let's brainstorm some other ideas together."

"Like what? I like my scissors shape, even if it has to be a little fatter than it was."

"But why not look at another idea or two in the abstract, just to get some creative juices flowing?"

"Such as?"

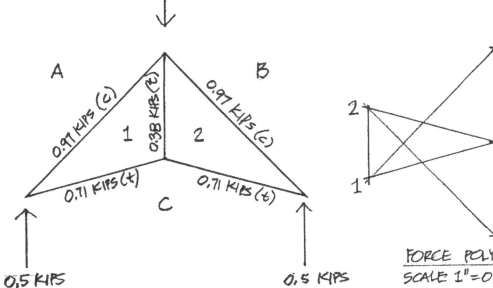

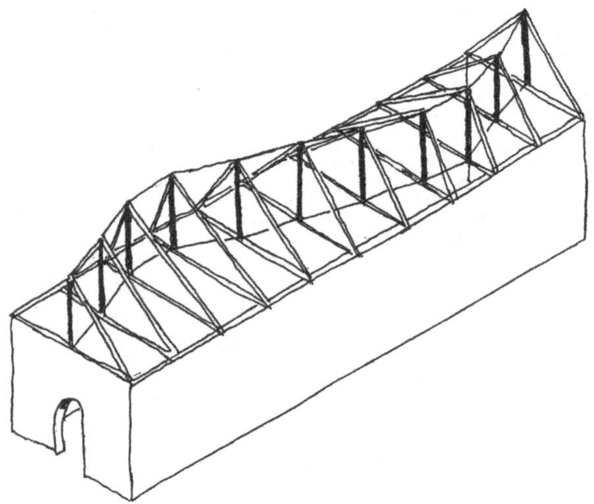

Figure 4.17

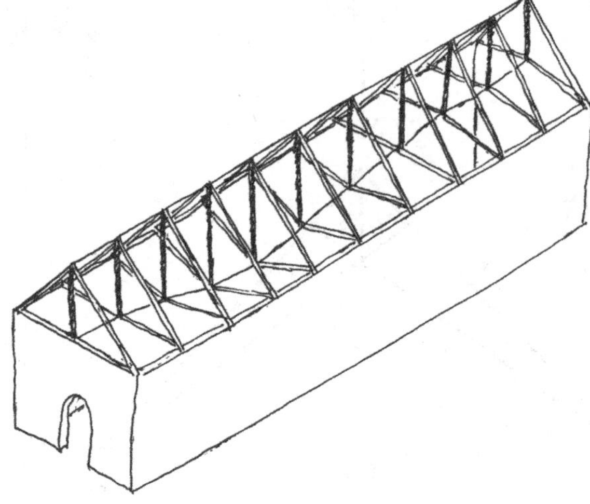

Figure 4.18

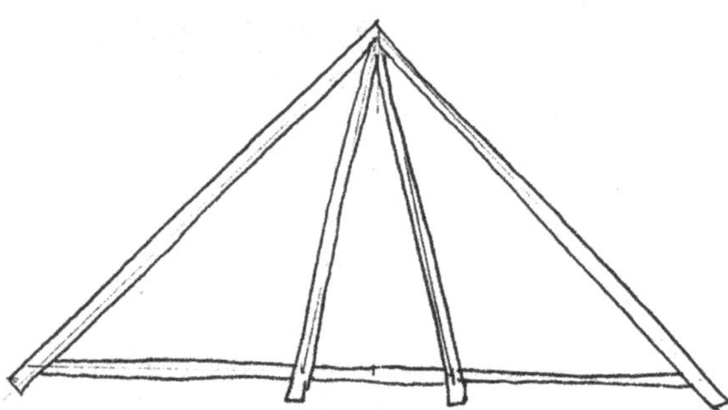

Figure 4.19

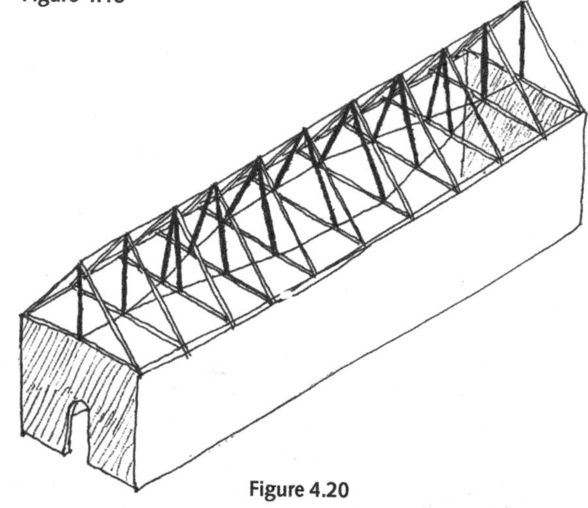

Figure 4.20

"What if we didn't make all the trusses the same? What if we did simple kingpost trusses, but let the kingpost move off center along some predetermined path from one end of the chapel to the other? The effect is almost like animation in a film. Hmmm . . . this is hard to draw!" Diane sketched a set of trusses in which the kingpost moved in an orderly progression that traced out a wave shape in the roof structure (4.17). *"This gives you not only a visual effect of motion in the kingpost, but also roof surfaces that warp in interesting ways."*

"Well, that's an ingenious idea, and I like the notion that the trusses play a more active role in the interior aesthetic, but I want to keep the roof symmetrical and simple."

"We could try moving the center node of the bottom chord up and down a bit either way, but not enough to raise member forces significantly (4.18)."

"That's better. The roof planes are simple and flat. I might go for something like that."

Bruce studied the diagrams in silence for a moment. Then he reached for his pencil.

"What about this?"

He drew a truss with two interior members that met at the top node (4.19).

"What is the advantage of the two interior posts over a single one?"

"They can move symmetrically from one truss to the next. Give me a minute to draw an idea for you. It's tough to put on paper, so you'll have to use your imagination a bit to understand it. I'll darken the members that move so you can see them better—there! Will this idea work?"

Bruce drew a picture of a chapel roof in which the two interior members of the trusses started tightly together at one end, gradually spread to a maximum separation at the middle of the space, and returned again to a single vertical, tracing out a lenticular shape in a horizontal plane over the heads of the worshipers (4.20).

"That's a very intriguing idea! All the trusses have reasonably efficient shapes, and the visual effect is

powerful. The effect might be stronger if we were to raise the center portion of the bottom chord just a bit above the level of the supports, enough to make it appear lighter but not so much that it increases the member forces too much (4.21)."

"Yes, that does look better. Hey, this is getting interesting! Let me try to do the analyses of these trusses myself," offered Bruce. "I'll do the two extreme cases (4.22, 4.23). First the one with the interior members close together."

Bruce worked slowly, figuring out the force polygon line by line.

"Now for the other extreme . . . " His pace quickened. "Hmm, the forces are practically the same in both trusses!"

"That's good. We can see just from the relative compactness of the force polygons that member forces are low in both of the trusses. Can you work out which members are in tension and which in compression?"

"Aw, Diane, just when the design is getting interesting, you want us to take time to figure out . . . "

"Don't worry; it's easy and doesn't take long at all. And it may help us improve the design. Just put your finger on the top node of the truss on the form diagram, and read the member names in clockwise order around that point. First you read B3. *And from* b *to* 3 *on the force polygon the force is pushing up and to the left against your finger."*

"It's in compression."

"And then we read the name of this next member clockwise around the joint. It's 3–2."

"A force going from 3 to 2 on the force polygon is pulling away from my finger: 3–2 is in tension. The same for 2–1."

Bruce worked quickly to identify the characters of the forces in the remaining members. His face brightened suddenly.

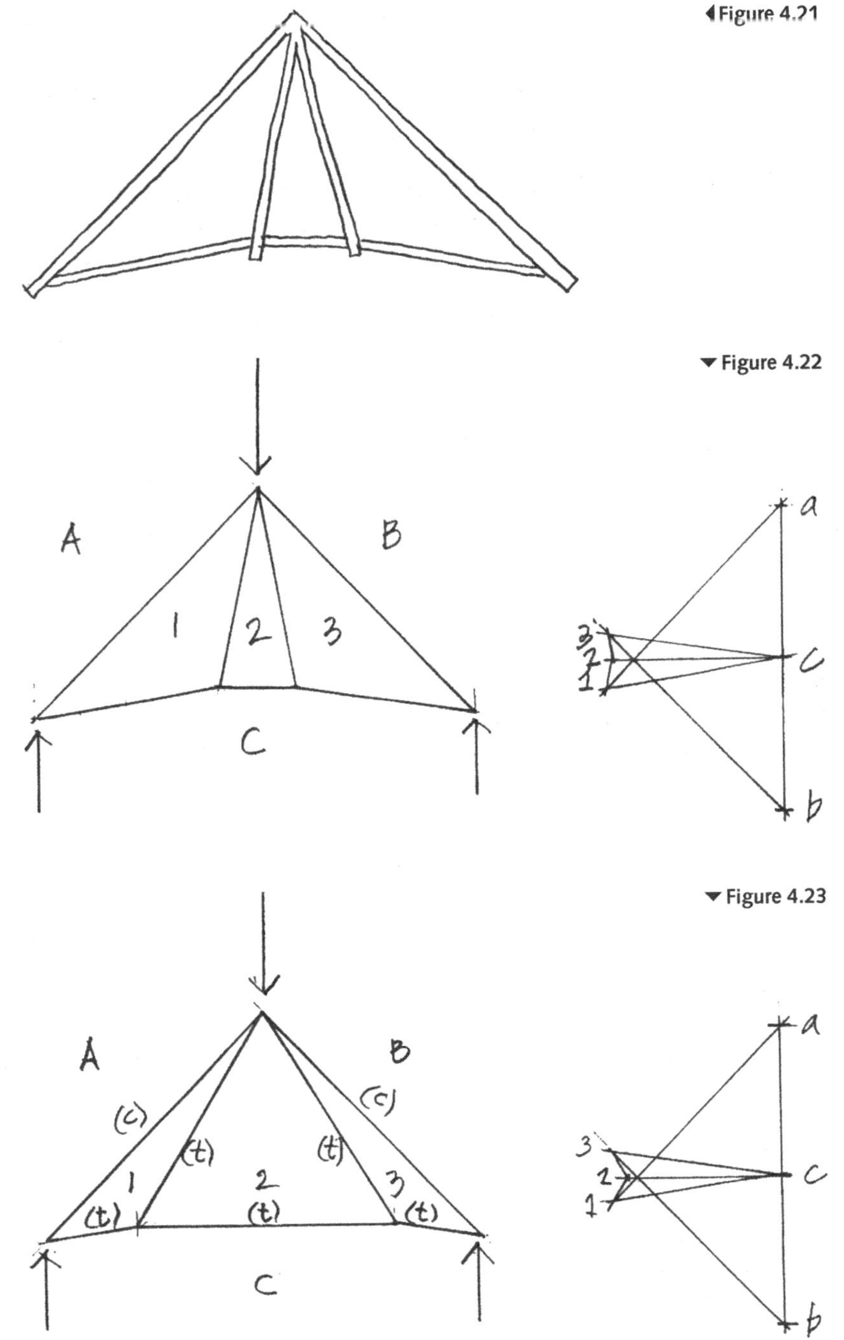

◀Figure 4.21

▼Figure 4.22

▼Figure 4.23

"Hey, there's really a use for what you've just put me through. I've found that only the two top chord members are in compression. Could I use chains instead of wood for all the other members? It would give a lot of texture and character to the trusses, and it would make clear to the observer which members are in tension."

"Probably, but I'll have to look at what happens when wind applies a lateral load to the roof. Wind can exert a suction on a roof surface and reverse the characters of the forces in the truss members. I'll have to check to be sure, but it doesn't seem likely with this geometry and with the stiff stone walls below. It would be exciting visually to use chain, and I see no structural problem with it. We'll want to use the best grade of chain, the kind used for slings and hoists. I'll look into it.

"We need to think about how we're going to detail these trusses. I've just been making a very rough mental estimate of the loads on them, which total about 3 kips at the apex of each truss. Maximum member forces seem to be in the range of 2 kips, which is pretty low, low enough that we can use 2-in. lumber for the top chords if we want to, although I would recommend 4-in. lumber just so the trusses look sturdy enough. Do we want to use nominal 4-in. lumber and join it with bolts and steel plates on the outside faces?"

"I was hoping we could make the trusses of two layers of 2-in. lumber and sandwich the metal connector plates between them, mostly out of sight. All that you'd see under most lighting conditions is the heads and nuts for the bolts."

Bruce sketched a connection for the top node of the truss (4.24).

"Okay. With the relatively low member forces that we're looking at on the force polygon, we'll need only two or three bolts in each member at joints, which makes things easy.

"There's another thing we need to think about: the bottom edges of the trusses need to have a bit of lateral bracing to keep them from moving back and forth. Any ideas?"

"Without a knowledge of how things are put together, good design is impossible."

—Wacław Zalewski

Bruce rummaged through the pile of sketches and pulled one out.

"Yes. How about using the big, boatlike shape of two chains in the horizontal plane that I drew on this sketch? (4.25). I think it's called a lenticular shape. The points of attachment of the chains would follow the opening and closing of the lower ends of the interior members of the trusses. They would brace the lower chord chains and help define the shape of the space, too."

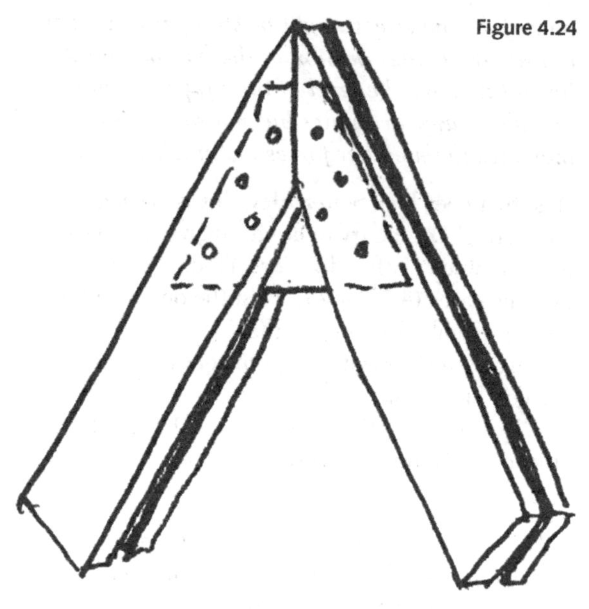

Figure 4.24

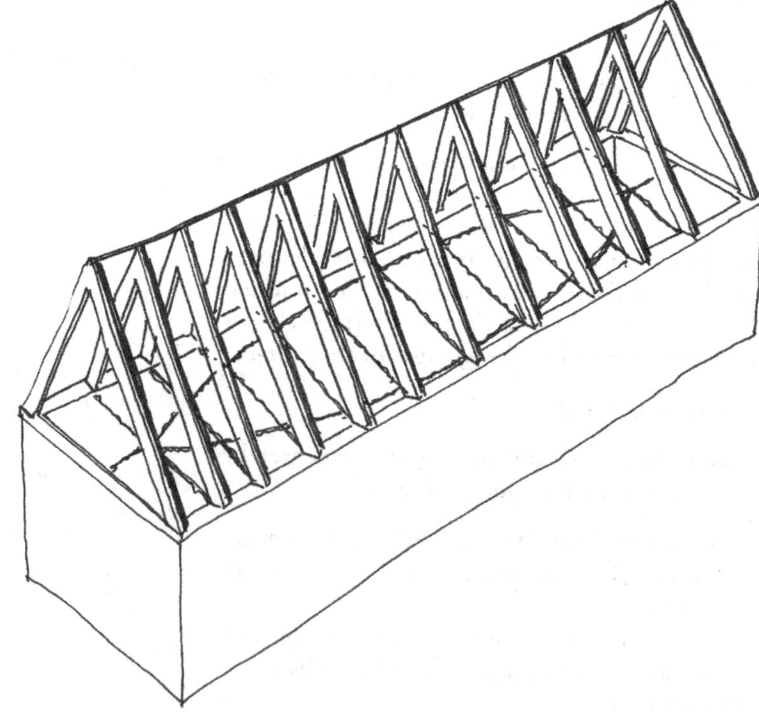

Figure 4.25

"That's exciting! Let's do it."

"I'd like to coordinate the lighting fixtures with the trusses. Maybe they could be big globes of glass with bare-filament bulbs inside. These could hang from the joints where the horizontal, lenticular chains are fastened to the lower chord chains. They would reinforce the lenticular geometry."

"Sure, good idea. And what are you going to do for daylighting?"

"Well, I was hoping the trusses wouldn't need too massive a connection to the stone walls so that there could be a line of clerestory windows between the roof and the walls. Is that feasible?"

"Probably, but I'll have to look in detail at how lateral loads are transmitted from the roof to the walls."

Now both designers grew silent, looking over the sketches they had made and searching for unsolved aspects of the design. Suddenly, Bruce reached for a roll of tracing paper and began to draw energetically.

"Tell me if this will work," he said. "Could we eliminate the center portion of the bottom chord chain in each truss, and instead use the chains that make a lenticular shape to provide the horizontal pull that was originally exerted by the lower chord chains? Each of the two lenticular chains would work like a suspension bridge cable lying on its side (4.26)."

Diane understood immediately.

"What an amazing idea! You've just made the structure fully three-dimensional! Yes, that should work. And it would be a really powerful way of shaping the central portion of the space. Let's look at what the forces in the lenticular chains will be. I can do a quick estimate: Let's see, each truss spans 22 ft, and the trusses are 8 ft apart. The total roof area per truss, measured in horizontal projection, is 22 ft times 8 ft, which is 176 sq ft. But the rafters carry the loads from half this area directly to the

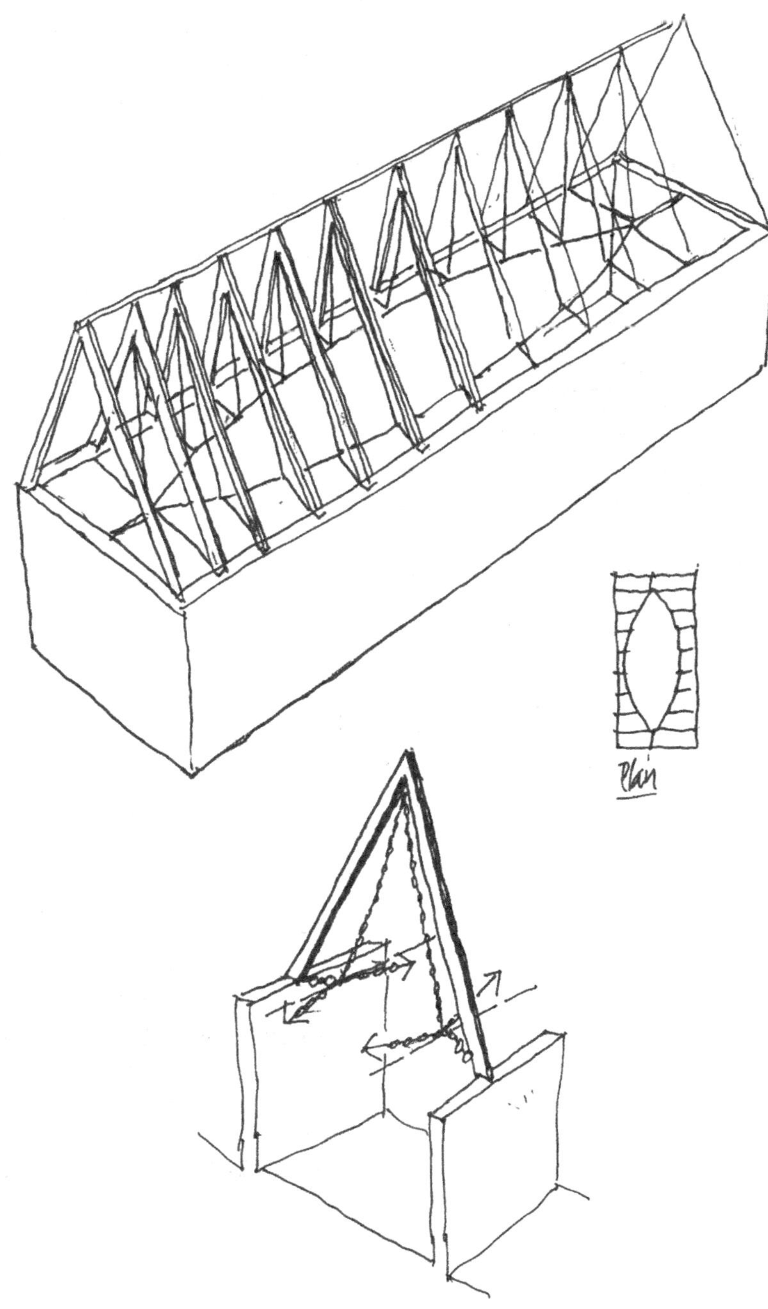

Figure 4.26

walls; the other half goes to the ridge beam, which is supported by the trusses. So only half of this area, 88 sq ft, is supported by each truss directly (4.27).

"The live load is estimated in this area of the country at 20 lb per square foot. The wood roof construction is relatively light—I would guess about 15 lb psf—so the total load at the apex of the truss is 88 sq ft times 20 plus 15, which works out to about 3,100 lb, which is 3.1 kips.

"For our analysis of the truss forces, we used a scale at which 2 in. equals the load at the top of the truss. We're now estimating that load at 3.1 kips. I'll use a ratio here: The force in the horizontal chain in your truss analysis scales at 1.15 in. on the force polygon. This means that the lower chord force is 1.15 in. over 2 in. times 3.1 kips. This comes to just under 1.8 kips. Each of the lenticular chains will have to exert

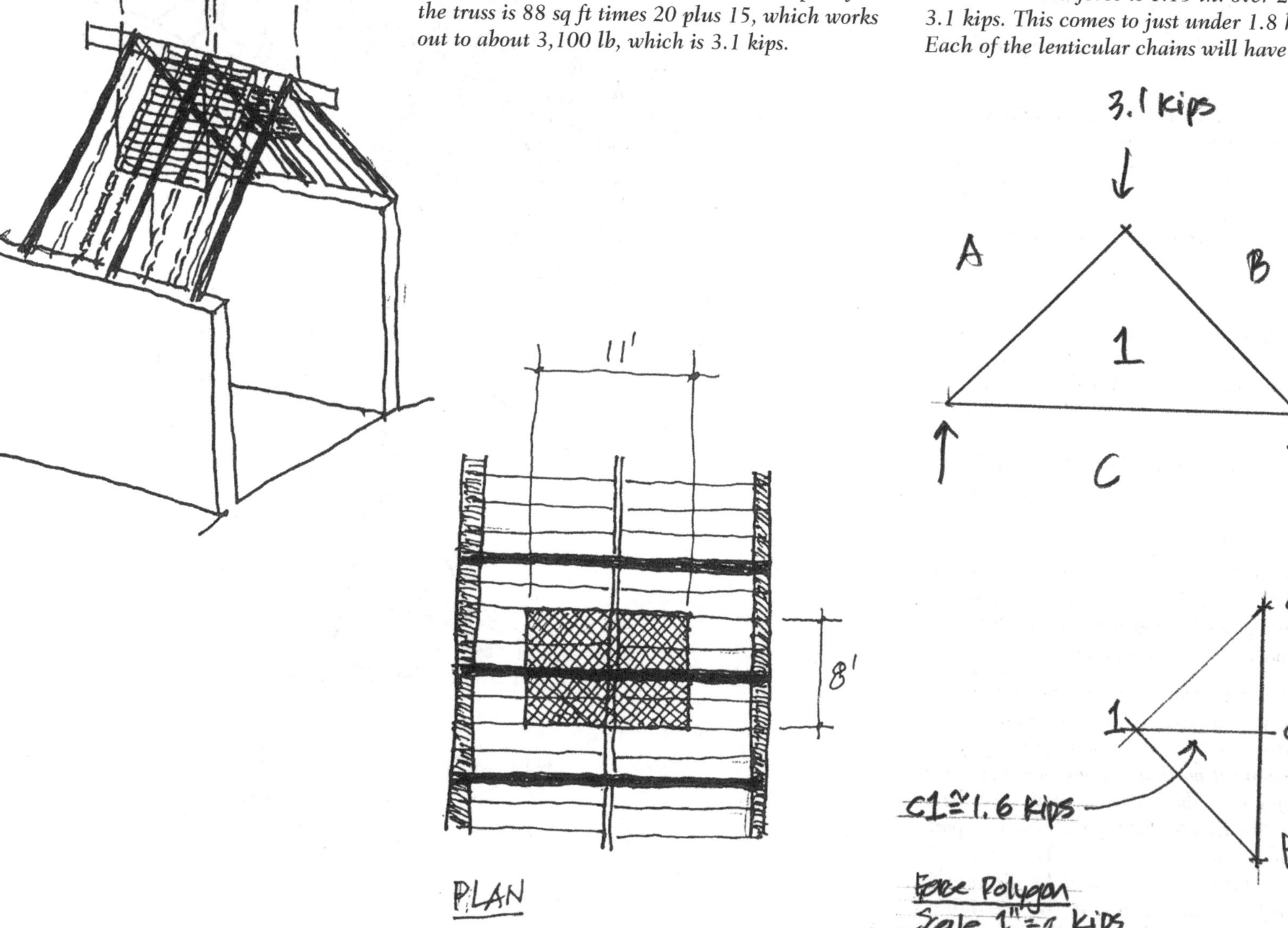

Figure 4.27

a horizontal force of about 1.8 kips at each node to replace the forces in the bottom chords that we've removed.

"I'll do a graphical solution to find the form and forces for one of the lenticular chains. The curve of each chain will be tangent to a parabola, so I can solve for its internal forces just as I would for a suspension cable for a bridge or a roof."

Diane labored for several minutes with the rolling ruler (4.28).

"Okay, the maximum force in the lenticular chains is only about 10 kips. I shouldn't have any trouble finding a chain with that much strength. But how am I going to support the ends of the chains, where there's a horizontal pull of nearly 17 kips to transmit to the end walls of the chapel?"

"Can't the heavy stone end walls resist that much horizontal force? We can add steel reinforcing bars inside the masonry."

"No, my feeling is that it would be just too much bending force for the walls to resist. But perhaps we can work out a way to anchor the chains to the corners of the building, where the longitudinal walls stiffen the end walls."

"I'll work on the plan geometry and see if this can be done. I've got an appointment in a few minutes at a construction site, but let's meet again next week to see if we can make everything work. I'll prepare some accurate drawings of our design. Can you phone me later today with some dimensional information on the chains?"

"Sure thing. Same day and time next week? At your place?"

"That works for me."

* * * * * * * * * *

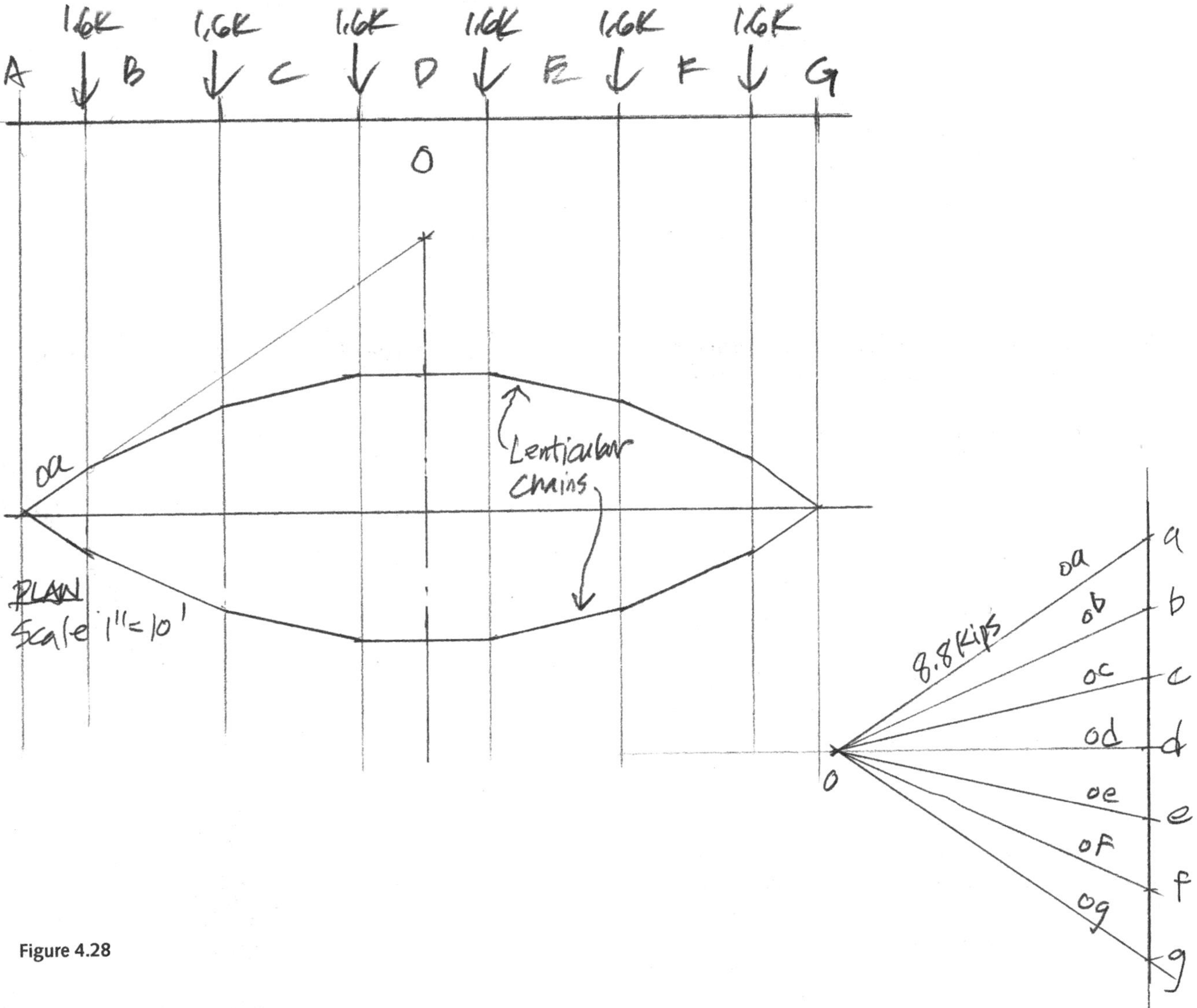

Figure 4.28

A week later, Bruce laid two new drawings of the chapel on his conference table (4.29, 4.30).

"You've put a lot of inspired work into this!" exclaimed Diane. "What an exciting space! And you've reconfigured the ends of the building to resist the horizontal pulls of the two chains. It looks great!"

"I made the angles in the walls so that the chains could be anchored in corners, where the walls are stiff because of their shape."

"That should do the job."

"I've also lifted the whole roof up to create a band of clerestory windows all around, as I mentioned last week. I'm proposing to connect the bottom ends of the rafters to a rectangular steel tube that will run all the way around the building at the top of the clerestory. The ends of the two chains will connect to this tube. Will that work structurally? I'm assuming that we will weld all the joints in the tube, and that it can act like a horizontal arch to resist the pull of the chains."

"Yes, I think that will work. I suggest that we make all the framing of the clerestory windows from rectangular steel tubes, the bottom sill and vertical mullions as well as the top. Large sections of it can be welded together in the steel fabricator's shop. These will be easy to truck to the site, hoist into place with a crane, fasten to anchor bolts embedded in the masonry, and weld to one another. If the welded joints aren't stiff enough to resist the wind loads that need to be transmitted from the roof to the walls, we can weld diagonal braces made of smaller steel tubes in some of the window openings. We can detail the windows so the glass will run right past the diagonals in a plane outside the bracing."

Diane added diagonals to Bruce's sketch (4.31).

"That was my thought, too. I started to sketch some details, but I don't know enough about how to connect chains to plates and to other chains."

"I've spent some time learning about chains and how to connect them. Chains aren't a very common component of structures and I haven't

Figure 4.29

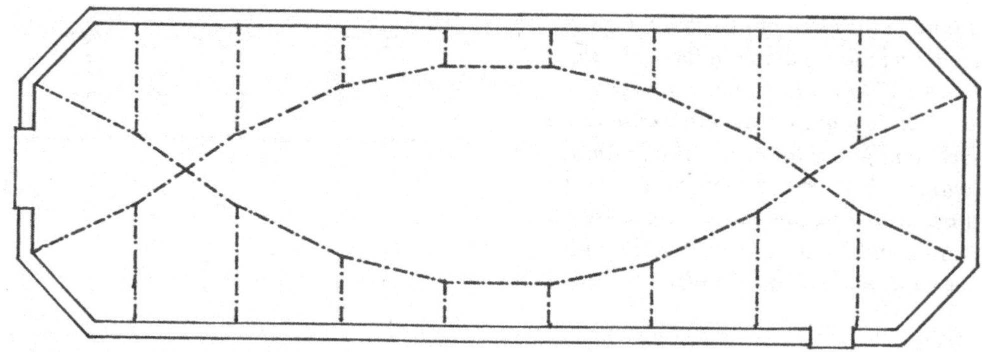

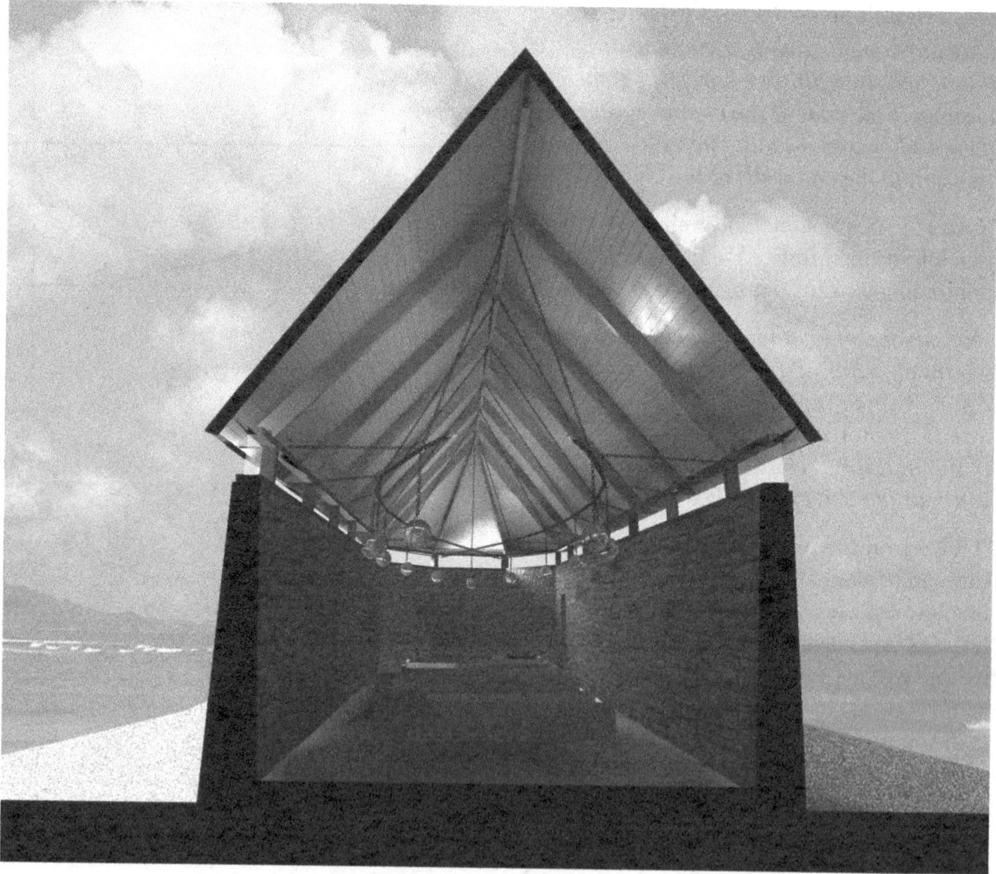

Figure 4.30

Design and image by Boston Structures Group.

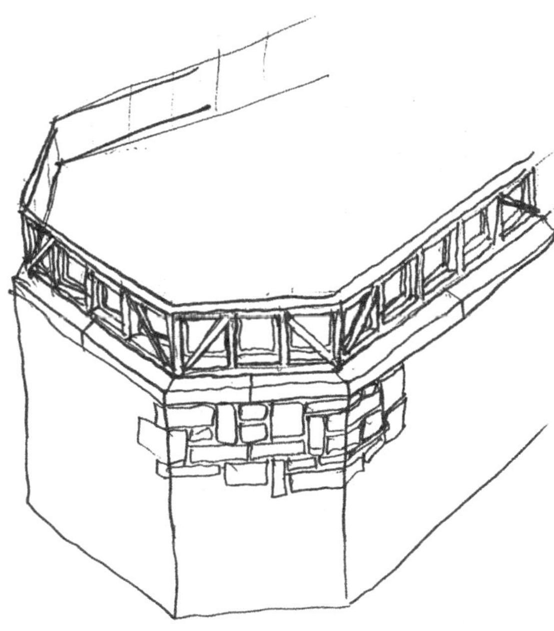

Figure 4.31

worked with them before. We'll want to use Grade 100 chain, the strongest grade. Within the trusses themselves, the highest force in any chain is 1,800 lb. Looking at the table of working load limits furnished by the chain manufacturer (4.32), a 9/32-in. Grade 100 chain can safely resist 4,300 lb of tension, which is a lot more than we need, but it's the smallest size chain available in that grade. The safety factor is 4, meaning that the chain won't break until it is loaded to about four times its working load of 4,300 lb.

"The maximum force in the lenticular chains is about 10,000 lb. The smallest chain that will safely resist this force is a 1/2-in. Grade 100 chain, whose allowable load is 15,000 lb, again with a safety factor of 4. Between the 50 percent overcapacity and the safety factor, we have a huge margin of security against failure of this chain, as we do in the trusses. I made a drawing that shows each chain full size (4.33). It may be helpful to us in working on connection details.

Grade 100 Chain

Size	Working Load Limit
9/32 in.	4,300 lb
3/8 in.	8,800 lb
½ in.	15,000 lb
5/8 in.	22,600 lb

(Chain sizes are approximate diameters of rods from which the chains are manufactured)

Figure 4.32

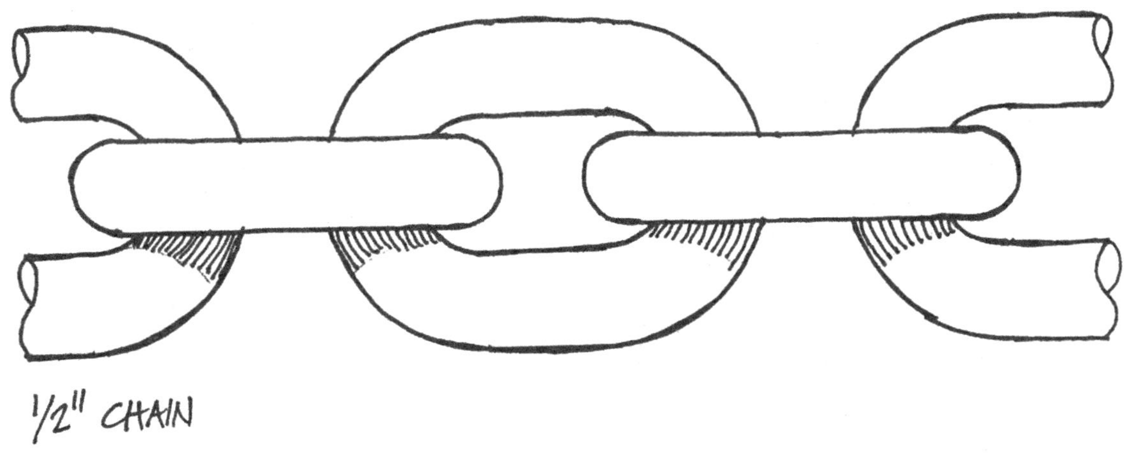

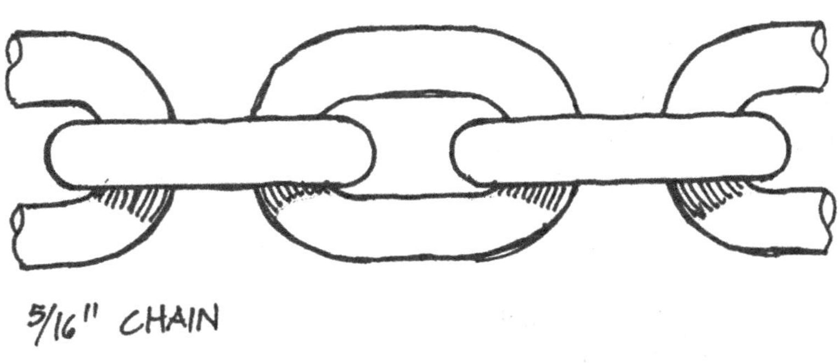

Figure 4.33

"The basic chain connection is made with a connecting link, which comes in two identical mating halves that are inserted into a link of the chain and into an eye bolt or a hole in a steel plate (4.34). After insertion, the pieces are pushed together and riveted shut by pounding their integral rivets with a heavy hammer.

"Although we have a huge surplus of strength in the chains, the connections are another story. For the chains within the trusses, we'll have to use a 5/16-in. connecting link, which has a working load of only 1,900 lb, just 100 lb more than the estimated tensile force in the truss member (4.35). For the lenticular chain, there's no connecting link strong enough to transmit a 10,000-lb force.

"Here's a preliminary sketch for a special welded connection to anchor the lenticular chain to the rectangular steel tubes at the ends of the building (4.36). It uses a large-diameter steel pin to connect the chain to two horizontal steel plates. The plates are welded to the steel tube that frames the top of the clerestory. The connection between the plates and the tube has to be really strong, so I'm beveling the edges of the tube and using a full-penetration weld, which will be as strong as the tubes themselves."

"Does all this beveling and welding get done on the construction site?"

"No, it needs to be done in the steel fabricator's shop, where they can do the work under controlled conditions and with good tooling. The framing for the clerestory, including these anchors, will be done in big sections in the shop. We'll make these sections as long as a truck can carry on the road. To connect the truss chains to the wood members, we'll sandwich a custom-made steel plate between doubled 2-in. wood members and fasten it securely with bolts. We'll cut a hole in the plate and attach the chain to the plate with

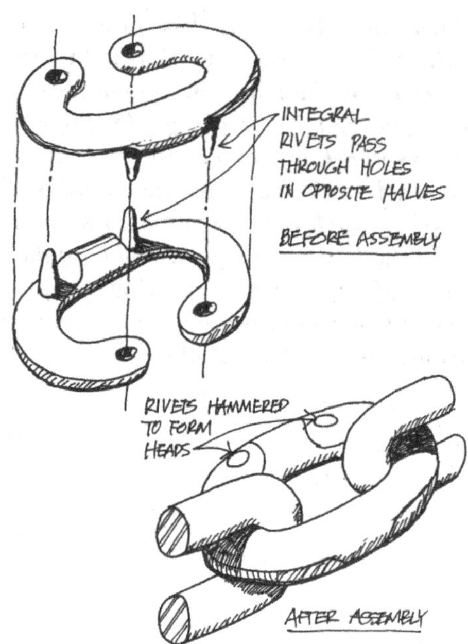

Figure 4.34

Connecting Links

Size	Working Load Limit
3/16 in.	750 lb
1/4 in.	1,250 lb
5/16 in.	1,900 lb
3/8 in.	2,650 lb
½ in.	4,500 lb
5/8 in.	6,950 lb

Figure 4.35

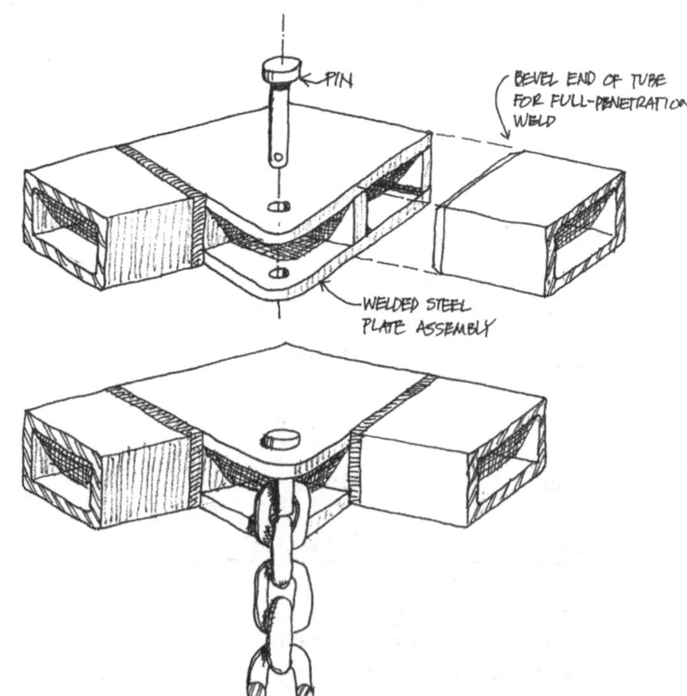

Figure 4.36

connecting links (4.37). For the connection of the ridge beam to the apex of the truss, I'm thinking of a custom-made welded connection, which you can see in the upper left corner of this same sketch. The upside-down tees support the ridge beam sections. They're welded to the plate that is used to bolt the rafters together.

"The chain-to-chain connections are the most difficult. If we were just fastening one smaller chain to the lenticular chain at each truss, I could use a 3/8-in. shackle, which has a working load of 2,000 lb (4.38, 4.39). But there's also another, smaller chain coming from above at each such junction. The forces in the smaller chains are not very large, and maybe I can work out a detail that replaces the pin in the shackle with an eye bolt (4.40). I would want to run a load test on this connection in a lab before using it in the actual structure. One last concern of mine is to provide a way to adjust the chain network to fine-tune all its parts with respect to tension and location. I'm proposing to do this with a turnbuckle on each portion of the lower chord chain in each truss (4.41). The turnbuckle that I would use has a jaw on each end that's similar to a shackle, so it's easy to splice it into the chain. The two rods in the turnbuckle have threads that run in opposite directions: One is a right-hand thread, and the other a left-hand thread. When you turn the body of the turnbuckle with a wrench, you either tighten or loosen the chain."

"Nice work. I like the whole package of details that you've proposed. It does the job physically, and it's aesthetically consistent.

"This is going to be a magnificent roof. It took the two of us working together to make it happen. When you put your first sketch on the table last week, I knew that we could make the design better, but I never imagined that it would get this much better!"

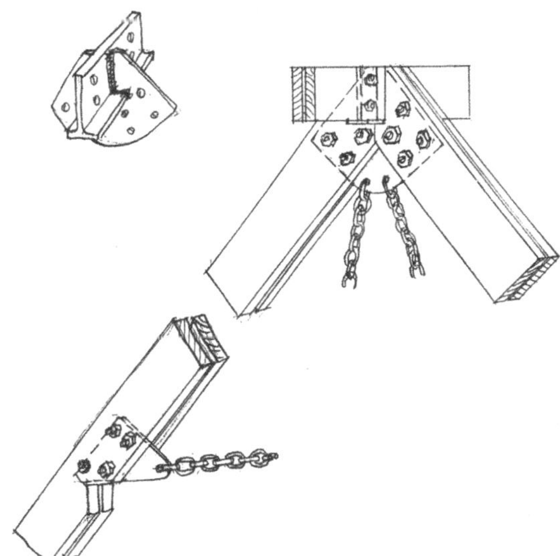

Figure 4.37

Duty-Rated Chain Shackles

Size	Working Load Limit
3/16 in.	670 lb
1/4 in.	1,000 lb
5/16 in.	1,500 lb
3/8 in.	2,000 lb
7/16 in.	3,000 lb
½ in.	4,000 lb
5/8 in.	6,500 lb
3/4 in.	9,500 lb
1"	17,000 lb

Figure 4.38

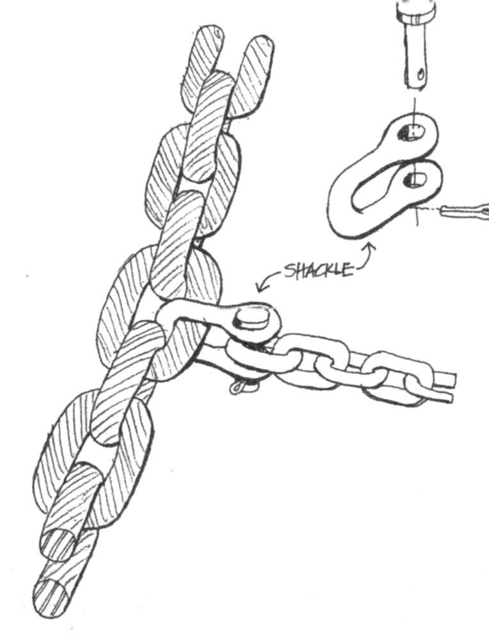

Figure 4.39

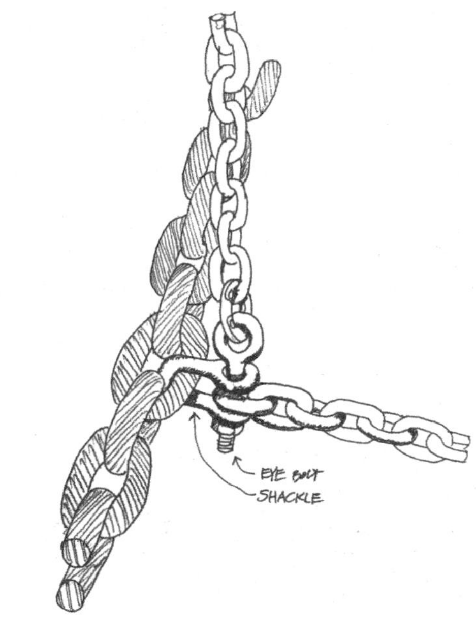

Figure 4.40

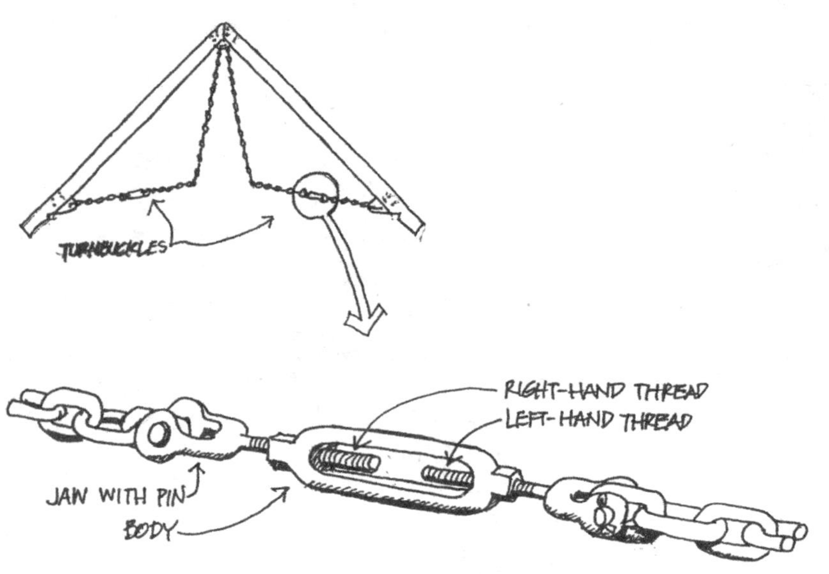

Figure 4.41

"I have to confess that I had no idea that we would end up doing what we've done. I really, really like how the structure of the chapel articulates the interior space (4.42)."

Bruce's smile changed to a sly grin.

"But Diane, why were you **so** insistent for **so** long on using those pathetic scissors trusses? Why did you find it so hard to give them up?"

He ducked just in time to avoid the ball of tightly crumpled tracing paper that came whizzing past his ear.

Figure 4.42

KARL CULMANN

Karl Culmann (1821–1881), a structural engineer and educator, was born near Bad Bergzabern in Germany. He was educated at the Karlsruhe Polytechnic and joined the Bavarian civil service in 1841, designing railroad bridges through an engineering apprenticeship. While developing his engineering skills he continued studying mathematics with Schnuerlein, and in 1847 he began developing his English-language skills in Munich in preparation for a study tour of engineering works in the United Kingdom and the United States. This tour (1849–1851) led him to develop analytical and comparative methods of truss analysis in graphical form. He published his collected work on graphic statics in 1865 as *Die graphische Statik*. As an educator, he chaired the engineering sciences department at the Federal Institute of Technology (ETH) in Zurich, from 1855 until his death in 1881. Having pioneered various graphical techniques of analysis and design, in part inspired by mathematical work of Jean-Victor Poncelet and others, Culmann shaped the ideas of generations of teachers such as Ritter, who taught Robert Maillart, and Lardy, who taught Christian Menn, as well as many engineering students, including Maurice Koechlin, who developed the 300-m tower design constructed in Paris by Gustave Eiffel. (See pp. 286–288.) Culmann is widely considered to be the father of graphic statics.

CHAPTER 5

Building on a Vertical Site

- *Moments of forces*
- *Equilibrium of nonconcurrent forces*
- *Graphical analysis of nonconcurrent forces*
- *Detailing and construction of a steel frame structure on a very difficult site*

A deep river gorge in Idaho is renowned for the richness of its bird life. Falcons, hawks of many types, ospreys, vultures, and bald eagles ride its air currents and prey on its small mammals and reptiles. We are designing an ornithological viewing pavilion that will be built on a vertical rock wall of the gorge to permit close-range observation of birds in flight and of their nests on the cliff below (Figure 5.1). Access to the pavilion will be by way of a tunnel in the rock that contains a stair and an elevator to the plateau above. As viewed in plan, the preliminary design for the building is an isosceles triangle that measures 20 ft along its short side, which will lie adjacent to the cliff face, and 30 ft from its apex to the short side (Figure 5.2). The roof, because it has generous overhangs for sun shading, is substantially larger than the floor.

Selecting a Structural Material

We have decided to frame the building with structural steel. A wood structure would be light in weight and easy to fabricate, but resistant to neither fire nor decay. A concrete building would be difficult to form and pour on the vertical cliff face and would be comparatively

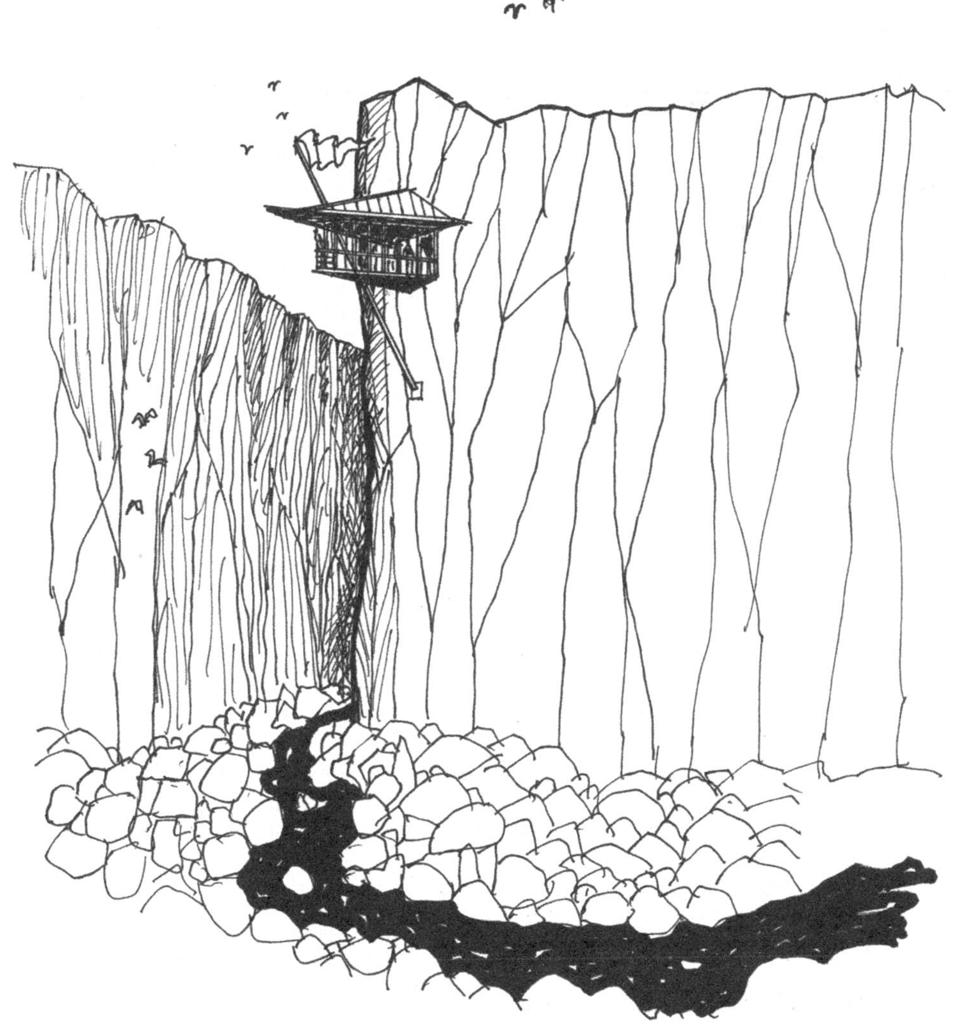

Figure 5.1 A sketch of the proposed pavilion.

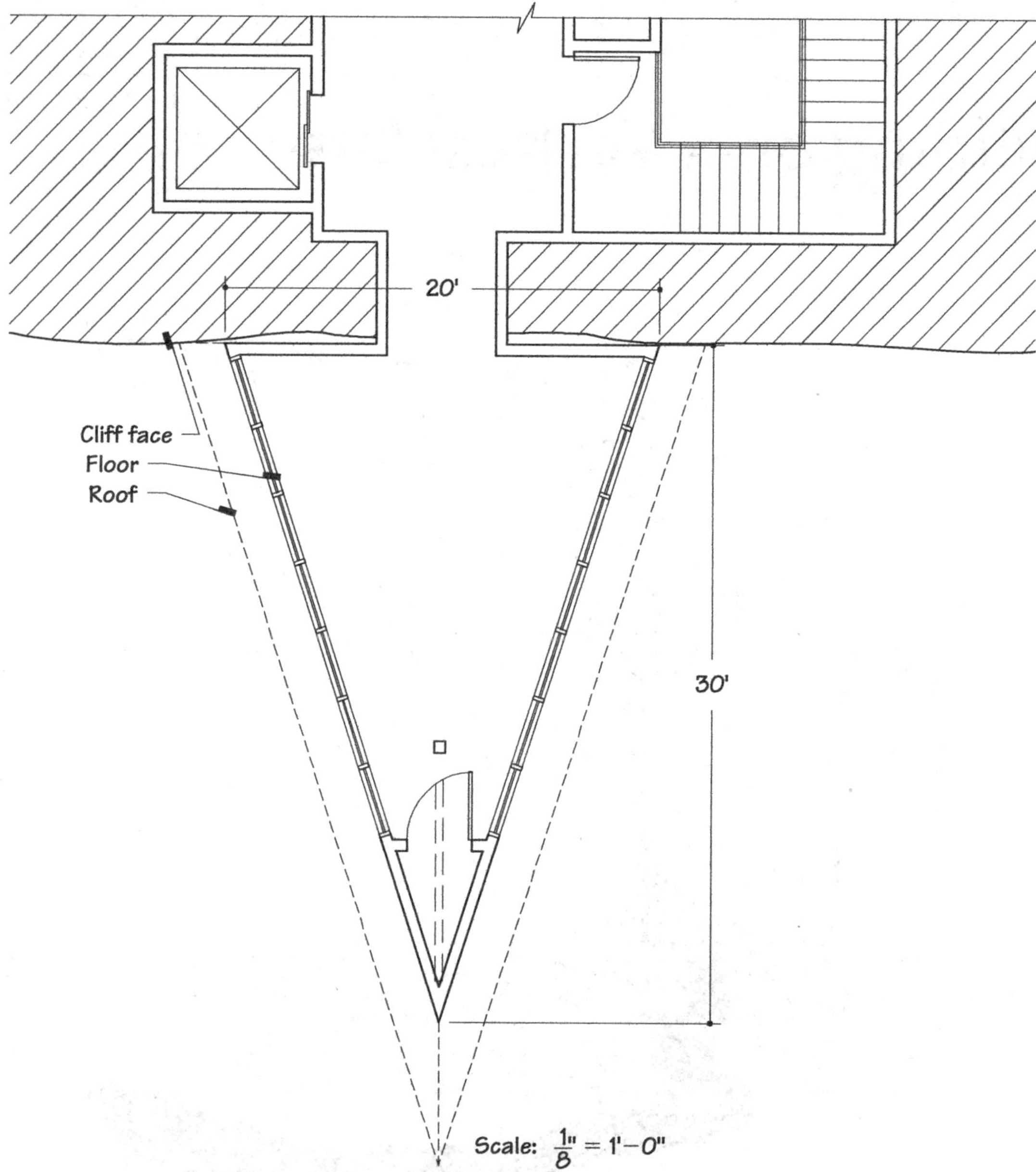

Figure 5.2 A floor plan of the pavilion.

heavy, requiring stronger foundations and greater expenditure of energy during construction than wood or steel. Steel building members are noncombustible and can be protected against the high temperatures of a fire with either spray-on insulation or an *intumescent coating*, a paintlike finish that swells when heated by a fire to form a thick, insulating char. A steel frame can be assembled on the plateau above the building site and lowered over the side in several large pieces by a mobile construction crane, thus reducing the amount of work that must be done on the vertical cliff.

SCHEMES FOR SUPPORT

We consider a number of alternative ways of building and supporting the pavilion, as shown schematically in Figure 5.3. Alternative (a) is to assemble the structure fully on the level ground at the top of the cliff while preparing foundation attachments on the cliff face. The structure is then lowered into place by a large mobile crane working from above. The two bottom corners adjacent to the cliff are hinged to foundations that provide vertical support but allow rotation. The two top corners are fastened to links, which have two pins each and can resist only horizontal forces. This combination assures that there will be no forces exerted on the structure or foundations that are caused by differences in thermal expansion between the cliff and the structure. This design is relatively easy to construct, but it requires heavy diagonal bracing within the walls of the structure.

Alternative (b) also utilizes the two hinges at the corners of the floor, but replaces the internal diagonal bracing with external diagonal struts that support the outer edge of the frame from below. It is a little more difficult to build than (a) because it requires that field connections be made at the outer edge, but its member forces will probably be lower. Alternative (c) is the same as (b) except that it adds members in a vertical plane near the cliff face to support the bottom ends of the diagonal struts. This simplifies construction by

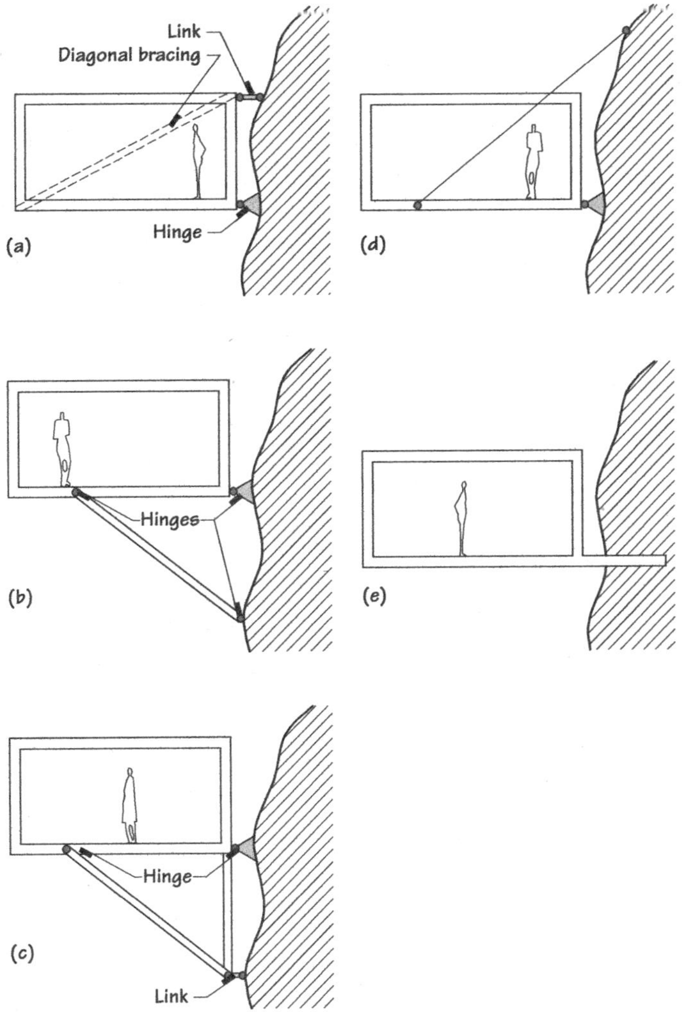

Figure 5.3 Section drawings showing some ways of supporting the pavilion on a vertical rock face.

requiring only two connections to be made on each side after the crane has lowered the structure down the cliff. It increases maintenance costs, however, because the additional members will need periodic painting and are in a place that is difficult to reach.

Alternative (d) is the same as (b) except that the diagonal struts below the floor are replaced by diagonal ties above the floor. Alternative (e) involves excavating two horizontal shafts into the face of the cliff, inserting steel beams into the shafts, shimming and bracing the beams in exactly the right positions, and grouting the shafts to embed the beams. This looks simple on paper, but it involves a lot of heavy, dimensionally precise work on the face of the cliff, which is dangerous and expensive.

DEVELOPING A SUPPORT SCHEME

After trying many options, we adopt a tentative design for the pavilion that is loosely based on alternative (b). Because of the unusual character of the site, we produce preliminary details for the building very early in the design process so that we can proceed confidently with the design (Figures 5.4, 5.5). The structural steel floor frame that we propose is drawn in Figure 5.6. A single long, steeply inclined strut angles out from the cliff below and meets the frame of the building to support its outer end. We propose to make this strut from a square steel tube. The attachment of the corners of the frame to the cliff is shown in Figure 5.7, and the intersection of the strut and the floor beams in Figure 5.8. The framing plan for the floor of the pavilion (Figure 5.5a) shows a beam at each face of the building and two interior beams. The maximum spacing of these four beams is determined by the maximum span of the corrugated steel decking they support. A poured concrete fill will be installed over the decking to produce a level floor surface. The roof is framed with light-gauge steel rafters and sheathed with fire-retardant plywood, which serves to receive the nails for attaching standing-seam copper roofing. All the weight of the roof is brought to the floor structure for support through the vertical steel *mullions*, the posts between the windows.

To proceed with development of the design, we must first determine the external forces that are necessary to support the building. The dead and live loads have already been estimated. The total weight of the building is about 71 kips (71,000 lb). This is made up of a total roof weight (live and dead loads) of 26 kips and a total floor weight of 45 kips. The floor weight is

Figure 5.4 A perspective drawing of the design for the pavilion.
Design and image by Boston Structures Group.

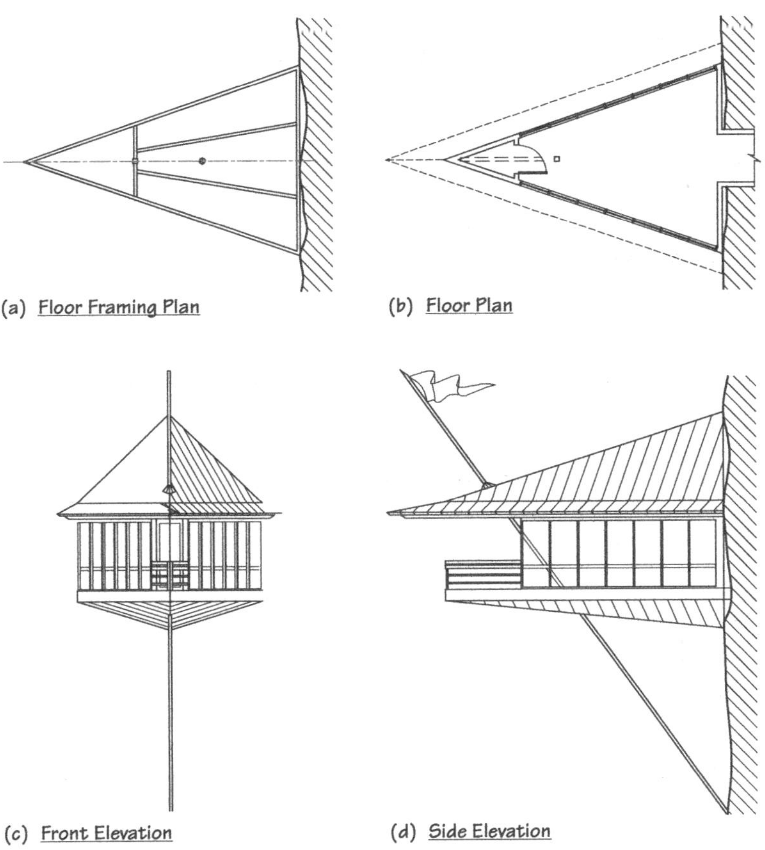

Figure 5.5 Four views of the pavilion design.

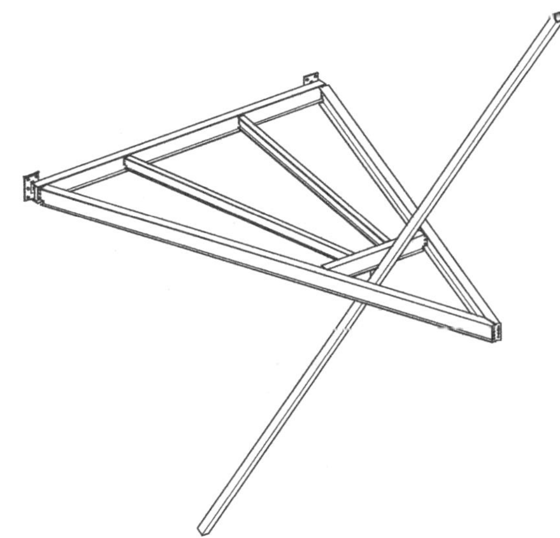

▲ **Figure 5.6** A perspective view of the floor frame for the pavilion.

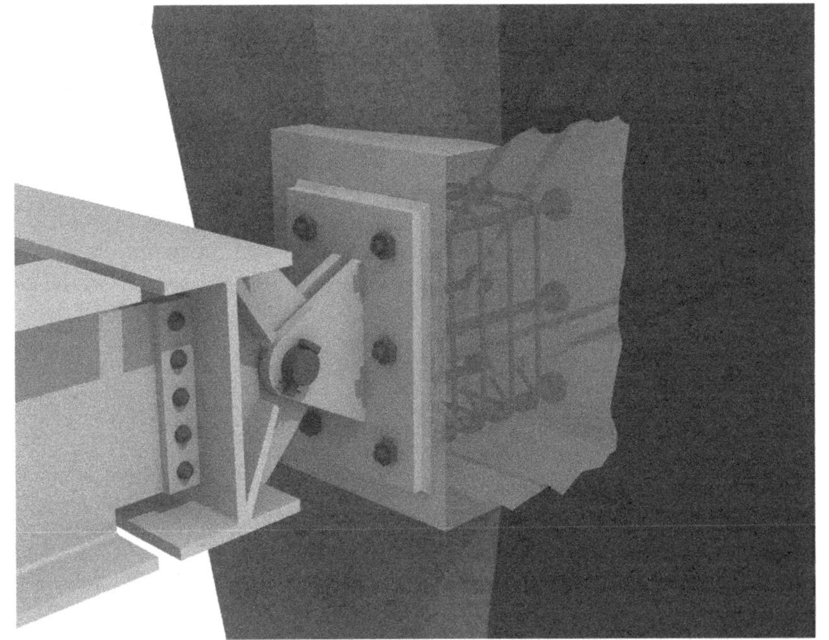

▶ **Figure 5.7** The floor frame is hinged to two steel plates anchored into the rock cliff. A rectangular pocket is excavated from the rock. Several holes are drilled from this pocket deeper into the rock. Steel reinforcing bars are inserted into the holes, then the holes are pumped full of grout. Next, the anchor plate and its button-headed bolts are held in place by a temporary wooden frame, and the pocket is grouted. After the grout has cured, it transfers force from the button heads of the bolts to the reinforcing bars and thence to the rock cliff. The hinge avoids forces caused by thermal expansion and contraction of the steel as it responds to changes in air temperature.

Figure 5.8 The diagonal strut, made from a square steel tube, supports the outer end of the floor and roof. A seat cut from a structural steel tee is shop-welded to the strut to support the wide-flange crosspiece that brings the loads from the floor frame. A plate welded to the strut and field-bolted to the beam prevents the beam from overturning. Despite all the bolts and welds, this is considered to be a pinned or hinged joint because it provides little resistance to twisting of the beam.

much larger than the roof weight because the building code mandates a live load estimate of 100 lb per square foot. This addresses the fact that at times the room may be tightly packed with people.

This weight is centered about the *centroid* of the floor plan. Because the floor plan is triangular, the centroid is approximately one-third of the distance from the rock wall to the tip of the building. In Figure 5.9a, for the purpose of determining equilibrium, we see this distributed load represented as a concentrated load at the centroid. An upward force is applied to the edge of the floor by the foundations at the face of the cliff. Because these two forces are not collinear (do not act along the same line of action), the structure is not in equilibrium, and will rotate downward into the canyon unless we take steps to bring it into equilibrium. In Figure 5.9b we have added the inclined strut to stabilize the building and prevent it from rotating.

Figure 5.10 is the start of a free-body diagram of the pavilion floor. It shows in section view the roof and floor loads as two concentrated forces that act at points a short distance apart. The centroid of the roof is farther from the cliff than that of the floor because the roof, with its overhangs, is substantially larger. We have resolved the inclined forces from the strut and the hinge at the cliff face into their horizontal and vertical components to facilitate a numerical solution.

In Chapter 2, we learned two expressions of static equilibrium that we can use to determine the external reactions at the cliff face and the inclined strut:

$$\sum F_v = 0$$

$$\sum F_h = 0$$

There are just two horizontal forces, Q_h and R_h. These are opposite in direction and must be equal to each other to be in equilibrium, but we do not know their magnitude. In the vertical direction, we have two gravity loads and two vertical components of reactions. Arbitrarily assigning a positive sign to

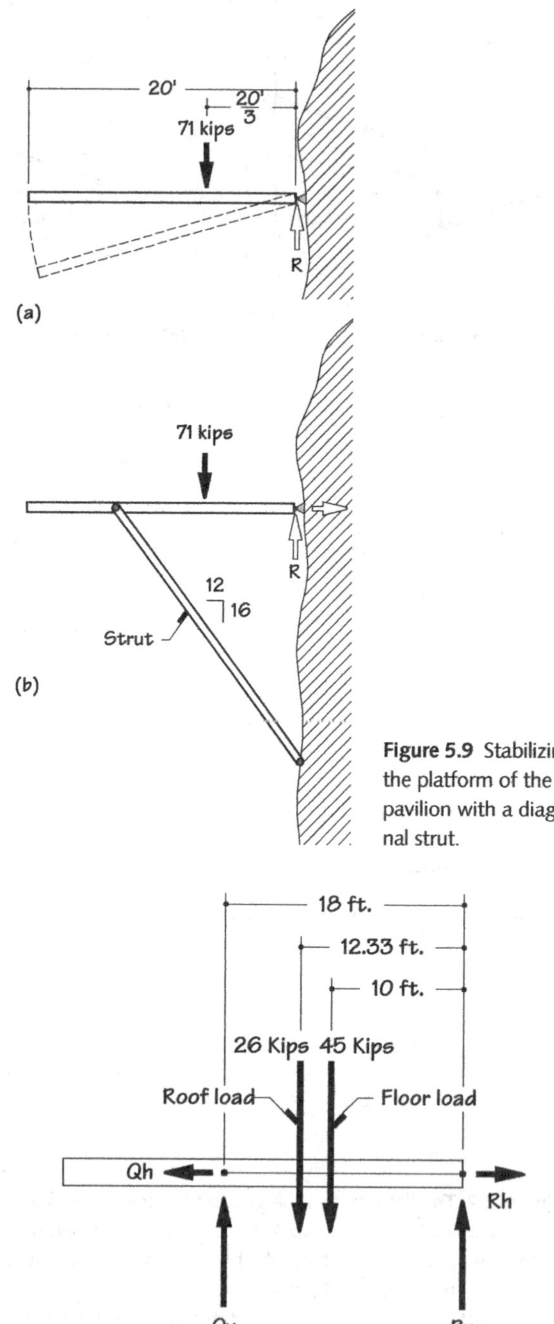

Figure 5.9 Stabilizing the platform of the pavilion with a diagonal strut.

Figure 5.10 A free-body diagram of the pavilion floor.

downward forces, we sum the forces in the vertical direction:

$$\sum F_v = 0 = 26 \text{ kips} + 45 \text{ kips} - Q_v - R_v$$

This is as far as we can progress toward evaluating the external forces on the building using two equations of static equilibrium. We need a third expression of static equilibrium to determine the direction, magnitude, and points of application of these forces. This expression concerns the equilibrium of moments of forces.

LEARNING FROM THE PLAYGROUND: MOMENTS OF FORCES

Children apply equal but opposing forces to the pushbars of a playground merry-go-round. Because these forces are not concurrent, they exert moments, and the device rotates (Figure 5.11). A *moment of force*, usually called a *moment*, is a measure of the capability of a force to cause rotation of a body around a selected axis of rotation. We quantify a moment, M, as the product of a force, P, and the perpendicular distance, d, from the line of action of the force to the axis of rotation about which we wish to find the moment:

$$M = Pd \qquad [5\text{-}1]$$

The perpendicular distance, d, which is also the shortest distance between the line of action of a force and an axis, is commonly referred to as the *moment arm*. In Figure 5.12, force P creates the same moment Pd with respect to the given axis, regardless of its location on its line of action.

Figure 5.11 A playground merry-go-round.

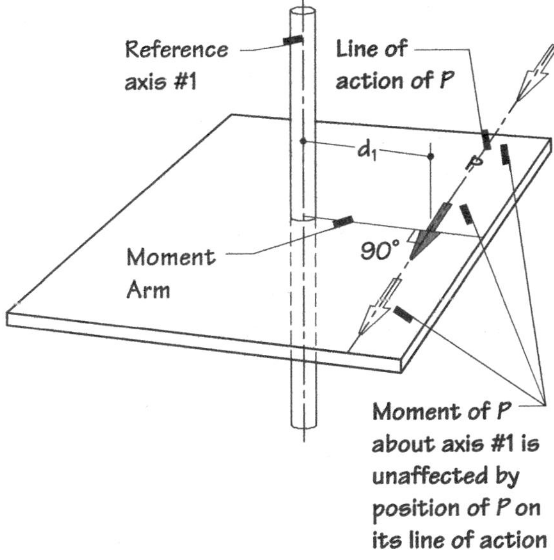

(a) Perspective

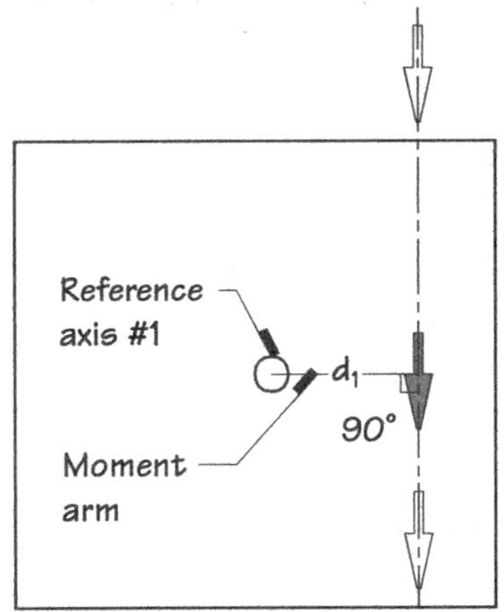

(b) Top View

Figure 5.12 Definition of a moment of force, M = Pd. Drawing (a) shows the force and axis in perspective. Drawing (b) depicts the same system in top view, where the reference axis shows as a point. This is the most usual view.

An axis of rotation may be thought of as resembling the centerline of a rotating axle or the shaft of a machine. When we represent a system of forces on a sheet of paper or computer display, an axis of rotation is usually perpendicular to the sheet or screen, and thus shows as a point. When we say we are taking moments "about a point," we understand that this point represents an axis of rotation, which is actually a line.

Consider the force *P* shown in Figure 5.13. With respect to axis *a*, the force exerts a clockwise moment, M_a, that is evaluated as follows:

$$M = Pd$$
$$M_a = (750 \text{ lb})(3 \text{ ft})$$
$$M_a = 2{,}250 \text{ lb} - \text{ft}$$

Notice that the moment arm in this case is measured along a line through *a* that is perpendicular to the line of action of *P*, not to some point on the vector itself.

A moment is always expressed in units of force times distance, in this case lb-ft. Other common units for moments are lb-in., kip-in., kip-ft, and N-m. It doesn't make any difference which units we adopt in evaluating moments, as long as they remain consistent throughout a computation. (In conventional units, liberties are often taken with the accepted practice of placing the force unit before the distance unit, so that lb-in., for example, is often called in.-lb).

A moment has either a clockwise or counterclockwise sense with respect to a given axis. We represent this sense as being positive or negative; there is no hard-and-fast convention for doing this. In this book we will usually assign a positive sign to clockwise moments and a negative sign to counterclockwise moments. What is important is to use the same convention throughout a calculation. The force *P* in Figure 5.14 is the same as it was in Figure 5.13, but it exerts a different moment with respect to axis *b* than it does with respect to axis *a*:

$$M_b = -(750 \text{ lb})(4.5 \text{ ft}) = -3{,}375 \text{ lb} - \text{ft}$$

The sign is negative because the moment is counterclockwise about axis *b*.

In Figure 5.15, we add additional axes to this picture. We could also evaluate the moment of force *P* about the axes represented by point *c*, point *d*, or any other point we might choose. Points *e*, *f*, and *g*, which lie on the line of action of the force, are of particular interest, because the moment arm of the force with respect to each of them is zero. This means that the force exerts no moment about any of these points, a phenomenon that we will put to good use shortly.

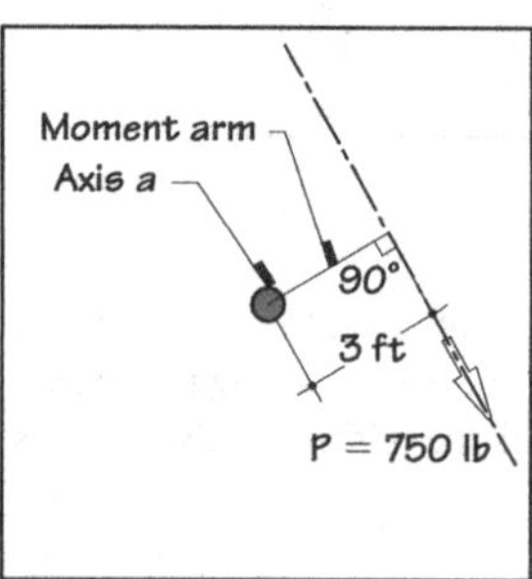

Figure 5.13 A moment arm is always perpendicular to the line of action of the force.

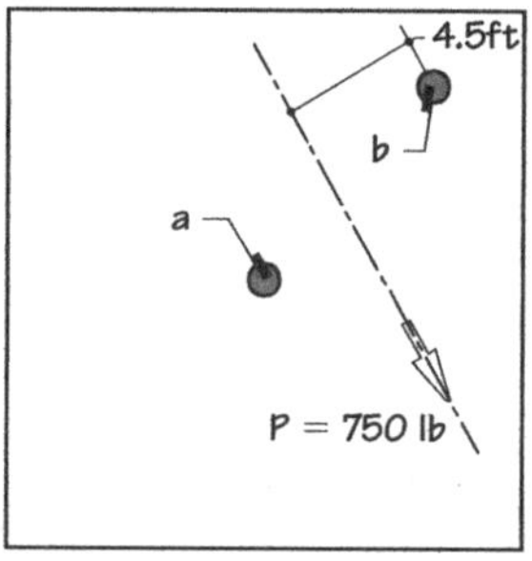

Figure 5.14 If we adopt clockwise moments as positive, force *P* exerts a positive moment about axis *a* and a negative moment about axis *b*.

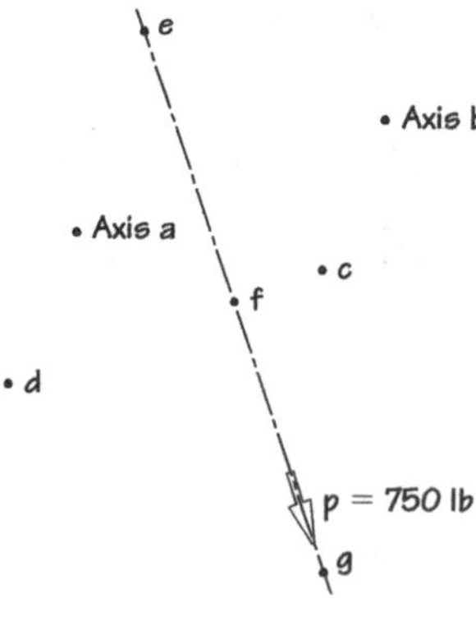

Figure 5.15 The moment of a force may be evaluated about any axis. With respect to axes *e*, *f*, and *g*, which lie on its line of action, *P* has no moment arm, and therefore exerts zero moment.

EQUILIBRIUM OF MOMENTS

Experimentation has shown that a body does not rotate if the sum of the moments of force that act upon it equals zero:

$$\sum M = 0 \qquad [5\text{-}2]$$

This is the third and final condition of static equilibrium for forces that act in a plane. To summarize all three expressions:

A body is in static equilibrium if:

- The sum of its external forces in the horizontal direction is zero.
- The sum of its external forces in the vertical direction is zero.
- The sum of its moments of external force about any axis of rotation is zero.

Symbolically, a body is in static equilibrium if:

$$\sum F_v = 0$$
$$\sum F_h = 0$$
$$\sum M = 0$$

In evaluating the equilibrium of any structure or part of a structure in which the external forces are nonconcurrent, we must employ all three expressions. The moments of force that we use in equation [5-2] may be evaluated about any point or axis that we wish to adopt, but within any single computation, all the moments for a given body must be evaluated about the same point or axis. It turns out, conveniently, that for any set of forces in equilibrium, if the sum of the moments about any one axis is zero, the sum of the moments about any other axis is also zero.

Another Lesson from the Playground: The Seesaw Analogy

In childhood, each of us learned intuitively about equilibrium of moments while playing on a seesaw or teeter-totter. A larger child and a smaller one can seesaw on equal terms by placing the smaller child farther from the axis. The larger child exerts a larger force at a shorter distance from the axis, and the smaller child achieves an equal but opposite moment by exerting a smaller force at a greater distance. In Figure 5.16, one child on the seesaw weighs 100 lb and the other only 50 lb. If the smaller child is seated 8 ft from the axis of the seesaw, at what distance must the larger child sit to bring the device into balance?

There are no horizontal forces in this system, which eliminates the need to sum forces in the horizontal direction. A summation of forces in the vertical direction tells us that the reaction at the axis of the seesaw is equal to the total weight of the two children, 150 lb. To determine the position of the larger child, we must sum the moments in the system and set their total equal to zero.

There is only one unknown, h, the distance of the larger child from the axis. To shorten the expression for static equilibrium of moments, we adopt a reference axis that is on the line of action of one of the three forces, which has the effect of eliminating one term from the equation that we are about to write. We choose to place this axis on the hinge of the seesaw. This removes the 150-lb reaction from the operation because it has zero moment arm with respect to this axis. Assuming clockwise moments as positive, we evaluate moments in this system:

$$\sum M = 0$$

$$(-100\ \text{lb})h + (8\ \text{ft})(50\ \text{lb}) = 0$$

$$h = \frac{(8\ \text{ft})(50\ \text{lb})}{100\ \text{lb}} = 4\ \text{ft}$$

The heavier child must sit 4 ft from the axis of the seesaw.

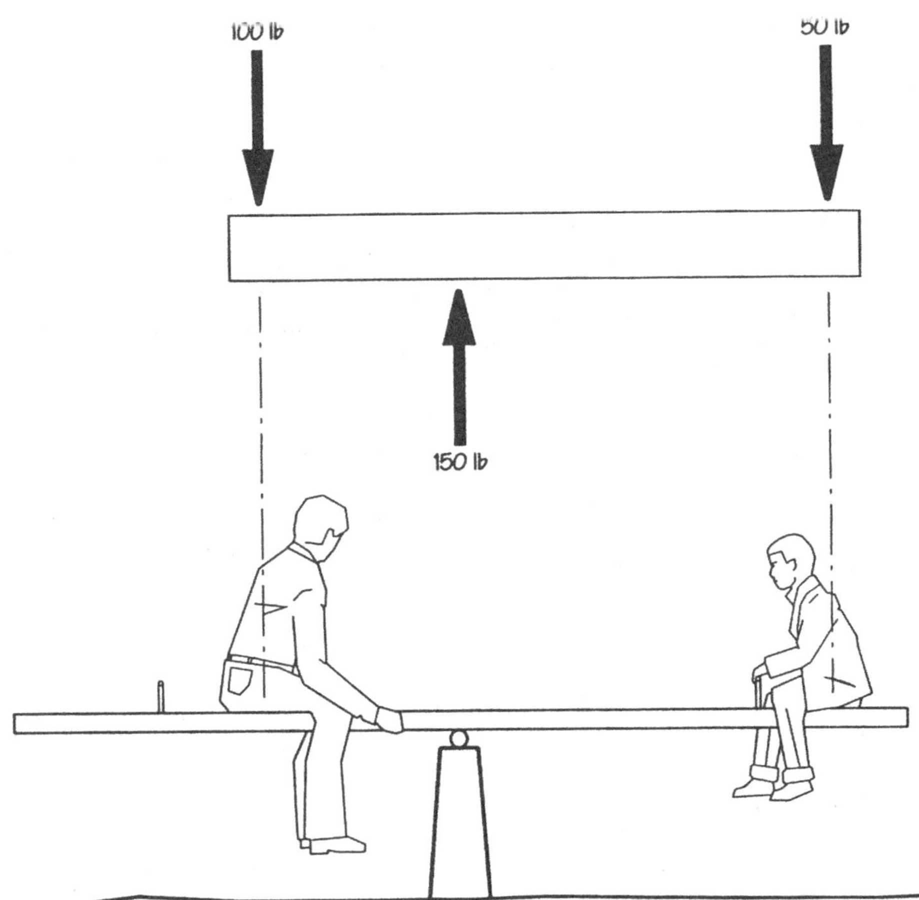

Figure 5.16 Children on a seesaw.

Each term in the expression that we set up here is a moment of force: The weight of the larger child, 100 lb, is multiplied by its distance from the axis, h. The weight of the smaller child, 50 lb, is multiplied by 8 ft, its distance from the same axis.

What happens if we select another axis about which to evaluate moments? Let's again eliminate a force by placing the axis on its line of action, in this case the weight of the smaller child. We define h' as the distance between the two children:

$$\sum M = 0$$

$$(150\ \text{lb})(8\ \text{ft}) - h'(100\ \text{lb}) = 0$$

$$h' = \frac{(150\ \text{lb})(8\ \text{ft})}{100\ \text{lb}} = 12\ \text{ft}$$

The smaller child is 8 ft from the axis of the seesaw, so the larger child must be (12 ft – 8 ft) = 4 ft from the axis, just as we discovered in the original computation. We arrive at the same result, no matter which axis we adopt.

Before tackling the problem of supporting the pavilion on the vertical face of a cliff, we will develop our familiarity with moments by means of several additional examples.

FINDING BEAM AND TRUSS REACTIONS

The most common use of moments of force is to evaluate the *reactions* of beams, trusses, and other structural spanning devices. Reactions are so named because they are forces that react to the loads placed on the structure in such a way as to maintain static equilibrium. In Figure 5.17, a wooden beam is subjected to a single load of 150 lb at a distance of 4 ft from its right support. The beam is supported by two vertical reactions near its ends; these are 12 ft apart. What is the magnitude of each reaction, assuming for the sake of simplicity that the beam itself is weightless?

We have available three expressions that we can use to find these reactions. First, the sum of the horizontal forces must be zero. There are no forces in the horizontal direction, so this condition is satisfied automatically. Second, the sum of the vertical forces must be zero. This means that the downward force of 150 lb must be balanced by upward forces that total 150 lb. Again we assume that downward forces are positive, and upward are negative:

$$\sum F_v = 0$$

$$150\text{ lb} - R_1 - R_2 = 0$$

$$R_1 + R_2 = 150\text{ lb}$$

This is as far as the first and second conditions of static equilibrium will take us. Now we must turn to the third condition to complete the solution: The sum of the moments about any axis must be zero. If we chose to take moments about an axis that does not lie on the line of action of one of the reactions, we would have to solve two simultaneous equations for the two unknowns, R_1 and R_2. Instead we select an axis that lies on the line of action of one of the unknown reactions, point 1, which results in a moment arm of zero for force R_1 and an equation with only one unknown, R_2. With respect to point 1, the 150-lb load has a moment arm of 8 ft, and R_2 has a moment arm of 12 ft. The 150-lb load exerts a clockwise, positive moment, and R_2 exerts a counterclockwise, negative moment. Thus:

$$\sum M_1 = 0$$

$$(150\text{ lb})(8\text{ ft}) - R_2(12\text{ ft}) = 0$$

$$R_2 = \frac{1{,}200\text{ lb-ft}}{12\text{ ft}} = 100\text{ lb}$$

Having found the value of R_2 so directly, we may find the value of R_1 with equal ease, either by taking moments about point 2, or by substituting into the expression $\Sigma F_v = 0$:

$$\sum M_2 = 0$$

$$R_1(12\text{ ft}) - (150\text{ lb})(4\text{ ft}) = 0$$

$$R_1 = \frac{(150\text{ lb})(4\text{ ft})}{12\text{ ft}}$$

$$R_1 = 50\text{ lb}$$

This completes our finding of the reactions on the beam. It is common practice to sum forces in the vertical and/or horizontal directions as a check on the correctness of our work. Assuming downward forces are positive:

$$\sum F_v = 0$$

$$150\text{ lb} - 100\text{ lb} - 50\text{ lb} = 0 \quad \text{check}$$

Perhaps you have noticed that this example is the seesaw example turned upside down.

Selecting the most advantageous axis about which to evaluate moments is the key to efficient solution of any problem involving two or more unknown forces. It is always possible to locate an axis on the line of action of at least one unknown force, thus eliminating that force from the initial computation, as we did in the previous example.

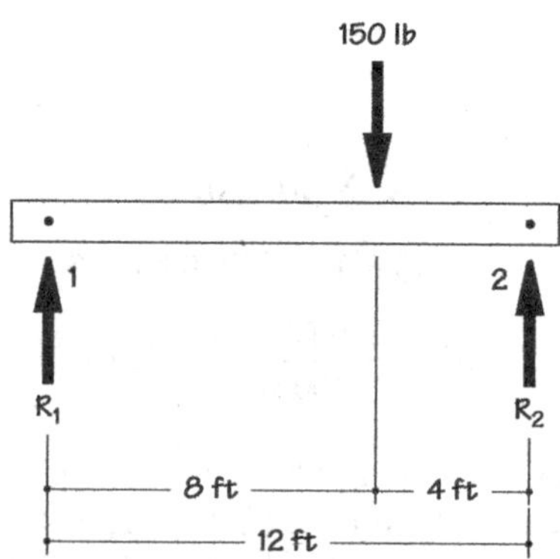

Figure 5.17 A beam with a single concentrated load.

FINDING THE REACTIONS ON A BEAM WITH A COMPLEX LOADING

Beam loadings in real structures are often complex. Consider a beam that supports a load of 2,000 lb that is concentrated at the end of an overhang, and a load of 6,000 lb whose action is distributed over two-thirds of the main span (Figure 5.18a).

The beam must also support its own uniformly distributed weight of 1,600 lb. What are the values of the two reactions, R_a and R_b?

For the purpose of finding the reactions, we replace each distributed load with its resultant, a single force of equal magnitude that is located at the center of the distributed load (Figure 5.18b).

We can find the solution to this seemingly messy problem with two simple equations, each of which contains only one unknown quantity. We set up each equation by summing moments about an axis that lies on the line of action of one of the reactions, thus eliminating one of the unknowns from the computation:

$$\sum M_a = 0$$

$$(6,000 \text{ lb})(4 \text{ ft}) + (1,600 \text{ lb})(8 \text{ ft}) + (2,000 \text{ lb})(16 \text{ ft}) - R_b(12 \text{ ft}) = 0$$

$$R_b = 5,733 \text{ lb}$$

$$\sum M_b = 0$$

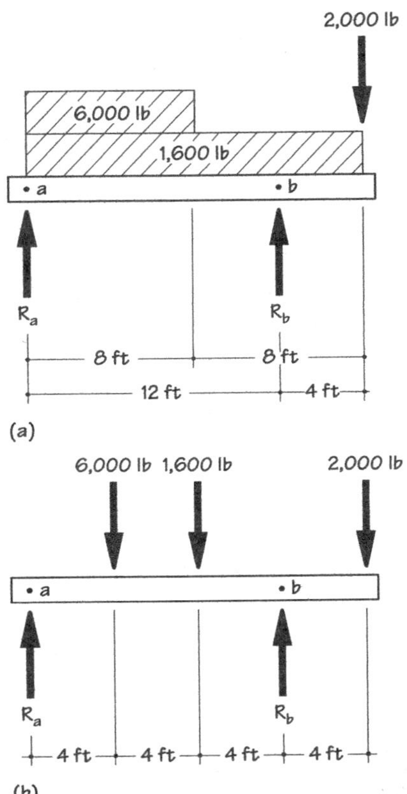

Figure 5.18 A beam with a complex loading. (a) The actual loading pattern. (b) Converting distributed loads to concentrated loads for the purpose of finding reactions.

$$12R_a - (8 \text{ ft})(16,000 \text{ lb}) - (4\text{ft})(1,600 \text{ lb}) + (4 \text{ ft})(2,000 \text{ lb}) = 0$$

$$R_a = 3,867 \text{ lb}$$

Check:

$$\sum F_v = 0$$

$$6,000 \text{ lb} + 1,600 \text{ lb} + 2,000 \text{ lb} - 3,867 \text{ lb} - 5,733 \text{ lb} \stackrel{?}{=} 0$$

$$0 \equiv 0 \qquad \text{check}$$

Our work is correct.

"A thought that structural design consists basically in performing computations is for a responsible engineer not less ridiculous than would be an attitude of a tennis player who watches the scoreboard instead of the ball, or of an airplane pilot who flies in the mountains on instruments only, without looking out of the window."

—Michael Dertouzos

Hinges and Rollers*

The type of support that is provided at each reaction of a truss, arch, or beam has an important effect on the distribution of forces throughout the member (Fig. A).

- A roller or rocker (1.1, 1.2) cannot transmit moment. It can transmit only compressive force, and it can do so only in a direction that is perpendicular to the surface on which it bears. The same effect can be achieved with a slide bearing (1.3), which depends on petroleum grease or slippery Teflon plastic between two metal plates to avoid transmission of lateral forces.
- A link (2.1), like a roller or rocker, cannot transmit moment. It can transmit either tensile or compressive force along its axis.
- A pin or hinge (3.1) also cannot transmit moment, but it can transmit a force in any direction.
- A fixed end (4.1) can transmit any direction and character of force, as well as moment.

When analyzing a simply supported spanning element such as a truss or beam, we usually show diagrammatically on the free-body diagram a hinge support at one reaction and a roller support at the other (Fig. B). This enables us to assume with confidence that the reaction at the roller is vertical. Any lateral component of the reactions must pass through the hinge. Thus, the problem is made statically determinate. A hinge-and-roller support condition also assures that there will be no forces placed on the structural element by thermal expansion and contraction, material shrinkage, or small movements in foundations.

(Continues)

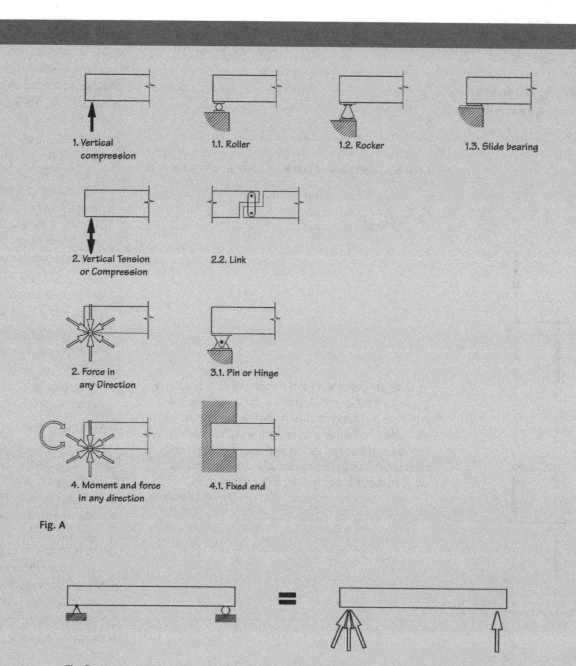

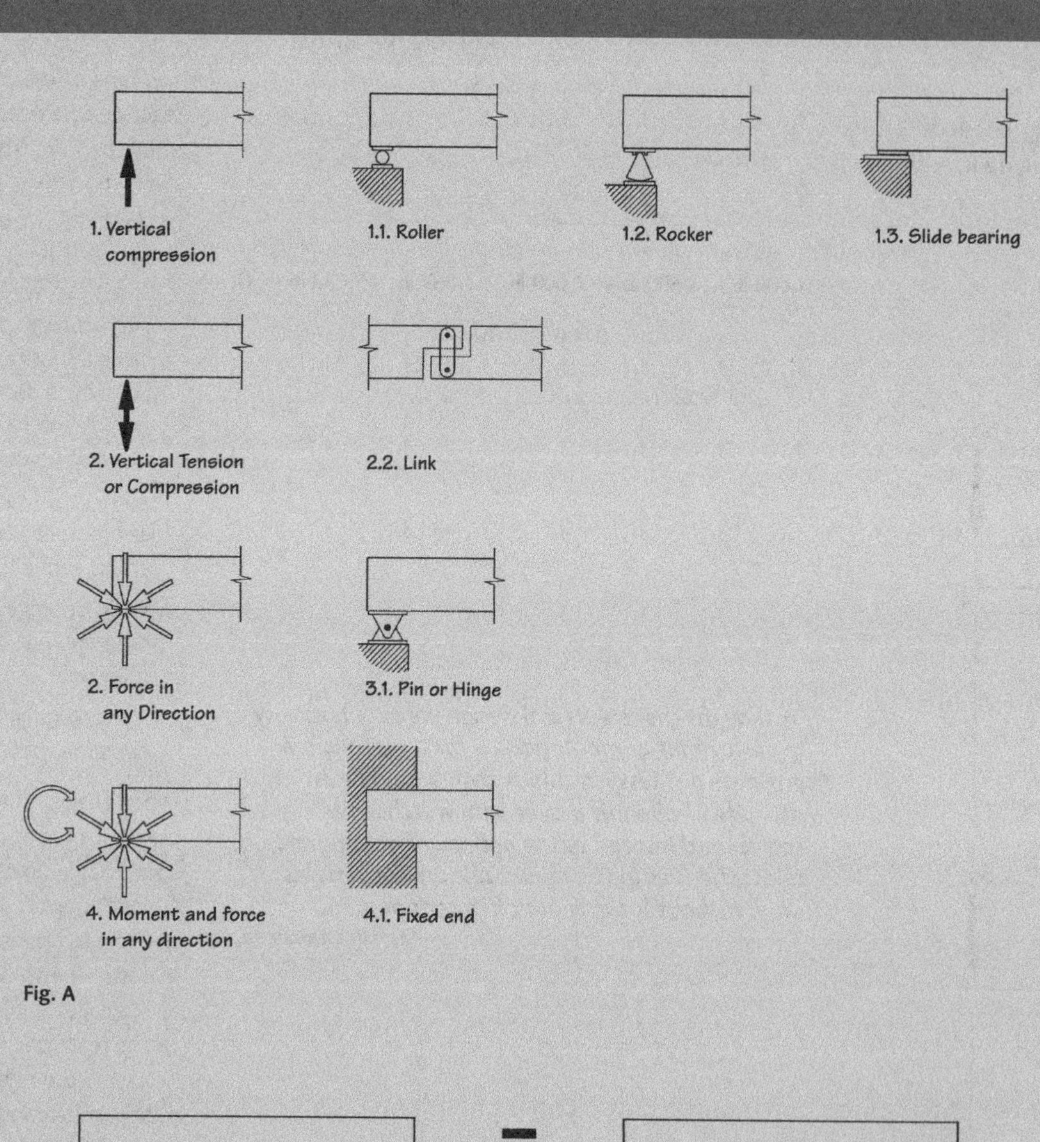
1. Vertical compression
1.1. Roller
1.2. Rocker
1.3. Slide bearing
2. Vertical Tension or Compression
2.2. Link
2. Force in any Direction
3.1. Pin or Hinge
4. Moment and force in any direction
4.1. Fixed end

Fig. A

Fig. B

To be certain that the conditions for which a beam or truss is designed are those that it will actually experience, rollers, slide bearings, hinges, and rockers are often translated literally into support hardware in bridge construction and in the longer-spanning elements of large buildings (Fig. C). Because of the high concentrations of forces that pass through very small areas of their material, these elements are invariably made of steel, regardless of the predominant material of the structure of which they are a part. By keeping an eye out as you pass under bridges and walk through very large enclosed spaces, you will discover a surprising variety of practical ways of creating these details.

Fig. C

The famous concrete hinges in Maillart's arch bridges function mainly through the flexing action of highly compressed steel reinforcing bars (Fig. D). The crossing of the bars at the hinge point reduces their resistance to bending almost to zero.

A fixed-end condition for a beam of any material may be created by embedding it deeply into a large, inert mass of masonry or concrete (Fig. E(a)). In steel construction, a beam whose flanges are fully welded to a stiff steel column is considered to have a fixed end (b). In concrete construction, fixed ends are easily created by placing steel reinforcing bars continuously through the connections (c). Except for cantilevers, structural elements with one or more fixed ends are statically indeterminate, which makes them somewhat more difficult to analyze than those with ends that are free to rotate. But fixed ends usually create

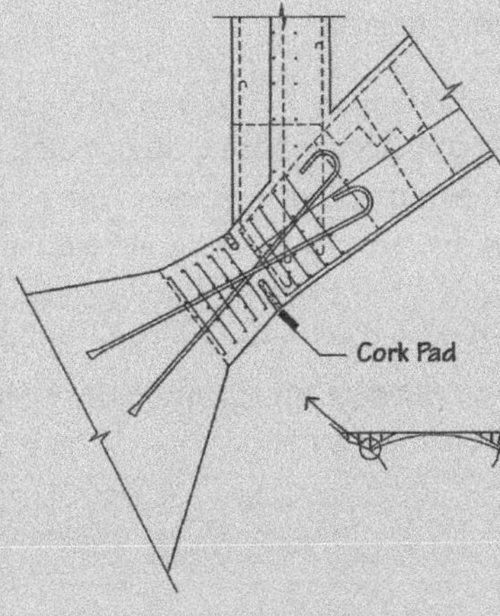

Fig. D

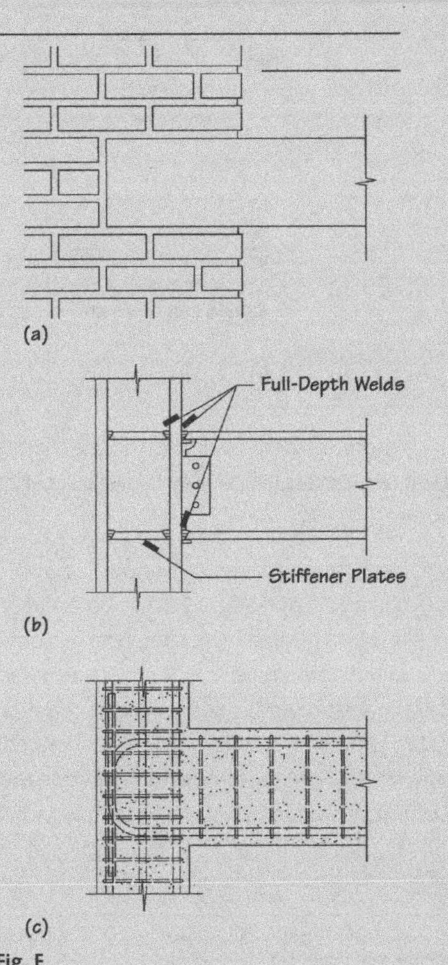

Fig. E

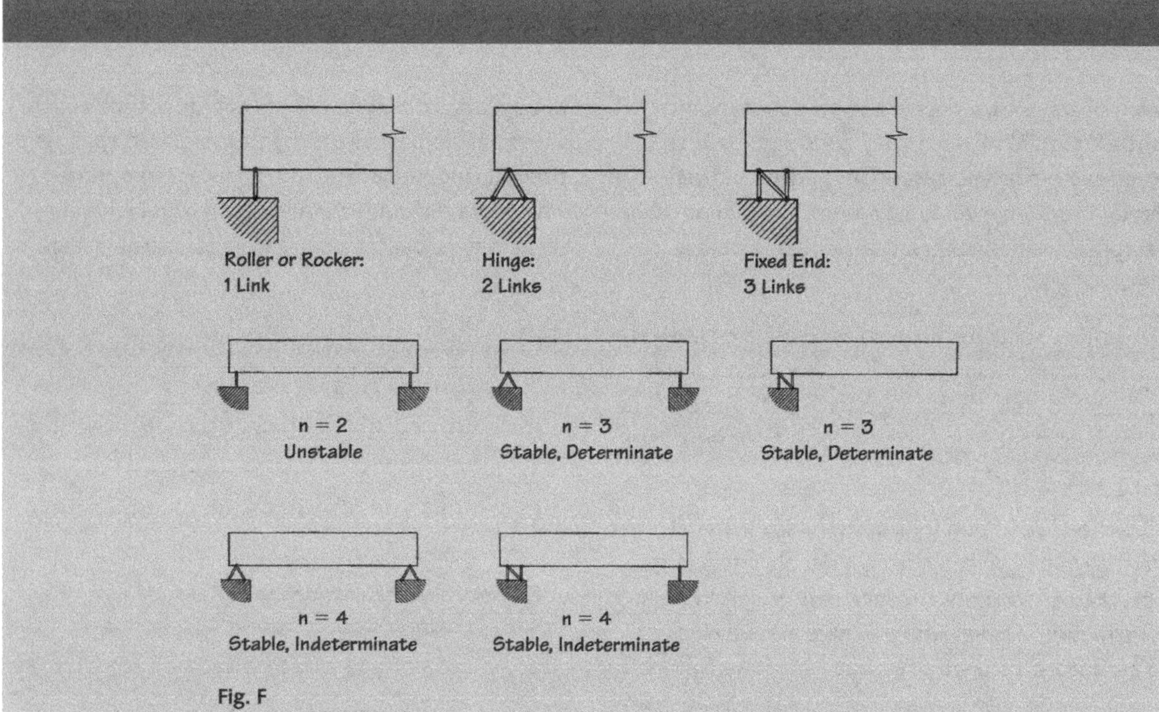

Fig. F

a much more efficient utilization of the material in a beam, which results in a lower overall cost for a structure.

It is helpful in understanding various support conditions to imagine that each is made up entirely of links (Fig. F). A roller, rocker, slide bearing, or link is equivalent to a single link. A pin is equivalent to two links. A fixed end is equivalent to three links. A stable support condition cannot be created with a total of only one or two links. If the total number of links that support a single span is three, the support is both stable and statically determinate. A support condition that totals four or more links is statically indeterminate.

Most beams, joists, rafters, and purlins in buildings span modest distances and are bolted, nailed, or welded to their supporting members with simple connections that, strictly speaking, are neither hinges nor rollers. Yet these common connections offer little restraint against rotation and act almost as hinges, thus avoiding any significant level of incidental forces in the members.

*From *Shaping Structures: Statics* by Wacław Zalewski and Edward Allen (New York: John Wiley & Sons, Inc.), 1998. Reprinted with permission.

FINDING REACTIONS GRAPHICALLY

Reactions may also be found graphically, a procedure that can be faster than a numerical determination when the loadings on a beam or truss are very complex. The steps to a graphical determination of reactions for any loading are as follows:

1. Draw accurately to scale a free-body diagram of the truss or beam.
2. Construct to another scale a load line that is made up of all the known forces on the truss or beam.
3. Adopt any convenient pole; draw rays; and parallel to the rays, draw a funicular polygon, either a cable or an arch, over vertical extension lines from the forces on the member.
4. Draw the closing string of the funicular polygon.
5. Draw a ray parallel to the closing string through the pole of the force polygon. This ray divides the load line into the two reactions.

In Figure 5.19, we have applied this method to the beam that we have just considered in Figure 5.18.

Arbitrarily chosen pole location *o* is used to generate the force polygon and funicular polygon. Because space C extends from the 1,600-lb load to the 2,000-lb load at the end of the overhang, and space D wraps around from the 2,000-lb load to the right reaction, segment *oc* of the funicular polygon reaches all the way to the right end of the funicular polygon, and segment *od* doubles back from the overhanging end to the right support. The closing string of the funicular polygon, *oe*, is drawn between the ends of the funicular polygon. Ray *oe* on the force polygon, drawn parallel to the closing string, divides the load line into segment *ae*, which measures 3,900 lb, and *ed*, 5,700 lb. These are the values of the reactions to within 1 percent of the theoretical values that we calculated earlier. If we were to do this graphical determination in a CAD program, we would arrive at exactly the same values as with a numerical solution.

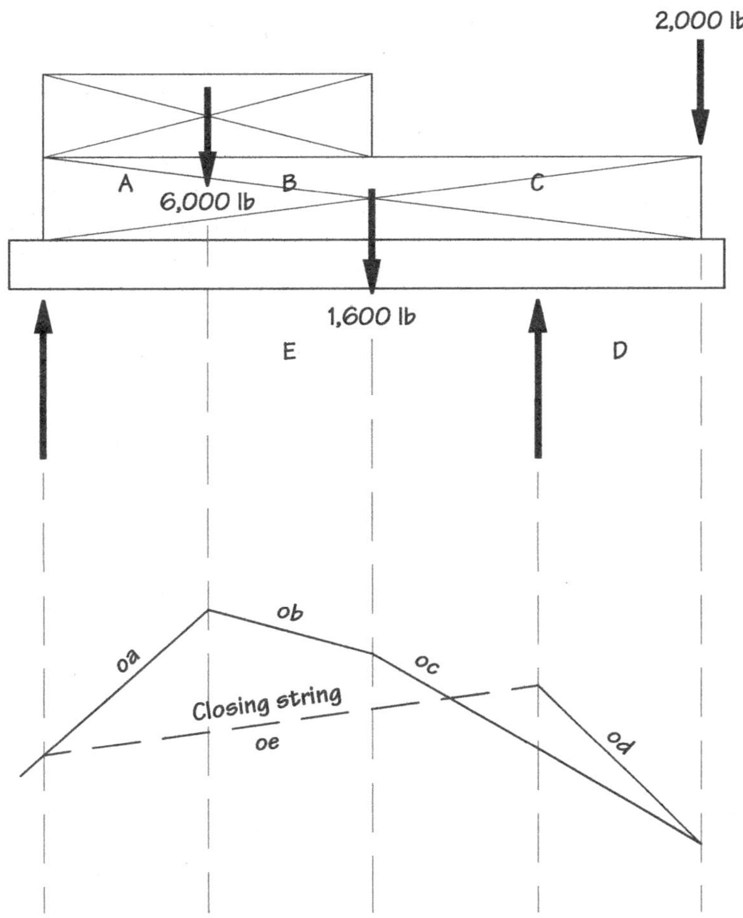

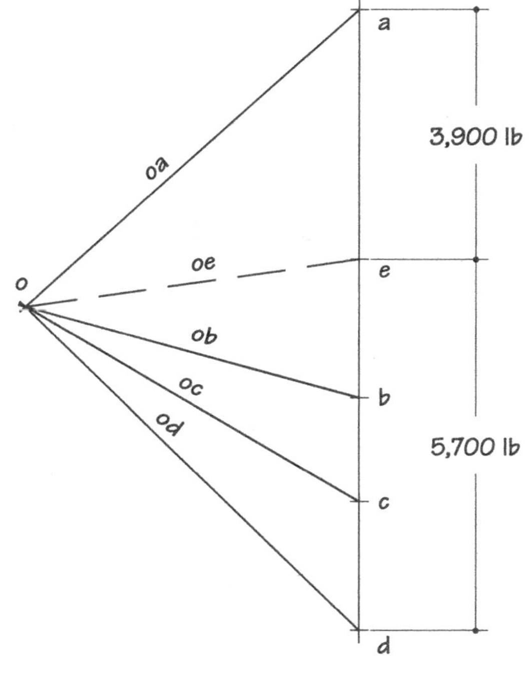

Figure 5.19 A graphical determination of reactions on the beam shown in Figure 5.18.

Trigonometric Functions*

We will make only rudimentary use of trigonometric functions in this book. The functions that we will use are the sine, cosine, and tangent. These are defined for any angle, θ, as follows, referring to the accompanying figure:

$$\sin\theta = y/r$$
$$\cos\theta = x/r$$
$$\tan\theta = y/x$$

The vertical component of any inclined force is equal to the force multiplied by the sine of the angle between the force and the horizontal. The horizontal component is equal to the force multiplied by the cosine of the same angle. If this is difficult for you to remember, then use only the cosine: Either component of a force is equal to the force multiplied by the cosine of the angle between the force and the component.

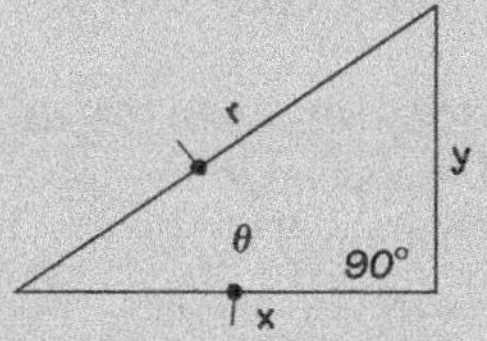

*From *Shaping Structures: Statics* by Wacław Zalewski and Edward Allen (New York: John Wiley & Sons, Inc.), 1998. Reprinted with permission.

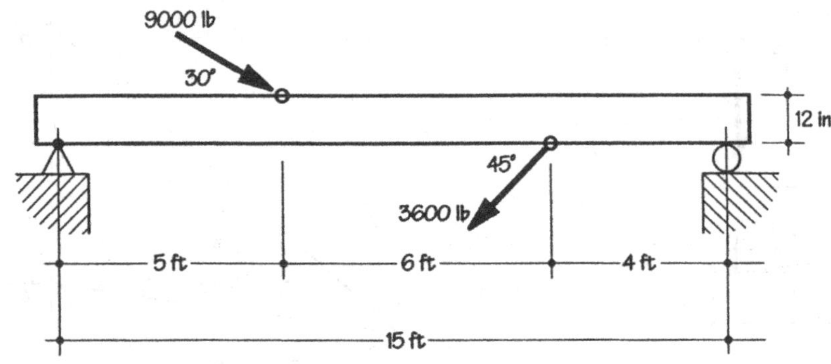

Figure 5.20 A beam with inclined loads.

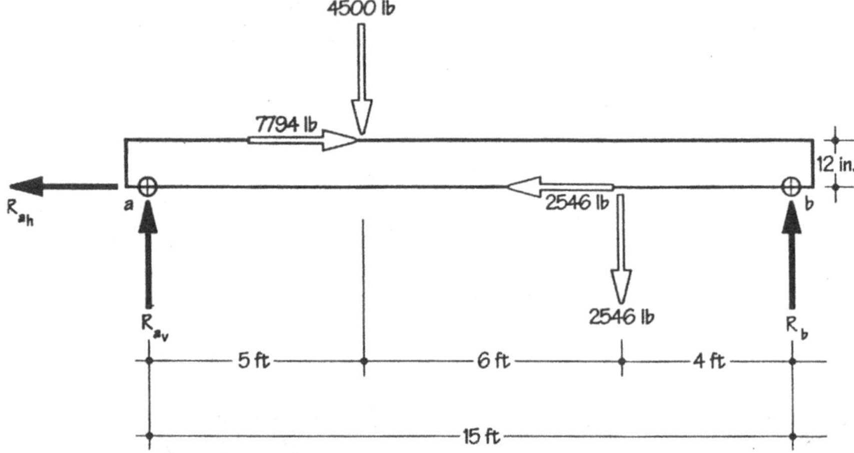

Figure 5.21 Resolving the inclined loads into their horizontal and vertical components.

FURTHER APPLICATIONS OF MOMENTS OF FORCE: FINDING REACTIONS ON A BEAM WITH INCLINED LOADS

Figure 5.20 depicts a beam that supports two inclined loads. One load is applied to the top of the beam, and the other to the bottom. The beam is 12 in. deep. One reaction is furnished by a roller, which can transmit force only in a vertical direction. The other reaction is through a hinge, which can transmit force at any angle.

To find the reactions, we must sum the moments of the inclined loads. There are two ways of doing this: One is to find the lengths of the inclined moment arms of these loads with respect to a selected point. The other is to resolve each inclined load into its vertical and horizontal components, and then to sum the moments of the components of the loads. Either method will yield the same result. For this example, we choose to resolve the forces into components because it makes the determination of the lengths of the moment arms much easier.

Figure 5.21 shows a free-body diagram in which the inclined loads have been resolved into their horizontal and vertical components.

The horizontal component of the 9,000-lb load was found by multiplying 9,000 lb by the cosine of 30°. The vertical component is equal to 9,000 lb times the sine of 30°. The components of the 3,600-lb load were determined in a similar way. The left-hand reaction has been resolved into horizontal and vertical components whose magnitudes are unknown.

We begin by summing moments about point *a* in the lower left corner of the beam. This point is a good axis about which to take moments because the lines of action of three force components, two of them of unknown magnitudes, pass through it and, thus, two unknowns are eliminated from the first step of the computation, leaving only one unknown force for which to solve. We are careful to include an expression for the moment caused by the 7,794-lb horizontal component of the top load:

$$\sum M_a = 0$$

$$(4{,}500\text{ lb})(5\text{ ft}) + (7{,}794\text{ lb})(1\text{ ft}) + (2{,}546\text{ lb})(11\text{ ft}) - R_b(15\text{ ft}) = 0$$

$$R_b = 3{,}887\text{ lb}$$

$$\sum M_b = 0$$

$$-(4{,}500\text{ lb})(10\text{ ft}) + (7{,}794\text{ lb})(1\text{ ft}) - (2{,}546\text{ lb})(4\text{ ft}) + R_a(15\text{ ft}) = 0$$

$$R_{av} = 3{,}159\text{ lb}$$

The remaining unknown quantity, R_{ah}, is found by summing forces in the horizontal direction. It is 5,248 lb, acting leftward on the beam. We may check the accuracy of our moment calculations by summing forces in the vertical direction:

$$\sum F_v = 0 = -3{,}159\text{ lb} + 4{,}500\text{ lb} + 2{,}546\text{ lb} - 3{,}887\text{ lb} = 0$$

$$0 \equiv 0 \qquad \text{check}$$

APPLYING MOMENT ANALYSIS TO A PORTION OF A STRUCTURE

If a structure is in static equilibrium, then any portion or segment of it must also be in static equilibrium. To illustrate the usefulness of this principle, let us apply what we know about moments to find the force in member *m* of the steel bridge truss shown in Figure 5.22.

We make an imaginary cut that passes completely through the truss in such a way that it intersects member *m*. We discard the portion of the truss to one side of the cut (we could throw out the portion to the right of the cut line or the one to the left; it doesn't matter). Then we construct a free-body diagram of the remaining portion of the truss (Figure 5.23).

On this diagram, we show the forces in the cut members as vectors of unknown magnitude but known lines of action. We assume a character, tensile or compressive, for each of them. It is not important whether the assumed characters are correct or not.

There are three of these vectors of unknown value, and a solution would appear at first glance to require fairly involved calculations. But the lines of action of two of the vectors, F_j and F_k, pass through joint 1, so we will sum moments about this point, leaving as the only unknown in this expression F_m, the force in member *m*:

$$\sum M_1 = 0$$

$$(100{,}000\ \text{lb})(36\ \text{ft}) - (100{,}000\ \text{lb})(12\ \text{ft}) + F_m(16\ \text{ft}) = 0$$

$$F_m = -150{,}000\ \text{lb}$$

We had assumed initially that F_m pushed to the left. The minus sign of the answer tells us that it pulls to the right instead. *m* is a tension member rather than a compression member.

We can use the same free-body diagram (Figure 5.23) to find force F_j in member *j*. To do so in a single step, we must take moments about the point through which the lines of action of the other two unknown forces pass, thus eliminating them from the computation. This point of intersection, 2, lies in the empty space to the right of the diagram. From the dimensions

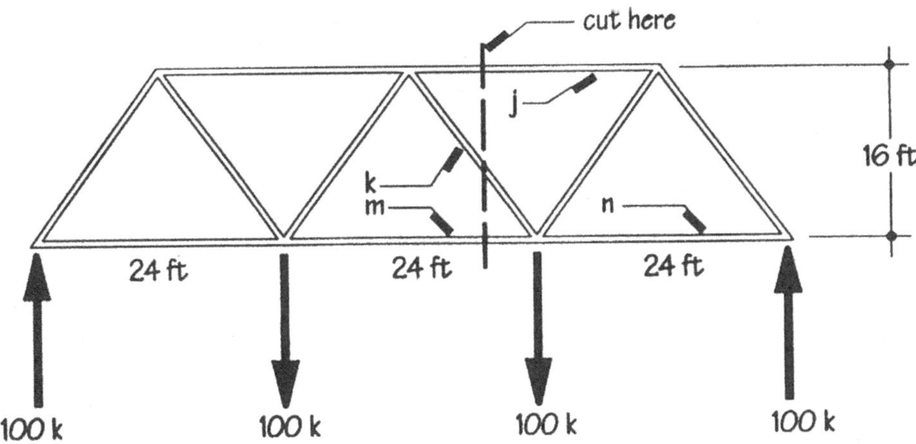

Figure 5.22 A steel bridge truss.

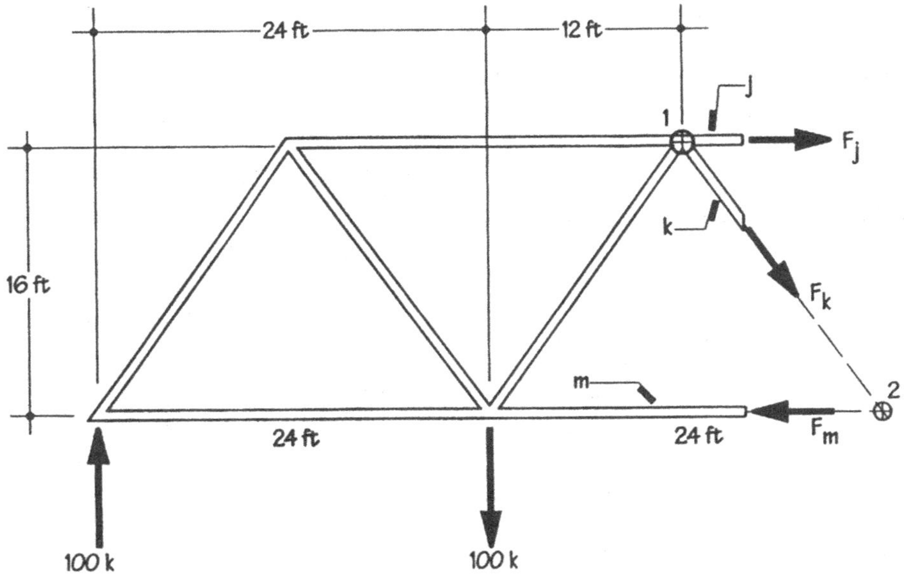

Figure 5.23 An imaginary cut through the bridge truss.

on Figure 5.22, we know that it lies at a distance of 24 ft from the adjacent 100-kip load, which makes it easy to set up the solution:

$$\sum M_2 = 0$$

$$(100{,}000 \text{ lb})(48 \text{ ft}) - (100{,}000 \text{ lb})(24 \text{ ft}) + F_j(16 \text{ ft}) = 0$$

$$F_j = -150{,}000 \text{ lb}$$

The minus sign tells us that we assumed the wrong direction for F_j, as we did for F_m; member j is compressed.

It is apparent that we could find the force in any other member by cutting completely through the truss along a line that intersects the member, selecting a point about which to take moments in such a way that only the member force we wish to find remains as an unknown, and following a similar procedure to a solution. This method of finding the forces in the members of a truss is known as the *method of sections*. The method of sections may be applied to finding internal forces in other types of structures as well.

SOLVING FOR THE FORCES ON THE CLIFF STRUCTURE

Moments of force are the primary tools we need to find the external forces that act on the observation pavilion on the wall of a river gorge. We also need a tool to find the *centroid* of any distributed load, the point through which it may be considered to act as a concentrated force.

Finding Centroids

The centroid of a triangle lies on a line from any vertex to the center of the opposite side at a distance from the opposite side of one-third of its altitude. This puts the centroid of the floor at one-third of the 30-ft length of its triangular floor plan, or 10 ft away from the cliff face. The centroid of the roof, which is 37 ft long, is 37/3 ft, or 12.33 ft, from the cliff face (Figure 5.24).

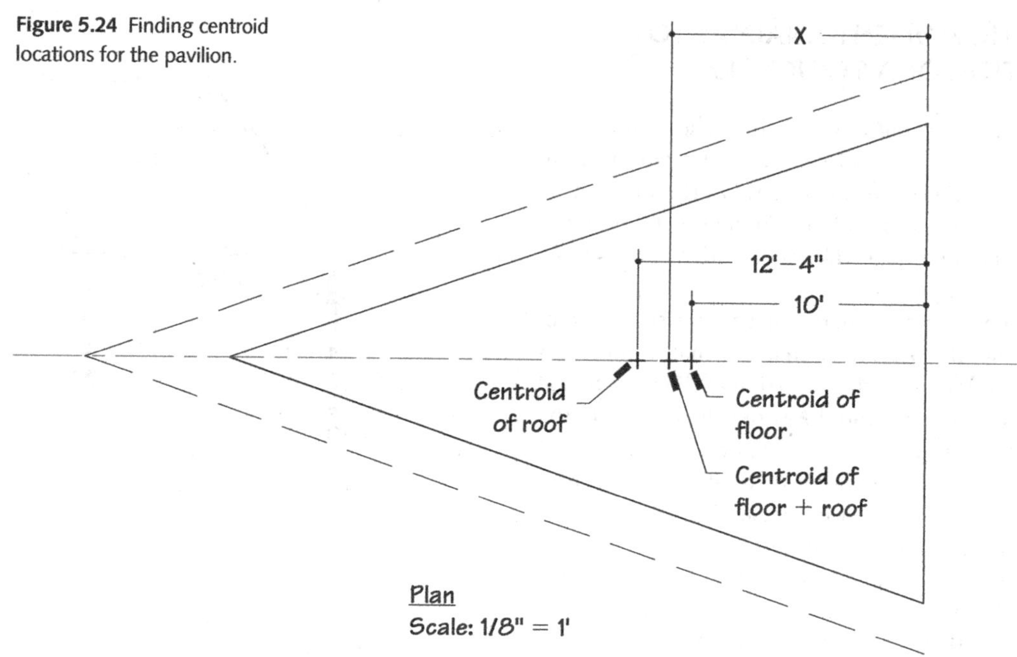

Figure 5.24 Finding centroid locations for the pavilion.

Now we need to find the centroid of the entire structure, the roof, and the floor acting together as a single entity. We can do this by working numerically:

1. We evaluate the moments of the roof weight and the floor weight with respect to the same arbitrarily selected axis. We choose as the axis in this case the short edge of the floor.
2. We add these moments to one another.
3. We set the sum of these two moments equal to a single moment with respect to the same axis. This single moment consists of the total weight of the floor and roof times an unknown moment arm, x, for which we solve (Figure 5.25):

$$M_{\text{roof}} + M_{\text{floor}} = M_{\text{total}}$$

$$(26 \text{ kips})(12.33 \text{ ft}) + (45 \text{ kips})(10 \text{ ft}) = (71 \text{ kips})x$$

$$x = \frac{(26 \text{ kips})(12.33 \text{ ft}) + (45 \text{ kips})(10 \text{ ft})}{71 \text{ kips}} = 10.85 \text{ ft}$$

The centroid of the weight of the entire structure is on the common centerline of the triangles at a distance of 10.85 ft from the short edge of the floor.

Finding the Other Forces in the Structure

Figure 5.26 is a free-body diagram of the whole pavilion structure, which is represented in side view as if it were a beam. It shows the 71-kip total weight of the pavilion acting downward at a point 10.85 ft from the edge near the face of the cliff, as we just determined. The inclined steel tube strut exerts a force Q at a distance of 18 ft from this same edge. We will work with Q in the form of its vertical and horizontal components, Q_v and Q_h, respectively. We will also resolve the reaction at the cliff face, Y, into its vertical and horizontal components, Y_v, and Y_h.

The angle of Q with the horizontal, θ, is given as 16 in. of rise per 12 in. of horizontal run. These two measurements are the legs of a right triangle.

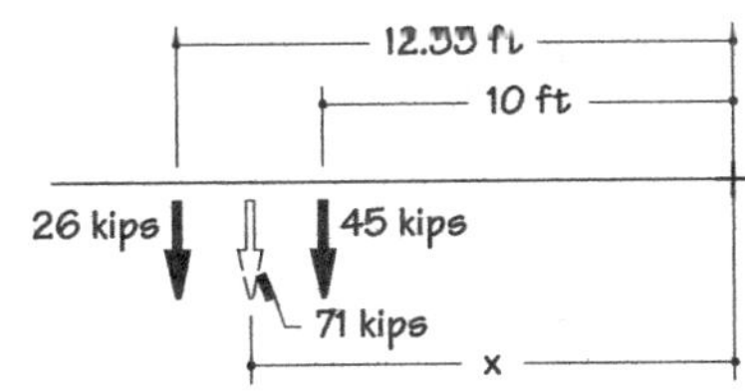

Figure 5.25 Finding the centroid of the structure.

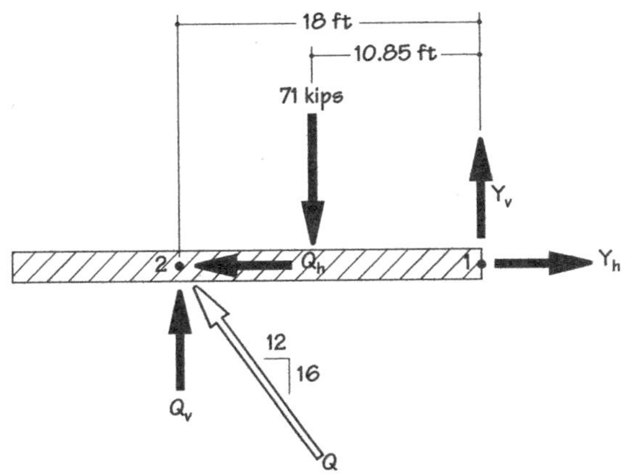

Figure 5.26 Finding the forces in the pavilion.

To calculate the trigonometric functions of θ, we must find the length of the hypotenuse of this triangle, which is the square root of the sum of the squares of the legs:

$$\text{Hypotenuse} = \sqrt{12^2 + 16^2} = 20$$

The sine of θ is 16/20, which is 0.8. The cosine is 12/20, which is 0.6. The tangent is 16/12, which is 1.33. We can convert θ to degrees by finding the arctan of 1.33, which is 53.06°. (Arctan is short for *arctangent*, which is the angle that has a given tangent, in this case 1.33.)

Returning to the free-body diagram in Figure 5.26, we evaluate moments about point 2, which eliminates three variables from consideration:

$$\sum M_2 = 0 = (7.15 \text{ ft})(71 \text{ kips}) - (18 \text{ ft})Y_v$$

$$Y_v = \frac{(7.15 \text{ ft})(71 \text{ kips})}{18} = 28.2 \text{ kips}$$

This force component is shared by two attachments to the cliff, each 14.1 kips. Next we evaluate moments about point 1, which again leaves only one variable:

$$\sum M_1 = 0 = (-10.85 \text{ ft})(71 \text{ kips}) + (18 \text{ ft})Q_v$$

$$Q_v = 42.8 \text{ kips}$$

As a check of our work, we can sum forces in the vertical direction:

$$\sum F_v \overset{?}{=} 0 = 71 \text{ kips} - 42.8 \text{ kips} - 28.2 \text{ kips} \equiv 0$$

check

To determine the remaining components of force at points 1 and 2, we can carry out more computations, or we can utilize the trigonometric functions of the angle θ:

$$Q_h = \frac{-Q_v}{\tan\theta} = \frac{-42.8 \text{ kips}}{1.33} = 32.1 \text{ kips}$$

Because there are only two horizontal forces on the free-body diagram, component y_h must be equal and opposite to Q_h in order to create equilibrium; its value is 32.1 kips, which is split between two points of attachment to the cliff, each carrying 16.05 kips.

The axial force in the strut, Q, is found from its components by means of the Pythagorean theorem:

$$Q = \sqrt{Q_v{}^2 + Q_h{}^2} = \sqrt{42.8^2 + 32.1^2} = 53.5 \text{ kips}$$

The inclined force transmitted to each of the two foundations at the cliff wall is found in similar fashion:

$$Y = \frac{\sqrt{Y_v{}^2 + Y_h{}^2}}{2} = 0.5\sqrt{28.2^2 + 32.1^2} = 21.4 \text{ kips}$$

A GRAPHICAL SOLUTION

A graphical solution to the same problem is remarkably simple and direct (Figure 5.27). The distributed load of the floor and roof is represented by a single downward vector of 71 kips at the centroid of the combined floor and roof loads. To determine the location of this vector, we construct a load line that is made up of the floor and roof loads. Then we adopt any convenient pole and draw rays to complete a force polygon (b). Parallel to these rays, we draw the segments of a funicular polygon, (c), on which the distance between the two loads, 2 ft–4 in., is plotted accurately to scale. We extend the lines of action of the first and last segments of the funicular polygon, *op* and *or*, until they intersect. The resultant of the two forces passes through this point of intersection on the funicular polygon. This is the centroid of the sum of the two loads. We scale the horizontal distance to determine that it is 10 in. to the left of the centroid of the roof load.

The free body of the pavilion, diagram (d) of Figure 5.27, has only three external forces acting upon it. We know the locations and directions of two of these forces: the 71-kip vertical load, which we have just found to be 10 in. to the left of the centroid of the floor load, and the diagonal force along the axis of the inclined strut. Extending the line of action of the floor and roof loads until it crosses the axis of the inclined strut, we find a point of concurrence through which the third force, which acts through the pin connection to the right, must also pass. (If the line of action of any of the three forces did not pass through the point of concurrence of the other two, the moments in this system of forces would not be in equilibrium).

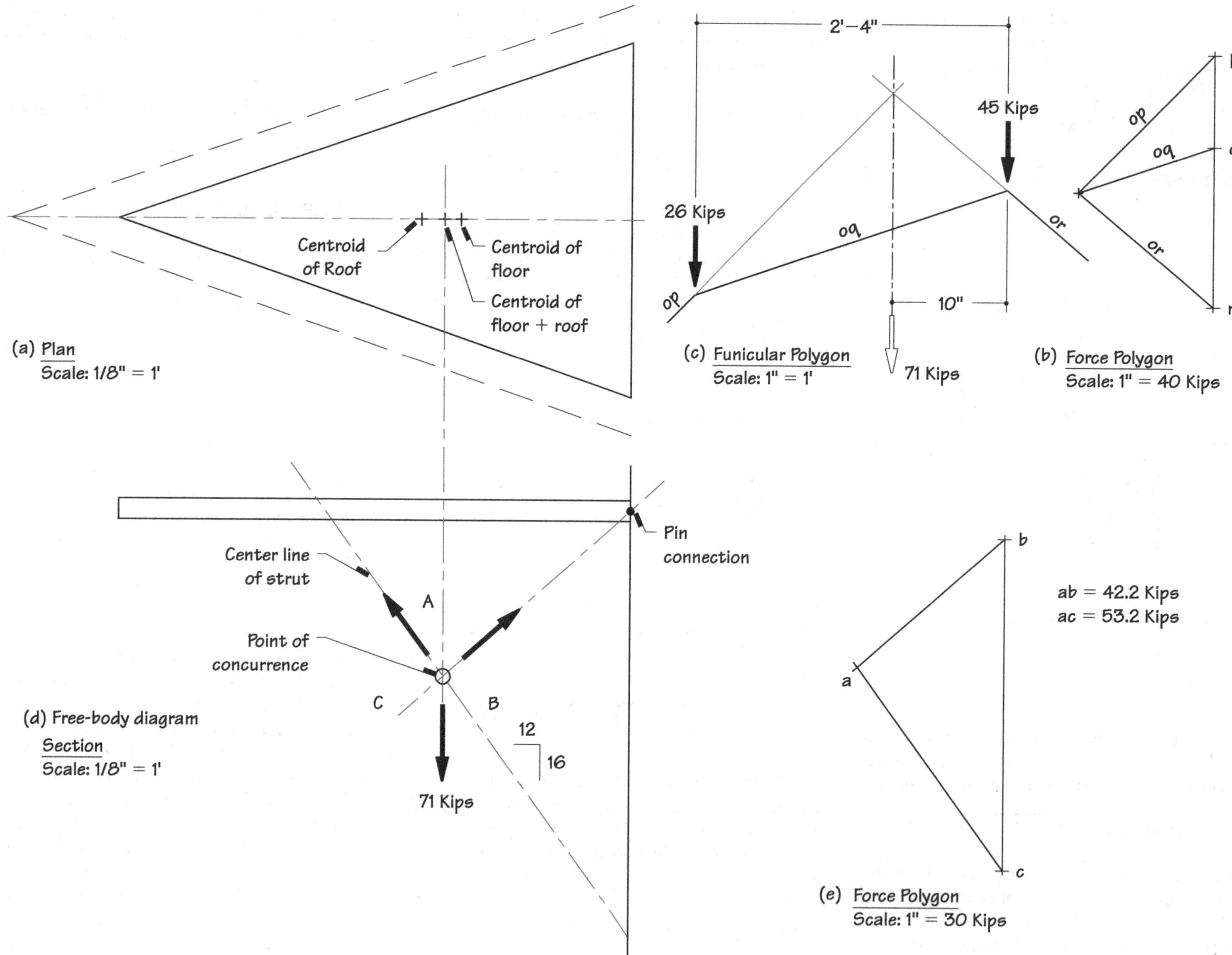

Figure 5.27 Graphical determination of the forces in the pavilion.

We use Bow's notation to label the spaces between these forces. Working clockwise around the point of concurrence, the 71-kip load is *bc*. As we move from *b* to *c* on the free-body diagram, the force pushes downward. Thus, we construct a load line to the right (e) that is 71 kips long at the designated scale, with *b* at the top and *c* at the bottom. Through point *b*, we construct line *ab* parallel to *AB*, and through point *c*, line *ca*. The two lines *ab* and *ca* intersect at *a*. We scale these lines to find the numerical values of the three forces: 53 kips for *ca*, which is the force in the inclined strut, and 42.6 kips for *ab*, which is the total force transmitted to the two foundations in the rock wall of the gorge. Both values are within 1 percent of those that we would find numerically. The angle of *ab* is already determined by its passing through the pin and the point of concurrence.

SIZING THE STRUT AND BEAMS

Although we have not yet learned to assign sizes to beams, we can give approximate sizes based on a rule of thumb: A simply supported steel floor beam should have a depth of about 1/20 of the span. For a roof beam, the proportion can be 1/24. The difference is due to the fact that floor beams generally carry heavier loads and that deflection (sagging) must be more closely controlled in floor beams than roof beams. Applying these proportions to the cliff structure is tricky, because the two major floor beams, the ones at the outside edges, carry heavy roof loads that are brought to them by the window mullions, which calls for an increase in their depth. At the same time, these beams overhang at the outer end, which allows the depth to decrease somewhat. But the overhang is rather long, which requires greater depth. In Chapters 16 and 17 we will learn how to assign a definite size to these beams despite all these complications. For now, taking all these factors into account, we will give the major beams an approximate depth of 1/20 of their overall length of 32 ft, which is about 19 in. Standard sizes of steel beams go from 8 in. to 18 in. in 2 in. increments, then from 21 in. to 36 in. in 3-in. increments. Accordingly, we round up the size to 21 in. The two interior beams span about 20 ft, so they can be 12 in. deep. The short girder that brings the loads from the floor beams to the inclined strut is atypical, in that it carries a heavy load over a very short span and can't be sized by a simple approximation. Pending calculations, we guess that it might be 18 in. deep.

The inclined strut can be sized approximately with the aid of the column tables in the AISC *Manual of Steel Construction*. There is a table specifically given to square tube columns. By reading the free length of the column, 30 ft, down the left side, then finding in this row a capacity in kips that equals or exceeds the load on the strut in our structure, which is 63 kips, we arrive at a steel tube size of 6 in. square. Although this is a safe size for this member, given its crucial importance in the support of the pavilion, we might wish to increase the size to 8 in. for additional security against buckling.

Redundancy

The stability of this structure depends primarily on just three of its elements: the diagonal tube and the two hinges that are attached to the cliff. If any of these should fail, the result would be a catastrophe that would possibly result in the loss of human lives as well as the structure. In talks with the owner of the pavilion, we have decided that such a failure cannot be tolerated. We must provide for the stability of the structure in such a way that if any main component of it should fail, there will be another element to take over its supporting role.

After much discussion, we design a simple, economical backup structure. Two stainless steel rods will tie connections on the two sides of the floor of the pavilion to special foundation plates high on the cliff. These rods will be tightened at the conclusion of construction until they are barely taut. If the diagonal steel tube should buckle or otherwise fail, these rods will assume its load and transmit it to the special foundations with only a slight subsidence of the structure. In a similar way, short steel rods attached to the floor frame near the two hinges will secure the frame to additional anchors in the cliff. All these newly added members are *redundant*, which is to say that they duplicate the roles of members already provided in the structure. Normally we do not provide redundant members in a structure, but redundancy is desirable in circumstances where total structural failure is likely and/or would have dire consequences. Following terrorist attacks on certain kinds of government buildings, it has become standard practice to design redundancy into the frames of such buildings so that if any single column is destroyed by a bomb or vehicle, the frame will still stand.

BUILDING THE OBSERVATION PAVILION

Construction of the pavilion is complicated by its being on a vertical site rather than a horizontal one. Without proper safety precautions, any mistake on the part of the builders could result in the free fall to the bottom of the canyon of a dropped tool, a mishandled component, an incautious worker, or the entire structure. A safety net will be deployed a short distance below the structure to catch any worker who might fall. This will be supported by cables attached to temporary outriggers on the floor frame. Additionally, every worker will be required to wear a safety harness. This will be tied to an elastic line that is anchored on the rock wall above the structure. In accordance with detailed provisions of the U.S. Occupational Safety and Health Act (OSHA), each steel floor beam will be equipped with a waist-high horizontal cable mounted on temporary vertical brackets. This serves both as a handrail for workers and a line to which each worker can connect his or her safety harness with a simple clip.

As much assembly of the pavilion as possible will take place on the plateau above so that the crane can handle it in several large pieces. Figure 5.28 diagrams a tentative procedure for erecting the building. In part (a), the process begins with workers being lowered from above on cables to install

Figure 5.28 Stages in the erection of the pavilion.

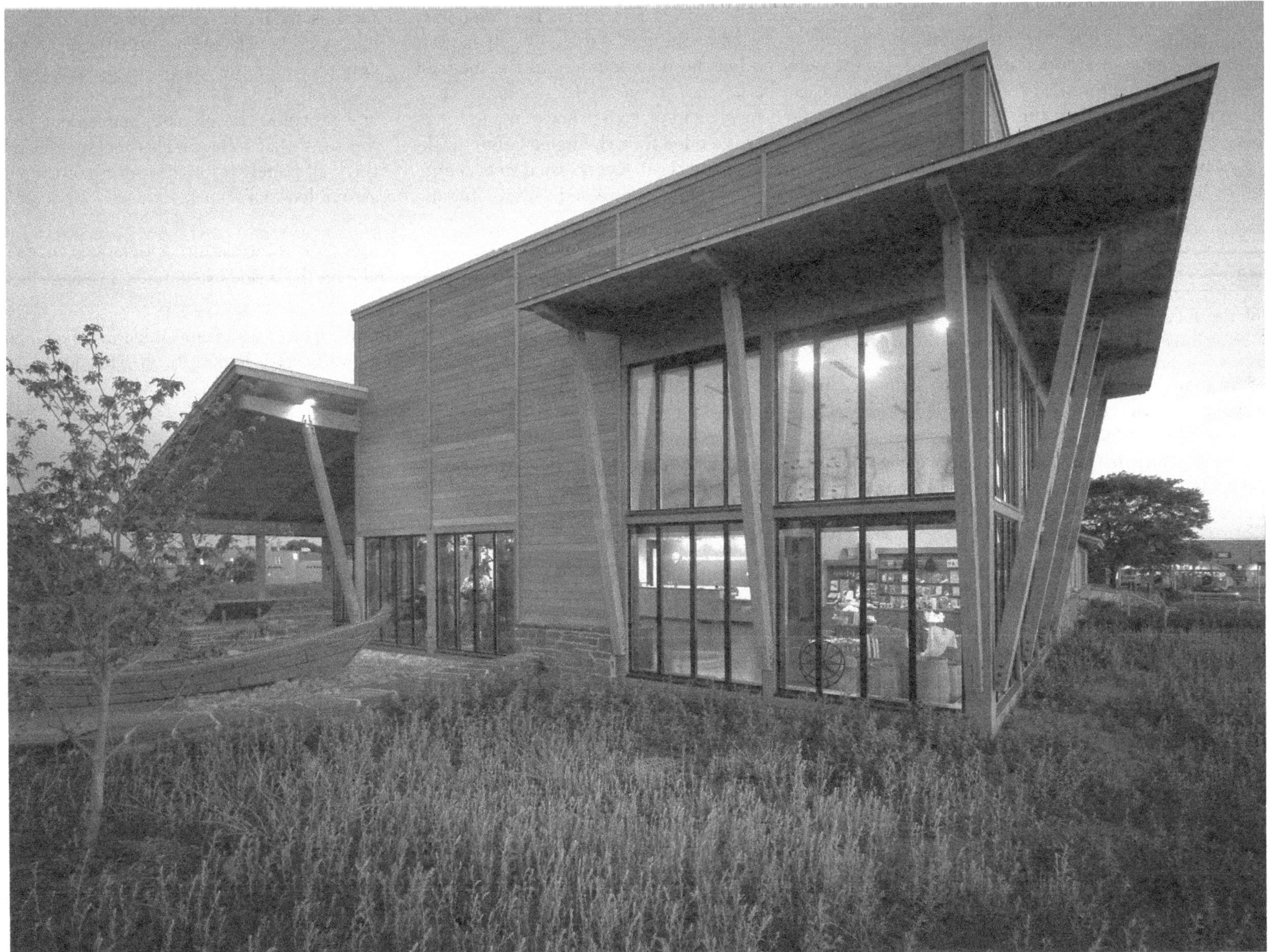

Figure 5.29 At Fort Stanwix National Monument in Rome, New York, the Marinus Willett Collections Management and Education Facility was designed by the team of architects and engineers at Einhorn Yaffee Prescott. In such a snowy climate, the potentially heavy loads on its various cantilevered roof areas are resisted by inclined struts. The forces in these struts were found by evaluating moments.

three foundations into the rock, one for the base of the inclined strut and two for the inside end of the floor platform. These are detailed in Figure 5.7. Worker access may be improved by temporary ladders, or by excavating the access tunnels from the plateau above early in the process. Part (b) shows the entire floor frame being lowered as a unit—note the temporary handrails that have been installed on the frame for worker protection. Two temporary cables anchored to the top of the cliff will support the outer end of the floor frame until the inclined strut can be lowered, connected to its foundation, and bolted securely in place, as shown in part (c). A safety net is suspended from the frame before workers resume their labors (d). A corrugated steel deck is attached to the beams, and welded wire reinforcing mesh is installed over the deck. Then the crane lowers concrete in large buckets. Workers distribute the concrete over the floor decking and trowel it into a smooth floor slab. This covers the corrugations and provides a level, safe, convenient platform for the work that follows. This includes installation of the wall panels (e) and lowering of the completely assembled roof (f).

Exercises

For each of the following exercises, decide whether a graphical or a numerical approach is more direct, and follow that approach to a solution.

1. Figure 5.30 shows four additional ways of supporting the pavilion on the cliff. In scheme (a), an internal tension rod is substituted for the inclined strut. Scheme (b) depicts three different inclinations for the inclined strut. Schemes (c) and (d) would place the structure in a different part of the gorge where support is available for a vertical column. Find the forces in the column, strut, or tension rod for each of these alternative designs.

2. Find the reactions for each of the beams in Figure 5.31. The self-weight of the beam is included in the distributed load in each case.

3. Find the forces in members *a*, *b*, and *c* of the theater roof truss in Figure 5.32.

4. The free-body diagram in Fig. 5.33 is a cross section that represents the forces that act on a garden toolshed. The downward vector of 2,250 lb represents the weight of the shed. The horizontal vector of 1,600 lb represents the resultant of the estimated maximum force of the wind. How much downward force is required at point *a* to keep the shed from overturning? What are the components of the reaction at the other corner of the shed?

5. Figure 5.34 shows a design for a cantilevered roof for a stadium grandstand. The sum of the live and dead loads for one bay of the roof is 21 kips. Find the magnitudes of the reactions R_1 and R_2.

6. Find the reactions at *a* and *b* on the welded steel frame in Figure 5.35. Ignore the weight of the frame.

7. The 12-ft cantilever beam in Figure 5.36 is embedded in a rectangular block of concrete that is 6 ft wide and weighs 30,000 lb. At what load, *W*, will the block begin to tip over?

Key Terms and Concepts

intumescent coating
mullion
centroid
moment of force
moment
M = Pd [5-1]
moment arm, *d*
$\Sigma M = 0$
reaction
sine (sin)
cosine (cos)
tangent (tan)
method of sections
redundancy

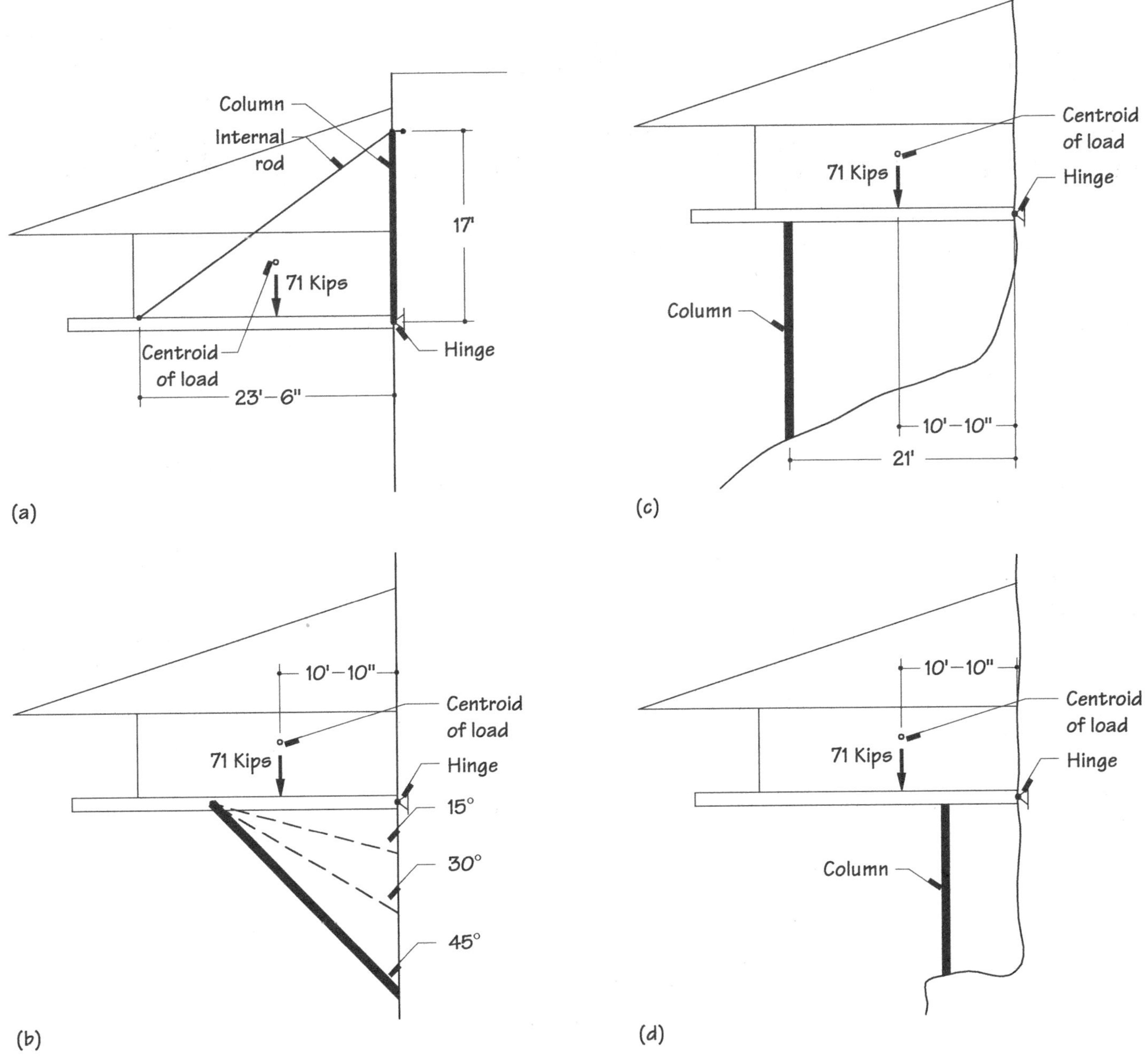

Figure 5.30 Additional ways of supporting the pavilion.

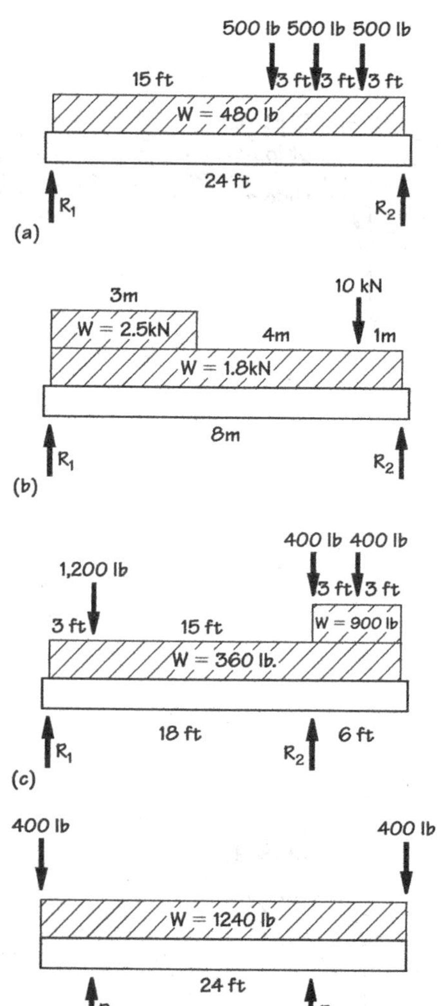

Figure 5.31

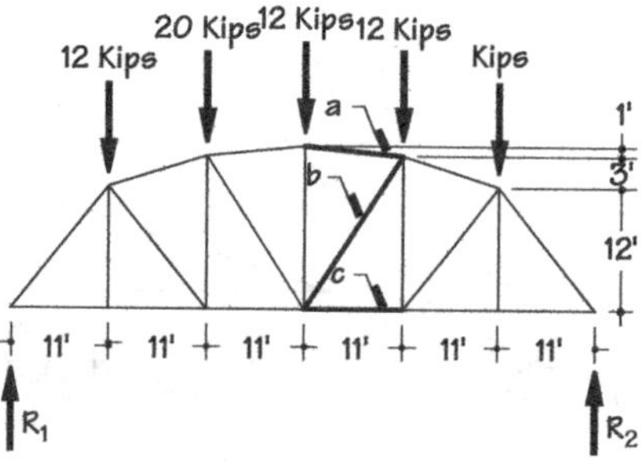

Figure 5.32 A roof truss for a theater.

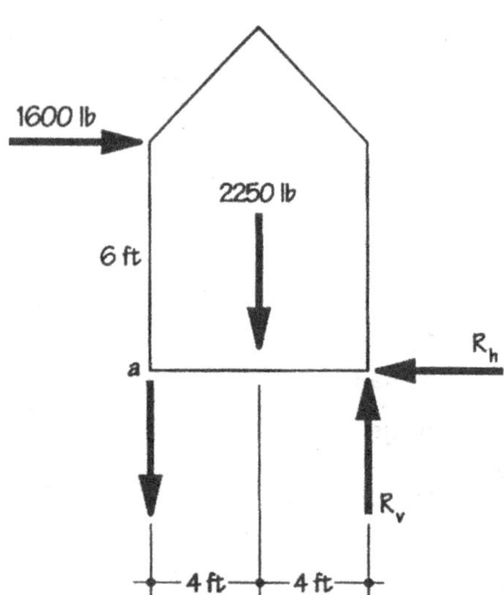

Figure 5.33 Free-body diagram of a garden toolshed.

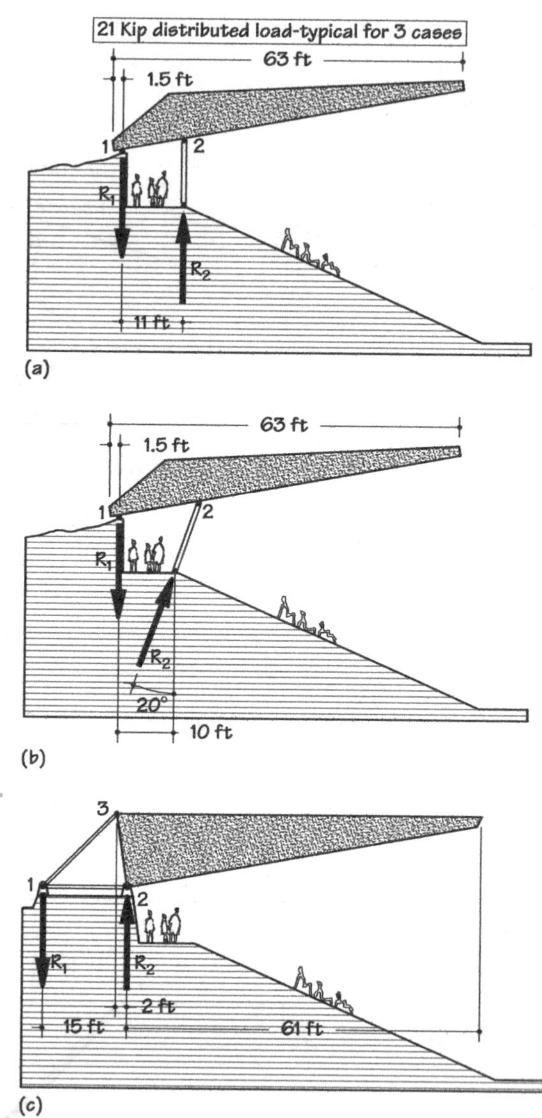

Figure 5.34 Three alternative roof designs for a grandstand.

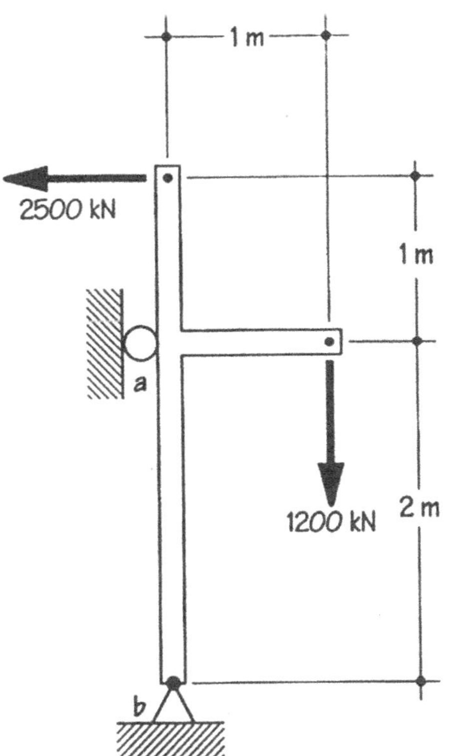

Figure 5.35 A welded steel frame.

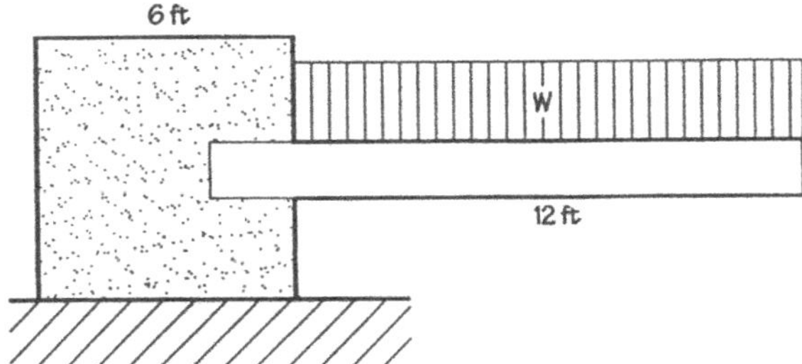

Figure 5.36

Women in Structural Design

The building design professions have been slow to add women to their ranks. The architecture profession began to open slightly to women a century ago, when Marion Mahony Griffin (1871–1961) began doing some of Frank Lloyd Wright's design work and renderings in Chicago, and Julia Morgan (1872–1957) became an important architect in California. Mahony Griffin was the second woman to earn an architecture degree at MIT and the first to be licensed to practice in Illinois. Morgan graduated in civil engineering and subsequently studied architecture at the Ecole de Beaux Arts in Paris. She designed more than 600 projects, the most famous William Randolph Hearst's San Simeon castle in California.

Today, enrollments in many schools of architecture are more or less evenly divided between men and women. A number of women practitioners have risen to prominence, though none has attracted attention as a designer of exemplary load-bearing structures, whether bridges or buildings.

Women engineers who design and build major structures are much rarer than women architects. Enrollments in university programs in structural and civil engineering are still predominantly, but not exclusively, male. The first woman to come to prominence in bridge construction was Emily Warren Roebling (1844–1903), who assumed greater and greater responsibility for the construction of the Brooklyn Bridge after her husband, Washington Roebling (1837–1926), the engineer for the project, was permanently disabled by caisson disease. It is difficult to know with certainty how much influence she had on the design of the bridge; indications are that it was considerable. She had not studied engineering, but apparently had an aptitude for the work of bridge-building and was a quick study. She made several trips a day to the site to guide construction. A newspaper of the day declared that she was "Chief Engineer of the Work," and noted that she was admired and respected by everyone connected with the project.

A female structural engineer who has attained international prominence as a designer of major structures today is Linda Figg. After graduating in civil engineering from Auburn University in 1981, she practiced with her father, Gene Figg (1938–2002), also a civil engineer, for 20 years and took over the firm upon his death. In the first quarter century of its existence, Figg Engineering and its predecessor firm, Figg and Muller, built $6 billion in projects and won more than 200 design awards. Their most celebrated projects include the cable-stayed Sunshine Skyway Bridge in Florida, the Natchez Trace Parkway in Tennessee, and the Blue Ridge Parkway in North Carolina.

A generation ago, a woman studying architecture or engineering was likely to be subjected to some amount of hazing and, in many cases, outright hostility by teachers and/or male students. Today, such inexcusably discriminatory behavior has largely disappeared and there is no reason why women should not do as well as men in the building design professions.

CHAPTER 6

Designing with Multipanel Trusses

- *Various methods of analysis for multipanel trusses*
- *Common truss configurations and their uses*
- *Developing and refining the forms of complex trusses based upon forces and connections*
- *Detailing and construction of a building with heavy timber trusses*

We have just signed a contract to design an assembly building for a children's summer camp in the Pocono Mountains of Pennsylvania. The owner envisions a simple wooden enclosure with a concrete slab floor, a raised wooden performance platform toward one side that is easily demounted and stored, and a column-free floor area about 40 ft by 60 ft (Figure 6.1). It will be used for many different types of events, including meetings, talks on nature and wilderness, drama productions, film showings, and indoor rope climbing and other rainy-day sports. Many of these activities will require fastening things to the ceiling—climbing ropes, gymnastic apparatus, theatrical lights—which has led us and the owners of the camp to agree on the desirability of spanning the space with wood trusses rather than solid beams. Trusses will also have the potential to create a much richer and more exciting interior space than beams.

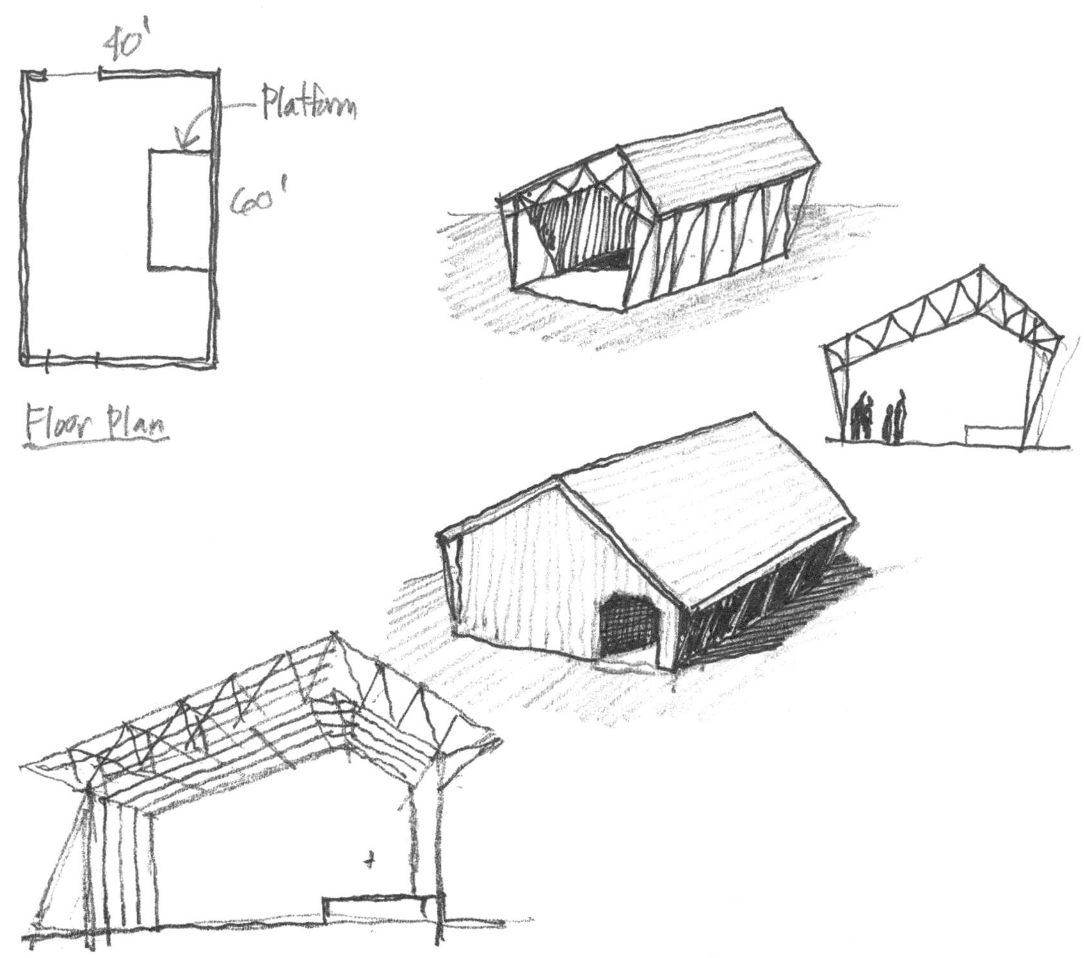

Figure 6.1 Early conceptual sketches for a summer camp building.

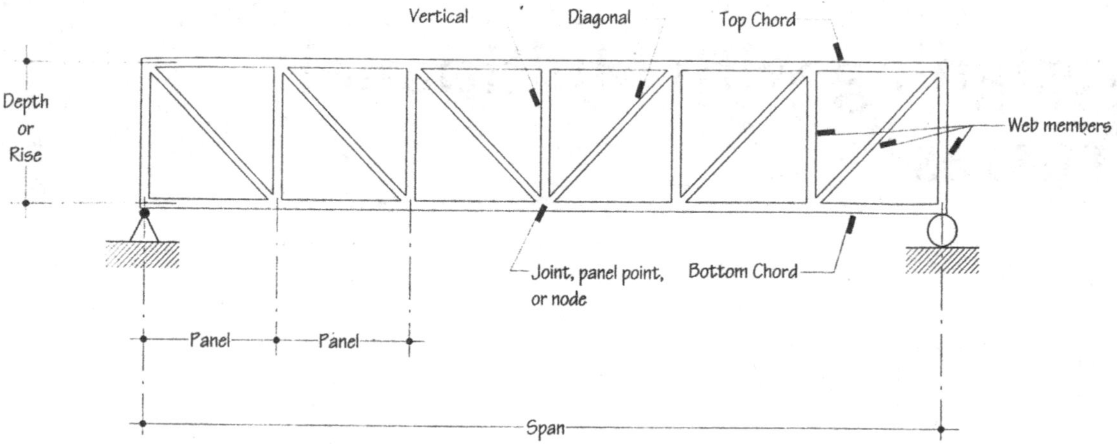

Figure 6.2 Terminology for trusses and their components.

In a series of meetings with the owners and groups of campers, we have made some very rough sketches of various ideas of what the building might look like. We would like to create a space that is higher over the performance platform and lower toward the back, away from the platform. We propose to do this with asymmetrical gabled *parallel chord trusses*. Some early design studies featured ideas that we've since abandoned, such as giving the trusses triangular legs so that the entire frame of the building is made up of trusses without separate columns or walls (Figure 6.3a). In reflecting on this idea, we realized that it makes each truss a two-hinged arch with its *hinges* at the foundations. A two-hinged arch is *indeterminate*, which

Figure 6.2 illustrates terminology pertaining to trusses.

- The top and bottom members are the *chords*.
- The members that connect the chords are the *web members*, which may be further classified as *verticals* and *diagonals*.
- Compression members may be called *struts*, and tension members, *ties*.
- Any portion of a truss that is bounded by adjacent verticals is a *panel*.
- The points at which members converge may be termed *joints, panel points*, or *nodes*.

We have checked the building code to be sure that we are legally permitted to make this building of wood. The International Building Code classifies the use as Occupancy Group A-3: Assembly–Miscellaneous. For this occupancy, it allows a single-story structure built of exposed wood, light frame construction to be as large in floor area as 6,000 sq ft, which is far larger than the 2,400 sq ft that we will build. We may therefore construct this building of wood.

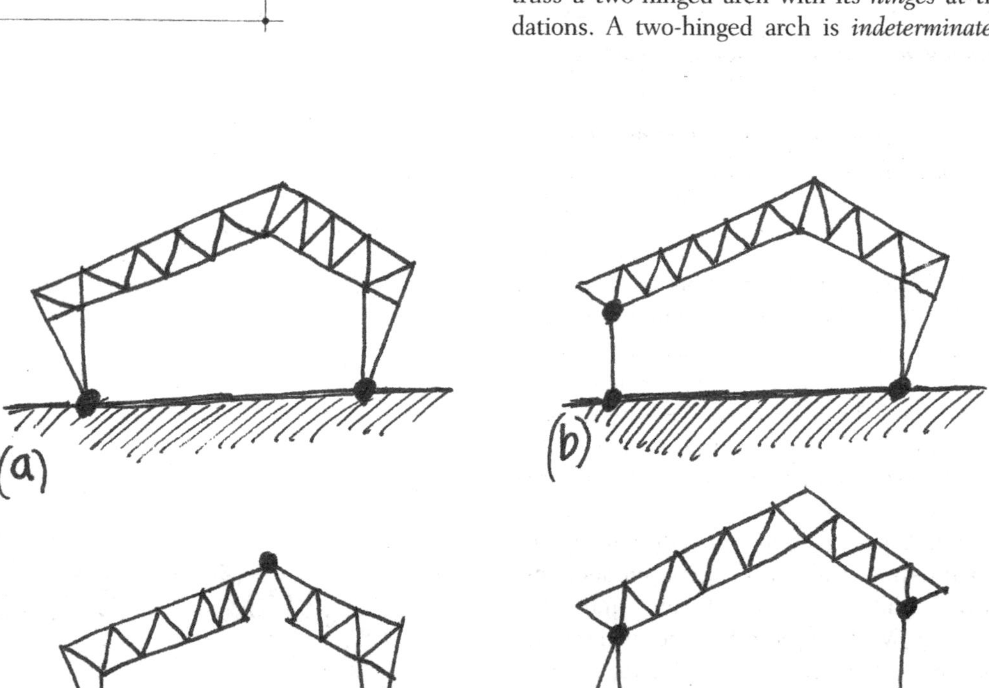

Figure 6.3 Sketches showing ideas for the camp building: (a) shows a two-hinged indeterminate example; (b), (c), (d) show three-hinged examples.

means that the three expressions of static equilibrium are insufficient to find the forces in its members. It also means that normal expansion of the wood during humid summer days would create stresses in the trusses that are difficult to quantify. We decided to avoid dealing with such problems by putting three hinges into each plane of trusses, which makes it *statically determinate*. We diagram several ways of doing this (Figure 6.3b, c, d).

Early sketches also show end extensions of the trusses that produce an overhang of the roof at each end. This is a desirable feature because it protects the columns and walls from rain. We decide to keep and enhance similar overhangs as we pursue the final design.

DEVELOPING THE DESIGN

Proportioning the Trusses

The depth of a truss is usually determined by approximate *depth-to-span ratios*, as shown below:

Truss Configuration: Minimum Depth-to-Span Ratio

	Steel	Wood
Parallel Chord	1:10	1:9
Gable/Triangular	1:6	1:4
Bowstring/ Lenticular	1:8	1:7
Joist Trusses	1:20	1:16

These are not rigid rules, but rather proportions that tend to produce trusses with reasonable levels of internal force and acceptable deflections. These guidelines suggest that for a parallel-chord wood truss we use a ratio of 1:9, which for our 40-ft span would be about 4.5 ft. We round this up to 5 ft to keep forces low.

Designing the Structure

As we do with all structures, we will develop the structural system from the top down, which is how a structure accumulates loads and conducts them to the ground. The topmost structural component is the deck. We propose to use wood tongue-and-groove *decking* (Figure 6.4). The interlocking tongues and grooves enable the planks to act as a unit in resisting loads: A load applied to one plank is transmitted through the tongues and grooves to be shared by the planks on either side. This load-sharing action also allows end joints between pieces of decking to occur anywhere in the roof, not just over supports.

We would like to use decking with a nominal 2-in. depth, which is actually 1–1/2-in. thick. In this depth, the decking can span about 5 ft. We don't want to place the trusses this close together, because it would require too many of them. Instead we will support the decking with beams called *purlins* that transmit the loads from the decking to the nodes of the trusses (Figure 6.5). The 5-ft allowable span of the decking thus becomes both the purlin spacing and the panel width for the trusses. The 40-ft truss span will be made up of eight panels, each 5 ft wide. Factors to consider in determining the spacing between the trusses include:

Figure 6.4 Tongue-and-groove decking.

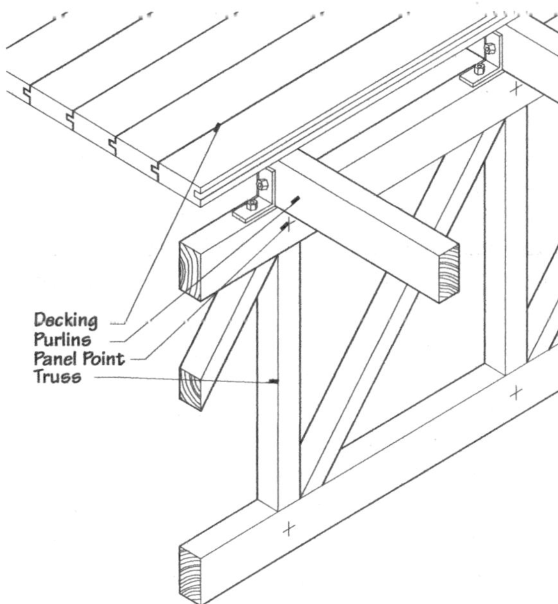

Figure 6.5 Purlins transfer loads from the decking to panel points of the truss.

- *Purlin depth*: Relatively deep purlins allow us to space the trusses farther apart and, therefore, to use fewer trusses.
- *Strength and weight*: Wider spacings result in larger tributary areas that require stronger trusses, which may be heavier and more difficult to make.
- *Visual intensity*: It is often desirable to maintain a certain visual intensity by keeping the trusses relatively closely spaced.

A rule of thumb for the depth of wood purlins is 1/20 of the span. Accordingly, 4 × 6 purlins, which are actually 5–1/2 in. deep, will span a maximum distance of about 9 ft. We decide to space the trusses 8 ft apart in order to balance these factors and achieve an appropriate visual intensity. This will also provide appropriately spaced lines of structure along which gymnastic apparatus, ropes, and theatrical lighting can be attached for camp activities.

Shaping the Trusses

Roof slopes, which are often referred to as *pitches*, are traditionally given in inches of *rise* (vertical dimension) per 12 in. (1 ft) of *run* (horizontal dimension). As noted earlier, this way of designating a slope is convenient for a builder because the angled cuts and sloping lengths for the framing components may be laid out rapidly and accurately by utilizing the rise and run measurements on the two legs of a *framing square* (Figure 6.6). A slope designated in degrees would require either sophisticated surveying instruments or a very large protractor to attain the same level of accuracy. We adopt tentatively a slope of 6 in 12, which is a little less than 30° and looks about right for our design.

We will keep the trusses well above head level at all points as a way of discouraging young campers from climbing on them. We consider tapering the trusses to make them deeper in the middle part of its span, where forces are highest. This would reduce the amount of material that they would use, but it would make almost every component of a truss different from all other components, which would complicate cutting and assembly operations and increase costs. We decide to keep a constant depth in order to standardize the truss components as much as we believe is reasonable.

To facilitate further experimentation with the shape of the truss, we begin laying it out with drafting instruments at a scale of 1/8 in. equals 1 ft (1:96). We would like to make the panels of the truss square, or nearly so, for maximum structural efficiency. Accordingly, we draw parallel vertical lines 5 ft apart; these represent the centerlines of the vertical members of the truss. We also pencil in top and bottom chord centerlines; these are 5 ft apart vertically and slope at 6 in 12. Then, working by trial and error, we refine our initial thoughts by trying several different truss shapes and proportions. Our goal is to arrive eventually at a form that looks handsome and is easy to construct. We sketch human figures to scale, both adults and children, on each drawing to help us judge the size and proportions of the building. We try two different locations for the peak of the roof and choose the one that puts three panels on one side of the peak and five on the other (Figure 6.7a, b). We also try several different heights above the floor for the trusses and settle on one that seems comfortable in relation to the human figures on the drawing.

As the design develops, we explore different arrangements for the internal truss members (Figure 6.8a, b). Because we are going to make the truss of wood, we choose to orient the diagonals so they are in compression. This will avoid tensile connections, which are often difficult to make in wood. A level, flat truss would have vertical and diagonal interior members. Our truss is sloping, which gives us the option of making the "verticals" truly vertical or perpendicular to the top and bottom chords. We decide that the perpendicular orientation will work better because it shortens the diagonals, which reduces the likelihood of their buckling (Figure 6.8b, c). Additionally, it will make the truss easier to lay out and assemble.

We consider the need to include three hinges in each truss plane. After sketching several alternatives, we decide to hinge one end of the truss to the tip of a triangular frame whose base is anchored to the foundation at two points so as to resist wind loads (Figure 6.8c). A second hinge will occur at the other end, where the truss joins a tall column. The third hinge will be at the base of the column. In actuality, we will not design true hinges for these three

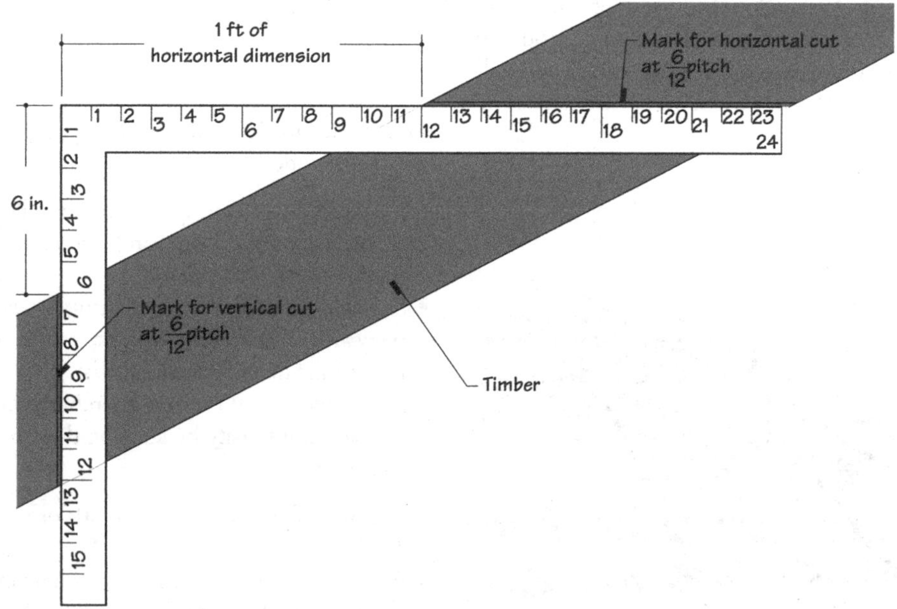

Figure 6.6 Using a framing square to lay out rafter cuts and lengths.

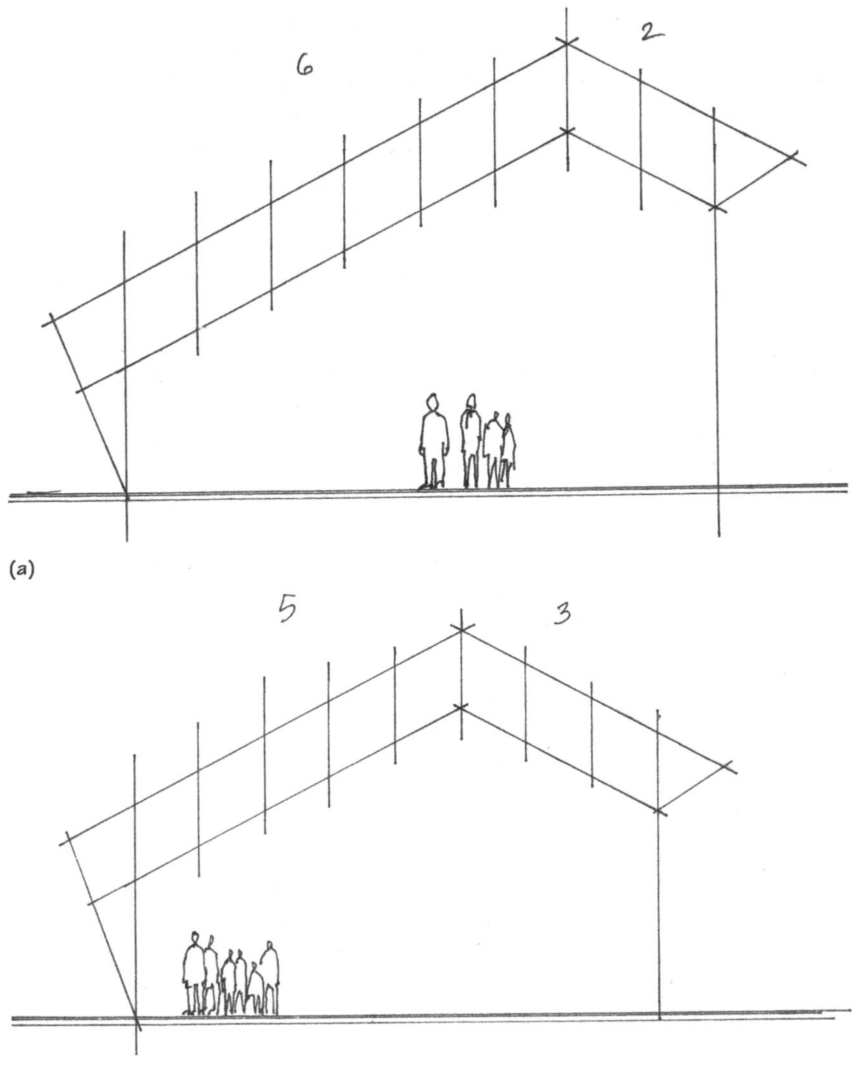

▲ **Figure 6.7** Sketches experimenting with different proportions and configurations: (a) Six panels seem to create too high a gable, so we choose to reduce the number to five (b).

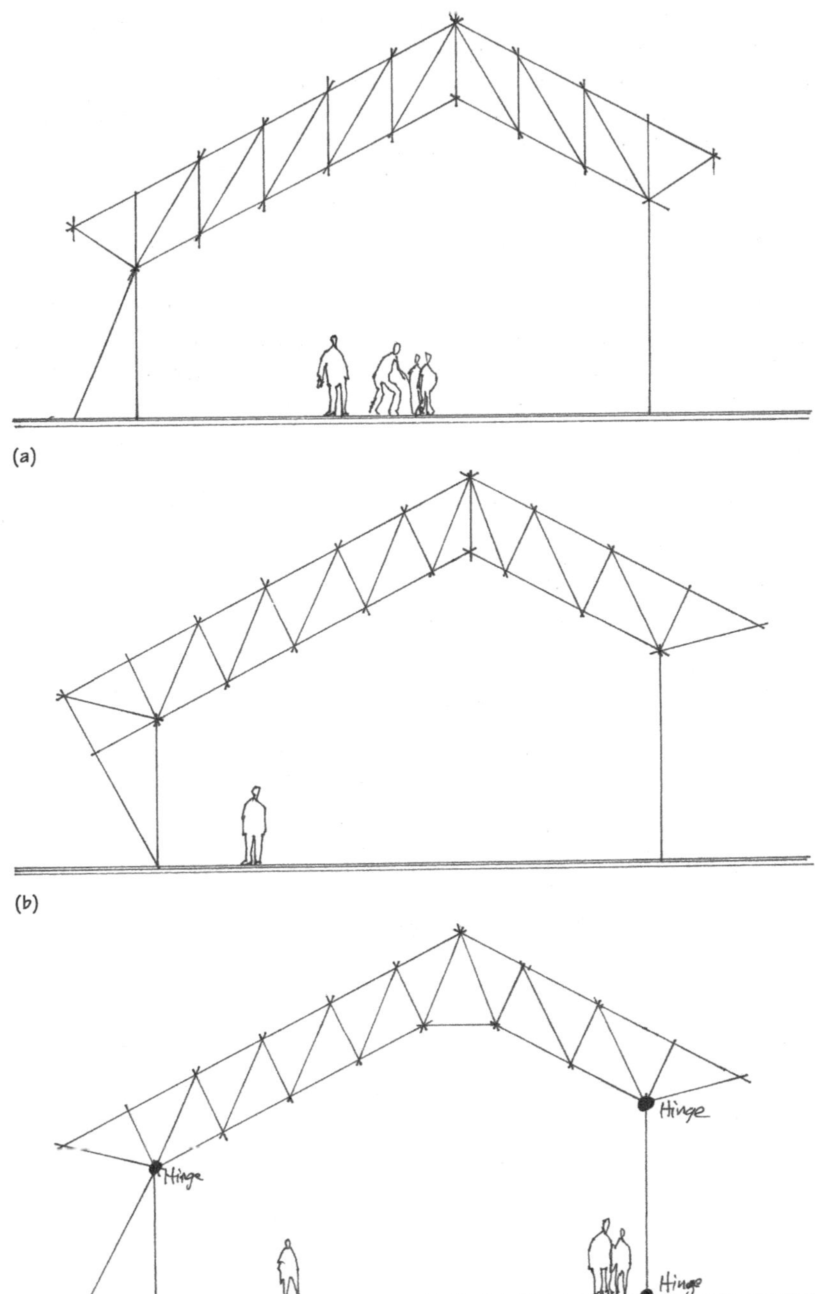

▶ **Figure 6.8** One option (a) is to use true verticals and diagonals that will be in compression. If we rotate the verticals to be perpendicular to the parallel chords (b) then the diagonals are shorter, but the area near the gable becomes congested. We refine this into a calmer configuration (c) so that the panel at the gable is a single triangle with a horizontal lower chord, and we determine the locations of the three hinges.

locations. The amount of movement that needs to occur to maintain equilibrium will be very small and will be easily accommodated by the normal amount of "play" in a bolted wood connection.

We decide to create generous, sheltering overhangs by extending the truss one panel beyond the support on each end. These overhangs will also have the beneficial effect of reducing the intensity of bending action in the main span of the truss.

It takes long, patient exploration and experimentation to arrive at a final layout for the truss. We reduce the forces in the members and joints where the truss changes direction at the ridge of the roof by putting in a level section of bottom chord, which has the effect of deepening the truss and simplifying its nodes at this critical location. Then we try several schemes for the layout of the panels with respect to the supports, finally arriving at a very simple, logical design (Figure 6.8c). We draw this form neatly to scale, still showing only the centerlines of the members. Now we are ready to determine the forces in the truss members, which will enable us to select member sizes and detail nodes. This requires that we become more familiar with trusses in general.

TRUSSES

A truss is made up of one or more triangles of short linear elements joined together so as to support loads across a span. Usually the elements all lie in a plane to make up what is called a *planar truss*, but sometimes they are arrayed in three dimensions to produce a *space truss*, also called a *space frame* (Figure 6.9). Whether in two or three dimensions, each member of a truss works axially, either in tension or compression. Because of the efficiency of *axially acting* members, trusses can span long distances and are economical of structural material. Trusses can span farther than beams and rigid frames, but not as far as cable structures and arches. The usual range of truss spans is from 20 ft to 300 ft, though spans longer than this are possible. Trusses are readily designed to carry heavy loads and unusual distributions of loads. A truss generally uses less material than a beam that would do the same job. However, the cost saving on material must be weighed against the additional labor required to make a truss.

An advantage of a truss over a cable or arch is its capability to sustain many different load distribution patterns without significantly changing its shape. For this reason, trusses are often used as deck structures in suspension bridges to distribute concentrated loads to the cables and to restrain the cables against changing shape as loading patterns shift. Arches are often trussed to give them increased efficiency and greater resistance to buckling and change of shape (Figure 6.10).

Trusses are often custom-designed, as in our camp building example, so as to give them shapes or structural properties appropriate for particular bridges or buildings. There are also many types of standardized trusses available "off the shelf" for use in floors and roofs, such as *open-web steel joists* (also called *bar joists*) and steel *joist girders* for use in industrial, commercial, and institutional buildings, and wooden *roof trusses* and *floor trusses* for residential-scale buildings (Figures 6.11–6.14). Standardized trusses are almost always designed for relatively light loadings that are uniformly distributed over the span.

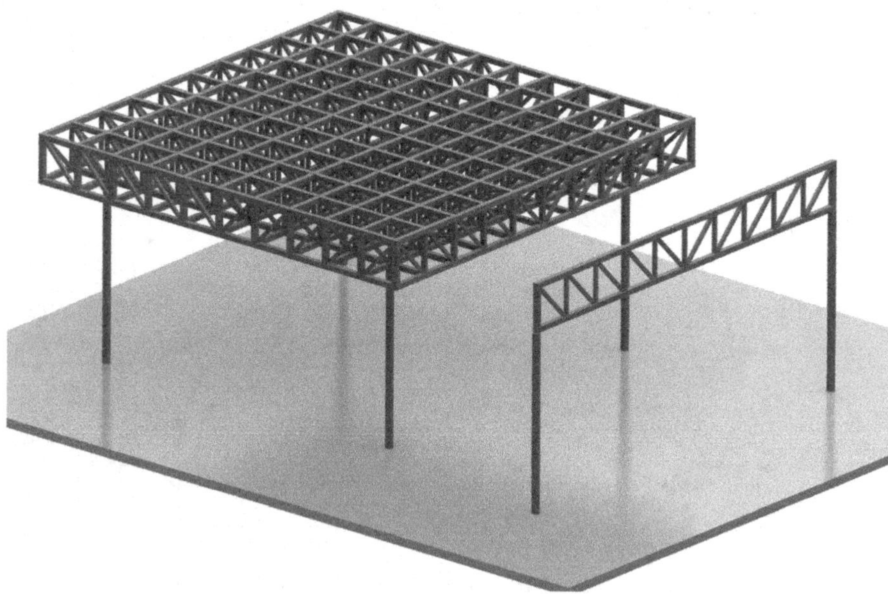

Figure 6.9 A three-dimensional space truss and a two-dimensional planar truss of similar configuration.

Trusses for Bridges

There are several ways to use trusses in bridges (Figure 6.15). A *through truss* bridge is one in which the vehicles or pedestrians pass between two deep trusses that are braced against one another over the top of the open passage. In a *pony truss* bridge, the passage lies between two shallow trusses that are not joined overhead. The trusses in a *deck truss* bridge are placed entirely below the deck.

◀**Figure 6.10** The arch of the Bayonne Bridge is restrained from changing shape by its steel trussing, which allows the suspended deck to be very thin. The span is 1,675 ft (520 m). The bridge connects Bayonne, New Jersey, with Staten Island, New York. Engineers: Ammann and Dana.

Photo courtesy of the Port Authority of New York and New Jersey.

▲**Figure 6.12** An iron worker attaches a joist girder to a column.

◀**Figure 6.11** Open web steel joists are supported by heavier joist girders, which conduct the loads to columns.
Figures 6.11 and 6.12 courtesy of Vulcraft Division of Nucor.

◀**Figure 6.13** These floor trusses (shown here being set up for a demonstration house in a parking lot) are made of sawn lumber members joined by toothed-plate connectors. The oriented strand board (OSB) web at each end of the truss allows workers to adjust the length of the truss with a saw, if necessary. Trusses are deeper than sawn joists or I-joists, but can span farther between supports and offer large passages for ductwork and pipes.

Photo courtesy of Wood Truss Council of America.

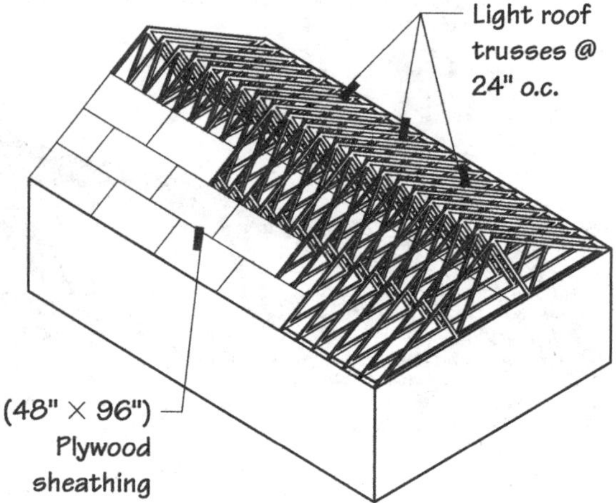

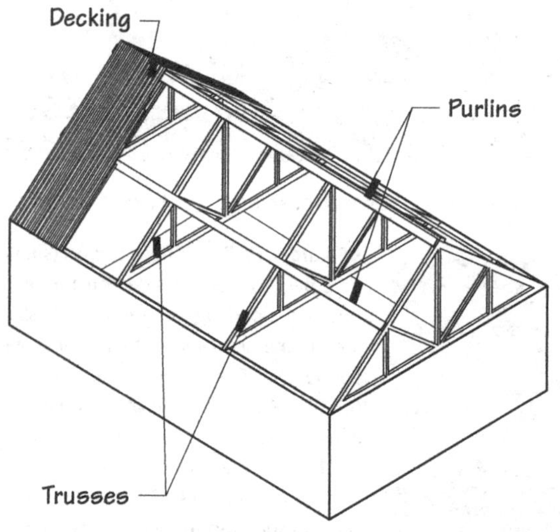

Figure 6.14 Two methods of using roof trusses: (a) closely spaced light wood trusses support plywood sheathing directly; (b) widely spaced heavy timber trusses carry decking by way of purlins.

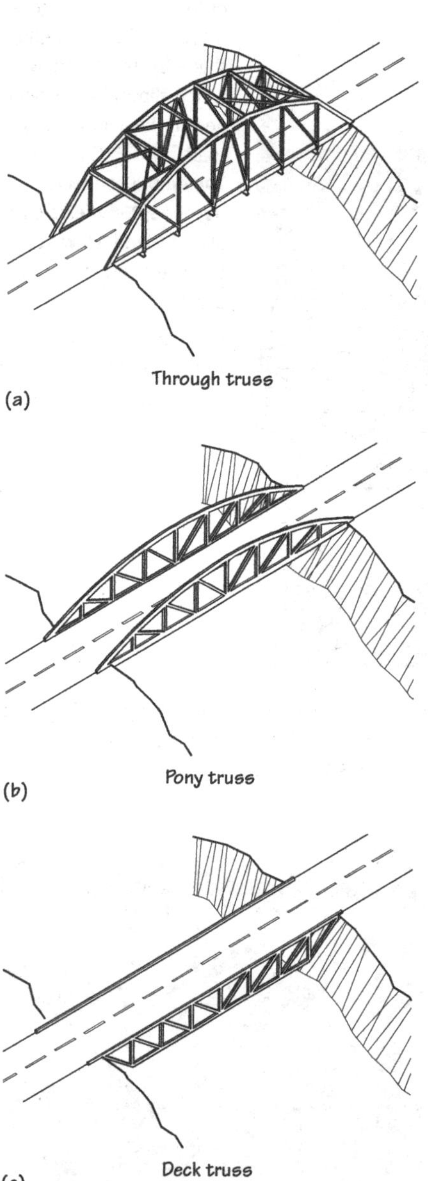

Figure 6.15 Three common ways to use trusses to support bridges: (a) through truss bridge, (b) pony truss bridge, (c) deck truss bridge.

Trusses in Buildings

Large trusses have several different kinds of uses in buildings (Figure 6.16). Often they are used directly to support floor or roof decks. Sometimes they are used within a building that is framed with ordinary beams and columns for special purposes such as supporting a roof over an auditorium or swimming pool, or cantilevering a balcony in a concert hall. *Transfer trusses* are used in situations where the vertical alignments of columns in a building must change. This can happen if a tall building has floors of apartments, which generally have short spans, over floors with the longer spans required by open office space. Another use for transfer trusses is to make the transition between column spacings in a parking garage and those in a building directly above. Transfer trusses are weighty and expensive because they carry such heavy loads. They also tend to be deep and to occupy space within a building that could otherwise be used for productive purposes. They should be avoided unless there is no reasonable alternative.

DESIGNING FRAMING SCHEMES THAT USE TRUSSES

Selecting a Truss Configuration

A variety of truss forms have been invented over the last two centuries. For most situations it is possible to find an appropriate truss design from among these standardized configurations. It is equally possible to create a new form when needed, as we are doing. Figure 6.17 illustrates a range of common truss configurations. Each has its particular advantages and disadvantages. The truss with the tensile diagonals is called a flat *Pratt truss*, after its inventors Thomas and Caleb Pratt, who created it in the 1840s. The Pratt design is an excellent choice for a steel truss, whose members tend to be very slender, because its long diagonal members are in tension and therefore are not subject to buckling. The vertical members are less likely to buckle because they are shorter than the diagonals and experience

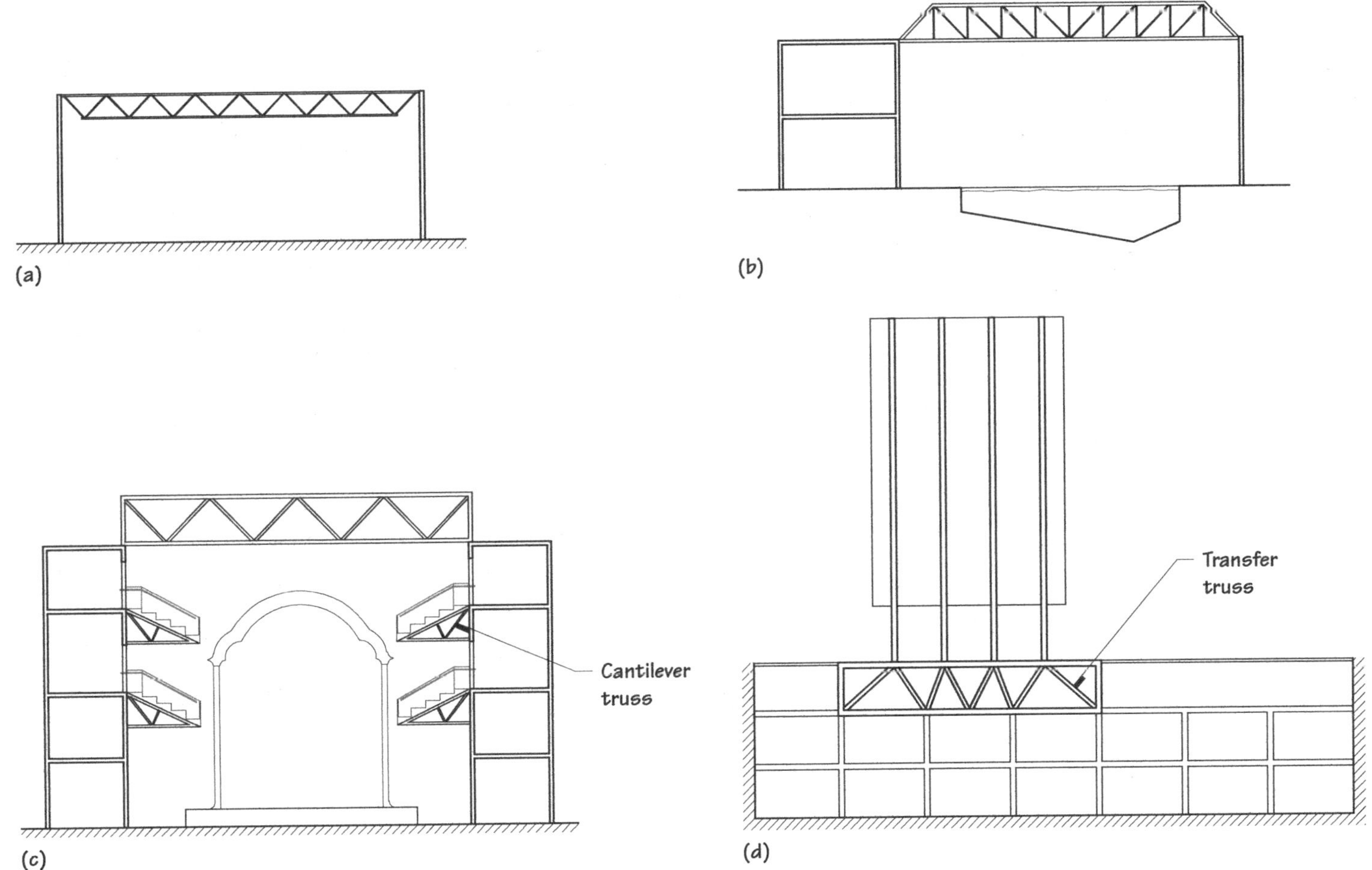

Figure 6.16 Sample uses of trusses in typical applications: (a) spanning over a warehousing area; (b) spanning over swimming and athletic areas; (c) an auditorium employs major Warren trusses for the roof span and cantilever trusses for the balconies; (d) a large building over a parking garage uses transfer trusses to mediate between the column spacing for the parking and that for the structure in the building above.

lower forces. The truss design with the compressive diagonals, called a flat *Howe truss*, is often preferred for heavy timber trusses. Whereas steel tensile members may be joined strongly with bolts or welds, bolted tensile joints in timber are relatively weak. The Howe configuration (also dating from the 1840s and named after farmer and inventor William Howe) allows the diagonal members to transfer their forces to the vertical and horizontal members by bearing directly against them; and timber members tend to be thick enough that buckling is less likely to be a problem than in steel members. A *Warren truss* and its triangular equivalent, the *simple Fink truss*, have large apertures that are ideal for the passage of heating and cooling ductwork. The Warren configuration also offers a pleasing appearance

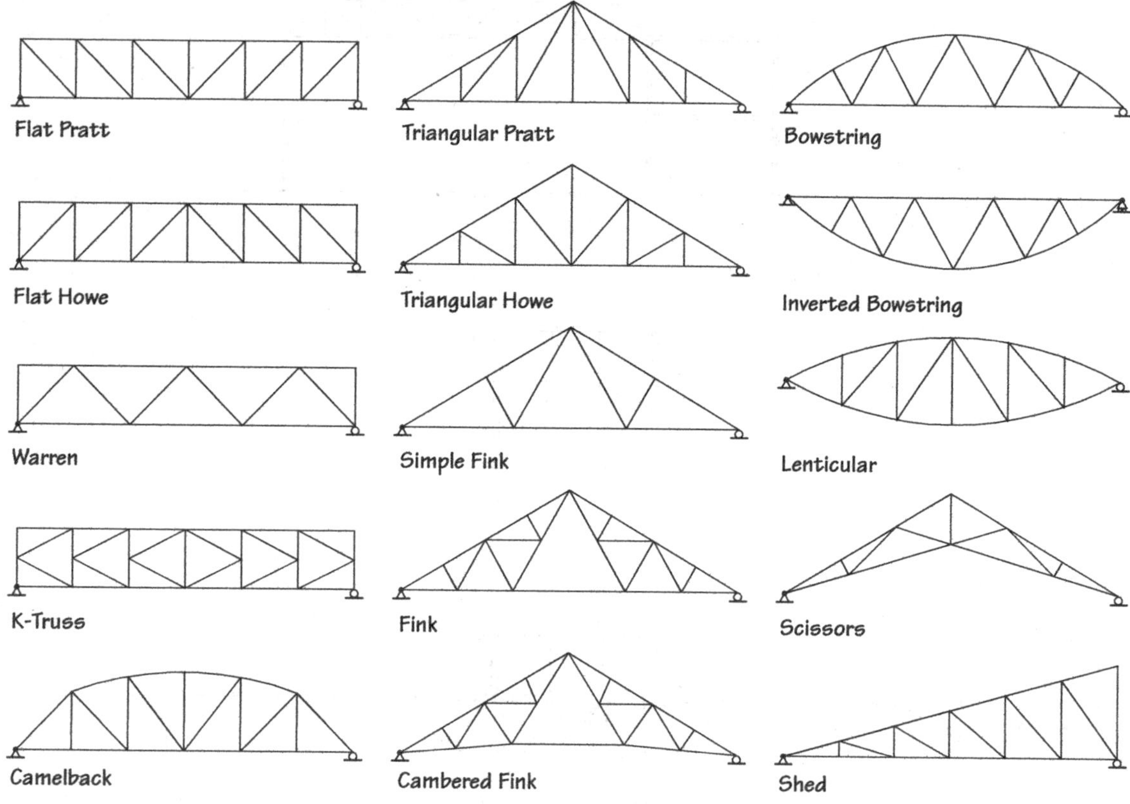

Figure 6.17 Common truss configurations.

and simplicity of fabrication that stems from the fact that its web members are all the same size and shape and are joined in the same way. The *Fink truss* allows roof purlins to bear at close intervals along the top chords. The *cambered Fink* design experiences somewhat higher internal forces than the regular Fink truss, in exchange for which it offers a higher interior space. This may be useful for a roof of a building that houses tall machinery, or it may be desirable because it imparts a more gracious shape to the interior space of a building.

The *scissors truss* is much beloved by architects for its agreeable spatial qualities, but as we learned in Chapter 4, the acute angles between the chords at the supports create high chord forces, which can lead to a heavy appearance and difficulty in designing the nodes. The *bowstring, inverted bowstring, lenticular*, and *camelback trusses* are all shapes that result in highly efficient structural performance. Under ideal loading conditions, the diagonal members in these four designs carry little or no force, and the top and bottom chords experience forces that are distributed much like those in a cable or arch throughout their length. We will learn how to derive the shapes of these efficient trusses in Chapter 10. The *K-truss* is another highly efficient form that we will discuss further in comparison to beam behavior in Chapter 17.

The exterior shapes of trusses are adapted to particular uses. The flat configurations are used for floors, flat roofs, and deck truss bridges. The camelback shape is designed especially for through-truss bridges, and can also be useful for high roofs. The bowstring design is suited for roofs with a curving surface that follows the top chord of the truss. The *triangular, shed*, and *scissors* trusses are intended for use in sloping roof structures.

We can design trusses for specific situations that are highly unusual in form (Figure 6.18), provided that we pay attention to making the truss entirely of triangles, furnishing sufficient depth in relation to span, offering purlin support at the required intervals, and avoiding members that converge upon one another at too small an angle, which creates very large forces in members and connections.

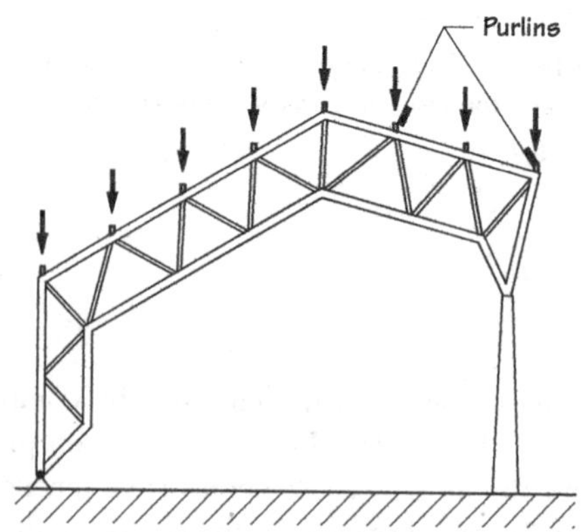

Figure 6.18 Trusses can be designed in unusual shapes.

TRUSSES IN VARIOUS MATERIALS

Often the choice of material for a truss is virtually automatic in the context of a particular design problem. A wooden building generally suggests wooden trusses, and a steel building, steel. In many cases, however, the choice will be made largely on the basis of building code requirements that pertain to fire safety. Light trusses made of wood, such as those used for roofs of houses, are made of nominal 2-in. wood members, which catch fire easily because they are so thin. They are permitted only in small buildings and may not be used in downtown areas, in tall buildings, or in buildings with large floor areas. Heavy timber trusses, whose members meet or exceed code-specified minimum thickness and depth dimensions, may be used in somewhat larger and taller buildings, because larger timbers are slow to ignite, burn slowly, and retain their strength for a considerable time during a fire.

Steel trusses do not burn. However, steel loses much of its strength at relatively low temperatures that are often reached in building fires. Accordingly, buildings that use steel trusses are restricted with regard to building use, height and floor area of the building, and the height of roof trusses above the top floor of the building. If steel trusses are covered with appropriate thicknesses of fire-resistant insulating material called *fireproofing*, they may be used in virtually any situation.

Aluminum is sometimes used in trusses in situations where the weight of the truss must be minimized or where corrosion is likely to be a problem. Aluminum self-protects against corrosion and weighs only a third as much as steel. Its disadvantages are that it is not nearly as strong or stiff as steel and it is much more costly.

Joining Wood Truss Members

Light, repetitive roof trusses and floor trusses are joined with *toothed plate* connectors that are pressed into the wood from both sides at each connection (Figure 6.19). Toothed plates make strong connections because their many closely spaced prongs penetrate the members in a dense array that interlocks with the fibrous microstructure of the wood.

Heavier wood trusses (also called *timber trusses* or *heavy timber trusses* in the United States) may be assembled in a variety of ways using nails, screws, bolts, or proprietary connectors. One option involves making the truss of multiple layers of relatively thin lumber with nails or bolts passing through the overlapping members to make the connections (Figure 6.20). This requires careful planning of how the layers relate to one another. There are stringent rules for bolt spacings in wood connections that sometimes lead to problems when member forces are high and a joint is not large enough physically to contain enough bolts to transfer the forces safely. Rules for nail spacing are much more relaxed, but load transfer capacity per nail is relatively low, and nailed connections are usually suitable only for small trusses with relatively lightly loaded members.

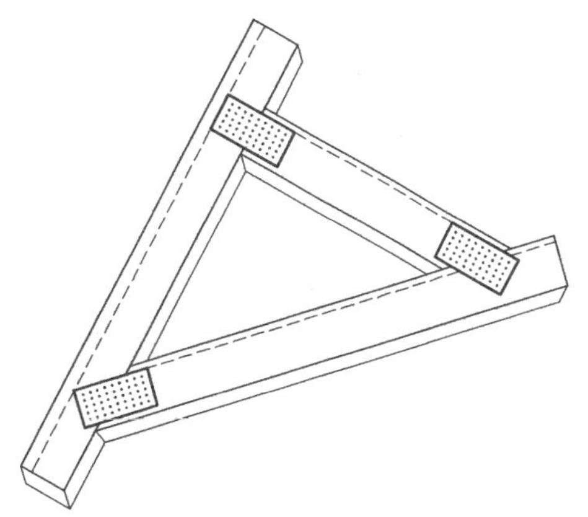

Figure 6.19 Steel-toothed plate connectors are embedded into both sides of wooden truss members by hydraulic presses.

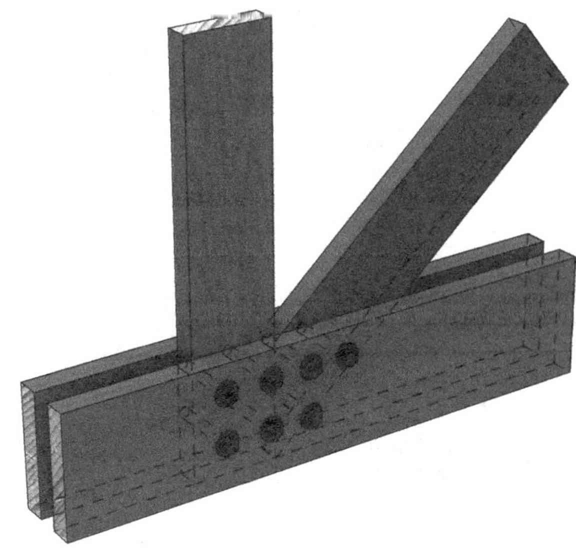

Figure 6.20 A three-layer truss composed of nominal 2-in. timber members connected by bolts.

Heavy timber trusses for buildings are most often assembled in a single layer, nominally 4 to 8 in. thick (Figure 6.21). To connect the components, steel *side plates* may be applied to both sides, and bolts passed through drilled holes in the plates and timbers. Alternatively, steel plates may be placed in slots at the ends of the timbers, so that only the ends of the bolts show on the faces of the truss (Figure 6.22). Another approach is to place steel plates in slots and connect them to the wood with proprietary steel *dowel* fasteners that drill their own paths through the timber and steel and remain in place (Figure 6.23). These dowels are smaller in diameter than bolts but larger than nails. The drill point on each dowel is hardened so that it can drill through at least a half inch total thickness of steel.

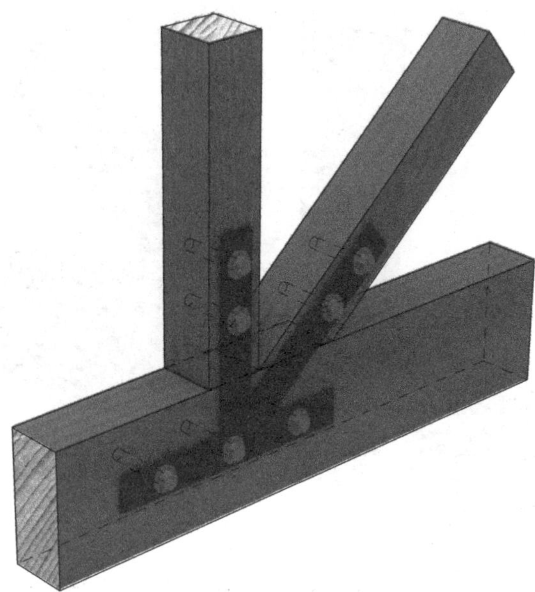

Figure 6.21 A single-layer heavy timber truss with side plates and bolts.

Figure 6.22 A bolted timber truss with splice plates recessed in slots cut in the members.

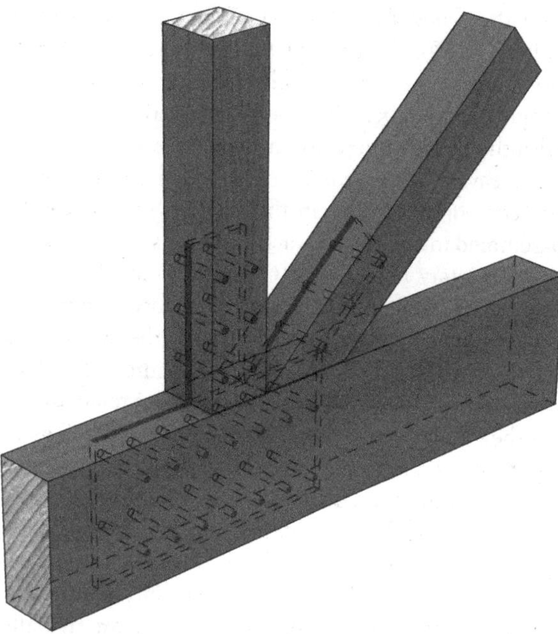

▲ **Figure 6.23** A truss with doweled connections. Special hardened steel dowels drill their own ways through the wood and steel and are left in place to create the connection.

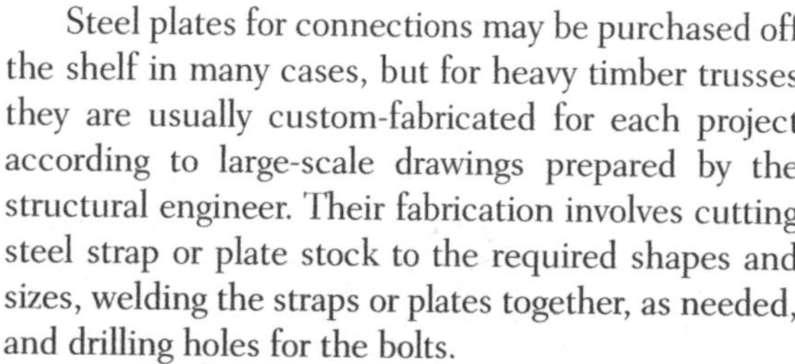

Steel plates for connections may be purchased off the shelf in many cases, but for heavy timber trusses they are usually custom-fabricated for each project according to large-scale drawings prepared by the structural engineer. Their fabrication involves cutting steel strap or plate stock to the required shapes and sizes, welding the straps or plates together, as needed, and drilling holes for the bolts.

Traditional heavy timber joinery, which transfers forces between members by direct bearing of one member upon another, is also possible (Figure 6.24a). Difficult tensile connections may be avoided by using steel rods for tensile members (Figure 6.24b).

▶ **Figure 6.24** A wood-to-wood compressive joint in a heavy timber truss; lag screws serve only to hold the member in alignment (a); steel rods can replace wood for tensile members.

Types of Steel Truss Detailing

There are many ways to construct trusses of steel members. A traditional method utilizes back-to-back steel angles for truss members. At the nodes, steel *gusset plates* are sandwiched between the angles; either bolts or welding may be used to make the connections (Figure A). For larger trusses, steel channels may be used instead of angles.

For large, high-capacity steel trusses, wide-flange shapes of the same depth are assembled with steel side plates, either welded or bolted (Figure B). Wide flanges may also be mitered and joined by welding (Figure C).

Steel trusses that will be exposed to view are often made of steel tubing, either round, rectangular, or square (Figure D). The tubes may be joined directly by welding; automated cutting machinery prepares the ends of the pieces so that they mate perfectly, after which the joints are welded and the welds are ground smooth. Another type of connection utilizes steel gusset plates welded into slots in the tubes (Figure E).

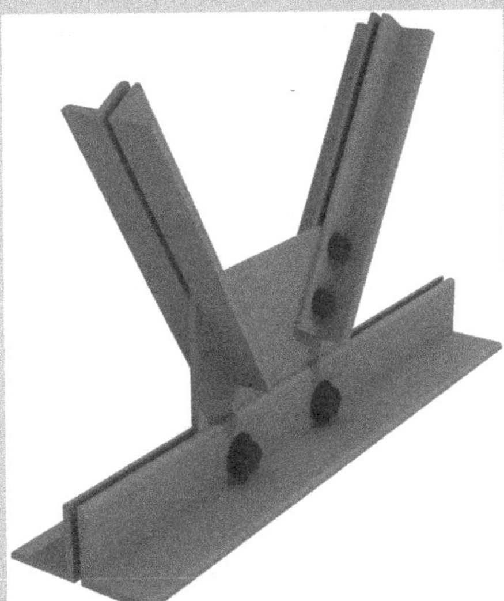

Figure A Sandwiched steel angle connection with gusset plate.

Figure B Steel connection with side plates.

Figure C Welded steel connection.

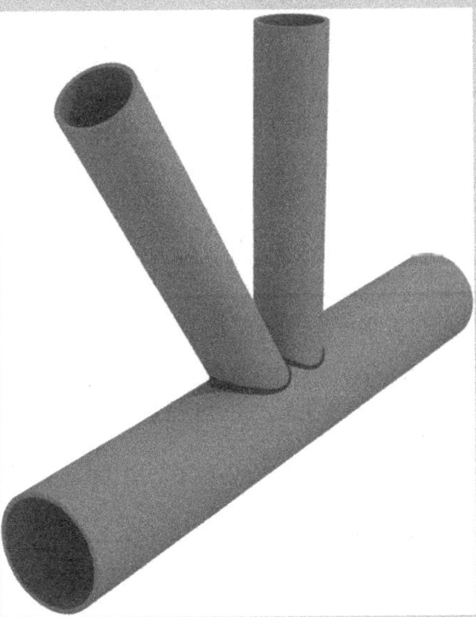

Figure D Welded steel tube connection.

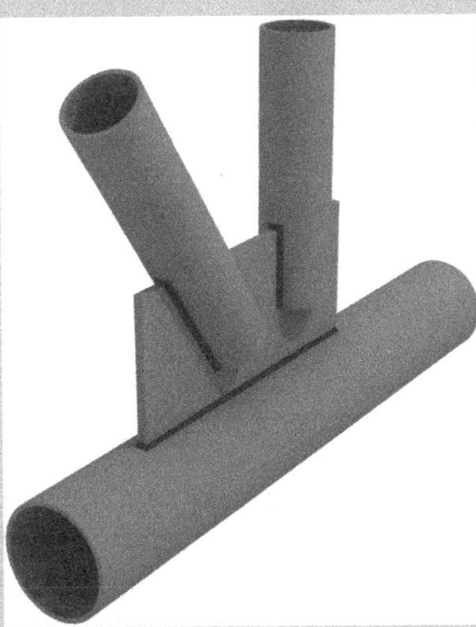

Figure E Steel tube connection with gusset plate.

FINDING FORCES IN A TRUSS

The forces in the members of a truss may be found either numerically or graphically. Numerical methods are summarized in the sidebar titled "Numerical Finding of Forces in Truss Members: The Method of Joints." For excellent lessons in graphical analysis of trusses, go to the following lessons on the supplemental site:

- Lesson 1 of "Form and Forces: Graphical Techniques"
- Demonstrations 2, 4, and 6 of "Active Statics"

In this book, we will use graphical methods exclusively, because they have the following advantages:

- Graphical analysis is easier and faster, especially for trusses with irregular forms.
- Graphical analysis is more transparent than numerical analysis at revealing patterns of forces in the truss at a glance.
- Graphical analysis makes it easier to evaluate the form of a truss, to see how it might be improved.
- Through graphical means, we are able to find efficient shapes for trusses, as we will explore further in Chapter 10.
- Starting in Chapter 14, graphical methods will enable us to create and analyze trusses that mimic the flow patterns of forces through solid structural components, and thus to discover what is happening inside beams, columns, load-bearing walls, and plates.
- As with our previous examples, if drawn in CAD, graphical analysis gives theoretically perfect accuracy. If drawn by hand at reasonable scale, numerical values for member forces are usually within 1 percent of theoretical values. This is considerably more precise than our live load estimates or actual variations in member forces caused by joint restraint and material anomalies.

"Concept comes before calculations."

—Anthony Hunt

FINDING FORCES IN A SIX-PANEL FLAT TRUSS

We will begin our examination of multipanel trusses by finding the forces in the members of a *simply supported* six-panel *flat Pratt truss* with 45° diagonals that slope downward toward the center of the truss. A vertical load of 1,600 lb is applied to each panel point along the top chord. The span is 48 ft.

Our analysis will follow the graphical procedure that we developed in Chapter 4. The lesson entitled "Multipanel Truss" on the supplemental site will help you to learn this method. We begin the project on Worksheet 6A by drawing an accurate form diagram of the truss at the upper left corner of the sheet (Figure 6.25). This is constructed to a convenient scale of length to length, 1/8 in. to the foot in this example, so as to represent accurately the shape of the truss and the slopes of its members. We draw vectors to represent the loads on the truss.

Next we find the two reactions on the truss and add their vectors to the form diagram. Because the loading is symmetrical in this case, we simply assign half the total load to each reaction. The form diagram is now a complete free-body diagram of the truss. Working clockwise and from left to right, we apply Bow's notation to the diagram, assigning uppercase letters to the spaces between external forces and numbers to internal spaces. By convention, the letter "I" has been omitted in this example to avoid confusion with the numeral "1."

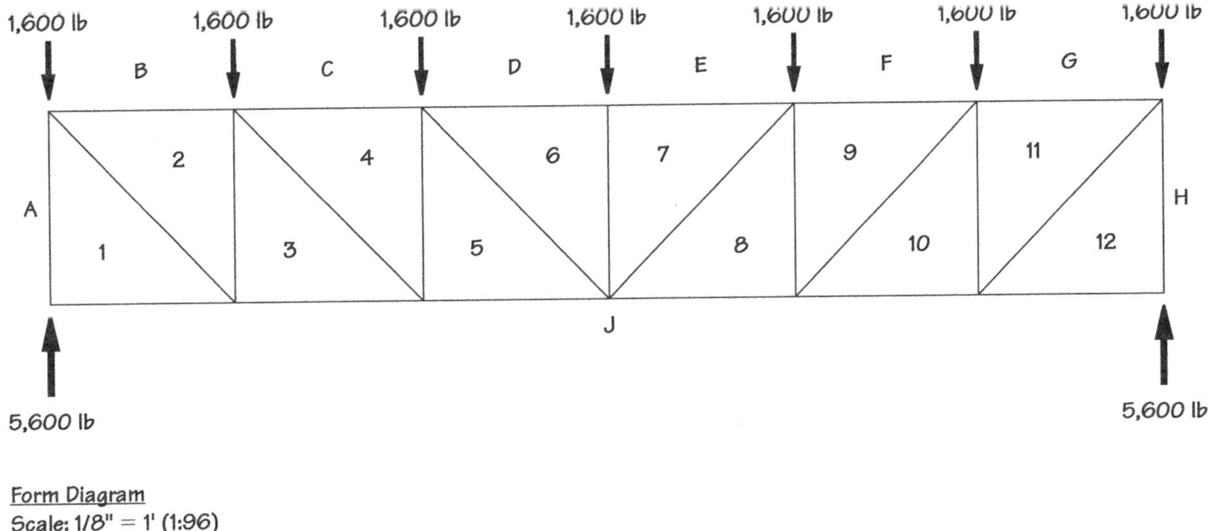

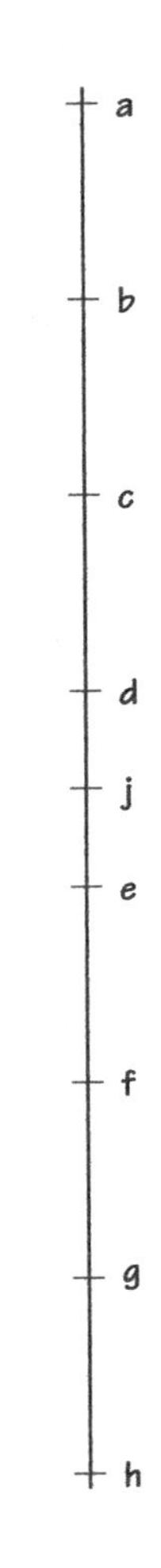

Figure 6.25 Worksheet 6A, showing a six-panel flat truss.

To the right of the form diagram, we begin the construction of a force polygon by plotting a load line to a convenient scale of length to force; here, 1 in. equals 2,500 lb (Figure 6.26). Using Bow's notation and working clockwise around the truss from the upper left, we tick off carefully measured increments of vertical length on the load line to represent each of the applied loads. This brings us to *h* at the bottom. The right-hand reaction is *HJ*, an upward-acting force that we plot on the load line as a segment that begins at *h* and extends upward to *j* at a location that is 5,600 lb above. Finally, we plot the left-hand reaction as *JA*, another upward force that closes the load line back to its point of origin. This completes our clockwise tour of the external forces. If *ja* does not scale to 5,600 lb, we have made an error somewhere in laying out the load line and must find and correct this error before proceeding. (A good way to avoid cumulative errors of measurement in the load line is to measure each of the loads from the end of the line rather than from the previous tick mark: Measure and mark *ab* as 1,600 lb, then *ac* as 3,200 lb, *ad* as 4,800 lb, and so on).

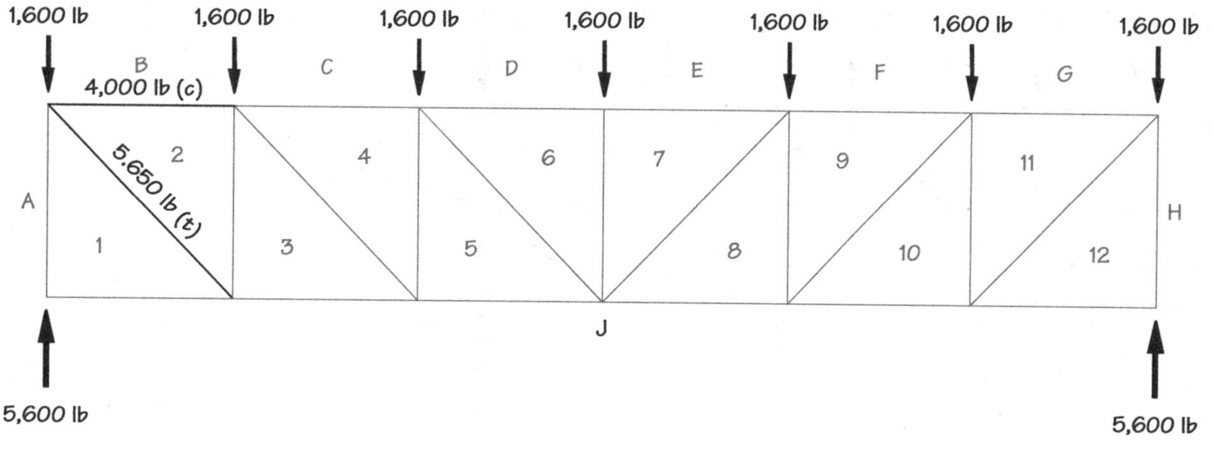

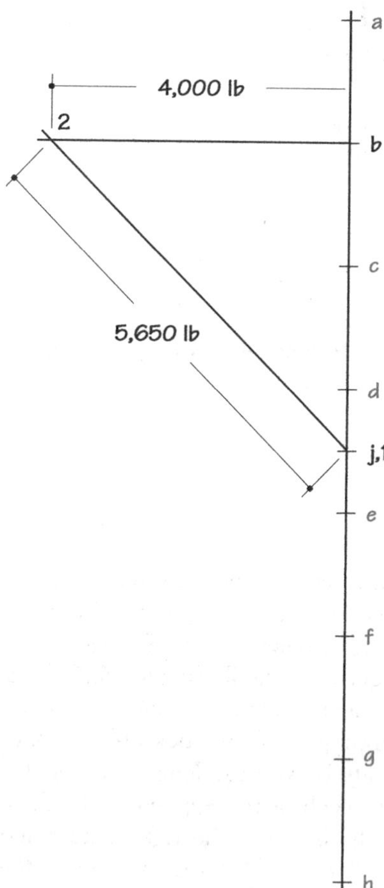

Figure 6.26

Examining the left end of the truss, we find that the only joint with fewer than three unknown forces is *A1J*, so this is where we begin our analysis of the members of the truss (Figure 6.26). On the force polygon, the forces in the two members that meet at *A1J* are represented by a vertical line segment, *a1*, that intersects a horizontal line segment, *j1*, at point *1*. Segment *a1* must pass vertically through *a*, which means that it lies along the load line, while *j1* must pass horizontally through *j*. These conditions can be satisfied only if point *1* lies precisely at *j*. Therefore, *j1* is a point rather than a line. It has zero length, meaning that *J1* is a zero-force member and could be eliminated from the truss. However, there is often a reason for having such a member, such as providing lateral stability to the building or furnishing support for a ceiling below.

Now that we have determined the length of *a1*, we are ready to solve for the forces at the upper left-hand joint, *AB2–1*. The two remaining unknown forces at this joint are in members *B2* and *2–1*. We construct lines *b2* and *2–1* parallel to these members on the force polygon; *b2* is a horizontal line through *b* on the load line, and *2–1* is a diagonal line through *1*. The point of intersection of these lines is the location of point 2. We can measure the lengths of the forces in *B2* and *2–1* to find the amount of force in these two members.

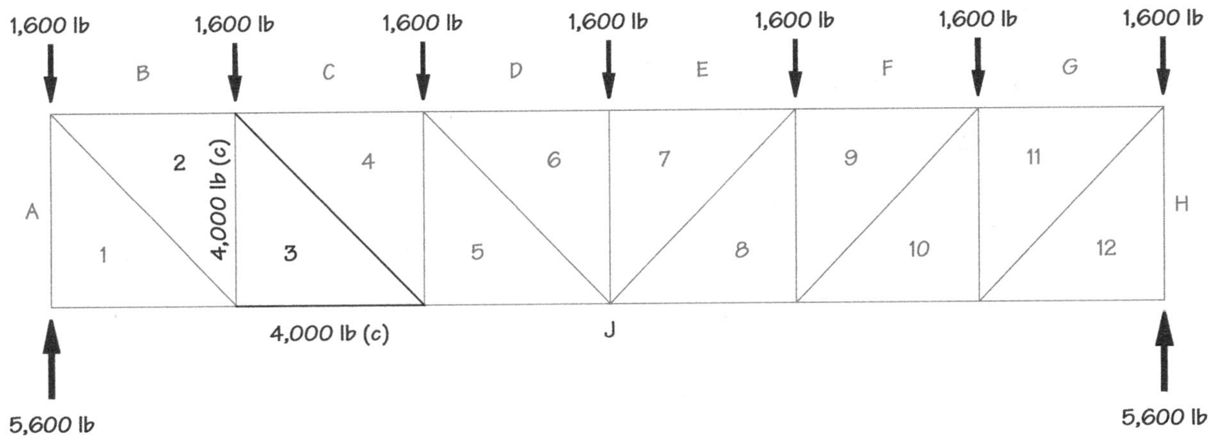

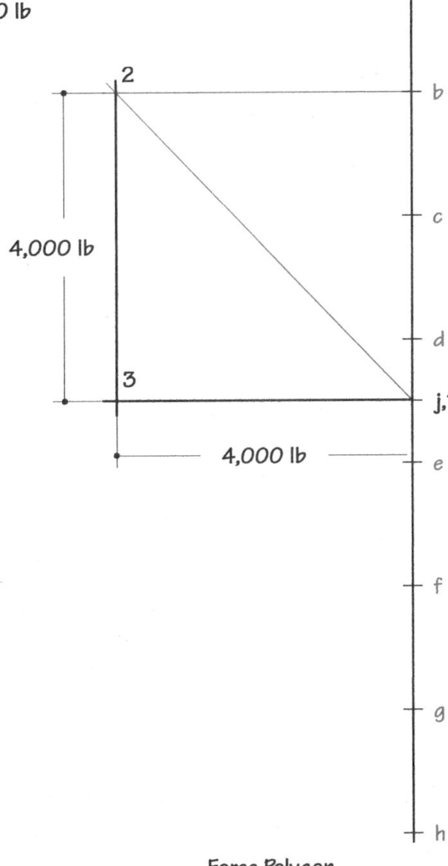

Figure 6.27

In Figure 6.27, we continue to find the forces in the truss by moving to the next joint that has only two unknown forces, which is *1–2–3J*. The unknown forces are in members 2–3 and *3J*; we plot lines 2–3 and *3j* on the force polygon parallel to these members to find point 3.

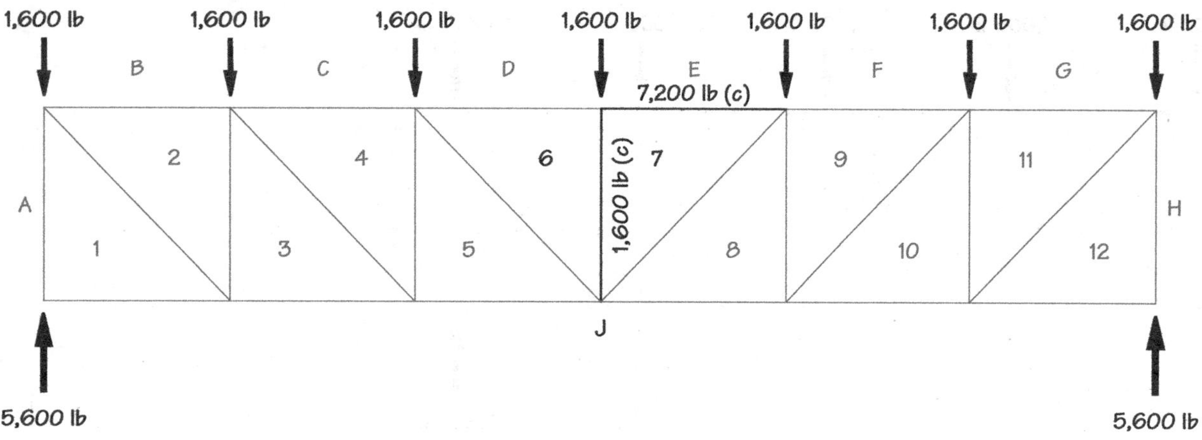

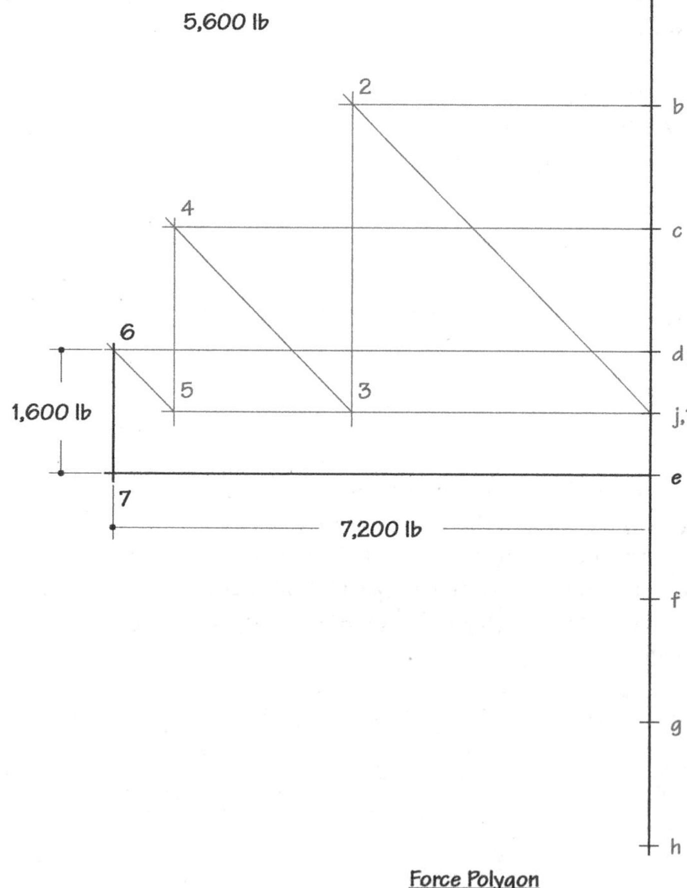

Figure 6.28

We repeat this process, moving joint by joint across the truss. We move each time to an adjacent joint that has only two unknown forces. **The second number in the name of the web member is always the same as the number in the name of the chord member that is considered at the same time. If the numbers were applied systematically left to right on the form diagram, the common number in the two member names at each step is always one higher than the number that was just added to the force polygon.** In Figure 6.28, the last number added to the force polygon was 6. Thus we know that the next pair of members that we must consider are 6–7 and a chord member whose name ends in 7, which can only be *E*7. When we plot the lines on the force polygon that represent these two forces, **their point of intersection is labeled with their common number.** In this way, Bow's notation guides us through the analysis of a truss in the proper order.

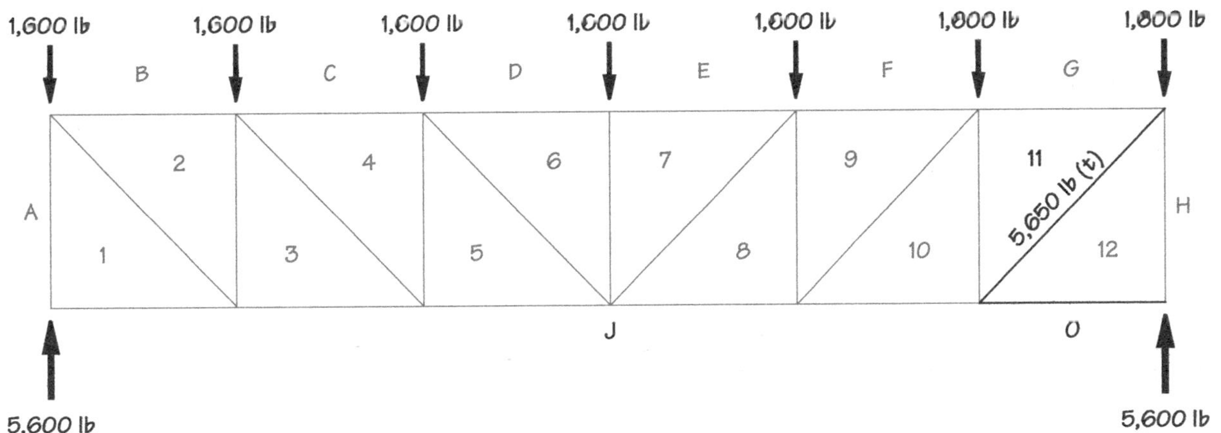

Figure 6.29

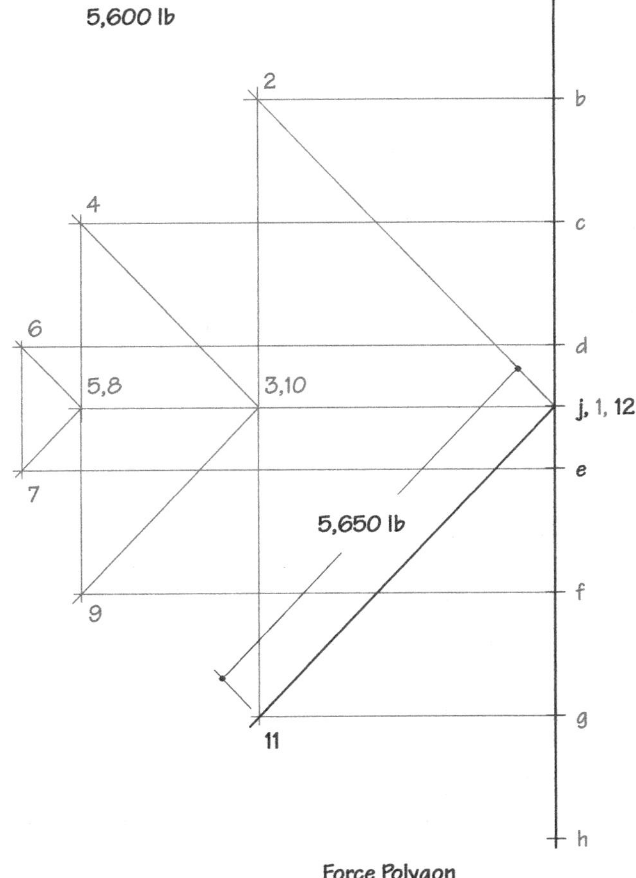

In Figure 6.29, we complete the construction of the force polygon. Points 5 and 8 turn out to share the same location, as do 3 and *10*, and *j*, *1*, and *12*. The last two forces that we plot are *j12*, which is zero, and *h12*. The diagram closes at *j*, indicating that our construction is probably correct.

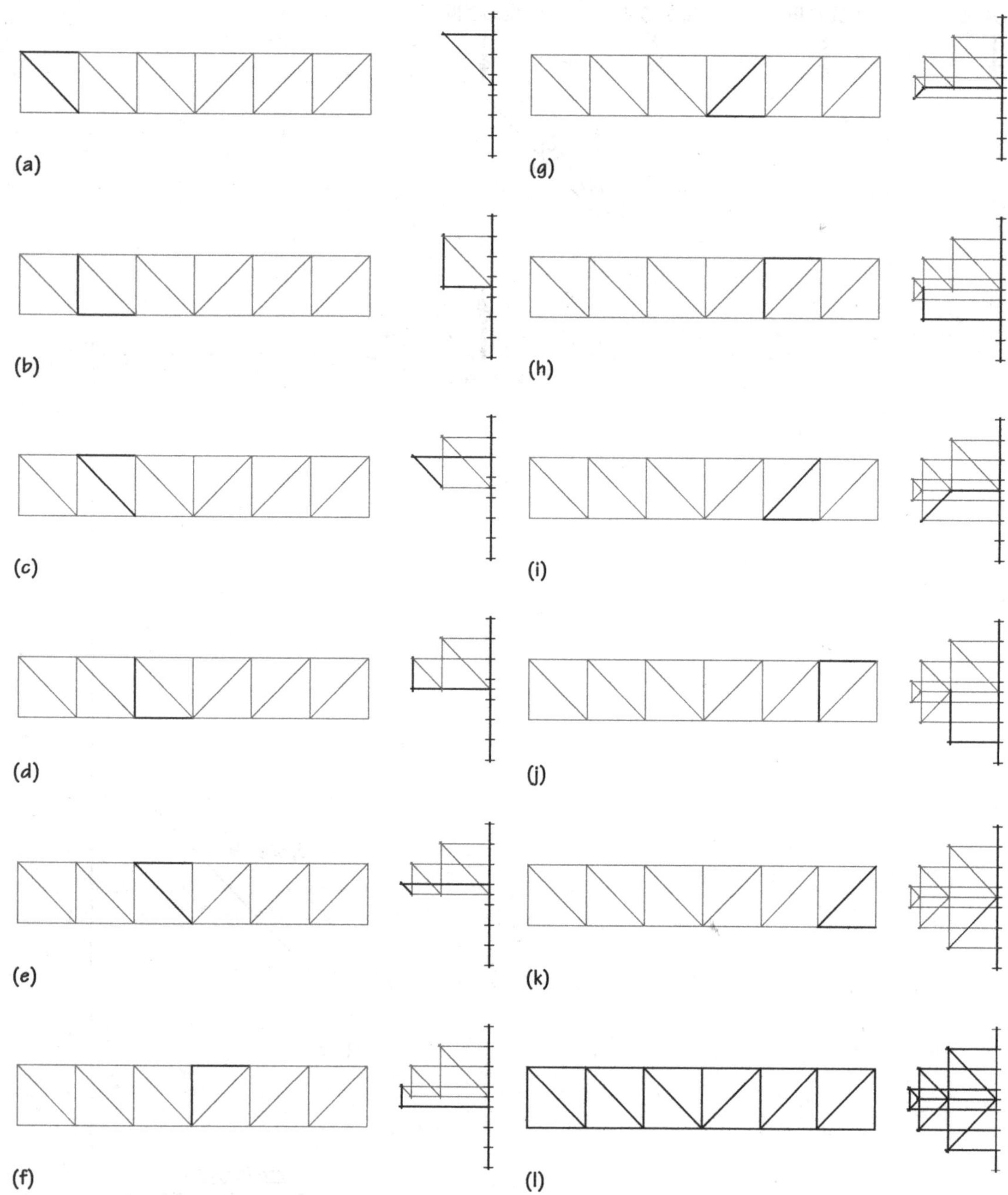

Figure 6.30 A summary of the steps in drawing the force polygon for a six-panel flat truss.

Figure 6.30 shows sequentially every step in the truss analysis that we have just completed.

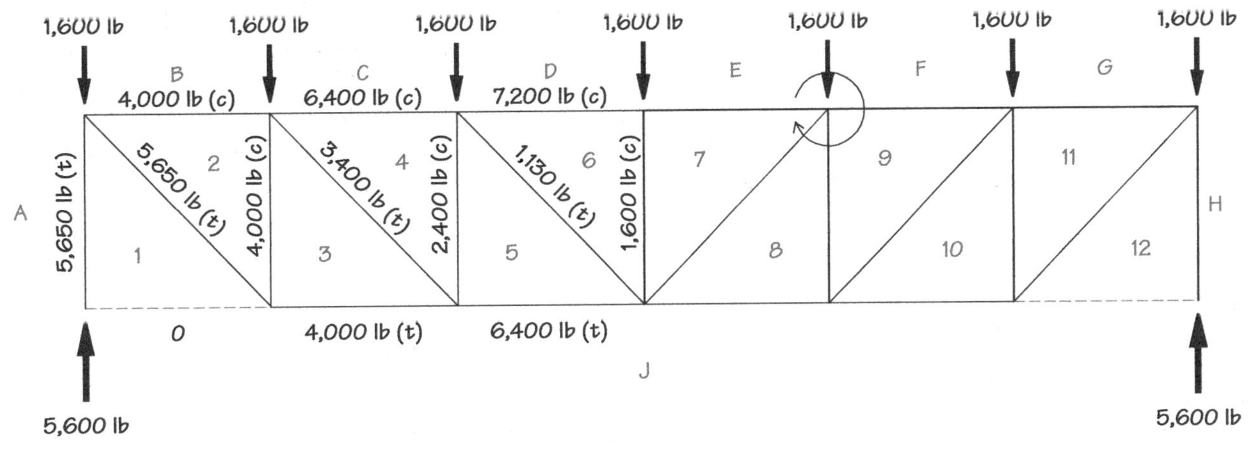

Figure 6.31 A summary of member forces and a determination of character of forces around node EF-987.

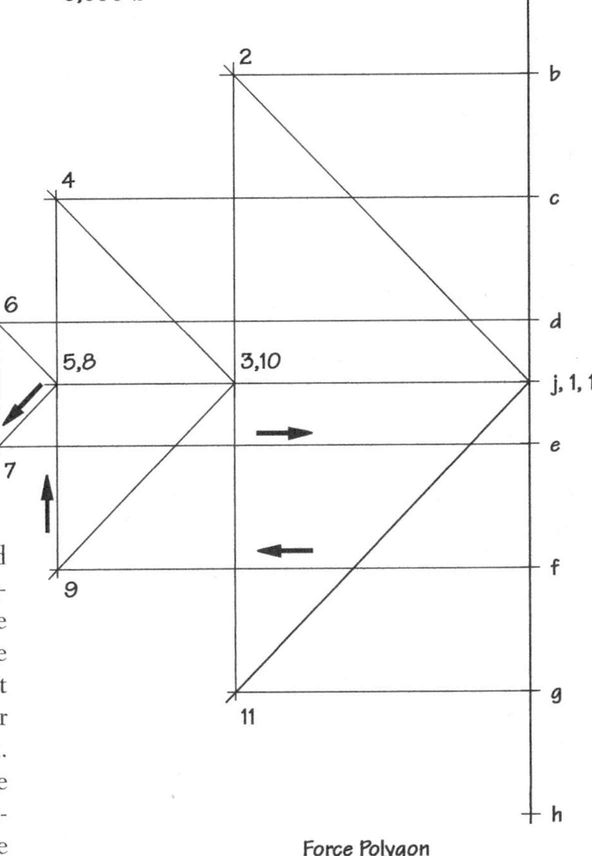

The last steps in the analysis are to measure the line segments in the force polygon to find their magnitudes, and to utilize Bow's notation as was done in Chapter 4 to determine their characters. Figure 6.31 shows the resulting information applied to half the truss. The values for the other half are mirror images of these values.

To review the method of finding the character of the forces in the members, let us examine the joint just to the right of center on the top chord of the truss, which is named *EF*9–8–7 in clockwise order (Figure 6.31). It helps to place the index finger of the left hand on this joint on the form diagram and to keep it there while proceeding. The top chord segment to the right of the joint, named in clockwise order, is *F*9. On the force polygon, a motion of the right index finger from *f* to 9 is leftward, meaning that member *F*9 pushes to the left on the joint where our left index finger lies and is, therefore, in compression. Similarly, going from 9 to 8 on the force polygon, we move upward, toward the left index finger, indicating a compressive force. Moving from 8 to 7 on the force polygon, we are pulling down to the left; 8–7 is in tension.

UNDERSTANDING THE BEHAVIOR OF THE SIX-PANEL TRUSS

Examination of the magnitudes of the forces in this truss shows that the forces in the top and bottom chords are least in the end panels of the truss and rise panel by panel to maximum values at the center. The forces in the web members vary in just the opposite manner: They are least in the center panels and reach their maxima in the end panels. This pattern is typical of uniformly loaded, simply supported trusses. In Chapters 16 and 17, when we study beam behavior, we will find that the forces inside solid beams follow a very similar pattern.

Figure 6.32 shows a way of visualizing the paths that loads take through this truss. At the top of this figure, we see that the center of this model is an inverted kingpost truss of two panels that supports a single load of 1600 lb at midspan. The member forces in this truss are indicated on it. Each thick, tapered member is a compressive strut, and each single-line member is a tensile tie.

In the middle diagram of Figure 6.32, each end of the two-panel inverted kingpost truss is supported on a vertical strut that also bears an additional 1,600-lb external load. These two struts are supported by a tie whose two sloping ends are held apart by a long horizontal strut. Taken together, all these members make up a four-panel truss. The four-panel truss is supported in turn by a construction made up of two more vertical struts that are held up by a long tie and horizontal strut, thus arriving at the full six-panel configuration, as shown in the bottom diagram.

The forces in the web members of these nested trusses are identical to those that we found for the original six-panel truss. The forces in the top and bottom chords of the three nested trusses can be added to arrive at the magnitude of the chord forces in the original truss. Thus, the bottom chord forces in the center panels of the original truss are 2,400 lb plus 4,000 lb, or 6,400 lb. The top chord forces for the center panels are 4,000 lb plus 2,400 lb plus 800 lb, or 7,200 lb. The chord forces for the remaining panels may be found similarly.

The center joint in the bottom chord, in addition to being pulled horizontally in each direction with a force of 6,400 lb, is also acted upon by two diagonal pulls of 1,130 lb each. The horizontal component of the 1,130-lb force is a pull of 800 lb. Added to the force in the lower chord, the total horizontal pull on the joint is 7,200 lb, which is equal to the maximum compression in the top chord.

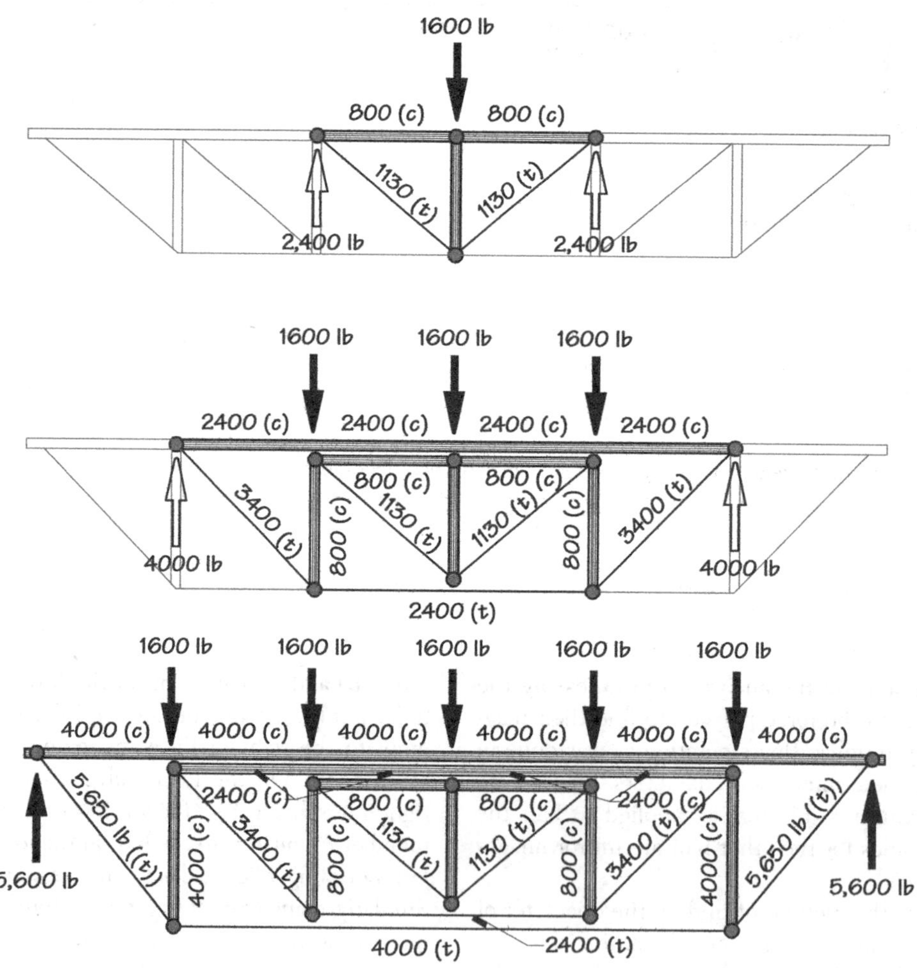

Figure 6.32 Visualizing the load paths through a flat truss using a series of nested kingpost trusses.

REVERSING THE DIRECTIONS OF THE DIAGONAL MEMBERS

What happens if the diagonals of this truss, instead of sloping downward toward the middle, slope upward instead? Figure 6.33 tells the answer. In each form diagram, the compressive members are shown as thick lines, tensile members as thin lines, and zero-force members as broken lines. When the directions of the diagonal members are reversed, the character of the forces in all the web members, both diagonal and vertical, reverses. The magnitudes of the forces, however, stay the same.

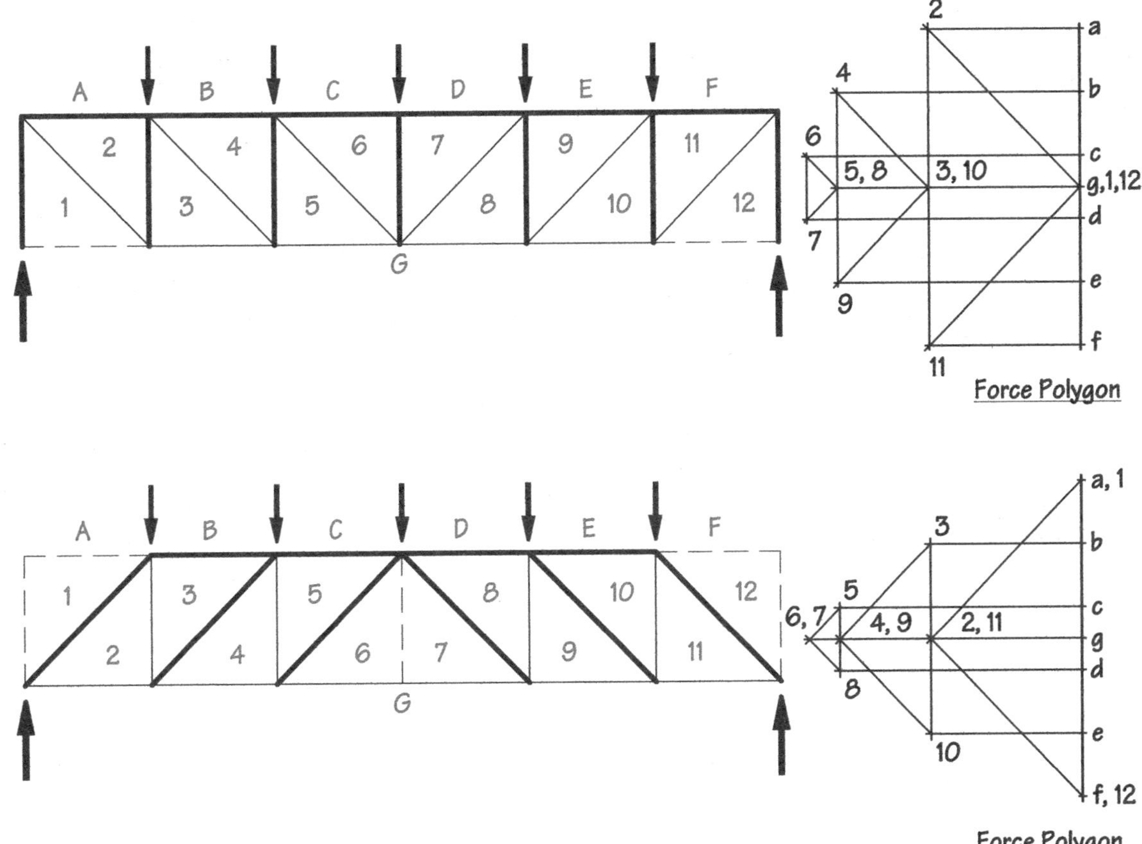

Figure 6.33 Reversing the direction of the diagonal members: a flat Pratt truss above, a flat Howe truss below.

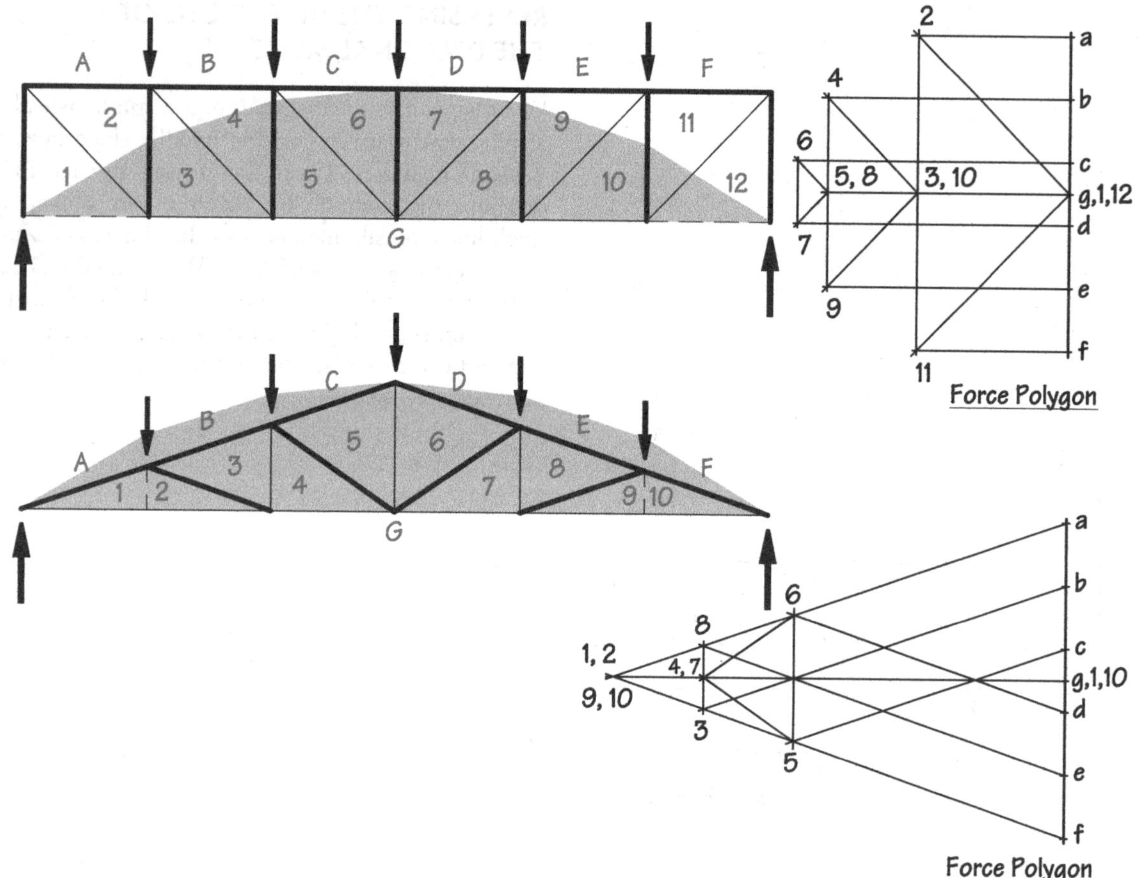

Figure 6.34 Comparing the actions and magnitudes of forces in flat and triangular trusses. The shaded area is a funicular shape for this loading. The direction of the web forces depends on whether the truss shape goes outside this area or not.

FLAT AND TRIANGULAR TRUSSES

For trusses that support roofs, a triangular outline is often used, with the slope of the roof establishing the slope of the top chords of the truss. Triangular trusses are sometimes called *gable trusses*, after the double-sloped gabled or hipped roofs they support. Does a triangular truss behave differently than a rectangular one? Figure 6.34 compares two trusses whose depth, loads, and orientations of diagonal members are identical and whose only difference is their external shapes. A glance at the magnitudes of the force polygons tells us that member forces are substantially higher in the triangular truss, a situation that can be overcome by increasing its depth. The indications of tensile and compressive members on the form diagrams tell us that the characters of the forces in the web members are opposite in the two trusses, even though the direction of inclination of the diagonals is the same. This leads to a somewhat confusing situation in the naming of trusses: While the parallel-chord truss shown in this figure is a flat Pratt truss, the triangular truss with the analogous inclination of diagonals is a triangular Howe truss. The naming follows the force configuration rather than the appearance: For a triangular truss to be a Pratt, which by definition has tensile diagonals, its diagonals must be inclined in the opposite direction from those in a flat Pratt truss. In Chapters 14 through 18, as we use truss analogies to visualize the flow of forces in beams, we will discover why forces in the diagonals behave in this way.

REDUCING THE DEPTH OF A FLAT TRUSS

Figure 6.35 depicts the left halves of three six-panel flat Howe trusses, each made of laminated wood members. All three trusses support identical loads of 1,600 lb at each panel point. The top truss is 3 ft deep, the middle one is 2 ft deep, and the bottom one is only 1 ft deep, as measured between the centerlines of the top and bottom chords. The forces in the members of each truss have been found by constructing its force polygon to the right, and each member has been given a thickness based purely on the magnitude of the force it must carry, assuming a uniform stress in all members of 1,500 psi and disregarding any potential for buckling of compression members. As is the usual practice in detailing trusses, the center axes of the members are made to coincide with the lines of the form diagrams of the three trusses.

It is apparent from the force polygons that the forces in the members of the shallowest truss are several times higher than in the members of the deepest one. In fact, as the depth of the truss approaches zero, the member forces rise more and more rapidly. If the chords of the shallowest truss were forced to lie entirely within the 1-ft depth rather than being centered on it, the truss would have to be solid wood. It would become, in other words, a wooden beam rather than a truss.

This demonstration brings out an important lesson: A truss needs sufficient depth to operate efficiently. In general, trusses must be deeper than beams to carry the same loads over the same span. In exchange for this disadvantage, however, a truss offers brilliant advantages: It uses less material than the beam, and trusses in general can span much farther than beams.

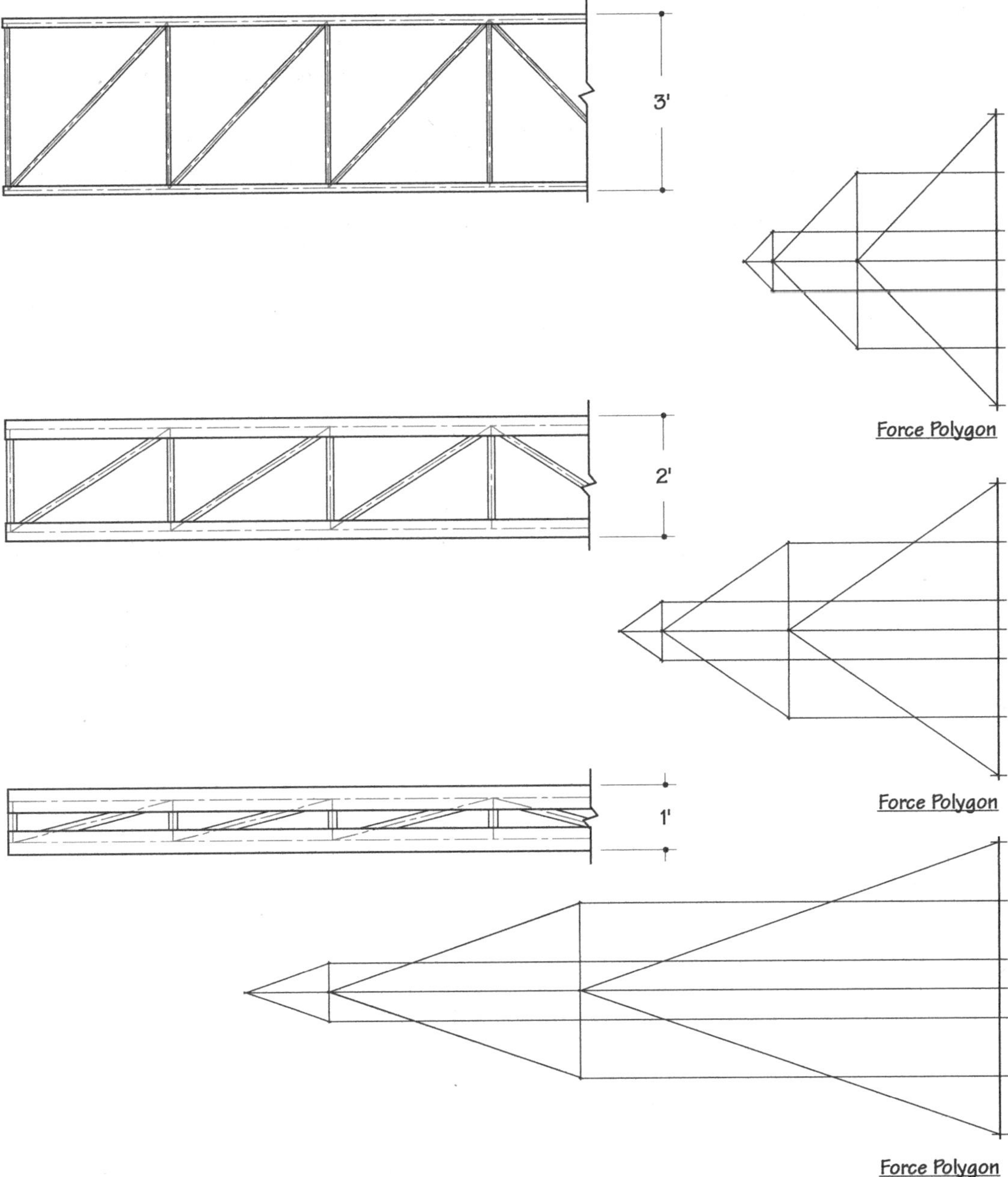

Figure 6.35 Reducing the depth of a truss increases member forces; the relative magnitudes of the trusses may be read at a glance from their force polygons.

A TRUSS WITH AN ODD NUMBER OF PANELS

So far, we have examined only trusses with an even number of panels. Figure 6.36 shows an analysis of member forces in a five-panel truss that has identical loads at its panel points. The unique feature of this truss proves to be that its middle diagonal, 5–6, is a zero-force member. If the uniform character of the loading is reliably constant, and if the truss is assembled in such a way that it derives significant stiffness from its joints (as it does when the top and bottom chords are single pieces that are as long as the truss), the diagonal may be omitted from the center panel; it is therefore shown as a dashed line in our analysis. This is the basis for floor truss designs in both wood and steel in which the diagonal is omitted in the center panel to allow for the passage of large ventilation ductwork. It also suggests that any web members in the center panel of a truss could be designed more for visual delight than for structural function—they could, as one example, form a circle or ellipse.

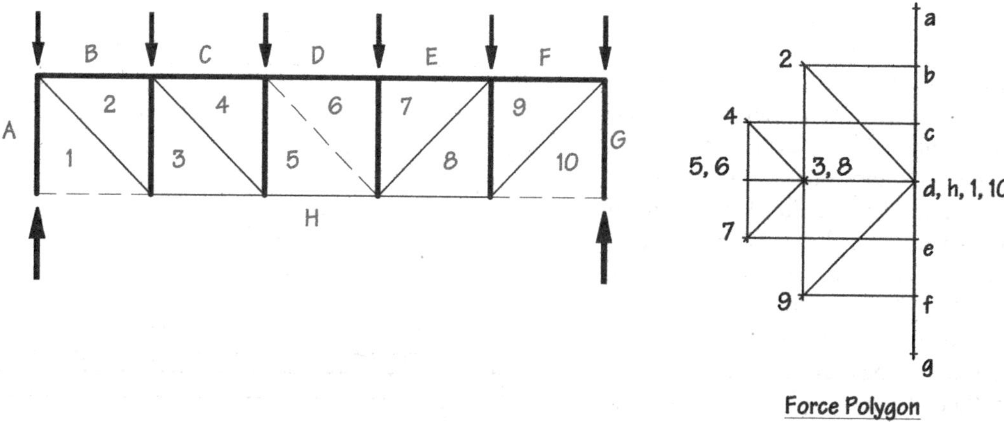

Figure 6.36 A truss with an odd number of panels.

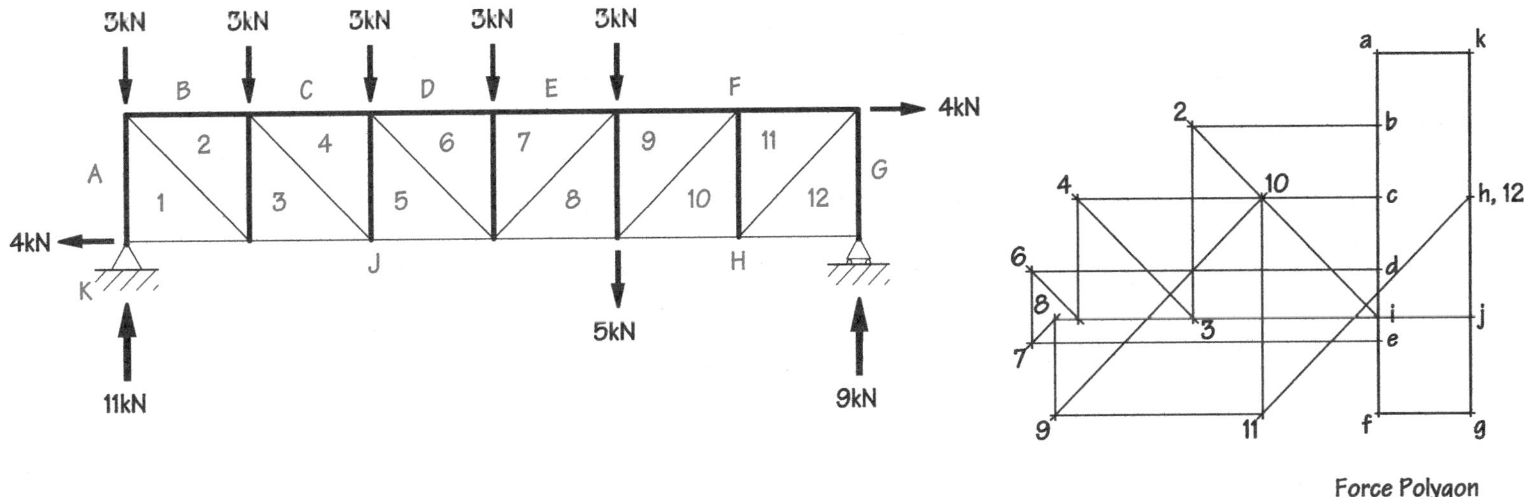

Figure 6.37 A truss with asymmetrical loading.

ASYMMETRICAL LOADING PATTERNS

The truss in Figure 6.37 is loaded very asymmetrically. It is subjected to a horizontal load at one end and a load suspended from the bottom of the truss, as well as a set of top loads that are applied at some panel points and not others. Because of the horizontal load, the reactions on this truss must be found by assuming that one of them passes through a roller and therefore must be vertical. This assumption having been made, the reactions are readily found by taking moments about each support. The resulting load line is a rectangle, *akgf*. The force polygon is asymmetrical but is easily constructed, and closes with segment *12g*. This example demonstrates that the graphical method of truss analysis is general and applies to any combination of loads. Inclined loads can be included either by resolving each of them into horizontal and vertical components, or, as is more commonly done, by including them as inclined segments in the load line, as we did in the previous chapter.

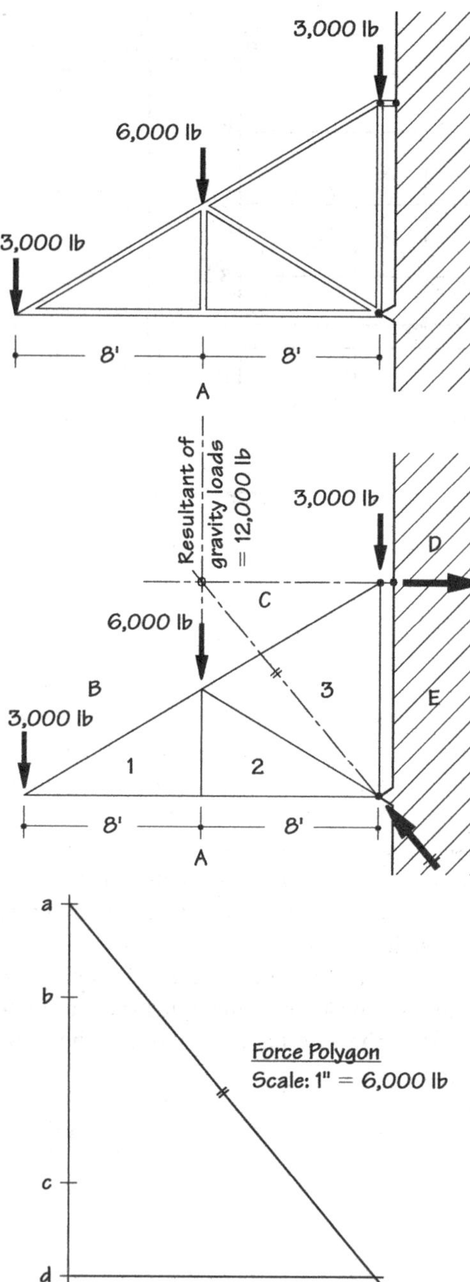

Figure 6.38 Finding the reactions on a cantilever truss.

A CANTILEVER TRUSS

To this point, we have examined trusses that are *simply supported*, that is, trusses that are held up by a reaction at each end. Figure 6.38 shows a truss that is designed to carry a projecting balcony of a concert hall. This is referred to as a *cantilever truss* because it is supported only at one end by a rigid wall or column. The upper support is a horizontal link that is hinged at both ends. The lower support is a hinge. What are the member forces in this truss, and what are the magnitudes and directions of the reactions?

We construct a combined form diagram and free-body diagram of the truss on which we indicate all the external forces that act upon it (Figure 6.38). Bow's notation helps us to identify these forces: *AB*, *BC*, and *CD* are the loads from the longitudinal floor beams of the balcony. *DE* is the top reaction. Because it occurs through a hinged link, it must act horizontally, but we do not know its magnitude. *EA*, the bottom reaction, can occur in any direction through the hinged connection, so we know neither its direction nor its magnitude.

We could find the magnitude and direction of the reactions by taking numerical moments, but let us pursue instead a graphical solution. We begin by plotting the external loads on a load line at a convenient scale. Vertical line segments *ab*, *bc*, and *cd* represent the loads on the truss. Force *de* we know to be horizontal, so we lay out a horizontal line through *d*; but we don't know how long segment *de* should be, so we cannot locate point *e*. Because we can't locate point *e*, we are also unable to draw line segment *ea*, which will terminate at point *a* at the top of the load line. We recognize now that the load line, rather than being just a vertical line, will be a triangle.

We complete the load line by means of a simple graphical operation: The line of action of the resultant of the three gravity loads passes through the central vertical member of the truss. The line of action of the horizontal reaction, *DE*, intersects the line of action of the resultant at a point that we label *n*. Because the truss is in equilibrium, the line of action of the remaining external force, *EA*, must also pass through *n*. This construction gives us the direction of line segment *ea* on the force polygon, which allows us to complete the load line, *ade*.

The remainder of the force polygon is easily drawn (Figure 6.39). We scale the diagram and use the clockwise convention of Bow's notation to assign magnitudes and characters of forces to all the members and reactions.

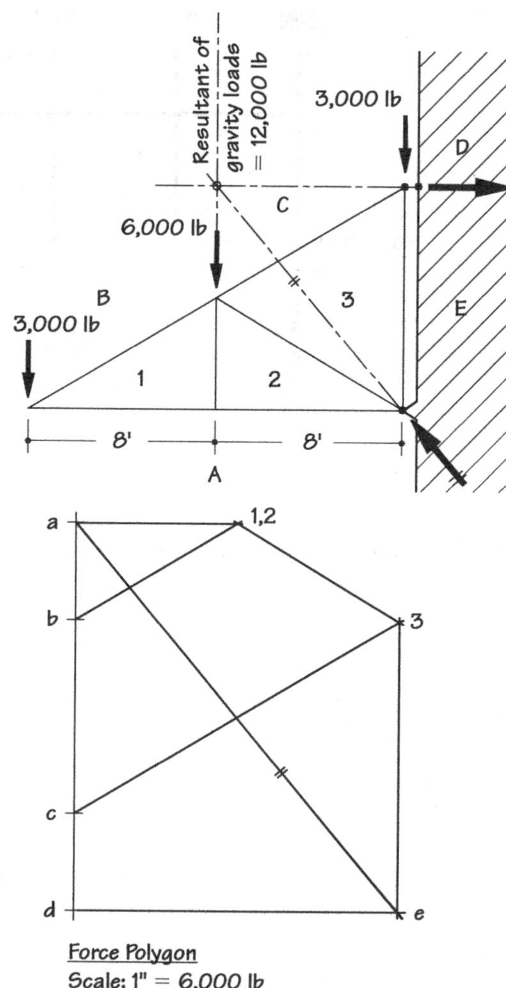

Figure 6.39 Analyzing the forces in a cantilever truss.

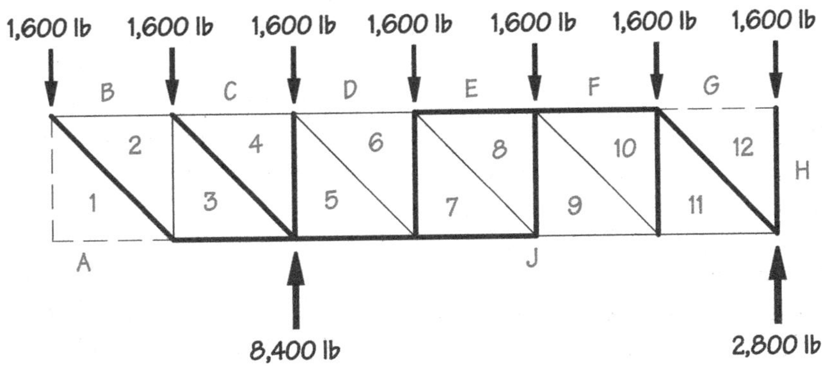

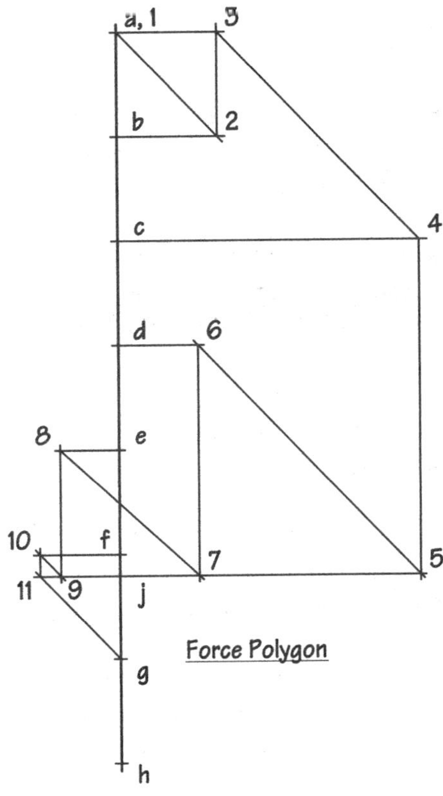

Figure 6.40 An example of an overhanging truss. We show compressive members in thick lines and tensile members in thin lines.

AN OVERHANGING TRUSS

Figure 6.40 illustrates the analysis of an *overhanging* truss, one that extends beyond one of its supports. The accompanying force polygon projects both to the right and to the left from the load line. The construction crosses the load line along diagonal 7–8. It is no coincidence that panel 7–8 on the form diagram is unique in being surrounded on all four sides by compression members, as indicated by thick lines. The panels to its right have a tensile chord along the bottom, and those to its left have a tensile chord along the top. There is a reversal in panel 7–8 of the direction in which the truss bends under load. The force polygon is very compact, indicating in a general way that this is a truss with low member forces. This efficiency stems partly from the fact that the truss is relatively deep in relation to its span, but it also indicates that the overhang has the effect of decreasing the forces in the members of the panels that lie between the two supports.

Numerical Finding of Forces in Truss Members: The Method of Joints

In addition to the graphical method, there are numerical methods for finding the forces in members of a truss. One of these, the method of sections, was demonstrated in Chapter 5. Another, the *method of joints*, is directly parallel to the graphical method, in that it solves for the forces in one joint at a time, working from left to right across the form diagram of the truss. Here is how the numerical method of joints is applied to a truss similar to the one that we have just analyzed graphically:

1. Bow's notation is not generally used in numerical solutions. Instead, letters are assigned to the nodes of the truss (Figure A). A member is named by the nodes at its ends: The leftmost segment of the top chord, for example, is called *AB* or *BA*.
2. We use moments to find the reactions on the truss. In this example, the loads are symmetrical, making it easy to assign values of 5,600 lb to both reactions. As with the graphical method, it is extremely important to be sure that the reactions are correct before proceeding. A lot of painstaking work will be lost later if the reactions are incorrect.
3. The left end of the truss is examined to find a node that has no more than two unknown forces acting upon it. In this truss, *N* is such a node. We draw a free-body diagram of it (Figure B).

   We adopt arbitrarily a convention that rightward- and upward-acting forces are positive. We apply the expressions of static equilibrium to this node:

$$\sum F_h = 0 = NM$$

$$NM = 0$$

$$\sum F_v = 0 = -NA + 5{,}600 \text{ lb}$$

$$NA = 5{,}600 \text{ lb}$$

   The positive sign of *NA* indicates that we have chosen the correct direction for the arrow in the free-body diagram. *NA* presses downward on the node; it is in compression. If we had drawn *NA* pulling up on the node, we would have arrived at a negative answer that tells us to reverse the vector arrow on the free-body diagram.
4. Now that we have found the force in member *NA*, node *A* has only two unknown forces. One of these is inclined at an angle of 45° (Figure C). In each equation, we multiply *MA* by the cosine of 45°, which is 0.707, to find its vertical or horizontal component:

$$\sum F_v = 0 = -1{,}600 \text{ lb} + 5{,}600 \text{ lb} - MA \cos 45^\circ$$

$$0.707 MA = 4{,}000 \text{ lb}$$

$$MA = \frac{4{,}000 \text{ lb}}{0.707} = 5{,}658 \text{ lb}$$

$$\sum F_h = 0 = (5{,}658 \text{ lb}) \cos 45^\circ - AB$$

$$AB = 4{,}000 \text{ lb}$$

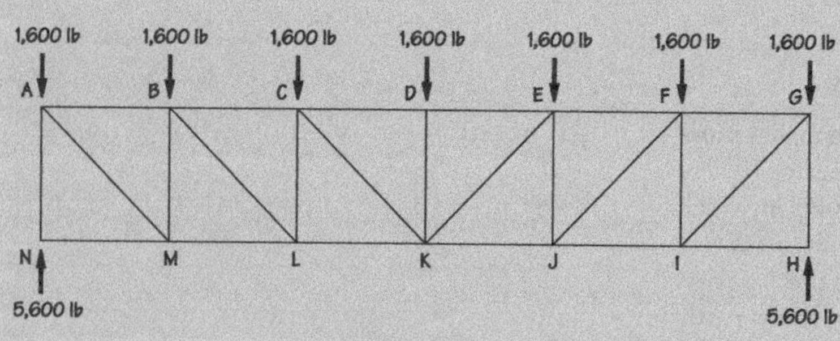

Figure A A form diagram of the truss.

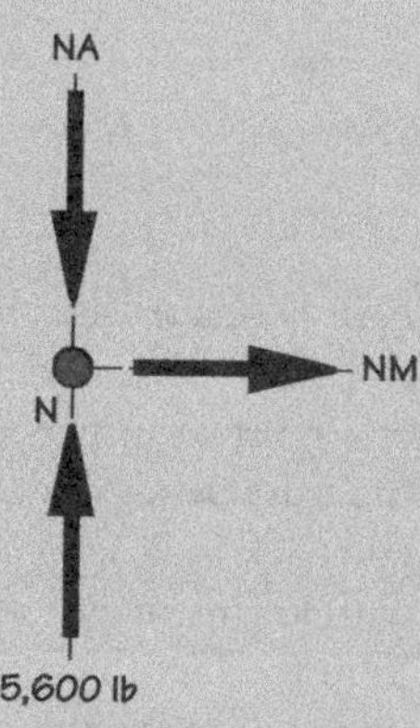

Figure B

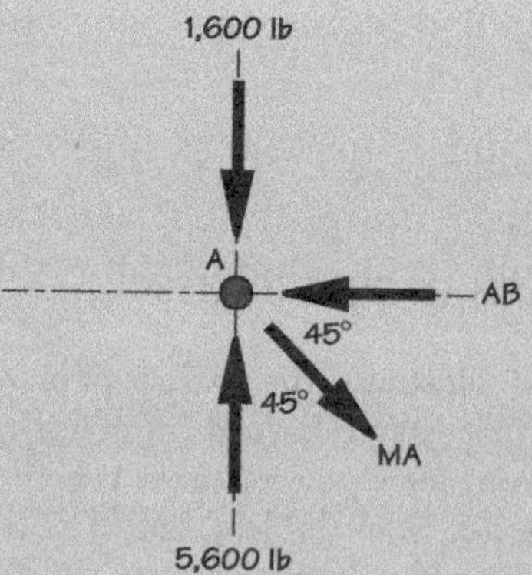

Figure C Vector diagram for numerical analysis.

5. We move next to node M (Figure D):

$$\sum F_v = 0 = (5{,}658\text{ lb})\cos 45^\circ - MB$$

$$MB = 4{,}000\text{ lb}$$

$$-(5{,}658\text{ lb})\cos 45^\circ - ML = 0$$

$$ML = -4{,}000\text{ lb}$$

The minus sign tells us that we assumed the wrong direction for ML. It actually pulls to the right.

6. In Figure E, we examine the forces at node B:

$$\sum F_v = 0 = -1{,}600\text{ lb} + 4{,}000\text{ lb} - LB\cos 45^\circ$$

$$LB = \frac{-1{,}600\text{ lb} + 4{,}000\text{ lb}}{0.707} = 3{,}395\text{ lb}$$

7. This leaves only two unknowns at node L (Figure F):

$$\sum F_v = 0 = (3{,}395\text{ lb})\cos 45^\circ - LC$$

$$LC = 2{,}400\text{ lb}$$

$$\sum F_h = 0 = LK - (4{,}000\text{ lb}) - (3{,}395\text{ lb})\cos 45^\circ$$

$$LK = 6{,}400\text{ lb}$$

8. This procedure is followed node by node until the forces in the last members of the right-hand end of the truss are found. If the work has been done correctly, these last forces will balance one another to create equilibrium. If the last forces are not in equilibrium, an error has been made earlier in the analysis, and the entire process must be checked to find it.

In two instances, these numerical solutions do not agree perfectly with the ones done previously by graphical means. For member MA the numerical solution is 5,658, compared to 5,650 for our graphical solution. For LB, the numerical solution is 3,395; the graphical, 3,400. These discrepancies are each well below 1 percent of the theoretical value.

There are several disadvantages to the numerical method. It is laborious and often very slow, especially if the truss is irregular in form. The purely numerical results that it gives are difficult to interpret in order to understand what is going on inside a truss, or to discover how to improve its form. Moreover, the apparent precision of the numerical method gives the illusion of a very accurate analysis, when in fact the calculations are invariably based on loading assumptions that are only educated guesses. In service, a truss is likely to undergo loadings that differ from the assumptions by significant amounts.

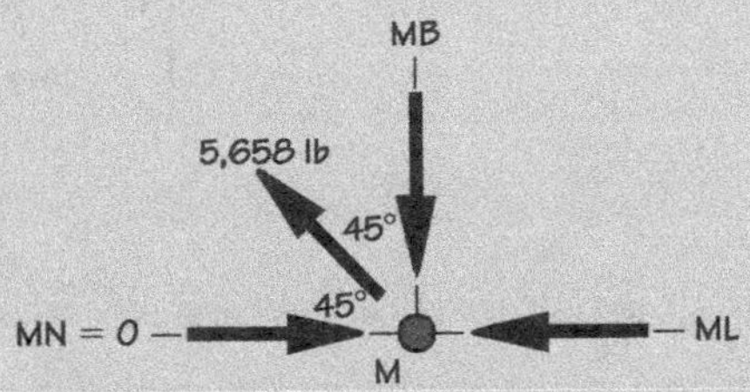

Figure D Vector diagram for numerical analysis.

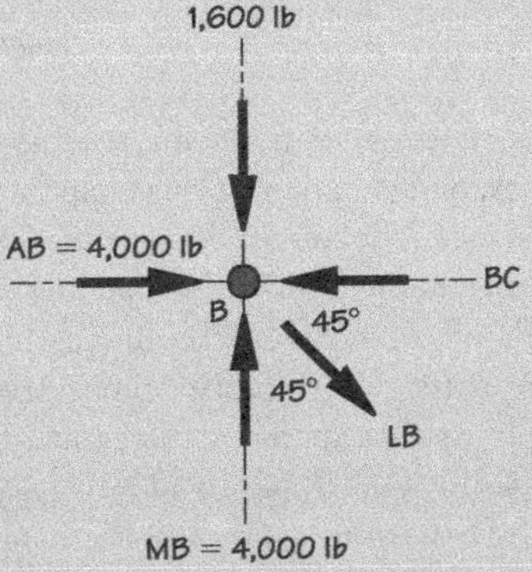

Figure E Vector diagram for numerical analysis.

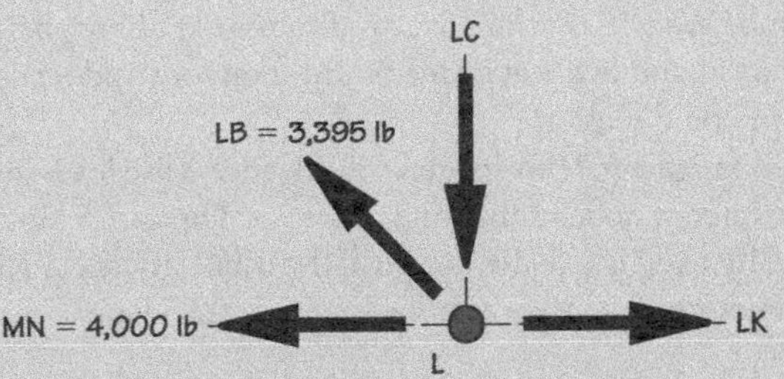

Figure F Vector diagram for numerical analysis.

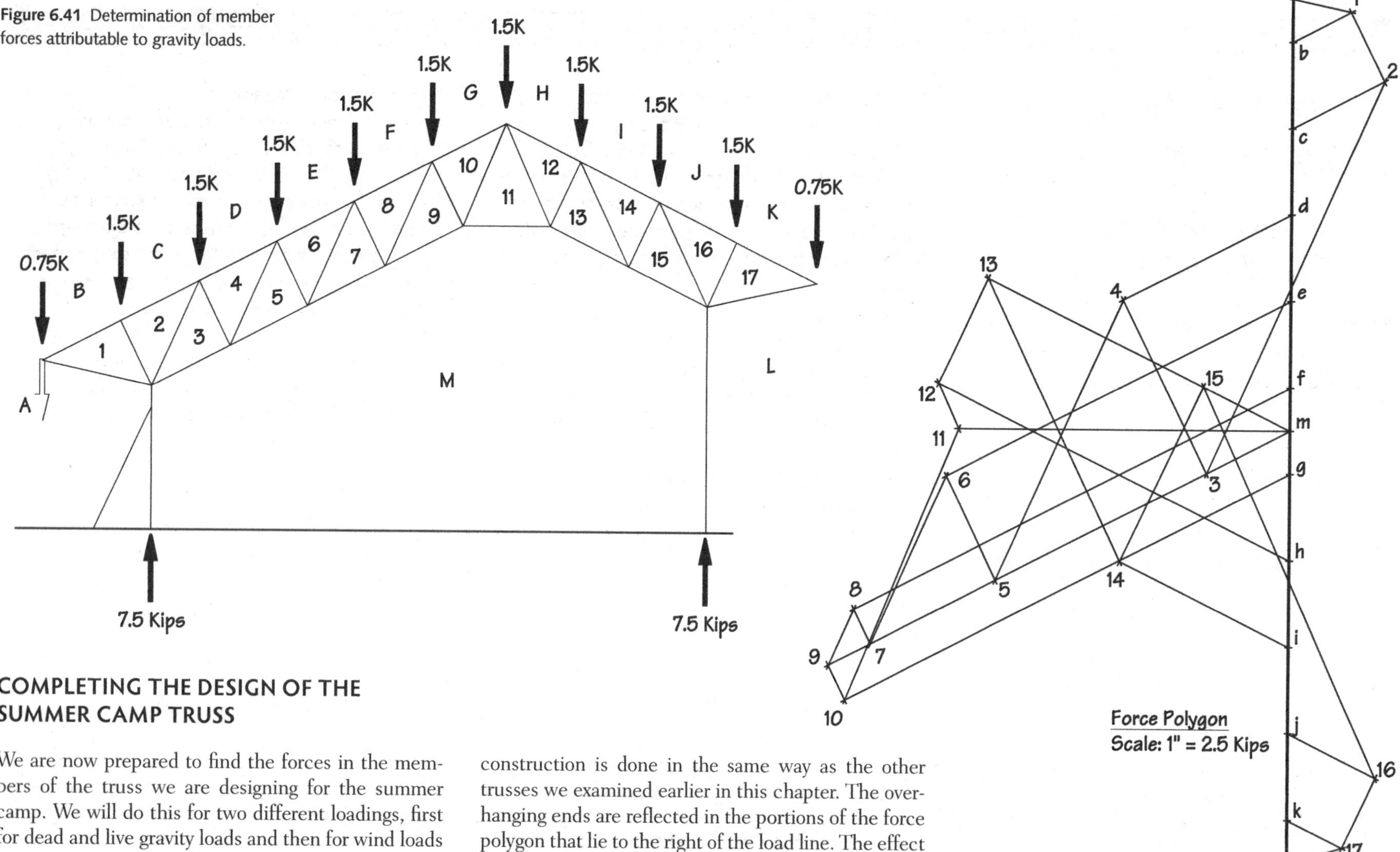

Figure 6.41 Determination of member forces attributable to gravity loads.

COMPLETING THE DESIGN OF THE SUMMER CAMP TRUSS

We are now prepared to find the forces in the members of the truss we are designing for the summer camp. We will do this for two different loadings, first for dead and live gravity loads and then for wind loads from one direction.

In Figure 6.41 we estimate the dead and live loads on one interior node of the truss. These add up to 1.5 kips. The first and last nodes have half the tributary area of an interior node, so they bear loads of only 0.75 kips.

Gravity Load Analysis

The gravity load force polygon (Figure 6.41) is complex because of the asymmetry of the truss, but its construction is done in the same way as the other trusses we examined earlier in this chapter. The overhanging ends are reflected in the portions of the force polygon that lie to the right of the load line. The effect of the overhangs is to reduce the forces in the main span of the truss. The relative compactness of the diagram tells us that member forces are not excessive; this is a direct result of our adopting an adequate depth for the truss and adding the overhanging ends. As shown in Figure 6.42, the largest forces are in chord members *F8*, 8.7 kips compression, and *M9*, 9.2 kips tension; the largest forces in diagonal members are in *15–16* and *2–3*.

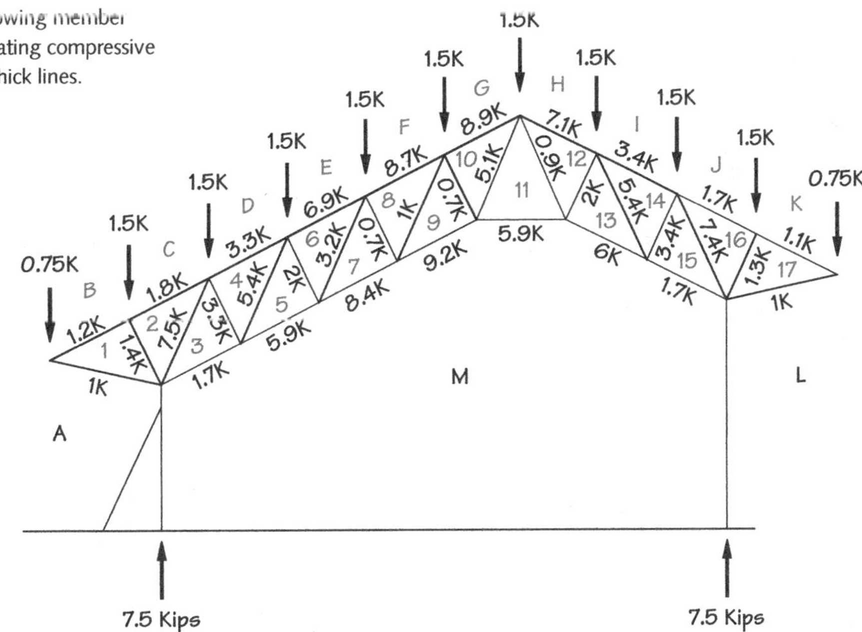

Figure 6.42 Showing member forces and indicating compressive members with thick lines.

Wind Load Analysis

The actual forces that the wind exerts on roof trusses are extremely complex and constantly fluctuating. The patterns of *wind forces* that are given in building codes for purposes of building design are necessarily simplified but still complex, requiring structural designers to analyze based on several different wind directions and to examine the effects of *outward pressures* (suctions) as well as *inward pressures*. It would take an entire chapter to explore a full analysis of this kind, so we will look only at one case. Figure 6.43 is an analysis of the actions of a wind from the right that is assumed to exert pressures perpendicular to the windward side of the roof, and suctions perpendicular to the leeward slope. For the moment, we disregard all gravity loads and analyze only for wind forces. The reactions are found graphically as follows:

1. The lines of action of the resultant vectors of the forces on each of the two roof slopes, R_1 and R_2, are drawn on the form diagram; they intersect at *y*.
2. A force polygon on these two vectors is drawn to the lower left. Its closing string is the resultant vector, *la*, of the wind load on both slopes.
3. This leaves three forces acting on the truss: the right reaction, the left reaction, and *la*, the resultant of the wind load on both slopes. We know the location and direction of the right reaction. Because it is applied through a column that is hinged at both ends, its line of action must lie along the vertical axis of the column.
4. The line of action of the total wind load on the roof, *la*, intersects the vertical line of action of the right reaction at *z* on the form diagram.
5. The line of action of the left reaction, *am*, must pass through the left hinge and also through *z*.

These constructions give us the lines of action of all three external forces on the truss: the right reaction, *lm*; the left reaction, *am*; and the resultant of all the wind forces, *la*. We also know the magnitude of one of them, the total wind load, *la*. We complete the force polygon to find the magnitudes of the two reactions. The right reaction, *lm*, is a mere 120 lb of tension. The left reaction, *am*, is also tensile; its magnitude is 2,350 lb. In simple language, the assumed pattern of wind loadings would lift off the roof if we do not take measures to hold it down.

These three forces make up a triangular load line for the determination of wind forces in the members of the truss. We subdivide the vectors for the loads on the two slopes of the roof into the forces at the individual nodes and apply Bow's notation. Then, working patiently and systematically, we complete the force polygon, which closes. In general, it shows that wind forces in the truss members are only about one-third as large as gravity forces, and often opposite in character.

If we were doing a complete analysis of the truss, we would analyze also the wind from the opposite direction. Then we would add the wind forces and gravity forces for all the members of the truss, using only the dead-load portion of the gravity loads, on the assumption that a maximum-force wind will blow snow off the roof. We would design each member and each connection for the worst-case combination of dead load plus wind load.

FINDING MEMBER SIZES

We have found the maximum compressive chord and diagonal member forces, and from these we will size appropriate members. The allowable compressive force in the truss members is found by starting with a handbook value of *allowable stress* in compression for the species and grade of wood that we will use. This value is based on laboratory testing of the strengths of a large number of wood specimens. Then we reduce this value to account for the length of the member and its potential for buckling (we will reexamine these topics in Chapter 19). Further adjustments of the allowable stress are made for the duration of the load and for

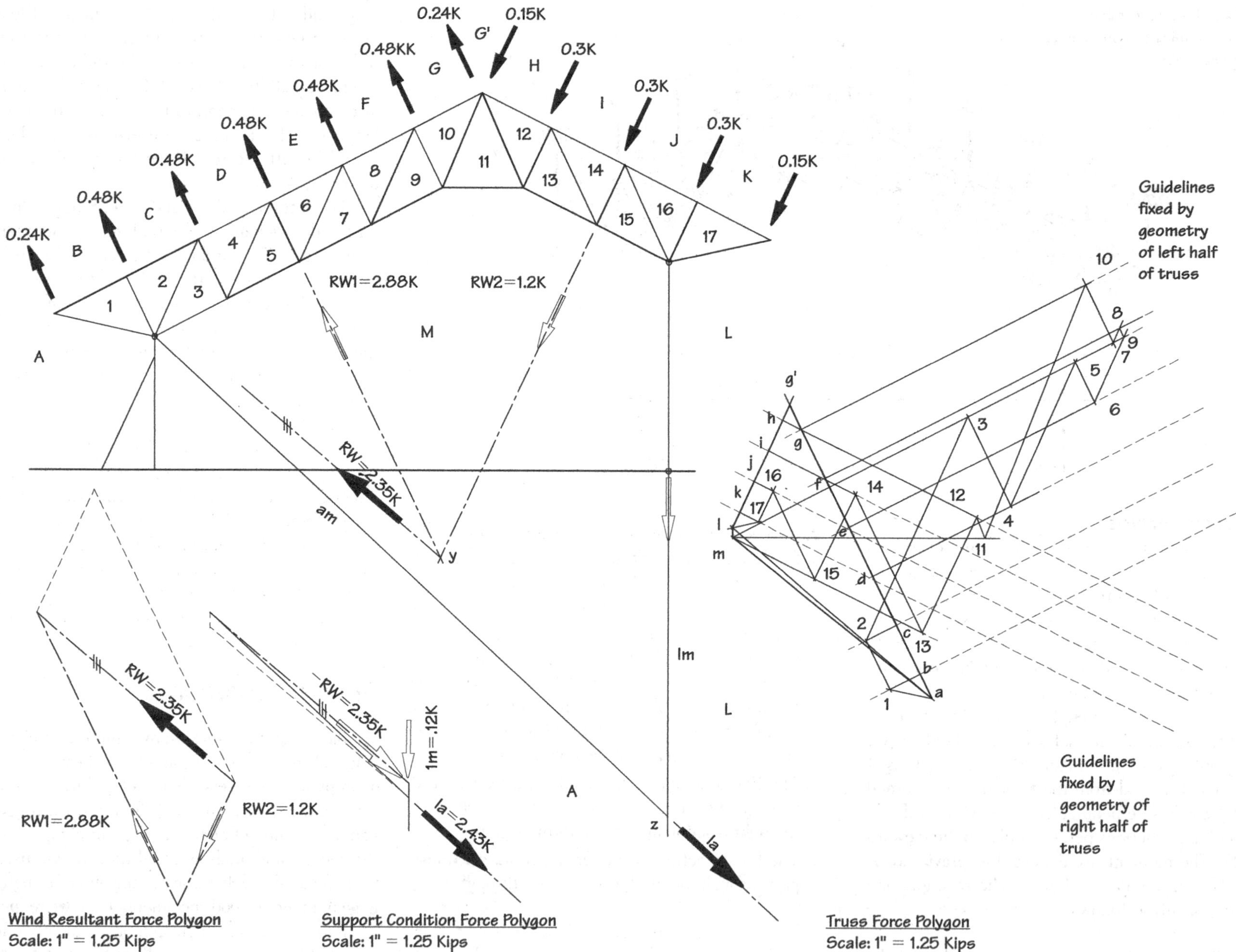

Figure 6.43 Determination of member forces attributable to a particular wind loading case.

such conditions of service as temperature and humidity. These factors are beyond the scope of this book, so to complete our example we will simply assume an allowable compressive stress of 900 psi. The required cross-sectional area of wood in a member is equal to its axial force divided by the allowable stress:

$$A_{req} = \frac{P}{F_{allow}}$$

For the most heavily loaded compressive chord member in the truss:

$$A_{req} = \frac{8.8 \text{ kips}}{900 \text{ lb/in.}^2} = 9.78 \text{ in.}^2$$

A 4 × 4, which is actually 3.5 in. square, has a cross-sectional area of 12.25 sq in. Since it has more than enough area, we could use 4 × 4s for the compressive chords and for the interior compressive members, none of which carry forces as large as the chord segment we have just examined.

Allowable tensile strengths of wood are tabulated separately from compressive strengths and are generally much lower. Tensile strengths do not need to be adjusted or reduced to account for buckling, though. Assuming a tensile strength of 600 psi, the most heavily loaded tensile member, *m*9, which carries a maximum of 9.2 kips, requires 15.3 sq in. of cross section. This is larger than a 4 × 4, but smaller than a 4 × 6, which has an area of 19.25 in^2.

If we wanted to create a truss that uses as little wood as possible, we would adopt the minimum size of lumber for each member. However, the design of the joints in such a truss would present many problems due to the varying dimensions of the pieces. To simplify assembly, we will use nominal 4-in. lumber for all the members of the truss. We decide to use 4 × 4s for all the interior members and 4 × 6s for all the chords. These will make a good-looking truss that has extra reserves of strength that will help it remain stable during the critical operation of hoisting it into position.

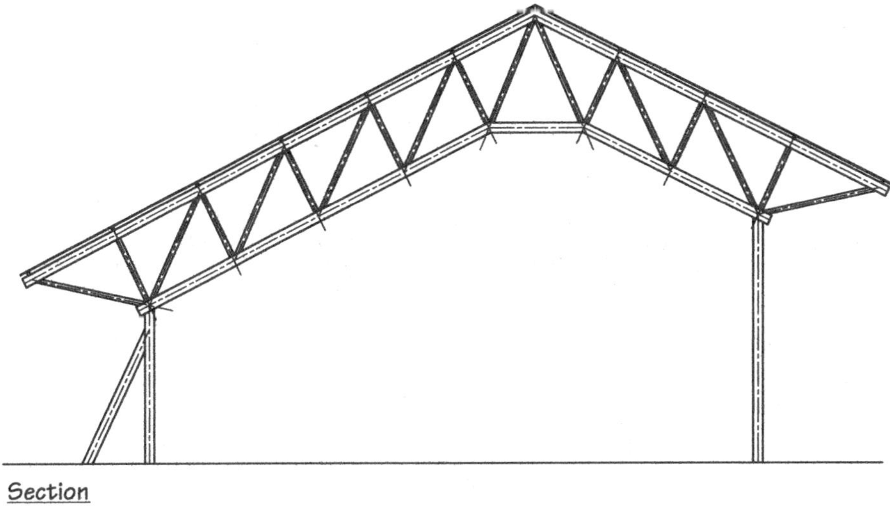

Figure 6.44 Scaled elevation drawing of the camp structure showing member thicknesses.

DETAILING THE TRUSS

We take another step toward completion of the design for the truss by constructing larger-scale drawings. Using drafting instruments or CAD, we draw first an overall elevation, as shown in Figure 6.44. The members are plotted to scale around their centerlines. The intersection of the centerlines at each node is called the *working point*. If we can make the centerlines of all the members that converge on each joint go through the working point, we have theoretically produced a truss in which all forces are axial. This assumption is not strictly true, for a variety of reasons:

- We use long, continuous pieces for the top and bottom chords. Because of their continuity, these members do not behave exactly as they would if the truss were made up of short members. In fact, they add strength to the truss through their own stiffness and strength.
- Our analysis assumes that the joints are perfect hinges. In reality, each joint has two or three bolts in it. These bolts, and the friction between pieces of wood that their tension creates, restrict rotational movement to some degree.
- A truss is seldom manufactured as perfectly as we would like; individual members may be a bit off in length or angle of cut, and bolts may not end up exactly where they are supposed to go.
- Drifting snow and wind pressures cause unusual loading patterns in the truss elements.

Nevertheless, we usually specify joint locations and fastener positions with 1/4-in. precision or better. If it is difficult to bring the centerlines of all the members at a joint to the same working point, it matters little whether we move a member a bit one way or the other to make things work dimensionally, because the truss has reserves of strength upon which to draw, reserves created by the continuity of the chords and the fixity of the joints.

Although we found that 4 × 6 chords are sufficient to carry the loads, they look too insubstantial in our scaled drawing. The design is not merely a result of our calculations, and particularly since the lower members have the added consideration of their

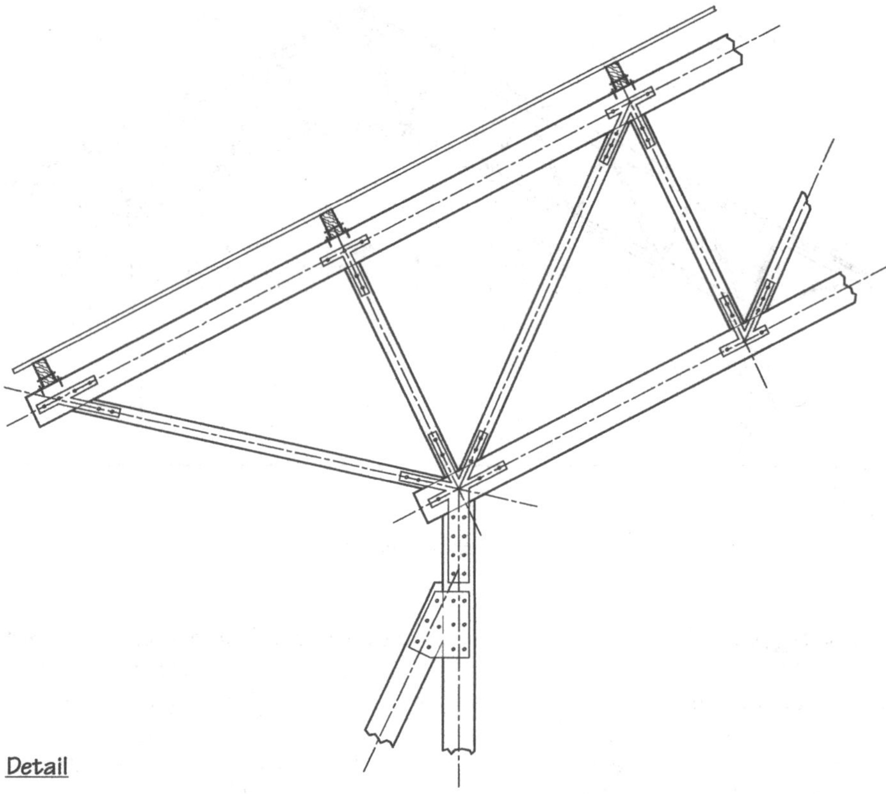

Figure 6.45 A scaled detail elevation showing connector plates at the left-hand connection. Notice that member centerlines converge at working points to avoid eccentric loadings.

prominent role in defining the spaces and activities of the camp goers, we decide to use 4 × 8s instead, keeping to 4 × 4s for most interior members. At larger scales still, we can show details of the connections (Figure 6.45). We decide to use bolts with welded steel strap plates on both sides of our trusses. The number and diameter of bolts at each node is dependent on many factors:

- The density of the wood: Denser wood transmits more pounds per bolt than less dense wood.
- The diameter of the bolts: Larger bolts transmit more force per bolt.
- The number of *shear planes* (interfaces between members) through which each bolt passes: A bolt through two shear planes transmits twice as much as a bolt through one.
- The dimensions of the lumber used in the truss: Thicker lumber puts more wood fiber against the bolt shank and transmits more force.
- The duration of the expected live load on the truss. Wood is stronger in resisting short-term loads, such as wind, than long-term ones, such as snow or stored goods.
- The moisture conditions in the building. Dry wood is stronger than wet wood.

Determining the number and spacings of bolts in each joint is not difficult: The bolts in a node are generally placed so that they are symmetrical about the centerlines of the members. This prevents the bolts from imparting bending forces to the columns and walls of the building. (Further information on bolting is available in sources listed at the end of this chapter.)

Bridging

The trusses we have designed are 40 ft. long and only 3–1/2 in. thick perpendicular to the plane of the truss members. They are very strong and stiff against vertical loads, but very weak against *out-of-plane forces*, lateral loads and buckling perpendicular to their planes. *Bridging* is bracing that is installed between trusses to maintain them all in their original planes, regardless of these forces (Figure 6.46). Bridging does not have to be nearly as strong as the trusses themselves, because its structural role is only that of keeping the trusses from moving sideways. We design a simple bridging scheme that is attached to the purlins and perpendicular truss members with *lag screws*, which are large, heavy-duty screws that are inserted into drilled holes by turning them with a wrench. Standard diameters of lag screws range from 1/4 in. to 1–1/4 in. We use lag screws instead of bolts in situations where it would be problematic to pass a bolt all the way through a joint, and install a washer and nut on the far side. We keep the lower ends of the bridging diagonals above the bottom chords of the trusses as a way of maintaining the visual dominance of the trusses.

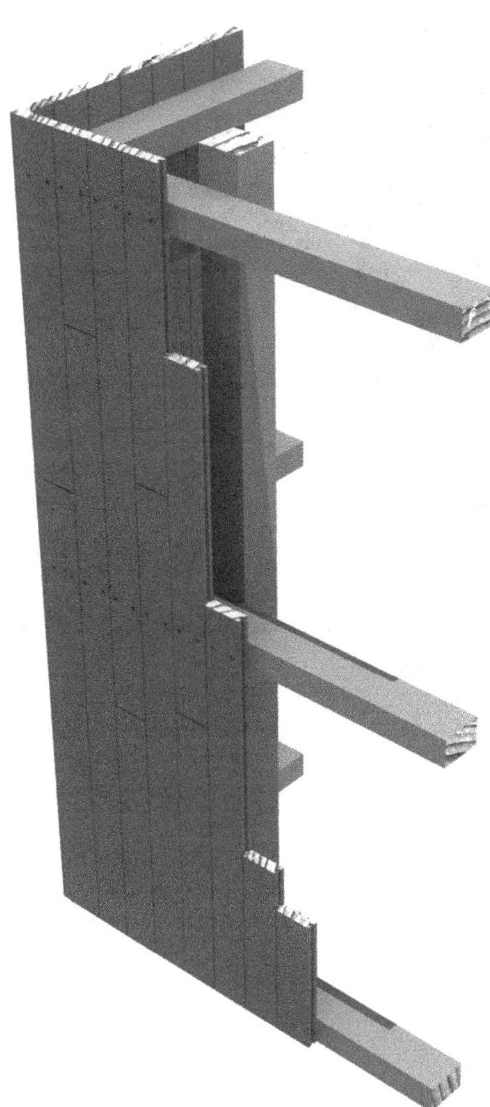

Figure 6.46 A detail of the wall construction.

Enclosing the Walls

The timber frame that we have created is beautifully patterned, but we must enclose it with walls to keep rain and snow out of the building and to protect the trusses against the decay that would occur if they were wetted frequently by storms. We make the walls in the simplest possible way: We add horizontal girts to the columns and nail vertical tongue-and-groove planks to the girts (Figure 6.46). The inside surface of the decking and the girts and braces make a beautiful pattern that we will leave exposed to the eye. Because this building is used only in summer and is not heated or cooled, we will not bother to insulate the walls or roof; and airtightness of the walls is not an issue.

We would like to end the line of trusses in a way that is visually satisfying. Though it is not difficult structurally to terminate a building, a visually satisfactory termination is not a trivial design problem. The system we are using to construct the hall does not inherently provide a formal way of terminating it at its open ends; its trusses could be used to produce a building of any length. Because there are few constraints on the design of the end walls, we can take advantage of the trusses' broad spans, which allow the freedom to create rather generous door and window openings. These openings could be made very large or complex, but for this site and program we use the proportions and patterning of the trusses just described to inform the division of the end walls and their wooden cladding. In Chapter 3 we terminated a corrugated barrel vault rather successfully with corrugated masonry walls. You may find it stimulating to design an endwall termination scheme for this building.

Lateral Stability of the Building as a Whole

We must brace the building against the lateral forces of wind and earthquake. The bridging between the trusses is not sufficient to keep the whole building from being blown over. In the short direction of the building, the inverted V supports can do the entire job of stabilization. In the long direction, we elect to add diagonal braces between the columns that support the trusses (Figure 6.47). These braces will remain exposed on the inside of the building as a part of its aesthetic. They will also help users of the building understand how it resists lateral forces.

The tongue-and-groove decking, because it is in the form of long, narrow strips of material, may not provide sufficient diaphragm action to transmit wind forces through the roof planes to the planes of bracing that are parallel to the wind. If this is the case, plywood panels may be nailed over the decking, or diagonal braces may be added beneath it to create wind trusses that lie parallel to the roof planes. The plywood panels may not expand and contract as much as the decking, which may lead to bulging of the plywood due to changes in humidity.

FABRICATING AND ERECTING THE TRUSSES

Although it would be possible to cut and assemble the trusses on the construction job site, it is much better to do it in a factory. The timbers can be kept dry so they don't swell before they are assembled. Bolt holes can be drilled with much greater accuracy. Level, flat floors and fixtures are available. Steel connectors can be kept dry and free of rust by being kept temporarily under the roof of a shop. All work is done conveniently and efficiently at floor level or bench level. The result is a set of prefabricated truss sections that are clean, dry, precise, and attractive. Each truss can be made in two sections that join at a node adjacent to the roof peak; this makes it possible to transport the sections to the building site on a flatbed truck trailer.

The truss sections are relatively light in weight, but each one is still far too heavy to be lifted and placed by muscle power. The manufacturer will bring to the site a mobile crane that will make quick, easy work of erecting the roof. First the columns will be raised, bolted to their foundations, and braced temporarily

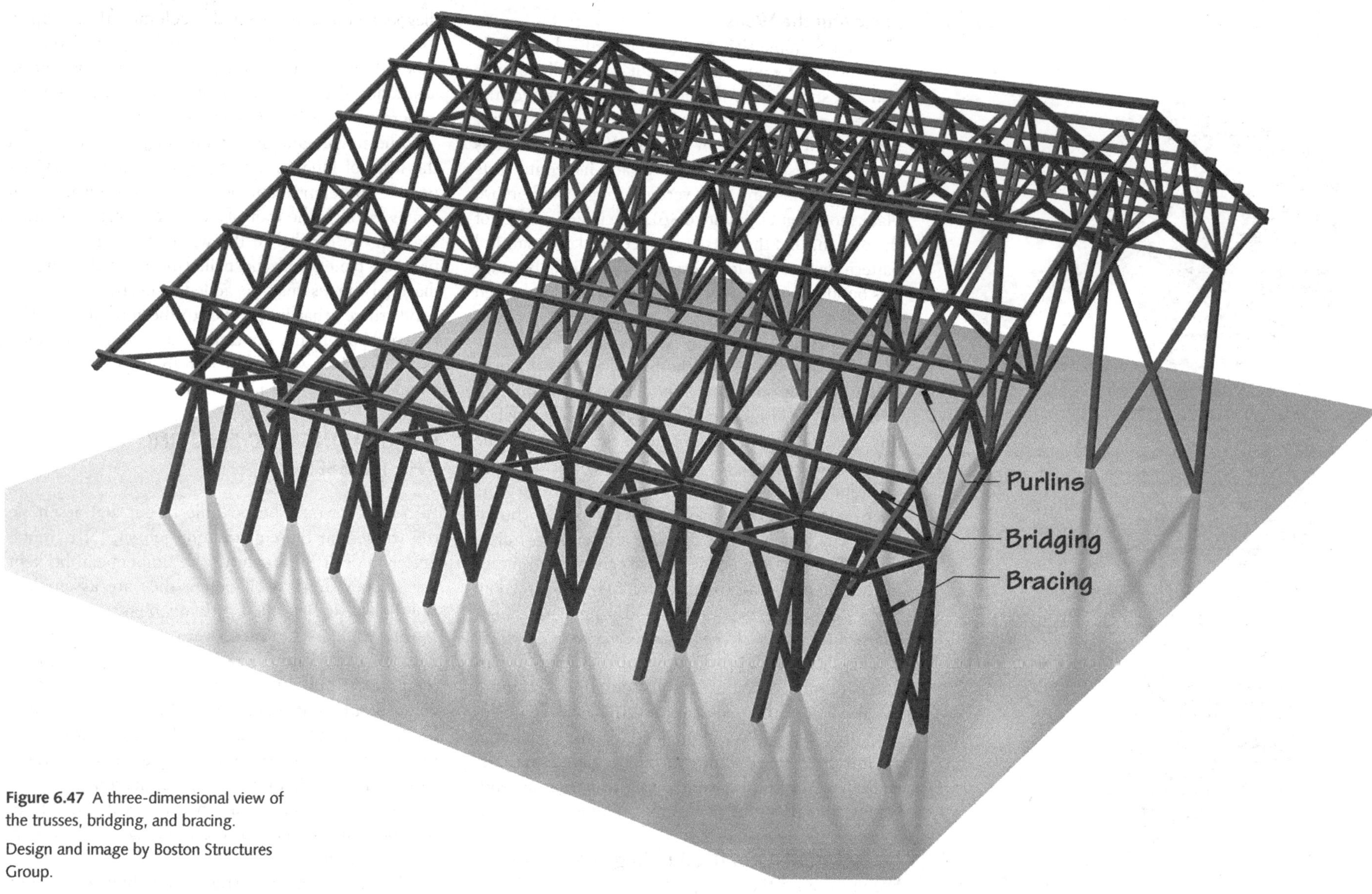

Figure 6.47 A three-dimensional view of the trusses, bridging, and bracing.

Design and image by Boston Structures Group.

Figure 6.48 A nineteenth-century Fink truss carries a train across a river. The highway bridge in the background is supported by wooden arches; it is covered by walls and a roof to keep the wooden structure dry and free from decay.

Photo courtesy Smithsonian Institution, Photo No. 41,436.

with timber diagonals. Then the trusses will be lifted, guided into place by workers with taglines, and bolted to the tops of the columns. Each truss will have to be braced with a number of temporary diagonals to prevent it from failing by buckling before the bridging and decking are applied. It may also be necessary to attach temporary stiffeners to the trusses to stiffen them while they are being raised and before the bracing is applied. The building will be completed with the application of roof shingles and siding to provide shelter without fully enclosing the space.

ANOTHER CHALLENGE

You are undertaking on your own the task of designing a bandstand roof for a public park. The function of the roof is to keep sun and rain off the musicians and to reflect sound to the audience that will be arrayed on the lawn outside. The required floor area of the bandstand is 600 ft^2, and this may be configured in any shape that is wider than it is deep from front to back. Assume that the floor is a flat wooden structure 4 ft above the ground, but do not spend time designing its structure. Concentrate instead on creating a trussed roof above that will be both beautiful and functional, considering its supports and shape, including overhangs. Assume a gravity live load of 20 psf; do not analyze for wind loads. Find the forces in the members and assign approximate sizes to them, providing for the roof's general lateral stability. You may want to consider using your repertoire of wood details if timber members are used, or evaluate whether steel trusses are more appropriate for your intentions and ideas for the structure over the performance space.

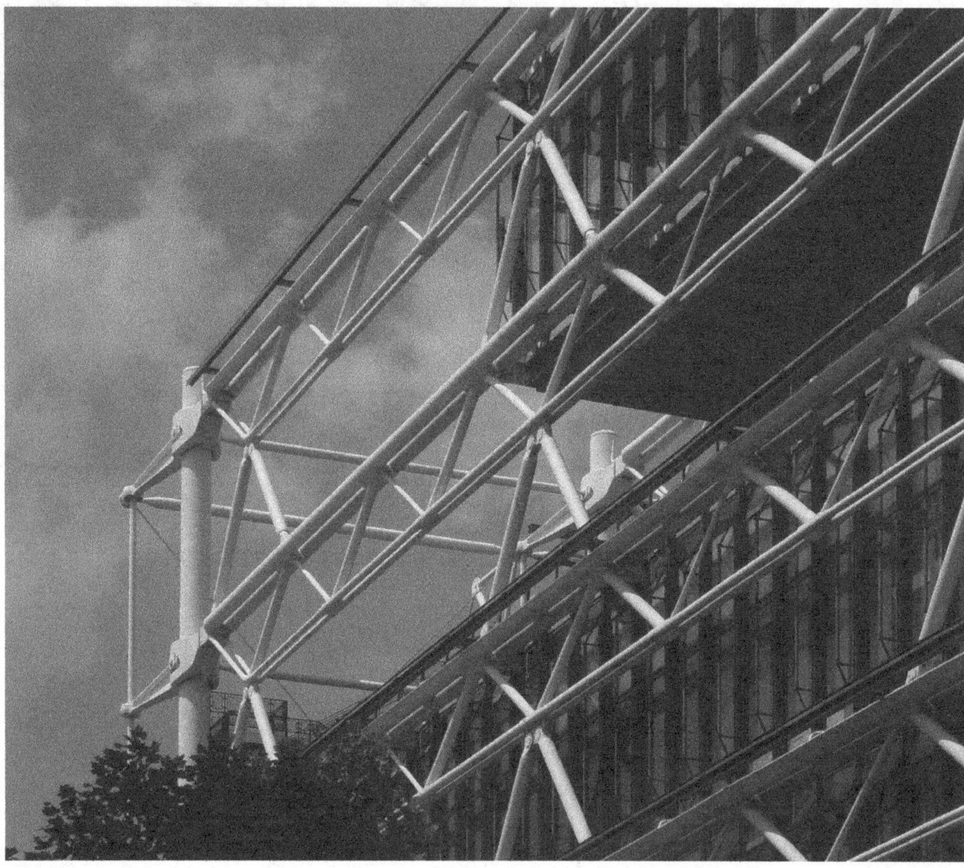

Figure 6.49 The floors and roof of the Centre Georges Pompidou in Paris are supported by Warren trusses 2.5 m (8.2 ft) deep that span 45 m (148 ft). Each top chord is a pair of 419-mm (16.5-in.) diameter steel tubes. A pair of 225-mm (9-in.) solid steel rods make up the bottom chord. Architect: Piano and Rogers. Structural engineer: Ove Arup and Partners.

Photo: David M. Foxe.

Exercises

1. Design a trussed roof for an art exhibition room that is 24 ft wide and 36 ft long, with walls that are uniformly 11 ft tall. Shape the wooden trusses in such a way that clerestory windows admit light to the space from one direction only. Assume that the total of live and dead loads is 50 lb per square ft of horizontal projection.

2. Find and compare the forces in the members of the gable trusses in Figure 6.50.

3. Figure 6.51 depicts a steel truss for a sloping footbridge. Find the forces in its members.

4. Determine the effects of the horizontal and vertical loads on the Warren truss in Figure 6.52.

5. Find the forces in the cantilever truss in Figure 6.53.

6. Prepare a preliminary design for a footbridge to span a distance of 42 ft between abutments on either side of a stream. The bridge will have an inside clear width of 44 in. Total live and dead loads have been estimated at 300 lb per foot of span. With the aid of a handbook of standard steel shapes, assign approximate sizes to the members, using square steel tubing with welded joints.

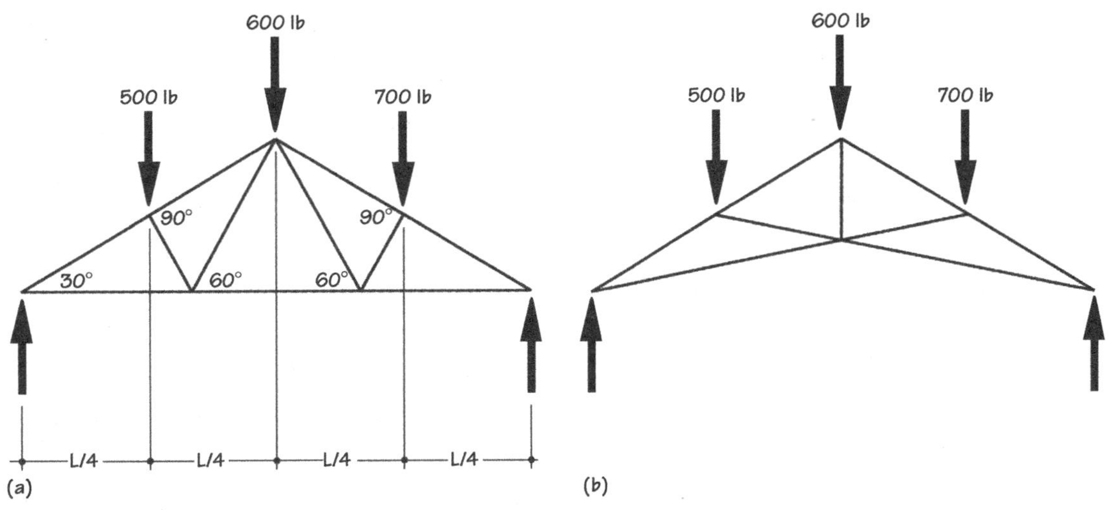

Figure 6.50 Two gabled trusses.

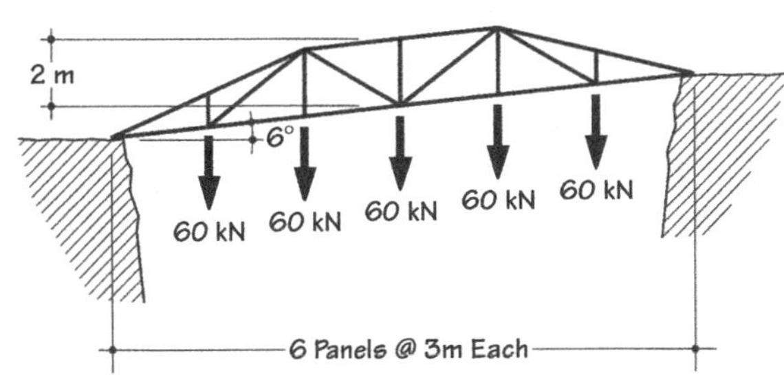

Figure 6.51 An inclined steel footbridge.

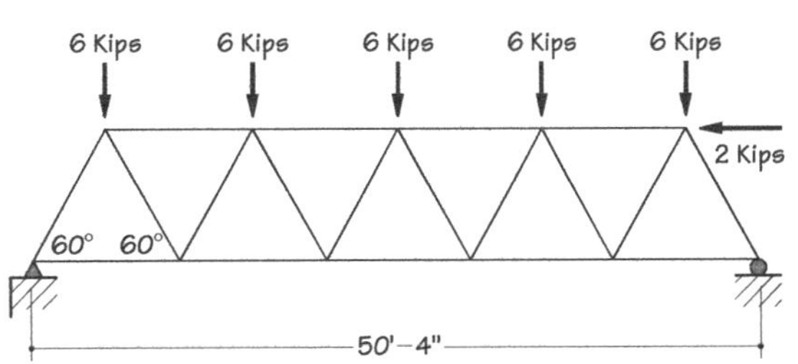

Figure 6.52 A Warren truss.

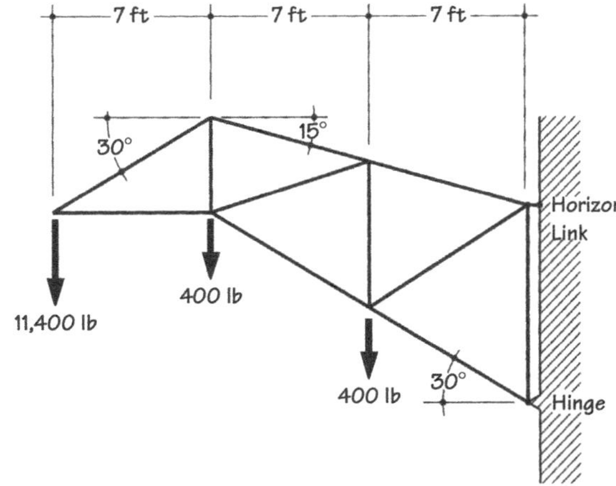

Figure 6.53 A cantilevered truss.

Key Terms and Concepts

truss
chord
web member
vertical
diagonals
struts
ties
panel
joint
panel points
nodes
International Building Code
parallel chord truss
hinge
indeterminate
statically determinate
depth-to-span ratios
decking
purlins
pitch
rise
run
framing square
planar truss
space truss
space frame
axial loading
open-web steel joists
bar joist
joist girder
roof and floor trusses
through truss
pony truss
deck truss
transfer truss
Pratt truss
Howe truss
Warren truss
simple Fink truss
Fink truss
cambered Fink truss
scissors truss
bowstring truss
inverted bowstring truss
lenticular truss
camelback truss
K-truss
triangular truss
shed truss
scissors truss
fireproofing
toothed plate
heavy timber
side plate
dowel
gusset plates
simply supported truss
flat truss
overhanging truss
wind forces; outward/inward pressures
allowable stress
working point
shear planes
out-of-plane forces
bridging
lag screws

Further Resources

Goetz, Karl-Heinz, Dieter Hoor, Karl Moehler, and Julius Natterer. *Timber Design and Construction Sourcebook.* New York, NY: McGraw-Hill, 1989. An international collection of imaginative timber buildings.

Goldstein, Eliot W. *Timber Construction for Architects and Builders.* New York, NY: McGraw-Hill, 1999. A comprehensive, eminently practical manual of timber construction, with emphasis on the creative phase of design, as well as the details.

www.strongtie.com: Simpson Strongtie manufactures probably a greater range of steel connectors for wood construction than any other company.

www.timberlinx.com: Manufacturers of an ingenious timber connection technology.

www.sfsintecusa.com: Manufacturers of self-drilling steel dowel connectors for timber construction.

CHAPTER 7

Designing a Fanlike Roof

- Extending graphical truss analysis to design fanlike structures both compressive and tensile (cable-stayed)
- Finding good forms and member forces for cable-stayed, fanlike, and treelike structures
- Design and detailing issues in steel tube construction

The sketches in Figure 7.2 are early ideas for a large roof under which vendors will assemble to sell fruits, vegetables, fish, meats, cheeses, baked goods, and other foodstuffs directly to the public. We propose to support the roof planes on structural elements that bear a resemblance to trees, such as those in the second and third columns of Figure 7.2. We would like to make these elements from round steel tubes. To develop this idea, we need to learn how to find a structurally appropriate form for the branching structures, how to find forces in their members, how large the tubes need to be, and how to detail and build the structure we design. The branched forms belong to a general class of devices that we will call *fanlike* structures, and which are actually a special class of trusses.

"We can design beautiful bridges when the flow of forces is logical."

—Michel Virlogeux

Figure 7.1 The Millau Viaduct in southern France was completed in 2004 after 38 months of construction, creating a gently curving 2,460-m-long roadway that is as high as 343 m (1,125 ft) above the valley below. The international project team of architects and engineers included French engineer Michel Virlogeux, architect Lord Norman Foster in London, and the engineering firm RFR in Paris.

Photo courtesy of Ben Johnson.

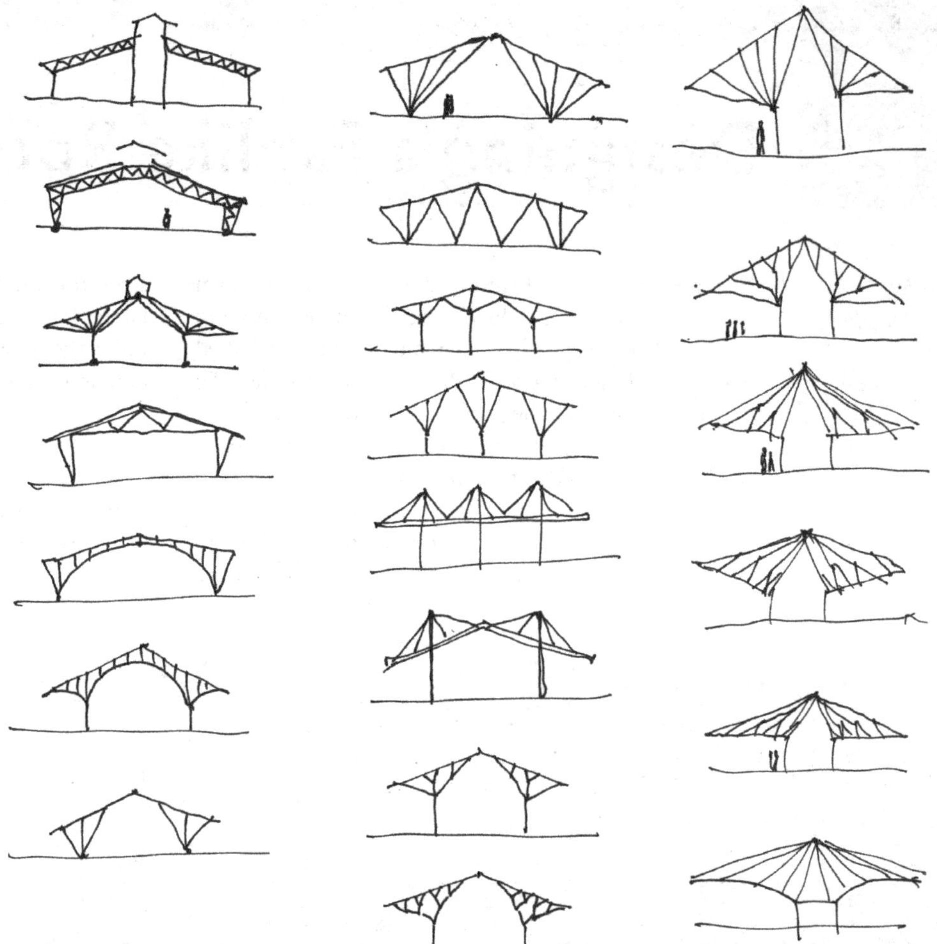

Figure 7.2 Conceptual sketches for the covered market roof structure.

FANLIKE STRUCTURES

Fanlike structures are named for their superficial resemblance to a traditional handheld fan. The most common type is the *cable-stayed structure,* a tensile form that designers use widely for bridges and roofs (Figures 7.1, 7.3). The compressive versions are comparatively rare and are very limited in scale because of the tendency of long compressive members to buckle.

The radiating members of a fanlike structure may all come to a point to form a *fan* configuration, but it is difficult to join so many members at a single place. This has led to the *semifan* or *half-harp* configuration, as well as the *harp*. Figure 7.4 illustrates that member forces in any of these patterns may be found by the same graphical method we use for trusses. Other factors being equal, forces are lowest in the fan configuration and highest in the harp. The *dendriform* (meaning branching or treelike) configuration has been used in several interesting structures in both tensile and compressive versions. Both the Active Statics program and the "Form and Forces Graphical Techniques" lessons included on the supplemental site include exercises in fanlike structures that you will find instructive and helpful.

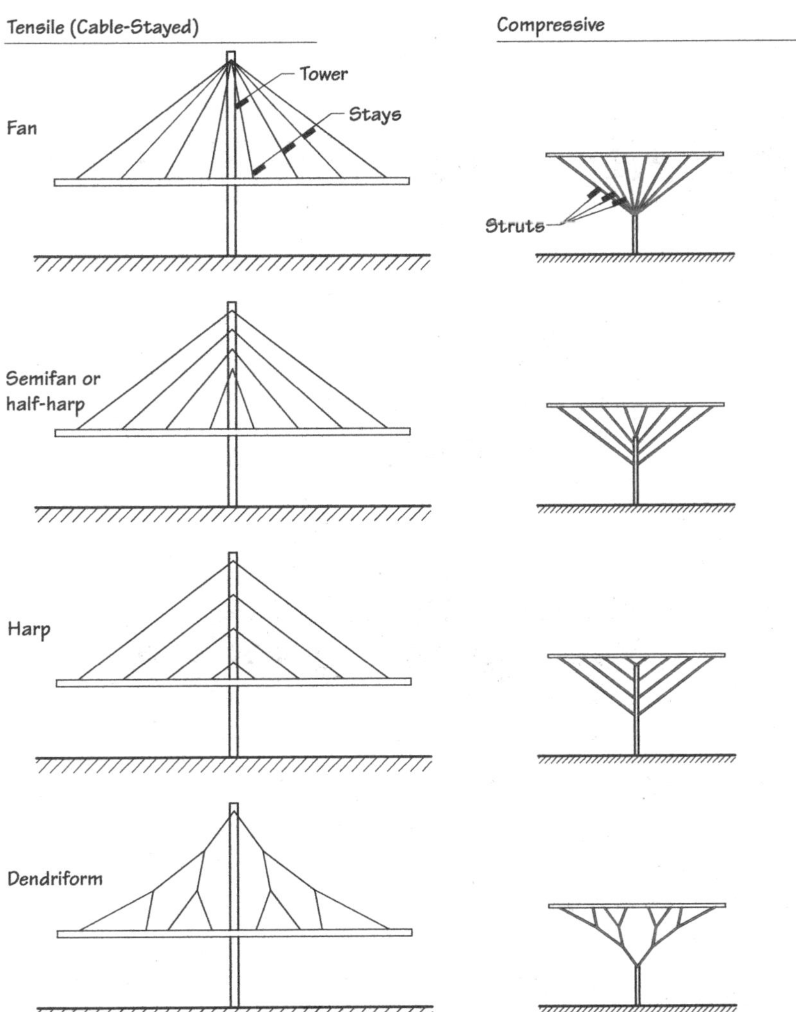

Figure 7.3 Fundamental types of fanlike structures, tensile on the left and compressive on the right. Because of buckling, compressive fanlike structures cannot be nearly as large as tensile ones. This scale disparity is even more pronounced than this drawing would indicate.

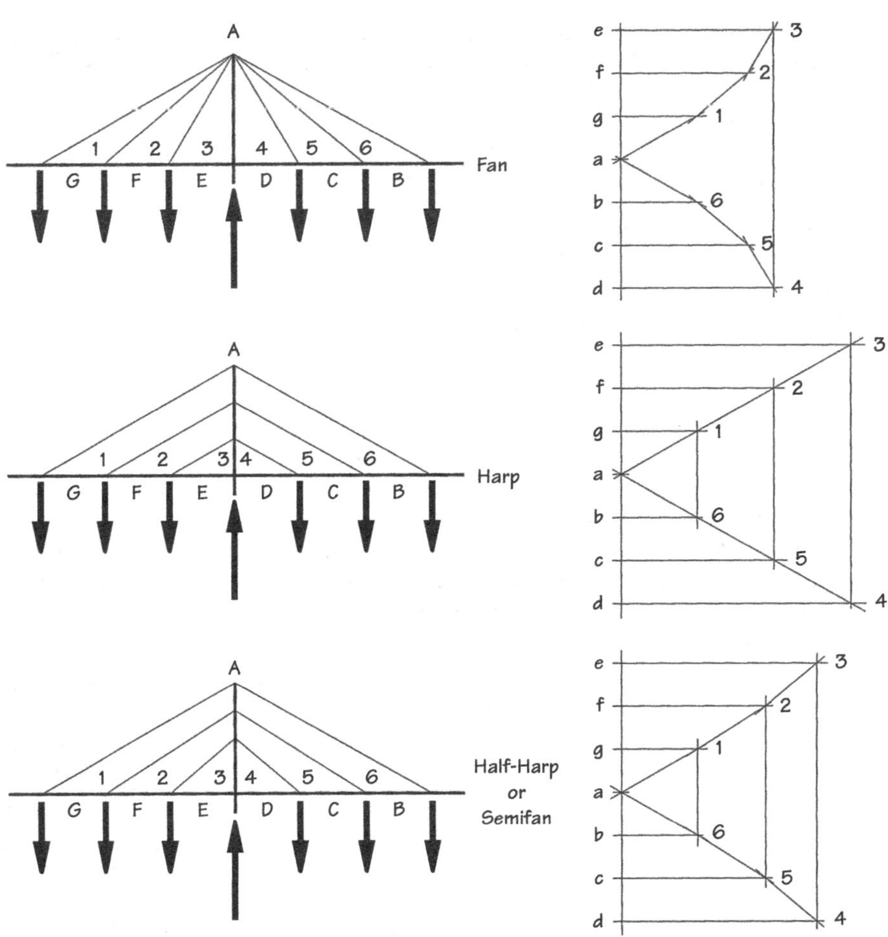

Figure 7.4 Graphical analyses of otherwise identical bridges with three different patterns of stay cables show the relative material efficiencies of the patterns. Each bridge is assumed to balance on a single reaction at its central tower, with no external forces at the ends.

CABLE-STAYED STRUCTURES

Figures 7.1, 7.5, 7.6, and 7.11 demonstrate a variety of cable-stayed bridges and roofs. Very long spans are feasible, although not nearly as long as those of suspension structures with funicular cable shapes. The longest span for a cable-stayed bridge at the time of this writing is 3,520 ft (1,088 m) in a bridge in Nantong, China. This is about half the record span for a suspension bridge. Cable-stayed construction is economical for bridge spans as short as 500 ft and is often practical for much shorter spans of both bridges and roofs. The most economical height for the *tower* (also called a *mast* or *pylon*) is between 0.2 and 0.25 of the span. It is usually assumed for purposes of preliminary design that a cable-stayed structure is supported entirely by its inclined *stays*, with little or no vertical force being transferred from the end of the span to its adjacent abutment or column. In actuality, the ends of the bridge or roof must be restrained so that they remain aligned with adjacent construction. As the design develops, forces must be taken into account at these junctions. Steel rods are less expensive and easier to connect than cables for small stayed structures. (The details and connections for rod structures shown in Chapter 1 are readily adaptable to fanlike configurations.)

We see from the horizontal lines on the force polygons in Figure 7.4 that horizontal forces accumulate in the deck of a cable-stayed structure and can be very large in the vicinity of the tower, especially if the stays are placed at shallow angles. The deck structures of long cable-stayed bridges are generally hollow box girders of steel or concrete, because the box configuration is highly resistant to buckling under these heavy compressive forces. Box girders are also excellent in resisting the torsion (twisting) that occurs in bridges that are supported by only one plane of stays when one side of the road is heavily loaded and the other is not. In smaller-scale bridges and roofs, ordinary beams of wood, steel, or concrete are often sufficient to support the deck.

Figure 7.5 The roof of the INMOS microprocessor factory in Wales is framed with shallow steel trusses. Stay rods fan out from central columns of steel tubing to support the trusses at the third points of their spans. The architects are Richard Rogers and Partners; the engineers are Anthony Hunt Associates. Photo courtesy of Pat Hunt.

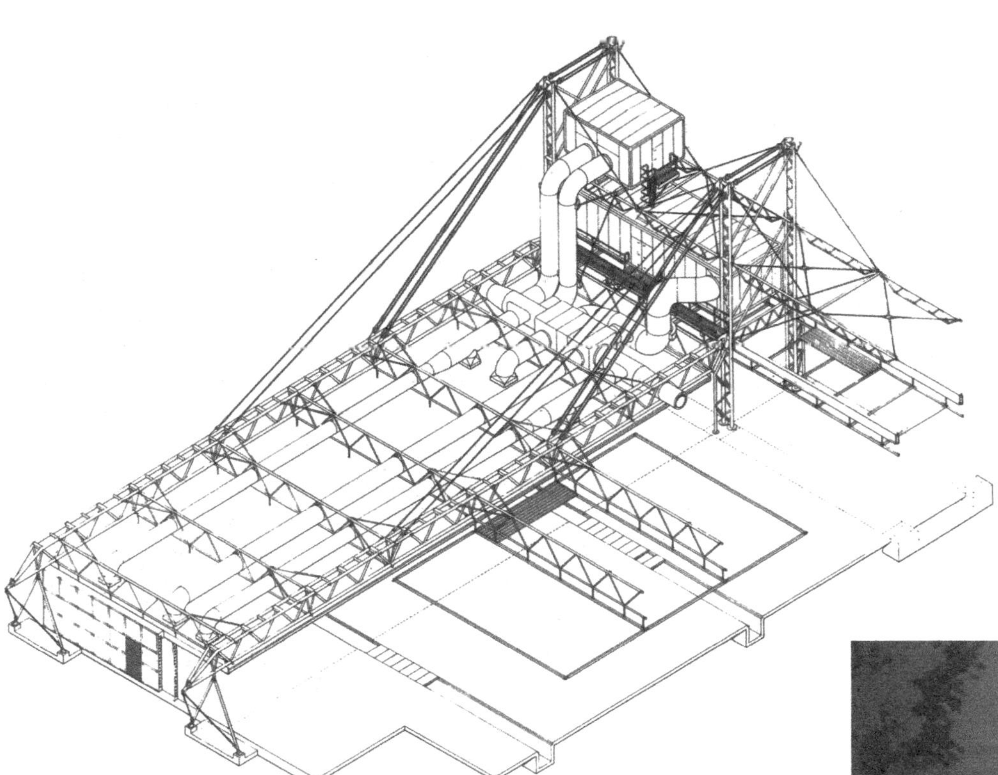

◂**Figure 7.6** A diagram of the INMOS roof discloses that each main truss is supported at four points. One end (left) bears on a pair of inclined struts. The other end bears on a trussed column. Two interior points of support are provided by inclined stays.

Source: Chris Wilkinson, *Supersheds: The Architecture of Long-Span, Large-Volume Buildings*. Oxford, UK: Butterworth-Heinemann, 2nd ed., 1996. Reproduced by permission.

▾**Figure 7.7** Architect Daniel Bonilla supported the roof of the Colombian Pavilion at 2000 Hanover Expo with treelike inverted pyramids made of teca wood.

Source: Alejandro Bahamón, *Sketch, Plan, Build: World Class Architects Show How It's Done*. New York: Harper Collins, 2005, p. 152ff.

Although the overall analyses of the forces in the stays, towers, and deck shown in Figure 7.4 are simple and straightforward, the full design process for a cable-stayed structure is complicated by a number of factors. Each stay stretches under load in an amount that is proportional to its stress and its length. Because the stays vary considerably in length, a heavy vehicle, when crossing a cable-stayed bridge, tends to cause a much larger deflection in the deck when it is distant from a tower than when close by, and a cable-stayed roof that is subjected to a uniform snow load tends to sag more at points distant from the towers than at points closer in. Each stay also sags slightly under its own weight, a factor that can be ignored during early stages of design but must be taken into account as the design develops. Every cable-stayed structure

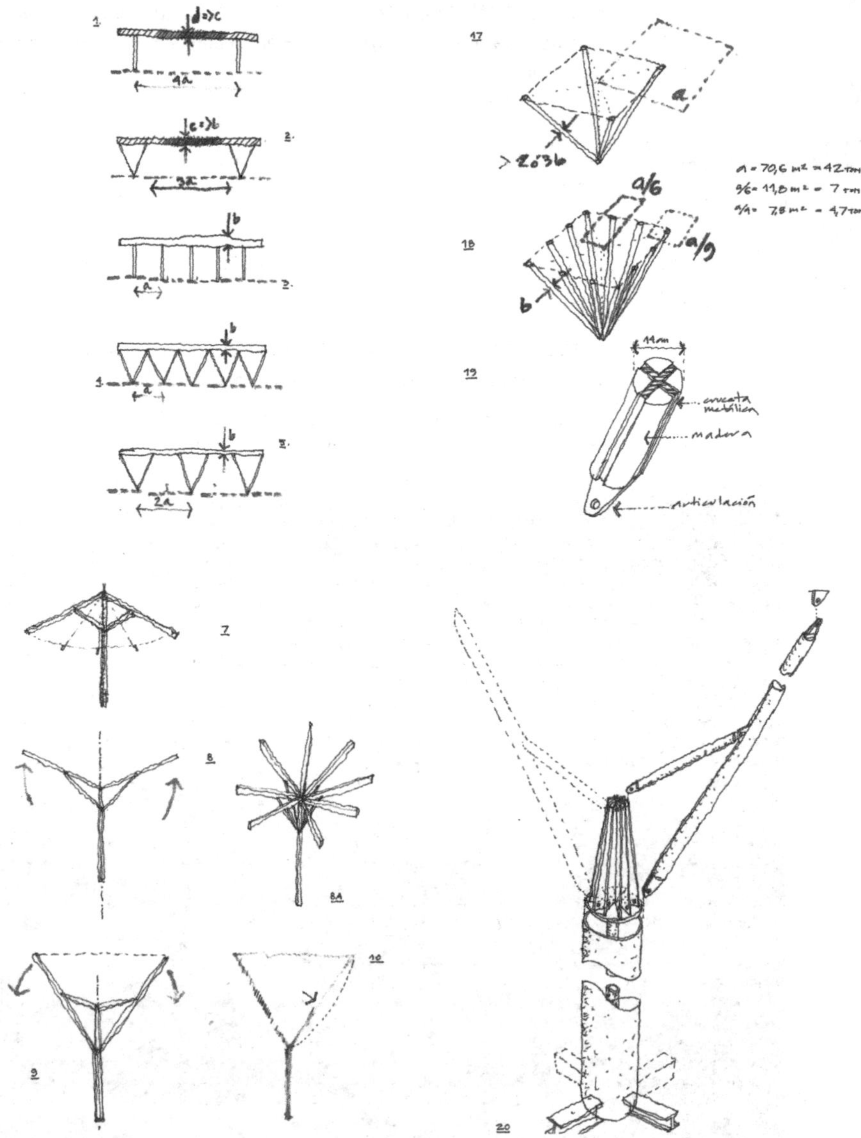

Figure 7.8 Design sketches for the Colombian Pavilion by Daniel Bonilla.

Source: Alejandro Bahamón, *Sketch, Plan, Build: World Class Architects Show How It's Done*. New York: Harper Collins, 2005, p. 152ff.

MICHEL VIRLOGEUX

French bridge designer Michel Virlogeux (b. 1946) studied in Paris and worked in Tunisia before joining the national French highway construction and design agency (SETRA). He served with this agency's technical team from 1974 to 1995 and then became an independent consultant. Among his more than 100 bridges is the well-known Normandy Bridge (Pont de Normandie) completed in 1995 between the cities of Honfleur and Le Havre, a span of over 2,800 feet (856 m)—at the time the longest in the world. He was also a consultant on the Millau Viaduct. In 2003, the International Association of Bridge and Structural Engineering recognized Virlogeux with its IABSE Award of Merit in Structural Engineering for "his major contributions leading to very significant progress in the field of civil engineering, in particular through the development of external prestressing, landmark cable-stayed bridges and composite structures."

should be designed to support its load safely even if any single stay is ruptured; this allows for accidental breakage and for maintenance replacement of cables. Oscillations of the structure under moving loads or wind loads must also be predicted and designed for.

A cable-stayed roof generally employs as many planes of stays as it requires to keep the cross spans of the roof deck components within reasonable limits. A cable-stayed bridge may be supported on one, two, or three planes of stays, depending on its width and the judgment of the designer. A single plane is often sufficient. It is usually placed along the center of the deck, between the opposing lanes of traffic, reducing the number of towers and cables and producing a bridge that often appears quite slender and daring. Bridge decks more than 120 ft wide have been supported successfully by a single plane of stays (Figure 7.9). At this width, the roadway must cantilever more than

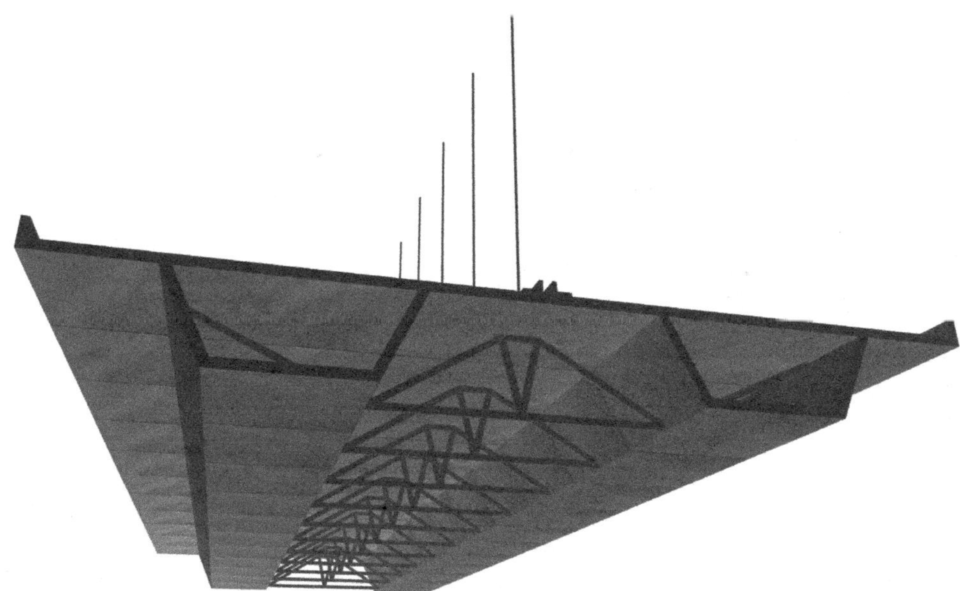

▲**Figure 7.9** A cutaway view from below of the deck of the Chesapeake and Delaware Canal Bridge, constructed in 1994 to the design of the Figg Engineering Group. The main span is 750 ft. The single central plane of cables supports a roadway that is 127 ft wide. Two box girders, each 12 ft deep, are made up of precast concrete segments that are held together longitudinally with posttensioned steel tendons. Precast concrete transverse trusses bring the loads of the roadway to the stay cables.

60 ft in each direction from the plane of the stays, and torsional resistance of the deck becomes important. In a bridge, the depth of a *box girder* that is supported by a single plane of cables is typically about one-tenth of the width of the deck.

Most cable-stayed bridges can support themselves throughout the construction process. The *balanced cantilever method* of erection, illustrated in Figure 7.10, is most common. Deck sections, typically 20 to 25 ft long and coordinated in length with the spacing of the stays, must be added symmetrically on both sides of the tower to maintain equilibrium at all stages of construction. The tower must have sufficient rigidity to resist overturning and torsion that may be caused by high winds and unbalanced loads during construction. In other situations, temporary supports may be needed (Figure 7.11).

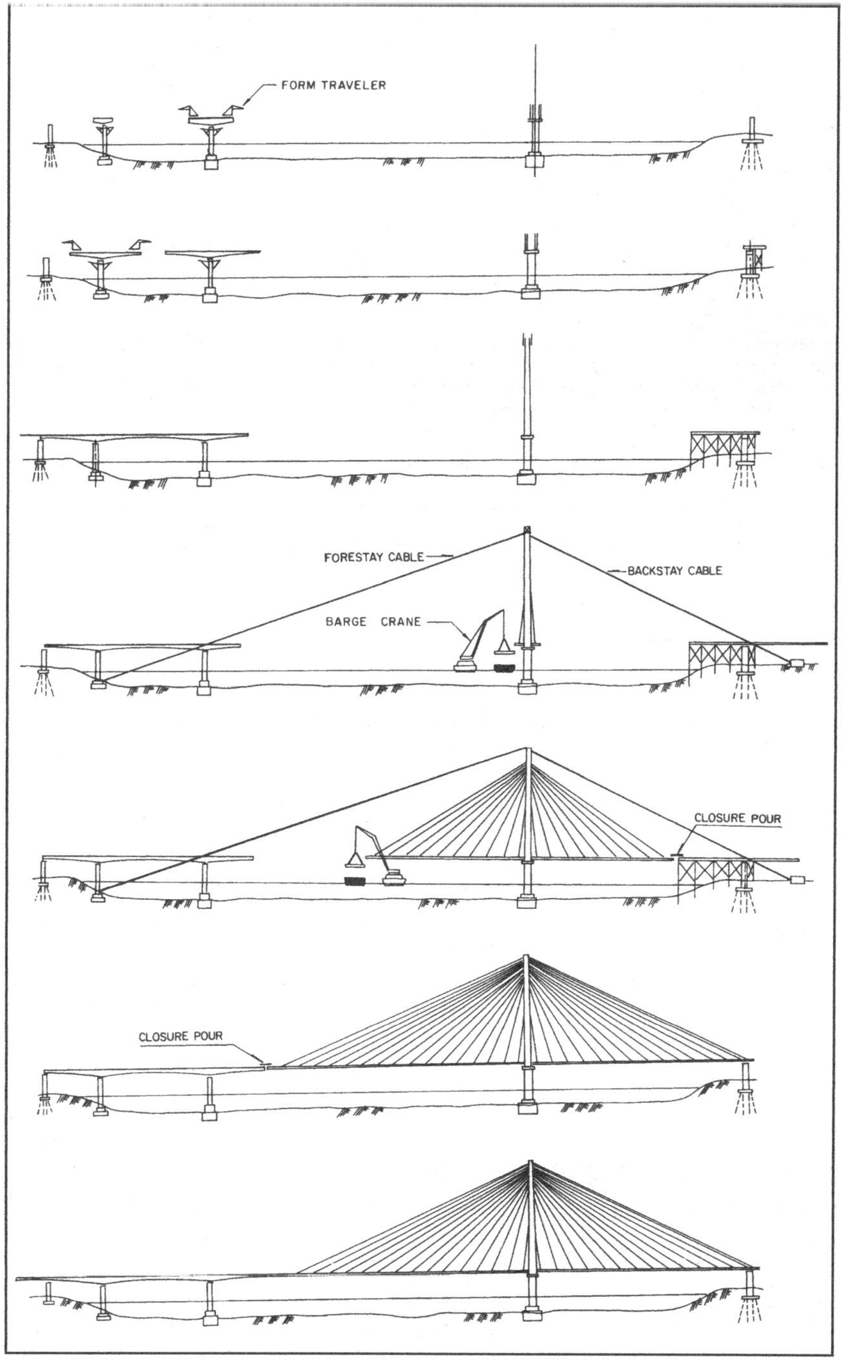

▶**Figure 7.10** The balanced cantilever method of erection as applied to the East Huntington Bridge between West Virginia and Ohio, designed by Arvid Grant and Associates, engineers, and built in 1987. The main span is 900 ft.

Source: *PCI Journal*, Precast/Prestressed Concrete Institute, Chicago, Illinois.

▲ **Figure 7.11** Temporary support towers were used in the construction of the Millau Viaduct. Photo courtesy of Ben Johnson.

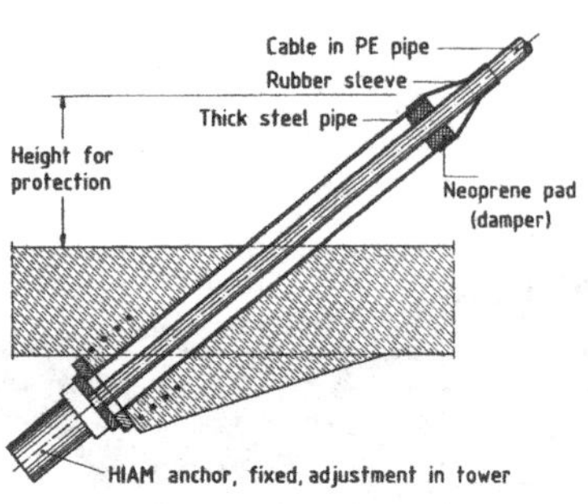

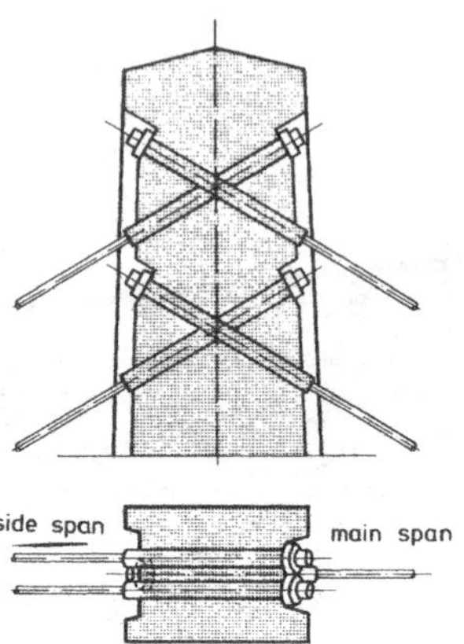

▶ **Figure 7.12** Typical details of a concrete cable-stayed bridge.

Source: *PCI Journal*, Precast/Prestressed Concrete Institute, Chicago, Illinois.

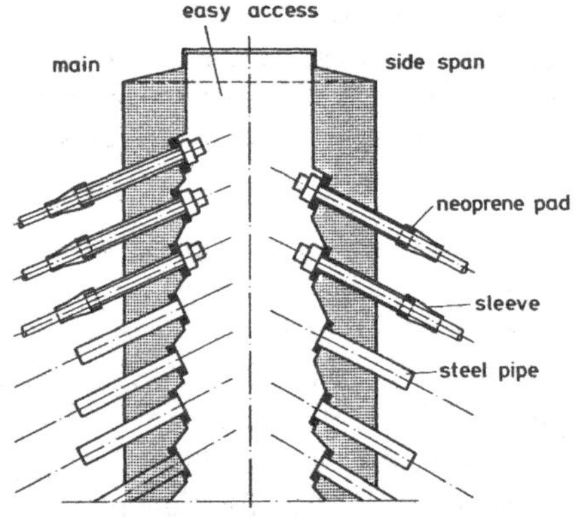

Figure 7.12 shows typical details for a cable-stayed bridge with a concrete tower. The deck is often precast in segments at a nearby casting yard. The deck segments are hoisted into place and joined with steel prestressing tendons that are threaded through longitudinal openings cast into the concrete. Alternatively, the deck may be cast in place. The stays are high-strength steel cables, usually encased in a plastic or metal covering that is filled with grout to protect against corrosion. After erection, small adjustments in stay lengths may be made at their anchors or at the tower, as provided for by the designer.

A CABLE-STAYED BRIDGE WITH COUNTERWEIGHT

The Alamillo Bridge in Seville, Spain, resists the pull of its single harp of stays with a heavily *counterweighted* tower (Figures 7.13 and 7.14). Just how heavy does this tower need to be? In Figure 7.15 we conceptualize a graphical method for answering this question. The form diagram (a) is based on the geometry of the actual bridge, but for the moment we simplify the analysis by assuming that there are only four stay cables. We divide the deck into four equal segments, with each of the four cables fastened to the center of one segment. We assume that the roller at the right end of the deck bears no load. The tower is similarly divided into four parts, each tied to a cable at its centroid. We assign a gravity load to each segment of the deck.

The force polygon, Figure 7.15b, is constructed by first drawing the partial load line, *ae*, that represents the deck loads. Starting with *ab4* and finishing with *de1–2,* we draw equilibrium polygons for the four nodes of the deck. The four segments of the sloping line *1a* represent the equal tensile forces in the four stays. The horizontal lines represent the axial compressive forces in the deck segments, all as indicated by Bow's notation.

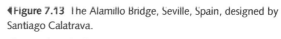

◀**Figure 7.13** The Alamillo Bridge, Seville, Spain, designed by Santiago Calatrava.

Photo: Edward Allen.

▼**Figure 7.14** Understanding the Alamillo Bridge: In a symmetrical cable-stayed bridge (a), the weights of the two spans balance one another. If one span were tilted up to become a counterweight (b), its weight would have to be increased to compensate for the reduction of moment arm. In the actual bridge (c), the tower and counterweight merge to become a single member.

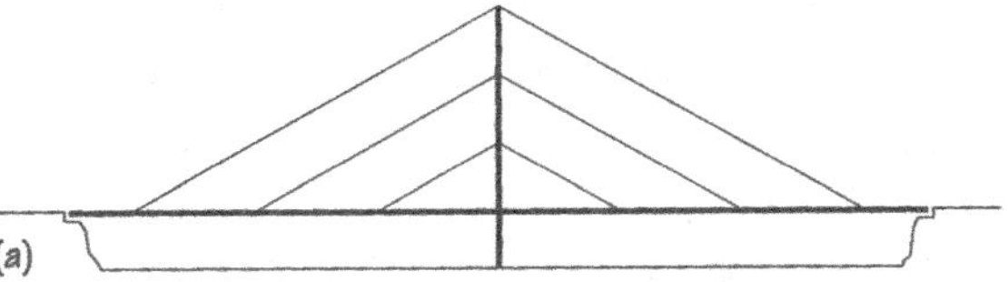

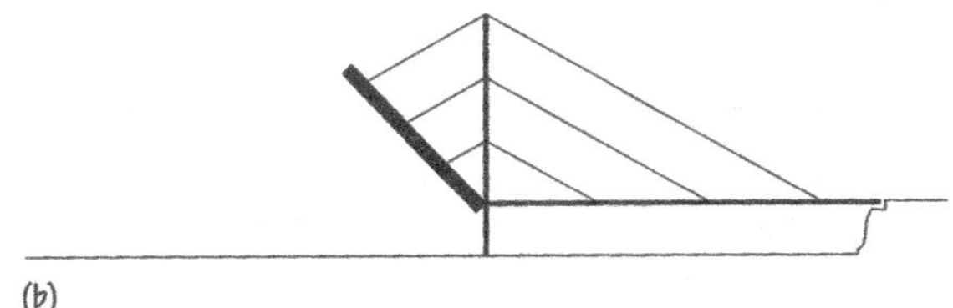

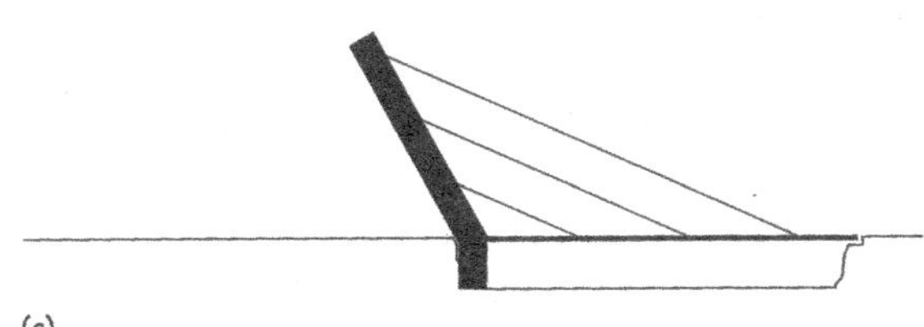

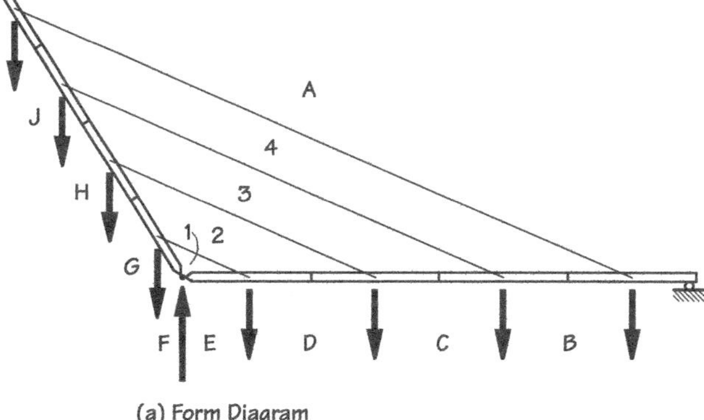

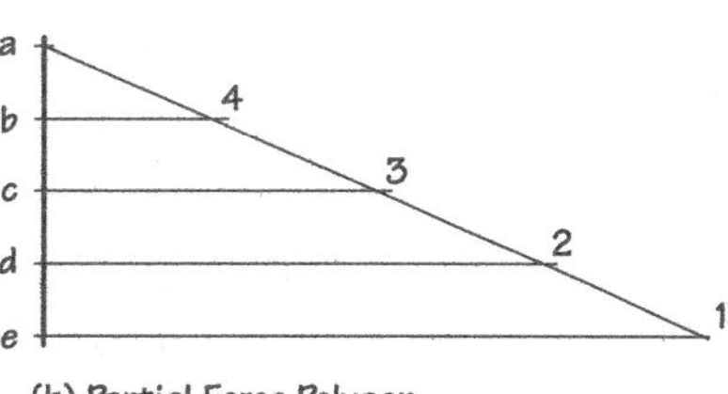

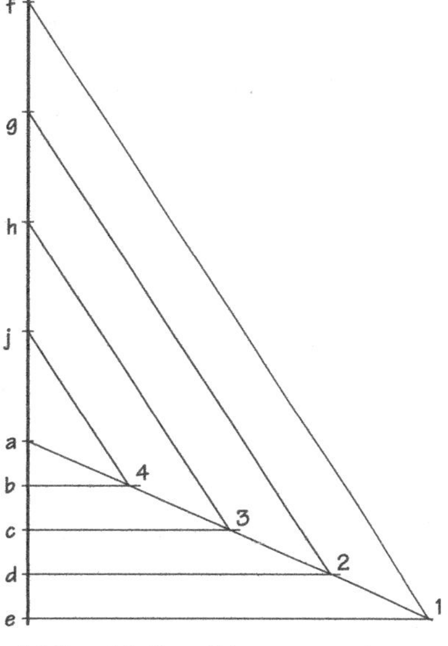

Figure 7.15 Simplified analysis of the Alamillo Bridge.

We complete the simplified analysis in Figure 7.15c by examining the forces that act on the sloping tower. Steeply sloping lines *f1* through *j4* are drawn parallel to the axis of the tower and represent the axial compressive forces in its four segments. They intersect a vertical extension of the original load line at points *f* through *j*, dividing it into the weights that are required in each segment of the tower to maintain the equilibrium of the bridge.

SANTIAGO CALATRAVA

Santiago Calatrava (b. 1951) studied art and then architecture in Valencia and earned a doctorate in engineering from the ETH in Zurich in 1981. His work derives formal inspiration from anatomy and nature, yet his designs are often based on graphical understandings of forces. His completed projects invariably go beyond bare solutions to engineering problems to express and dramatize the solutions' forms. He frequently includes in his buildings major elements that physically move or transform or that appear to be in a state of suspended animation. After winning the 1982–1983 competition to design a Zurich railway station, he designed and built, among many other projects, a range of pedestrian bridges in Barcelona, Seville, Bilbao, and other locations, and additional railway stations in Lucerne, Lisbon, and Lyon. Some of his more recent projects are abstractions of how the human torso twists and bends in various poses; like architects and engineers since Leonardo, Calatrava uses anatomical proportions to inspire forms and connections, even incorporating moving appendages as sunshades or entry gates. Since his first American work, the Milwaukee Art Museum expansion, opened in 2001, Calatrava's bridges and sculptural architectural designs have been proposed for an ever expanding list of sites in the United States, from Dallas to Lower Manhattan. The widespread popular appeal of Calatrava's works has broadened the public appreciation of structural expressionism. "Calatrava understands that even people with no architectural or engineering training have an intuitive understanding of the built physical environment. . . . [T]hrough his use of our common-sense knowledge to read latent forces and potential movement, Calatrava invites the viewer to reflect, contemplate, and dream, and thus to become a part of the creative process" (Alexander Tzonis, *Santiago Calatrava: The Poetics of Movement*, New York: Universe Publishing, 1999 p. 230).

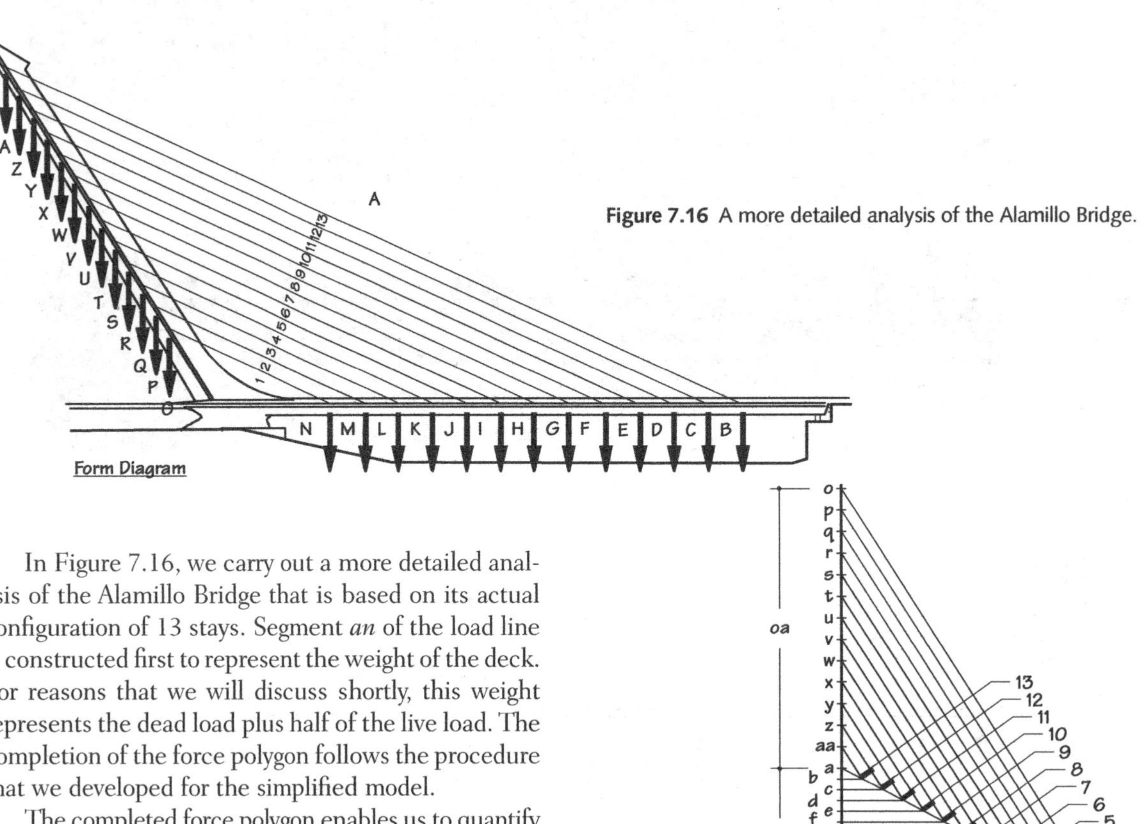

Figure 7.16 A more detailed analysis of the Alamillo Bridge.

In Figure 7.16, we carry out a more detailed analysis of the Alamillo Bridge that is based on its actual configuration of 13 stays. Segment *an* of the load line is constructed first to represent the weight of the deck. For reasons that we will discuss shortly, this weight represents the dead load plus half of the live load. The completion of the force polygon follows the procedure that we developed for the simplified model.

The completed force polygon enables us to quantify the forces in the actual bridge relative to the total weight of the loaded deck, *an*. The maximum compressive force in the deck, *n1*, is about 2.2 times the total deck weight. Each stay experiences a tension that is equal to about one-fifth of the total deck weight. The total weight of the tower, *oa*, is about 2.5 times the weight of the deck. The maximum force in the tower, *o1*, occurs at the base and is equal to about 4.2 times the deck weight.

All these conclusions are based on the assumption that the entire bridge is delicately balanced on a hinge at point *1–no* when it carries traffic uniformly distributed across its span at half the maximum intensity. The reality, however, is more complicated. The right-hand end of the bridge must be attached to its abutment to keep the roadway smooth and level at the junction of the approach road and the deck. The actual tower is not hinged at its base, but is rigidly joined to a very large foundation. Given the large cross-sectional area of the tower, the rigidities of this joint and of the tower itself are able to play major roles in stabilizing the bridge under varying live loads. If the weight of the tower were designed to balance the full dead load plus half the maximum live load, the tower would experience moderate bending in one direction when the bridge was free of traffic, and in the other direction when traffic is bumper-to-bumper. The graphical approach allows us, if we wish, to experiment freely with different loading assumptions, and with different angles, heights, and weights of towers.

TWO ALPINE BRIDGES

The bridge in Figure 7.17, high in the Swiss Alps, uses fans of cables encased in triangular concrete walls to support the roadway; the concrete casings protect the cables from weather. The tall, slender towers and the graceful curvature of the underside of the deck combine with the palpable tautness of the stays to give this bridge an extraordinarily light, soaring appearance.

Figure 7.18 is a photograph of another, older Swiss bridge that is supported by fanlike compression members of reinforced concrete below the deck. If we hold this picture upside down, we see that this structure is essentially a compressive analog of the bridge in the preceding photographs. The compressive version is necessarily much shorter in span because of the tendency of long compressive members to buckle, but the principles on which the two designs are based are much the same. In the same region as these is another compressive example executed in timber (Figure 7.19).

(a)

(b)

▶**Figure 7.17** Two photographs of the Ganter Bridge, Simplon Pass, Switzerland (1980), designed by Christian Menn. The main span is 174 m and the higher tower is 150 m tall.

Photo courtesy of Dr. Chris H. Luebkeman.

▶**Figure 7.18** The Simme River Bridge, Garstatt, Switzerland, designed by Robert Maillart and built in 1940.

Photo courtesy of ETH-Bibliothek, Zurich.

CHRISTIAN MENN

Christian Menn was born in 1927 and studied in Chur, Switzerland, and then at the ETH in Zurich, earning his diploma as Bauingenieur in 1950. After military service and engineering apprenticeships he was a research associate with Professor Pierre Lardy at the ETH; Menn became a full professor in 1971 and retired in 1992. He opened his own engineering office in Chur in 1957, and has focused almost exclusively on bridge construction. His work builds on the ETH's graphical traditions, further honing and developing strategies that Maillart pioneered. Menn's first completed bridges in Crestawald (1958) and Croet (1959) demonstrate both curved and segmented articulations of funicular arches. After completing his well-known span at Reichenau and the dramatic double viaduct at Biaschina in Italy, with parallel parabolic beam profiles between supports, he created the innovative inverted fan at the Ganterbruecke (1980), where the deck is supported by tensile reinforcements angled from above. Tensile fanlike strategies are evident in his theoretical 3,000-m span proposal that uses a composite of cable-stayed and suspension strategies. Aside from these proposals for extreme spans, most of his research has focused on problems and challenges of typical engineering practice such as striving to better analyze materials and minimize weathering and corrosion. He is recognized as continuing the fine qualities of Swiss bridge building abroad. He consulted on the Leonard P. Zakim/Bunker Hill Bridge in Boston, a large cable-stayed design completed in 2003.

Figure 7.19 Another recent creative use of fanlike supports in compression is the Vals Rhein Bridge by engineer Jurg Conzett, who studied at the ETH in Zurich and now practices in Switzerland.

Photo courtesy of Michael Ramage.

DENDRIFORM TENSILE STRUCTURES

The roof of the Patscenter manufacturing facility in Princeton, New Jersey, is suspended on steel rods from a linear series of steel pipe A-frames (Figures 7.20, 7.21). The junctions of the rods and pipes are expressively detailed with circular steel plates. In analyzing the section drawing of the building (Figure 7.21), we notice that the outermost rods (*A1* and *A9*) on each half of the central A-frame are connected to points that are already supported by columns. Therefore we designate them zero-force members. We infer that on each half, only the short rods (*1–2*, *2–3*, *7–8*, *8–9*) near midspan actually support the roof beam, a conclusion that is borne out by the much smaller diameters of the two longer rods in the photograph. The function of the other rods (*A1*, *A9*, *3–4*, and *6–7*) is to keep the suspended circular plate and, therefore, the roof beam from moving excessively if snow or wind should load the span unevenly, and to restrain the position of the ring. The connections at the ring are based on thin steel plates straddled by the clevises at the ends of the rods. Rod lengths may be adjusted by turning threaded turnbuckles on the rods. The relative compactness of the force polygon may be attributed to the generous height of the A-frame, which helps keep member forces low.

▶**Figure 7.20** The Patscenter manufacturing facility, Princeton, New Jersey. The architect is Richard Rogers, and the architect of record, Kelbaugh and Lee. The structural engineer is Ove Arup Partners; Peter Rice, lead designer.

Photo courtesy of Kelbaugh and Lee.

▼**Figure 7.21** Analysis of the Patscenter roof.

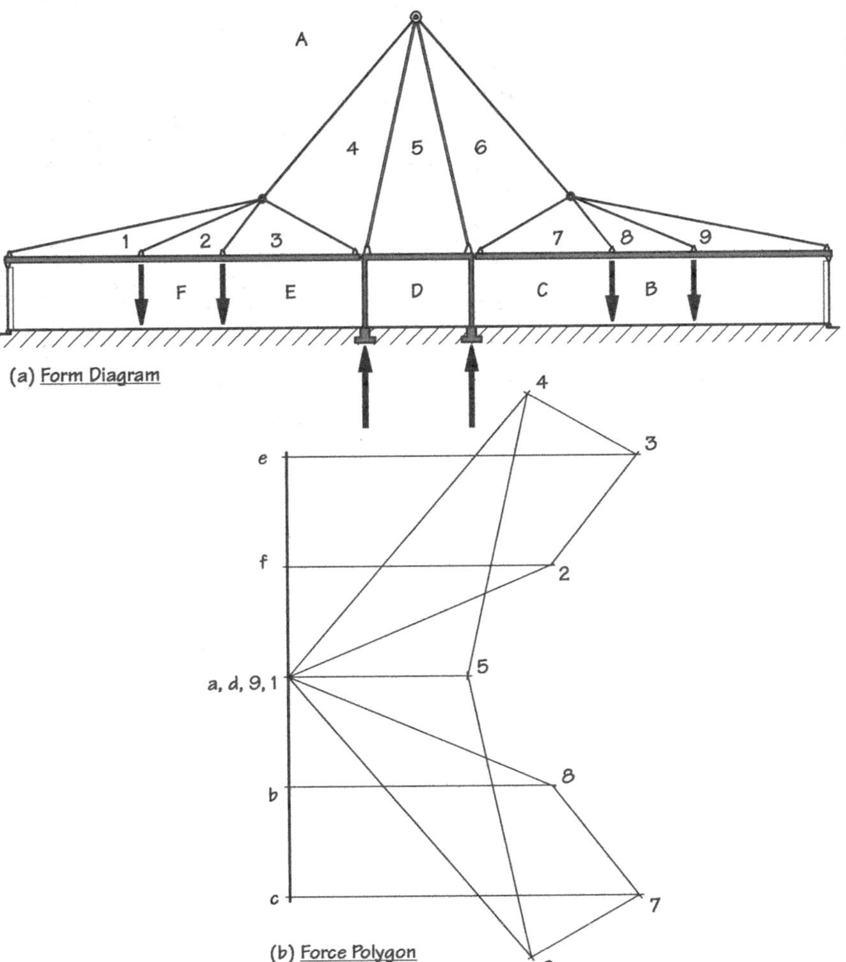

CABLE STAYS IN THREE DIMENSIONS

Stay cables need not be confined to planes. The roof diagrammed in Figure 7.22 shelters a hall for 1,000 diners, yet is supported from only two columns by three-dimensional arrays of stay cables. The roof plane is framed with a grid of steel beams running in perpendicular directions. Downward-pulling stay cables and perimeter columns stabilize the structure against wind uplift and asymmetrical loads.

The Ruck-a-Chucky Bridge is an unbuilt design for a California river crossing in rugged terrain. Jammed into a tight canyon, the road makes a U-turn on the bridge itself (Figure 7.23). The steep rock cliffs on either bank offer anchorages for numerous cables without the need for towers. In this virtuoso performance, engineer T. Y. Lin designed the locations and inclinations of the stays so that they produce longitudinal forces in the deck that are carried along the curved axis of the bridge to its abutments. Because no two cables lie in the same plane, we would not even attempt analysis of this bridge by graphical means, but our prior experience with graphical analyses of fanlike structures helps us understand how this graceful bridge works.

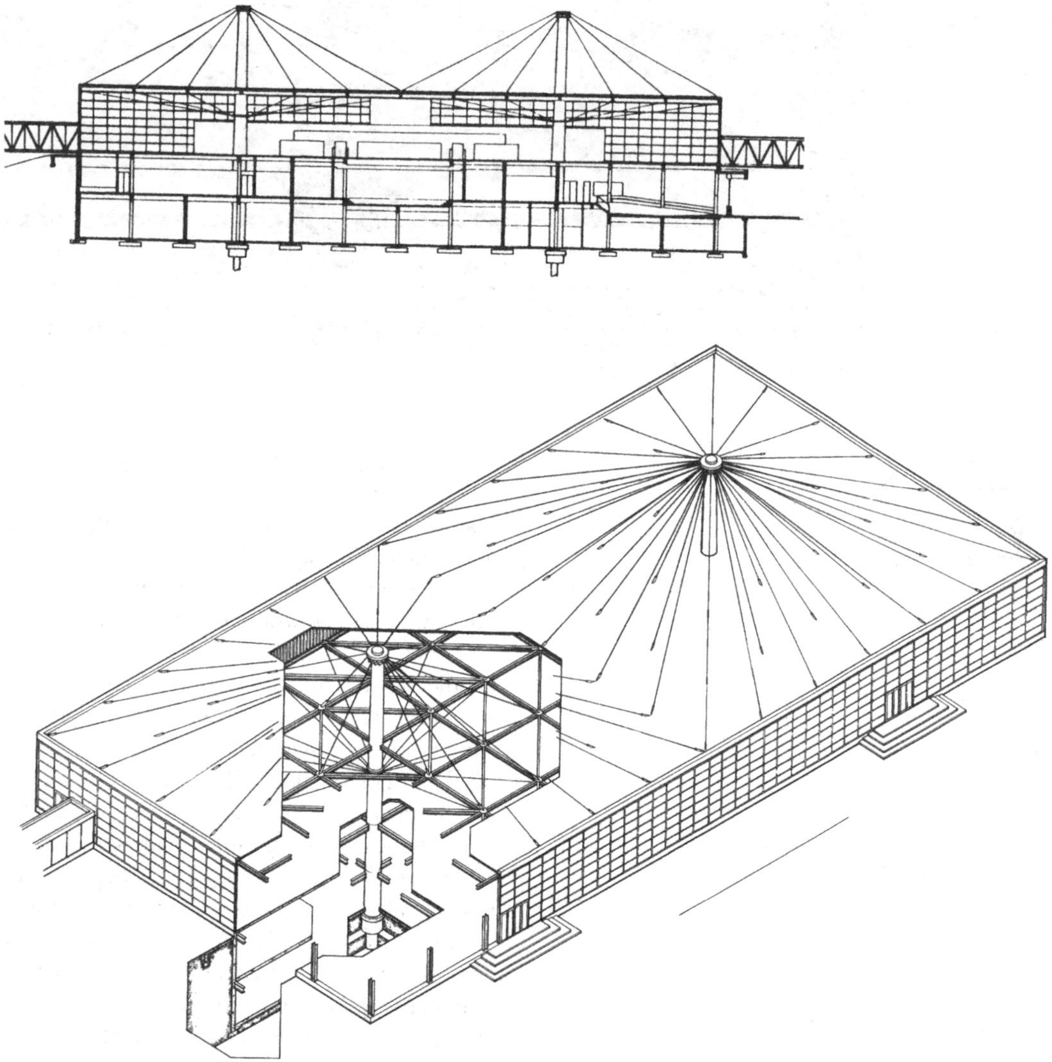

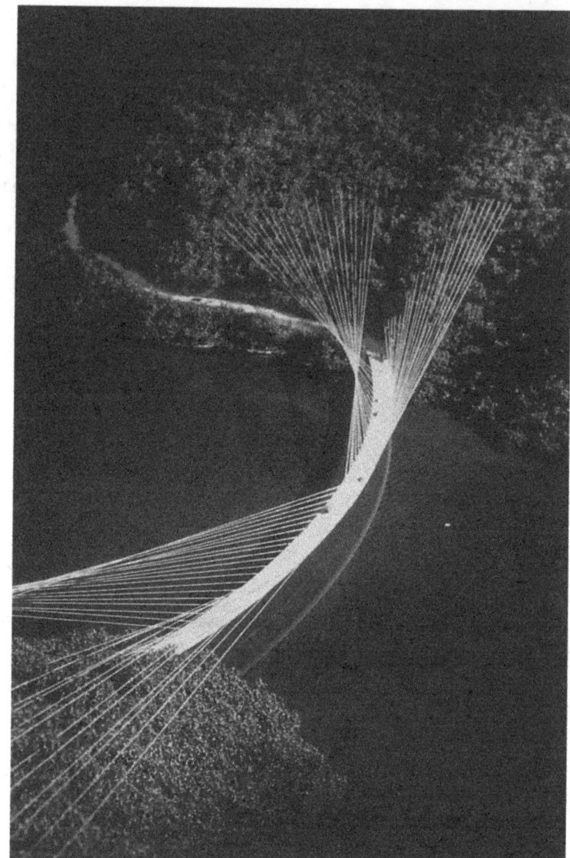

Figure 7.23 Aerial view of a model of the Ruck-a-Chucky Bridge project.

Photo courtesy of the designer, T. Y. Lin.

Figure 7.22 Diagrams of the Baxter Laboratories dining hall, Deerfield, Illinois. The architects and engineers are Skidmore, Owings and Merrill.

Source: Andrew Orton, *The Way We Build Now: Form, Scale, and Technique* By permission of the publisher, Chapman and Hall. Reproduced by permission.

Fanlike tensile structures reveal their behavior to us through their forms (Figures 7.24). Their cables and towers are visible conduits of forces, resulting in highly expressive shapes that most people find pleasing and satisfying.

COMPRESSIVE FANLIKE STRUCTURES

The compressive fans that architect Alvar Aalto designed for the Town Hall of Saynatsalo, Finland, in the twentieth century were not without precedent (Figure 7.25). The nineteenth-century English engineer Isambard Kingdom Brunel built a number of railway bridges in which the track is supported by fanlike arrangements of timbers on top of stone masonry piers (Figure 7.26). These represent conceptually an inversion of the cable-stayed bridge. Their action is analyzed in Figure 7.27. Clockwise reading of joint names confirms that all the timbers in the fan are in compression. Forces are low because the timber struts are steep and the spans are short.

▲**Figure 7.24** The 2004 Olympic Stadium in Athens, Greece, designed by Santiago Calatrava to support canopies over the seating via a fanlike arrangement of cables connecting to longitudinal arches.

Photo courtesy of Inge Kanakaris-Wirtl.

◀**Figure 7.25** Smaller compressive fanlike support under the roof of the meeting chamber that Finnish architect Alvar Aalto designed for the Town Hall in the small village of Saynatsalo.

Photo courtesy of Scott Waddell, intern architect, EYP/Architecture and Engineering.

Figure 7.26 A nineteenth-century timber railway bridge in Britain, designed by engineer I. K. Brunel.

Photos courtesy of Great Western Railway Museum, Swindon, England.

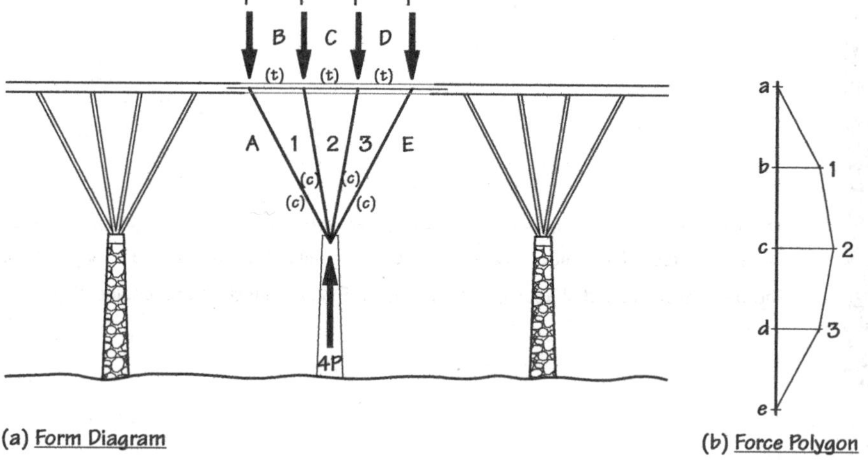

(a) Form Diagram

(b) Force Polygon

Figure 7.27 Analysis of one span of the bridge in Figure 7.26.

The lesson "Designing a Fanlike Structure" on the supplemental site is an important exercise in manipulating the form of a structure to minimize member forces while developing an exciting appearance. The optimization is done through a simple but surprisingly powerful analysis that deals with only three forces. This three-force analysis is applicable to many kinds of structural problems and will be helpful in understanding the remainder of this chapter.

DEVELOPING THE DESIGN OF THE MARKET ROOF

Having assimilated this background information on fanlike structures, let us return to the design of a roof for a produce market, the project explored in conceptual sketches at the beginning of this chapter. The town has provided a flat urban site measuring 100 by 288 ft, all of which is to be under roof. The market building will be a single space without any interior partitions. Toilets are already provided in a small building on an adjoining site. This allows us to concentrate our efforts on designing the roof itself. The town has asked that daylighting and natural ventilation be provided to maximize comfort and minimize energy expenditures. The fire chief has suggested a steel frame structure with fire suppression sprinklers to minimize chances of a conflagration if some cartons should catch fire in a market stall.

Determining Building Code Provisions

We check the applicable building code, which for this project is the International Building Code, to determine which structural materials we can use. The market is classified by the code as Occupancy Group M, Mercantile. Our building will have a single story with 28,800 sq ft of floor area. The least fire-resistive types of construction that the code permits for a building of this size and occupancy with an automatic sprinkler system are heavy timber and exposed steel. Precast and site-cast concrete are also permitted. Because the market building will not be heated, the sprinkler system will have to be a "dry" system, in which there is normally no water in the pipes to freeze and burst them during cold weather. If a fire should break out, the flow of water to the sprinkler head or heads in the vicinity of the fire will be activated automatically.

To maintain maximum flexibility of space in the market, we want to keep the number of columns to a minimum. Yet there is not a hard-and-fast requirement that the space be free of columns. The town's program for the structure notes that it is important that it be a landmark that will draw shoppers not just because the food is good and prices are low, but also because it is a memorable space to shop.

Finding a Concept and a Shape for the Market Roof

We have made many early sketches of various types of roof structures that might fulfill this mandate. We keep coming back to the ones that were inspired by trees (Figure 7.2). These range from highly simplified concepts to more elaborate ones that mimic fairly closely the multiple branchings of trunks, limbs, and twigs. However, our trees, unlike real ones, will be two-dimensional.

We also have in mind an image of nineteenth-century market buildings with corrugated metal roofing. Metal roofing requires a slope in order to shed water. We are thinking of using a gable roof, which has two opposing, sloping planes that meet at a ridge.

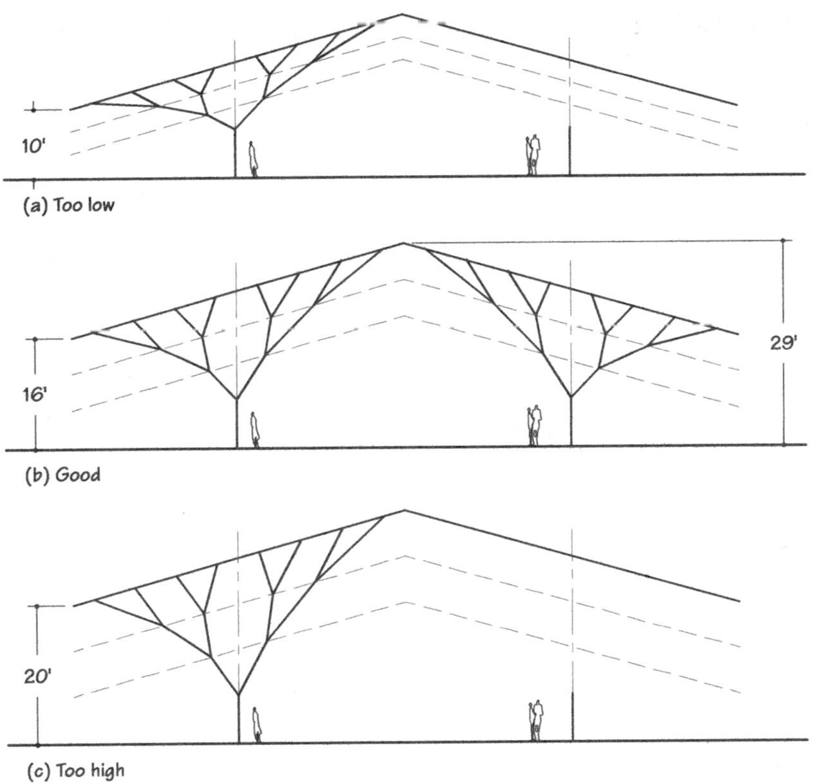

Figure 7.28 Investigating the scale and proportions of the market roof, using scaled human figures.

FINDING FORM FOR DENDRIFORM COMPRESSIVE STRUCTURES

The two-dimensional tree shapes that we favor from among the many sketches provide eight points of support to each rafter (Figure 7.28). If a purlin is placed at each of these points, the purlin spacing is a little over 8 ft. A quick check of a steel roof decking catalog tells us that the decking needs to be only 2 in. thick to achieve this span. The metal itself is a small fraction of an inch thick; the 2-in. overall thickness is achieved by corrugation.

We give some attention to how many tiers of branching members are needed to achieve the tree-like appearance that we have in mind (Figure 7.29). We try several alternatives on tracing paper overlays of the cross section of the market and decide that three tiers would look best. We consider also the proportions of the interior space. How high should the low point and high point of the roof be? How steeply should the roof slope? We would like to keep the eaves low, to give maximum protection from windblown rain, but can we fit three tiers of branches under a low roof? We try a range of heights and slopes on section overlays, always with human figures drawn to scale, to assess various possibilities (Figure 7.28). We settle finally on a design whose eaves are 16 ft high, with the roof planes rising to a 29-ft peak. The eaves are a little higher than we would like, but if they were any lower, the trees would become too squeezed in their vertical dimension. We have purposely dimensioned the trees so that the first branching occurs only 7 ft above the floor, high enough to prevent head-bumping but low enough that an adult can reach up and touch the lowest branches. It is also high enough to make it difficult for young children to climb the trees.

Finding the Form for the Trees

To channel forces axially through the branching members of a tree, we must arrange them in such a way that the axis of each member passes through the center of the tributary area that it supports. This process involves the following steps, which are illustrated in Figure 7.29:

1. We lay out a section view of half of the structure (Figure 7.29a). We draw lines to represent the floor and the bottoms of the purlins, adopting tentatively a roof slope of 15°. We add three intermediate lines parallel to the line of the purlins to divide the structure into the three equal-height tiers of branches. Below these tiers is a zone in which the trunks of the trees will be located. We draw vertical lines right and left, 50 ft apart, to indicate the boundaries of the roof surface. We draw the vertical centerline of the half-roof. This line is also the axis of the trunk of the tree, a location about which the gravity loads will balance. The trunk will occupy only the zone adjacent to the floor.
2. We decide to double the number of members at each branching point, starting from the top of the trunk and moving upward. Thus, in each tree the trunk will branch into two members in the bottom tier. These two will branch into four in the middle tier, and the four into eight in the top tier. It would be possible to branch into three, four, or more members at each tier, but it seems from our sketches that double branchings will give a pleasing visual complexity and treelike appearance without excessive cost and congestion of members. To lay out the bottom tier of branches, we mark the center of each half of the rafter. The axis of each branch begins at the top of the trunk and passes through the center of one half of the rafter (Figure 7.29b). However, we use only the portion of this axis that lies in the bottom tier.
3. Next we divide each half of the rafter in two, dividing the roof into four portions (Figure 7.29c). In the middle tier, we draw a line connecting the center of each portion of the roof surface to the upper end of the nearest branch in the tier below. The portion of each of these lines that lies in the middle tier is the axis of a member.
4. We carry out a similar operation for the top tier to provide eight points of support for the half-roof (Figure 7.29d).

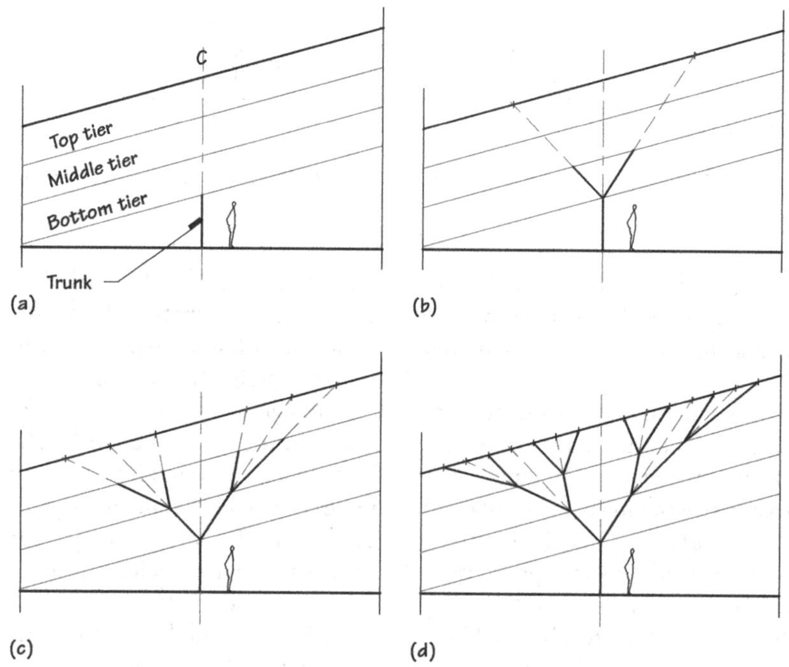

Figure 7.29 Finding a form for the tree such that its members are in static equilibrium.

Our first impression of this layout is that it is satisfyingly treelike. It appears to be quite reasonable in scale as we imagine ourselves taking the places of the figures we have drawn. Its visual complexity is pleasing, perhaps because the complexity is soon sorted out into a simple system by the eye of the viewer. The angles at which forces are supported by its members do not appear to be ones that will result in excessive internal forces.

This latter judgment needs to be backed up by an analysis of the intensities of member forces. To do this, we must determine the values of the gravity loads. The half-structure is 50 ft wide, so each of the eight loads on the diagram of the structure will have a tributary width of 50 ft divided by 8 loads, which is 6.25 ft.

We make a tentative decision to use 12-in.-deep steel wide-flange shapes for the purlins. An economical purlin span is 24 times the depth, which is 24 ft for a 12-in. depth. This dimension will be the spacing between the planes of trees, unless we choose later to alter this spacing for formal or technical reasons. The tributary area for each point of purlin support is 6.25 ft times 24 ft, 150 sq ft. For preliminary design purposes, we will assume a dead load of 30 psf and a live load of 20 psf, for a total load of 50 psf. The total load per point of purlin support is 150 sq ft multiplied by 50 psf, or 7,500 lb (7.5 kips).

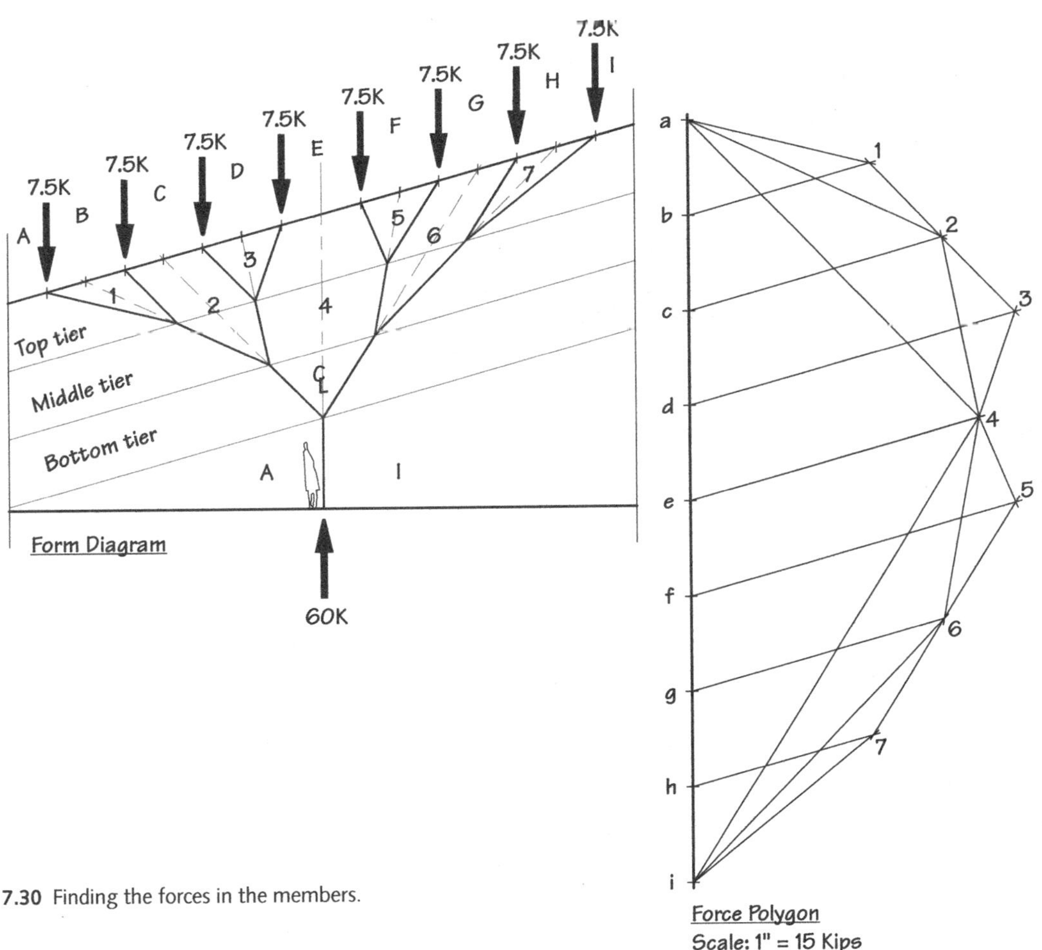

Figure 7.30 Finding the forces in the members.

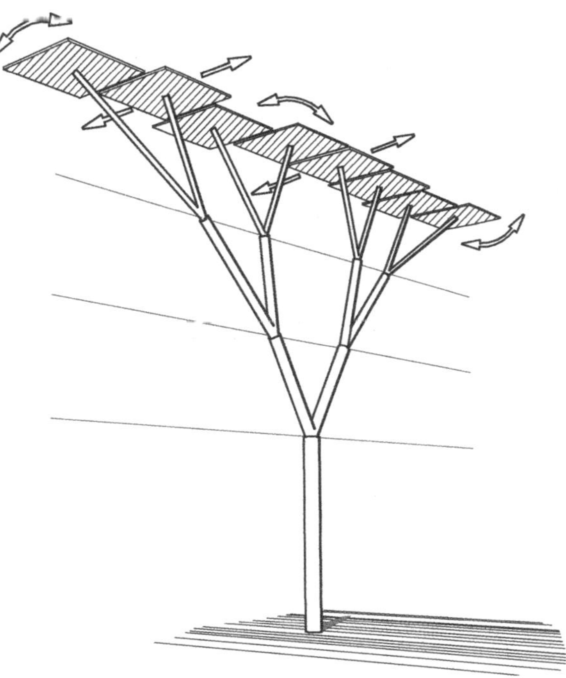

Figure 7.31 In a real tree, the tips of the branches are structurally independent and move freely in the wind.

We find forces in the members as if the tree were an ordinary truss (Figure 7.30). We apply Bow's notation and construct a force polygon. The process is interesting because it involves analysis of three different tiers of branches in three superimposed force polygons. The line *a–1–2–3–4–5–6–7–i* on the force polygon represents all the members in the top tier of branches. The line *a–2–4–6–i* represents the middle tier. And the line *a–4–i* gives forces for the bottom tier, which has just two branches. The accurate nesting of these three force polygons verifies that we have constructed a good form for the tree, one in which all forces caused by gravity loads are axial.

This structure is fundamentally a truss, even though it does not consist entirely of triangles. If we were to insert additional members so that the truss is fully triangulated, these members would prove to have zero force under the loading pattern we have assumed. From the slender proportions of the force polygon we can tell that member forces are low, even before we assign numerical quantities to any of them.

This structure looks like a tree. However, it doesn't resemble a tree in its structural actions, because the tips of its branches are connected together. If the tips were not connected, and each tip supported an independent rectangle of roof surface, and if the trunk were rigidly fixed to the floor, then this structure would behave like a tree, with each branch moving independently in the wind (Figure 7.31). If this were done, however, it would be difficult to make the roof watertight, and the deflections of the long, cantilevered branches would be very large. In trees, these

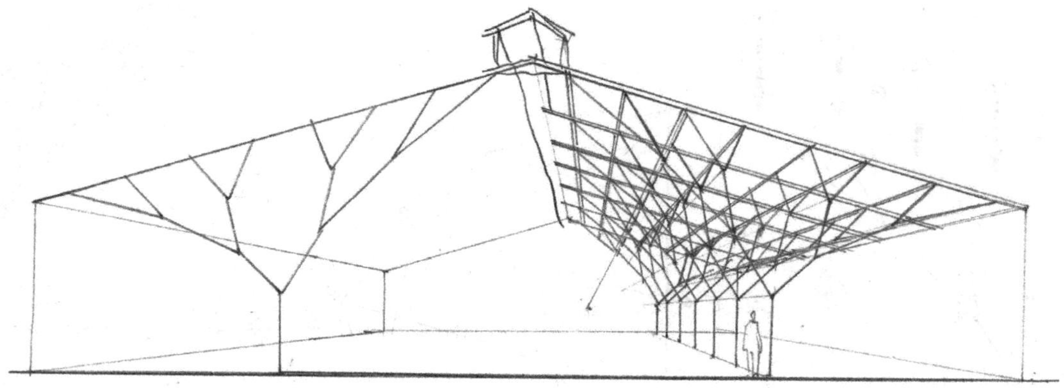

Figure 7.32 A study perspective of the market roof

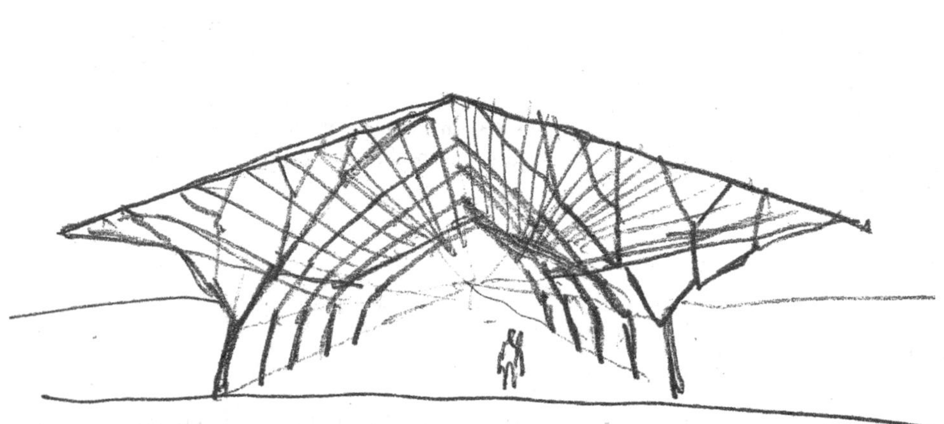

Figure 7.33 A sketch showing inclined columns.

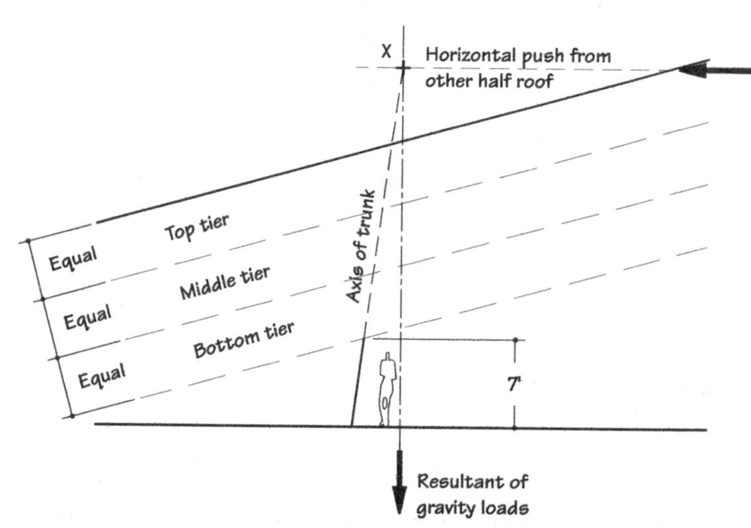

Figure 7.34 Finding the form of the tree: establishing the slope of the trunk.

large deflections are desirable because they help the tree to shed high wind and snow loads without breaking. In a building, they would be disastrous, because floors would bounce, furniture would slide across the room, and roof sections would wave like handkerchiefs in the wind.

A FORMAL REFINEMENT

We draw a full cross section of the structure and project a portion of it in perspective to judge the visual effect of the trees (Figure 7.32). They look good, but somehow the structure seems less energetic than we were hoping. An idea occurs to us: What if we were to lean the trees in each pair slightly toward each other? A quick sketch of the idea (Figure 7.33) looks promising.

This new layout involves several further decisions: How steeply should the trees lean? And how will they balance the horizontal forces that are generated by their leaning? Some experimentation on tracing paper

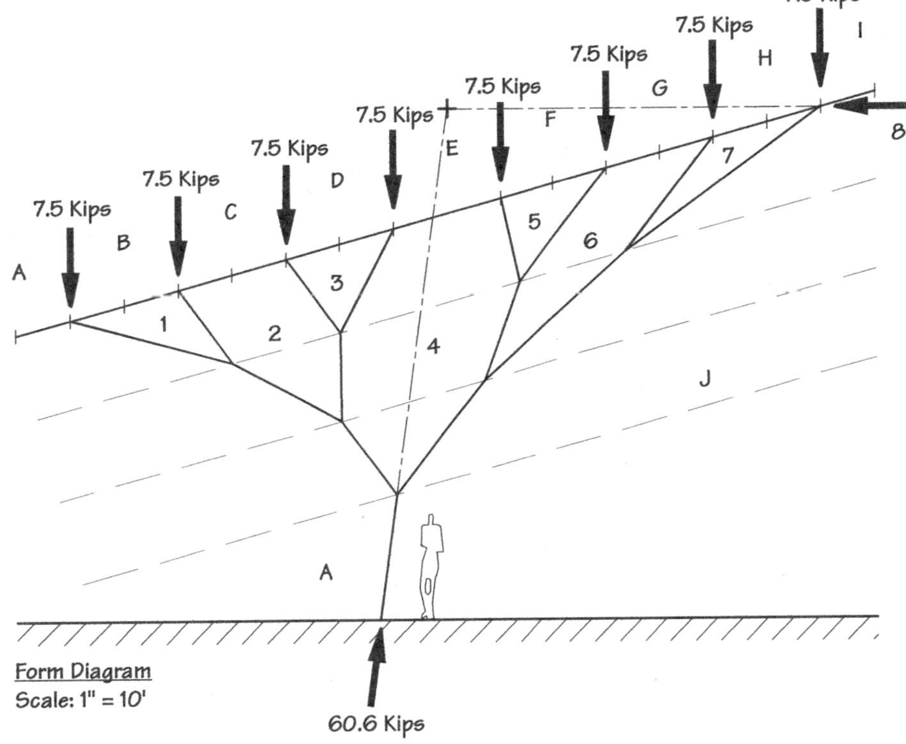

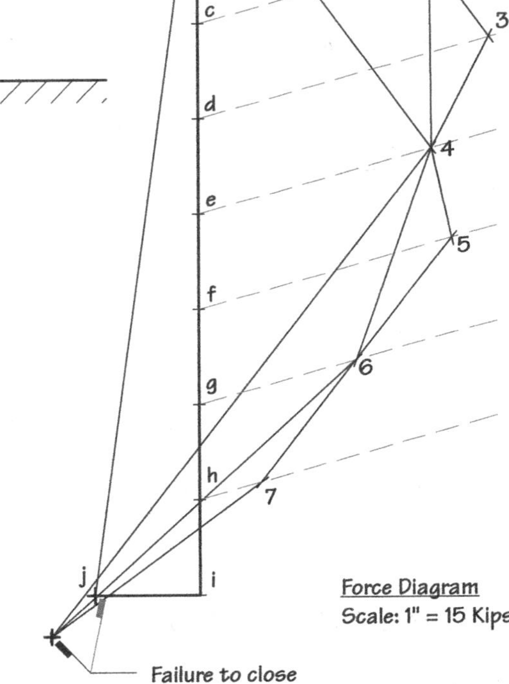

Figure 7.35 Finding a form for the inclined tree such that its members are in static equilibrium.

establishes the lean. To avoid complications, we will transfer the horizontal force through a hinge that lies at the level of the tip of the topmost branch. (If this transfer were done at the tip of the rafter, it would introduce a nonaxial force into the system). To find the axis of the trunk, we draw the line of action of the resultant of all the gravity loads. This is a vertical line through the center of the half-roof (Figure 7.34). Then we add the line of action of the horizontal push from the other half of the roof. This goes through the hinge. There is only one additional force on the half-roof: the oblique, upward push of the trunk. For the system to be in equilibrium, the line of action of this force must pass through the intersection of the other two external forces.

We make an accurate diagram and undertake a graphical analysis of this structure (Figure 7.35). The load line is a triangle, *aij*. We encounter a problem in the graphical solution: The force polygon does not close. Checking back through the procedure we have followed, we see that everything is working fine until we get to the set of branches to the right of the trunk axis. After some thought, we realize that in making the branch layout we did not take into account the horizontal thrust at the top hinge. The branches to the left of the trunk are unaffected by the thrust, but those to the right must be oriented in such a way that they act axially when subjected to the combination of the thrust and the gravity loads.

To solve this problem, we work first with the force polygon, which already includes the horizontal thrust, *ij*, in its triangular load line (Figure 7.36). The vectors for the branches in the left-hand portion of the tree, which are unaffected by the thrust, are constructed as before. We draw the vectors for the forces in the right-hand branches so that they intersect one another at the proper points and close the force polygon. When the force polygon has been completed, we return to the picture of the tree and draw the branches in its right half parallel to their corresponding vectors on the force polygon. Two of the branch intersections occur just above the sloping tier lines that we first established, but the tree remains attractive nevertheless.

DEVELOPING THE TREE STRUCTURE

As a next step in the design process, we will assign approximate sizes to the members that are longest and/or most heavily loaded. This will give us an indication of whether the structure can be made of reasonably sized pieces of material. These sizes will be refined later as analyses are made of lateral and unbalanced loadings, but they are close enough for present purposes.

The longest and most heavily loaded member in the top tier is 7*j*, which is about 14 ft long. The force in this member, as given by the force polygon, is 17 kips. The *Manual of Steel Construction* contains selection tables for steel compression members of various shapes. These tables take into account both material stress and buckling potential. We propose to use steel pipes. Pipes are available in diameters of 3, 3.5, 4, 5, 6, 8, 10, and 12 in., and in three weight ranges: Standard, Extra Strong, and Double

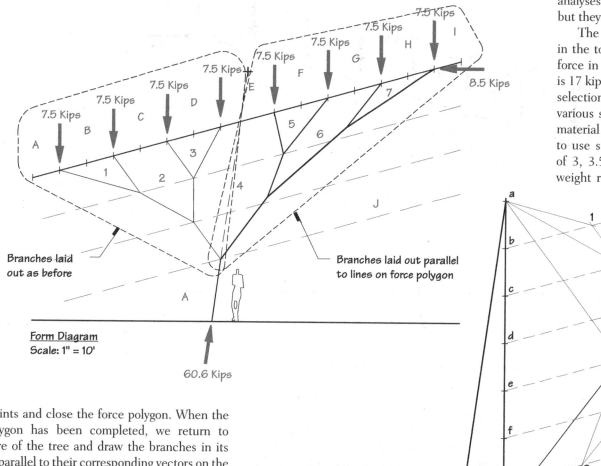

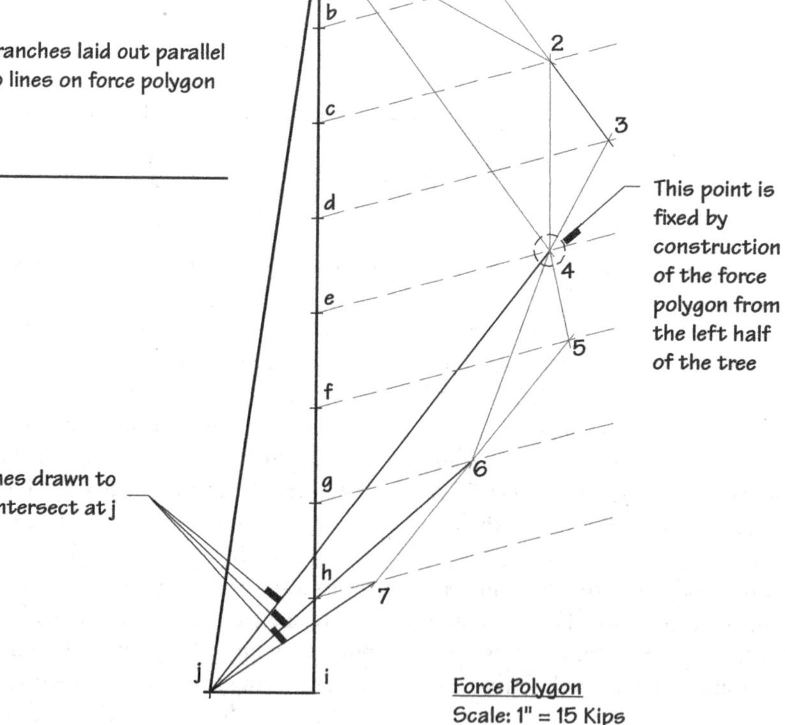

Figure 7.36 The statically correct form for the inclined tree is found by completing the force polygon first, then laying out the branches of the tree so each is parallel to its vector in the force polygon.

Extra Strong. (Standard pipe in this diameter has a wall that is 0.216 in. thick. Extra Strong pipe has a 0.3-in. wall. The third type, Double Extra Strong, has a 0.6-in. wall.) All three weights of pipe have the same outside diameter, which often makes it possible to maintain a given "look" of a member while changing its load-bearing capacity.

Entering the table for steel pipes with a force of 17 kips and a length of 14 ft, we determine that a 3-in. diameter, Standard pipe is sufficient for all members in the tier. Dropping down to the middle tier of branches, we again find that a 3-in. pipe is sufficient; and the same applies to the bottom tier. This sameness of required member sizes can be explained by the fact that although lower branches carry higher forces, they are shorter than the longest members in the higher tiers and, therefore, less likely to buckle.

The trunk is 7 ft long and carries a load of 61 kips. The load tables tell us that this requires either a 3-in. diameter Extra Strong pipe or two Standard 3-in. pipes. We have assigned these sizes based on balanced gravity loads alone. The trees will often be subjected to unbalanced snow loads and wind loads, which will require further study before the design is made final. The largest anticipated forces in the pipes will almost certainly be larger than the ones we have found in our simplified analysis. We will also need to study the buckling potential in long combinations of members, such as *4j*, *6j*, and *7j*. Some lateral bracing at the nodes may be needed. However, it seems likely that we will be able to retain the pipe diameters that we have chosen, using heavier weights of pipe where necessary.

DEVELOPING THE DETAILS

We think about potential details for the branch junctions. In larger structures made of steel pipes, custom-made steel castings have often been used for joints. These would probably be too costly for this modest structure. It occurs to us that in actual trees, small twigs grow from branches that are larger in diameter, which grow from

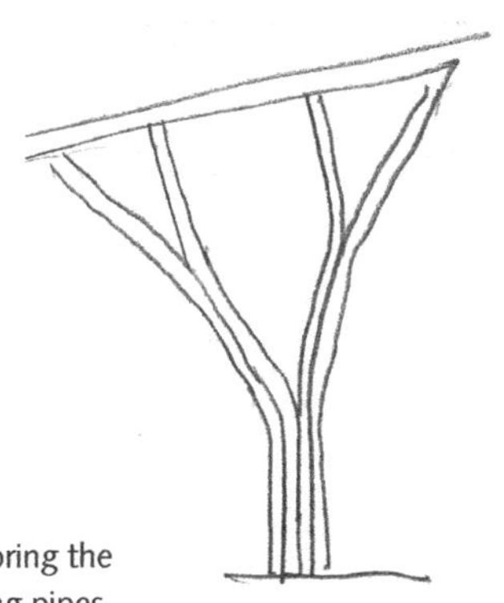

▸**Figure 7.37** Exploring the idea of accumulating pipes.

still larger branches, and so on until the ground is reached with a sturdy trunk. We could emulate this in a more formal way by starting with eight separate pipes in the top tier, each supporting a purlin. We could join these into four pairs of pipes, each pair welded together in parallel, in the middle tier, and two groups of four parallel pipes each in the bottom tier, finishing with a trunk that is made up of all eight pipes running in a parallel array. Where pipes change direction, we will simply bend them into a curve of comfortable radius. The bent portions of the pipe will experience eccentric forces, but we expect more detailed analysis to show there is sufficient excess capacity in each pipe to resist these forces successfully. This approach holds the promise of looking more sturdy and presenting an even more interesting geometry and texture than a single-pipe tree (Figure 7.37). There are steel fabricators that specialize in bending structural shapes, for whom precision bending of these small-diameter pipes will be an easy task.

If the bent pipes are nested tightly together and welded into a single component, any slight irregularities in straightness or curvature will let light pass between the pipes in a ragged, unattractive, chaotic pattern. We can avoid this problem, and make assembly of the trees easier at the same time, by inserting steel spacers between adjacent pipes to create intentional, inch-wide slots. Slight irregularities in the pipes will not be discernable if this is done, and the regular light

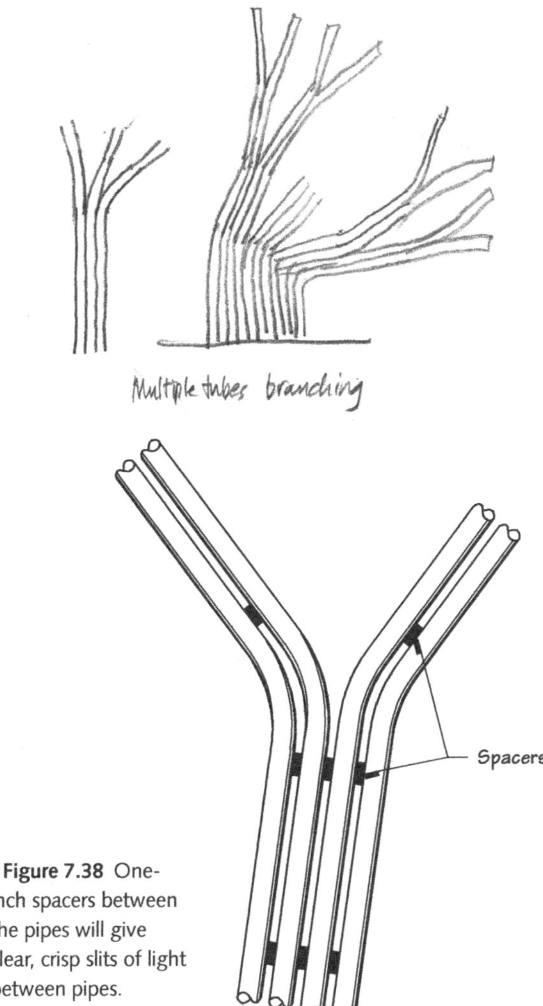

▸**Figure 7.38** One-inch spacers between the pipes will give clear, crisp slits of light between pipes.

patterns of the inch-wide slots should enhance the appearance of the structure considerably. We indicate tentatively spacers made of 1/2-in. steel plate, each 1 in. by 2 in. These would be inserted and aligned every 2 ft or so, the exact pattern for the entire tree to be worked out on paper prior to assembly (Figure 7.38). A tree-size template will be built horizontally on the floor of the fabricator's shop. This will include vertical tabs or blocks to align the pipes, and seats to support

▼**Figure 7.39** Adding longitudinal braces to stabilize the roof.

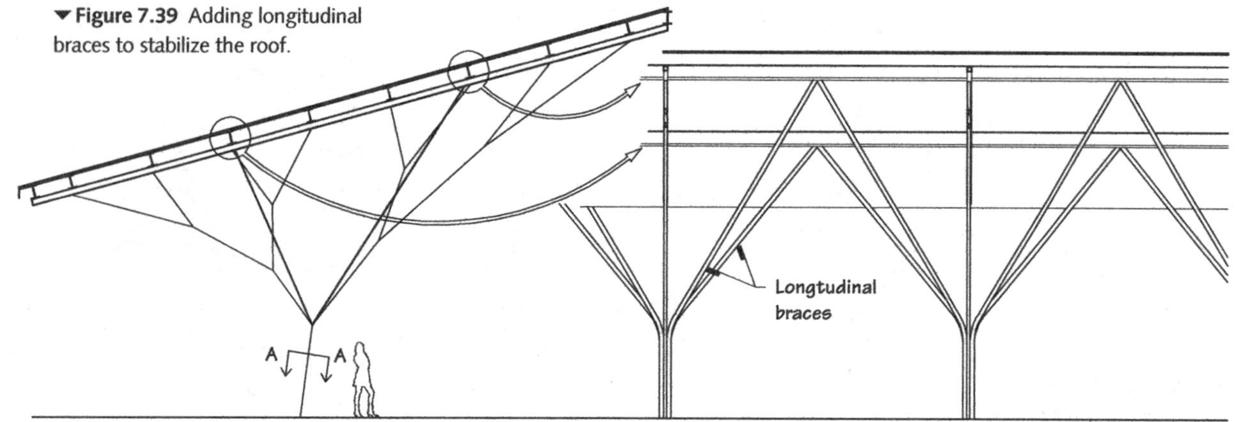

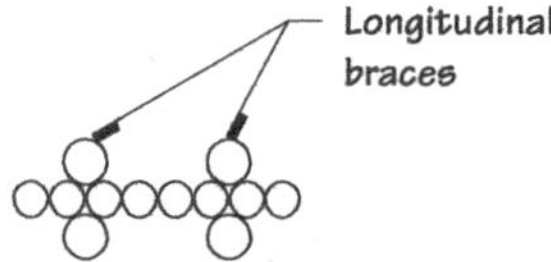

(c) Cross Section AA
(Through Trunk)

the spacers until they have been welded. We note that a tree will be too large to transport by truck, so we will work with the fabricator to divide the trees into shop-fabricated portions that can be trucked to the site and assembled there.

The pairs of trees will form three-hinged arches that are stable against lateral forces in the short direction of the building. The structure will also need longitudinal bracing. In creating this bracing, we would like to continue with the tree motif rather than introduce another geometric theme into the design. After much experimentation, we decide to do this by bringing pipes from the floor alongside the primary pipes, then obliquely from the tops of the trunks to the centers of the purlins to create a set of longitudinal K-braces (Figure 7.39). A brace need not occur at every purlin—we decide in a preliminary way to bring braces only to the third purlins in from the ridge and the eave. This bracing will also serve to prevent buckling of the trees in their weak direction by restraining lateral movement at the top of the trunk.

We are not prepared at this time to assign sizes to the braces, but once drawn in a 3-in. diameter, they look to us to be too slender in relation to their length. We increase the braces' diameter to 6 in., subject to later analysis in detail. We tuck the bottom ends of these braces in among the primary pipes of the trunk.

To this point we have been carrying in mind solutions to the provision of daylight, ventilation, and shelter around the edges of the building from wind-driven rain and snow. Now it is time to put these solutions onto paper and integrate them with the design of the structure. We propose to provide daylighting and ventilation by means of a long, transparent roof monitor with louvered sides at the peak of the roof, over the hinges.

Vendors and shoppers at the edges of the building are exposed to wind-driven rain and snow unless we provide walls of some type to prevent wind from moving at full force through the interior of the building. We propose walls of steel decking supported by exposed, treelike framing made of steel pipes (Figure 7.40).

If we do not insulate the roof, it will become very hot on sunny days and cause thermal discomfort for the shoppers and vendors below, via direct radiational heating. We make a note to provide several inches of rigid insulation board in the roof.

In trying to sketch in three dimensions how the interior space of the market will look, we find it almost impossible to keep track of all the pipes that are flying through space at a variety of angles. Freehand perspectives are not precise enough to give an accurate impression of how the space will look, so we construct a quick, approximate solid model on the computer and print a perspective view (Figure 7.41). We find the resulting visual patterns satisfying.

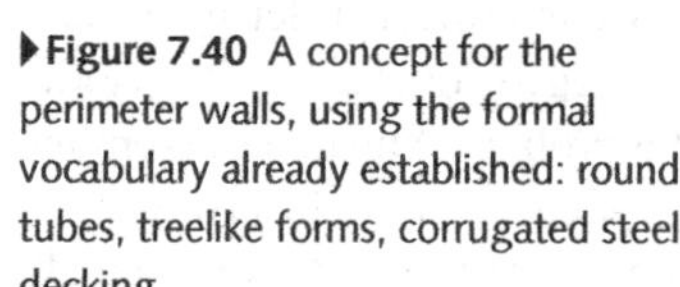

▶**Figure 7.40** A concept for the perimeter walls, using the formal vocabulary already established: round tubes, treelike forms, corrugated steel decking.

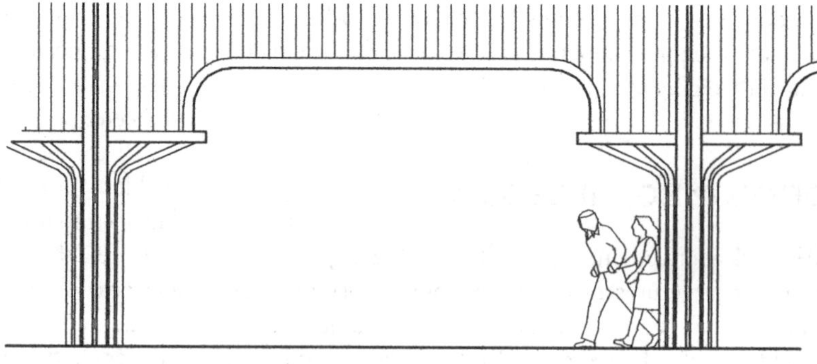

Partial Elevation
Scale: 1/8" = 1'

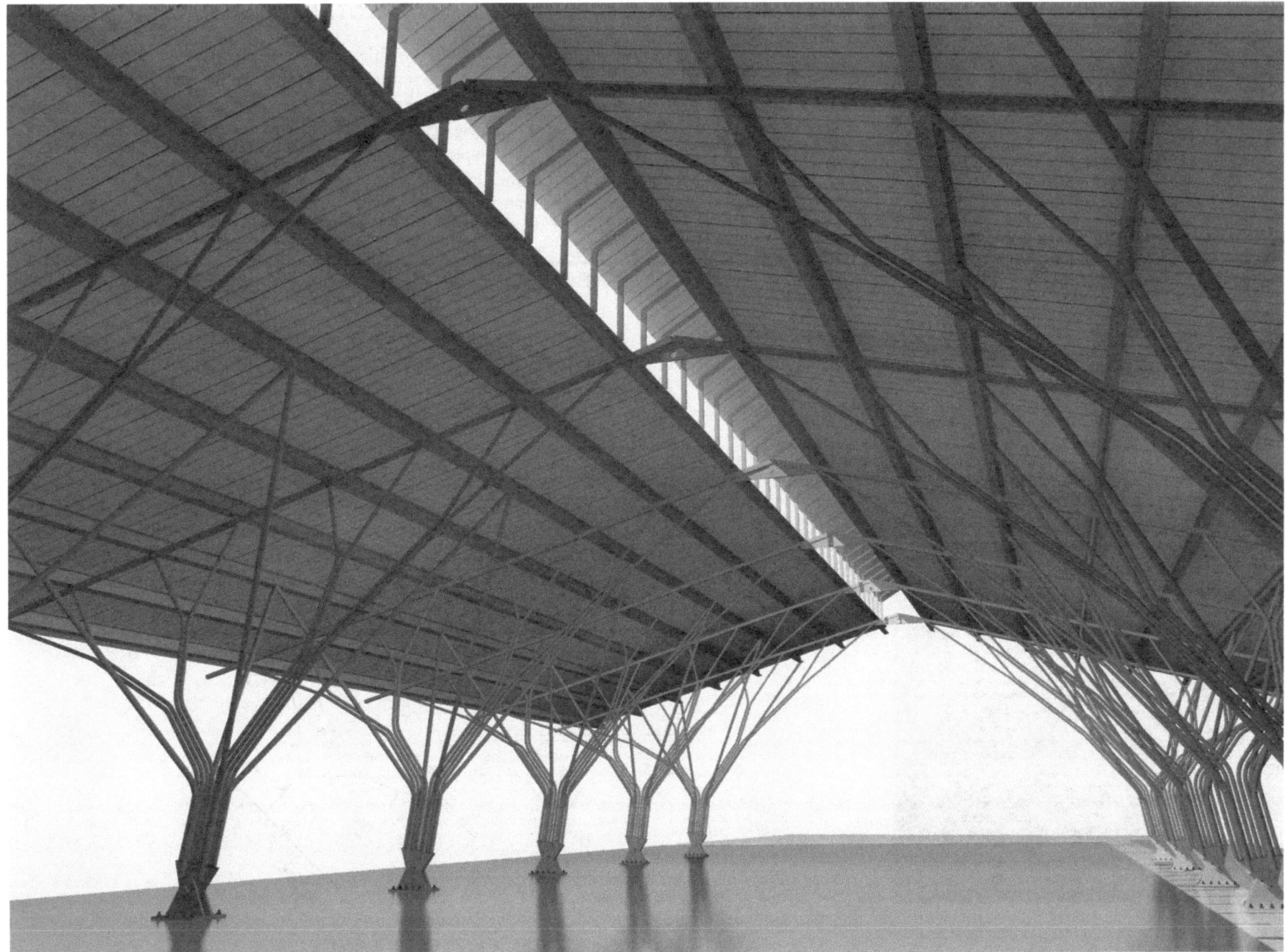

Figure 7.41 An interior view of the market roof we have created.

Design and image by Boston Structures Group.

Figure 7.42 Architects Van Gerkan Marg and Partners created three-dimensional steel trees for the roof structure of the Stuttgart Airport.

Photo: Edward Allen.

THREE-DIMENSIONAL DENDRIFORM STRUCTURES

We have developed the design of a tree structure that lies in a plane. With only a bit more work, we can design three-dimensional trees like those in the Stuttgart Airport (Figure 7.42). To do so, we first lay out a typical tree by aiming the branches in each tier at the centers of the areas they support. Then we generate enough auxiliary views to give the true size and shape of every branch in the tree (Figure 7.43). This sets the stage for two-dimensional graphical analyses to determine the member forces.

ANOTHER CHALLENGE

Although we are pleased with the dendriform structural system that we have developed for the covered market, we would like to try a cable-stayed solution to the same problem and compare the two schemes before deciding which to build. You have been appointed to lead the design team in preparing this design. You may use any material that you wish for the compressive elements and the roof deck structure—wood, concrete, steel. You are free to take inspiration from any of the structures shown in this chapter, or to develop an original form of your own invention.

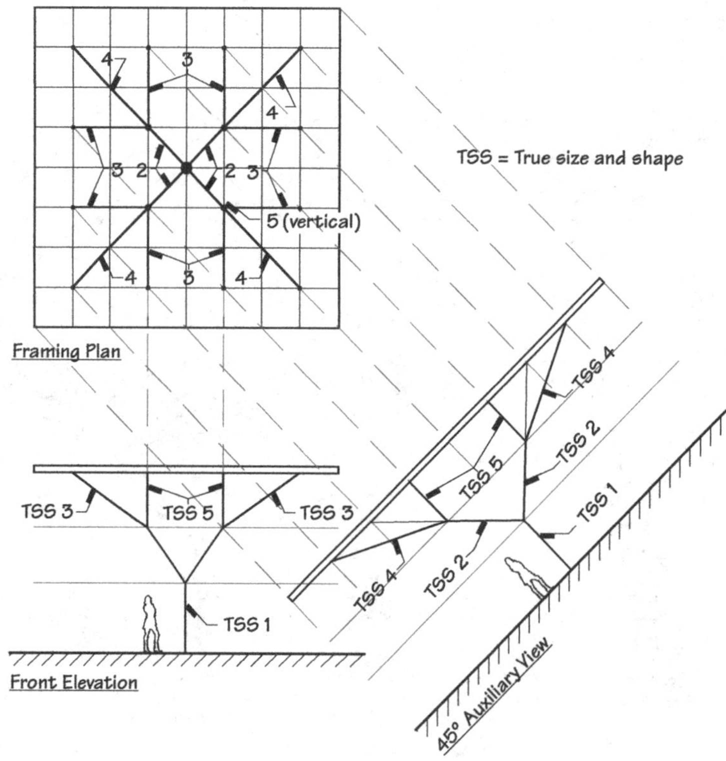

Figure 7.43 Using an auxiliary view to help find good form for a three-dimensional tree.

Exercises

1. We observed in Figure 7.21 that members 3–4 and 6–7 restrained the position of the steel rings. If these members were omitted, what would be the resulting form the structure would have the tendency to take? What are the advantages and disadvantages of subtracting these members? What about adding other members?

2. The National Park Service requests a "signature" bridge to mark the entrance to the canyon trail for which we designed a number of bridges in Chapter 1. The proposal is to create a fanlike design spanning 120 ft, as sketched in Figure 7.44. The topography leaves limited space for a tower and backstay. (A central tower is out of the question because of the depth of the canyon.) As shown in Figure 7.45, we have started by using five pairs of stays to support two side beams at intervals of 24 ft, starting at 12 ft from each end. We use a semifan pattern to facilitate connections to the tower. This form is arbitrary: We simply drew a structure that seemed right in its shape and proportions. Your task is to analyze its performance and determine whether and how its form can be improved.

From the initial graphical analysis shown on Figure 7.45, we see that a considerable force, *cd*, accumulates in the deck and must be transmitted to the soil at the right-hand end of the bridge. We also notice that the tower and backstay forces, *cb* and *ab*, respectively, are extremely high relative to the total load on the bridge, *da*. Using Worksheet 7A from the supplemental site (reproduced here as Figure 7.45), how could we change the inclination or height of the mast and backstays to lower the forces and optimize the design without losing its visual character?

We would like to use rectangular steel tubes and either rods or cables. At the base, we develop a sketch detail for the junction of the tower, deck, and cliff (Figure 7.46a). At the end of the deck farthest from the tower, we develop a detail that does not transmit any load to the cliff, but will restrain the bridge from moving laterally or upward. What other considerations would you apply to this design based on wind and uplift forces?

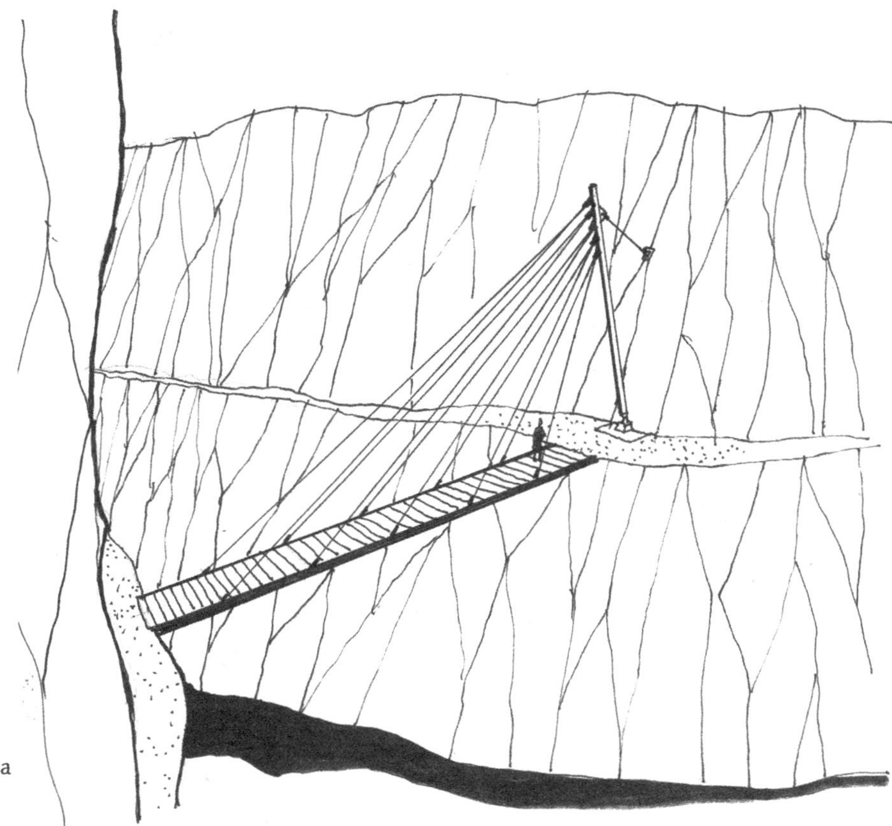

Figure 7.44 An early design sketch for a cable-stayed pedestrian bridge.

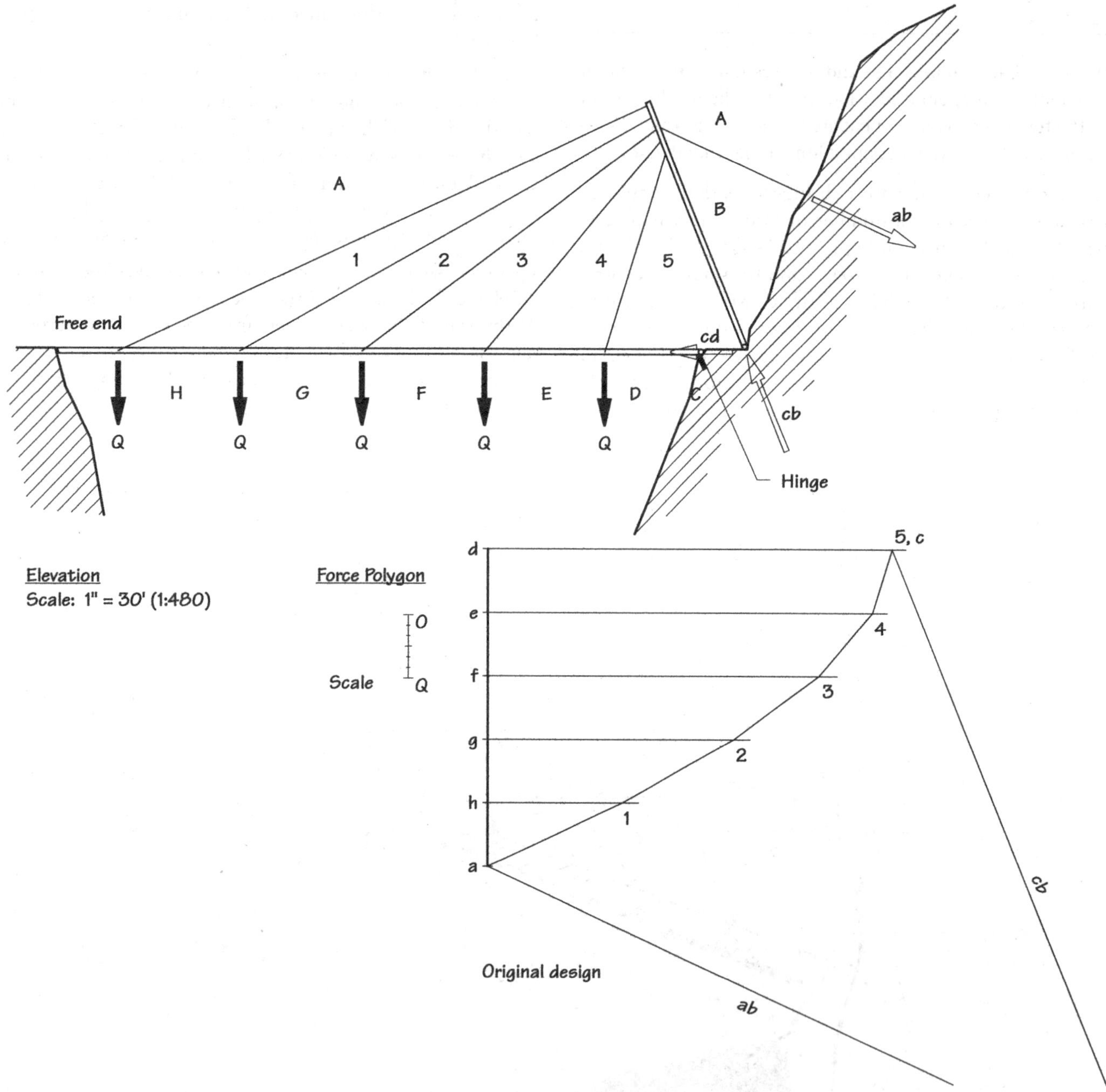

Figure 7.45 Graphical analysis of the original configuration for the pedestrian bridge.

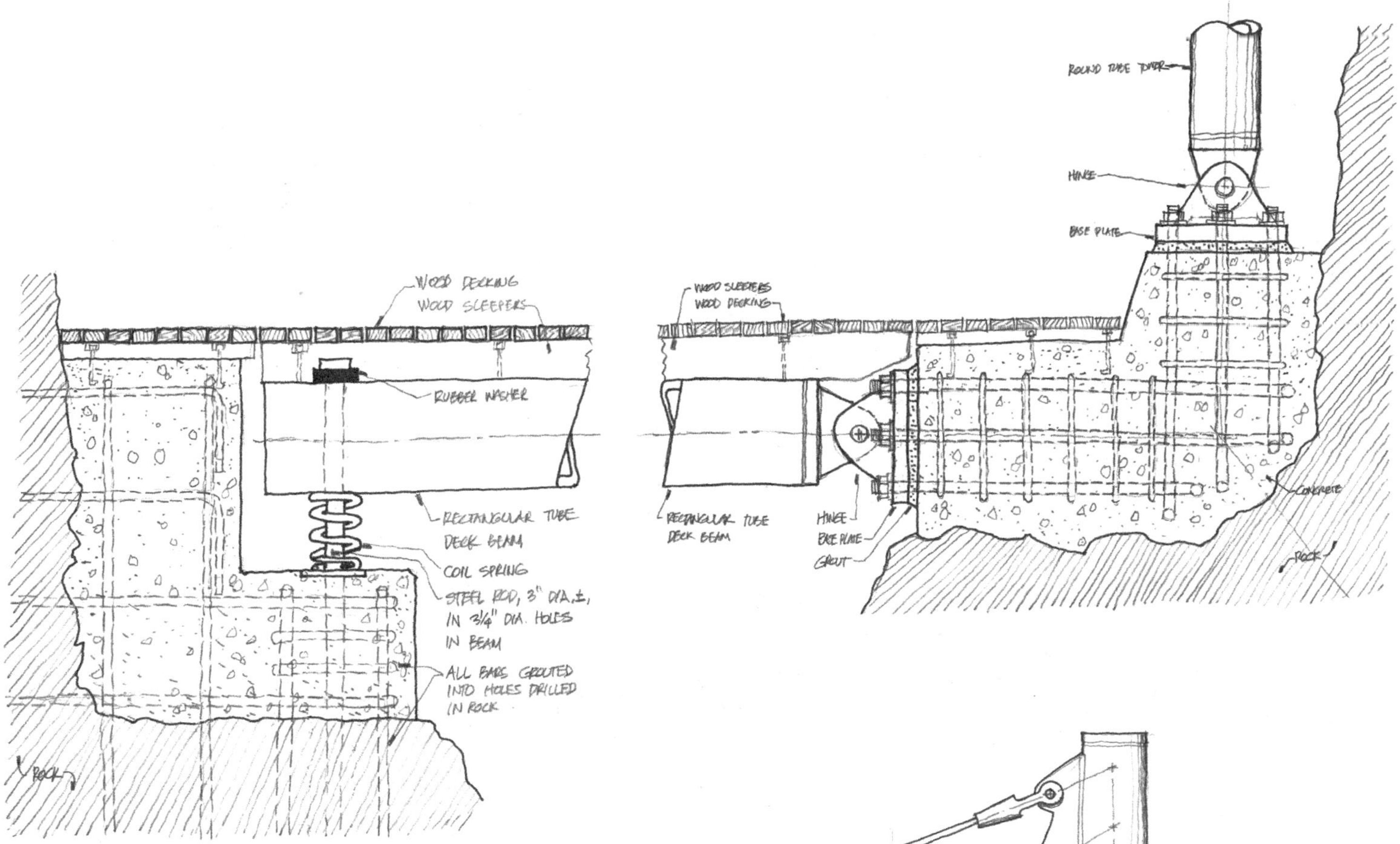

(a)

Figure 7.46 Preliminary sketch details for the pedestrian bridge: (a) Where the tower and deck meet and their forces are brought to earth, both members are hinged to a massive block of concrete. The concrete is heavily reinforced to avoid failure under large compressive forces. A wood walking deck is attached to the steel tube beams. The free end of the footbridge (left) is restrained from lateral movement by heavy vertical steel rods that pass through slotted openings in the beams. A steel spring below the beam allows some movement of the deck with changes in temperature and load.
(b) A sketch detail for the top of the tower. A semifan pattern is used to avoid conflict of the stay cable connections with one another. A pair of towers that rise from their base in a very narrow V may be required to accommodate the two planes of stay cables. The connecting plates are welded securely to the steel tube tower. At right, a sketch detail for the attachment of a stay cable to the deck beam. The cable is fastened to a threaded steel rod with a tensile socket that has an internal screw thread. This connection is protected from weather by a rubber boot. The rod passes through an oblique pipe that has been inserted into the tubular beam and welded there. At the bottom of the pipe, the load is transferred from the rod to the beam by a washer and nut.

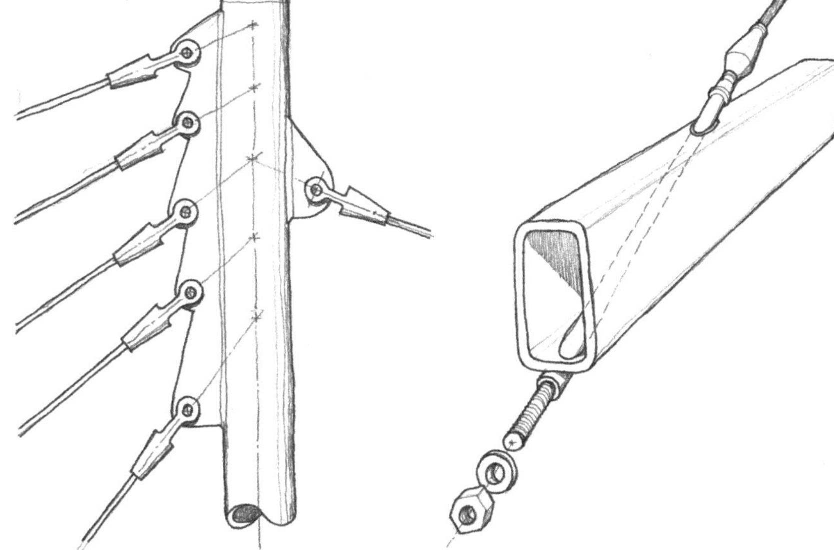

(b)

▶**Figure 7.47** The British architect Nicholas Grimshaw collaborated with Atkins Civil Engineers and the contractor Alfred McAlpine to create this 476-ft bridge over the River Usk in Newport City, United Kingdom. Its 16-ft-wide deck for foot and bicycle traffic is supported by a very unusual arrangement in which the towers are not on the axis of the bridge. The small inset sketch is a plan view that shows the relationship of the towers, cables, and bridge deck.

Photo courtesy of John Wilson.

Key Terms and Concepts

fanlike structures
cable-stayed structure
fan
semifan
harp
half-harp
dendriform
tower
mast
pylon
stay
box girder
balanced cantilever erection
compressive fan
counterweighted structure

Further Resources

Harris, James B., and Kevin Pui–K Li. *Masted Structures in Architecture*. Oxford, UK: Butterworth Architecture, 1996. Most of the structures presented in this book are fanlike structures of cables or rods.

Menn, Christian (English translation by Paul Gavreau). *Prestressed Concrete Bridges*. Basel, Switzerland: Birkhäuser, 1986. A master of bridge design devotes a substantial portion of this book to design procedures for cable-stayed bridges.

Pollalis, Spiro N. *What Is a Bridge? The Making of Calatrava's Bridge in Seville*. Cambridge, MA: MIT Press, 1999. The author of this book worked in the Calatrava office during the design and construction of the Alamillo Bridge. Here he gives detailed information on every aspect of its design and assembly.

www.bridgepros.com/projects/Millau_Viaduct: Documentation of the Millau Viaduct.

www.greenvillebridge.com: The longest bridge over the Mississippi River.

www.johnweeks.com/cablestay: A complete registry of North American cable-stayed bridges, with a link to a similar site in Europe.

www.china.org.cn/china/photos/2008–07/01/content_15914098.htm: The world's longest-span cable-stayed bridge.

CHAPTER 8

Designing Unreinforced Masonry

Contributing Authors: JOHN A. OCHSENDORF and PHILIPPE BLOCK

- *Understanding, designing, and detailing traditional unreinforced masonry*
- *Stability of masonry vaults with ties, engaged and flying buttresses*
- *Load tracing and kerns*
- *Graphical analysis of arches of predetermined shape*
- *Design and formal vocabulary of funicular masonry arches and vaults*

An archaeological excavation in the Roussillon region of southern France has uncovered a well-preserved mosaic floor from an ancient Roman villa. The local authorities would like to construct a roof to provide a visitor's center for the site and to protect the mosaic from the elements. The Roussillon region has a long tradition of vaulted construction in brick masonry. This prompts us to pursue a design solution composed entirely of unreinforced brickwork, so as to provide a long-lasting, elegant shelter for the mosaic floor. Having visited the vaulted brick winery in Spain from 1919 by architect Cèsar Martinell (Figure 8.1), we are confident that we can design a soaring brick structure that will be an elegant complement to the mosaic. The mosaic floor is rectangular and will require a 12-m span. The topography of the site is such that one side of the new building will rest on an existing earthen embankment (Figure. 8.2).

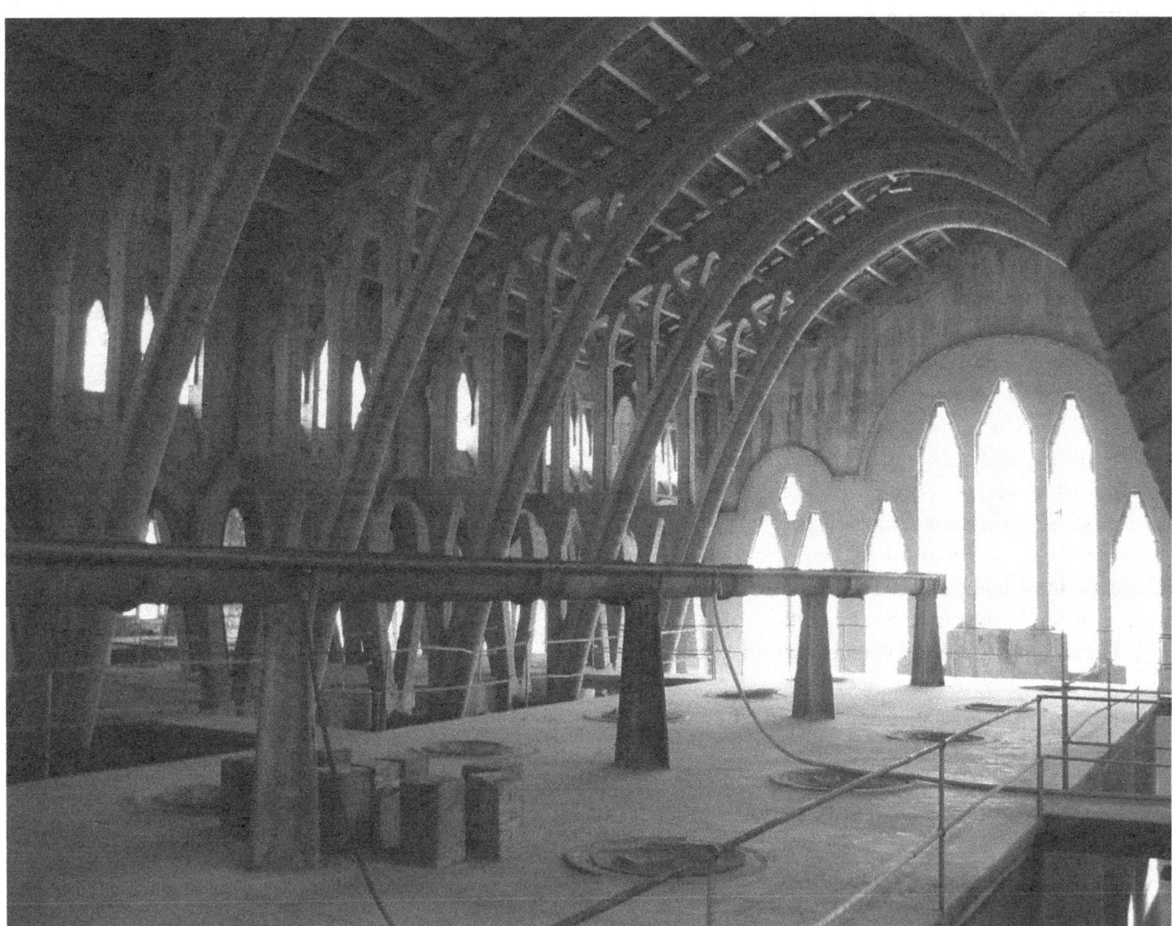

Figure 8.1 Vaulted brick winery by architect Cèsar Martinell, Tarragona, Spain, 1919. Photo courtesy of Michael H. Ramage.

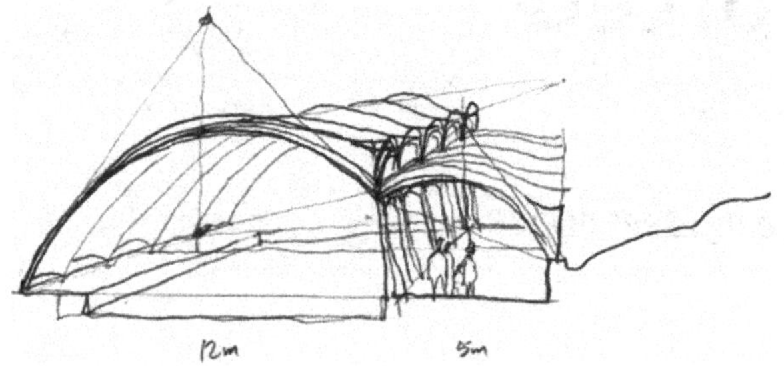

Figure 8.2 Preliminary design sketch for the masonry structure over the archaeological site with mosaic floor.

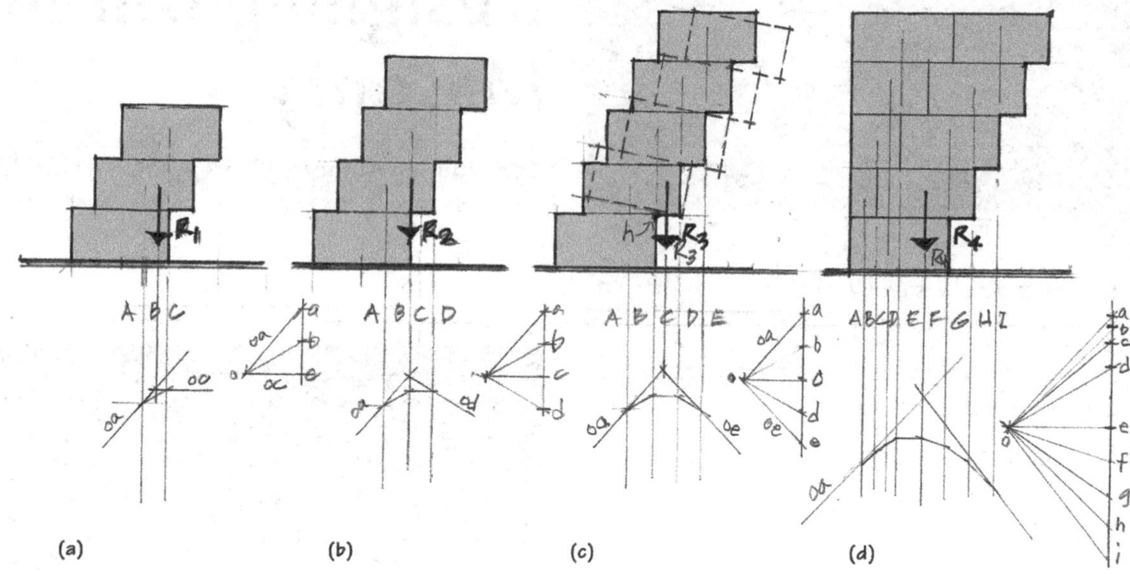

Figure 8.3 Stability of corbel: (a) three blocks in stable equilibrium; (b) four blocks at the limit of stability; (c) five blocks in an unstable configuration; (d) added masonry as backweight to ensure stability.

By using local brick, the project can employ local labor and provide a stimulus for the regional economy. Local materials minimize energy requirements for transportation. Clay bricks have low overall embodied energy and are manufactured of inert, nonpolluting materials. Furthermore, by using brick without any internal steel reinforcing, we can ensure a long-lasting, low-maintenance roof. This is because steel bars in reinforced concrete and reinforced brick structures are prone to corrosion over long periods of time. This could lead to disintegration of the brickwork and rust stains in our structure that could damage the mosaic. The attractive color and pattern of the brickwork eliminate the need for applied interior finishes and their associated costs and environmental impacts.

The tradition of masonry construction extends back thousands of years, to the mud brick and stone buildings of our earliest ancestors. Most of the great buildings of the world are constructed of masonry. The material stresses in masonry structures are very low, and failure is more likely to occur due to an unstable form rather than a lack of compressive strength. Traditional design methods are based on rules of proportion and geometry, which are appropriate for structures with low stress values.

An *unreinforced masonry* structure must be shaped so that it does not rely in any way or under any loading condition on tensile forces. If the form is incorrect, tensile forces will occur and the building will not stand. We will find a correct form for our structure by using two methods: chain modeling and graphic statics.

"The human race built most nobly when limitations were greatest and therefore when most was required from imagination in order to build at all. Limitations seem to always be the best friend of architecture."

—FRANK LLOYD WRIGHT

CORBEL AND THOLOS

The *corbel* is the simplest and most primitive device for spanning with masonry. It is built simply by projecting each *course* of bricks or blocks outward a short distance over the course below (Figure 8.3). In theory, a course could project a distance of up to half the length of the masonry unit (brick or block); beyond this, the unit would tip and fall over the edge. However, in order to minimize tensile stress and make the work of the mason easier, it is wise not to project a unit more than about half its height. This produces a corbelled bracket or opening at an angle of approximately 65° to the horizontal.

To remain stable, a multicourse corbel must be *backweighted* with masonry so that it is not overbalanced at any course. In Figure 8.3a, the center of mass of the two projecting courses lies along the line of action of their resultant weight, R_1, which passes within the end of the bottom course, showing that the construction is stable. In part (b), the resultant weight of the three projecting courses lies just at the end of the bottom course, making the construction liable to tip.

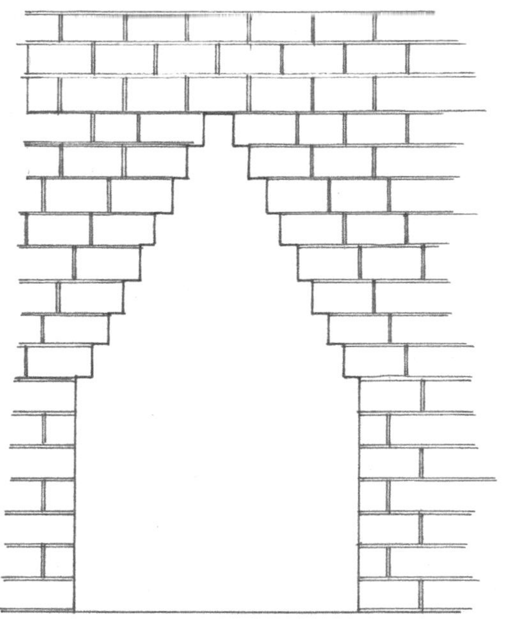

Figure 8.4 Mirroring two corbels to span a space.

(a)

(b)

Figure 8.5 (a) Corbelled ornament on a building in Natick, Massachusetts; and (b) corbelled brick supports for a roof corner and corbelled window openings, Barcelona, Spain.

Photos: Edward Allen.

Adding a course in part (c), the resultant weight passes outside the bottom course, producing a mechanism that is clearly unstable. In part (d), we can remedy this situation by adding masonry to the back of the construction. This brings the resultant weight safely back inside the bottom course, and stability is restored. Notice that full-length masonry units are used to form every projection, with units cut to length as needed in the interior of the masonry. In each of these four examples, the location of the center of mass has been established with a force polygon and funicular polygon, as shown here and as demonstrated on p. 132.

Corbelling can be doubled in mirror-image fashion to create openings in walls, as seen in Figure 8.4. This construction does not exert horizontal thrust unless it is insufficiently backweighted, in which case the two corbels will lean against each other. This sets up an arching action that has an accompanying thrust. A corbel is often called a "false arch," but if the two sides are leaning against each other for support, then it is actually a "true arch," which exerts horizontal thrust. The corbel technique is limited to short spans. The most common use of corbelling is in ornamental brickwork (Figure 8.5).

A *tholos* may be conceptualized as a conical corbel, but in reality its action is more complicated than this (Figure 8.6a). Because the tholos is not backweighted, it exerts a radial outward thrust, and its circular courses tend to collapse inward toward the center of the construction. This tendency is resisted by full-circle horizontal arching action in each course, in which the arch forces on either side of any stone lie at angles such that their resultant is an outward thrust that is equal to the inward force exerted by the inclined masonry. Both the corbel and the tholos may be laid either with or without mortar. The largest known tholos, an ancient tomb in Greece from 1250 BC, spans 14.5 m (48 ft).

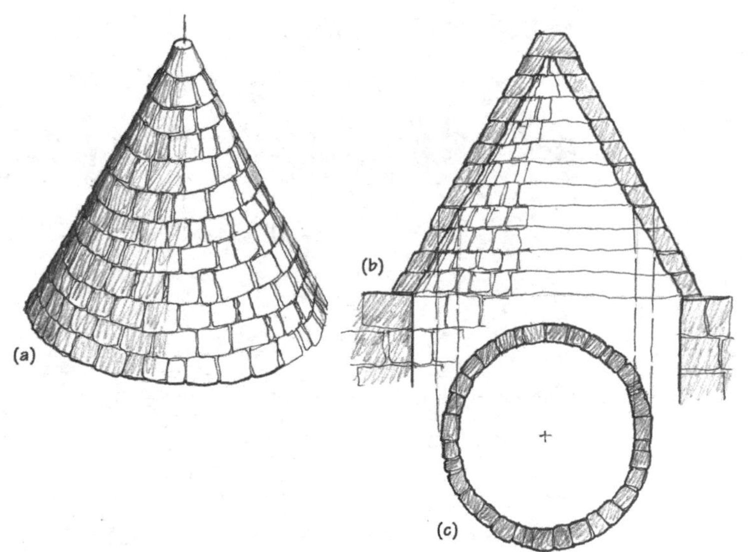

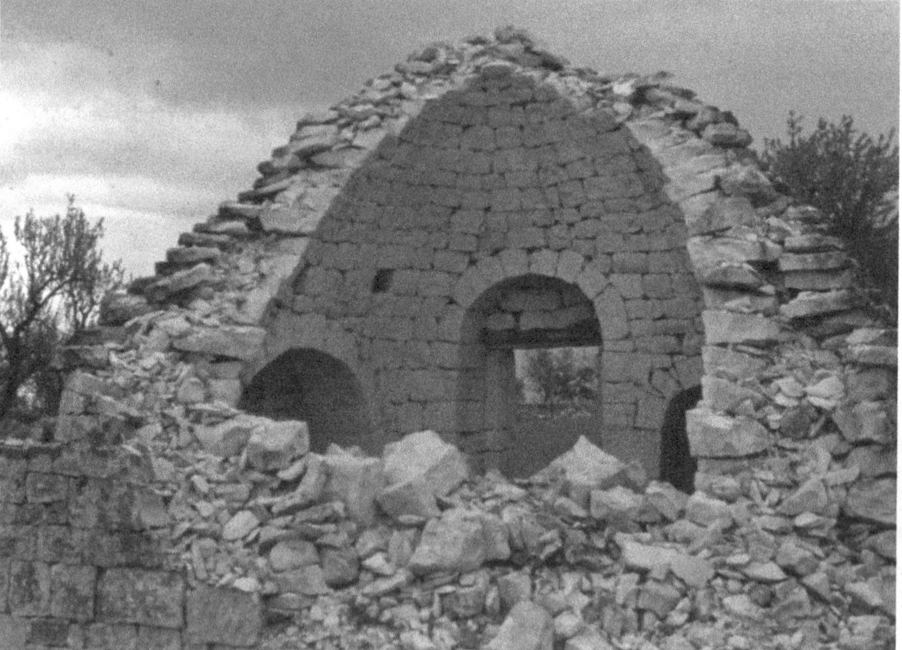

Figure 8.6 (a) Conical tholos where hoop forces in each ring prevent the stones from falling inward; (b) *trulli* houses in southern Italy made from tholos structures of small irregular stone blocks; (c) a partially collapsed *trullo* reveals its tholos construction.

Photos: Edward Allen.

MASONRY ARCHES: ROBERT HOOKE'S GUIDING PRINCIPLE

Much longer distances may be spanned in masonry by utilizing arch action rather than corbeling. In 1675, English scientist Robert Hooke (1635–1703) discovered "the true Mathematical and Mechanical form of all manner of Arches for Building," which he summarized with a single phrase: "As hangs the flexible line, so but inverted will stand the rigid arch." Hooke described the relationship between a hanging chain, which forms a catenary in tension under its own weight, and an arch, which stands in compression (Figure 8.7). Both the hanging chain and the arch must be in equilibrium. Generalized, *Hooke's principle* signifies that the funicular shape that a string or chain takes under a set of loads, if rigidified and inverted, is an ideal shape for an arched structure to support the same set of loads. In the centuries that followed, this simple idea has been used to understand and design numerous important structures.

To understand the application of Hooke's principle, consider the arch of randomly irregular stone blocks shown in Figure 8.8. Because masonry can resist only compressive forces, the arch can stand only if a path of compressive forces is shown to lie entirely within the masonry. Each *voussoir*, or stone, in the arch has a known mass and centroid. A model of the arch could be constructed with a piece of string supporting small bags of sand to represent the weight of each block. The resulting shape of the string is the path of the tensile forces necessary to support these weights. By pulling on the ends of the string with different values of horizontal force, an infinite number of funicular solutions can be found for the same loading condition. This is equivalent to moving the pole of the associated force polygon horizontally, which adjusts the level of horizontal thrust in the system.

Equilibrium in a masonry arch can be visualized by means of a *line of thrust*, a theoretical line that represents the path of the resultants of the compressive forces through the structure. If the thrust line strays

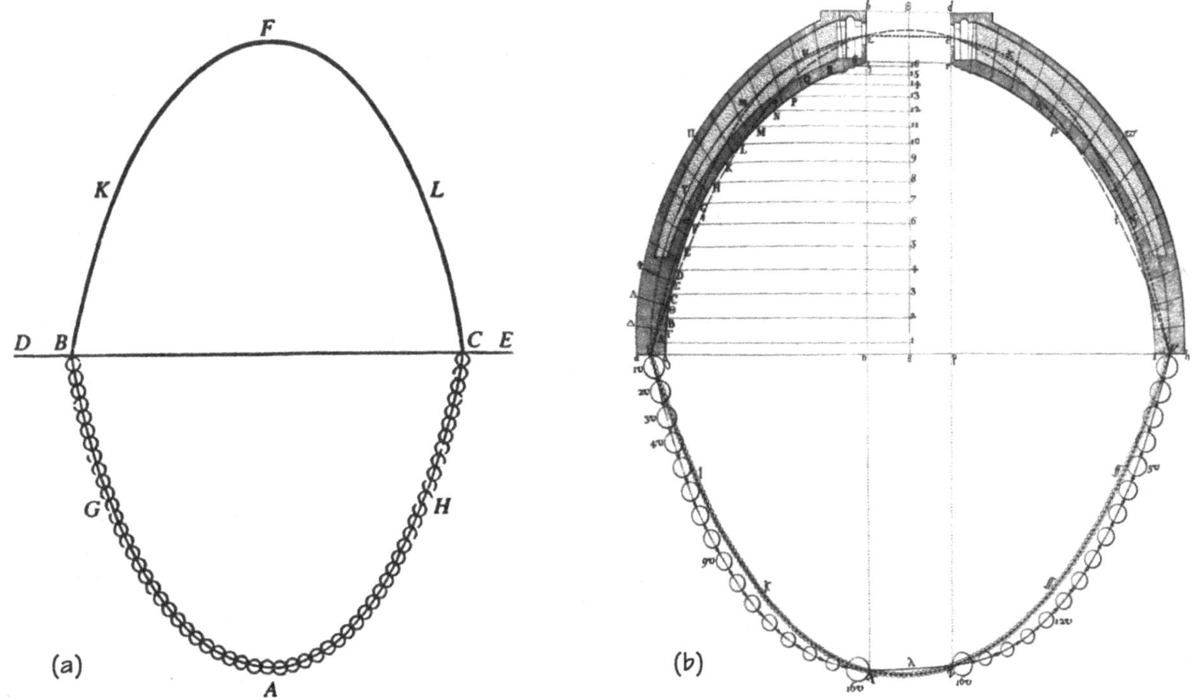

Figure 8.7 (a) Hooke's hanging chain in tension with the corresponding inverted arch in compression; (b) analysis of the cracked dome of St. Peter's in Rome by Giovanni Poleni (1683–1761) using Hooke's principle.

Image from Poleni, 1747.

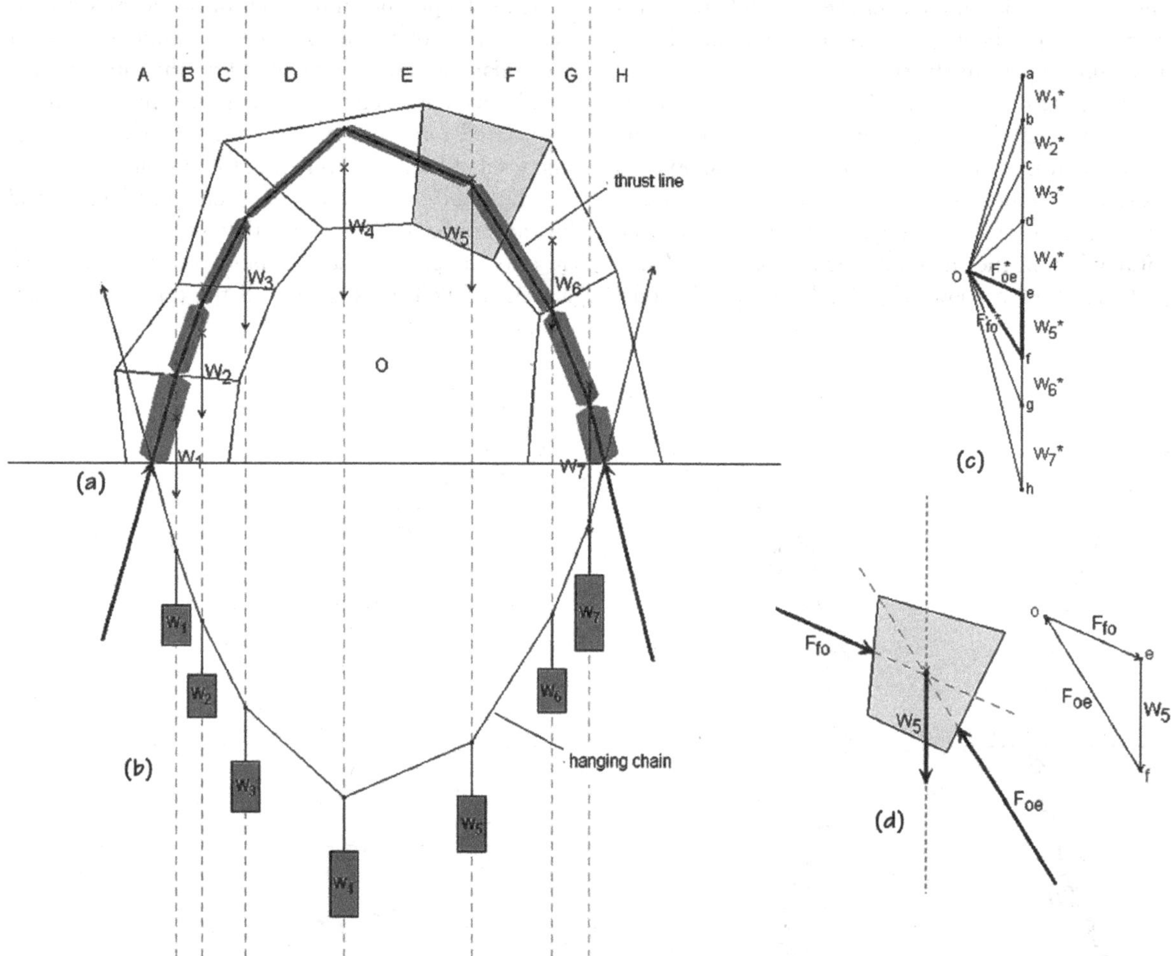

Figure 8.8 Random arch with (a) possible internal line of thrust; (b) its inverse, a hanging string with weights proportional to the weights of the voussoirs; (c) the corresponding force polygon; (d) one of the arch voussoirs with a closed triangle visualizing the equilibrium of the forces that act on it.

outside the section, compressive forces must travel through the air, which is only possible if the material can resist tension. Although we have drawn only one path, the stone arch of Figure 8.8 has an infinite number of possible thrust lines that lie within the masonry: It is statically indeterminate. This means that multiple equilibrium solutions are possible, with each solution corresponding to a different compressive line of thrust inside the masonry.

The line of thrust for any arch can be found by using either a physical hanging model or graphic statics. Either method will provide the geometry of the thrust line and estimates of the forces throughout the arch. Each individual segment of the arch is held in place by the compressive forces applied to it from adjacent segments. In this manner, the weight of each portion of the arch is carried down to the supports in compression. The equilibrium of a single block in the arch is represented by the bold triangle shown in the funicular polygon of Figure 8.8. It is interesting to note that the blocks at the center of the arch support lower forces than the blocks closer to the support. In fact, the central stone of an arch, called the *keystone* because it is often the last stone put in place, has the smallest value of compressive force acting on it.

Though an infinite number of compressive thrust lines may be found in a typical masonry arch, the geometry of the arch will establish the minimum and maximum horizontal force that is possible within the arch (Figure 8.9). If asked to assess the safety of a historical arch, the analyst can determine the range of possible thrust values, though the exact internal value of force is known only to the arch. However, if support movements occur, then the arch will adjust to these movements by forming hinges. Such hinges make the arch statically determinate because a single thrust line can be found that passes through the hinges. A small outward movement of the supports will lead to the state of *minimum thrust* (Figure 8.9b) and a small inward movement of the arch supports will lead to the state of *maximum thrust* (Figure 8.9c). The minimum (or passive) thrust state

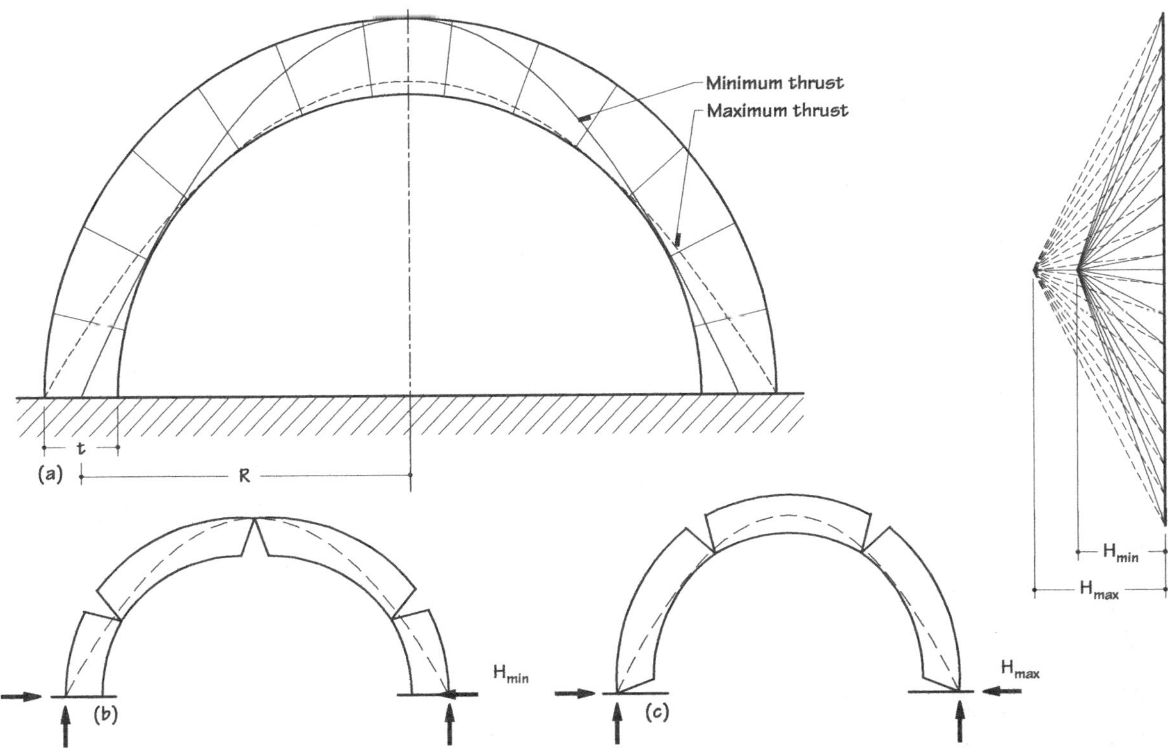

Figure 8.9 (a) Minimum and maximum horizontal thrust values in a semicircular masonry arch; (b) inward movement of the supports leads to the minimum thrust state; and (c) outward movement of the supports leads to the maximum thrust state.

Figure 8.10 Relationship between the location of the thrust line and the assumed internal compressive stress distribution in the masonry section: (a) uniform compressive stress [$x = b/2$]; (b) entire section is in compression with minor eccentricity of the thrust line [$b/3 < x < b/2$], linear elastic assumption of stresses due to mortar; (c) entire section in compression with variable stress distribution [$b/3 < x < b/2$]; (d) thrust line at kern of a rectangular section [$x = b/3$]; (e) thrust line outside of the middle third of a rectangular section [$x < b/3$]; (f) thrust line acting at or near the edge may lead to formation of a hinge.

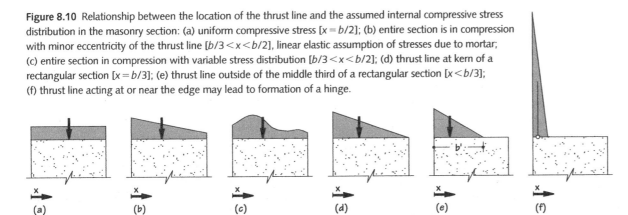

represents the least amount the arch can push horizontally on its neighboring elements, as a function of its self-weight and shape. The maximum (or active) state of thrust represents the largest possible horizontal force that this arch can provide. The challenge of vaulted masonry structures is to control thrust and bring it safely to earth within the fabric of the masonry.

What is occurring locally within particular points in an arched structure? A voussoir feels forces from three directions: gravity load pushing down on it from above, and oblique forces from the stones on each side. The sum of the vertical components of the two oblique forces must equal the gravity load, as represented by a force polygon that is a closed triangle. At each section of the arch, the force that is centered on the thrust line applies compressive stress locally to the material. If the thrust line acts along the centers of the voussoirs, uniform compressive stress acts across the section (Figure 8.10a). If the thrust line develops eccentricity and moves away from the centers of the voussoirs, the compressive stress distribution changes, and one side of the voussoirs experiences greater compression than the other. This may be represented as a linearly varying stress contour, based on the assumption of elastic behavior of the material (Figure 8.10b). Mortar helps to distribute the internal forces over the entire interface between voussoirs. Dry stone arches (arches constructed without mortar) have rough contact surfaces that may cause local stress concentrations (Figure 8.10c). If the thrust line is located at the one-third point of a rectangular section (Figure 8.10d), the compressive stress at the far edge will be reduced to zero, rendering ineffective the material at that edge. If the thrust line approaches the edge of the masonry, then higher compressive stress occurs on a smaller area of the masonry (Figure 8.10e). If the thrust line reaches the edge of the masonry, it causes much higher stresses in compression and may also create a hinge (Figure 8.10f). A stable arch may develop up to three hinges, but four hinges or more will lead to collapse.

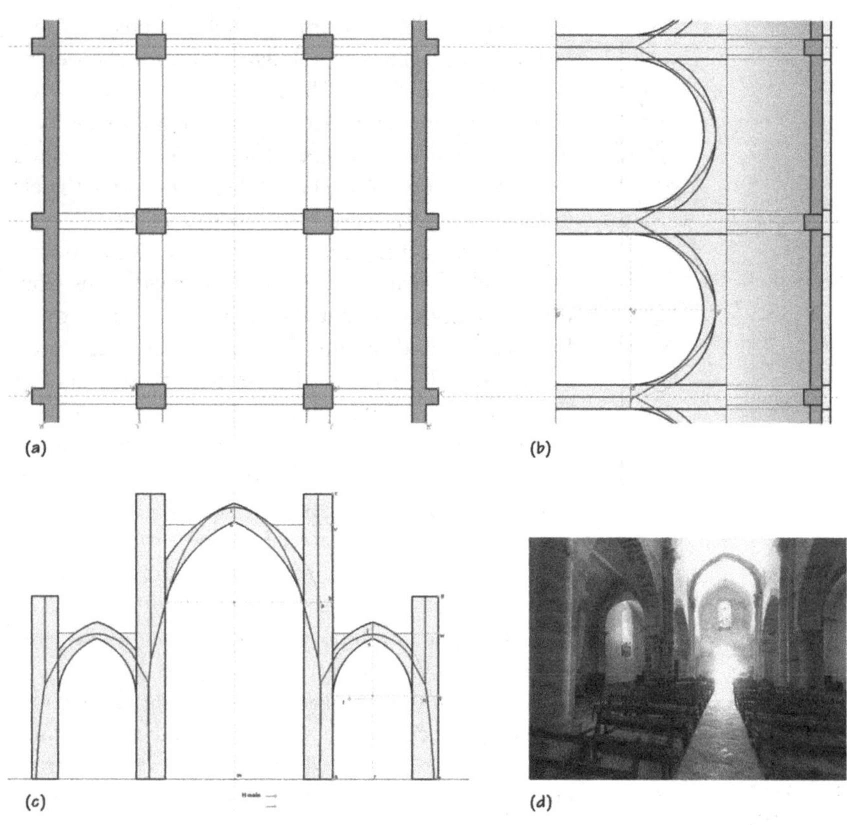

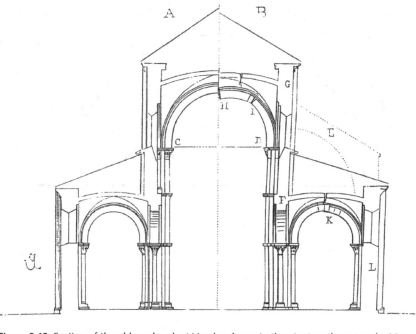

Figure 8.12 Section of the abbey church at Vezelay drawn in the nineteenth century by Viollet-le-Duc. It is shown in its ideal undeformed state (left) and in its deformed state at the time it was drawn (right).

Figure 8.11 Romanesque church in central France: (a) partial plan of church; (b) longitudinal section of church showing possible thrust lines; (c) lateral section through central nave and side aisles with thrust lines; and (d) interior view.

Photo courtesy of Andrew Tallon.

Arches shaped to contain the funicular path of compressive forces can span space and create architecture. The forces must lie within the masonry all the way to the foundations, and supporting buttresses may become necessary as the arches are raised higher above the ground.

THE QUEST FOR HEIGHT

Though the arch was used in Egypt thousands of years earlier, the builders of the Roman Empire vastly extended its use in architecture. Extruding the arch into the third dimension, the Romans constructed barrel vaults supported by masonry walls and buttresses. When medieval builders throughout Europe began to develop vaulted masonry buildings in the eleventh century AD, they drew on the simple cylindrical barrel vault as an effective means of covering space. As these vaults were constructed higher and higher above the foundations, they required increasingly more innovative *buttressing* solutions.

In the Romanesque era, masonry vaults were constructed more frequently than timber roofs, because they were more permanent and fire resistant to fire (Figure 8.11). In a church with side *aisles*, the longer spans of the central *nave* produce higher values of horizontal force than the smaller spans and forces of the side aisles. In this situation, the central nave often acts in a state of minimum horizontal thrust, while the side aisles act in a state of maximum thrust, as in the famous abbey church at Vezelay, France (Figures 8.12, 8.13).

In the Gothic period, master masons, driven by the desire to build higher and to open up the walls for larger windows to admit natural light, created the tallest and most daring structures ever built in masonry.

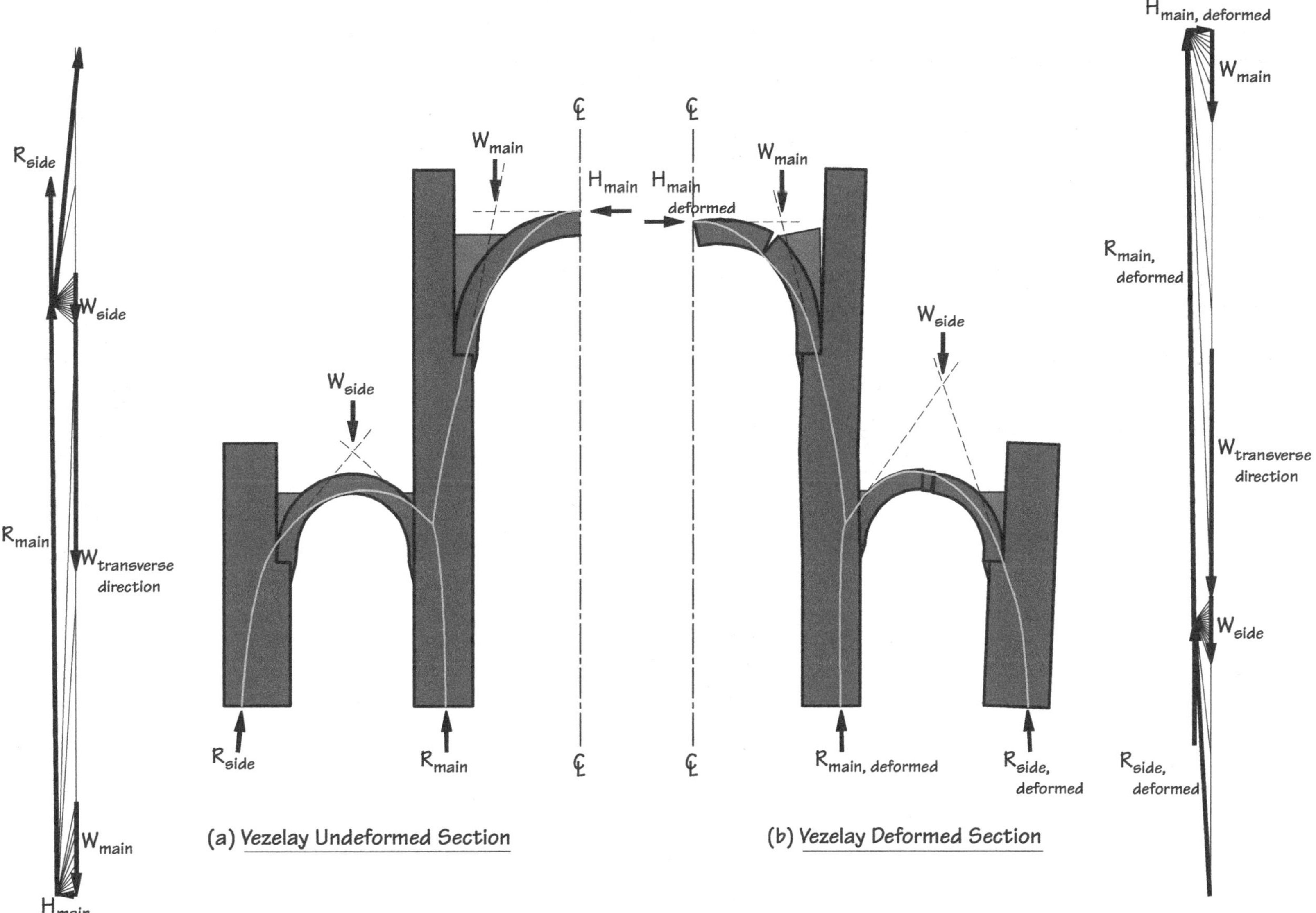

Figure 8.13 Approximate thrust lines and corresponding force polygons through the abbey church of Vezelay: (a) the original, undeformed section; and (b) the section as deformed by foundation movement and structural deflections. The force polygons indicate that vertical forces predominate and horizontal forces are proportionately small.

They developed *flying buttresses*, detached piers connected by inclined "flying" arches, to stabilize the high Gothic vaults and to channel the thrust downward to the ground, while avoiding obstruction of the aisles and allowing natural light to enter the nave through the vast windows (Figure 8.14).

As cathedrals became taller, lateral wind loads became increasingly significant and the flying buttresses assumed another important role: that of bringing wind loads to the ground. In the Gothic era, pointed arches opened up larger areas for glazing and approximated the catenary shape more closely than semicircular arches, reducing the horizontal thrust of the high naves and allowing interior columns to become taller and more slender (Figure 8.15). These delicate stone skeletons pushed the limits of the geometrical design methods that had served for simpler structural forms.

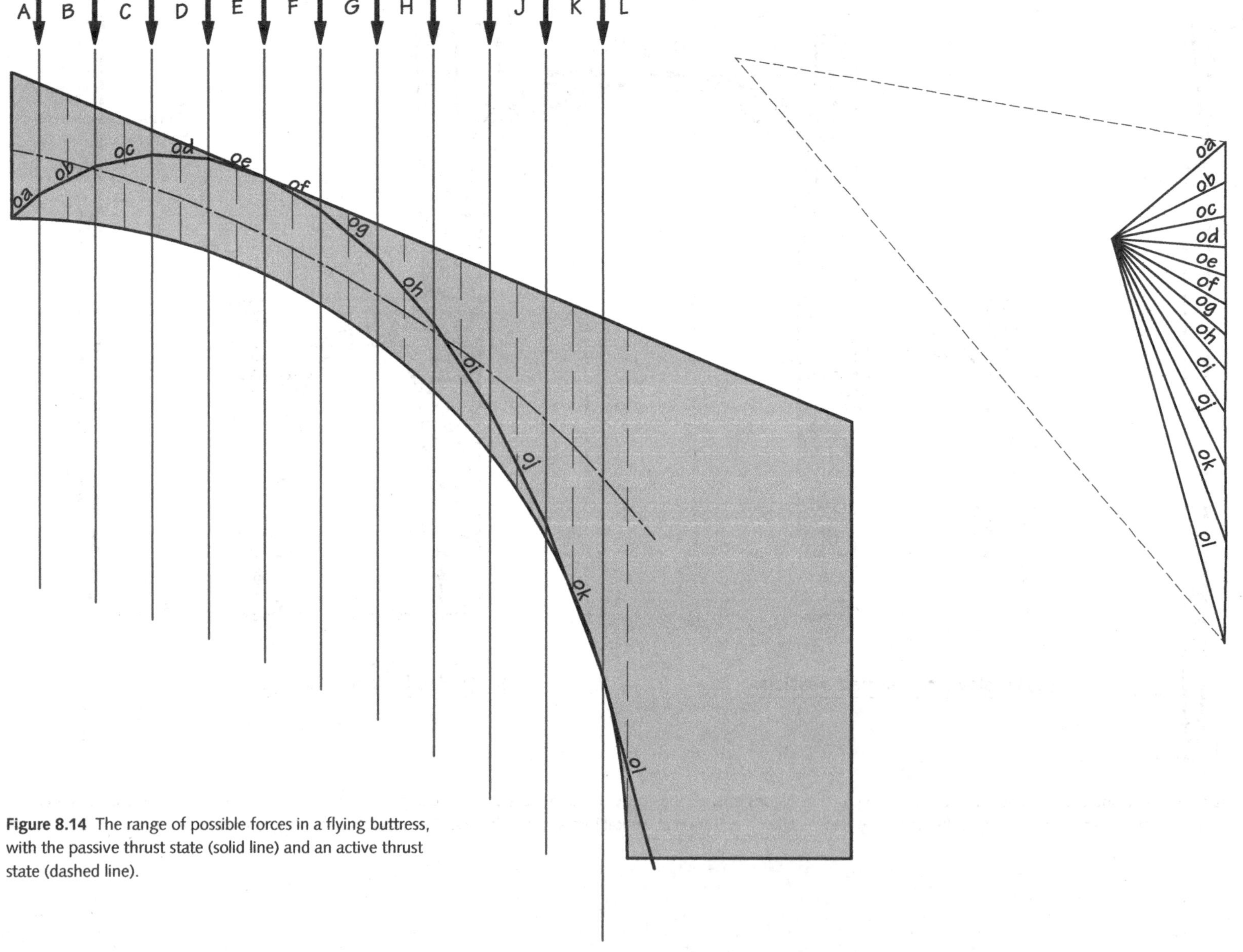

Figure 8.14 The range of possible forces in a flying buttress, with the passive thrust state (solid line) and an active thrust state (dashed line).

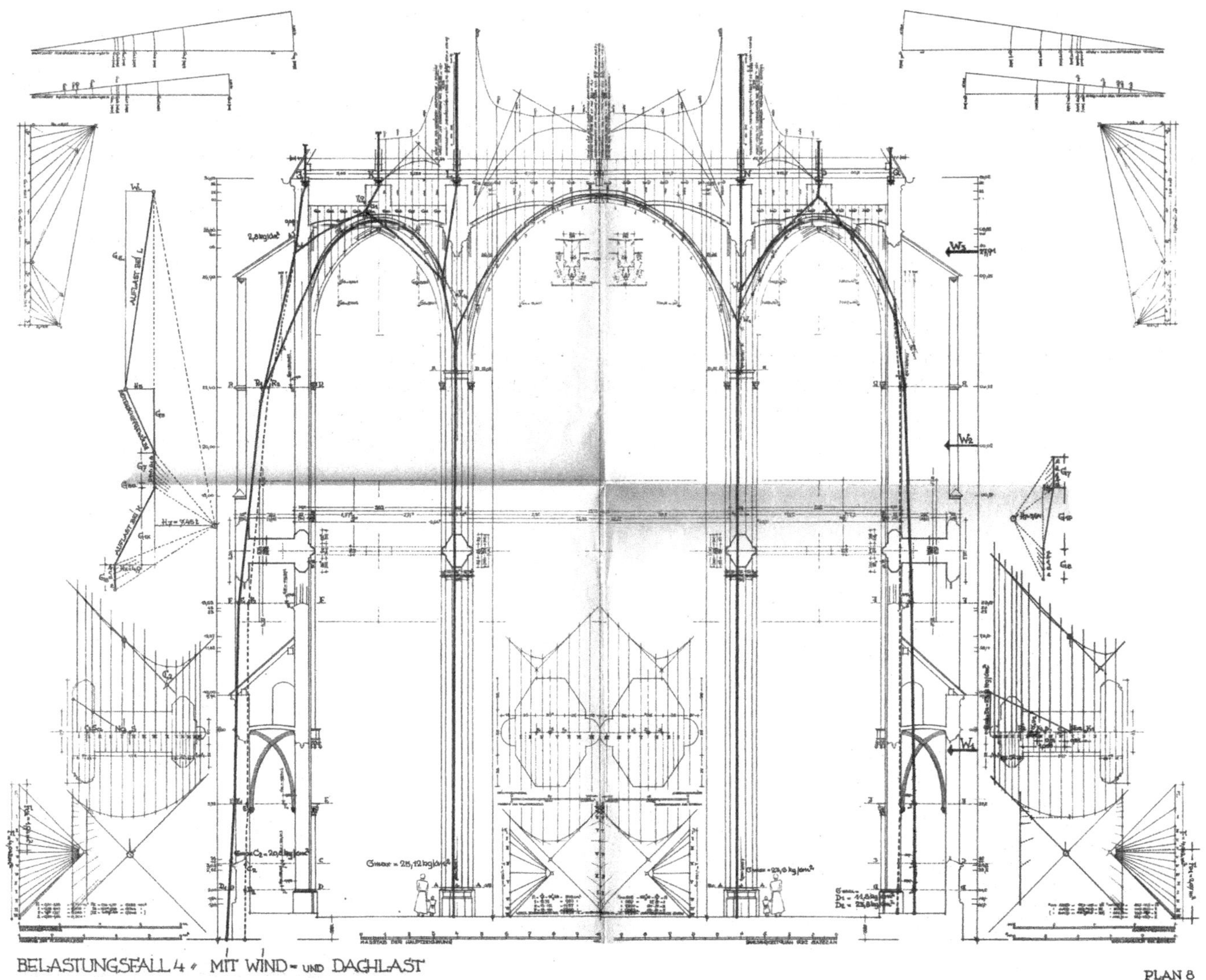

Figure 8.15 Thrust line analysis of a Gothic section by Zorn (1933). In this analysis, the weight of the roof structure and the horizontal forces imposed by the wind are included. (This image was scanned from Zorn, E., *Statische Untersuchung der St. Martinskirche in Landshut*, Ph.D. dissertation, Universität München, Germany, 1933.)

MASONRY BUTTRESSES

Classical masonry structures have vertical columns and piers that are generally incapable of resisting any substantial lateral thrust from arches or vaults. Although exposed iron or steel tie rods are an economical way of resisting thrust, they are visually inharmonious. A more satisfactory solution to the thrust problem from a visual standpoint is to deploy masonry in such a way that its dead weight deflects the inclined thrust line from the arch or vault along an ever steeper path until it passes to the foundations of the building, still safely contained within the mass of the masonry. Such a construction is called a *buttress*.

A buttress is usually shaped visually, then analyzed to discover if it works. An elementary example of this analysis procedure is shown in Figure 8.16. Here we see a drawing of an arched *flying buttress* that passes an inclined thrust of 15,000 lb from a vault that is off the picture to the left to a vertical masonry pier. The pier in this example is made up of three broad rectangular blocks of masonry. Its breadth is disproportional to its height by Gothic standards, but it serves better for this example because it avoids a confusion of overlapping lines in the drawing.

Our task is to find the path of the thrust line through this buttress design. For maximum safety, this line must pass entirely within the *kerns* of the various buttress sections so as to avoid inducing tensile stresses into the masonry. (We will take up the topic of kerns in greater detail in Chapter 00. A kern is defined as the portion of a cross section of material within which the application of a perpendicular force will not result in tension in any part of the section.) The kerns of the three sections of the pier are shaded in each case. Because the component blocks are rectangular, the kern is the middle third of each horizontal section. In part (a) of Figure 8.16, we are given, in addition to the inclination and magnitude of the thrust from the buttress arch, the weights of the three blocks that make up the pier. A load line is constructed to the right, consisting of an angled vector *oa* representing the thrust from the arch plus three vertical segments, *ab*, *bc*, and *cd*, which represent the weights of the three blocks that make up the pier.

Vector *ob* is the resultant of the vault thrust, *oa*, and the weight of the topmost pier block, 6,000 lb. When we translate this vector to the diagram of the buttress, it must pass through the intersection of the lines of action of its two component forces, the vault thrust and

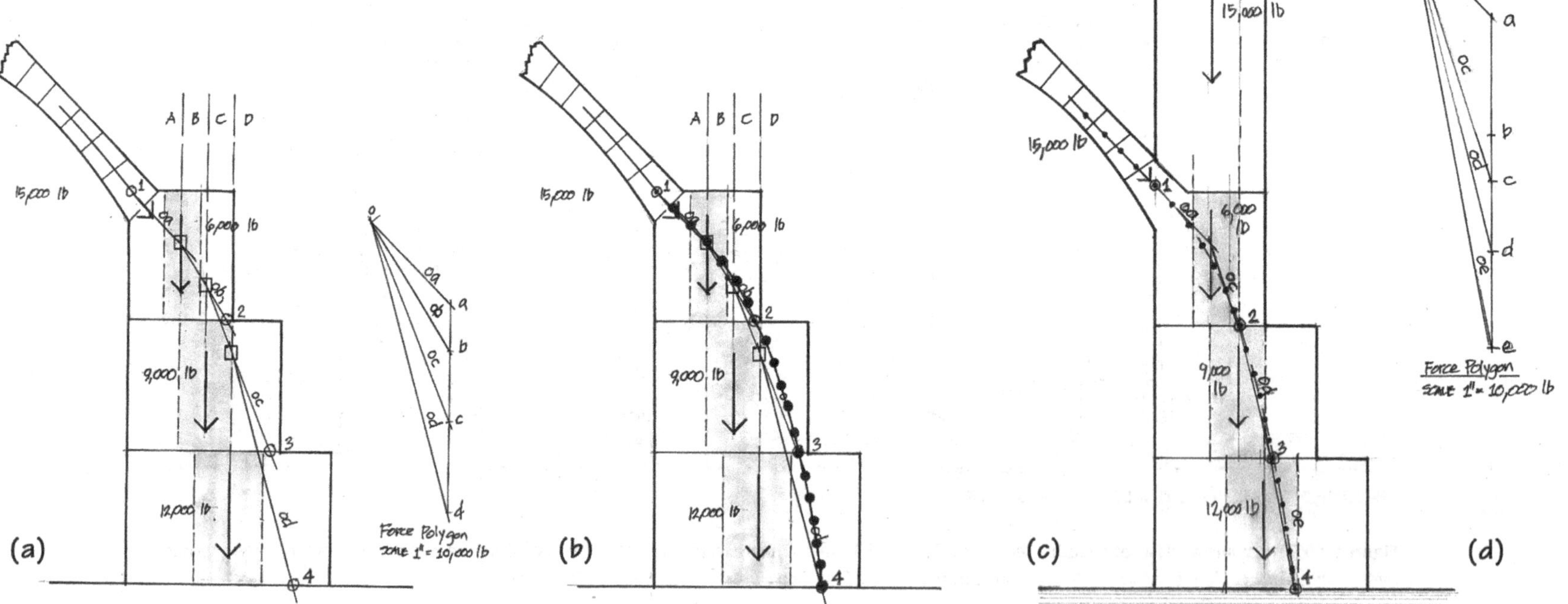

Figure 8.16 Graphical construction of a thrust line in a stepped buttress; at right, an extra surcharge from a pinnacle stabilizes the buttress by keeping the thrust line in the safe middle third area (hatched gray) of the buttress section.

the 6,000-lb weight. This location is marked by a small square in the top pier block on the drawing. From here, we construct *ob* parallel to ray *ob* so that it extends to the upper face of the block below at an intersection that we circle and label 2. (Point *1* has been previously marked on the thrust vector from the arch where it passes through the imaginary top left corner of the top block.) Point *2* lies on the thrust line within the buttress. The next step is to use the force polygon to find the resultant, *oc*, of the arch thrust and the weight of the top and middle blocks. On the diagram of the buttress, this vector must pass through the intersection of its two components *ob* and *oc*, which is marked with another small square below the first one in the upper block. It is extended to the bottom of the middle block, which it intersects at circled point 3. Point 3 also lies on the thrust line of the buttress. Finally, we draw resultant *od* of the thrust from the middle block and the weight of the bottom block. This passes through the point of intersection of these two forces, which is marked with another square, and is extended until it meets the ground at point *4*, which lies on the thrust line.

In Figure 8.16b, a smooth curve has been drawn to connect points 1–4. This is the entire thrust line and has been marked with a series of black dots to make it prominently visible. This line lies almost entirely outside the kerns of the three blocks that make up the buttress pier and passes alarmingly close to the two inside corners of the pier profile. The buttress would stand, but it leaves little room for error, and tension cracks are likely to open on the edge of the pier farthest from the thrust line.

In Figure 8.16c, we try a strategy that was universally used by Gothic builders: We add a heavy pinnacle to the pier. Because the pinnacle bears only its own weight, it has often been thought to be purely ornamental, but, in fact, such pinnacles generally play a significant structural role. In this example, the weight of the pinnacle, *ac*, has the effect of deflecting vectors *oc* through *oe* into much steeper angles than in the previous buttress. The thrust line passes outside the kern of the pier only for a short distance at point 3. A small addition of pinnacle weight should correct this slight defect in the design.

Similar analyses of actual church buttresses follow these same simple steps, but the diagrams become more densely packed with a tangle of lines because of the slenderness of the pier, and it becomes important to work carefully to avoid errors or confusion.

FROM ARCHES TO VAULTS

All elements of a masonry structure, no matter how complex, must be in equilibrium in three dimensions. Gothic builders became proficient in creating increasingly intricate arrangements of arches and vaults. They introduced *rib vaults*, which allowed much lighter construction than Romanesque barrel vaults. In rib vaults, the compressive forces flow to the ribs, while the webs between the ribs are filled by thinner, lighter shells of masonry, reducing the weight and thrust of the vaults and the weight of material required for the buttresses.

To consider the structural actions of more complex geometries in three dimensions, we may divide the vault into a series of intersecting arches (Figure 8.17). A sensible way to visualize the arches in a three-dimensional vault is to follow the lines of steepest descent, imagining the paths that water would take in

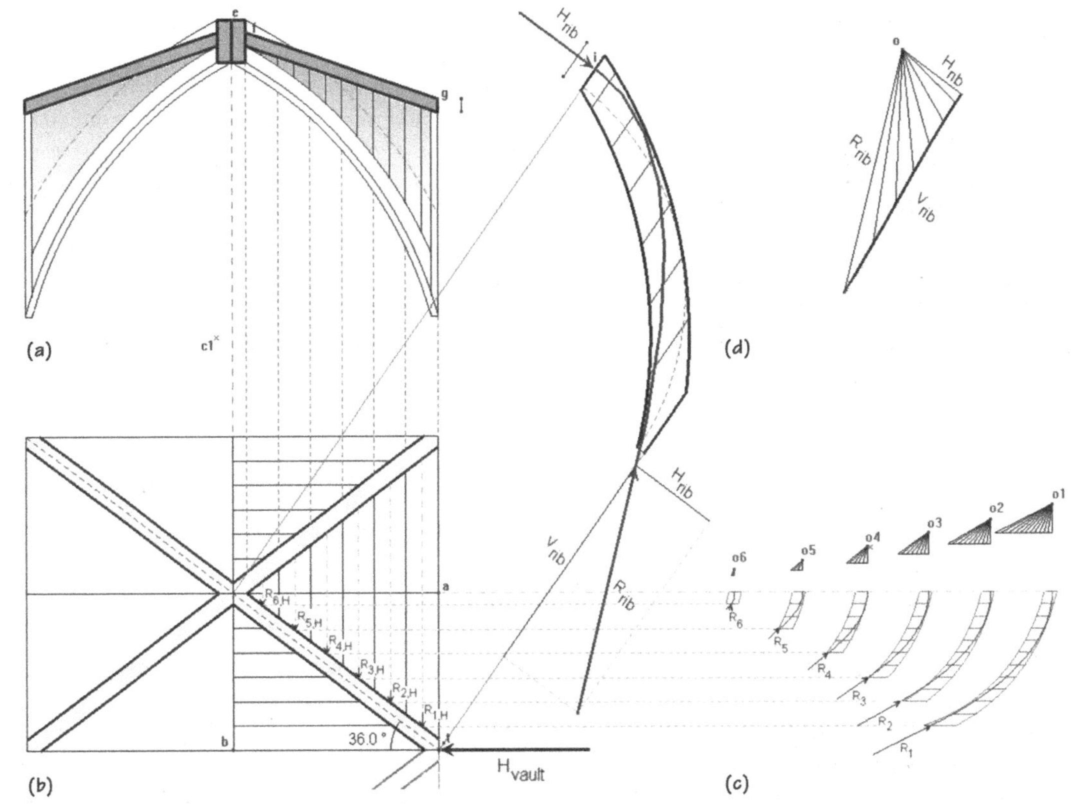

Figure 8.17 Graphical analysis of the forces in a ribbed quadripartite vault: (a) cross section; (b) plan view; (c) arch sections span between the main ribs; and (d) the rib profile with a safe thrust line and its corresponding force polygon. The loads on the main rib come from the resultants of the series of web arches.

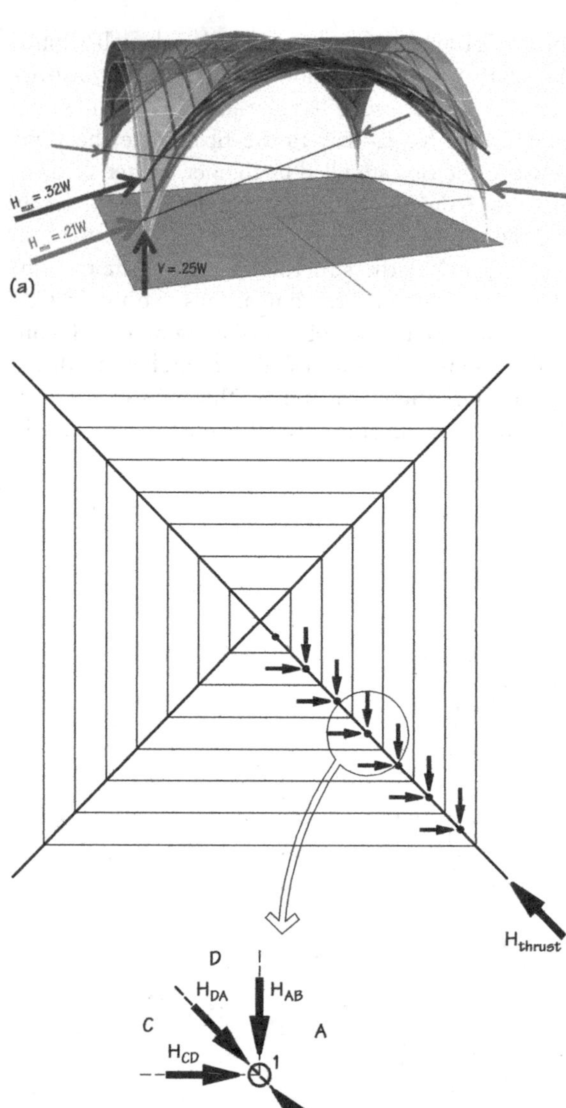

Figure 8.18 Graphical analysis of the forces in a groin vault: (a) 3D visualization of the global minimum and maximum horizontal thrust state; (b) top view of the network of arches representing the 3D behavior of the vault and a thrust diagram demonstrating equilibrium of a node within the vault.

flowing down the contours of the vault. These paths are parallel to the imaginary slices that we make in dividing the vault. For simplified analysis of a *quadripartite vault*, also known as a groin vault, one that is made up of four distinct *web* areas supported by masonry ribs across its diagonals, we may divide each web into parallel arches. The ribs bring forces to the columns at each corner, and the web arches span between the ribs. The thrusts of the arches of adjacent webs coming together in the ribs are linked through geometry: The force resultant needs to be in the direction of the stone rib.

For a quadripartite vault, the equilibrium of all thrust values of the combining arches can be visualized in a diagram representing the horizontal equilibrium, as seen in plan (Figure 8.18). This is a simplified approximation of behavior of the structure, but it is effective and safe because it neglects beneficial three-dimensional effects. For a quadripartite vault, all forces go to the supports in each of the four corners. The vertical component at each corner is one-quarter of the total weight of the vault *W*. As with an arch, a vault can contain a range of possible thrust values within its thickness. For the vault of Figure 8.18, the horizontal thrust at each corner varies between 21 and 32 percent of the total weight of the vault. We label the spaces around a node connecting different arches in Figure 8.18b and demonstrate its horizontal equilibrium in the *thrust diagram*. The resultant thrust value at the corners of the vault can be found by measuring the outside segments of the thrust diagram.

MASONRY DOMES

Masonry domes have created some of the most grandiose spaces ever conceived. A common simplification in the design and analysis of masonry domes is to ignore circumferential forces and divide the dome into a series of wedge-shaped arches that lean against each other along radial lines (Figures 8.19). This is a safe but conservative approach. In actuality, domes also contain circumferential *hoop* forces. (In fact, they contain an infinite variety of forces in every direction, but it is reasonable to approximate this behavior with its radial and circumferential components.) The hoop forces act in compression in the upper portion of a hemispherical dome. Below an angle of approximately 52° from the vertical, the hoop forces in a hemispherical dome are tensile rather than compressive.

Figure 8.19 illustrates a three-dimensional graphical analysis of a hemispherical masonry dome by William S. Wolfe in his book *Graphical Analysis: A Textbook on Graphic Statics* (1921). The hoop forces are fixed at the values needed to keep the thrust line on the center surface of the dome. These values can be found using the following graphical construction.

We start by dividing the dome into pie slices in plan (Fig. 499) and then in radial pieces in section (Fig. 500). Fig. 497 shows in simplified form what we have done. Next, we find the centroids of all pieces in section, estimate the weights of the pieces, and construct a load line from these weights (Fig. 501).

We draw a horizontal line from A at the top of the load line to the right. Through points B through S, we draw lines parallel to the corresponding segments of the section (Figure 500). These intersect the horizontal line through A at points 1, 2, 3, etc.

The small arrows in Fig. 499 are aligned in the directions of the hoop forces (circumferential forces) that act on each segment of the dome. Parallel to the first pair of these arrows (P_1, P'_1), we draw lines through A and 1 to intersect at a'. These two lines can be scaled to give the hoop forces at the top of the dome. Continuing this operation, from the top down, we find hoop forces for successive segments of the dome.

At segment 10, these hoop forces diminish to zero. Below this point, the spiky triangles of hoop force are negative in value, reflecting the reversal of hoop stress that occurs in an actual dome at about 52 degrees from the vertical (identified on Wolfe's drawing as section Y-Y). Above Y-Y, the rings of the dome are compression rings, and below, they are tension rings.

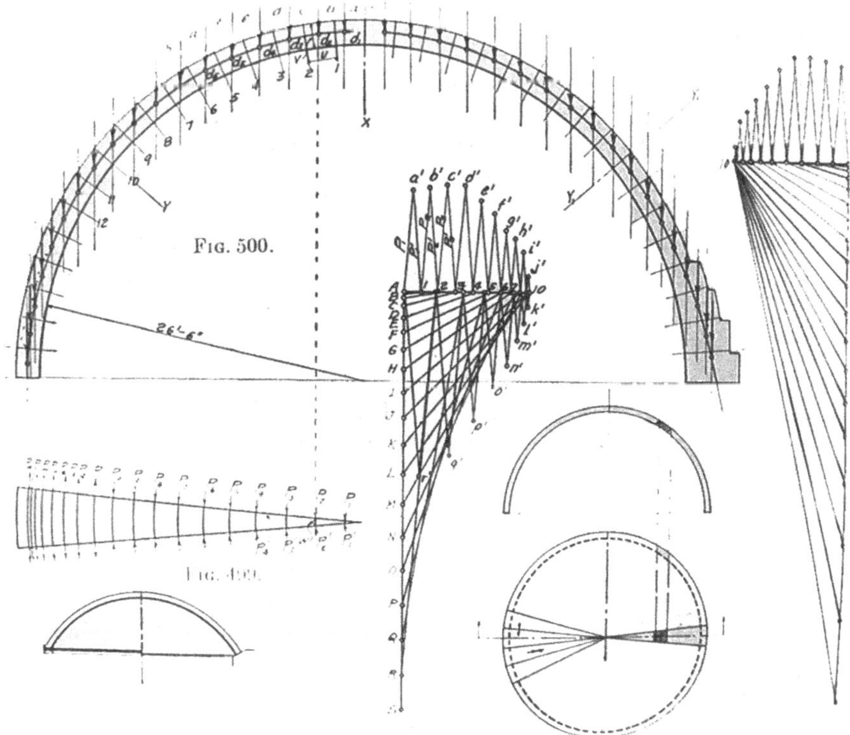

◀**Figure 8.19** Graphical analysis of a masonry dome (Wolfe, 1921).

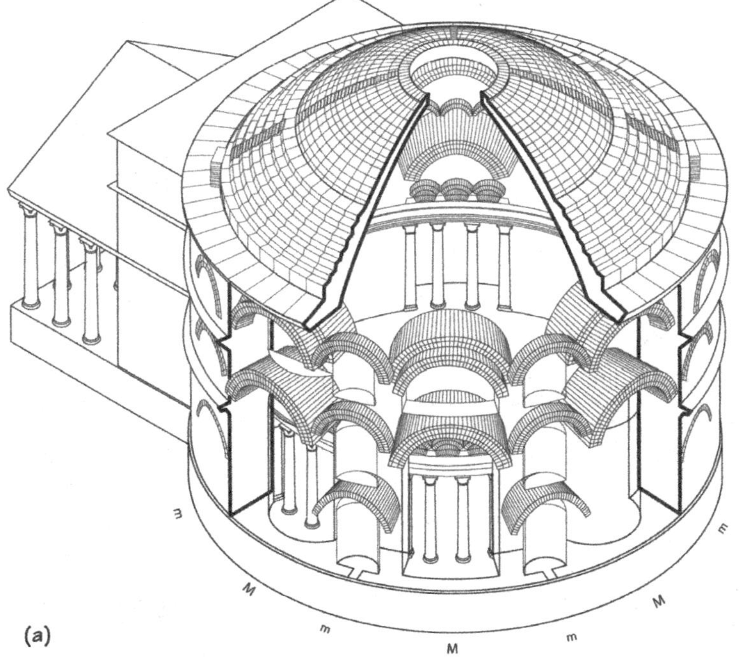

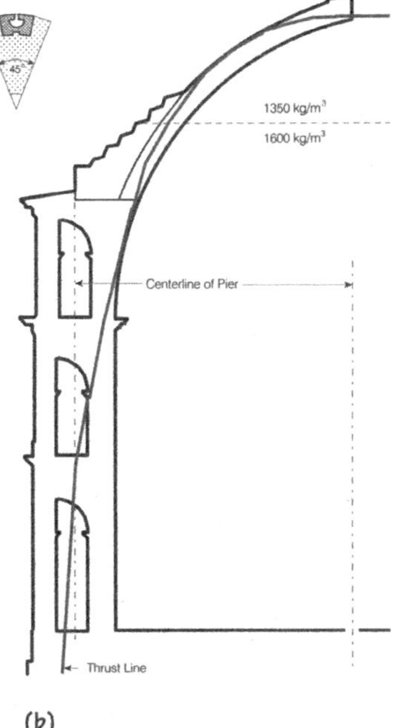

▼**Figure 8.20** (a) Axonometric drawing of the structure of the Pantheon dome; and (b) thrust line of section through dome and buttress wall.

Drawings courtesy of Lynne Lancaster.

A two-dimensional arch will collapse if any voussoir is removed. But in a dome, forces flow in three dimensions, allowing for many additional load paths. Rounded holes that are small relative to the size of the dome can be introduced in almost any location. Many classical domes, for example, feature a set of small, arched windows around the bottom, or dormers in higher locations. A horizontal circular hole can be introduced into the top of a dome, creating an opening known as an *oculus*. Forces flow around the oculus in a local compression ring. This ring is circular, the funicular form for radial loading. The most famous oculus is that of the Pantheon in Rome, whose dome was cast in unreinforced concrete and thus acts as an unreinforced masonry dome. The clear span of the dome is 43 m (143 ft), and the diameter of the oculus is 8.3 m (27 ft) (Figure 8.20).

In the twentieth century, the Guastavino Company used graphic statics to design hundreds of thin

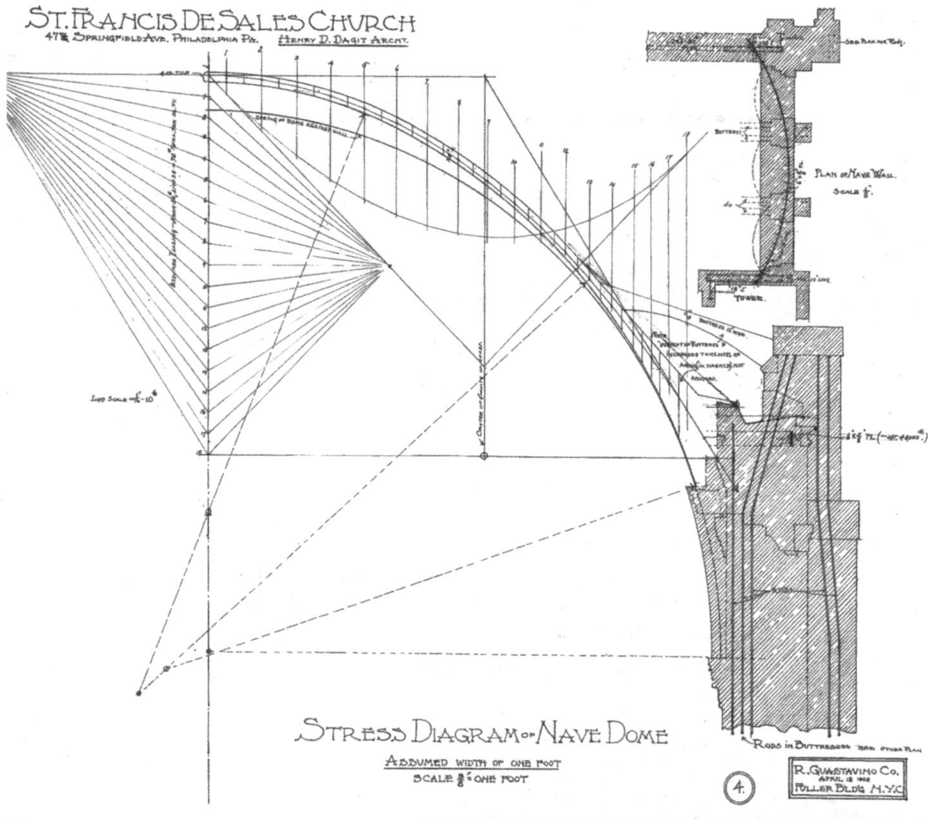

(a)

(b)

Figure 8.21 Two domes by the Guastavino Company: (a) St. Francis de Sales Church, Philadelphia, 1908; (b) inner dome of the Elephant House in the Bronx Zoo, 1909, with numerous openings for natural light.

Drawing courtesy of Guastavino/Collins Collection, Avery Library. Photo courtesy of Michael Freeman.

shell tile domes that were subsequently built. In some cases, they added flying buttresses to resist the outward thrust of the dome, as in the church of St. Francis de Sales in Philadelphia (Figure 8.21a). Their structures were characterized by excellent craftmanship, decorative tile finishes, and elaborate arrays of openings to admit natural light, as in the Elephant House of the Bronx Zoo (Figure 8.21b).

FUNICULAR VERSUS GEOMETRICAL DESIGN IN MASONRY

The task of the designer of an unreinforced masonry structure is to find a shape for it such that all parts of the structure will remain in compression under all foreseeable loading conditions. To do this, the designer has two basic options. One is to use *classical* geometry, which is composed of vertical walls and columns supporting arches, vaults, and domes that are made up of circular arcs of constant radius. The other is to use a *funicular* geometry governed by the lines along which forces flow through structures (Figure 8.22). Structures with classical geometries are easier to lay out and build, but they use more material in forcing the structural thrust lines to fit within a predefined geometrical section. In contrast, funicular geometries locate all material close to the thrust line and thereby use less material; but funicular arches, with their constantly changing angles and radii, are somewhat harder to lay out and build than classical arches.

Architect Antoni Gaudí (1852–1926) and others of his time in the Barcelona area, working from a rich local tradition of masonry vaulting, created their buildings from complex arrangements of funicular arches and vaults whose shapes were derived both from hanging chain models and graphic statics. Their expressive, exciting structures demonstrate solutions to the inherent challenges of funicular geometries. Because the self-weight of masonry is the dominant load, a funicular form is often designed to correspond closely to the thrust lines due to dead load only. We will follow this assumption as we return to our development of a

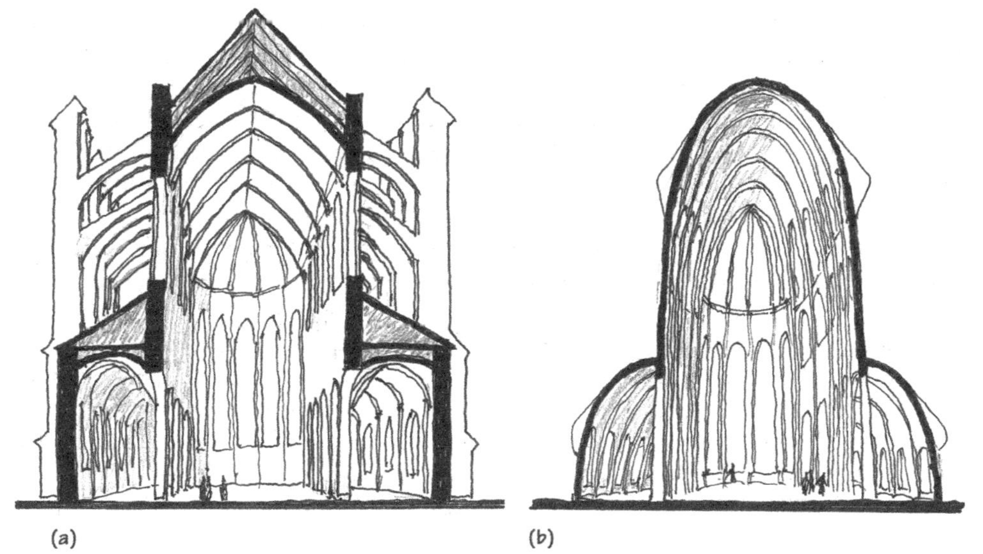

Figure 8.22 Classical (a) versus (b) funicular geometry for a masonry structure.

funicular design for the brick vault over the mosaic floor in southern France.

HANGING MODELS

An easy and powerful way to begin designing a funicular masonry structure is by experimenting with hanging chain models, using any of a number of small chains that are available in hardware stores. Though a bare chain does not generally represent the actual loads acting on the real structure, its form is a good approximation for that of a structure with a uniformly distributed dead load. Small weights can be added to the chain to mimic any actual load distribution. If we are working in two dimensions, a sheet of paper is mounted on a vertical surface, and the chain is hung over the sheet of paper, allowing us to trace the line of the chain. A chain model facilitates fast exploration of the infinite possibilities of structural form and gives insight into the influence of the support conditions. We will use hanging chain models for the initial design exploration of the vault, as shown in Figure 8.23, and then follow with more precise graphical methods.

INITIAL FORM-FINDING EXPERIMENTS

Our experimentation, as documented in Figure 8.23, begins with a single catenary, which corresponds to a single funicular vault (a). The supports for this shape can be on the same level or different levels. If the span is kept constant, a longer chain produces a higher vault shape with lower forces, and a shorter chain produces a lower vault with higher forces. We do not find that any shape and proportion of single vault is satisfactory for the roof over the ancient mosaic. Next we try dividing this vault into two equal spans (b), resulting in a single plane of vertical support piers or walls at the center. The equal spans do not give any particular importance to the mosaic floor; we would like to build a longer span over the floor to recognize its importance, and use a shorter span for auxiliary purposes. In (c), we change the support conditions to create two unequal arch spans,

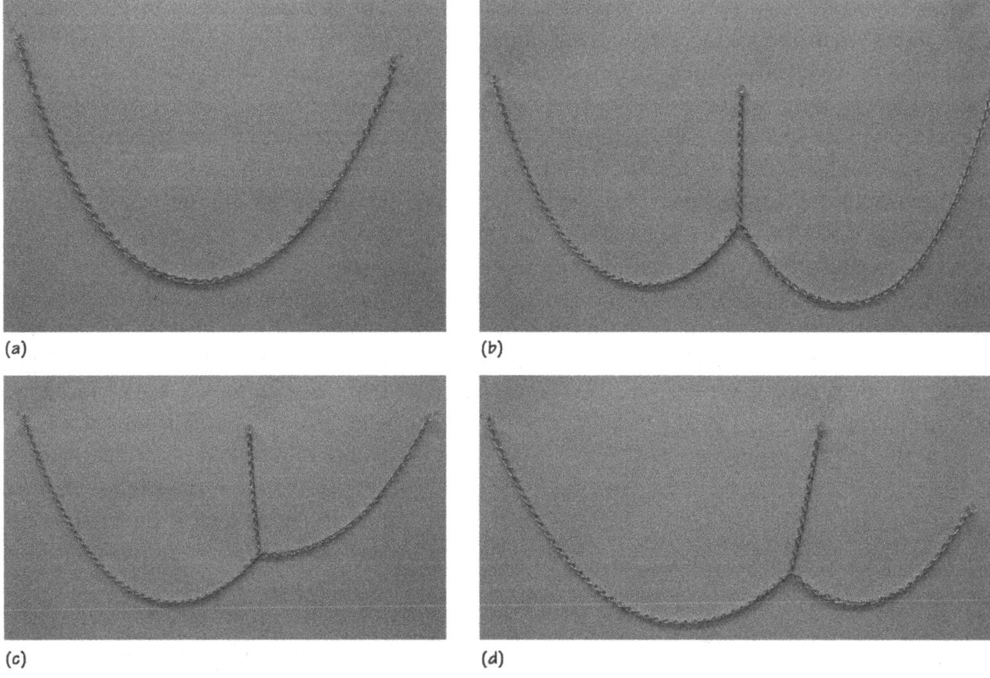

Figure 8.23 Hanging chain explorations of possible sections for a vaulted masonry building. Photo courtesy of Philippe Block.

and the chain adapts to show a sloping internal pier. The inclination of the pier, as determined by the hanging chain, is governed by the relative proportions of the two spans. We refine this in part (d) to reflect the actual site condition, in which the outer support for the smaller vault is higher than the other two supports in order that it may clear a low retaining wall and rest on a higher bank along the rear edge. The result shows two unequal spans buttressing each other in an asymmetrical configuration that is stable. This solution provides a large hall to shelter the mosaic floor, with an adjacent, smaller gallery to display related archaeological artifacts and explain the history of the site. We like the relative proportions of the model, as well as the graceful curves of its vaulting, and will proceed with the design on this basis.

Developing the Design of the Vaulted Brick Roof

For more detailed development of our design for the vaulted brick roof, we switch to graphical analysis. This allows us to model the varying load conditions easily and provides an accurate determination of the internal forces in the structure. First, we estimate the loads. Uniformly spaced equal loads are a good first guess for a vault of constant thickness. For our vault, the total width is 20 m. Because the ratio of the vault spans is 12:5, we divide this width into 17 segments (with 17 point loads). We find that dividing this span into 17 segments (with 17 point loads) is suitable to devise the geometry of its form. For a vault with a thickness of 14 cm, the self-weight of a 1-m-wide strip is about 0.14 m × 2000 kg/m^3 = 280 kg/m^2. This results in loads of 280 kg/m^2 × 1 m × (20/17) m = 330 kg for each of the point loads in the strip.*

To convert the shape of the hanging chain to its compressive equivalent (Figure 8.23d), we mount paper on a tackboard and hang the chain model over it. We trace the form of the chain onto the paper. Then we use this tracing, inverted, as the basis for a graphical analysis, which will result in a more precisely defined shape and numerical values of force (Figure 8.24). We start with the main span by constructing a funicular shape through three points: the boundary nodes *1* and 2 and a third point chosen at the crown of the chain solution. Because the curve of the chain is more or less parabolic, we can construct this curve with the simple construction used in Chapter 2.

Once the main arch is constructed, the inclination of the buttress through node 2 and the shape of the arch of the side aisle (passing through nodes 2 and 3) are fixed. In order to guarantee equilibrium for each arch, their outer rays have to intersect at the lines of action of their respective resultants, W_{main} and W_{side}. For global equilibrium, the outer rays of the entire system—that is, both arches combined—also need to intersect on the line of action of the global weight resultant, W_{total}. We can find the pole of the force polygon for the side arch easily, because we know the direction of its outer rays, from which the funicular shape can be drawn directly.

So far we have found the shape of the vault that is funicular for the dominant loading case—that is, under self-weight only. We now need to design for asymmetric live loads such as snow, accidental point loads, or wind. There are several possible approaches that we may follow from this point. The first is to choose an initial constant thickness for the section and then check to see if the thrust lines of all loading cases stay within the middle third of the chosen section to ensure that the masonry remains in compression throughout. A second approach is to add stiffeners or diaphragms, which locally provide more depth for the thrust line to pass through. The vault can be thinner overall compared to the first approach, but stiffeners may be visually unappealing. The third approach is to optimize the section by generating an envelope of all thrust line solutions and then to build up the masonry section of varying thickness to safely contain this envelope. A fourth option could be to create the extra depth needed to accommodate the thrust lines under all loading cases by undulating the masonry surface.

The last two approaches allow for a more expressive structural design, but it is necessary to make some choices to limit the envelope of the thrust values. To sculpt the supports, we choose to have a thinner section at midspan, hence dictating that all solutions pass through a single point at midspan. We can account for live loading by superimposing asymmetric loading on parts of the structure to account for the effects of wind or snow. For an arch, the critical live loading usually acts on one half of the span, roughly equivalent to applying a large concentrated load at the quarterpoint of the arch. In an earthquake zone, the influence of horizontal ground accelerations can be considered by analyzing a mortarless model of the masonry structure on a tilting plane to approximate the seismic loading. The tangent of the angle of tilt is equal to the horizontal acceleration of the strongest expected earthquake. Fortunately, the Roussillon region of France is not subject to strong seismic events, so seismic loading can be neglected for this design.

We also analyze a loading consisting of the live load plus the dead load. Since there are again an infinite number of possible shapes that are in equilibrium with the new set of loads, we choose to continue our previous approach, minimizing the depth of the section at midspan of the main vault, as well as minimizing the width of the support at node 3. This means we want all solutions under all asymmetric loading cases to stay within the middle third of the 14-cm segment of the main arch at midspan and to pass through node 3.

The loads in the sections where live loads are superimposed become (280 + 150) kg/m^2 × 1 m × (20/17) m = 457 kg for a 1-m-wide strip. Figure 8.25a superimposes live loads on the dead load due to self-weight for just the left half of the main span; and (b) on the right half of the main span. These two load cases are judged to be the most critical.

*There are two conventions currently in use for force and stress calculations in metric units. This chapter uses the older and simpler of the two, which assumes that kilograms are units of force and that centimeters are an acceptable unit of distance. The newer convention, which is presented in the next chapter, recognizes that the kilogram is actually a unit of mass, not force, and must be converted to newtons of force by being multiplied by the acceleration of gravity. To avoid confusion of units, it uses only millimeters and meters, not centimeters.

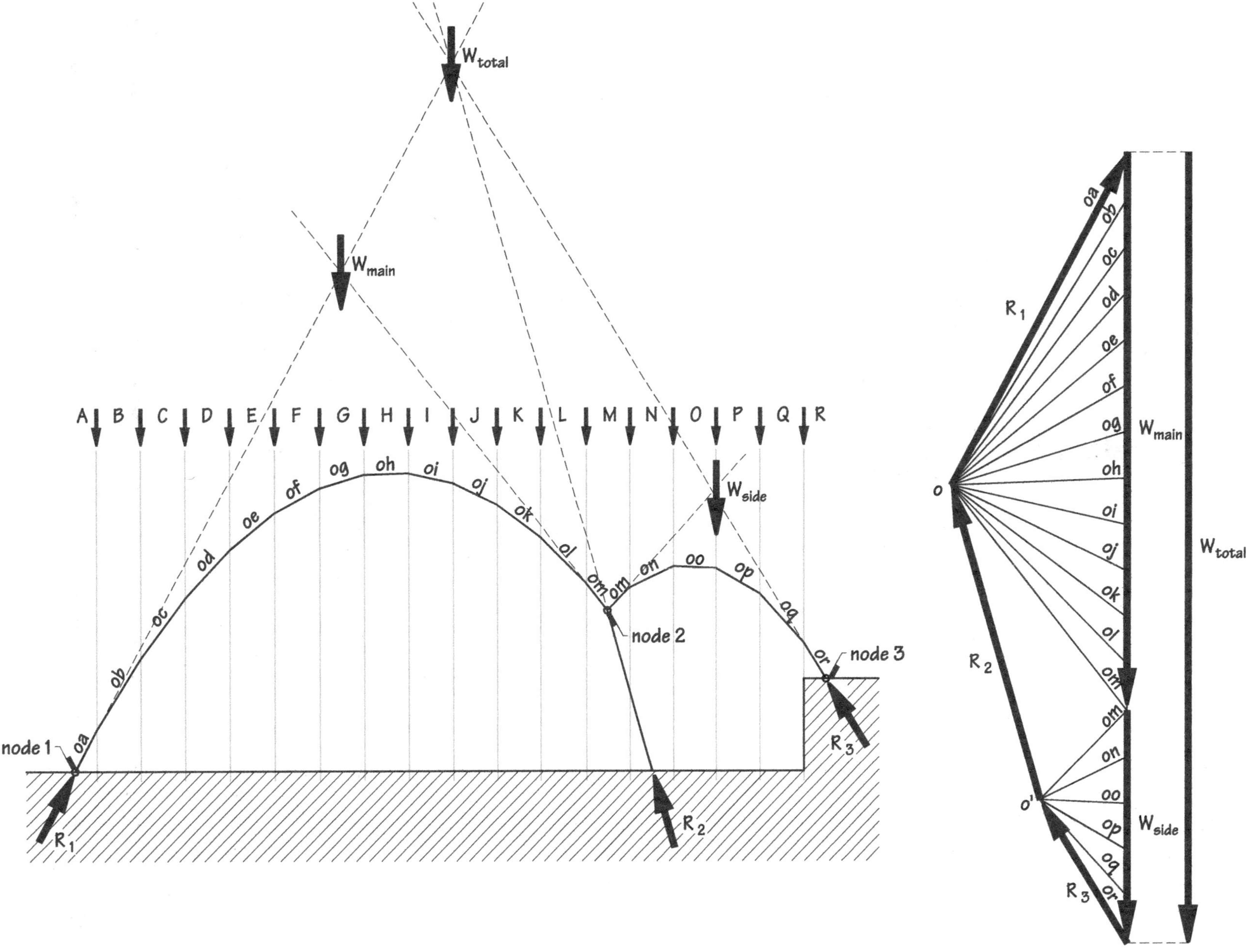

Figure 8.24 The funicular design found from the hanging chain model is translated using graphic statics.

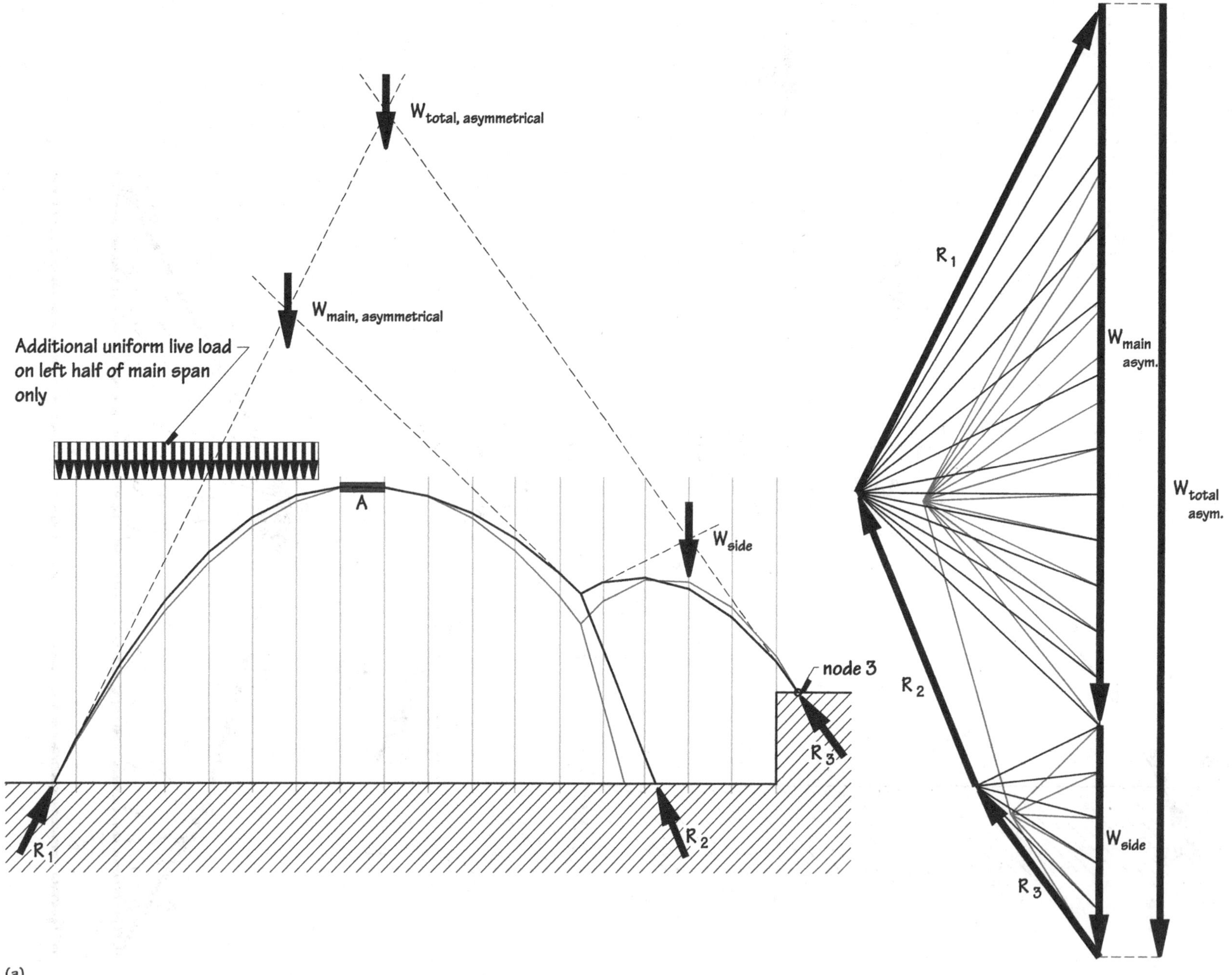

(a)

Figure 8.25 Graphical solution for asymmetric live loading, applied on only (a) the left and (b) right half of the main span, superimposed onto the estimated dead load.

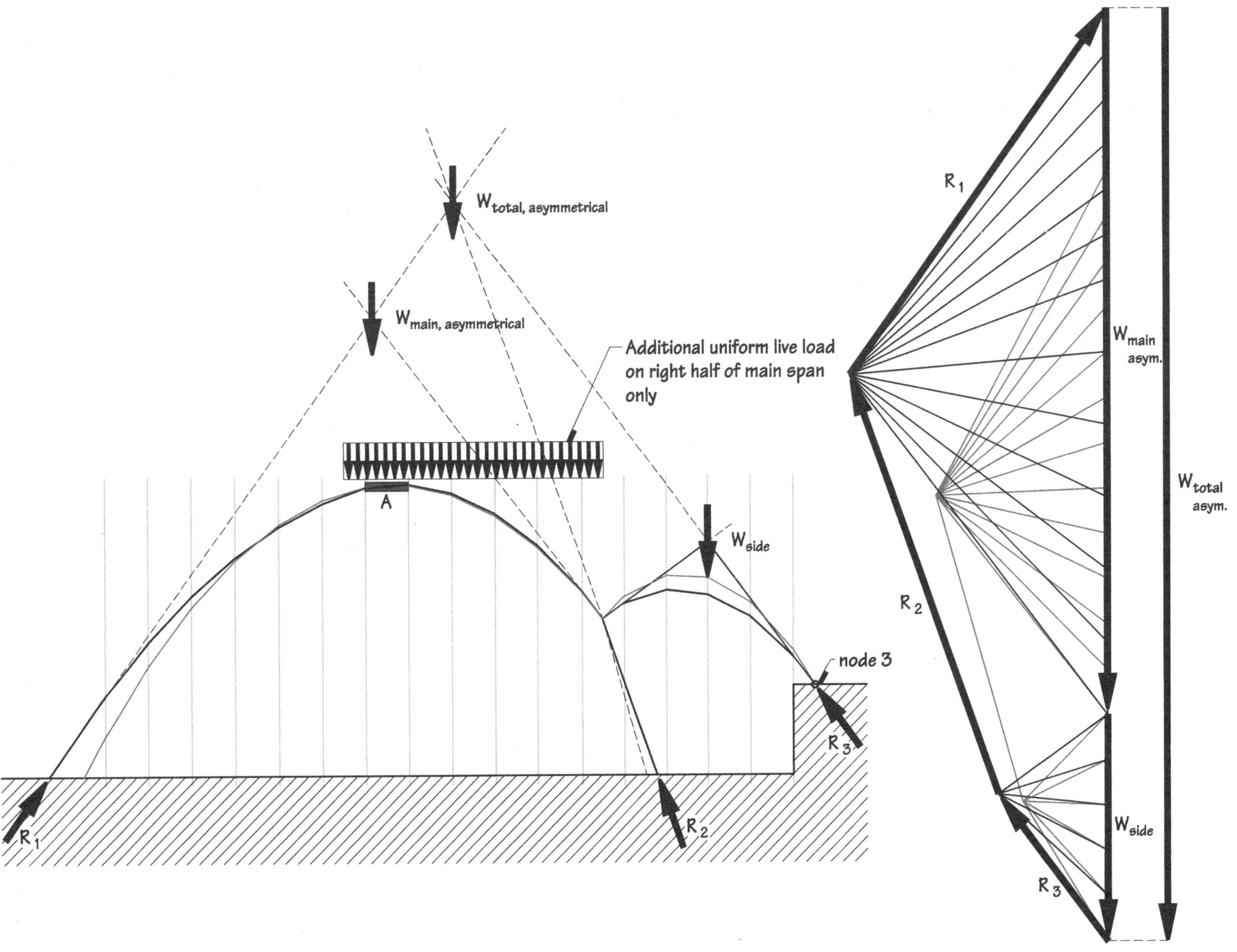

(b)

Figure 8.25 *(Continued)*

Figure 8.26a displays all of the various equilibrium solutions in one drawing. From this, we trace the envelope of all solutions. This envelope will become the middle third of the final sectional profile of our design. Notice that the asymmetric loading cases on the side aisle are not checked, because it is clear that in this case, the depth of the side arch, due to the asymmetric loading cases on the main arch, is enough to take all loading cases.

Instead of thickening the vault section to match the envelope of all solutions, which would use a vast amount of masonry, the necessary depth can be achieved by undulating or corrugating the masonry surface (Figure 8.26c–d). This allows the masonry shell to retain its relatively small thickness of 14 cm while having an effective depth that is much greater, and it opens to us some spatially interesting strategies to extend the vault in the third dimension, an art of which Eladio Dieste was a master (Figure 8.27).

Finally, we want to estimate the stresses in the material to ensure that they are within safe limits. Looking at Figure 8.25a, we see that the largest force will occur at point *1* when the live loading acts on the left half of the main arch. We find the force by measuring the length of the longest vector in the force polygon in (a), which gives approximately 3,960 kg. The stress acting on the 1-m-wide strip then becomes 3,960 kg / (14 cm × 100 cm) = 3 kg/cm^2, which is well below the crushing stress of a typical brick (~150 kg/cm^2). The safety factor against crushing is greater than 50, illustrating that the stresses in the brick are very low indeed.

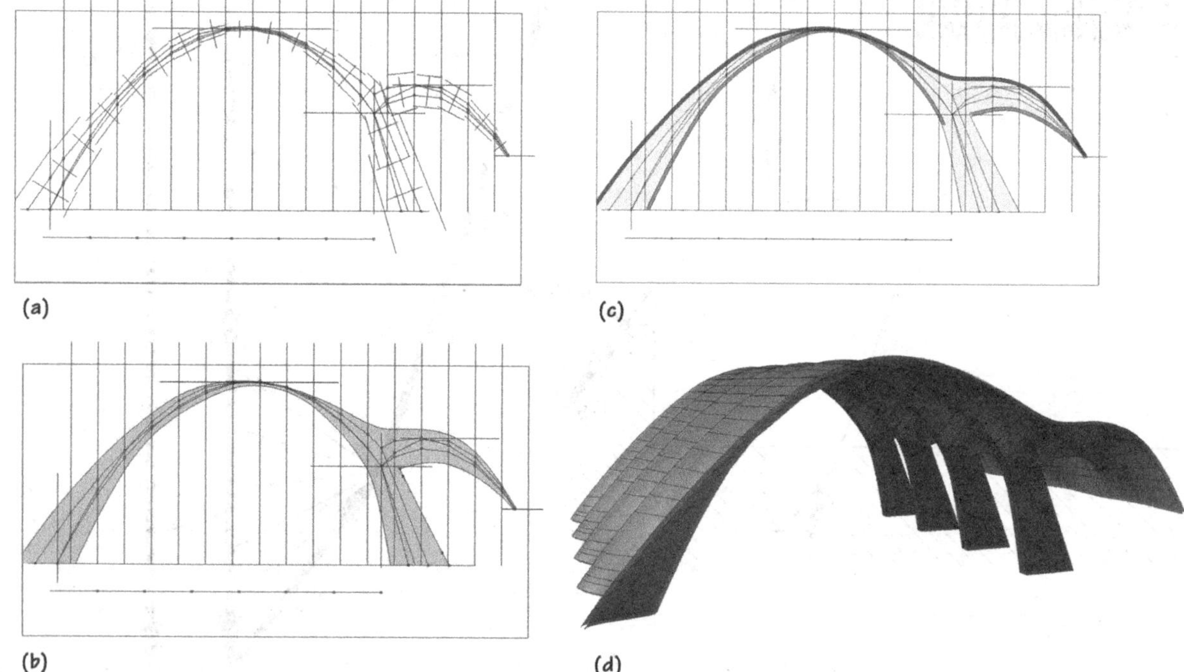

Figure 8.26 (a) Offsetting the bounding box of all loading cases to guarantee all solutions to stay within the middle third of the final section, shown in (b); (c) the necessary depth provided by an undulated vault of constant thickness (d).

EXTENDING THE DESIGN TO THREE DIMENSIONS

Until now, our design exploration has considered a two-dimensional section of the vaulted building. Now we must consider how to extend this exciting two-dimensional form into three dimensions. The first option is a full extrusion: The initial section is extruded into the page to create a barrel vaulted hall, as in Figure 8.28a. However, this would create a dark interior with poor air circulation. Since the stresses in the material are low, we can open up the vault by inserting funicularly shaped openings in the transverse direction (Figure 8.28b). This makes the structure much lighter visually and more architecturally interesting but would require extensive formwork to support the vault during construction and may not be stable under live loads. A third option (Figure 8.28c) is to create brick arches in the form of the two-dimensional section, and then to vault between these arches with brick vaults, which would result in an undulating form.

▲ **Figure 8.27** One of Dieste's grain silos in Vergara, Uruguay; it is only one brick thick. The shape was created by undulating a catenary profile in the third dimension. See also Figures 11.45 and 11.46.

Photo: Edward Allen

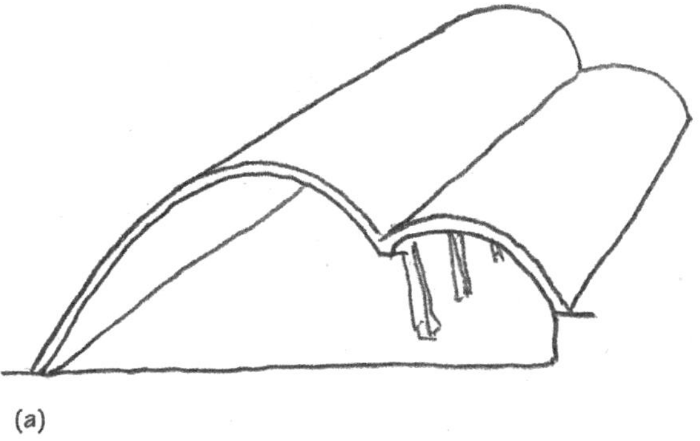

(a)

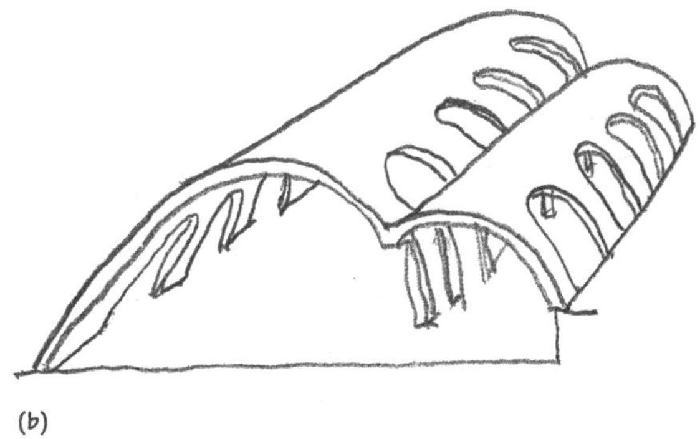

(b)

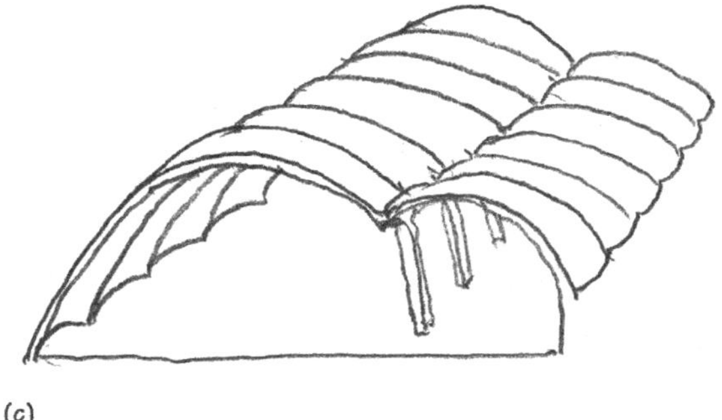

(c)

Figure 8.28 Alternatives for extending the vault design into three dimensions.

To construct brick vaults between parallel arches, we may consider one of several different vaulting methods (Figure 8.29). Mediterranean tile vaulting laminates multiple layers of thin ceramic tiles to create structural vaults with minimal centering required during construction. This type of construction flourished in medieval Spain and has long been practiced in the Roussillon region of France. Thus, it is culturally appropriate for the new building, and it could help to revive a local masonry vaulting tradition. For our building, tile vaulting could be used to create complex curving forms with upturned edges to maximize daylighting and ventilation, using individual bricks to sculpt the vault supports.

To further increase the resistance of the vault to unbalanced loadings, we elect to give it secondary curvature in the form of a series of shallow barrel vaults at right angles to the spanning direction of the main vaults. This greatly increases the effective depth of the main vaults.

We must stabilize the parallel arches against out-of-plane forces such as wind. At the final arch on each end of the building, the vault thrust is not balanced by an adjacent vault and needs to be buttressed. Steel tie rods running from one end of the structure to the other could be introduced to restrain this thrust, but they would compromise the appearance of the brick vaults and create a long-term maintenance problem because of corrosion of the steel. Another solution would be to erect masonry buttresses at the ends of the structure. These could assume any of several shapes (Figure 8.30). Leaning the final bay inward at each end is another alternative that would provide an elegant structural solution, although it would be fairly complicated to construct.

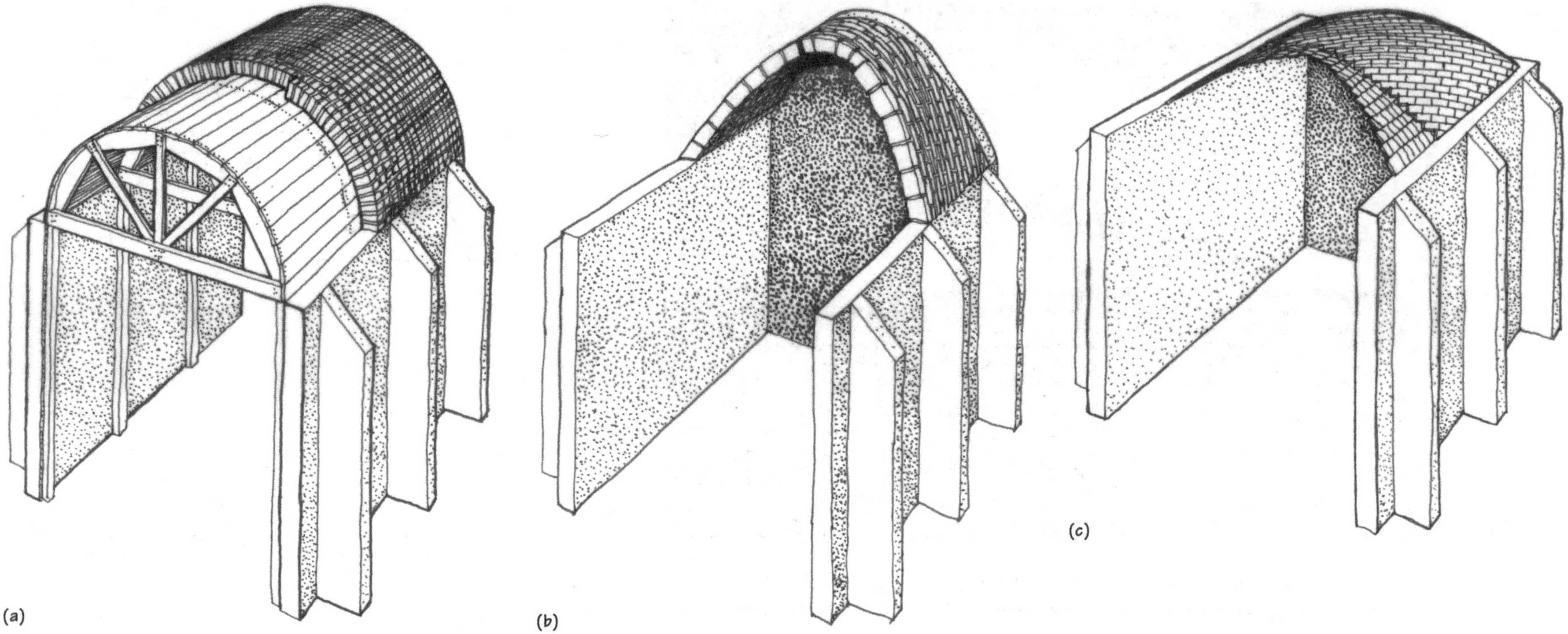

(a) (b) (c)

Figure 8.29 Three methods of brick vault construction: (a) northern European vaults, constructed with extensive wooden centering; (b) pitched brick vaults built in North Africa and the Middle East without centering; and (c) Mediterranean laminated tile vaults constructed without centering.

Drawing: Edward Allen

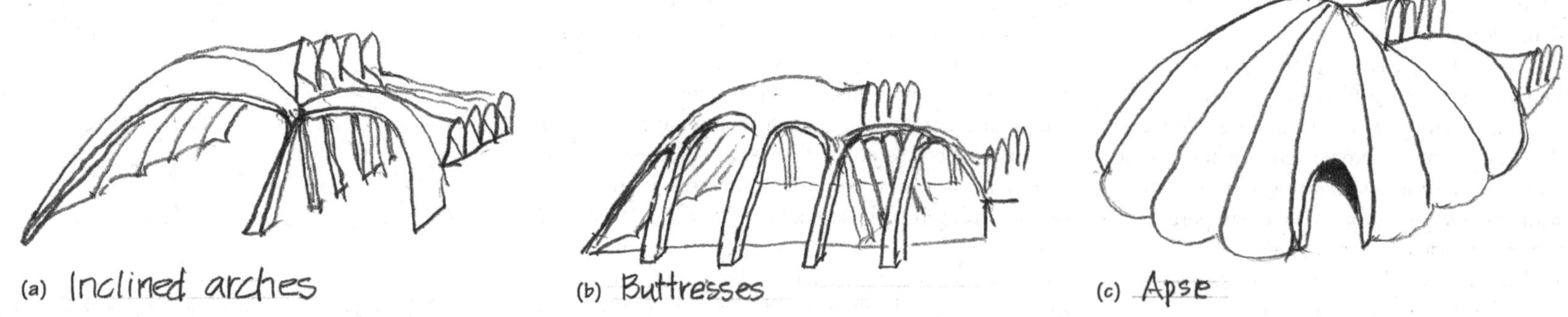

Figure 8.30 Options for buttressing the final arch in masonry.

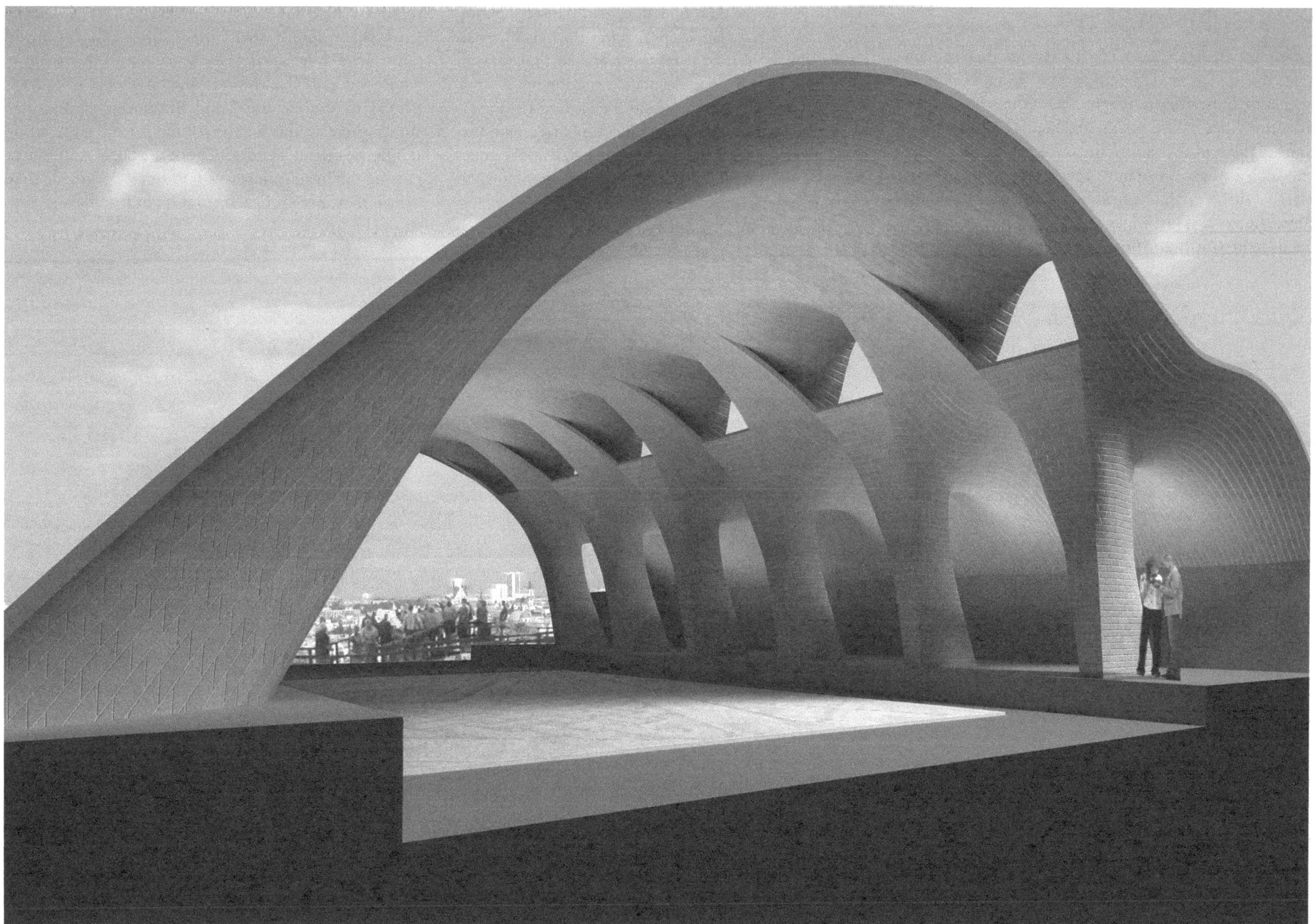

Figure 8.31. Rendering of possible final design for the vault. The form was found from the thrust lines developed in this chapter, sculpted into three dimensions with CAD software. Design and image by Boston Structures Group.

COMPLETING THE DESIGN

There are many aspects of this design that call for careful shaping and detailing, not from structural necessity, but rather to create a structure that is confidently sculpted and neatly finished. The raised portions of the roof that house the clerestory windows are one such aspect: These must merge smoothly with the main vaults in such a way that rainwater drains freely from the roof. The brickwork of the inclined piers needs to be sturdy and beautiful, with the bed joints at right angles to the direction of thrust, to limit shearing action. We must also keep in mind that visitors will tend to put their hands on the piers, so that we will want to provide a pleasant tactile experience.

Brick and tile masonry lend themselves to decorative patterns that exploit the small units to create textures, patterns, and shadows (Figure 8.32). We must consider the extent to which we might employ such devices in this structure.

Masonry vaulting has not been used very much in the United States in recent years because of the relatively high labor costs involved in the intricate work that vaulted structures require. In countries with lower wages, such as Mexico and other Latin American states, architects and engineers have continued to design and build unreinforced masonry vaulting by traditional methods, often with stunningly beautiful results. There are also contemporary examples of innovative buildings worldwide that utilize masonry arches and vaults in fascinating new ways (Figure 8.33).

Figure 8.32 This window in Seville is spanned with a combination of corbelling and arching; projecting bricks above the arch offer shelter from rain.

Photo: Edward Allen.

◀**Figure 8.33** Structural stone arches support the roof of the San Giovanni Rotondo church dedicated to Padre Pio. Designed by Renzo Piano, Italy, 2004.

Photo: Edward Allen.

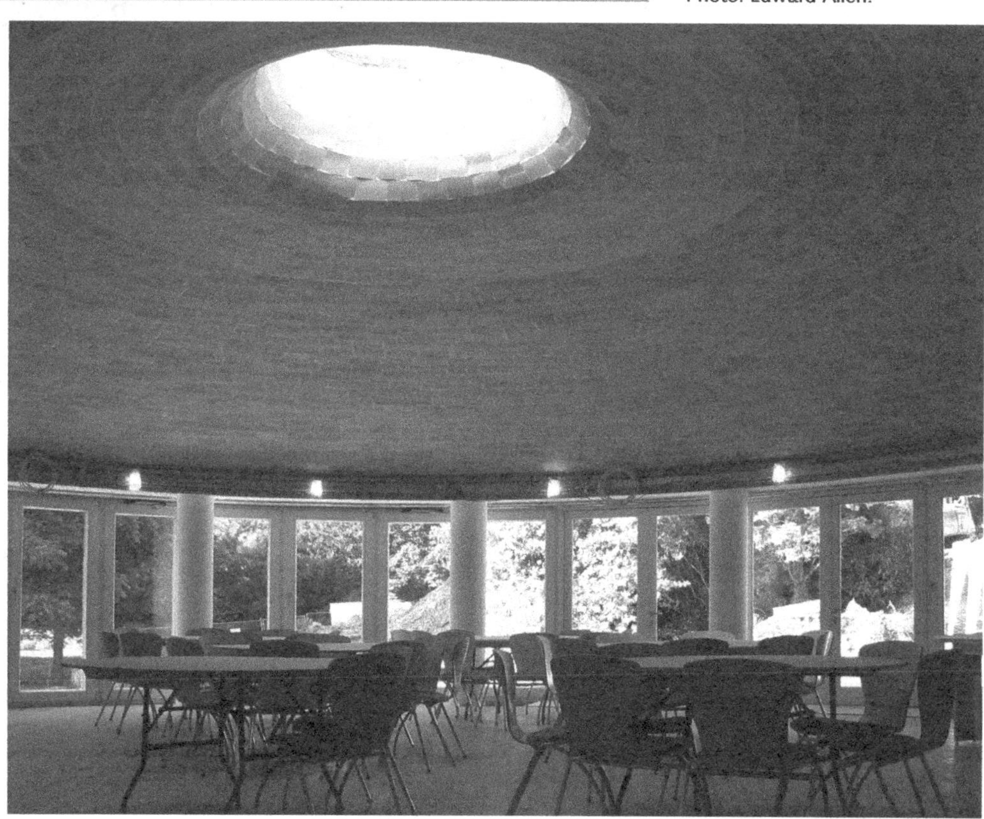

▶**Figure 8.34** Tile vaulted domes support a green roof in the Pines Calyx Building, by Helionix Designs, Dover, England, 2006.

Photo courtesy of Michael H. Ramage.

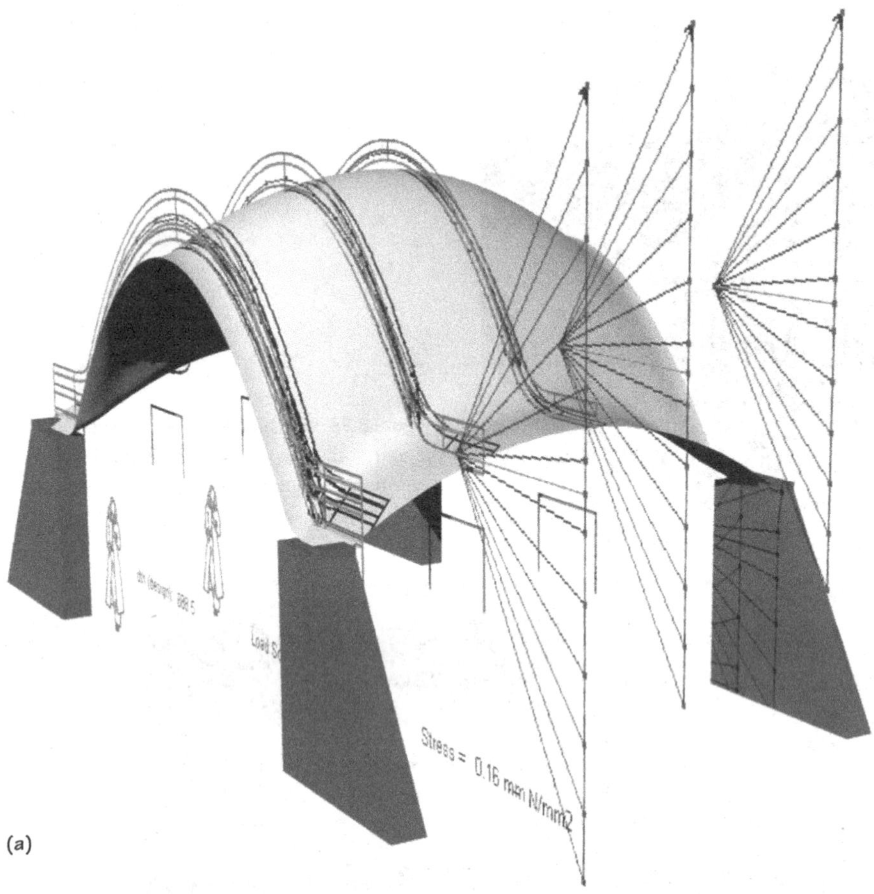

(a)

(b)

(c)

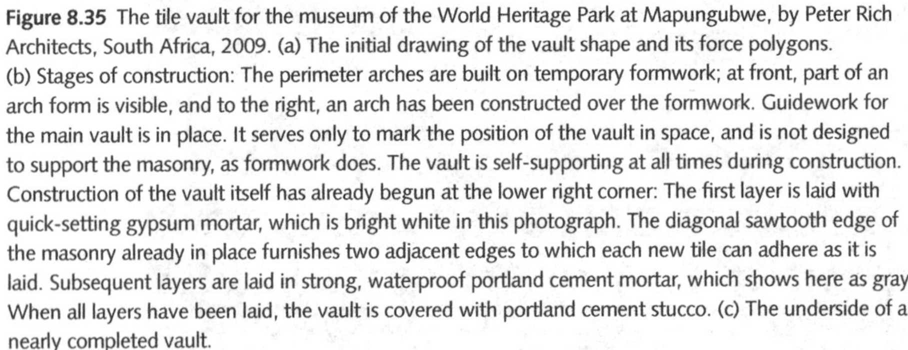

Figure 8.35 The tile vault for the museum of the World Heritage Park at Mapungubwe, by Peter Rich Architects, South Africa, 2009. (a) The initial drawing of the vault shape and its force polygons. (b) Stages of construction: The perimeter arches are built on temporary formwork; at front, part of an arch form is visible, and to the right, an arch has been constructed over the formwork. Guidework for the main vault is in place. It serves only to mark the position of the vault in space, and is not designed to support the masonry, as formwork does. The vault is self-supporting at all times during construction. Construction of the vault itself has already begun at the lower right corner: The first layer is laid with quick-setting gypsum mortar, which is bright white in this photograph. The diagonal sawtooth edge of the masonry already in place furnishes two adjacent edges to which each new tile can adhere as it is laid. Subsequent layers are laid in strong, waterproof portland cement mortar, which shows here as gray. When all layers have been laid, the vault is covered with portland cement stucco. (c) The underside of a nearly completed vault.

Photo courtesy of James Bellamy.

Figure 8.36 Free-form stone vault designed using graphical equilibrium methods in three dimensions, by Escobedo Construction and Philippe Block.

Figure 8.37 Michael Butrim, then a student of architecture at the University of Washington, designed this brick-vaulted museum of unreinforced brick masonry to house an ancient Egyptian wooden boat. He decided to forgo the use of buttresses by determining graphically the paths of the forces and providing masonry along these paths. (a) Longitudinal section. (b) Exterior perspective. (c) Interior view.

ANTONI GAUDÍ

Antoni Gaudi (1852–1926) was a Catalan architect who worked in and around Barcelona. His complex and often colorfully ornamented curved surfaces grew from technical traditions of Catalan masonry. Gaudí's masterwork, still under construction, is the immense Sagrada Familia temple in Barcelona. Here, from 1884 until his death in 1926, he took over construction of a neo-Gothic work already underway and transformed it with his new approach. As a result of his lifelong search for a truly natural architecture, he believed that structural forms should be derived from funicular lines rather than predetermined geometries such as vertical Gothic piers and buttresses. Gaudí designed his inclined piers and arches both by graphic statics and by inverted hanging models. He said in an interview, "I found the funiculars for the [Sagrada Familia] in a graphical manner and those of the Colonia Guell by experiment. But the two procedures are the same, one is the brother of the other." Later Spanish architects such as Jose Lluis Sert saw great potential in his exploration of curved surfaces. Sert wrote, "We cannot go on building our cities solely of edifices that look like boxes and are inspired exclusively by the system of beams and pilasters. . . . The continuing evolution of modern architecture will probably lead to an ever greater appreciation and importance of Gaudí's later experiments." (M. Ragon, "Historia de la arquitectura," *Rome*, 1974, vol. 1, pp. 266–267.)

Exercises

1. From Roman times until the present, a popular type of bridge for short spans has been the earth-filled stone arch bridge (Figure 8.38). Bridges of this type are found throughout the world. The arches are built of stone masonry, almost invariably in semicircular form. Spandrel walls of stone are built on each side from the arches up to the level of the roadway, creating a large vessel of masonry that is then filled with compacted earth and paved. A structural analysis of such a bridge must take into account the dead load of the earth fill, which varies considerably across the arch span. Find a plausible thrust line for dead load plus a live load of 100 psf in the arch of the bridge shown here. Assume a weight for stone and earth of 130 pounds per cubic foot. Comment on the suitability of the semicircular shape for an earth-filled arch. Could there be a wedging action that also plays a role in the structural behavior of this bridge? Can you suggest a more suitable shape?

2. Using Worksheet 8A on the supplemental site, propose a strategy to roof a house with brick vaulting.

Key Terms

unreinforced masonry
corbel
course
backweight
tholos
Hooke's principle
voussoir
arch
line of thrust
keystone
minimum thrust
maximum thrust
buttress
aisle
nave
flying buttress
kern
pier
rib vault
quadripartite vault
classical and funicular geometry

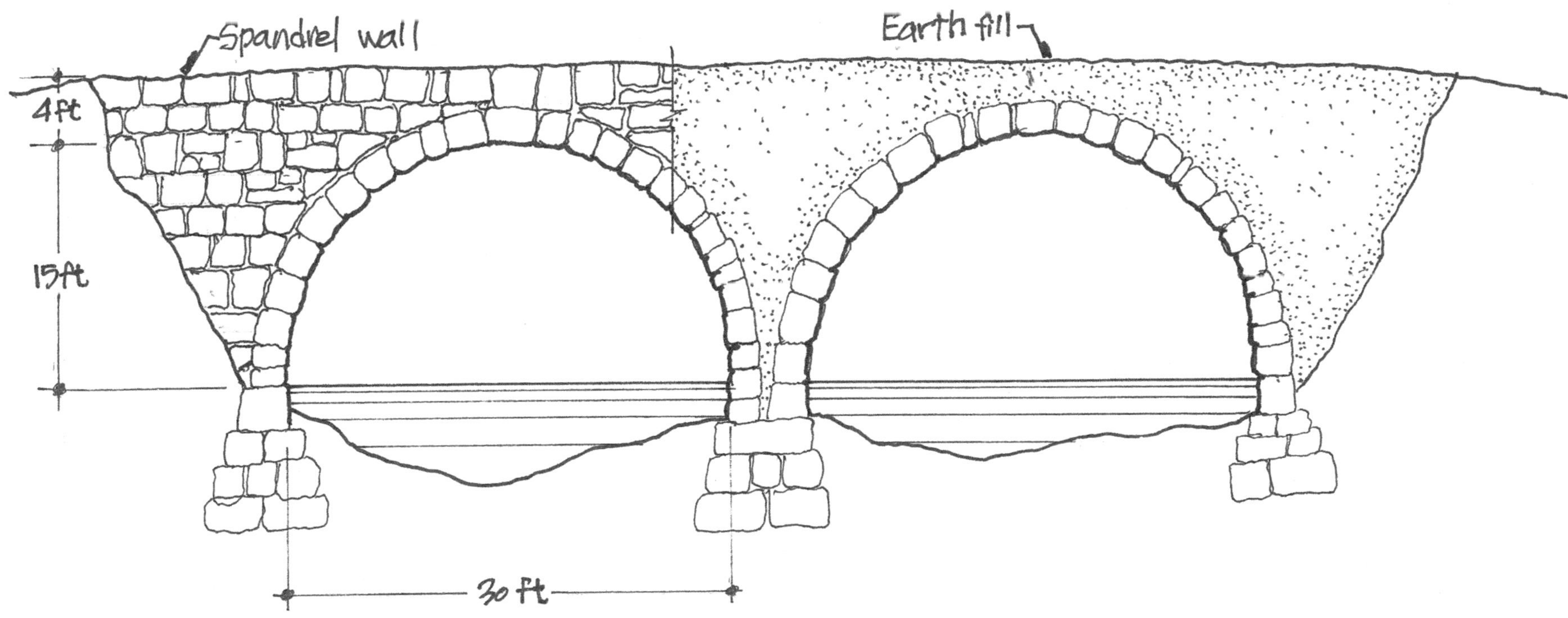

Figure 8.38 Partial elevation (left) and partial longitudinal section of an earth-filled bridge.

Further References

Anderson, Stanford (ed.), *Eladio Dieste: Innovation in Structural Art.* New York: Princeton Architectural Press, 2004. With sumptuous color photographs and essays on various aspects of his work, this is the definitive volume on Eladio Dieste and his buildings in reinforced masonry.

Heyman, J., *The Stone Skeleton: Structural Engineering of Masonry Architecture.* Cambridge, UK: Cambridge University Press, 1995. This is the best introduction to the function of historic masonry structures, written by an engineer and pioneer in the field.

Huerta, S., *Arcos, bóvedas y cúpulas: geometría y equilibrio en el cálculo tradicional de estructuras de fabrica.* Madrid: Instituto Juan de Herrera, 2004. Though not yet available in English translation, this book provides the best overview of the design methods and science of traditional masonry construction.

Lancaster, L., *Concrete Vaulted Construction in Imperial Rome.* Cambridge, UK: Cambridge University Press, 2005. This award-winning book offers an overview of the materials, construction techniques, and structural behavior of Roman vaults and domes.

Ochsendorf, J., *Guastavino Vaulting: The Art of Structural Tile.* New York: Princeton Architectural Press, 2009. This book provides a rich visual and technical overview of the structural tile vaulting constructed by the Guastavino Company.

http://web.mit.edu/masonry: Research group in masonry structures at the Massachusetts Institute of Technology.

www.guastavino.net: Resources on Guastavino tile vault construction.

CHAPTER 9

Master Lesson: Designing a Concrete Shell Roof for a Grandstand

- *Equilibrium in three dimensions of a composite structure; combining funicular vaults and trusses*
- *Architectural and engineering interactions in designing forms and construction processes*
- *Working in SI (metric) units*

Diane's excitement came over the telephone even before she spoke.

"Hey, Bruce, a letter just arrived inviting me to enter a competition for the design of a structure in Costa Verde. Work is a little slack here at the moment, so I've got time to do it. I'm hoping that you can work on it with me."

"From the sound of your voice, it must be something terrific! What is the building?"

"It's a roof to cover the grandstand seats of their new national soccer stadium. It's relatively modest in scale and simple in its requirements, which means that aside from gravity and wind, there are few constraints on the design. And they're looking for something delightful and innovative that will focus world attention on their country. That means that it will be good publicity for its designers, too."

"Won't hundreds of firms enter? If so, it could be just a waste of our time."

"That's part of what's so good about it. They are inviting just six firms to enter, of which mine is one. They saw our mariner's chapel published in a magazine and liked it, so they put me on the short list."

"One in six is good odds when you factor ability into it. I'm in. Your office or mine?"

"Well, by coincidence, I'm calling on my cell phone from just outside your office door. I walked over to tell you in person, but your door was locked, so I called. How come the door isn't open?"

"Because it's eight o'clock in the evening, and we closed at five-thirty. But here I come to let you in."

Diane was apologetic as she stepped inside.

"If you're working late, maybe you're too busy to do this competition."

"I'm never too busy for a project with this kind of potential. It intrigues me. I think we can do a great job on it, and it could get us some good press. Tell me the program."

"It couldn't be simpler. They are looking for a straight run of grandstand seating with a column-free roof to keep sun and rain off spectators. The roof will have to cantilever 17 m from a line at the top of the seats. The length isn't fixed at the moment, but will probably be about 120 m."

"That's all? No toilets, no concession stands, no box seating for the prime minister?"

"The roof is all we have to do for the competition. The seats will rest directly on a sloping bank of earth."

"Okay. Do you have sketches of your ideas?"

"I haven't put any of them on paper yet, because I want to work with you from the beginning. The possibilities are endless."

FIRST IDEAS

"What materials should we be considering? Steel, concrete; maybe a synthetic fabric roof?"

Diane seized a pen and a roll of paper.

"All of the above. We should generate ideas in every material. Fabric and cables could be good. The long-span capability of the cables would even permit us to span the entire length of the stands from the ends (9.1)*."*

"Could we also use a longitudinal cable but move the masts inward (9.2)?"

"That would make the cables self-anchoring, eliminating the backstays. Another way to cantilever would be with steel trusses. We could shape them so they are deepest at the pylons, where forces are highest (9.3)*."*

"It might be fun to give the fulcrum more expressive emphasis in the form and details of the roof."

Bruce sketched a tiny perspective to illustrate the idea (9.4).

Figure 9.1

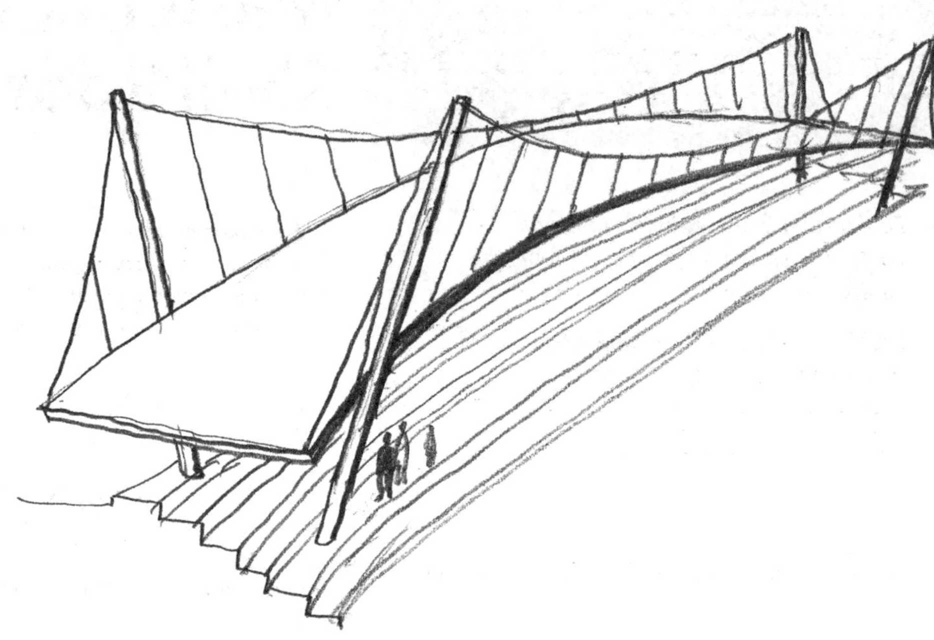

Figure 9.2

Figure 9.3

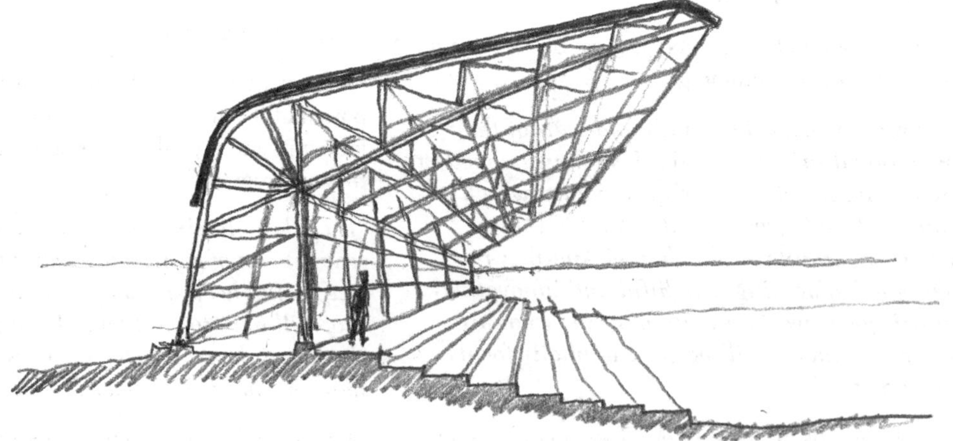

Figure 9.4

Figure 9.5

"We could also span the long direction of the grandstand with trusses (9.5)*."*

"The trouble with any system that spans the long way is that it puts columns right in the field of view of some of the spectators, even if they're only at the ends. The columns would also get in the way of future expansion of the stands. A cantilever seems to be the way to go."

"Just to get still more ideas on the table, let's look at some concrete shell solutions, too. Many of the skilled guys who worked on Felix Candela's magnificent shells in Mexico a half century ago (9.6) *came from Costa Verde. The Costa Verdeans continue to have a strong tradition of doing high-quality concrete work at reasonable prices."*

"This sounds like a rare opportunity to do a concrete shell roof. They seem to be economical only in countries where labor is inexpensive. Could we do something like this?"

Bruce took his pencil from his pocket to sketch a single-curved concrete surface held back by cables and masts (9.7).

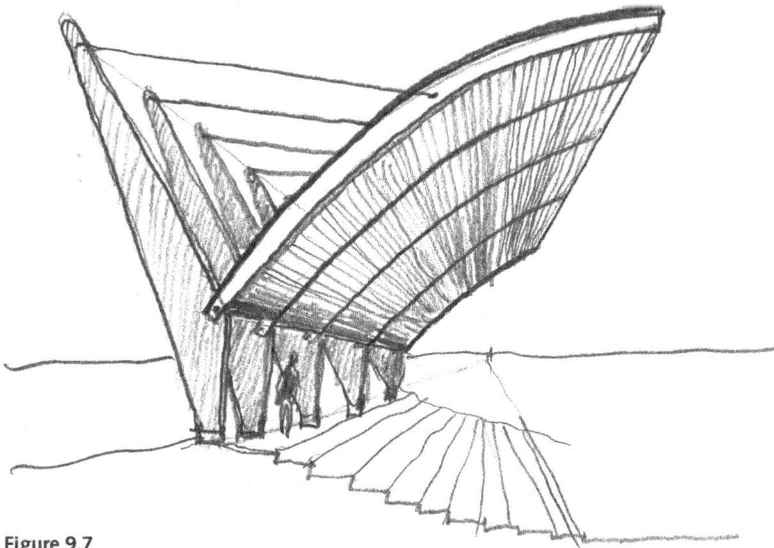

Figure 9.7

Figure 9.6 Workers on the roof of the Exchange Hall (La Bolsa de Valores), Calle Uruguay, 1955, engineered by Felix Candela.

Photo from Colin Faber, *Candela the Shell Builder*, New York: Reinhold Publishing, 1963.

"Yes, we can do something like that, *but with some modifications. For one thing, the cables need to pull tangentially to the surface, otherwise they would introduce bending forces into it and it would have to get a lot thicker and heavier to resist them. There's also a tremendous bending force applied to the mast by the lower edge of the shell. We'd want to find the line of action of the resultant of the forces in the mast and the shell at this intersection, and use that as the axis for the lower end of the mast to eliminate the bending* (9.8)."

> ***"Analytical procedures in [structural] mechanics should be so simple and flexible that they should draw in the mind a picture of a structure in action."***
>
> —Hardy Cross

"There's another thing we should consider regarding this type of structure: A single-curved shell such as this would need to be relatively thick to resist deformations along its straight axis. We should be looking for a way to fold the shell or give it a double curvature instead of only single curvature (9.9), *so that it can stay thin."*

"Like this (9.10)?"

"Almost. You added curvature in the longitudinal direction of the grandstand but eliminated it in the perpendicular direction."

Bruce started sketching (9.11) and wondered aloud:

"How big would those shells have to be? Let's see: They have to cantilever 17 m. They could be narrow in the other dimension if we wanted, maybe even just 5 or 6 m."

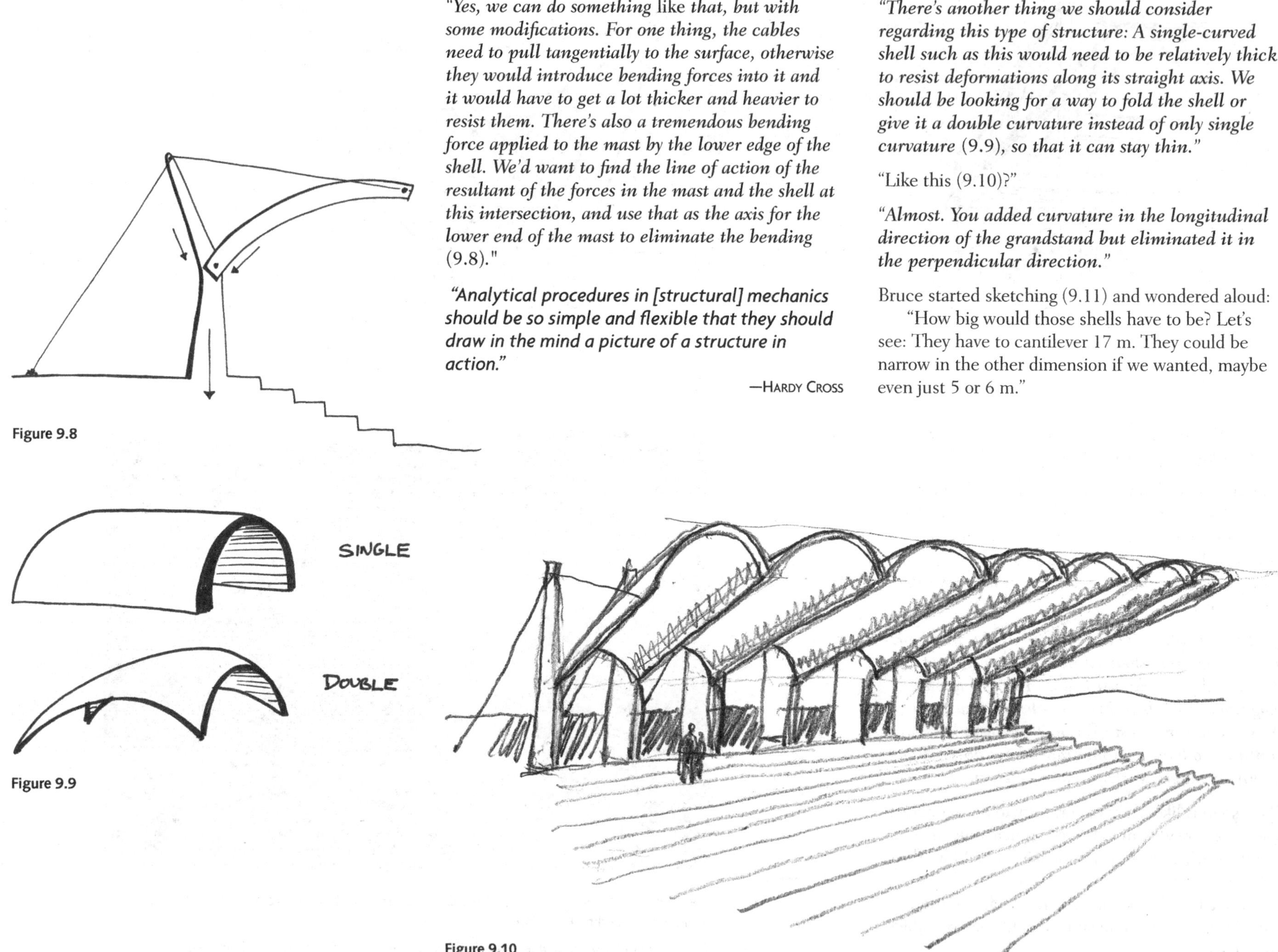

Figure 9.8

Figure 9.9

Figure 9.10

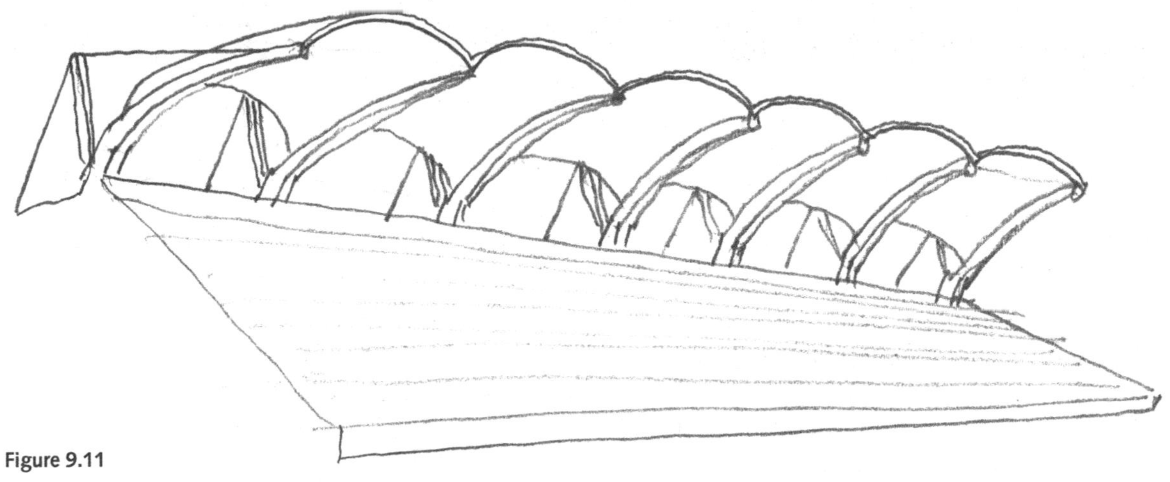

Figure 9.11

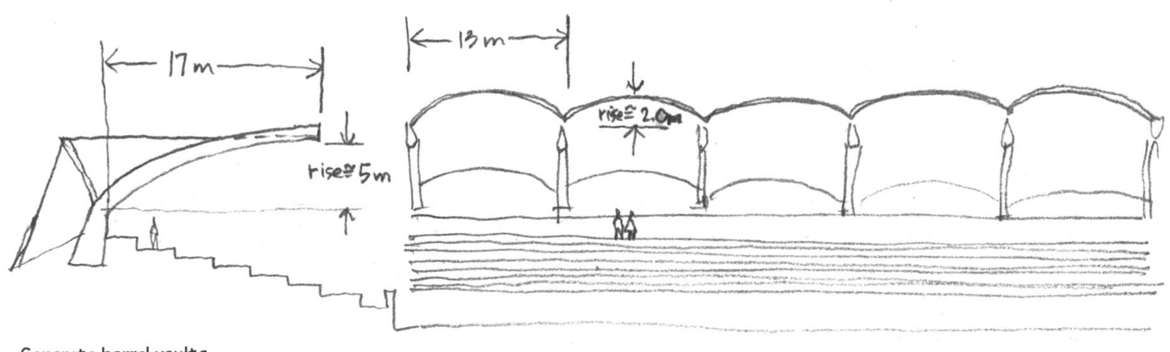

Concrete barrel vaults
Cantilever arches, tied back

Figure 9.12

"True, but if they're narrow, we have to put in a lot more foundations than we would if they were wide. I'd say we should use a generous span for the shells in the longitudinal direction, maybe about 40 ft, which is roughly 13 m. This is a trivial span for the shells, and it would keep the foundation work to a minimum (9.12)*."*

"How much rise do the shells need?"

"I would use a rise of about 15 percent of the shell span and use the same ratio for the arches based on the full span for a complete arch of 34 m, rather than just the 17-m half-arch cantilever in this design. The rise of the shell span is 2 m and the rise of the arch is 5 m based on this rule of thumb."

Diane continued sketching a dimensioned set of freehand drawings to record these numbers.

Bruce reached across the table to add human figures to Diane's drawing.

"I always like to have people on my drawings so I can feel how big the spaces are. I know that your drawing is not to scale, so I based their heights on the 2-m rise of the vaults."

"Your scale figures tell us that this is a large, spectacular structure! Do you like the scheme?"

"Yes, a lot. How about you?"

"I'd say that at the very least, it's worth developing to the point that we know what its proportions are and what it looks like. If it's still looking elegant and almost weightless at that point, I'd be tempted to make it our competition-winning scheme. Say, where has the evening gone? Do you want to keep going for awhile, or call it a night?"

"I'd like very much to keep working with you, but unfortunately I have to get these payroll tax forms in the mail tomorrow, and I don't even understand them yet, let alone have the figures ready to put into them. We'd better stop."

"As I said earlier, I don't have a lot of work in the office right now. I have time to develop the idea to the point that we will know its sizes and shapes and proportions. Then I'll bring it back to show to you, and we can go from there."

"If it's all the same to you, I'd like to be in on the entire process, to see how you're going to do it. It would satisfy my curiosity, and it would mean that we could make design decisions as we go. I could be at your office any time after ten tomorrow morning."

"My place at ten. Perfect! Good night, Bruce!"

SI Units of Measurement

The United States is the only industrialized country in the world that still uses the ancient and inconsistent units of measurement that are part of our English heritage. Elsewhere, SI units, a streamlined version of the metric system of measurement, are used. To hasten the conversion of the U.S. building industry to SI units, the U.S. government requires their use on all federal building projects. The basic units of the SI system are the meter (m) for length, the kilogram (kg) for mass, and the second (s) for time. The millimeter (1/1,000 of a meter, abbreviated mm) is the preferred subdivision of the meter. To avoid confusion, the centimeter (1/100 of a meter) is not used in SI. Area is measured in square meters (m^2) or square millimeters (mm^2), and acceleration in meters per second per second (m/s^2). The SI unit of force, $kg \cdot m/s^2$, is called a *newton*, abbreviated N. (Notice that in SI notation, units that are multiplied by one another are separated by a dot, as in $kg \cdot m$).

Three standard prefixes are commonly applied to units used in SI structural calculations: *milli-*, *kilo-*, and *mega-*. Milli- always means one-one thousandth. Kilo- means one thousand, and mega- means one million. Most forces in building structures are many newtons in magnitude, so they are usually expressed as kilonewtons (kN) or meganewtons (MN). A kilonewton is 1,000 newtons, and a meganewton, 1,000,000 newtons. Preferred practice in SI computations is to eliminate the commas that we use to divide large numbers into groups of three digits, and to replace the commas with spaces. Thus, a meganewton is properly represented as 1 000 000 newtons. Most countries customarily use a comma as a decimal point instead of a period. In this book, we work interchangeably in both conventional and SI units, so to avoid confusion we will use a period as a decimal point in both systems of measurement.

The unit of stress in the SI system is the *pascal*, abbreviated Pa. One pascal is equal to one newton of force per square meter. As with newtons, structural calculations are usually carried out in kilopascals (kPa) or megapascals (MPa).

In calculating with conventional units, we customarily use units of pounds to represent both force and mass. This is ambiguous. Strictly speaking, force equals the mass of a body times the acceleration of gravity. The SI system is unambiguous in this regard: The force that gravity exerts on a mass is equal to the mass in kilograms times the acceleration of gravity. In physics this relationship is expressed by the equation $P = Ma$, where P represents force (push or pull), M, mass, and a, acceleration. The acceleration of gravity at the surface of the earth in SI units is approximately 9.8 meters per second per second (m/s^2). If you are not accustomed to thinking in SI units, the following approximations may be helpful to you:

LENGTH

The handiest figure to keep in mind, and a very close approximation, is that 100 millimeters equals about 4 in. This is especially useful because both 4 in. and 100 mm are preferred dimensional modules for construction. One foot is three modules long, or approximately 300 mm. A standard sheet of plywood is 4 ft by 8 ft, which is 12 modules by 24, approximately 1,200 by 2,400 mm. One meter is approximately 40 in., or 3 ft–4 in. A millimeter is so small, about the thickness of a dime, that except when working with detailed dimensions of precision-crafted components, it is good practice in designing and constructing buildings to work to the nearest 50-mm dimension, which is about 2 in. Remember that in SI centimeters are not used, only millimeters and meters. Dimensions on construction drawings are generally given in mm only. A dimension of 44 500 may be read either as 44,500 mm or 44.5 m.

AREA

One square meter is equal to about 10.76 sq ft. For really quick mental calculations, you can think of this as 10 sq ft per square meter; this results in an inaccuracy of about 8 percent. If you use 11 sq ft per square meter in your computations, your error will be only about 2 percent.

MASS

A kilogram of mass is equal to about 2.2 lb. To convert kilograms to pounds in your head, multiply the number of kilograms by 2, then add another 10 percent. Thus, to convert 1,450 kilograms to pounds, first multiply by 2 to get 2,900 lb, then increase this number by 10 percent, which is 290 pounds, for a total of 3,190 lb. To convert pounds to kilograms, multiply the number of pounds by 0.45; or divide by 2 and subtract 10 percent.

FORCE, WEIGHT, LOAD

One newton is the weight of an average apple, a fact that is easy to remember because we associate Sir Isaac Newton's theory of gravitation with a falling apple. One pound of force is equal to about 4.5 newtons (there are four or five apples in a pound). In this book we also calculate loads and forces in kips (short for kilopounds), which are units of 1,000 lb. A kip, being a kilopound, is equal to approximately 4.5 kilonewtons.

STRESS, PRESSURE

One pascal can be visualized as the weight of one apple distributed over 1 sq m of surface area. This is a very small pressure indeed: The apple weighs less than a quarter of a pound, and a square meter is nearly 11 sq ft. In fact, a single sheet of paper exerts a pressure of a little less than 1 Pa on a desktop. A book with 300 pages puts a pressure of about 200 Pa on a table, if it is lying flat. Structural analysis is generally done in kilopascals or megapascals. A kilopascal (kPa) is the pressure exerted on a tabletop by a stack of five average hardcover novels, about 0.145 lb per square inch. A megapascal (MPa) is a thousand times larger, approximately 145 psi; 100 kPa is a very close approximation of atmospheric pressure at sea level.

DEVELOPING THE IDEA

As Bruce entered Diane's conference room the next morning, she had just finished setting up her laptop and arranging papers on the table.

"Do you still like the scheme that we hatched last night?"

"Yes. I'm eager to move ahead with working it out to the point that we know it's feasible. Most of this work will require your structural expertise, so you should take the lead while I serve as observer, cheerleader, and expert heckler."

"I'm going to think out loud as I work, Bruce. That will allow you to follow what I'm doing, none of which is very mysterious or complicated."

"Sounds good to me. Full speed ahead!"

"First let me review the idea in its entirety: We're building a sunshade and rain shelter over a grandstand at the National Stadium of Costa Verde. The competition program says that a strong limestone bedrock is found everywhere on the site about a meter below the surface, which gives us a stable foundation for just about any type of structure we'd like to do. The seating will be constructed directly on a sloping bank of earth and rock. The roof structure idea that we're both excited about at the moment consists of a series of cylindrical concrete barrel vaults that are supported by cantilevered concrete half-arches (9.11, 9.12). The thrust at the upper end of each half-arch is balanced by the pull of a horizontal tie. The other end of each tie is fastened to the top of an inclined concrete strut, from which a second, steeply inclined tie is anchored to a foundation in the ground. Another foundation transmits the compressive force from the half-arch and strut to the ground.

"I'm going to assume that we will build with concrete whose ultimate strength is approximately 25 megapascals (MPa). For the arches and struts we will use an allowable stress of 40 percent of this value, which is 10 MPa. This is an average value for the composite action of concrete and reinforcing steel that is suitable for preliminary design.

"In finding form and forces for this structure, we'll work on the barrel vaults first, then the arches, then the ties and struts, and finally the foundations. This top-to-bottom sequence allows us to follow the path of the loads as they accumulate from the topmost element through the various members and pass into the earth.

"The minimum practical thickness for the barrel vaults is determined by the diameters of the steel reinforcing bars that they contain, plus the thickness of concrete cover within which the bars must be embedded to protect them from corrosion and fire. The smallest standard size reinforcing bars, 10M, will be sufficient. A 10M bar is 11.3 mm in diameter. We will install bars in both the circumferential and longitudinal directions in the vault, creating an orthogonal grid of steel to minimize cracking that might otherwise occur in any direction from such forces as concrete shrinkage and temperature expansion and contraction. The reinforcing will also help the vault resist unforeseen localized loadings such as might occur if workers pile a stack of heavy roofing materials on a small area of the vault.

"Where the bars cross one another, they create a total thickness of steel of 22.6 mm (9.13). We don't know yet which code requirements are applicable in Costa Verde, but they probably follow the Standard Building Code Requirements of the

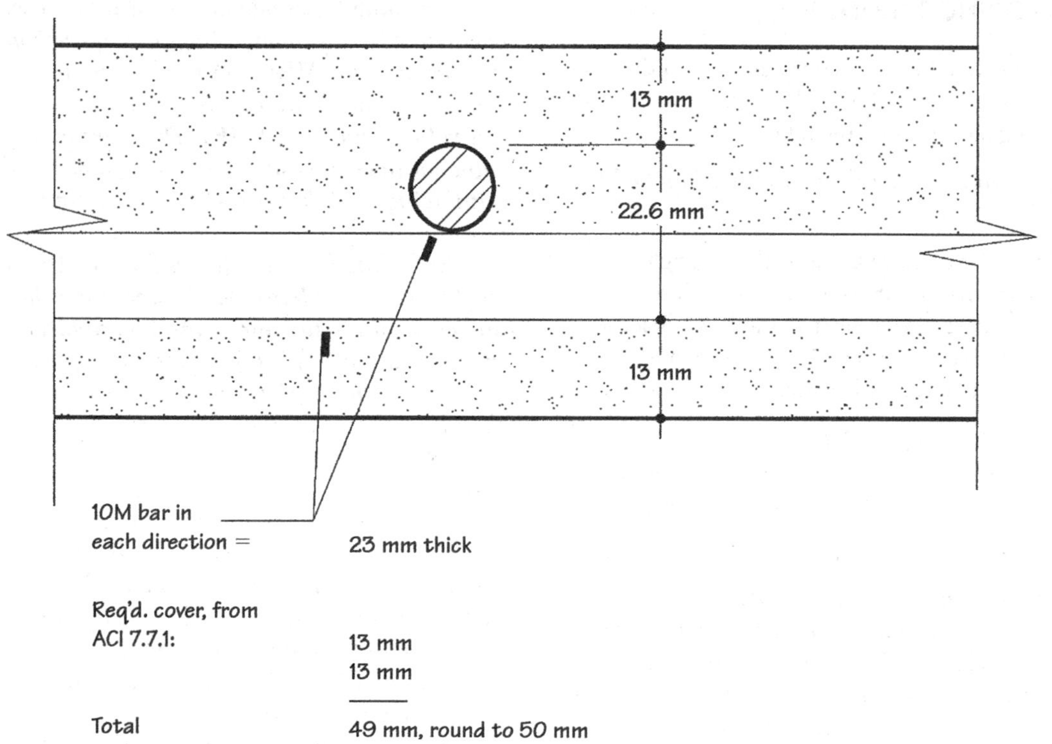

Figure 9.13

American Concrete Institute, which specify that for concrete shells with bars of this diameter, a minimum concrete cover of 13 mm is required on each side of the reinforcing. A sketch of the reinforcing bars and minimum cover shows that the least possible thickness for the vaults is about 50 mm, which is about 2 in. But a shell this thin is very difficult to make: Even a slight inaccuracy in the bending of the bars or the curvature of the formwork would result in a structure that does not meet minimum cover requirements and whose shape differs significantly from the assumed geometry. Experience suggests that a minimum practical thickness for shells is 60 mm. We'll adopt a thickness of 80 mm to provide a cushion against construction imperfections. This will make the builder's task sufficiently less exacting that it will probably result in a lower contract price, even though it uses more concrete than a shell of minimum thickness."

"That's still only about 3 in. of thickness!"

"Will you read me the dimensions of the vaults again?"

"They span 13 m, measured from centerline to centerline of the cantilevered arches, and rise 2 m between the arches. The half-arches themselves reach out 17 m from the foundations at the top of the grandstand and rise 5 m."

"I'm thinking that the half-arches need not be discrete ribs. Instead we'll simply thicken each intersection where two vaults come together to create an integral rib."

"Why? How?"

"Like this:"

Diane produced a small sketch, a section through the intersection of two vaults (9.14).

"We'll just add some concrete fill in the valley between the vaults. It will make the vaults simpler and cheaper to form, and it will give a cleaner, sleeker look to the form of the roof. While we're at it, we'll also eliminate the sharp edge on the underside of the vault intersection by making a flat surface that is, oh, say, 750 mm wide, to avoid the problem of trying to cast a flawless sharp edge in concrete."

"It will definitely look cleaner this way. A sharp intersection would be difficult to keep perfectly straight, and it would be vulnerable to damage during construction."

"The filled valley has another advantage: Because it's so broad, it effectively reduces the span of the vaults to about 12.4 m."

"I'd say we should keep the 2-m rise, though, because it gives a nice visual proportion to the vaults."

"I agree. Now, these vaults are actually double-curved, because the cantilevered arches that support them give them a secondary curvature in a direction perpendicular to their primary curvature. The secondary curvature imparts additional strength and stiffness to the vaults and makes their exact analysis somewhat more involved.

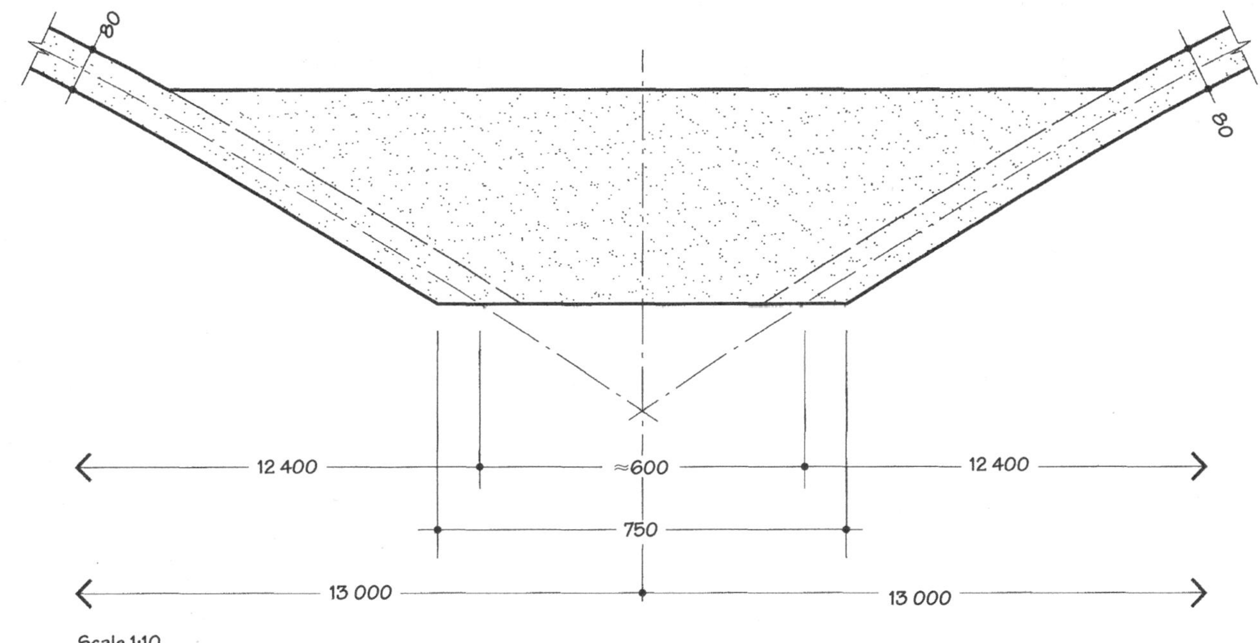

Figure 9.14

For preliminary design, however, we can make the conservative assumption that each vault acts only in one direction, from half-arch to half-arch.

FINDING FORM AND FORCES FOR THE VAULTS

"To confirm the form and thickness of the vault, we'll do a preliminary, simplified analysis in which we will examine a strip of it that is 1 m wide. This strip acts as an arch. To estimate the loads on the horizontal projection of a square meter of its surface, I have to figure both dead load and live load. The dead load, which is the self-weight of the arch, is based on the density of concrete. I'm going to make the conservative assumption that the live load per unit area is about the same as it would be for a building in a temperate zone of the United States."

Diane recorded some numbers neatly on a sheet of graph paper:

Dead load = (0.08 m)(2,400 kg/m^3) = 192 kg/m^2
Live load from building code = 120 kg/m^2
Total load = 312 kg/m^2
The force exerted by this load = (312 kg/m^2)(9.8 m/s^2) = 3.06 kN/m^2

"Remember that this is the total load per square meter, not for the whole arch. We know that the loads are distributed uniformly over the surface of the vault. To facilitate a graphical analysis, however, we'll treat them as if they are divided into 10 discrete, concentrated loads. The span of 12.4 m divided by 10 gives us 1.24 m of span for each segment. Each segment is represented by a concentrated load at its centroid. This places the first and last loads 0.62 m from the ends of the span, with the other loads occurring at 1.24-m intervals between. The magnitude of each load is:

$$P = (3.06 \text{ kN/m})(1.24 \text{ m})(1\text{m}) = 3.8 \text{ kN}$$

"Now I'm ready to find form and forces for the vault."

Carefully offsetting parallel lines while drafting on her laptop, Diane drew the force polygon and funicular polygon (9.15). Knowing that the curve

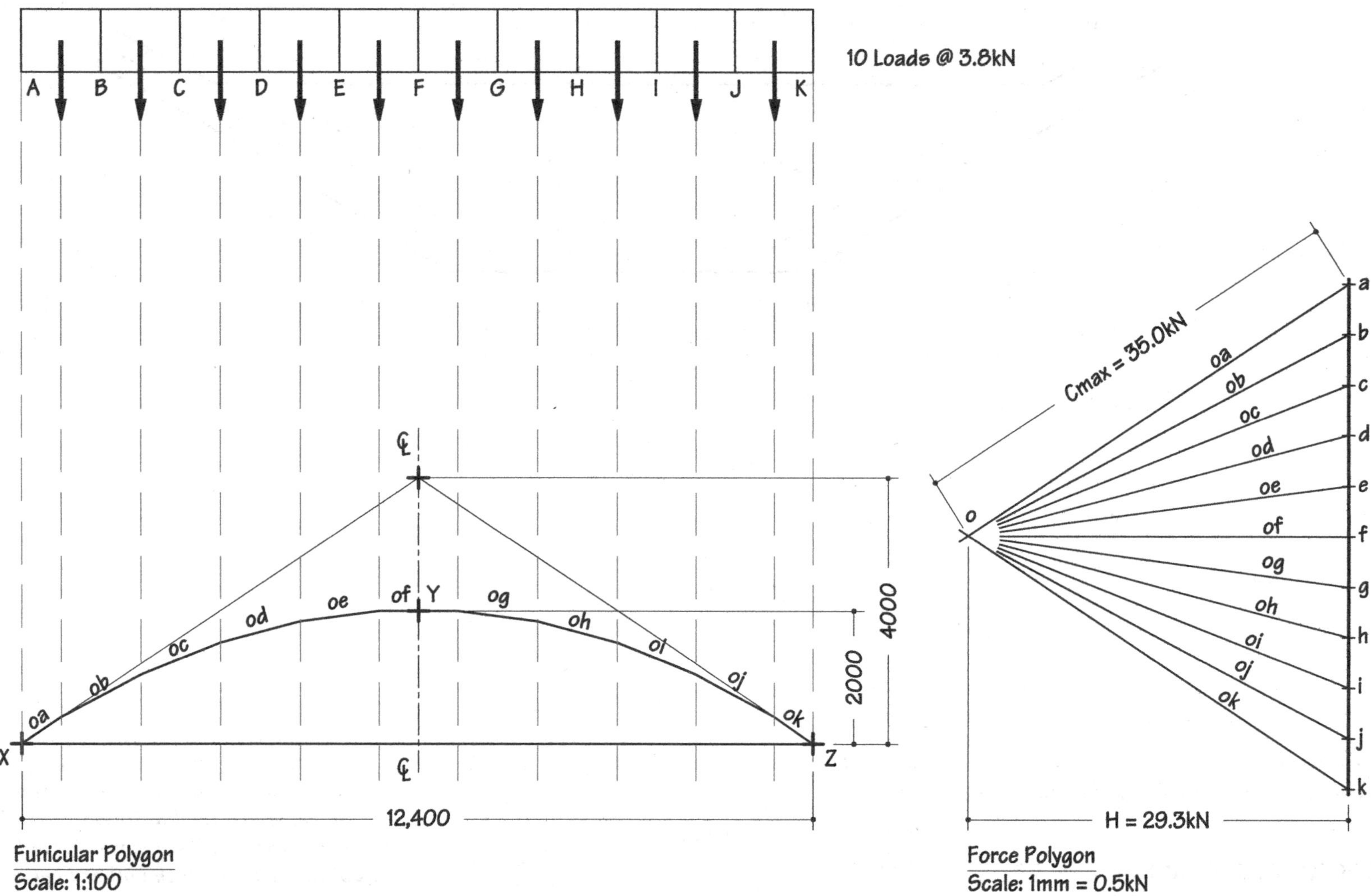

Figure 9.15

would be a parabola, she found the pole directly by drawing the first and last funicular segments, *oa* and *om*, each along a line that starts from a support and passes through a point on the centerline of the polygon that lies twice as far from the closing string as the desired rise. Rays *oa* and *ok* on the force polygon are drawn parallel to these segments to find the pole.

She scaled the completed force polygon to learn that the maximum compressive force in the 1-m-wide arch is 35 kN and the horizontal thrust is 29.3 kN. Bruce was following the whole process intently.

"Okay, this gives us a good estimate of the forces in the vault. Now let me figure out the maximum stress in the vault: It's equal to the maximum force in the vault divided by the cross-sectional area of a 1-m-wide strip:

$$f = \frac{P}{A} = \frac{35\text{ kN}}{(1\text{ m})(0.08\text{ m})} = 0.44\text{ MPa}$$

"Let's see, that tells us that the average stress in the concrete is 0.44 MPa, which is only about 5 percent of the allowable stress. How can it be so small? That can't be right!"

"But it is. Forces are typically very low in structures that are based on funicular geometry. When the form of a vault is right, the forces are all axial and they're very small. Despite this low stress, experience has shown that it's wise to stiffen the free edges of each vault to protect them against load concentrations caused by wind pressures, construction incidents, and, in climates like ours, drifting snow. When such load concentrations occur in the interior region of the vault, they tend to be less serious than at a free edge because of the spreading of the load to adjacent material all around the point of application. In addition, any local tendency for the vault to buckle in its interior regions is suppressed by the stiffness of the surrounding surface. Along a free edge, a thin vault lacks this load-spreading, mutually supportive quality. A reinforced concrete rib three times as thick as the vault, which comes to 240 mm in this case, is usually adequate to stiffen a free edge."

"Just as I'm getting excited that we're creating such a thin shell, you turn around and tell me that we have to put a fat, ugly edge rib on it!"

"Fortunately, the rib can be recessed from the free edge by half a meter or so and still do its job. This usually makes the rib invisible to viewers below and preserves the elegant slenderness of the visible edge of the vault (9.16). *We'll slope the sides of the rib at 30°. This permits a smoother flow of forces between the rib and the vault and facilitates the placement of the concrete during construction. It also permits easier installation of a waterproof membrane on the roof. If this vault were single-curved, it might also require stiffening ribs in its interior regions; but our vault, with its double curvature, will probably not need them.*

"We also have to deal with the lateral thrust of these vaults. We found in our graphical analysis that each meter-wide strip of vault exerts a horizontal thrust of about 29 kN when it is fully loaded."

"Don't the lateral thrusts of the vaults cancel one another out? At each valley, one vault is pushing to the left, and the other to the right. The resulting horizontal force is zero."

"That's true, except at the two ends of the structure. The horizontal thrust at the outside edge of the last vault is not balanced by that of an adjacent vault, and must be resisted in some way. Usually, the easiest, least expensive way to do this is with horizontal steel tie rods. These rods must extend from one end of the roof to the other, passing through all the vaults, in order to balance the two end thrusts against one another."

"That's deplorable! The rods will look just plain awful. Besides, they will interfere with the erection and removal of formwork for the vaults."

A sly smile crept over Diane's face.

"I agree with you on all points. But there's a way around this problem. If we add a cantilevered half-vault at each end of the roof, this places the line of unbalanced thrust and the resulting tie rods across the crowns, or tops, of the vaults, where the rods will not be seen (9.17).

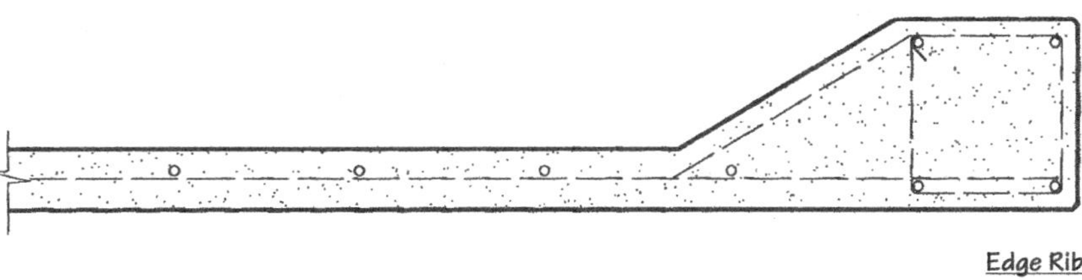

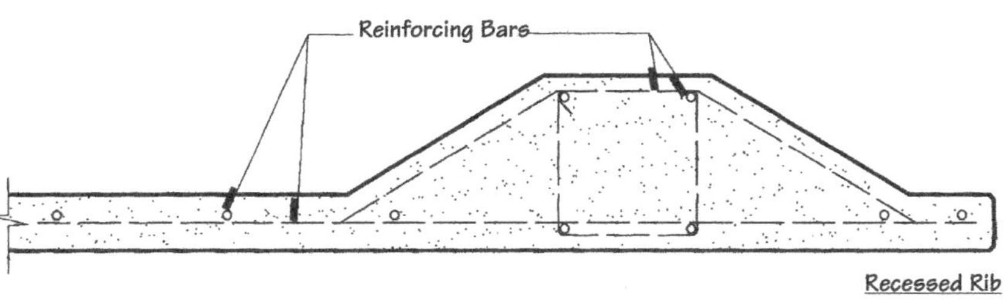

Figure 9.16

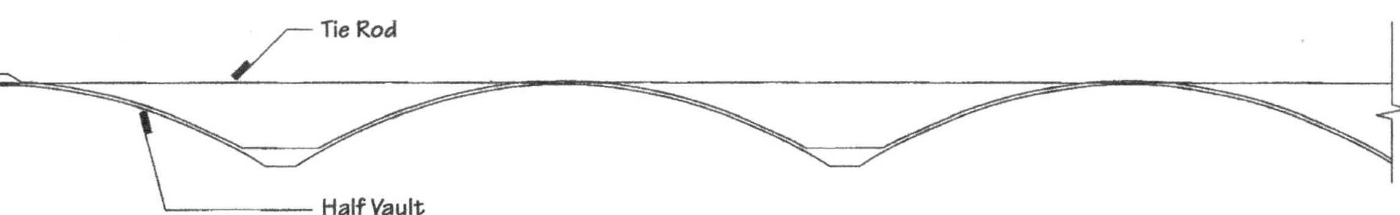

Figure 9.17

This scheme is also advantageous because it permits a roof of the required total area to be constructed with one fewer cantilevered arch, which will save money. And the winglike half-vaults increase the apparent lightness of the roof."

"As always, Diane, you amaze me!"

"If we installed, oh, say, five tie rods across the roof, each would have to resist the thrust of a strip of vault that is 3.4 m wide, 1/5 of the 17-m span of the cantilevered arches. We will use mild steel bars with an allowable stress, F_t, of 150 MPa. We size these bars as follows:

$$\text{Tensile force per bar} = T = \left(\frac{17\text{ m}}{5}\right)(29\text{ kN/m}) = 99\text{ kN}$$

$$\text{Required area of steel} = \frac{T}{F_t} = \frac{99\text{ kN}}{150\text{ MPa}}$$
$$= 0.66 \times 10^{-3}\text{ m}^2 = 660\text{ mm}^2$$

"Now we look in a table of standard sizes of round steel bars and we select the smallest size that exceeds 660 mm² in area. This is a 30M bar, which is 29.9 mm in diameter and has a cross-sectional area of 700 mm²."

"That's about 1.2 in. in diameter—not too big. You make it look so easy and simple."

"The simplest methods are often the best."

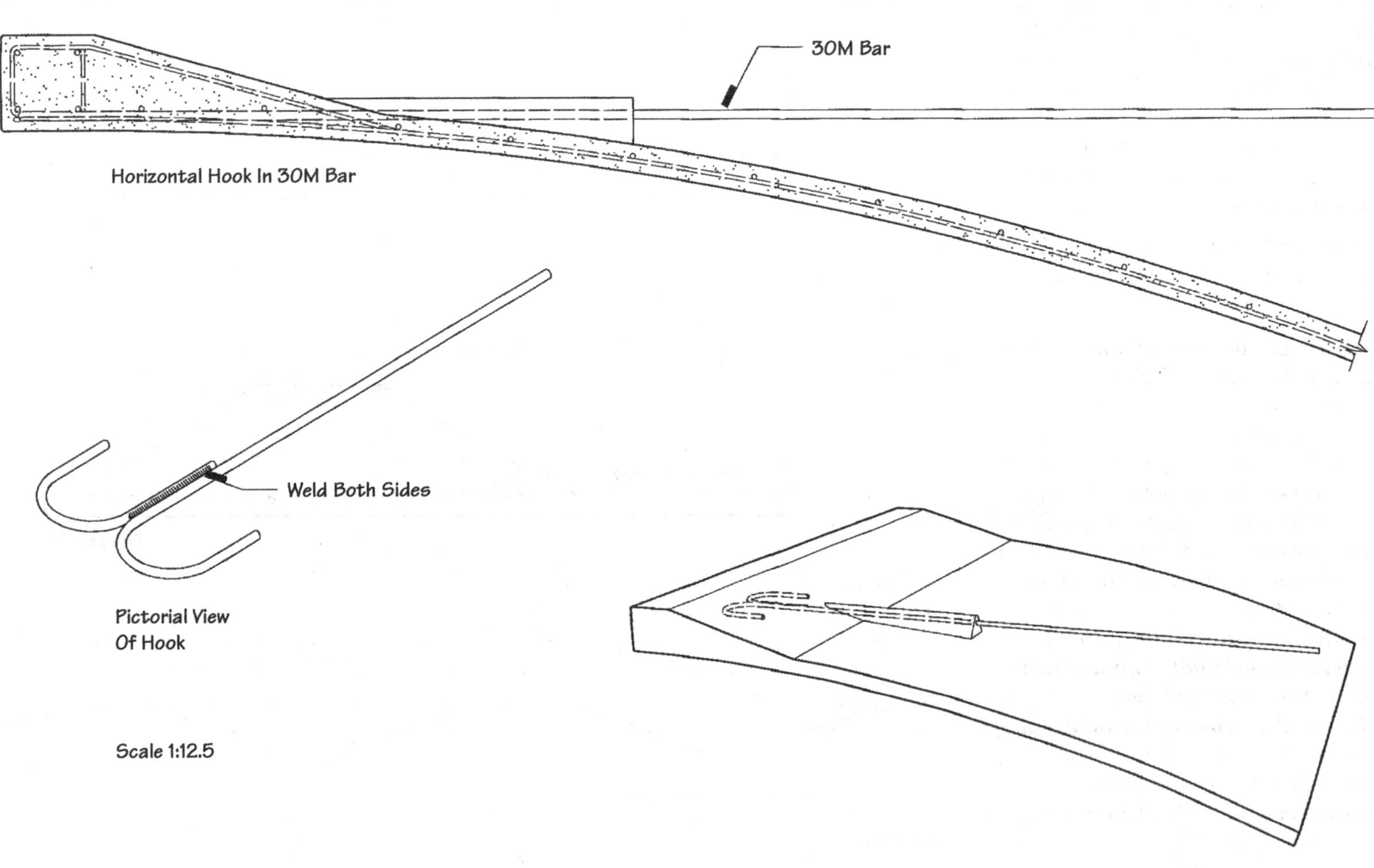

Figure 9.18

Settling back into her chair, Diane pulled her sheets of sketches and calculations together in front of her.

"Let's finish detailing the tie rods. At each end, we must anchor the tie rod to the concrete edge of the vault. The vault is only 80 mm thick, but its free edge must be stiffened with a 240-mm rib. Let's make a scaled drawing of this (9.18). To avoid bending moments in the vault, the 30M tie rod must be anchored to the concrete at the center of the vault thickness. As we draw the grid of reinforcing bars in the vault, we notice that the tie rod interferes with the positions of the last several longitudinal bars near the free edge. We can move these bars up slightly so that they pass over the tie rod. To maintain the required cover of concrete over these bars, we extend the taper of the rib.

"A logical way to anchor the tie rod would be to attach it to a steel plate at the edge of the vault. The vault is so thin, however, that it would be difficult to embed a plate of sufficient size. Instead, we can transfer the force at the end of the rod into the concrete by forming the rod into a U-bend of standard dimensions, called a hook. The hook should lie horizontally in the center plane of the vault to avoid the creation of bending forces. To create a symmetrical pull on the rod, we'll weld a second hook to the first one in a mirror-image arrangement."

"What do we do to protect the exposed portions of the tie rods from corrosion?"

"Paints must be renewed every few years, so for easier maintenance and greater reliability we will probably use galvanized rods, which have a heavy zinc coating."

FINDING FORM AND FORCES FOR THE CANTILEVERED ARCH

"Let's move on to the finding of form and forces for the cantilevered arch. Would you like to have a stab at it?"

"Sure! Let's see—we conceived the cantilevered arch as being level at its free end. This means, it seems to me, that we may consider it to be half of a parabolic arch on a level base."

"Yep. Keep going."

"To begin the graphical solution, I'm going to divide the 17-m span of the half arch arbitrarily into 10 intervals of 1.7 m and estimate the load on each of its segments (9.19). We already determined that the total load of a 1-m strip of vault is 38 kN. Each arch supports half of this load, 19 kN, from the vault that bears on it from each side. This totals 38 kN per meter of arch length. We must add to this an approximate self-weight of the arch itself. When I scale the dimensions of the added concrete from your sketch (9.14), I find that its cross-sectional area is about 0.44 m^2. Hand me that sheet of paper and I'll calculate the loads on a 1.7-m-long section of the arch:

Vault load, D.L. + L.L.: (38 kN/m)(1.7 m) = 64.6 kN

Self-weight of arch:

$(0.44\ \text{m}^2)(1.7\ \text{m})(2{,}400\ \text{kg/m}^3)(9.8\ \text{m/s}^2) = 17.6\ \text{kN}$

"Now I have to add the live load on a portion of the broad valley between the shells. This load is supported directly by the arch without first passing through the shells. On your earlier sketch (9.14) you give the width of this portion as being about 0.6 m.

Live load on 0.6 m strip of arch =
$(120\ \text{kg/m}^2)(0.6\ \text{m})(1.7\ \text{m})(9.8\ \text{m/s}^3) = 1.2\ \text{kN}$

Total load per 1.7-m segment of arch =
64.6 kN + 17.6 kN + 1.2 kN = 83.4 kN

We round to 84 kN."

"There. I think that's right."

"Good work. Now can you find the form and forces for the arch?"

"Okay, I'll set up a side view of the arch at a convenient scale, maybe 1:100. Then I'll divide the 17-m span of the arch into 10 segments, place a vector representing a load of 84 kN in the center of each segment, and construct the load line accordingly."

Bruce drew industriously for a couple of minutes.

"Okay, I have the span divided into 10 segments, and I've constructed the load line (9.19). I want the arch to be level at its free end. This means that its crown, represented by the topmost segment of the funicular polygon, is going to be labeled *ok*, and it will be level (9.20). Because the arch is parabolic, a line tangent to the arch at its support will intersect a vertical line through the crown of the arch at a height of 2*s*, which for this arch is 10 m, above the baseline. Thus we're able to begin the construction of the final funicular polygon by drawing its first and last segments, *oa* and *ok*. This enables us to draw the first and last rays of the force polygon. These intersect to determine the pole location, enabling us to construct the curve of the arch and determine the forces in it (9.20)."

As he finished the construction, Bruce added a scale human figure to it.

"Amazing! I'm imagining myself as being this figure. The space feels great! What a soaring roof we've made!"

"Did you say a sorry *roof?"*

"No, **soaring**!"

Diane was giggling uncontrollably. Finally she wiped her eyes and measured the force polygon that Bruce had just completed.

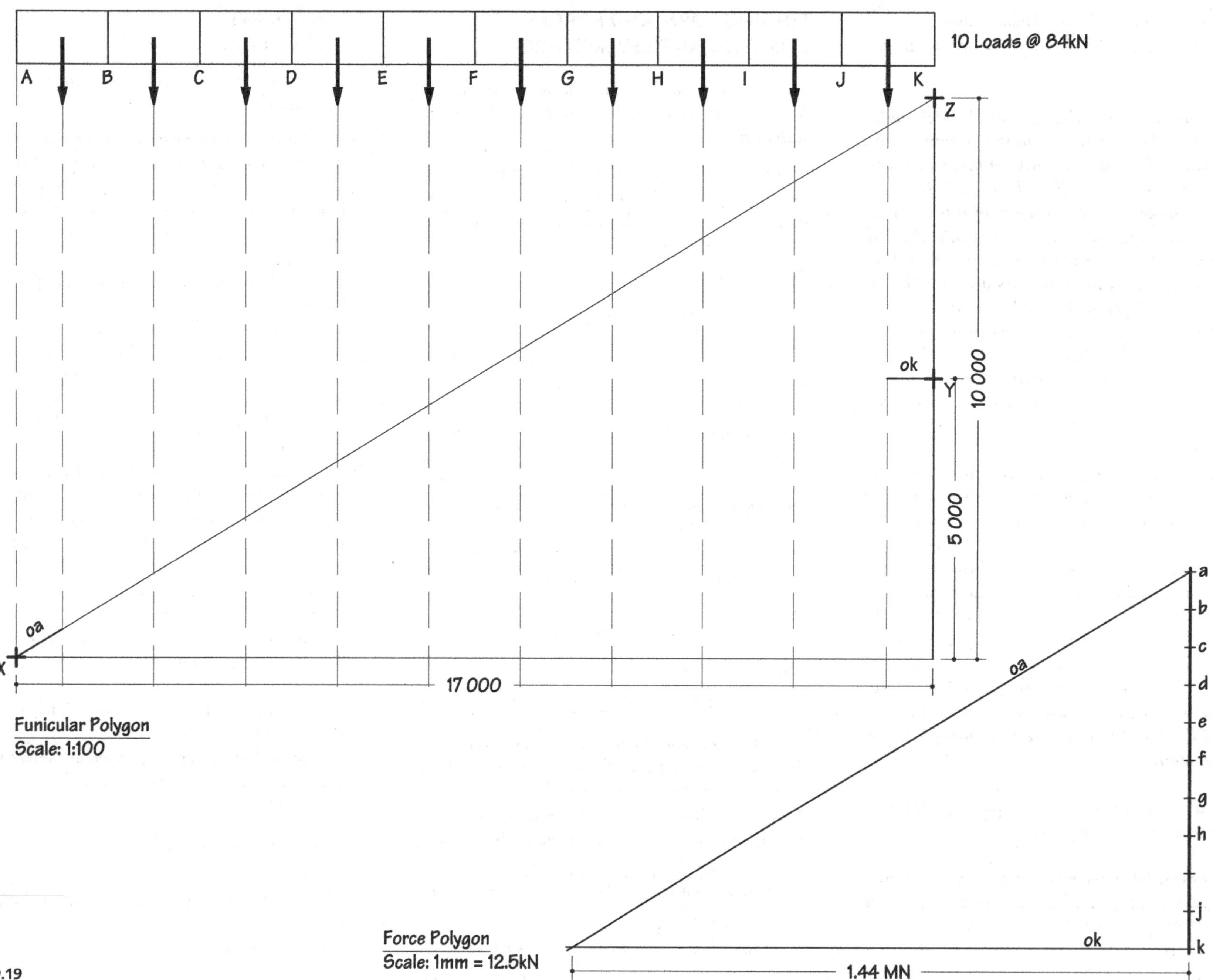

10 Loads @ 84kN
A
B
C
D
E
F
G
H
I
J
K
Z
ok
Y
10 000
5 000
oa
X
17 000
Funicular Polygon
Scale: 1:100
a
b
c
d
e
f
g
h
j
k
oa
ok
Force Polygon
Scale: 1mm = 12.5kN
1.44 MN

Figure 9.19

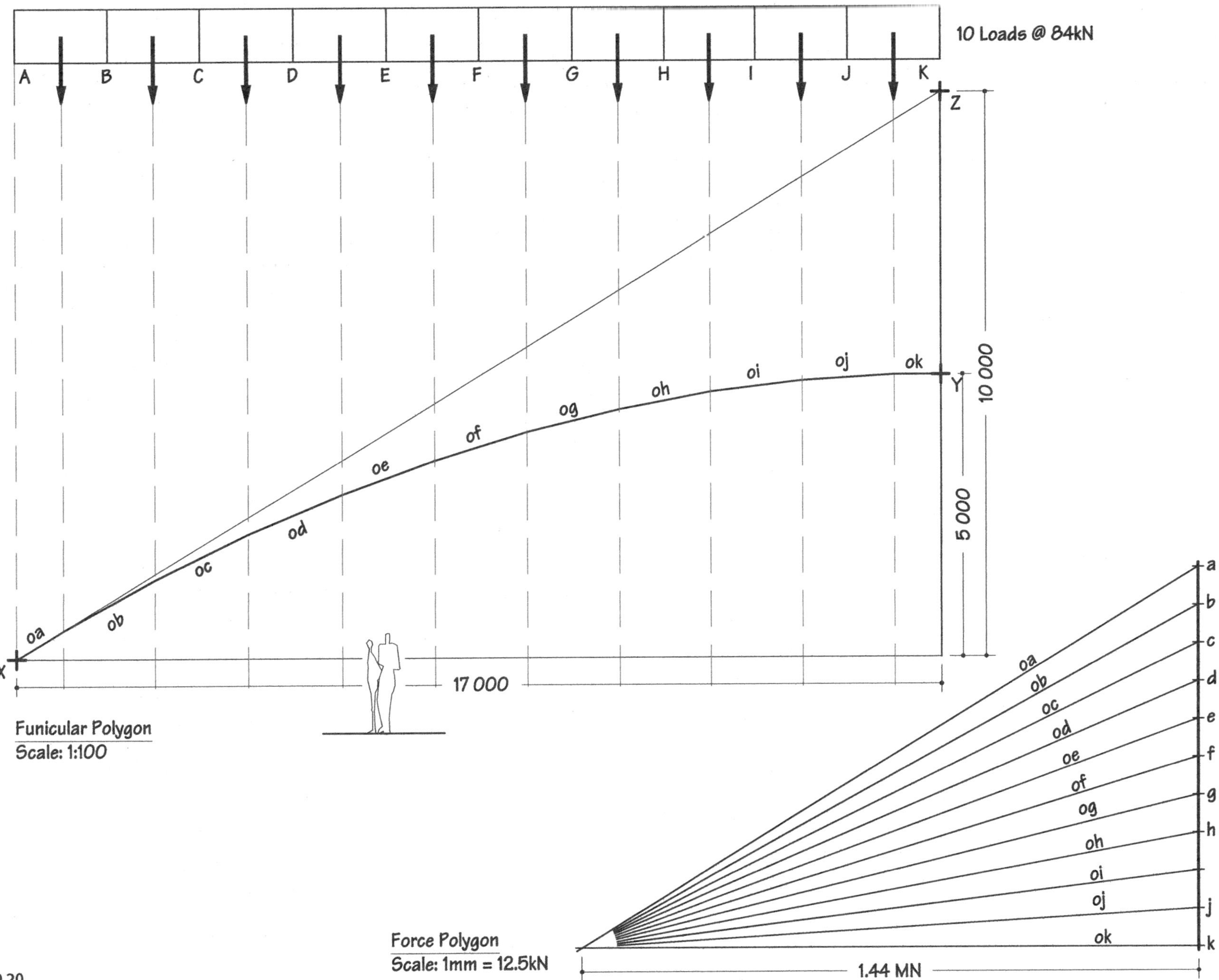
10 Loads @ 84kN
A
B
C
D
E
F
G
H
I
J
K
Z
Y
X
oa
ob
oc
od
oe
of
og
oh
oi
oj
ok
10 000
5 000
17 000
Funicular Polygon
Scale: 1:100
a
b
c
d
e
f
g
h
j
k
Force Polygon
Scale: 1mm = 12.5kN
1.44 MN

Figure 9.20

"The maximum force in the arch, oa, scales as 1.66 MN. The force at the upper end, which is also the force in the horizontal stay cable, is approximately 1.44 MN. We can scale the rise of the arch at each interval from the centers of the line segments on the funicular polygon."

SIZING THE ARCH

"To determine the required cross sectional area of concrete at the base of the arch, we'll use the same allowable stress in the concrete that we used before, 10 MPa:

$$A_{req} = \frac{P}{F_c} = \frac{1.66\ \text{MN}}{10\ \text{MPa}} = 0.166\ \text{m}^2$$

"Our early detail (9.14) provides a cross-sectional area of about 0.44 m² of concrete in the arch, more than twice as much as is required. On the other hand, the depth of 0.4 m that we show in this drawing is too shallow for a freestanding arch of this span, which would be likely to buckle. However, in our design the arch is not freestanding, but is integral with the vaults on either side in a V-shaped section, which will probably prove to be plenty stiff against buckling."

DESIGNING THE STRUT AND TIES

"That takes care of the vaults and arches. We need to investigate the size of the steel rod that will pull back against the free end of the half-arch. Our arch analysis (9.20) shows that it carries a maximum force of 1.44 MN, which is quite a lot. I imagine we'll want to use a high-strength steel posttensioning tendon for this."

"Actually, we'll be better off using ordinary mild steel rods. It's rather counterintuitive. As live loads on the roof increase and decrease, the tie will elongate and shorten. To protect the structure from damage, we would like to minimize this movement. The amount by which a length of steel stretches under an increased load is directly proportional to the increase in the stress in the steel, regardless of the allowable strength of the steel. We could keep the diameter of the tie relatively small by using a high-strength steel posttensioning tendon, as you suggest; but for a given change in load, a smaller-diameter tie would experience a larger variation in stress, and therefore a larger change in length, than a larger-diameter tie made of lower-strength steel. To control fluctuations in the length of the tie, we'll make it of mild steel, whose allowable tensile stress is 150 MPa. The required area of steel in the tie is:

$$A_{req} = \frac{P}{F_c} = \frac{1.44\ \text{MN}}{150\ \text{MPa}} = 0.0096\ \text{m}^2$$

"The ends of the tie will be threaded to receive a nut that will transmit the force to a steel bearing plate that will spread the force over a large area of concrete so as not to exceed the allowable strength of the concrete. The threaded ends permit fine-scale adjustments of the structure during and after construction. To account for the reduction in the working area of the round steel tie by the threads, we'll add 15 percent to the above value to arrive at a required gross area for the tie of 0.0110 m², or 11 000 mm². This area can be provided by a single steel bar 120 mm in diameter, or two bars, each of them 90 mm in diameter."

"Those are **huge,** Diane! You're saying we need a single round bar almost 5 in. in diameter, or two bars each more than 3–1/2 in. in diameter. Must they be so big?"

Bruce formed circles of his thumbs and forefingers to show these dimensions full size.

"Yes. But consider their size in relation to the size of the arch and the vault. A pair of 90-mm bars would look big sitting on your desk, but insignificant in size against an arch that's cantilevering 17 m and a vault that's 13 m wide."

"I guess you're right."

"Now we need to work out the inclined strut and tie that bring the force from the tie into the earth. The tie from the end of the half-arch is horizontal. If the inclined strut bisects the angle between the horizontal tie and the tie that goes to the foundation, the force will be the same in both ties."

"Hmm, I never thought of that. And if the forces are the same, we can use the same-diameter rod for both."

"If we were to incline the strut at 45°, the rod to the ground would be vertical. This might look pretty good."

Bruce converted her words to a sketch and was pleased. Diane, in the meantime, prepared a scaled layout of the roof structure and a force polygon that determined the forces in its members (9.21).

"How did you do that?"

"It's just a graphical truss analysis. It's a pretty versatile technique. Even though this may not appear to be a trussed structure at first glance, it is a truss that is balanced on its apex."

"What is the 840-kN force, and how do you know where it's applied?"

"It's the total of live and dead loads for one half-arch, and it's applied at the middle of its span. In other words, it's the resultant of all the loads on the half-arch."

"Got it. Now we know from this diagram the forces on the two foundations, as well as the forces in

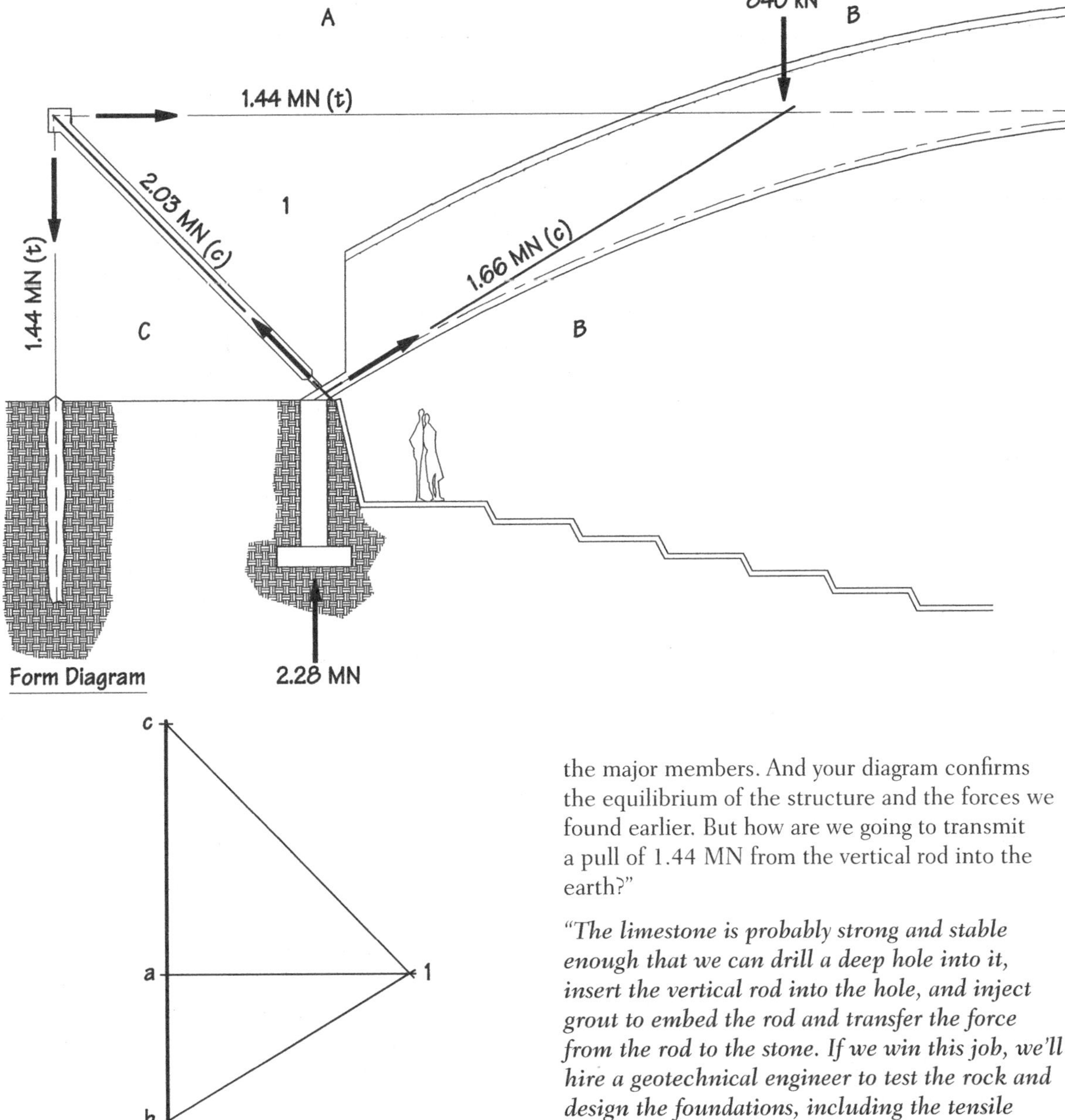

Figure 9.21

the major members. And your diagram confirms the equilibrium of the structure and the forces we found earlier. But how are we going to transmit a pull of 1.44 MN from the vertical rod into the earth?"

"The limestone is probably strong and stable enough that we can drill a deep hole into it, insert the vertical rod into the hole, and inject grout to embed the rod and transfer the force from the rod to the stone. If we win this job, we'll hire a geotechnical engineer to test the rock and design the foundations, including the tensile foundations."

Now Diane was doing arithmetic on a pad of graph paper, with the aid of a pocket calculator.

"At an allowable concrete stress of 10 MPa, the strut would have to be 0.203 m² in cross-sectional area, which is 451 mm square. To minimize the risk of buckling and increase the appearance of strength in the strut, we might adopt a section that is 500 mm square. I need a few minutes to work out some odds and ends; would you see what you can do to develop the details of the strut?

For a time, each worked independently, sketching and doing simple math as needed to complete the preliminary shaping of the structure. When they resumed their meeting, Bruce was chuckling to himself.

"Take a look at these strut details that I've sketched (9.22). The pieces practically fell into place by themselves. The strut is 500 mm square and inclined at 45°. It comes to a level head that is 900 mm square. The head provides flat faces against which each of the ties can be anchored. Because the vertical tie is exposed to vandalism, we'll make it sturdy by using a single, 120-mm-diameter bar. To simplify the connection of the ties at the head of the strut, we can use a pair of 90-mm-diameter bars for the horizontal tie; this avoids interference of the rods as they pass through the head. The bars go through greased steel pipe sleeves that are embedded in the concrete, with the double horizontal bar straddling the single vertical bar. We'll need washers and steel bearing plates to spread the force from each tie over a sufficient area of concrete such that the actual stress in the concrete doesn't exceed the allowable stress of 10 MPa. I worked out a minimum size of a typical plate."

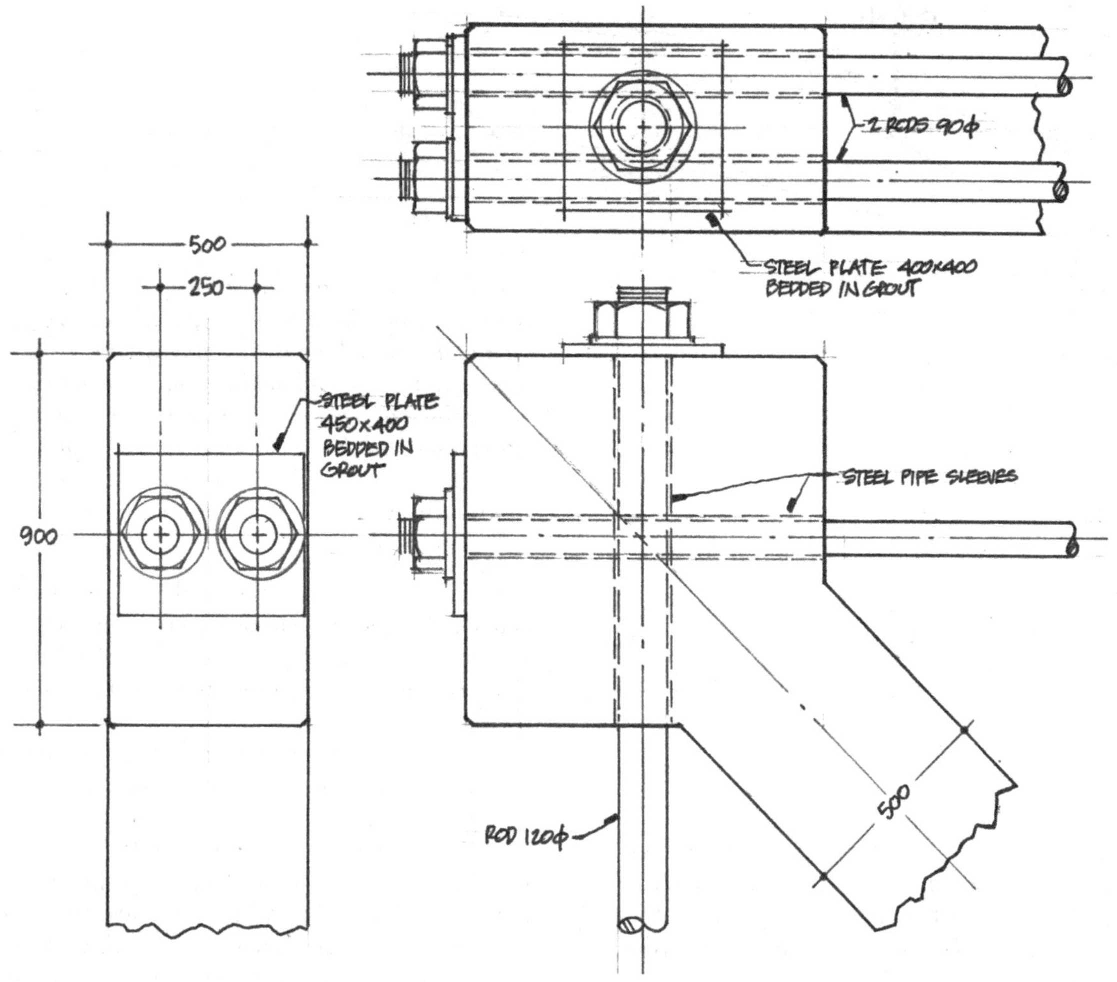

Figure 9.22

Bruce showed a neatly lettered calculation on a sheet of graph paper.

"Then I added area to the plate to replace the concrete that's missing where the bars penetrate:

$$A_{gross} = 144\ 000\ \text{mm}^2 + 2\pi r^2 = 144\ 000\ \text{mm}^2 + 2\pi\left(50\ \text{mm}\right)^2 = 159{,}700\ \text{mm}^2$$

"I used a radius for the bars of 50 mm, rather than their actual 45 mm, to account for the pipes and a clearance between the rods and the pipes. I'm assuming that to ensure full contact between the bearing plates and the concrete, each plate will be bedded in grout.

"At the base of the strut, we need to have a hinge to allow the strut to move back and forth a few millimeters each way in response to temperature and load changes. The simplest kind to make is probably the kind that Robert Maillart often used in his Swiss bridges in the early twentieth century, such as the Salginatobel Bridge (9.23). The reinforcing bars cross one another at the joint to minimize their bending resistance, but they still retain their compressive strength, which is what transfers the force from the strut to the foundation assembly. In our design, rubber pads eliminate most of the concrete, allowing considerable flexibility in this connection (9.24)."

"Nice details! Well done! I especially like the way you've avoided interference in the head of the strut by using two bars horizontally and a single bar of the same area vertically. We'll anchor the horizontal bars to the outer end of the arch with a similar detail (9.25). This connection could be left exposed, or it could be concealed within a grout-filled pocket in the end of the arch.

"The horizontal tie bars will sag under their own weight, and this sag may be enough to be unsightly or disturbing. We can estimate the amount of self-sag by using this equation:

$$S = \frac{wL^2}{8T} \qquad [9\text{-}1]$$

where:

S is the sag of the bars under their own weight,
w is the self-weight of a 1-m length of tie bar,
L is the free length of the bars, and
T is the tensile force in the bars."

"I looked up the self-weight of a 90-mm-diameter bar, which is 490 N/m. The free length of each tie bars is about 20 m, and its total tension is 0.72 MN. Hmm . . . my figures say that the total sag for a tie bar is:

$$S = \frac{(490\ \text{N/m})\,(20\ \text{m})^2}{8\,(0.72\ \text{MN})} = 0.017\ \text{m} = 17\ \text{mm}$$

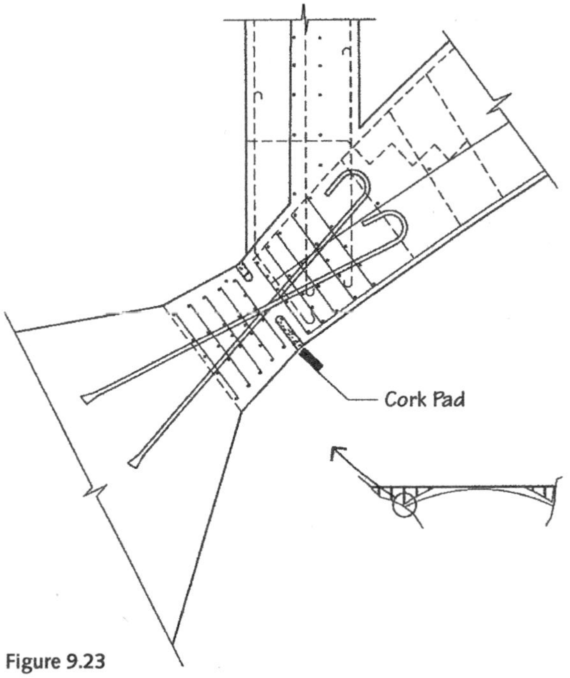

Figure 9.23

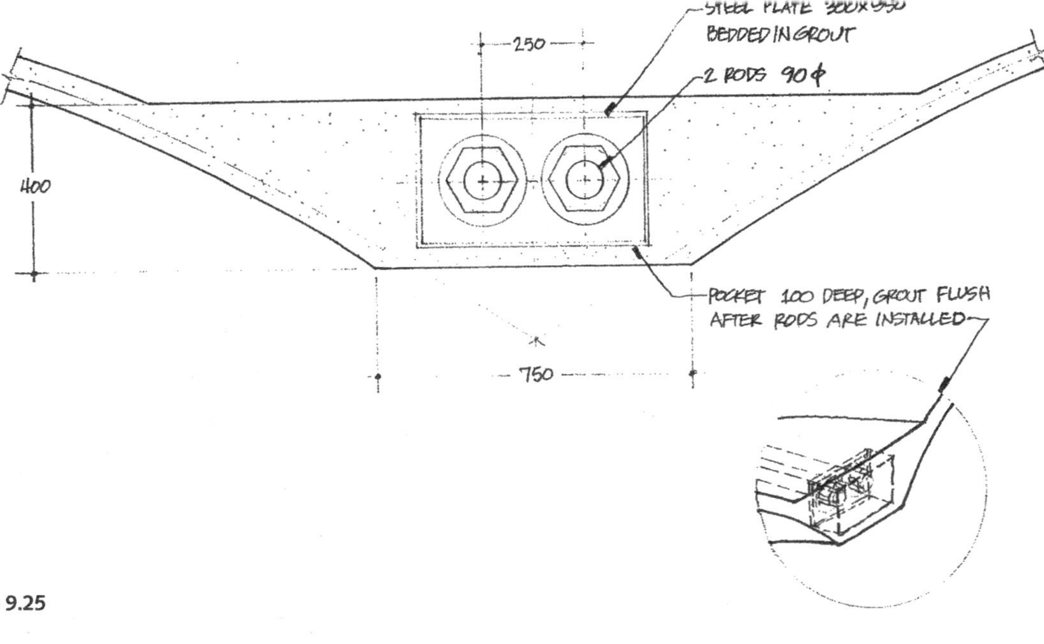

Figure 9.25

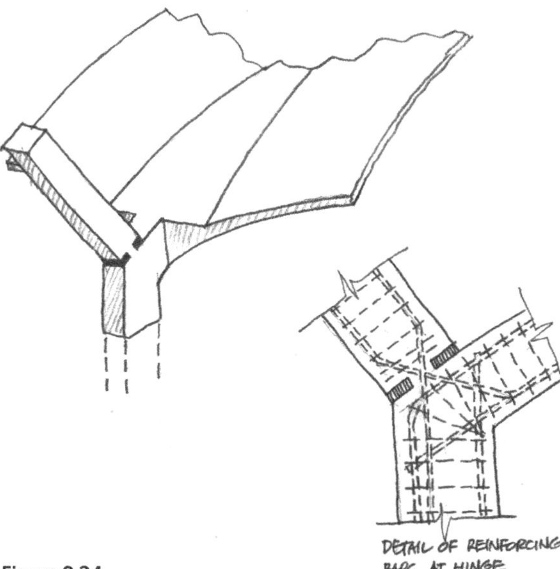

Figure 9.24

"This is less than 20 percent of the diameter of the bar. Under dead load only, the tension will be about 40 percent lower, so the self-sag will be about 40 percent higher, a total of 24 mm. This will be imperceptible. No problem!"

Diane went on to explain that she had sized the stem of the foundation, which transmits the forces of both the arch and the inclined strut down to the footing, on the basis of the 2.28-MN force found in her graphical analysis (9.21). The calculated strut size was 477 mm square, which looked too slender and joined badly to the 500-mm square strut. Instead, she sized the stem so it would join smoothly to the strut and arch and look appropriately sturdy, 500 mm in both thickness and depth (9.22). To get a preliminary idea of the size of the footing under the base of the arch, Diane used a rule-of-thumb allowable stress value of 1.0 MPa that is given for soft limestone in the building code:

$$A_{req} = \frac{P}{F} = \frac{2.28\ \text{MN}}{1\ \text{MPa}} = 2.28\ \text{m}^2$$

$$\sqrt{2.28\ \text{m}^2} = 1.51\ \text{m}$$

The footing will be a block of concrete about 1.5 m square, which is not unusually large.

"If we win the competition, I'll also ask our geotechnical engineer to work out the depth, dimensions, and details of the foundations, including the drilled and grouted backstay anchor in the bedrock."

"What if the subsoil for this structure were a soft clay instead of rock?" asked Bruce.

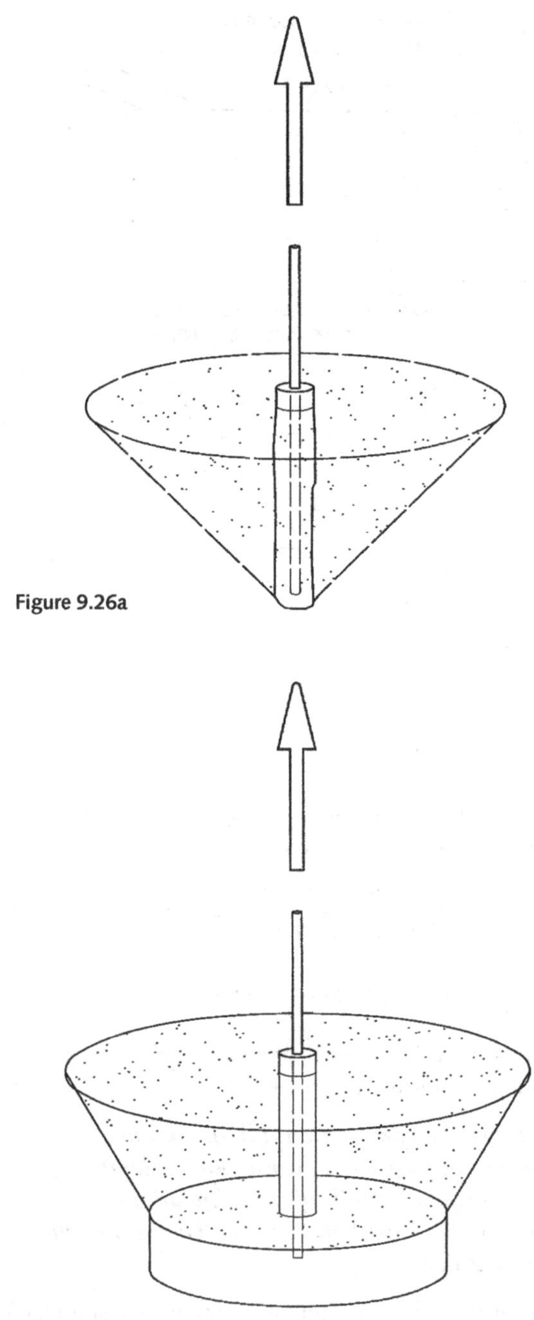

Figure 9.26a

Figure 9.26b

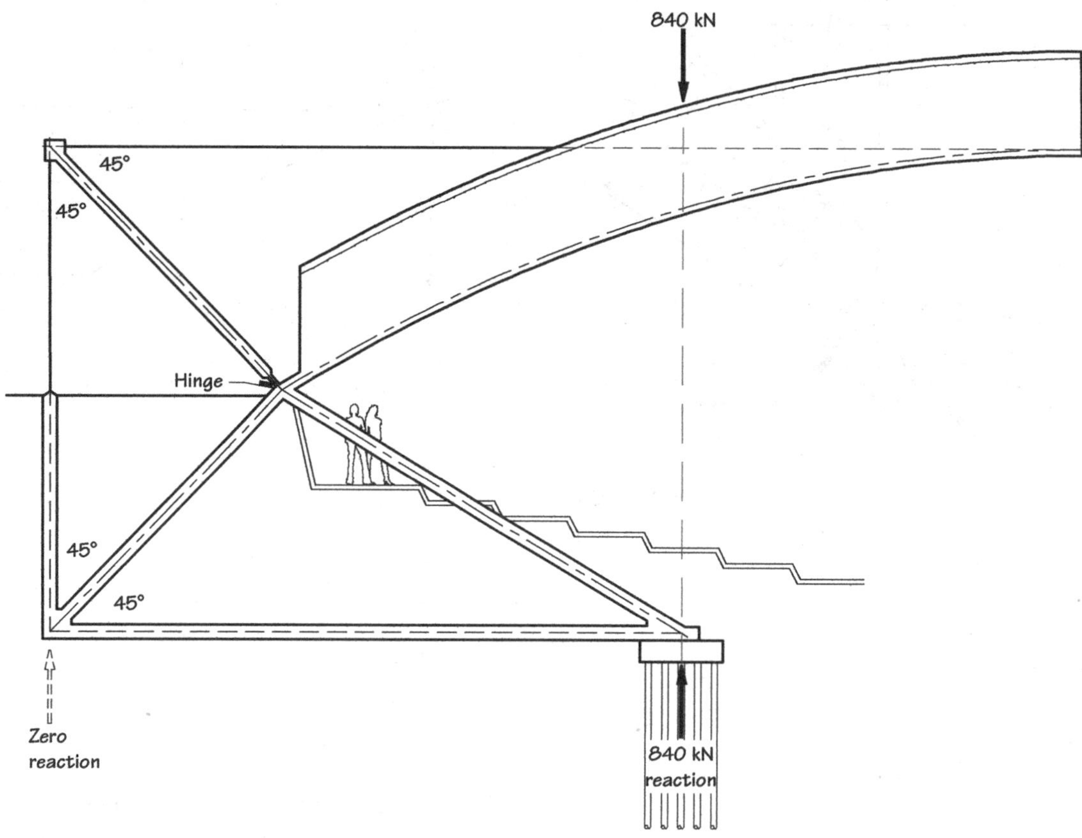

Figure 9.27

"A drilled and grouted backstay anchor (9.26a) probably wouldn't be feasible in soft clay. One alternative in this case would be a dead-man anchor, which is a disk of concrete that depends on breadth rather than depth for its effectiveness (9.26b). The weight of the truncated cone of soil on top of the disk accounts for most of the weight of the anchor.

"There's another way we could cope with soft soil: An underground system of struts and ties—a subterranean truss, really—could bring both the tensile and compressive loads in the structure to a single foundation that lies on the line of action of the resultant of all the loads on the structure (9.27). We can analyze this frame graphically to find its member forces, and we could also develop an alternative that does not obstruct the walkway at the top of the bleachers (9.28). But I doubt that we're going to want to construct something this elaborate and costly."

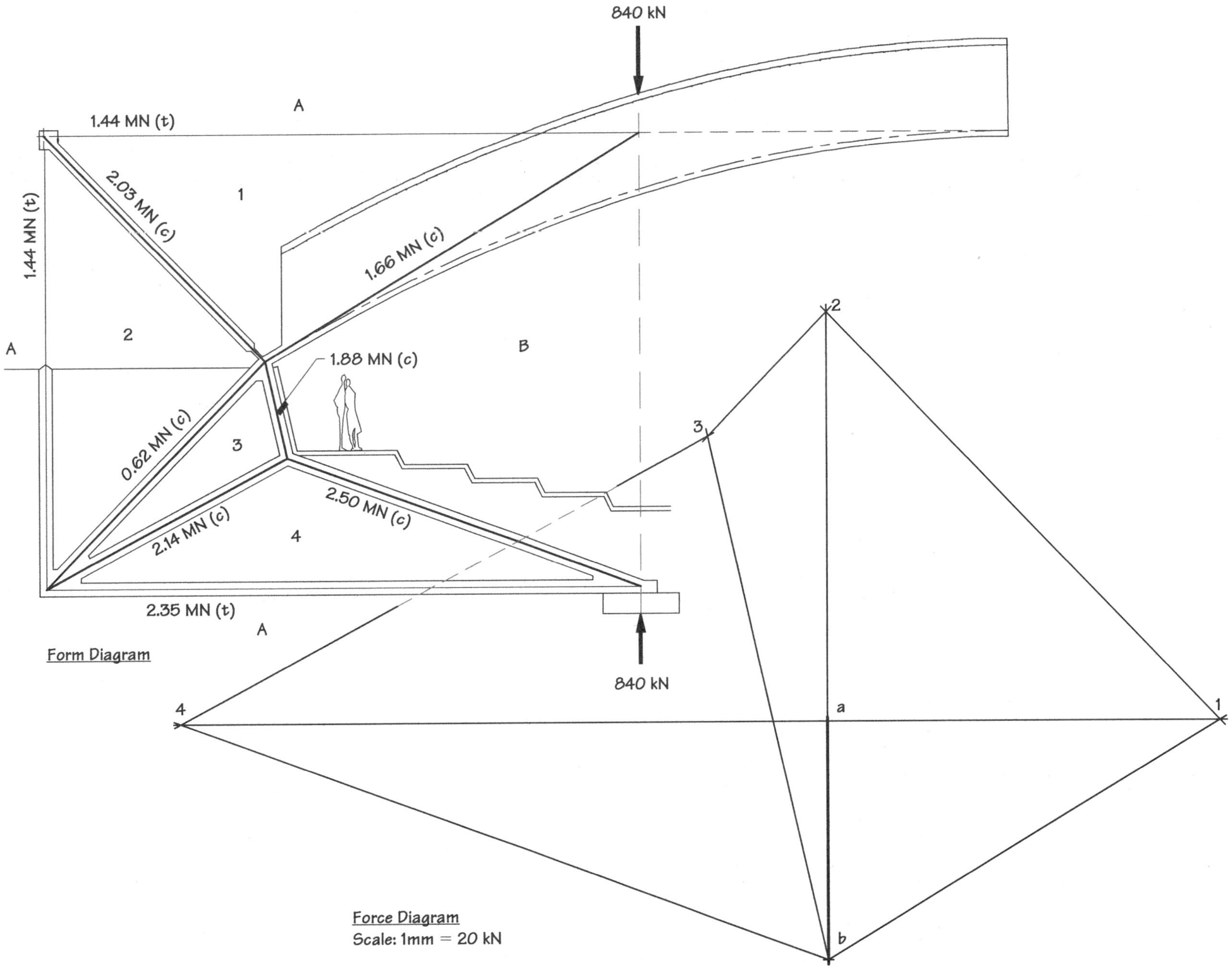
840 kN
A
1.44 MN (t)
2.03 MN (c)
1
1.44 MN (t)
1.66 MN (c)
2
A
1.88 MN (c)
B
0.62 MN (c)
3
2.50 MN (c)
2.14 MN (c)
4
2.35 MN (t)
A
Form Diagram
840 kN
2
3
4
a
1
b
Force Diagram
Scale: 1mm = 20 kN

Figure 9.28

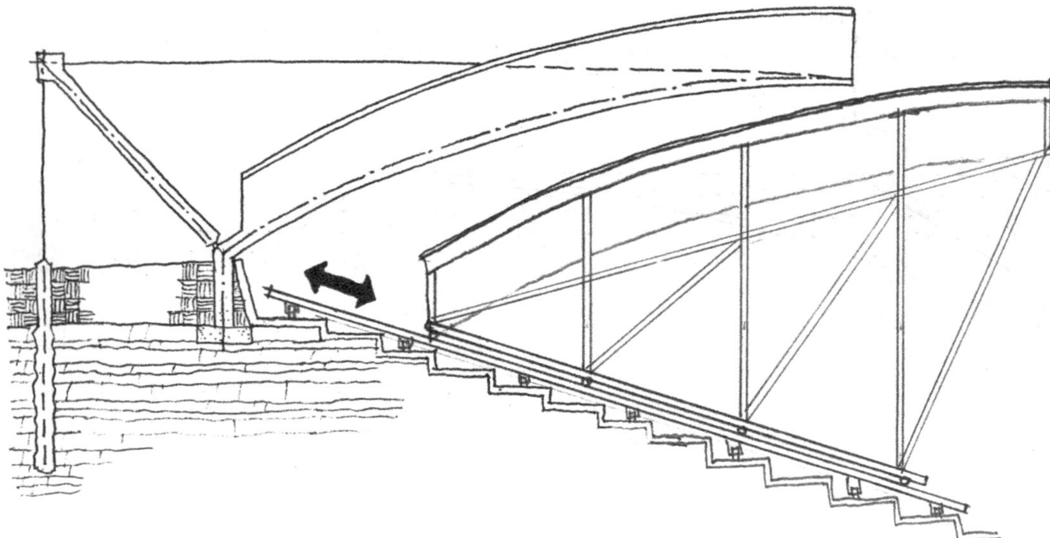

Figure 9.29

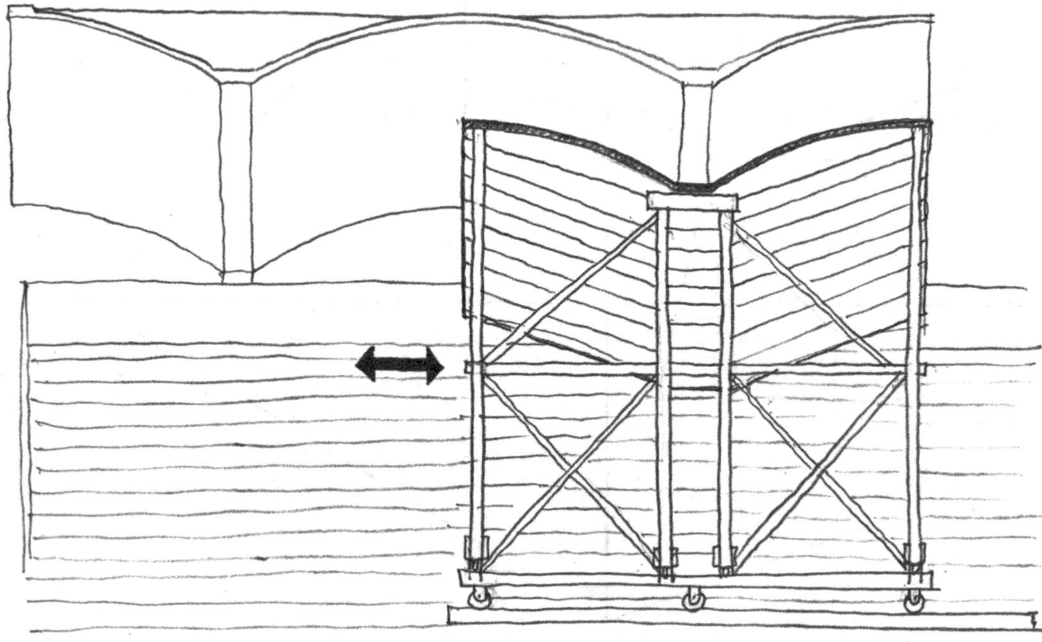

Figure 9.30

Figure 9.31

FORMING THE CONCRETE

"I've been thinking ahead to how we'd build this roof," offered Bruce. "Because it's repetitive in form, it could be constructed most economically with a single bay of formwork that can be used repeatedly. With this in mind, we could evolve a design for a form that is supported on a wheeled framework (9.29, 9.30). To move from one bay to the next, the framework would be rolled on tracks along the steps of the bleacher seats. To allow this motion to occur, the form also rolls on sloping tracks that allow it to be dropped below the bottoms of the arches, then to be pushed up again to the proper height for pouring the next bay. It's apparent in looking at the motion of the formwork that our decision to move the tie rods to the crown line of the vaults was a good one."

"That's what I was just thinking. Because the roof will be constructed one vault at a time, it will be necessary to anchor each tie bar with a hook at the crown of each vault, rather than running continuous bars the full length of the roof. The curved reinforcing bars from within each vault will be left projecting out of the edge of the vault crown in each pour. These will be overlapped with the curved bars in the next pour and spliced by embedding them in the concrete. This will knit the entire line of vaults into a single, monolithic structural unit (9.31)."

FURTHER WORK

"Well, Diane, I think we've got the winning design. Its shape is efficient and elegant, its members are proportioned according to the forces that they will have to resist, and we've worked out a practical way to construct it. Best of all, it's a rather spectacular roof, the kind of structure that tends to catch a design jury's attention."

"I agree. It's got spunk. It would be a showcase for Costa Verdean concrete work, too, which is a point that I hope will not be lost on the competition jury.

"If we win, we'll have a lot of detailed work to do before it can be built. We've shaped and sized all the concrete members in such a way that, in theory at least, they are subjected only to compressive forces and don't require tensile reinforcing. But we'll have to provide a grid of bars within the vaults to resist cracking from forces caused by temperature change, concrete shrinkage, and unforeseen loading conditions. For similar reasons, we'll put longitudinal bars in the arches, struts, and columns. These longitudinal bars are always surrounded by smaller-diameter ties that resist the tendency of compressed concrete to expand and burst in directions perpendicular to the longitudinal compression (9.32).

"We'll also need to examine several other aspects of the design. One is the potential for the wind to lift and vibrate the roof. The dead load of the vaults and arches is more than the upward pressure that would be exerted by the strongest likely wind, but winds of various velocities and directions might cause this sail-like surface to oscillate and twist in such a way that large dynamic forces would occur. Another aspect requiring investigation is the resistance of the structure to overturning, like a line of dominoes, in a direction perpendicular to the planes of the half-arches. For this to happen, the vaults would have to flex and break. The vaults are probably stiff enough to prevent this possibility, but if this does not prove to be the case, we may have to stiffen the inclined stems of the foundations, or add diagonal bracing or stiff walls between them."

A day later, Bruce walked unannounced into Diane's office and unrolled a rendering of the grandstand roof (9.33).

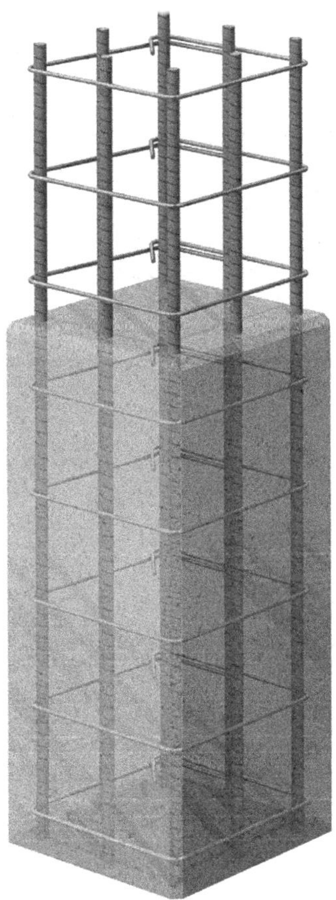

Figure 9.32

Courtesy Concrete Reinforcing Steel Institute.

"This drawing can be the key element in our presentation. I like this design a lot, and I think the jury will, too."

"What a nice surprise! Good work! How's your Spanish?"

"Muy mal! But that will change if we win . . . "

Figure 9.33

Design and image by Boston Structures group.

Figure 9.34 Roof of the Municipal stadium in Florence, Italy (1929–1932), designed by Pier Luigi Nervi.

Source: From Pier Luigi Nervi, *Structures*, New York: F. W. Dodge Corporation, 1956.

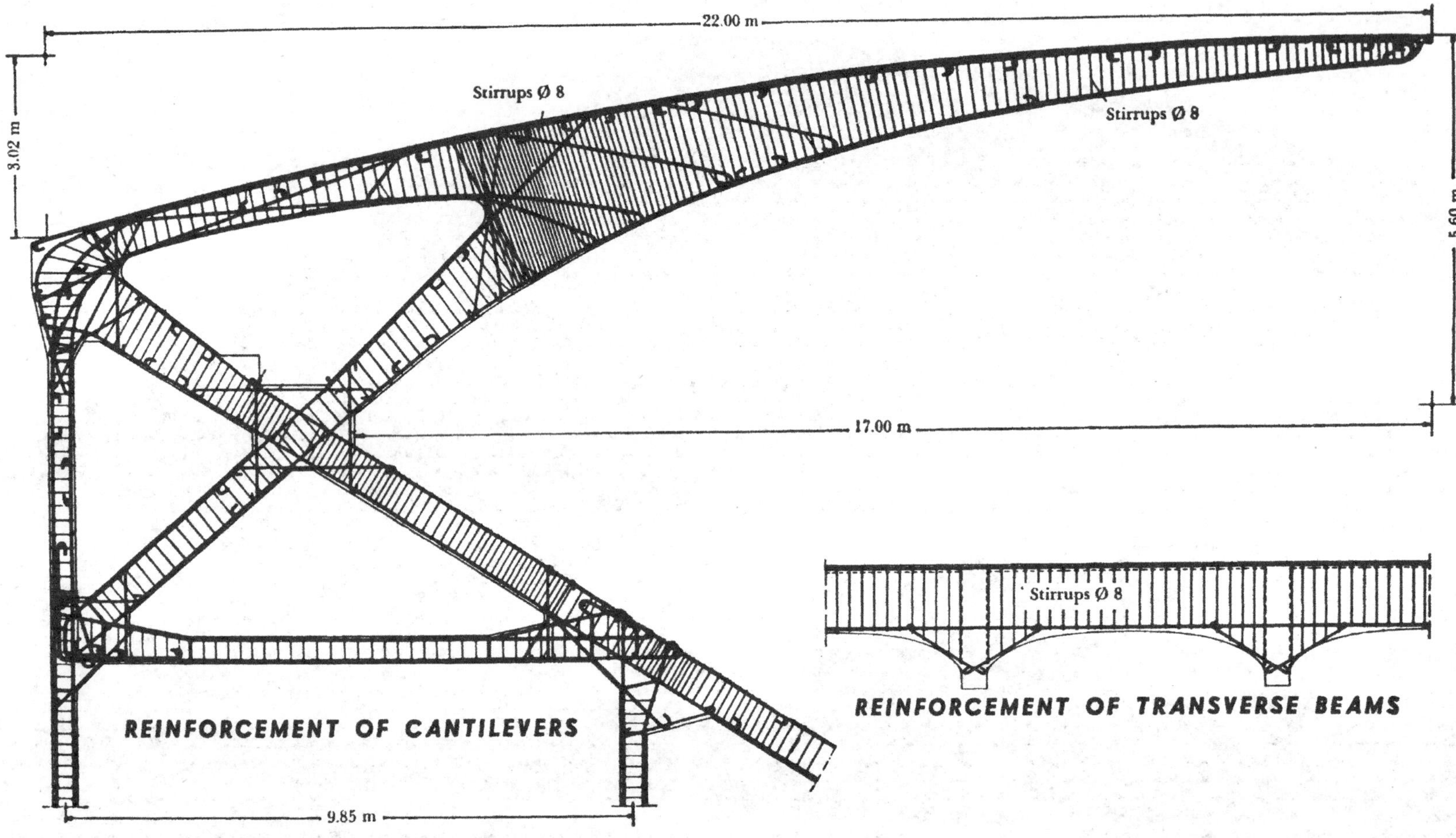

Figure 9.35 A section through the structure of the Florence stadium, showing the steel reinforcing bars in the concrete. The member that slopes down toward the right serves to support the stadium seating, as well as to act as an element of the roof structure.

Source: From Pier Luigi Nervi, *Structures*, New York: F. W. Dodge Corporation, 1956.

Figure 9.36 (a) The stadium roof at the Zarzuela Hippodrome in Madrid, Spain, 1935, designed by Eduardo Torroja. The cantilever distance is about 13 m (42 ft), and the vault thickness at the upper edge is 50 mm (2 in.). Notice the vertical backstays at the rear of the roof. Torroja avoided horizontal tie bars by warping the vault surfaces into hyperboloids that undergo tensile force along the crown lines. (b) A construction photograph shows the internal reinforcing bars, which are placed along the internal lines of tensile force in the structure, as Torroja drew in his sketch below. In Chapters 14 and 17, we will learn how to draw flow patterns of forces like this for any structure.

Source: From Eduardo Torroja: *Structures of Eduardo Torroja*, New York: F. W. Dodge Corporation, 1958.

(a)

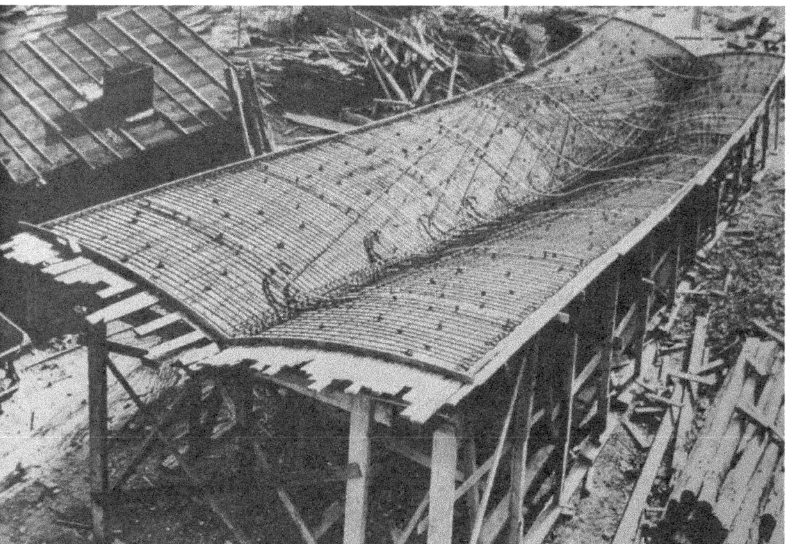

(b)

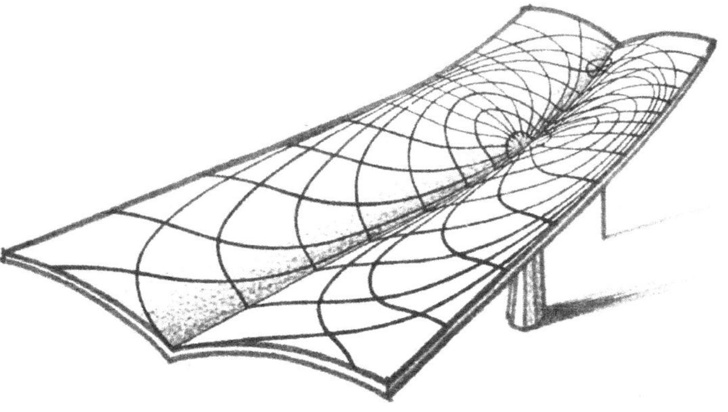

DISTRIBUTION OF STRESSES

EDUARDO TORROJA

The son of a mathematician who specialized in projective geometry, Eduardo Torroja (1889–1961) was a Spanish engineer who is best known for innovative concrete shell designs. Inspired in his youth by Catalonian brick vaulting techniques, Torroja applied his creativity to reinforced concrete. His Hippodrome for a racecourse at Zarzuela (1935) and his roof for the Market of Algeciras (1933) were two of his most exuberant early works, using doubly-curved concrete surfaces and delicately tapered cantilevers. He also created highly articulate steel-framed hangars and other structures. He founded the Technical Institute of Construction and Cement in 1949, and continued designing and collaborating on various churches and other buildings into the 1950s. He was one of the few modern builders who designed and built aqueducts throughout his career. Torroja built all of his work in his native Spain, and later served as a visiting professor at universities such as Princeton, Harvard, MIT, and North Carolina State University.

CHAPTER 10

Designing Efficient Trusses

- *Reversing the graphical process to synthesize shapes of constant-force trusses and arches*
- *Rapid assessment of truss efficiency by comparing force polygons*
- *Typical forms of constant-force trusses*

We are designing a steel roof structure for an exhibit hall in a science museum. We hope to design elegant trusses that will have a high-tech feel appropriate to the use of the hall (Figure 10.1). The span is 90 ft, and the load-bearing masonry wall that will support one end of the trusses is 9 ft higher than the wall at the other end (Figure 10.2).

A major factor in the visual fascination of a trussed roof is that we see the trusses arrayed in complex, constantly changing geometric overlappings as we move through the space below them. This effect is magnified if the trusses are closely spaced (Figure 10.3). The length of the hall is 125 ft, which we divide tentatively into 10 spacings of 12.5 ft between each truss. Based on our early sketches of different forms, we will see if this spacing gives the desired visual effect, and change it if necessary (Figure 10.4).

Rather than give a predetermined shape to the trusses, we will attempt to discover a shape that is highly efficient in its use of materials. One of the best ways to make a truss efficient is to shape it so that either its top or bottom chord will have constant force throughout its length under the loading for which it is designed. When this is done, the constant-force chord utilizes its material at full capacity throughout

Figure 10.1 The roof over the new concourse at Piccadilly Railway Station in Manchester, England (2002), improves the station's image and connections to the city. ETFE translucent panels bring in daylight through the single-pitched roof, which is supported by spidery constant-force trusses. (Architect, planner, and MEP design: BDP. Structural engineer: URS.) Photo: David M. Foxe.

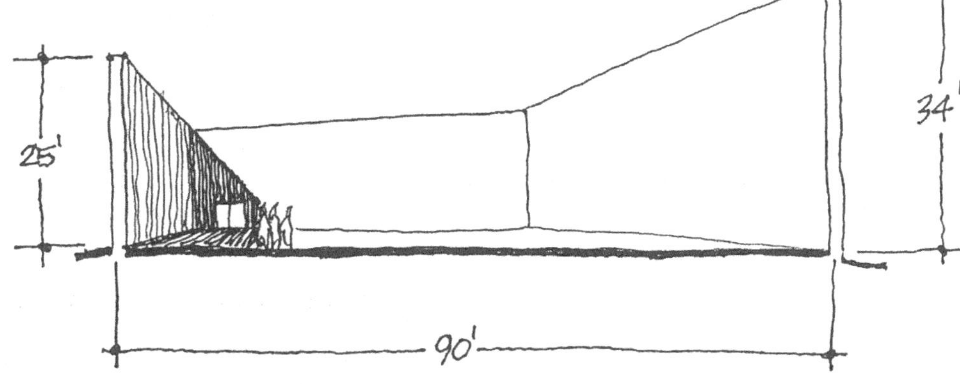

Figure 10.2 The walls of the museum exhibit hall.

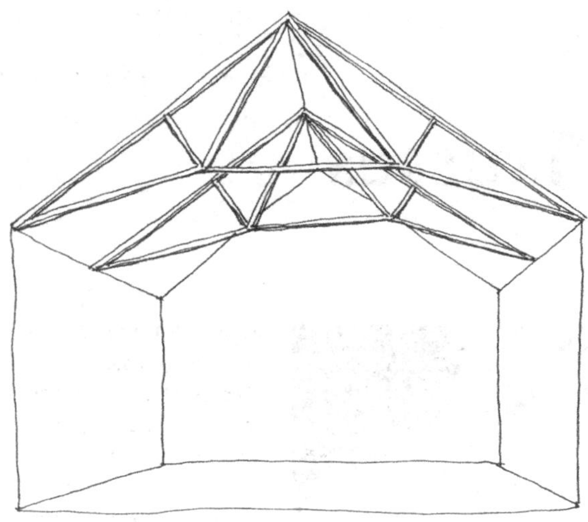

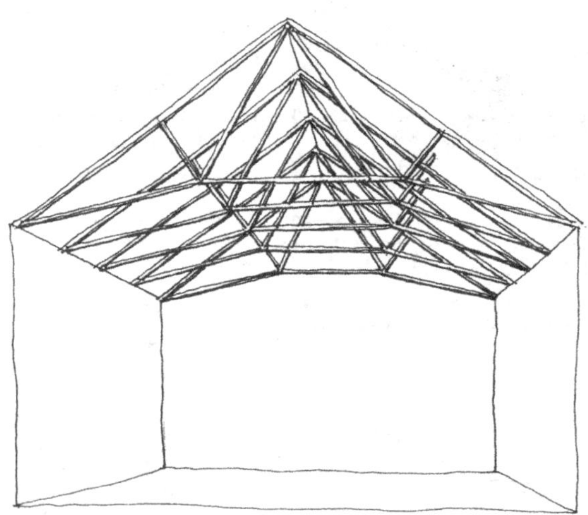

Figure 10.3 The visual interest of trusses is often dependent on a relatively close spacing.

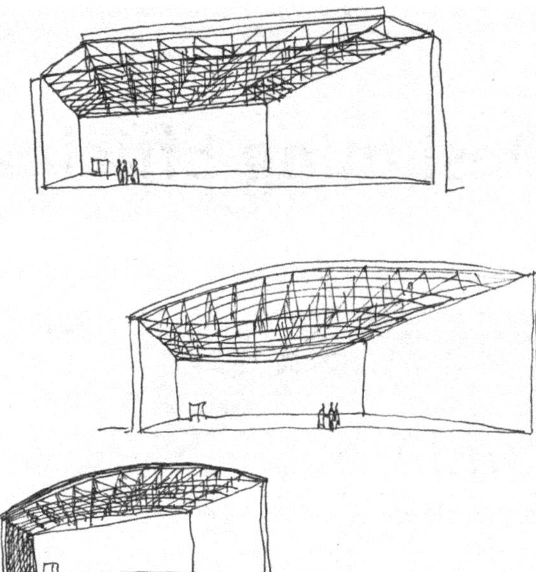

Figure 10.4 Initial sketches for the roof of the museum.

its length when the truss is fully loaded, as do the web members. The forces in the segments of the other chord, which does not have constant force, do not vary much from one to another. Furthermore, in many cases the diagonal web members can be eliminated. All this adds up to considerable material saving over conventional trusses.

For the museum roof, we might, for example, use steel rods for the bottom chord and shape the truss so that all the material in the rods is working to its full allowable strength under the design loading. Can we derive a shape for a truss that will have this property? And will it result in an attractive truss?

FINDING THE FORM OF THE TRUSS

Working at the drawing board with Worksheet 10A, taken from the supplemental site, we divide the top chord of the truss into nine panels, each 10 ft long (Figure 10.5). Each node of the top chord will support a purlin. We have already calculated the tributary area supported by each top node of the truss and multiplied it by the assumed load per unit area to find that the estimated load is 7.5 kips per node. We will try a design in which the lower chord is made up of two steel rods, each 1–1/2 in. in diameter, which we think will appear slender but still be readily visible. The allowable stress in the ordinary mild steel of these rods is 24,000 psi.

Cambering the Truss

In setting up the design solution, we decide on a purely formal basis to give the top chords of the trusses a pronounced upward camber to create the illusion that they carry their loads effortlessly, and to impart a more pleasant feel to the space below. We create the camber by first deciding on the rise that we would like between the end of the truss, where it is zero, and the middle of the span. By trial and error, we decide on a rise of 30 in., which is 1/36th of the span. We decide that the most graceful curve for the camber will be a parabola. We could lay out a parabola by graphical means, but this parabola will be so flat that a graphical construction will be difficult to carry out. Instead, we will make use of a simple mathematical expression that gives the height of a parabola above its closing string at any distance, x, from its left end:

$$Y_x = 4s\left(\frac{x}{L} - \frac{x^2}{L^2}\right) \qquad [10\text{-}1]$$

where:

Y_x is the height of the parabola at distance x from the left end,

s is the maximum vertical distance from the parabola to its closing string, and

L is the horizontal dimension of the parabola.

Figure 10.6 shows how this expression is applied to finding the coordinates of the parabolic camber. These numbers can be furnished to the steel fabricator

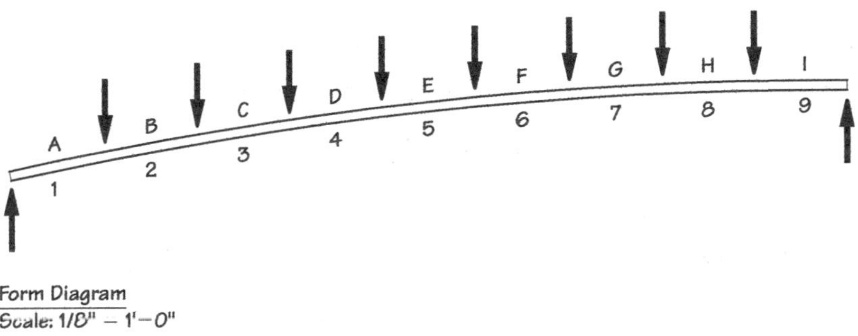

Figure 10.5 A reduced copy of Worksheet 10A for the museum truss design.

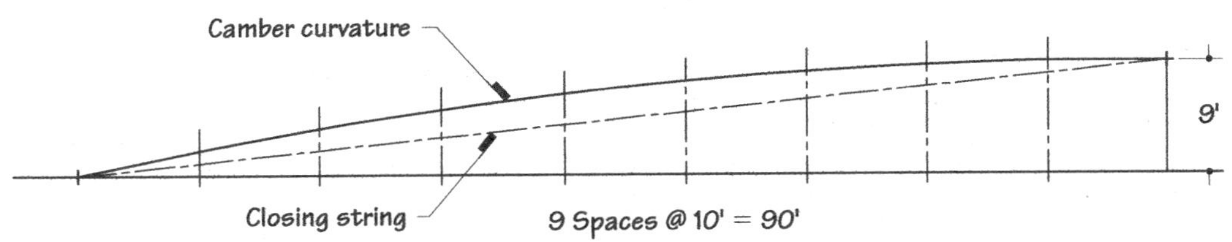

Figure 10.6 The cambered shape of the top chord of the museum trusses is generated as a very shallow parabola.

to use in the layout and construction of the trusses. Later we will consider whether it is more economical to make the top chord of segments as shown, or of a single, bent member whose curve passes through these points.

The finding of the overall form of this truss would appear to be a fairly involved problem, with the ends of the truss at different levels, an arbitrarily curved top chord, and a requirement for constant force in the bottom chord. In fact, we will discover that its solution is rather straightforward; but before we attempt it, we will learn how to do it by working through some simpler examples of a very powerful design technique that invariably yields structural forms that are both elegant and efficient.

A GRAPHICAL METHOD FOR FINDING FORM FOR A CONSTANT-FORCE TRUSS

Drawing (a) in Figure 10.7 shows a loading pattern for a top-loaded truss. We would like to find a form for this truss such that the force in the top chord will be a constant 26,000 lb throughout its length, thus allowing a single piece of material of uniform size to serve for this member. The top chord is to be straight and level; the form of the bottom chord is unknown.

Bow's notation facilitates the graphical solution. The load line is constructed in the usual manner. Then a line is drawn parallel to the load line at a horizontal distance of 26,000 lb to the left of it. The force polygon is constructed in steps (a) through (d) in such a way that all the horizontal line segments that represent the forces in the segments of the top chord end at this vertical line. These intersections determine the inclinations of the various segments of the bottom chord, which are added one by one to the form diagram, generating the shape of the truss. All the segments of the bottom chord have the letter *G* in their names, so all the lines on the force polygon that represent the forces in them must pass through g on the load line. At each step, the construction of the lines on the force polygon precedes and guides the construction of the form of the truss.

All the diagonals turn out to be zero-force members. This is because the force in the bottom chord could not be constant otherwise. If there were force in a diagonal member, the horizontal component of this force would be transferred to the chord, creating a difference in force from one panel to the next.

The forces in the other members are found by scaling the lengths of the corresponding line segments in the force polygon. How efficient is this truss in its utilization of material? The top chord has the same force throughout, so it utilizes its material at 100 percent of capacity under a full load. The interior members can be sized so that each is fully stressed throughout. And the bottom chord member least utilized has a force that is 87 percent as great as the most utilized member.

Constant-force trusses of this shape have been used in such structures as the Shiosai Bridge in Japan (Figure 10.8) and the Alamodome roof in San Antonio, Texas (Figures 10.9, 10.10). A number of recent buildings employ trusses of this shape as window mullions for large expanses of glass, where their chief role is to resist horizontal wind pressures on the glass (Figure 10.11).

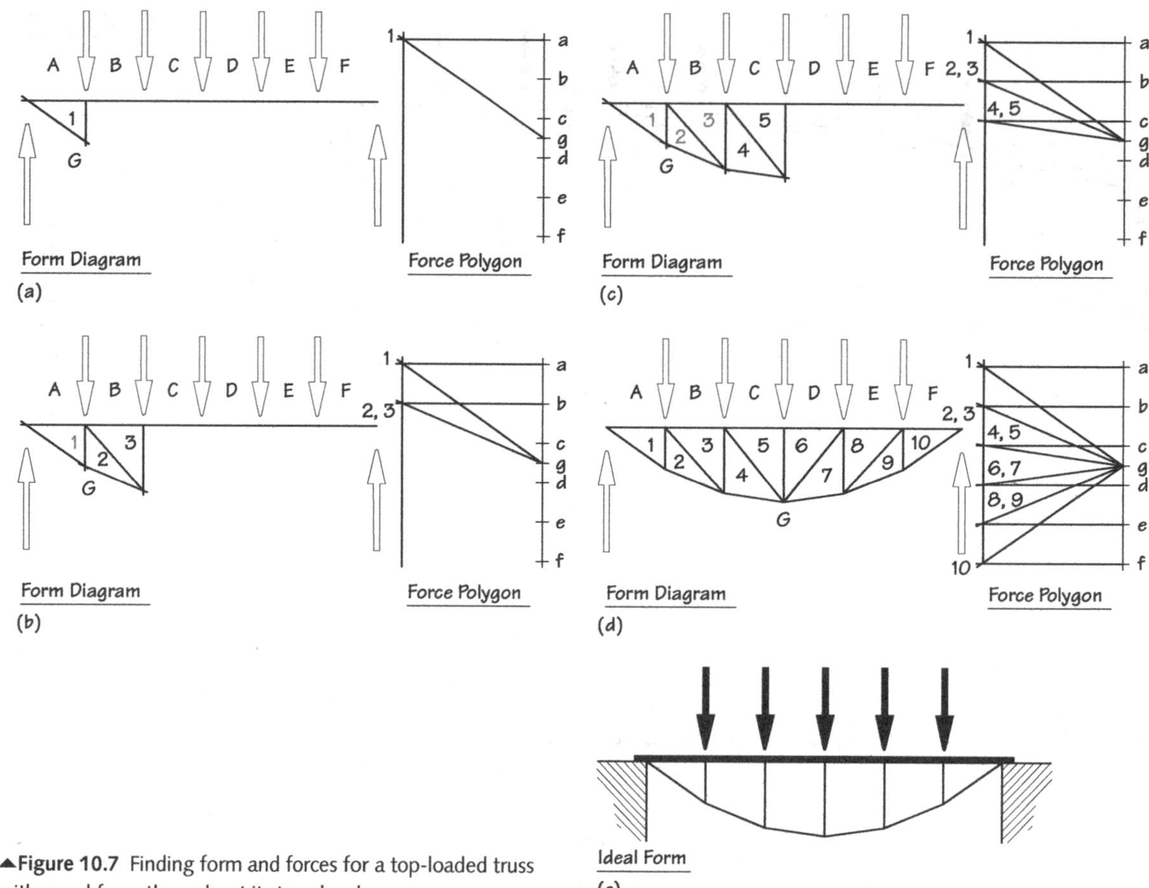

▲**Figure 10.7** Finding form and forces for a top-loaded truss with equal force throughout its top chord.

Figure 10.8 The Shiosai Bridge, in Japan, with a clear width of 3 m (10 ft), is used by pedestrians and cyclists. It is made of concrete and high-strength steel posttensioning tendons. The longest span is 61 m (200 ft). Diagonal members have been omitted.

Photo courtesy of the owner, Shizuoca Prefecture. Contractor: Sumitomo Construction Company, Ltd.

▶ **Figure 10.9** The Alamodome in San Antonio, Texas, constructed in 1993, is a huge arena that seats 65,000 people for football games. The main roof truss in the center of the photograph spans 378 ft. Its funicular bottom chord is made of steel cables. Its top chord is a steel wide-flange shape that is 3 ft deep. The truss supports sloping, parallel-chord steel trusses over the seating area, and together with its twin, off the photo to the right, 10-ft-deep trusses over the playing field, which were installed after the photograph was taken. (Structure designed by Marmon Mok.)

Photo courtesy of Vulcraft Division of Nucor Corporation, manufacturer of the parallel-chord trusses.

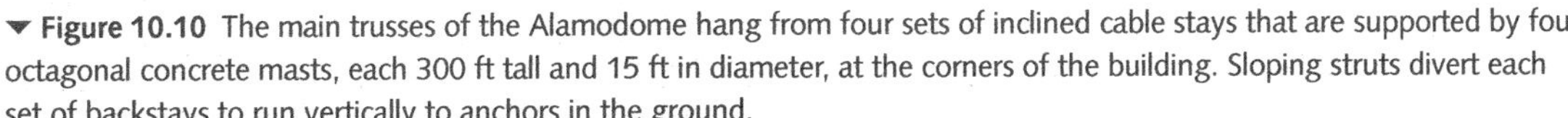

▼ **Figure 10.10** The main trusses of the Alamodome hang from four sets of inclined cable stays that are supported by four octagonal concrete masts, each 300 ft tall and 15 ft in diameter, at the corners of the building. Sloping struts divert each set of backstays to run vertically to anchors in the ground.

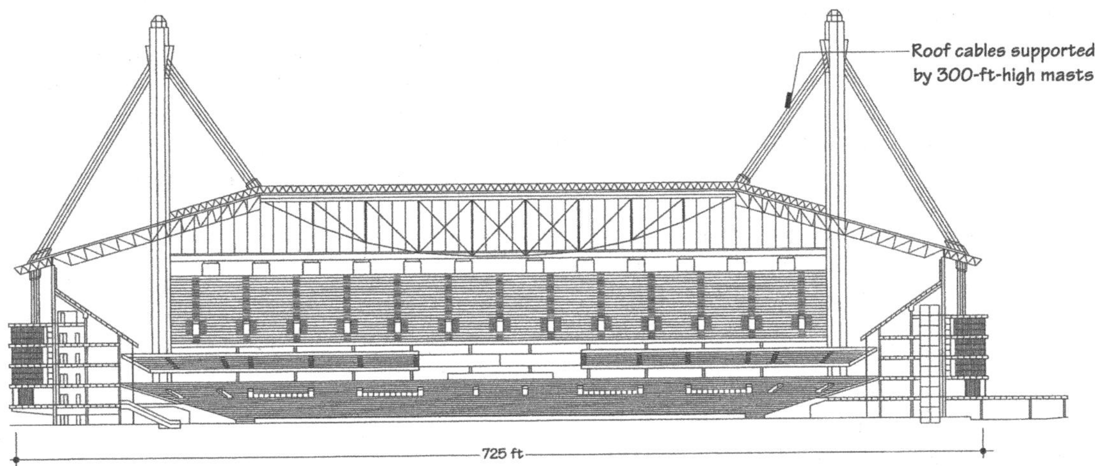

▲ **Figure 10.11** Vertical constant-force trusses with funicular outer chords stiffen a glass wall against wind loads at the Kansai International Airport in Osaka, Japan. Each vertical joint between sheets of glass is supported by mirror-image trusses inside and out. The roof trusses, triangular in section and made of steel pipes with welded joints, do not follow funicular lines. Architects and engineers: Renzo Piano Building Workshop and Ove Arup and Partners.

Photo courtesy of John Edward Linden/Arcaid.

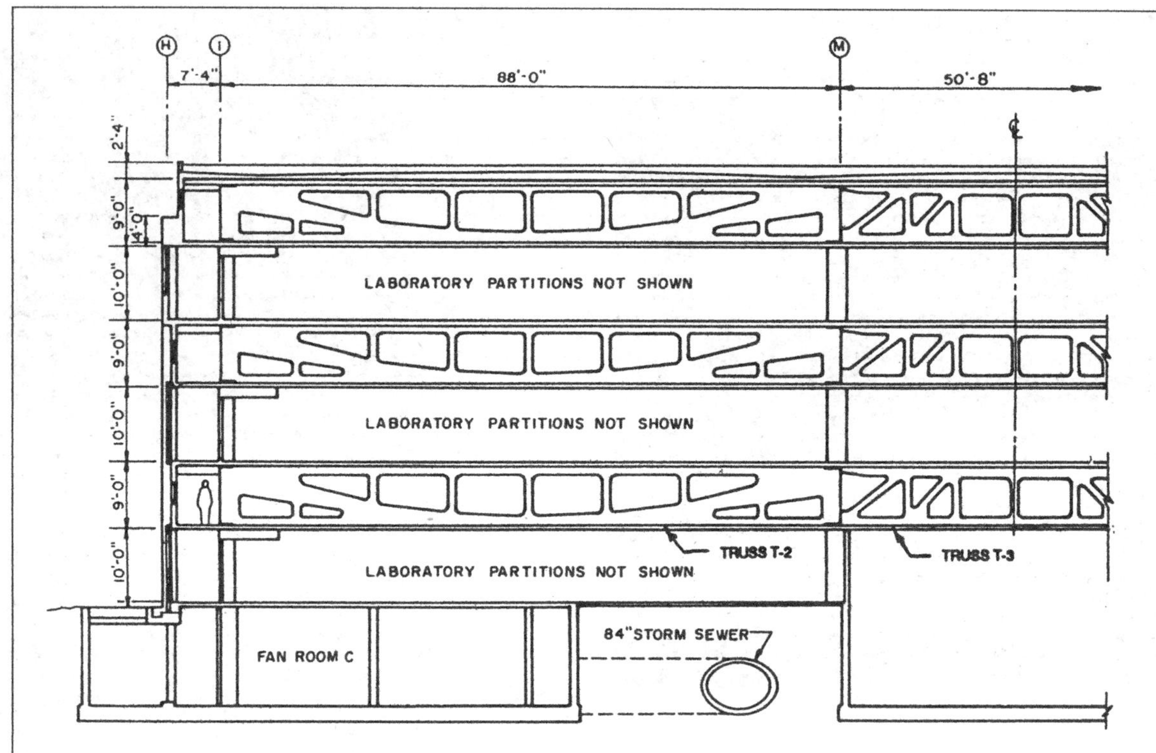

Figure 10.12 Laboratory floors of the Ciba-Geigy Life Science Building in Summit, New Jersey, built in 1992, rest on precast concrete constant-force trusses. The funicular bottom chord of each truss consists of steel posttensioning tendons encased in concrete. Below this chord hangs a horizontal semistructural member of concrete that supports a level ceiling below. The trusses, each 9 ft deep and 88 ft long, provide column-free laboratory space, as well as a generous horizontal zone for piping, wiring, and ductwork.

Photo courtesy of Weidlinger Associates, New York.

Figure 10.13 Each truss for the Ciba-Geigy Life Science Building was cast on its side. The smooth, bundled strands in this photograph are plastic-sheathed steel posttensioning cables that follow the funicular line of the bottom chord. The rest of the internal elements are steel reinforcing bars.

Photo courtesy of Weidlinger Associates, New York.

In the buildings among these examples, diagonals were added to the ideal form to resist nonuniform loadings. Figures 10.12 to 10.14 illustrate a precast concrete floor truss design that does not utilize diagonals, but like the Shiosai Bridge, relies instead on the stiffness of its steel-reinforced concrete members and joints to resist incidental forces caused by asymmetrical loads. A level bottom chord that has no significant role in the overall strength and stiffness of the truss has been added to connect to a flat ceiling.

A BOTTOM-LOADED CONSTANT-FORCE TRUSS

If equal loads are applied along the bottom chord of a truss that has a level, constant-force top chord, a form emerges in which all internal members carry zero force (Figure 10.15). The ideal form of the resulting truss (b) is that of a funicular suspension cable with a compression strut to resist its horizontal pull. The force polygon is a mirror image of the diagram that one would use to find the form and forces for a hanging cable.

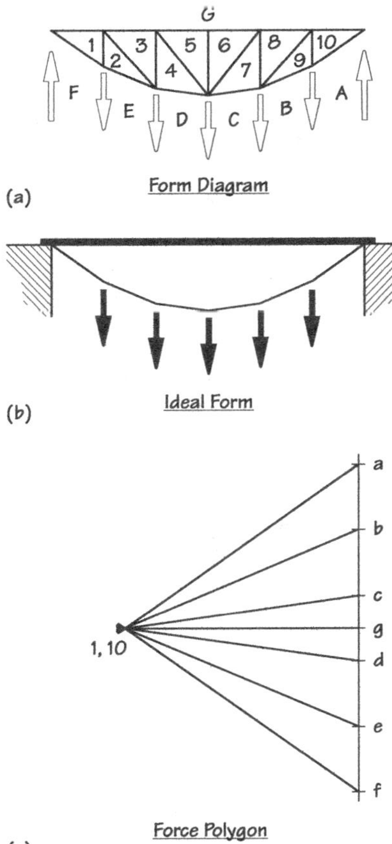

Figure 10.15 Finding the form of a bottom-loaded truss with a constant force in its top chord.

Figure 10.14 Each truss weighs 43 tons. The short reinforcing bars that project from the edges of the truss will be overlapped with similar bars from the floor, ceiling, and column elements before the concrete is poured. When cured, the concrete thus unites all the members into a strong, single-piece construction. Architects: Mitchell/Giurgola. Engineers: Weidlinger Associates.

Photo courtesy of Weidlinger Associates, New York.

If the depth of the truss in Figure 10.15 is decreased progressively in relation to its span, and if the sizes of the tensile and compressive members are proportioned to the forces that they experience, we arrive at the form of a longitudinally compressed beam that incorporates a funicularly curved tendon (Figure 10.16). This is similar to the form of a posttensioned concrete beam that is designed for a uniformly distributed load, and offers a simple way in which the behavior of such a beam may be analyzed and understood.

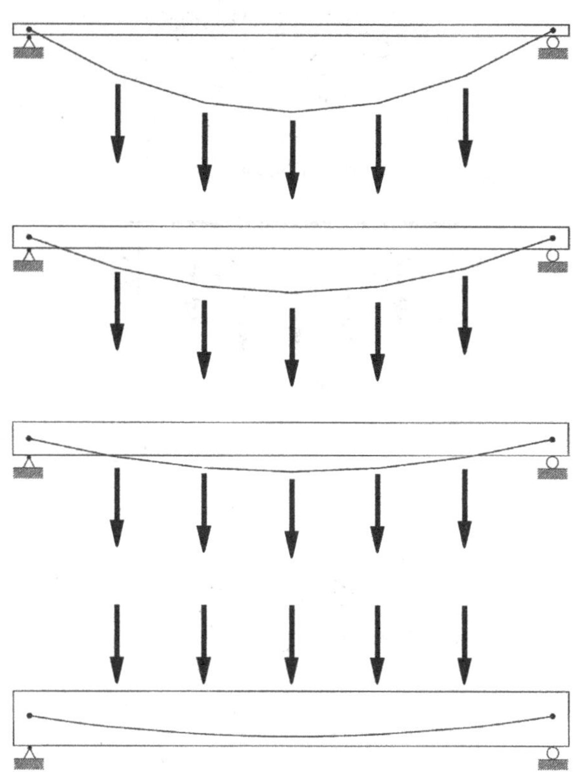

Figure 10.16 As the depth of the truss in Figure 10.13 is gradually decreased, its member forces rise. The concrete top chord, which is in compression and must resist buckling, grows very thick. The bottom chord may be made of very high-strength steel cables so as to remain slender. The limiting case is a form similar to that of a posttensioned concrete beam.

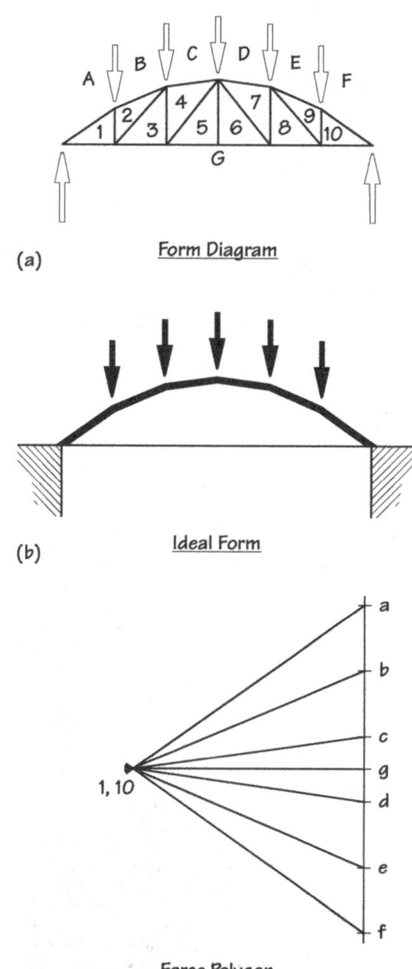

◀ **Figure 10.17** Finding the form of a bowstring truss, which is a top-loaded truss with a constant force in its bottom chord.

▲ **Figure 10.18** Steel bowstring trusses support the roof of an elementary school.

Photo courtesy of Vulcraft Division of Nucor Corporation.

Figure 10.17 shows the inversion of the form of the truss in Figure 10.15, an elegantly simple truss whose ideal form (b) is that of a tied funicular arch. The force polygons for the two examples are identical, although in Bow's notation their letters correspond to letters that are differently located on their respective form diagrams. With the addition of diagonals, this becomes the highly economical *bowstring truss* of wood or steel that is widely used in roof structures of industrial and commercial buildings (Figure 10.18). For ease of fabrication, a segment of a circle is often used as the shape for the top chord instead of the ideal shape, which is a parabola. This results in a negligible loss of efficiency that is reflected in the small forces that occur in the web members of the truss under a uniform loading.

A further exploration of this line of investigation is shown in Figure 10.19. The truss is bottom loaded, but is constructed to have a straight bottom chord with constant force throughout. The resulting form is that of an arch with slender tensile verticals, which transmit the applied loads to the arch, and a horizontal tie that resists the thrust of the arch. This form is widely used in *tied arch* bridges.

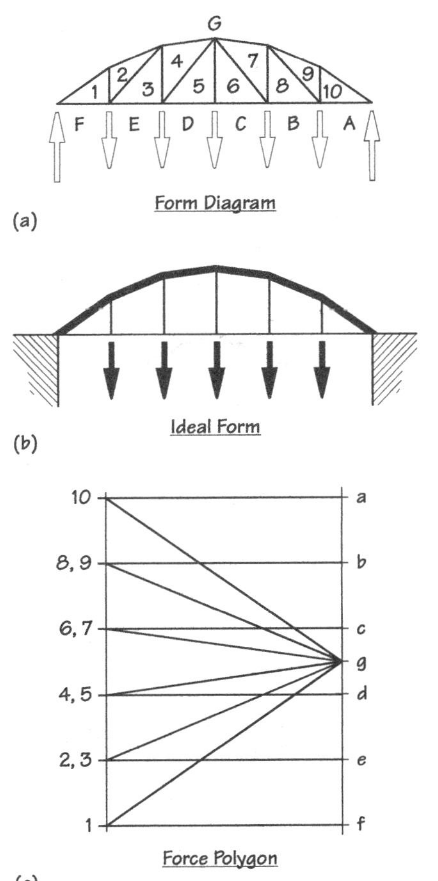

Figure 10.19 Finding the form of a tied arch, a bottom-loaded truss with constant force in its bottom chord.

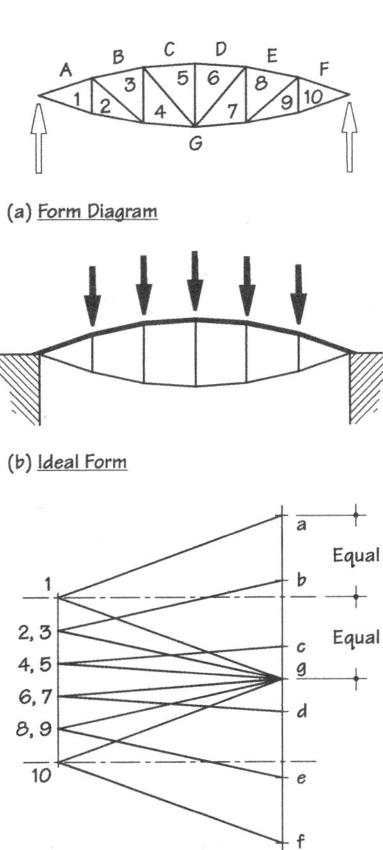

Figure 10.20 Finding the form of a lenticular truss.

▲ **Figure 10.22** This late-nineteenth-century lenticular bridge still carries traffic in western Massachusetts.

Photo: Edward Allen.

▶ **Figure 10.21** The Royal Albert Bridge at Saltash, England, was designed and built by Isambard Kingdom Brunel in 1859. It is an early example of the use of lenticular trusses. Each truss spans 455 ft and has a midspan depth of 62 ft. The top chord is a tube, elliptical in cross section, made of wrought-iron plates riveted together. Each bottom chord is a chain of long wrought iron links.

Photo courtesy of the Institution of Civil Engineers, London.

ISAMBARD KINGDOM BRUNEL

Isambard Kingdom Brunel was born in 1806. Working for his engineer father, he became engineer in charge of work on the Thames Tunnel project in London at the age of 20. After several construction challenges that delayed for years the tunnel's completion, I.K. became a prolific civil engineer in his own right, designing bridges, the Great Western Railway, and the eventual completion of the Thames Tunnel in 1843. Brunel combined a talent for making proposals on a grand scale with the promotional skill to argue successfully for their construction. His pioneering design for the Royal Albert Bridge at Saltash used lenticular trusses with a single compressive tube and paired tensile cables on either side of the track below. Before his death in 1859, Brunel worked on fanlike timber viaducts, railway terminals, prefabricated construction systems, steamship design and construction, and a variety of other transportation engineering projects.

A LENTICULAR TRUSS

A *lenticular truss,* also called a *Pauli truss* after its inventor, the nineteenth-century German engineer Friedrich August von Pauli, has the unique property that within each panel, the forces in the top and bottom chords have the same absolute value, but are opposite in character. The shape is generated from the force polygon (c) in Figure 10.20. In each panel of the truss, the inclinations of the top and bottom chord segments are made equal, as shown. Lenticular trusses were widely used in the nineteenth century for road and railway bridges (Figures 10.21, 10.22). More recently, they have been proposed as an efficient means for carrying tension hangers that support multiple floors from the top of a high-rise building (Figure 10.23).

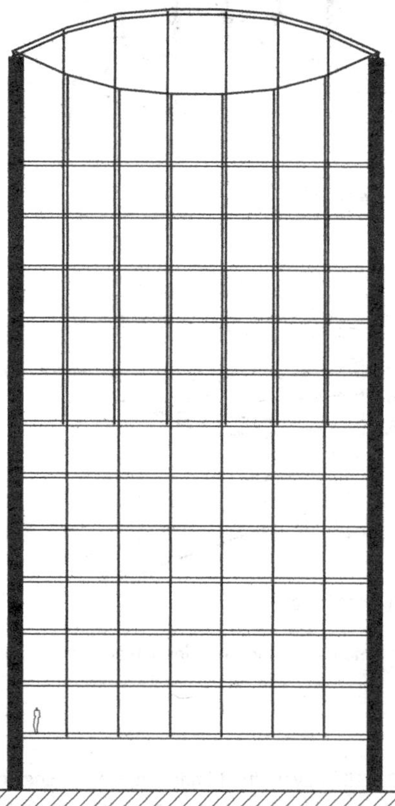

▲ **Figure 10.23** Lenticular trusses supported by elevator and stair towers can furnish economical support for a tall building. Half the building's floors are hung from the top chord, and half from the bottom chord, thus balancing the forces in the truss.

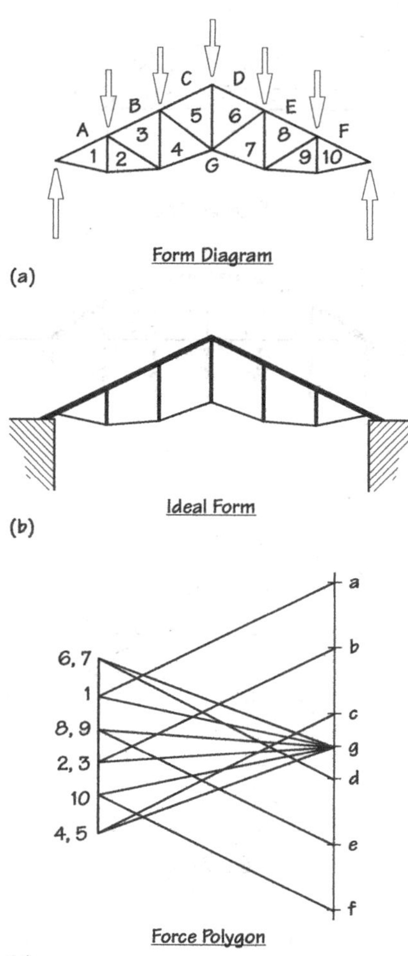

▲ **Figure 10.24** Finding the form of a constant-force gable truss.

▶ **Figure 10.25** Constant-force gable trusses in the Magazzini Generali warehouse at Chiasso, Switzerland. Robert Maillart designed the structure in 1924. Concrete struts in the long direction of the building prevent out-of-plane movement of the trusses. The detailing of the cantilevered roof overhang and columns is particularly expressive.

Photo courtesy of ETH-Bibliothek, Zürich.

A CONSTANT-FORCE GABLE TRUSS

Gable trusses may be optimized in the same general manner as flat trusses. Figure 10.24 shows the shaping of a gable truss in which the force is constant throughout the top chords. The inclination of the top chords is given by the desired pitch of the roof that is supported by the truss. A vertical line is constructed to the left of the load line at a distance that yields the desired force in the top chords; this distance is measured along lines *a1*, *b3*, *c5*, *d6*, *e8*, and *f10*, whose inclinations are the same as those of the top chords. The form of the bottom chord is determined by the lines that radiate from *g* on the force polygon. Concrete roof trusses of this somewhat unusual form, without diagonals, were used by Robert Maillart in a warehouse at Chiasso, Switzerland (Figure 10.25).

EFFICIENT CANTILEVER TRUSSES

Figure 10.26 illustrates the shaping of a cantilever truss that carries six identical top loads while maintaining a constant force in its level bottom chord. As with the other trusses in this chapter, the form of the truss is derived from the form of the force polygon. The verticals and diagonals in this truss carry no forces under the ideal loading condition. The ideal form of the truss is that of a funicular cable held away from the wall by a strut that has constant axial compression throughout.

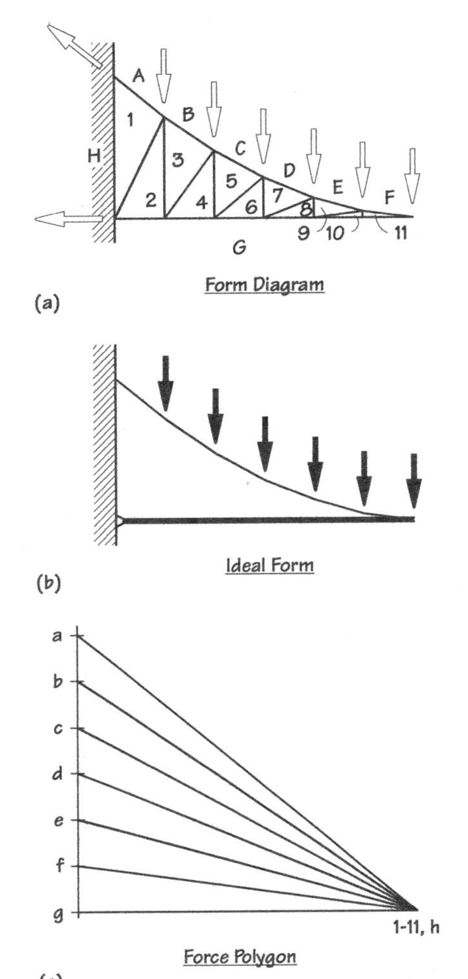

▲ **Figure 10.26** Finding the form of a top-loaded, constant-force cantilever truss.

GUSTAVE EIFFEL

Gustave Eiffel was born in 1832 of German parents. He moved from Dijon to Paris in 1850 to study at the Polytechnic. He earned a place at the Ecole Centrale des Arts et Manufactures, gaining a chemical engineering diploma. This led to employment in the field of metallurgy. Later he worked for a French rail organization, where he led its research department at factories in Paris. In 1868 he set up a limited partnership with a young but wealthy civil engineer, Theophile Seyrig. In this new office Eiffel won acclaim for devising economical bridges constructed with limited numbers of parts. By 1875 he was designing the new bridge over the Douro River in Portugal and a railway station in Budapest. His office went on to design larger, bolder bridges and viaducts at Garabit and Tardes, and even the interior trusses that support the body and upstretched arm of the Statue of Liberty (1883–1886).

The 1000-ft tower in Paris that now bears his name was long imagined as a temporary structure for the 1889 exposition. Eiffel and his chief designer Maurice Koechlin envisioned a tower of tapering trusses shaped as a vertical cantilever. The tower was completed in 1889, along with restaurants and amenities for tourists on its various elevated platforms. It remained the only tower in the center of the French capital until decades after World War II. It has earned a place in Parisian culture, inspiring countless paintings, musical tributes, paper models, souvenirs, and other imitations and descriptions of its iconic form. Eiffel eventually retired to conduct experiments in his other interests of aerodynamics, astronomy, and meteorology, many of them done from his observatory high in the tower, until his death in 1920.

The truss in Figure 10.27 is the cantilevered equivalent of a lenticular truss. Its orientation on the page is that of a tower that is subjected to lateral wind forces. Its form is generated by a force polygon that has been constructed in such a way that the left and right (or top and bottom, depending on how you see it) chord forces are identical in magnitude in each panel. The resulting form suggests the shape of the Eiffel Tower, a structure that was designed using graphical methods (Figures 10.28 to 10.30). This form of tower is very efficient in resisting wind forces by means of nearly constant internal forces throughout its height.

CONSTANT-FORCE TRUSS FORMS: THE GENERAL SOLUTION

Most of the examples given to this point have been level, symmetrical trusses with symmetrical gravity loadings. The method that has been used, however, is general, and may be applied to inclined and irregular loading and support conditions. Figure 10.31 shows an inclined truss with varying loads, one of which is nonvertical, applied at irregular intervals. The force polygon has been manipulated to produce a truss form that has constant force throughout its top chord. Because of the nonvertical load, the hinged end reaction is inclined, and the resulting load line is a quadrilateral. All the lines that represent the forces in the segments of the top chord on the force polygon have been constructed to the same length, which produces an inclined internal member in the ideal truss. This construction is shown here to make the point that it is possible to find a form for a truss with almost any desired characteristic by using these simple graphical methods.

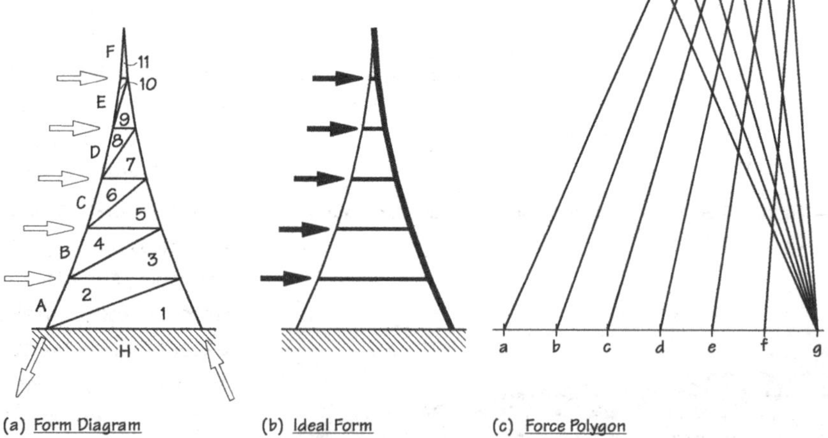

Figure 10.27 The form of this tower is the cantilevered equivalent of a lenticular truss. The left and right chords in each panel experience forces of equal magnitude in response to horizontal wind loads.

Figure 10.28 The Eiffel Tower, designed by Gustave Eiffel and Maurice Koechlin for the 1889 Universal Exposition in Paris, was by far the tallest structure in the world at the time of its construction. With such an efficient shape, its structure is astonishingly light: If its members were all melted down into a solid block as large as its base, the block would be only 2.5 in. high. If a cylinder were built that would contain the tower, the air inside the cylinder would weigh more than the tower.

Photo: David M. Foxe.

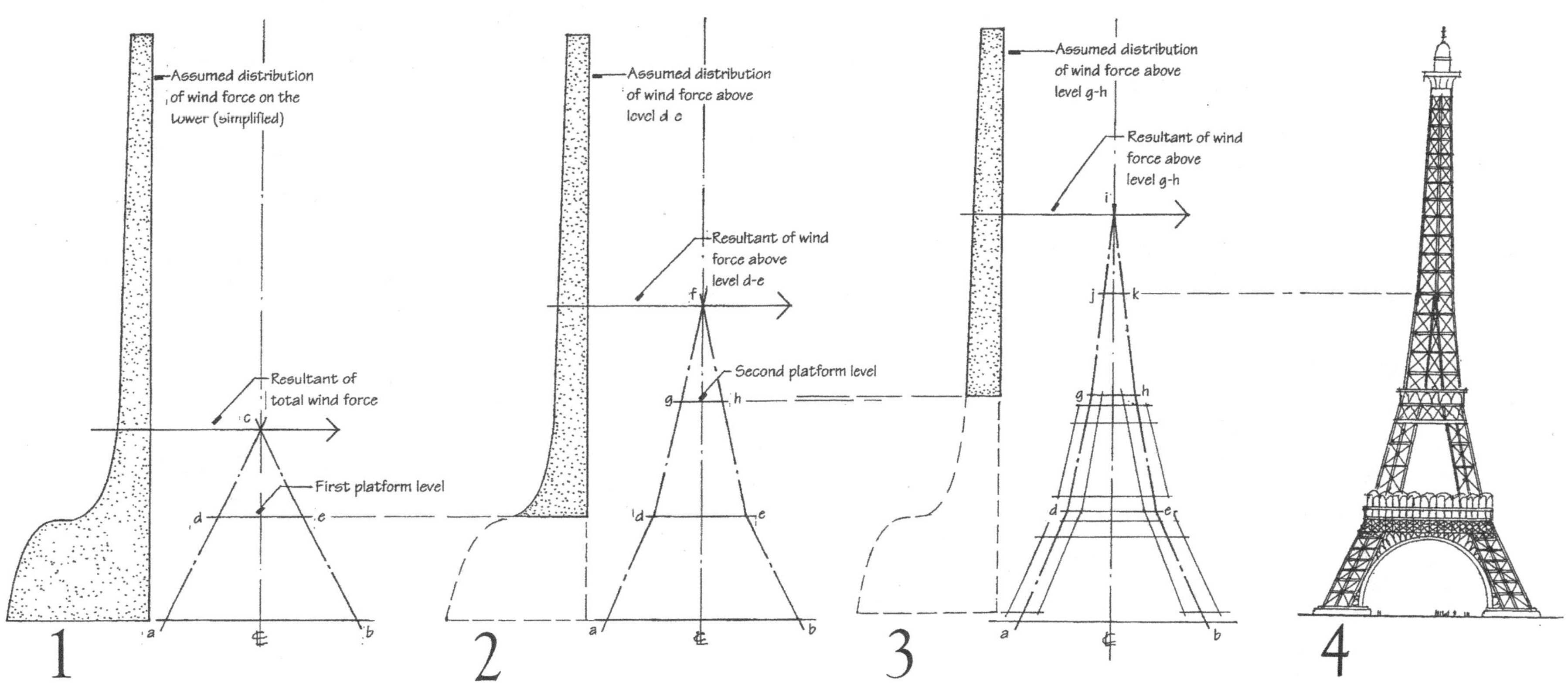

Figure 10.29 Koechlin's method for finding the form of the tower is based on the assumed distribution of wind forces, along with assumptions of the effective area of the tower. Wind force per unit area is much higher at the top of the tower than at the ground, but the shape of the Eiffel tower presents large areas to the wind near the base and smaller ones higher up. In the first step, the overall stability is assured by checking that the centerlines of the piers intersect on the resultant of the wind force on the entire tower (1). Koechlin then established the height above the ground of the lowest platform (2). Disregarding the wind load below this platform, he found the centroid of the remaining wind load and drew the centerlines of the tower piers above the platform so they intersected on the line of action of the wind centroid. In step 3, a second platform was placed, and the operation was repeated for the load and piers above this platform. The resulting tower form (4) needs no diagonals in its lower panels.

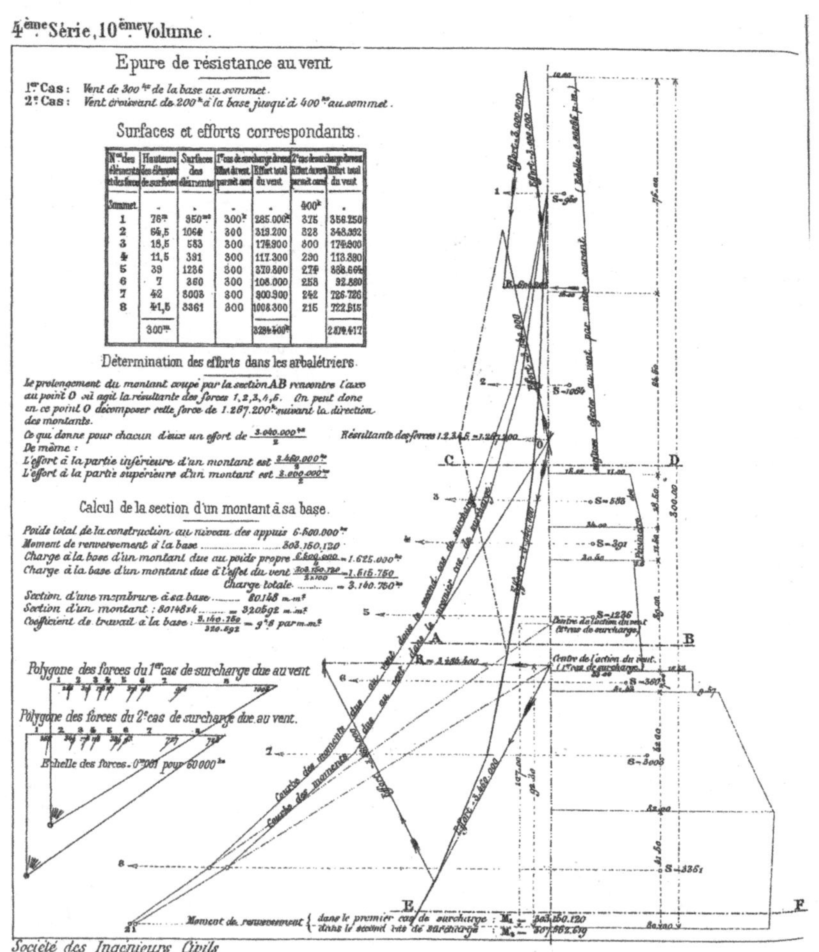

Figure 10.30 The profile to the right of the centerline on this actual page of Koechlin's graphical calculations is the assumed distribution of wind forces on the tower, and to the left is a graphical determination of the angles of the piers of the tower.

Source: Gustave Eiffel, *La Tour de trois cent metres*, Chapter III, Paris: Impremerie Mercier, 1900.

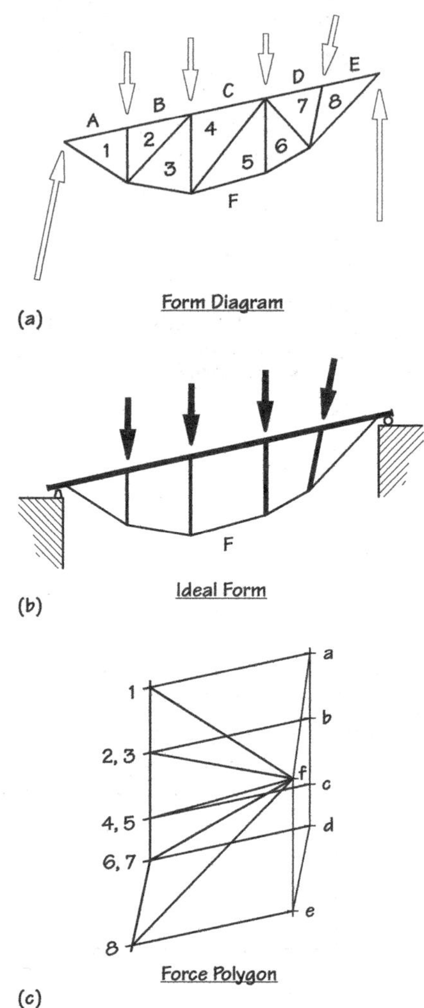

Figure 10.31 Finding the form of a constant-force truss with a sloping top chord and an irregular set of loads.

SUBOPTIMAL TRUSS FORMS: THE CAMELBACK TRUSS

In many situations, an external constraint is placed upon the form of a truss. Such is the case with a bridge truss whose portals at each end must be tall enough to clear the vehicles on the roadway or track that passes through the bridge. Figure 10.32 demonstrates the shaping of a *camelback* truss, a form frequently seen in through-truss road and railway bridges. The heights of members *1-2* and *9-10* are fixed by vehicle clearance requirements, thus determining the inclinations of top chord segments *G-1* and *G-10*, and the inclinations of *g-1* and *g-10* in the force polygon. For the remainder of the truss, the construction of the force polygon precedes the construction of the form diagram at each step. The four center segments of the top chord are configured so that they carry equal forces. This allows them to be the same size, which simplifies fabrication and increases overall structural efficiency.

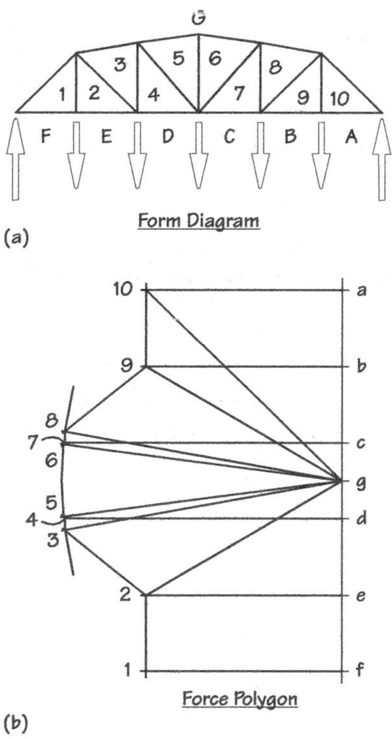

Figure 10.32 Finding the form of a camelback truss.

VISUALIZING FORM IMPROVEMENTS IN TRUSSES OF NONOPTIMAL SHAPE

An important advantage of the graphical method of truss analysis over numerical or computer analyses during early stages of design is that the force polygon furnishes ample, easily discernable clues as to how the form of an arbitrarily shaped truss might be improved. Consider the *scissors truss* (a) in Figure 10.33, which supports a gable roof while maintaining a lofty, soaring interior space. A comparison of the length of the load line with that of the lines that represent the higher member forces in the truss reveals that some member forces are roughly twice as high as the total external load. If this is to be a welded steel truss,

(a)

(b)

(c)

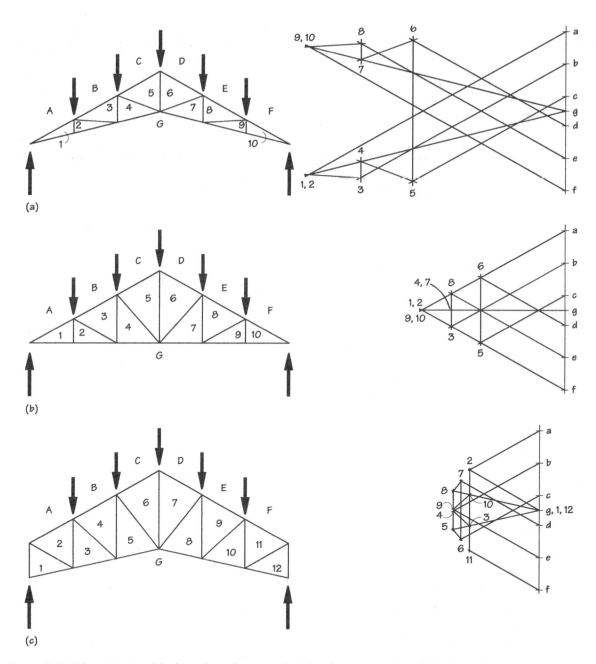

Figure 10.33 Suboptimization of the form of a roof truss, in which the relative compactness of the force polygons is a rough measure of the efficiency of the trusses.

these high forces might be of comparatively little consequence; but if the truss is to be made of wood, it is likely that some of the connections will need so many bolts or timber connectors that they will be impossible to make. In examining the force polygon further, we find that the member forces are so large because the lines that represent the forces in the ends of the top and bottom chords (*a-1* and *g-1*, for example) meet at so sharp an angle. If these two lines met at a less acute angle, their lengths would be considerably shorter.

Acting on this clue, we might flatten the bottom chord to increase the angle between the chords, producing a triangular truss (b). Even without measuring, we can see by comparing this force polygon with that of the scissors truss that this strategy has practically halved the maximum chord forces. This is good, but the lofty, soaring quality of the enclosed space has been lost. How can we get it back, without returning to a truss form that has excessive member forces?

Realizing that the maximum chord forces occur at the ends of the truss, we could increase still further the angle between the top and bottom chords at the very ends, but pull the bottom chord back up in the middle panels so as to give a more pleasing shape to the enclosed space (c). Comparing the three force polygons, we perceive instantly by eye that the forces in this truss are by far the lowest of any of our three designs. Perhaps this third design contains too much interior volume to be economical or desirable—no matter, we can try other alternatives that retain the basic form of the third truss but reduce its overall height somewhat, because we are now in a position to guess that their member forces will probably not exceed those of the triangular truss option.

This type of experimentation lies at the heart of the structural design process. It is facilitated by the rapidity of the graphical method of analysis and by the ease with which generalizations may be made about the overall performance of each truss simply by noting the relative compactness of the force polygon. Numerical analyses tend to take longer, and the bare numbers they yield are of little help in figuring out how to improve the form of the truss.

FINDING A TRUSS FORM THAT HAS CONSTANT FORCE IN THE CURVING CHORD

Examination of the completed force polygon in Figure 10.7 suggests that one might easily find a form for a truss in which the force is constant throughout the curving bottom chord rather than the straight top chord, a condition that would allow the efficient use of a rod or cable for the bottom chord. This derivation is shown in Figure 10.34. The lines on the force polygon (c) are constructed first for each pair of members, then the corresponding lines on the form diagram (a). To begin, we notice in the form diagram that all bottom chord segments have the letter *g* in their names. This means that all of their corresponding vectors will radiate from point *g* on the load line. Working to the same scale as the force polygon, a compass is set to a radius equal to the desired force in the bottom chord, and an arc is swung about

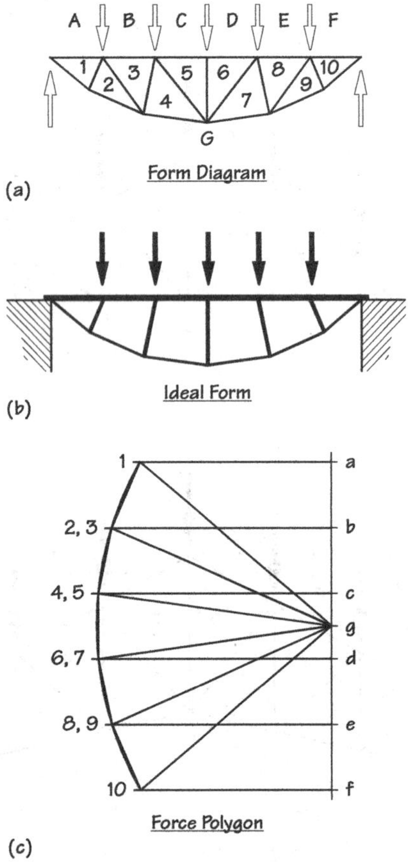

Figure 10.34 Finding the form of a truss that has constant force in its curved bottom chord.

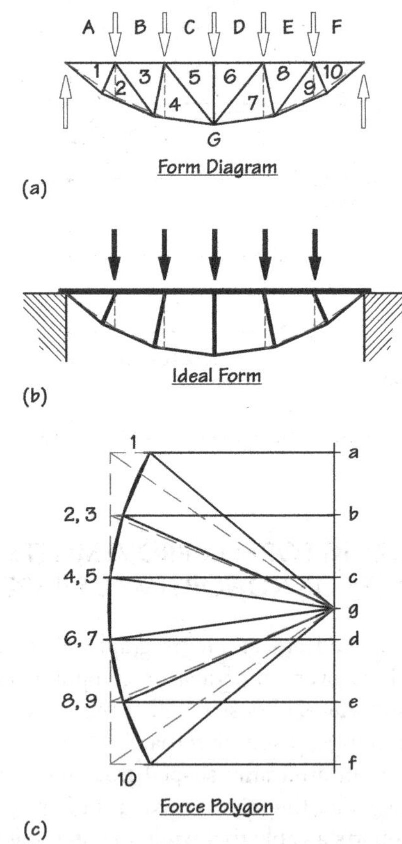

Figure 10.35 Comparison of form and forces in two constant-force trusses. On the force polygon, the solid lines are the vectors for the truss with constant force in its curving bottom chord. The broken lines are those for a truss with constant force in its level top chord.

point *g* on the load line. The intersections of this arc with the horizontal lines that represent the forces in the top chord segments are the locations of the numbered points in the force polygon. Except at the centerline of the truss, all the internal members are inclined. Half of them carry zero force under the ideal loading condition and may be eliminated to arrive at the ideal form (b).

Figure 10.35 demonstrates that member forces are lower in this truss than in a truss of the same depth with constant force throughout its top chord. This highly efficient form apparently was first discovered by the American engineer George Pegram; he used it in 1894 for the slender, graceful steel roof trusses of the train sheds in the St. Louis Union Station (Figure 10.36). Their span, 141 ft, was the longest of any roof truss in the world at that time. Figures 10.37 to 10.40 show some other constant-force trusses.

Figure 10.36 Steel roof trusses of the train sheds at the St. Louis Union Station, designed by George Pegram in 1892-1894.

Photo: Edward Allen.

Figure 10.37 Engineer Michel Virlogeux achieved constant tension in the four steel strands that form the bottom chord of this bridge truss by inclining the V-shaped struts at appropriate angles. The deck acts in compression as the top chord of the truss.

Photo courtesy of Michel Virlogeux.

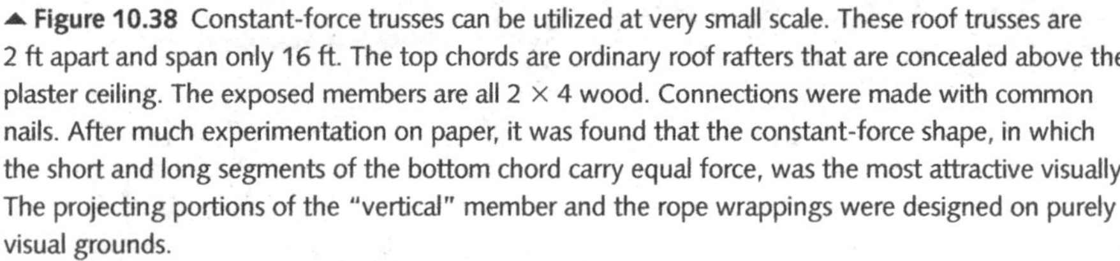

▲ **Figure 10.38** Constant-force trusses can be utilized at very small scale. These roof trusses are 2 ft apart and span only 16 ft. The top chords are ordinary roof rafters that are concealed above the plaster ceiling. The exposed members are all 2 × 4 wood. Connections were made with common nails. After much experimentation on paper, it was found that the constant-force shape, in which the short and long segments of the bottom chord carry equal force, was the most attractive visually. The projecting portions of the "vertical" member and the rope wrappings were designed on purely visual grounds.

Photo and architect: Edward Allen.

(a)

(b)

▶ **Figure 10.39** Constant-force trusses can also be useful at very large scale. These steel trusses (a) were designed to support the heavy column loads of a 15-story laboratory building that was subsequently constructed above them on Roosevelt Drive in Manhattan. The polygonal top chord of each truss is shaped so that it is funicular for the particular loads and spacings of the line of columns that it carries. This results in considerable variation of form from one truss to the next. The truss members, as seen in (b), are heavy wide-flange steel shapes, welded at the joints. Despite their considerable weight, these optimally shaped trusses, by replacing the inefficient plate girders that had been designed earlier for this project, saved $1 million worth of steel. (Trusses designed by Ysrael Seinuk for Cantor/Seinuk Partnership.)

Photo courtesy of Bernstein Associates.

Figure 10.40 Constant-force trusses with an arbitrarily shaped top chord in an atrium of the Van Abbe Museum, Eindhoven, The Netherlands. (Architect: Abel Cahen)

Photo: David M. Foxe.

DESIGNING THE TRUSSES FOR THE MUSEUM EXHIBIT HALL

Having learned from these numerous examples how to find the form of constant-force trusses, we return now to the truss design problem introduced at the beginning of this chapter. The roof trusses that we are designing for the science museum exhibit hall are essentially the same configuration as Pegram's trusses, and we can follow a similar procedure to find their form and forces. In this regard, you may find it helpful to review the tutorial lesson on Designing Constant Force Trusses on the supplementary site.

We start in step 1 with the given information: a span of 90 ft, 9 panels of 10-ft width, a 7.5-kip load at each node, and a slightly cambered top chord whose polygonal shape is a shallow parabola (Figure 10.41). We apply Bow's notation to the form diagram, with the letter *J* applying to the entire space beneath the truss. We assign a number to each space within the truss. For the purpose of analysis, knowing that any diagonals will have zero force under the uniform loading, we will not bother to insert diagonals. Thus, a single number will suffice to identify each panel space of the truss. (We may insert diagonals at a later stage of design to resist forces caused by nonuniform loadings.)

The second step is to draw lines on the force polygon parallel to the segments of the top chord, using Bow's notation to tell us where each line attaches to the load line. The allowable force in the bottom chord is equal to the cross-sectional area of steel in the chord times the allowable stress of 24,000 psi. The area of one of the 1–1/2 in.-diameter bars that we have tentatively selected is 1.77 sq in. Therefore, the allowable force in the bottom chord is 2 rods times 1.77 sq in. times 24 kips per square inch, which is 85 kips.

All the segments of the bottom chord have the letter *J* in their names. On the force polygon, the lines that represent their forces must all pass through *j*. In step 3, we set a compass for a radius of 85 kips to scale and draw an arc about point *j* on the load line. Where this arc intersects line *a1* is point *1*. As shown in step 4, we draw line *j1* on the force polygon and a line parallel to it on the form diagram from the leftmost node of the truss. We do not yet know the length of this line.

Next, as shown in step 4, we draw a line from *j* on the force polygon to intersect line *b2* at point 2. The short line segment *1-2* on the force polygon gives us the angle of the interior strut between spaces *1* and 2. We draw this strut on the form diagram. Its intersection here with *j1* is also the point from which lower chord segment *j2* departs.

We continue with this process, working from the force polygon to generate the form diagram, until the entire form of the truss has been constructed, in step 5. We find it to be a graceful shape that is especially attractive when seen as a group of trusses closely spaced (Figures 10.42).

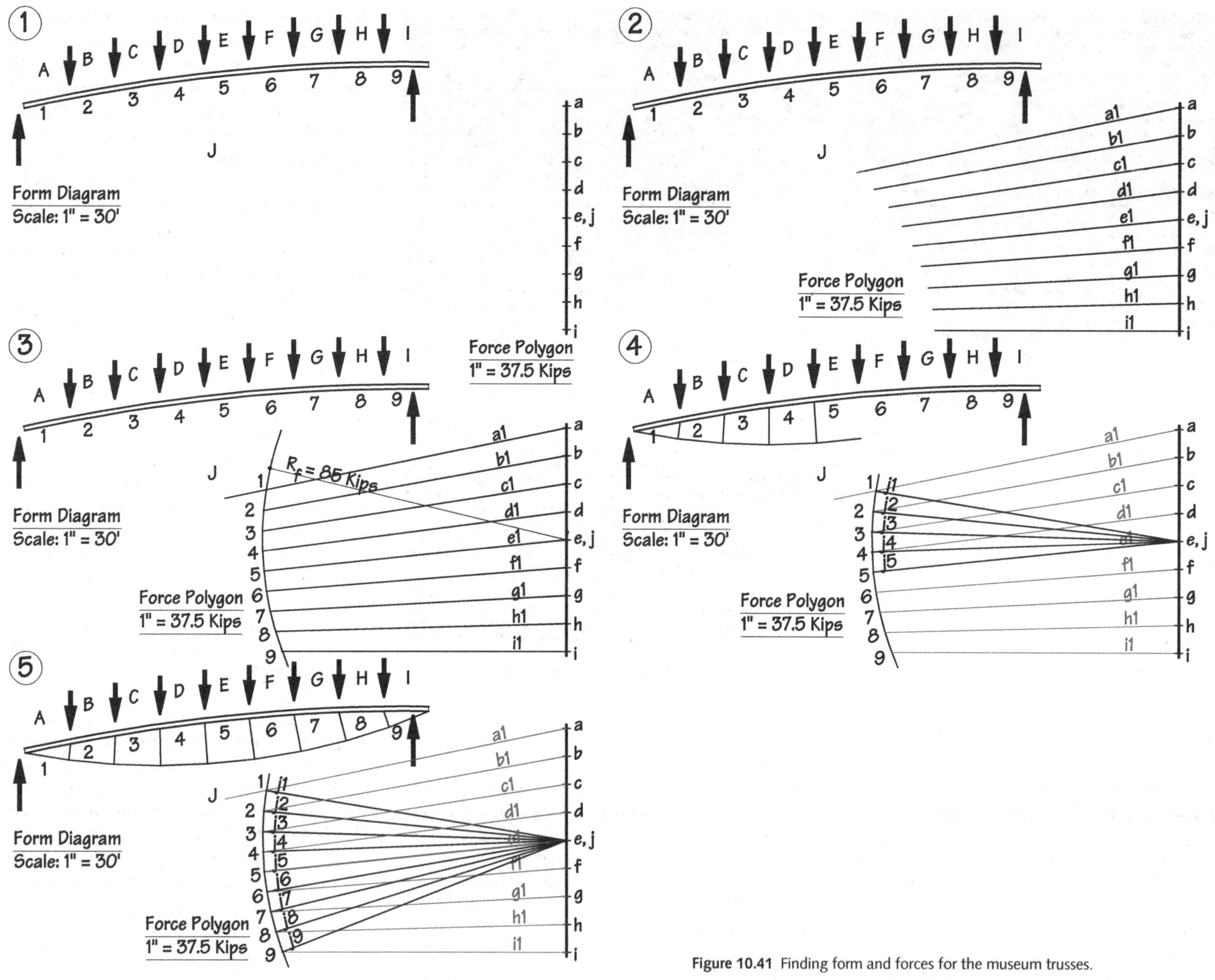

Figure 10.41 Finding form and forces for the museum trusses.

Figure 10.42 A view of the interior of the museum hall.

Design and image by Boston Structures Group.

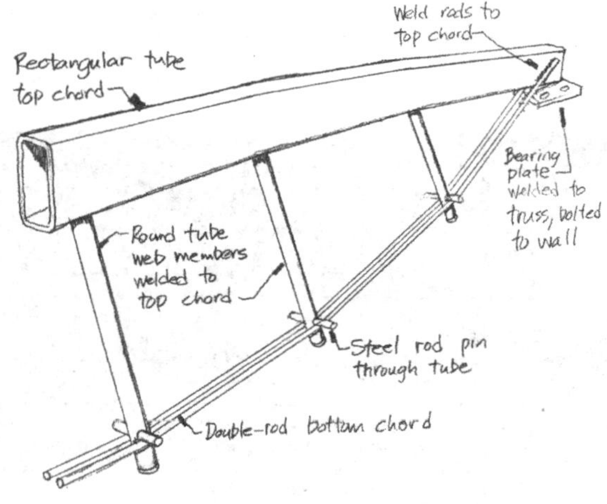

(a)

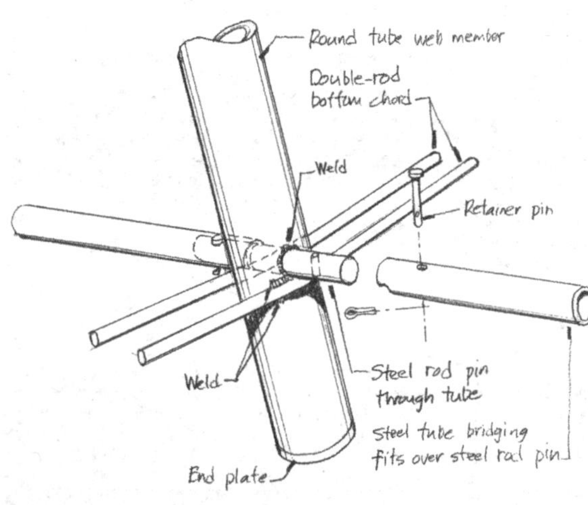

(b)

▲**Figure 10.43** Preliminary sketches for details of the museum trusses. Steel rod pins through the round tube web members serve a dual purpose: They transfer force between the bottom chord and the web members, and steel pipe bridging between the trusses slips over the pins, where it is held by retainer pins. The bridging assures that the trusses stay planar and do not deflect laterally.

▸**Figure 10.44** A pictorial view of the constant-force arch bridge. Design and image by Boston Structures Group.

We develop and sketch preliminary ideas for the details for the truss (Figure 10.43). Each truss is about the size and proportions of a large open-web steel joist, which is simply welded together and doesn't have any internal hinges or joints to relieve stresses caused by temperature or structural deflections. This tells us that we probably don't need any special joints within our trusses, either. We will get two price estimates on the top chord, one for a chord welded together from short segments of straight tubing, and the other for a bent tube, then adopt the more economical design. In either case, the web members will be smaller, round tubes, with simple welds to connect them to the top and bottom chords. Where the rods of the bottom chord meet the tubular web members, a steel rod that passes through the web member transfers the force.

Longitudinal *bridging* will be needed to prevent the lower chord from moving out of plane and causing failure. After much experimentation with various types of bridging, we hit on a scheme of using round tubes for bridging at each node. The tube simply slips over the projecting end of the steel rod. It is cut at each end to fit neatly around the rod that serves as the bottom chord, and is held in place by a small retainer pin that passes through corresponding holes in the rod and tube (Figure 10.43b).

We decide each truss will be assembled lying on its side in the fabricator's shop. Probably it can be fully assembled in the shop and brought to the building site on a special flatbed truck, but it may be necessary to transport each truss in halves that will be welded together on site. During lifting, the top chord is likely to buckle laterally unless it is restrained by a stiff lifting frame that is attached to it temporarily. After the roof structure is complete, the top chord, which is in compression, will be braced against lateral buckling by the roof decking that bears on it; and on this basis it can be quite a small rectangular tube.

ANOTHER CHALLENGE

The general technique that has been developed in this chapter can often be applied to structures other than trusses. Consider the following scenario: You've

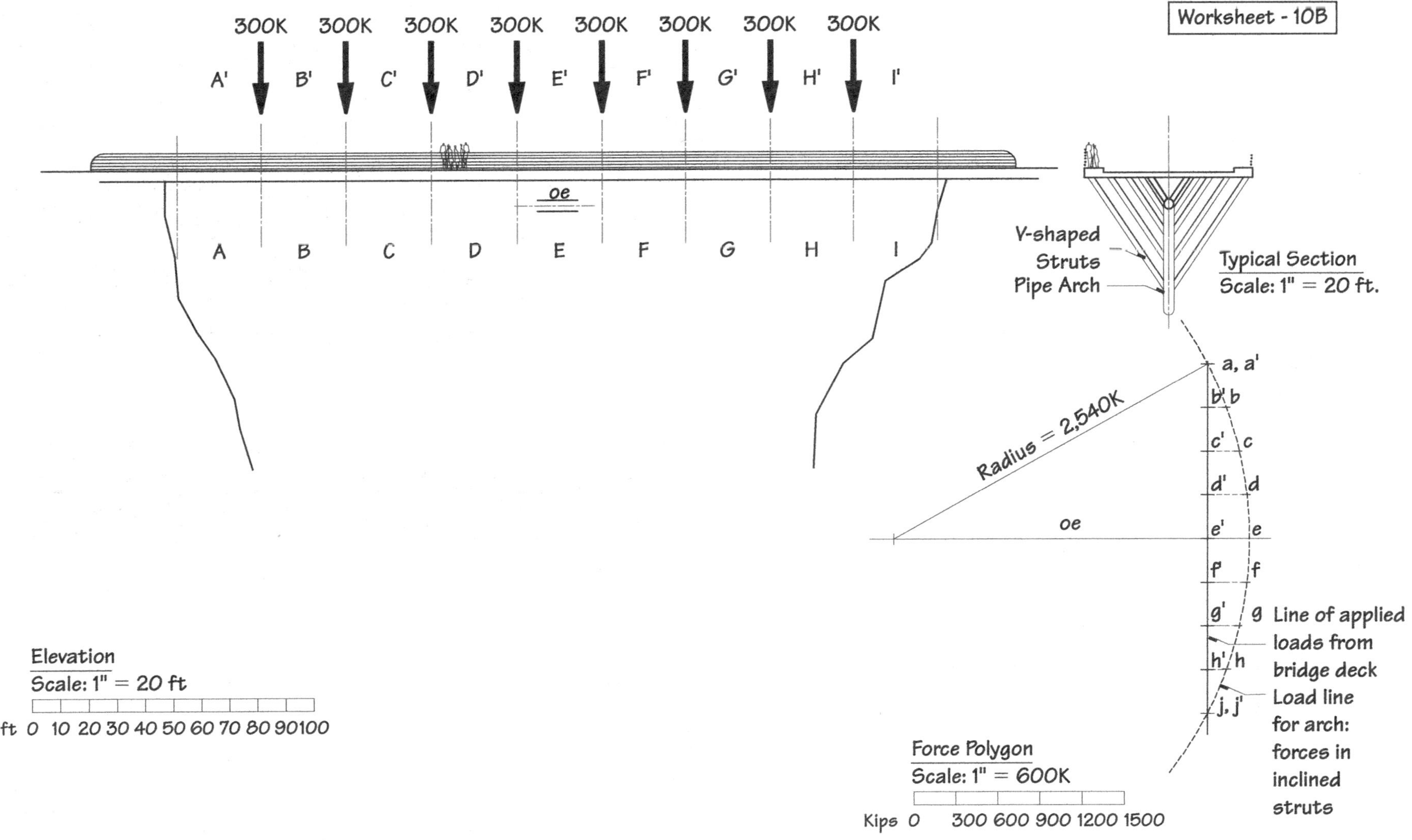

Figure 10.45 A reduced copy of a Worksheet 10B for finding form and forces for a constant-force arch bridge.

entered a competition for the design of a two-lane road bridge that spans 180 ft. Your idea is to support the deck with a single arch made of straight segments of steel pipe 30 in. in diameter that are welded together at each node (Figure 10.44). The loads are brought from the deck to the arch by V-shaped steel pipe struts of 18 in. diameter. You would like to shape the bridge so the pipe arch will be loaded throughout its length to its full allowable load, which you previously determined to be 2,540,000 lb (2,540 kips). Now you must find the shape of the arch and the inclinations of the V-supports such that the arch will have this characteristic. You decide to place the center section of the arch, *oe,* parallel to the deck and a few feet below it.

This design problem is laid out on Worksheet 10B, which is on the supplemental site (Figure 10.45). This bridge is much like the concrete arch bridge that we designed in Chapter 3. The main difference between the two projects is that the concrete arch experiences significantly higher compressive stress at its ends than in the

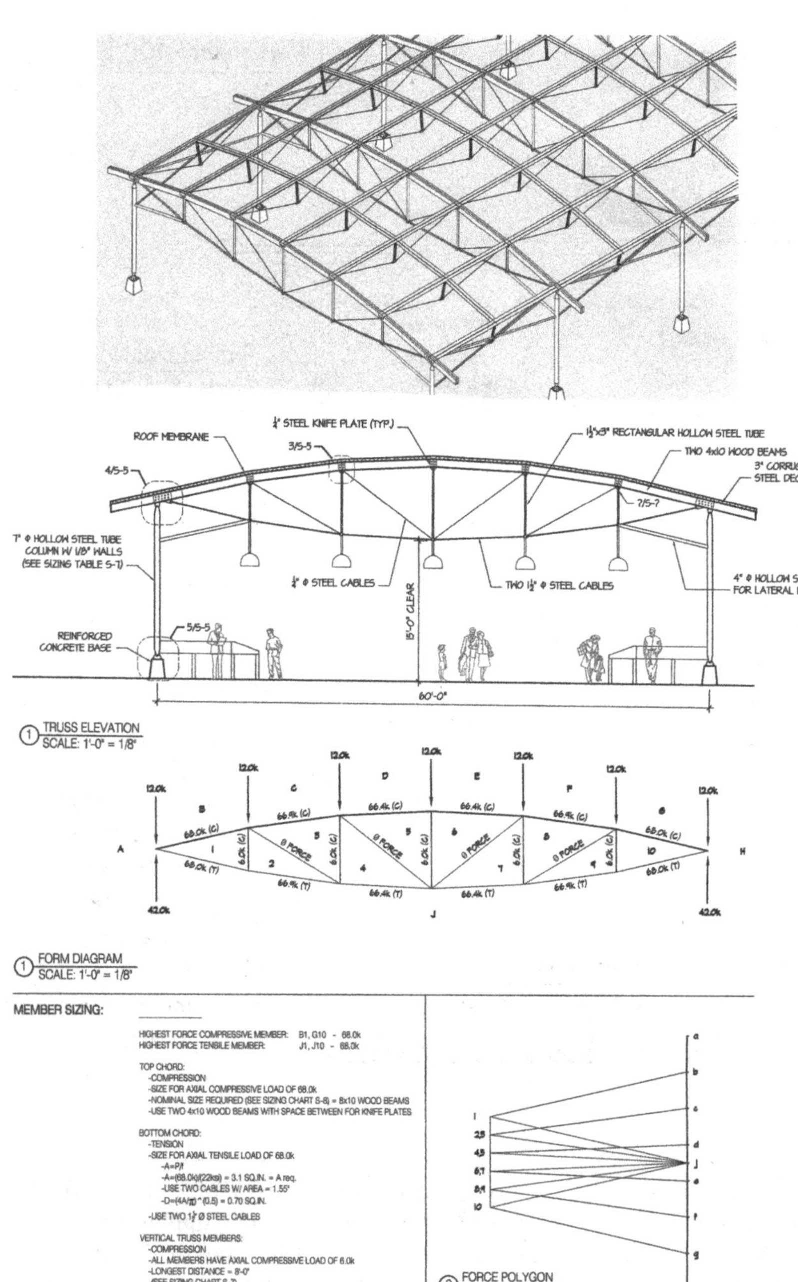

(a)

(b)

◀ **Figure 10.46** Bryan Watzin and Alyse Riggin, students at the University of Maryland, used constant-force trusses to support this roof. The drawing (a) and interior perspective (b) also show the additional angled struts that provide lateral stability.

Image courtesy of Bryan Watzin and Alyse Riggin.

middle, whereas this arch will have constant force throughout.

The worksheet already contains a free-body diagram of the bridge with all the external forces shown and Bow's notation applied. A load line, *ai*, has been set up, on which the distance *ai* represents the total gravity load on the bridge, the sum of forces *ab, bc, cd,* and so on. There are just two other external forces that act on the bridge, the reactions at the ends of the arch. We have specified that these will be 2,540 kips each to match the capacity of the steel tube. The left arch reaction, *oa,* will be represented by a line 2,540 kips long that passes through *a* on the load line. The right reaction, *oj,* also has a value of 2,540 kips. By setting a compass for this value and drawing arcs around centers *a* and *i,* we determine the pole location, *o.*

◀**Figure 10.47** The retractable roof of the University of Phoenix Stadium in Arizona is supported by two gigantic lenticular trusses that each span over 700 ft. (Architects: Peter Eisenman and HOK Sport; structural engineers: TLCP; contractor: Hunt Construction.)

Photo courtesy of Jen Liewer, Glendale, Arizona, Office of Tourism.

▼**Figure 10.48** Vivian L. Reynolds, then a student at the University of Oregon, won the ACSA/STI Student Design & Engineering Challenge Award of Excellence in 1997–1998 for this project. A market enclosure for the Nuevo Mercado de la Encarnacion in Seville, Spain, the design uses a three-hinged trussed arch "spine" along the axis of the site and constant-force Pegram trusses for the purlins. The outside ends of the purlins follow a curve that runs contrary to the curve of the arch, thus producing the intriguing warpage of the roof structure.

Image courtesy of Vivian L. Reynolds.

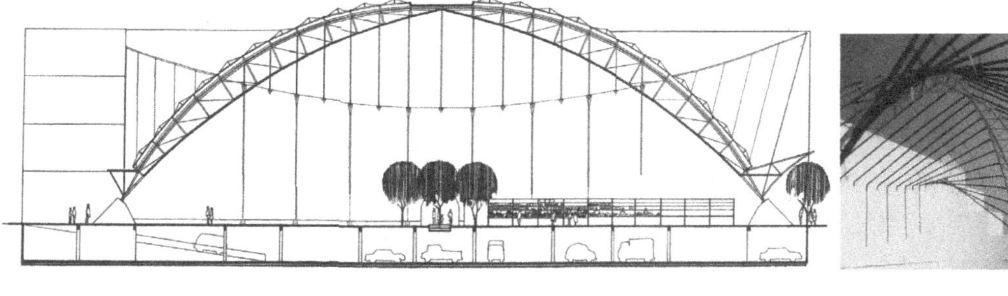

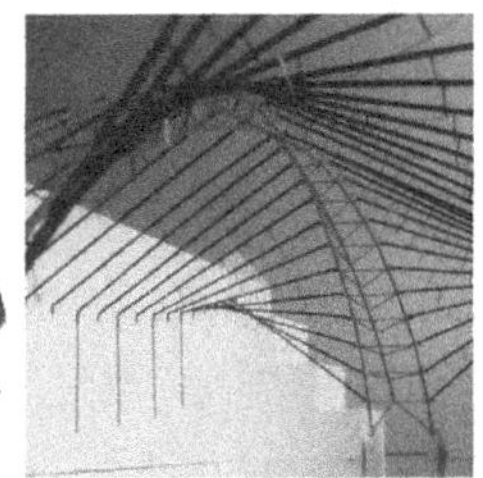

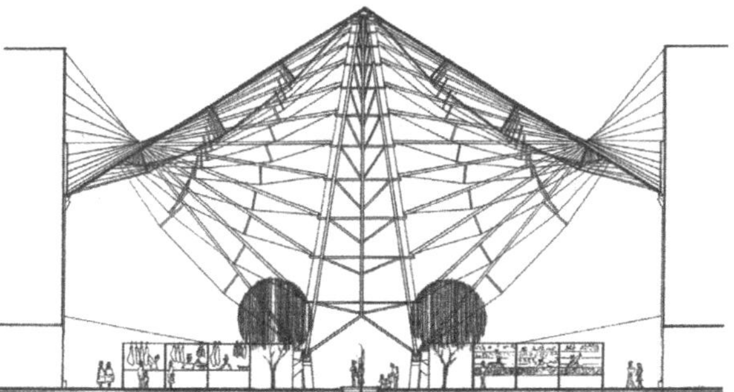

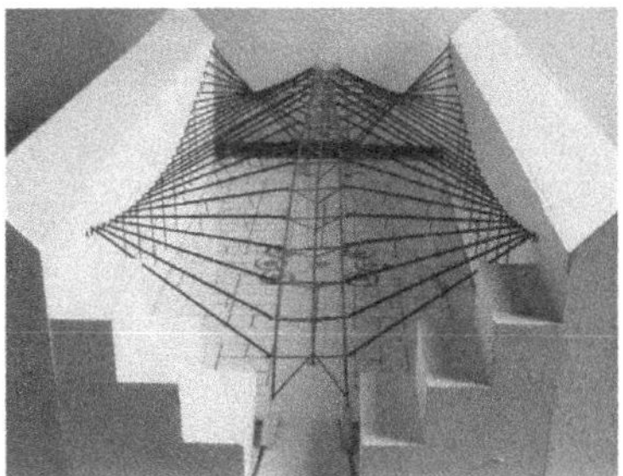

All the vectors that represent the forces in the pipe segments will run from the pole to an arc of radius 2,540 kips drawn around the pole.

Because the interior members of the bridge slope, they will impart horizontal components of force to the bridge deck. These will be represented by horizontal vectors on the force polygon that pass through the lettered points on the load line. We draw these lines *b'b*, *c'c*, until we reach *h'h*.

The vectors that represent forces in the interior members will all pass from *o* to the lettered points on the curve adjacent to the load line. The vectors for the arch segments will all run from the pole to the lettered points on this curve. The inclinations of the segments of this curve will be parallel to the interior members of the structure, and their lengths will be proportional to the forces in these segments.

Exercises

1. A six-panel, parallel-chord truss supports a gravity load of 6 kN at each node along the top chord. The span is 12 m. Find a depth for this truss such that the maximum chord force is 36 kN.

2. A seven-panel truss supports a gravity load of 1,000 lb at each node of the bottom chord. An additional vertical load of 4,000 lb is applied to the bottom chord node that lies just inside the right-hand support. Shape this truss in such a way that its level, straight top chord has a uniform force of 7,000 lb throughout its length.

3. The straight bottom chord of an eight-panel truss lies at an angle of 15° to the horizontal. Each joint along the top chord is subjected to a gravity load of 1,500 lb. Shape this truss so that the force is constant at 12,000 lb throughout the bottom chord.

4. A cantilever truss of five equal panels has a straight top chord that slopes down from the wall at an angle of 15° to the horizontal. Three bottom loads of 10 kips each are applied to the outermost joints. Shape this truss so that its top chord has a tensile force of 40 kips throughout its length under this loading.

5. A 10-panel bowstring truss supports nine gravity top loads of 6 kN each on its interior nodes. Find a shape for this truss such that it will have a constant force in its bottom chord of 42 kN. Construct and analyze a second bowstring truss of the same maximum depth, similarly loaded, whose top chord is a segment of a circle. Compare the member forces in the two trusses. Are they significantly different?

Key Terms and Concepts

bowstring truss

camelback truss

constant-force arch

constant-force truss

lenticular truss

Pauli truss

Pegram truss

scissors truss

tied arch

CHAPTER 11

Designing Restraints for Funicular Structures

- *Tensile and compressive strategies of restraint to resist change of shape*
- *Effects of unbalanced loads on structures*

Most people have an intuitive ability to recognize the proper relationship between the form of a hanging cable and the loads that are applied to it. It takes only a glance at the cable forms in Figure 11.2 to conclude that they are more or less correct. But even a child is likely to perceive immediately that the cable forms in Figure 11.3 are absurd, because they contradict our common sense and our instinctive knowledge of funicular forms. From earliest times to the present day, unschooled builders in many regions of the world have erected funicular compression structures of stone, brick, and mud, giving vivid testimony to the human instinct for recognizing and putting to practical use the directions along which internal forces flow in solid bodies. Funicularly shaped structures, whether cables, tents, arches, domes, vaults, or combinations thereof (Figure 11.1) transmit forces with a forthright simplicity that leads not merely to a high degree of technical efficiency but also to a satisfying perception since they are elegant and harmonious.

Today's structural materials are several times stronger in compression and hundreds of times stronger in tension than those used by the unschooled builders. We are able to build structures of relatively low self-weight that span distances and support loads many times larger than in any previous era. As we have noted in earlier chapters, for structures with the

Figure 11.1 The corrugated roof of the Supersam market in Warsaw is made up of alternating arches and cables of equal curvature. The pull of each cable is equilibrated by the push of an adjacent arch, so that the ends of the roof may be supported by simple columns, without stay cables or buttresses. The corrugations act as sloping trusses to resist changes of shape due to nonuniform loadings.

Photo: Collection of Wacław Zalewski.

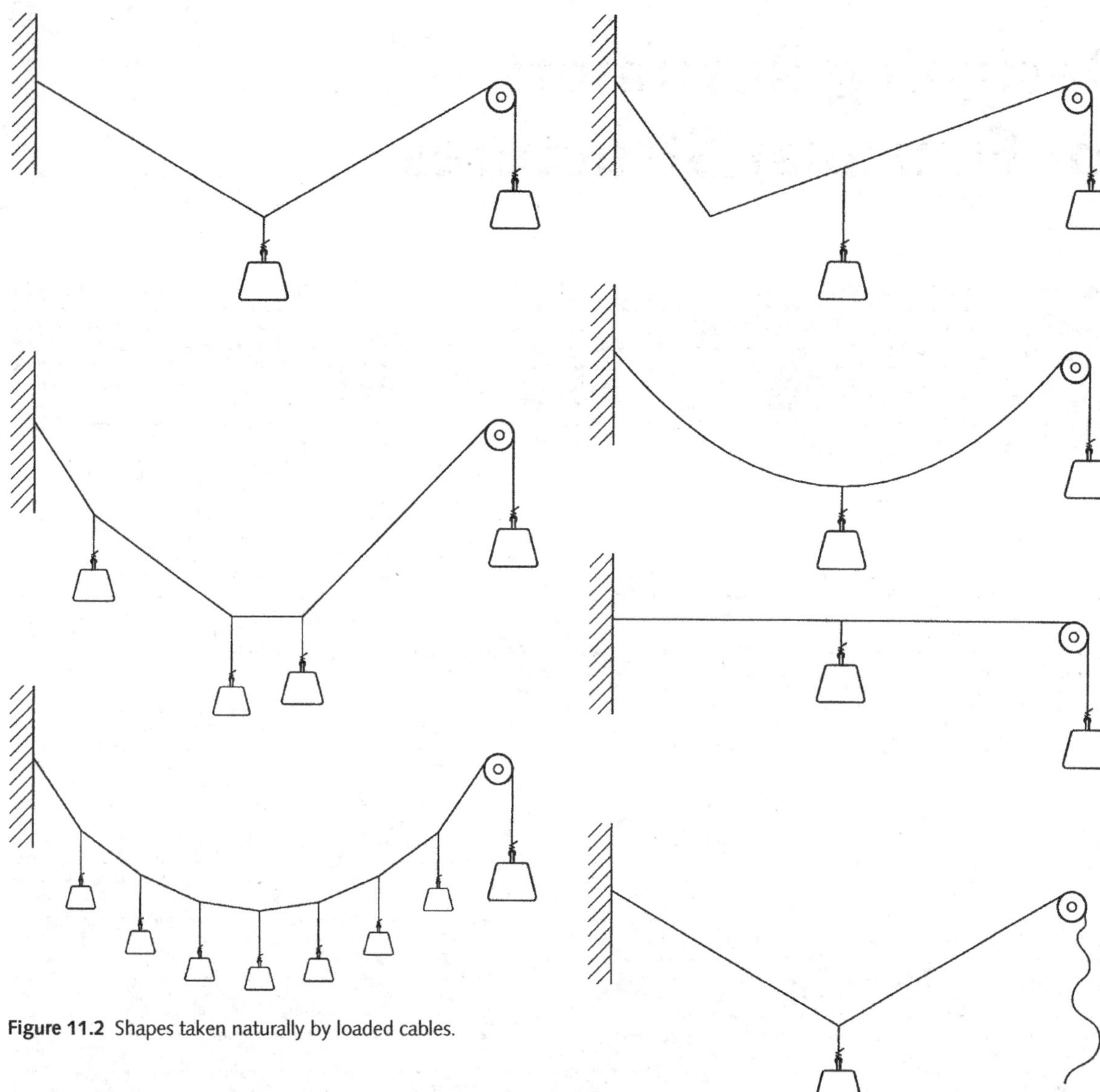

Figure 11.2 Shapes taken naturally by loaded cables.

Figure 11.3 Shapes that cables cannot take.

longest spans, we invariably choose funicularly shaped cables spun from high-strength steel wires. The prodigious load-carrying capacity of a hanging cable results not only from the high strength of the material, but also from the capability of the flexible cable to develop a strictly axial response to any pattern of loading by assuming a shape that is funicular for that pattern. In this way, all the material in a cable works to resist the axial effect of the external load. This self-adjusting action also presents us with a problem, however: In nearly all of the suspended structures that we design, we cannot permit the cable to change its shape as its loading patterns change, because such changes of shape would make the structure unfit for human use. Consider a heavy railway locomotive that is moving across a hanging bridge (Figure 11.4): The main suspension cables, if unrestrained, will change shape constantly to assume a maximum curvature at the point where they bear the load of the locomotive. In so doing, they will cause undulations in the deck that will make it impossible for the locomotive to proceed, and that may well lead to the total disintegration of the bridge.

The true art of designing a funicular arch or cable structure lies not so much in finding the basic form, which is simple enough to do, but in developing a suitable means to *restrain* the funicular members against changes of shape that are caused by reasonable loadings for which the members are not funicular. Wind creates pressure on the windward side of a curved or sloping roof and exerts suction on the leeward side, then changes direction, creating constantly shifting loading patterns, none of which matches the loads for which the supporting arch or cable was shaped. Wind can scour snow off one portion of a roof, leaving it without any live load, and deposit snow in heavy drifts on other portions. Floor loading patterns change with every change of furnishings in a room, and with the daily migrations of the occupants of a building. Bridge decks are sometimes empty of vehicles, sometimes full, and most often, are loaded with vehicles in random locations. Irregular loadings

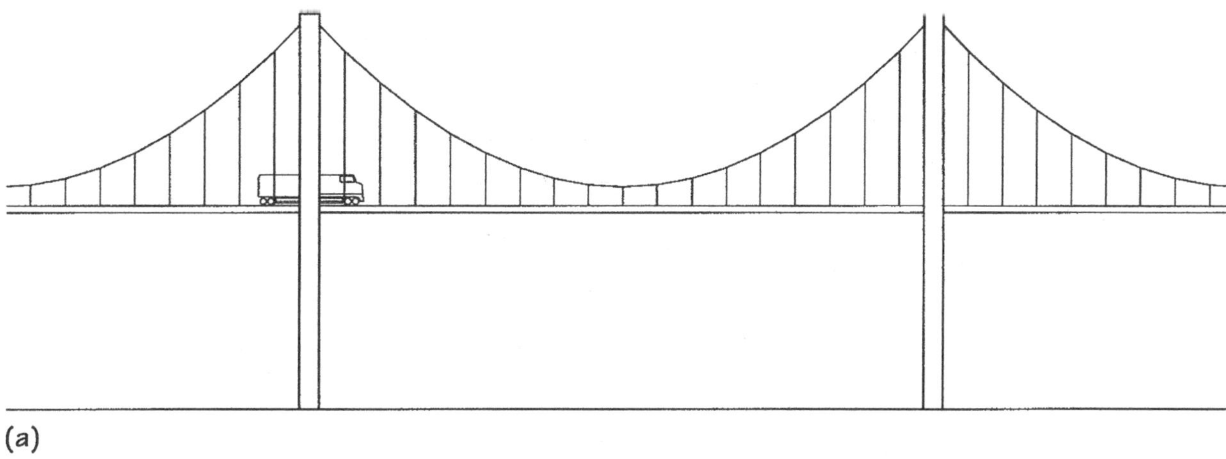

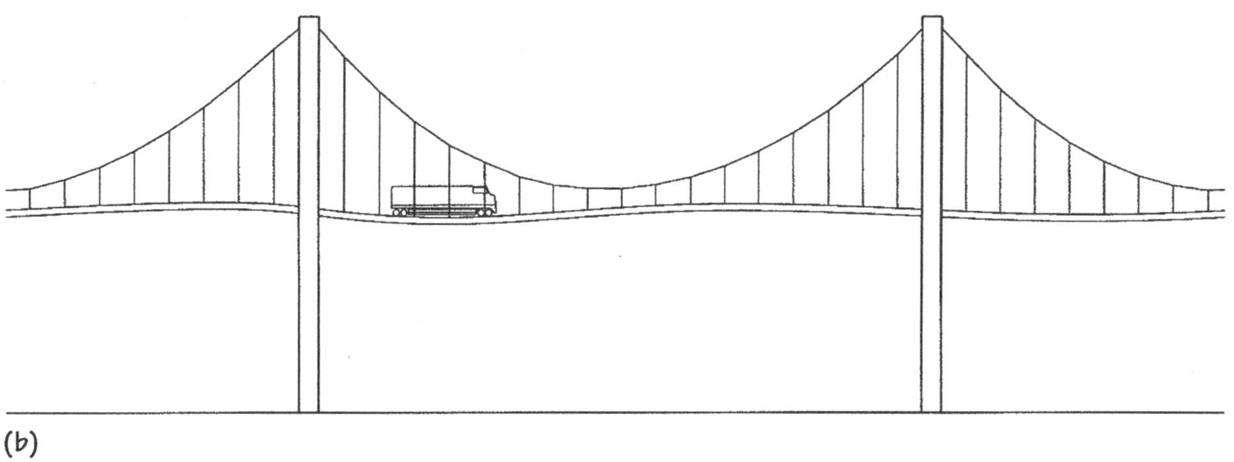

Figure 11.4 Deformation of an unrestrained hanging bridge by a heavy locomotive.

may also be created by vibrations induced by wind or earthquakes. No arch or cable can be given a shape that is funicular for all such conditions. Instead, we must base the shape on the predominant loading pattern, which is most often the dead load, and provide structural restraint to assist the funicular element in supporting other patterns of loads.

This problem and several of its solutions have been alluded to in previous chapters. Our purpose here is to conceptualize and summarize the full range of potential solutions to the restraint problem and to illustrate how they have been employed in a variety of actual structures. Figure 11.5 shows a number of ways of restraining a hanging cable by using auxiliary cables. The purpose of the auxiliary cables in each example is

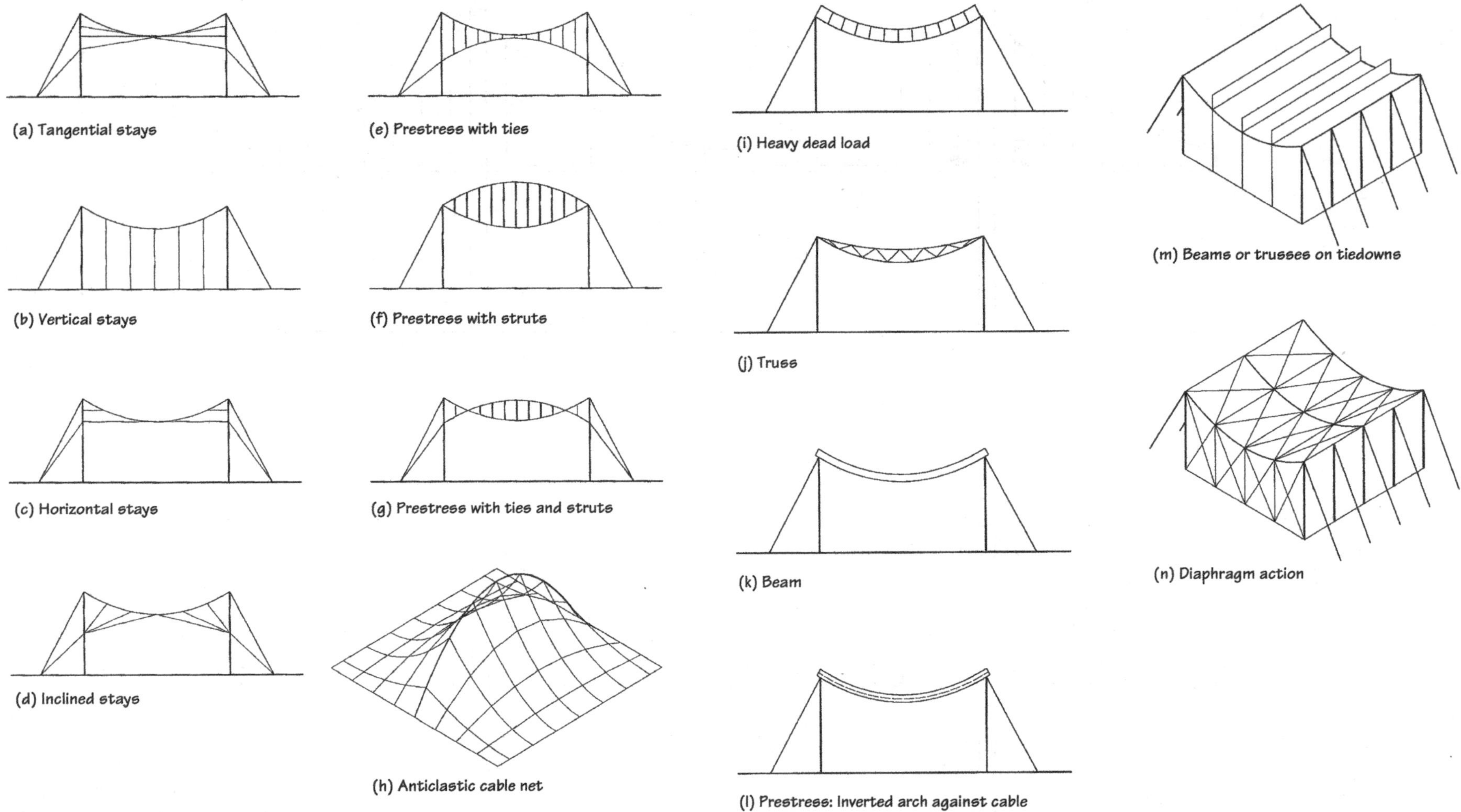

Figure 11.5 Restraining hanging structures using cables.

Figure 11.6 Restraining hanging structures using means other than cables.

to restrain the primary cable from changing its shape when its loading pattern changes. The options in Figure 11.6 address the same problem, but include elements other than cables. Figure 11.7 relates to the problem of restraining a planar arch, and Figure 11.8 shows still other alternatives that present themselves when the arched structure assumes a third dimension to become a vault, dome, or shell.

Many structures combine a flat floor or roof deck with a funicular supporting element, either an arch or a cable. Figure 11.9 shows that this combination opens further possibilities for restraint, some based on stiffening the funicular member, some on stiffening the deck, and some on adding diagonal braces in the spaces between the deck and the supporting member.

The diagrams in this chapter present a wide range of potential solutions to the restraint problem. They may be used to review options when confronting a particular design. Rather than discuss in the abstract each option in the diagrams, however, it will be more productive and enjoyable to view how the designers of a number of actual structures have employed them.

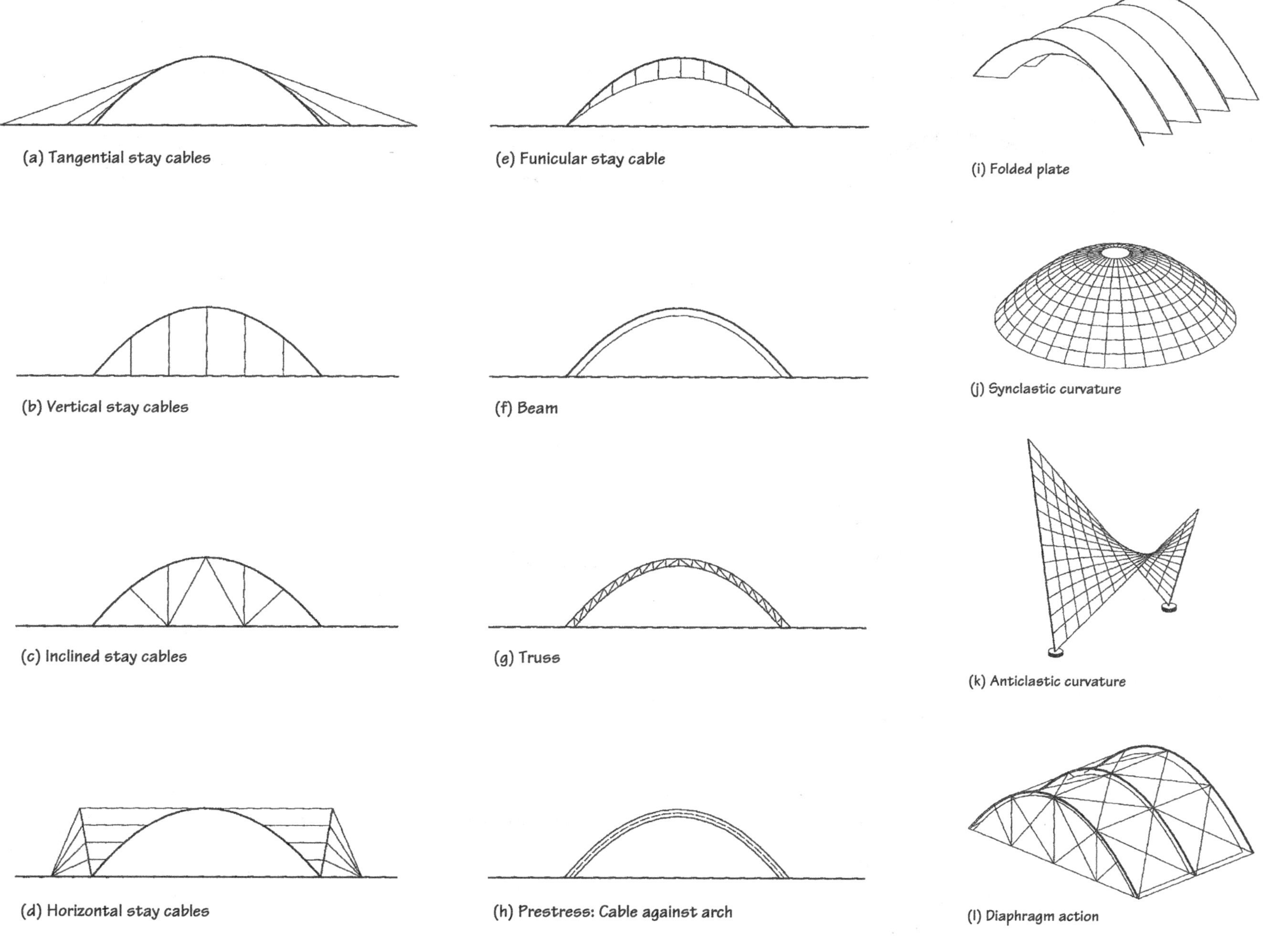

Figure 11.7 Two-dimensional means for restraining arches.

Figure 11.8 Three-dimensional means for restraining arches.

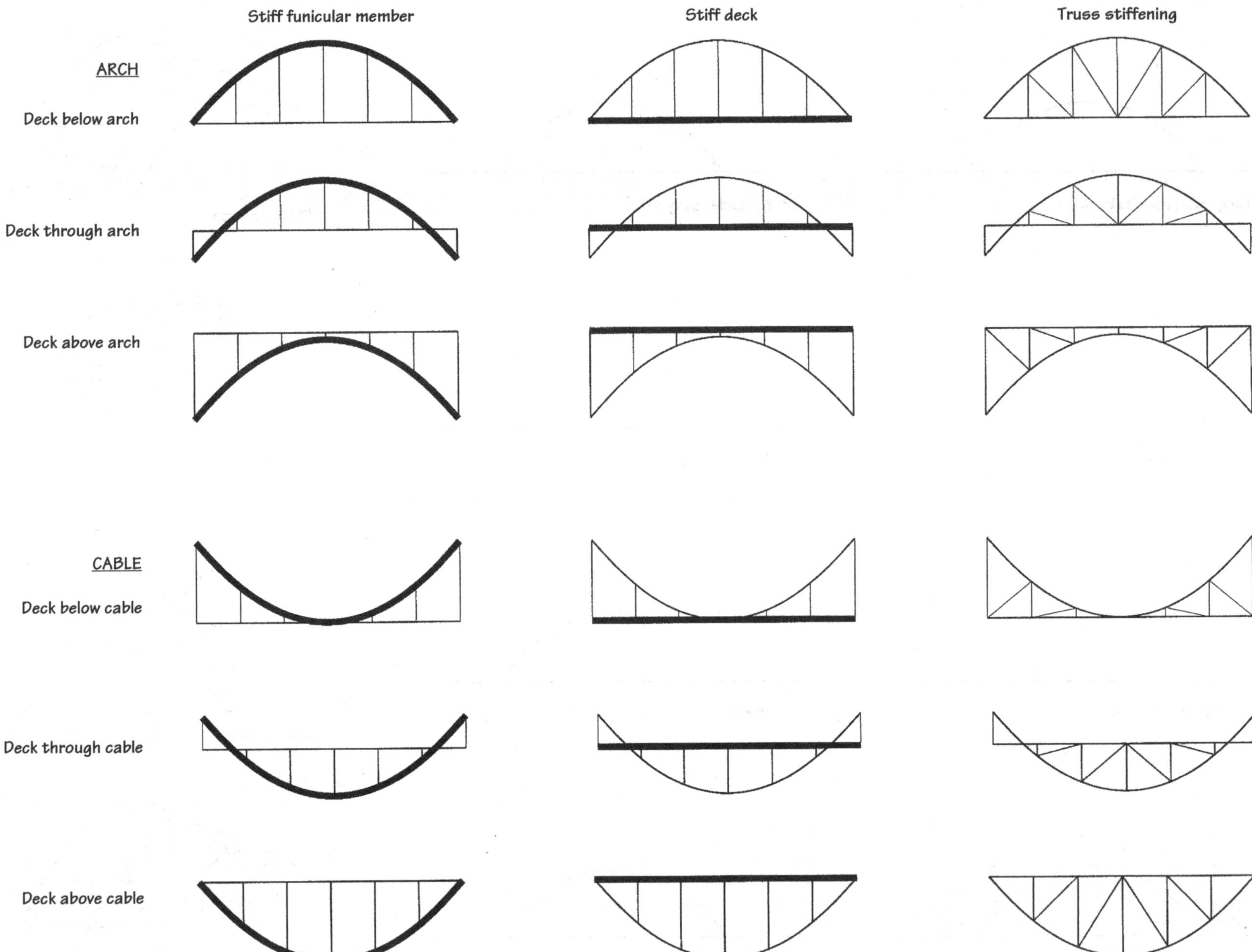

Figure 11.9 Means for restraining funicular members in structures that include a flat deck.

RESTRAINT BY STAYS AND STRUTS

Figure 11.10a shows the shape of a cable that supports a uniformly distributed load. In (b), we see the effect of applying a live load to only the left half of the cable: The right half becomes straight, while the left half takes on a greater curvature than before. Point C, which was formerly in the middle of the span, has moved to the left. If the live load shifts to the right half of the cable only, (c), the entire shape reverses, and point C moves to the right. A logical response to this situation is to install horizontal stay cables that prevent horizontal displacements of point C at midspan (Figure 11.10d). If different loadings occur on the two halves of the main cable, the stay cable on the less loaded side of the span intervenes with a pulling force that corresponds to the difference in loads.

Although this simple restraint system will reduce greatly the changes in the shape of the main cable under nonuniform loads, it cannot prevent changes due to loads that are localized in an area that does not correspond to a half-span. By adding *tangential stays* at suitable intervals across the whole span, as diagrammed in Figure 11.11, we can make the main cable as rigid as we wish against any pattern of loads, no matter how random. When the loading pattern is compatible with the shape of the main cable, the stays are inactive, but they react instantly to any change in loading conditions.

In a similar manner, stay cables in several other patterns can also serve to restrain a suspension cable (Figure 11.5) or an arch (Figure 11.7a–e). Compression struts can replace the stay cables in any of these patterns. As an example of this, consider a concrete bridge on the Italian Autostrada del Sole that is supported by funicular arches (Figure 11.12). Although parabolic in its larger outline, each arch is actually a polygon whose vertices coincide with the points at which the vertical columns bring the deck loads to the arch. Horizontal concrete struts between these

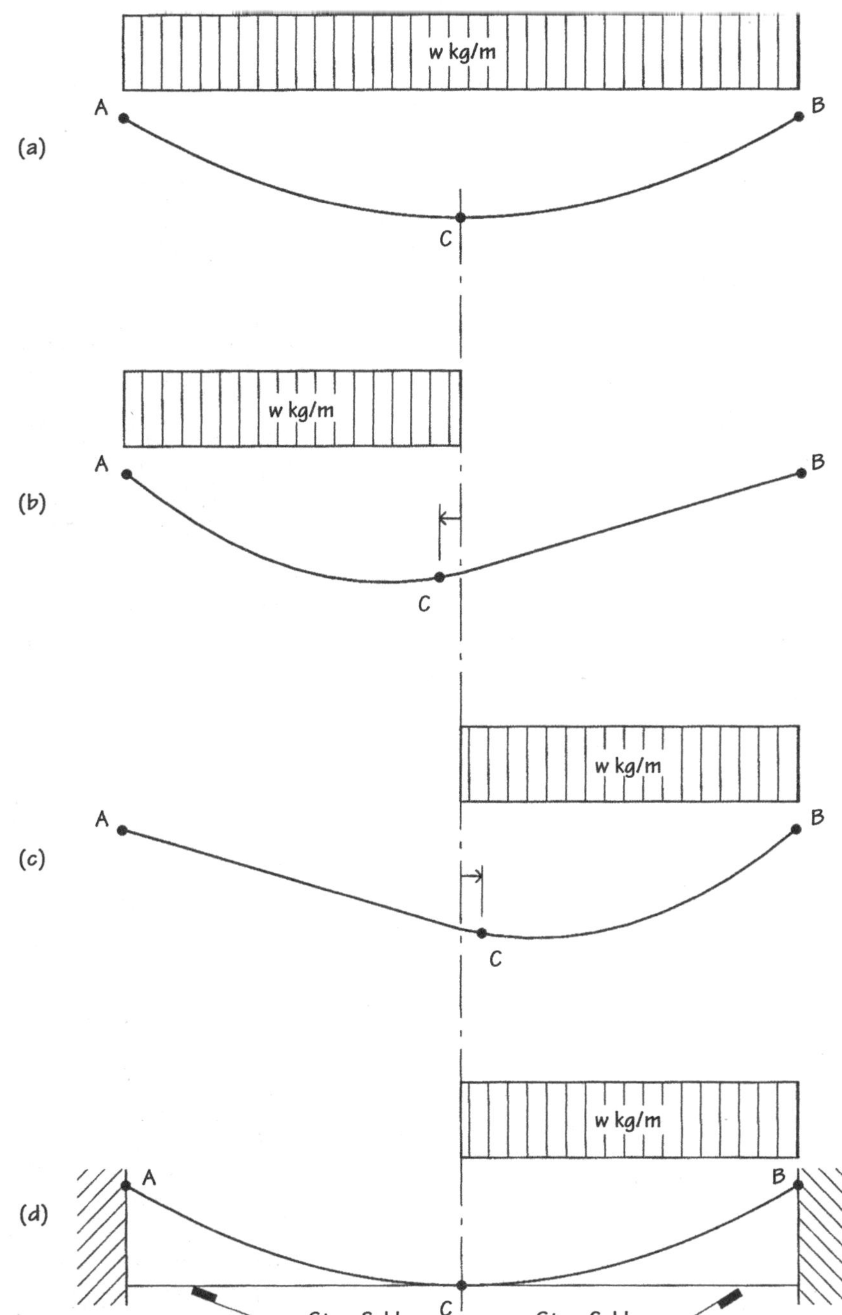

Figure 11.10 Restraint of a hanging cable using horizontal stay cables.

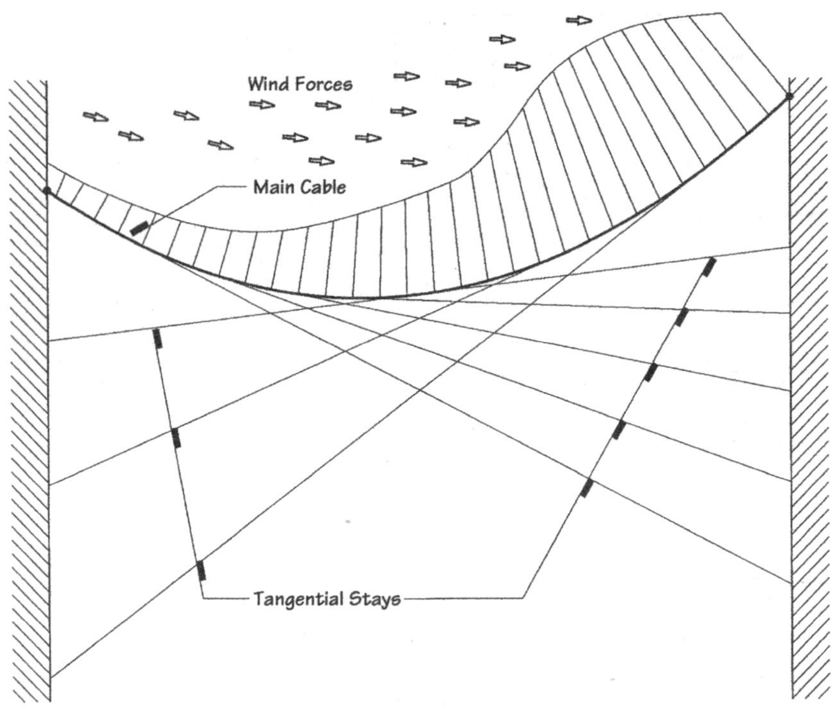

▲ **Figure 11.11** Restraint of a hanging cable using tangential stay cables.

▲ **Figure 11.12** Bridge on the Autostrada del Sole between Bologna and Firenze, Italy, 1960. Engineers: Arrigo Carè and Giorgio Gianelli.

Photo from the collection of Fritz Leonhardt. Reproduced by permission.

vertices restrain the arches from changing shape as heavy vehicles move across the spans. It is instructive to compare the forms of these arches above the top line of horizontal struts with the arch form of the Salginatobel Bridge, Figure 11.30.

The four parallel steel arches of the Broadgate Office Building in London are each restrained by two inclined steel stays (Figure 11.13). Analysis by the structural engineers of the building showed that these two stays alone, when considered together with the stiffness of the arch itself, were sufficient to prevent excessive arch deflections under any anticipated shift in loading.

The strategy employed at Broadgate invites comparison with the restraint system employed at

▶ **Figure 11.13** Broadgate Office Building, London. The building is carried across a railroad yard by steel arches. Architects and engineers: Skidmore, Owings & Merrill.

Photo: David M. Foxe.

Figure 11.14 The floors of the Federal Reserve Bank in Minneapolis are carried across a 270-ft span by parabolic cables, with hangers below and struts above. Architects: Gunnar Birkerts and Associates; structural engineers: Skilling, Helle, Christiansen, Robertson.

Photo courtesy of Balthazar Korab Ltd. Photography.

the Federal Reserve Bank in Minneapolis (Figure 11.14), which like Broadgate has a base that only bears on the site at the two ends of the building's length. Designed by architect Gunnar Birkerts and engineers Skilling, Helle, Christiansen, and Robertson, the floor beams above the cables are supported by columns, and those below, by hangers. The cables are restrained from changing shape by stiffening trusses at the top of the building, which also act as struts to resist inward components of force at the ends of the cables.

RESTRAINT BY PRESTRESSING CABLES

The circular roof of the Utica Municipal Auditorium, diagrammed in Figure 11.15, is a so-called *bicycle wheel* structure. The gravity loads are supported by a lower set of radial cables that span between a central tension ring and a compression ring at the top of the perimeter wall. (A compression ring is a full-circle horizontal arch. Its circular shape is funicular for the inward radial loading exerted by the cables). To restrain these cables against movement caused by wind uplift, vibrations, and asymmetrical snow loads, an upper set of radial cables apply downward forces through vertical tubular steel struts to prestress the lower cables. The sags of the two sets of cables are different, which prevents resonant vibrations of the roof. A parallel-cable prestressed roof that works on similar principles but utilizes ties between the cables rather than struts is illustrated in Figure 11.16.

Anticlastic curvature of a three-dimensional cable net is another way of restraining cables with prestressing forces. In the arena roof of Figures 11.17 and 11.18,

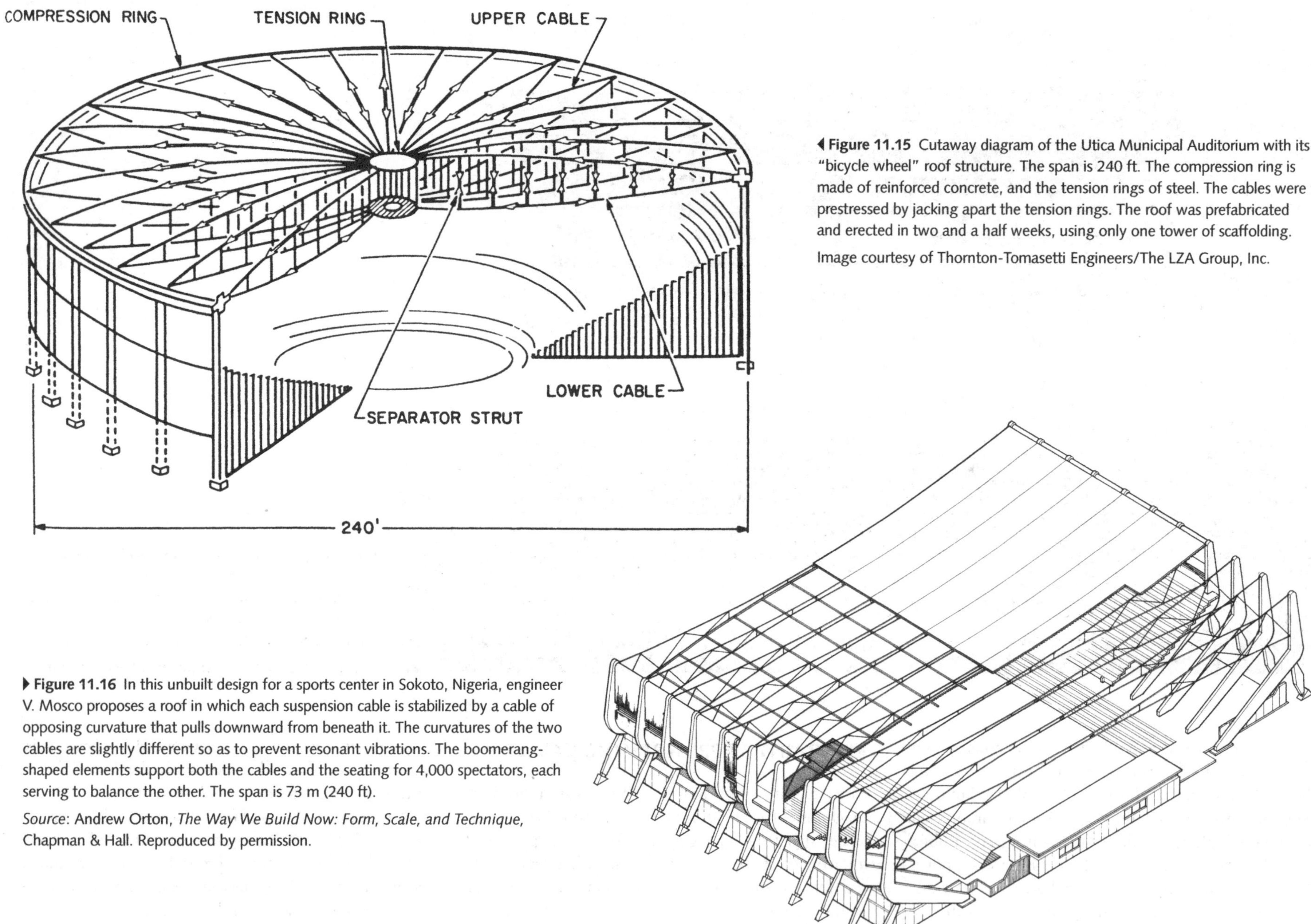

◀ **Figure 11.15** Cutaway diagram of the Utica Municipal Auditorium with its "bicycle wheel" roof structure. The span is 240 ft. The compression ring is made of reinforced concrete, and the tension rings of steel. The cables were prestressed by jacking apart the tension rings. The roof was prefabricated and erected in two and a half weeks, using only one tower of scaffolding.

Image courtesy of Thornton-Tomasetti Engineers/The LZA Group, Inc.

▶ **Figure 11.16** In this unbuilt design for a sports center in Sokoto, Nigeria, engineer V. Mosco proposes a roof in which each suspension cable is stabilized by a cable of opposing curvature that pulls downward from beneath it. The curvatures of the two cables are slightly different so as to prevent resonant vibrations. The boomerang-shaped elements support both the cables and the seating for 4,000 spectators, each serving to balance the other. The span is 73 m (240 ft).

Source: Andrew Orton, *The Way We Build Now: Form, Scale, and Technique*, Chapman & Hall. Reproduced by permission.

▸ **Figure 11.17** The hanging roof of the Ingalls Hockey Rink, Yale University, built 1956–1959 by Eero Saarinen, architect, with structural engineers Severud-Elstad-Krueger.

Photo: Edward Allen.

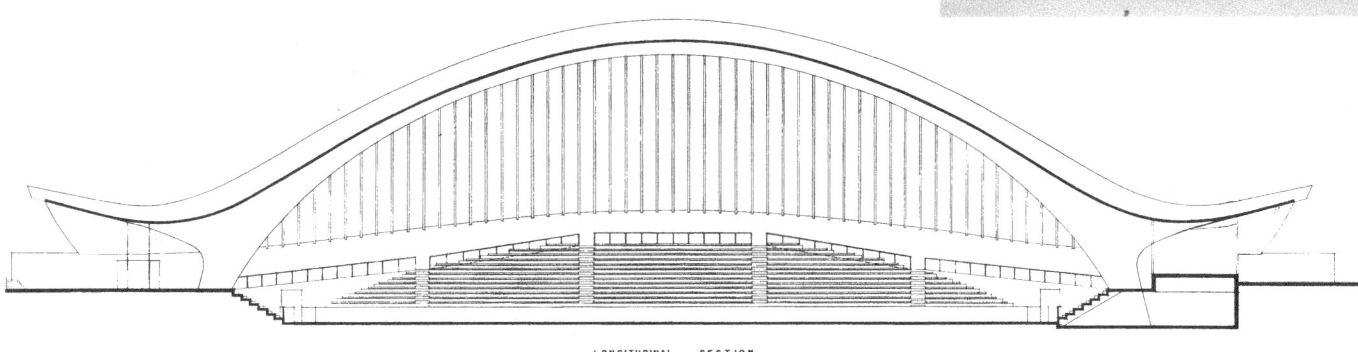

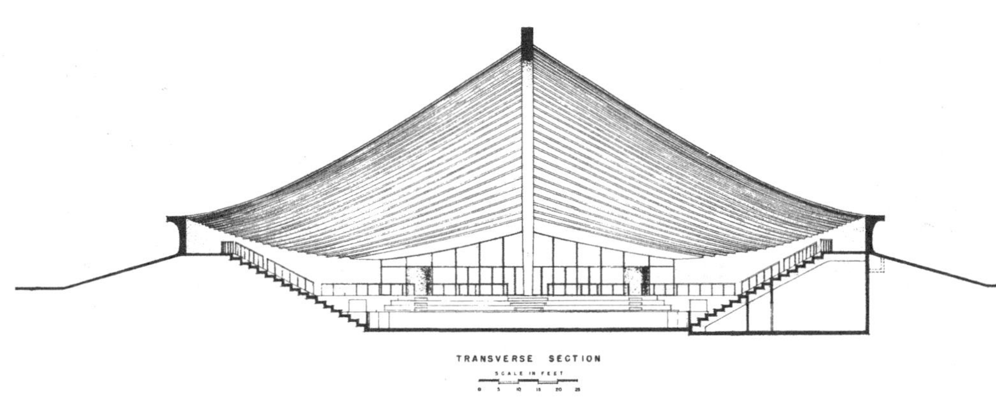

◂ **Figure 11.18** Section drawings of the Ingalls Rink. The arch spans 230 ft (70 m). The maximum width of the building is 180 ft (55 m).

Source: Eero Saarinen, *Eero Saarinen On His Work*, New Haven, CT: Yale University Press, 1962. Reproduced by permission.

a longitudinal parabolic arch of reinforced concrete supports transverse load-bearing cables that span to curving perimeter walls. Longitudinal cables pull downward on the load-bearing cables to restrain them. This principle is more easily seen in another arena roof, Figure 11.19, in which the opposing curvatures of the two sets of cables are more pronounced. The cables and fabric membranes of the tent roof photographed in Figures 11.20 and 11.21 are tensioned into anticlastic surfaces that are as poetic as they are rigid.

▶**Figure 11.19** Sports Arena for 8,000 spectators, Maracaibo, Venezuela, 1967. Designed by the Ministry of Public Works and Wacław Zalewski.

Photo: Collection of Wacław Zalewski.

▲**Figures 11.20 and 11.21** Pier 6 Concert Pavilion, Baltimore, 1992. FTL Architects; Buro Happold and M.G. McLaren, engineers.

Photo Copyright 1989, Durston Saylor.

Figure 11.22 Stress ribbon footbridge, Prague-Troja, Czechoslovakia, 1984. The main span is 96 m (315 ft), with a sag of only 1.86 m (6.1 ft). Dopravni stavby, engineers.

Photo courtesy of Jiri Strasky, PhD, PE.

Figure 11.23 Dulles Airport, Chantilly, Virginia, under construction in 1962. The span is 160 ft (49 m). Architect: Eero Saarinen; engineers: Ammann and Whitney.

Photo courtesy of Balthazar Korab Ltd. Photography.

RESTRAINT OF A CABLE BY AN INVERTED ARCH

It is theoretically possible to replace a hanging cable in any structural system with its inverted shape in the form of an arch. In the *stress ribbon* footbridge in Figure 11.22, the prestressing cable in the system shown in Figure 11.16 is replaced by what is, in effect, an upside-down concrete arch that follows the same curvature as the suspension cables. The cables prestress the arch and the arch prestresses the cables, creating a rigid structure. To avoid excessive inclinations of the bridge deck, the sag is minimal and the cable forces are extremely high, requiring strong end anchorages.

A much higher sag ratio was used in the stress ribbon roof of the Dulles Airport terminal building near Washington, DC (Figure 11.23), leading to more modest cable forces. As in the stress ribbon bridge, the inverted arch of the concrete roof deck serves to restrain the cables. The massive, outward-leaning concrete columns make a gesture of balancing the inward pull of the roof, creating a visually powerful architectural expression that reflects the forces in the structure.

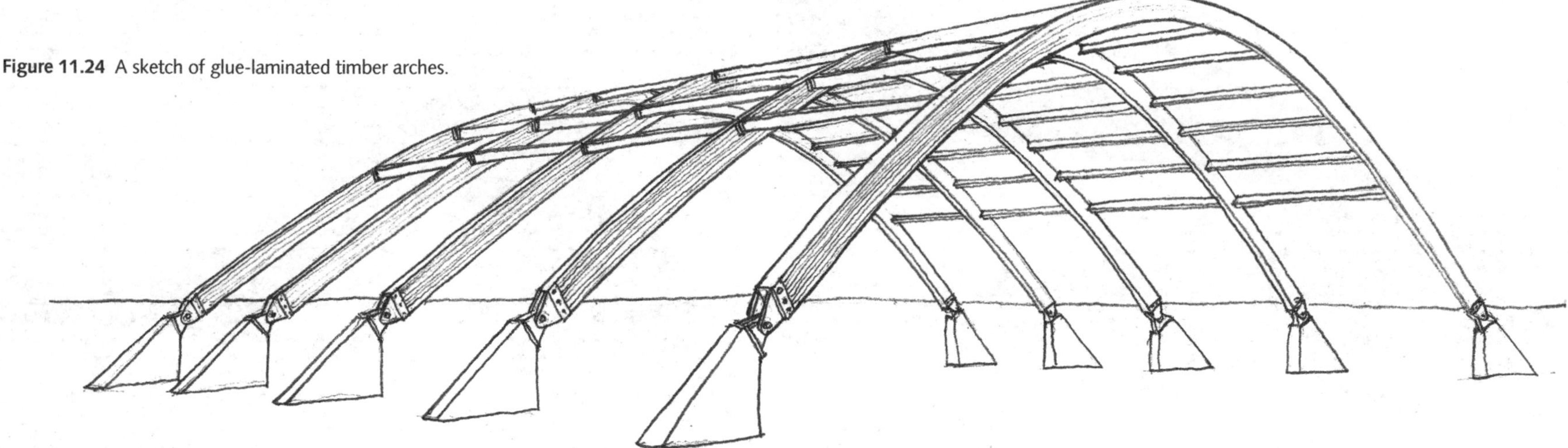

Figure 11.24 A sketch of glue-laminated timber arches.

RESTRAINT BY STIFFENING THE FUNICULAR MEMBER

Arches for long spans are nearly always made of laminated wood, steel, or reinforced concrete, all of which are materials that are inherently resistant to bending. This stiffness is frequently employed to resist changes of shape of the arch. The laminated wood roof arches in Figure 11.24 are designed to withstand both axial compression and the maximum expected bending moment due to asymmetrical snow and wind loads. The parabolic reinforced concrete barrel vault in Figure 11.25 does not need to be very thick to resist axial loads, but deep concrete ribs have been added to stiffen the roof against nonuniform loadings; this is similar to what we explored in the design process of Chapter 3. The steel arches in Figure 11.26 are trussed to restrain them from changing shape under moving loads.

Figure 11.25 U.S. Army hangar, Rapid City, South Dakota. The clear span is 340 ft (104 m), and the thickness of the concrete shell varies from 5 to 7 in. (125 to 180 mm). Engineers: Roberts and Schaefer Co. Photo of Stedman & Dyson, structural engineers.

In Figure 11.27, we study once again the shapes taken by a cable under a uniformly distributed load, (a), and loads distributed on either half of the cable only, (b) and (c). If auxiliary cables were added to create the form shown in (d), the curving cables would be able to maintain their shapes under any of the loading conditions shown. In an actual structure, the presence of an unvarying dead load would suggest replacement of the straight cable segments with ones that are curved funicularly for the dead load only, thus arriving at the basic form of the suspension members in the bridge shown in Figure 11.28. In this structure, the designer has also stiffened the funicular members by making them into steel trusses. Hinges at the supports and the apex allow for the system to move slightly in response to temperature changes and foundation settlement.

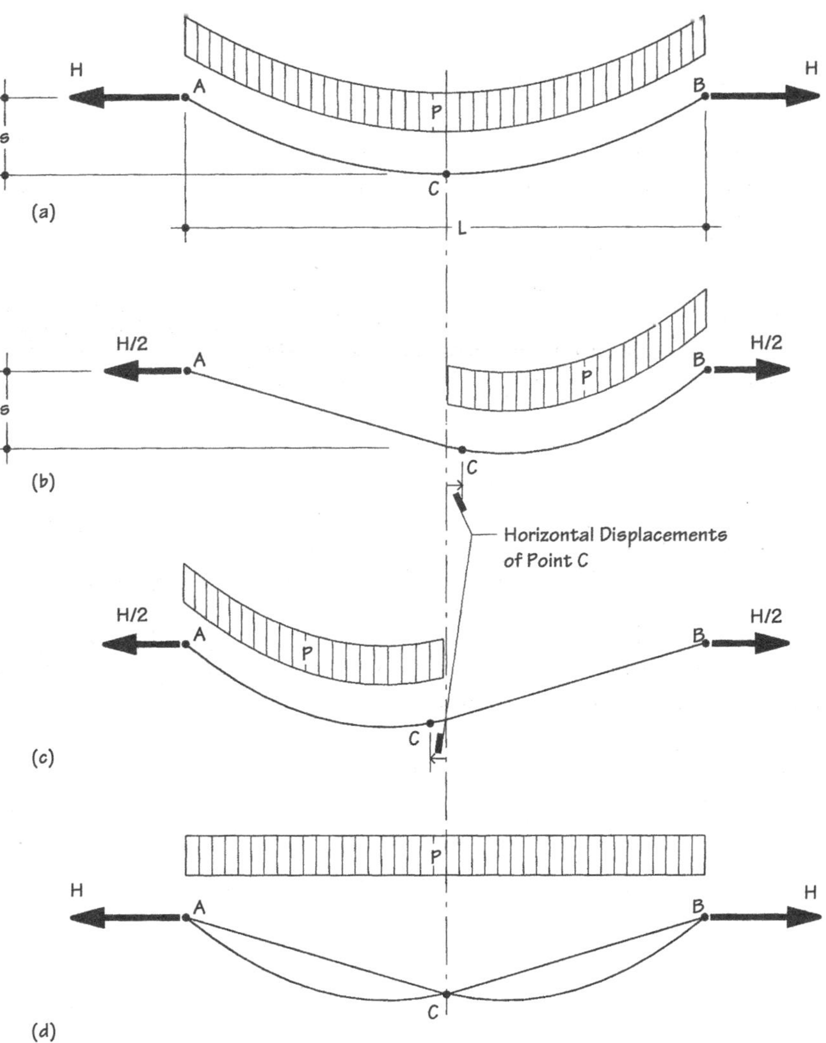

Figure 11.27 Restraint of a cable using a double-cable configuration.

Figure 11.26 The New River Gorge Bridge, built in Fayette County, West Virginia, in 1977, spans what was at the time the longest distance of any arch in the world, 1,700 ft. The deep, stiff, trussed construction of the arch allows the deck trusses to be shallow.

Photo courtesy of Michael Baker Corporation.

If Figure 11.28 is viewed upside down, its form resembles that of the famous Salginatobel Bridge, Figure 11.29, whose graceful shape originated from a similar line of reasoning. Robert Maillart designed this bridge using the same graphical methods that are presented in this book (Figure 11.30). Figure 11.31 shows that the crescent-shaped concrete stiffening walls that converge at the three hinges of this bridge are integral to an arch structure that takes the shape of an inverted double T (sections *a–a* and *b–b*). This configuration is often referred to as a *box arch*. The pressure line of a uniform loading on the bridge, shown clearly as a dashed line in Figure 11.30, runs within the hollow space of the open-topped box, at about a third the height of the crescent at every point on the span. If the live load is concentrated on the opposite half of the bridge only, the pressure line drops slightly; and if the live load is all concentrated on the same half, it rises slightly, but it always remains well within the confines of the crescents. Because the bridge is shaped so intelligently, its stresses remain very low regardless of the loading condition, and the steel reinforcing bars, none of which is larger in diameter than a human thumb, play little role except to resist temperature and shrinkage stresses.

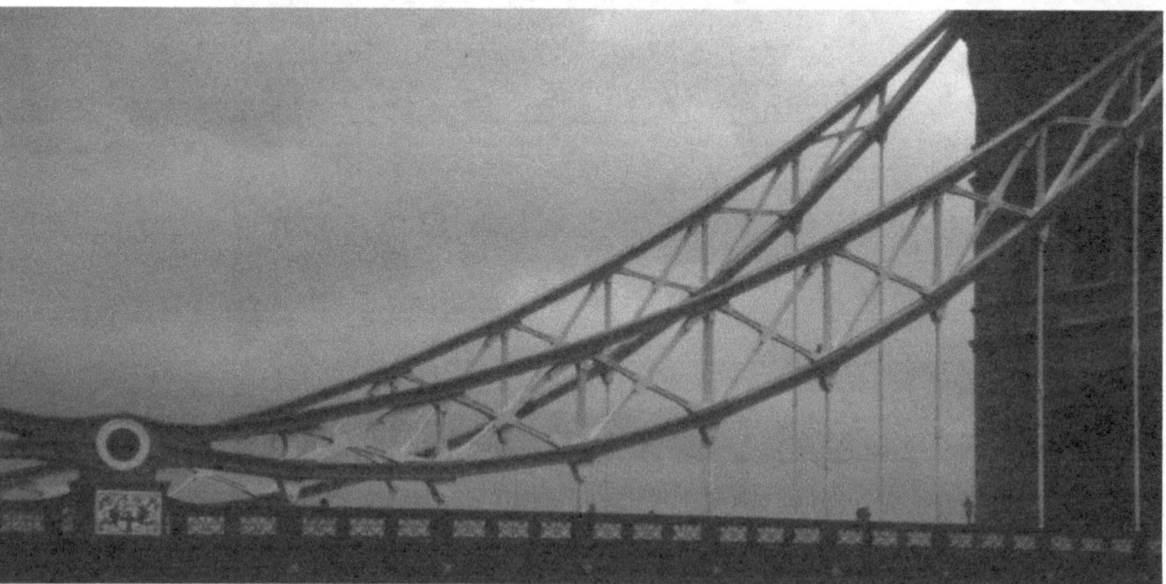

Figure 11.28 Tower Bridge, London, 1886–1894, John Wolfe Barry, engineer. The main span is 270 ft (82 m).

Photo Copyright, Will & Deni McIntyre, Photo Researchers, Inc.

▲ **Figure 11.29** Salginatobel Bridge, Schiers, Switzerland. Robert Maillart, engineer, 1930. The span is 90 m (295 ft).

Photo courtesy of ETH-Bibliothek, Zurich.

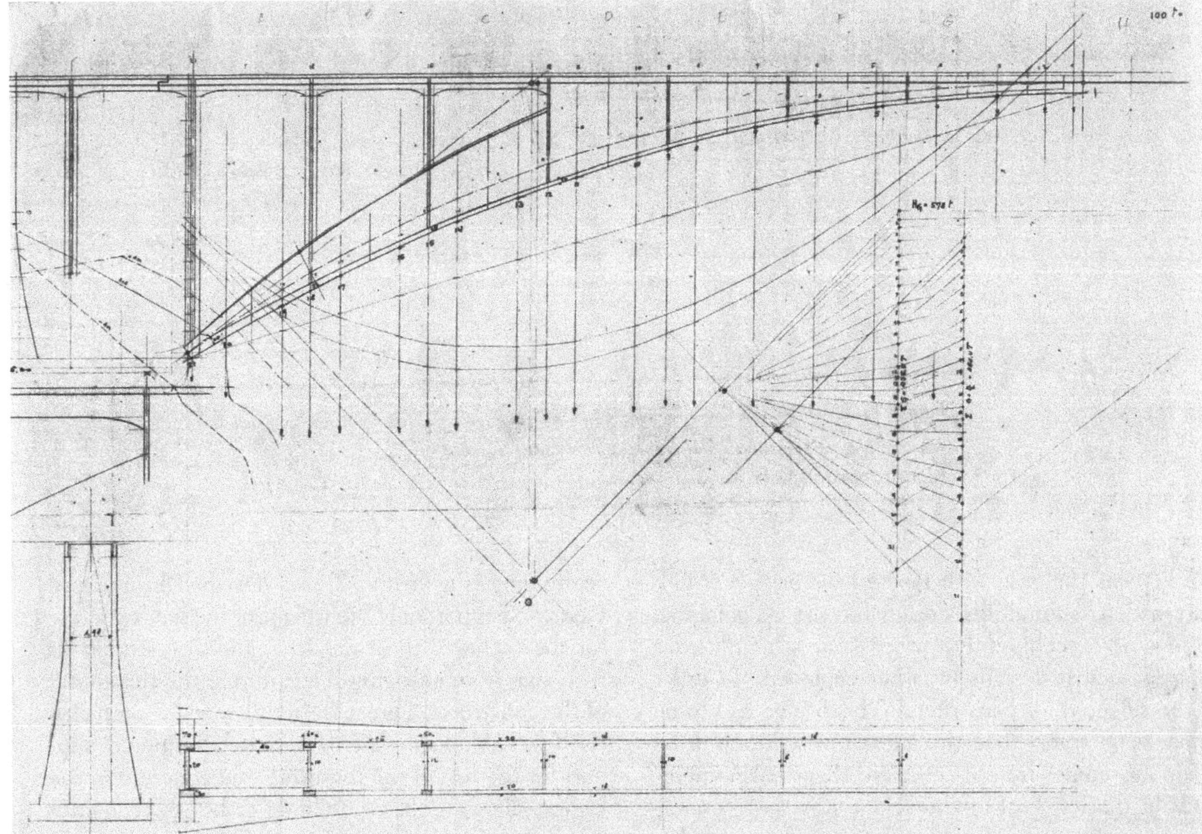

▶ **Figure 11.30** One of Maillart's design development drawings for the Salginatobel Bridge, from the Maillart Archives, ETH, Zurich.

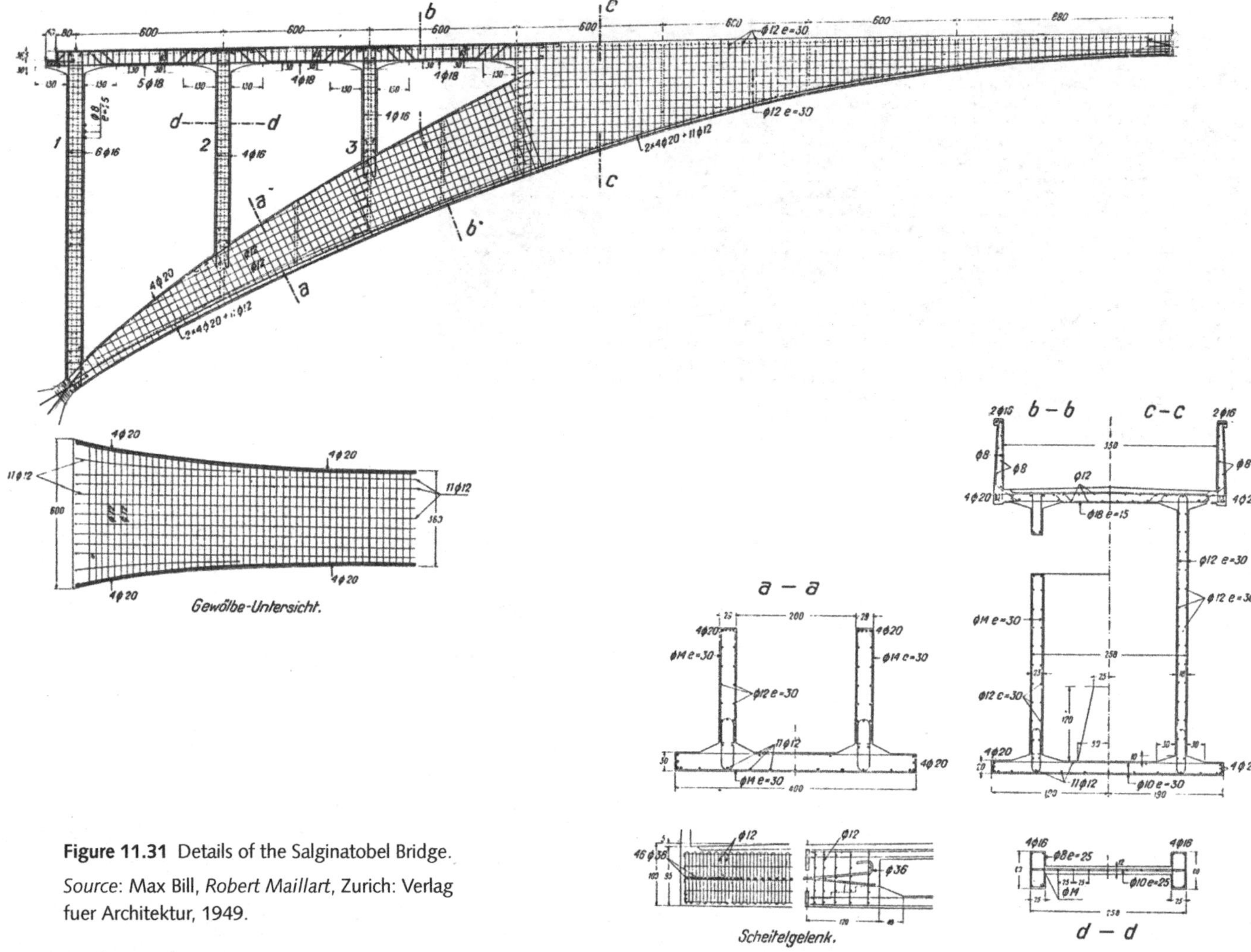

Figure 11.31 Details of the Salginatobel Bridge.
Source: Max Bill, *Robert Maillart*, Zurich: Verlag fuer Architektur, 1949.

As was the case with most of his bridges, Maillart had to submit his design for the Salginatobel Bridge to a competitive process in which it was judged against designs by other engineers. In order to be selected for construction, his bridge had to be more economical than the alternatives. Much of its economy comes from its efficient shape. Also important in the low cost of the bridge was the economy of its construction process. The ingenious wooden scaffolding (Figure 11.32) was designed by Richard Coray to support only the weight of the wet concrete for the bottom slab of the arch, and to restrain this arch slab from changing shape during the remainder of the construction process. In this way, the arch slab itself was able to provide the required temporary support for the rest of the formwork and concrete in the bridge, allowing the scaffolding to be much lighter and less costly than usual.

RESTRAINT BY STIFFENING THE DECK

The most common way of restraining the cables in a suspension bridge is to deepen the deck into a *rigidity beam*, which in most cases is actually a truss. The rigidity of the beam enters into action only when the bridge is loaded in a manner that is incompatible with the shape of its cable; otherwise, a cable subjected to loads compatible with its shape deforms

Figure 11.32 Scaffolding to support the concrete formwork for the Salginatobel Bridge.

Photo courtesy of ETH-Bibliothek, Zurich.

much less than the beam and, therefore, absorbs all such loads. The only role of the rigidity beam is to absorb excessive loads in certain regions of the bridge and carry them to less loaded regions. This relocation of loads makes the vertical pulling action on the cables compatible with their parabolic shape.

Figure 11.33 illustrates the nature of the stabilizing effect of a rigidity beam on the shape of a cable of a bridge that is subjected to a single, large load such as a locomotive, without taking into account any dead load. The beam transforms the single load into a distributed set of equal vertical pulls that are compatible with the shape of the cable (a). All the

Parabolically Shaped Cable under Uniform Down Pull

Uniform Pull on the Cable

(a)

Parabola

(b)

The negative and positive areas of the moment diagrams are made equal.

Diagrams of Approximate Bending Moments in the Rigidity Beam

(c)

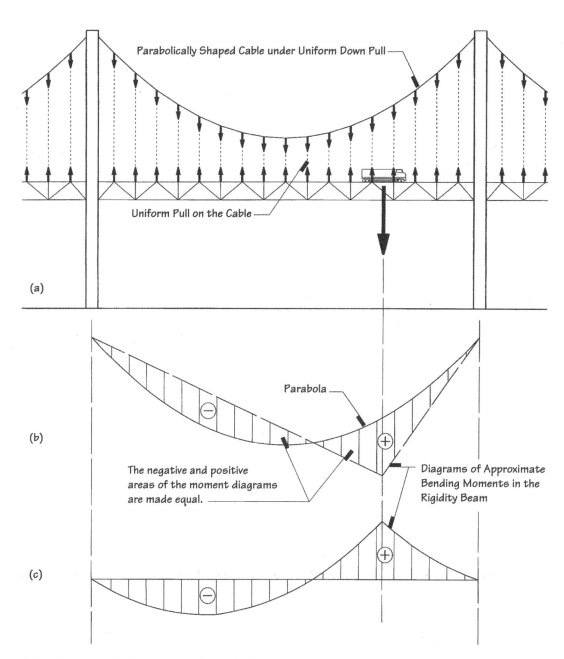

Figure 11.33 Determining the bending moments in a rigidity beam.

differences between the actual loading and the loading that corresponds to the shape of the cable are absorbed by the beam. An approximate diagram of the intensity of the bending moments in the beam may be constructed by superimposing a shape that is funicular for the single load on the shape of the cable in such a way that the negative and positive areas between the shapes are equal (b, c). In reality, the uniformly distributed dead load of the deck is sufficiently large that it contributes a great deal to the stabilization of the shape of the cable and considerably reduces the role of the rigidity beam.

The application of rigidity trusses to a hanging roof is illustrated in Figures 11.34 and 11.35. This factory building was designed by Pier Luigi Nervi to house a very long machine for making paper. It was anticipated that the factory would be expanded over time by adding more such machines side by side, and it was important not to obstruct the space between the machines with columns. The concrete heads of the columns are shaped in such a way that each cable is anchored to a flat surface that lies perpendicular to its axis.

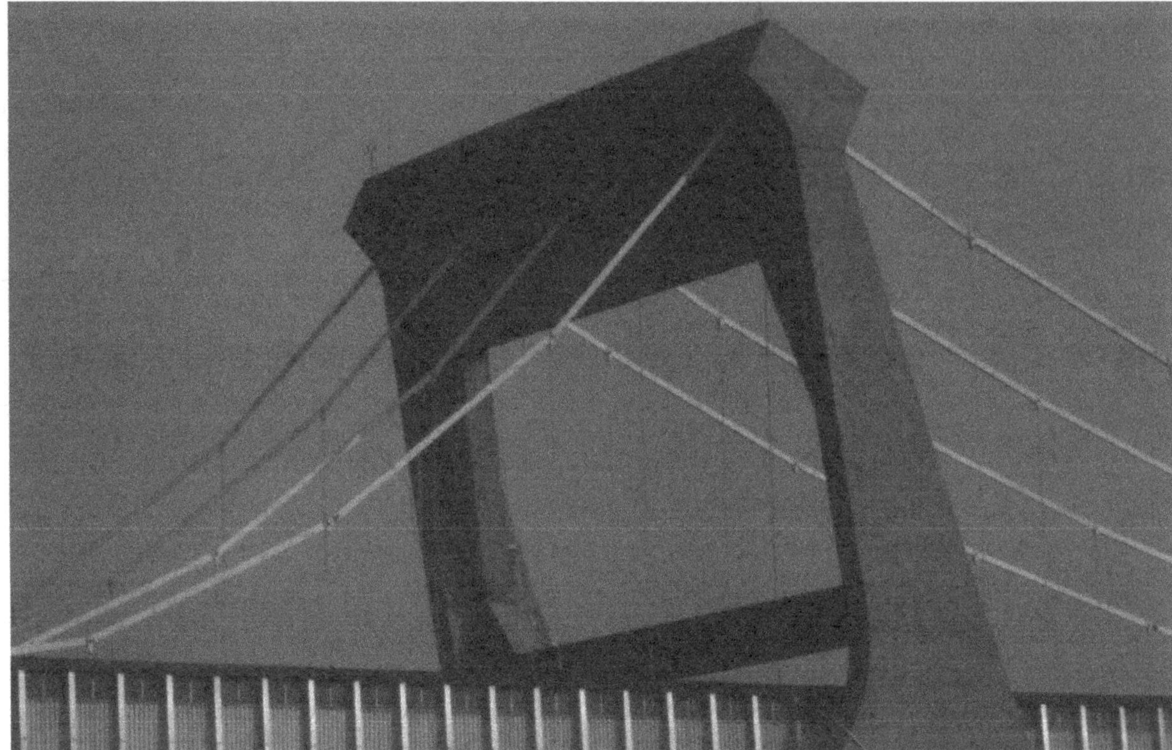

Figure 11.34 Burgo Paper Mill; Pier Luigi Nervi, engineer. Photo courtesy of Dr. Chris H. Luebkeman.

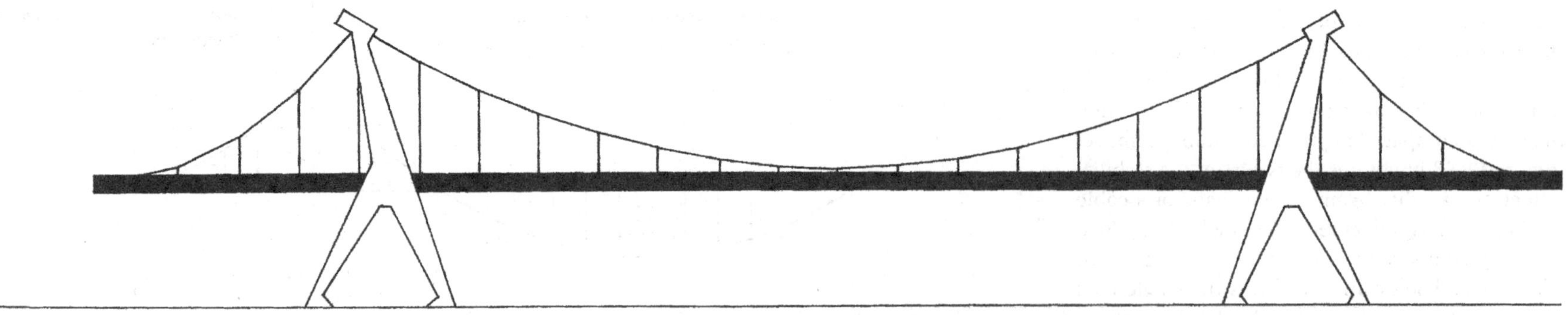

Figure 11.35 Burgo Paper Mill; Pier Luigi Nervi, engineer. The solid black area indicates the trussed rigidity beam (Drawing by Edward Allen).

The principle of the rigidity beam is applied to arched structures in the form of the *deck-stiffened arch* (Figure 11.36). Robert Maillart built many of his shorter-span bridges as deck-stiffened arches; one of these is pictured in Figure 11.37. Notice that the arch itself is a thin slab, designed for axial forces only, that follows a funicular profile. The deck is a deep reinforced concrete rigidity beam.

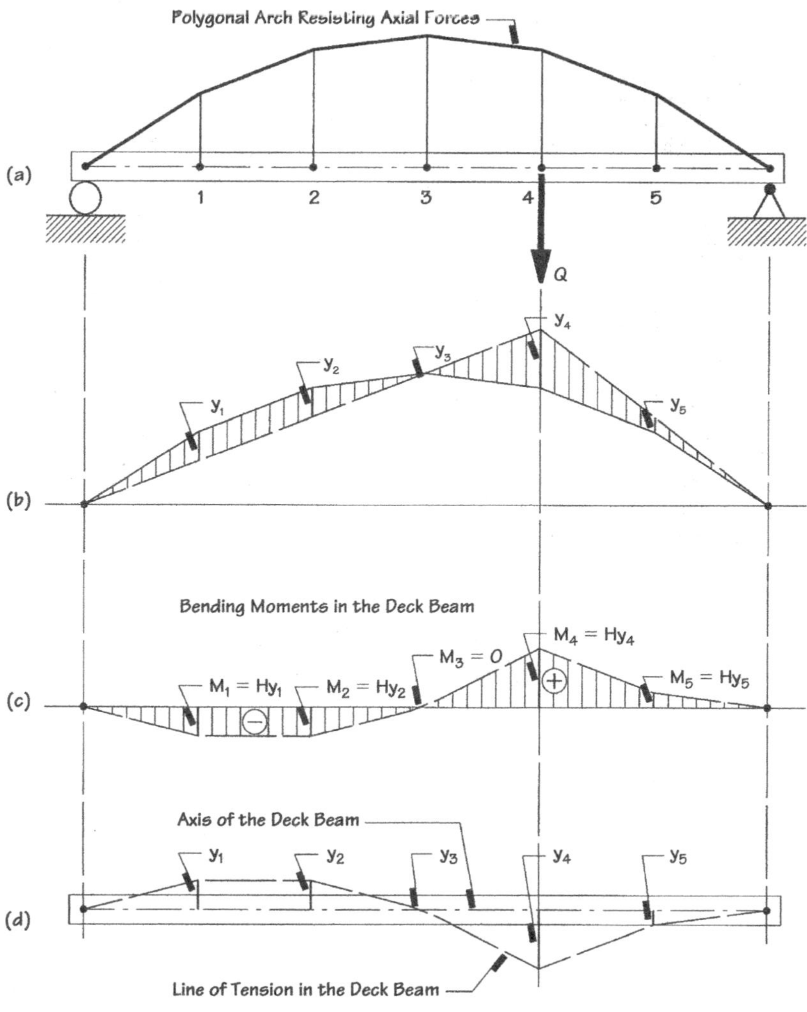

Figure 11.36 Moments in a deck-stiffened arch.

Figure 11.37 Schwandbach Bridge, Switzerland, 1933; Robert Maillart, engineer. The arch slab is only 200 mm (8 in.) thick and spans 37.4 m (123 ft).

Photo courtesy of ETH-Bibliothek, Zurich.

RESTRAINT BY TRUSSING THE FUNICULAR MEMBER AND THE DECK

The bridges in Figure 11.38 are supported by very slender steel arches. The arches are restrained against changing shape by adding diagonal members between the arches and the shallow deck, to create a very rigid structure. With pinned connections at both ends, these bridges function as restrained arches, and their form is completely logical. If one end were put on rollers, however, the arch action would disappear and the bridge would function as a truss in bending. In this case, the most efficient form for the bridge would be a parabolic truss whose depth varies from zero at the supports to a maximum at midspan, just the opposite of the actual curvature of these bridges. But here another factor comes into play: The canyon is very deep, making temporary support from below impossible. The trussed arch, being deep at the canyon wall, is ideally shaped to act as a cantilevered truss during construction. It can be built out from each side of the canyon until the two constructions meet, at which time its supports can be modified to make it act as an arch. The ideal parabolic truss, with its minimum depth and hinge and roller supports, is much more difficult to construct.

RESTRAINT BY DIAPHRAGM ACTION

Restraint of a cable roof by diaphragm action is illustrated in Figure 11.39. Cables support a shallow concrete deck. Although the thickness of the curved concrete of a hanging roof is too small to be effective in preventing displacements of the cables in a direction perpendicular to its surface, the same slab, if it acts as a unit, is extremely rigid in the direction tangential to its surface and is able to act in that direction as a very stiff beam. Thus, if we secure the curved edges of the solid deck of the auditorium to rigidly braced sidewalls at midspan (a), the great surface rigidity of the deck will not allow lateral movements of the cables embedded within (b). The restraint by these properties of the surface as a

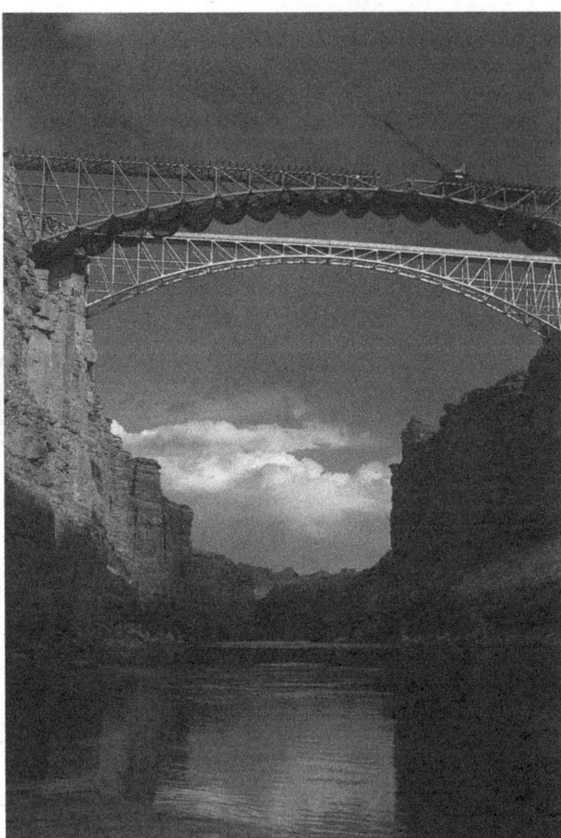

Figure 11.38 Navajo Bridges, Grand Canyon, Arizona. The bridge in the background spans 616 ft (188 m). It was built in 1929 by engineer R. A. Hanson. The new span of 726 ft (221 m, foreground) was completed in 1995 by engineers Cameron and Associates. Because the depth of the canyon at this point is 457 ft (142 m), temporary scaffolding to support the bridges during construction was not a practical possibility. The trussed configuration made it possible to construct each bridge by cantilevering from the supports at both ends.

Photo courtesy of Richard Strange Photography.

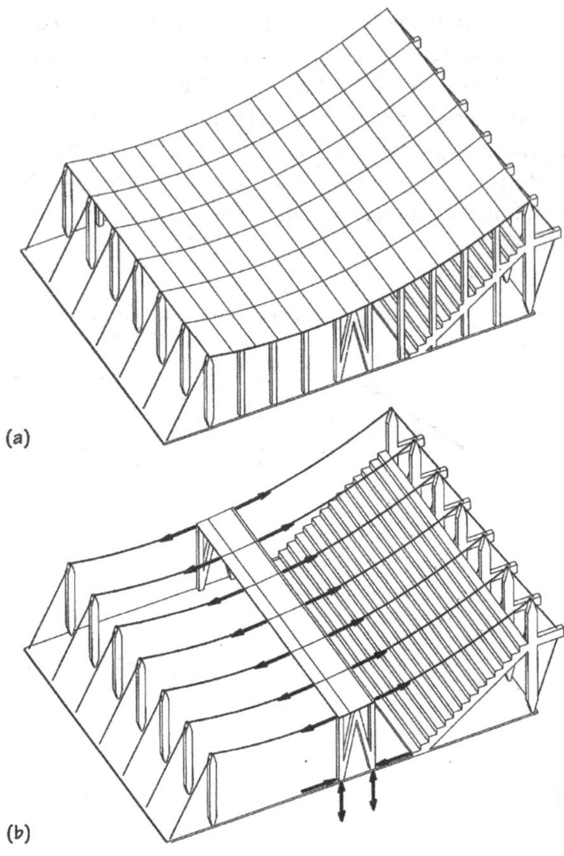

Figure 11.39 The effect on the roof cables of sidewall bracing and surface action in the roof deck. The strip of roof deck between the braced wall panels acts as a horizontal beam to resist lateral displacements in the main cables.

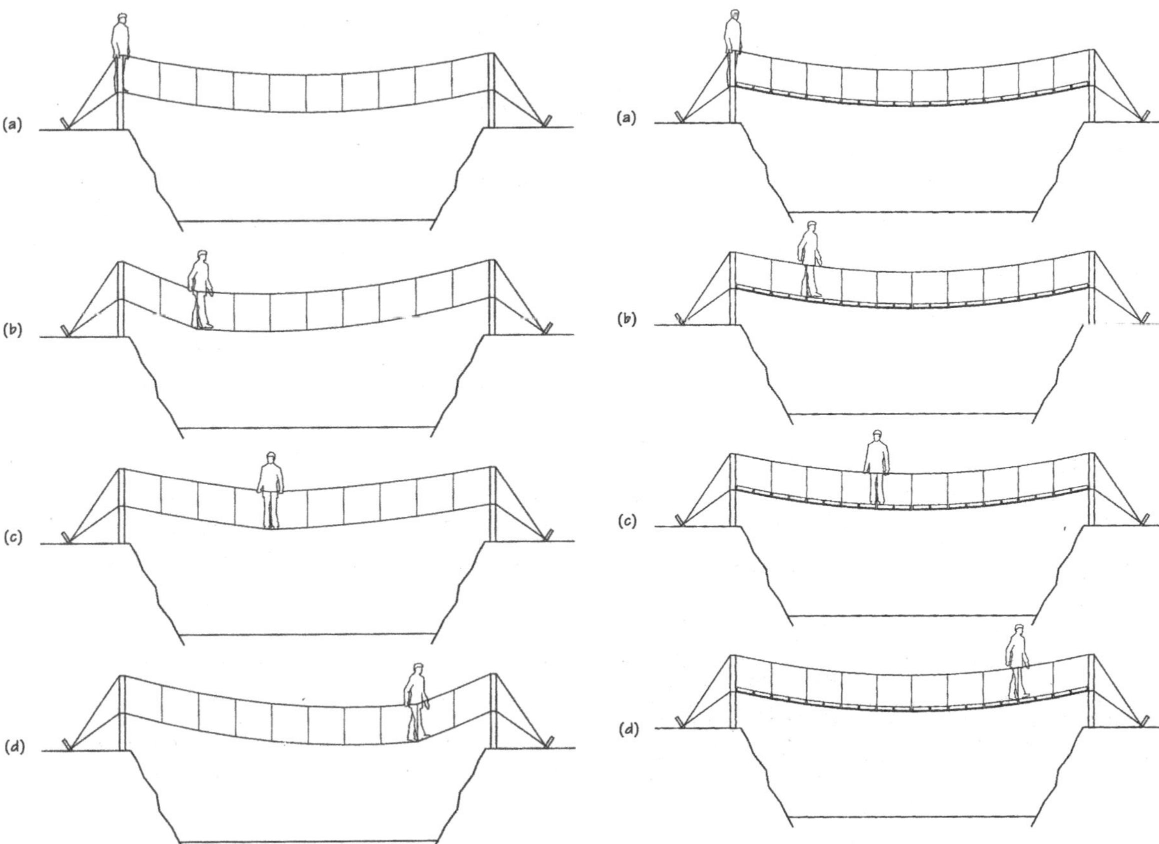

Figure 11.40 Crossing a river on a lightweight hanging bridge.

Figure 11.41 The effect of adding a heavy deck to the hanging bridge.

diaphragm will restrict any significant distortions to the cables' shapes. Though the more heavily loaded parts of the cables will be tensioned more than their less loaded parts, the shape of the cables will be unaffected because the portion of the roof slab between the loads of different magnitudes will act as a rigid surface beam that is restrained from moving by the rigid sidewalls. To act in this way, the roof deck must be made as a single continuous slab rather than separate panels or strips. The sidewalls may be braced as shown or they may be rigid planes of concrete that act as diaphragms, much like the surface action of the roof slab.

Dead load can also be used to restrain a cable structure from excessive changes in shape. Consider a very lightweight suspension footbridge. (Figure 11.40). The weight of your body is large in relation to the weight of the bridge. As you advance across the bridge, its shape changes radically with each step. In a wilderness footbridge this behavior is tolerated by able-bodied hikers, but the analogous changes of shape in a large roof or other structure due to varying wind and snow loads could be disastrous. If the bridge had a heavy deck made of large timbers placed across the suspension ropes, your weight would be small in relationship to the dead load of the deck, and changes of shape would be minimized (Figure 11.41).

RESTRAINT BY FOLDED PLATE STIFFENING

Pier Luigi Nervi stiffened the thin concrete vaults of his Turin Exhibition Building by folding them into corrugations (Figures 11.42–11.44). The folds increase the effective depth of the vaults many times over and avoid the need for stiffening ribs. The detail section in Figure 11.44 shows the ingenuity of the construction: The roof was prefabricated as a set of short elements, each 2.5 m wide, made of what Nervi called "ferro-cemento," a very thin, almost fibrous construction that consisted of multiple, closely-spaced layers of fine wire mesh impregnated with portland cement plaster. Lateral diaphragms of the same material prevent the thin sections from buckling. After these prefabricated elements were placed on temporary scaffolding, longitudinal reinforcing bars were installed over the ridges and valleys, and concrete was poured in these two regions to knit the elements into a single, strong roof shell.

Figure 11.42 Turin Exhibition Hall, 1949. Pier Luigi Nervi, engineer.

PIER LUIGI NERVI

Pier Luigi Nervi (1891–1979) graduated as a civil engineer in Bologna, Italy, in 1913. Throughout his career he created elegantly patterned designs executed in reinforced concrete, extending and improving this versatile material for a variety of uses and load configurations. He formed his own firm, Nervi and Nebbiosi (1920–1932), in Rome, and won early municipal stadium design competitions due to the cost efficiency of his designs. Nervi also served as a contractor; the firm that he formed in 1932 (Nervi and Bartoli) bid successfully on many of his own competition-winning designs and constructed the projects using techniques of Nervi's own devising. He was a pioneer in the prefabrication of concrete building components. The scarcity of steel and ready availability of labor in Italy motivated his development of strategies for minimizing extraneous reinforcement for greater economy. His own reinforced concrete system, known simply as "ferro-cemento," was used for an exhibition hall in Turin. This famous "Salone B," erected in nine months in 1948–1949, demonstrated the visual and spatial potential of his approach. It was roofed with precast concrete units less than 2 in. thick. Nervi was instrumental in the design of the UNESCO headquarters in Paris (with Marcel Breuer) and the tapered Pirelli skyscraper in Milan (with Gio Ponti). By 1960 his Palazzo and Palazzetto dello Sport were completed for the Olympics in Rome. Late in his life Nervi completed the Washington Bus Station in New York City (1963), the Tour de la Bourse in Montreal (1964), and other projects from New Hampshire to California. One of his last works was the Cathedral of Saint Mary of the Assumption in San Francisco, with the Italian-American architect Pietro Belluschi.

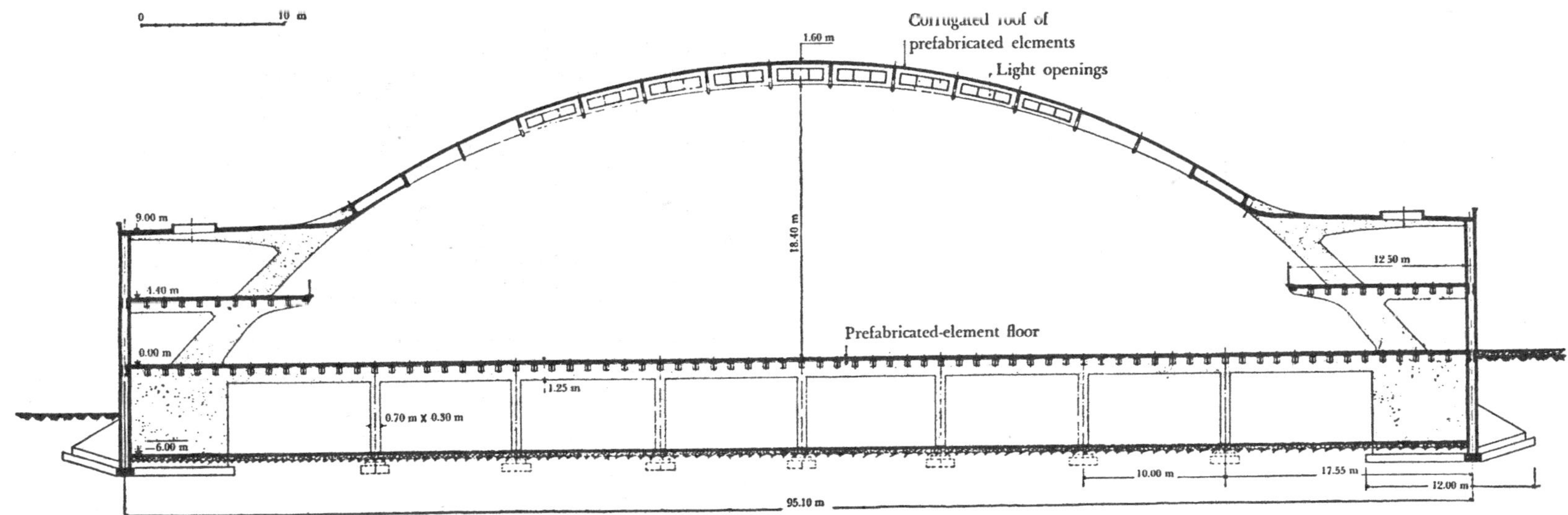

Figure 11.43 Cross section, Turin Exhibition Hall, 1949. Pier Luigi Nervi, engineer.
Source: Pier Luigi Nervi, *Structures,* New York: F.W. Dodge Corp., 1956.

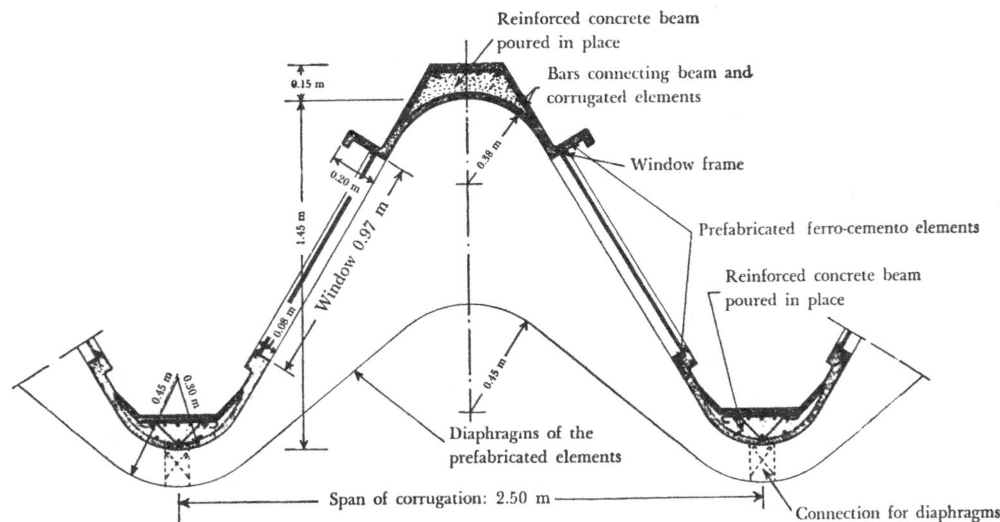

Figure 11.44 Detail of vault, Turin Exhibition Hall, 1949. Pier Luigi Nervi, engineer.
Source: Pier Luigi Nervi, *Structures,* New York: F.W. Dodge Corp., 1956.

The rice storage silo by Eladio Dieste (Figures 11.45, 11.46) is a thin parabolic vault made of hollow clay tiles. Reinforcing bars in the mortar joints between the tiles strengthen the vault considerably, but its sinusoidal corrugations make it highly resistant to changing shape when subjected to the shifting pressures of external winds and internal piles of rice.

The Supersam market in Warsaw, Poland (constructed in 1962, demolished in 2006–2007) employs a more complex type of folded-plate stiffening in which tensioned and compressed elements are balanced against one another (Figure 11.1). Figure 11.47 illustrates the evolution of the structural concept as designed by the Buro Bistyp office (including Wacław Zalewski), along with other architects and engineers: Two retail spaces, divided from each other by a central structure for storage and food preparation, could be roofed with separate hanging roofs (a). To eliminate the diagonal backstays from the central

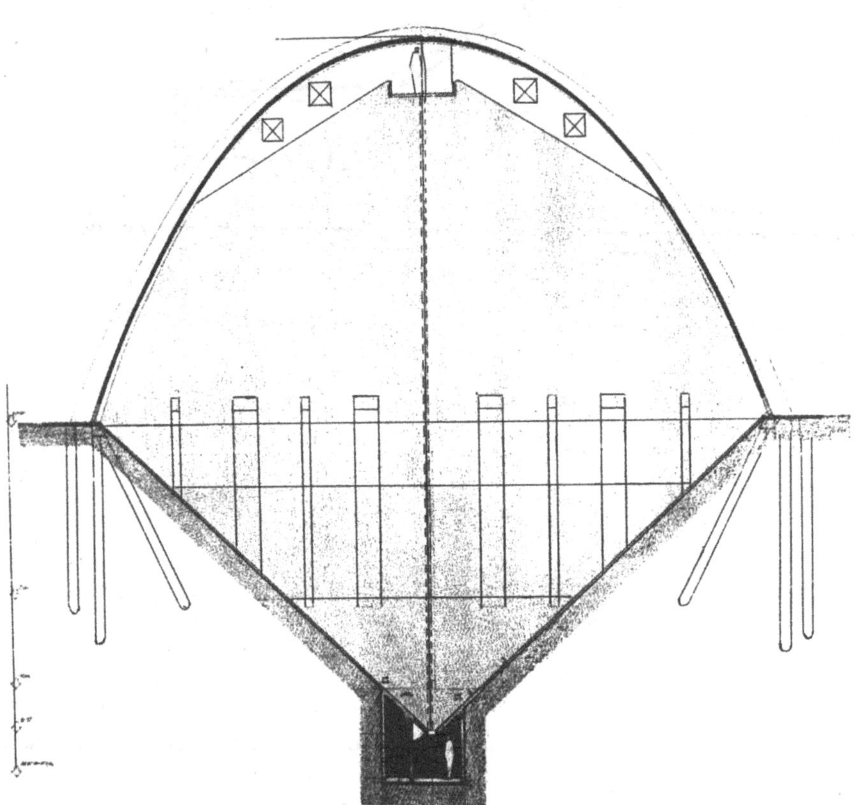

Figure 11.45 Cross section, rice silo, Vergara, Uruguay. Eladio Dieste, engineer. Courtesy of Dieste & Montanez S. A.

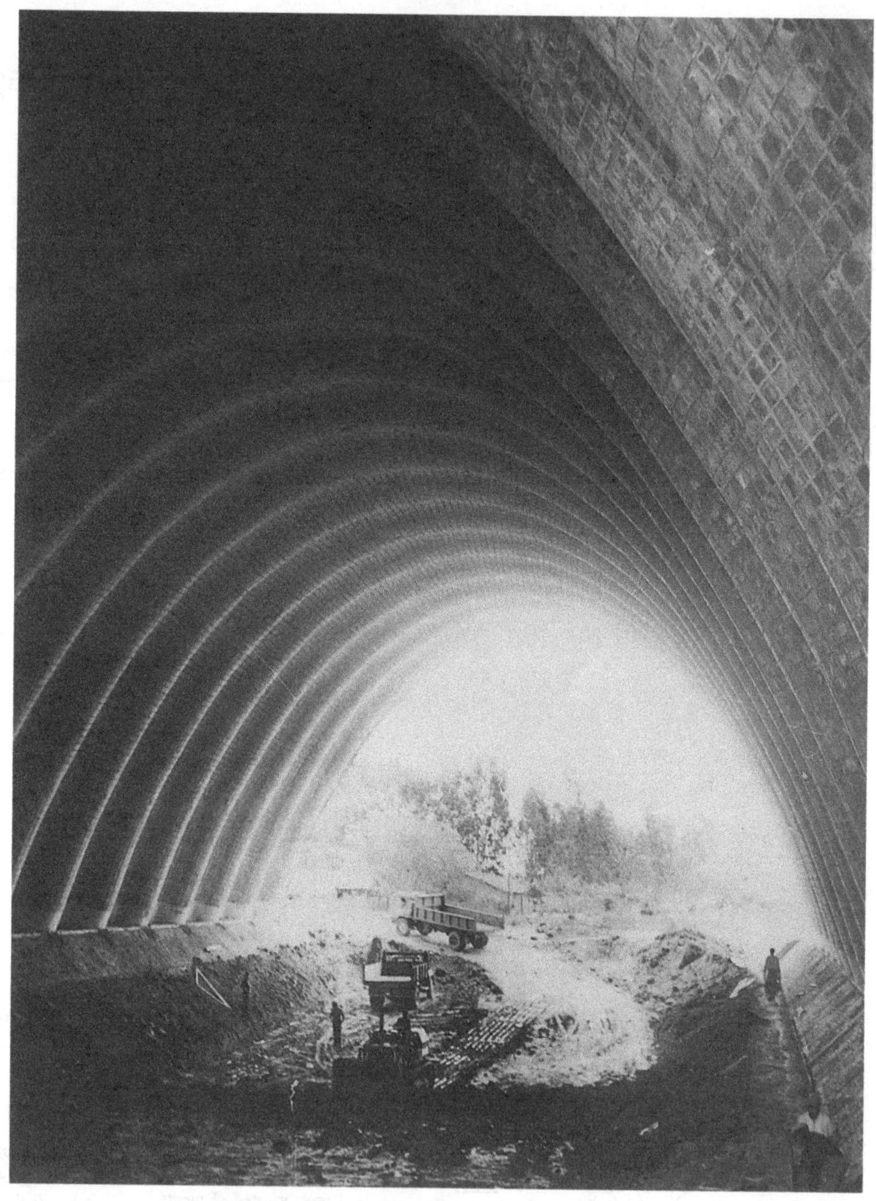

Figure 11.46 Rice silo, Vergara, Uruguay. Eladio Dieste, engineer. Photo courtesy of Dieste & Montanez SA.

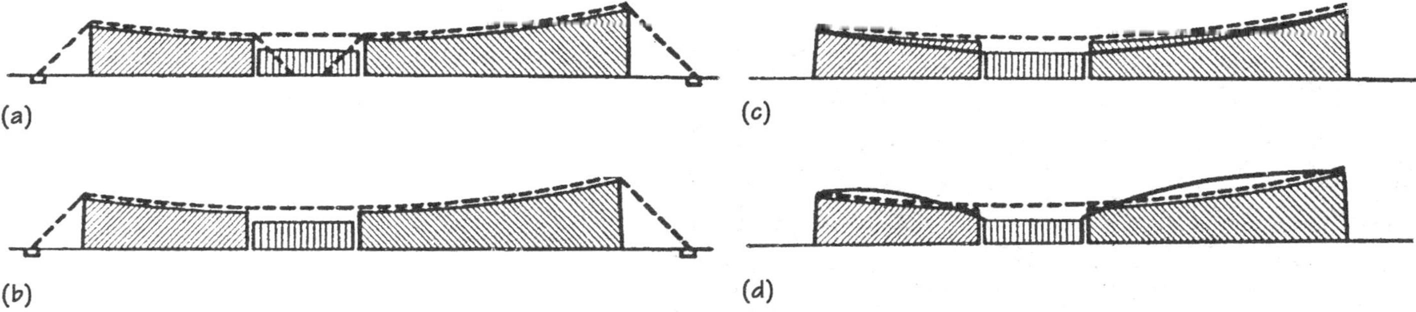

▲ **Figure 11.47** The concept of the Supersam roof.

Image: Collection of Wacław Zalewski.

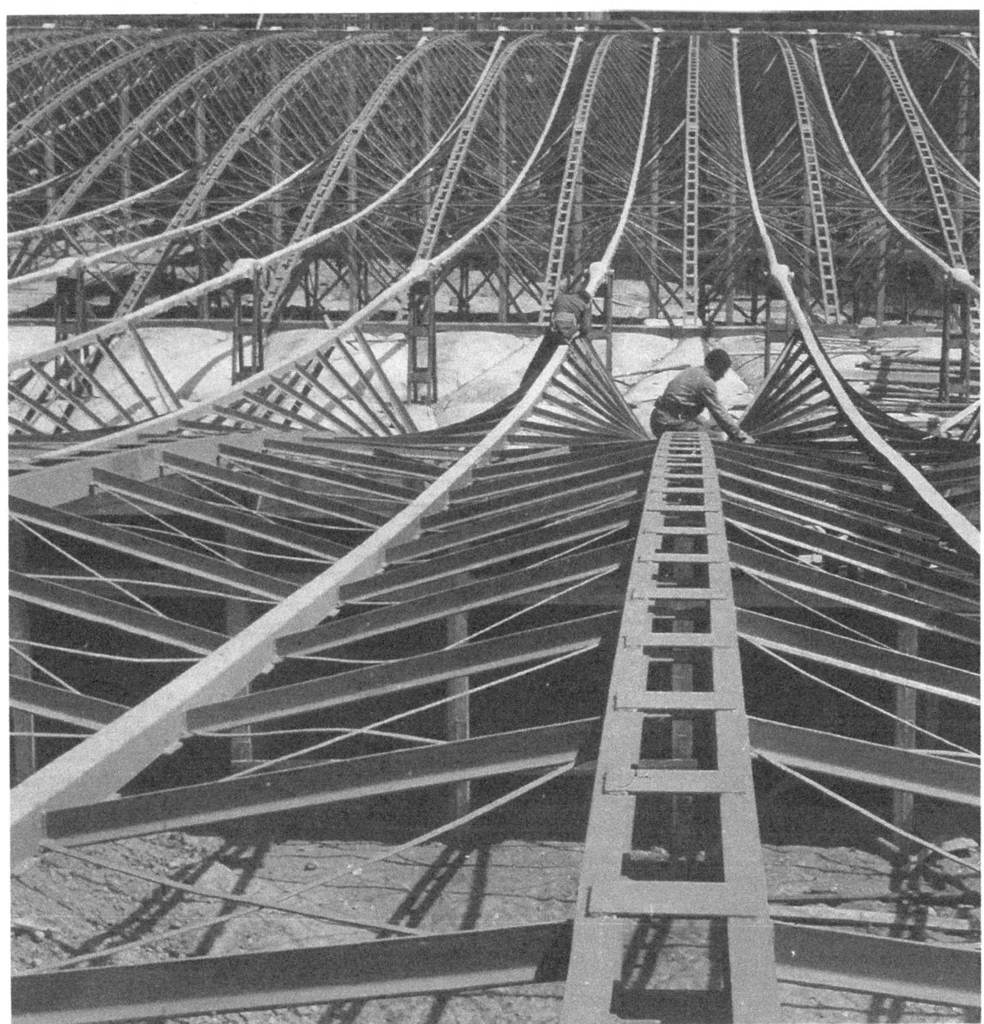

▶ **Figure 11.48** Construction photograph of the Supersam roof in Warsaw, Poland, c.1961.

Photo: Collection of Wacław Zalewski.

area, the roof cables could be made continuous (b). The outside backstays could also be eliminated by adding compressive struts that are almost horizontal to equilibrate the pull of the cables (c). To arrive at the final design, the struts were curved to become arches that support half the roof load directly (d). The alternation of cables and arches produces the folded plate pattern shown at the opening of this chapter in Figure 11.1. Figure 11.48 shows the construction: Each arch consists of a pair of steel channels. Another pair of steel channels provides a path for each cable. Short lengths of steel angle connect the arches and cables to frame the surfaces of the folded plate. The steel framework was prefabricated in large sections that were erected on temporary supports with the aid of a crane. Then the cables were threaded through the framework and tensioned with hydraulic jacks. The roof was covered with sheet metal on the outside and wood on the inside (Figures 11.49, 11.50). Triangular steel frames on the roof of the central structure prevent lateral movement of the cable under asymmetrical loadings.

◀**Figure 11.49** The interior of Supersam, showing the wood slats on the underside of the roof and the clerestory lighting, shortly before the building was demolished in 2006–2007.

Photo: David M. Foxe.

▶**Figure 11.50** Cables and arches alternate in the Supersam roof to create a folded-plate structure; the triangular supports over the service area at the center restrain the cables from lateral movement.

Photo: Collection of Wacław Zalewski.

◀**Figure 11.51** The Barajas Airport in Madrid (Richard Rogers, architect, 2006) has a roof structure that combines bending and funicular action. Its form is an approximation of the funicular form for the loading; this results in reduced bending stresses in the stiff members, which in turn resist the deformations that would occur if the structure were purely tensile.

Photo courtesy of Creative Commons license. Photo by Usuario Barcex.

▶**Figure 11.52** The laminated wood elements of the graceful Essing stress-ribbon footbridge in Bavaria were manufactured along funicular lines. Because the depth of the elements in relation to their span is insufficient for them to act primarily as beams, they function instead as wooden tensile members that have enough bending resistance to provide restraint against changing shape when loading patterns vary. The bridge was constructed between 1978 and 1986 to the design of Richard Dietrich.

Photo courtesy of Nicholas Janberg, Structurae.

WACŁAW ZALEWSKI

Polish-American engineer and educator Wacław Zalewski (VAHTS-wahff zah-LEFF-skee) was born in 1917 in a part of the Polish empire that is within present-day Ukraine. In 1935 he began his studies of structural engineering in Warsaw. Just before he was to receive his degree in 1939, German armies invaded and occupied Poland, making further academic work impossible. Joining the Polish underground army, and thus frequently forced into hiding, he used these interludes to reflect on his studies and read extensively about structural behavior. He soon looked beyond the narrowly mathematical curriculum he had been provided in engineering school to develop a strong interest in how the flow patterns of forces through structures might suggest more efficient structural forms.

In 1944, Zalewski took part in the ill-fated Warsaw Uprising against the Nazis. He escaped capture, but two members of his immediate family were killed by German bombs. In 1947, after earning his master's degree in civil engineering, he was able at last to take up work as a designer of structures. As his first projects were built, including shell-roofed factories and municipal structures, he developed another aspect of his philosophy of engineering: a strong concern for minimizing the difficulty and cost of construction. The dual goals of shaping structures according to their internal forces and designing efficient processes for their construction have been primary themes in Zalewski's work throughout his academic and professional careers. By 1962 he had completed a wide range of work, including the Supersam commercial building in Warsaw and the preliminary scheme for the Spodek sport hall in Katowice, two of the most iconic works of postwar Polish design. After earning a doctorate in 1962 from the Warsaw Polytechnic, he accepted an invitation to teach and practice at the Universidad de los Andes in Merida, Venezuela. In 1966, he joined the MIT Department of Architecture, where he taught as a tenured professor until his retirement in 1988. He retained his connections in Venezuela for many years, however, and continued to design structures there, including the Venezuelan pavilion for the 1992 World Exposition in Barcelona, Spain. He was awarded an honorary doctorate for his professional achievements by the Departments of Architecture and Civil Engineering of the Warsaw Polytechnic in 1998.

Zalewski's ongoing career as a designer of innovative structures is documented in an exhibition of his work designed by the same team of authors as this volume; the exhibit has been shown since 2006 at MIT, Roger Williams University, the University of Maryland, the Department of Civil and Environmental Engineering at Stanford University, and in several locations in Poland. In describing his design methods, Zalewski has stated that "The intellectual delights of . . . analytical procedures are very different from the sensuous pleasures of giving a structure its shape. . . . Geometry is the mathematics of structural imagination."

Exercises

1. Sketch five other ways of restraining the concrete arch slab of the Salginatobel Bridge against the effects of asymmetrical loadings (Figures 11.29–11.31). Write a paragraph discussing the advantages and disadvantages of each. What procedure would you use to erect each of your designs?

2. Find the minimum force under full live load in a cable in the stress ribbon bridge shown in Figure 11.22. Use the dimensions given in the figure legend. Assume that there are six cables. The live load is 4.0 kN/m^2. The dimensions of the deck section are 3.8 m by 0.3 m.

3. Working graphically, determine whether the inclination of the columns of the paper mill shown in Figures 11.34 and 11.35 is such that the columns are subjected only to axial forces under a uniform roof loading.

4. Sketch four different ways of restraining a cylindrical concrete shell roof that is 6 in. thick, rises 40 ft, and spans 175 ft.

Key Terms and Concepts

anticlastic curvature
bicycle wheel structure
box arch
deck-stiffened arch
inverted arch
restraint by diaphragm action
restraint by folded plate stiffening
restraint by prestressing
restraint by trussing
restraint of a funicular element
restraint with stay cables or struts
rigidity beam
sag ratio
stress ribbon
synclastic curvature
tangential stays

CHAPTER 12

Designing Shell and Membrane Structures

Contributing Author: MICHAEL H. RAMAGE

- *Form-finding techniques applied to shell, tent, pneumatic, and membrane structures*
- *Material constraints and opportunities*
- *Detailing lightweight structures*

King's College in Cambridge, England, one of the institutions that make up Cambridge University, is famous for its chapel, a Gothic masterpiece of masonry vaulting (Figure 12.2). During springtime each year a large number of students and their families congregate in Cambridge to celebrate their graduation. The college needs an outdoor pavilion on a site adjacent to the chapel that can serve year after year on this occasion and others like it to shelter the numerous visitors from rain, wind, and sun.

We have been asked to design a membrane structure that will provide shelter for 200 people and that will harmonize with the structure of the chapel. The 200 people will need about a square meter of ground area each, which comes to 200 m^2. We will allow another 100 m^2 for a catering and sound stage area, for a total of 300 m^2 of covered area. The cables and masts for the roof may well fall outside this area, but we must design them so that they will not restrict access into and out of the pavilion.

Figure 12.1 Like the petals of a giant flower, tensile structures arranged in a huge ring shade the grandstand of King Fahd Stadium in Riyadh, Saudi Arabia. Masts are 58 m (190 ft) high. Architects: Ian Fraser, John Robertson Partners; roof designer and structural engineer: Geiger Berger Associates.

Photo courtesy of Horst Berger.

MEMBRANE STRUCTURES

A *membrane structure* is one that consists primarily of a taut surface of textile *fabric* (Figure 12.1).

Figure 12.2 The vaults of King's College Chapel, Cambridge, England, which were constructed from the fifteenth to the sixteenth centuries.

Photo courtesy of Michael H. Ramage.

Figure 12.3 Stretching a membrane in two dimensions.

Photo: David M. Foxe.

Figure 12.4 A membrane held taut in space with four hands.

Photo: David M. Foxe.

Like a cable, fabric crumples when it is subjected to compressive force. When pulled in only one direction, the fabric becomes *taut* in that direction but does not extend outward to become a surface. In order to be an effective tensile surface, it needs to be pulled in two opposing directions simultaneously. Two of us can model this phenomenon easily with a square piece of fabric from 20 to 50 cm on a side. (Stretch fabric is best, T-shirt fabric is almost as good, and nearly any fabric will work.) We grasp diagonally opposite corners with our left hands and pull the fabric taut (Figure 12.3). Now we pull the other two corners taut until most or all of the wrinkles disappear from the surface. Finally, we maintain our pull on the fabric while we both move our left hands down toward the floor and our right hands up toward the ceiling. We will find that we have created a simple, elegant membrane structure (Figure 12.4).

Figure 12.5 A fabric and string model of the simplest membrane structure has two high points and two low points.

Photo courtesy of Michael H. Ramage.

Figure 12.6 A scallop-shaped shell roof for a textile factory in Łodz, Poland, designed by Wacław Zalewski (built 1960, demolished 2007).

Photo: Collection of Wacław Zalewski.

THE ELEMENTS OF A MEMBRANE STRUCTURE

A membrane structure is articulated using *masts* (also known as poles), *cables*, and specially tailored sheet(s) of fabric held in tension (Figure 12.5). The curvature of the fabric surface in opposing directions is called *anticlastic* curvature; most membrane structures are anticlastic. (Air-supported structures are an exception; see pages 350, 351.) The tension in the fabric is referred to as *pretension* or *prestress*. Pretension is a way of putting stress into the membrane structure before it is loaded by external forces, such as wind or snow. The masts that push upward and the cables that pull downward combine to pretension the membrane.

As we saw in Chapters 1 and 2, shallow cables have higher tension in them than deeply sagging cables with the same load. The same is true for fabric: For a fabric surface of shallow curvature to maintain its rigidity under a variety of loads, there must be higher forces in the fabric before the load is applied. Without the curvature and pretension, the fabric would develop unsightly wrinkles and flap in the wind. With it, a properly shaped and stressed membrane becomes a fully rigid, gracefully curved, lightweight structure.

SHELL STRUCTURES

Conceptually, a chain hanging in tension can be inverted to become an arch in compression. Fabric membrane structures have their inversions in shells, which are thin structural surfaces that act primarily in axial compression (Figure 12.6). Like tensile structures, shells are often designed as funicular shapes for the dominant load case (usually the dead load), but in compression rather than tension. Shells, unlike membranes, can be designed to resist bending and combinations of tensile and compressive stresses. Geometric shapes such as sections of spheres, hyperbolic paraboloids, and regular polyhedra are also commonly used (see the sidebar, "Questions of 'Perfect' Geometries").

Shells are usually made of concrete, but can also be built using brick, steel, wood, plastics, and glass. Unreinforced masonry shells have been built around the world for thousands of years (see Chapter 8), but these can carry loads efficiently only in axial compression.

FINDING THE FORM OF THE PAVILION

With our understanding of how fabric must be tensioned in two directions, we can begin to define the form of the pavilion for King's College. We will make the basic plan a rectangle 10 m by 30 m, using tall

Questions of "Perfect" Geometries

Since their description by ancient Greek mathematicians, the regular convex polyhedra known as "Platonic solids" (tetrahedron, cube, octahedron, dodecahedron, icosahedron) have been objects of great fascination for designers and scientists (Fig. A). As the faces of these and other polyhedra are further subdivided into triangles (a process known as *triangulation*), the resulting shapes begin to approximate spheres. Spherical geometries can have many desirable characteristics, among them that the surface of a sphere encloses the most internal volume with a given surface area, and each point on the surface has the same curvature in every direction. Throughout the twentieth century, visionary designers such as R. Buckminster Fuller used spheres and triangulated spherical space frames (known as "geodesic" spheres) to imagine and construct a wide variety of buildings such as the United States Pavilion at Expo '67 in Montreal, Quebec (Fig. B).

The spatial efficiency of a sphere and the fascinating geometries of the Platonic solids have motivated many attempts to use these shapes for buildings. Except for certain large-scale geodesic domes, these attempts have generally failed. Thousands of geodesic domes were built at small scale in the 1970s as houses, nearly all of which have since been abandoned. Their builders found that indeed, the geodesic frames were quick and economical to build, but getting beyond the raw frame was problematic. The cutting of sheet materials to cover the polygonal faces of the domes was exceedingly wasteful and thus costly. Making the domes watertight proved to be almost impossible. Windows and doors had to be custom made. Kitchen cabinets, bathrooms, beds, and refrigerators did not fit easily into the round floor plan with sloping, faceted walls. Later expansion of

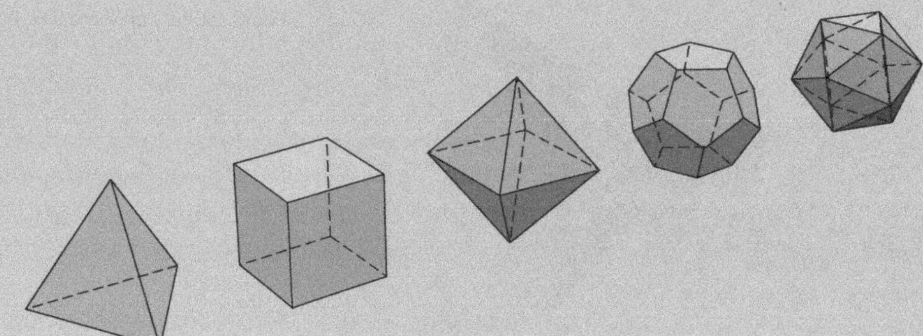

Fig. A Platonic solids.

Fig. B The United States Pavilion for Expo '67 in Montreal, Canada, designed by R. Buckminster Fuller.

the house was difficult at best. Those who tried to house themselves in buildings based on Platonic solids fared no better, facing similar challenges to those who sought to inhabit geodesic domes.

These difficulties are not unique to these geometric shapes. Similar problems occur any time that we try to stuff human lives and activities into predetermined shapes and volumes. We tend to need vertical walls, rectangular rooms, orthogonal framing that is easy to connect and easy to change and expand. The Platonic solids have many virtues, but there is no reason to believe that they should be suitable as shapes of enclosures for human habitation. From the decades of experimentation with lightweight shells, domes, and membranes at various scales, the primary surviving technology is the anticlastic fabric membrane. Because membranes, unlike domes, can be designed and adapted to almost any formal geometries and site constraints, they have persisted and even flourished, taking a place alongside conventional systems of construction as possible selections for many kinds of uses.

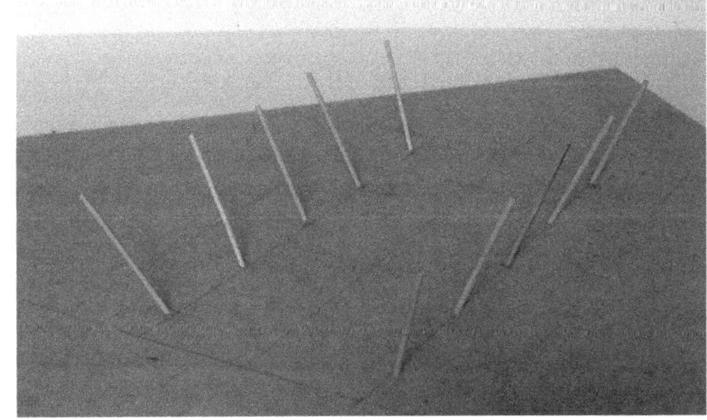

◀ **Figure 12.7** Model making: placing the support masts and locating the tie-down points.

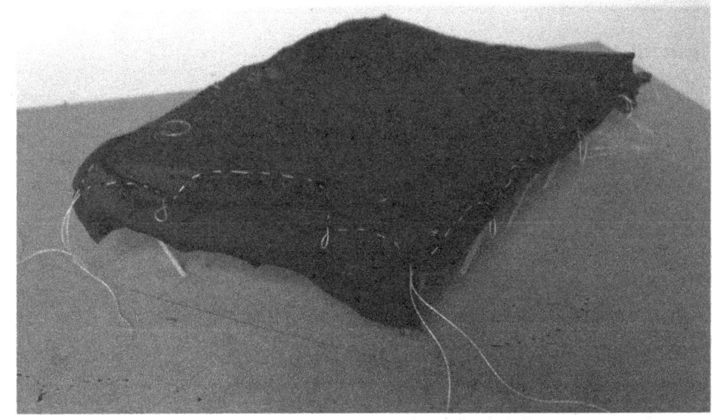

▶ **Figure 12.8** Model making: sewing the edge cables.

masts in compression to hold up the high points of the fabric. Cables will be attached to the lower edges of the fabric to secure it to the ground. Because the pavilion will be put up and taken down each year, we will construct it in repeating bays of similar structure, each 10 m wide by 5 m long. This will allow it to be erected and taken down by a small crew and stored in reasonably-sized bundles. Through its repetition of similar modules, it will also give a rhythm to the structure.

Drawing the subtle curves of a membrane structure is difficult. Even experienced designers rely heavily on physical and computer models, as will we. The masonry fan vaults of King's College Chapel, although they transfer their load to the ground by means of compressive forces only, will serve as the inspiration for our pavilion, which will rely primarily on tensile forces. We can't actually turn the chapel upside down, but look again at Figure 12.2, this time upside-down. We'll use a similar central junction of tensioned fans to create a structure reminiscent of the grand nave of the chapel. Regularly spaced masts toward the outside will push the fabric up, and cables at the periphery will pull it down. The way in which we align and cut the fabric will also define the form. We will use cables at the seams between fabric panels to gather the forces.

We've made enough decisions to be able to produce a physical model of the design to see how the fabric responds to the parameters we've defined. Fabric that stretches easily in both directions is best for modeling; pantyhose fabric is ideal. The first step is to place both the support masts and the tie-down locations on the model base (Figure 12.7). Next we draw the arcs of the edge cables on the fabric and sew a strong thread along these arcs. This thread will mimic the action of edge cables when we tension the form. We then stretch the fabric over the supports. At first, the sheet does not take on the form of the membrane structure (Figure 12.8). But as we adjust the tensions in the edge cables and apply increasing downward pull, the form gradually emerges, and we can evaluate the structure we have created with the given masts and tie-down locations (Figure 12.9). We will want to make many changes in the model, experimenting to arrive at the

Figure 12.9 Model making: stretching the fabric.

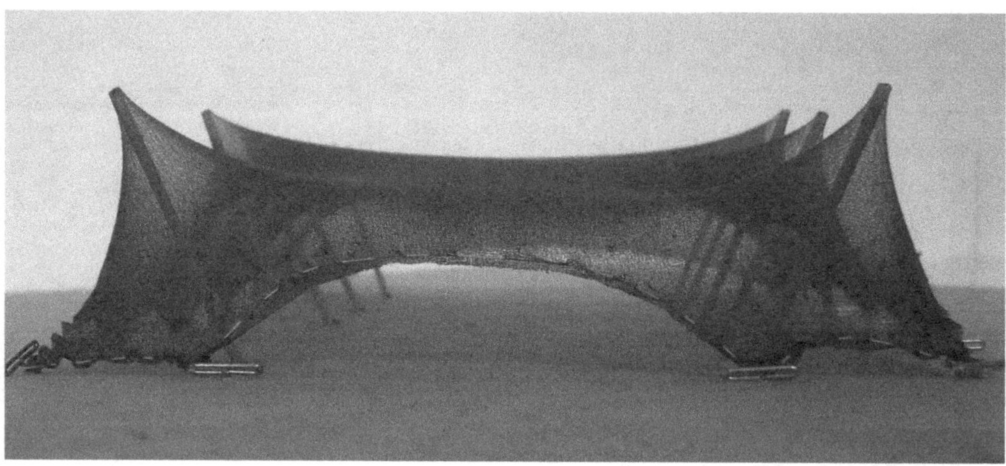

Figure 12.10 Model making: view through completed model.

most natural, attractively proportioned shape that we can produce (Figure 12.10). Finally, we trim the fabric and add cables across the structure to divide the pavilion into panels for easier assembly and disassembly. An important thing for us to keep in mind throughout this process is to maintain sufficient curvature in the membrane that it can be kept taut and rigid with relatively low forces. If it becomes too flat, forces rise, and the likelihood of wind-induced fluttering increases.

We can generate a similar model in the computer using software designed for finding the form of fabric structures (Figure 12.11). We have chosen to use Formfinder Light, a free program that may be acquired on the web at http://www.formfinder.at/main. Formfinder is also sold in a full version that is more powerful. The first step, as with the physical model, is to draw the supporting structure. In this drawing we define distinct locations for the end connections of edge cables and the high points of the fabric at the top of the masts. Working from the parameters we provide, the software lets us quickly test a variety of ideas. This allows us to see a range of configurations that are possible using the same supports (Figure 12.12). In evaluating these alternatives, we need to verify again that there is enough curvature in every part of the shape

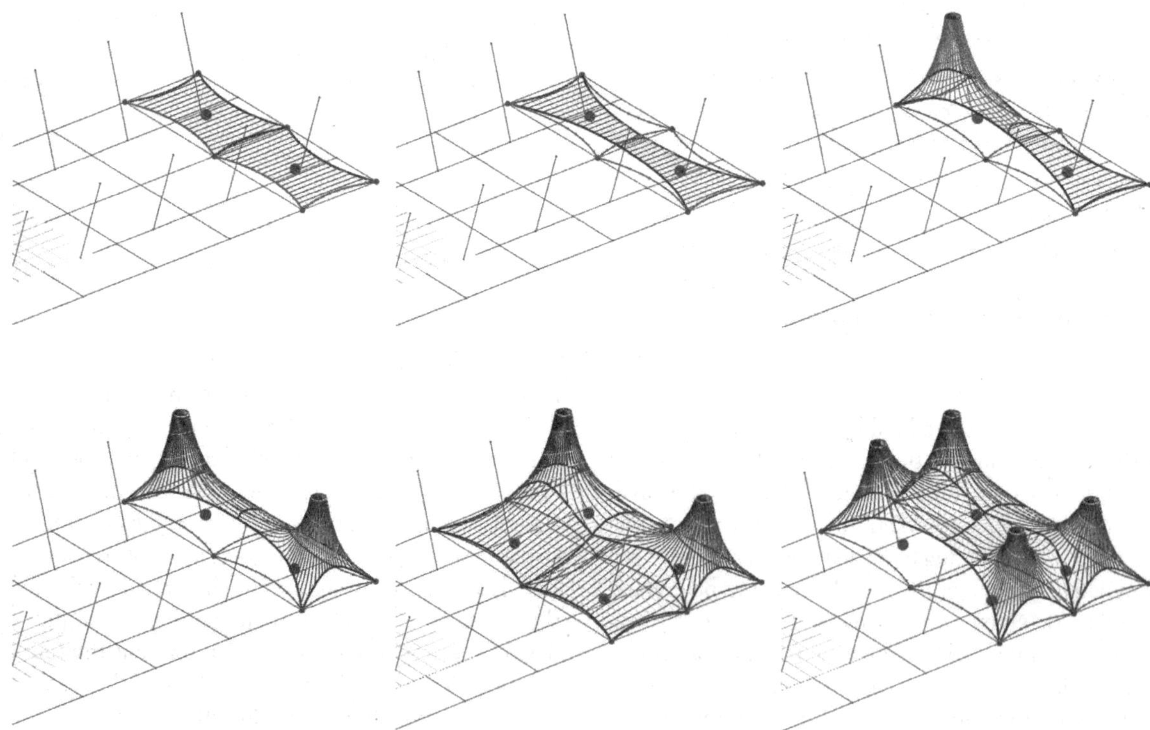

Figure 12.11 CAD model making in Formfinder Light: analogous digital process for modeling a similar structure.

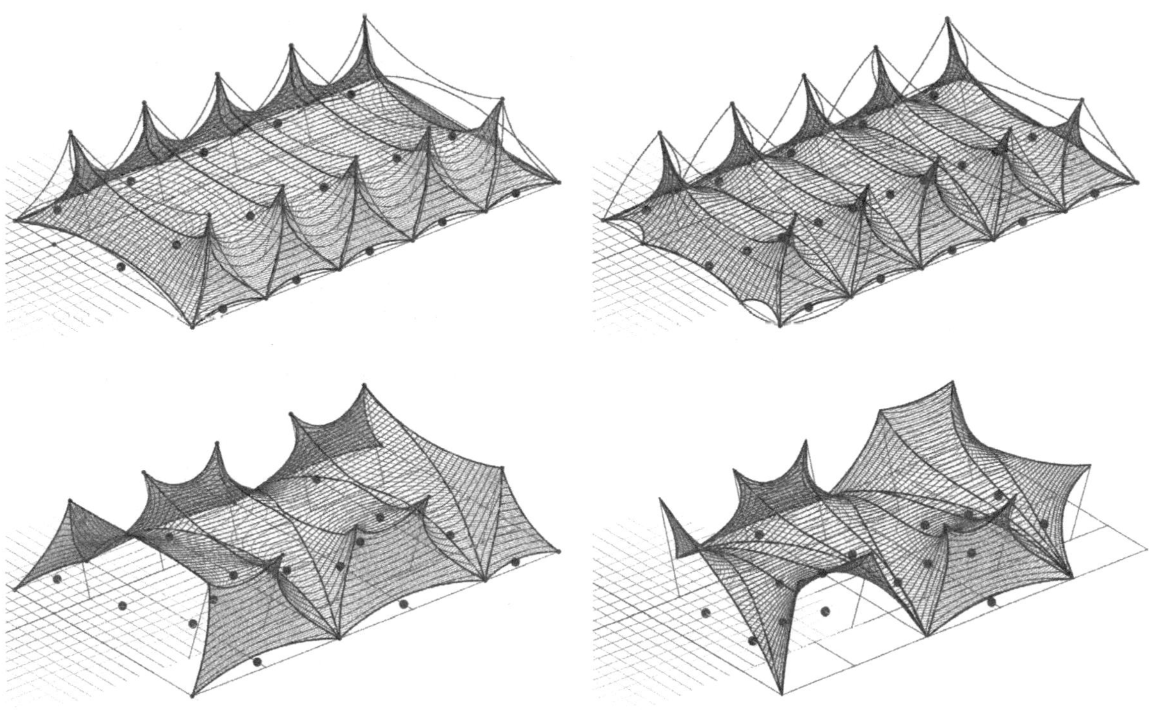

Figure 12.12 CAD model making in Formfinder Light: variations in membrane shape on the same supports.

FREI OTTO

Frei Otto (b. 1925) is recognized internationally as a master of innovative structures. He studied architecture at the Technical University of Berlin. He was drafted into the German army as a pilot and imprisoned in France, but completed his studies in 1948. His 1954 doctoral dissertation on suspended roofs led to his influential collaborations with Behnisch, Schlaich, and other designers on the Olympic Stadium in Munich (1972) and dozens of other permanent structures, temporary pavilions, and experimental designs. He founded the Institute for Lightweight Structures at the University of Stuttgart, where he taught from 1964 to 1990. He notes that, "The whole natural world is built from a single constructional detail: a casing filled with fluid." He cautions against designing to look "futuristic," noting that, "I'm simply interested in doing something new, and when one succeeds in that, it points in the direction of the future anyway."

to keep the fabric taut without excessive pretension. After considering many alternative designs, we select for further development a scheme with radial membranes over the masts and cables between them.

FINDING THE FORCES IN THE MEMBRANE

Now that we have defined the form, how do we calculate the forces? We know that the masts are in compression and the fabric and all the cables are in tension, but how much? If we go back to our original square piece of cloth, and reduce it to its simplest configuration, two pieces of string, we can see how to begin calculating the forces (Figure 12.13). The two strings define a point in space where they cross, and fix its location. (If we take away any one of the four string

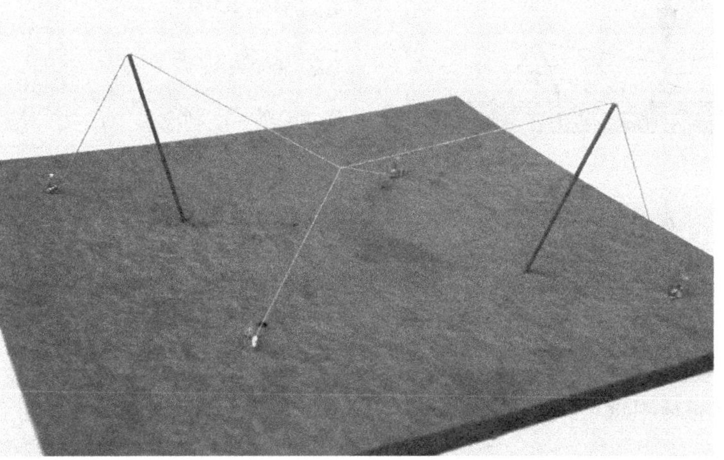

Figure 12.13 Two taut, crossed strings define a stable point in space.

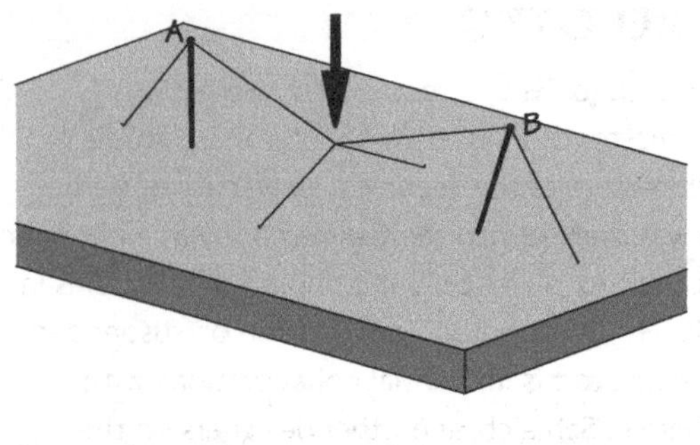

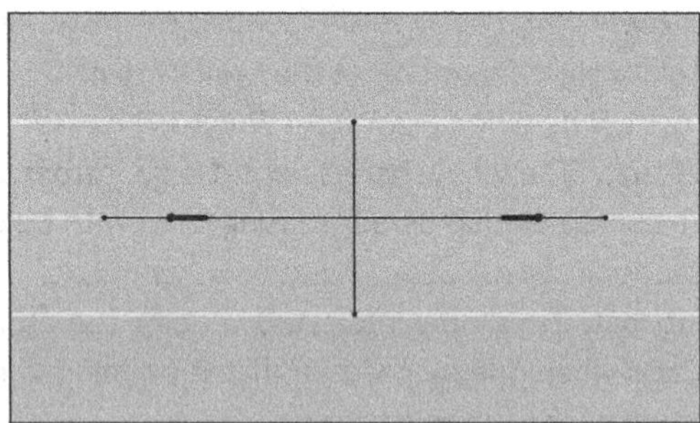

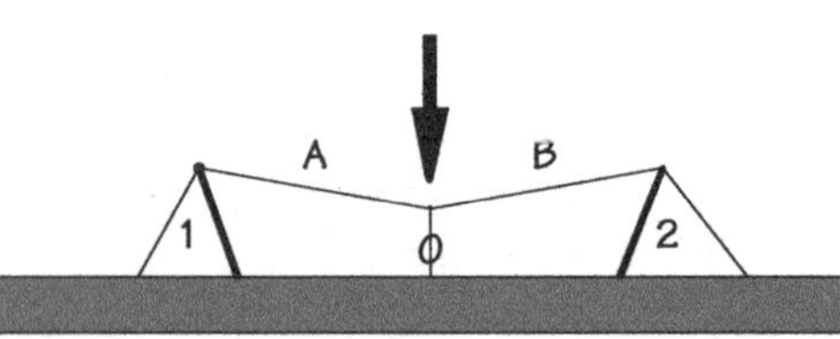

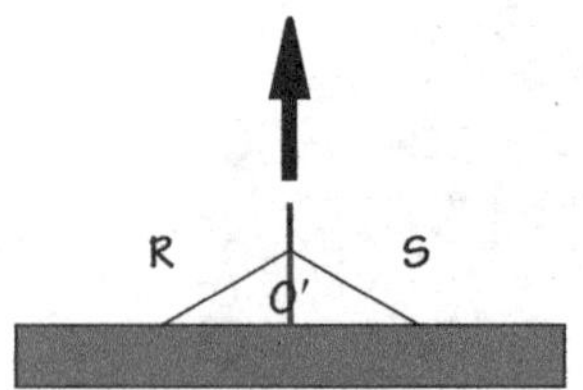

Figure 12.14 Axonometric, plan, and section drawings of two taut, crossed strings.

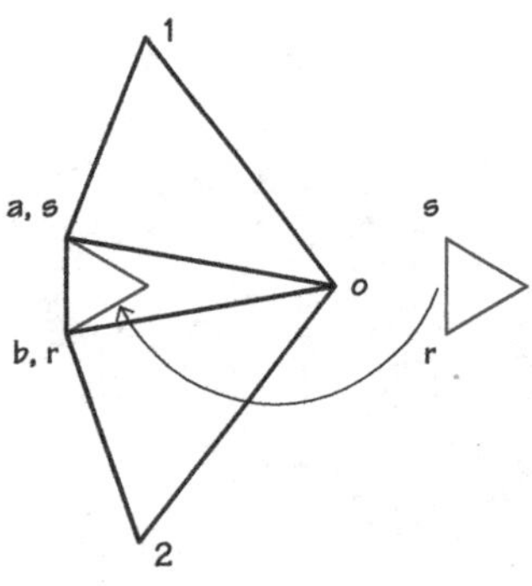

Figure 12.15 Composite force polygons for the two strings and their masts.

segments, the point will no longer be fixed in space.) This structure must be able to satisfy the equations of static equilibrium, so the sum of the forces in the *X*, *Y*, and *Z* directions must be zero. We don't need to solve for equilibrium of moments: A moment is equivalent to a force couple of tension and compression. Because the elements of a tensile structure can't resist compression, there are no moments in the membrane.

In our string model, we can analyze a section cut through both masts. The force polygon is shown in Figure 12.15. A perpendicular section gives us the two strings pulling downward, with an upward force equal to the first downward force. Since the forces are the same, but in opposite directions, we can draw them on the same force polygon, where the load line is the equilibrium force between the perpendicular lines (Figures 12.14 and 12.15). Mathematically, we can solve the system of forces at the intersection of the cables with the equations shown (Figure 12.16).

If we add cables to the basic system, as shown in Figure 12.17, we begin to develop a *cable-net* structure, the precursor of membrane structures. The Olympic

$$P_{up} = -t_1 \sin\alpha$$
$$P_{up} = -P_{down}$$
$$P_{down} = t_1 \sin\alpha$$
$$P_{down} = -t_2 \sin\beta$$
$$t_1 \sin\alpha = t_2 \sin\beta$$

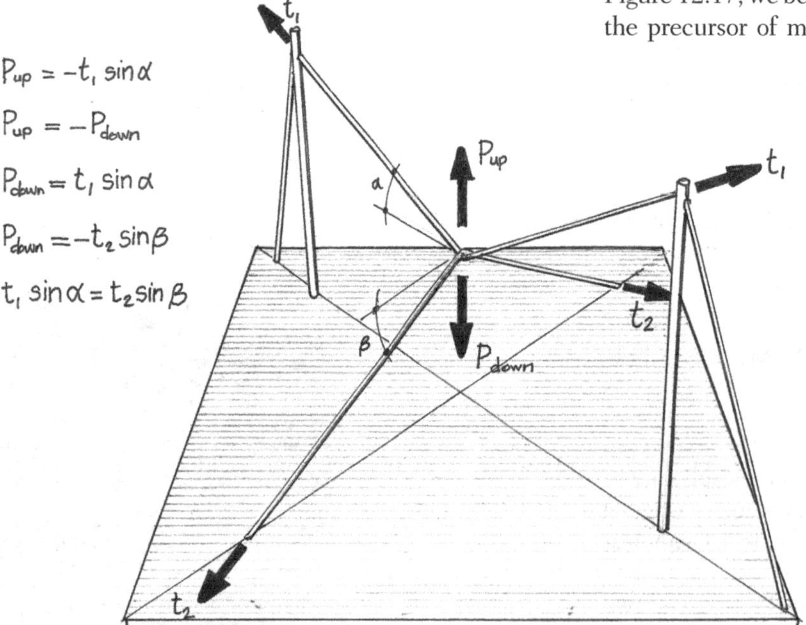

Figure 12.16 Equilibrium equations for the point at which the two strings cross.

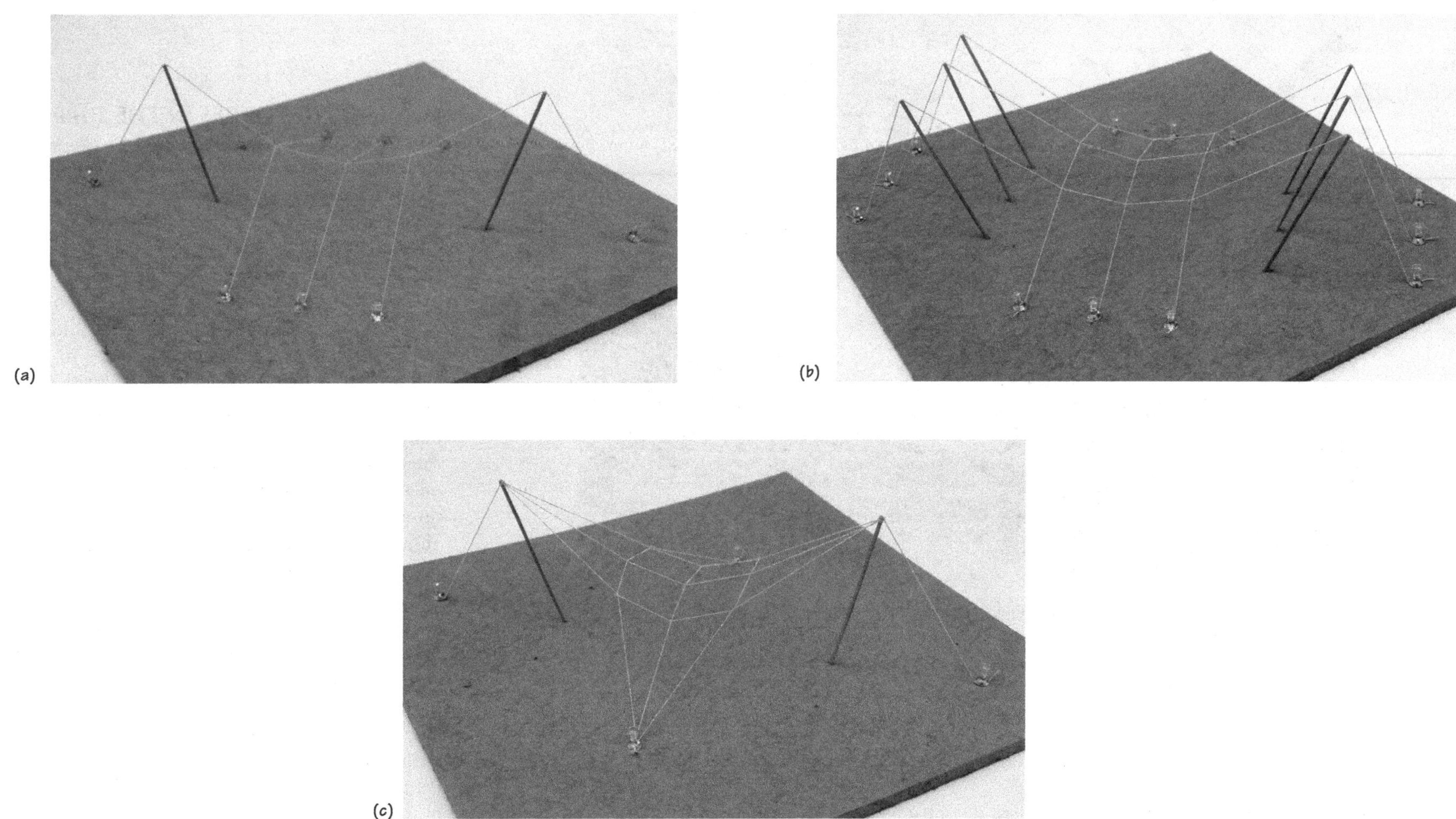

Figure 12.17 Development of a cable net from two crossing strings into a network that can support a surface. (a) A single string pulls up on three down-pulling strings. (b) With three strings pulling up and three down, a saddle-shaped surface begins to emerge. (c) In this variation, just two masts are required.

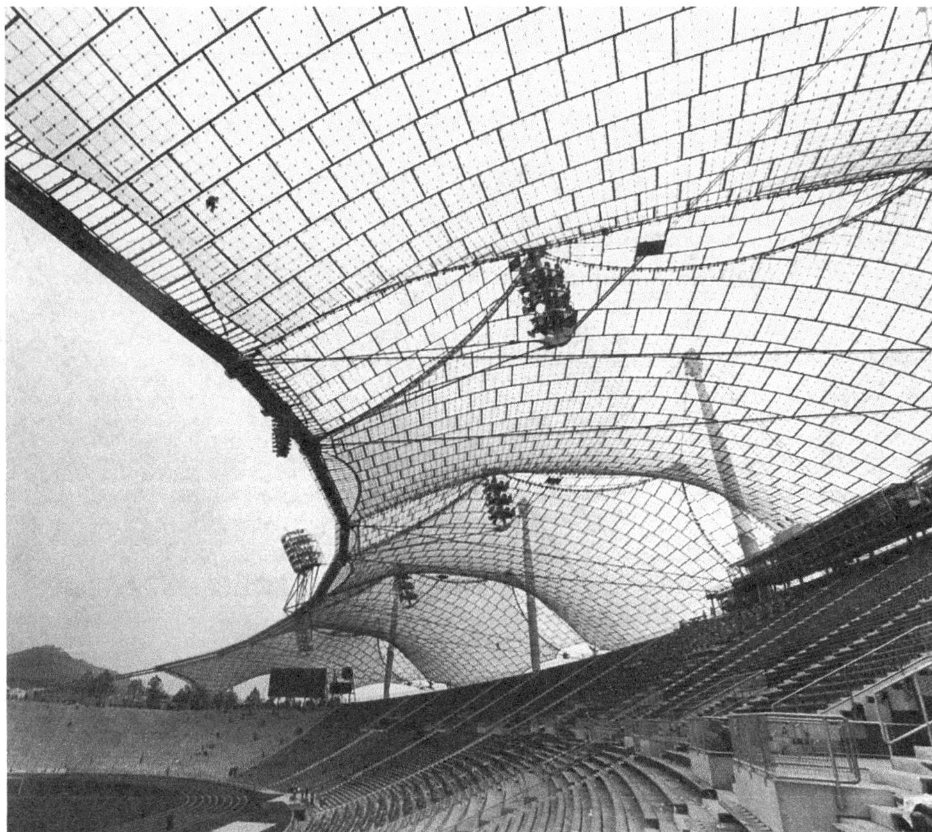

Figure 12.18 The Olympic Stadium roof in Munich, Germany, is made of steel cables and transparent acrylic plastic panels. For scale, notice the worker seen through the roof at the upper left. Architects: Frei Otto, Ewald Bubner, and Behnisch and Partner.

Photo courtesy of the Institute for Lightweight Structures, Stuttgart.

Stadium in Munich, which is based on investigations by the architect Frei Otto, is the largest and best known of these early tension structures (Figure 12.18).

Because membrane structures are defined by anticlastic curvature, at every point on the surface there will be a tensile force curving downward and a perpendicular tensile force curving upward. These forces must be in equilibrium, just like the strings in the first simplified model, Figure 12.16. Forces are calculated in planes that are perpendicular to each other, usually referred to as the U and V directions. By repeating this analysis at many points along the surface, we can find the forces in the membrane. This is tiresome to do by hand, especially considering that the mathematics of these points are highly interactive, leading to many simultaneous equations. Computers are well suited to the many repetitive calculations that this entails, and many programs that use a variety of algorithms are available.

FINDING THE FORCES IN THE SUPPORT STRUCTURE

We still need to decide on the arrangement of the edge cables, how to anchor them to the ground, and what material to use for the masts. The forces in the membrane are brought to the ground in compression through masts and in tension through cables along the edge of the fabric. Adjusting the pitch of the masts will alter the forces in the same way as demonstrated in Chapter 2, but with the added complexity that we are using the membrane as a backstay, and it might be most advantageous for the masts to lean in three dimensions. Depending on the forces, we could make the masts of aluminum, wood, or steel, but we are predisposed toward aluminum because it is lightweight and corrosion-resistant (see Chapter 13). We want our structure to give many years of service with minimal maintenance. For efficient use of material, we want the masts to experience axial loads only. The physical and digital models allow us to see the direction the fabric will pull, and inform us of the suitable lean angles for the masts. We learn from close examination of the models that the corner masts should lean away from the structure (toward the corners) in both directions, while the center masts only need to lean out perpendicular to the main axis of the structure. As we saw in the force polygons, the masts are heavily loaded—they must support both gravity loads and the prestress forces in the membrane, as well as the vertical components of the backstay forces.

THE MATERIAL OF THE MEMBRANE

A wide range of materials is available for membrane structures, from standard woven fabrics to highly specialized polymer foils. Most use a woven cloth that has been coated with a synthetic material; the cloth provides the structural strength while the coating keeps the fabric airtight and water resistant. The three most commonly used materials for membrane structures are *PTFE-coated fiberglass fabric, PVC-coated polyester fabric*, and *EFTE foil*.

PTFE is the synthetic fluorpolymyer polytetrafluoroetheylene, widely known as Teflon™. It is the material of projects such as the Hajj Terminal, Figure 12.19. It is more expensive than the other coated fabrics but it has a longer life span and remains clean longer because of the slippery character of Teflon.

PVC-coated polyester fabric is often used for seasonal and temporary structures that open and close, because it folds well. It has also been used for permanent structures such as the Marschweg Stadium Roof in Germany, Figure 12.20. PVC-coated polyester is also less expensive than other membrane fabrics, but at the time of this writing it does not meet U.S. building code requirements for noncombustible materials and can be used only in smaller structures.

The previously described fabrics are typically white with varying degrees of translucency, and are used in large stretched anticlastic membranes. ETFE (ethylenetetrafluoroethylene) foil is transparent (but can be printed with patterns or colors) and is most widely used in inflated cushionlike panels held within

Figure 12.19 Constructed of a PTFE membrane, the world's largest roof structure covers the Hajj Terminal in Jeddah, Saudi Arabia, a colossal airport facility that is used to facilitate the travel of vast numbers of Muslim faithful during a short period of annual pilgrimage. Architects: Skidmore, Owings & Merrill; roof designer and structural engineer: Geiger Berger Associates.

Photo courtesy of the photographer, Horst Berger.

Figure 12.20 The PVC canopy of the Marschweg Stadium integrates membrane structures with funicular stabilizing cables. The structure was designed by engineers Schlaich Bergermann and architects von Gerkan Marg.

Photo copyright © Oliver Heissner; www.oliverheissner.com.

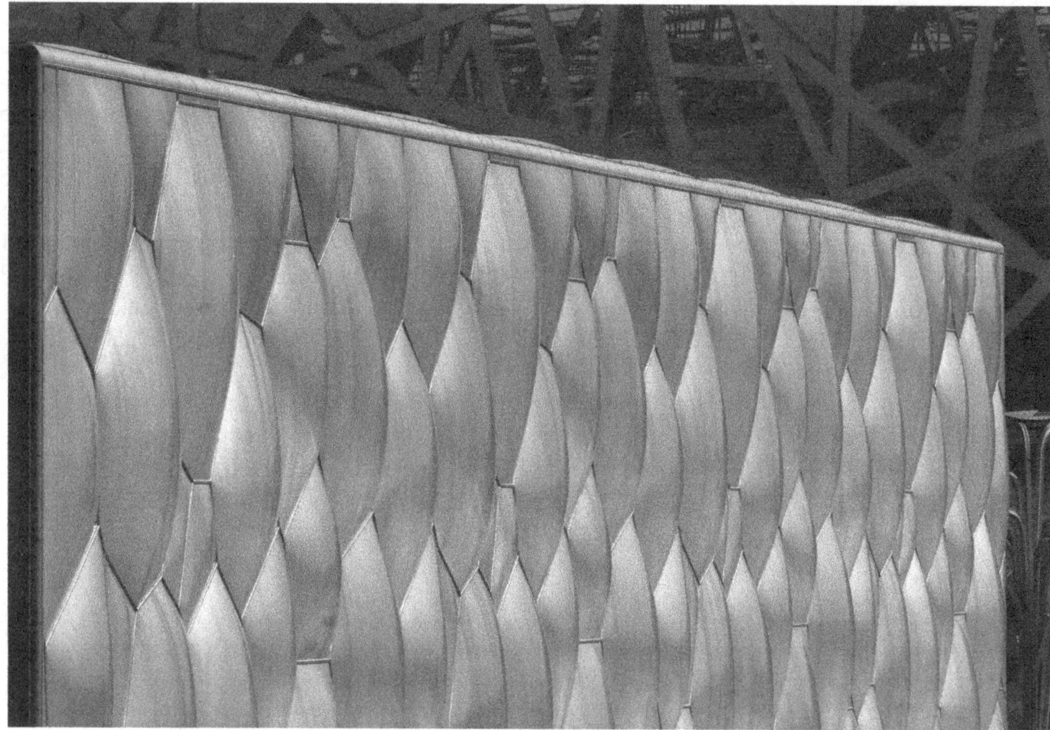

Figure 12.21 ETFE pillows used in the outer skin of the Water Cube for the Beijing Olympics are held between steel framing members, arranged in a repeating tessellation of polygons.

Photo courtesy of Sean McGowan.

a rigid primary structure, as has been done in the Chinese National Aquatics Center ("Water Cube"), which is shown in Figure 12.21.

We will choose PVC-coated polyester fabric for the pavilion because the structure is temporary and the membrane will be folded and unfolded many times.

ENVIRONMENTAL FACTORS

Though a single layer of fabric has little resistance to the flow of heat, its insulating qualities can be improved considerably with a fabric liner that is suspended about a foot below the structural fabric. A fabric structure can also achieve substantial energy savings through selective use of translucency and reflectivity. Translucency can be used to provide natural illumination, gather solar heat in winter, and cool the space at night in summer. A highly reflective fabric can reduce solar heat gain and conserve electricity that would otherwise be used for artificial cooling.

Stretched fabric surfaces are highly reflective of sound. Tensile membranes tend to disperse sound because of their anticlastic convex curvature. Air-supported structures and other synclastic membranes tend to focus sound. An acoustic inner liner can be installed to control sound reflection and help create good hearing conditions.

HORST BERGER

Horst Berger is a prolific engineer and builder of tensile fabric structures. From the Hajj Terminal in Jeddah for which he collaborated with Fazlur Khan and SOM (see page 341), to the Denver International Airport finished in 1994, Berger has expanded the scale and technology of how thin membranes can safely and beautifully enclose space. Yet Berger also believes that this approach is deeply rooted in the animal skin-covered tents and other structures from long ago. In contrast to what he terms the "brute-force-energy-waste approach" of much industrial building, he has developed membrane configurations anchored by cables and masts for a wide range of programs and locations worldwide. In his 1996 book on light structures, Berger sums up how form is a driving factor within his integrated approach:

> Curvature, following scientific laws, is a critical aspect of the structure. Consequently, the shape of the structure cannot be arbitrary but derives from the structural function. Form and function are one. Art and engineering are inseparable. The continuous fabric surface which is an integral part of the structure, serves also as the enclosure, separating the interior space from the outdoor environment, keeping out water and wind, reflecting most of the sun's heat, transmitting natural light, controlling the intrusion and reverberation of sound . . . and this clear and purposeful shape of the structure defines the space it encloses and gives the building its identity. . . . This integrated approach to building design is largely foreign to the segregation and specialization which pervades the design and construction process today, a result of the scientific advances of the industrial age. It resembles much more the ways of the pre-industrial architect. (Horst Berger, *Light Structures—Structures of Light*, Basel/Boston: Birkhauser, 1996, p. 3)

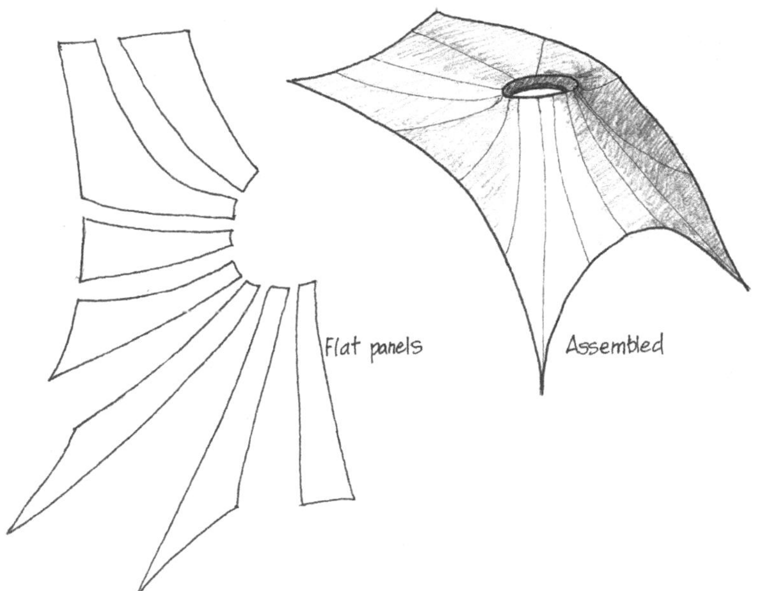

◀ **Figure 12.22** A sketch of one bay of the King's College pavilion showing the cutting patterns needed to create the three-dimensional membrane from two-dimensional fabric.

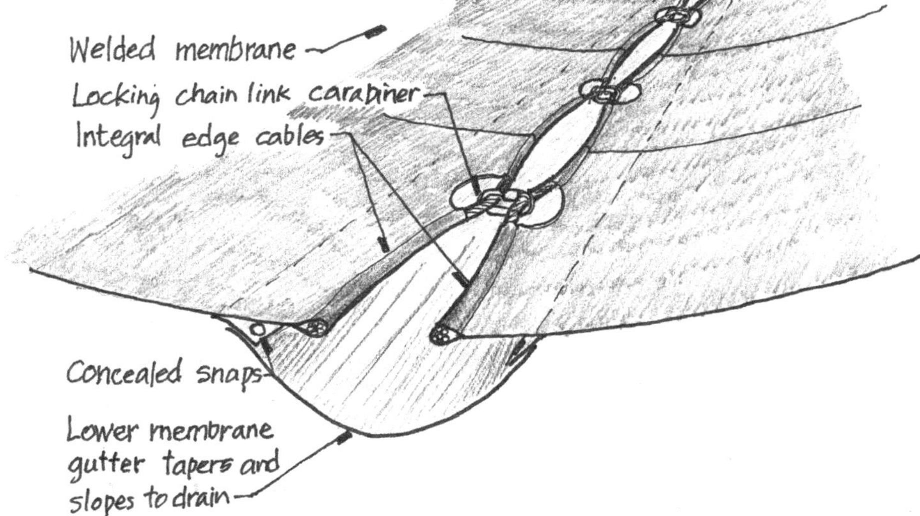

▶ **Figure 12.23** Adjacent bays of fabric are joined by steel connecting links between the two edge cables. A fabric gutter below the open seam catches and drains rainwater. Snaps allow the gutter to be opened for cleaning.

CUTTING PATTERNS

Our pavilion has five similar bays. The two end bays are mirror images of each other, and the three middle bays are identical to one another. Each of the five bays will be made up of multiple panels of fabric cut from two-dimensional sheets using a *cutting pattern*. Cutting patterns are developed by unrolling the shape from the 3D model of the project into flat shapes. Figure 12.22 shows one bay and its unrolled elements. These pieces will be welded together in the factory (a high-temperature process that makes a continuous integral connection between multiple fabric layers), but each bay must be rejoined to its neighbor each time the pavilion is erected. This is done with metal clips that join the edge cables of adjacent bays to one another. Because this detail is not watertight, a fabric gutter is fastened below the joint (Figure 12.23).

Erecting the pavilion involves joining the five bays of fabric on the ground, loosely anchoring the edge cables to the foundations, erecting the masts, and finally, tensioning the edge cables to arrive at a properly stressed, stable form.

DETAILING THE MEMBRANE

The critical membrane details occur at the tops of the masts and at the edge cables. The top of the mast collects all the forces in the fabric, so the stresses here tend to be high. The fabric can't actually come together at a point, because this would result in very high membrane forces that would rip the fabric. We need to design a ring for this location to gather the forces from the fabric and transmit them to the mast. It is usually necessary to reinforce the membrane in this region with multiple layers of fabric

Figure 12.24 Panel joints come together at the top of the mast. Where stresses are higher the fabric is reinforced in multiple layers.

Photo courtesy of Michael H. Ramage.

Figure 12.25 The Truck Depot for the Munich Office of Waste Management, completed in 1999, designed by architects Ackermann and Partner with engineers Schlaich Bergermann and Partner, covers 8,400 square meters. The tops of the conoid membranes are held on masts supported by tension rods; because there are no continuous compressive paths to the ground, this is a tensegrity structure.

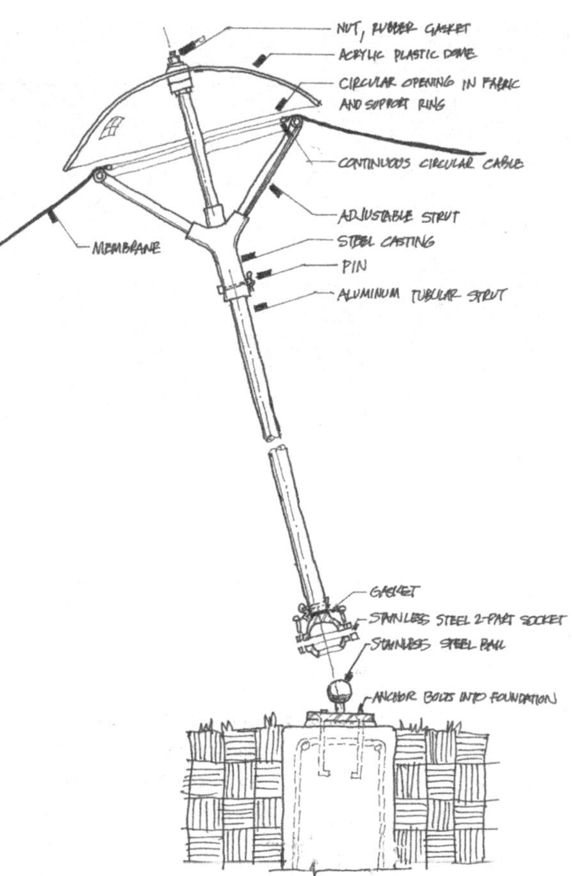

Figure 12.26 Forces from the fabric are gathered in a circular cable supported by a ring of metal tubing at the top of the mast. A domed plastic cap keeps rain away from the opening. At the base of the mast a two-part ball-and-socket joint facilitates construction and provides free movement. The lower collar of the socket prevents the mast from lifting off the base.

(Figure 12.24). The ring leaves the area around the top of the mast open, so we'll need to put a cap over it to keep the weather out, using a solution similar to that developed by architects Ackerman and Partner and structural engineers Schlaich Bergermann and Partner in their membrane-roofed truck depot for the Munich Office of Waste Management (Figure 12.25). In this project, the fabric around the perimeter of the hole is hemmed around a small circular cable. The circle of cable rests on a slightly larger circle of round metal tubing at the top of the mast. The tension in the fabric pulls the cable ring tightly against the tube support to create a stable load-bearing connection (Figure 12.26). Our structure, like all fabric structures, will tend to move more under wind loads than other types of long-span structures, so the masts need to be hinged for relatively large amounts of free movement in every direction.

The edge cables will need to be tightened considerably to prestress the fabric. This means that we will incorporate connections that have the potential for a large amount of adjustment built into them. The force at the bottom of each mast will be typically transferred downward into the foundations, but we need to account for the possibility that uplift caused by a high wind could reverse the forces. Since the span between masts is greater across the space than along its length, most of the movement will be across the width of the pavilion. However, we will need to provide for some movement in the other direction as well. A simple pin joint would allow for most of the necessary movement in the structure, but because the pavilion will be erected and taken down frequently, we will opt for a ball-and-socket

Figure 12.27 Cables run through sleeves at the edge of the membrane and are fixed to a steel plate to transfer the forces to the edge connection and the mast. The clamping action of the bolts and plates are important to spread the force over a large enough perimeter of fabric to reduce the stresses on the membrane to acceptable levels. The fitting by which it joins the connection on the mast allows for rotation, and the nuts allow for tightening and adjustment of the rods and the membrane. The stainless steel rods and fork connections are similar to those used in Chapter 1.

Photo courtesy of Michael H. Ramage.

Figure 12.28 The form of the Denver International Airport combines saddle and radial forms to echo the forms of the surrounding mountains. Architects: C. W. Fentriss, J. H. Bradburn & Associates; roof designer and structural engineer: Severud Associates, Horst Berger, principal consultant.

Photo courtesy of Horst Berger.

joint. This can act as a hinge in any direction, which will make assembly easier (Figure 12.26).

The last critical details relate to how the edge cables are attached to the fabric and how they are anchored to the foundations. The attachment to foundations is similar to that of the cable structure in Chapter 2, but with larger allowances for adjusting the length of the cables, and thereby their tension. Attachment of the cable to the fabric is usually done by means of clamps or sleeves. To avoid stress concentrations, these are designed to distribute the force over a wide area of fabric rather than to a single point. For simplicity and a clean appearance, we decide to pass the edge cables through a simple sleeve sewn (or welded) into the fabric (Figure 12.27).

MEMBRANE VARIATIONS

We have designed a stretched fabric membrane with radial forms supported by masts, but we could have used the same configuration of supports to design a ridge-and-valley structure, or even one with saddle shape (Figure 12.28). It is also common to stretch the fabric by connecting it to a rigid arch of steel or laminated wood, or to support it from overhead masts (Figure 12.29).

Figure 12.29 The Schlumberger Research Center in Cambridge, England, by architect Michael Hopkins (1979–1981) uses overhead masts to pull the membrane taut.

Photo courtesy of Michael H. Ramage.

GRAPHICAL ANALYSIS OF A CONE MEMBRANE

As we have seen, it is difficult to find form and forces for complex membrane configurations by hand, but we can approximate forces in some of the simpler forms using graphical techniques with which we are already familiar. For example, we can find forces for a radial cone membrane similar to the ones in Figure 12.24 or 12.28 by first deciding how high the mast will be and how far out the edge cables will be anchored (Figure 12.30a), which gives us a closing string (Figure 12.30b). The membrane is radial, so we can divide the height into a suitable number of circular hoops that will pull inward. The membrane will be prestressed, so we don't need to deal with any external loads, just those induced by stretching the fabric. The tension in a radially loaded circular arc is equal to the load per unit length of cable multiplied by the radius. In this case, we know the tension, because a typical prestress for membrane fabric is 1 kN/m, with which we can determine the inward pull at each hoop point, which works out to be π multiplied by the prestress. We will round this to 3 kN/m.

We have drawn the closing string as a straight line from the ground anchor to the top of the mast and we have established where the hoops lie on that string, so we can now draw the load line as a series of horizontal 3 kN forces. Then we establish a trial pole and a set of rays, from which we construct a trial funicular polygon (Figure 12.30b). We construct a ray parallel to the closing string of the trial funicular polygon (shown as a broken line) to establish the centroid of all the forces on the load line. From its point of intersection with the load line, we draw a line parallel to the final closing string. The intersection of this line with the vertical line of the mast is the final pole. This lets us develop our final funicular polygon, from which we can measure the force in the mast. We have to remember to multiply it by 2, since there is an equivalent semicircle of fabric on the other side, for a total force in the mast of 28 kN. Adjusting the

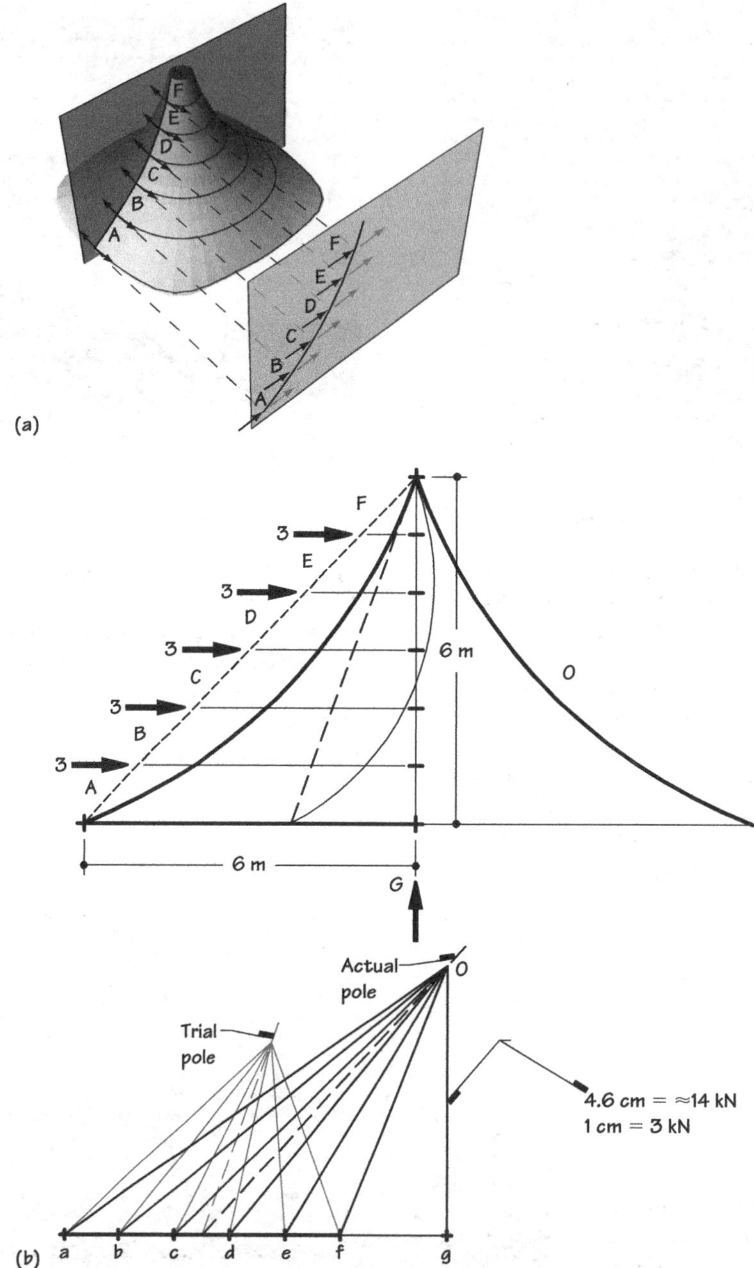

Figure 12.30 (a) A three-dimensional diagram of a radial membrane; (b) load line, trial pole, and funicular form for the membrane. The complete membrane fully surrounds the mast, so the mast loads are doubled.

location of the funicular pole can indicate the effect of changing the amount of prestress on the force in the mast.

CONCRETE AND MASONRY SHELLS

As we stated initially, a *shell* is the inverted, compressive equivalent of a tension membrane. There are as many possible shapes for shells as there are architects and engineers who design them, but most fall into a few categories. Shells with single curvature, as we saw in Chapter 3, are relatively straightforward to design and construct, but they are more susceptible to buckling than shells with double curvature, so they must be corrugated, folded, or ribbed to add stiffness.

Double curvature opens up a world of possibilities, ranging from simple domes to complex combinations of *hyperbolic paraboloids* (Figure 12.31). The double curvature gives a wider variety of possible load paths for the forces that result from different loading conditions. It also imparts greater depth to a structure, giving the designer greater freedom in shaping the shell. But significant constraints to the form remain, including ones that relate to buckling and ease of construction.

The Spanish/Mexican architect Felix Candela was an imaginative, extremely prolific shell builder.

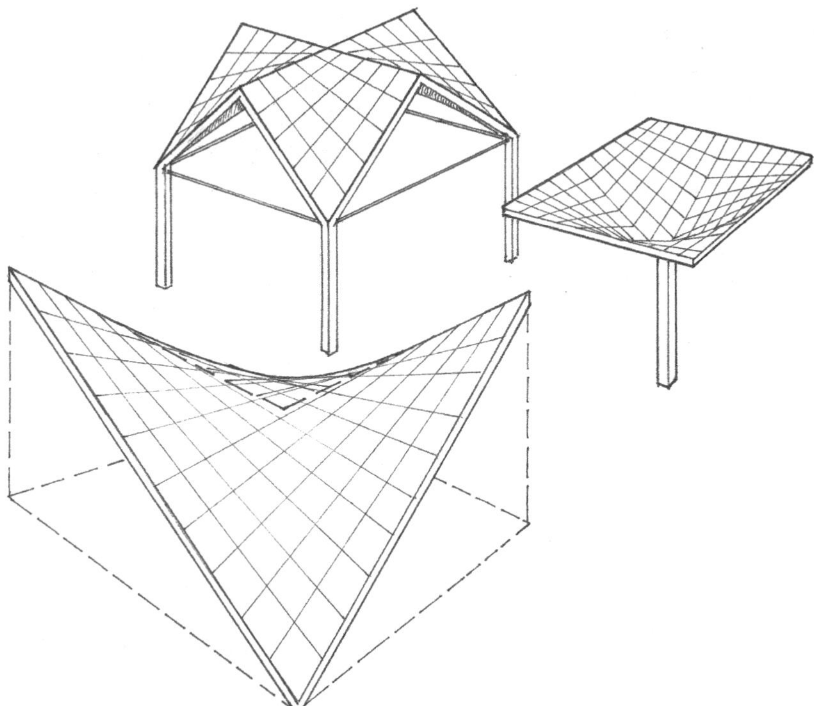

Figure 12.31 Hyperbolic paraboloids are generated as surfaces ruled by straight lines, which facilitates construction of their formwork; they can be combined in many configurations to form anticlastic shapes for shells.

FELIX CANDELA

Felix Candela (1910–1997) was educated as an architect in his native Madrid, Spain. A champion skier in his youth, he took an interest during school in how structural calculations predict strength and collapse. After fighting in the Spanish Civil War and being captured, he was sent to Mexico in 1939, where he continued to develop his interests in reinforced concrete. There he rapidly acquired a reputation as a fluent designer, contractor, and builder of thin concrete shells. Candela pioneered innovations in double-curvature surfaces, chiefly hyperbolic paraboloids. He insisted on designing structures that correspond directly to how they transfer forces, rather than shaping the form arbitrarily and then trying to fit shells or surfaces to conform. Nonetheless, his structural exuberance is apparent in the tour-de-force Xochimilco restaurant (1958) with its dramatic vaults and rotational symmetry. In the beginning, he built vaults primarily for factories and other utilitarian uses. These led to increasingly complex and sculptural public and ecclesiastical buildings, notably the Iglesia de la Virgen Milagrosa in Navarte (1955). Nearly all of the more than 300 structures Candela completed were built during the 1950s and early 1960s. He lived in the United States from 1978 until his death. For all of Candela's mathematical ability, he tended to emphasize design over calculation, as he stated in the 1963 biography compiled by Colin Faber: "[S]cience goes on analyzing . . . but art, the synthetic process, pools many things together so as to get the complete vision."

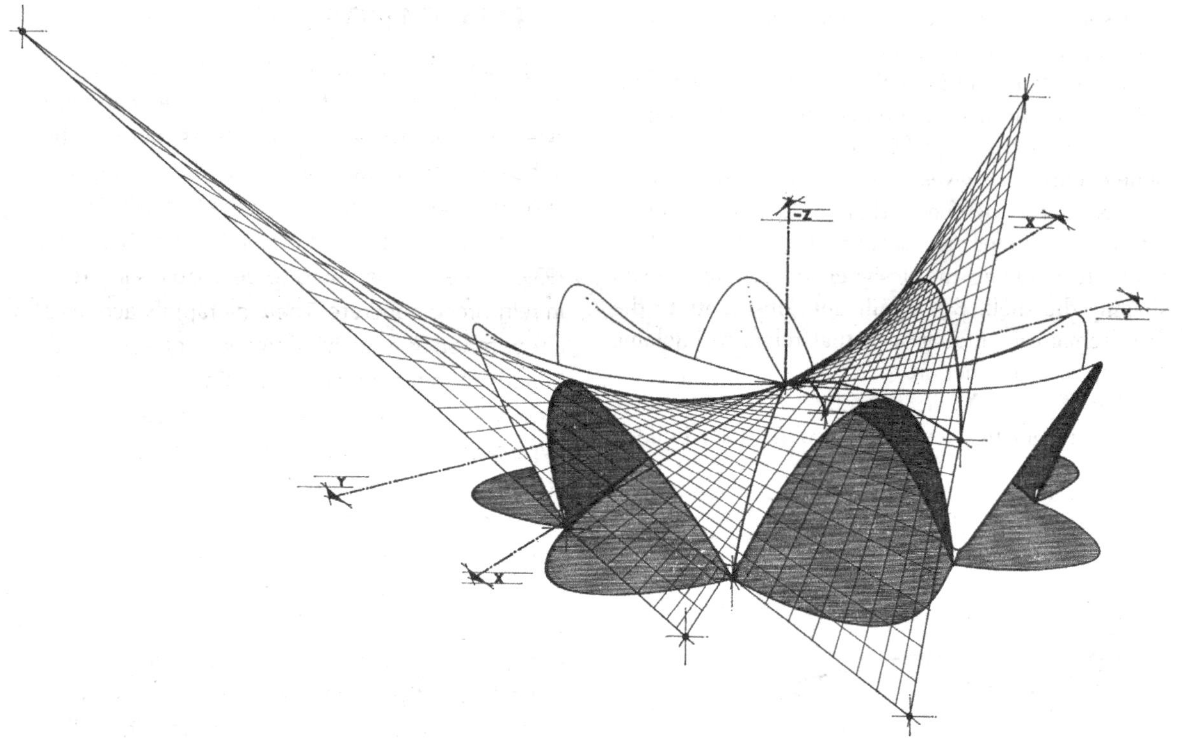

Figure 12.32 The roof of the restaurant Los Manantiales in Xochimilco, Mexico, constructed in 1958 by architect Felix Candela, is a concrete shell in the shape of three intersecting hyperbolic paraboloids. Notice the skillful way in which Candela combined the shapes and truncated them to produce the gracefully curving shape.

Photo courtesy of Javier Yaya Tur, La Fundación CV Ciudad de las Artes y las Ciencias.

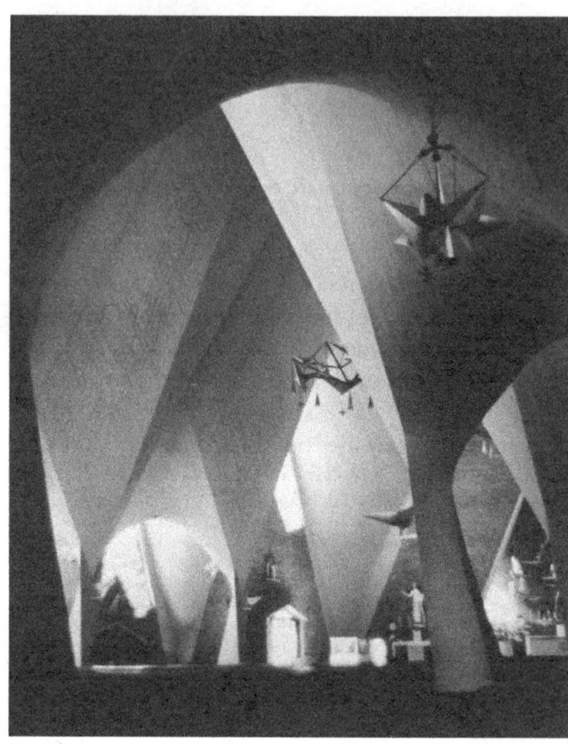

Figure 12.33 The Iglesia de la Virgen Milagrosa in Narvarte, Mexico, is a virtuoso performance in the use of hyperbolic paraboloids; Candela designed and built it in 1953–1955.

Source: Colin Faber, *Candela/The Shell Builder*, New York: Reinhold, 1963.

Nearly all his shells were made up of ruled surfaces, which are defined by straight lines, so that their formwork was relatively easy and economical to build. The hyperbolic paraboloid, which is a hyperbolic combination of opposing parabolic surfaces, is one such form, seen in his Xochimilco restaurant and other projects (Figures 12.32, 12.33).

The Swiss engineer Heinz Isler (b. 1926) has pioneered the use of hanging fabric models to find form and load paths for concrete shells (Figure 12.34). Measurements taken from his models serve as the basis for many of his projects. Construction of Isler's shells could be difficult because their shapes are not easily defined, but Isler has succeeded in making them economical through clever reuse of formwork.

ANALYSIS

Structural analysis of shells is a crucial part of their design. Model building plays an important part in this, as we can use inverted tensile models to suggest shapes for structures in compression. This is fun and informative to do in the design studio, and it can also be simulated on the computer to great effect (Figure 12.35). An important difference between the upturned hanging models of fabric for compression shells and tensioned membrane structures is that the hanging models derive their shape from gravity-induced dead loads, while membrane structures find their form through the equilibrium of their prestressing forces. The finding of forces by means of membrane theory is a highly developed and specialized branch of engineering, dealing with stresses, bending, and buckling.

Figure 12.34 The Norwich Sports Village Hotel, Norfolk, England, by Heinz Isler (1991) is a repeating series of thin-shell vaults spanning 48 m each.

Photo courtesy of Michael H. Ramage.

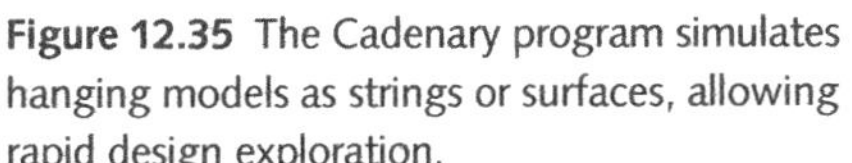

Figure 12.35 The Cadenary program simulates hanging models as strings or surfaces, allowing rapid design exploration.

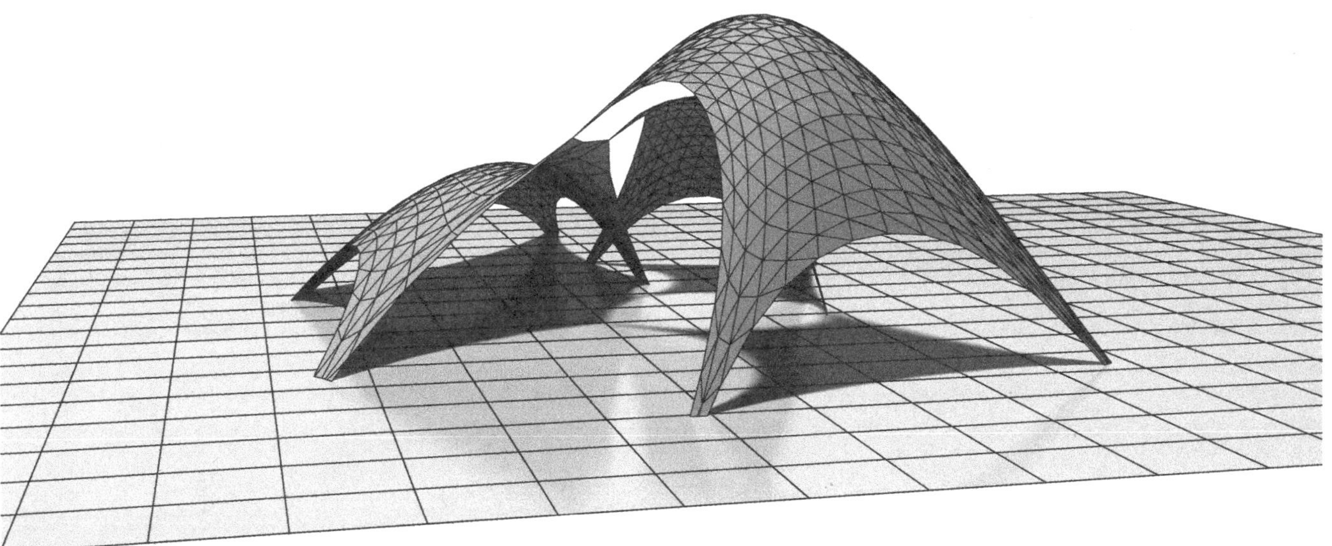

PNEUMATIC STRUCTURES

Air-supported structures are made of fabric that is stretched in two directions and held up by positive air pressure within the space enclosed by the membrane (Figure 12.36). The pressure is supplied by the fans that heat, cool, and ventilate the building. The required air pressures are so low that they are scarcely discernable by people entering or leaving the building, but they are high enough (5 to 10 lb per square foot, or 0.25 to 0.50 kPa) that they would make ordinary swinging doors impossible to open. For this reason, revolving doors, whose operation is unaffected by internal pressure, and which maintain a continual seal against loss of air, are usually used for access in these structures.

The fabric of an air-supported structure is prestressed by its internal air pressure to prevent flutter. A downward-pulling cable net is often employed to shape the structure. The fabric spans between the cables, and the fabric and the cables pull up on the foundations with a total force that is equal to the internal air pressure multiplied by the horizontal area of ground within the pressurized space. The supporting elements and foundations must be designed to resist this uplift. Wind causes suction forces to occur on many areas of an air-supported structure, which results in additional tension in the fabric and cables.

The downward forces from wind or snow load on an air-supported structure are resisted directly by the internal air pressure pushing outward against them. Theoretically, this places no force in the membrane, but in actuality, external loads vary from one part of the structure to another due to drifting snow or the dynamics of the wind, and tearing of the fabric can ensue. In geographic areas where snow loads are larger than acceptable internal pressures, snow must be actively removed from the roof. Failure to do so has led to unplanned deflations of several air-supported roofs.

In theory, air-supported structures are not limited in span. In practice, flutter and perimeter uplift forces restrict their span to a few hundred meters, but this is sufficient to house entire sport stadiums. For safety, the outer edges of most air-supported roofs are placed at a level that is well above the floor level within. Thus, if the roof should deflate because of fan failure, inadequate snow removal, or air leakage, the roof fabric will hang in suspension at a height well above the floor of the building.

SHELLS AND MEMBRANES REVISITED

A large number of both shells and membranes were constructed for a wide range of building programs in the twentieth century. Tensile membranes continue to proliferate, but shells are seldom built today. One reason for this is that the economies of material in thin-shell construction have been offset by the expense of labor to construct their complex formwork. Another reason is that the wide variety of temporary and permanent applications of tensile structures has led to their incorporation in combination with other systems, such as trussed and cable-stayed components.

But the material innovations that we have already discussed have been themselves a major reason that tensile membranes have flourished, sometimes even as enclosure elements for domed or shell-like compressive forms (Figure 12.38). The capability of single- and double-layer membranes to allow specific translucencies to block or transmit radiant heat and conserve heat gain, to accommodate natural ventilation and thus achieve energy savings over conventional enclosures, are all innovations made possible by new fabrication technologies and by the inherent properties of the materials themselves.

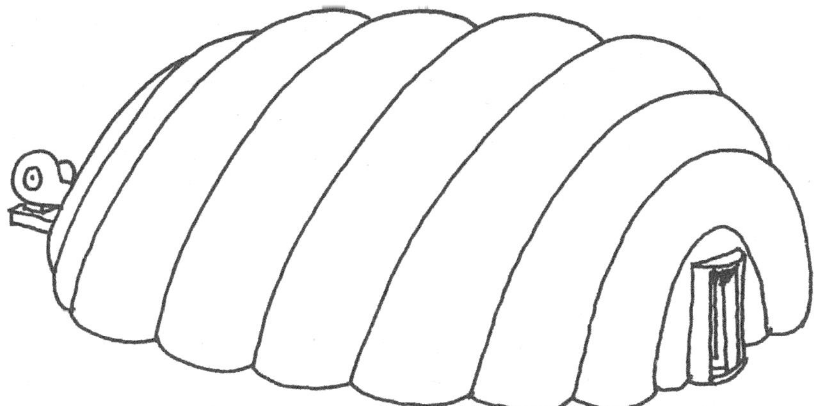

Figure 12.36 Sketch of an air-supported structure. The structure is fundamentally a large bubble that is held up by air pressure in the occupied space beneath. Cables pull down on the membrane to induce small-radius double curvature that resists membrane flutter.

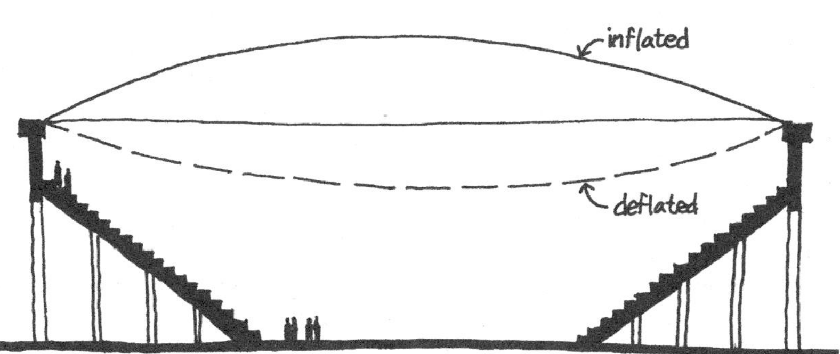

Figure 12.37 This section shows how an air-supported structure can keep occupants safe even if the membrane should collapse.

Figure 12.38 The Eden Project, Cornwall, England, uses ETFE pillows as insulation and skin. Creative Commons license. Photo by S. Murray.

Exercises

1. Construction was started more than a decade ago on a bandstand in a city park. For political reasons, the project was cancelled shortly after it began, leaving five concrete post footings in a regular pentagonal pattern. A circle drawn through these footings would have a diameter of 32 ft. Now the project has been resurrected. The city has commissioned you to design a concrete shell roof for the bandstand. In discussions with city representatives, you are being asked to use the five footings to support a roof made of five identical concrete hyperbolic paraboloids. Develop a shape for this roof in plan and section. Use the drawing technique from Figure 12.31 to indicate the generating lines for the shell surfaces. You may make the shells as tall as you wish, but be sure to leave sufficient headroom for passage of musicians and other users.

2. You're designing a group of a dozen cottages to be aligned along the beach at a seaside resort in the Caribbean. You have talked the owner into an innovative scheme that features a tentlike roof on a single mast for each cottage. The roof serves only to keep off sun and rain. Wooden structures will be built beneath each roof to provide bathrooms, kitchens, floors, outer walls, partitions, and other amenities. Mosquito netting will be used to span between the rigid walls and the flexible membrane. Use pantyhose or T-shirt fabric to develop the form of a typical cottage. Build a model that makes clear how the fabric roof and rigid elements join one another. Model or draw in perspective the appearance of the group of cottages.

Experiment at large scale or full scale with a few yards of stretch fabric and a ball of strong twine. Work with the uncut fabric for a while to develop initial ideas. For vertical support, work within a grove of small trees, or use lengths of bamboo or wood or steel electrical conduit tubing. Buy or make tent pegs to hold things down. You might also work in your room, tying the fabric to backs of chairs, ends of beds, or plastic gallon jugs filled with water. (Do not tie anything to lighting fixtures!) Your goal is to produce a fabric enclosure that is pleasing to inhabit. After a period of experimentation, cut and sew the fabric to tailor it to your design, then finish the structure and invite your friends to see it. Make measured drawings of the structure at a scale of 1 in. to the foot (1:12 or 1:10) or larger.

3. Make an inverted hanging model of a concrete shell roof of your design. A good way to start is to place a rigid base of plywood, OSB, or homasote across the backs of two upright wooden or metal chairs. Attach cotton string or T-shirt fabric to the underside of the base with push pins. The fabric will produce full surfaces directly. The string will have to be draped back and forth in many directions, or tied into a grid configuration, to produce surfaces. You may find it useful to insert rigid struts such as matchsticks or bamboo skewers into your hanging structure to get the shape you want.

As you close in on a shape that you would like to create, it may facilitate your work to cut a large hole in the board, using a hand-held power jigsaw. This will give you good access to both the outer and inner surfaces of the model. Make the cutout the exact shape and size of the ground plane of the roof, lowering the fabric or string net through the hole and pulling it up and down until you like the shape.

To rigidify the model, try one of the following:

a. On a cold winter day, saturate the fabric or string with water, then take it outdoors, hang it in its desired position, and allow it to freeze.

b. Saturate the fabric or string with white glue slightly diluted with warm water. This will drip, harden, and make a mess that is difficult to remove, so cover the floor and furnishings with newspapers or plastic drop cloths.

c. Saturate the model with a runny mix of plaster of Paris. Plaster of Paris hardens very, very quickly, so you may wish to purchase and use a set-retarding admixture.

When the model has been made rigid, turn it over. This is the shell you have designed. All the elements that were tensile when it was a hanging model are now compressive. Any matchsticks or other rigid elements in the original model are now acting in tension.

Key Terms and Concepts

membrane
fabric
taut
mast
cable
anticlastic curvature
prestress
pretension
Platonic solids
triangulation
cable net
PTFE-coated fiberglass fabric
PVC-coated polyester fabric
EFTE foil
cutting pattern
shell
hyperbolic paraboloid
pneumatic structures /air-inflated structures
air-supported structures

Further Resources

Bechthold, Martin. *Innovative Surface Structures.* New York, NY: Taylor and Francis, 2008. This volume discusses recent developments in structural surfaces in tension and compression.

Berger, Horst. *Light Structures—Structures of Light.* Basel/Boston: Birkhauser, 1996. This book presents the concepts and strategies of Berger, a pioneer of advanced contemporary membrane structures. Simple membrane design software "surfaceform" is available from www.HorstBerger.net.

Faber, Colin. *Candela/The Shell Builder.* New York, NY: Reinhold, 1963. A comprehensive monograph on the shells of Felix Candela, with details of their structure, design, and construction.

Koch, Klaus-Michael, with Karl J. Habermann. *Membrane Structures.* Munich/New York: Prestel Verlag, 2004. *Membrane Structures* presents the technology and design of this structural type and a useful collection of case studies.

Lewis, W.J. *Tension Structures: Form and Behavior.* London: Thomas Telford, 2003. This book contains details of the mathematics and computation used for complete engineering of membrane structures.

www.birdair.com: Bird-Air has been involved with the design and construction of many significant membrane structures.

www.cadenary.com: Cadenary software offers the opportunity to construct digital hanging models of strings or surfaces.

www.formfinder.at: This software allows simple exploration of membrane forms, and contains a gallery of projects and details.

CHAPTER 13

Structural Materials

- *Granular materials*
- *Solid materials*
- *How materials break*
- *Transmission of forces in solid materials*
- *Characteristics of a good structural material*
- *Common structural materials*
- *Concepts of stress and strain*
- *Factors of safety*

Structures are dependent on materials that have the necessary capacities and properties to bear their loads. Most structures for buildings and bridges are made of wood, masonry, steel, or concrete. Aluminum, stainless steel, various plastics, and glass play secondary structural roles. New, stronger materials that are based on fibers of glass, carbon, or aramid are gradually becoming practical. What qualities do these materials possess that make them suitable for use in structures? Each has its own attributes we must learn and secrets we must discover in order to design safely and imaginatively with it.

GRANULAR MATERIALS: LESSONS FROM THE BEACH

We can learn some of the secrets of structural materials by reflecting upon our experiences with building sand castles on the beach (Figure 13.1). Sand generally

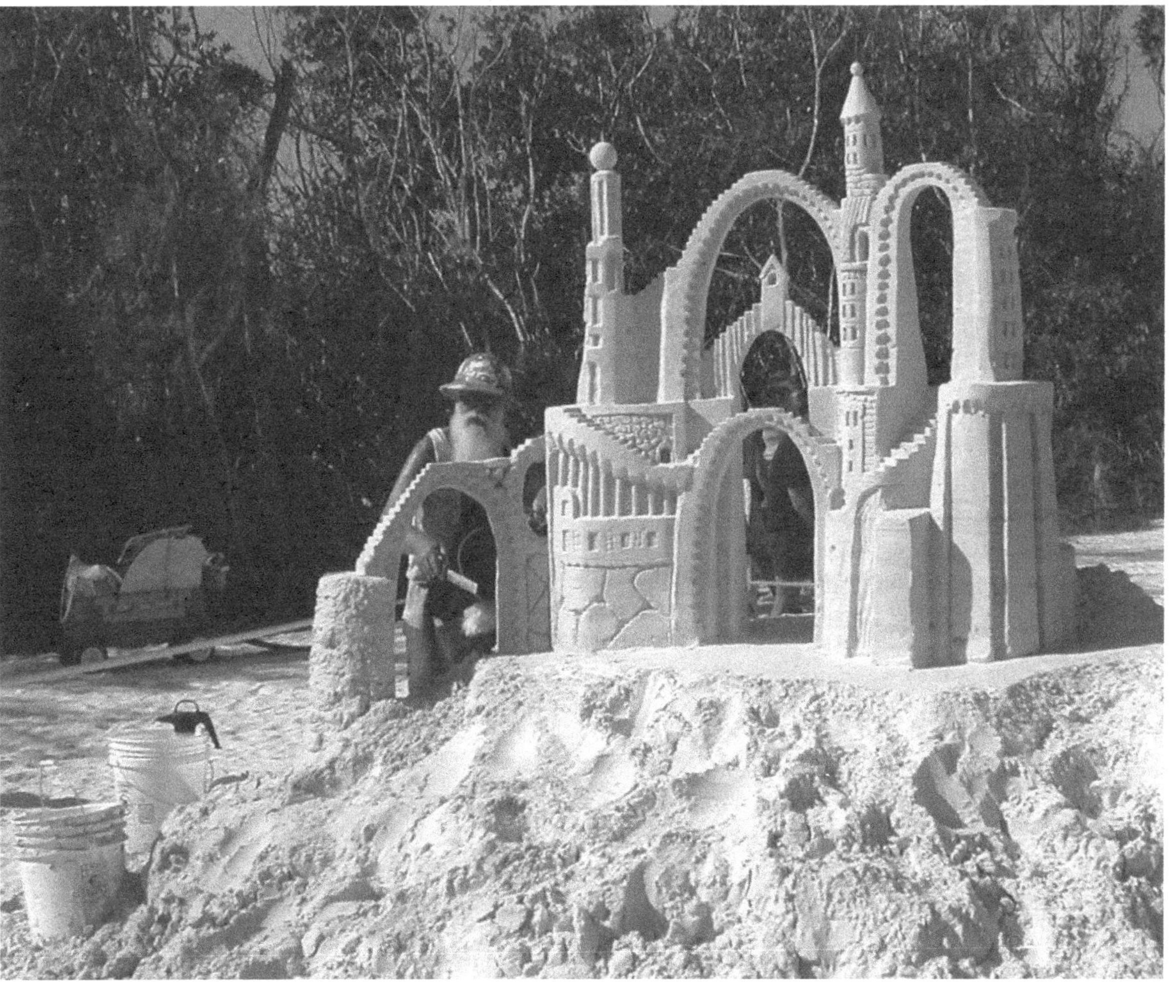

Figure 13.1 Sandcastles on the beach.

Photo courtesy of Rev. Leslie Penrose, JustHope.org.

consists of small, angular particles of quartz (silicon dioxide). Imagine four buckets side by side (Figure 13.2): The first one contains dry sand. The second bucket contains sand saturated with an excess of water, whereas the sand in the third bucket is moistened just enough to coat all its grains with water. The fourth bucket has no bottom in it, and contains dry sand.

When we invert the first bucket, the dry sand pours out of it into a conical pile whose slopes grow to a maximum inclination known as the *angle of repose* (Figure 13.3a). Any sand that we add to the pile after the angle of repose has been reached will trigger a small avalanche that will bring the pile back to the same angle.

Dry, granular materials like sand experience *internal friction* that is created by the coarseness and angularity of the individual particles. Internal friction produces forces that counteract the sliding tendency of granules on slopes. When the frictional forces just balance the sliding tendencies of the granules, the mound of material reaches its angle of repose, which is more or less constant for each material. A material with a higher internal friction has a higher angle of repose. A material with a very low internal friction, such as a quantity of small steel balls, will flow almost like water and will never accumulate into a pile.

Piled, dry sand can support weight. We could flatten the top of the conical pile of sand that we have just created and place a bucket filled with water in the middle of the flattened area to apply a downward force. If the force is not too large, the sand will bear it without distress. If the force is too large, the sand will redistribute itself in response to the pressure, allowing the bucket to sink.

If we invert the second bucket, the saturated sand disperses like a watery soup (Figure 13.3b). The excess water has flooded the pores between the granules and acts as a lubricant, turning the sand into a semiliquid *slurry* that flows readily. Sand that contains an excess of water is said to be in a *quick condition*, meaning that it acts more like a liquid than a granular solid. It will not support even a small load, but it presents an important lesson because quicksand is fairly commonly encountered in excavations for buildings: It occurs where groundwater rises up through the sand and transforms it into a quivering, jellylike material. Vibrations from excavation machinery exacerbate the problem. Quicksand can be remedied by stopping the flow of water or providing adequate drainage to remove the excess water from the sand. As soon as the soil is drained, it becomes stable and can bear substantial loads. *Silt,* which is soil that is made up of granular particles considerably smaller than grains of sand, is also capable of becoming quick.

If we invert the third bucket carefully and lift it away, the damp sand that it leaves behind retains the

Figure 13.2 Four buckets of sand: (a) dry sand; (b) sand completely saturated with an excess of water; (c) moist sand; (d) dry sand in a bucket that has no bottom.

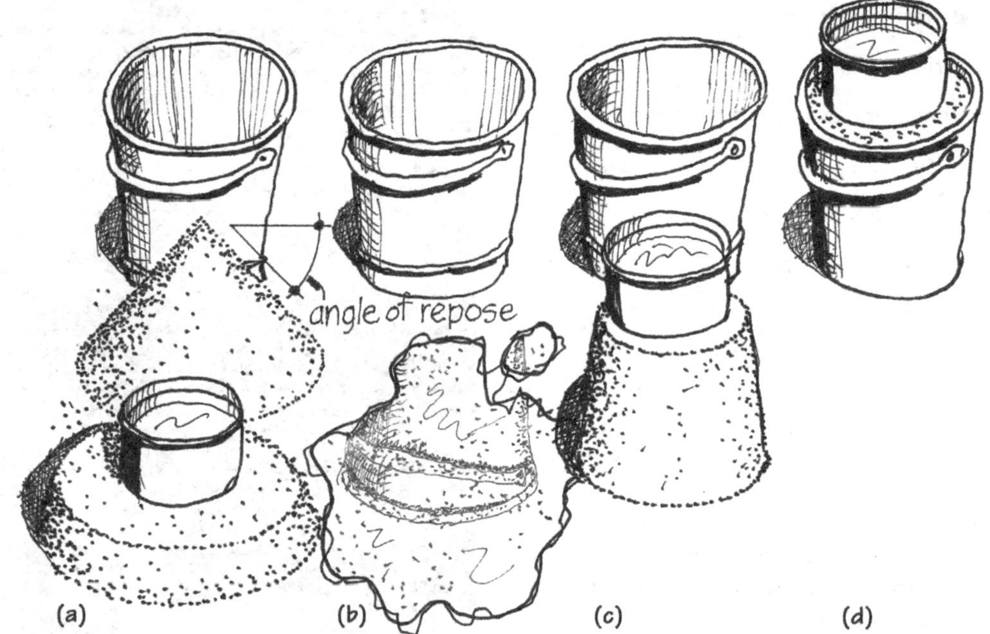

Figure 13.3 (a) When the dry sand is turned out of its bucket, it forms a conical pile with a characteristic angle of repose. If flattened, the pile can support a weight. (b) The saturated sand makes a gritty puddle. (c) The moist sand coheres and retains the shape given it by the bucket. (d) The bottomless bucket confines the dry sand so that it is able to support a considerable load.

shape of the bucket (Figure 13.3c). The inclination of the sides of the pile of damp sand greatly exceeds the angle of repose of dry sand. In fact, we can even cut sand away with a shovel or knife to make the sides vertical, or remove sand from the bottom to dig a tunnel from one side to the other. This is why damp sand is the preferred material for sand castles. It can exhibit this superior performance because it is held together by the cohesive action of thin films of water that just coat the granules and span the gaps between them. The *surface tension* of the water pulls together adjacent grains of sand and bonds them into a fairly cohesive mass that has a small but useful amount of tensile strength.

The fourth bucket, the one that has no bottom, contains dry sand that would reshape itself into a fragile conical pile if we lifted the bucket. But with the bucket in place around it, the sand can support a surprisingly heavy load (Figure 13.3d). We could even stand and exert all of our weight on it; the sand will support our weight without experiencing any substantial deflection or flow. The dry sand in this bucket is no different from the sand that we poured out of the first bucket, but the bucket provides *confinement*, a pushing inward from without.

Material that is pushed or pulled in two different directions experiences *biaxial stress* (Figure 13.4). Confinement of the sand by the bucket, together with the application of a load to the top of the sand, goes one step further to establish a *multiaxial stress field* that compresses the sand in all directions. The lateral compression introduced by the confining force works to increase the strength of the material against the load that acts on it. Its effect is the same as that of the thin film of water that pulls a mass of sand together from within: In either case, the granules are prevented from sliding so that they can act together to support a load.

Confinement by the walls of a bucket is much stronger than the weak cohesive pull of the water film in damp sand. But if we were to substitute for the water film a strong cementing substance such as epoxy plastic or *portland cement*, the cementing substance, once cured, would exert a cohesive pull that might be equal or superior to the confining push of the bucket.

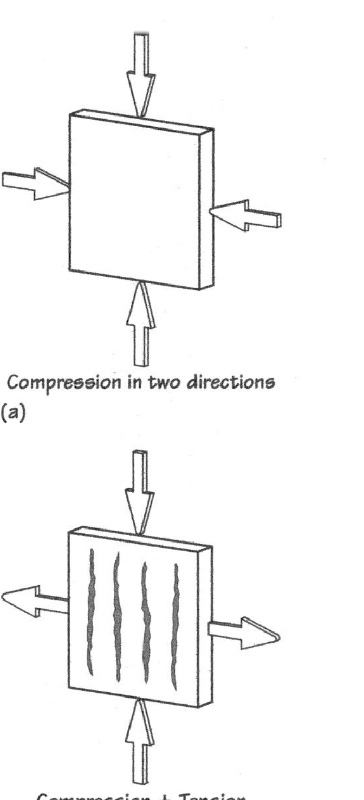

Figure 13.4 Biaxial stress. Compressive stress along two perpendicular axes strengthens the material. Tensile stress along one of the axes tends to pull the material apart and weakens it.

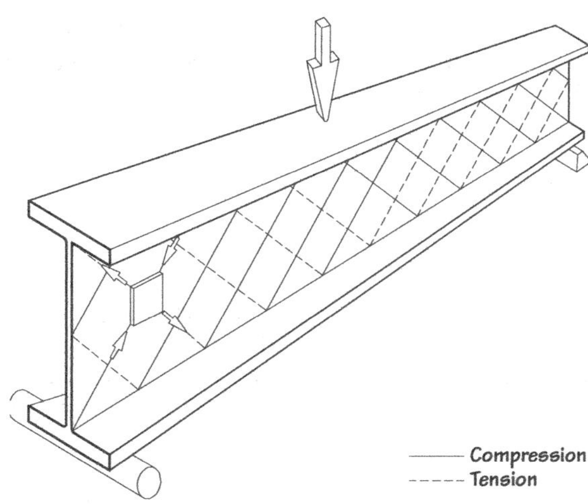

Figure 13.5 The web of a steel wide-flange beam is in a state of biaxial stress, tensile in one direction and compressive in the other. The allowable stress in the web is, therefore, only about two-thirds of that in the flanges, which experience uniaxial stress only.

Confined sand is a rather good soil on which to place building foundations. It has a moderately high allowable stress under a footing, and its properties are little affected by water, even by saturation, so long as the water is stagnant and confinement is provided by surrounding soil.

If the lateral force in a biaxial stress field is tension rather than compression, it weakens the material by pulling apart its granules or crystals. Such a state of biaxial stress exists in the webs of beams, where diagonal forces of tension and compression cross one another at right angles, reducing the strength of the material in this part of the member (Figure 13.5). This biaxial stress reaches a maximum value near the supports of the beam, where web forces are highest; we will reencounter this phenomenon in Chapter 17.

A reinforced concrete column illustrates the effects of both *confinement* and *cohesion* between particles (Figure 13.6). The granules of aggregate in concrete are held tightly together by needlelike crystals of hardened portland cement that exert a strong inward-pulling action within the mass of the column (Figure 13.6a). This action may be enhanced by adding short fibers of high-strength material to the concrete mixture. The aggregate granules are also held by the external, confining effect of the vertical reinforcing bars and closely spaced steel spiral or ties that wrap around the vertical reinforcing bars (Figure 13.6b). The combined effect of the cement crystals and the confining steel is to make the column far stronger than either of them acting alone. Grid reinforcing in layers is another option that can have a similar net effect as external confinement; the spiral pushes from without, whereas the grid pulls from within the column itself (Figure 13.6c).

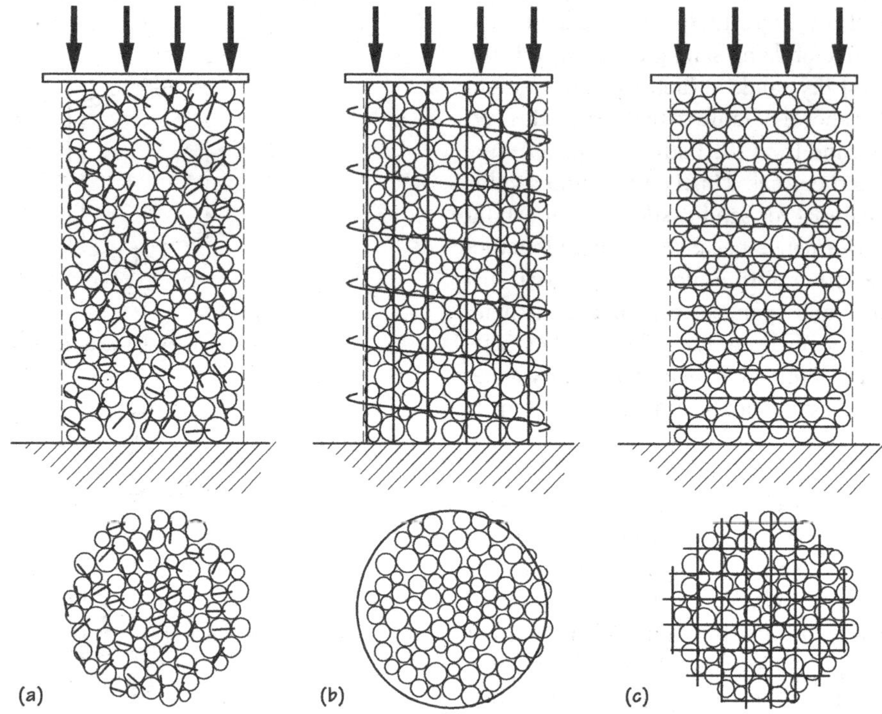

▸**Figure 13.6** Three ways of strengthening a granular material: (a) Short fibers mixed into the material add tensile strength by tying the particles together. (b) Confinement may be provided by means of an external cage around the material, such as the steel spiral and vertical bars of a typical concrete column. (c) Layers of mesh or fabric provide confinement, which strengthens the material.

◂**Figure 13.7** Eight concrete-filled steel pipes, each 7.5 ft in diameter, act as columns for the core of this tall building in Seattle. Each pipe provides confinement for the concrete that it contains, increasing its strength dramatically despite a total lack of steel reinforcing bars.

Photo courtesy of Skilling Ward Magnusson Barkshire.

Some tall buildings are supported by *composite columns* that consist of a cylindrical steel shell that is filled with concrete. Composite columns up to 10 ft in diameter have been used in buildings of about 60 stories (Figure 13.7). No reinforcing bars are used in the concrete except at points where beams and girders bring their loads to the column. The strength of the column results from a combination of the compressive strength of the concrete and the confining effect of the steel shell.

Internal friction and cohesive forces that include the bonding force of water impart structural capabilities to earthen materials to the extent that we can build earthen embankments to support roadways, railroads,

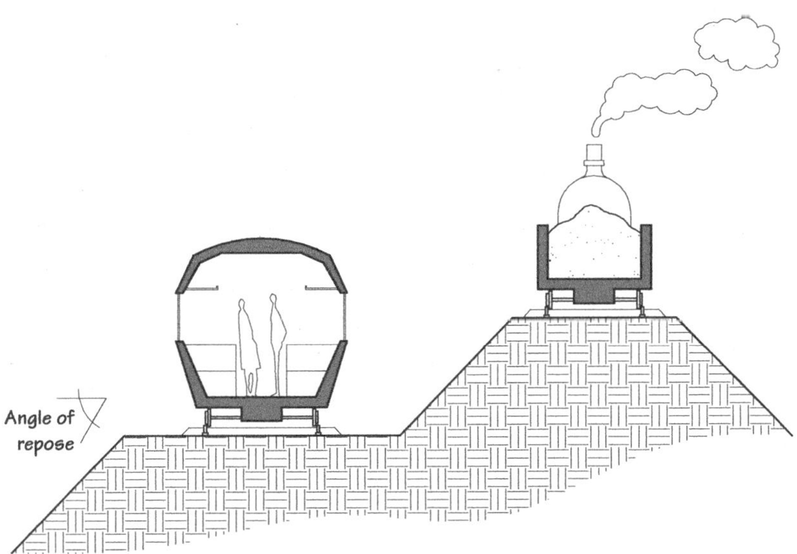

Figure 13.8 For soil stability, embankments should be designed with slopes less than the angle of repose of the material.

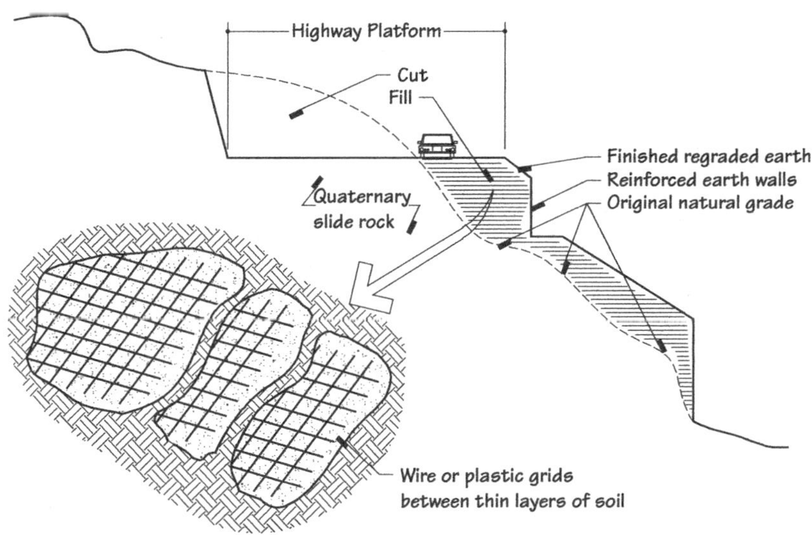

Figure 13.9 Multiple horizontal geogrids made of galvanized metal or durable plastics can be inserted between thin layers of compacted earth to provide confinement that is not governed by angle of repose.

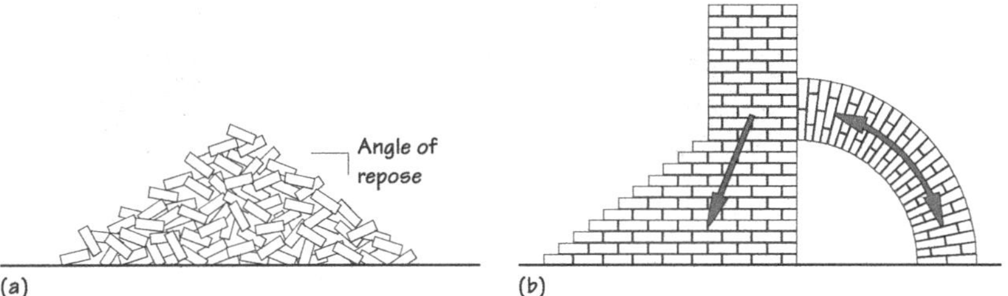

Figure 13.10 Rectangular granules such as bricks behave much like dry sand unless they are stacked in orderly horizontal layers, whereupon they become self-stabilizing. Bricks in an arch are stable in part because their broad surfaces are perpendicular to the line of thrust.

and even buildings (Figure 13.8). Such embankments must be constructed of suitable soils (avoiding, for example, clay soils that become semiliquid when saturated with rain), and the angles of the slopes must be shallower than the angle of repose. Steeper slopes may be stabilized by placing multiple layers of steel or plastic mesh horizontally between thin layers of compacted soil (Figure 13.9). The mesh acts in tension to confine the soil, thereby mimicking the actions of roots of trees and plants that have stabilized slopes since the beginning of time.

If a truckload of bricks is dumped in a heap, the randomly oriented bricks will exert a considerable internal friction and will form a conical pile with an angle of repose that is characteristic of the particular bricks (Figure 13.10a). If we had previously coated the bricks with a slippery plastic, or if we had rounded off the sharp edges and corners of all the bricks, the angle of repose would be lower. On the other hand, if we stack the bricks so that their largest surfaces are perpendicular to the directions of compressive forces, even without using mortar we can construct a variety of durable walls (Figure 13.10b). This is because in the act of stacking the bricks at right angles to the paths of forces, we minimize or eliminate the tendency of the bricks to slide past one another. If we perversely constructed a column whose courses of bricks sloped at a 45° angle, it could easily

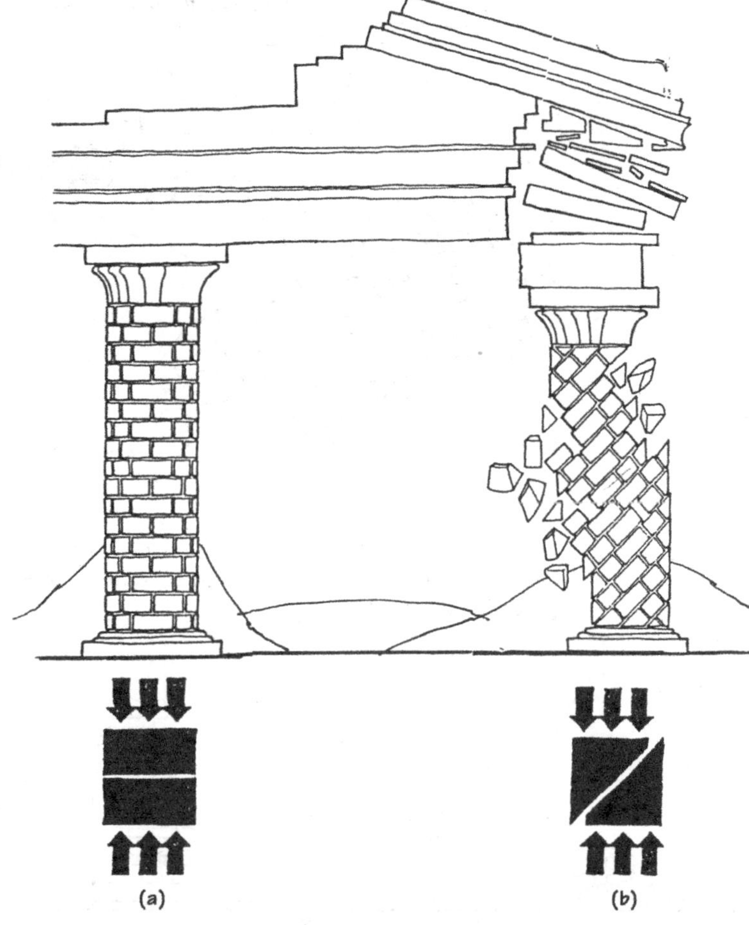

Figure 13.11 (a) A column in which the broad surfaces of the bricks are horizontal is strong and stable. (b) If the joints were to be laid in diagonal planes, the column would disintegrate under load.

Drawing by John R. Freeman, AIA.

be destroyed by a sliding action of the courses under the vertical load (Figure 13.11).

Every sand castle eventually disintegrates. This fact of life can have several causes. We can jump on top of the castle, applying a load so large that the cohesive forces of the water films cannot hold the granules together. We can let it dry out, which deprives the granules of the tensile force exerted by the water film and allows the castle to slump into conical piles of dry sand with the characteristic angle of repose. Or we can leave the castle to confront alone the erosion of wind and rain, or to face the incoming tide, which floods its fragile fabric with water that lubricates its granules and brings about its immediate collapse.

SOLID MATERIALS

Buildings are made of solid materials, ones that have at least enough tensile strength to hold together while being handled by workers and machines. Sand is present in masonry mortar and concrete, but it is made solid by a portland cement binder. For the purpose of filling utility trenches with a stable material, concrete can be formulated to be no stronger than the soil in which it is placed. This material, called *flowable fill* or *controlled low-strength material (CLSM),* hardens in a few hours, does not settle over time, and can be excavated like normal soil at some future date when the building is changed or demolished. At the other end of the spectrum, concrete can be produced in compressive strengths that approach that of structural steel. But even this extremely high-strength concrete is vulnerable to cracking, and once it has cracked, its tensile strength is zero. Stone, bricks, and concrete, which are united by mortar to form *masonry*, behave similarly to concrete.

Wood consists of tiny longitudinal tubes of cellulose that are bound together by *lignin*, a natural cementing substance. Parallel to these tubes, wood is very strong in both tension and compression. Perpendicular to the tubes, wood is very weak.

Metals like steel and aluminum are made up of tiny crystals that are very strong in both tension and compression. Steel is stronger, stiffer, and less expensive than aluminum, which is why we use it for structural frames of buildings and bridges.

HOW MATERIALS BREAK

While we can visualize quite easily the ways that sand castles made of small particles and water collapse, we need to investigate several general mechanisms in order to comprehend how other materials break. The key to our understanding of conditions leading to the failure of a solid material under load was provided in the 1920s by A. A. Griffith. Griffith postulated that the mechanism of fracture consists of the levering and prying effects of small, usually invisible *fissures* that permeate the bodies of all common materials. Figure 13.12 illustrates Griffith's fracture mechanism by showing what happens inside a sheet of brittle material when it is pulled in any direction. An existing fissure in the material opens to provide powerful leverage to the pulling action (a). When this happens, the internal bonds at the very tip of the fissure are subjected to much higher tension than other bonds in the vicinity (b). When these highly-tensed bonds break, the tension is immediately transferred to a new layer of bonds. A chain reaction ensues, which results in an overall tearing action and eventual parting of the material (c). As a crack develops across a solid body, there is progressively less material to resist the tension, and this hastens the chain reaction.

The splitting potential of a small fissure is closely related to the sharpness of its tip. It follows that the susceptibility to failure of a brittle material that has a notch or tear in it can be reduced considerably by drilling a small, round hole at the tip of the notch or tear (Figure 13.12d). The hole, because of its rounded shape, has the effect of spreading the stress at the tip of the fissure over a much larger area of material and a much larger number of internal bonds. In analogous fashion, when a groove is milled into a brittle material such as stone, the groove is given a rounded profile rather than a square one. Such measures, known as *crack stoppers*, are widely used in industry. The accumulations of stress in solid materials that can lead to these tensile failures will be among the behavior that we investigate further when we consider the flow of forces in solid bodies (Chapter 14).

A BALL-AND-SPRING MODEL OF THE TRANSMISSION OF FORCES IN SOLID MATERIALS

The interactions under an external load of the particles in a solid material can be visualized with a simple mechanical model that is a cube made up of nine hard balls (Figure 13.13) connected by a system of vertical, horizontal, and oblique springs that can be compressed or tensed. The balls, eight at the corners of a cube of space and one at its center, represent the hardness of the crystals or grains of a material and account for its rigidity. In contrast, the connecting springs—with varying

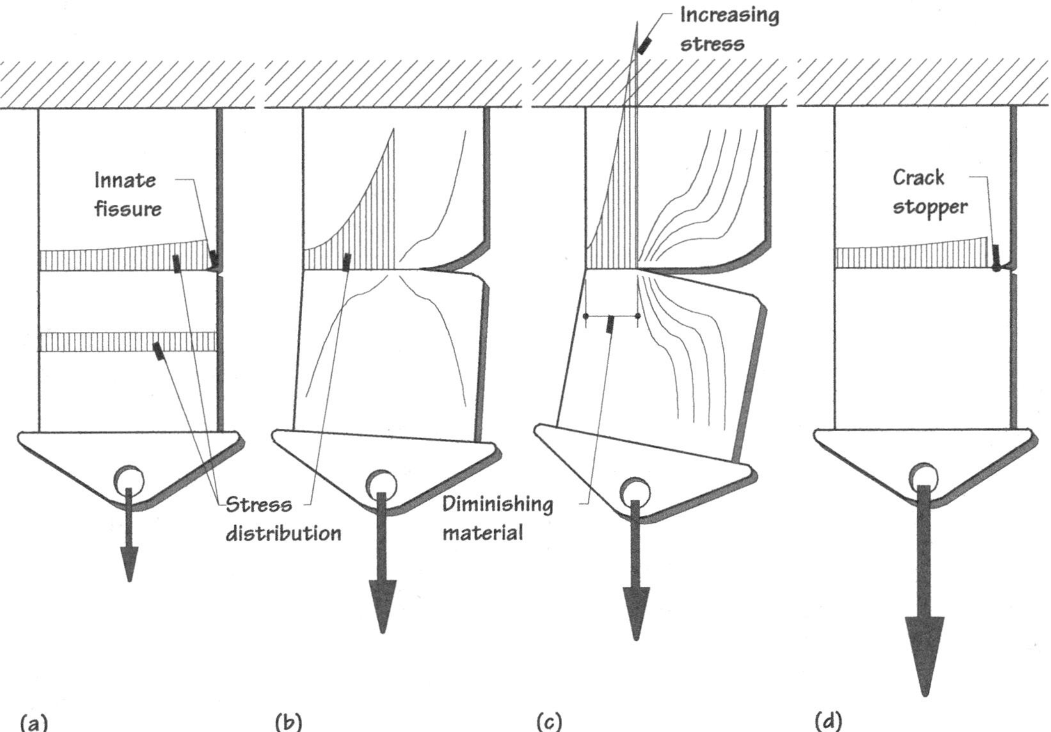

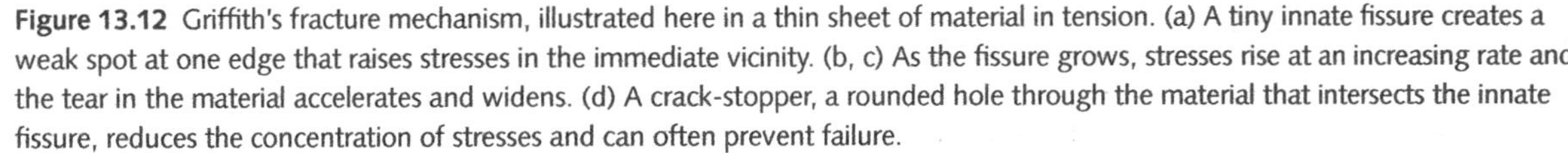
Figure 13.12 Griffith's fracture mechanism, illustrated here in a thin sheet of material in tension. (a) A tiny innate fissure creates a weak spot at one edge that raises stresses in the immediate vicinity. (b, c) As the fissure grows, stresses rise at an increasing rate and the tear in the material accelerates and widens. (d) A crack-stopper, a rounded hole through the material that intersects the innate fissure, reduces the concentration of stresses and can often prevent failure.

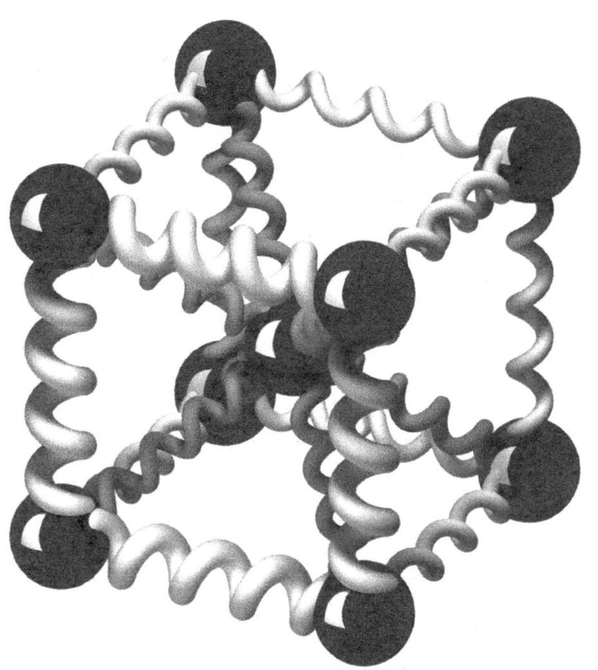

Figure 13.13 A ball-and-spring model can demonstrate the microscopic behavior of material under stress. The balls represent hard granules or crystals of material; the springs represent the bonds between them.

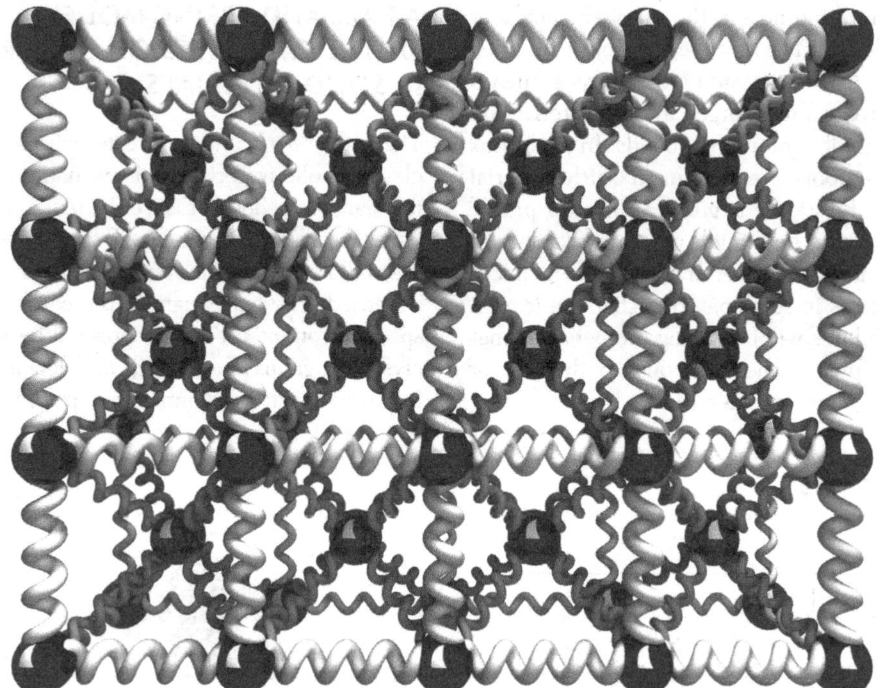

Figure 13.14 A larger mass of material behaves much like a large number of balls and springs connected in orderly fashion.

resistances to stretching or compressing—reflect the deformability and resiliency of various materials. Any mass of material may be seen as being composed of very large numbers of such ball-and-spring elements (Figure 13.14). When this mechanism is pressed down, its vertical and oblique springs are compressed and grow shorter. Its horizontal springs are stretched by the horizontal components of force in the oblique springs. The vertical pressure on the mechanism results not only in a vertical squeezing, but also a lateral expansion induced by the diagonal springs' attempts to resist deformation (Figure 13.15). For analogous reasons, a vertical pull on the mechanism produces a vertical stretching and lateral contraction.

These actions illustrate the *Poisson effect*, named after the French investigator S. D. Poisson (1781–1840). When any material is compressed in one direction, its contraction in that direction is always accompanied by smaller but proportional expansions in the perpendicular directions. When it is tensed in one direction, its stretching in that direction is always accompanied by contractions in the perpendicular directions. The Poisson effect can be seen by pressing downward on a block of foam rubber and observing the bulging of the foam around the sides of the block (Figure 13.16), or by pulling on a strip of foam rubber, which produces lateral shrinkage.

The same ball-and-spring model also demonstrates that lateral forces have their greatest effect on the oblique springs, some of which are stretched while others are compressed. When subjected to a lateral force, the model as a whole deforms from a cube into a rhomboid shape, as can be simulated with a block of foam (Figure 13.17). In this situation, each lateral face deforms from a square to a rhombus, and the internal springs can be visualized as having biaxial tension and compression (Figure 13.18).

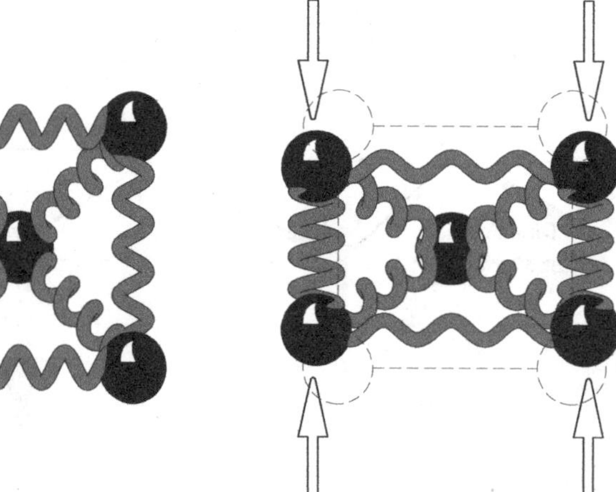

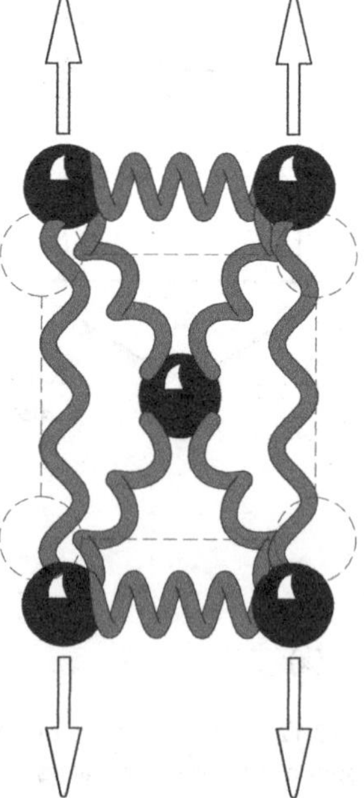

Figure 13.15 The Poisson effect is created by the diagonal springs in the model.

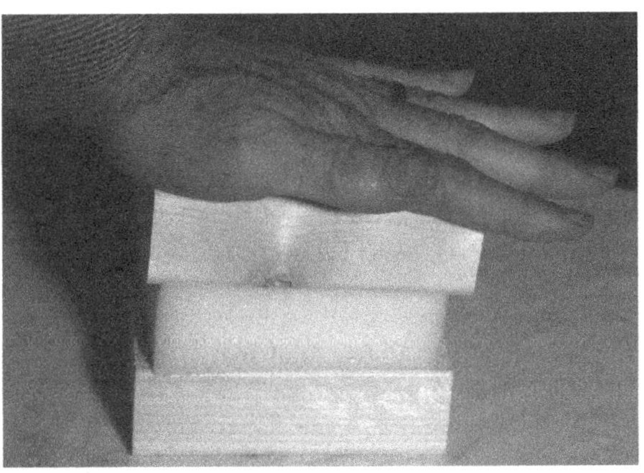

Figure 13.16 The Poisson effect is illustrated by the bulging of a block of foam rubber squeezed between blocks of wood.

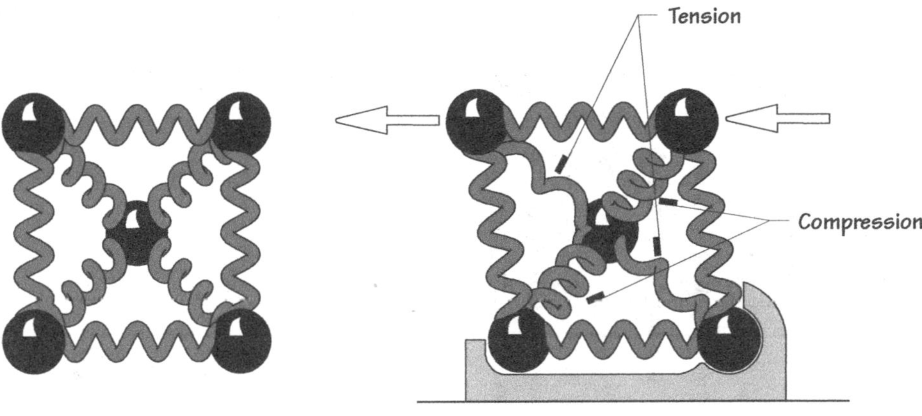

Figure 13.18 When a block of material is subjected to shearing loads, the diagonal springs are stretched in one direction and squeezed in the other.

Figure 13.17 When a block of foam rubber is subjected to a shearing action, the circles on its surface deform into ellipses. The direction of the long axes of the ellipses is the direction of principal tension, and the short axes indicate the direction of principal compression.

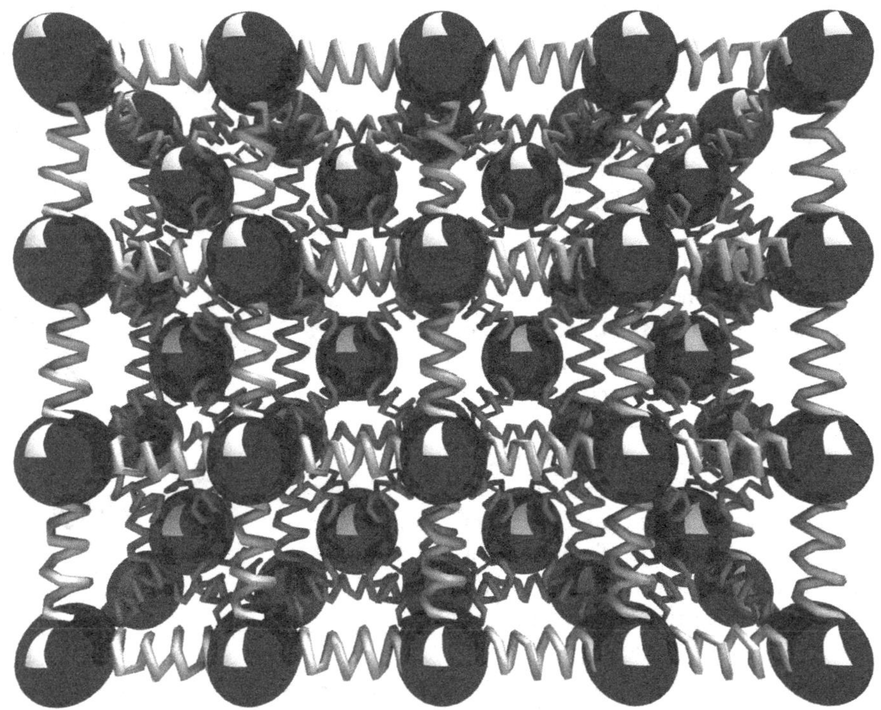

Figure 13.19 A ball-and-spring model of a brittle material features closely spaced balls with short, weak springs.

The relative sizes of the balls and the *stiffnesses* of the springs and their arrangements in the model can be proportioned in various ways to mimic the behavior of any material. Figure 13.19 shows a portion of a model with short, relatively weak springs that are much stiffer in compression than in tension. This model behaves

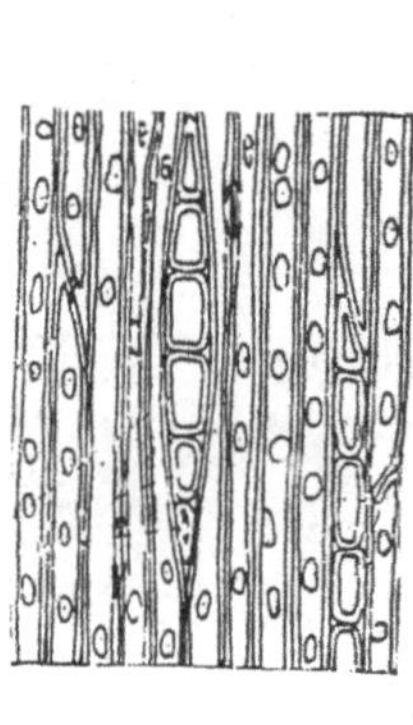

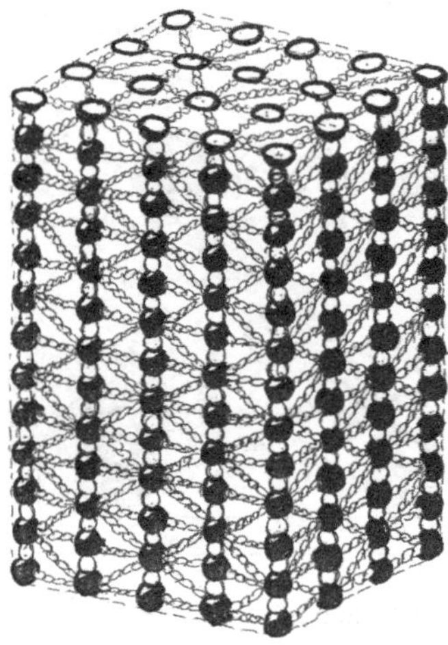

◂**Figure 13.20** The isotropic behavior of wood (left) is modeled with balls that are closely spaced and stiffly sprung parallel to the grain, but widely spaced and loosely sprung perpendicular to grain.

analogously to such materials as stone and concrete, which exhibit relatively high resistance to compression but are weak when subjected to tension.

The fibrous structure of wood can be represented by a model in which the vertical springs are like very stiff links, to emulate the strength of the cellulose tubes in the wood. The springs in the other directions, which represent the weak bonds of lignin, are soft (Figure 13.20).

Griffith's mechanism of fracture can be envisaged by means of a ball-and-spring model in which a connecting spring is missing (Figure 13.21). It is easy to visualize the additional stress that the absent connector creates in the surrounding connectors.

The ball-and-spring model is very versatile. You may find it intriguing to invent models that simulate the structural behaviors of familiar materials such as rubber, steel, and glass. We can also use the model to envision new combinations or configurations of material, such as the combination of ordinary sand with cementitious adhesives, or the addition of short, strong glass fibers to a concrete mixture. The actual molecular structure of the material may or may not be similar to this configuration; it is not intended to reflect the actual bonding structure. It is merely a simplified representation that makes it easy for us to understand the relative structural performances of various materials.

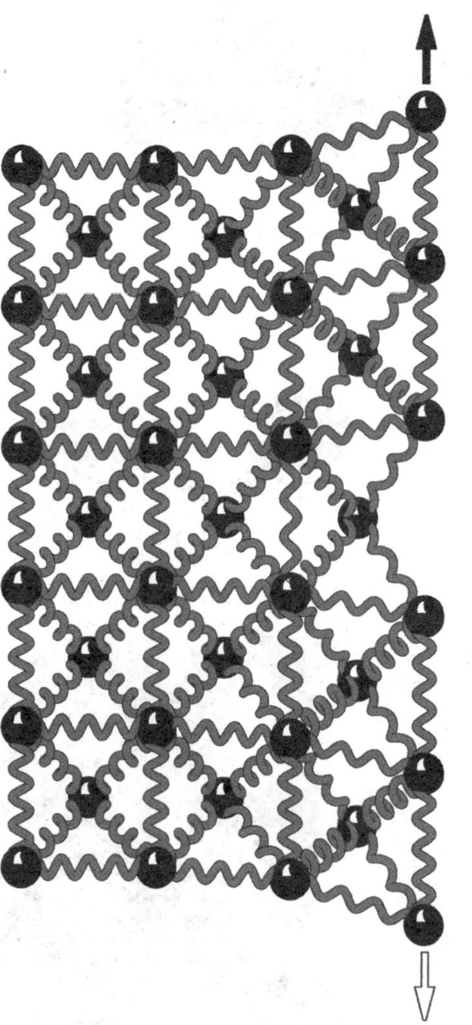

▴**Figure 13.21** The beginning of Griffith's mechanism of fracture may be visualized as the tearing of one spring at the edge of a body of material.

THE CHARACTERISTICS OF A GOOD STRUCTURAL MATERIAL

Strength

It is evident that a structural material needs to be strong enough to bear its own weight, the dead load and live loads that we expect it to carry, and short-term overloads such as those caused by wind gusts or earthquakes. Ideally, every structural material would be strong in both tension and compression, like steel and wood. But two very useful materials, concrete and masonry, are strong only in compression. We combine them with steel reinforcing bars to produce structures that have the necessary strength in tension as well as compression. In centuries past, we built masonry buildings without tensile reinforcing by configuring their structures in such a way that they experience only compressive forces (Chapter 8).

Stiffness

In addition to *strength* (having resistance to breaking), a structural material must also be *stiff* (resistant to deformation). Steel is both strong and stiff, while rubber may be strong, but not as stiff. Structural components of buildings need stiffness: If they deform too much when loaded, nonstructural components such as glass and plaster will crack and break. Beams, joists, rafters, and slabs must be made of stiff materials so they do not deform nor sag too much under load. A beam that sags excessively can create a roof surface that traps water, causing additional unexpected loads, or causing a floor to slope instead of being flat. Floors that are insufficiently stiff may be strong enough to carry their loads safely, but still feel unstable underfoot as they sag and vibrate; we will reexamine these issues in Chapter 17.

Steel is a very stiff material, yet even a steel beam sags when it is loaded. Concrete and wood are neither as strong nor as stiff as steel, so that when we make beams of these materials, we must use more material to achieve the same rigidity.

Earlier in this chapter we referred to the relatively low stiffness and relatively high cost of aluminum. But aluminum is very useful nevertheless. Because it self-protects against corrosion, is easy to form into intricate shapes, accepts a wide range of attractive finishes, and is easy to fasten together, it is widely used in window frames and for the framing of *curtain walls*, nonload-bearing exterior walls that are supported by the primary frame of the building. In a curtain wall or other large window assembly, the aluminum frame acts primarily to support glass and other wall materials against the lateral pressures and suctions of the wind. For this it requires a certain degree of stiffness, though not as much as a floor structure requires (Figure 13.22).

Although some types of glass fibers are stronger than steel, they are not nearly as stiff; they can resist high stresses without breaking but they deform excessively. Accordingly, the load-bearing capacity of structural elements made of glass-fiber-reinforced plastics is often limited by stiffness rather than strength.

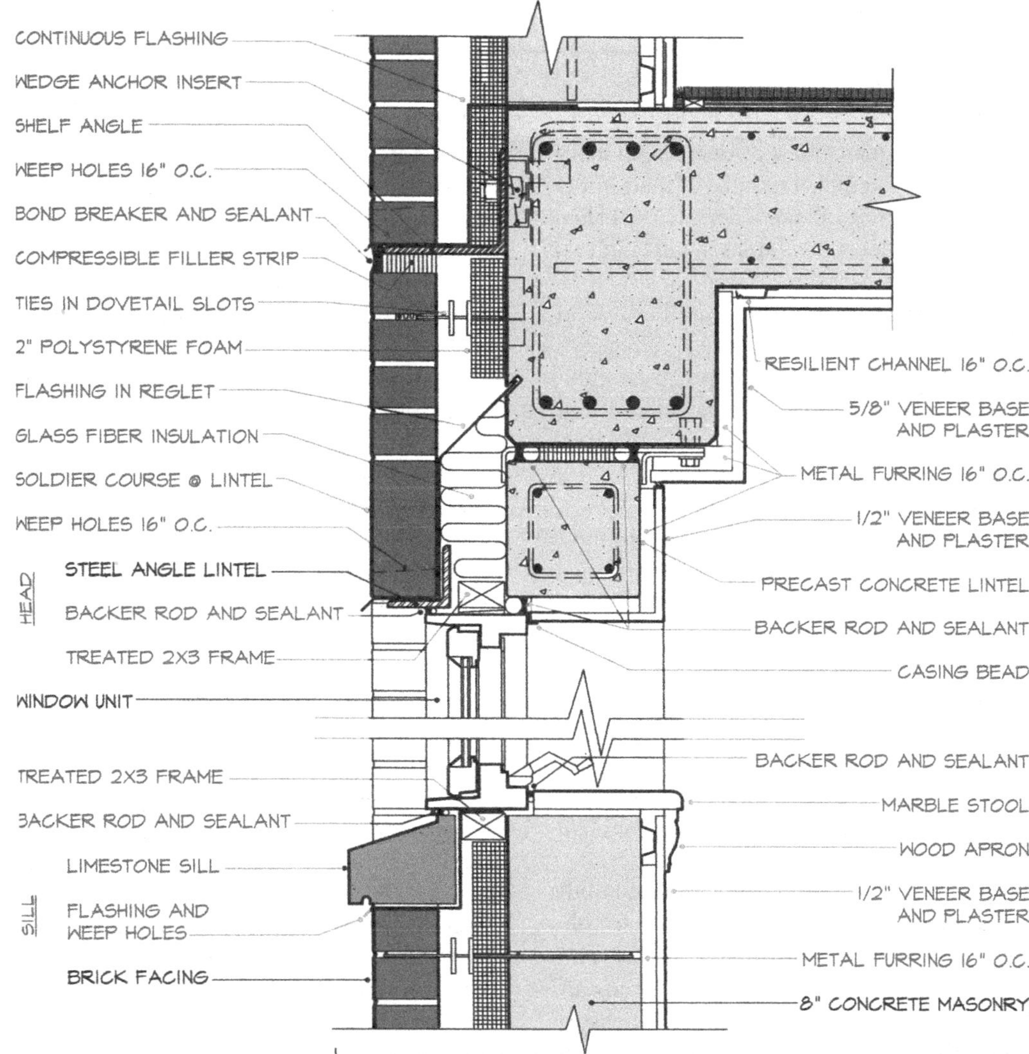

Figure 13.22 This vertical section detail shows the dozens of materials required to make a typical school or office building wall that is faced in brick. These materials need to be selected, assembled, and sometimes designed even to create the relatively simple appearance of this wall. The angle lintel is steel, which is the only material strong enough and stiff enough to carry the load of the brick facing in its tight location in such a way that will be nearly invisible from the exterior. The steel is galvanized to prevent rust; the zinc galvanizing coating will self-heal if scratched or damaged. Brick was chosen as the facing material because brick masonry units are durable, noncombustible, available in attractive colors, and will weather well over time. The bricks will absorb little water and will last for a century or more; the joints will need to have the old mortar raked out and replaced with fresh mortar every 50 to 100 years. Concrete masonry is a lower-cost material than brick, and is available in larger-sized units that are easily assembled with less labor for locations where bulk and compressive strength are needed. It appears in this detail in the backup wall that supports a membrane air barrier and the brick veneer against wind loads. The window unit is framed with vinyl-clad wood, which was chosen for its stiffness, machinability, and low thermal conductivity. The vinyl was formed into shaped sleeves that slip tightly onto the wood window frame pieces to protect them from weathering and give a good appearance that does not need painting. The vinyl sleeves are heat-welded at the corners so that there are no cracks through which water can penetrate.

Ductility

Ductility is the capability of a material to be reshaped by stretching or squeezing without losing its strength. A ductile material is characterized by its capability to engage many bonds simultaneously in the task of resisting tearing in the region surrounding the tip of a fissure. The same force that can rupture the few bonds at the tip of a fissure in a brittle material is unable to break the many bonds at a similar location in a ductile material.

The difference between brittle and ductile behavior in a material is exemplified by placing a hardened steel ball on the surface of a piece of window glass and pressing the ball into the surface with a hydraulic jack. The glass is *brittle*, and shatters into many small pieces before the ball is able to penetrate it. When a steel plate is subjected to the same test, it exhibits ductile behavior: As the force is increased, the ball is pushed farther and farther into the steel plate, leaving a permanent indentation without causing cracks to occur or the plate to disintegrate.

Ductility enables a structure to redistribute its internal forces so as to draw into its overall resisting action other, initially less stressed parts of a structure. Thus ductility of a structural material not only prevents and warns against early, sudden collapse of a structure, but also extends its resisting capabilities. Aluminum and steel are ductile, whereas concrete and masonry are brittle—they have little tensile strength and they tend to fail without warning if they are placed under tensile stress.

If a structure becomes severely overloaded and structural failure is inevitable, we want to be warned of its impending failure. If overloaded, a steel or wood beam sags visibly to alert us to its distress long before it breaks. Concrete beams and slabs are designed to be *underreinforced*, which means that their tensioned regions are purposely made weaker than their compressive ones. If an overload occurs in an underreinforced beam, the reinforcing bars in the tensile regions of the beam, which are ductile, will stretch considerably before the compressed concrete fails, thus giving warning of impending failure by means of progressive sagging of the member and a series of widening cracks across its bottom surface. If the beam were overreinforced, the stiff but brittle concrete would fail before the steel, giving little or no warning before collapse. We might think of an overreinforced concrete beam as behaving like a piece of peanut brittle, and an underreinforced one like a soft chocolate bar with a caramel filling: When we bite into peanut brittle, it fractures immediately and irregularly. When we bite a soft chewy chocolate bar, its fracture is pleasingly gradual and predictable.

Creep Resistance

Wood, concrete, and many plastics deform gradually and irreversibly over a period of months or years under normal levels of stress, a phenomenon that is called *creep*. Creep causes concrete columns in tall buildings to shorten significantly over time. A wood or structural concrete floor sags slowly over the years because of creep. At normal levels of stress, creep diminishes gradually and eventually ceases. Creep can be minimized by keeping stresses relatively low. Steel is not subject to creep at normal temperatures.

Fatigue Resistance

If we bend a paper clip back and forth many times, the wire eventually breaks. This is because of *fatigue*, the embrittlement of metal by repeated cycles of stressing and relaxation. When some metals (most prominently steel) are deformed again and again at room temperature, their crystalline structure is reworked into smaller and smaller units, which causes the metal to become progressively stronger but more brittle. Metal fatigue can occur even at relatively low levels of stress when the stress is applied and removed over a span of millions of cycles. Fatigue is not usually a factor in the frames of buildings, but in structures such as bridges, whose traffic loads come and go thousands of times each day, and airplanes, which are buffeted endlessly by strong air currents and stretched cyclically by cabin pressurization and depressurization, fatigue must be taken into account. Wood, concrete, and masonry are not susceptible to fatigue.

Reliability

When we use a structural material in a beam, slab, or column, we must be able to do so with reasonable certainty that it will perform as we expect. This means that the quality of structural materials must be tested during manufacture and installation to ensure reliability. Pieces of lumber are inspected and, in many instances, are subjected to physical tests of strength and stiffness in the sawmills where they are produced. Each piece of lumber is stamped with a grade that indicates its strength and stiffness. In the steel mill, samples taken from batches of molten structural steel are subjected to chemical analysis, and a certificate of quality is furnished with each batch of finished steel members. Concrete and masonry structures are essentially manufactured on the construction site, so that strength testing must be done by local laboratories on samples of material that are taken as the materials are put in place.

Sustainability

There is increasing interest in using materials with a low impact on the natural environment. One class of low-impact materials comprises those that are used in their natural state, such as rammed earth, adobe, logs, fieldstone, and straw bales. Another class includes those that are recycled or reused: Most structural steel is manufactured from scrap metal. Aluminum is recycled at a very high rate. Concrete may be ground up and used as aggregate for new concrete.

The amount of energy used to manufacture and ship materials, and the environmental pollutants given off in these processes, must also be taken into account. The manufacture of portland cement, the binder in concrete, uses large quantities of energy and emits large amounts of carbon dioxide and particulate matter. Structural steel that is manufactured from ore is also an energy-intensive product with by-products that pollute earth, air, and waters. Structural steel manufactured from scrap steel, as most steel is in the United States, uses much less energy and emits far less pollution.

Wood is the least energy-intensive material commonly used in construction. At the end of its useful lifetime, a wood member left on the ground will decay and become once again a part of the soil, furnishing energy and nutrients for new trees.

Isotropy

Steel and concrete are essentially *isotropic*, which means that they exhibit the same structural properties regardless of the direction in which they are stressed. Wood and fiber-reinforced plastics are *anisotropic*: Their structural properties are very different when measured parallel to their fibers than when measured perpendicular to them. In a typical wood species, for example, the allowable compressive stress parallel to the grain is about three times as much as the allowable compressive stress perpendicular to the grain. Allowable tensile stress perpendicular to the grain of wood is so low that it is not even listed in wood design tables. This quality of isotropy must be considered, particularly in situations where materials are subjected to varying loads in different directions, to ensure that anisotropic materials are fabricated and installed with their grain in the proper orientation.

Resistance to Fire

Fires in buildings are common. It is important that every building resist collapse caused by fire at least long enough for its inhabitants to escape safely. A building framed with slender wood joists, studs, and rafters burns readily, for which reason building codes do not allow this type of construction to be used for very large buildings or even small buildings in central cities. Thicker pieces of wood are much slower to catch fire than thinner wood members, and because of their larger mass, they do not burn as rapidly. Consequently, building codes allow somewhat larger buildings to be framed with heavy timbers than with light framing.

Steel framing, because it is *noncombustible*, would appear to be highly resistant to fire. Unfortunately, however, steel begins to lose strength and can fail to support a load at temperatures well below its melting point that are reached in building fires of low to moderate intensity. Steel framing in small buildings may be left exposed to view, but building codes require that steel members in medium- to large-sized buildings be protected by any of a group of fire-resistant insulating materials that are collectively called *fireproofing*.

Concrete is noncombustible and much more resistant to fire damage than bare steel, but when exposed to fire, its crystalline structure of cementing compounds gradually breaks down and the concrete eventually crumbles. Bricks, which are products of fire, are the most fire resistant of structural materials, but their mortar joints, which are essentially concrete, are subject to damage at elevated temperatures, and the bricks themselves may begin to disintegrate from thermally induced forces in a prolonged, hot fire.

Smoke and other combustion products are generally very toxic. The amount of such products that a material can generate during a fire, and their relative toxicity, are increasingly regulated by law.

Thermal Stability

Every material grows longer when heated and shorter when cooled. The amount by which a material changes dimension with a change of 1° in temperature is its *coefficient of thermal expansion*, which is measured as in./(in./°F) or in corresponding units such as mm/(mm/°C). The coefficients of expansion of masonry materials are relatively low; those of aluminum alloys, relatively high; and those of plastics, very high. Steel and concrete have expansion coefficients that are moderate and similar to one another. Wood is unique in this regard: Dimensional changes caused by changes in humidity are so large that thermally induced changes of dimension are small by contrast and are usually ignored. A structure in any material, if it is fully enclosed within a heated and cooled building, is subject only to minor variations in temperature and humidity and is generally considered to be dimensionally stable. Elements of a structure that are exposed to the outdoors will grow or shrink by substantial amounts with changes in temperature.

Economy

There are metals such as tungsten and titanium that are stronger than steel, but they are generally so much more costly that we seldom use them in buildings or bridges. Red maple is a stronger, stiffer wood than Douglas fir, but it is far more expensive because red maple trees are relatively rare and have short, crooked trunks, whereas fir trees are plentiful and have long, straight trunks that are easily sawed into lumber. Concrete can be formulated to be almost as strong as steel, but costs much more in this formulation than concrete of ordinary strength. The costs of a material itself, and of working it and putting it in place in a building, must be reasonable if we are to use it.

Durability

A structure must be resistant to attack by water, chemical agents, the ultraviolet wavelengths of sunlight, decay, wood-destroying insects, corrosion, cycles of freezing and thawing, and other forces that might shorten its life. Accordingly, steel must be painted or plated with zinc (in a process known as *galvanizing*) to keep it from rusting. Wood must be either kept dry, treated with chemical preservatives, or painted to keep it from decaying. Wood that is fully submerged in freshwater, including wood supporting piers and decades-old foundation pilings that are driven down into the groundwater table, are safe from decay because the water prevents the decay-causing organisms from getting air. Concrete that is exposed to the weather must be very dense in order for it to resist water penetration and damage caused by freeze/thaw cycles, unless it is painted. In places where concrete is exposed to salty water, such as oceanfront buildings, or road bridges in snowy climates, the steel reinforcing bars within it are coated with epoxy to keep them from corroding.

COMMON STRUCTURAL MATERIALS

Wood comes from the trunks of trees. The trunk is sawed into rough planks that are dried to remove excess water and planed to make them smooth and true to dimension. Each piece is graded for quality, either by visual inspection or by high-speed, continuous testing machines that flex it between rollers and record its resistance. Allowable strengths for wood are tabulated by species and grade in structural handbooks.

With the cutting of the last old-growth forests, a steadily increasing proportion of construction lumber is produced from rapidly grown, younger trees whose trunks are smaller in diameter and have a higher percentage of knots than old-growth trees. To better utilize these smaller trees, and to reduce the amount of wood that is wasted in sawdust and shavings in the sawmill, more and more wood structural members are being manufactured from wood veneers (thin sheets of wood) or long shreds of wood fiber that are bonded together with very strong, waterproof glues.

An examination with a hand lens will reveal that wood consists of parallel tubes of stiff cellulose that are bound together by lignin, a soft cementing substance. The long axes of the tubes run parallel to the long axis of each piece of lumber, and give wood its visible "grain" (Figure 13.20). Wood is markedly anisotropic, strong when loaded parallel to its grain, weak perpendicular to its grain. For further information on wood construction, see Chapters 1, 4, 6, and 17.

Masonry is a composite construction of *masonry units* and *mortar*. As we saw in the end walls of the athletic facility in Chapter 3, the most common types of masonry units are *stones, bricks,* and *concrete masonry units* (*CMUs;* also called *concrete blocks*). Mortar is a cementitious mixture that is placed between the masonry units to act as cushion, sealant, and adhesive. Chapter 8 covers unreinforced masonry construction in greater detail.

Structural steel is iron with a carbon content of about three-tenths of 1 percent. It is very ductile. It is made into *structural shapes* such as *wide-flange shapes, channels,* and *angles* by being squeezed between shaped rollers while it is very hot but not molten. Structural steel is used by itself in steel framing, and for plates that connect wood or precast concrete structural elements in frames made of those materials. Steel is also used for reinforcing bars for concrete structures. In structures, steel has entirely replaced *cast iron,* which was used historically, but is very brittle because of its high content of carbon and impurities; and *wrought iron,* which is ductile but labor-intensive and expensive to manufacture. For more detail on steel frame construction, see Chapters 5, 18, and 22.

Concrete is made of *aggregates*, water, and *portland cement*. The aggregates make up the bulk of the mixture. They consist of *coarse aggregates*, which are larger particles of crushed stone or gravel, and *fine aggregate,* which is sand. The relative proportions and diameters of coarse and fine aggregates are determined so that the fine aggregates just fill the voids between the particles of coarse aggregate. The portland cement, activated by water, *cures* by hydration to become a binder that completely coats all the aggregate particles and cements them together into a solid, strong mass. Various *admixtures* are often used in concrete mixes for such purposes as improving the workability of the wet mixture, accelerating its curing reaction, and increasing the strength of the cured concrete.

Because it has little tensile strength, concrete is almost always *reinforced* with round steel bars that add tensile strength where it is needed, or *prestressed* by stretching special high-strength steel strands and bonding or anchoring them to the concrete so that they compress the concrete before a load is applied. These practices are covered in greater detail in Chapters 3, 9, 20, and 21. Recent innovations with concrete have focused on introducing short fibers into the concrete mixture to create tensile strength throughout the material rather than only through the rebar.

NO MATERIAL IS UNIFORM

We tend to think of structural materials as being continuous, homogeneous substances, although we know that, in fact, they are aggregations of particles of various shapes and sizes, even if the particles aren't large enough (like grains of sand) to be perceived as such. Scientific investigation has revealed that every material, whether gaseous, solid, or liquid, is made up of very small elementary particles, atoms and molecules whose sizes are on the order of 10^{-9} m—10 million times smaller than the thickness of a dime—which are held together by electrostatic forces. The bonds between the elementary particles in any of these materials are extremely strong, but this strength is not reflected in a correspondingly high strength of the material as a whole. This is due to the fact that materials are not orderly assemblies of molecules, but rather random agglomerations of separate, small particulate clusters of molecules—crystals, grains, or fibers. Each such cluster, besides being weakened by its own internal defects, is surrounded by discontinuities, impurities, and material imperfections of various kinds. Generally speaking, bonds between adjacent clusters are not as strong as the bonds inside them. Therefore, the effective strength of solids is determined by these weaker bonds.

THE CONCEPT OF STRESS

While the structural materials in buildings reflect their molecular properties, we generally need ways of dealing with them macroscopically. The French mathematician and physicist Agustin Cauchy (1789–1857) introduced the concept of stress as a way of simplifying complex actions in structural bodies so that they might be studied readily. We first became acquainted with the concept of stress at the very beginning of this book, where it was defined in Chapter 1 as the axial force on a member divided by the cross-sectional area of the member:

$$f = \frac{P}{A}$$

Now that we have become acquainted with the microscopic behavior of structural materials, we must examine this concept more closely. As defined by this expression, *stress is a statistical quantity that reveals the average intensity of the actual internal forces that act on small areas within the material of structures*. It is a resultant stress, the vectorial sum of all the randomly oriented particle-to-particle stresses in the body, and represents their actions in a mathematically manageable way. Figure 13.23a shows in diagrammatic form how the forces might actually act within a cross section of an axially compressed element. Part (b) of this same figure shows the statically equivalent diagram of uniform stress that represents in simplified form the play of the actual forces in this element.

As another way of conceptualizing stress, consider a cubic ball-and-spring model that is compressed uniformly in the vertical direction (Figure 13.24). Examining its square cross sections, all the micropushes in the members that are cut by the horizontal plane 1–1 can be represented in part (b) of Figure 13.24 by a uniform state of stress in that section. At the same time, we see in part (c) that along a vertical plane, there are pulls in the horizontal springs that are balanced by the opposing horizontal components of the compressive forces in the diagonal springs. The resultant of all these horizontal actions is an average horizontal force of zero. We see from this that the absence of stress over a certain area of material does not necessarily mean that there are no actual microforces in that area but rather that such microforces, if they exist, are in equilibrium with one another. We can also see evidence of the Poisson effect, that any uniform compressive action in one direction produces uniform compressive stress and shortening in that direction, accompanied by elongations and zero stress in the perpendicular direction. These diagrams help to explain why the failure of a brittle material such as concrete, brick, or stone, begins

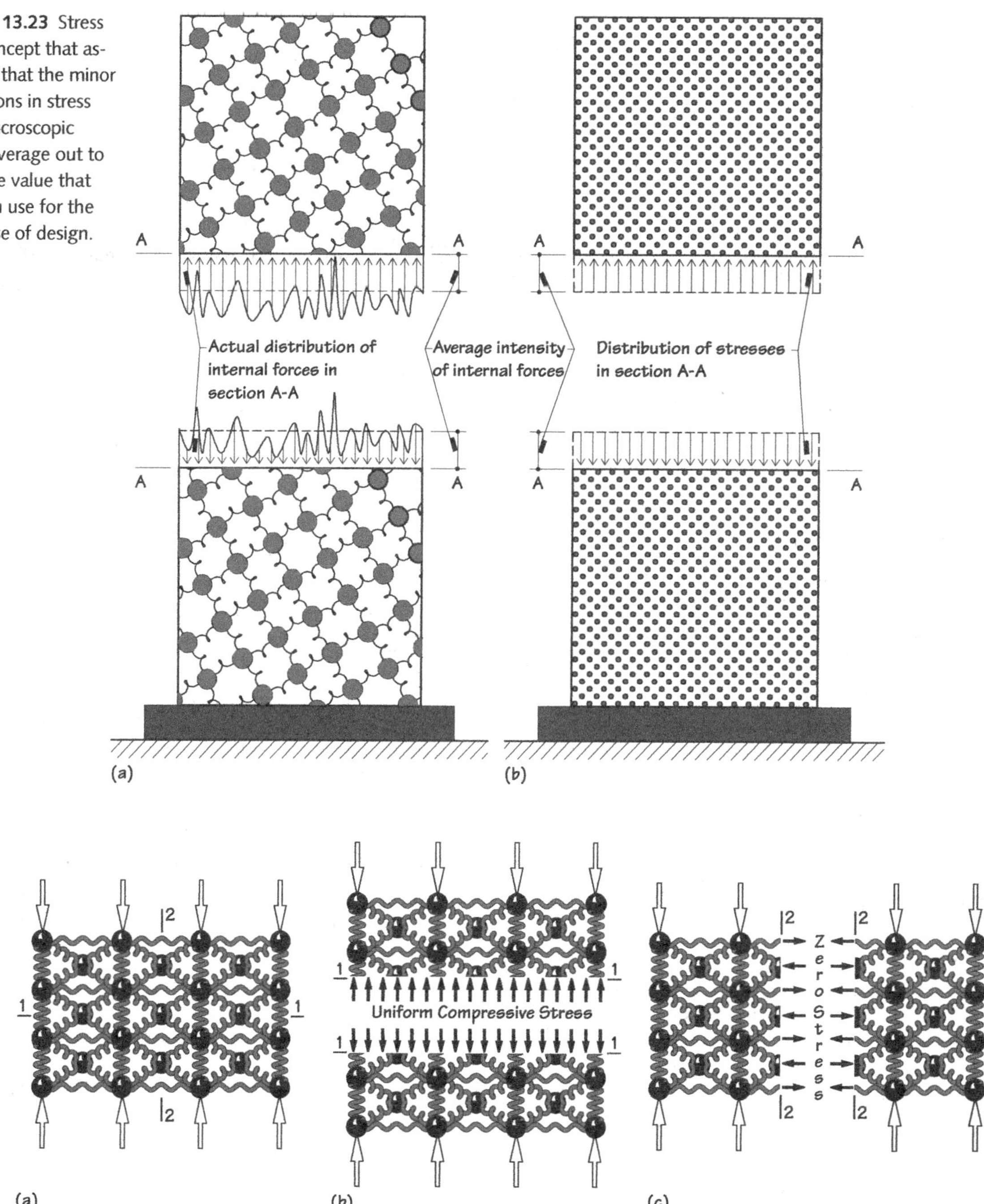

Figure 13.23 Stress is a concept that assumes that the minor variations in stress at a microscopic level average out to a single value that we can use for the purpose of design.

Figure 13.24 When a block of material is subjected to compressive loads, the diagonal springs exert microforces perpendicular to the direction of principal stress. Because half of these forces are tensile and half compressive, they cancel one another, leaving only the principal stress.

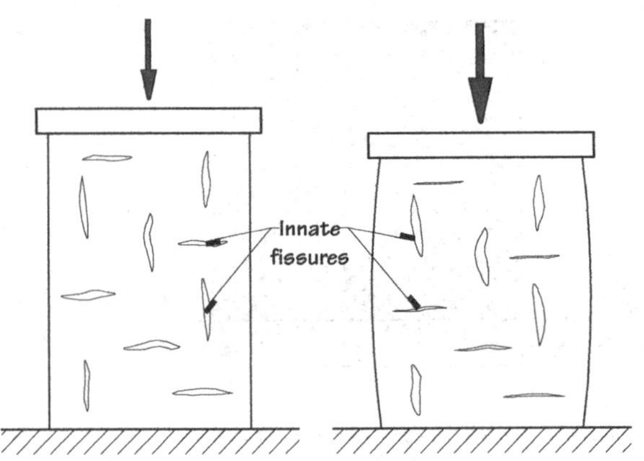

Figure 13.25 Innate fissures in a block of material affect its mode of failure when it is tested for strength.

with the formation of cracks parallel to the direction of the main compressive force (Figure 13.25).

It should be apparent from these observations that numerical methods of structural analysis, if dissociated from physical understanding of what the numbers actually represent, can lead to a misunderstanding of many important structural phenomena. Thus, even a basic phenomenon and quantity such as "stress" is a highly simplified description of a very complex set of physical actions.

STRESSES AND STRAINS

The actions of forces on solid materials are always accompanied by deformations of the materials. The concept of *strain* was introduced to represent the intensity of deformations in materials. Strain, *s*, is defined as the change in the length of a structural element, ΔL, divided by the original length of the element, L (Figure 13.26):

$$s = \frac{\Delta L}{L} \qquad [13\text{-}1]$$

The units of strain are in./in. or mm/mm. Strain is therefore a dimensionless quantity.

The linear relationship of stress and strain was discovered independently by the English scientist Robert Hooke (1635–1703) and the French physicist E. Mariotte (1620–1684). Working with springs and beams, they found that deformations in structural bodies are proportional to the forces that act on them. They also discovered that the deformations disappear when the forces are removed—the bodies return to their original shapes and dimensions. *Hooke's law*, also known as the *law of elasticity*, states that strain is inversely and linearly proportional to stress:

$$E = \frac{f}{s} \qquad [13\text{-}2]$$

where:

E is the modulus of elasticity,

f is the stress in the material, and

s is the strain in the material at the given stress, f.

The modulus of elasticity, which is constant for a given material, is also called *Young's modulus*, after Thomas Young (1773–1829), an English scientist who did research on the phenomenon of elasticity of materials. The units of E are pounds per square inch (lb/in.^{2} or psi) or pascals (Pa). The higher the modulus of elasticity, the stiffer the material.

The modulus of elasticity of a material is determined by mounting a small sample of the material in a testing machine that subjects the sample to steadily increasing levels of either tensile or compressive stress while simultaneously recording the deformations of the material (Figure 13.27). A graph of stress to strain is constructed from these measurements, with the vertical axis representing stress and the horizontal axis, strain (Figure 13.28). The modulus of elasticity is the slope of the straight-line portion of the curve.

If the force on a sample of ductile material such as steel or aluminum is increased until the sample ruptures, the curve will follow a straight, sloping line through the *elastic range* of the material until a stress known as the *yield point* is reached. (Within the elastic range, any strain in the material disappears if the load is withdrawn, and the material returns to its original shape and dimension.) With further increases in the force beyond the yield point, and with accompanying increases in strain, the relationship between stress and strain changes radically. The material begins to flow plastically (that is, it deforms irreversibly) with little or no increase in its resistance. The values of stresses remain close to the yield stress, and the material continues to sustain a load, but the strain continues to increase until the sample finally ruptures completely at the *ultimate strength* of the material. A brittle material, by contrast, simply breaks without warning at the limit of its elastic range.

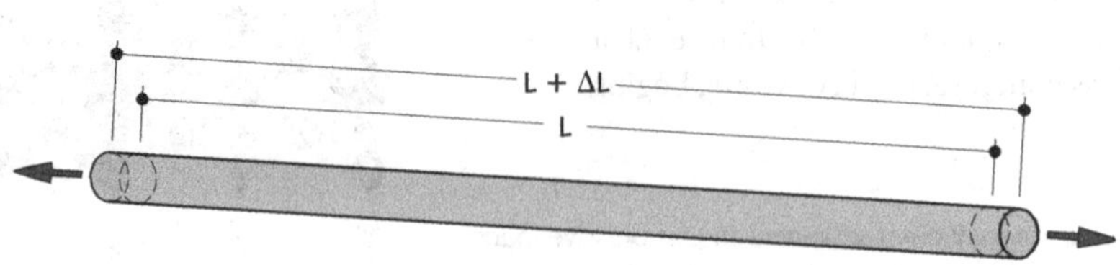

Figure 13.26 Strain is a lengthening or shortening of an element in response to axial stress.

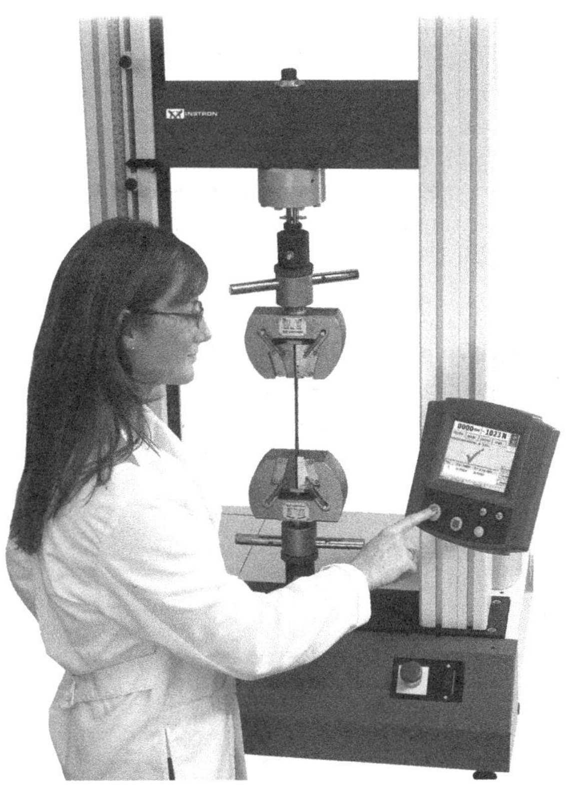

Figure 13.27 Materials are tested for strength on instruments such as this one, which applies an increasing force to a sample of the material while simultaneously plotting a curve of stress versus strain.

Photo courtesy of Instron Corporation.

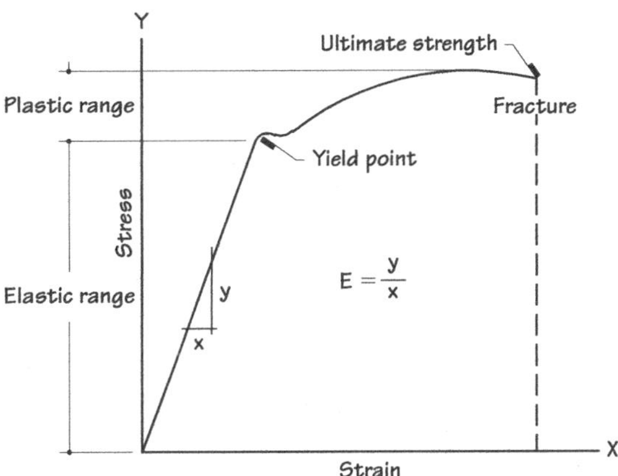

Figure 13.28 A stress/strain curve for structural steel is produced by a testing machine that plots stress versus strain as the sample is loaded slowly. The elastic range of stress is represented by the steeply climbing straight-line portion of the curve. If the load is removed from the sample in this range of stress, the sample will exhibit elastic behavior by returning to its original size and shape. At the upper end of the elastic range, the slight dip in the curve indicates that the yield point is reached: The material undergoes plastic deformation, after which it cannot return to its original size and shape. The plastic deformation, however, hardens the material, causing it to reach higher stresses than at the yield point. Eventually, as the testing machine continues to pull on the sample, the fracture load is reached, at which the material pulls apart and has no further strength.

CLAUDE LOUIS MARIE HENRI NAVIER

Claude Louis Marie Henri Navier (1785–1836) was a French academician whose mathematical investigations laid the foundations for modern forms of numerical analysis. Raised by his uncle, a civil engineer named Emiland Gauthey who emphasized traditional empirical methods of design, Navier entered the École Polytechnique in Paris, where he studied with Fourier and other mathematicians. After graduating, Navier edited his late uncle's papers and built theoretical methods of analysis through scholarship and teaching. In contrast to other contemporaneous builders who strove to improve suspension bridge design through empirical testing, such as Finley in Pennsylvania and Telford in England, Navier developed the first correct mathematical method to find the forces in a suspension bridge. He sought to account for factors such as vibration, elasticity, and temperature variation that were not previously predicted. Navier's innovations allowed him to propose the stone arch Pont des Invalides at the very low height-to-span ratio of 1:17. After construction difficulties and delays, which caused contractual and political disputes, the partially constructed bridge was demolished in 1826. Yet this same year he published the first essentially correct book on structural calculations, derived from work by Coulomb, Marriotte, and other mathematicians. He contributed greatly to the fields of engineering and fluid mechanics, including the Navier–Stokes equations that describe relationships of fluid momentum and viscosity, for which he developed the correct form even before the physical properties of such fluids were understood.

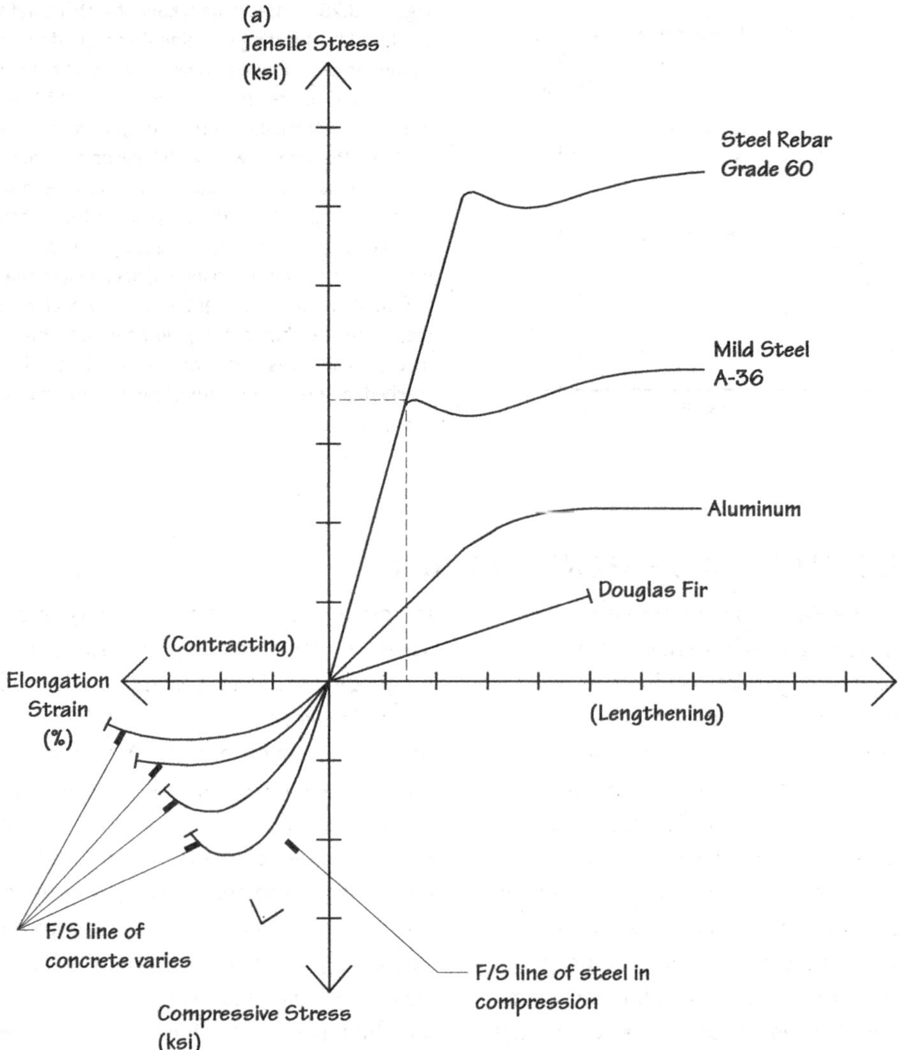

13.29 Stress/strain curves for several materials. By convention, tensile stress lies in the first quadrant, and compressive stress in the third.

The deformations of common structural materials are not usually visible to the unaided eye, but they can be measured precisely in laboratory testing machines. The moduli of elasticity of these materials are on the order of a thousand times larger than their allowable strengths. Typical stress/strain curves for a few common structural materials are shown in Figure 13.29.

Quantifying Strains in Structural Elements

The modulus of elasticity enables us to predict how much a structural element will deform under load. If a column 14 ft tall is made of a species of wood that has an elastic modulus of 1,600,000 psi, how much will it shorten under a load that stresses it to 1,200 psi? We find the answer by first substituting for the terms of equation [13-2]:

$$E = \frac{f}{s}$$

$$s = \frac{f}{E} = \frac{1,200 \text{ psi}}{1,600,000 \text{ psi}} = 0.00075 \text{ in./in.}$$

Then we substitute actual values for the terms in equation [13-1]:

$$s = \frac{\Delta L}{L}$$

$$\Delta L = sL$$

$$\Delta L = (168 \text{ in.})(0.00075 \text{ in./in}) = 0.126 \text{ in.}$$

The compression caused by the given load shortens the column by about 1/8 in.

If a structural steel tie member 12 ft long is subjected to its full allowable load, how much does it stretch?

$$s = \frac{f}{E} = \frac{24 \times 10^3 \text{ psi}}{29 \times 10^6 \text{ psi}} = 8.28 \times 10^{-4} \text{in./in.}$$

$$s = \frac{\Delta L}{L}$$

$$\Delta L = sL$$

$$\Delta L = (144 \text{ in.})(0.000828) = 0.12 \text{ in.}$$

FACTORS OF SAFETY

Most structures are designed to function with full design live loads at stresses that are 40 to 60 percent of their yield strengths, depending on the reliability of the material. These correspond to factors of safety of 2.5 to 1.67, respectively. These factors of safety give structures considerable reserves of strength within the elastic range to resist exceptional occurrences such as being run into by a vehicle, being in the path of a tornado, or having a crane drop an air compressor or a bundle of steel on them during construction. Even so, the possibility remains that a wind or earthquake of unusual magnitude may strike the structure, for which reason stresses may stray into the plastic range in some of its members. When this occurs, the building will be deformed permanently in some degree, but it will not collapse unless internal stresses in its frame exceed the ultimate strength of its framing material. Thus, plastic behavior provides an additional margin of safety above that normally furnished by the factor of safety that is incorporated into the allowable stress.

At the time of this writing, structural members made of fibers of glass, carbon, or aramid embedded in a plastic matrix are being used in experimental structures, mainly pedestrian bridges, although several highway bridges have also been built. Much will be learned from these structures regarding strength, stiffness, durability, long-term performance, and fire resistance, information that will soon enable us to use these miraculously strong, light materials in buildings.

SUMMING UP

This chapter has introduced some fundamental concepts of structural materials, including their desired qualities, their actual qualities, and the actions that take place within materials that give them their strength. We have examined the ball-and-spring theoretical model that represents in simplified form the character of the internal actions of solid and granular materials, and the physical mechanisms of these actions. We have learned to work with the modulus of elasticity to quantify the changes of dimension that are caused by stress, and we have made some comparisons among the common structural materials.

It is likely that within your lifetime you will encounter at least one major new material in the building industry, whether as a volume of unfinished substance available for your own creativity (like sand in a bucket) or within a manufactured product. The criteria described in this chapter present some initial ways to understand the possibilities of such a material, and to reconsider traditional materials in new applications.

Exercises

1. A wood column is 5.5 in. square in cross section and 12 ft long. Its modulus of elasticity is 1.3×10^6 psi. How much will the column shorten under a compressive load of 36,000 lb?

2. A high strength steel rod 0.45 in. in diameter and 25 ft long is subjected to a tensile force of 16 kips. How much does it stretch?

3. Draw a ball-and-spring model that represents the microstructure and behavior of each of the following materials:

- **a.** Foam rubber (such as is used in a mattress)
- **b.** Cotton cloth (such as is used in textile fabrics)
- **c.** Polyethylene plastic (such as is used in flexible bags and sheets)
- **d.** Limestone (such as is used for stone façades of buildings)

Annotatc cach modcl to cxplain how it represents its material.

4. You are in the Peace Corps as a volunteer in an unfamiliar part of the globe. Upon your arrival, your supervisors tell you that you are expected to come up with a new way of using locally available materials to build walls and roofs for schools that can resist frequent minor earthquakes. These walls and roofs must also insulate against excessive heat loss during the occasional weeks of cold weather when school is usually cancelled because the buildings have no heating equipment. Steel and cement are expensive and difficult to obtain. Available materials include:

- Clay and silty mud
- Bamboo in diameters up to 6 in. and lengths to 22 ft
- Stratified limestone that is easily broken out of a quarry with crowbars
- Cypress trees that have trunks up to 4 ft in diameter and 40 ft long

Simple tools are also available: shovels, crowbars, saws of various kinds, including a pit saw apparatus for manual sawing of logs into boards.

Diagram a system that utilizes some or all of these materials to build classrooms 24 ft square. Draw large-scale details of major joints.

Key Terms and Concepts

angle of repose
internal friction
slurry
surface tension
capillary action
internal friction
quick condition
biaxial stress
multiaxial stress field
confinement
cohesion
composite columns
flowable fill
controlled low-strength material (CLSM)
fissure
Griffith's fracture
crack stopper
ball-and-spring model
Poisson effect
stiffness
strength
curtain walls
ductility
brittleness
reinforcing
underreinforced, overreinforced conditions
creep
fatigue
isotropy
anisotropy
heavy timbers
noncombustible
coefficient of thermal expansion
wood
masonry
structural steel
structural steel shapes
wide-flange
channel
angle
cast iron
wrought iron
concrete
aggregates
portland cement
curing
admixtures
prestressing
strands
pretensioning
posttensioning
stress
strain
Hooke's law
law of elasticity
modulus of elasticity
Young's modulus
yield point
ultimate strength
factor of safety

$$s = \frac{\Delta L}{L} \quad [13\text{-}1]$$

$$E = \frac{f}{s} \quad [13\text{-}2]$$

CHAPTER 14

Master Lesson: Designing with the Flow of Forces

- *Trajectories of principal stresses*
- *Strut-and-tie modeling; truss modeling*
- *Three patterns of force flow; applications of basic patterns to any structural element*
- *Use of graphical truss solutions to find forces in truss models*

"I've got just the design tool for you!"

"How so, Diane?"

"Well, I see these drawings you've brought me, showing shapes for concrete wall panels, and you said you want me to figure out where the critical stresses are in them, and find equations to calculate how big the stresses are, right?

"Yes."

"I can help you, but to answer that second part of your question, I don't have equations to do that."

"Wait!" said Bruce, looking puzzled. "You just said you have just the design tool for me, and now you're saying that you don't."

"I said I don't have ***equations.*** *But I do have a really elegant design tool that can do the job, one you can apply to lots of design strategies."*

"To other panel designs?"

"It's a technique that can help you in many different situations. Not just in figuring out stresses in concrete, but in all kinds of projects in all materials. It will help you know where to add material, where to subtract material, where to cut holes in a structure (14.1). *It's the ultimate shaping tool. Its use is instrumental in creating some of the structural details that are such an elegant part of today's best structures. And it will help you understand the behavior of your structures better."*

"Do I have enough math background to do this?"

"You don't really need any more math than we have already used together. We'll start with qualitative diagrams—the quantitative part comes only at the end, and it's done with graphical truss analysis."

"Truss analysis? Are you telling me that there are trusses in these wall panels? They're solid masses of concrete!"

"You'd probably never suspect that there are trusses lurking inside them. But in an important way we can show how it's true—there are invisible trusses in every structural body. You just have to discover their shapes and the loads on them, and if necessary, solve for their member forces. Then you'll have the basis for shaping the solid body and proportioning its parts."

"I'm still mystified, but you have piqued my curiosity. Let's give it a try. This is a rather offbeat project, and I need your help. How much do you know about concrete tilt-up construction?"

"Not very much," admitted Diane. *"I've never actually worked on a tilt-up building. I know how the process works in a general way, but that's about it."*

"Well, the project for which I've been starting sketches is an experiment for Grainger Tilt-Up Construction.

Figure 14.1
Photo: David M. Foxe.

Figure 14.2

Rob Grainger, the owner, has been taking me to see their projects, both finished buildings and buildings under construction. They build mainly warehouses, factories, and shopping centers. They also do the occasional school, church, or office building."

"What is he asking you to do?"

"He wants me to generate fresh architectural ideas that they can use to expand their market. Most tilt-up buildings are rather dreary looking. Architects and builders attempt to add excitement with applied colors and patterns, applied surface materials like tiles or thin bricks, and imaginative fenestration schemes. Rob thinks it would be more interesting to look for fundamentally new ways of shaping the panels, rather than just playing with surface finishes."

"That's an exciting challenge! What do you need from me?"

"Well, I find myself sketching some pretty unusual panel shapes, like asymmetrical L-shapes and T-shapes, and panels with various shapes of holes in them. Some of them have edge notches. And in most cases they have to hold up some rather heavy roof loads."

Bruce fanned out an array of sketches on the table showing various panel shapes (14.2).

"I need to know what's feasible and what's not. And if something is feasible, I need to know how much steel reinforcing is needed and where to put it."

"Some of these are pretty complicated. Architects never seem to do the easy, simple thing. Why is that?"

"Don't blame me this time—this was Rob's idea. But I have to admit that I like unusual projects that expand my thoughts and capabilities, and Rob has the imagination to appreciate that. And you and I tend to work on slightly offbeat projects like this one."

"Yes, I do. They are fun and they stretch our abilities, as you've said."

TILT-UP CONSTRUCTION

"Isn't tilt-up construction just a matter of pouring and finishing a floor slab, then casting wall panels on top of the slab, curing the panels, and hoisting them up onto wall footings?"

"That's the essence of the process. Here are diagrams and photos of how it **usually** works (14.3, 14.4,

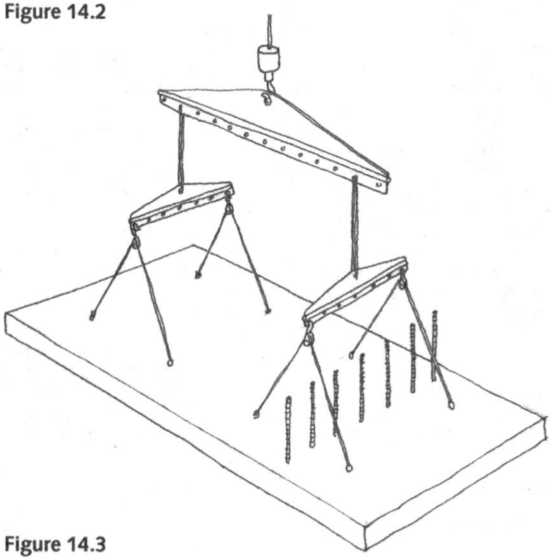

Figure 14.3

Figure 14.4

Photo courtesy of Portland Cement Association, Skokie, Illinois.

14.5, 14.6). After the site is prepared, a floor slab is cast, finished smoothly, and cured. But an area of slab all around the perimeter of the building is omitted for the moment. Strip footings are formed and poured for the walls. Wall panels are cast on the floor slab and cured; then the panels are lifted and placed on the footings. Telescoping steel pipe diagonal braces are installed temporarily to keep the panels upright. Finally, the roof structure is constructed, the slab around the perimeter is poured and finished, and the braces are removed."

"I get it—the perimeter trench allows the panels to be set directly on the footings, and to attach to the floor slab with rebars that stick out of the inside surface of the panels. How are the panels connected to one another?"

"Typically, with small weld plates at the roof line. The roof acts as a diaphragm to hold the tops of the wall panels in alignment. The vertical joints between panels are made weathertight with a sealant.

"Can Grainger build only single-story buildings with tilt-up?"

"No, they can do two stories quite readily, even three or four, but most of their work is single-story."

"Are the panels cast with the outside surface up, so they only need to be tilted up to get them in position?"

"No, they're almost always cast face-down, for many reasons. A major one is that it's much easier to get a good finish on the bottom side of the panel than on the top. For example, a surface cast against a very smooth, steel-troweled floor slab looks like it has been steel troweled itself, but there's no additional troweling cost, as there would be if the panel were cast face-up. Also, with face-down casting, rubber form liners can give any desired pattern or texture to the outside surface of the panels. Besides, lifting attachments (14.5) need to be cast into the top face, and they don't want them appearing on the outside of the building."

Figure 14.5

Photo courtesy of Muse Concrete.

"That all makes sense. How big are tilt-up panels, typically?"

"The most economical sizes are in the range of 400 to 500 sq ft, with heights between 22 and 30 ft. Heights up to 80 ft have been cast and erected successfully."

"That's a tall wall to tilt up! It must have to be really thick to avoid breaking when it's lifted."

"If the panels are unusually tall or full of openings, a steel strongback, which is a custom-designed frame of wide-flange beams, is attached to each panel in turn to stiffen it during lifting. Once the panel is in place and braced, the strongback is removed and attached to the next panel. Typically these panels are 5–1/2 to 7–1/2 in. thick, so height-to-thickness ratios usually run from 40 to 50. But I'm itching to get on with this—can we look at some of my panel shapes and then get back to your detailed questions later?"

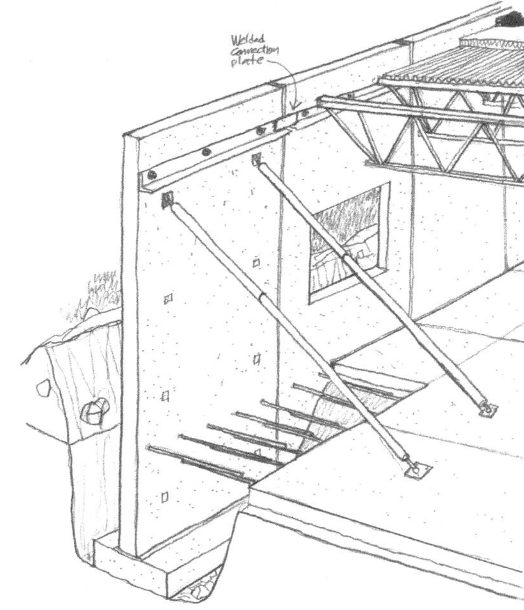

Figure 14.6

"Good idea—let's do that. I'm rather impatient to see what you've created."

Bruce selected one of his sketches.

"How are we going to apply this mysterious method to this panel?"

"We're going to draw the pattern in which forces flow through the panel."

"That sounds intriguing, but hard to predict."

"It's actually not hard at all for most situations. The flow pattern is a really good basis for shaping the panel for optimum structural performance. And on the basis of the flow pattern we can construct an imaginary truss that is a good approximation of the flow pattern. Finally, we can analyze the truss to determine the forces within the panel."

"By 'analyze,' you mean with a force polygon?"

"Yes. I'll demonstrate."

CONSTRUCTING FLOW PATTERNS

Diane unrolled a layer of tracing paper over Bruce's diagram of a sample panel. With deft strokes of her pen she added to it a set of straight and curving lines, some of them broken and some solid (14.7).

"This is the flow pattern."

Bruce peered closely.

"How'd you do that?"

"I'll show you the process. Then you can plot the flow patterns for any panel shape that you can imagine. You'll see that you can use it to understand what happens around openings and slots and notches, and that it can be applied to everything from giant dams to small connector plates. And it's fun, too!"

"Do you mean this design tool can help find good shapes for all kinds of solid structural bodies, like . . . well, steel gusset plates for trusses, and masthead details, and hinge elements, and . . ."

"Yes, that's what I mean. Here's what I did to arrive at the flow diagram that I showed you. I began by making your panel shape into a free-body diagram, by adding external loads and reactions. Then I looked at the forces around the edges of the panel—they are all concentrated forces in this case. From the point of application of each of them, I drew a radiating fan of lines. For a concentrated load, these lines represent the dispersal of the force into the body of the panel. For a concentrated reaction, they represent a gathering together of forces within the panel in order to conduct them out of it. Then I connected the fans to one another with straight lines through the body of material to complete a diagram of the flow of primary forces. And finally, wherever the lines change direction, I added lines of secondary force perpendicular to the lines of primary force. I'm using solid lines to indicate compressive forces,

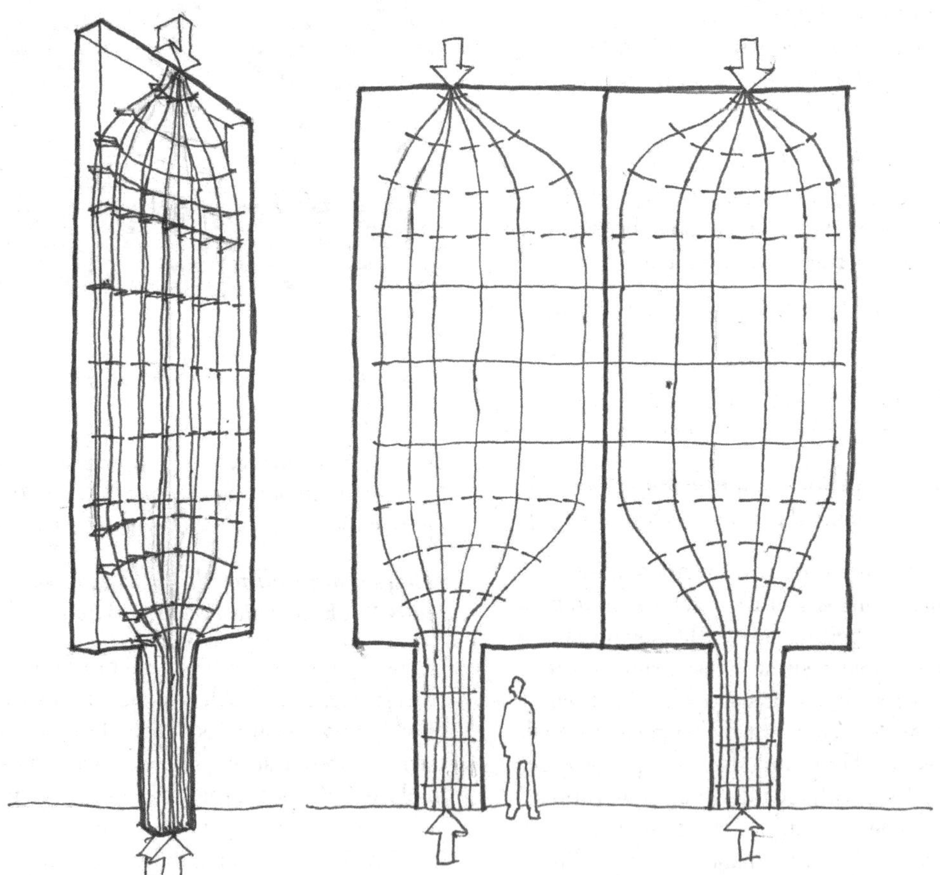

Figure 14.7

and broken lines, which look like they're being pulled apart, for tensile forces. But I'm getting ahead of myself. Let's back up so I can explain what's happening."

"It is not difficult to draw a logical sketch of a network of internal forces in a structure if a little thought is given to the basic principles and interest taken in the approach to such problems."

—Eduardo Torroja

FLOW OF WATER AND FLOW OF FORCES

Diane took from her bookshelf a loose-leaf binder that bristled with index tabs.

"In spare moments, I've been creating some drawings for the structures class I teach that help to explain this phenomenon. We can begin with water flowing in a river."

"Do forces really flow through a structure in the same way as water flows through a river?"

"Not quite, but water flow is a useful analogy for force flow. Most forces in buildings are static, meaning that nothing moves or flows through a body of material in the literal sense, but the forces follow patterns that we perceive as being like those we observe in flowing liquids. When water flows through a narrow channel, its currents all flow in parallel. This is analogous to the parallel pattern of flow of forces."

Diane indicated a drawing of parallel flow (14.8a).

"Where a narrow channel of water discharges into a sea, its currents disperse in a pattern that looks like a handheld folded paper fan. This is analogous to the fan pattern of flow of forces, which occurs when a concentrated force is applied to a large body of material (14.8b). A fan of this type is known as a half-plane fan.

"If the channel discharges into the corner of a square harbor, it disperses in a quarter-plane fan pattern. This tangential introduction of water into the harbor causes some eddy currents along the harbor wall at right angles to the channel. This behavior is analogous to the reversal of stress in the corresponding area of a quarter-plane fan of forces (14.8c). We could even imagine two half-plane fans joining at midstream in a canal to form a full plane fan (14.8d)."

Diane grabbed a tablet of paper, on which she drew a tall rectangle.

"Let's back up for a moment and apply these flow patterns to a simpler example than the one I just sketched. You can think of this rectangle as a wall panel that has a roof structure resting on top of it. The roof applies a uniformly distributed load to the top edge of the panel. The bottom edge rests on a concrete strip footing. How do you think the forces flow through this panel?"

"This must be a trick question. It seems obvious to me that the forces will follow parallel paths through the wall. But I'm sure there's more to it than that."

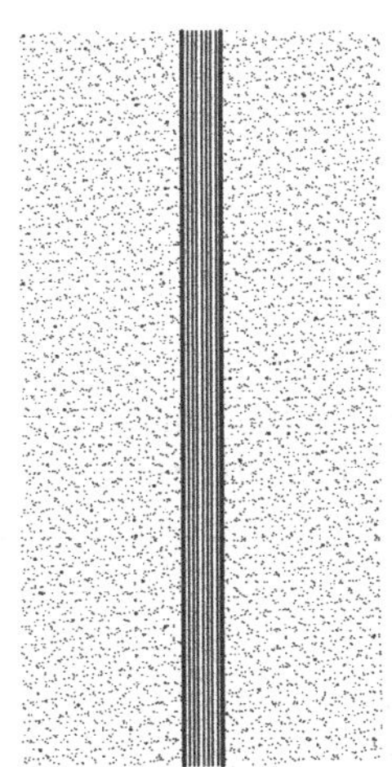

(a) Parallel Flow

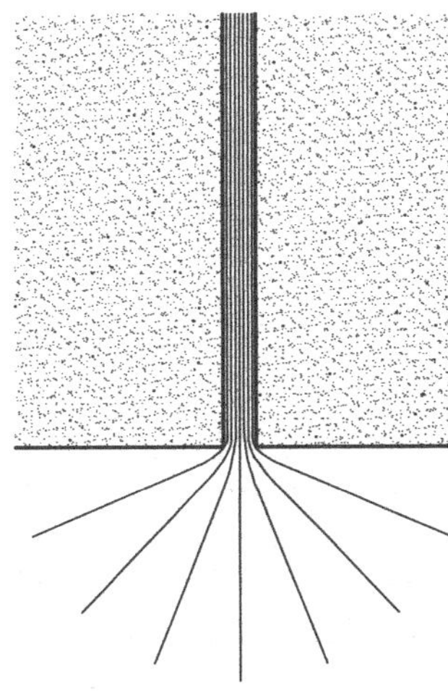

(b) Half-Plane Fan

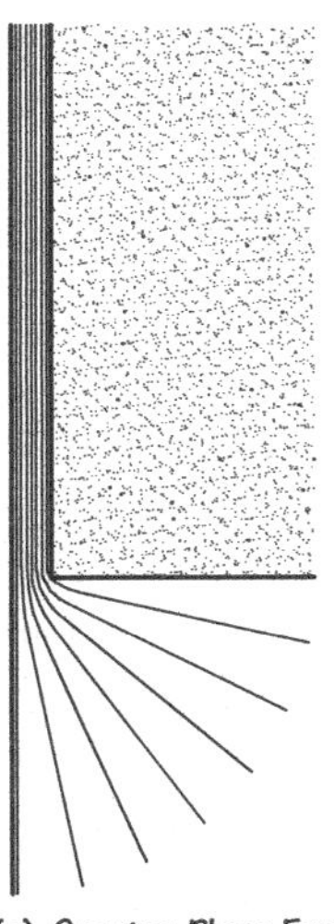

(c) Quarter-Plane Fan

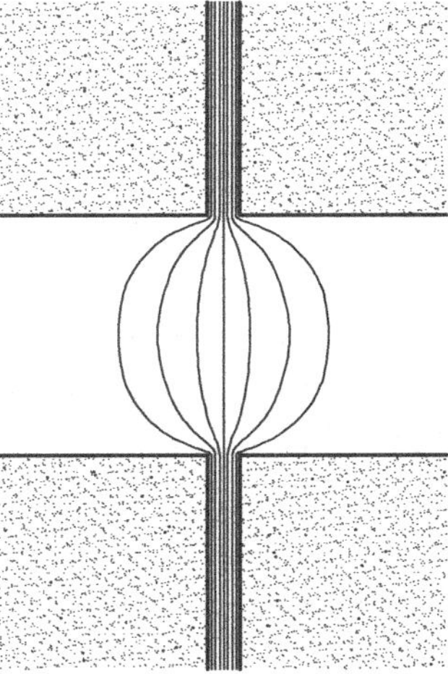

(b) Full-Plane Fan

Figure 14.8

"There isn't. It's the parallel pattern of flow (14.9). *Oh, there are some very small secondary forces running crosswise, caused by irregularities in the material. We represent these secondary forces by lines perpendicular to the main direction of flow. But the directions of the primary forces are all parallel and vertical. What we're calling flow is the pattern of the directions of the* principal stresses *in the material. A principal stress is the maximum stress that occurs at a given point in a structural body. The flow lines that we're drawing are often called* trajectories of principal stresses, *or just* stress trajectories. *But we need to keep in mind that these lines represent directions of stresses, not intensities. Stresses can and often do vary along the length of a single trajectory line. The intensity of stress is indicated in a general way by the spacing of the trajectories—the closer the lines are spaced, the higher the stress."*

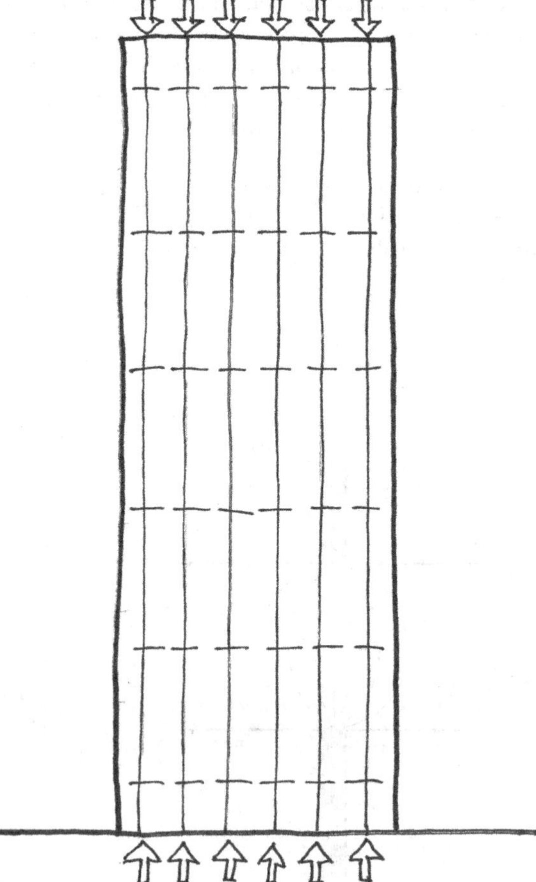

Figure 14.9

"Let me see if I understand this: If I had a magnetic compass that could indicate the direction of maximum stress at any point in a structural body, and if I followed the direction that the needle pointed until I had traveled from one side of the body to another, my path would be a stress trajectory?"

"That's right. Just one more thing before we go on: The lines that I'm drawing, the trajectories, merely indicate a few lines that represent the directions of an infinite number of paths within the object. They aren't the only paths along which forces flow."

"Design [of structures] is far wider in scope [than their numerical analysis]. It is an art, not just a set of calculations. . . . Consideration must be given at an early stage to the flow (or path) of forces. . . . The most revealing feature of a flow of forces is that it enables the structural behavior to be visualized and the dominant structural action to be identified."

—D. J. Fraser

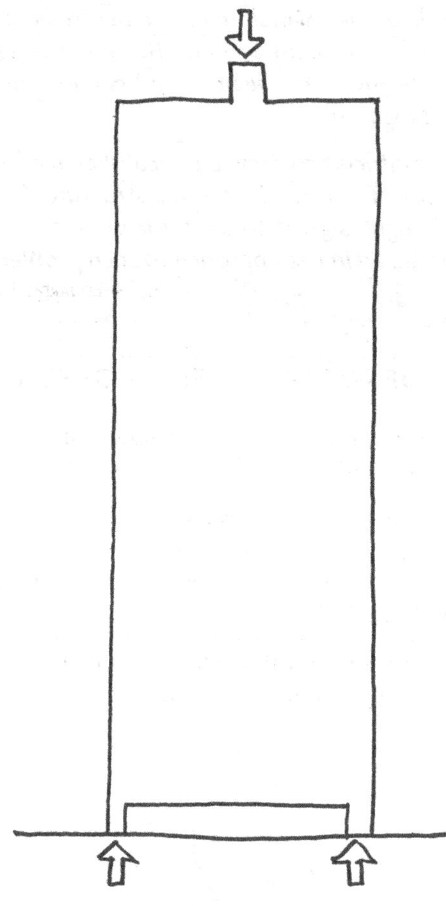

Figure 14.10

FLOW PATTERNS AT CONCENTRATED LOADS

"Now, suppose that the load on this tall wall comes from a beam that rests on the center of the top edge of the panel. And let's further suppose that the bottom edge of the wall is supported only at the two corners (14.10). *What do you think happens here?"*

"The load is concentrated rather than distributed on the top edge of the wall. The forces must spread out from the place where the beam bears until they fill the entire width of the panel."

"And that's just what they do."

Diane sketched a set of lines that radiated from the end of the beam into the panel (14.11).

"This is the fan pattern *of flow. If you imagine the material of the panel as being like a network of balls and springs, you can visualize how the forces fan out from the point of application* (14.12). *This can result from*

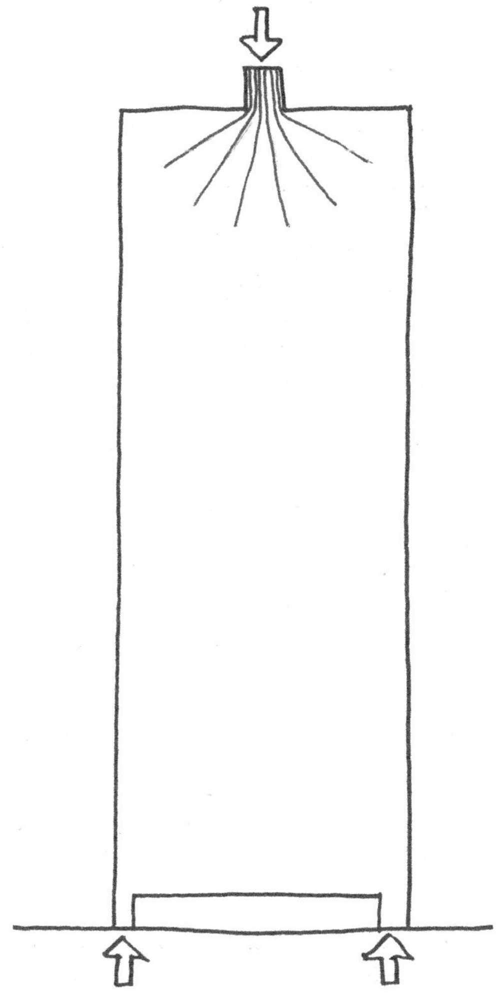

Figure 14.11

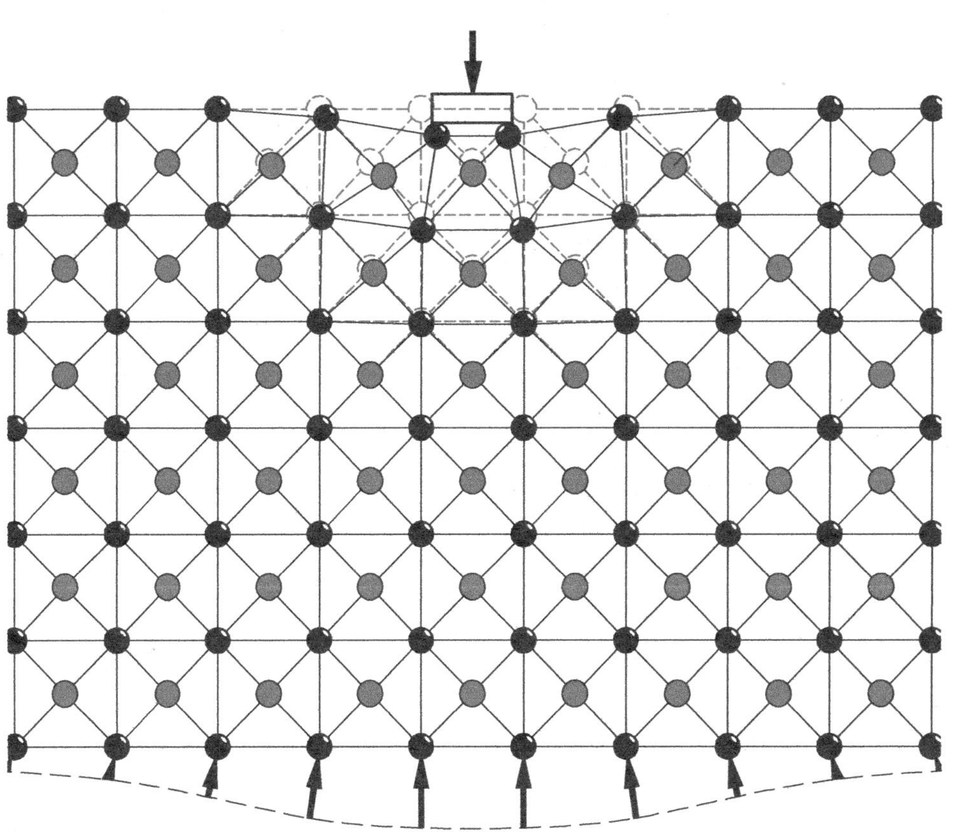

Figure 14.12

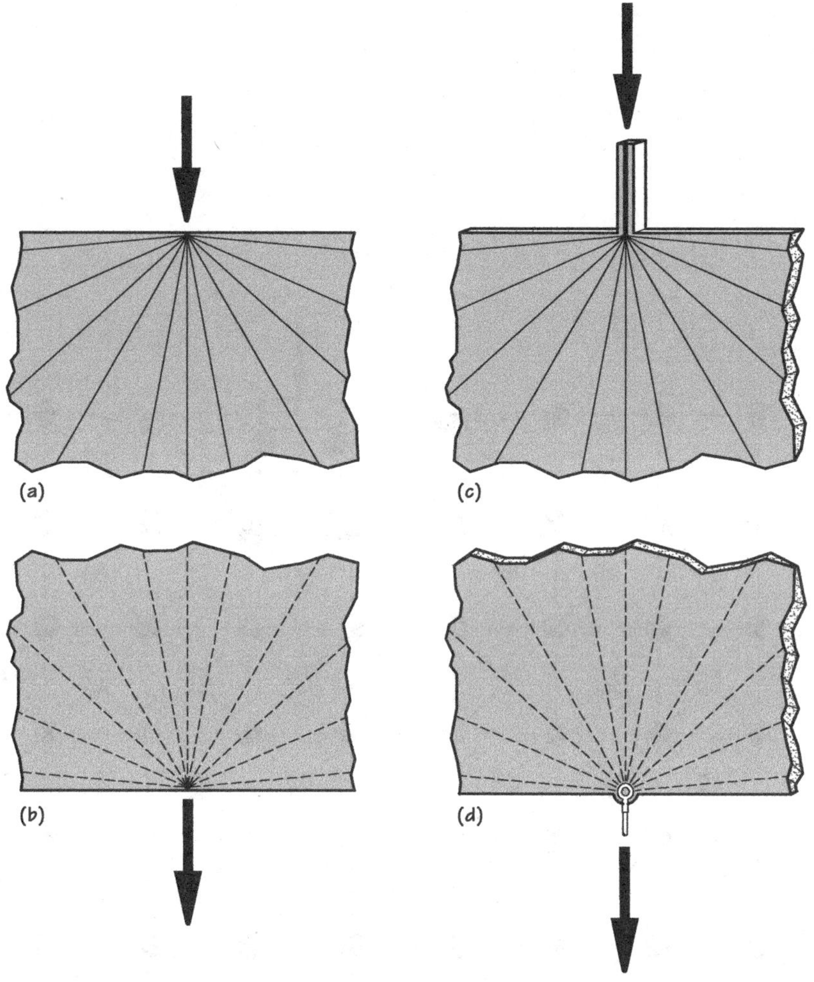

Figure 14.13

many kinds of loads, in compression or in tension (14.13)."

"There must be dozens of flow patterns that you have to learn."

"Actually, there are only three of them, and we've seen two of them already, fan and parallel! The third flow pattern is called lattice, *and we won't need that one for most of these walls that you've sketched."*

"You mean that we only need these two patterns, fan and parallel, to understand how forces flow in these walls?"

"Yes."

"Excellent! I didn't realize it would be so simple. Let's move on to the next wall."

"Not until we finish with this one. There's more to it that I need to explain. Here's a diagram that shows in five steps how to draw a complete flow diagram for this wall (14.14). *Focus on the downward-acting forces from the bottom of the beam; they fan out into the top of the wall panel within a very short distance. In order for them to change direction from the vertical external force to the various directions of the fan, there must be secondary forces at right angles to them to push or pull them into the new direction. There are no external forces to equilibrate with pulling forces in this region of the wall, so the secondary forces must be compressive, pushing out on the primary forces in a symmetrical pattern that is self-equilibrating.*

"When the forces in the fan approach the vertical edges of the panel, they must change direction a second time. They turn downward and become parallel flow, as you can see in step 3. *And in order to make that turn downward, there must be self-equilibrating forces that pull them inward, toward the center of the wall. The principle is the same as in arch or cable structures. For an arch or cable to change direction, there must be a secondary push or pull that acts on it from outside its axis* (14.15). *So we look for curvature of the trajectories, and wherever we see it, we add lines of secondary force perpendicular to the trajectories."*

"You're indicating that the fan is changing to a parallel pattern of flow with the assistance of secondary tensile forces that draw the primary trajectories inward. How do I know that this is true? Couldn't a set of compressive forces from outside the fan squeeze it into the parallel pattern?"

"If there were compressive forces pushing inward from within the body but from outside the fan, they would need equal and opposite external forces on the vertical edges of the body to maintain static equilibrium, and there are no such external forces in this example. On the other hand, tensile forces in the middle of the body can create static equilibrium by pulling equally on each side. So the secondary forces must be tensile in this region."

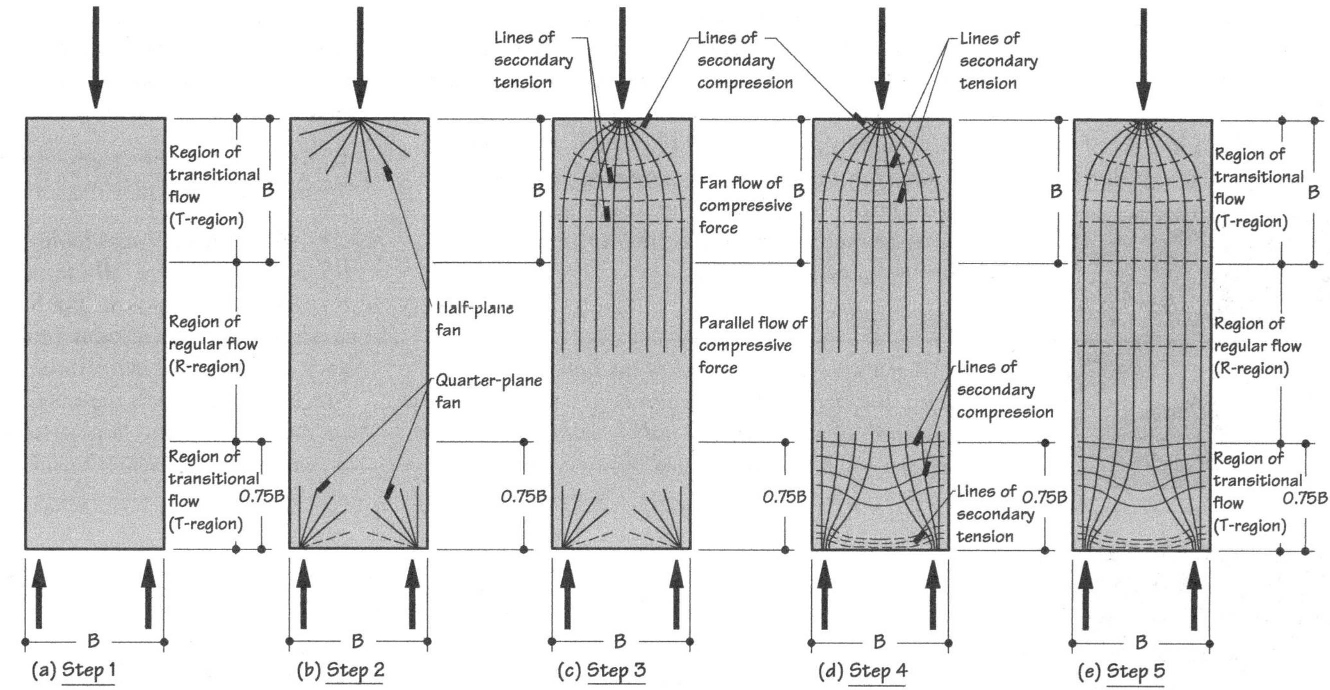

Figure 14.14

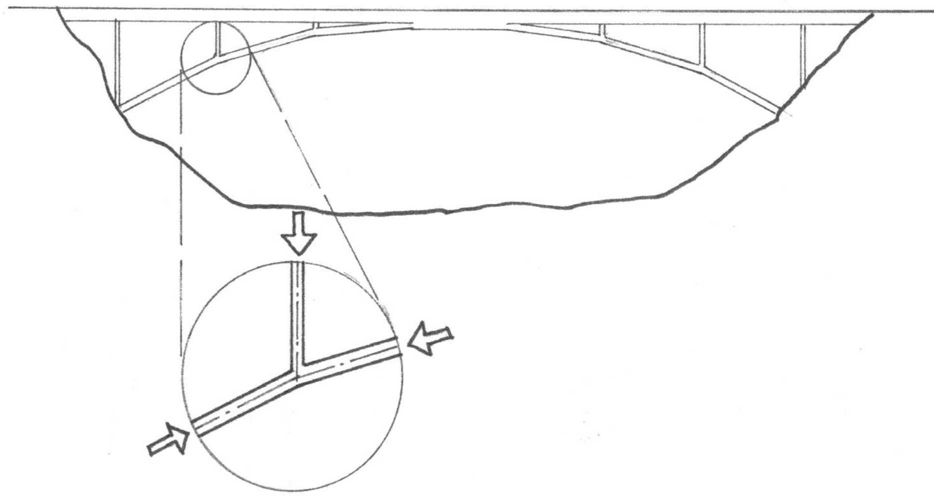

Figure 14.15

SAINT-VENANT'S PRINCIPLE

"Now we need to know where in the wall this transition from fan to parallel flow occurs. Does the fan happen very abruptly at the top, or does it extend far down into the wall? A French researcher named Barré de Saint-Venant figured out the answer to this question in the middle of the nineteenth century. Here's how he did it."

Diane picked up a cylindrical piece of foam.

"I use this foam to demonstrate Saint-Venant's principle in the class I teach at the university: If I grip the foam in my hand and squeeze it, only the foam within my grasp and very close to my hand changes shape. The rest of the piece is unaffected (14.16). *But if I place the foam piece across between two*

piles of books that support its ends, and push down on its middle, the entire piece changes shape."

"So?"

"In each case, I subjected the foam to a set of forces in equilibrium. When I squeezed it, equilibrium was created by the opposing forces exerted by my fingers and thumb. When I supported it across two piles of books, equilibrium resulted from my push in the center and the two reactions at the ends furnished by the books. In both cases, the portion of the body affected by the system of forces in equilibrium was no larger in any dimension than the maximum distance d *between the forces. That's Saint-Venant's principle."*

"Wait, explain that again."

"When I squeezed the foam in my hand, the maximum distance between the forces in equilibrium was the width of my hand, and only a small local area of the piece of foam was stressed by my squeeze. When I supported the foam piece on two books near its ends and pressed in the middle of it, the maximum distance between forces was the distance between the books, and the entire piece changed shape."

"Can you give me an example of what this means?" Diane opened to a new diagram. (14.17).

"Ah—here's what I was looking for. It shows five different metal bars, all identically loaded in axial tension or compression. Each bar has an end condition that is different from the others. Each has end regions of transitional flow—I call them T-regions*—in which the particular end condition has an effect on the flow pattern that is particular to that end condition. Outside those T-regions*

(a)

(b)

(c)

Figure 14.16

Photo: David M. Foxe.

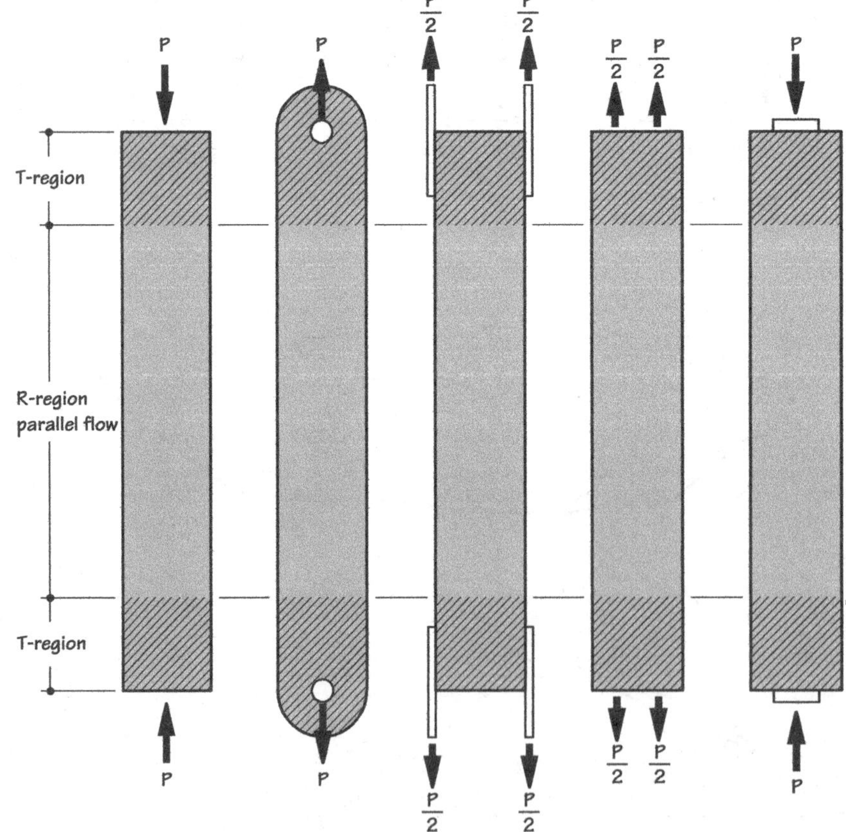

Figure 14.17

the flow in all the bars is identically parallel, and does not depend in any way on the end conditions. The length of all the regions of transitional flow is the same—it's equal to the maximum distance between the self-equilibrating forces at each end. This maximum distance is equal to the width of the bar. Parallel flow is the regular pattern of flow for this situation, and it occurs throughout the R-regions, *the regions of regular flow.*

"Let me pause to explain the terminology. In the engineering literature, these regions are sometimes called 'R-regions' *and* 'D-regions,' R *standing for regions of regular flow and* D *for regions of disturbed flow. I've adopted the name* 'transitional flow' *instead of* 'disturbed flow' *because the flow in such a region is not actually disturbed, but is making a well-ordered transition from one regular pattern to another.*

"I'm also using a different line convention than is used in engineering papers and texts. They use solid lines for tensile trajectories and broken lines for compressive trajectories. To me, broken lines look like lines that have been stretched and are pulling apart, so I use them for tensile forces, and solid lines for compression. I think that my conventions that are more intuitive and easier to remember."

"Okay, I understand and I agree with you. But back to Saint-Venant's principle: How does it apply to this wall?"

"The regular flow pattern for a deep wall loaded at the top is parallel. But because we applied the load at a single point, the forces must first spread out in a fan in order to fill the width of the wall before they can become parallel. This fanning out is transitional flow, and takes place in a T-region. This region of fan flow is maintained in equilibrium by the parallel flow in the main body of the wall and the concentrated force at the top of the wall. The maximum distance between any of these forces is the distance between the left and right edges of the distributed parallel flow within the panel. This distance is the same as the width of the wall. So Saint-Venant's principle tells us that the vertical distance occupied by the fan can be no larger than the width of the wall."

"Why is it important to know how big the fan is?"

"Because the secondary tensile forces that turn the fan into parallel flow are substantial enough that we have to provide steel reinforcing bars in the concrete to resist them. We have to put the steel in the right place. Saint-Venant tells us where. Also, we need the dimensions of the fan to be able to construct the truss model that will represent the forces in this wall."

"Ah, I'm beginning to catch on! But how do we know how **much** steel to put in at that place? Regardless of anything else, a panel is generally reinforced throughout with a single grid of #4 or #5 rebars spaced 12 to 16 in. apart in both directions. That's just to deal with lifting stresses, wind loads, and unusual loadings that occur during construction. I imagine that in many cases this is all that's needed, but how do we know?"

"Now we do have an equation for this!"

Diane opened her binder to an equation with an accompanying diagram (14.18).

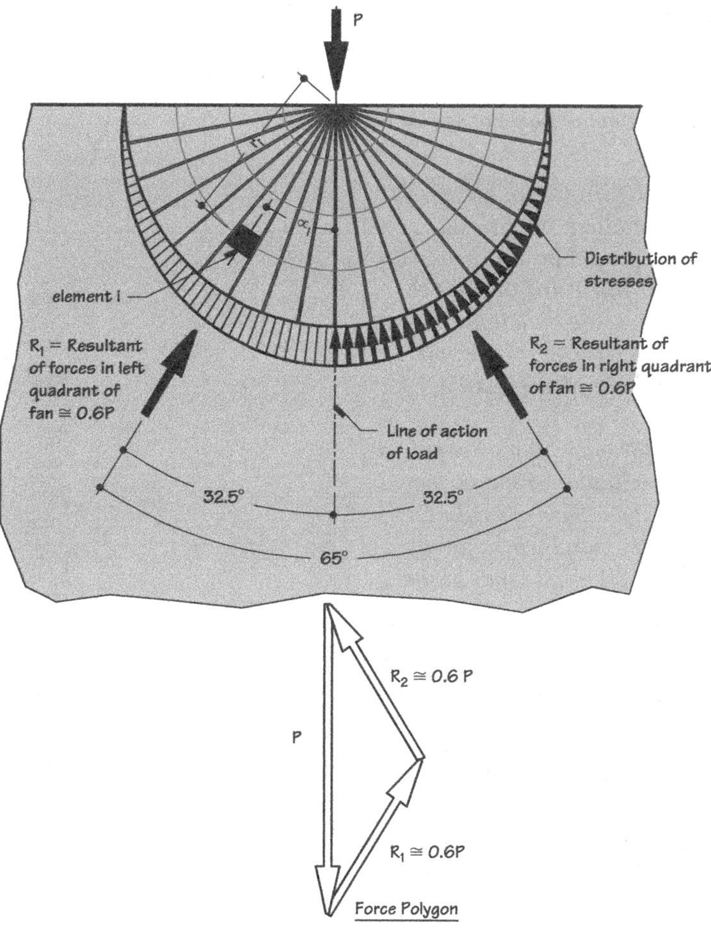

Figure 14.18

"The stresses in a fan were worked out by Saint-Venant's student, Joseph Valentin Boussinesq, and a co-worker of Saint-Venant, Alfred-Aimé Flamant. This expression, the Boussinesq-Flamant equation, gives the stress at any point in a fan:

$$f_{ri} = \frac{2P\cos\alpha}{\pi t r_i} \qquad [14\text{-}1]$$

where:

f_{ri} is the stress at selected element i,

P is the external force applied at the top of the fan,

α_i is the angle between the line of action of the applied force and the ray of the fan that passes through i,

t is the thickness of the wall, and

r_i is the radial distance from the point of application of P to element i.

"This expression says that the stresses in a fan pattern of forces are highest along the line of action of the external load, and they diminish with increasing angles from that line until they reach zero at an angle of 90° to the line of action. As the forces fan out, they also diminish in proportion to their distance from the point of application of the external force.

"This equation works for loads that are applied at angles other than perpendicular to the surface (14.19). *It even describes the effects of loads tangent to the surface* (14.20), *and works for an external load that pulls as well as one that pushes."*

"I see how this expression can give us the stress at any point in the fan. But how does it help us quantify the secondary force in the region where the fan changes to parallel?"

"We build an imaginary truss that is analogous to the flow pattern. Here's how: It can be shown with the help of this equation that the resultant of all the forces in each half of a half-plane fan is about 0.6P, where P is the external downward

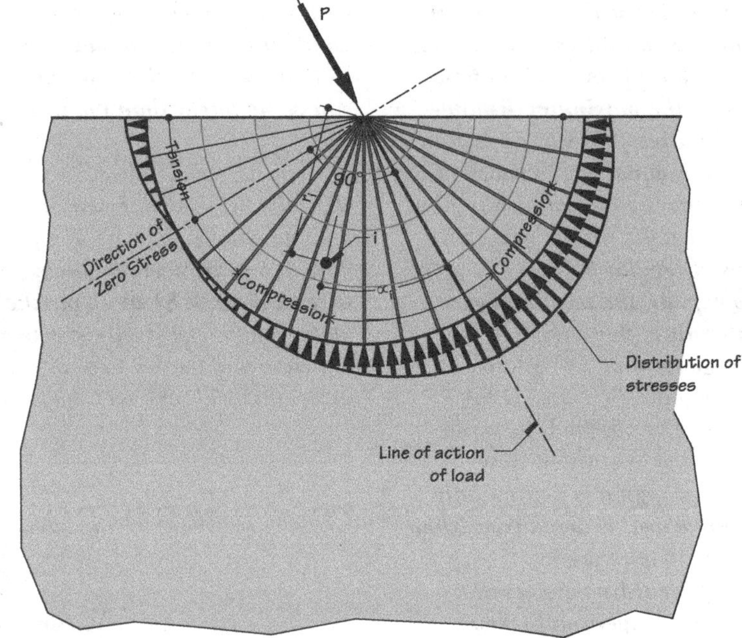

Figure 14.19

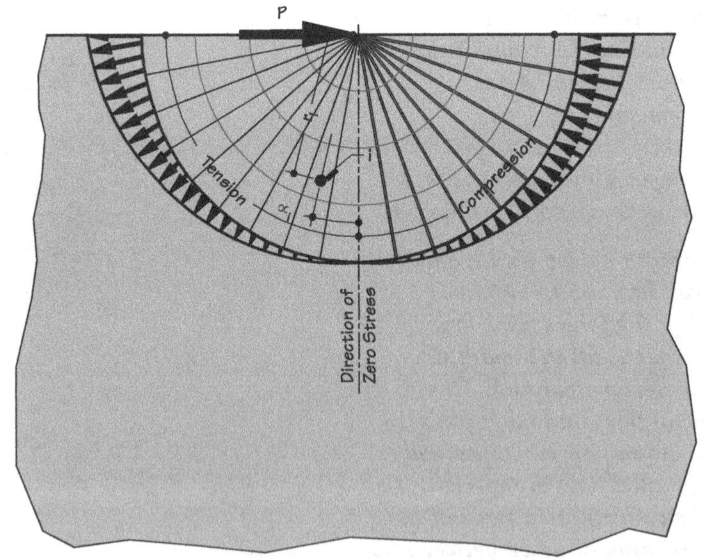

Figure 14.20

force at the top of the fan (14.18). *And the angle between the resultants in the two halves is about 65°. In our diagram, we replace the fan with two imaginary struts, each representing one of the resultants. The struts are 65° apart."*

Diane pointed to another illustration in her book (14.21).

"To further simplify our analysis, we can replace the parallel flow in the wall with two struts, each representing the total force in half the width of the wall, which is 0.5P. Each strut is located at the centroid of its half of the wall, which is the quarter point of the width. What's missing? What else is needed to put this structure that we've developed into equilibrium?"

"A horizontal tie where the sloping struts join the vertical struts."

"Precisely!"

"And that horizontal tie represents the secondary tensile forces in the flow pattern?"

"Bravo! Now we've reduced the fan and parallel flow at the top of the wall to a single-panel truss. And we can solve easily for the forces in the truss members by making a force polygon from those resultants, just as we would do for any truss (14.21). *We scale vector 1–2 on the force polygon to find that the tie experiences a force of about 0.32P. It's close enough if we call this 0.3P or P/3."*

"I'm impressed. That's quite a chain of logic, and it gets us to an answer to my question. But how good is the answer? You made some gross simplifications and approximations along the way."

"Surprisingly, the value we've found in this way is sufficiently accurate for almost any purpose. Given the low level of certainty that we have about live-load assumptions, there's seldom a need for a more

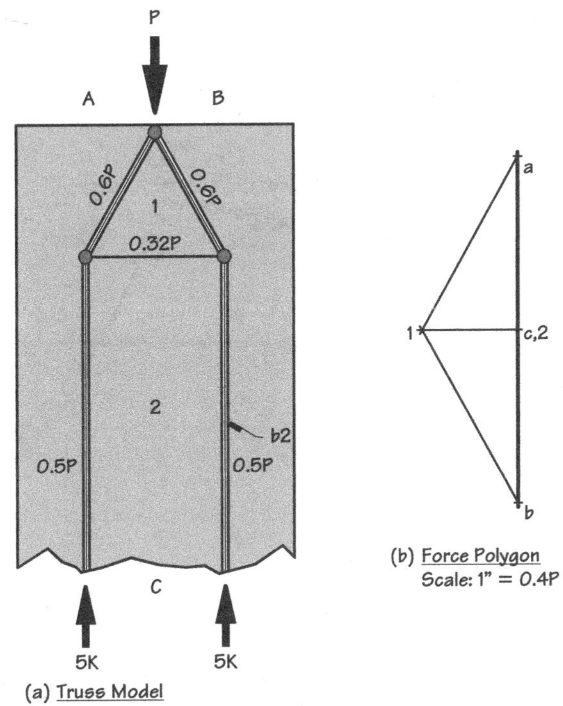

Figure 14.21

accurate determination than this method can give us. In our case, if P is 100 kips, the horizontal force at this point in the wall is about 32 kips. If we use grade 60 rebars, which have an allowable strength of about 36 ksi, we need 0.9 sq in. of steel, which can be provided by a single #9 bar. Or you could use three #5 bars, which total about 0.9 sq in., to spread the force over a larger area of the wall.

"This simplified way of finding forces in a solid body is called strut-and-tie analysis. *It's also widely known as* truss analysis. *It's a universal method for finding approximate values for the forces in any solid body of material, such as a wall, a connecting plate, or a foundation. It has been widely accepted in the engineering profession, especially as a tool for determining forces in structures whose behavior can't be reduced to a simple mathematical formula."*

Strut-and-Tie Modeling

Systems for the identification, depiction, and analysis of flow patterns inside solid bodies of material have been developed independently in many locations by different practitioners. The use of truss analogies for deep beams and other concrete elements can be traced back as early as Ritter's analyses published in 1899, which were followed by the work of a host of other Swiss and German practitioners and theoreticians. This general approach has been known as "flow of forces" since the 1950s in Poland. Through the pioneering work of Jörg Schlaich and his coworkers, the approach of visualizing forces and representing them with trusses has become widely known since the 1970s as strut-and-tie modeling (or STM). As one of the major codifications of this approach, Schlaich and his colleagues Kurt Schafer and Mattias Jennewein at the University of Stuttgart published "Toward a Consistent Design of Structural Concrete" (*PCI Journal, May/June 1987*). This paper traces the history of the strut-and-tie model and proposes generalized approaches for analyzing and designing any concrete structure, along with the reinforcement and prestressing within. STM is now utilized for both theoretical and applied engineering of structures by engineers and scientists throughout the world.

FORCES AT THE BOTTOM OF THE WALL

"Now we need to look at what happens at the two lower corners. This diagram shows that a fanlike pattern of flow exists at each of the two supports (14.22). In fact, it's a quarter-plane fan like we saw earlier (14.8c), and it forms wherever we load a rectangular wall or plate at one corner. It's an intriguing pattern because it includes a substantial area of tensile force along the edge perpendicular to the line of action of the external force. This tensile force is why it's dangerous to drive a vehicle too close to the edge of a foundation excavation, or to build a building right on the edge of a cliff. In either situation, this tensile force can cause the brittle soil or rock along the vertical edge to break away."

"Fascinating!"

"At the lower edge of the wall, the tensile forces in the quarter-plane fans act to spread the corners apart, so we need to put horizontal reinforcing bars in this region. A little higher up, in the upper regions of the quarter-plane fans, secondary compressive forces push the radiating lines of force toward the parallel direction that they follow in the main body of the wall. We need to find out how large these forces are."

"I imagine we do this by completing the truss model of the wall to include these areas. But I don't see how to do it."

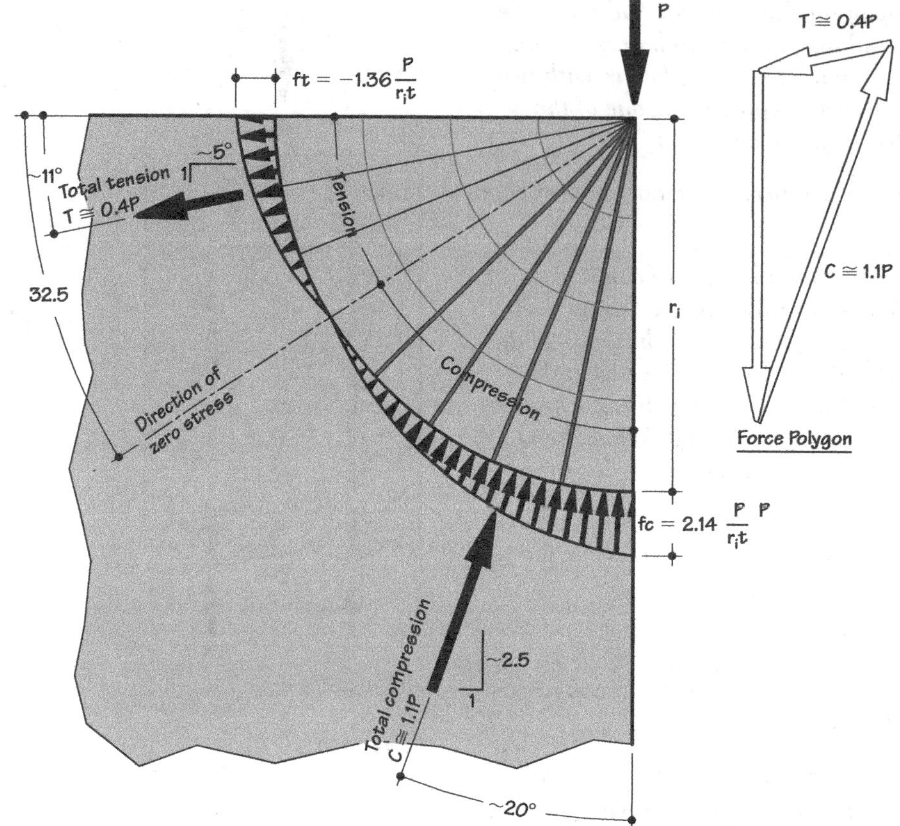

Figure 14.22

"It's actually pretty easy. We examine the diagram of forces in a quarter-plane fan, looking particularly at the resultants that are shown with the large vector arrows. In each corner of the wall, we show a strut and a tie for the two major resultant vectors. We take these angles from the diagram of the quarter-plane fan (14.22). Each strut slopes at 20° from the vertical and the ties at 11° from the horizontal. The struts connect to the two vertical struts we've already drawn (14.23). The ties slope up toward the middle of the wall and meet at the centerline. They need an upward force at this intersection to maintain this position, so we add two sloping tie members to the nodes in the struts to provide this force."

FINDING FORCES IN THE TRUSS MODEL

"Now we can solve for the forces in the entire wall in one graphical operation, using a force polygon. This overall pattern, the combination of the fan and parallel patterns, is often called a bottle pattern, *for obvious reasons. By the way, the same distribution pattern and secondary*

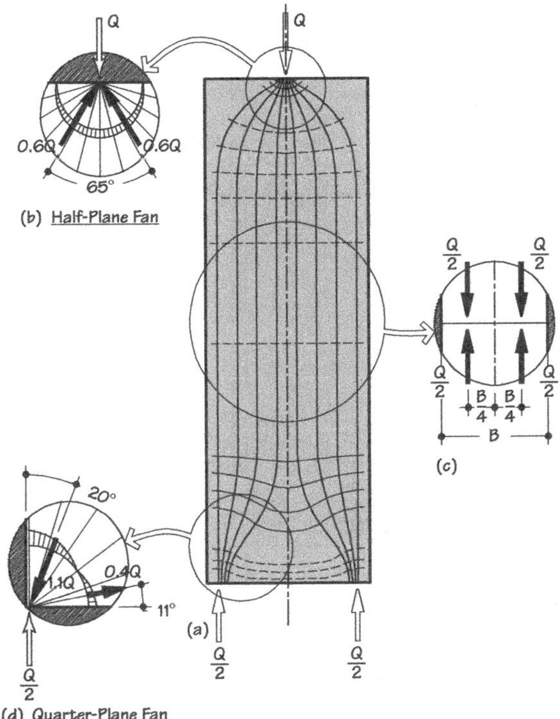

Figure 14.23

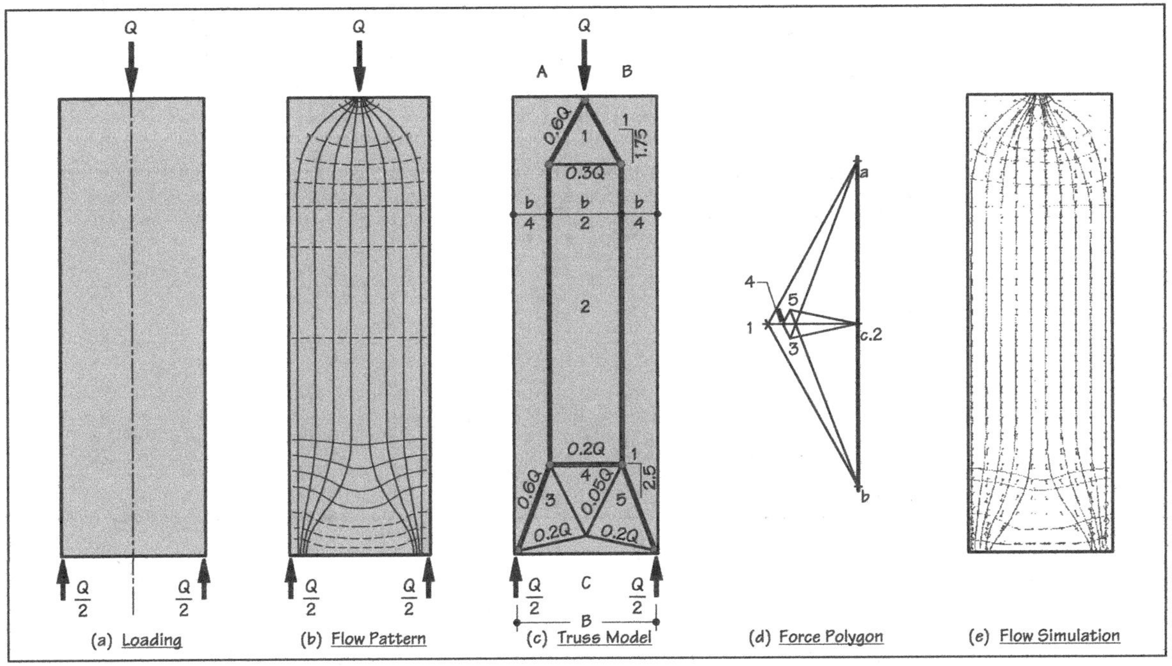

Q
A
B
0.6Q
0.3Q
0.2Q
0.05Q
0.2Q
0.2Q
1.75
2.5
C
Q/2
B
(a) Loading
(b) Flow Pattern
(c) Truss Model
(d) Force Polygon
(e) Flow Simulation

Figure 14.24

forces are found if the wall or plate is loaded in tension instead of compression, but of course, the characters of all the forces are reversed.

"This is part of a summary drawing showing everything we need to know about this deep wall (14.24). At the left is a diagram of the wall and its external loads. Next is the flow diagram that we've just drawn. After that, the reduction of the flow lines to a simplified truss model. The top part of this we evolved a few minutes ago, based on the properties of a half-plane fan. The bottom part derives from the geometry of flow in a quarter-plane fan. In this case, we show the sloped struts and ties not through angles in degrees but through equivalent approximations in rise and run.

"To the right of that is a force polygon that solves for the forces in the truss model. By scaling this diagram, we can learn the values of the forces that must be resisted by reinforcing bars, which in turn allows us to select the number and size of bars for each location. And finally, at the far right, we see a computer simulation of the flow in this wall. It was done by my colleagues Bashar Altabba and Nicole Michel, who made a number of these simulations for many different situations using a program called ANSYS. Their work was underwritten by the HNTB Corporation. The flow pattern is indicated by a

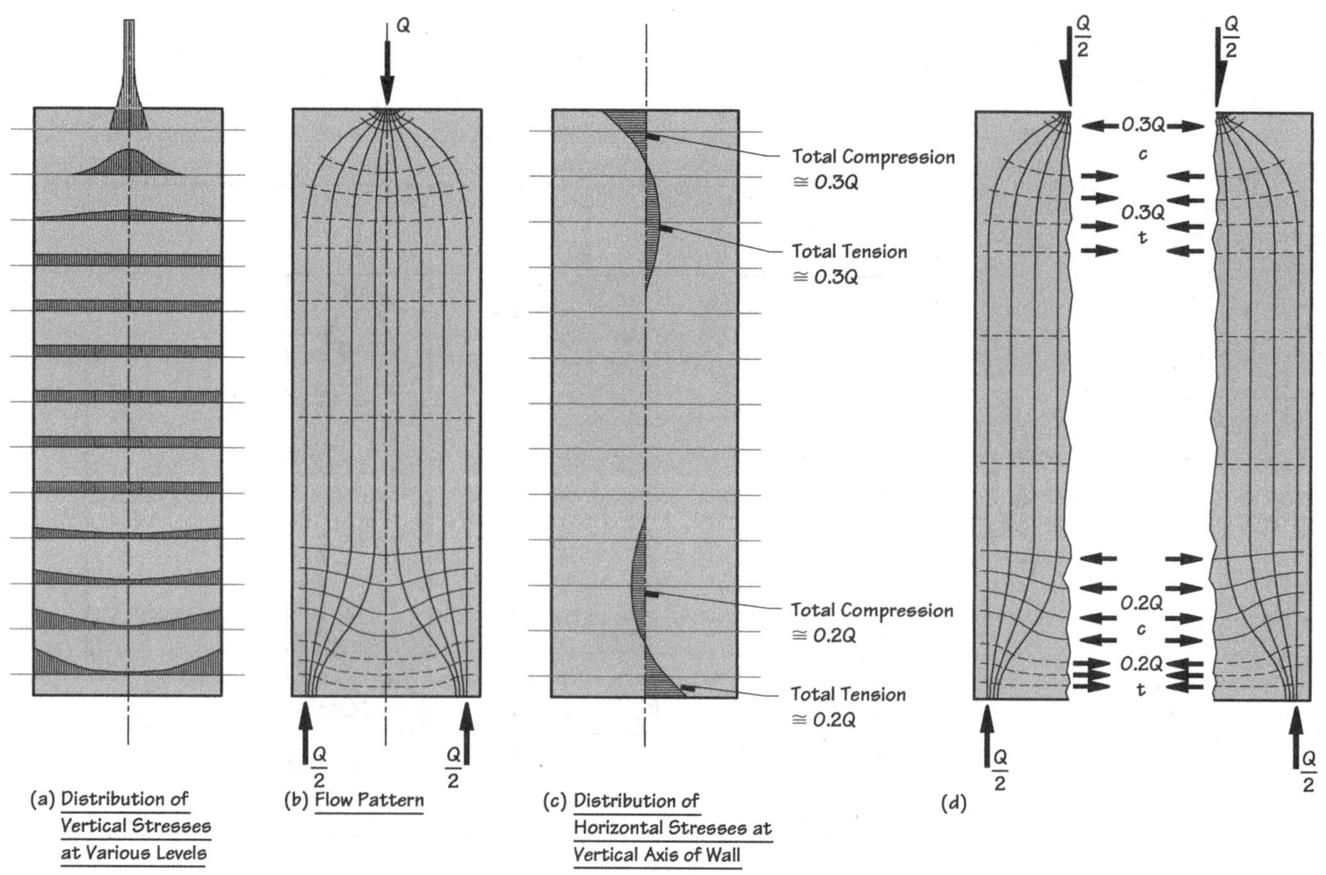

Figure 14.25

regular grid of marks. If there's just a dot at each grid point, there is no force flow in the area. Tick marks at a grid point indicate the directions and magnitudes of the principle forces at that point. The length of a tick mark is proportional to the intensity of the force at that point, and the direction of the arrowheads indicates tension or compression. You can see immediately that the ANSYS analysis confirms the flow pattern that we sketched by hand. We can also extend these results and see the distributions of horizontal and vertical stresses in the wall (14.25), *as another way of visualizing the accumulation of different forces within the wall.*

"Flow analysis often enables us to give more efficient shapes to structural bodies. It's obvious in a deep wall with a concentrated load at the center of its top edge that we can eliminate the material that lies outside the flow patterns in the 'shoulders' of the wall."

ECCENTRICALLY LOADED DEEP WALLS

Bruce had a question:

"What if I want to load the top edge of a deep tilt-up wall panel at some point other than its center? Maybe at its quarter point, or even at the corner?"

"Then things get really interesting!"

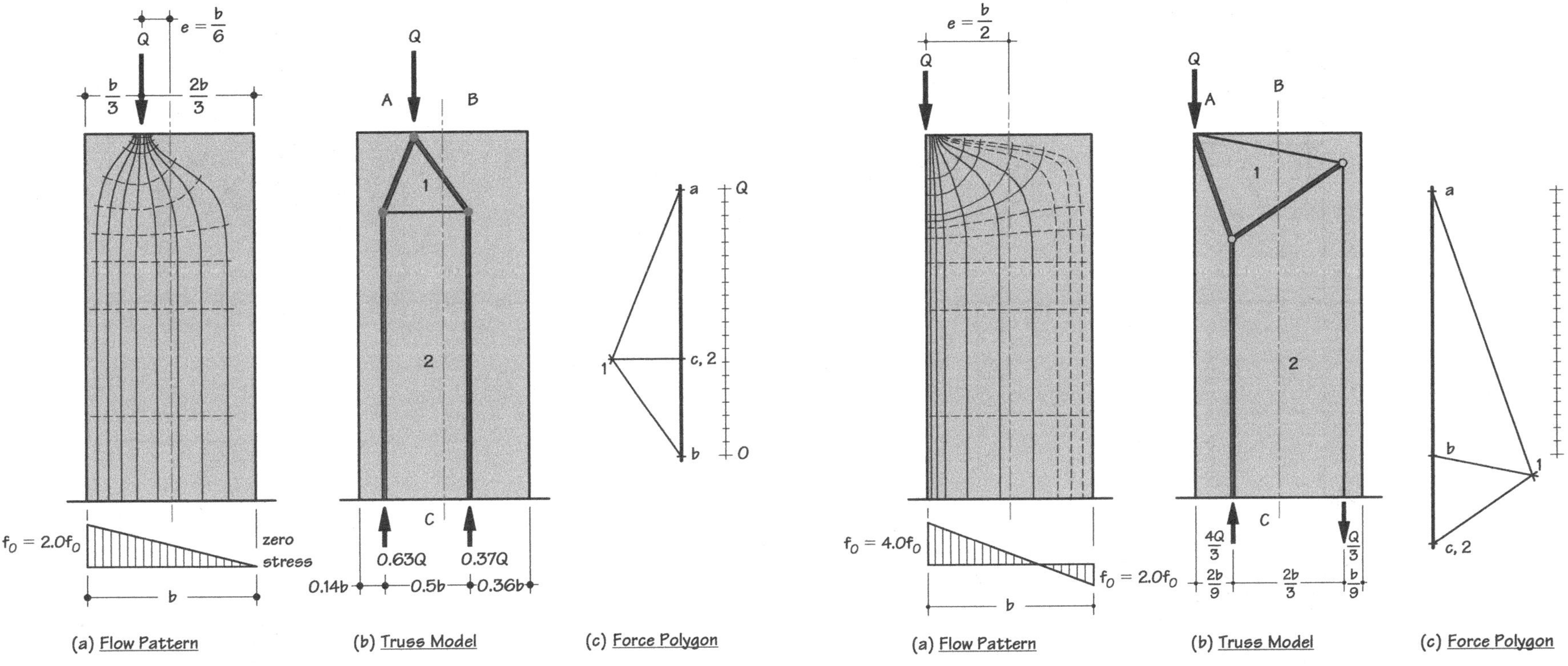

(a) Flow Pattern (b) Truss Model (c) Force Polygon

Figure 14.26

(a) Flow Pattern (b) Truss Model (c) Force Polygon

Figure 14.27

Diane opened to a page that showed another truss model of a deep wall (14.26).

"Here's a diagram of force flow in a wall that's loaded eccentrically. It assumes support all across the lower edge of the panel, such as you would have if the panel sat on a strip footing. You can see right away that this eccentricity places higher stresses on the side of the wall that is nearer to the line of action of the applied force, and lower ones on the other side. There's a linear distribution of the forces in the R-region. This is indicated by the flow lines in the R-region, which are closely spaced at the vertical edge nearer the line of action of the load, and more widely spaced on the other edge. With this load applied at the third point of the top edge, notice how the stresses are distributed across the width of the wall: at the edge farther from the load, there is zero stress. At the nearer edge, the stress is double the value for an axially loaded wall.

"If the load moves outside the middle third of the wall, a portion of the wall on the side away from the load goes into vertical tension (14.27). *This is a very interesting overall pattern: There are some fairly large secondary compressive forces that act in a diagonal orientation near the top of the panel to push the primary tensile forces toward the edge of the wall. This entire flow pattern is easy to understand if you compare it to the spars and cables of a tall construction crane with a counterweight* (14.28)."

"We would have to put vertical reinforcing in the tensile zone of this wall. Wouldn't we also need to tie that side of the wall down to the earth, to keep it from leaning in the direction of the loaded edge?"

"Yes, we would. Loads in the middle third of the wall result in a wall that is in vertical compression all across its width, whereas a load outside the middle third causes tension. The middle third of a wall is one example of a geometric property of any

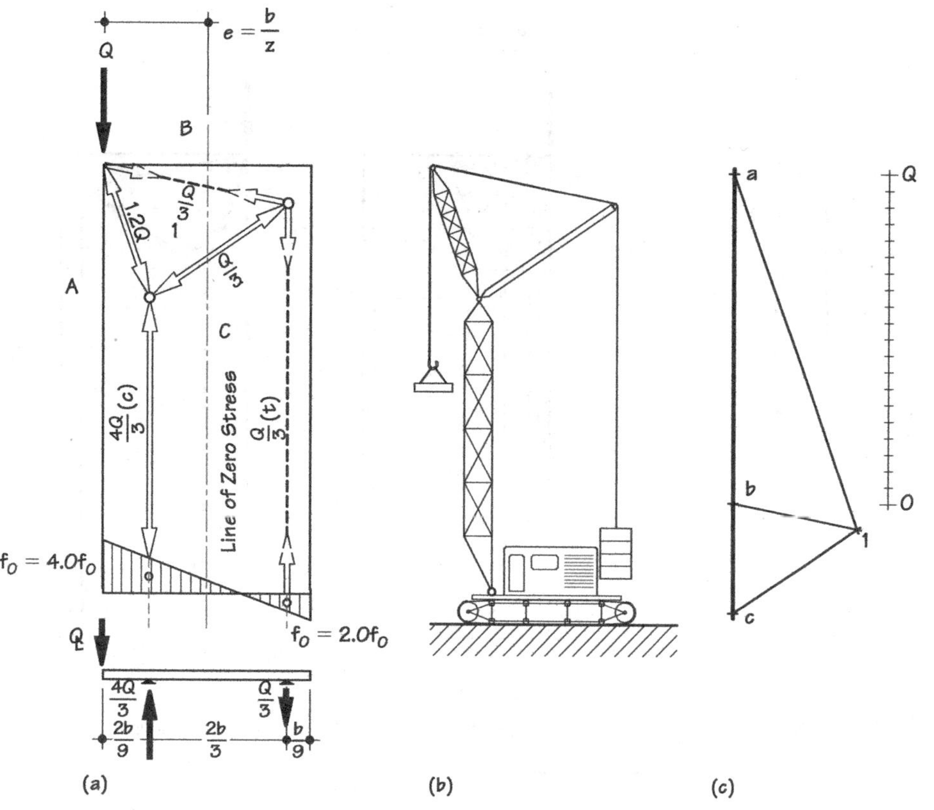

Figure 14.28 (a) (b) (c)

section that is known as the **kern** *of the section. If a compressive load is applied outside of the kern, the kern being the middle third in the case of a wall, tensile forces will occur on the other side of the kern.*

"The kern is a very useful concept in concrete, masonry, and many other materials and systems. If we imagine a masonry wall that is loaded outside its kern, cracks will appear on the edge of the wall opposite the load. If a column rests outside the kern of a footing, the side of the footing opposite the column will rise, and the footing will rotate and possibly fail (14.29). *The kerns of various shapes can be derived geometrically, and they're tabulated in many structures reference books* (14.30). *You can also find the outline of a kern*

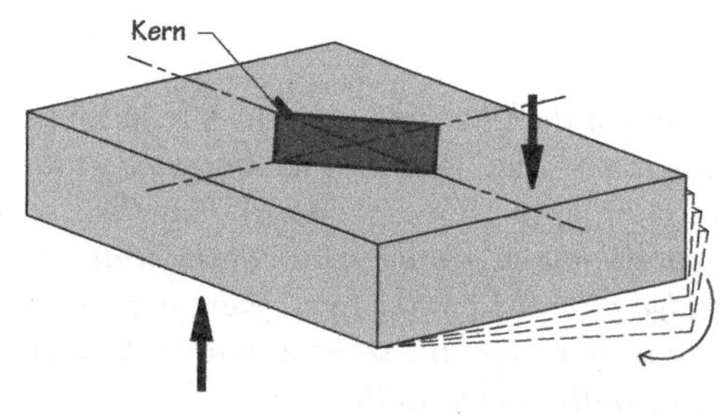

Figure 14.29

experimentally with a model of its shape—here's a photo of how it's done, using a block of foam rubber to represent the soil, and a rigid block for the footing (14.31)."

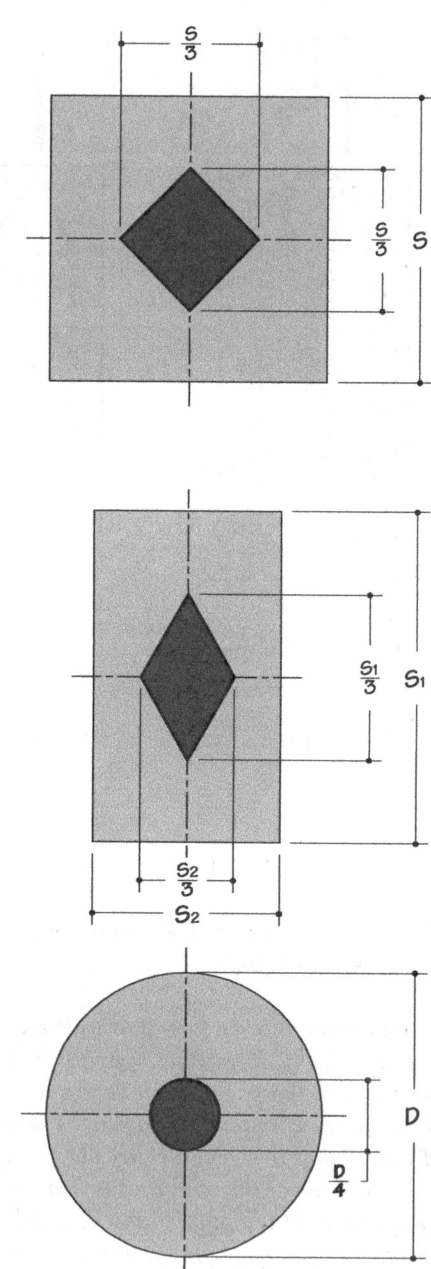

Figure 14.30

Figure 14.31

Photo: David M. Foxe.

LOOKING AT MORE WALL PANELS

"Shall we explore the ideas for tilt-up wall panels now?"

Bruce laid sketches on the table.

Diane sorted through the several pages and selected one.

"Yes, let's see. . . . This one is easy but interesting (14.32). *You've shaped some panels so they taper gradually from full width at the top to a relatively narrow base, leaving high-peaked window openings between. What does your intuition tell you about how forces might flow through these shapes?"*

"It looks to me like there would be parallel flow in the top of a panel, then the lines would converge in a sort of fan pattern through the tapered portion of the panels, and become parallel again at the bottom." Bruce sketched the pattern as he described it (14.33).

"Yes, that's what would happen. The tighter spacing of the lines at the bottom of the panel indicates a higher stress than at the top, which you would expect just because the cross-sectional area of the panel is reduced. What about secondary forces?"

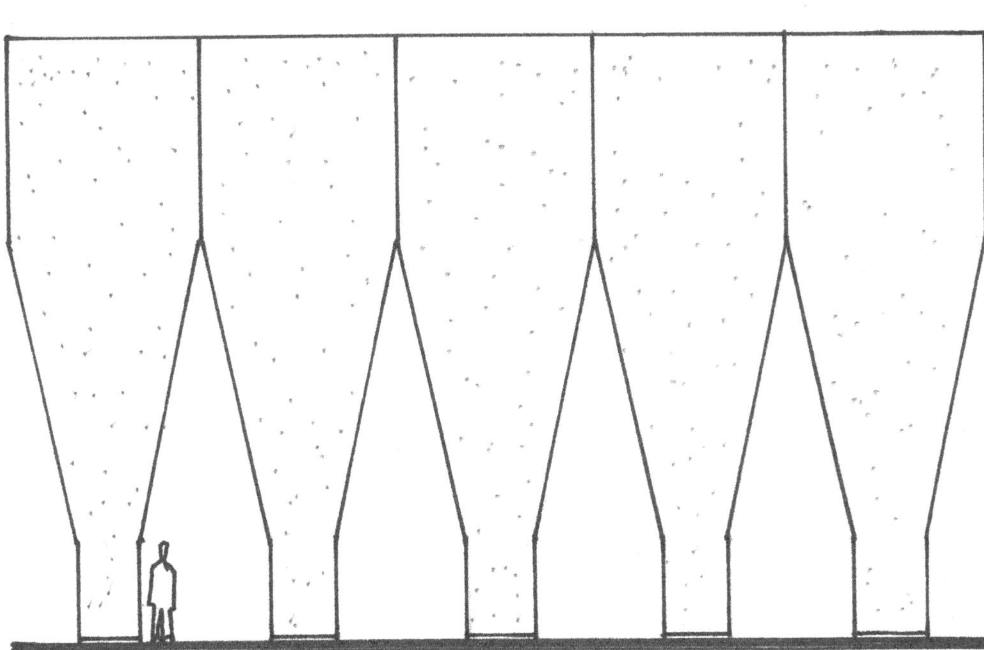

Figure 14.32

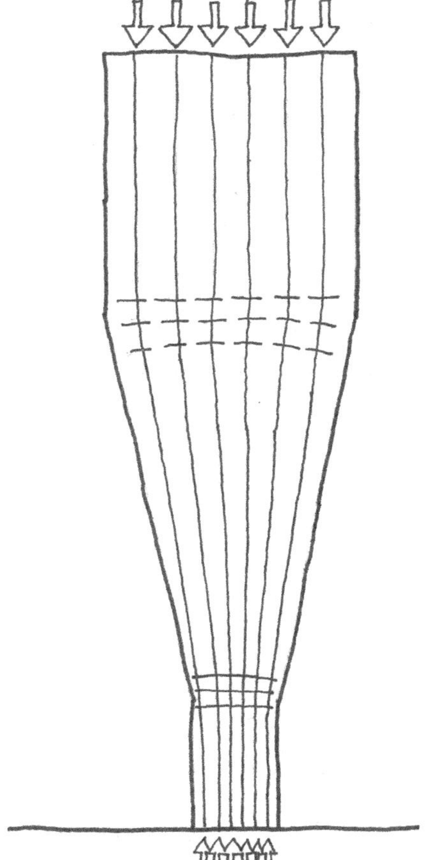

Figure 14.33

"Umm. . . . There must be secondary tension to pull the forces together where they converge at the top of the tapered section, and secondary compression to push the forces out so they become parallel again near the bottom."

He added these lines onto the diagram (14.33).

"Right again. Because the taper is so gentle, these forces are not large. How would you determine how large they are?"

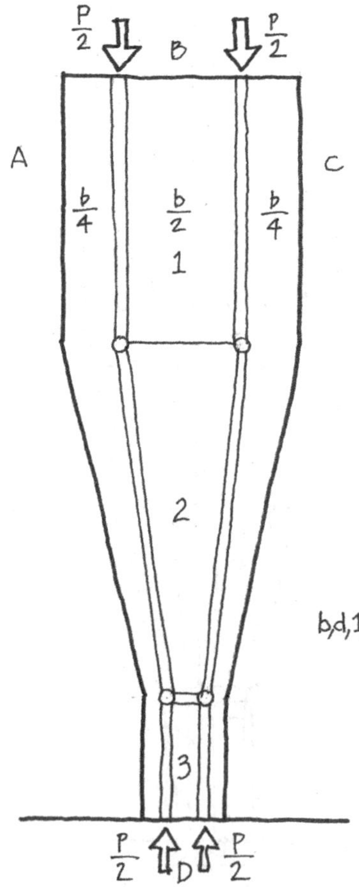

Figure 14.34

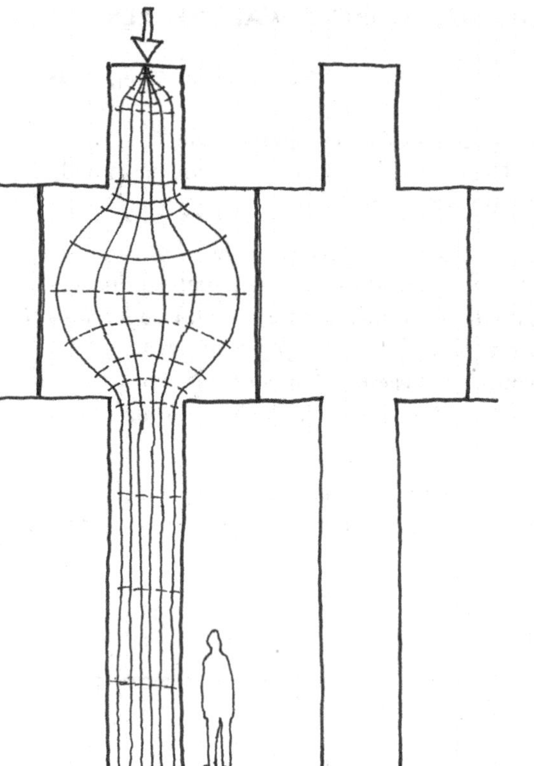

Figure 14.35

"I'd construct a strut-and-tie model and analyze it. Can you stand by to help while I try to do it?"

"Sure. Let's keep it simple by using only two vertical struts. We could use as many as we want, but two are usually sufficient."

"Because we're using two struts, each strut represents the forces in half of the wall, so each should be located at the middle of its half of the wall. Then we add a horizontal tie at the top of the tapered section, and a horizontal strut at the bottom (14.34).

"And finally, we add Bow's notation and draw the force polygon. By scaling the force polygon, we can see the tie force is only about 1/8 of the load on the wall, and the horizontal strut has the same amount of force as the tie, but compressive rather than tensile. This panel shape should work very well."

"I agree. The forces in it are very low. But some of these other walls will have higher secondary forces."

◀Figure 14.36

FORCE FLOW IN LONG WALLS

"Let's go back to one of your earlier sketches, one with panels that are narrower both above and below, with a broader area in the center, which will have a pattern that looks like this (14.35). To understand why such patterns happen in these kinds of panels, let's look at an exaggerated version first, like this one where you show tilt-up panels as long spandrel walls with horizontal strips of windows between (14.36). The upper panel supports itself on narrow concrete mullions."

"Let's look at the middle horizontal band of panels in your sketch. Each panel carries two concentrated loads from above, and is held up by two directly opposite forces from below. Tell me what you think the forces do in these panels."

"Saint-Venant's principle would seem to be the key here: We have self-equilibrating forces top and bottom. The area of the panel that the forces will occupy can be no larger in any dimension than the distance between the forces. That distance is the height of the panel. So for each opposing pair of forces there is a square region of the panel that can be affected (14.37a)."

"Good so far. What happens when a concentrated force is applied to the edge of a large planar body?"

"It creates a fan pattern of force flow. So I can draw two fans between each opposing pair of mullions. Like this . . . (14.37b). The fans must join each other somehow. It seems that the radiating lines of force will have to curve around to join each other . . . (14.37c)."

"That's exactly what they do. What sorts of secondary forces must there be to create these curving paths of primary forces?"

"There will have to be a small area of horizontal compression next to each concentrated force to spread the vertical forces into radiating lines . . . and then there will have to be horizontal tensile forces in the rest of the pattern to make the primary lines of compression curve toward one another (14.37c)."

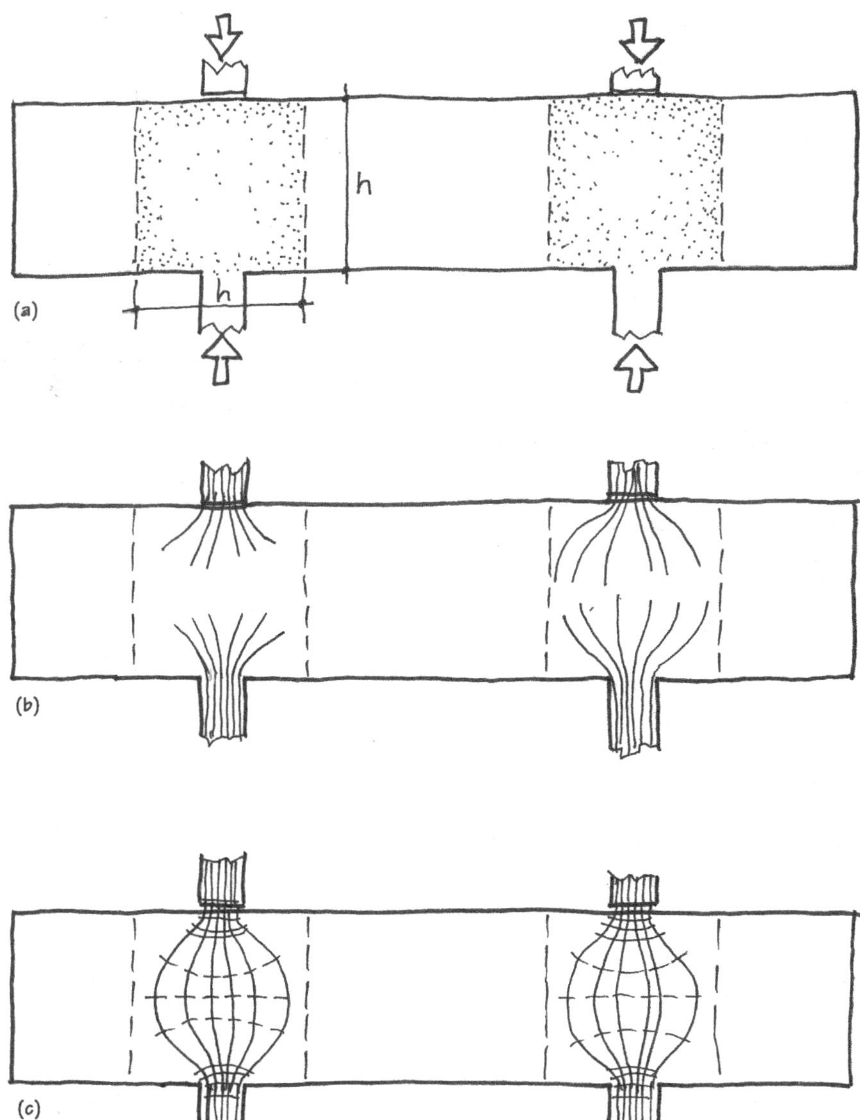

Figure 14.37

Diane opened to another page in her binder (14.38).

"This pattern is based on two half-plane fans. From their geometric properties, I can make a truss with two compressive struts 65° apart radiating from each point of force application, and a tie across the middle. Then I apply Bow's notation, draw a load line, and complete the graphical analysis. This shows that we need enough reinforcing steel across the middle of the panel to resist a tensile force that is about 0.64 times the external force."

"It appears that the overall pattern fits neatly into an imaginary round disk," observed Bruce.

"That's true, there will be only very minor forces outside the disk. I call this a long wall pattern. *There are many interesting variations of it, as you can see in my book* (14.39–14.42). *The ones with two forces opposing two forces, and one force opposing two, you could pretty well guess. The one with a compressive force and a tensile force on each side takes a bit more thought* (14.41). *It's intriguing because some of the lines of primary force cross over to become lines of secondary force in the other half of the pattern. What we're seeing here for the first time is just a hint of the third pattern of flow, which is the* lattice.*"*

"What's going on in this situation?" asked Bruce, pointing to another long-wall example in Diane's binder (14.42). "It looks like this is verging on a lattice pattern, too."

"So it is. It's not a configuration that we encounter frequently in everyday work, but it's of some interest because of the pattern's elegance and unusual qualities; the form of the trajectories is that of a minimum-weight cantilever truss known as a Michell structure *(Chapter 17)."*

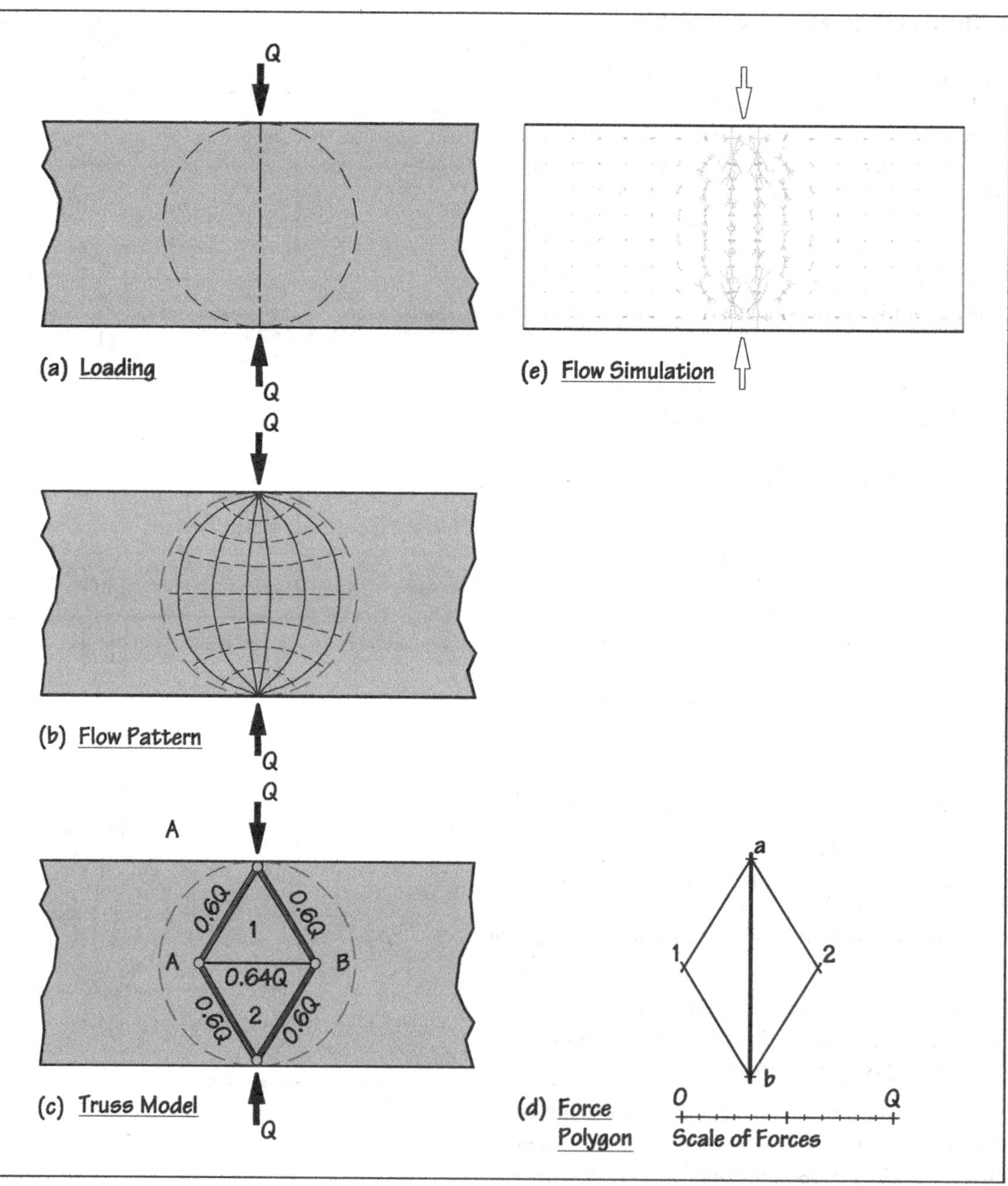

Figure 14.38

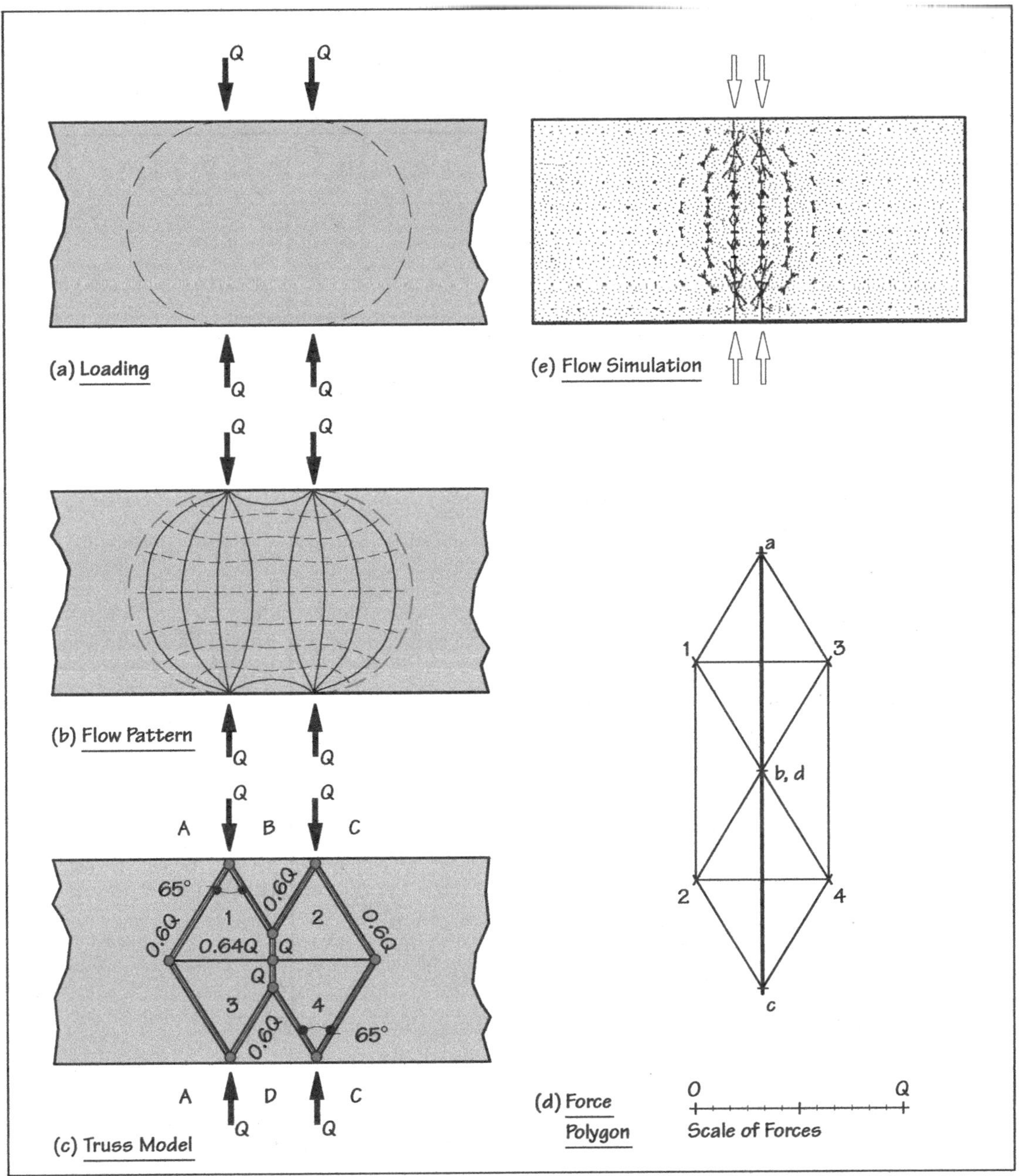
Q
Q
(a) Loading
Q
Q
(e) Flow Simulation
(b) Flow Pattern
A
B
C
65°
0.6Q
1
2
0.64Q
Q
3
4
D
(c) Truss Model
a
1
3
b, d
2
4
c
(d) Force Polygon
0
Scale of Forces

Figure 14.39

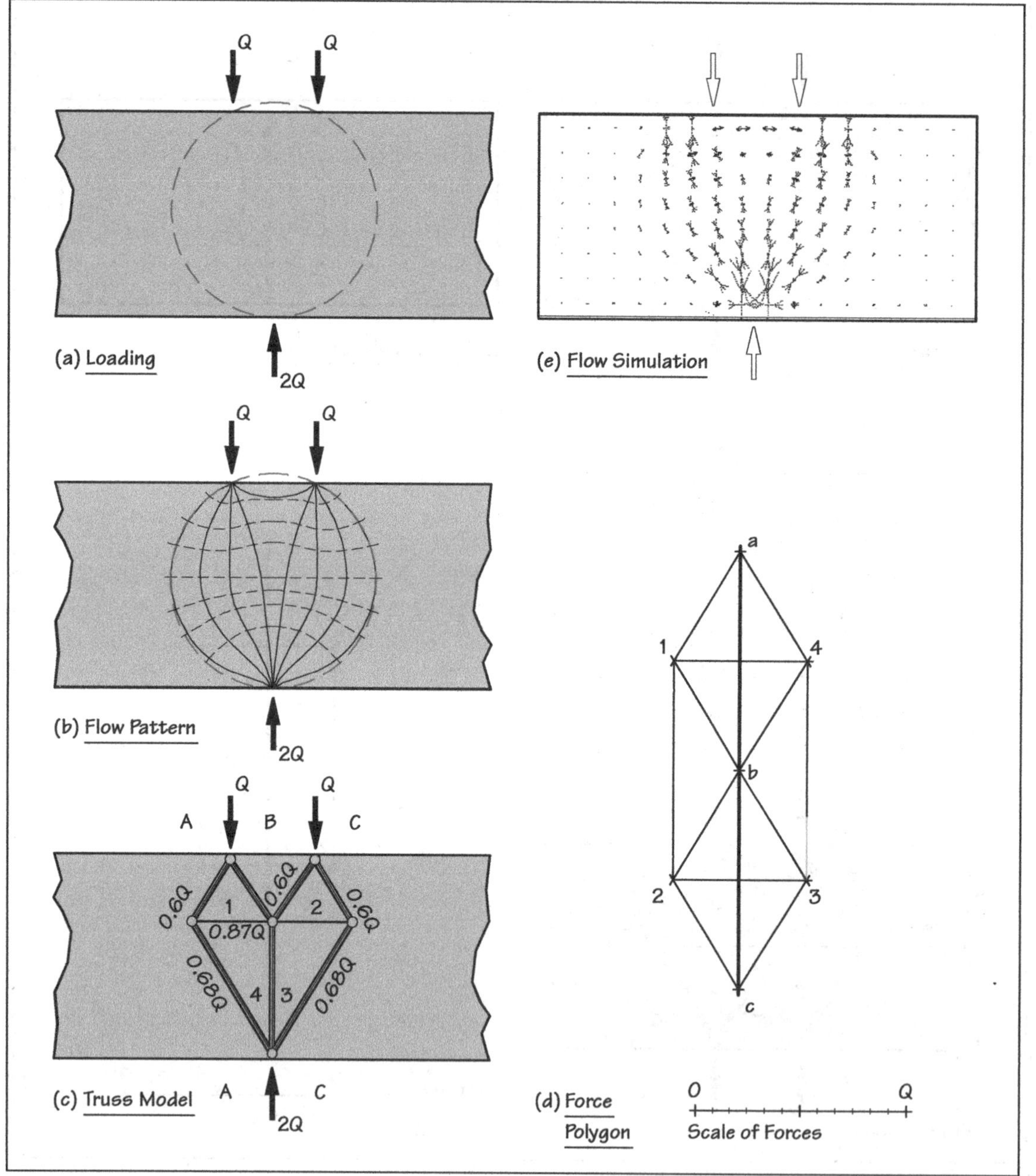
Q
Q
(a) Loading
2Q
(e) Flow Simulation
Q
Q
(b) Flow Pattern
2Q
Q
Q
A
B
C
0.6Q
0.6Q
0.6Q
0.6Q
1
2
0.87Q
0.68Q
0.68Q
4
3
(c) Truss Model
A
C
2Q
a
1
4
b
2
3
c
(d) Force Polygon
0
Q
Scale of Forces

Figure 14.40

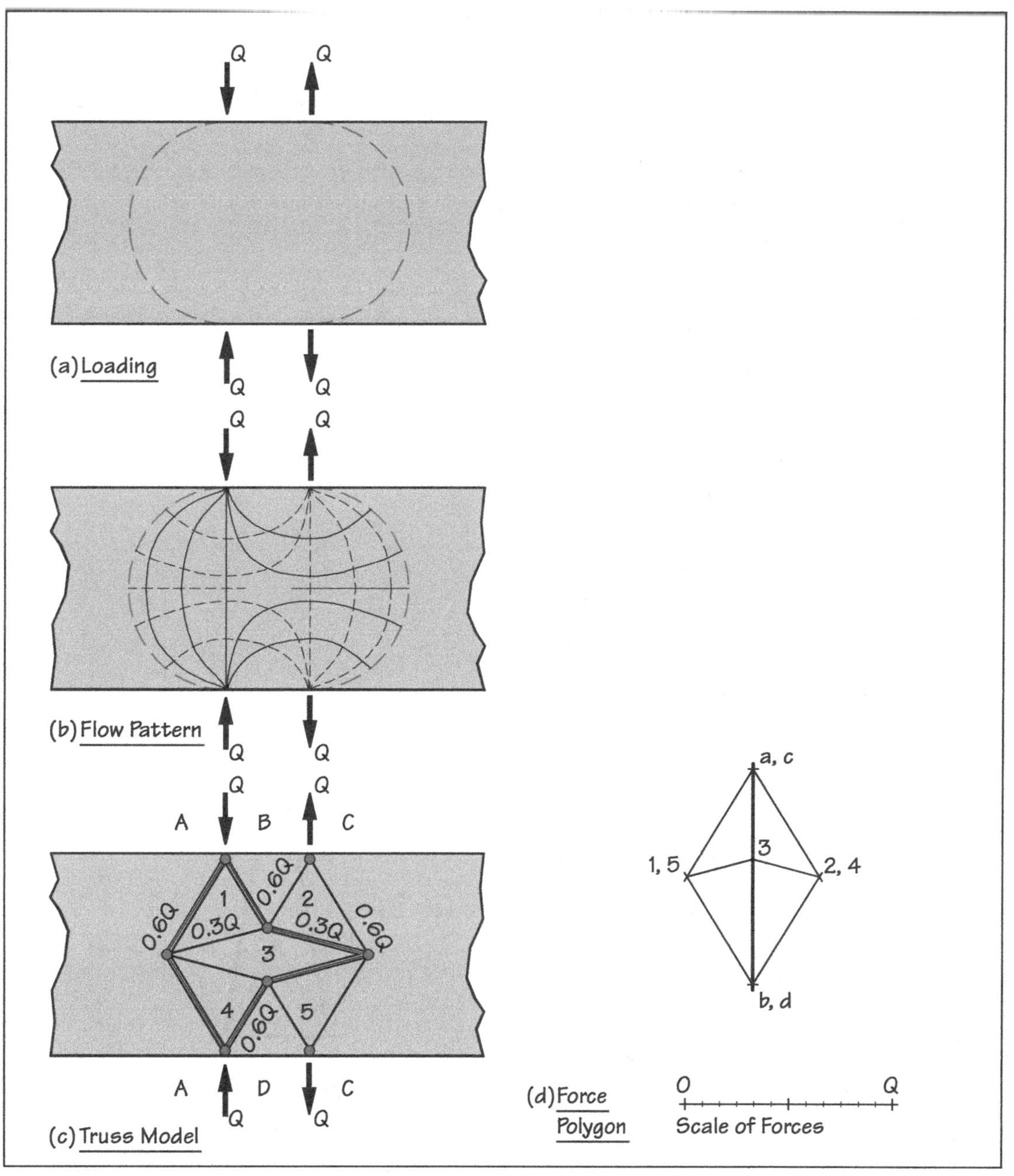
Q
Q
(a) Loading
Q
Q
Q
Q
(b) Flow Pattern
Q
Q
Q
Q
A
B
C
1
2
3
4
5
0.6Q
0.3Q
0.6Q
0.3Q
0.6Q
0.6Q
A
D
C
Q
Q
(c) Truss Model
a, c
1, 5
3
2, 4
b, d
(d) Force Polygon
0
Q
Scale of Forces

Figure 14.41

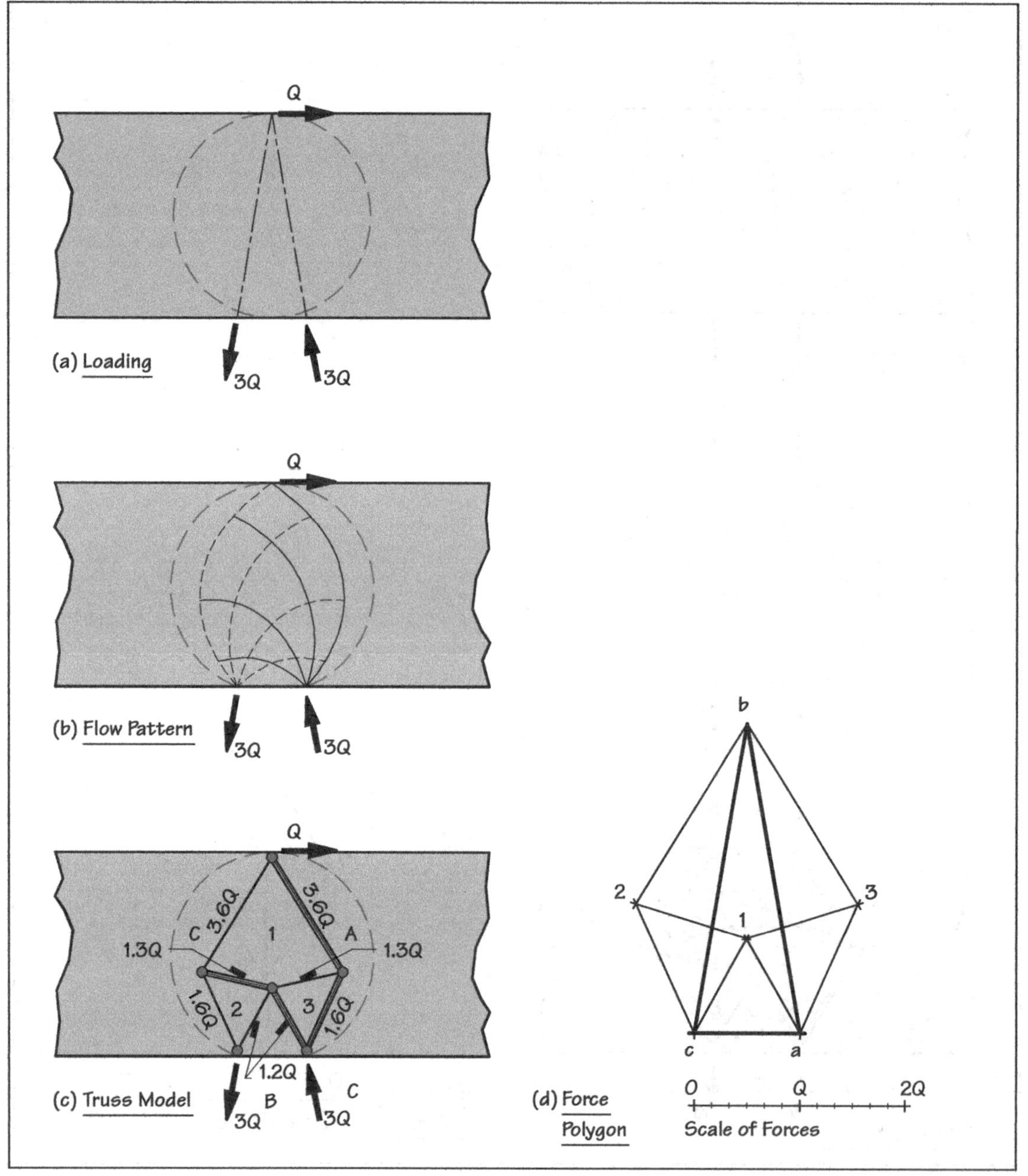
Q
(a) Loading
3Q
3Q
Q
(b) Flow Pattern
3Q
3Q
Q
3.6Q
3.6Q
C
1
A
1.3Q
1.3Q
1.6Q
2
3
1.6Q
1.2Q
B
C
(c) Truss Model
3Q
3Q
b
2
3
1
c
a
(d) Force Polygon
0
Q
2Q
Scale of Forces

Figure 14.42

"I think I see now what the flow pattern will be in my panels with the larger area in the middle. It will be a disk pattern just like we've seen in the long wall, as you sketched. It does seem a little odd, however. Why doesn't the force just flow in a narrow stream of parallel, vertical forces across the broad part of the panel?"

"A structure will always behave in the way that requires least 'work.' It's called the principle of least work, in fact, but the 'work' that a structure does is difficult to visualize: It's the sum of all its small changes of dimension times the forces that cause those changes of dimension. A structure always deploys its forces in such a way that it minimizes this work. This notion explains why structures behave as they do. In your bulging wall panel pattern, the total work required to channel the forces across the bulge in a narrow band is more than the work required to channel them across a broader area and create the disk pattern (14.43)."

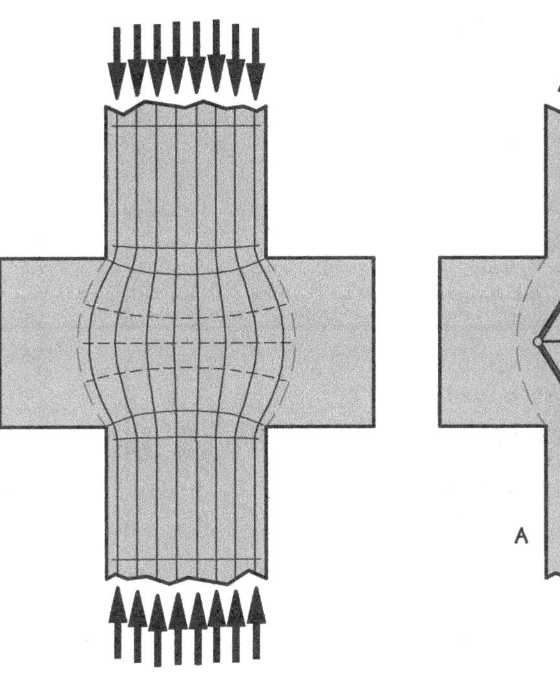

(a) Flow Pattern

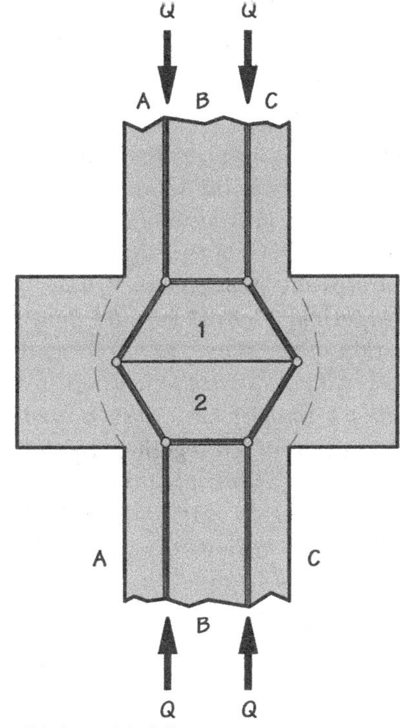

(b) Truss Model

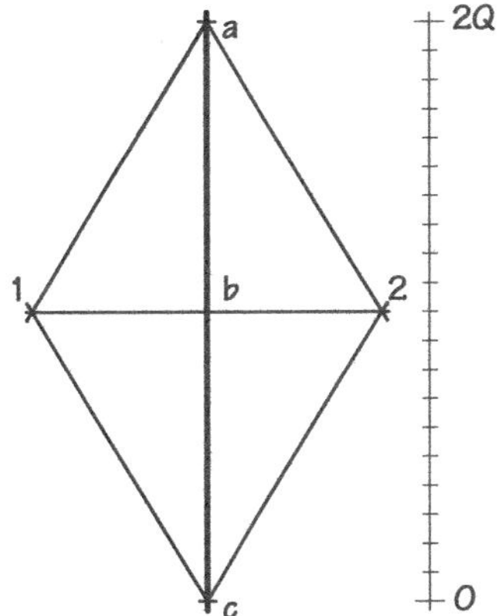

(c) Force Polygon

Figure 14.43

"I'm interested to learn what forces will do in these T-shaped wall panels," Bruce said, showing another drawing to Diane (14.44a).

She paused for a moment to think.

"I'm trying to imagine the best way to explain this one. If we try to apply Saint-Venant's principle to this shape, we find that most of the shape consists of T-regions, regions of transitional flow. The exception is the stem portion of the tee, which will experience mostly parallel flow. In the broad portion of the shape, the flow would like to be parallel, if I can attribute feelings to the panel; but the trajectories have to start turning immediately so as to bunch together where the stem of the tee begins. Probably the best way to figure out what is going on is to imagine this as the shape of a channel of flowing water. The water will start in a broad channel then funnel into a narrow one."

Diane drew the pattern over one panel as she described it.

"That makes sense. But you've drawn only the lines of primary force. Let's add the lines of secondary force, which always act perpendicular to the lines of primary force. Hmm—we're getting another small lattice!"

"Yes, almost! We're seeing the beginnings of a true lattice. The two arms of the T-shape are acting as stubby cantilever beams, and most beams experience lattice flow. If the arms were a little longer, we'd see true lattices developing. Another feature to notice is how the primary trajectories bunch together around the inside corners of the shape. This bunching indicates high stress levels at the sharp inside corners (14.44b). *We could ease the flow, and also the level of stress, by rounding these corners."*

Bruce pawed through his pile of papers on the table and displayed one of them triumphantly to Diane.

Figure 14.44a

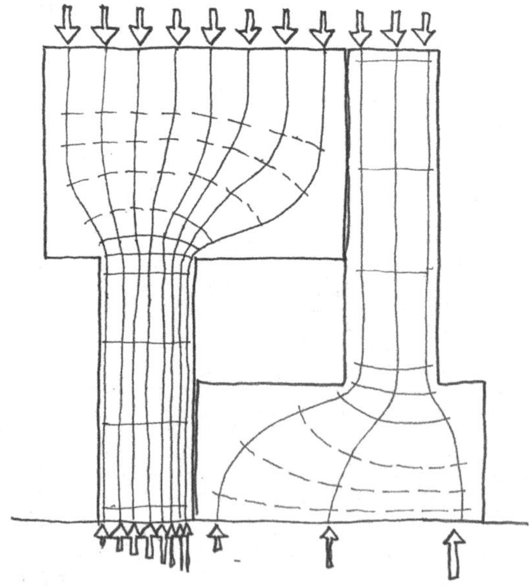

Figure 14.44b

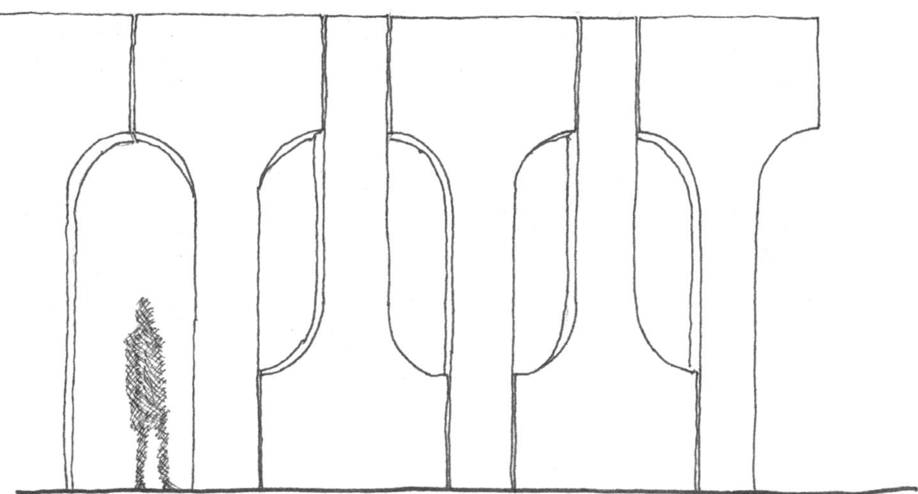

Figure 14.45

Figure 14.46

"That's what I was thinking when I designed this panel shape. Now I can add the lines of force flow, and they are quite simple. After a while, this becomes rather intuitive (14.45)."

"With those large radii for the inside corners, you've reduced stresses considerably. It also reminds us of how the evenly distributed loads across the top will be unequally distributed when they reach the bottom."

OPENINGS AND NOTCHES

Bruce pulled out his last sheet of drawings and laid it in front of Diane.

"I'm really interested to learn about what kinds of shapes are good for openings in wall panels, which ones will work well. Here are some general examples I was thinking about (14.46)."

"Architects love to design holes and openings! Well, Bruce, we can start intuitively. Based on what we've discussed, which of the five openings do you think will raise stresses the least?"

"I'd have to say the football-shaped one in the middle."

"How did you make that judgment?"

"I imagined all the openings as rocks of the same shapes in a stream of water. The water slips right around the football shape without much turbulence."

"That's a good way to think about it. You're right."

"The circular opening is next best. The football shape turned sideways must be pretty bad—it's not only broad, but it also presents very sharp corners to the flow in the narrow passages on either side of it."

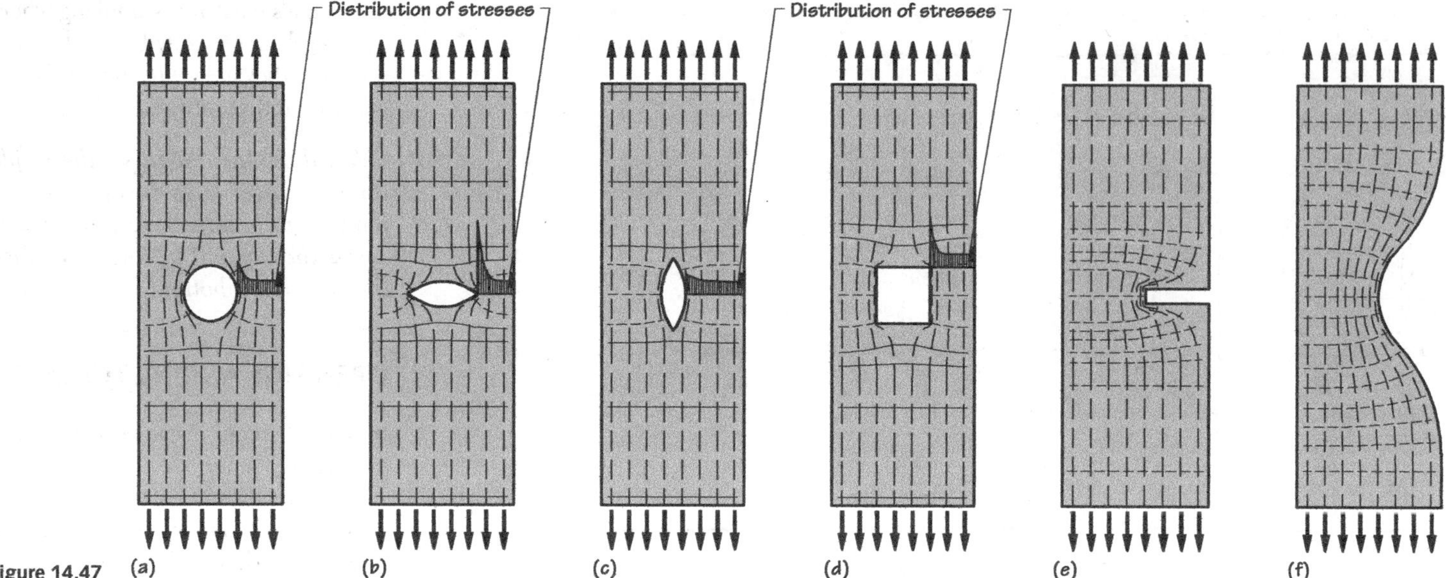

Figure 14.47

"The horizontal rectangular window is bad, too, but it's frequently done because it's relatively simple to compensate for the high corner stresses with steel reinforcing. The slot in the edge of the rightmost panel is the worst opening on this page. It cuts deeply into the panel and it has sharp corners. It also creates substantial bending moments in the panel. You should avoid using it."

She showed him a set of drawings from her binder that illustrated the flows in similar panel shapes (14.47).

"Even a more gently shaped cut that penetrates deeply into the panels will have high forces (14.47f).

"You'll notice that any openings in a panel, regardless of shape, tend to repel forces that pass by. We can use water flow analogies for these too, again recognizing the extent of the transitional areas as given by Saint-Venant's principle (14.48).

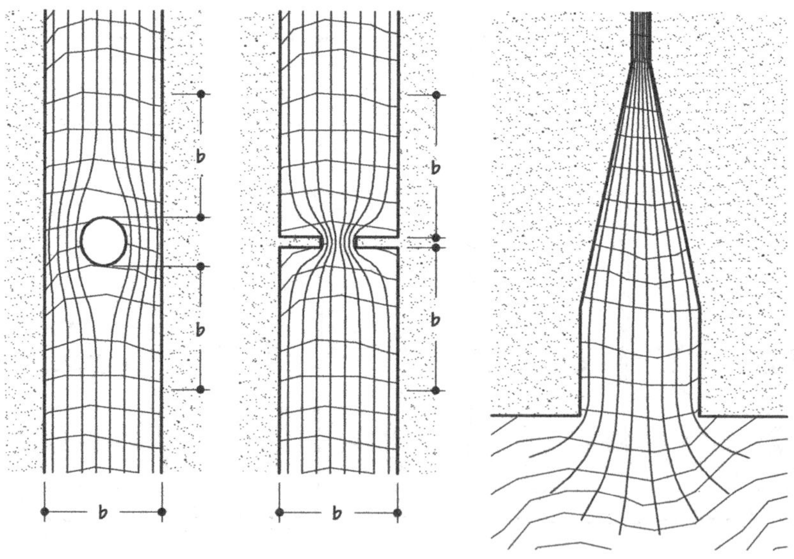

Figure 14.48

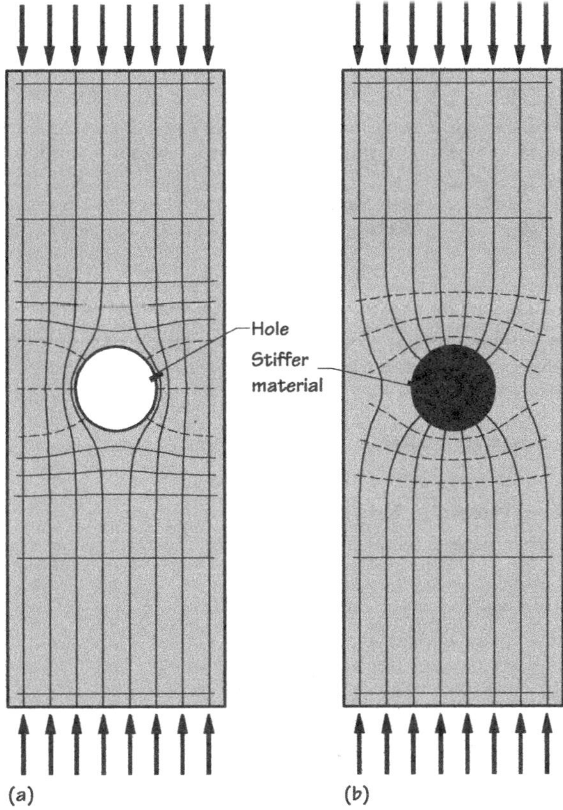

Figure 14.49

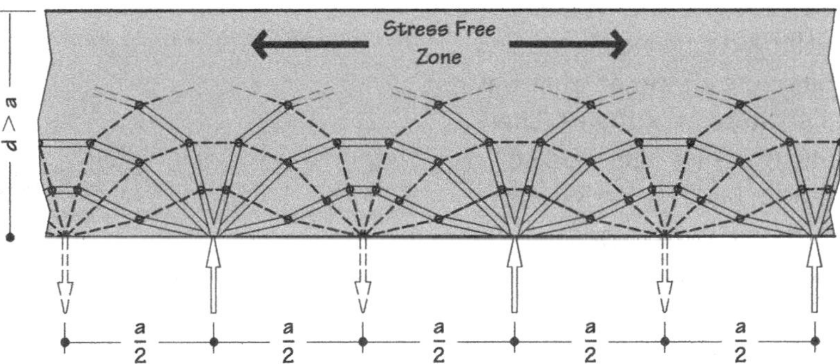

Figure 14.50

But here's something you might not expect: If instead of making a hole, we cast into a concrete wall a disk of very dense granite or steel, any material that is stiffer than concrete, the stiffer material will actually attract lines of force instead of repelling them (14.49)."

"I suppose that situation could even come up inadvertently if a concrete wall were cast around a large-diameter, thick-walled steel pipe. The pipe had better be strong enough to carry a large share of the load that's coming down through the wall!"

"Exactly. And the flow of forces may give clues as to the forces that building components are subjected to during transport and construction, not just in their final configuration."

"The designer must literally get inside his structure and feel the way the structure wants to respond to the force influences from the outside. When this is done, the designer will know instinctively where the areas of distress might logically be."

—Raymond Di Pasquale

TILT-UP CONSTRUCTION REVISITED

"One bit of information that I remember from my brief exposure to tilt-up construction in engineering school is that in most cases the most critical load on the panels, the one for which they must be designed, is the lifting force that occurs as the panel is just coming free from the floor slab."

"Right, there's a partial vacuum between the panel and the floor that has to be filled with air at that instant. A bond-breaker compound, which is an oil or wax or silicone that keeps the fresh concrete from adhering to the floor, is sprayed onto the floor slab before the wall panels are cast, but even so, a momentary high force occurs. Sometimes wedges are driven under an edge to break the vacuum before the crane begins to lift the panel. The risk of breaking the panel at the moment of lifting is minimized by using multiple lifting points on each panel, and by a harness of cables and pulleys that assures that each lifting

JÖRG SCHLAICH

German structural engineer Jörg Schlaich, born in 1934, grew up near Stuttgart and worked as a joiner before enrolling in engineering studies and attending architecture classes at what was then the Technical Institute of Stuttgart (later the University of Stuttgart). He later studied structural engineering in Berlin under Werner Koepcke, who emphasized mathematical approaches, in contrast to the pragmatic tendencies at the University of Stuttgart. He attended graduate school at Case Institute of Technology in Cleveland and earned his doctorate under Fritz Leonhardt at Stuttgart. Practicing with Leonhardt, he designed concrete towers and hyperbolic paraboloid structures, and led the Munich Olympic Stadium project with architect Günter Behnisch. He later followed Leonhardt as professor of concrete structures at the University of Stuttgart. Schlaich's experience and skepticism about the assumptions associated with structural calculations of typical concrete structures led him to develop with his students a theoretical methodology for deciphering the internal behavior of prestressed and reinforced concrete. This new approach, now known as "strut-and-tie method," describes structural members as having regions of different force configurations that can be modeled and analyzed as a series of compression struts and tensile ties. These enable us to visualize and understand deep beams and other members with complex loads and areas where behavior is discontinuous, as we have seen in this chapter.

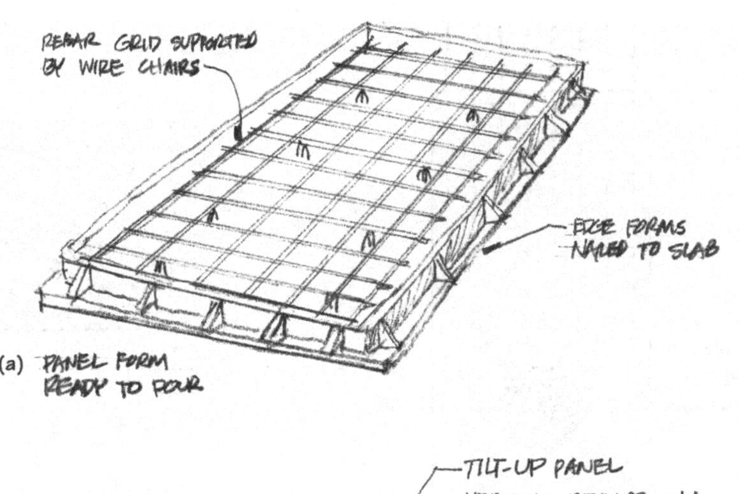

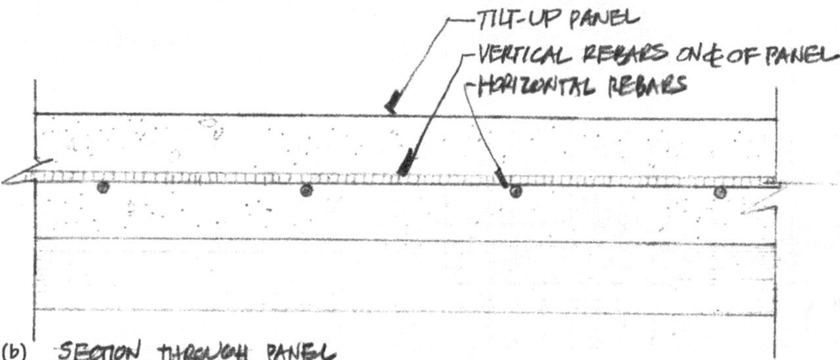

Figure 14.51

point receives exactly the same force as all the others when the crane lifts the panel (14.3, 14.4). It's pretty ingenious how these harnesses work: simple but effective. Of course, the lifting points have to be laid out on the panel so they have equal tributary areas."

"What sorts of roof decks are usually used with tilt-up walls?"

"Well, on the West Coast, wood joists and plywood are most common. Elsewhere, open-web steel joists and corrugated steel decking. Precast concrete planks are also used."

"It's a fairly intricate process. Why is tilt-up so popular?"

"Because it's relatively inexpensive. The savings come primarily from the simplicity of the formwork, which usually consists only of edge forms for the panels (14.51)."

THE MEETING ENDS

"This has been a really good session for me," said Bruce. "I feel as though I know a lot more now about what goes on inside structural elements."

"You're definitely up to speed on this subject. And we both know a lot more about the issues around panel construction than before. There's one important thing we haven't touched on, however. That's the self-weight of the wall. A tilt-up concrete wall

will weigh 20 kips or more, depending on its size and thickness. At the top of the wall, the self-weight is small and has little effect on flow patterns from concentrated loads. But lower down, the weight of the panel begins to be an important factor in the flow pattern, and often even the dominant factor."

"How do I take it into account?"

"The easiest way is to add the force from the panel's self-weight to the vertical force at any given level in the wall. For instance, if we're analyzing a deep wall that carries a beam reaction of 20 kips at the top and sits on its two bottom corners, its self-weight won't affect the top fan region very much. But forces in the two quarter-plane fans at the bottom should be worked out on the basis of the total of live and dead loads for the panel, not just the live load. If the panel weighs 25 kips, then each of the reactions at the lower corners should be 20 plus 25, divided by 2, which comes to 22.5 kips at each corner.

"By the way, perhaps you've noticed that the primary flow in these panels is made up of parallel and fan patterns. The third pattern, the lattice, is important in understanding bending in beams (Chapter 17), *but it doesn't appear in most other types of structures."*

Diane looked at her watch, then rose from her chair.

"The morning has flown by and I have to get on with other tasks. We've spent a lot of time discussing ***how*** *to diagram flows of forces without talking very much about* ***why*** *it's important to be able to do it."*

"Well, it's been important to me to learn how my ideas for new wall shapes would work. And force-flow analyses give me a way of doing that."

"Yes, that's one important function of the technique. There's another function that's equally important: Through an understanding of flow patterns, we can shape structural elements to utilize materials efficiently and express the ways in which they work. Efficient material utilization saves money and resources. On top of that, expression of force flow is a key aspect of structural elegance. We can see that in many scales of structures large and small that we admire (14.52–14.54)."

"Strut-and-tie method not only turns beam elements into trusses but also carries the same ideas over to such otherwise mathematically intractable elements as loading or reaction points, frame corners, corbels, and openings. The entire structure becomes alive and an integral whole."
—DAVID BILLINGTON

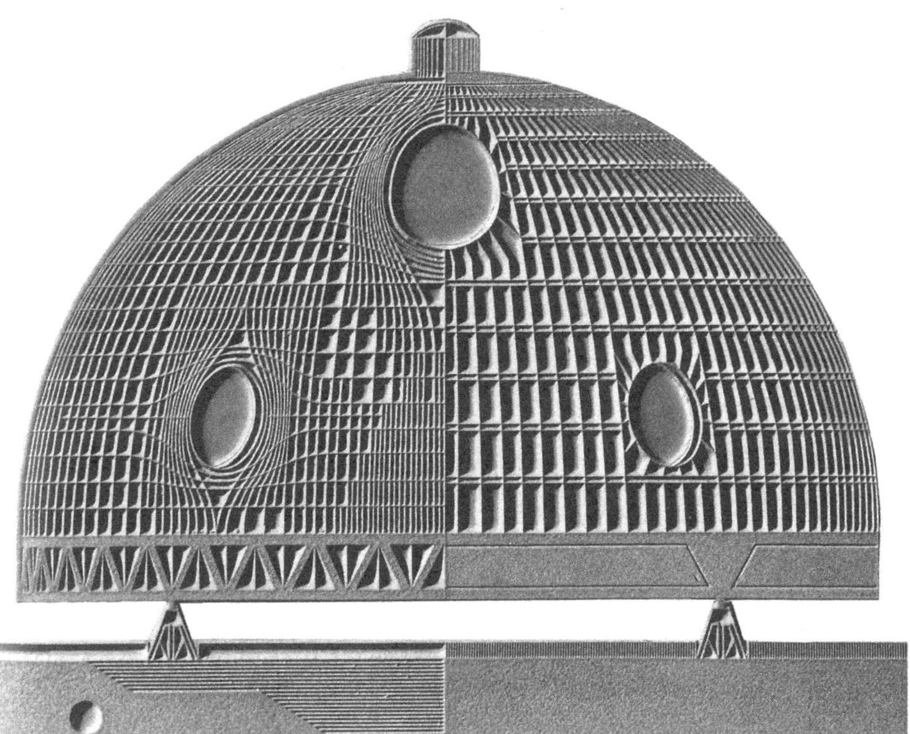

14.52 Spherical design proposal.
Image courtesy of the architect, Eduardo Catalano.

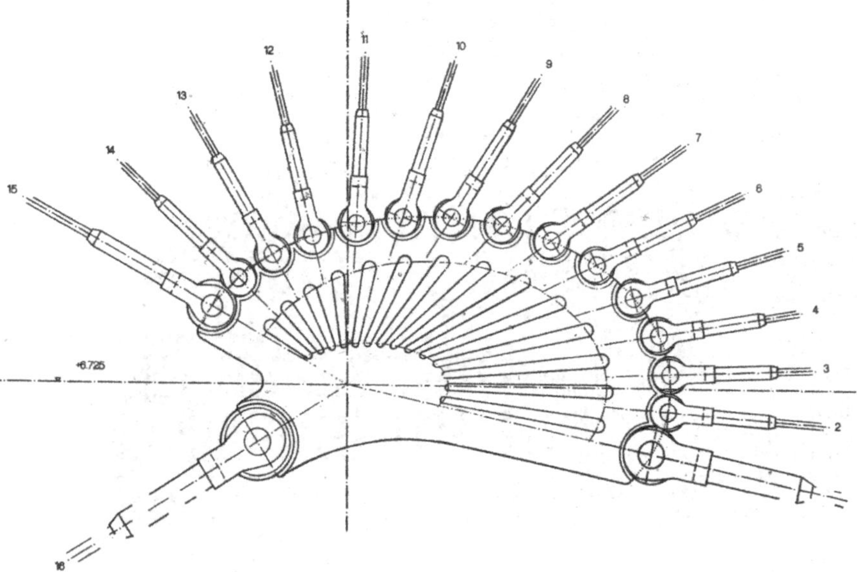

14.53 Drawing and photograph of tensile plate connection for the spa roof structure at MineralBad Canstatt in Germany.

Images courtesy of the engineers, Schlaich Bergermann and Partner.

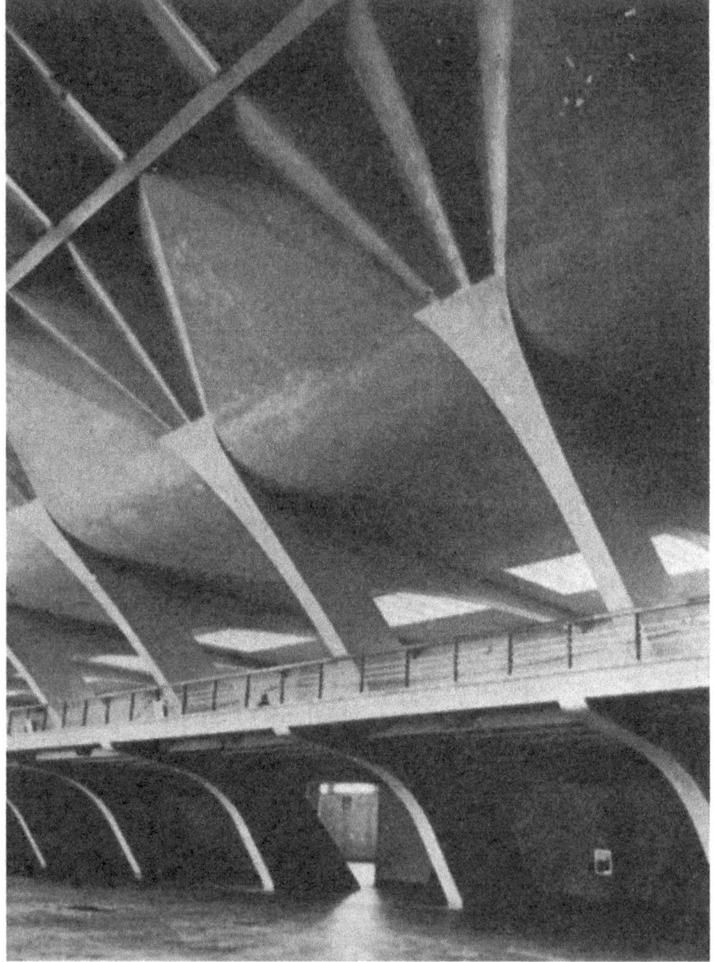

14.54 The fan pattern of flow is reflected in these buttresses of the Turin Exhibition Building by Nervi (see pp. 324 and 325).

Source: Pier Luigi Nervi, *Structures*, New York: F.W. Dodge Corp., 1956.

Exercises

1. Diagram the flow of forces in the circular plate that connects the rods of the suspension bridges in Chapter 1. Show both primary and secondary forces, and distinguish tensile forces from compressive ones. Propose a new shape for the plate that will be more efficient and more expressive of what is happening structurally within it.

2. Repeat Exercise 1, but this time for the plate at the top of the mast of the inter-city bus terminal in Chapter 2.

3. Diagram the flow of forces in the concrete panel with a hole as shown in Figure 14.1, given that it supports a continuous roof load. What is the effect of changing the radius of the circular hole?

4. Propose alternative wall panel designs to improve upon what Bruce and Diane have sketched. What opportunities for shaping the panels would be appropriate for different building types, roof load patterns, and interior uses?

Key Concepts and Terms

tilt-up construction

lifting points

lifting harness

strongback

bond breaker

flow of forces

flow lines

stress trajectories

parallel pattern

fan pattern

lattice pattern

half-plane fan

quarter-plane fan

Saint-Venant's principle

$f_{ri} = \frac{2P\cos\alpha}{\pi t r_i}$ [14-1]

truss modeling

strut-and-tie modeling

deep wall

long wall

eccentric load

kern

primary forces

secondary forces

principle of least work

Further Resources

Schlaich, Jörg, Kurt Schäfer, and Mattias Jennewein. "Toward a Consistent Design of Structural Concrete," *PCI Journal,* May/June 1987, pp. 75–150. This is the landmark paper that first published a simple approach to diagramming the flow of forces in structures.

Liang, Qing Quan. *Performance-Based Optimization of Structures.* London and New York: Spon Press, 2005. This book demonstrates the use of a computer program that automatically generates strut-and-tie models for structural bodies.

Menn, Christian. *Prestressed Concrete Bridges.* Translated into English by Paul Gauvreau. Basel, Switzerland: Birkhäuser Verlag, 1986. A noted bridge designer discusses every aspect of concrete bridge design and construction, often using truss models to demonstrate force flow and help design reinforcing patterns.

Note: There are numerous, and frequently expanded, Web sites on the subject of strut-and-tie modeling.

CHAPTER 15

Designing a Bay of Framing

- *Configuring building frames in three dimensions; laying out a framing plan*
- *Understanding bays, decking, joists, beams, girders, slabs, columns, and framing materials*
- *Load tracing for gravity and lateral loads*
- *Bracing to resist lateral loads*
- *Criteria influencing design of bays in very tall buildings where lateral loads predominate*
- *Integration with vertical transportation, life safety and egress planning, mechanical systems*

The primary purpose of a building structure is to support surfaces for human use: roofs to protect the inner spaces of a building from weather, floors to provide dry, level platforms that are often stacked to multiply available ground space, and walls to enclose the building. The surfaces of most buildings are supported by systems of beams and columns (Figure 15.1). A building structure made of beams and columns is referred to as a *trabeated* ("**tray**-bee-ate-ed") structure. This distinguishes it from an *arcuated* ("**ark**-you-ate-ed") structure, which is based on arches (Figure 15.2). Columns are often called *posts*, and trabeated systems *post-and-beam* systems.

A *column* is a vertical member that resists vertical loads (Figure 15.3). It acts axially (longitudinally), and like other longitudinally acting structural forms,

Figure 15.1 A warehouse roof structure of laminated wood members illustrates the elements of post-and-beam framing: Beams are attached to girders with metal connectors. Columns are visible at the lower right, along with an expanse of installed decking. Lengths of wood decking are stacked at the top of the picture, ready for installation.

Photo courtesy of American Institute of Timber Construction.

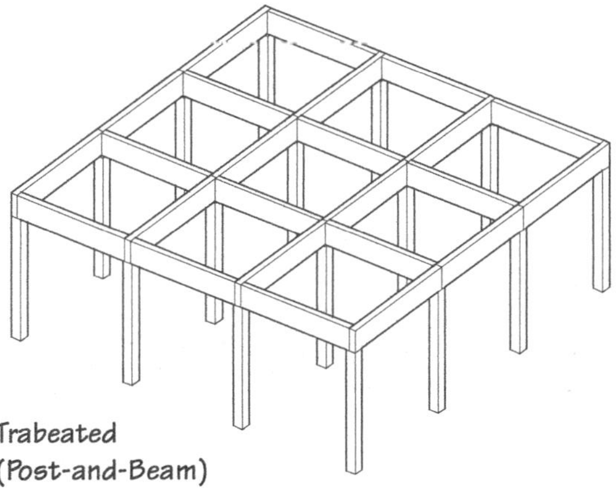

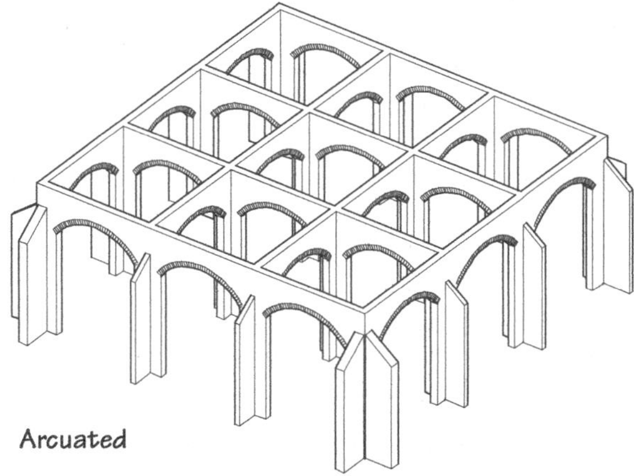

Figure 15.2 Isometric views of trabeated and arcuated structures.

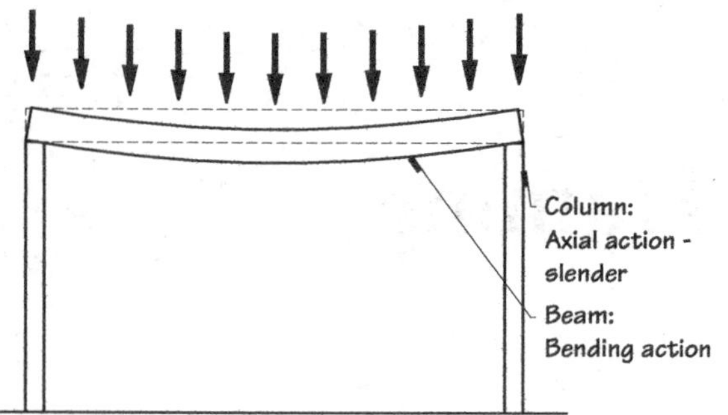

Figure 15.3 A beam supported by two columns.

it is efficient in its utilization of structural material and can be rather slender. (In many situations, however, columns are eccentrically loaded and must resist transverse actions as well as longitudinal; we will take up this topic in Chapter 19.) For simplicity of terminology, *load-bearing walls*, usually called simply *bearing walls*, are included in this chapter under the general category of columns. They may be thought of as columns that are short in one horizontal direction but very long in the other.

A *beam* is a member that acts in bending to resist transverse loads, that is, loads applied perpendicular to its axis (Figure 15.3). It does this through a fascinating pattern of internal forces, the lattice pattern, The lattice pattern does not utilize structural material as efficiently as the parallel pattern in columns, so a beam must be rather deep and heavy as compared to the columns that support it.

Despite their relative inefficiency, we use beams more than any other type of spanning device. This is because they have certain practical advantages:

- At short spans, beams are shallower than other structural devices capable of carrying the same load; thus they occupy little vertical space in a building, compared to cables, arches, and trusses. This saves construction costs associated with increased overall height of a building, larger areas of exterior cladding materials, and increased fuel cost for heating and cooling a building with a larger skin area.
- Beams resolve their forces internally, exerting no external thrust or pull, like those of arches and cables. In this they are similar to trusses.
- Like trusses, but unlike arches and cables, a beam is able to accept a wide variety of loading conditions without significantly changing shape.
- Beams are slender linear elements that are easy to warehouse, ship, and handle on the construction site.
- Beams are easily manufactured because of their prismatic shapes (shapes that are constant throughout the length of the member). Straight, prismatic members are the natural products of sawmills, steel rolling mills, and extrusion processes for precast concrete planks.

Beams and columns are made of wood, steel, or concrete, in many different forms. We will discuss some of the more common ones in the chapters ahead. Columns (and very occasionally, beams) can also be made of masonry, either brickwork or stonework. Regardless of the material, we usually frame our buildings by combining beams and columns to form *bays*.

"It is inconvenient to live and work on surfaces which are not flat and level, and in modern life it is often absolutely necessary to superimpose one surface on top of another. We cannot, therefore, completely abandon right angles and straight lines in favor of Nature's curves. . . . What we can and should do is to understand that her use of curves is merely the expression of a principle of structural continuity; and this latter quality is what distinguishes her designs. We should study her principles, not attempt to copy her shapes. These are rich and bountiful, displaying everywhere the means whereby architects and engineers can achieve beautifully efficient form.

—Fred Severud, in "Turtles and Walnuts, Morning Glories and Grass," *Architectural Forum*, September 1945

BAYS

The simplest possible bay, the space between columns on a given level of a structure, is a rectangular volume bounded by four columns, two beams, and structural *decking* that spans between the beams (Figure 15.4). For bays in the range of sizes that we generally use, about 12 ft to 40 ft on each side, this arrangement would require decking that is very deep and expensive. To reduce the decking span to a practical dimension, we usually add a layer of framing to create bays like the ones in Figure 15.5, in which beams are spaced as dictated by the spanning capability of an economical thickness of decking. The beams rest on other beams called *girders*, which convey all the loads to the columns. (A girder

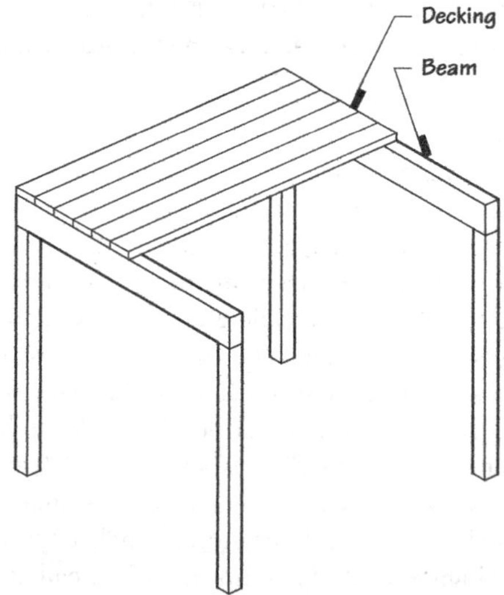

Figure 15.4 A bay of framing, using thick decking elements.

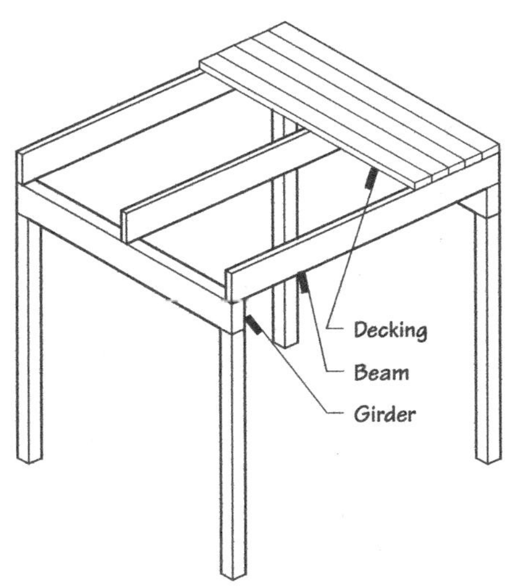

Figure 15.5 By utilizing girders to support beams, thinner decking may be used. By adding more beams, decking spans may be adjusted to any value.

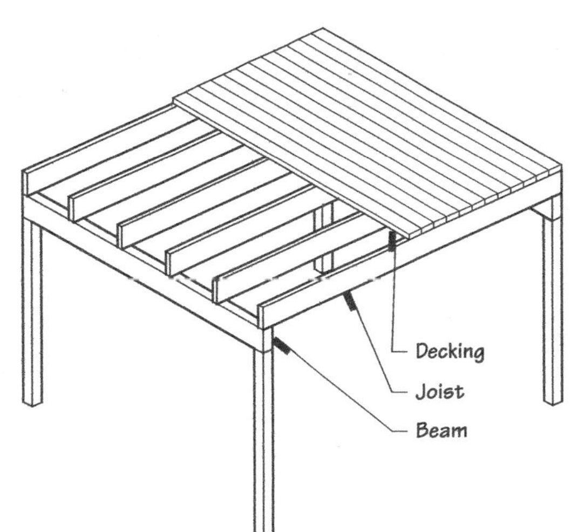

Figure 15.6 Joists are slender, closely-spaced beams that permit the use of very thin decking.

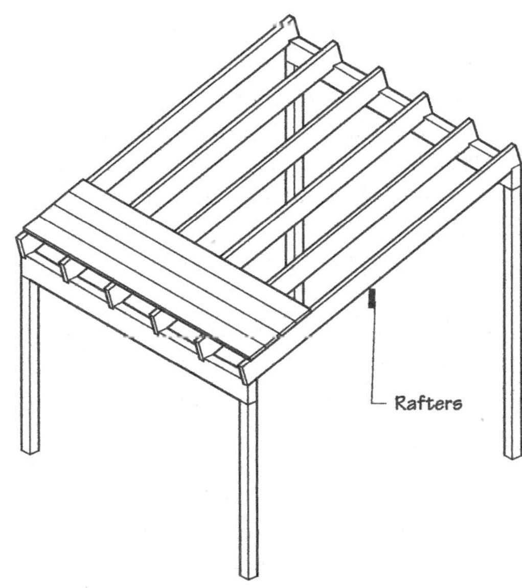

Figure 15.7 Rafters are joists or beams that follow the inclination of a roof.

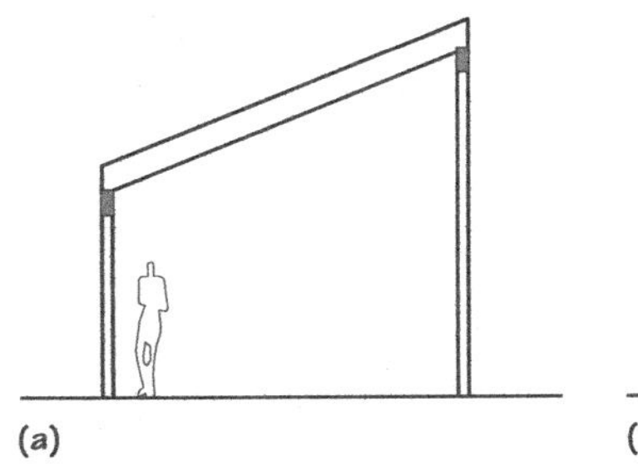

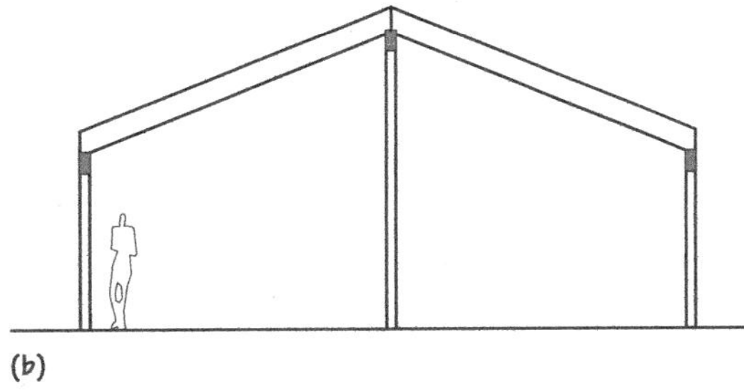

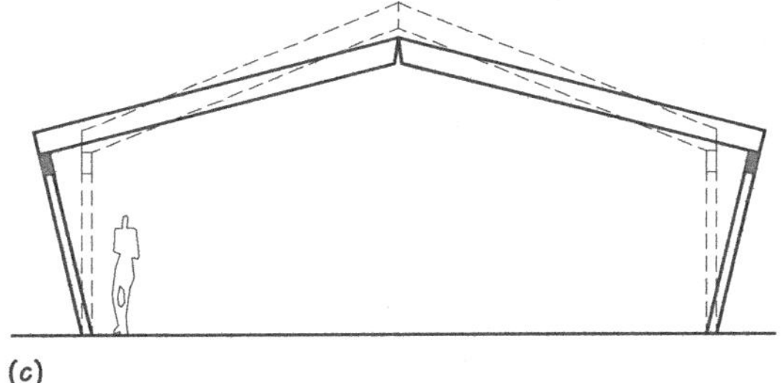

Figure 15.8 Rafters in (a) and (b) are supported at both ends and exert no horizontal thrust. The rafter pair in (c) does not have a ridge beam or horizontal tie; it constitutes a simple arch that exerts horizontal thrust.

is simply a larger beam whose primary job is to support other beams rather than to support decking directly.) Another common framing strategy is to support very thin decking on closely-spaced, slender members, called *joists*, if they are in a floor or flat roof (Figure 15.6), or *rafters*, if they are in a sloping roof (Figure 15.7). The joists may be supported directly on beams that bear on the four columns or on beams that are supported by girders. Rafters do not exert any lateral force if they are supported at both ends, as they are in a shed roof. It is only when rafters lean against one another, such as at the crown of a truss (a configuration in which they act as a simple arch) that they exert a lateral thrust (Figure 15.8).

A bearing wall may be substituted for two columns and a beam (Figure 15.9). Some buildings are built using bearing walls throughout, without columns. Hotels and dormitories are often structured this way, using walls of masonry or precast concrete panels that enclose the small, unchanging rooms that are characteristic of these types of buildings, and also provide vertical support for the floors and roof. Columns are more appropriate than bearing walls for buildings that may change over time, because they allow the internal spaces of the building to be enclosed in nonbearing partitions that are easily reconfigured.

Wood light-frame construction and the analogous system of framing that utilizes light gauge sheet-steel studs and joists are both essentially bearing-wall systems. Buildings that utilize these systems are not usually laid out in regular bays, but are planned with intricate and often irregular spacings to produce the desired arrangement of rooms. The load-bearing walls of these systems are actually closely-spaced arrays of very slender columns—the columns being restrained against buckling by the sheet materials applied inside and out to the walls (Figure 15.10).

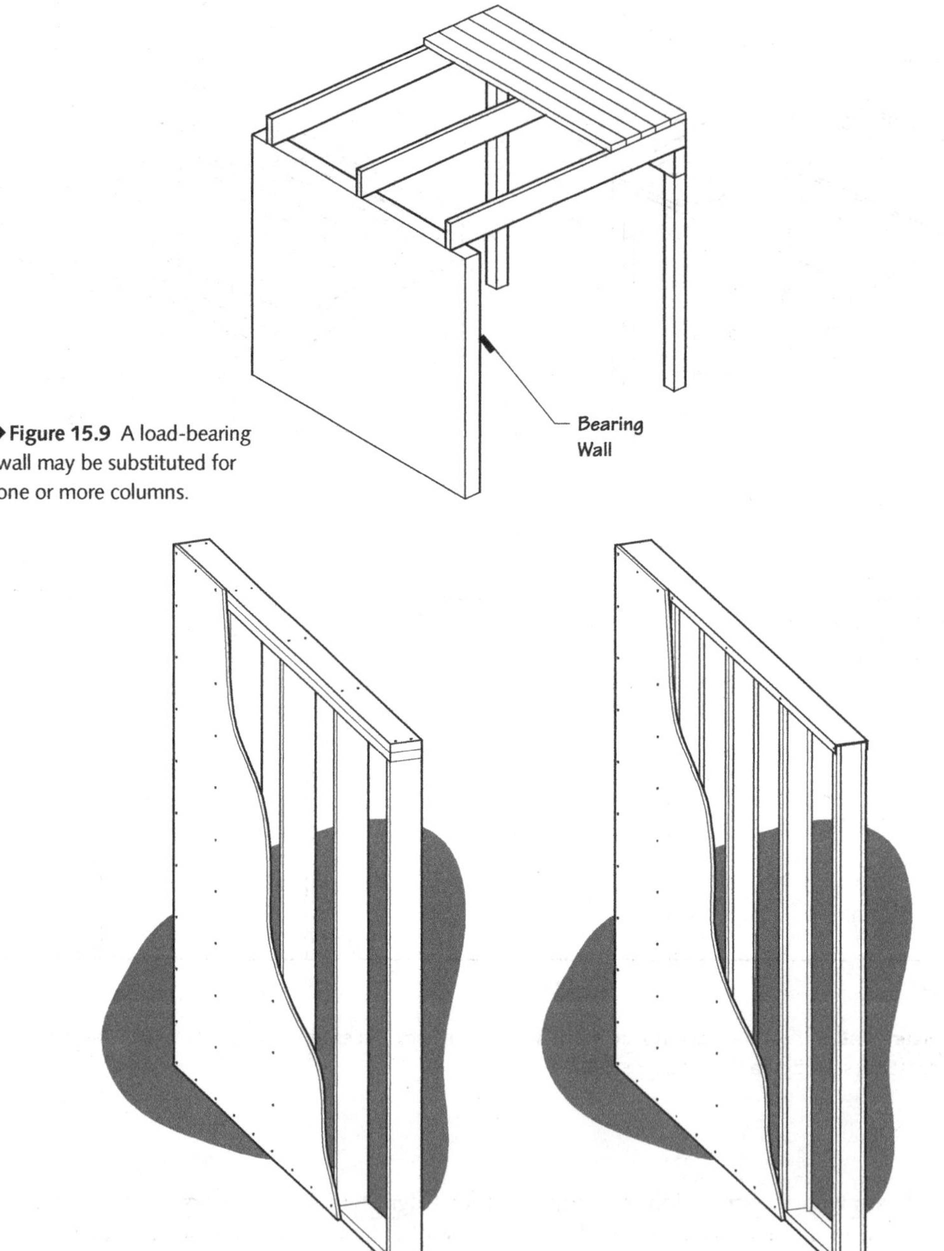

▶**Figure 15.9** A load-bearing wall may be substituted for one or more columns.

Figure 15.10 Bearing walls made of light framing are composed of many small, closely-spaced columns called studs that are braced by sheet materials applied to their faces.

LOAD TRACING

The work of a bay of framing is to conduct loads safely to the foundations and into the earth beneath the building. A beam on two columns, when subjected to a single, concentrated force, divides the force and carries a portion of it to each column, through which it flows to the foundations. If the force is applied at the center of the beam, half the force flows through each column (Figure 15.11). If the force is applied elsewhere on the beam, the distribution of the force to the columns may be determined by evaluating moments about any convenient axis (Figure 15.12). The routes followed by forces through a structure are called *load paths*.

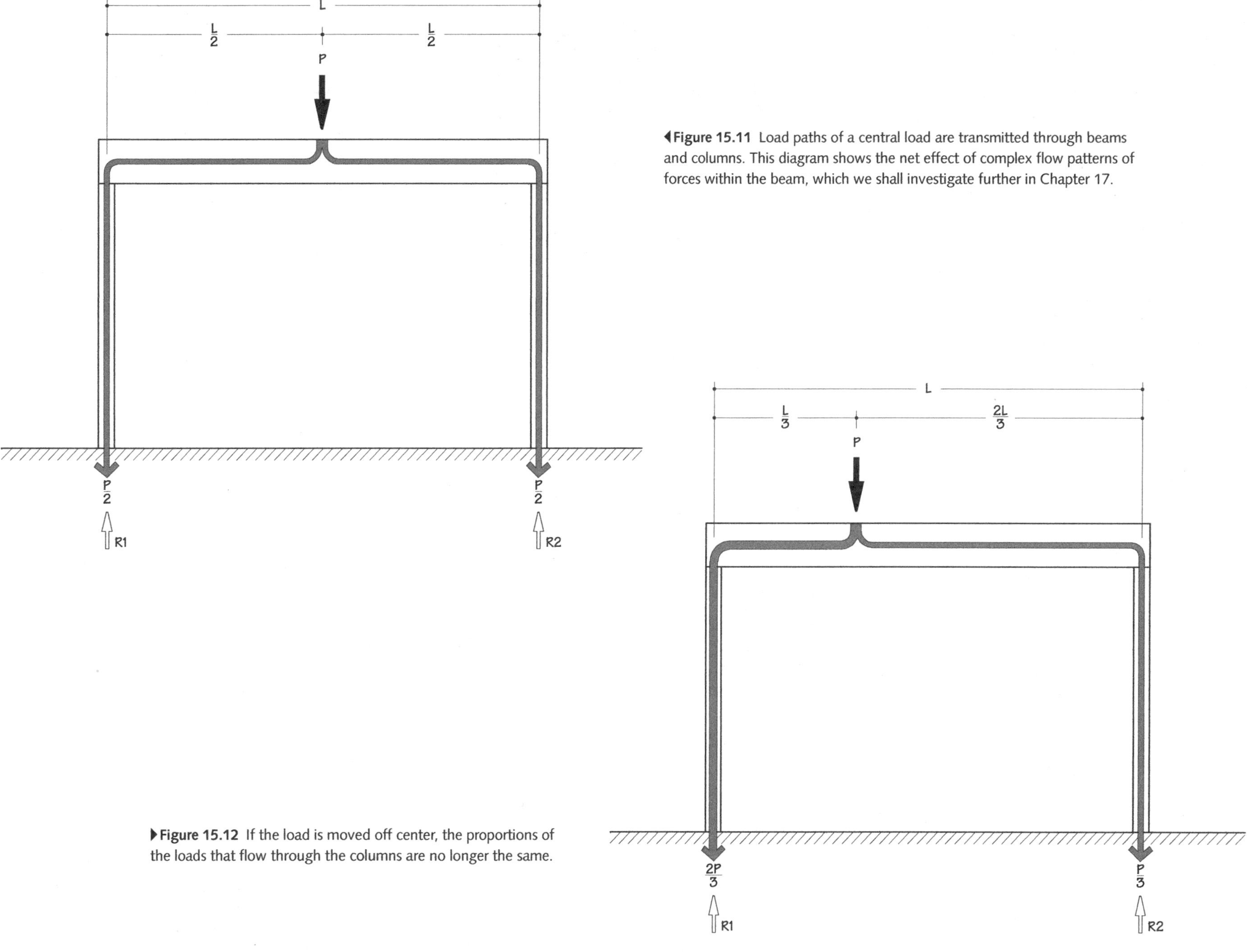

◀**Figure 15.11** Load paths of a central load are transmitted through beams and columns. This diagram shows the net effect of complex flow patterns of forces within the beam, which we shall investigate further in Chapter 17.

▶**Figure 15.12** If the load is moved off center, the proportions of the loads that flow through the columns are no longer the same.

We can visualize this in three dimensions. If a thick decking material, such as precast concrete hollow-core planks, is mounted on a pair of beams (Figure 15.13), the distribution of the force to the columns is easily determined. Even in a relatively simple beam-girder-deck system (Figure 15.14), the distribution of the forces becomes comparatively complex, with load paths in some cases splitting and then recombining lower in the system. Worksheet 15A on the supplemental site provides further experience for you to trace load paths on bays of framing.

"The purpose of structure is to channel the loads on the building to the ground. This action is similar to that of water flowing down a network of pipes. Columns, beams, cables, and other structural elements act as pipes for the flow of the loads."

—Mario Salvadori

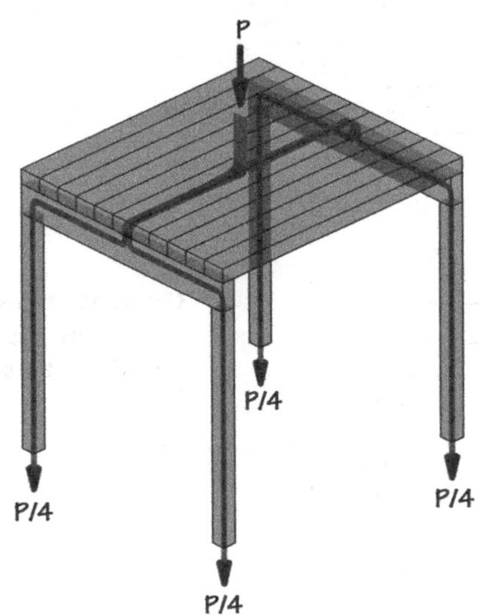

Figure 15.13 Load paths for a central load on a simple bay of framing.

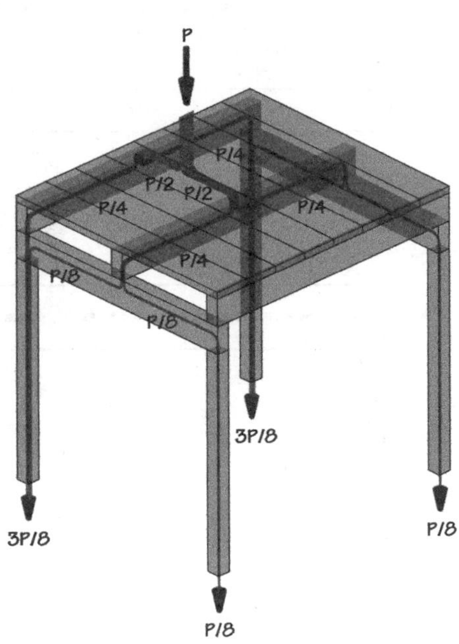

Figure 15.14 Asymmetrical loading of a bay of framing produces complex load paths.

LATERAL LOADS

To this point, we have considered a bay of framing only in its role of resisting gravity loads. It must also resist lateral (horizontal) loads caused by wind or seismic events. If a lateral load is applied to a bay of framing with ordinary joints, the bay will deform and collapse (Figures 15.15, 15.16). If we brace the same system with a sufficient number of diagonal members in appropriate locations, it can resist lateral loads (Figure 15.17). The *chevron bracing* shown here is a common pattern that is both efficient and convenient. Its efficiency stems from two basic causes: Its two members are relatively short and therefore less likely to buckle

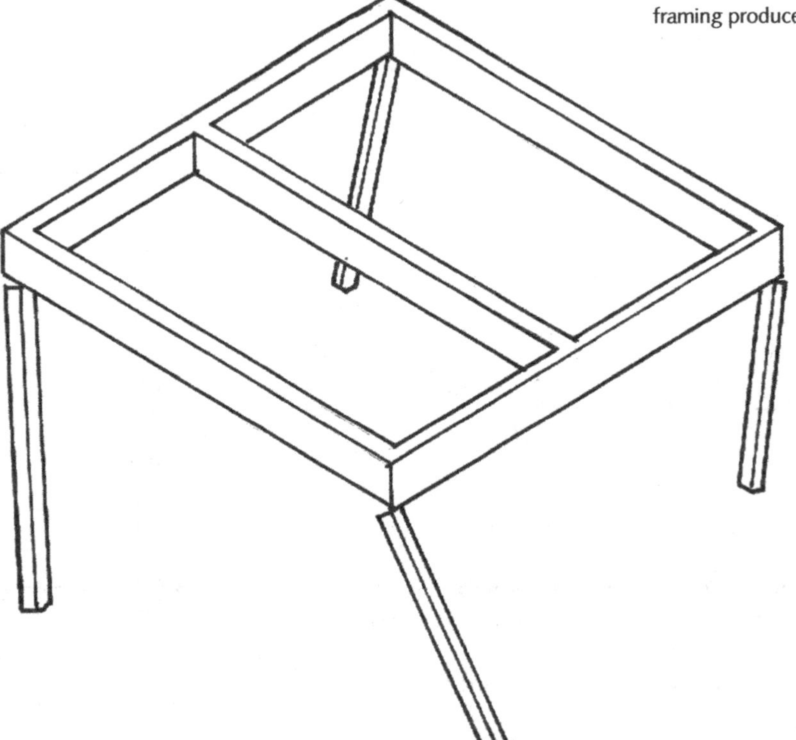

Figure 15.15 An unbraced bay of framing will often collapse with a twisting motion.

than long diagonal braces, and it utilizes material well because its members and the surrounding beams and columns form a panel of a vertical K-truss, a very efficient configuration. The convenience of chevron bracing relates to the way it provides a central opening in a wall or partition for a door or corridor. Chevron bracing alone can resist lateral loads in buildings up to about 45 stories tall, and with assistance from other systems of lateral bracing, it can go much higher.

In Figure 15.18, we see a variety of common bracing patterns. The single *diagonal brace* (a) is effective, but it is very long, which increases its susceptibility to buckling when it is in compression. If it is in an interior wall, it also obstructs passage of a doorway or corridor. The same disadvantages apply to crossing diagonal braces (b). This *cross-bracing* may be made of cables or rods, which work only in tension. A lateral force from the right will be resisted by one of the cables, and the other will be slack. A lateral force from the left will load the cable that was slack under the force from the right, and leave slack the cable that was formerly in tension.

If the upper ends of a chevron brace (c) are separated, as in drawing (d), a lateral load induces bending action in the beam. This is one example of *eccentric bracing*, which is useful in areas of high seismic risk because the flexing of the beam absorbs energy from the building as it rocks back and forth, helping to damp the oscillations.

If chevron braces are moved up near the tops of the columns, they become *knee braces* (e). The effect of knee braces is to make the beam/column joints rigid. This allows the system to resist lateral loads by imposing bending actions on both the columns and the beams of a building. The sizes of the columns and beams must be increased to enable them to resist gravity loads and lateral-load-induced bending simultaneously.

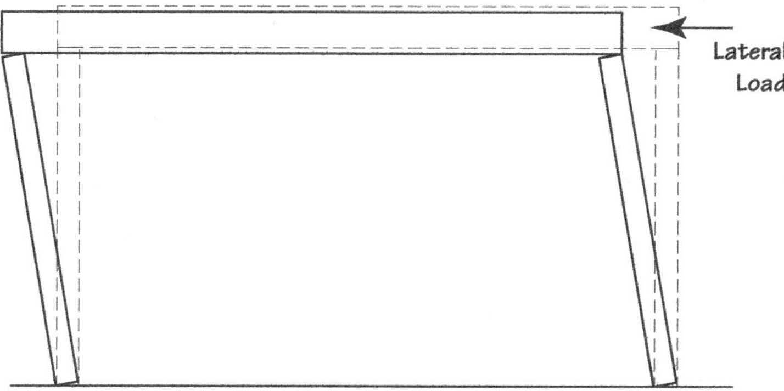

Figure 15.16 A lateral load tends to push over a beam and columns.

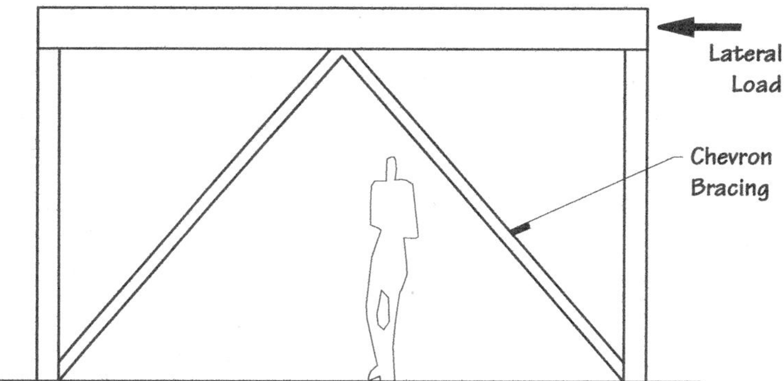

Figure 15.17 Any of a number of patterns of diagonal bracing can stabilize the beam and columns.

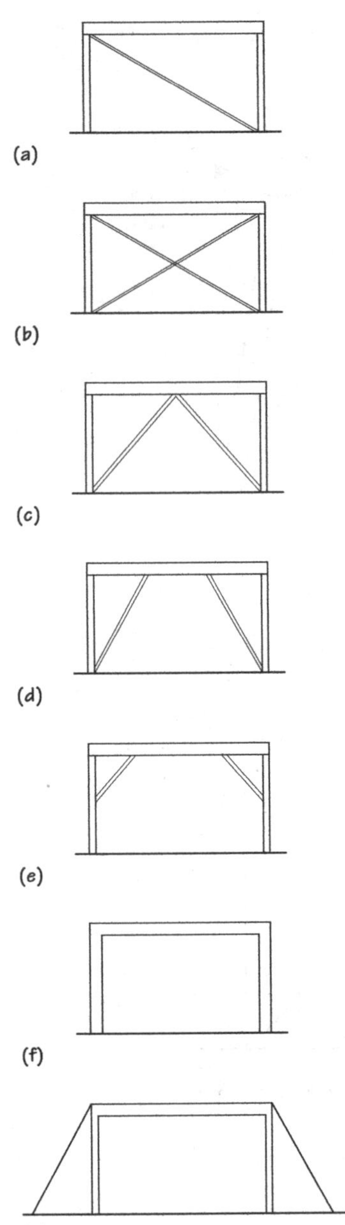

Figure 15.18 Common patterns of bracing: (a) single diagonal brace; (b) cross bracing; (c) chevron bracing; (d) eccentric bracing; (e) knee bracing; (f) rigid joints; (g) external bracing.

Rigid Joints

Rigid joints can be used to resist lateral forces on a building (Figures 15.18f and 15.19). It is easy to make beam/column joints rigid in steel frames by using welds that are detailed to be as strong as the members that they join. In nearly all reinforced concrete frames, steel reinforcing bars pass continuously through the joints, making them rigid automatically.

Rigid joints are harder to achieve in wood than in steel and concrete, even though trees themselves grow effortlessly as continuous structures with rigid joints. When we cut up a tree, we destroy this rigidity. To achieve it

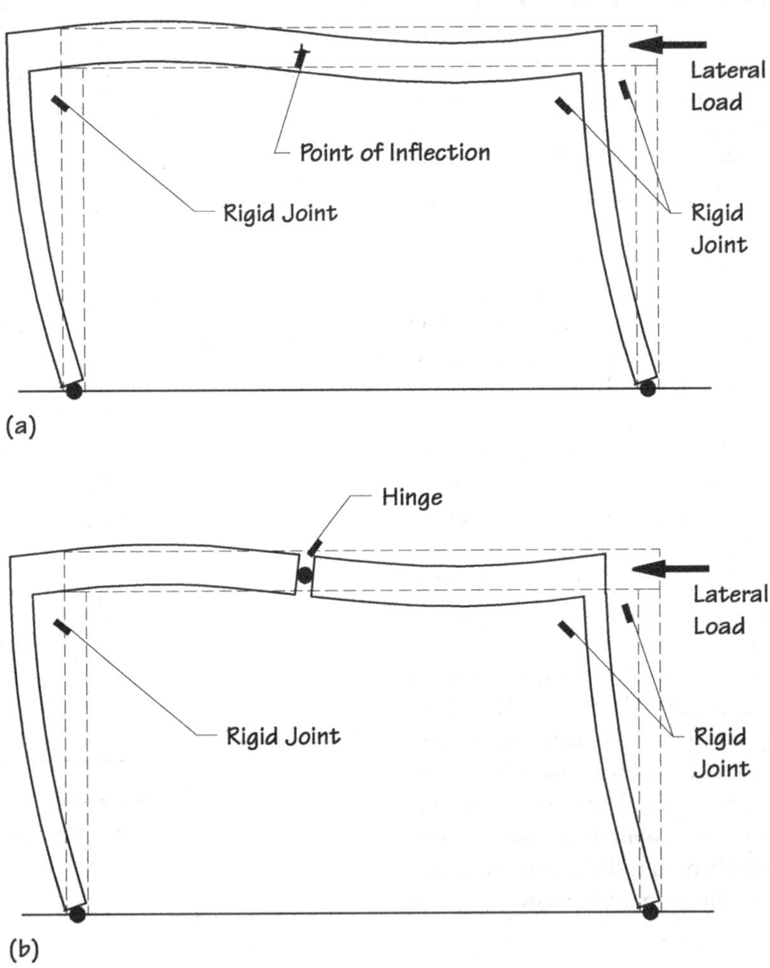

Figure 15.19 (a) An exaggerated depiction of the deformation of a frame with rigid beam-column joints. The base joints of the columns are hinged. (b) A hinge may be inserted at the point of inflection, where the curvature of the beam changes from positive to negative, without altering the performance of the frame.

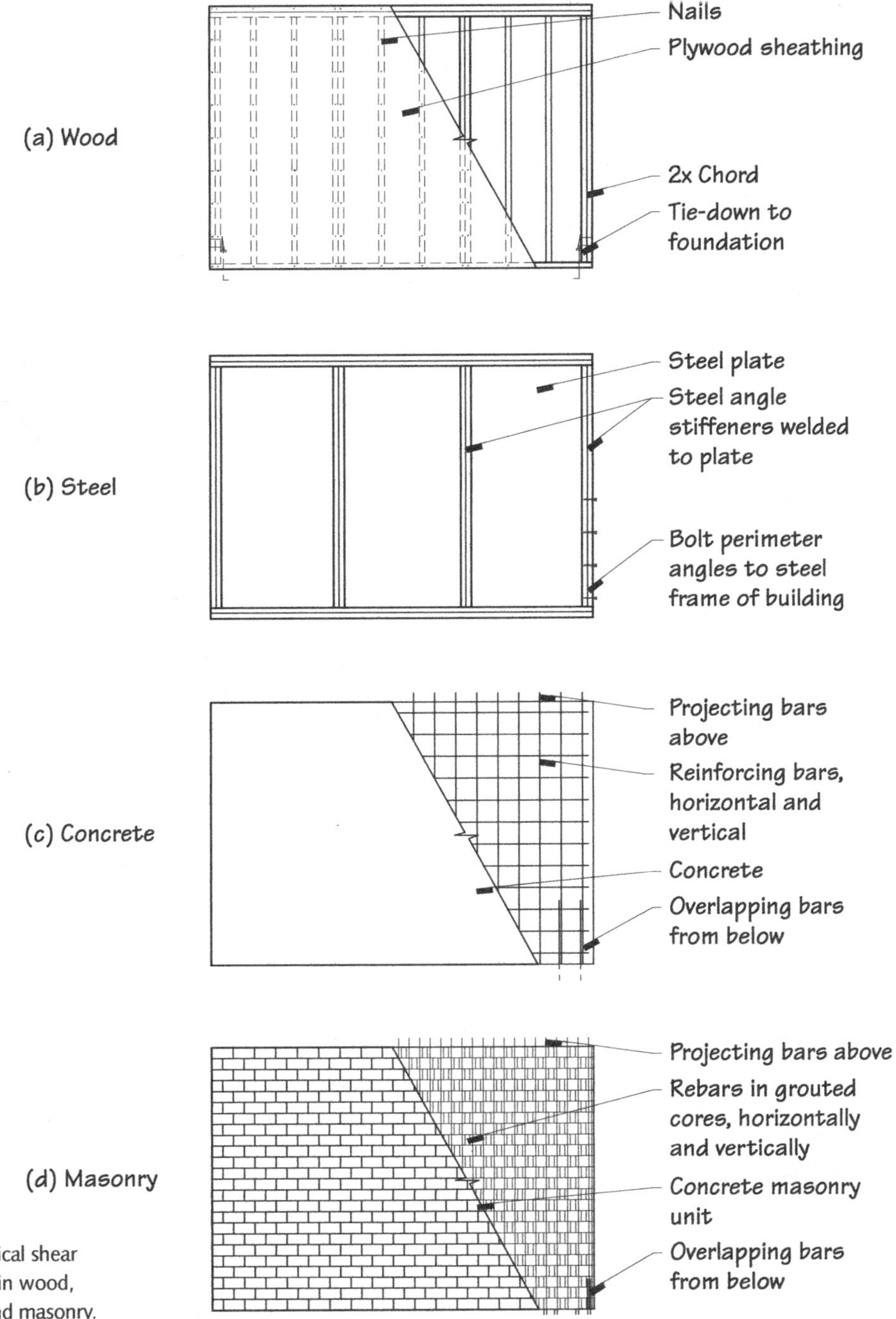

Figure 15.20 Typical shear wall construction in wood, steel, concrete, and masonry.

again, we must either build up laminated wood joints or use elaborate fastening or adhesive technologies.

To derive full advantage from the bracing action of rigid joints in any material, it is necessary to make the beams and columns as stiff as the joints. Rigid joints are capable of bracing buildings up to 30 stories high.

External Bracing

External bracing, shown in part (g) of Figure 15.18, is not common, but it can be useful in applications such as bracing a wall of an aircraft hangar that contains a door almost as large as the wall, and it deserves wider use by imaginative designers. It is essentially the same as the backstays used in tensile structures such as the one in Chapter 2, but it can also be formed with compressive struts rather than tensile elements.

Shear Walls

Shear walls, which are walls designed and constructed to be rigid against forces that act in their planes, are an alternative to bracing and rigid joints in the frame of a building. They may be made of wood, concrete, steel, or steel-reinforced masonry (Figure 15.20). They act as stubby, vertically cantilevered beams. Where these walls must act continuously from one floor to the next, they are joined securely at each floor line so they act as a single wall.

A shear wall is essentially a deep, vertical cantilevered beam. It does its work by means of diagonal tension and compression in the entire area of the wall, as well as vertical tension and compression in the *chords*, which are the vertical edge members of the wall (Figure 15.21). The chords are analogous to the flanges of a steel beam. We will encounter this pattern of crossing diagonal forces again as we look at flanged beams in Chapters 17 and 18, where we will explore it in depth.

Unless the building is heavy enough to prevent the ends of its shear walls from lifting in response to high lateral forces, the chords of a shear wall must be tied vertically to the foundation (Figure 15.22). Shear walls can brace buildings more than 50 stories tall, but special bracing strategies are required for extremely slender or supertall buildings where lateral loads predominate. We will return to questions of lateral forces and bracing several times in succeeding chapters.

FLOOR AND ROOF DIAPHRAGMS

Vertical planes of bracing, whether diagonals, rigid joints, or shear walls, work together with *floor and roof diaphragms* to stabilize the building. A diaphragm is a plane of floor or roof decking that acts to transmit the force of the wind or a seismic event to the vertical planes of bracing in a building. It may be thought of as a very deep wide-flange beam lying on its side (Figure 15.23). Sloping roof planes may also serve as diaphragms. Wind pressures on a wall of the building are transmitted by bending action in the wall structure to the edge of the diaphragm. The diaphragm transmits these forces to the building's vertical planes of bracing that lie most nearly parallel to the direction of the wind.

Like a wide-flange beam, a diaphragm must have both a web and flanges, although in a diaphragm, as in a shear wall, the flanges are called chords. The web may be a reinforced concrete floor or roof slab, a plane

Figure 15.22 A hold-down or tie-down for a wood shear wall.

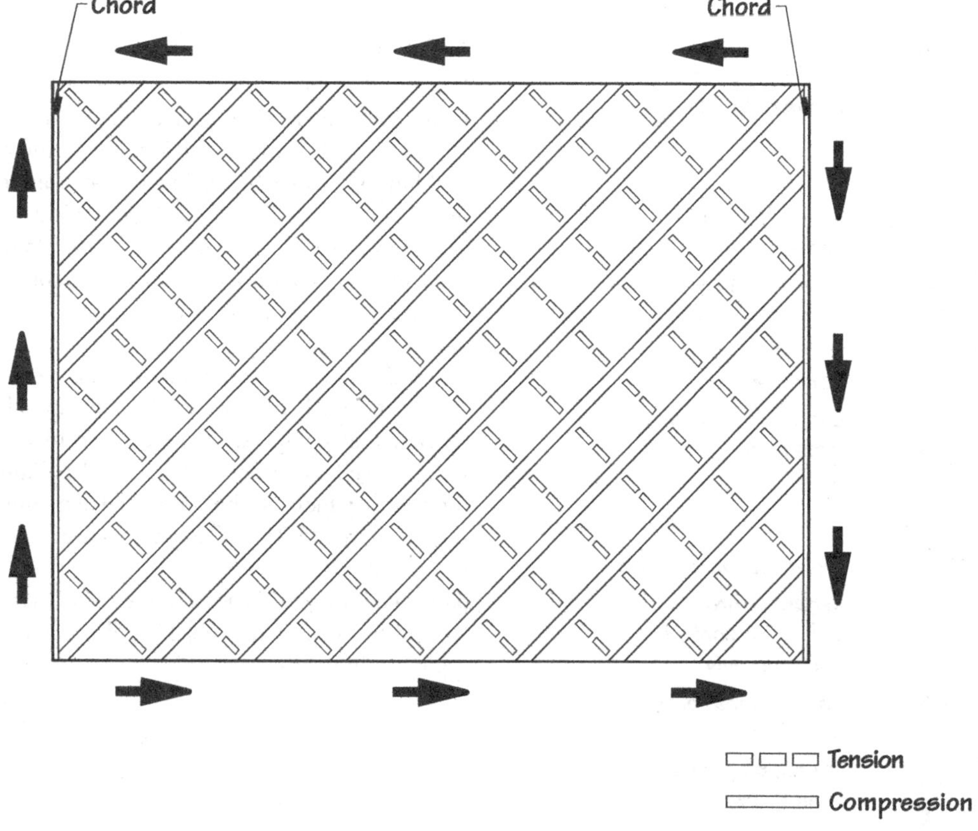

Figure 15.21 Forces within a shear wall flow along diagonal paths in the web area, and axially in the chords.

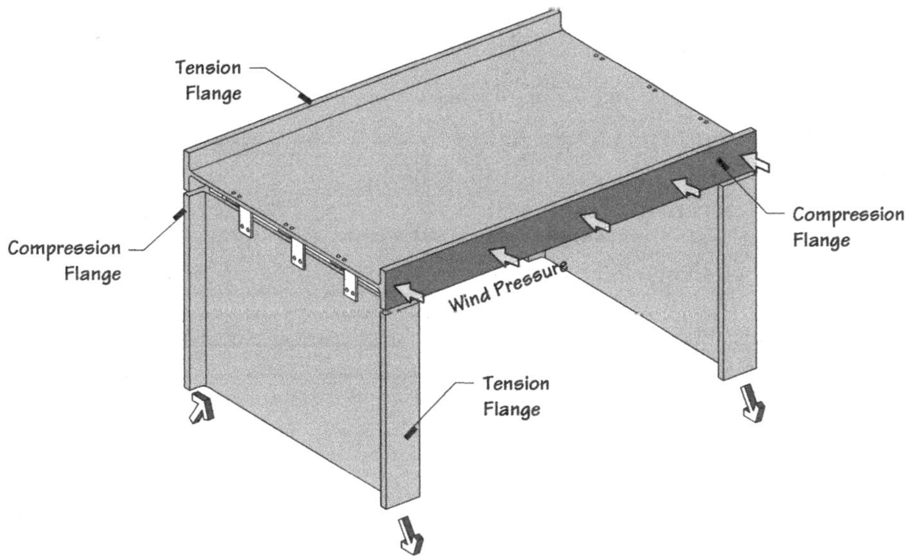

Figure 15.23 The combined action of shear walls and a roof diaphragm may be envisioned as that of three very deep steel beams with small flanges.

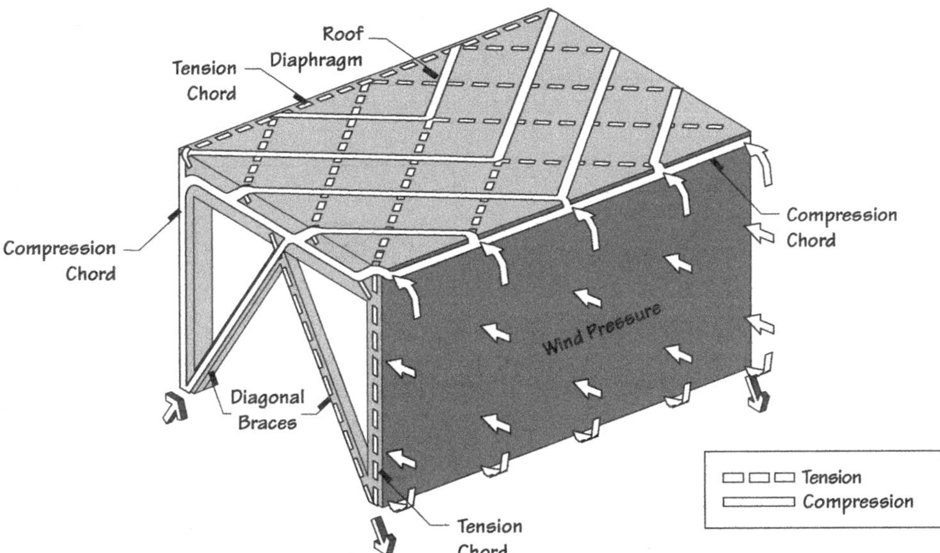

Figure 15.24 Half the wind pressure on a wall is transmitted to the ground in a single-story structure. The other half is transmitted up to the edge of the roof diaphragm by the wall framing. The diaphragm resists these forces by means of diagonal internal forces that transmit the forces to braced panels that lie in the same direction as the wind.

of steel decking welded together at the seams, a plywood floor or roof deck, or a deck sheathed with diagonal boards. Because a diaphragm is generally very deep in relation to its span (as deep as the building itself), the chords are often very small, and frequently they do double duty, serving another function such as a beam or girder. In a concrete building, the chords are usually the concrete beams at the edges of the floor or roof. Similarly, the chords for a diaphragm of steel decking are usually the steel beams at the edges, or they may be steel angles that are added along the edges. A plywood or wood diaphragm uses the joists along two of its edges as its chords, and the wood top plates of the walls or the header joist (rim joist) along the other edges.

Because winds can come from any direction, there must be chords on all edges of a floor or roof diaphragm. A wind that comes from an oblique direction is resisted by the chords on all the edges, with the chords that are closest to the direction of the wind doing a larger proportion of the work than those more nearly perpendicular to the wind.

Diaphragms must be detailed so that they are sufficiently strong and rigid for the roles that they play in the stability of a building. In plywood diaphragms, this often involves using thicker sheets of plywood than would be used for subflooring alone, nailing the edges of the sheets that lie perpendicular to the joists to wood blocking that keeps the edges from lifting when strong lateral forces stress the wall, and using larger nails than usual at closer spacings than usual, especially around the edges of the sheets. Nailing of the plywood to the chord members is particularly critical. Similar precautions are taken in other materials to fasten edges securely.

Figures 15.24 and 15.25 show how horizontal diaphragms act together with shear walls and braces to stabilize a single-story building. Half the force on the windward face of a building is transmitted to the edge of the floor, and half to the edge of the roof. The roof diaphragm accepts its half of the force and transmits it to planes of bracing or shear walls, which conduct it to the foundation and the ground.

A house or other small building, framed with wood or light-gauge steel studs and joists, more often than not has sufficient uninterrupted areas of plywood or other wood panel products in its exterior walls and roofs and floors to resist lateral loads. However, it is a good idea to check to be sure that every such building does indeed have sufficient areas of shear wall and diaphragms, that these areas are properly nailed, and that they are securely anchored to the foundations. This is especially important if the building has large windows or floor openings, which may eliminate so much plywood that the structure is unstable.

PLACING PLANES OF VERTICAL RIGIDITY IN PLAN

Planes of bracing or shear walls must be distributed in a balanced pattern on the floor plan of a building. In Figure 15.26, the right column shows floor plans on which vertical planes of lateral resistance, either shear walls, braces, or rigid joints, are distributed well. Those in the left column have various problems. In (a), there is no bracing in one entire face of the building. If the building is tightly anchored to its foundation, this arrangement will work, but a more symmetrical pattern of shear walls or bracing will work better and more reliably. The shear walls in plan (b) are too short, which will lead to very high chord forces and difficulty in preventing overturning of the walls. Plan (c) has plenty of shear walls, but they are placed far off center in the building. Figure 15.27 demonstrates what happens in such an arrangement: The resultant of the wind force passes through or near the centroid of the floor plan. When the center of lateral resistance is distant from the line of action of the resultant of the lateral forces, a couple is created that will twist the building, a condition known as *torsional instability*.

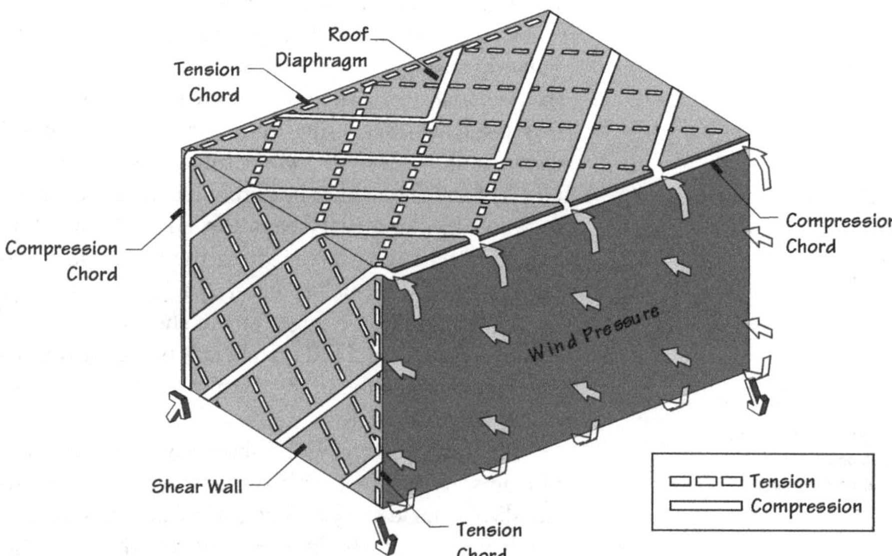

Figure 15.25 If shear walls are substituted for diagonal braces, the flow pattern in the walls is similar to that in the roof diaphragm.

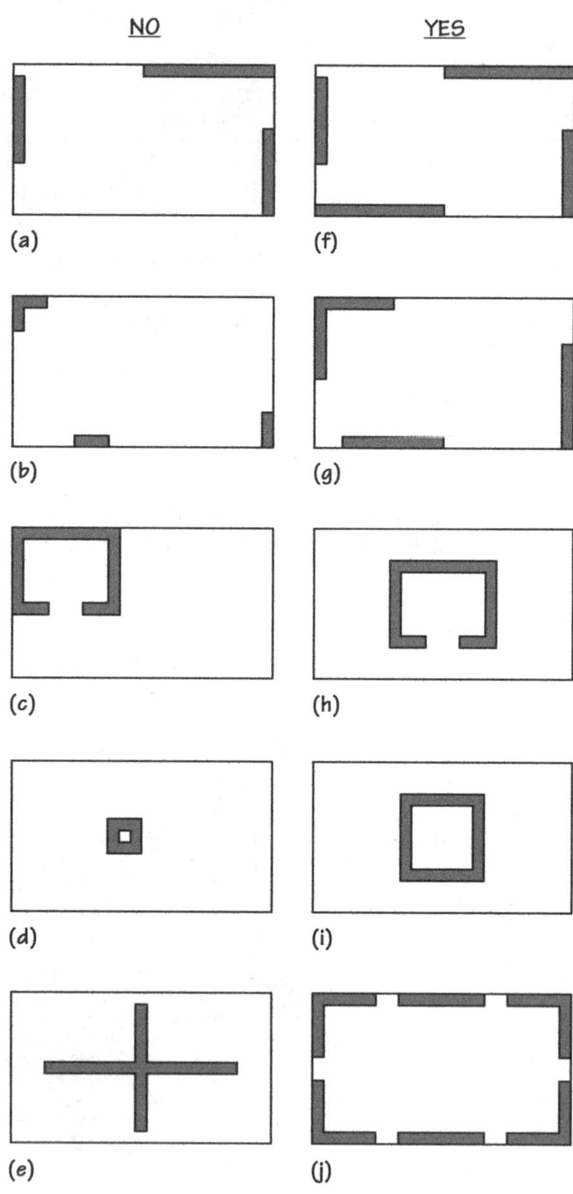

Figure 15.26 Bad and good placement of shear walls or bracing, as seen in plan view.

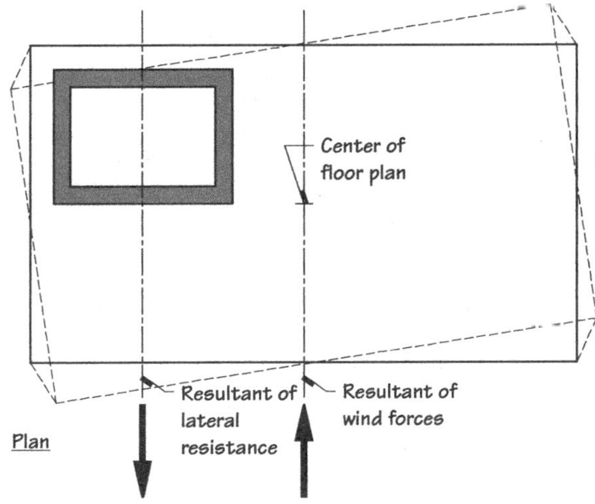

Figure 15.27 Asymmetry of placing lateral resistance elements, as seen in plan, can lead to twisting of the building.

Building plan (d) in Figure 15.26 has a symmetrical arrangement of shear walls, but the walls are too short in their horizontal dimensions. Stresses will be high in these walls, and hold-down fasteners will be subjected to very high forces. Figure 15.26(e) looks good at first glance, but the X-shaped arrangement of shear walls or bracing has no torsional resistance and will allow the building to twist. Short perpendicular shear walls at the ends of the walls would eliminate the problem.

MULTIPLYING THE BAY OF FRAMING IN THE HORIZONTAL DIRECTION

Most buildings are much larger than a single bay of framing. In Figure 15.28, 20 bays of framing have been laid out in a four-bay by five-bay arrangement. Shear walls (or planes of bracing) have been placed around two rectangular areas of the building. They are not perfectly balanced, but they are near enough to being balanced that they will still work well. The roof diaphragm acts to transmit wind loads from the exterior walls to these interior shear walls.

This is a very common type of arrangement. Usually the areas enclosed by interior shear walls or planes of bracing are used for such functions as stairways and elevators; toilet rooms; vertical shafts for pipes, wires, and ductwork; and storage and work rooms. Sometimes the bracing is left exposed as a feature of the architecture.

Figure 15.29 shows the same general plan of four-by-five bays, but with chevron bracing in perimeter faces of selected bays. The arrangement is not symmetrical, but it does place four bays of bracing in each principal direction. In accordance with the principle of transmissibility, the action of this frame in resisting lateral loads will be symmetrical. A rigid roof diaphragm is a necessity for both of the buildings diagrammed in Figures 15.28 and 15.29.

Shear walls do not have to extend to the corners of a building. In fact, roof loads on walls are lowest at corners, so that tie-downs are usually required at

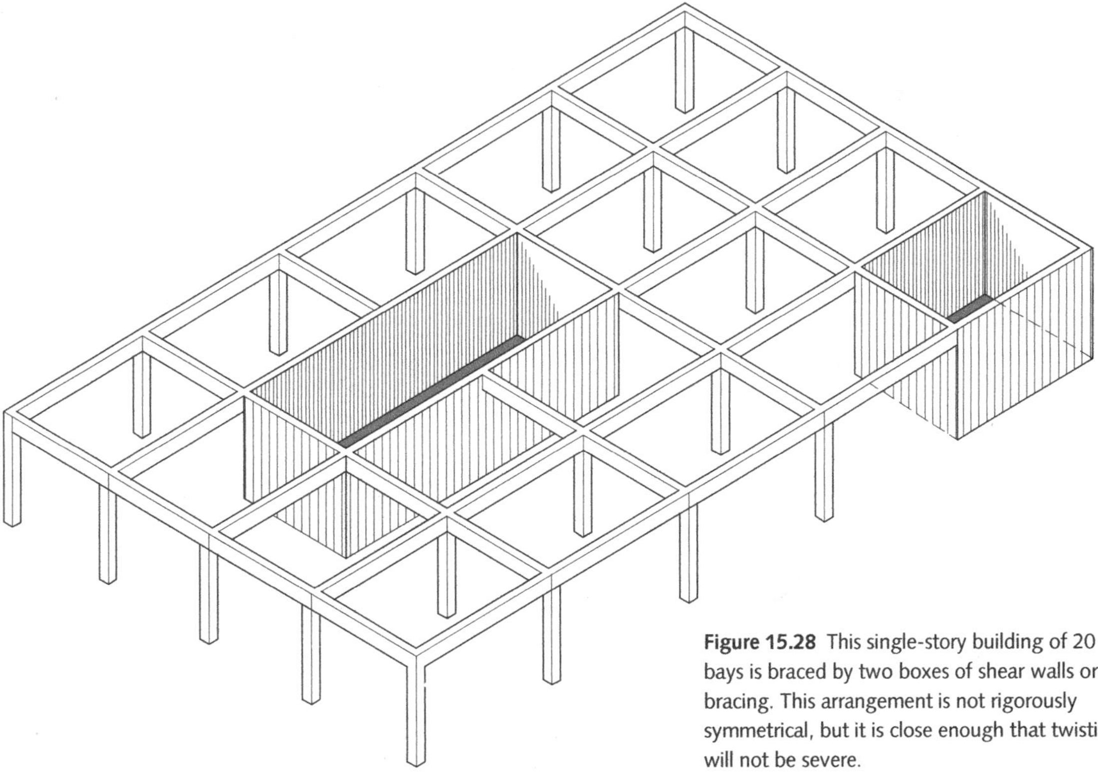

Figure 15.28 This single-story building of 20 bays is braced by two boxes of shear walls or bracing. This arrangement is not rigorously symmetrical, but it is close enough that twisting will not be severe.

corners, whereas shear walls that are away from the corners sometimes bear enough dead weight of roof that tie-downs are not needed.

MULTIPLYING THE FRAMED FLOOR IN THE VERTICAL DIRECTION

Imagine that we lift up the entire building frame of Figure 15.29, slip another, identical frame underneath it, and support the upper floor frame with the lower one (Figure 15.30a). Nothing changes within the frame that we have moved up: Both its vertical and horizontal forces remain the same. Beam, girder, and deck loads at both levels are unaffected by the two-story arrangement. However, the vertical elements of the frame that was inserted beneath must deal with gravity and lateral forces for both the ground level and the floor above. On the ground floor, column loads are doubled by the roof and floor loads that come from above. The diagonal braces on the lower floor must work to resist the wind loads that act on this floor, and also those that come from the floor above.

We can create a three-story building frame by lifting the two floors together and tucking a new one underneath (Figure 15.31a). All of the horizontal elements of the structure remain the same, but now the ground-floor columns and braces must accept and transmit accumulations of forces from two floors above. Column loads at ground level are three times those at the third level (assuming that the intensity of roof loads is the same as that of floor loads). The loads on lateral bracing accumulate similarly from top to bottom.

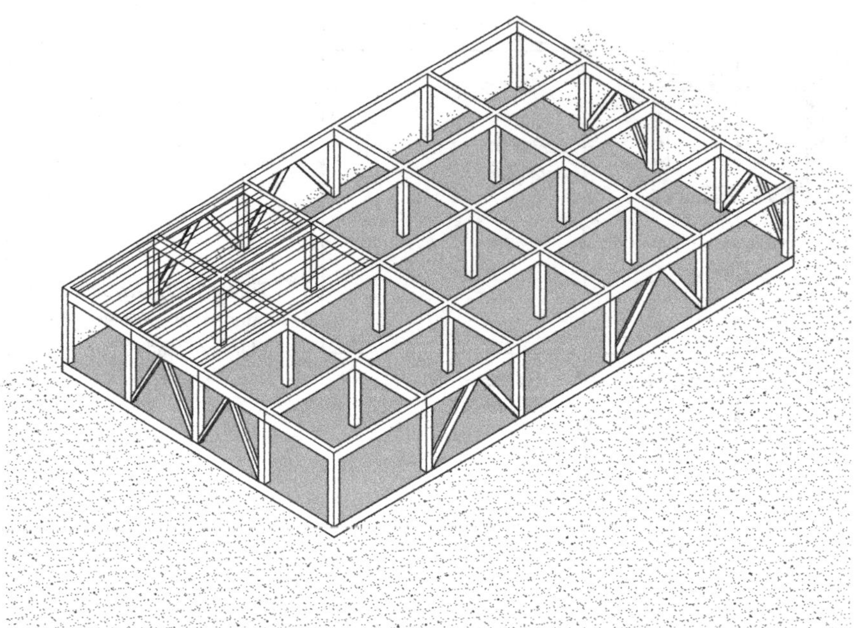

Figure 15.29 A single-story frame with well-placed chevron bracing.

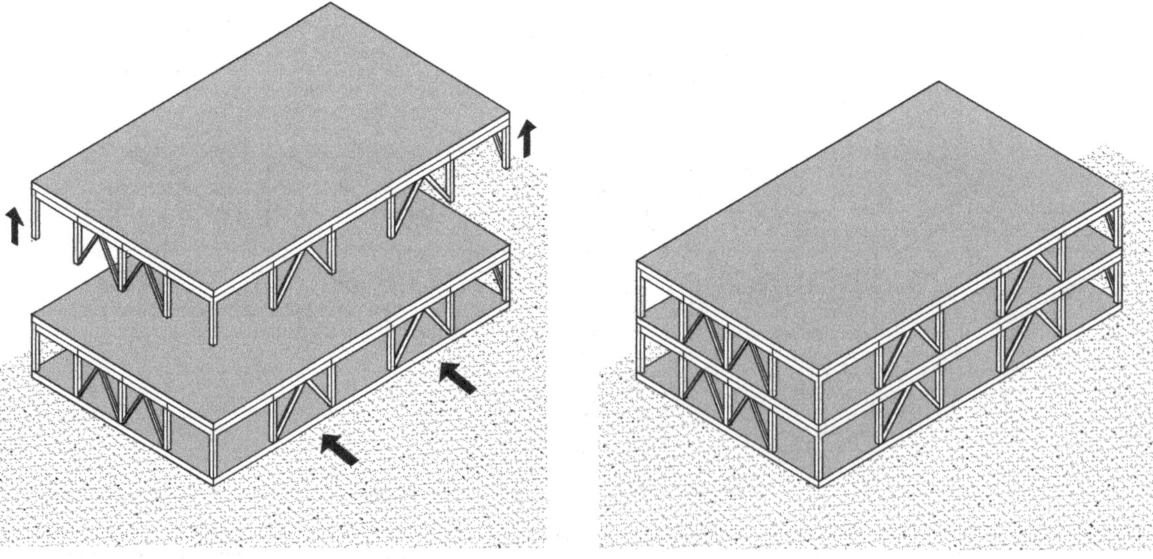

Figure 15.30 If the single-story frame is placed atop a similar frame to make a two-story frame, the forces on the beams and girders remain the same, but the forces on the columns and bracing are larger on the lower floor than on the upper.

WIND TRUSSES

What began as a single panel of chevron bracing in the single-story building has now become a three-panel K-truss, cantilevering vertically from the foundations to resist lateral loads. The vertical chords of this truss are columns that must also support vertical gravity loads from the roof and each of the floors. In Figure 15.32, we diagram a vertical bay of chevron bracing and indicate all the loads, both vertical and horizontal, that act on it. Then we apply Bow's notation and analyze it as a truss. Heavy lines on the form diagram indicate compression members, and light lines, tension members. Examination of the forces in the members shows some interesting trends: As we have already noted, column gravity loads accumulate from top to bottom, resulting in higher axial forces at ground level than at the top floor level. But if the columns were involved only in resisting gravity loads, their forces would be 15 kips at the top level, 30 at the middle level, and 45 at the ground. Instead, they run higher than this on the side of the truss away from the wind forces, and lower than this on the side near the wind forces. What is happening, of course, is that wind forces are creating loads on the wind truss, which must be resisted by forces in the members of the truss. The member forces in the truss must be added to the forces caused by gravity, as we have done in this analysis. Columns that are included in wind trusses must be larger than those that transmit gravity loads only in other areas of a building.

If we were to continue inserting floors under the building, we would soon find ourselves looking at a 10- to 20-story structure. Both gravity loads and lateral loads would accumulate from top to bottom, with the result that columns and braces would have to be much larger on the ground floor than at the top. But the loads on the parts of the frame that are only locally involved in lateral force resistance—namely the decking, girders, beams, and braces of the floors and roof—would be the same as for a single-story building.

As these forces accumulate, the overall action of bays of framing can become quite complex. As we saw in Figure 15.19, a frame structure with rigid joints will deform under lateral loads. There are many ways of modeling this behavior computationally, but this can also be understood through analogies involving simpler elements working together (Figure 15.33). For example, a tall uniform rigid frame subjected to lateral loading (a) deforms similarly to a tensioned cable that is loaded transversely (b). Similarly, the shear wall (c) acts as a cantilevered rotationally restrained vertical beam (d). Therefore, we can understand the complex deformation as a composite of the two (e, f). These types of analogies, which can be demonstrated in models (see also Figure 19.12), are effective for deepening the understanding and intuition of the designer involved with laying out bays of framing and evaluating the benefits of each configuration.

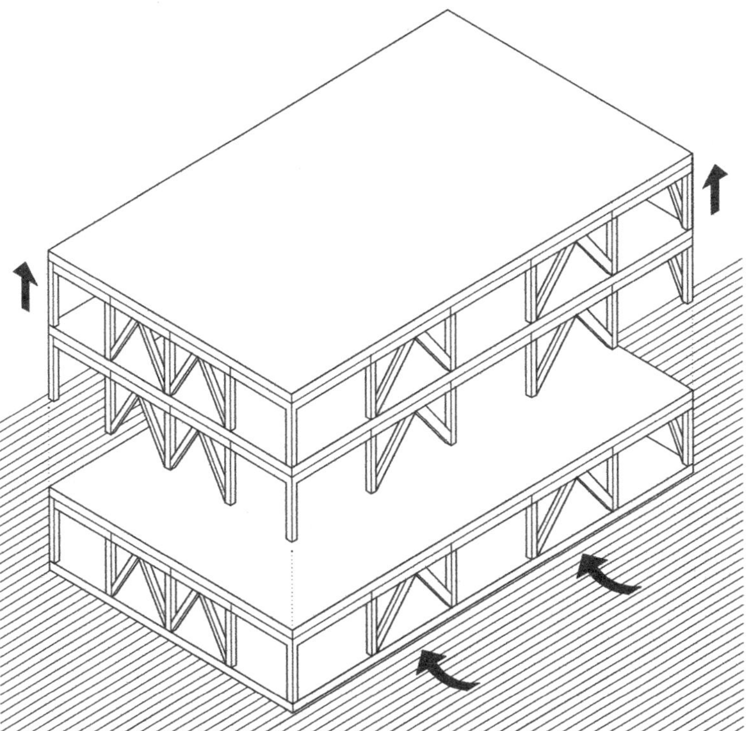

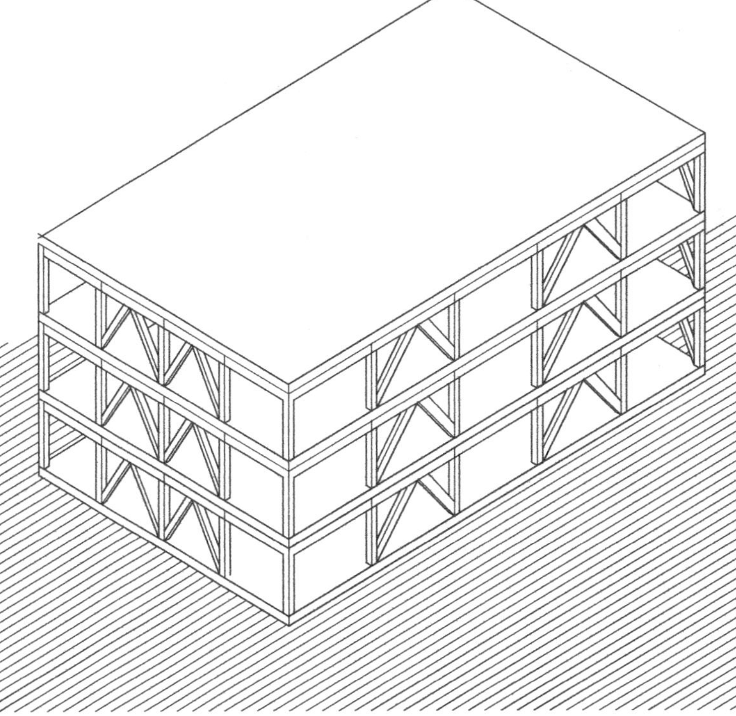

Figure 15.31
The process of raising and inserting floors of framing can be continued, up to the height at which ground-floor member forces become too large to resist.

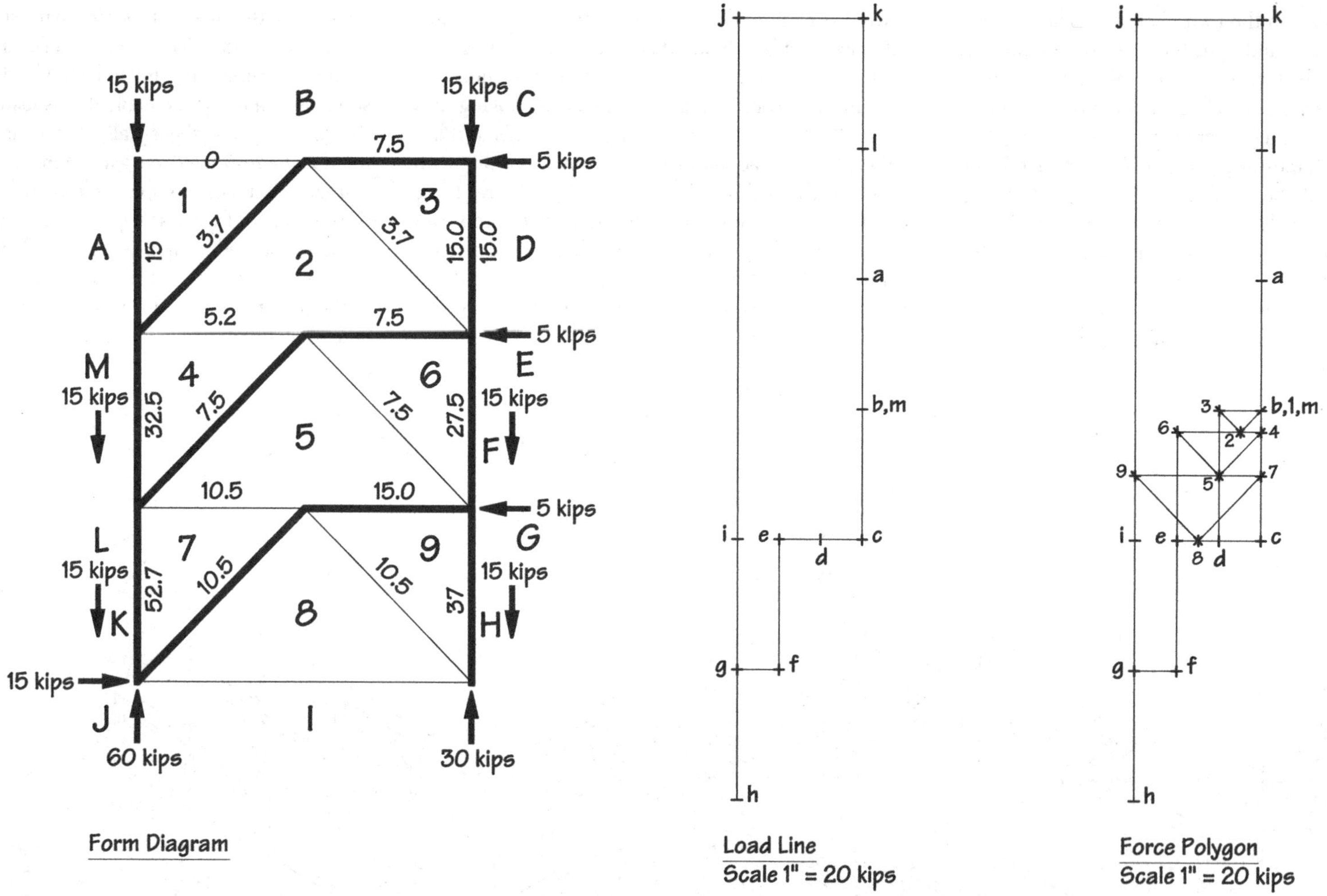

Figure 15.32 Analysis of a three-story wind truss. The load line is shown independently of the completed force polygon for the sake of clarity.

Common Planning Weaknesses in the Design of Building Framing

William L. Thoen, P.E.*

For nearly 50 years I have been pleased to provide structural consulting services to architects on building projects throughout the United States and the Mideast, ranging in size from smaller than a house to as large as a city. Most of the preliminary designs an architect brings to me for structural services are pretty well thought out in terms of appropriate column spacing and allowance for beam depths, and have suitable locations to accommodate the structural frame. In subsequent discussions an appropriate framing scheme usually develops without a great deal of conflict. Sometimes, knowing what the architect is trying to achieve, a unique structural arrangement becomes obvious, and if the architect can incorporate that in his or her plans, a strikingly new form evolves.

Having said that, there are some common weaknesses that I see frequently in these preliminary designs. They relate to:

- Building stability and lateral bracing,
- Vertical organization of the structural frame,
- Tolerances between the structural frame and the architectural finish,
- Site considerations, and
- Floor vibration and comfort performance.

LATERAL BRACING

If the architect has thought about lateral forces at all, he or she will often say, "Please keep all the lateral bracing in the core," as if that were the end of the matter.

If core bracing is used alone, the width or depth of the core becomes the *structural depth* of the building against lateral forces, regardless of how wide or how long the building is. Accordingly, a slender core becomes like a flagpole or mast that braces the entire building, and is often too slender for acceptable sway performance of taller structures. In addition, lateral forces that are eccentric with respect to the core may twist the building back and forth uncomfortably because the core alone cannot provide sufficient torsional stiffness. Even though the building may have sufficient lateral *strength*, the inability of the core alone to provide sufficient *stiffness* can result in undesirable building motion, slapping of elevator cables against sidewalls, sloshing of water in toilet bowls, swinging doors, binding windows, squeaks, groans, and mal-de-mer. It is more efficient and effective in most cases to put lateral bracing devices in the perimeter walls rather than the core. This greatly increases the effective structural depth of the lateral bracing and foundations.

Another popular but ineffective location for lateral bracing is the exterior wall corner bays of the building, which are the worst exterior wall locations because the corner columns are the most lightly loaded and therefore have the least gravity weight to offset overturning uplift.

VERTICAL ALIGNMENT

A common planning weakness that I have often seen is structural frame discontinuity in the vertical direction. Think of a building with a number of floors of apartments at the top, above a number of floors of commercial offices, with ground-floor retail spaces and basement parking underneath. Each occupancy has its own optimum structural bay size, which, if rigorously applied, results in massive transfer girders or story-deep trusses at each change of occupancy. These are extremely expensive and should be avoided by planning a single, efficient structural bay that can be made to work for all the occupancies. Frequently, the most demanding occupancy in this regard is the parking, where columns must be located such that automobiles can maneuver and park without sheet metal damage.

TOLERANCE

The need for dimensional tolerance between the structure and the architectural interior and exterior finishes is often not considered. The actual depth of a steel column may be as much as 2 in. larger than the nominal depth. Splice plates, connections, and bolts can make the structural cross section even deeper; and fireproofing, where required, adds to that. Base plates, because of welding and area requirements, will be larger than the column they support, and commonly sit atop a bed of grout, adding considerably to the space that must be allotted for them.

Concrete building frames are ordinarily built to dimensional tolerances such as plus or minus 1 in. in the location of a wall plane, and often exceed such tolerances. Remember, too, that concrete has a way of hardening up at inconvenient times. A slightly misplaced wall or anchor bolt will have to be accommodated somehow.

The detailer of a building should provide dimensional "float" (tolerance) between the structure and the architectural finish when preparing preliminary sketches, especially where concrete work joins the superstructure.

SITE CONSIDERATIONS

Site locations and constraints may influence the choice of structural module or type. Most architects practicing within a region are aware of its special requirements. Hurricanes (Southeast), earthquakes (West Coast), tornadoes (Midwest), expansive clays (Texas), permafrost (Alaska), and extreme temperature or humidity variation (Mideast) are special requirements associated with particular locales. Sometimes, local conditions such as availability of materials or lack of skilled labor will govern the design vernacular.

As important, site constraints or subgrade conditions may strongly affect the structural system and even the architectural form. On good soils, the structure can be founded on simple footings. Where the building location is underlain with organic material, soft clays, and the like, special foundation systems are required, and differential settlements and control of groundwater may have to be considered. These may influence the choice of the superstructure system, including column spacing, to achieve an optimal system.

FLOOR VIBRATION AND SERVICEABILITY

Today's buildings are lighter and more gossamer than their ancestors. With modern high-strength materials, composite construction, and lightweight concretes, floor spans can be made longer; and *stiffness,* rather than *strength,* often governs the structural depth. As a consequence, floor vibration, cambering, and careful deflection control become important factors for occupant comfort, especially in large, column-free spaces without the damping influence of partitions. Often, floor vibrations are not sensible to walkers, but become intolerable to a person sitting, as in an office. All too often, long, shallow-span floors are envisioned. Inevitably, these must be deepened or otherwise stiffened or damped against excessive vibration.

LEARNING TO DESIGN BUILDING FRAMING

A good way to learn these areas of structural planning (and structures in general) is to choose a local building of interest and study its structure. How have the architect and engineer collaborated to make it successful? What constitutes the lateral bracing system? Where is it located and why? What were the site constraints, if any, and how do they influence the design? What is the column grid module and what is the floor system depth in relation to its spans?

If a student studies two or three built projects a semester, each typifying a type of building that is likely to be encountered in practice, and if the student keeps a notebook of sketches and notes relative to each type of building, then he or she will have studied structural solutions in the context of the architectural problem. This notebook will also be a useful reference in architectural or engineering practice.

*William L. Thoen is a structural engineer who works primarily in New England. He was a principal for many years at LeMessurier Consultants, where he was involved in such landmark projects as King Khalid Military City (Saudi Arabia), the Dallas–Fort Worth Regional Airport Terminal Facilities, the Anchorage, Alaska Performing Arts Center, and the Miami–Dade County Office Building.

Exercises

1. A business owner needs a new single-story warehouse. In plan, it will be a rectangle 117 ft by 221 ft. The minimum acceptable bay dimensions are 30 ft by 33 ft. The larger bay dimension may run in either the long or short direction of the building. Work out a floor plan showing column locations that meet these criteria. Assume that you are using a decking material that can span a maximum of 8 ft. Draw and dimension a typical bay, including beams, girders, and decking. For economy, create as many identical bays as possible and make the beams run in the longer direction of the bay. Show dimensions to the nearest 1/4 in.

2. Assuming that the decking forms an adequate roof diaphragm, show a system of shear walls or braces that will resist the lateral loads on the warehouse in exercise #1.

3. Trace the paths taken by the given load through the bay shown in Figure 15.34. Calculate the percentages of the load that flow through each member.

4. Figure 15.35 shows a sketch by engineer Anthony Hunt for a house in Hampstead, England, designed by architect Sir Michael Hopkins and his wife Patty, showing the proposed configuration of exposed lateral braces. Propose three other appropriate systems for resisting lateral loads. What are the advantages of each? Which do you expect would use the least material?

Notice how Hunt's sketch contains a requirement that the edge of the floor structure and decking to be kept thin behind the glazing, yet the sketch also proposes relatively deep trusses. To achieve a thin edge, what are two alternate configurations for framing the house to minimize the exterior thickness dimension of the floor and deck? What do you believe is the limiting or constraining factor in this regard, and why?

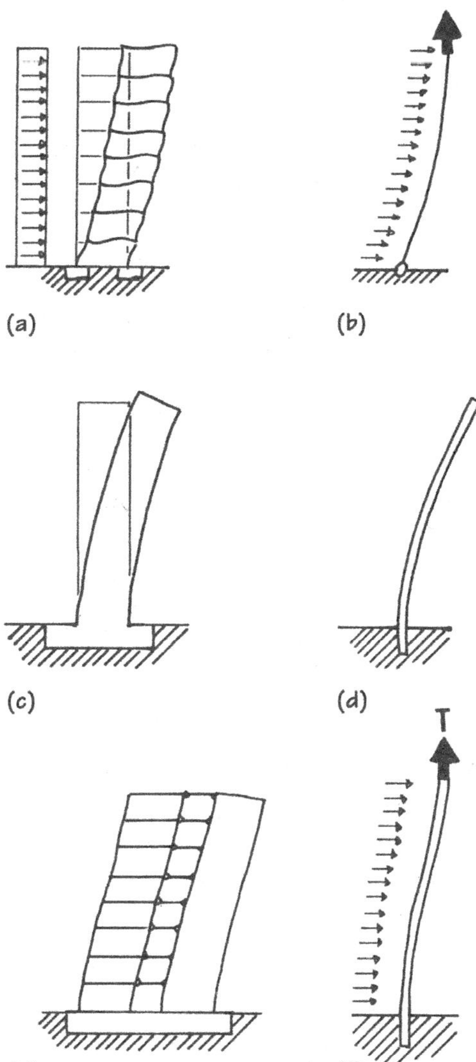

◀ **Figure 15.33** A diagram of the behavior of lateral load resistance systems, using analogies to a tensioned cable and a cantilevered beam. Figure 19.12 also demonstrates this behavior, using a simple paper model to show deformations of a rigid frame under lateral load.

Source: E. Traum and W. Zalewski, "Analogy to the Structural Behavior of Shear-Wall Systems," *Journal of the Boston Society of Civil Engineers*, October 1970.

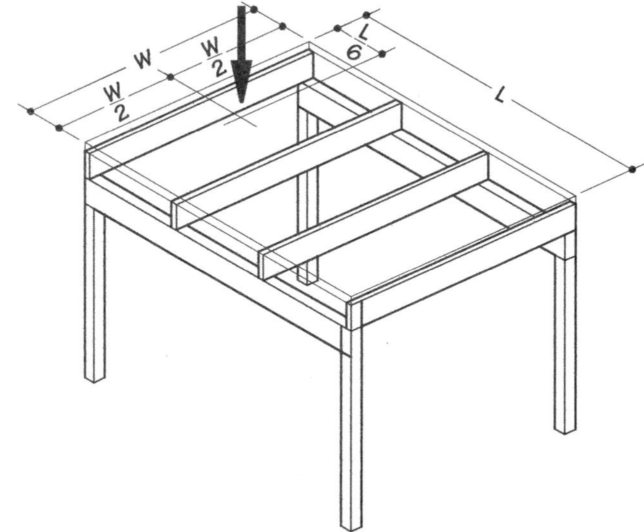

▲ **Figure 15.34** An asymmetrically placed load on a bay of framing.

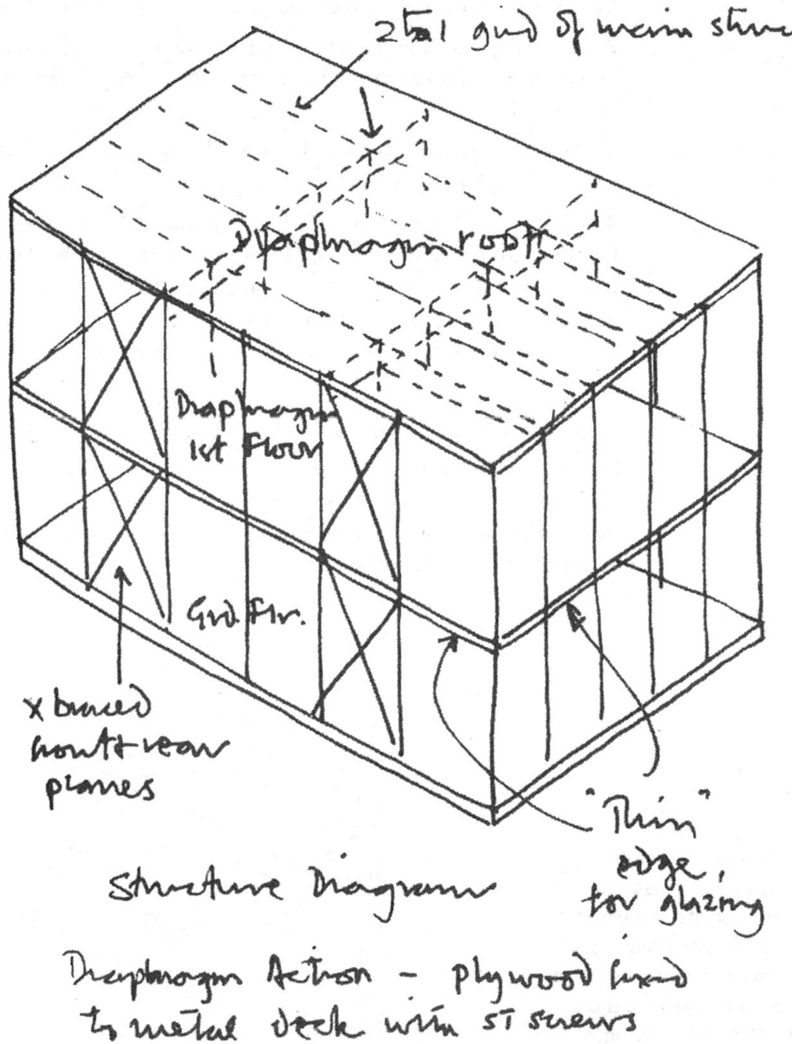

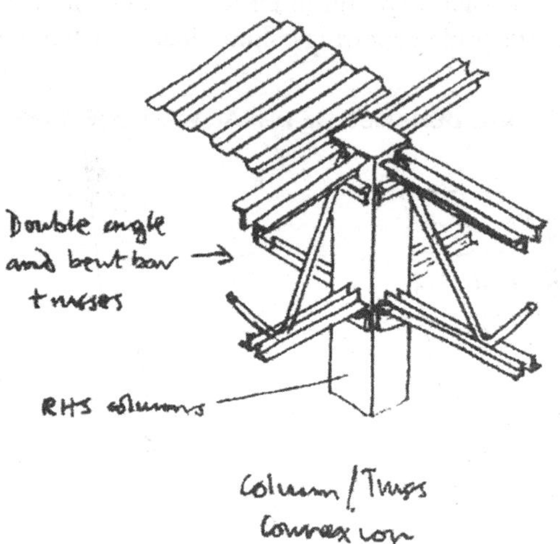

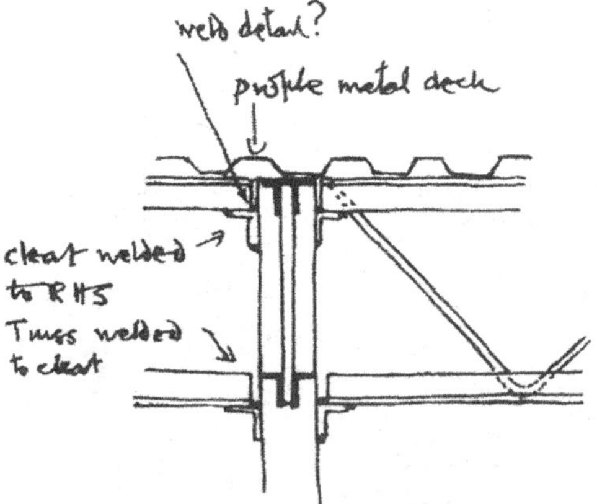

Figure 15.35 Sketch by Anthony Hunt for the Hopkins House, 1976, Hampstead, England.

Image courtesy of Anthony Hunt Associates.

Key Terms and Concepts

column
load-bearing wall
bearing wall
beam
bay
trabeated
joist
rafter
load path
load tracing
chevron bracing
knee bracing
cross bracing
arcuated
post
post-and-beam
bay
decking
girder
external bracing
rigid joint
diaphragm
shear wall
chord of a diaphragm
torsional instability
wind truss

Further Resources

Guise, David. *Design and Technology in Architecture,* Revised Edition. New York: Van Nostrand Reinhold, 1991. This volume contains a wide range of useful case studies on the framing strategies of notable twentieth-century skyscrapers, offices, and other buildings, including how their structural systems coordinate with the mechanical services.

Ambrose, James, and Dimitry Vergun. *Simplified Building Design for Wind and Earthquake Forces* (3rd ed.) New York: Wiley, 1997. The early chapters of this book review the means at our disposal for resisting lateral forces on buildings, and the later ones show simple analysis and design procedures.

CHAPTER 16

Bending Actions on Beams

- *Analysis of external load patterns on structures; quantifying and simplifying external loadings*
- *Bending moments and vertical forces*
- *V and M diagrams; relationship to force polygons and funicular polygons*
- *Graphical and semigraphical constructions*

How big does a beam need to be? This is not always an easy question to answer (Figure 16.1). Consider the variety of beams shown in the small structure of Figure 16.2. Free-body diagrams of the beams labeled (1) through (6) in Figure 16.2a are shown in Figure 16.2b. The beams labeled (1), (2), and (4), all have identical main spans. The first two support the same load, *W*, but in (1) this load is concentrated at midspan, and in (2) it is uniformly distributed over the entire span. In (4), the load is 20 percent larger to match the lengthening of the beam with an overhang that is 20 percent of the span. In which of these three examples is the bending action most intense? To find out, we must be able to take into account the magnitude of the load, the distribution pattern of the load, the span of the beam, and the way in which the beam is supported. In this chapter, we will learn how to find two simple quantities for any beam, *vertical force* and *bending moment*, that take all these factors into account. These will make it easy for us to assign sizes to beams, as we will do in the chapters that follow.

Figure 16.1 Various loading conditions are evident in the exposed beams of the Les Abouts house in Saint-Edmond-de-Grantham, Quebec, Canada, by Atelier Pierre Thibault.

The bays of roof framing depicted in Figure 16.2a further demonstrate the diversity of loadings and support conditions of beams used in buildings. The beam marked (1) is a girder, which bears a single, concentrated load from a beam that rests on it at midspan. Each girder, like every beam, must also support its own weight, which is uniformly distributed over its length. Beams (2) support loads from roof decking and self-weight that are both uniformly distributed over their entire span. Beam (3) is a girder that carries concentrated loads at its *third points* in addition to its own weight. Beams (4) have *overhanging ends* and support uniformly distributed loads. Beams (5) are *cantilevers*, which carry uniform loads and are supported at only one end. Beam (6) is *continuous* over its middle support, rather than simply supported; its

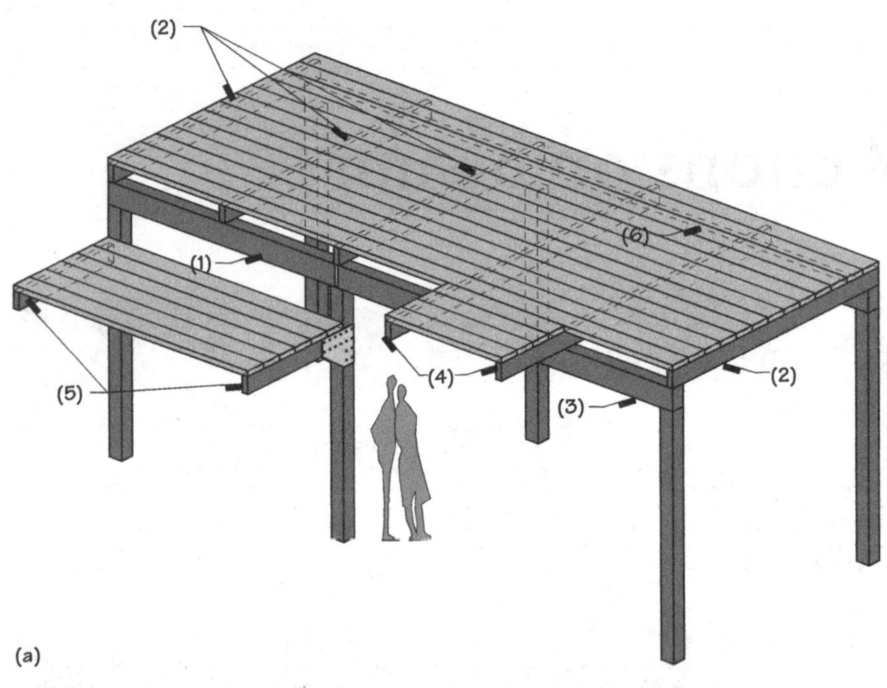

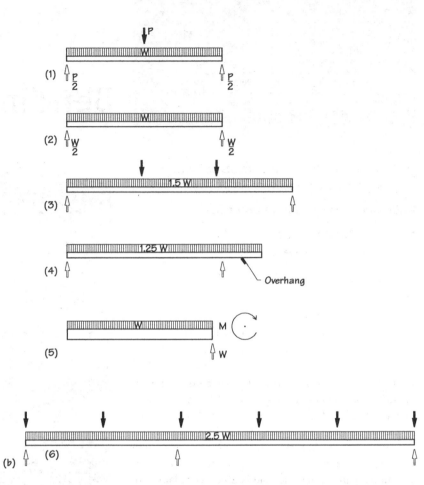

Figure 16.2 Even a small, simple structure (a) contains a large variety of support and loading conditions for beams (b).

concentrated loads are applied at uniform intervals over its span. Figure 16.2b isolates each of these beams as a free body. These are just a few examples of the unending combinations of loading and support conditions that we must consider when assigning sizes and shapes to beams.

LONGITUDINAL AND TRANSVERSE LOADINGS

When a *longitudinal* force is applied along the axis of a structural member, the member is placed in either tension or compression and grows slightly longer or shorter while retaining its linear shape (Figure 16.3a). When a *transverse* force is applied to a member, the member is placed in *bending,* and becomes curved (Figure 16.3b).

The determination of the effects of bending actions on cables, arches, and trusses is relatively simple, as we have learned in earlier chapters, because these types of structures translate bending actions into axial forces in their members. The member forces in an arch or cable may be found by constructing a fan-shaped force polygon and its associated funicular polygon (Chapters 2 and 3). Those in a truss are found by drawing a force polygon made up of lines parallel to the truss members (Chapters 4 and 6). With respect to beams, the process is slightly more involved, yet it is closely related to that for designing funicular members, as we will discover shortly.

FINDING VALUES OF VERTICAL FORCES AND BENDING MOMENTS

In Figure 16.4, we consider a simply supported beam of span L that supports a concentrated load, P, at midspan. We will make a series of imaginary vertical cuts

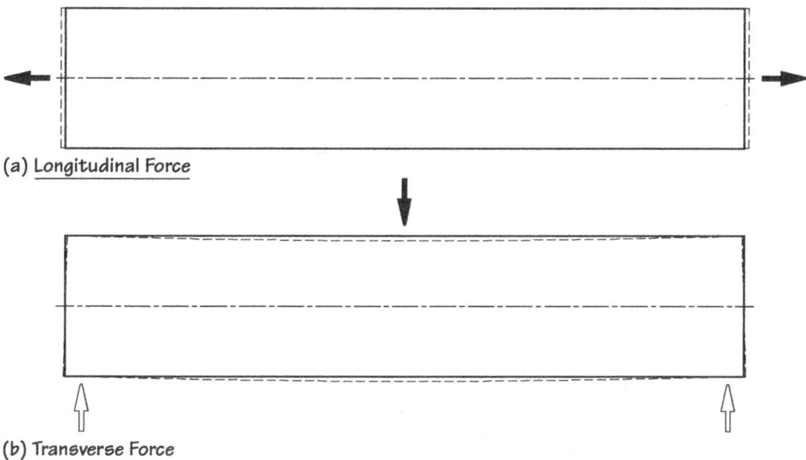

Figure 16.3 Longitudinal and transverse forces applied to beams.

at intervals of $L/8$ through the beam; for now, we will ignore the weight of the beam itself.

Having made the vertical cuts, we construct free-body diagrams of successive portions of the beam and find the forces necessary to maintain static equilibrium in each portion. At Cut 0, which is made at the left-hand support, the only given force acting on the segment is the left-hand reaction, which acts upward and has a value of $P/2$ (Figure 16.4). By summing vertical forces at the cut section and setting the sum equal to zero, we find that there must be a downward vertical force, V_0, of the same magnitude in order for the segment to be in static equilibrium. There are no horizontal forces or moments at this section.

At Cut 1 (Figure 16.5), a summation of vertical forces again shows that there must be a vertical force,

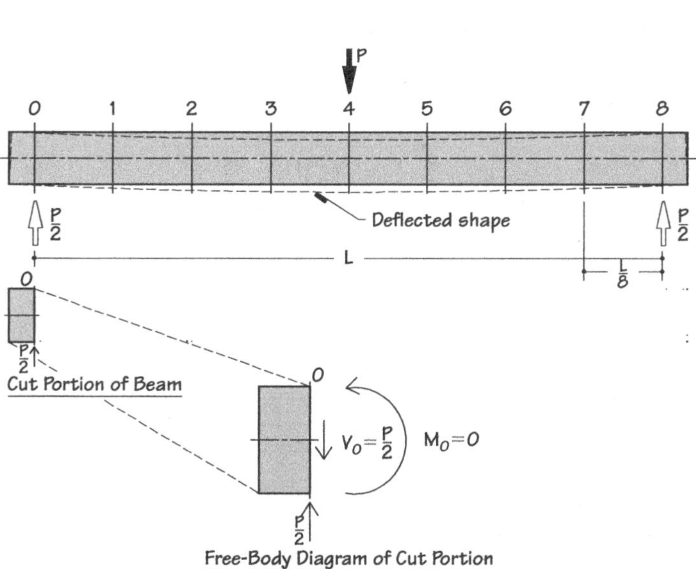

Figure 16.4 Analysis of forces on successive sections of a beam, step 0.

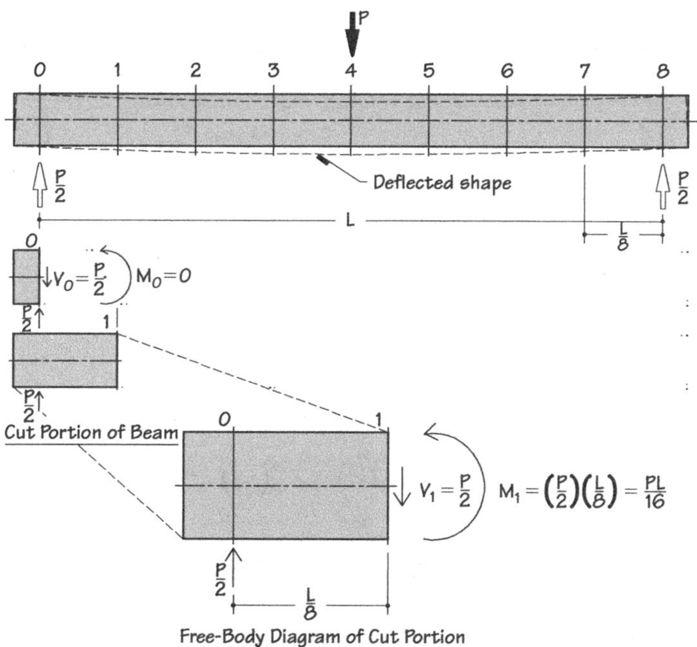

Figure 16.5 Analysis of forces on successive sections of a beam, step 1.

V_1, of magnitude $P/2$ at the cut face. But now there is a distance between this force and the equal but opposite vertical force of the left-hand reaction. The two forces create a clockwise couple whose moment is $P/2$ times the distance between the forces, $L/8$, which comes to $PL/16$. To resist this moment, there must be a counterclockwise moment of the same value at this section, which we indicate with a circular arrow.

At Cut 2 (Figure 16.6), the vertical force is still $P/2$, but now our moment calculation indicates that with the increase in length of the moment arm, a counterclockwise moment of $PL/8$ is needed to maintain equilibrium. At Cut 3, similarly, we find a moment of $3PL/16$.

At Cut 4, which is taken at midspan, we encounter a downward external force, which is load P. To establish equilibrium of vertical forces, we must add V_4, which is an upward force of $P/2$, to the free-body diagram. When multiplied by its moment arm of $L/2$, it creates a clockwise moment of $PL/4$, which must be balanced with a counterclockwise moment of the same value at the cut section.

As we move from midspan toward the right-hand support in successive steps to complete our analysis (Figure 16.7), the vertical force remains constant at minus $P/2$, and the moment diminishes to zero at the support.

Cut Portion of Beam

Figure 16.6 Analysis of forces on successive sections of a beam, steps 2 to 4.

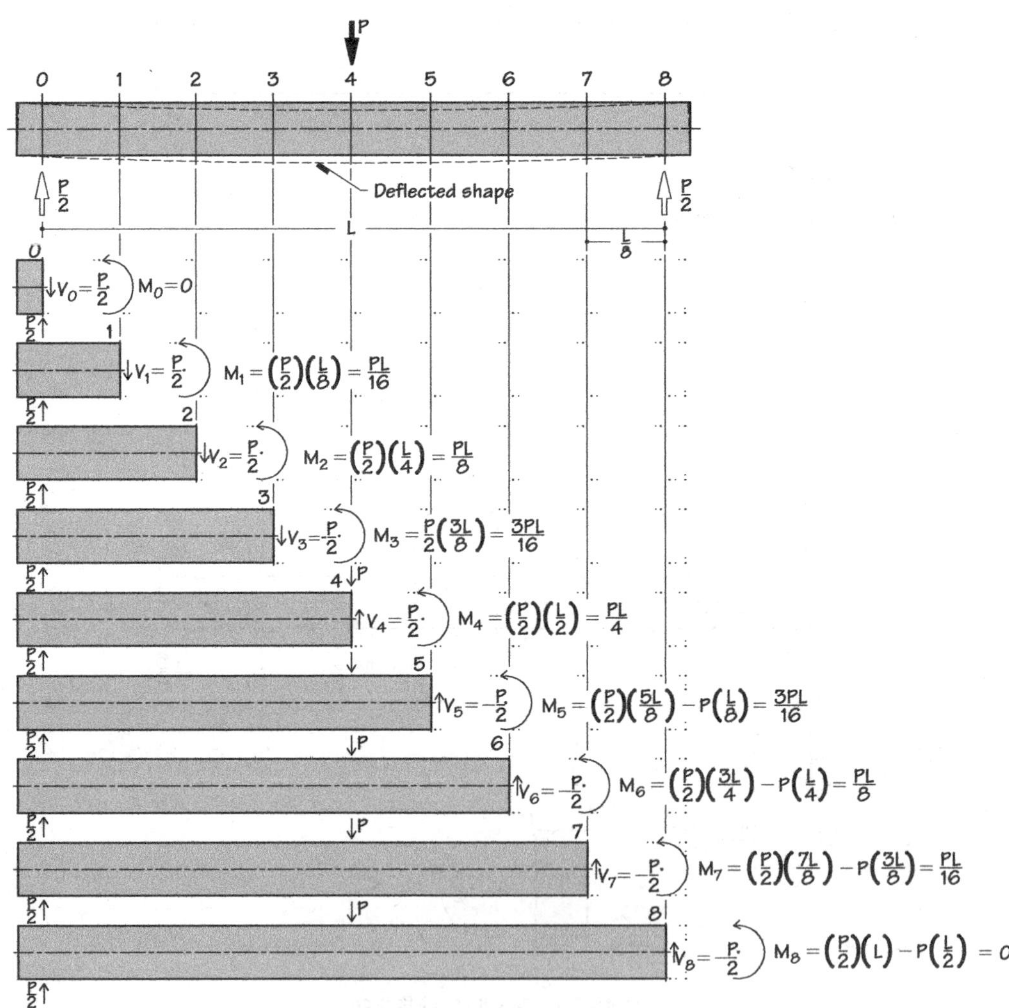

Figure 16.7 Analysis of forces on successive sections of a beam, steps 5 to 8.

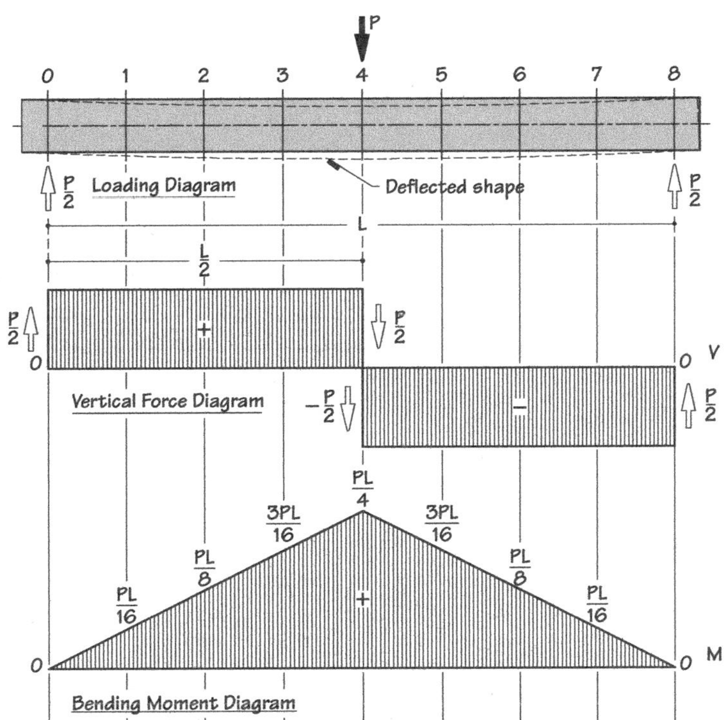

Figure 16.8 A summary diagram of loading, vertical forces, and bending moments.

In Figure 16.8, we graph the values that we have found for V and M, the vertical force and moment, respectively, aligning the graphs carefully below the loading diagram. In drawing the graph of V forces, we note that the line moves up and down to follow the directions of the external forces: up at the left reaction, which is also up, then down at the load P, which pushes down, and finally, back up to zero with the upward push of the right-hand reaction. V is constant and positive at a value of $P/2$ for the left half of the beam, and switches to negative values of the same magnitude in the right half. M increases linearly from 0 at the left support to $PL/4$ at midspan and then diminishes to zero at the right support.

M is called the *bending moment* because it is a measure of the intensity of bending action that is created at each vertical plane in a member with this pattern of loads. V is the *vertical force* that acts at each plane. Both V and M are created by the action of the applied load, in this case the load concentrated at midspan.

The graph of values of V is the *vertical force diagram*. The graph of the values of M is called the *bending moment diagram* or simply the *moment diagram*. The alignment of these two graphs below the loading diagram greatly facilitates their construction. It is the standard way of representing external bending actions on a beam.

V is usually referred to in structure books as *shear*, and the V diagram as the *shear diagram*. However, it is inaccurate to refer to V as "shear" (see pages 469 and 470), so we will call the diagram the *vertical force diagram*.

In the next chapter, our determination of internal stresses in beams will be based on these two quantities, vertical force and bending moment.

"Shear action is not the third elementary structural action. It is a combination of tension and compression."

—MARIO SALVADORI

GRAPHICAL CONSTRUCTION OF *V* AND *M* DIAGRAMS

Constructing V and M diagrams by evaluating equilibrium at a series of cut sections, as we have just done, is laborious and time-consuming. In practice, it is seldom done except within the invisible workings of structural software. It is much quicker when working by hand to construct these diagrams graphically or semigraphically.

The graphical means by which we construct V and M diagrams is closely related to the graphical construction of force polygons and funicular polygons, which we learned in the early chapters of this book. In Figure 16.9, we begin a graphical construction of the V and M diagrams for the same beam that we have just examined, one with a single, concentrated load at the center of the span. The first step is to draw the loading diagram accurately to a convenient scale, and below it and to one side or the other, to construct a force polygon for the loading on the beam, also at a convenient scale. There is no relationship between the scales at which the two drawings are constructed; one represents linear measurements of a beam and the locations of the loads on it, the other represents the magnitudes of external forces that are applied to the beam. The pole for the force polygon may be located arbitrarily, but it is convenient to locate it so that the closing string vector, *oc*, is horizontal, and to adopt a perpendicular pole distance that is equal to the total load on the beam, or half the total load, or some other round number. For this example, we have made this distance equal to P, the external load.

We continue the construction by drawing the V diagram, the graph of vertical forces. The vertical dimensions are projected off the load line of the force polygon. With the help of Bow's notation, we plot the intersections of horizontal lines from the load

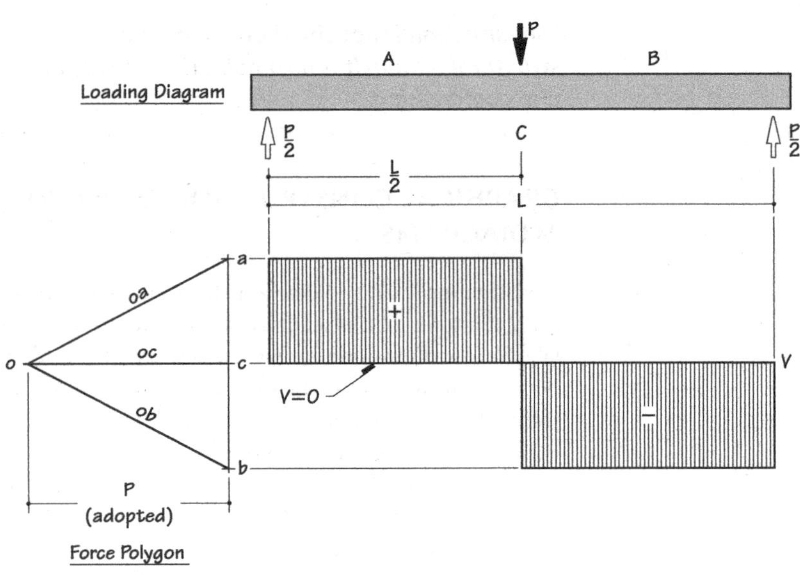

Figure 16.9 Starting a graphical construction for the same beam.

line with corresponding vertical lines from the form diagram. The path of these intersection points is the *V* diagram.

The bending moment diagram, *M*, is aligned vertically beneath the loading diagram and *V* diagram (Figure 16.10). It is constructed like any funicular polygon, with its segments parallel to the rays of the force polygon that are drawn from the pole location that we selected. The *M* diagram represents the intensities of the moment couples that we found at each vertical section as we sliced our way across the beam.

Numerical values for the bending moment at any point on the span may be obtained by multiplying the height of the moment curve above the baseline at that point by the perpendicular pole distance of the force polygon. This numerical interpretation of the graphical solution works because the bending moment that is exerted by a funicular cable at any given point on its span is equal to the vertical distance of the cable from the closing string at that point times the horizontal component of the force in the cable. The horizontal component of force in the cable is the same as the perpendicular pole distance. The units are feet or inches for the cable distance, and pounds or kips for the pole distance, giving moment values in pound-feet, pound-inches, kip-feet, or kip-inches.

The height of the peak of the *M* diagram above its closing string scales as *L*/4 on the diagram we have just drawn. Earlier we established the perpendicular pole distance as *P*. Thus, the maximum moment that acts on a beam with a concentrated load at midspan is the height of the *M* diagram, *L*/4, times the pole distance, *P*, which comes to *PL*/4. This is identical to the value that we found by cutting sections and evaluating moments numerically. Similar graphical constructions can be used to find bending moments for any loading condition.

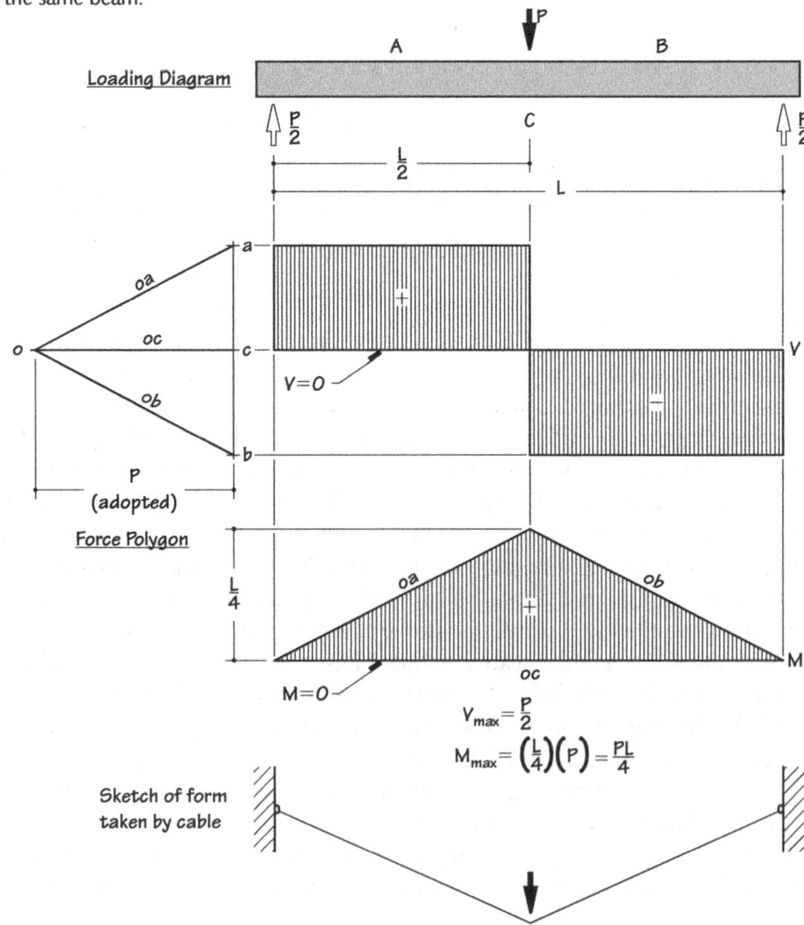

Figure 16.10 Completing a graphical construction for *V* and *M* diagrams.

V and M for Cables and Arches

The bending moment diagram is a function of factors external to the beam—a loading pattern and a set of support conditions—and not of the internal workings of the beam, which we will address in the next chapter. In fact, it represents the values of bending moment for **any** structure that carries this load across this span, whether a truss, an arch, or a cable.

If we cut a series of vertical sections through a simple cable structure, just as we cut them for a simple beam, we will find that we need vertical components of cable force at each cut to maintain equilibrium, just as we did for a beam (Figure 16.11). The horizontal components of cable force form force couples, and therefore moments, with the horizontal component of the end reactions. The moment of each couple is equal to the horizontal component of cable force, H, which is constant throughout the length of the cable, times the distance between the line of action of this component and the horizontal component of cable force. The same relationships are true for a funicular arch.

The value that we find graphically for the bending moment remains the same regardless of the pole distance that we choose, and regardless of whether the curve of moment values has a horizontal or sloping closing string. The graphical construction automatically compensates for these variables and always gives the same answers.

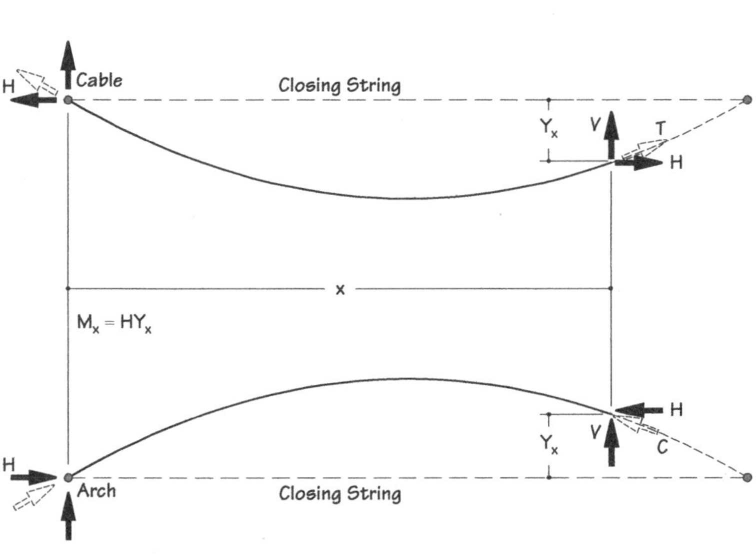

Figure 16.11 Diagram of vertical components of force required to maintain equilibrium in a cable or arch.

FURTHER EXPLORATIONS OF V AND M USING THE GRAPHICAL METHOD

We will consolidate our knowledge of the graphical method and broaden our acquaintance with V and M values for various loading conditions by constructing several more examples.

In Figure 16.12, we develop V and M values for a beam with a single concentrated load at its quarter

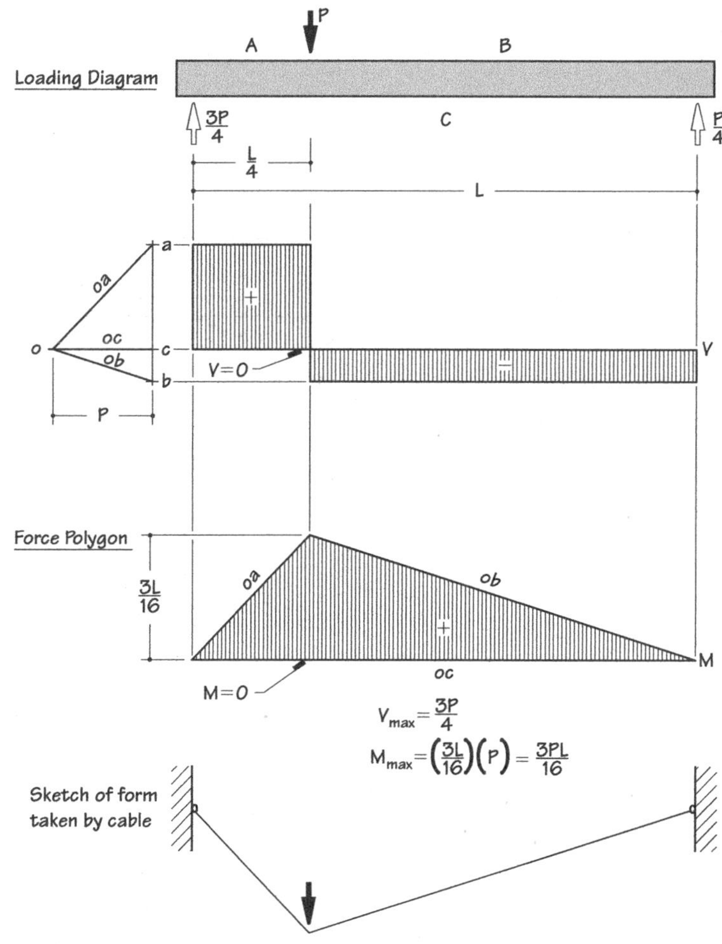

Figure 16.12 Graphical construction of V and M diagrams for a single load asymmetrically placed.

point. (We continue for the time being to disregard the self-weight of the beam.) The two reactions are found by evaluating moments. Ray *oc*, which represents the closing string of the moment diagram, is made horizontal on the force polygon to produce a level base for the moment diagram. The slopes of the *M* diagram are parallel to the corresponding rays on the force polygon.

Figure 16.13 shows the graphical derivation of *V* and *M* values for a beam that is loaded symmetrically at its third points. A notable property of this arrangement is that the portion of the beam span between the loads has a constant bending moment and no vertical force. When a beam is tested for strength in a laboratory, this loading is often used because its maximum moment is applied to a substantial length of the beam, making the beam equally likely to break at a number of points, and vertical force is not a factor in the breaking of the beam.

In Figure 16.14, we revert to a single load, but this time we place it at the end of a cantilever. The loading diagram, in order to be in equilibrium, has a two-part reaction at the wall: a vertical force of *P* and a counterclockwise moment of $-PL$. The closing

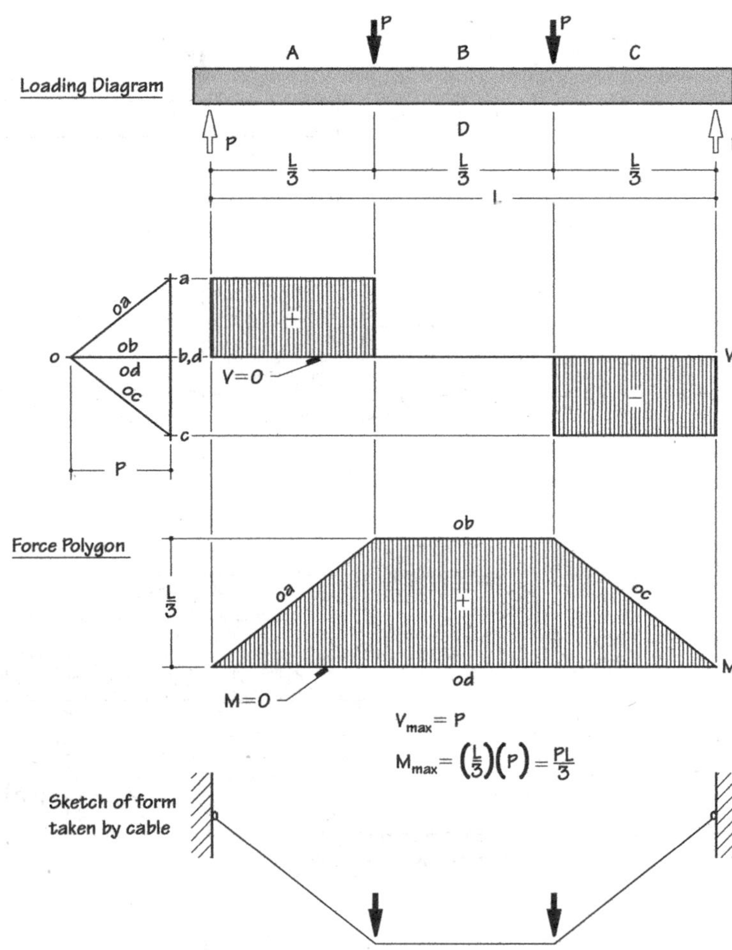

Figure 16.13 Graphical construction of *V* and *M* diagrams for concentrated loads at the third points of the span.

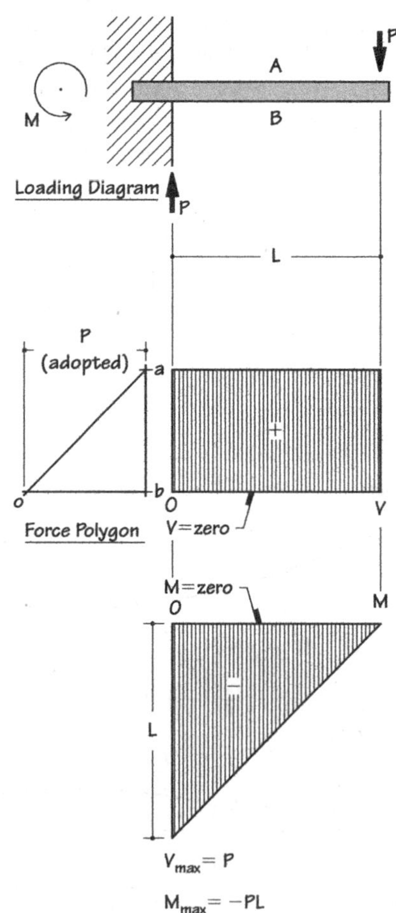

Figure 16.14 Graphical construction of *V* and *M* diagrams for a cantilever beam with a concentrated load at the end.

string, *ob*, is made horizontal, and a pole distance of *P* is adopted. The bending moment values are negative and vary linearly from zero at the load to −*PL* at the face of the embedment of the beam.

Figure 16.15 shows the construction of *V* and *M* diagrams for a uniformly distributed load on a simply supported span. The load is broken arbitrarily into increments, each represented by a vector at its centroid. The *V* diagram is drawn by projecting lines horizontally from the load line as before, and plotting a line through the intersections of these lines with the corresponding vertical lines from the loading diagram. *W*/2 is adopted as the pole distance and the *M* diagram is constructed from the rays of the force polygon. A horizontal projection of a lettered point from the load line intersects a vertical line from the center of the corresponding space on the loading diagram. For spaces *B* and *C*, we have shown this horizontal projection. For space *A*, the projection intersects the vertical line at the reaction because *A* is a half space. The maximum bending moment is *WL*/8, half of what it would be if the same load were all concentrated at midspan. In Figure 16.16 we extend this method to a cantilever beam with a

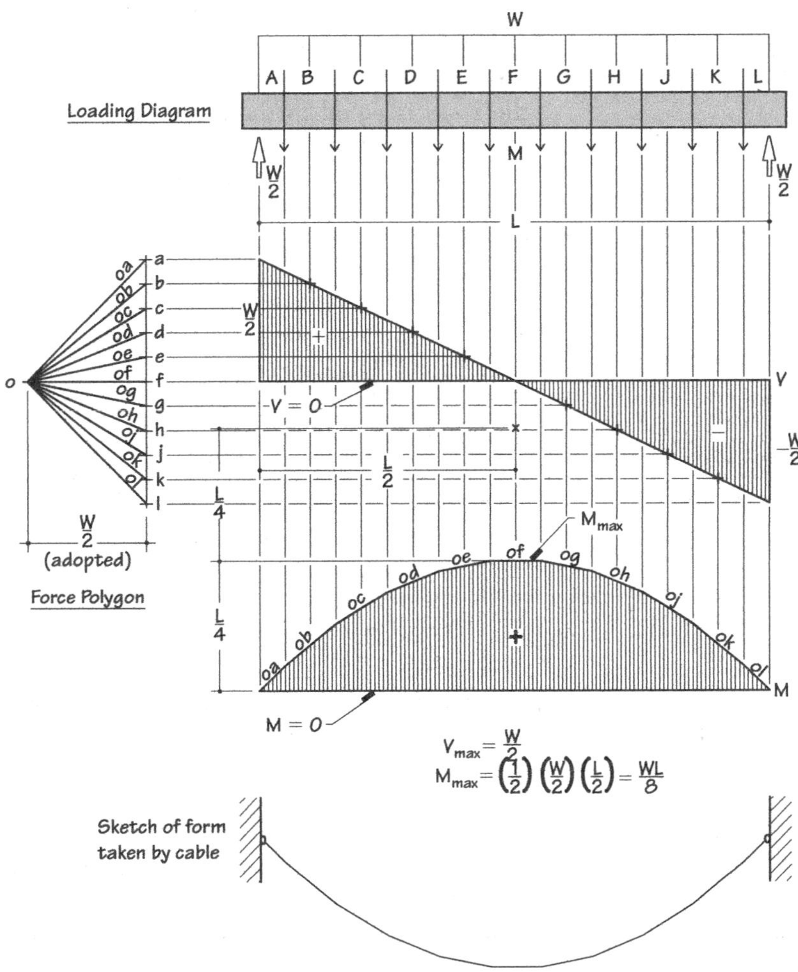

Figure 16.15 Graphical construction of *V* and *M* diagrams for a uniformly distributed load on a simply supported span.

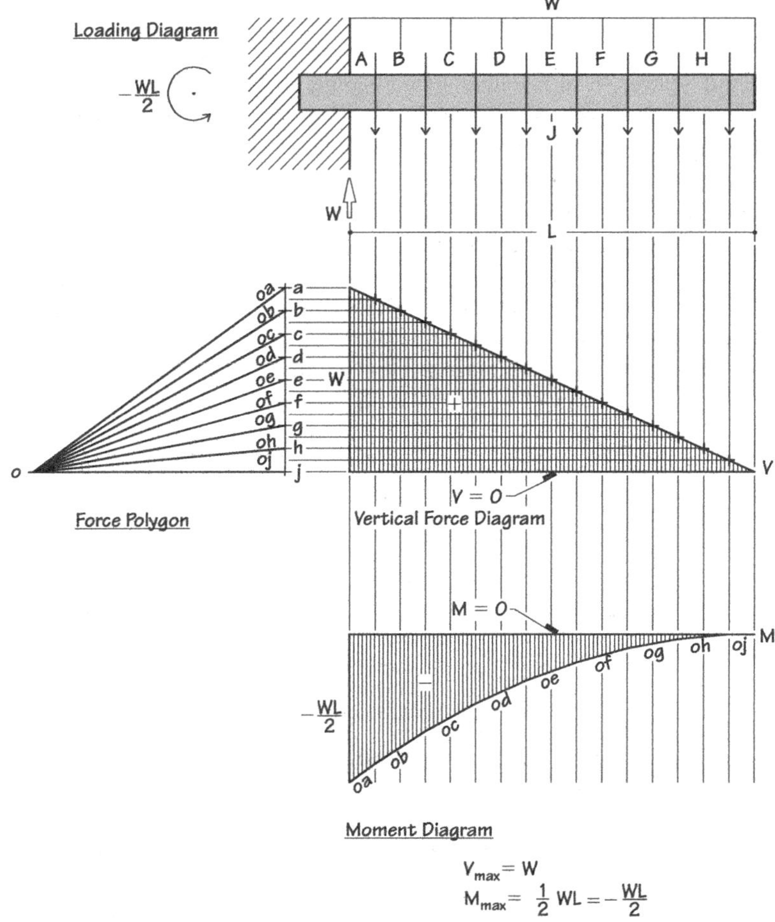

Figure 16.16 Graphical construction of *V* and *M* diagrams for a uniformly distributed load on a cantilever beam.

distributed load, whose bending moment is again half of that for the same load concentrated at the end of the span.

SEMIGRAPHICAL CONSTRUCTION OF *V* AND *M* DIAGRAMS

In everyday practice, completely graphical constructions of *V* and *M* diagrams are seldom used. Instead, we use the faster and easier *semigraphical* method. Semigraphical construction is based directly on graphical construction, but is done freehand with the aid of numerical calculations and some physical relationships between the *V* and *M* diagrams that we have already learned from graphical solutions. We can apply these semigraphical methods by clarifying the mathematical and geometric relationships we have just found in the previous examples.

How the Loading Diagram, *V* Diagram, and *M* Diagram Are Related

The lines on the *V* and *M* diagrams that we have just drawn, like all graphs of mathematical functions, are referred to as *curves*, even if they are straight lines. Curves of mathematical polynomial functions are classified according to the exponent that produces them (Figure 16.17).

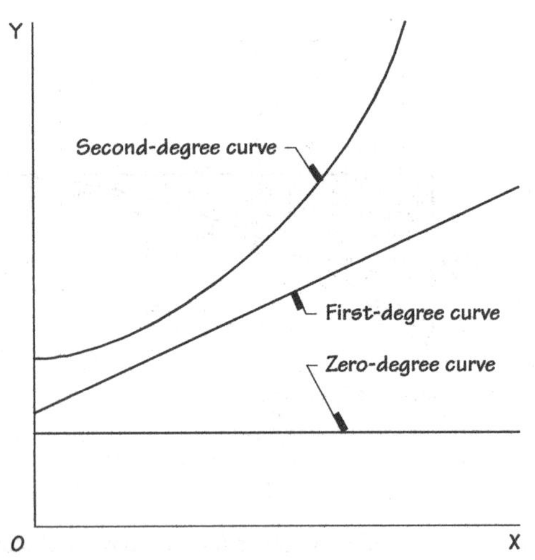

Figure 16.17 Degrees of mathematical curves.

- A straight horizontal line represents a constant value, which is the graph of a variable raised to the zero power. It is a *zero-degree curve*.
- A sloping straight line represents a variable raised to the first power; it is a *first-degree curve*.
- A parabola is a curve that represents a variable raised to the second power; it is a *second-degree curve*.

These three degrees of curve serve for most cases of vertical force and moment diagrams. To summarize:

$y = x^0 = 1$	Graphs as a horizontal straight line	Zero-degree curve
$y = x^1 + c$	Graphs as a sloping line	First-degree curve
$y = x^2 + c$	Graphs as a parabolic line	Second-degree curve

As shown on Figure 16.17, these expressions may include constants labeled *c* depending on their location with respect to the *x*- and *y*-axes.

As we look back over the *V* and *M* diagrams we have just drawn, these classifications help us to discern several very useful relationships among the loading diagram, *V* diagram, and *M* diagram:

1. **The *V* diagram curve is always one degree higher than the curve of the loading diagram. The *M* diagram curve is always one degree higher than the *V* diagram curve and two degrees higher than the loading diagram.** In the case of the beam shown in Figure 16.8, the level, straight line of the *V* diagram is a zero-degree curve, and the sloping straight line of the bending moment diagram is a first-degree curve. In Figure 16.15, the loading diagram is a zero-degree curve, the *V* diagram a first-degree curve, and the bending moment diagram a second-degree curve.
2. **The value represented by the *M* diagram at any vertical section is equal to the area beneath the portion of the *V* diagram to the left of that section.** For example, the height of the bending moment diagram at midspan in Figure 16.15 is equal to the area beneath the *V* diagram to the left of midspan. The shape of this portion of the *V* diagram is triangular, so its area is half the product of its base and altitude. The base is *L*/2. The altitude is *P*/2. Half their product is *PL*/8, the maximum bending moment for this loading.
3. **The value of the *V* force at any point in the span is equal to the slope of the bending moment diagram at that same point.** In Figure 16.15, the slope of the bending moment diagram at midspan is zero, which corresponds to a value of zero for the *V* diagram at this point. From the measured height of the *M* diagram and from our knowledge of the properties of parabolas, we know that the slope of the *M* diagram at the left support is *L*/2, which corresponds to the value of the vertical force at this plane, *W*/2.
4. **A positive value of *V* force corresponds to an ascending line in the bending moment diagram, and a negative value of *V* force to a descending moment line.** In Figure 16.8, the slope of the *M* diagram is positive until midspan. At this point, values of *V* become negative, and the bending moment curve begins its descent back toward its closing string.
5. **A maximum bending moment, either positive or negative, always occurs at a point in the span where the *V* force has a value of zero.** Check it out on any of the diagrams in this chapter. It's always true.
6. **The shape of the bending moment diagram for any loading is analogous to the shape that a flexible cable would take under the same loading (Figure 16.18).** In the United States, it is customary in drawing *M* diagrams to invert this shape to its "arch" configuration, which corresponds to positive values of bending moments, but many

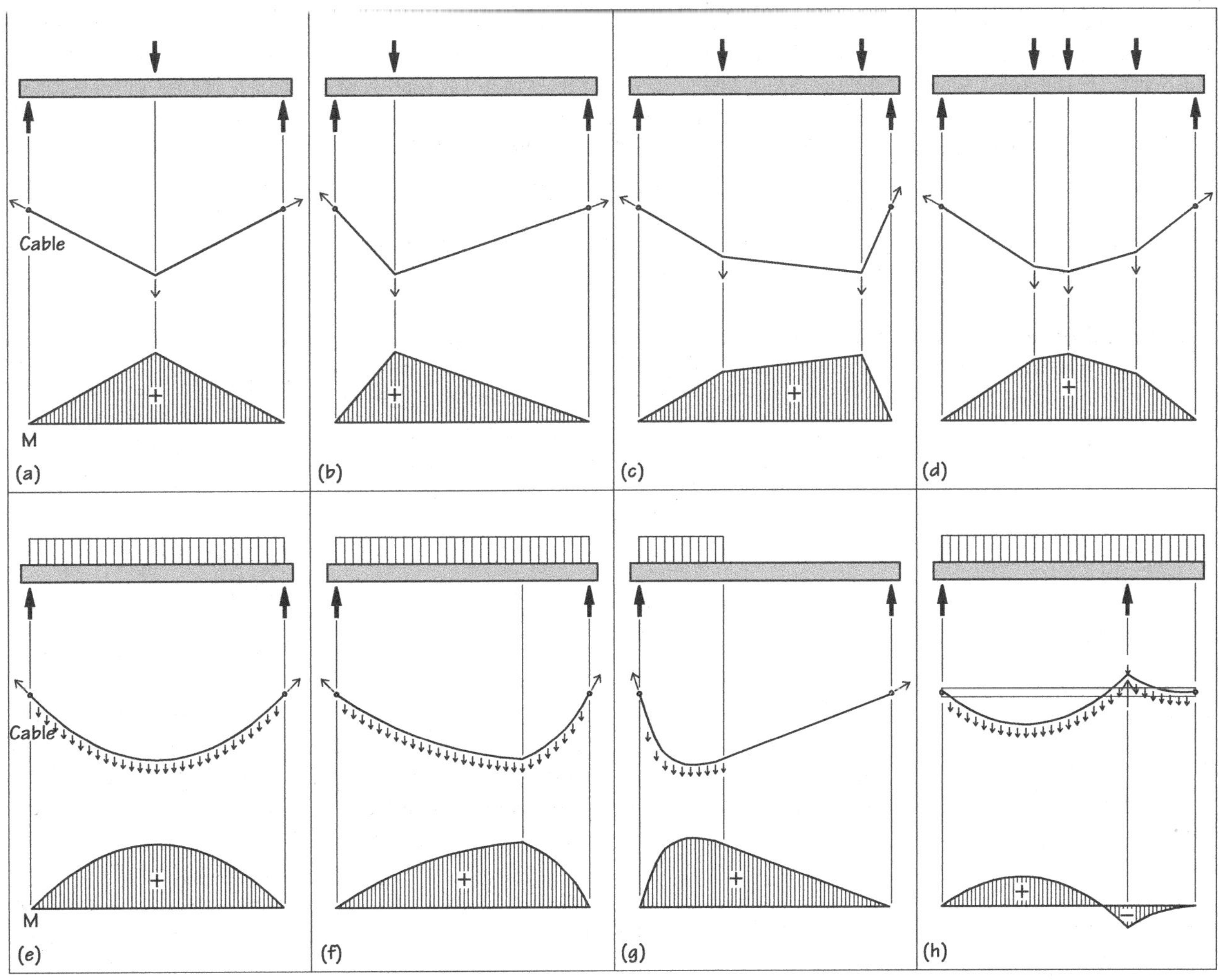

Figure 16.18 The shape of a moment diagram is always the inversion of the shape taken by a hanging cable with the same support and loading conditions.

structural designers, especially in Europe, prefer to keep the moment diagram in its "cable" configuration for easier visualization. In either case, it is often helpful to begin the process of constructing V and M diagrams by sketching the shape a cable would take under the given loading. If the final bending moment diagram does not resemble this shape, the work should be checked to determine whether an error was made in the detailed determination, or perhaps in the initial sketch of the cable.

The reader who has studied calculus will have deduced by now that the V graph is the integral of the loading diagram, and the M graph is the integral of the V diagram. (If the M graph is integrated, the resulting curve gives the slope of each part of the beam. If it is integrated a second time, it becomes the deflected shape, which is the shape taken by the axis of the beam when it is subjected to the given loading). It follows that the V diagram is the first derivative of the M diagram, and the loading diagram is the second derivative.

Drawing *V* and *M* Diagrams Semigraphically

The beam in Figure 16.19 carries a load of 10,000 lb that is uniformly distributed over half the span. The beam's self-weight, which is estimated at 100 lb per foot, applies to the entire span. What are maximum values of *V* and *M* for this beam? And where on the span do they occur?

The solution begins with evaluating moments to find the reactions, which are 8,500 lb at the left end, and 3,500 lb at the right end. **If the reactions are incorrect, a good deal of time and effort will be wasted in trying unsuccessfully to produce *V* and *M* curves. Double-check reaction values before proceeding further.**

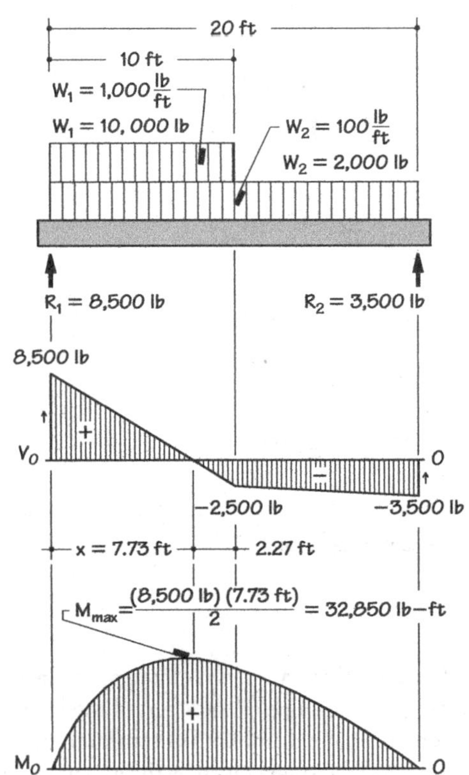

Figure 16.19 Semigraphical construction of *V* and *M* diagrams for a beam with two distributed loads.

We draw the *V* diagram first, working from left to right. The loading pattern begins at the left with the upward reaction of 8,500 lb, which we represent with a freehand line that rises above the baseline. We write a value of 8,500 lb at the top of the line. This written figure substitutes for our inability to scale the line, which is only crudely drawn.

As we move rightward, the curve descends from this value because of the downward action of the distributed loads. The applied load acts with an intensity of 1,000 lb per ft, and the self-weight, 100 lb per ft. Together, their intensity is 1,100 lb per foot of span. This is the rate of descent of the *V* curve, which is a straight, inclined line, a first-degree curve. It intersects the *x*-axis of the *V* diagram at a distance *x* from the left support equal to its initial height, 8,500 lb, divided by the rate of descent of the line, 1,100 lb per foot of span:

$$x = \frac{8{,}500\text{ lb}}{1{,}100\text{ lb/ft}} = 7.73\text{ ft}$$

The *V* curve continues to descend at this rate until it reaches the center of the span, where it intersects the centerline at a point 2,500 lb below the baseline of the diagram. This figure is determined as the left-hand reaction, 8,500 lb, minus 10 ft of span times 1,100 lb per foot:

$$V_{CL} = 8{,}500\text{ lb} - (10\text{ ft})(1{,}100\text{ lb/ft}) = -2{,}500\text{ lb}$$

The curve continues its descent over the right half of the span, but at a reduced rate because there is no live load on this half. This portion of the *V* diagram starts at a distance below the baseline of 2,500 lb and descends for 10 ft at a rate of 100 lb/ft to reach the right end of the beam at a value of –3,500 lb, which, like all values in semigraphical construction, we note numerically next to the curve. This is equal to the right-hand reaction, which closes the *V* diagram by pushing the curve back to zero. This closure is an indication that our work to this point is probably correct.

The *M* diagram curve must be one degree higher than the *V* diagram, which makes it a parabola. It will reach its maximum value where the *V* diagram is zero, at 7.73 ft from the left end of the beam. The value of the maximum bending moment is equal to the area under the *V* diagram to the left of this point, which is a triangle:

$$M_{max} = (0.5)(8{,}500\text{ lb})(7.73\text{ ft}) = 32{,}850\text{ lb-ft}$$

We determine by inspection that the maximum vertical force, V_{max}, is 8,500 lb and occurs at the left reaction. These two figures, M_{max} and V_{max}, are all that we need to proceed with the determination of the size of the beam, which we will learn to do in the next chapter.

Another Example of the Semigraphical Method

Figure 16.20 depicts an *overhanging beam*. The overhang is one-quarter of the main span. The entire beam is uniformly loaded at a rate, *w*, of 0.8 kips per foot, which includes the self-weight of the beam. What are the maximum values of *V* and *M*, and where do they occur?

The determination of the reactions is crucial, as always. Note that the load is given as a load per foot of span, *w*. This is first converted to the total load, *W*, by multiplying it by the loaded length of 30 ft. *W* comes to 24 kips. We evaluate moments about the supports to determine that the reactions are 9.0 kips at the left end and 15.0 kips at the right. The loading diagram is a zero-degree curve, so the *V* diagram will be a sloping line, which is first-degree. It begins with an upward vertical line of height 9.0 kips at the left end. As we move to the right from this point, the curve slopes downward at a rate equal to the load per foot of span, 0.8 kips. We divide 9.0 kips by 0.8 kips to find that it reaches a value of zero at a distance of 11.25 ft from the left support. It continues to descend at the same rate for 12.75 ft, to reach a minimum value of –10.2 kips at the right-hand support. The upward reaction of 15 kips brings it to a positive value of 4.8 kips.

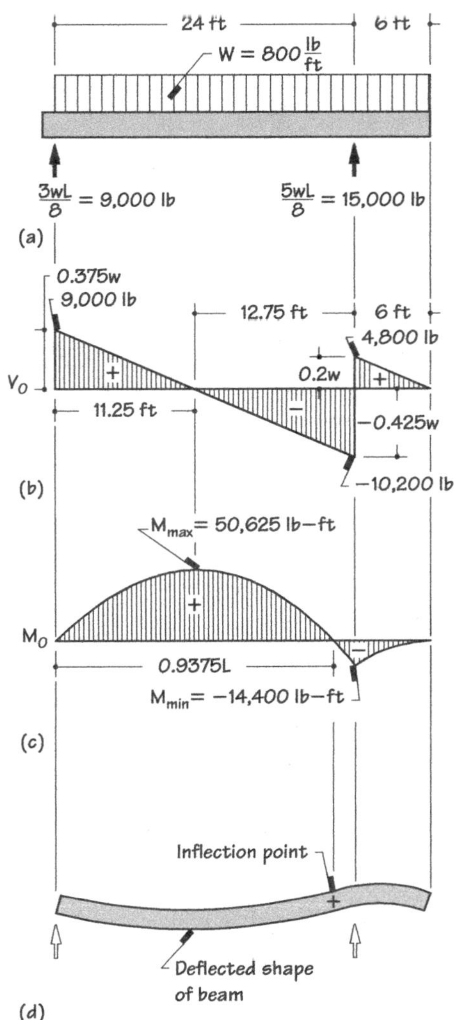

Figure 16.20 Semigraphical construction of V and M diagrams for a beam with an overhanging end and a uniformly distributed load.

Confusion About Units

Distributed loads on beams may be expressed in either of two ways, total load for the entire load, *W*, or load per unit of span length, *w*. This can lead to confusion if you are not careful to determine which you are working with in a given example. The uppercase *W* is simpler to deal with in many situations. The lowercase *w* is not only the load per unit of length but also the rate of descent of the V diagram, which can be handy in other situations. The relationship between the two is simply $W = wL$. Even here, however, we must take care that the unit of length used with *w* is the same as that used for *L*. If *L* is in inches, then *w* must be in pounds or kips per inch of span.

Greater confusion sets in when expressions are given for bending moment. The maximum bending moment for a beam with a uniformly distributed load may be given as either $WL/8$ or $wL^2/8$. In using the latter expression, we must take care that units are consistent: If we work with *L* in inches, then *w* must be given in load per inch of span, and the answer will be in lb-in. or kip-in.

The same confusion occurs with deflection formulas, all of which contain either of two terms, WL^3 or wL^4. These terms are interchangeable if we give *L* in inches and *w* in load per inch of span.

From here it descends at a rate of 0.8 kip per foot for 6 ft to close at zero.

We know that the bending moment diagram must be a parabola, which is a second-degree curve, one degree higher than the vertical force diagram. Using a semigraphical construction, the curve rises from zero at the left-hand support to reach a maximum value where the *V* diagram has a value of zero, which is 11.25 ft from the left end of the beam. It then descends symmetrically, to cross the baseline at a distance of 22.5 ft from the left end, 1.5 ft short of the right reaction. It reaches bottom at the right reaction. To the right of this point, the V diagram is a positive triangle. This triangle has its maximum height to the left, so that as one moves rightward, the *M* diagram climbs quickly at first, as larger increments of area are traversed on the *V* diagram, then more slowly, to reach zero height at the end of the beam overhang.

The maximum moment can occur at either of two points where the value of *V* is zero. One such point is near the middle of the main span. The value of the bending moment at this point is equal to the triangular area under the *V* curve to the left of this point. This area is equal to half the product of the base, 11.25 ft, and the altitude, 9.0 kips, which comes to 50.6 kip-ft. The other point is the right-hand support, where the moment is negative. We can find its value by subtracting from 50.6 kip-ft the area of the large negative triangle on the *V* diagram. This area is half of 12.75 ft multiplied by a negative value of 10.2 kips, which comes to –65.0 kip-ft. 50.6 minus 65.0 is –14.4 kip-ft, which is the bending moment at the right-hand support. We can check this value by finding the area of the *V* diagram to the right of this point: It is half of 4.8 kips times 6 ft, which is also 14.4 kip-ft.

The point on the span where the bending moment is zero is an *inflection point*, where the beam reverses its curvature. The reversal of bending in this region acts to decrease the intensities of bending across the main span, including the maximum bending moment. If the beam were simply supported over a span of 24 ft, without the overhang, its maximum bending moment, as we found in Figure 16.15, would be *WL*/8, which works out to 57.6 kip-ft, substantially more than the 50.6 kip-ft of the same beam with a 6-ft overhang.

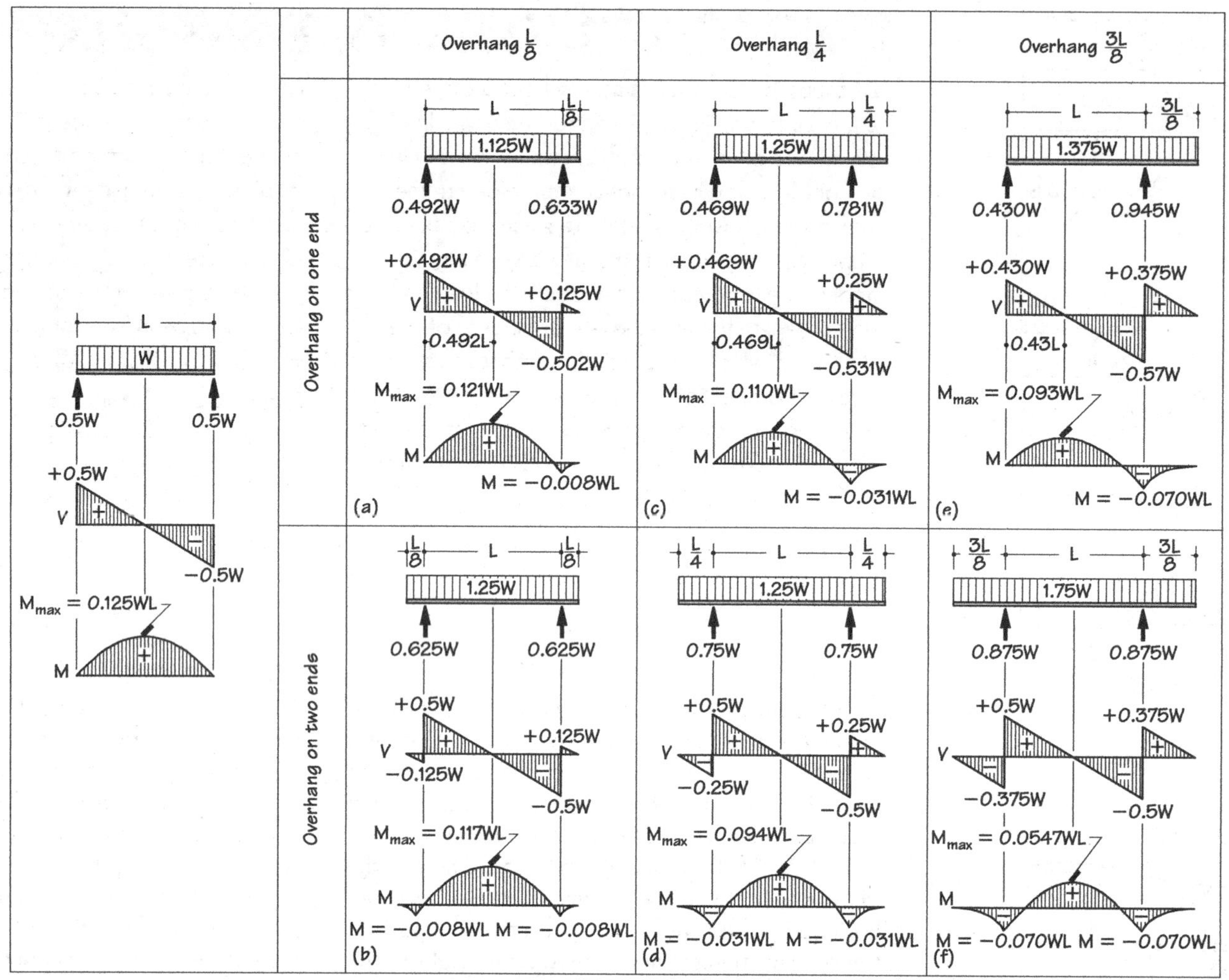

Figure 16.21 Effects on maximum *V* and *M* values of different lengths of overhangs on beams.

OVERHANGS

Overhanging beams are often employed in framing to reduce maximum bending moments and beam sizes. Figure 16.21 is a trial-and-error investigation of the effects on maximum *V* and *M* values of different lengths of overhangs on beams. The top row is for an overhang on one end, and the bottom row for overhangs at both ends. The overhang would be optimal if the negative bending moment at the support were equal to the positive moment in the main span, which would result in maximum economy by stressing the beam material to its maximum at both points on the span. For a single overhang, this will occur at an overhang length of a bit more than three-eighths of the main span. For a double overhang, it happens when the overhangs are slightly less than three-eighths.

CONTINUOUS SPANS

A one-piece beam that spans across three or more supports is said to be *continuous*. Because of the reversal of bending that occurs in continuous beams, they experience significantly lower maximum bending moments than the simply supported beams that we have been considering. This permits the use of smaller beams, with a consequent reduction in cost.

Continuous beams are *indeterminate*, which means that we can't find their reactions by using only the expressions of static equilibrium; we must also take into account the relative deflections of the continuous spans. While the derivation of bending moments in indeterminate members is beyond the scope of this book, we can benefit from examining the work of others on continuous spans. In Figure 16.22a we observe that the maximum bending moment in a beam that is continuous over two spans is the negative moment at the interior support, which is more than 70 percent larger than the positive moments. Looking at three continuous spans in part (b) of this illustration, we see that the positive moments in the two end spans are relatively close in value to the maximum negative moments over the supports; however, the positive bending moment in the middle span is very small.

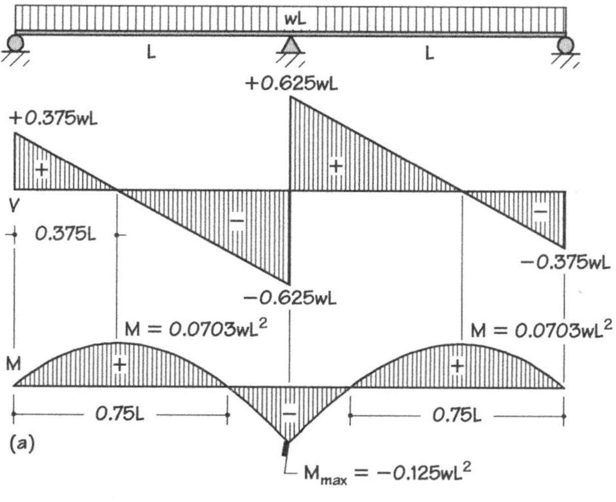

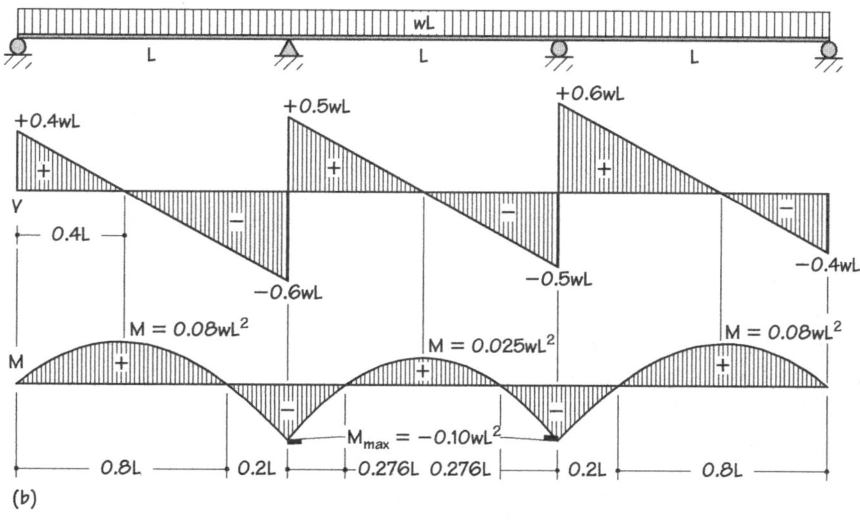

Figure 16.22 *V* and *M* diagrams for beams continuous over two and three spans.

Indeterminate Beams Become Determinate

In Figure 16.23, we add hinges at points of inflection to beams that are continuous over two and three spans.

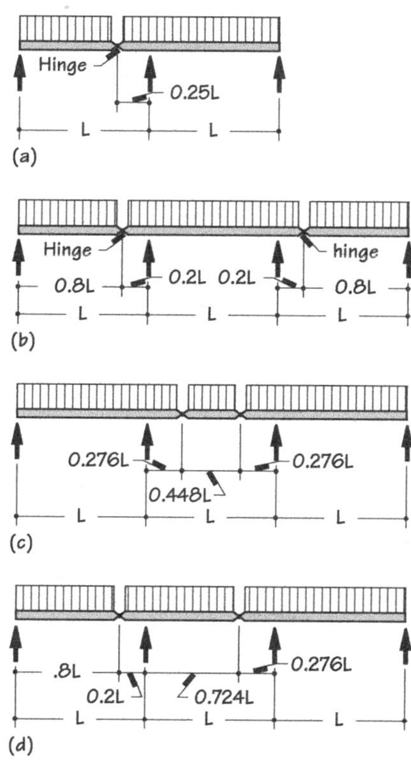

Figure 16.23 Continuous beams with hinges located at the points of inflection, as found in Figure 16.22, are determinate and efficient, and will experience the same bending moments as if they were continuous.

In each case, this converts the indeterminate beam into a series of determinate ones. Because bending moments are zero at points of inflection, the hinges do not alter the distribution of bending moments in the beams. This strategy is useful in situations where very long beams would be difficult to handle on the construction site, or where we wish to allow the beams to respond more directly to changes in load distribution while retaining the advantages of beam continuity. Some ways of joining beams at points of inflection are shown in Figure 16.24.

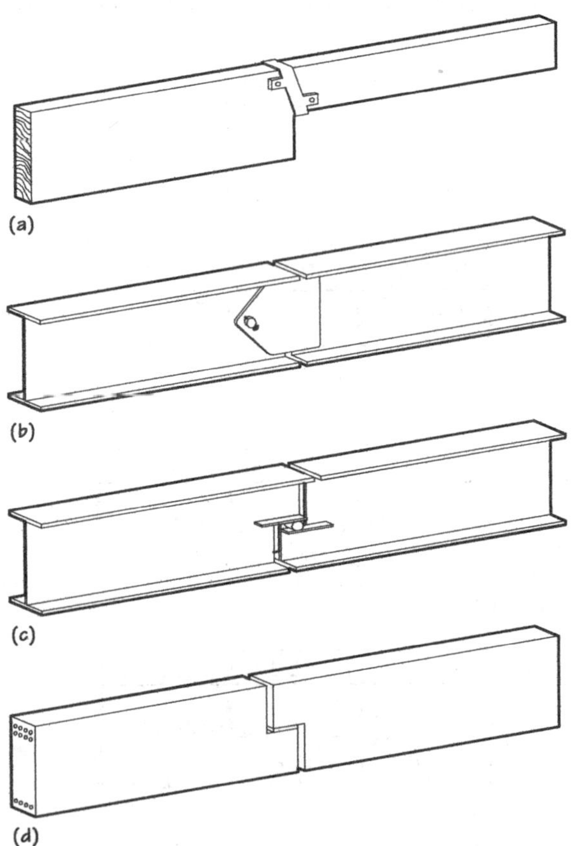

Figure 16.24 Details of hinges in beam spans: (a) steel strap seat used for laminated wood beams; (b) and (c) structural steel connections; (d) dapped ends in precast concrete beams.

ENCASTERED BEAMS

A beam end that is deeply embedded in concrete or masonry is said to be *encastered*. The encastered end is prevented from rotating by its embedment. This permits us to cantilever a beam from a masonry or concrete wall, as we did in Figures 16.14 and 16.16. It also allows the creation of beams with one end encastered and the other end propped, and beams with both ends encastered (Figure 16.25). Both these situations are statically indeterminate. In both cases, the embedment results in a large reduction in maximum bending moments.

V AND *M* VALUES FOR MANY BEAMS

There is no need to construct *V* and *M* diagrams for beams with common loading and support patterns, because many handbooks have extensive tables of *V* and *M* diagrams and equations for a broad range of situations. A sampling of these values is given in Figure 16.26.

In situations where two or more loads act on the same beam, time and work can be saved by simply adding the *V* and *M* values for the two loads. For example, if a beam supports both a uniformly distributed load and a concentrated load at midspan, the maximum bending moment in the beam is the sum of the handbook values for the two loadings, $WL/8$ for the uniform load, and $PL/4$ for the concentrated one. This procedure is called *superposition*. It works best for symmetrical loading situations, but with sufficient care it can also be applied to asymmetric ones.

"Very rough calculations are enough to get the approximate forces and dimensions [of structures]. Many engineers these days run a large number of computer calculations before they have a clear picture of the structure and its important details. That is wrong . . ."

—Fritz Leonhardt

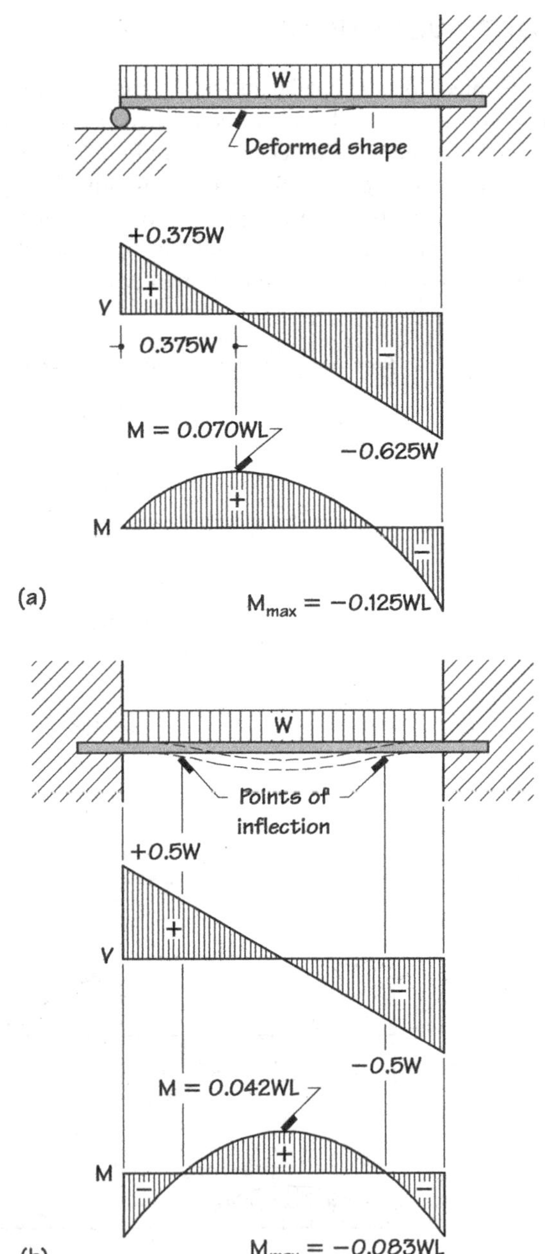

Figure 16.25 Beams with encastered ends: (a) propped beam; (b) beam with both ends fixed.

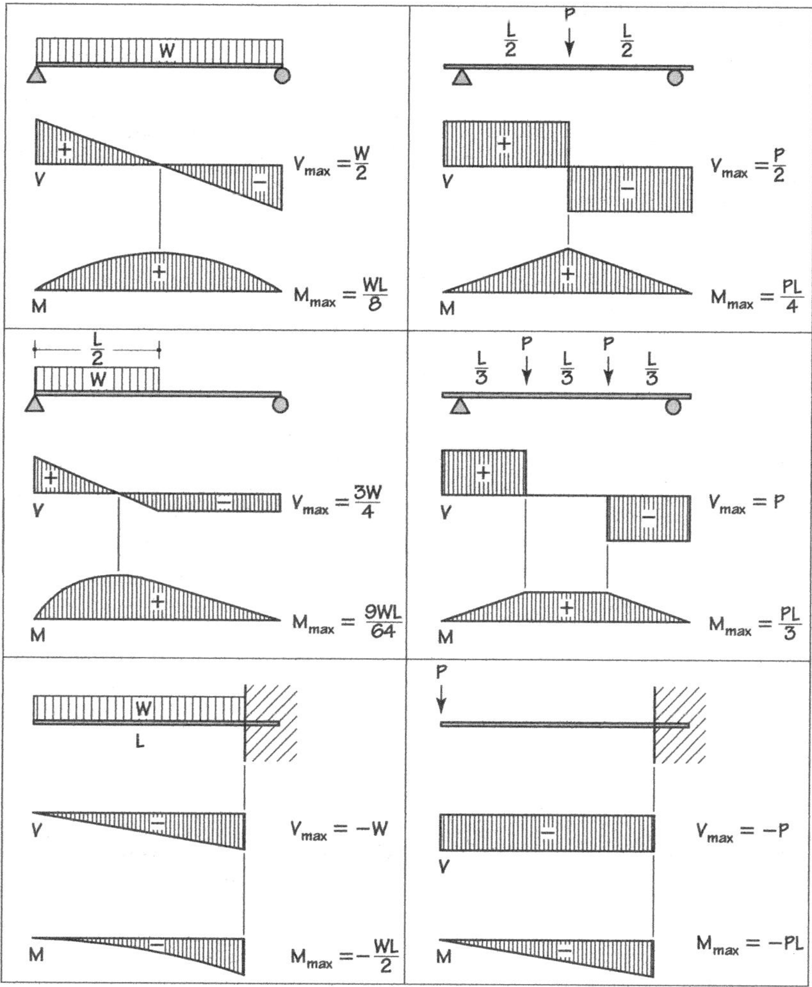

Figure 16.26 Vertical force and bending moment diagrams for some common situations of load and support.

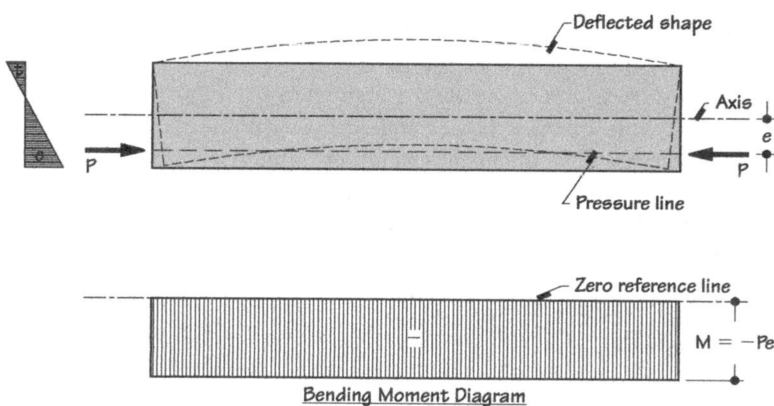

Figure 16.27 A beam with an eccentrically located longitudinal load.

BENDING MOMENTS IN LONGITUDINALLY LOADED MEMBERS

Bending moments can occur in structural elements that are loaded longitudinally. Figure 16.27 shows a compression strut of rectangular cross section in which the *pressure line* between the external loads is offset from the axis of the member by an eccentricity, *e*. This causes the strut to curve away from the pressure line. If the eccentricity is more than one-sixth of the depth of the strut, there will be tensile stresses on its convex side. If the lateral deflection of the strut is very small, the bending moment created by the eccentric loading may be considered to have the same value throughout the length of the member. However, if the deflection is large, the axis is bent sufficiently to increase the eccentricity of the loading, and the bending moment increases by an amount proportional to the distance of the bent axis from the original straight axis. This distance is greatest in the center of the length of the member and diminishes toward the ends. This behavior can lead to an accelerating increase in eccentricity and eventual buckling of the member. A tensile member, on the other hand, tends to straighten under load, which has the effect of decreasing its eccentricity and reducing its bending forces to a minimum.

Looking back at the cable roof in Chapter 2 and the arched concrete shell roof in Chapter 3, the cables tend to perfect their own forms under load, whereas the shell must be thickened by corrugation to resist the tendency of eccentric loadings to destabilize it by the chain of events described in the previous paragraph.

Figures 16.28 to 16.30 demonstrate instances in which a member has a curved shape to begin with. If opposing forces are applied along the axis between the ends of any of these members, bending moments are established. The values of these moments are represented by a moment diagram whose shape is identical to the shape of the curved axis of the member. These diagrams show why it is usually not optimal to curve a column, strut, or mast: Forces and stresses within the member rise from the modest values encountered in axially loaded members to the high values found in members in bending.

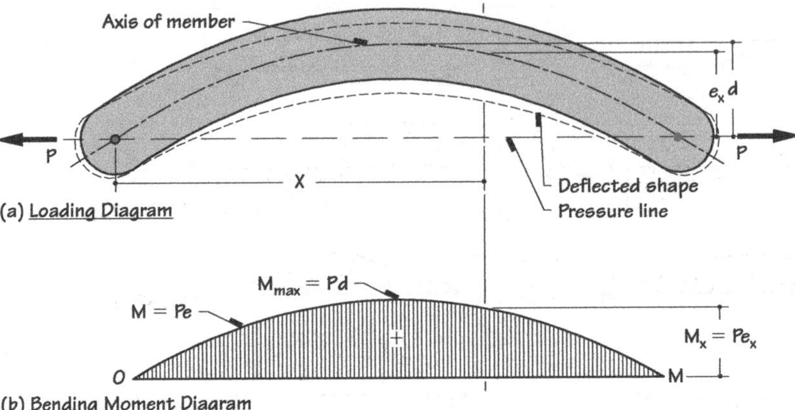

Figure 16.28 Bending moments in a curved tensile member. The tensile forces in this example tend to straighten the strut and reduce its eccentricity, which is very safe. If the forces were reversed to place the member in compression, they would tend to increase the eccentricity of the member, which would increase its stresses, which would again increase its eccentricity, in what could become a snowballing process of total destabilization and failure of the member.

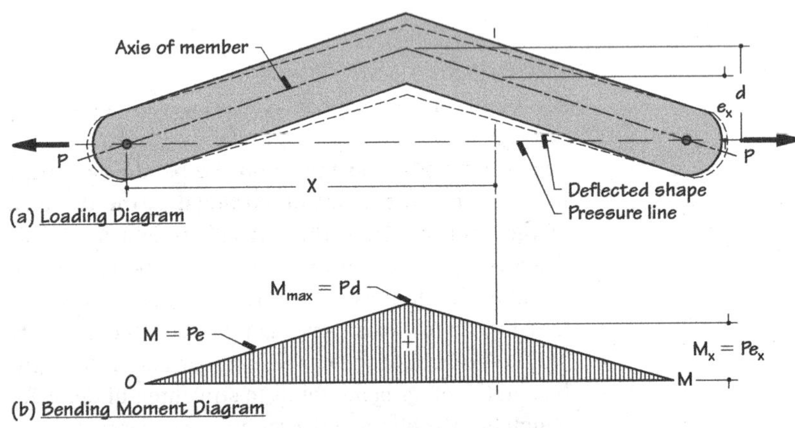

Figure 16.29 Bending moments in an eccentrically loaded tensile member.

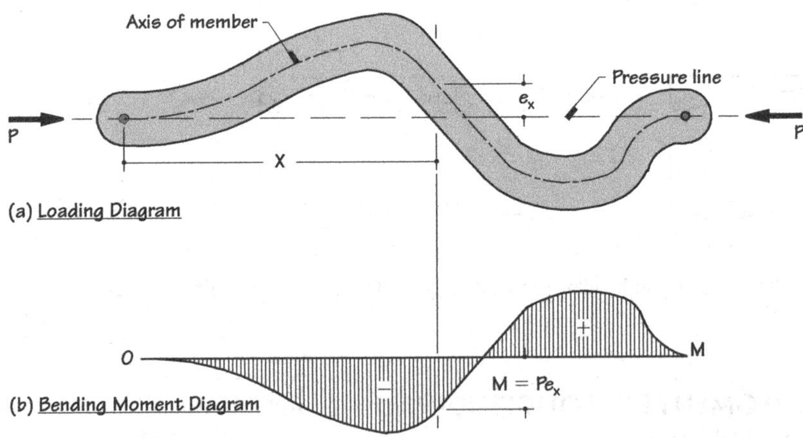

Figure 16.30 Bending moments are as easily determined in struts or ties of complex arbitrary shape as in simply curved members.

LOOKING AHEAD

How big does a beam have to be? This is the question we asked at the beginning of this chapter. We have developed the first part of the answer to the question: V and M diagrams enable us to predict the maximum intensity of bending action that will be exerted upon any beam, taking into account the magnitude of the load, the distribution pattern of the load, the span of the beam, and the way in which the beam is supported. In the chapters that follow, we will use these two quantities to find required sizes for beams.

What about the three beams with which we began this chapter? Which is subjected to the strongest bending action? Now that you are equipped to find the maximum values of bending moment and vertical force for each of them, you can answer this question for yourself.

Figure 16.31 The addition of a new glass-roofed atrium for the Morgan Library in New York City (Renzo Piano Building Workshop, 2006) features continuous beams over the tops of columns made of four welded-steel angles that transmit roof loads for the joists and glazing units separately from the stone façade of the adjacent building. Stiffener plates have been added to the beams at the points of maximum moment to prevent buckling.

Photo: David M. Foxe.

Figure 16.32 This simply supported beam supports a pedestrian bridge at the Cite Internationale complex in Lyon, France, completed in 1996 by Renzo Piano. Its form is shaped in profile to resemble its bending moment diagram, which gives it unique properties we will take up further in Chapter 22.

Photo: David M. Foxe.

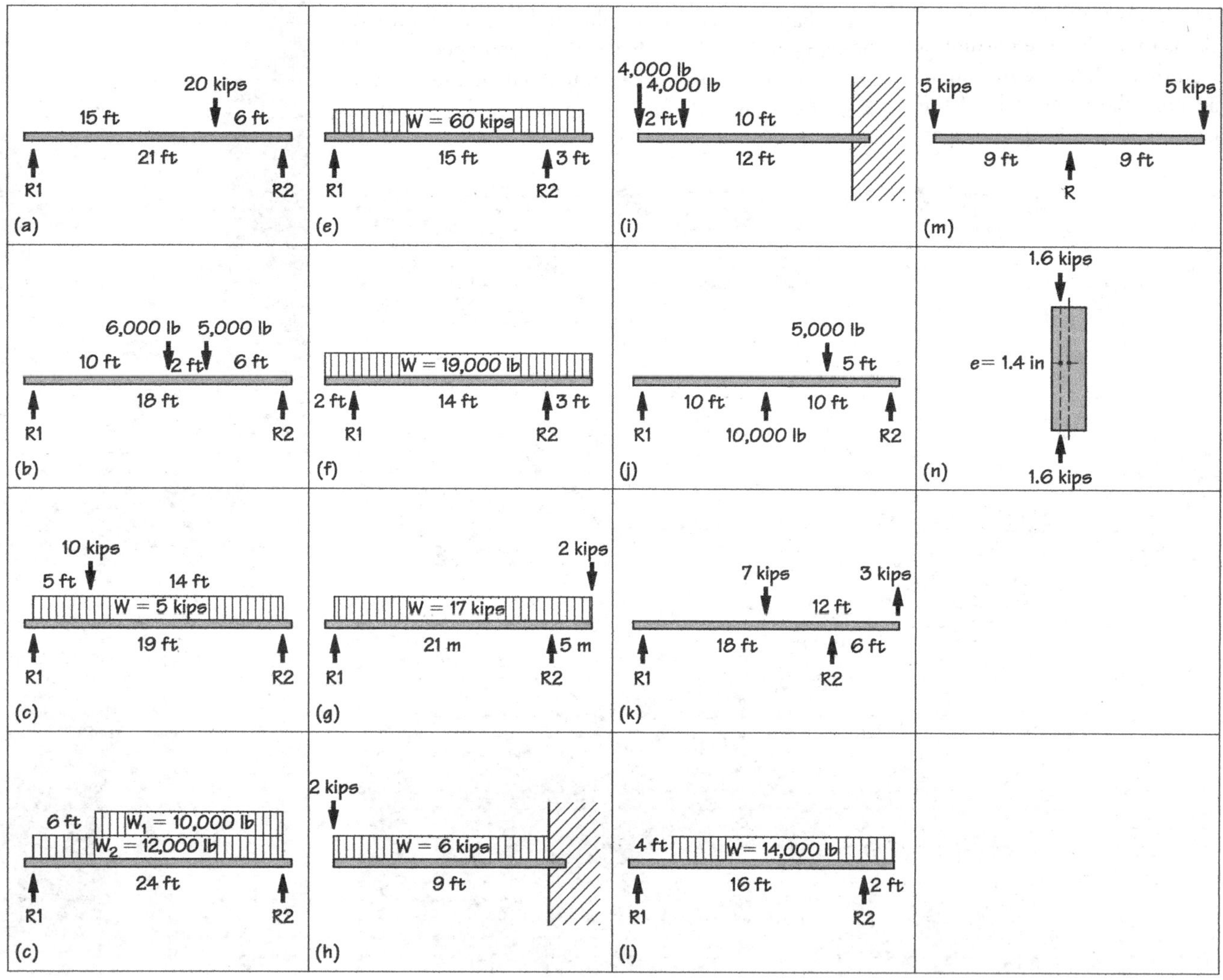

(a)
20 kips
15 ft
6 ft
21 ft
R1
R2
(e)
W = 60 kips
15 ft
3 ft
R1
R2
(i)
4,000 lb
4,000 lb
2 ft
10 ft
12 ft
(m)
5 kips
5 kips
9 ft
9 ft
R
(b)
6,000 lb
5,000 lb
10 ft
2 ft
6 ft
18 ft
R1
R2
(f)
W = 19,000 lb
2 ft
14 ft
3 ft
R1
R2
(j)
5,000 lb
5 ft
10 ft
10 ft
R1
10,000 lb
R2
(n)
1.6 kips
e= 1.4 in
1.6 kips
(c)
10 kips
5 ft
14 ft
W = 5 kips
19 ft
R1
R2
(g)
2 kips
W = 17 kips
21 m
5 m
R1
R2
(k)
7 kips
3 kips
12 ft
18 ft
6 ft
R1
R2
(c)
6 ft
W_1 = 10,000 lb
W_2 = 12,000 lb
24 ft
R1
R2
(h)
2 kips
W = 6 kips
9 ft
(l)
4 ft
W= 14,000 lb
16 ft
2 ft
R1
R2

Figure 16.33

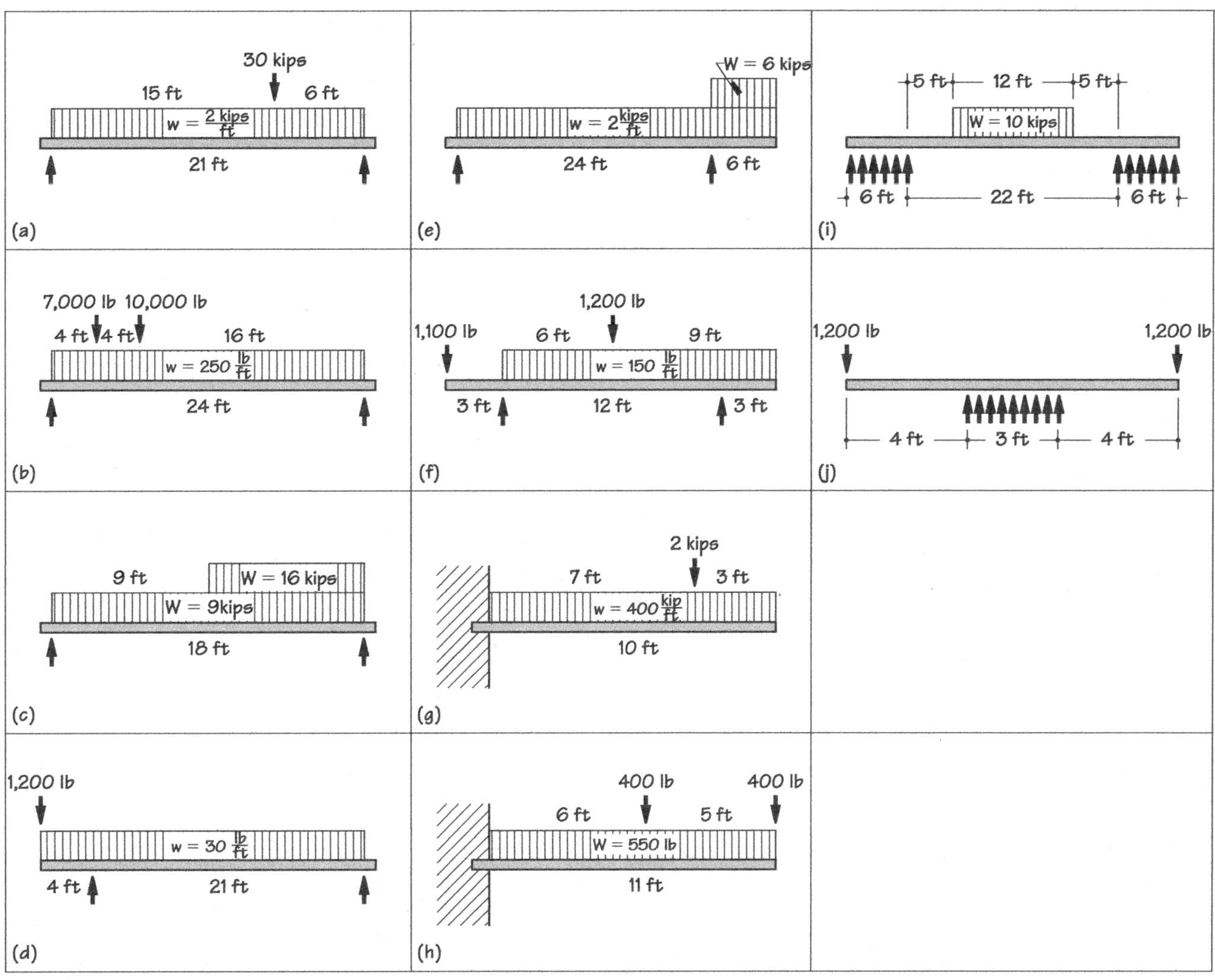
30 kips
15 ft
6 ft
w = 2 kips/ft
21 ft
(a)
W = 6 kips
w = 2 kips/ft
24 ft
6 ft
(e)
5 ft
12 ft
5 ft
W = 10 kips
6 ft
22 ft
6 ft
(i)
7,000 lb 10,000 lb
4 ft
4 ft
16 ft
w = 250 lb/ft
24 ft
(b)
1,200 lb
1,100 lb
6 ft
9 ft
w = 150 lb/ft
3 ft
12 ft
3 ft
(f)
1,200 lb
1,200 lb
4 ft
3 ft
4 ft
(j)
9 ft
W = 16 kips
W = 9kips
18 ft
(c)
2 kips
7 ft
3 ft
w = 400 kip/ft
10 ft
(g)
1,200 lb
w = 30 lb/ft
4 ft
21 ft
(d)
400 lb
400 lb
6 ft
5 ft
W = 550 lb
11 ft
(h)

Figure 16.34

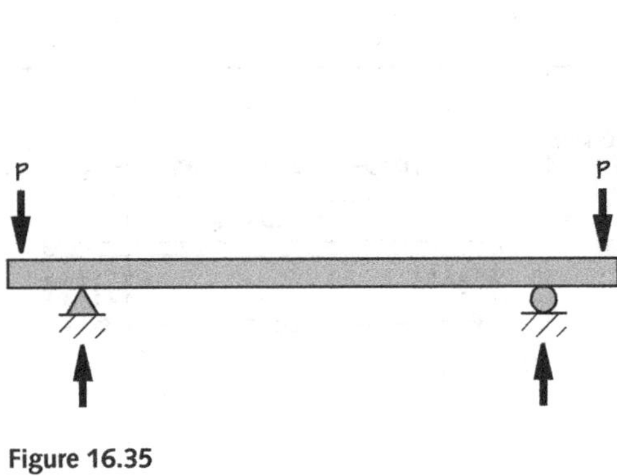

Figure 16.35

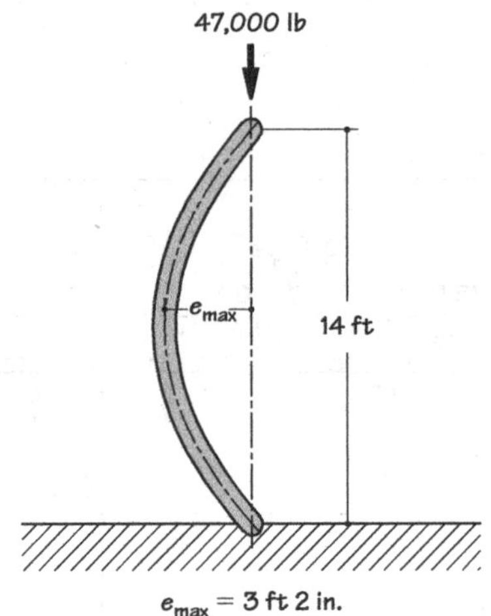

Figure 16.36

Exercises

1. Draw *V* and *M* diagrams and find maximum values of these two variables for selected examples in Figures 16.33 and 16.34, also available as Worksheets 16A and 16B on the supplemental site. You may work either graphically or semigraphically.

2. Draw *V* and *M* diagrams for the beam shown in Figure 16.35. Explain the unique qualities of this beam and loading.

3. Find the maximum bending moment for the curved, tusk-shaped column in Figure 16.36.

Key Terms and Concepts

vertical force, *V*

bending moment, *M*

third points

overhanging ends

cantilever

continuity of beams

longitudinal and transverse forces

vertical force diagram

bending moment diagram

moment diagram

shear, shear diagram

concentrated load, *P*

distributed load

distributed load per unit of span length, *w*

total distributed load, *W*

semigraphical method

degrees of curves: zero, first, second, third

indeterminate

point of inflection

encastered beam

superposition

pressure line

eccentricity

Further Resources

American Institute of Steel Construction. *Manual of Steel Construction*. Chicago, updated frequently. This comprehensive volume gives full dimensional and structural data on every kind of steel shape in every conceivable use.

Goldstein, Eliot W. *Timber Construction for Architects and Builders*. New York: McGraw-Hill, 1999. An architect renowned for his heavy timber buildings gives data and advice on every aspect of the subject.

CHAPTER 17

How Beams Resist Bending

- *Resistance mechanisms of beams*
- *Lattice pattern of flow of forces*
- *Deflection calculations*
- *Development of mathematical expressions for bending stresses and web stresses in rectangular beams*
- *Designing bays of wood framing*

Figure 17.2 depicts a simple outdoor deck made of wood. To construct this deck, we need to lay out a framing plan for it and assign sizes to its beams and joists such that these members will neither sag excessively nor break under expected loads. In the previous chapter, we learned to reduce the external actions of any beam loading, no matter how complex, to simple diagrams of vertical forces and bending moments, from which we can learn the maximum values of these two variables. In this chapter, we'll discover how a beam of rectangular cross section resists vertical forces and bending moments, and how to equate the maximum values of external vertical force and bending moment with a beam's internal forces of resistance. This will give us the tools we need to assign appropriate sizes to any rectangular beam, including the members of the wood deck and even the beams shown in Figure 17.1. In the next chapter, we will learn how to perform these same operations for beams of any shape, including steel wide-flange beams and custom-designed shapes.

Figure 17.1 This innovative use of laminated wood beams, by architects Bucholz McEvoy with the engineering firm RFR, serves as the roof structure for the welcome and security pavilion at Leinster House in Dublin, Ireland.

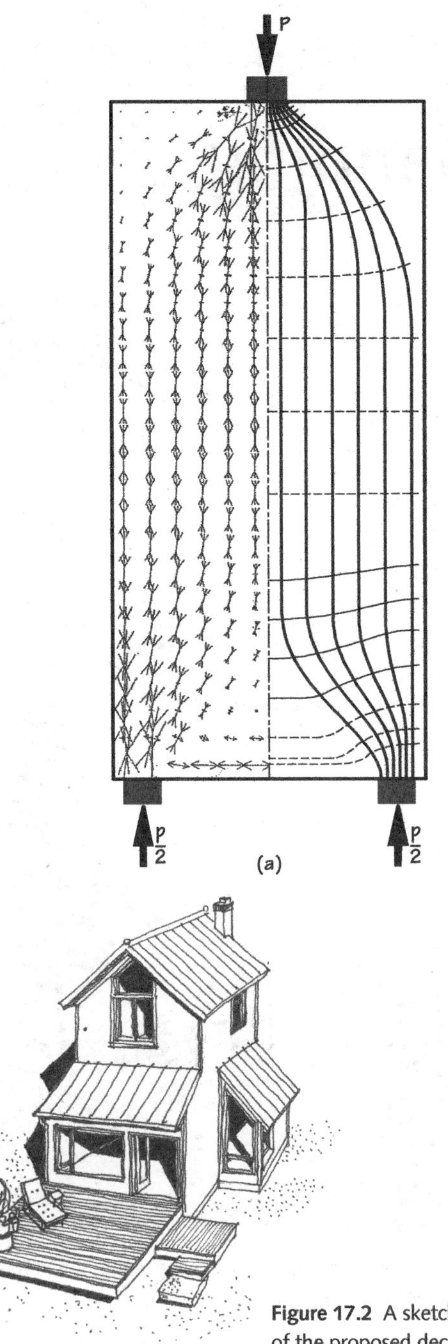

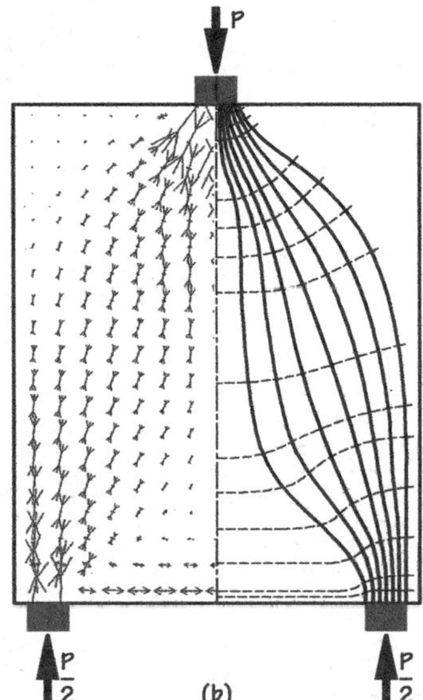

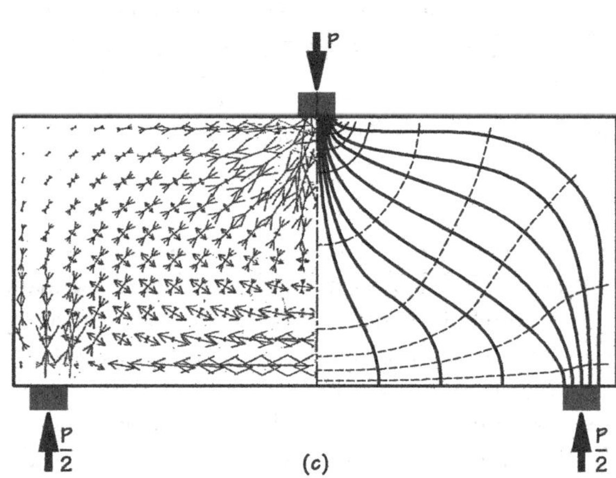

Figure 17.3 The flow of forces in five walls of decreasing depth.

ANSYS image courtesy of Nicole Michel and Bashar Altabba for HNTB Engineering.

Figure 17.2 A sketch of the proposed deck.

WALLS BECOME BEAMS

Figure 17.3 shows patterns by which forces flow in five walls that are identical in every way except for gradually decreasing depths and gradually increasing spans. Each is supported at its two lower corners. Each carries a single, concentrated load that is applied at the center of its top edge. As in Chapter 14, the pattern of force flow in each wall has been modeled by a computer simulation (ANSYS) whose graphical output is shown in the left half of each diagram. In the right half of each, lines of principal stresses have been plotted from the computer output.

The wall that is shown in Figure 17.3a acts as a very deep beam, one with a *depth-to-span ratio* of 2.5 to 1. A region of compressive half-plane fan flow develops immediately under the load. This leads to a region of parallel flow in the middle portion of the wall. In the bottom region of the wall, the trajectories of parallel flow split so as to converge through two quarter-plane fans on the supports at the bottom corners. Horizontal tensile forces at the bottom of the wall resist the horizontal components of the inclined compressive forces in the two fans.

When the depth of this wall is reduced to 1.5 times its span, the region of regular parallel flow in the

Figure 17.3 (Continued)

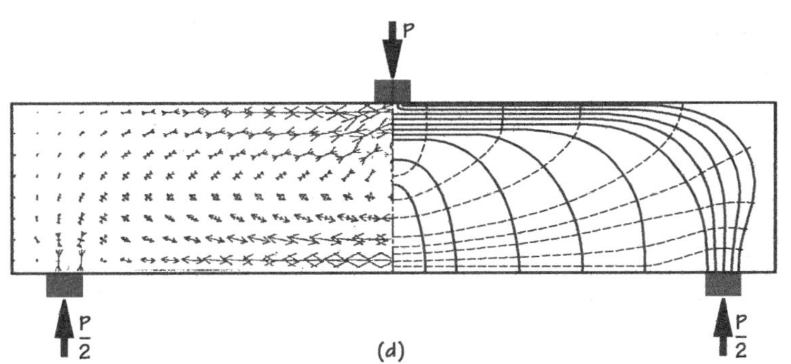

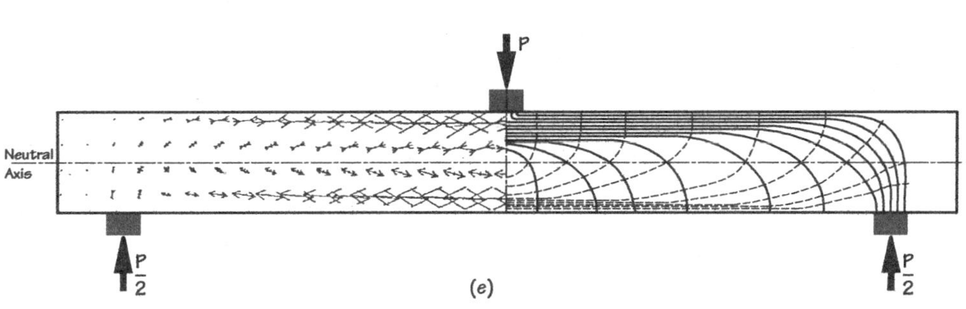

central region of the wall disappears (Figure 17.3b). Now the internal flow pattern is made up of three smoothly-merging fans that radiate from the load and the two reactions.

In Figure 17.3c, the depth of the wall is further reduced to about 50 percent of its span. At this depth, the compressive portions of the two corner fans lean toward each other and meet at the top of the wall, where they merge with the compressive forces that fan out from the place of application of the load. The upper part of this wall acts much like an arch, with the horizontal tensile forces in the lower part acting against the spreading tendency of the arch.

In Figure 17.3d the depth of the wall is reduced to one-quarter of the span. Horizontal forces within the wall clearly predominate over vertical forces. In addition to the three fans associated with the places of application of external forces, a lattice pattern of flow is discernable throughout most of the beam.

With its depth-to-span ratio of 1:8, the "wall" in Figure 17.3e is actually a beam of nearly normal proportions. Its predominant pattern of flow is lattice. The lattice may be interpreted as a series of arches, flattened to fit within the beam, combined with a mirror-image set of flattened cables. The outward thrust of the arches is balanced by the inward pull of the cables. At the ends, where bending moments are small, quarter-plane fans generated by the concentrated forces of the reactions dominate the flow pattern. Within a short distance of the supports, these fans merge with the lattice. The external load concentrated at midspan causes a local disturbance of the lattice that is negligible in comparison to the intensity of the longitudinal forces within the lattice in this region.

In practice, most beams have depth-to-span ratios that range from 1:12 to 1:24. Their flow patterns differ from the pattern in the shallowest beam in Figure 17.3 only in the sense that because of their lesser

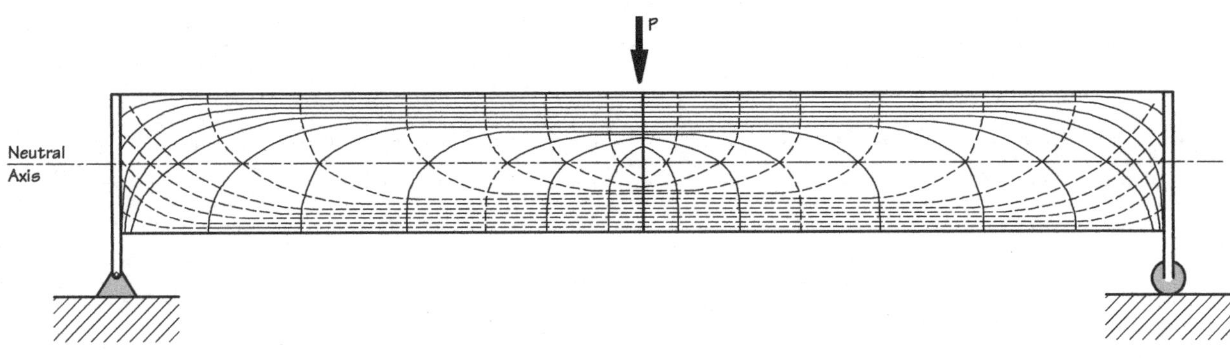

◀**Figure 17.4** There are no regions of transitional flow in a beam if each of the external forces is applied to the entire cross section of the beam.

▼**Figure 17.5** Comparisons of the relative efficiencies of seven alternative truss designs, all of the same depth and supporting the same load.

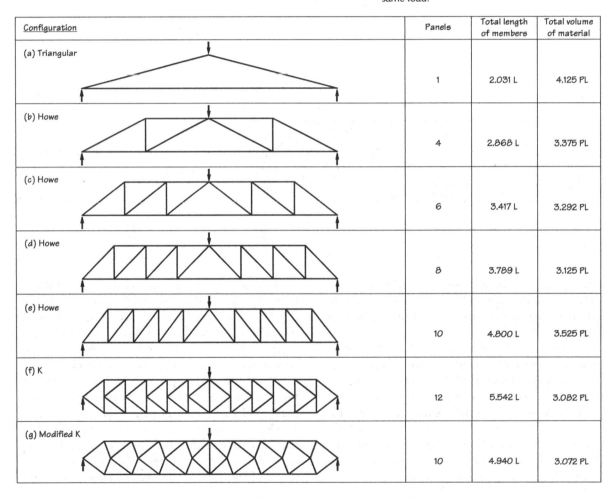

Configuration	Panels	Total length of members	Total volume of material
(a) Triangular 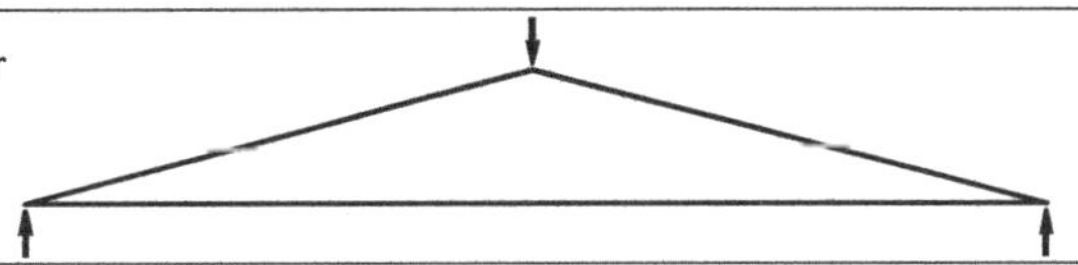	1	2.031 L	4.125 PL
(b) Howe 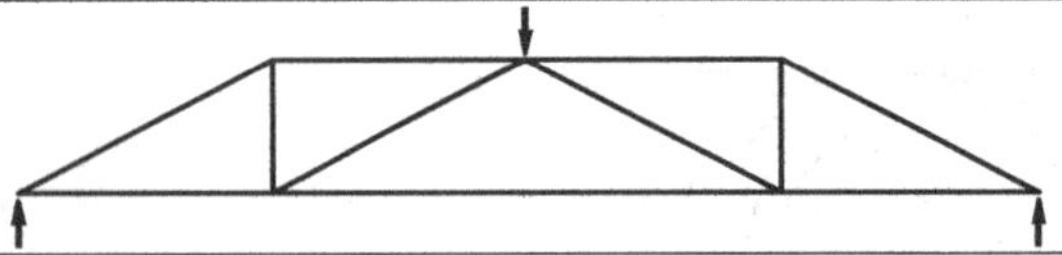	4	2.868 L	3.375 PL
(c) Howe 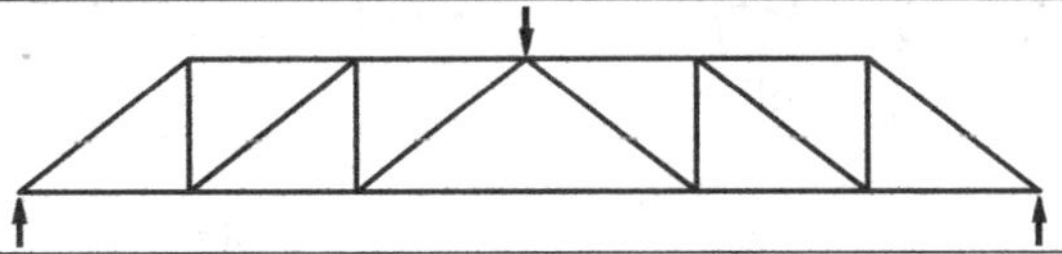	6	3.417 L	3.292 PL
(d) Howe 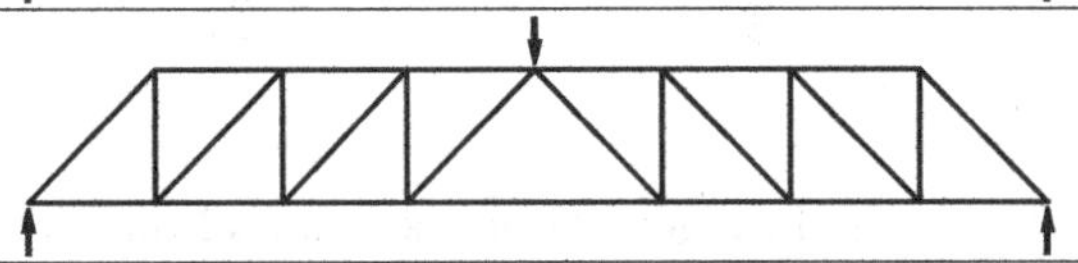	8	3.789 L	3.125 PL
(e) Howe 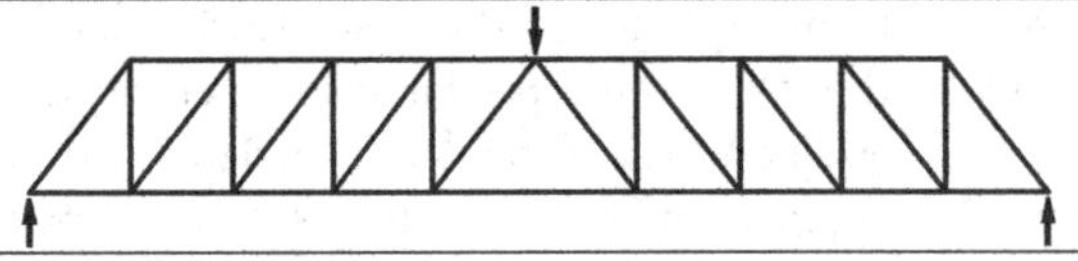	10	4.800 L	3.525 PL
(f) K 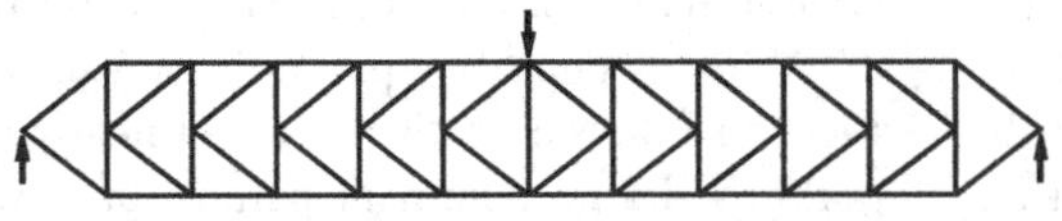	12	5.542 L	3.082 PL
(g) Modified K 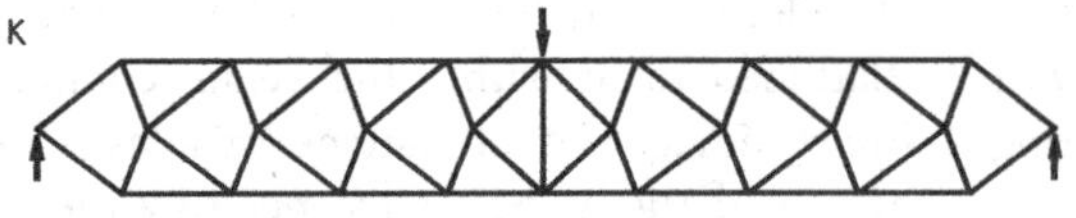	10	4.940 L	3.072 PL

depth, lattice flow occupies a larger proportion of the length of the beam.

Figure 17.4 shows a beam in which the external forces—the applied load and the two reactions—are applied by vertical steel plates glued to the full cross section of the beam. The plates, of which we see the edges in this view, distribute the forces uniformly over vertical sections of the beam instead of concentrating them on the upper and lower edges. This eliminates the regions of transitional flow so that the entire length of the beam is a single R-region of lattice flow.

WHY THE LATTICE PATTERN OF FLOW PREDOMINATES IN PRISMATIC BEAMS

As the walls in Figure 17.3 grow progressively shallower, and finally become a beam, why do their flow patterns change from fan-and-parallel flow to lattice flow? Why doesn't the flow in a beam follow a simpler pattern?

Figure 17.5 suggests the answer to these questions. It is a comparison of the relative efficiencies of material utilization in seven alternative truss designs, all of which are proportioned the same as the beam in Figure 17.3e: Each has a depth-to-span ratio of 1:8 and supports a single load at midspan. Zero-force members have been omitted. These seven designs approximate a number of different internal flow patterns that conceivably might exist in a beam of similar proportions, from a single-panel triangle to a modified-K configuration that closely resembles a lattice pattern.

To facilitate comparison, the efficiency of each truss is measured by its theoretical volume of material. This volume has been calculated for each truss by multiplying the length of each truss member, expressed as a decimal fraction of the span of the truss, *L*, by the force that the member carries, which is expressed as a decimal fraction of the applied load, *P*. It is assumed that stresses in all members are numerically equal to the same allowable stress, f_{allow}. Buckling of compression members has not been considered, because buckling is not likely to occur in the mass of solid material of the rectangular beam that we are modeling.

The single-panel triangular truss in Figure 17.5a has a theoretical volume of material of 4.125*PL*. Trusses (b) through (e) are all Howe trusses with various numbers of panels. The theoretical volume of material in truss (b), with four panels, is 3.375*PL*. This means that truss (b) contains substantially less material than truss (a), which suggests that the inclinations of the compression members in truss (a) are too shallow, creating excessively high member forces. The steeper angles of the diagonals of truss (b) result in substantially lower member forces; (b) is a more efficient truss, even though the total length of its members is about 40 percent more than that of truss (a).

Trusses (c) and (d) have six and eight panels, respectively, which results in progressively steeper inclinations of diagonals and progressively lower member forces. The total volume of material continues to drop as more panels are added, until the eight-panel truss in (d) contains about one-quarter less material than the single-panel truss in (a). However, the 10-panel truss in Figure 17.5e contains more material than the four-, six-, or eight-panel trusses. A truss of eight panels, with its 45° diagonals (d), seems to be the most efficient Howe truss at this depth-to-span ratio.

The member layouts in the last two trusses in Figure 17.5 mimic the lattice pattern of force flow that we have observed in beams of similar proportions. Truss *f* is a *K-truss*, which has the interesting property that the upper half of each vertical member is in tension, and the lower half in compression. This results in a pattern of compression members that is similar to the "arches" that we observe in the lattice pattern of flow, and a mirror-image pattern of tension members that resemble the curved "cables." The volume of material in this truss is lower than that of any of the Howe trusses, even though its total length of members is almost half again more than that of the eight-panel Howe design.

The last truss, (g), is a modified K-truss in which the verticals have been bent to create a pattern of members that resembles even more closely the flow lines in a lattice. This is the most material-efficient truss of the seven. Figure 17.6 shows how a modified K-truss can be conceptualized as a nested series of

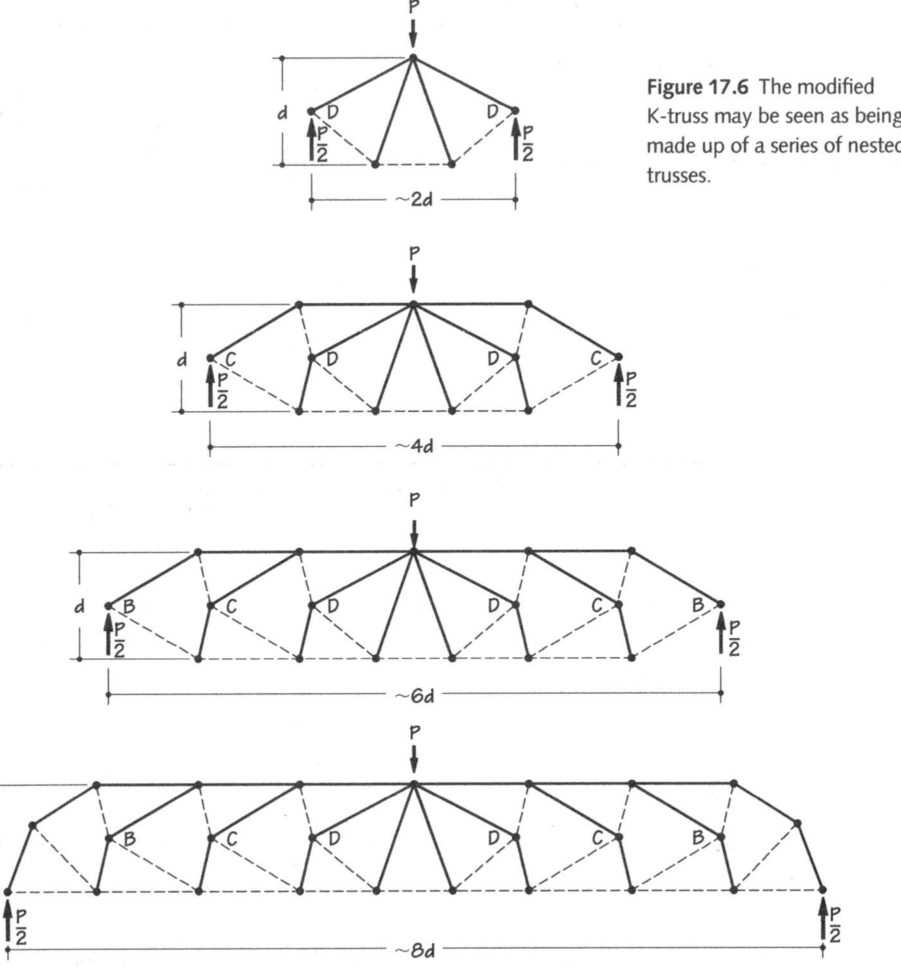

Figure 17.6 The modified K-truss may be seen as being made up of a series of nested trusses.

trusses, each containing within it all the trusses that lie above it in the diagram.

These analyses suggest that for a given ratio of depth to span, there is a close similarity between the arrangement of members in the most material-efficient truss and the patterns of the lines of forces in a solid beam that is similarly loaded. This similarity demonstrates the *principle of least work*, according to which the flow of forces in any structure always organizes itself to provide the necessary resistance to external forces with the least expenditure of elastic energy. Beam forces flow in lattice patterns because these patterns utilize material most efficiently under the external constraints imposed by beams.

FLOW OF FORCES IN A UNIFORMLY LOADED BEAM

To this point, we have looked only at beams that support a single load concentrated at midspan. When a beam whose proportions are identical to the beam in Figure 17.3e is subjected to a load of the same magnitude that is uniformly distributed over the entire span rather than concentrated (Figure 17.7), the flow within the beam follows a lattice pattern that, though not identical to the one for the concentrated load, is so similar as to be indistinguishable from it at first glance. However, in Figure 17.8, an analysis of modified K-trusses subjected to the same two loadings reveals large differences in the magnitudes of the forces carried by the analogous members of the trusses. A comparison of the *V* and *M* diagrams for the two loadings shows that the value of the *V* force produced at each vertical section along the span by the single load is the same, whereas *V* forces caused by the uniformly distributed load vary linearly from zero at midspan to a maximum at the supports. The maximum bending moment for the distributed load is half that for the same load concentrated in the middle of the span.

A comparison of the force polygons for the two trusses demonstrates these differences. The forces in the web members of the truss with the single load do not vary from one panel to the next, whereas the web forces in the uniformly loaded truss vary considerably, from maximum values at the supports to minimum values at midspan. Under both loadings, forces in the top and bottom chords range from low at the supports to high at midspan. Overall, forces in both the truss and the solid beam are half as large when the load is distributed equally to all the nodes rather than concentrated at midspan, as can be observed in the relative sizes of the two force polygons.

EVALUATING STRESSES IN BEAMS OF RECTANGULAR CROSS SECTION

To design a beam that will carry its load safely, we must be sure that at no point in the beam do the values of stresses that are caused by that load exceed the allowable (safe) stress in the material of which the beam is made. In beams, the evaluation of stresses in the swirling, intersecting lines of force in a lattice pattern becomes simple if we resolve the main internal forces into their vertical and horizontal components.

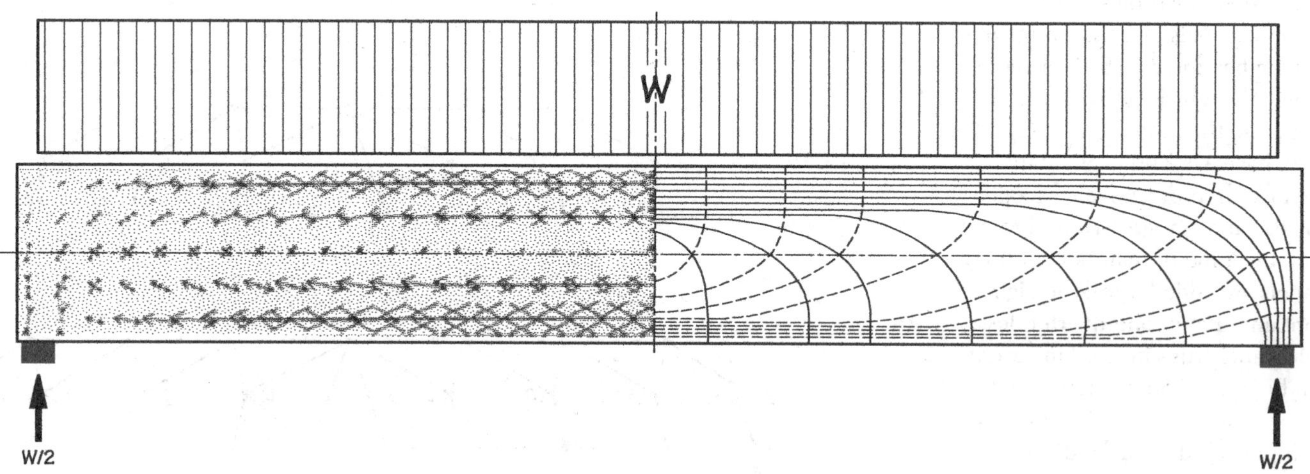

Figure 17.7 The flow pattern in a uniformly loaded beam is scarcely distinguishable from that of a beam loaded only at midspan.

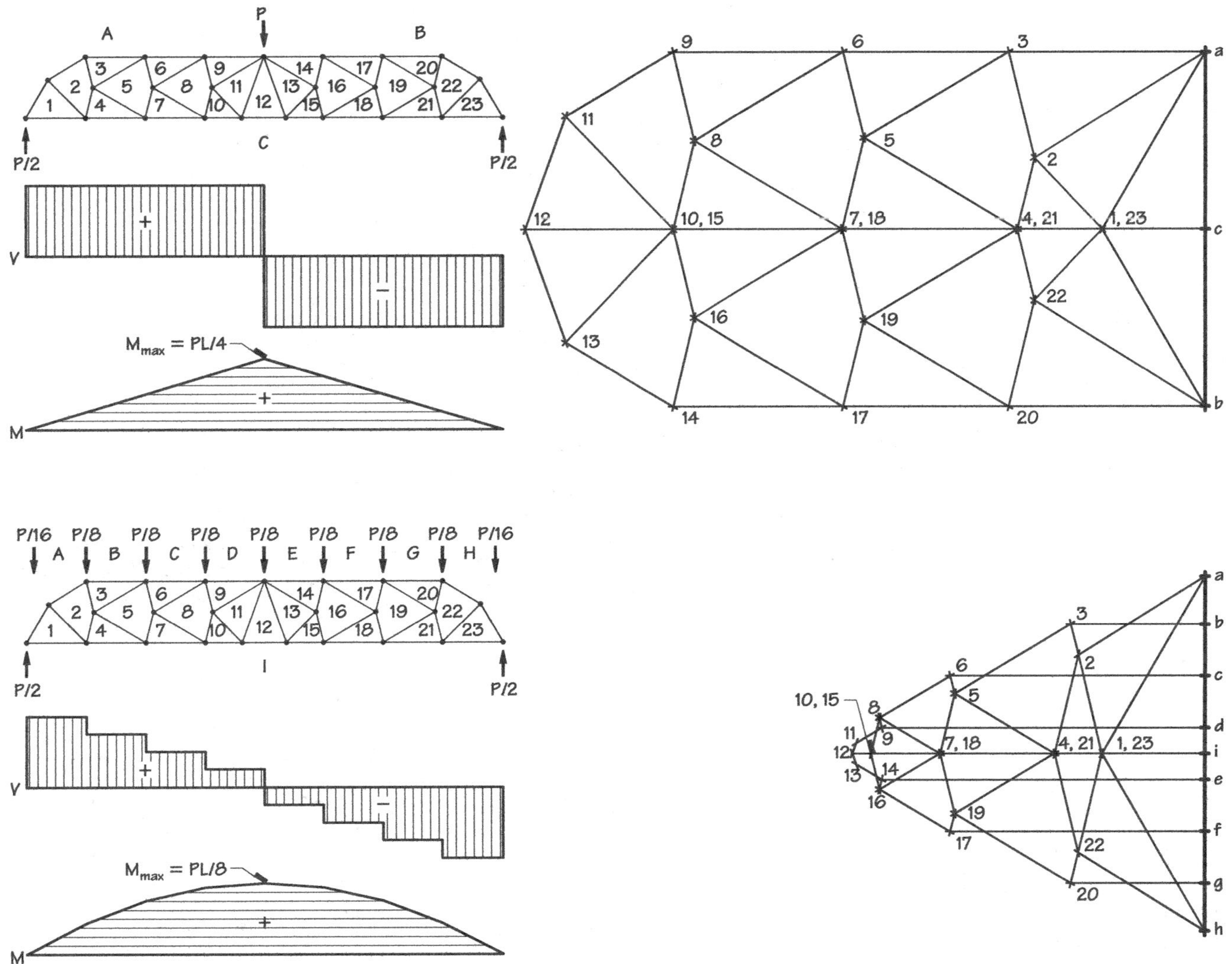

Figure 17.8 Analyses of two modified K-trusses of identical shape. The upper one bears a load concentrated at midspan, the lower one the same load distributed over its top nodes. The member forces differ by a factor of 2.

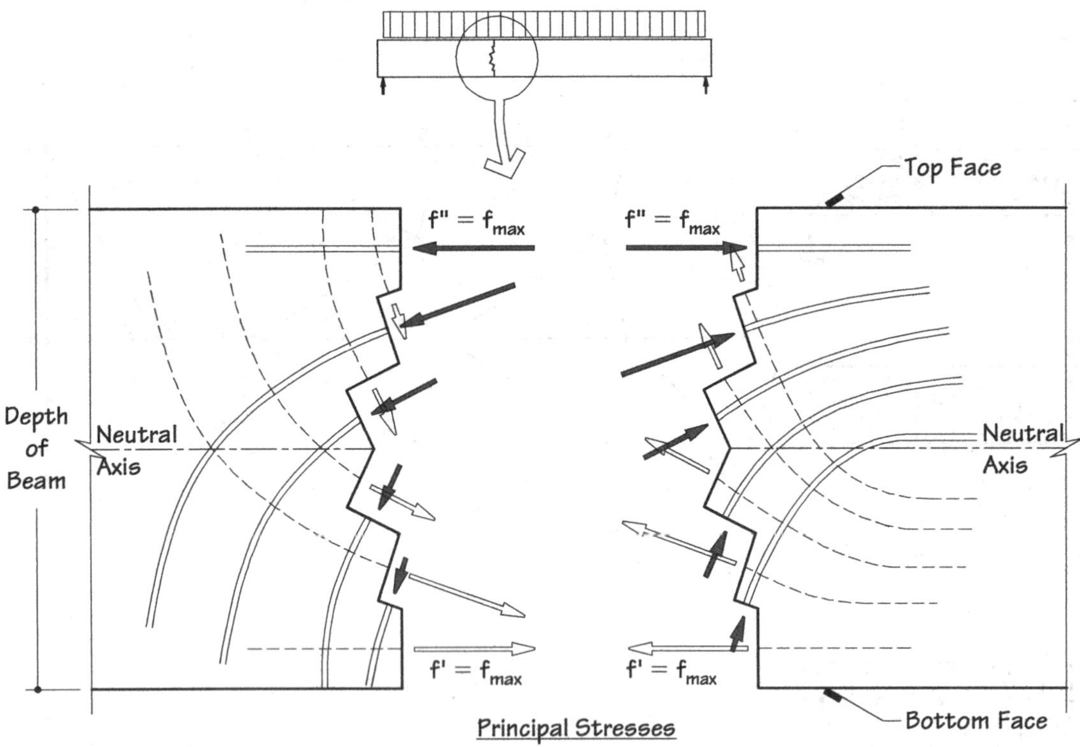

Figure 17.9 A beam cut a quarter-span with facets parallel and perpendicular to the directions of interior forces.

This allows us to develop straightforward quantitative expressions that are easily used in everyday practice for assigning sizes to beams.

In Figure 17.9, we cut through a loaded beam of rectangular cross section at the quarter point of the span with an imaginary surface made up of facets that are carefully oriented to be everywhere perpendicular to the directions of principal stress. Along these facets, the compressive forces are maximal at the top face of the beam and diminish to zero at the bottom face. The tensile forces are maximal at the bottom and zero at the top. The orientations of the forces of each kind vary over a range of 90°.

In Figure 17.10, we cut the beam at the same location as before, but with a smooth, vertical plane

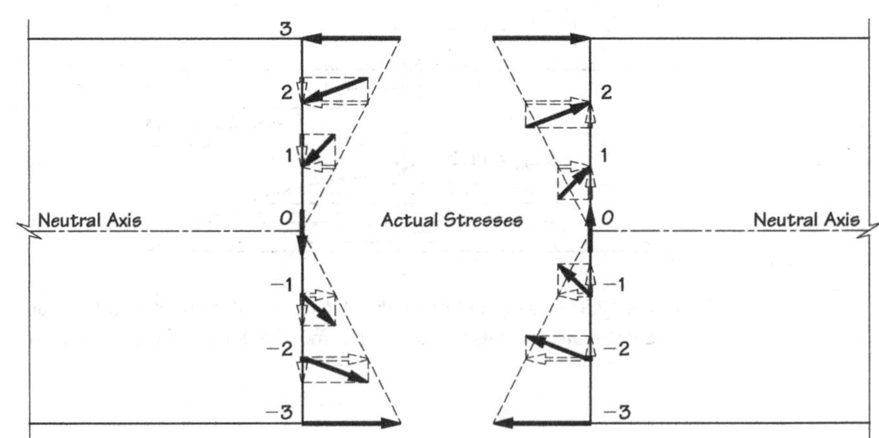

Figure 17.10 A smooth cut at quarter-span reveals the horizontal and vertical components of the interior forces.

rather than a faceted one. In this plane, we resolve the force in each of the inclined lines of principal force into its longitudinal and vertical components. A startlingly clear pattern emerges (Figure 17.11): The longitudinal components vary linearly from a maximum value of compression at the top face of the beam through zero at its midheight to a maximum value of tension at the bottom face of the beam. The vertical components vary according to a parabolic distribution: They are maximal at midheight and zero at the top and bottom faces.

A model beam that is made of a rectangular prism of soft foam rubber illustrates vividly this linear distribution of the longitudinal components of internal force (Figure 17.12). When the beam is bent, ruled lines on the front of the beam that were originally vertical remain straight, but their top ends are now much closer together than their bottom ends.

For the vertical lines to remain straight after the beam has deformed, there must be a linear distribution of longitudinal stress on its cross section. By observing the deformations of the foam rubber beam, we deduce that stresses are highest at the top and bottom faces, and diminish linearly to zero at the midheight of the beam. This verifies the stress distribution shown in Figure 17.11. We note further that the longitudinal stresses in the upper half of the beam are compressive, and that those in the lower half are tensile. We call the horizontal midline of the beam the *neutral axis* (abbreviated N.A.). In reality, this axis is not a line, but a horizontal plane that passes completely through the beam, which is why it is sometimes referred to as the *neutral plane*.

Figure 17.13 shows that the longitudinal components of force in a simply supported beam vary from a maximum at the point of maximum bending moment to zero at the supports. The vertical components of internal force are zero at the point of maximum bending moment and reach maximum values in the vicinity of the supports, where external V forces are maximal. Notice that the forces in the members

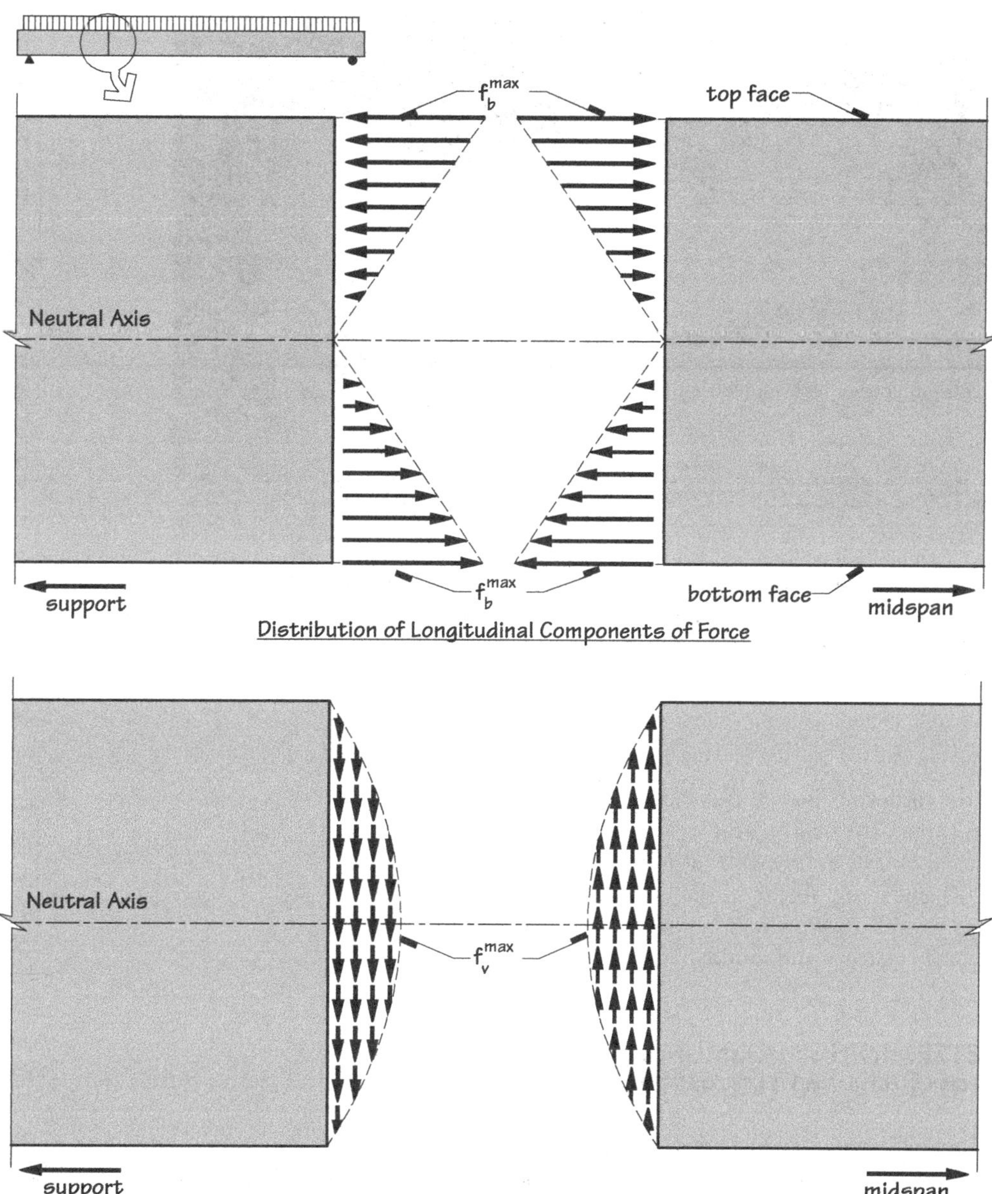

Figure 17.11 The distribution of horizontal and vertical components of internal force at quarter-span.

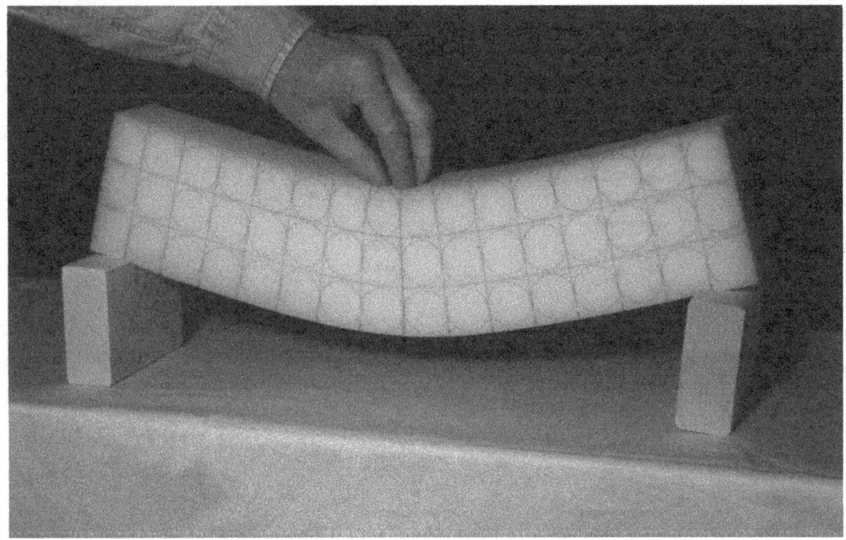

Figure 17.12 A loaded beam made of foam demonstrates that vertical plane sections of a beam remain planar after the beam is loaded, and that the top half of the beam is in compression and the bottom half is in tension.

Photo: David M. Foxe.

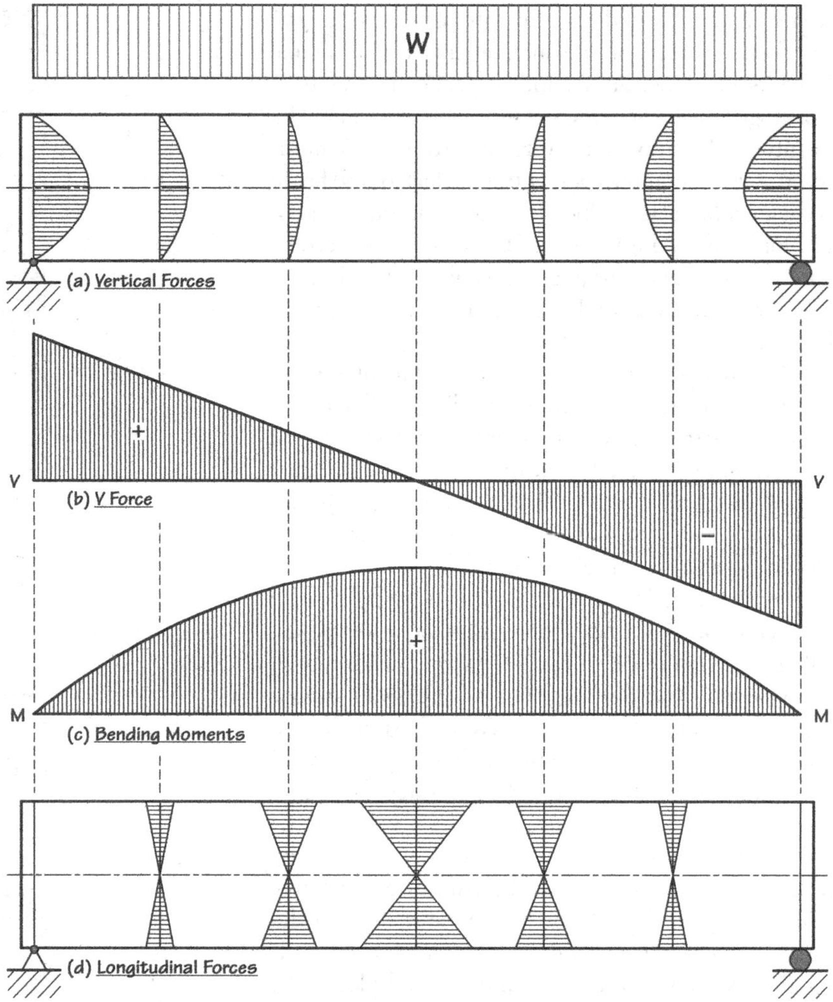

Figure 17.13 The distribution of vertical and longitudinal components of force in a uniformly loaded rectangular beam, together with the *V* and *M* diagrams.

of the uniformly loaded truss in Figure 17.8b follow this same pattern: Longitudinal forces in the top and bottom chords are maximal at midspan and minimal at the ends; and forces in the web members, analogous to web stresses in a beam, are maximal at the ends of the truss and minimal at midspan.

DETERMINING MAXIMUM LONGITUDINAL STRESS IN A LATTICE PATTERN

Now we'll examine the stresses that are caused by the two sets of components of the actual internal forces in a rectangular beam, beginning with the longitudinal components. Figures 17.14 and 17.15 represent the intensities of the longitudinal stresses exerted on the rectangular section of the beam as two wedge-shaped *stress blocks*, one of them a block of compressive stresses above the neutral axis of the beam, and the other of tensile stresses below. The triangular profile of each block is a graph of the linear variation of stress from zero at the neutral axis to a maximum value at the extreme top or bottom edge of the beam. The volume of each block represents the stresses multiplied by the area of the beam cross section over which they act; it is the total compressive or tensile force exerted by the internal resisting action of the beam.

To simplify our work, we will focus for the moment on these two total forces: TF_c represents the total compressive force in the top wedge, and TF_t the total tensile force in the bottom one. Each total force acts at the centroid of the stress block that it represents. It is evident

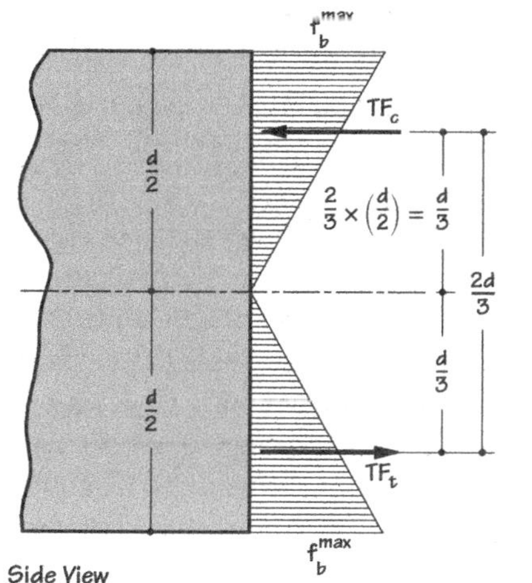

Figure 17.14 A side view of the stress blocks for a rectangular beam.

from the symmetrical deformations of the foam rubber beam in Figure 17.12 that the tensile and compressive stress blocks, and therefore the total forces, are equal in size. Together, the two total forces constitute a couple of equal, oppositely oriented forces whose moment is the resisting moment of the beam at that plane.

To arrive at a value for each total force, we must find the volume of the stress blocks that they represent. The height of each block, $d/2$, is half the depth of the beam. The width of each block, b, is the width of the beam. The length of each stress block at the top and bottom faces of the beam is equal to the maximum longitudinal stress in the beam, $f_b$max. The length of the block at the neutral axis is zero. Because the profile of each block is triangular, the vertical position of the line of action of the total force is at two-thirds of the height of the block, which is $d/3$. The *moment arm of internal forces* or *arm of resisting moment* is the distance of $2d/3$ between these two total forces.

The total force exerted by each stress block in a beam of rectangular cross section is equal to the volume of the wedge:

$$TF = \frac{1}{2}\left(f_b^{max}\right)\left(\frac{d}{2}\right)(b) = f_b^{max}\left(\frac{bd}{4}\right)$$

The moment exerted by a couple is equal to either of its forces multiplied by the perpendicular distance between the forces. Accordingly, the resisting moment of the beam, M_R, is equal to the total force represented by one stress block multiplied by the moment arm of internal forces, $2d/3$:

$$M_R = f_b^{max}\left(\frac{bd}{4}\right)\left(\frac{2d}{3}\right)$$

Simplifying,

$$M_R = f_b^{max}\frac{bd^2}{6} \qquad [17\text{-}1]$$

where

M_R is the resisting moment of the beam,
f_b^{max} is the maximum longitudinal stress in the beam,
b is the width of the beam, and
d is the depth of the beam.

Equation [17-1] is a general expression for the resisting moment of any beam of rectangular cross section. The quantity $bd^2/6$ is constant for any given rectangular beam, and is known as its *section modulus, S*. The units of a section modulus are in.^{3}, mm^3, or cm^3. Thus, equation [17-1] becomes:

$$M = f_b^{max}S \qquad [17\text{-}2]$$

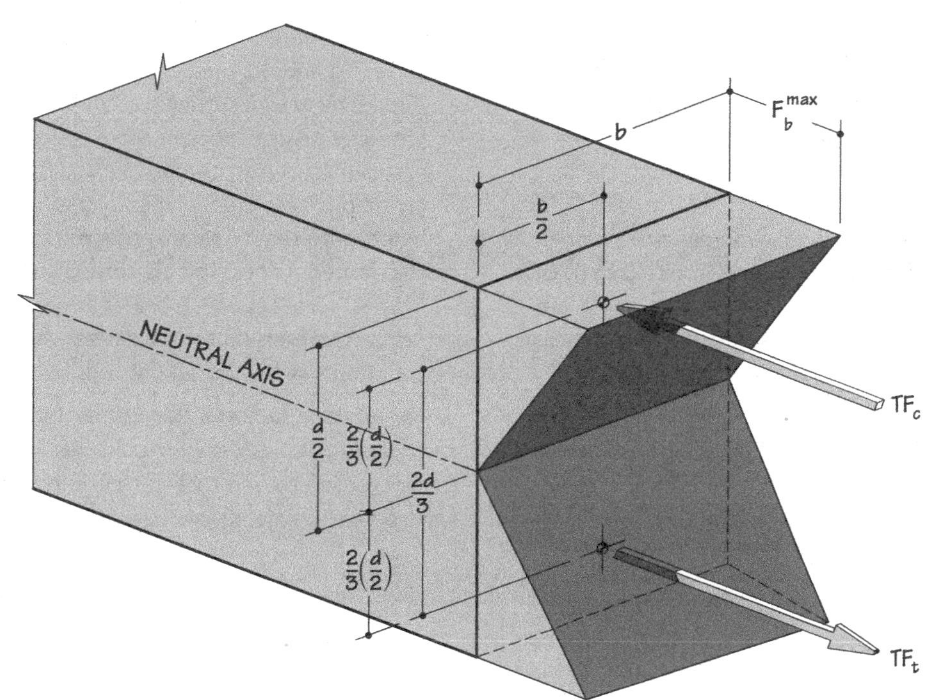

Figure 17.15 A three-dimensional view of the stress blocks for a rectangular beam.

Why Beams Are Inherently Inefficient and Why We Use Them Anyway

A uniformly loaded, simply supported beam experiences a maximum bending moment only at midspan. At midspan, maximum bending stress is developed at only the extreme top and bottom faces of the beam. When designing a structure, we select a beam whose size is such that the longitudinal stress at these two points of maximum stress, f_b, does not exceed the allowable stress in the material of which the beam is made. Usually we use a prismatic beam, one whose shape and section modulus are constant throughout its length, even though for a uniformly distributed load the average bending moment for all sections along its span is only two-thirds of the maximum bending moment.

As we have seen, the bending stress in vertical sections of the beam varies linearly from maximum compression at the top face and maximum compression at the bottom face to zero along the neutral axis. Thus, the average tensile and compressive bending stresses in vertical sections of a rectangular beam are only half the maximum stress.

Multiplying the two-thirds that represents the average bending moment in the beam by the one-half that represents the ratio of average bending stress in a beam to the maximum stress, we find that on average, the material of a simply supported, uniformly loaded, prismatic beam or rectangular cross section works to only about one-third of its capacity. Two-thirds of the strength of the material in the beam is wasted. Under a single, concentrated load at midspan, the waste of material is 75 percent. These performances may be contrasted with that of the material in an axially loaded structure, such as a cable or arch, which is 100 percent utilized under full load.

Because of this inefficiency, the maximum spans that we can attempt with beams are rather modest in comparison with the spans that we can create with trusses, cables, or arches. As the span of a beam grows longer, the self-weight of the beam becomes a larger and larger portion of the total load, until at the limiting span, the beam can barely carry only its own weight, leaving no capacity to support a live load.

Despite this structural inefficiency, we use beams far more frequently than any other spanning devices, because they are efficient in other important ways:

1. Beams are more efficient in their utilization of space and headroom within a multistory building than other types of spanning devices. A steel beam that is only 1 ft (0.3 m) deep easily spans 20 ft (6 m), whereas a cable or arch structure for this same span would have to be several times as deep. Furthermore, the beam has flat, horizontal faces both above and below, to which a level floor and flat ceiling may be directly attached.
2. The longitudinal tensile and compressive forces within a beam balance one another, leaving no external thrust to be transmitted to the rest of the building structure, whereas an arch or cable exerts a thrust or pull that must be resisted by additional structural devices such as backstays and buttresses.
3. A beam can carry a wide variety of loading patterns without perceptibly changing shape. If you walk from one end of a beam to the other, your moving weight subjects the beam to large variations in bending moments, yet the beam remains essentially straight and horizontal, with imperceptible deflections. By contrast, if you were to walk from one end of a small-diameter hanging cable to the other, the cable would undergo major changes in its geometry unless elaborate measures were taken to stabilize it.
4. Prismatic beams are easy to manufacture and distribute. Sawmills produce lumber by fastening a log to a rail-mounted carriage and passing it repeatedly by a cutting blade. This process produces prismatic beams more easily and naturally than any other shape. Rolling mills create prismatic steel shapes by passing hot steel billets between rollers that squeeze them into the desired shapes. This also produces prismatic beams. Precast concrete beams are produced in flat casting beds that are most easily adapted to creating straight, prismatic shapes.

Taking all these factors into consideration, we use beams far more frequently in our structures than any other type of spanning devices, even though beams are inherently wasteful of material.

WHY THE VARIATION IN TOTAL FORCES CREATES THE LATTICE PATTERN

Under any of the more usual loading conditions, the bending moments on a simply supported beam are largest at or near the middle of the span and diminish with distance from this point to become zero at the supports. The beam responds to these external moments with resisting moments that are created by two groups of internal longitudinal forces, tensile in one half of the beam (the bottom half if the beam is simply supported and supports a downward load) and compressive in the other half. The resultant of each group of forces is separated from that of the other group by a moment arm, thus forming a couple. The value of the couple, which is the product of the moment arm and one resultant force, is the *resisting moment* of the beam. For a beam to be in static equilibrium, the resisting moment must equal the applied or external moment.

In a prismatic beam, which is one that does not change shape or dimension along its length, the length of the internal moment arm between total longitudinal forces remains constant throughout the span. This means that in order for the internal moments to vary, the total longitudinal forces in a prismatic beam must vary in unison with the changing values of bending moments.

Because the total longitudinal forces are maximum at the point of maximum bending moment, their values on either side of this point on the span must be smaller. To accomplish this, a portion of the longitudinal force veers away from the horizontal and begins a swooping journey across the depth of the beam. This force follows a steeper and steeper path as it approaches the neutral axis of the beam, crosses the axis at an angle of 45°, and continues its ever-steeper journey to terminate perpendicular to the opposite face of the beam. It has a value of zero at this termination, because all its energy has been expended in meeting and equilibrating the forces of opposite character that it encountered in its mirror-image pattern. Both tensile and compressive trajectories behave in this way. Except for the transitional regions of flow near the supports, this same process of portions of the total force veering away and diminishing to zero is repeated along the full span, so that the total longitudinal force in a prismatic beam remains proportional to the external bending moment at every point.

"Bending is the most expensive stress."

—Antoni Gaudí

FINDING THE MAXIMUM BENDING STRESS IN A RECTANGULAR BEAM

To create a convenient expression for finding the maximum value of longitudinal stress, which is called *bending stress*, in a beam, we divide both sides of equation [17-2] by S, to arrive at:

$$f_b^{max} = \frac{M_{max}}{S} \qquad [17\text{-}3]$$

For a beam of rectangular cross section, this becomes:

$$f_b^{max} = \frac{6M_{max}}{bd^2} \qquad [17\text{-}4]$$

As an example of how this expression may be applied, consider a wood beam of rectangular cross section whose span, L, is 16 ft, and which supports a uniformly distributed load, including its own weight, of 250 lb/ft. Its width, b, is 5.5 in. Its depth, d, is 11.5 in. What is the maximum bending stress in the beam?

First we must determine the value of the maximum bending moment, M_{max}. Because the loading is simple and symmetrical, we do not bother to construct V and M diagrams, but use the formula for maximum bending moment in a uniformly loaded beam instead:

$$M_{max} = \frac{wL^2}{8} = \frac{(250\text{ lb/ft})(16\text{ ft})^2}{8} = 8{,}000\text{ lb-ft}$$

Then we employ equation [17-4], taking care to multiply the bending moment by 12 in./ft to convert it to units of lb-in. so that the units are consistent:

$$f_b^{max} = \frac{6M_{max}}{bd^2} = \frac{6(8{,}000\text{ lb-ft})(12\text{ in./ft})}{(5.5\text{ in.})(11.5\text{ in.})^2} = 792\text{ psi}$$

Notice that the beam depth is squared in equation [17-4], whereas the width is not. This explains why a rectangular beam placed on edge is much stronger than the same beam placed flat. If the beam whose maximum stress we just calculated were placed flat instead of on edge, its section modulus would be only half as much, and the bending stress within it would double. In general, when we design a beam, we make it as deep and narrow as possible, because material used to increase its depth is utilized much more efficiently than material used to increase its width.

DETERMINING MAXIMUM WEB STRESS IN RECTANGULAR BEAMS

So far, we have developed expressions for evaluating bending (longitudinal) stress in rectangular beams. Bending stresses are greatest at the top and bottom edges of a beam at points of maximum bending moment. Now we turn our attention to the stresses that reach maximum values at the neutral axis of the beam near the supports. The region of a beam that lies between the top and bottom edge regions is called the *web*, and the stresses that occur in this region we will call *web stresses*.

We found earlier in this chapter that vertical components of stress in beams vary from values of zero at the top and bottom faces of the beam to a maximum value, f_v^{max}, at the neutral axis. The distribution of these values over an imaginary vertical plane within the beam follows a parabolic curve. Over the length of the beam, maximum values of web stress occur near the supports, and there are no web stresses at midspan if the beam is loaded symmetrically.

The total internal vertical force, exerted by these stresses in a rectangular beam, V_{int}, is equal to the volume of a stress block that is parabolic in profile (Figure 17.16). Its height is d, the depth of the beam, and its thickness is b, the width of the beam. The maximum length of the parabola, which lies along the neutral axis, is f_v^{max}.

The area under a parabola is equal to two-thirds of the product of its base and altitude. Thus, for a rectangular beam:

$$\text{Total Internal } V \text{ force} = V_{int} = \frac{2}{3} f_v^{max} bd$$

For a beam to be in static equilibrium, this **internal** V force must be equal and opposite to the **external** V force at this point on the span, V_{ext}, the value of which may be taken from the V diagram:

$$V_{ext} = \frac{2}{3} f_v^{max} bd$$

Rearranging terms,

$$f_v^{max} = \frac{3V_{ext}}{2bd} \qquad [17\text{-}5]$$

where:

f_v^{max} is the maximum web stress at the neutral axis of a given section,

V_{ext} is the external vertical force at that section,

b is the width of the beam, and

d is the depth of the beam.

Equation [17-5] applies only to beams of rectangular cross section. The quantity bd in the denominator is equal to A, the cross-sectional area of a rectangular beam. Thus:

$$f_v^{max} = 1.5\frac{V_{ext}}{A} \qquad [17\text{-}6]$$

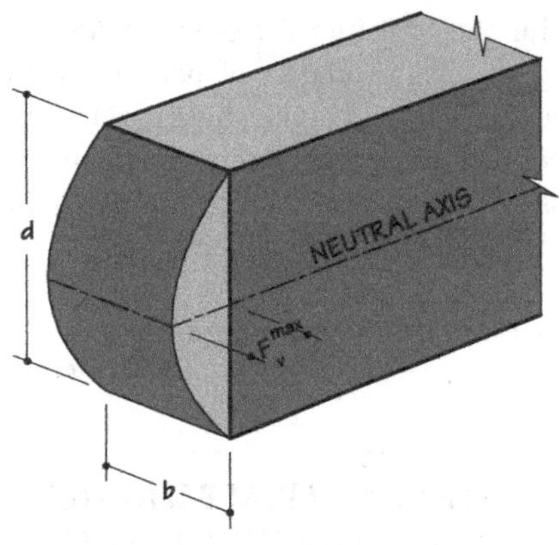

Figure 17.16 The parabolic stress block for vertical components of force in a rectangular beam.

where:

A is the cross-sectional area of the beam.

V_{ext} generally has its maximum value at a support or at the point of application of a concentrated load. However, equations [17-5] and [17-6] are applicable only to the lattice pattern of flow, which occurs only in the R-regions of a beam. An R-region normally does not extend all the way to a beam's supports or points of application of concentrated loads. There is at each such point an R-region whose horizontal dimension is not greater than the depth of the beam, in which flow is transitional because of the squeezing action of the support or load on the surface of the beam. Thus, equations [17-5] and [17-6] are valid only for the portion of the span of a rectangular beam that lies no closer than distance d to each support or concentrated load.

We will illustrate this with an example: Suppose that we wish to find the maximum web stress in the rectangular beam whose maximum bending stress we found earlier; its span is 16 ft and it supports a uniform load of 250 lb/ft. Its dimensions are 5.5 in. wide by 11.5 in. deep.

The maximum value of V force, 2,000 lb, is found over each of the supports. However, the maximum web stress that occurs within an R-region is found at a distance d from each of the supports. At this location, the value of V_{ext} is found by deducting from 2,000 lb the portion of the load that lies within distance d of the support:

$$V_{ext} = 2{,}000 \text{ lb} - \left(\frac{11.5 \text{ in.}}{12 \text{ in./ft}}\right)(250 \text{ lb/ft}) = 1{,}760 \text{ lb}$$

Thus, the maximum web stress in the R-region of the beam is:

$$f_{max} = \frac{3V}{2bd} = \frac{3(1{,}760 \text{ lb})}{2(5.5 \text{ in})(11.5 \text{ in.})} = 41.7 \text{ psi}$$

The usual procedure for sizing a beam is to find a trial size on the basis of the maximum bending stress, then to check the maximum web stress. If the web stress exceeds the allowable, the cross-sectional area of the beam must be increased sufficiently to reduce the maximum web stress as required.

Is *V* Force the Same as "Shear?"

The V force diagram for a beam loading is commonly called a "shear" diagram, and the term "shear stress" is universally used to refer to web stresses in beams. Although these uses of the term "shear" are incorrect, as explained in the accompanying sidebar, they are universally used and deeply embedded in the engineering literature.

CHECKING BEARING STRESS IN WOOD BEAMS

Where the bottom face of a wood beam rests on a column or wall, its fibers are compressed in a direction perpendicular to the grain. Wood is weak against stresses in this direction, and every wood beam should be checked to be sure that it will not crush where it comes in contact with its support. This is very easy to do: The bearing stress is equal to the beam

The Myth of Shear in Beams

If we hold a paperback book loosely in our hands and flex it, its pages slide past one another. If we grip the pages tightly together so they cannot slide, and then flex the book again, the book is many times stiffer than it was when held loosely. This and similar demonstrations have long been used to support the claim that there is horizontal shear in beams and that it plays an important part in contributing to their strength.

Our understanding of the flow of forces in beams enables us to see that so-called shear in a beam is actually a combination of oblique principal tensile and compressive stresses. These oblique stresses have their maximum effect at the neutral axis of the beam near the supports. If we cut through a beam in this area with an imaginary horizontal or vertical plane, we find the horizontal and vertical components of the oblique forces that are commonly construed to be "shear." It is true that a wood beam, because of its highly directional microstructure of hard, strong, longitudinal cellulose fibers embedded in a much softer matrix of lignin, may fail by sliding or shearing parallel to the direction of the fibers. But in the case of a concrete beam, whose material is strong in compression and weak in tension but not otherwise directional in its properties, a so-called shear failure manifests itself as diagonal cracks that run perpendicular to the diagonal directions of principal tensile forces near the ends of the beam. These "shear" failures are actually pure tensile failures.

Any material at the neutral axis of a beam, whether the beam is made of steel, concrete, aluminum, or wood, becomes more susceptible to failure because of simultaneous tension in one direction and compression in the other. Figure A explains why this is so: A small cube of material that is squeezed by a pair of opposing forces bulges slightly due to the Poisson effect (a). If this cube is squeezed simultaneously by pairs of opposing forces in both its principal directions, its material grows slightly stronger. This is because each pair of compressive forces opposes the Poisson effect caused by the other by confining the material of the cube so that it cannot bulge. However, if the cube is simultaneously stretched by a pair of tensile forces in one direction and squeezed by a pair of compressive forces in the other, each pair exaggerates the Poisson effect caused by the other and seriously diminishes the resistance of the material (b). This is why allowable web stresses, generally misnamed "shear" stresses in the literature, are substantially lower than allowable longitudinal stresses. In steel, the allowable maximum web stress is less than two-thirds of the allowable tensile and compressive stresses in the flanges. In a typical wood species, because of the directional structure of the grain and the weakness of wood perpendicular to the grain direction, the allowable web stress is only 7 to 10 percent of the allowable tensile and compressive forces in bending.

At the neutral axis of a beam, an imaginary cube of material is squeezed by compression forces along one axis and stretched by tensile forces along the other (Fig. C). Resolved into their horizontal and vertical components, these diagonal forces have been seen erroneously as representing a sliding or shearing action, hence the term "shear." If a beam is divided into independent horizontal or vertical layers, like the pages of the book that we flexed, a shearing action will be observed between the layers. But in a real beam, there are only pushes and pulls, not shear.

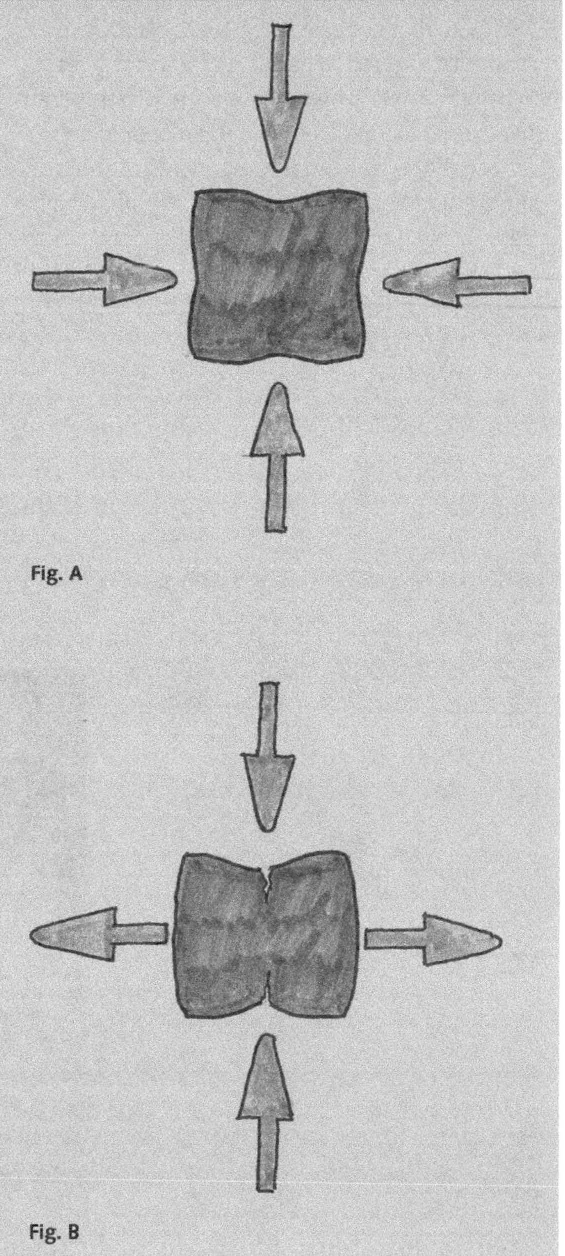

Fig. A

Fig. B

The foam rubber beam in Fig. D has cardboard cover plates glued to its top and bottom faces. When the beam is bent, these cover plates, because they are so much stiffer than the rubber foam, attract all the horizontal components of stress at the top and bottom of the beam. The weak, highly deformable rubber acts as a web that connects the cover plates. When a load is applied to this beam, the circles on the vertical face of the web deform into ellipses whose major and minor axes indicate the directions of principal tension and compression. It is clear that these principal stresses are diagonal. Noted engineer and teacher Mario Salvadori writes in his book *Why Buildings Stand Up* (W.W. Norton & Company, Inc., 1980), "It might be rightly thought that shear action is a new and different type of structural action and that there are three elementary structural actions rather than two . . . . This is not so . . . shear is structurally equivalent to tension and compression at right angles to each other and at forty-five degrees to the shears."

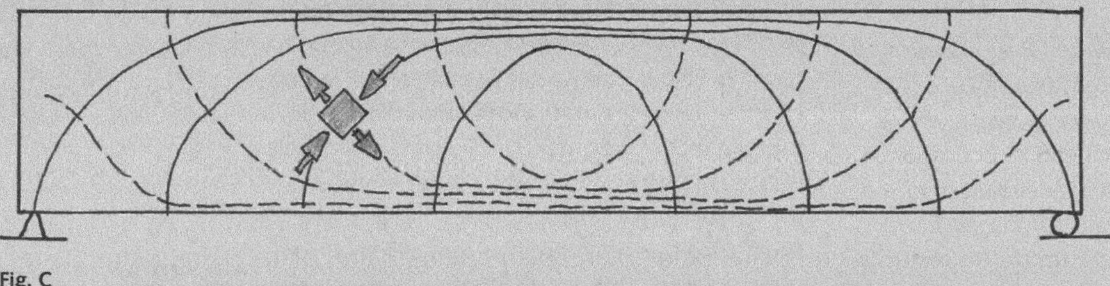

Fig. C

Fig. D

reaction divided by the area upon which the beam rests (Figure 17-17):

$$f_{c\perp} = \frac{R}{bl_B} \qquad [17\text{-}7]$$

where:

$f_{c\perp}$ is the compressive bearing stress perpendicular to grain,
R is the reaction,
b is the width of the beam, and
l_B is the length of beam that rests on the support.

For southern pine, the allowable bearing stress perpendicular to grain, $f_{c\perp}^{\text{allow}}$, is tabulated in engineering handbooks as 625 psi. Referring once more to the beam whose bending and web stresses we have calculated, the beam reaction is 7,107 lb. We calculate the required length of bearing as follows:

$$f_{c\perp}^{\text{allow}} = \frac{R}{bl_B} = \frac{7{,}100 \text{ lb}}{3.125\, l_B} = 625 \text{ psi}$$

Solving for l_B, we find that the minimum length of beam that must contact the supporting column or wall is 3.64 in. To allow for normal dimensional tolerances in construction, this dimension should be rounded up to 4 in. or more on the construction drawings.

If a beam is supported by bolting it directly to the side of a column, only the portion of the beam's cross section that lies above the lowest bolt hole is effective in resisting web stresses (Figure 17.18). Additionally, a bolt provides a relatively limited area of bearing against the wood of the beam. For these reasons, it is usually difficult and often impossible to support a wood beam on bolts alone. Various off-the-shelf metal connecting devices are available to make solid, safe connections between beams and the members on which they bear (Figure 17.19). Architects and engineers often design special metal connectors for exposed connections, ones that harmonize with the architectural aesthetic. Another way to make this connection is to bolt a wood bearing block to the column, placing the grain of the block in a vertical orientation (Figure 17.20). The block may be as tall as needed to accommodate the required number of bolts. A bolt acting parallel to the grain of the wood, as it does on this block and the column, exerts substantially more force than it would if it were acting perpendicular to grain in the beam itself, which helps to reduce the required number of bolts.

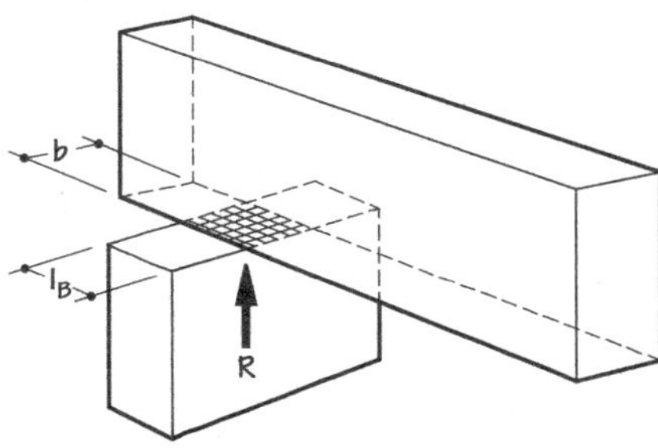

Figure 17.17 The shaded area represents the bearing area of a beam as it rests on a column, a wall, or another beam.

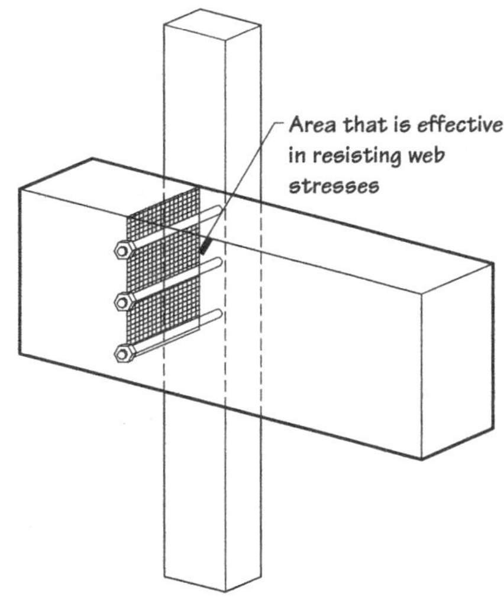

Figure 17.18 If a beam is bolted to the side of a column, only the shaded area is effective in resisting vertical forces. Thus, the capacity of this type of connection is severely limited.

DEFLECTIONS OF BEAMS

When a bending moment is applied to a simply supported beam, the material in the top half grows shorter in response to longitudinal compressive stresses, and the material in the bottom half grows longer in response to longitudinal tensile stresses. The extreme fibers of the beam, those at the very top and bottom edges, change dimension the most, whereas the fibers at the neutral axis do not change dimension at all. The result of these changes of length is that the beam assumes a curvature and *deflects* (sags).

Usually, beam deflections are so small as not to be readily apparent to the eye, but they can be problematic nevertheless. They can cause brittle finish materials such as plaster, glass, and stone to crack, and floors to feel bouncy and insecure underfoot. Deflections of beams that support a flat roof can create a low spot in the roof surface in which water collects and from which it does not drain. A pond forms in the low spot. As the pond grows, its increasing weight causes further beam deflection that traps still more water (Figure 17.21). This makes the pond heavier, causing yet more deflection and attracting even more water. This vicious circle of *progressive collapse* ends with the roof failing structurally when the weight of the ponded water overstresses the roof beams or a roof member buckles under the excessive load.

Deflections of beams are limited by both building codes and the designer's judgment. A typical maximum allowable live-load deflection for floor beams or for beams supporting brittle finishes such as plaster ceilings is 1/360 of the span (L/360). Roof beams that do not support brittle materials may be allowed to deflect

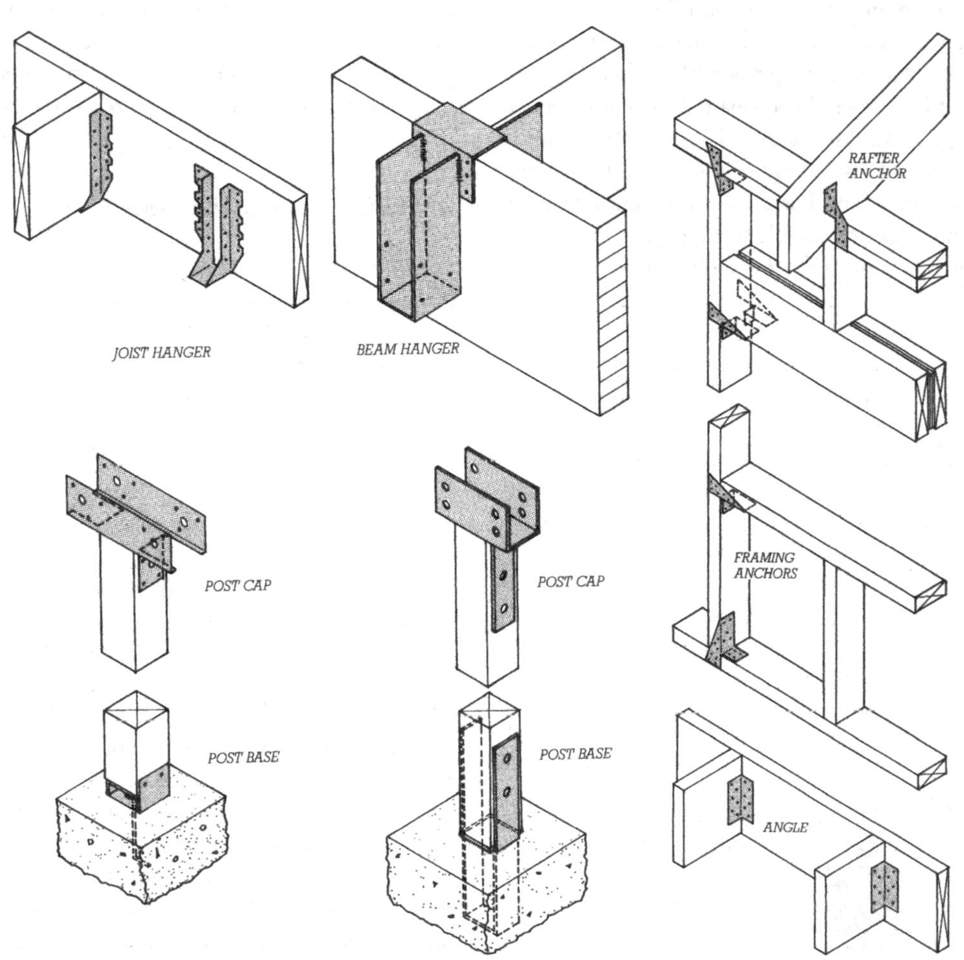

Figure 17.19 Some typical metal devices for connecting beams to columns and girders. Each is designed to support a beam loaded to capacity.

From Edward Allen and Joseph Iano, *Fundamentals of Building Construction, Materials and Methods,* 5th ed. Hoboken, NJ: John Wiley & Sons, Inc., 2009.

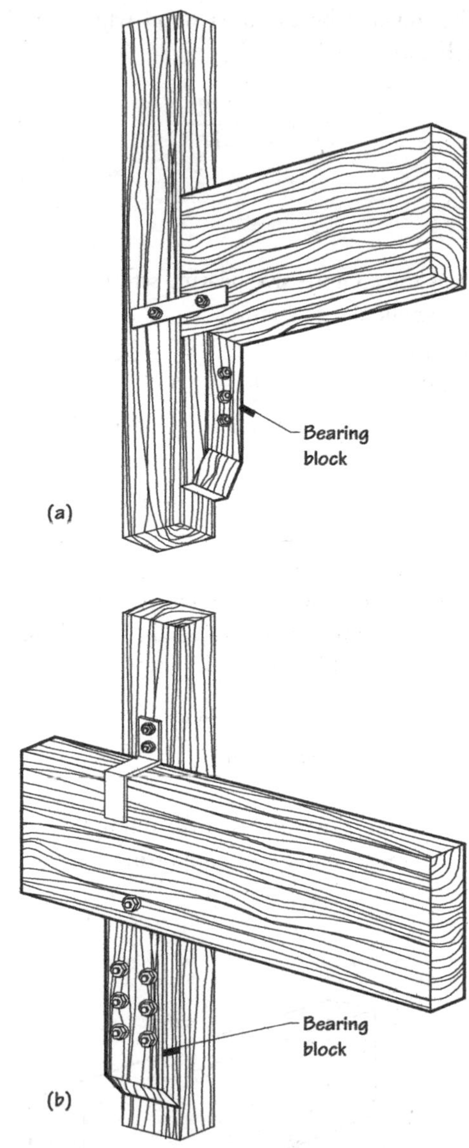

Figure 17.20 Two simple ways of providing full-capacity support for a wood beam where it bears on a column. Bolts pass through the beam only near its bottom edge; this is to assure that the beam will not hang directly on bolts after the wood shrinks.

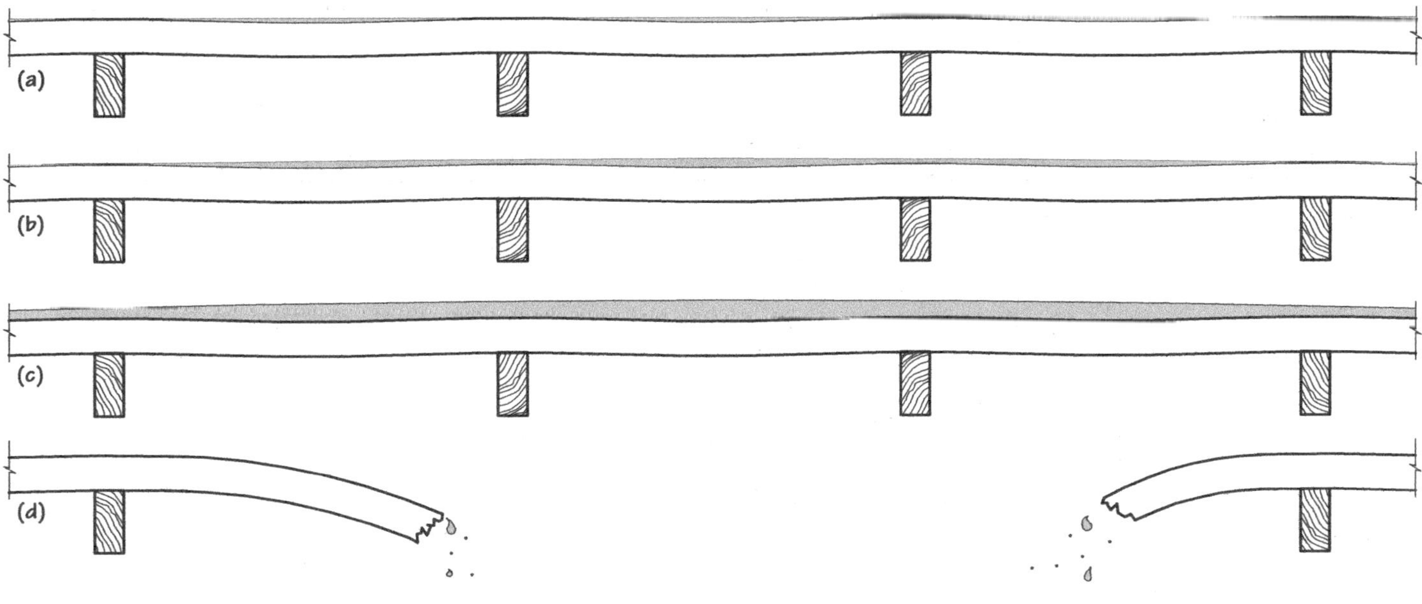

Figure 17.21 Progressive collapse of a flat roof caused by deflections of the roof beams: (a) Small puddles form in the low points of the roof. (b) The deflections cause more water to collect. (c) Soon the puddles have become a pond that gathers water still more rapidly and from a wider area of the roof. (d) The overloaded beams fail.

by *L*/240 or *L*/180. A wood-framed floor designed to a maximum deflection of L/360 will in many cases feel bouncy as one walks across it, even though it is strong enough to support its load safely. A stiff, solid-feeling wood floor structure can be achieved by designing its members for deflections not to exceed *L*/480.

Estimating Beam Deflections

Beam deflection, abbreviated **Δ**, is measured in inches or millimeters. Deflection increases with increasing load, *P*, *W*, or *w*, and also with increasing span, *L*. Working to resist deflection are the stiffness of the material of the beam, as measured by its modulus of elasticity, *E*, and the inherent resistance to bending of the beam's shape and size, which is expressed by its *moment of inertia, I*. Thus any expression for estimating the deflection of a beam has a load, *P*, *W*, or *w*, in the numerator, along with the span, *L*. The denominator contains *E* and *I*.

The moment of inertia, *I*, is a section property that is a measure of the stiffness of a beam. It is a constant for any section. It is closely related to section modulus, *S*, which is a measure of strength. For a rectangular beam section:

$$S = \frac{bh^2}{6}$$

$$I = \frac{bh^3}{12}$$

$$I = S\left(\frac{h}{2}\right)$$

Values of *I* for every structural material and shape are tabulated in tables of section properties, such as the ones for wood members reproduced in Figure 17.25. We will examine moments of inertia in more detail in Chapters 18 and 23.

The derivations of expressions that give close estimates of deflections for beams may be found in standard texts. The most commonly used of them is for the maximum deflection of a simply supported, uniformly loaded beam:

$$\Delta_{max} = \frac{5}{384}\frac{WL^3}{EI} \qquad [17\text{-}8]$$

where:

Δ_{max} is the maximum deflection of the beam, which occurs at midspan,
W is the total uniformly distributed load on the beam,
L is the span of the beam,
E is the modulus of elasticity of the beam material, and
I is the moment of inertia of the beam section.

In conventional units of measurement, *L* must be in inches to give a result in inches. Notice that *W* is the **total** load. If we wish to use the **load per unit of span**, *w*, instead, it must be expressed in load per **inch** of span in the following expression:

$$\Delta_{max} = \frac{5}{384}\frac{wL^4}{EI} \qquad [17\text{-}9]$$

As an example of the use of equation [17-8], consider a glue-laminated floor beam whose cross-sectional dimensions are 6–3/4 in. by 17–7/8 in. The handbook value for the moment of inertia of this beam is 3,213 in.^{4}, and its modulus of elasticity, E, is 1.8 million psi. It spans 18 ft and supports a uniformly distributed load of 25,800 lb. How much will this beam deflect under this load? Does this deflection satisfy a maximum deflection criterion of $L/360$?

$$\Delta_{max} = \frac{5}{384}\frac{WL^3}{EI} = \frac{5}{384}\frac{(25,800 \text{ lb})(216 \text{ in.})^3}{(1.8 \times 10^6 \text{ lb/in.}^2)(3,213 \text{ in.}^4)} = 0.59 \text{ in.}$$

$$\frac{L}{360} = \frac{(18 \text{ ft})(12 \text{ in./ft})}{360} = 0.6 \text{ in.}$$

The estimated deflection falls just within the $L/360$ criterion of 0.6 in.

Figure 17.22 gives formulas for maximum beam deflections for a number of common support and loading conditions. These equations apply to beams of any shape and material, except for nonhomogeneous beams such as reinforced or prestressed concrete.

The principle of superposition applies to deflections, as it does to bending moments. Thus, the maximum deflection of a simply supported beam that supports a concentrated load at midspan, as well as a load uniformly distributed over the entire span, may be estimated as the sum of the deflections calculated for each of the loads.

FINDING MEMBER SIZES FOR A WOOD DECK

Now we are equipped to tackle the problem posed at the beginning of the chapter: to design the supporting structure of a wood deck, 16 ft square in plan, that is to be attached to an existing house. The house will support one edge of the deck (Figure 17.2). The code-specified live load is 40 lb per square foot. The decking will be preservative-treated 6-in.-wide southern pine boards that are 3/4 in. thick. These require joists spaced 16 in.

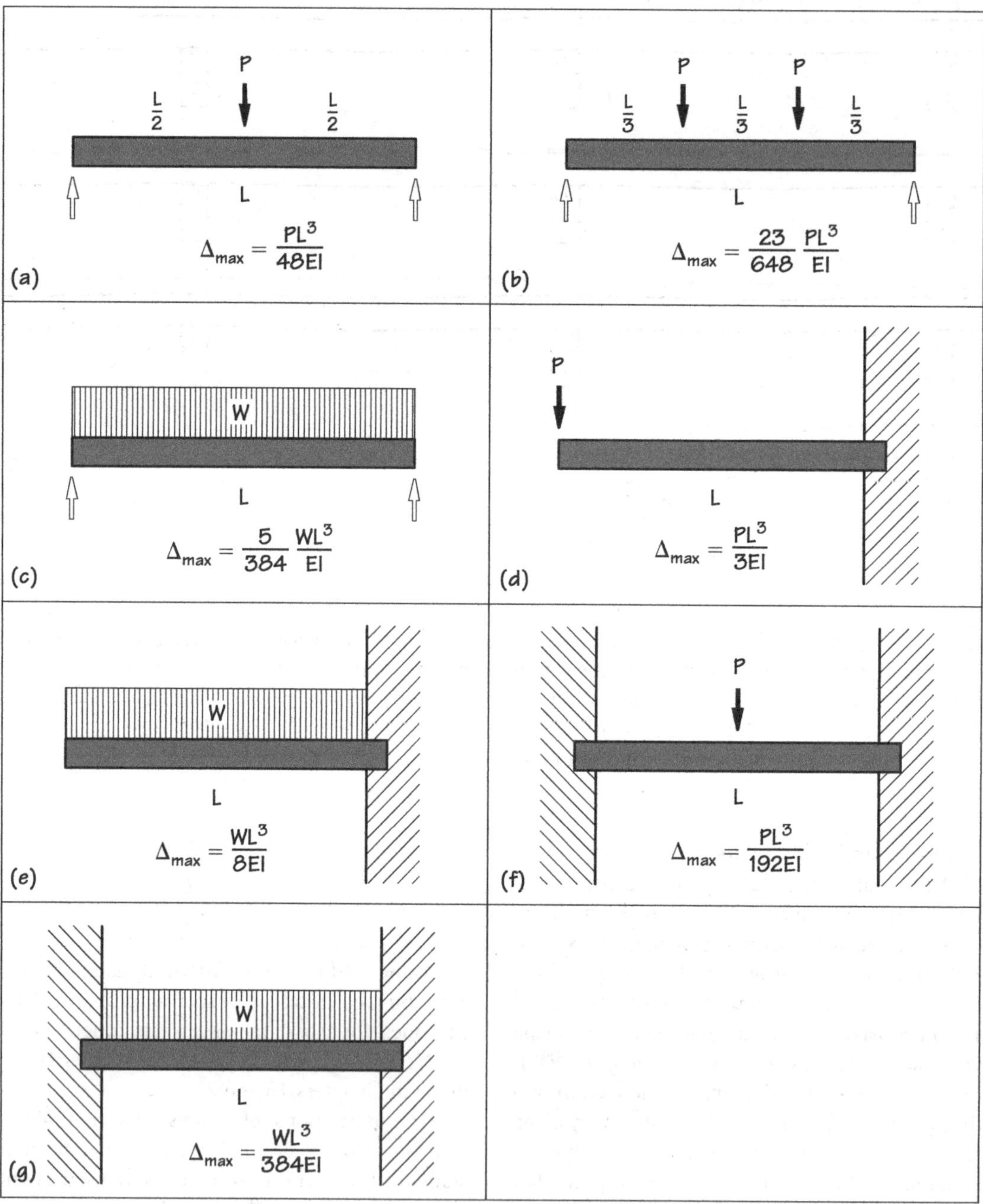

Figure 17.22 Deflection formulas for some common beam loadings.

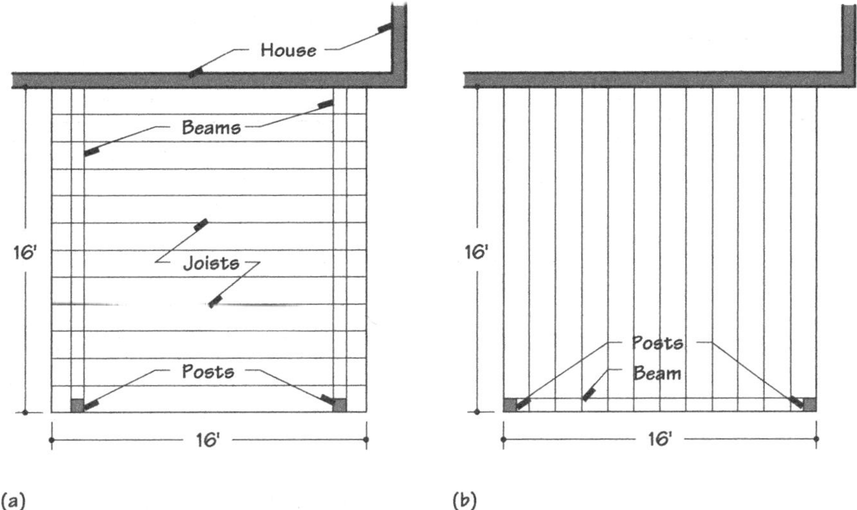

Figure 17.23 Two alternative framing plans for the deck.

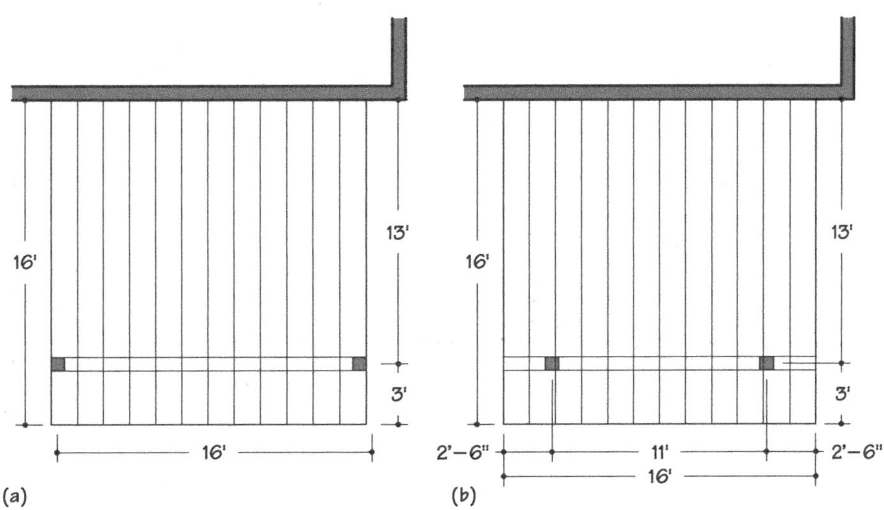

Figure 17.24 Moving the joist and beam supports to reduce bending moments.

apart. For joists and beams, we will also use southern pine that is preservative treated. The allowable bending stress, F_b, is 1,200 psi. The allowable web stress, F_v, is 90 psi. The modulus of elasticity, E, is 1.2 million psi. The wood weighs about 36 lb per cubic foot.

We experiment with various ways of framing the deck (Figure 17.23). If we run the joists parallel to the wall of the house (a), they will require support from two beams that lie perpendicular to the wall. If the joists are perpendicular (b), only one beam will be required. We choose the one-beam solution.

Joists spanning 16 ft will ordinarily have to be 12 in. deep. Is there a way we can use smaller joists instead? Yes. We can move the beam that supports the outer ends of the joists closer to the house. A distance of about 20 percent of the span is about right (Figure 17.24a). This reduces the bending moments in the joists substantially and will probably permit use of shallower joists.

Similarly, we can economize on beam material by moving its supports inward so that the beam overhangs about 20 percent of the main span, roughly 30 in., on each end (Figure 17.24b).

Standard sizes and section properties for wood and wood products are found in tables issued by lumber industry organizations (Figure 17.25).

ASSIGNING SIZES TO THE MEMBERS OF THE DECK FRAME

Robert Dermody, a registered architect who has degrees in both structural engineering and in architecture, performs the calculations that start on page 477 to find the required sizes of the structural members of the deck. He works carefully and neatly so that his calculations may be understood and verified by colleagues and building officials. He begins by drawing a dimensioned diagram of the frame and listing the design values that he will use on the pages that follow (Figure 17.26a).

Notice that Dermody's solution is based on an orderly application of the equations that we developed earlier in the chapter.

SECTION PROPERTIES OF STANDARD DRESSED (S4S) SAWN LUMBER

Nominal Size b x d	Standard Dressed Size (S4S) b x d inches x inches	Area of Section A in²	X-X AXIS Section Modulus S_{xx} in³	X-X AXIS Moment of Inertia I_{xx} in⁴	Y-Y AXIS Section Modulus S_{yy} in³	Y-Y AXIS Moment of Inertia I_{yy} in⁴	Approximate weight in pounds per linear foot (lb/ft) of piece when density of wood equals: 25 lb/ft³	30 lb/ft³	35 lb/ft³	40 lb/ft³	45 lb/ft³	50 lb/ft³
1 x 3	3/4 x 2-1/2	1.875	0.781	0.977	0.234	0.088	0.326	0.391	0.456	0.521	0.586	0.651
1 x 4	3/4 x 3-1/2	2.625	1.531	2.680	0.328	0.123	0.456	0.547	0.638	0.729	0.820	0.911
1 x 6	3/4 x 5-1/2	4.125	3.781	10.40	0.516	0.193	0.716	0.859	1.003	1.146	1.289	1.432
1 x 8	3/4 x 7-1/4	5.438	6.570	23.82	0.680	0.255	0.944	1.133	1.322	1.510	1.699	1.888
1 x 10	3/4 x 9-1/4	6.938	10.70	49.47	0.867	0.325	1.204	1.445	1.686	1.927	2.168	2.409
1 x 12	3/4 x 11-1/4	8.438	15.82	88.99	1.055	0.396	1.465	1.758	2.051	2.344	2.637	2.930
2 x 3	1-1/2 x 2-1/2	3.750	1.563	1.953	0.938	0.703	0.651	0.781	0.911	1.042	1.172	1.302
2 x 4	1-1/2 x 3-1/2	5.250	3.063	5.359	1.313	0.984	0.911	1.094	1.276	1.458	1.641	1.823
2 x 5	1-1/2 x 4-1/2	6.750	5.063	11.39	1.688	1.266	1.172	1.406	1.641	1.875	2.109	2.344
2 x 6	1-1/2 x 5-1/2	8.250	7.563	20.80	2.063	1.547	1.432	1.719	2.005	2.292	2.578	2.865
2 x 8	1-1/2 x 7-1/4	10.88	13.14	47.63	2.719	2.039	1.888	2.266	2.643	3.021	3.398	3.776
2 x 10	1-1/2 x 9-1/4	13.88	21.39	98.93	3.469	2.602	2.409	2.891	3.372	3.854	4.336	4.818
2 x 12	1-1/2 x 11-1/4	16.88	31.64	178.0	4.219	3.164	2.930	3.516	4.102	4.688	5.273	5.859
2 x 14	1-1/2 x 13-1/4	19.88	43.89	290.8	4.969	3.727	3.451	4.141	4.831	5.521	6.211	6.901
3 x 4	2-1/2 x 3-1/2	8.750	5.104	8.932	3.646	4.557	1.519	1.823	2.127	2.431	2.734	3.038
3 x 5	2-1/2 x 4-1/2	11.25	8.438	18.98	4.688	5.859	1.953	2.344	2.734	3.125	3.516	3.906
3 x 6	2-1/2 x 5-1/2	13.75	12.60	34.66	5.729	7.161	2.387	2.865	3.342	3.819	4.297	4.774
3 x 8	2-1/2 x 7-1/4	18.13	21.90	79.39	7.552	9.440	3.147	3.776	4.405	5.035	5.664	6.293
3 x 10	2-1/2 x 9-1/4	23.13	35.65	164.9	9.635	12.04	4.015	4.818	5.621	6.424	7.227	8.030
3 x 12	2-1/2 x 11-1/4	28.13	52.73	296.6	11.72	14.65	4.883	5.859	6.836	7.813	8.789	9.766
3 x 14	2-1/2 x 13-1/4	33.13	73.15	484.6	13.80	17.25	5.751	6.901	8.051	9.201	10.35	11.50
3 x 16	2-1/2 x 15-1/4	38.13	96.90	738.9	15.89	19.86	6.619	7.943	9.266	10.59	11.91	13.24
4 x 4	3-1/2 x 3-1/2	12.25	7.146	12.51	7.146	12.51	2.127	2.552	2.977	3.403	3.828	4.253
4 x 5	3-1/2 x 4-1/2	15.75	11.81	26.58	9.188	16.08	2.734	3.281	3.828	4.375	4.922	5.469
4 x 6	3-1/2 x 5-1/2	19.25	17.65	48.53	11.23	19.65	3.342	4.010	4.679	5.347	6.016	6.684
4 x 8	3-1/2 x 7-1/4	25.38	30.66	111.1	14.80	25.90	4.405	5.286	6.168	7.049	7.930	8.811
4 x 10	3-1/2 x 9-1/4	32.38	49.91	230.8	18.89	33.05	5.621	6.745	7.869	8.993	10.12	11.24
4 x 12	3-1/2 x 11-1/4	39.38	73.83	415.3	22.97	40.20	6.836	8.203	9.570	10.94	12.30	13.67
4 x 14	3-1/2 x 13-1/2	47.25	106.3	717.6	27.56	48.23	8.203	9.844	11.48	13.13	14.77	16.41
4 x 16	3-1/2 x 15-1/2	54.25	140.1	1086.1	31.64	55.38	9.42	11.30	13.19	15.07	16.95	18.84
5 x 5	4-1/2 x 4-1/2	20.25	15.19	34.17	15.19	34.17	3.516	4.219	4.922	5.625	6.328	7.031
6 x 6	5-1/2 x 5-1/2	30.25	27.73	76.26	27.73	76.26	5.252	6.302	7.352	8.403	9.453	10.50
6 x 8	5-1/2 x 7-1/2	41.25	51.56	193.4	37.81	104.0	7.161	8.594	10.03	11.46	12.89	14.32
6 x 10	5-1/2 x 9-1/2	52.25	82.73	393.0	47.90	131.7	9.071	10.89	12.70	14.51	16.33	18.14
6 x 12	5-1/2 x 11-1/2	63.25	121.2	697.1	57.98	159.4	10.98	13.18	15.37	17.57	19.77	21.96
6 x 14	5-1/2 x 13-1/2	74.25	167.1	1128	68.06	187.2	12.89	15.47	18.05	20.63	23.20	25.78
6 x 16	5-1/2 x 15-1/2	85.25	220.2	1707	78.15	214.9	14.80	17.76	20.72	23.68	26.64	29.60
6 x 18	5-1/2 x 17-1/2	96.25	280.7	2456	88.23	242.6	16.71	20.05	23.39	26.74	30.08	33.42
6 x 20	5-1/2 x 19-1/2	107.3	348.6	3398	98.31	270.4	18.62	22.34	26.07	29.79	33.52	37.24
6 x 22	5-1/2 x 21-1/2	118.3	423.7	4555	108.4	298.1	20.53	24.64	28.74	32.85	36.95	41.06
6 x 24	5-1/2 x 23-1/2	129.3	506.2	5948	118.5	325.8	22.44	26.93	31.41	35.90	40.39	44.88
8 x 8	7-1/2 x 7-1/2	56.25	70.31	263.7	70.31	263.7	9.766	11.72	13.67	15.63	17.58	19.53
8 x 10	7-1/2 x 9-1/2	71.25	112.8	535.9	89.06	334.0	12.37	14.84	17.32	19.79	22.27	24.74
8 x 12	7-1/2 x 11-1/2	86.25	165.3	950.5	107.8	404.3	14.97	17.97	20.96	23.96	26.95	29.95
8 x 14	7-1/2 x 13-1/2	101.3	227.8	1538	126.6	474.6	17.58	21.09	24.61	28.13	31.64	35.16
8 x 16	7-1/2 x 15-1/2	116.3	300.3	2327	145.3	544.9	20.18	24.22	28.26	32.29	36.33	40.36
8 x 18	7-1/2 x 17-1/2	131.3	382.8	3350	164.1	615.2	22.79	27.34	31.90	36.46	41.02	45.57
8 x 20	7-1/2 x 19-1/2	146.3	475.3	4634	182.8	685.5	25.39	30.47	35.55	40.63	45.70	50.78
8 x 22	7-1/2 x 21-1/2	161.3	577.8	6211	201.6	755.9	27.99	33.59	39.19	44.79	50.39	55.99
8 x 24	7-1/2 x 23-1/2	176.3	690.3	8111	220.3	826.2	30.60	36.72	42.84	48.96	55.08	61.20
10 x 10	9-1/2 x 9-1/2	90.25	142.9	678.8	142.9	678.8	15.67	18.80	21.94	25.07	28.20	31.34
10 x 12	9-1/2 x 11-1/2	109.3	209.4	1204	173.0	821.7	18.97	22.76	26.55	30.35	34.14	37.93
10 x 14	9-1/2 x 13-1/2	128.3	288.6	1948	203.1	964.5	22.27	26.72	31.17	35.63	40.08	44.53
10 x 16	9-1/2 x 15-1/2	147.3	380.4	2948	233.1	1107	25.56	30.68	35.79	40.90	46.02	51.13
10 x 18	9-1/2 x 17-1/2	166.3	484.9	4243	263.2	1250	28.86	34.64	40.41	46.18	51.95	57.73
10 x 20	9-1/2 x 19-1/2	185.3	602.1	5870	293.3	1393	32.16	38.59	45.03	51.46	57.89	64.32
10 x 22	9-1/2 x 21-1/2	204.3	731.9	7868	323.4	1536	35.46	42.55	49.64	56.74	63.83	70.92
10 x 24	9-1/2 x 23-1/2	223.3	874.4	10270	353.5	1679	38.76	46.51	54.26	62.01	69.77	77.52

SECTION PROPERTIES OF GLUED LAMINATED TIMBER

WESTERN SPECIES (based on 1-1/2" thick laminations)

Net Finished Dimensions b x d inches x inches	Number of Laminations	Area of Section A in²	X-X AXIS Section Modulus S_{xx} in³	X-X AXIS Moment of Inertia I_{xx} in⁴	Y-Y AXIS Section Modulus S_{yy} in³	Y-Y AXIS Moment of Inertia I_{yy} in⁴
2-1/2 x 6	4	15.00	15.00	45.00	6.25	7.81
2-1/2 x 7-1/2	5	18.75	23.44	87.89	7.81	9.77
2-1/2 x 9	6	22.50	33.75	151.9	9.38	11.72
2-1/2 x 10-1/2	7	26.25	45.94	241.2	10.94	13.67
2-1/2 x 12	8	30.00	60.00	360.0	12.50	15.63
2-1/2 x 13-1/2	9	33.75	75.94	512.6	14.06	17.58
2-1/2 x 15	10	37.50	93.75	703.1	15.63	19.53
2-1/2 x 16-1/2	11	41.25	113.4	935.9	17.19	21.48
2-1/2 x 18	12	45.00	135.0	1215	18.75	23.44
2-1/2 x 19-1/2	13	48.75	158.4	1545	20.31	25.39
2-1/2 x 21	14	52.50	183.8	1929	21.88	27.34
2-1/2 x 22-1/2	15	56.25	210.9	2373	23.44	29.30
2-1/2 x 24	16	60.00	240.0	2880	25.00	31.25
2-1/2 x 25-1/2	17	63.75	270.9	3454	26.56	33.20
2-1/2 x 27	18	67.50	303.8	4101	28.13	35.16
3-1/8 x 6	4	18.75	18.75	56.25	9.77	15.26
3-1/8 x 7-1/2	5	23.44	29.30	109.9	12.21	19.07
3-1/8 x 9	6	28.13	42.19	189.8	14.65	22.89
3-1/8 x 10-1/2	7	32.81	57.42	301.5	17.09	26.70
3-1/8 x 12	8	37.50	75.00	450.0	19.53	30.52
3-1/8 x 13-1/2	9	42.19	94.92	640.7	21.97	34.33
3-1/8 x 15	10	46.88	117.2	878.9	24.41	38.15
3-1/8 x 16-1/2	11	51.56	141.8	1170	26.86	41.96
3-1/8 x 18	12	56.25	168.8	1519	29.30	45.78
3-1/8 x 19-1/2	13	60.94	198.0	1931	31.74	49.59
3-1/8 x 21	14	65.63	229.7	2412	34.18	53.41
3-1/8 x 22-1/2	15	70.31	263.7	2966	36.62	57.22
3-1/8 x 24	16	75.00	300.9	3600	39.06	61.04
3-1/8 x 25-1/2	17	79.69	338.7	4318	41.50	64.85
3-1/8 x 27	18	84.38	379.7	5126	43.95	68.66
5-1/8 x 6	4	30.75	30.75	92.25	26.27	67.31
5-1/8 x 7-1/2	5	38.44	48.05	180.2	32.83	84.13
5-1/8 x 9	6	46.13	69.19	311.3	39.40	101.0
5-1/8 x 10-1/2	7	53.81	94.17	494.4	45.96	117.8
5-1/8 x 12	8	61.50	123.0	738.0	52.53	134.6
5-1/8 x 13-1/2	9	69.19	155.7	1051	59.10	151.4
5-1/8 x 15	10	76.88	192.2	1441	65.66	168.3
5-1/8 x 16-1/2	11	84.56	232.5	1919	72.23	185.1
5-1/8 x 18	12	92.25	276.8	2491	78.80	201.9
5-1/8 x 19-1/2	13	99.94	324.8	3167	85.36	218.7
5-1/8 x 21	14	107.6	376.7	3955	91.93	235.6
5-1/8 x 22-1/2	15	115.3	432.4	4865	98.50	252.4
5-1/8 x 24	16	123.0	492.0	5904	105.1	269.2
5-1/8 x 25-1/2	17	130.7	555.4	7082	111.6	286.0
5-1/8 x 27	18	138.4	622.7	8406	118.2	302.9
5-1/8 x 28-1/2	19	146.1	693.8	9887	124.8	319.7
5-1/8 x 30	20	153.8	768.8	11530	131.3	336.5

Figure 17.25 Dimensions and section properties for wood structural elements: sawn lumber and glue-laminated timbers. Courtesy of American Forest and Paper Association, and American Institute of Timber Construction, respectively.

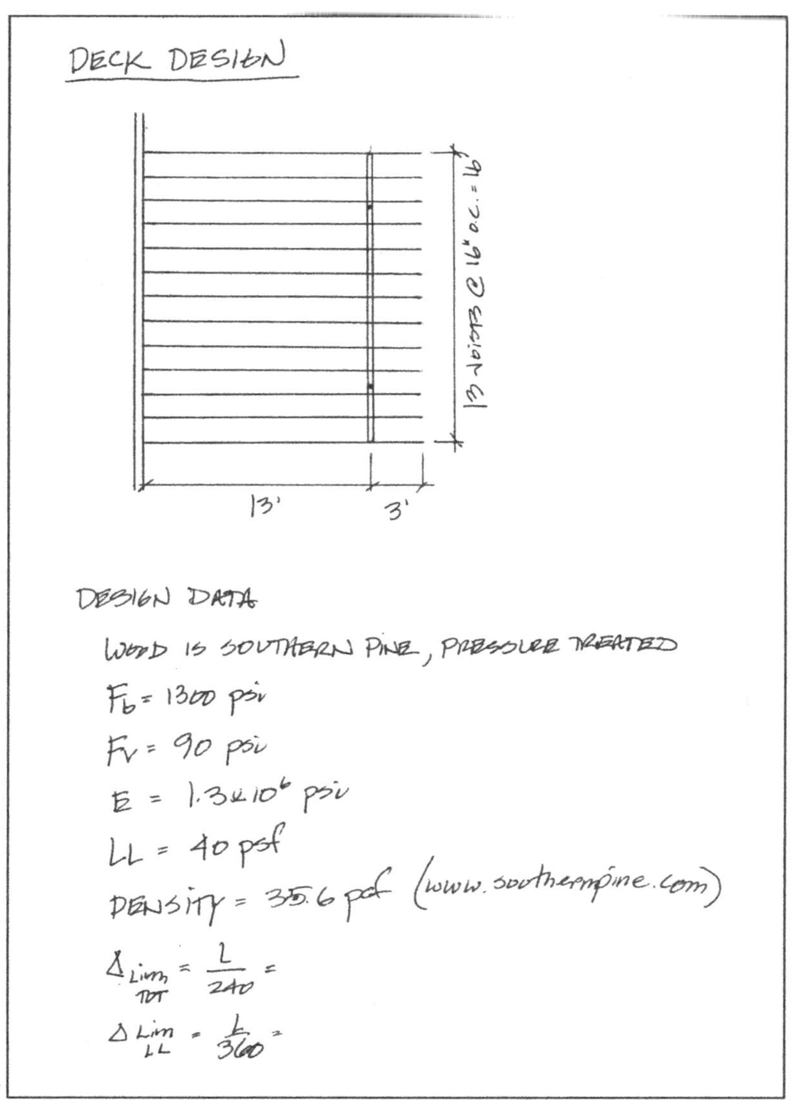

Figure 17.26a As a first step, Dermody shows the framing plan and lists the design values for the wood he will use.

Figures 17.26 a-k courtesy Prof. Robert J. Dermody.

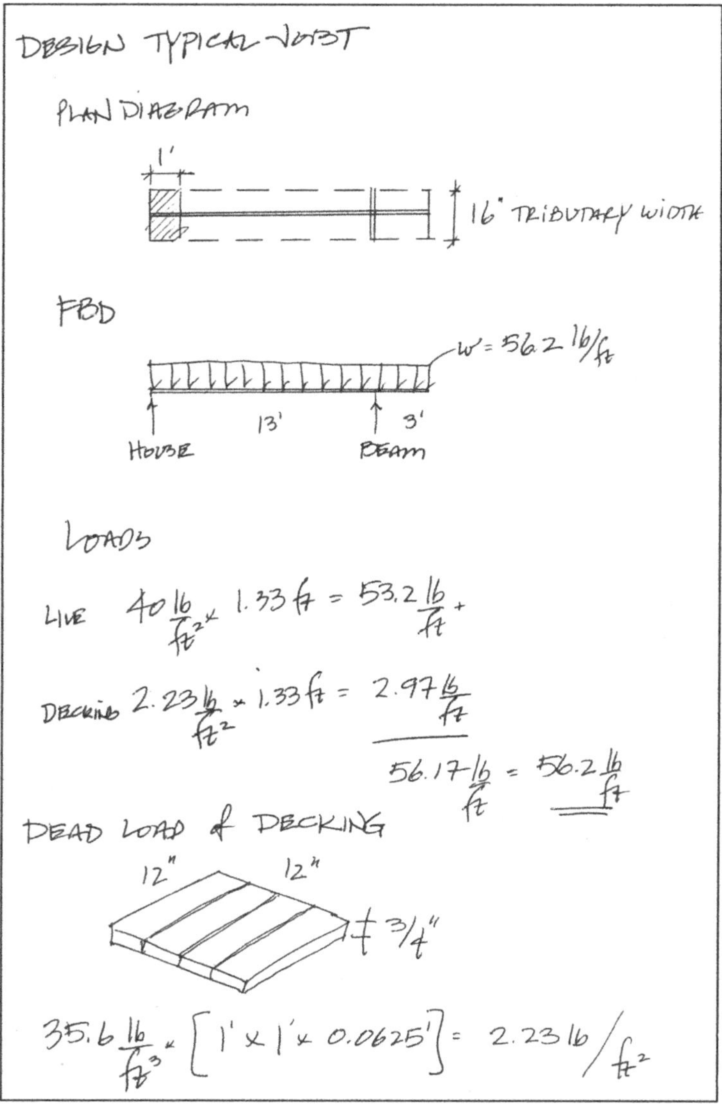

Figure 17.26b Next, Dermody calculates the live load for one joist, along with the dead load of the decking. The width of the tributary area of the joist is 16 in., which is 1.33 ft.

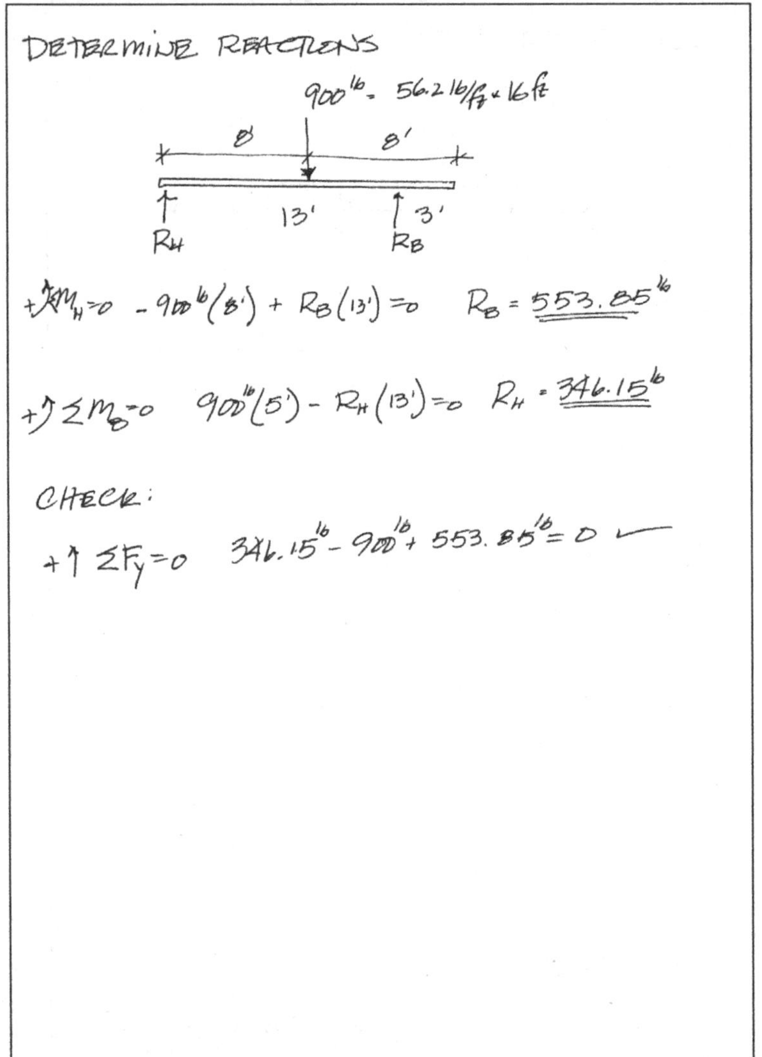

Figure 17.26c He evaluates moments to find the reactions on the joist. The swooping arrow at the start of each line loops around a plus sign, indicating that he is adopting counterclockwise as the positive direction of moments. He writes two moment equations, each using the point of application of one of the reactions as the axis. This yields the two reactions directly. As a check of accuracy, he adds the two reactions to the load on the joist and finds that the sum is equal to the total load.

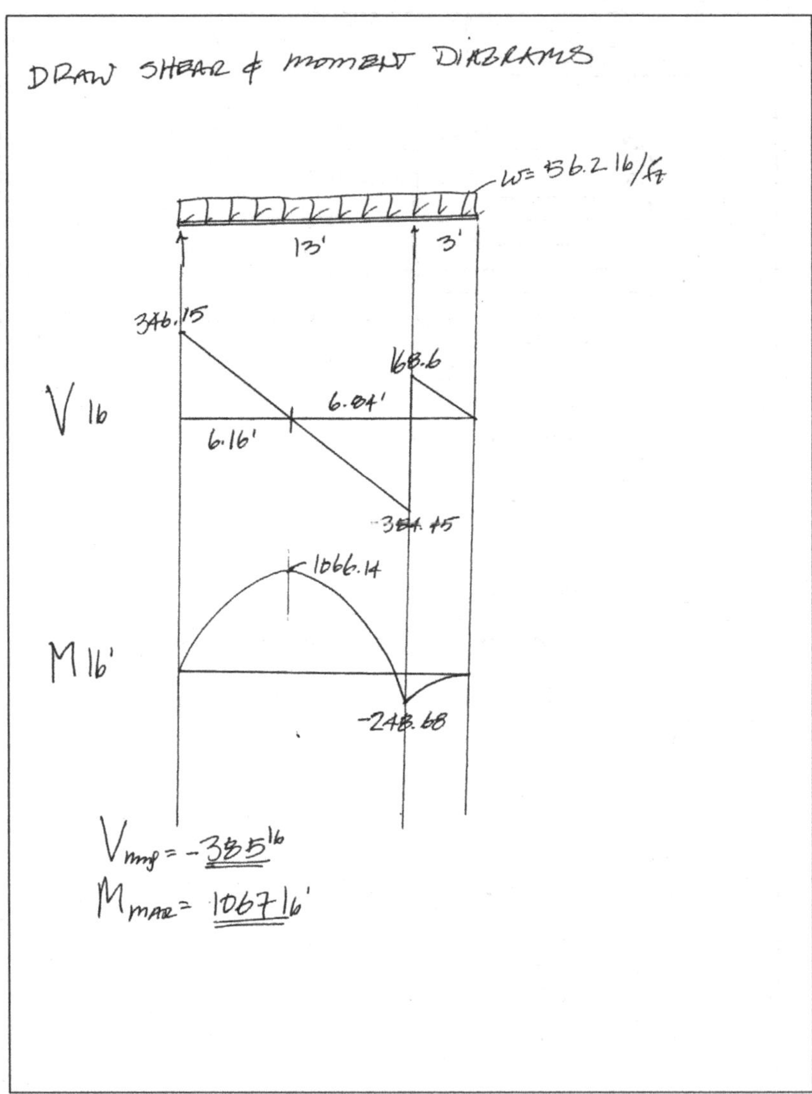

Figure 17.26d Using V and M diagrams, Dermody finds the maximum bending moment in the joist to be 1,067 lb-ft, and the maximum vertical force to be –385 lb. He rounds values for convenience.

SIZE JOIST

$M_{max} = 1066\ lb\text{-}ft$

$S_{req'd} = \frac{M_{max}}{F_b} = \frac{1066\ lb\text{-}ft\ (12\ in/ft)}{1300\ lb/in^2} = 9.84\ in^3$

$S_{req'd} = 9.84\ in^3$

$V_{max} = 385\ lb$

$A_{req'd} = \frac{1.5\,V_{max}}{F_v} = \frac{1.5\,(385\ lb)}{90\ lb/in^2} = 6.42\ in^2$

$A_{req'd} = 6.42\ in^2$

TRY 2x8

$S_{ACT} = 13.14\ in^3$

$A_{ACT} = 10.88\ in^2$

INCLUDE SELF WEIGHT of 2x8

$(1.5'' \times 7.25'' \times 12'') = \frac{130.5\ in^3}{1728\ in^3/ft^3} = 0.08\ ft^3$

$0.08\ ft^3/ft \times 35.6\ lb/ft^3 = 2.69\ lb/ft \approx 2.70\ lb/ft$

Figure 17.26e He assigns a tentative size to the joist. This is done by dividing the maximum bending moment by the allowable stress in bending, to find the required section modulus. Then he evaluates the maximum web stress. He consults a wood design handbook to find a joist size that has both a section modulus and a cross-sectional area equal to or greater than required values. At this point, he adds the self-weight of the joists he has tentatively selected to the total load, and recalculates.

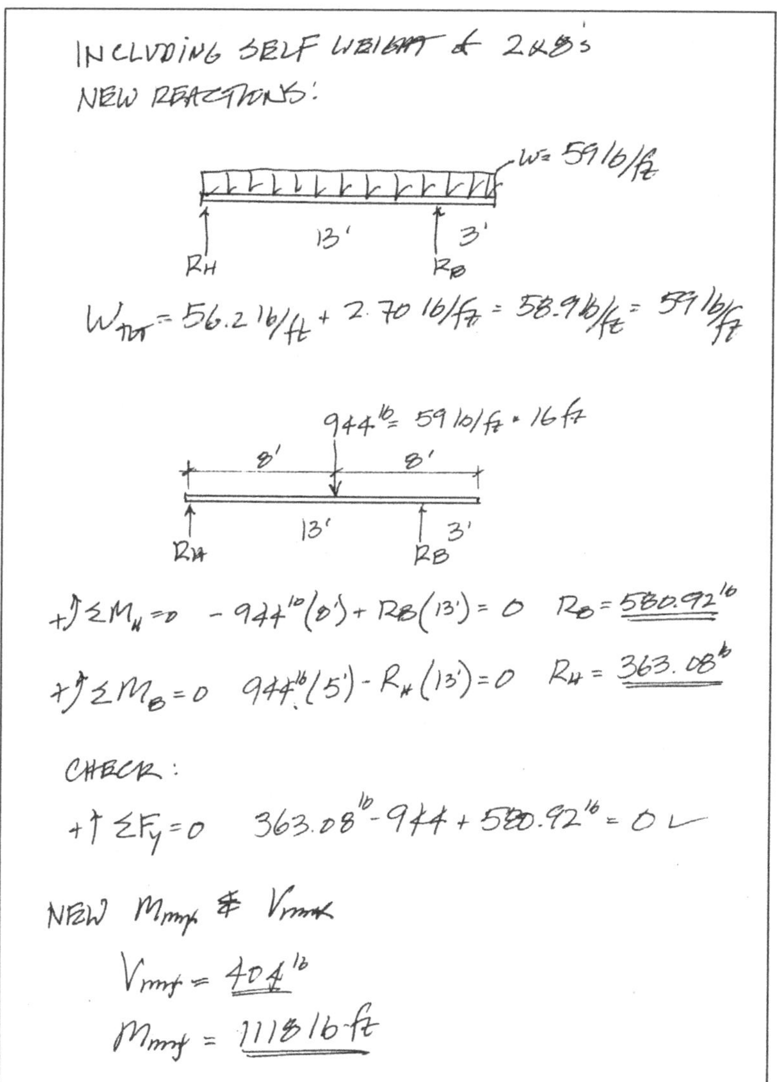

Figure 17.26f His recalculation continues on this page. An alternate way of arriving at the same result would be to estimate the size and weight of the joist and include them in the computation from the start. If the estimated size turns out to be correct, then the resizing can be avoided. If the estimated size is too small, he must recalculate using the actual weight of the joist.

RE-SIZE JOIST

$M_{max} = 1118$ lb-ft

$S_{req'd} = \frac{M_{max}}{F_b} = \frac{1118 \text{ lb-ft} (12 \text{ in/ft})}{1300 \text{ lb/in}^2} = 10.32 \text{ in}^3$

$V_{max} = 404^{lb}$

$A_{req'd} = \frac{1.5 V_{max}}{F_v} = \frac{1.5(404^{lb})}{90 \text{ lb/in}^2} = 6.73 \text{ in}^2$

2x8 WORKS IN BENDING & SHEAR:

$S_{act} = 13.14 \text{ in}^3 > 10.32 \text{ in}^3$ OK ✓

$A_{act} = 10.88 \text{ in}^2 > 6.73 \text{ in}^2$ OK ✓

Figure 17.26g The selected joist size, 2×8, is adequate in bending stress and web stress.

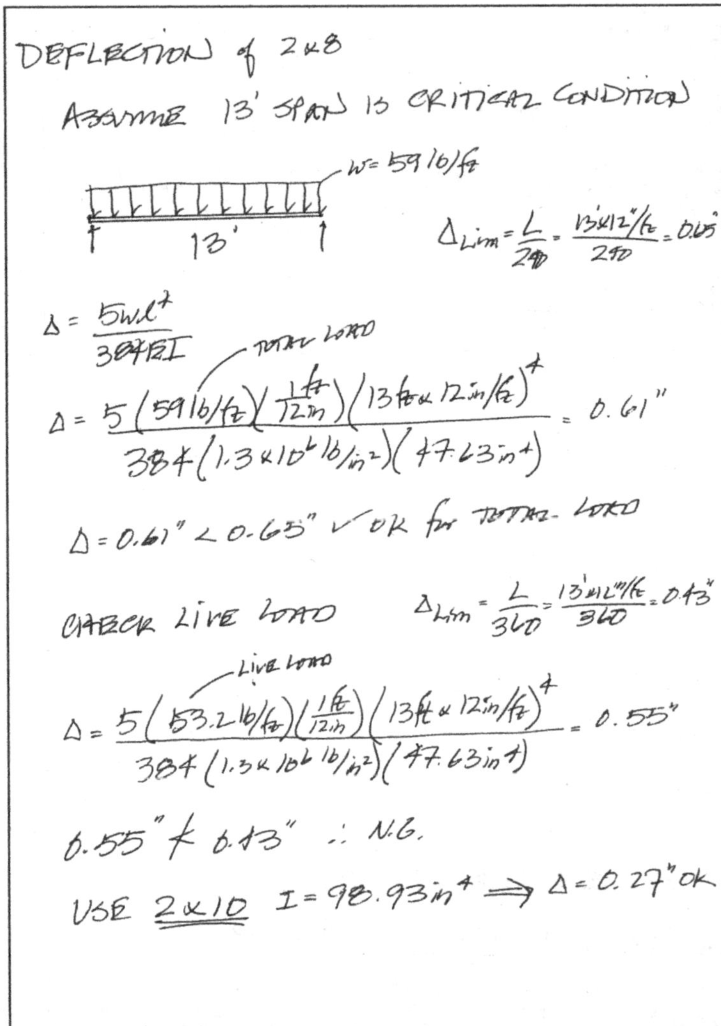

DEFLECTION of 2x8
ASSUME 13' SPAN IS CRITICAL CONDITION
w = 59 lb/ft
13'
Δ Lim = L/240 = 13'x12"/ft / 240 = 0.65"
Δ = 5wℓ⁴ / 384EI
TOTAL LOAD
Δ = 5(59 lb/ft)(1 ft/12 in)(13 ft x 12 in/ft)⁴ / 384(1.3x10⁶ lb/in²)(47.63 in⁴) = 0.61"
Δ = 0.61" < 0.65" ✓ OK for TOTAL LOAD
CHECK LIVE LOAD
Δ Lim = L/360 = 13'x12"/ft / 360 = 0.43"
LIVE LOAD
Δ = 5(53.2 lb/ft)(1 ft/12 in)(13 ft x 12 in/ft)⁴ / 384(1.3x10⁶ lb/in²)(47.63 in⁴) = 0.55"
0.55" ≮ 0.43" ∴ N.G.
USE 2x10 I = 98.93 in⁴ ⇒ Δ = 0.27" OK

Figure 17.26h Now Dermody checks the deflection of the 2×8 joist. He assumes that the critical condition occurs when there is no load on the overhanging portion of the joist. There are two reasons to make this assumption: (1) It is conservative, in that the dead load of the overhanging portion will decrease the deflection of the main span slightly; and (2) an expression for the deflection of a beam with overhang is complicated and takes longer to solve than that for a simple span. He checks deflections against two different criteria: one for total load, with a maximum permissible deflection of $L/240$, and another for live load only, with a maximum of $L/360$. The live-load deflection is excessive, more than can be accounted for by the simplifying assumption, so he adopts a 2×10 joist instead of a 2×8. Deflection has proven to be the limiting factor in selecting the joists.

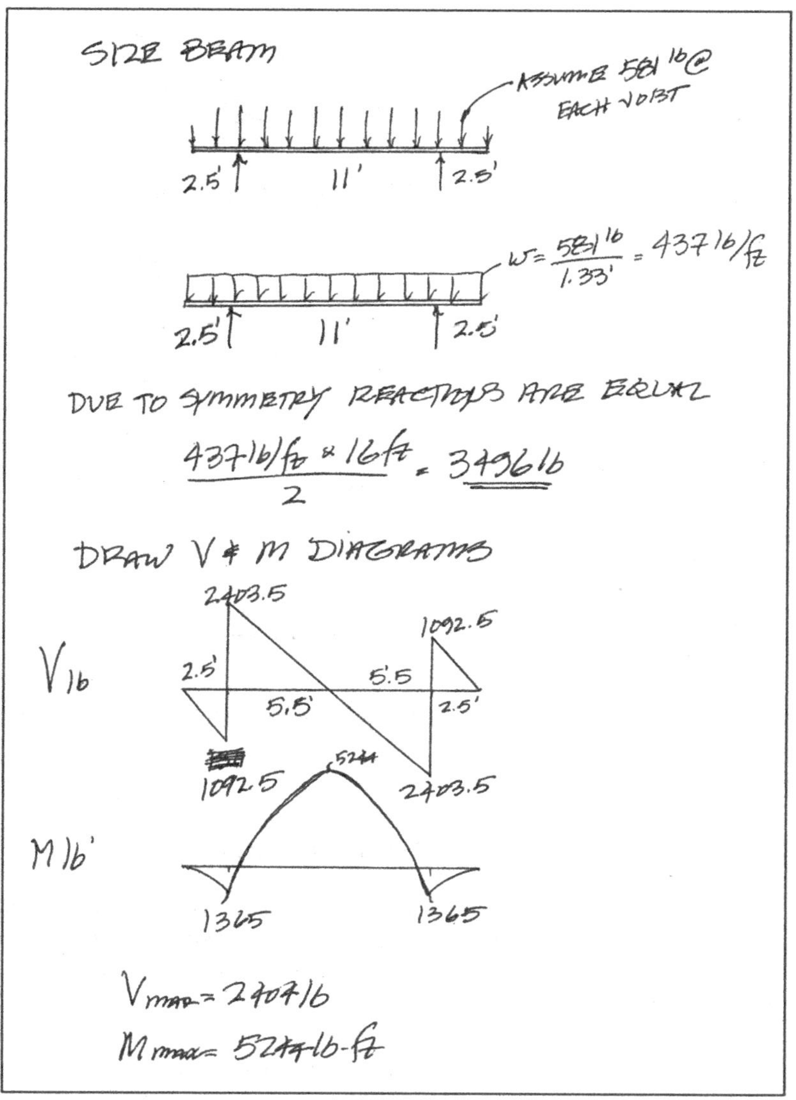

Figure 17.26i The beam computations follow the same procedure as that used for the joist.

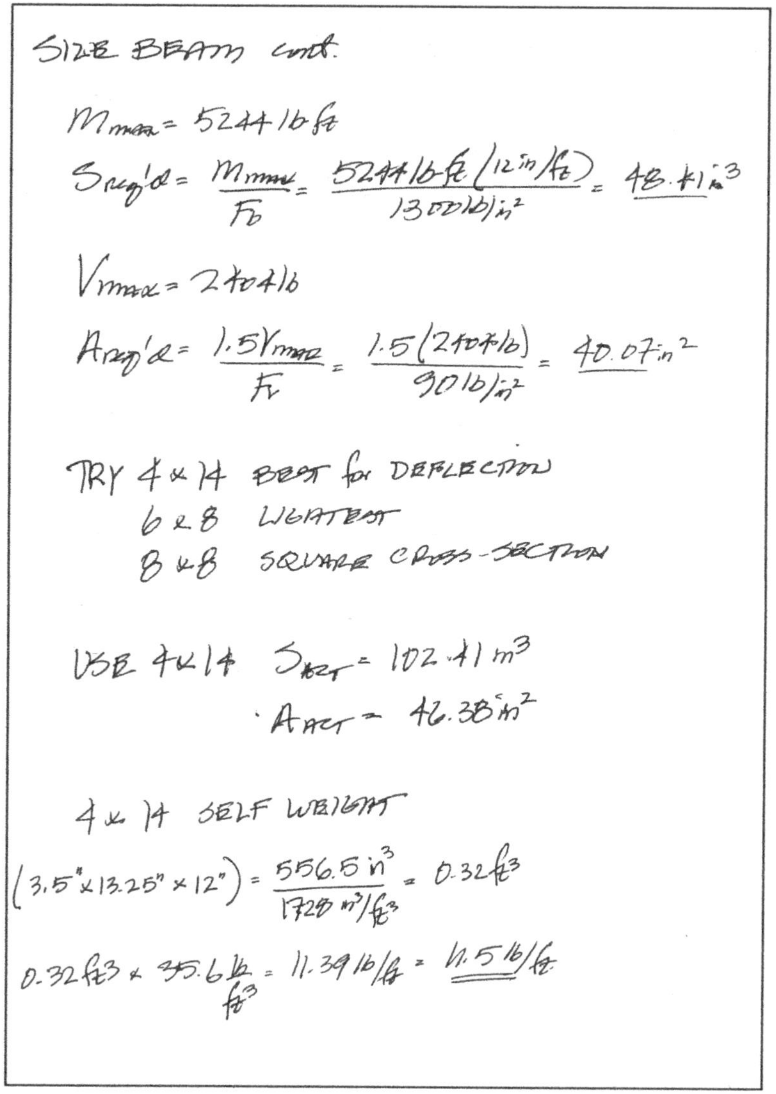

SIZE BEAM cont.

$M_{max} = 5244 \text{ lb-ft}$

$S_{req'd} = \frac{M_{max}}{F_b} = \frac{5244 \text{ lb-ft} (12 \text{ in/ft})}{1300 \text{ lb/in}^2} = 48.41 \text{ in}^3$

$V_{max} = 2404 \text{ lb}$

$A_{req'd} = \frac{1.5 V_{max}}{F_v} = \frac{1.5 (2404 \text{ lb})}{90 \text{ lb/in}^2} = 40.07 \text{ in}^2$

TRY 4×14 BEST for DEFLECTION
6×8 LIGHTEST
8×8 SQUARE CROSS-SECTION

USE 4×14 $S_{ACT} = 102.41 \text{ in}^3$
$A_{ACT} = 46.38 \text{ in}^2$

4×14 SELF WEIGHT

$(3.5" \times 13.25" \times 12") = \frac{556.5 \text{ in}^3}{1728 \text{ in}^3/\text{ft}^3} = 0.32 \text{ ft}^3$

$0.32 \text{ ft}^3 \times 35.6 \frac{\text{lb}}{\text{ft}^3} = 11.39 \text{ lb/ft} = 11.5 \text{ lb/ft}$

Figure 17.26j In the handbook table shown in Figure 17.25, Dermody finds three different beam sizes that satisfy the requirements for bending stress and web stress. He selects the one that is stiffest, 4×14.

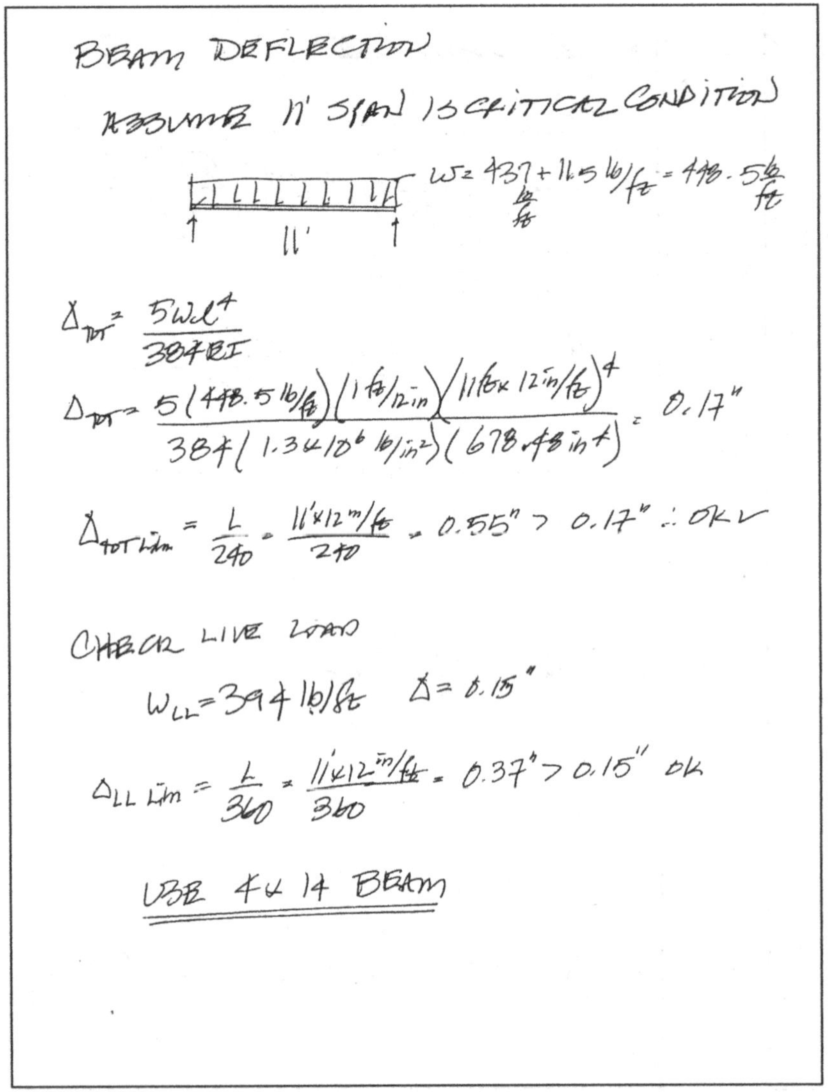

BEAM DEFLECTION

ASSUME 11' SPAN IS CRITICAL CONDITION

$w = 437\ \frac{lb}{ft} + 11.5\ lb/ft = 448.5\ \frac{lb}{ft}$

11'

$\Delta_{TOT} = \frac{5wl^4}{384EI}$

$\Delta_{TOT} = \frac{5(448.5\ lb/ft)(1\ ft/12\ in)(11\ ft \times 12\ in/ft)^4}{384(1.3\times10^6\ lb/in^2)(678.48\ in^4)} = 0.17''$

$\Delta_{TOT\ Lim} = \frac{L}{240} = \frac{11' \times 12\ in/ft}{240} = 0.55'' > 0.17''$ ∴ OK ✓

CHECK LIVE LOAD

$w_{LL} = 394\ lb/ft \quad \Delta = 0.15''$

$\Delta_{LL\ Lim} = \frac{L}{360} = \frac{11' \times 12\ in/ft}{360} = 0.37'' > 0.15''$ OK

USE 4×14 BEAM

Figure 17.26k Dermody checks the beam deflection, making the conservative assumption that the overhanging ends of the beam are not loaded. The 4×14 beam passes all tests and he has now completed the task of sizing all the members.

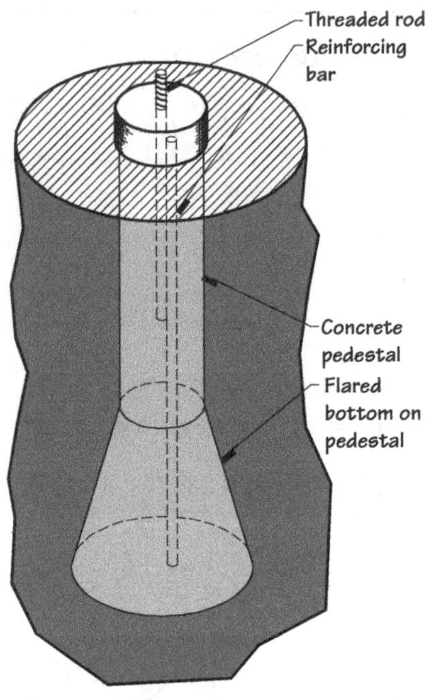

Figure 17.27 Each foundation for the deck is made of a concrete pedestal flared at the bottom to increase its bearing area on the soil and hold the deck down against wind uplift.

DETAILING THE DECK

The deck is founded on two round concrete pedestals, each constructed in a hole dug to the depth necessary to avoid soil freezing in winter (Figure 17.27). The bottom of the hole is enlarged to provide sufficient bearing area for the expected load. The enlargement also protects the deck and foundations from being lifted by wind forces. A paperboard tube a foot in diameter, waxed or plastic-coated so that concrete will not stick to it, is cut to length, placed in the hole, and supported temporarily with scraps of lumber. A reinforcing bar is placed vertically in the center of the tube, and a long anchor bolt or threaded rod is wired to it. The anchor bolt must be located with fair accuracy in order for it to align with the hardware for the beam, so measurements are taken and the bolt is held in position with wires or a wooden template. Then the tube is filled to the top with concrete and the top edges of the concrete cylinder are beveled with a mason's trowel to remove any sharp protrusions and give a neater appearance.

A day or two later, the paperboard tube is unwound from the concrete pedestal and discarded. The hole around the pedestal is backfilled with compacted soil. A galvanized sheet metal post base is bolted to the top of each foundation. Although it is intended to hold a post, it will serve our purpose, attaching the beam firmly to the foundation, very well. The post base is designed so that it can accommodate a bolt that is an inch or two out of place and still end up in the right location. The beam is leveled carefully, marked, drilled, and bolted or nailed to the post base.

Meanwhile, the attachment to the house is being prepared, as detailed in Figure 17.28. Galvanized steel joist hangers are nailed to the header joist at locations 16 in. apart. Corresponding joist locations are also measured and marked on the top of the beam. The joists are laid in position, checked to be sure that they are level, and shimmed if necessary to bring them all into a flat, level plane. Diagonal measurements establish that the deck is a perfect square. Then the joists are nailed to the joist hangers and to galvanized steel framing clips that anchor them down to the beam. A header joist finishes off the outer edge of the deck. The decking is fastened down with galvanized or stainless steel nails or screws driven by a nail gun or screw gun.

FURTHER NOTES ON WOOD STRUCTURES

Traditionally, wood has been used for joists, rafters, and beams in the form of rectangular, prismatic shapes of lumber sawn directly from tree trunks. Shapes analogous to steel wide-flange shapes would be more efficient in their use of material, but they would be difficult to make in a traditional sawmill, and their thin webs would be weak against web forces.

The lumber market has changed dramatically in recent years because of the scarcity of old-growth forests that are available for harvest, and the ensuing rise

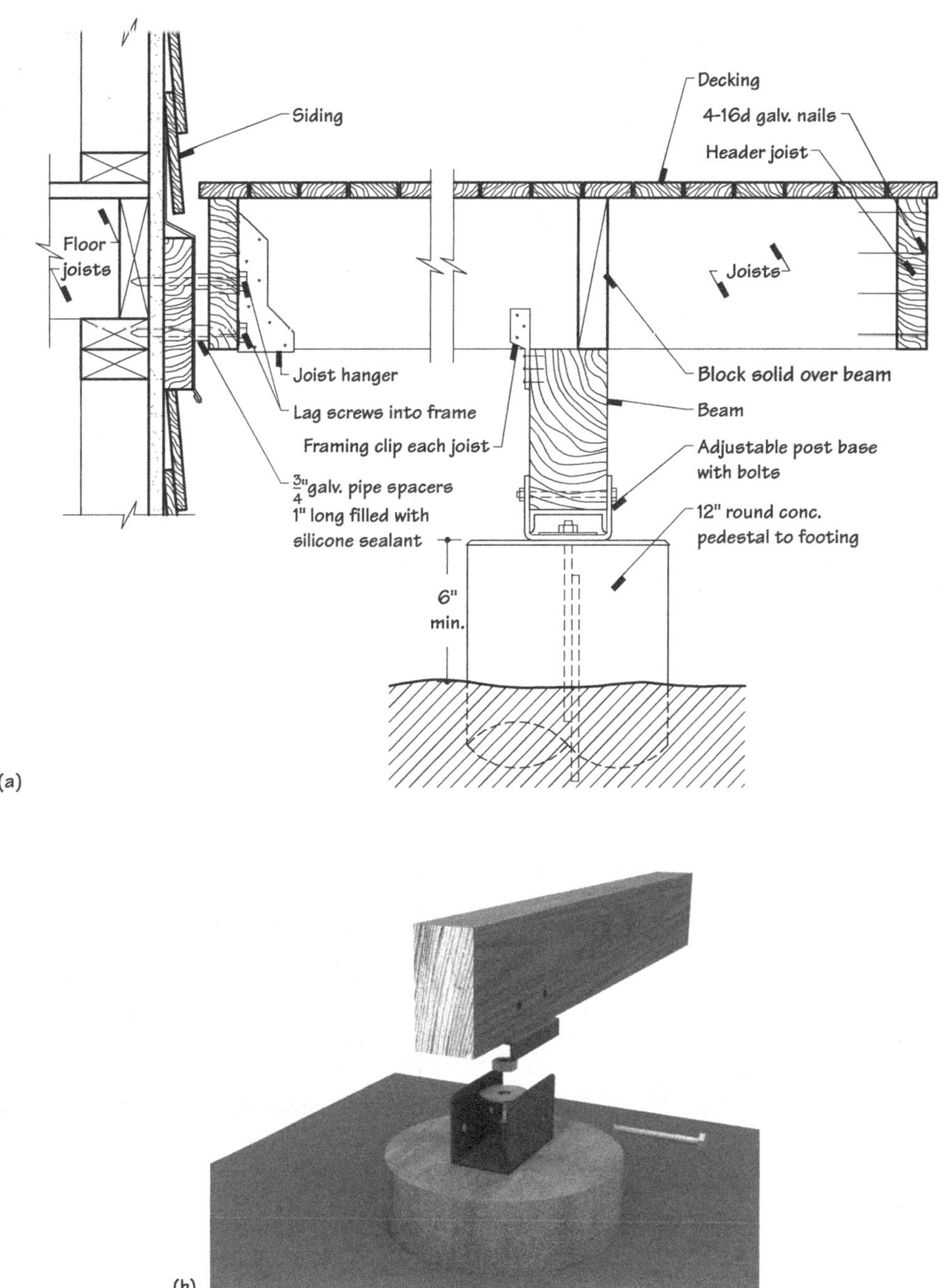

Figure 17.28 Details of the deck.

in price and decline in quality of lumber in general. A number of structural products manufactured from wood fiber have been developed, tested, approved by code agencies, and brought to market. These are based on either very narrow strips of thin wood veneers, once used only for plywood, or long shreds of wood. The veneer-based products are slightly stronger, but the shreds represent a much more sustainable approach to the utilization of trees because they can be made from branches, small trunks, crooked trees, mill scraps, and the rounded exterior slabs that are normally discarded when sawing lumber from round logs.

Wood *I-joists* are similar in principle to wide-flange steel shapes (Figure 17.29). The flanges are built up of wood veneers glued securely together. These flanges are stronger than solid lumber because the knots and other defects have been cut out of the veneers. A groove is milled into the flange pieces to receive a glue-coated edge of a web that is made either of plywood or oriented strand board (OSB). (Plywood is produced by gluing together sheets of veneer. OSB is made from adhesive-coated shreds of wood that are placed in thin layers, combed to orient the shreds in structurally desirable directions, pressed tightly together, and cured by the application of heat.) The plywood or OSB of the webs is more resistant to diagonal web stresses than solid lumber.

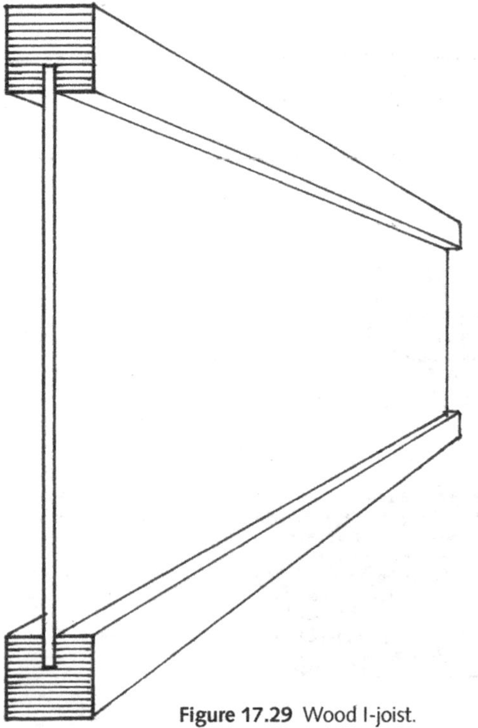

Figure 17.29 Wood I-joist.

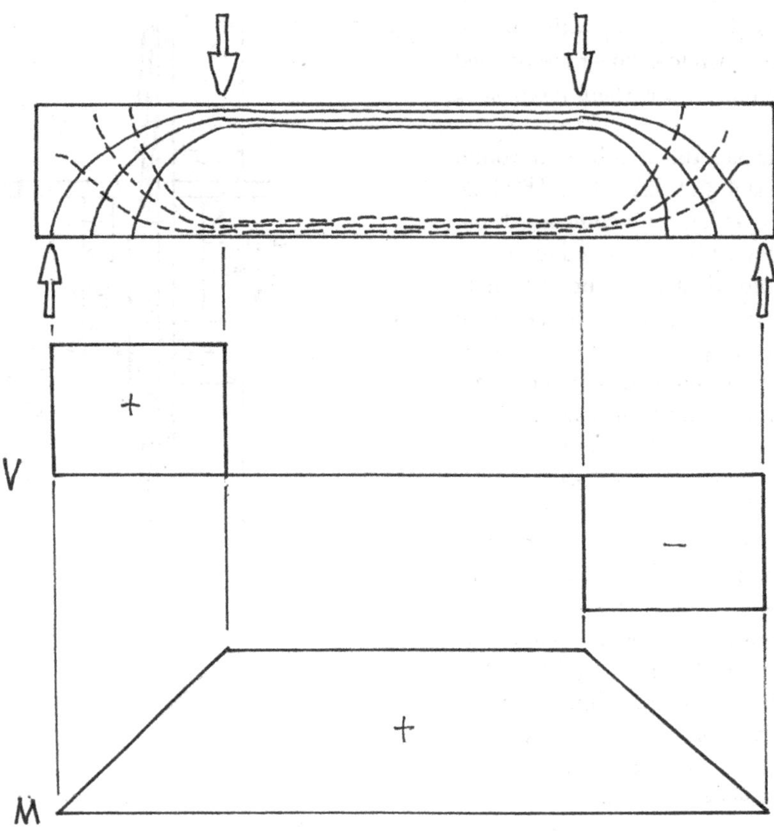

Figure 17.30 Flow of forces in a prismatic beam with a region of constant moment.

I-joists have a number of advantages over solid wood joists. They are very stiff. They can be produced in much longer pieces and greater depths than are economical or practical in solid lumber. They are lighter and easier to carry than solid joists. They are straighter and more dimensionally stable in changing humidity. When properly used, they produce a stronger, stiffer, quieter floor than solid joists. They are not suitable for outdoor use such as our deck, however.

Rectangular wood beams have also undergone a revolution. Until recently, we had a choice of sawn wood beams or beams that were glue-laminated from smaller, squared pieces of lumber. Beams are now available that are built of wood veneers or shreds of wood glued and pressed together. These are stronger and stiffer than solid wood beams, more dimensionally stable, and often more economical.

SHAPING BEAMS FOR GREATER EFFICIENCY

If we examine the flow of forces in a rectangular beam that is loaded at its quarter points, as in Figure 17.30, we find that although there is lattice flow, as expected, in the first and last quarters of the beam, flow in the center half of the span is parallel. The moment diagram for this loading shows why this is so: The bending moment is constant through the middle half of the beam. The constancy of the bending moment is matched by the constancy of the longitudinal beam profile, so that the longitudinal trajectories do not need to veer off to change the resisting moment in this region. Energy is not being expended in reducing the forces in trajectories, as it is in a lattice pattern. As a result, the beam is acting with increased efficiency, utilizing its material more fully. The behavior of this beam is verified by a foam beam loaded at its quarter points (Figure 17.31). There are no web stresses in the middle half, only a linear distribution of longitudinal tensions and compressions.

This behavior can be extended to any loading pattern by shaping the beam's longitudinal profile to match the bending moment diagram. If the depth of the beam is everywhere proportional to the bending moment, the internal flow will be parallel rather than lattice. Consider the beam in Figure 17.32, which has a triangular profile for its middle quarters. When it carries a single load at its center, its flow pattern is parallel rather than lattice in the triangular portion of the beam, because the depth in this portion is everywhere proportional to the bending moment. The end quarters, which do not follow the shape of the moment diagram for this loading, show substantial diagonal tension and compression. The principle extends to multiple concentrated loads and distributed loads (Figure 17.33). Nonworking material can be eliminated from most such beam forms, further increasing their efficiency.

How efficiently do these funicular-profile beams utilize material? Earlier we noted that overall efficiency for a prismatic beam with a uniformly distributed load is about one-third. In a beam of equal span with a parabolic profile, the material will be working, on average, to nearly two-thirds of its capacity.

Caution is required in shaping beams in this way. If a beam is always loaded in the same pattern, then we can shape the profile for parallel flow. But if another loading pattern is applied to this beam, then lattice flow, often disorderly, will ensue, and stresses may become intense in portions of the beam. Funicular-profile beams should be checked to be sure that they are configured to resist every conceivable loading pattern.

In Chapter 22, we will develop a structure whose beams are shaped to resemble their bending moment diagrams.

Figure 17.31 The circles in the center half of the span of this foam beam have not distorted when the beam is loaded at its quarter points. This shows that there is parallel flow throughout this portion of the beam. The circles in the end quarters have become diagonal ellipses, indicating lattice flow.
Photo: David M. Foxe.

EXPLOITING CONTINUITY: GERBER BEAMS

Beams that are continuous over two or more spans have substantially lower bending moments than simply supported beams. But long beams are often difficult to transport and handle on the construction site, and foundation subsidence and normal temperature expansion and contraction can cause unanticipated and sometimes destructive stresses in them.

These disadvantages can largely be overcome by adding hinges to continuous beams at points of inflection, which are also points of zero bending moment (Figure 17.34). If there is no bending moment at a given location on the span of the beam, then adding a hinge at this point does not alter the behavior of the beam. If one goes a step farther to shape the longitudinal profiles of the component beam segments to match the bending moment diagram, an efficient, highly expressive beam is created. This concept, which may be applied to solid beams and trusses alike, was patented in 1866 by the Bavarian engineer Heinrich Gerber (1832–1912).

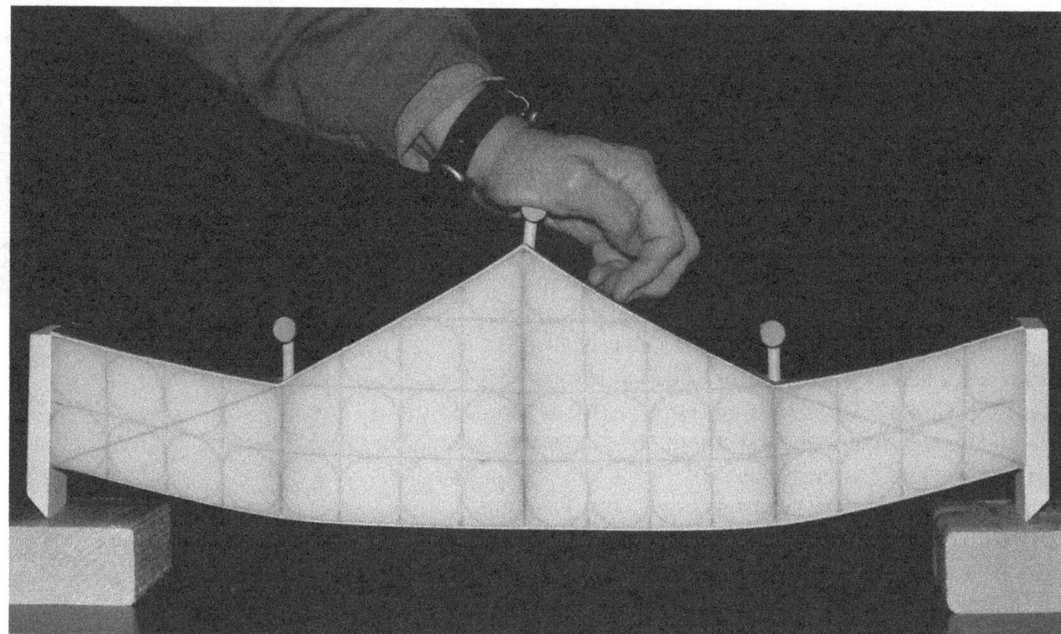

▶**Figure 17.32** A load at midspan does not induce lattice flow in the triangular portion of the beam, only in the prismatic ends.
Photo: Edward Allen.

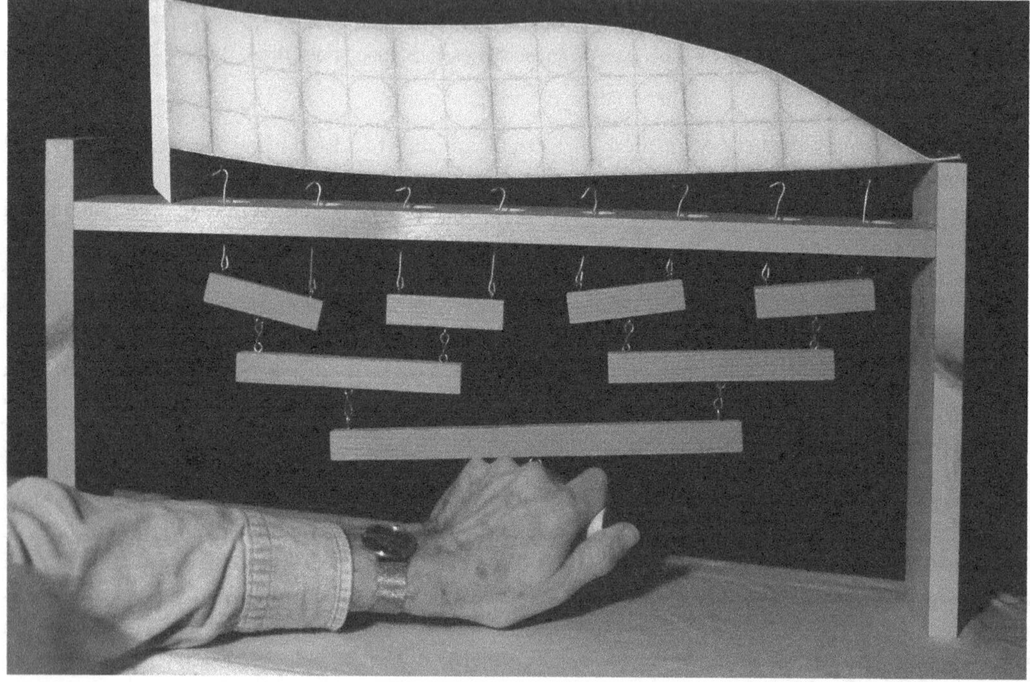

Figure 17.33 This beam is loaded with a harness beneath that distributes the overall load equally to eight loading points. The undistorted circles in the half of the beam that is shaped like the parabolic moment diagram for a uniform loading indicate parallel flow everywhere in this half. The distortion of the circles into diagonal ellipses in the prismatic half indicate lattice flow.
Photo: David M. Foxe.

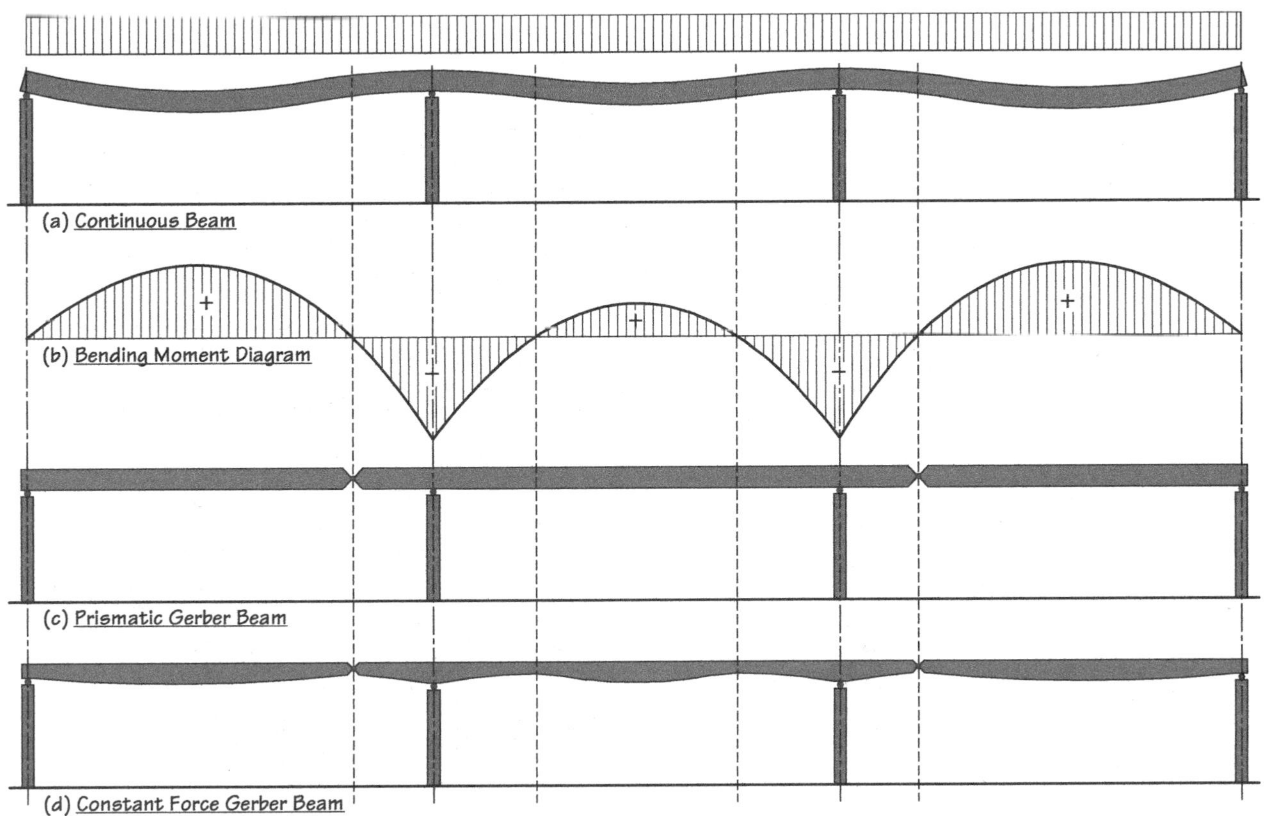

Figure 17.34 Gerber beams are provided with hinges at points of zero bending moment to gain the efficiency of continuous beams with shorter pieces of material. They may also be shaped to resemble the bending moment diagram.

MICHELL STRUCTURES

A century ago, the Australian mathematician and educator J. H. Michell (1863–1940) derived forms that are theoretically of minimum weight for resisting a point load with a planar structure. These bulbous patterns are identical to the flow patterns established in plates of infinite extent by similar loading patterns (Figure 17.35). It is not immediately obvious that these are the most efficient forms possible, but analysis shows that it is true (Figure 17.36). Their depths and the slenderness of their members are deterrents to their wider use, but proposals have been put forward for wind bracing of tall buildings whose form is based on Michell's shapes (Figure 17.37).

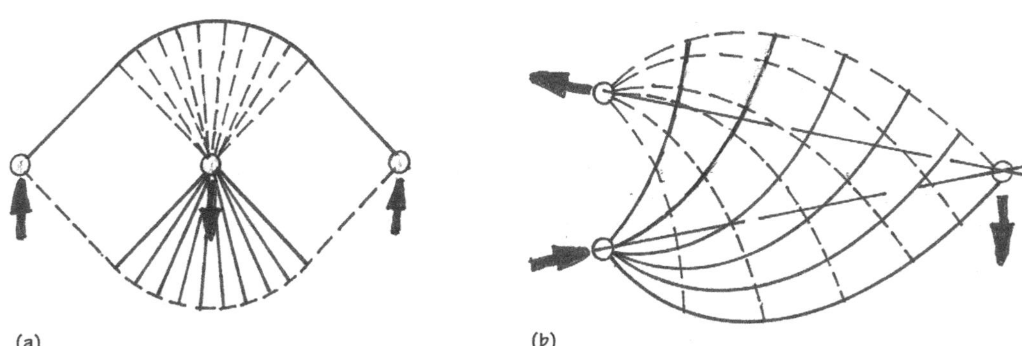

Figure 17.35 Two Michell beams: (a) for a simply supported beam with a single load at midspan, and (b) for a cantilevered beam with a single load at the tip.

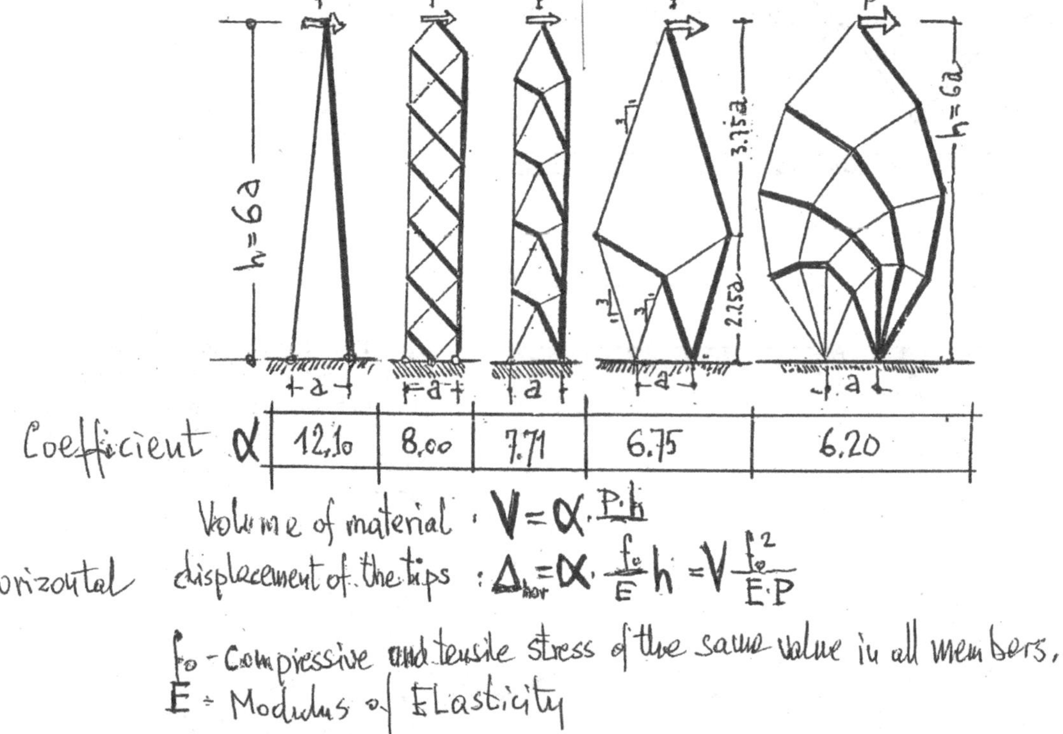

Figure 17.36 An analysis by Wacław Zalewski of five different configurations for an end-loaded cantilever truss. The coefficient alpha is an index of the material efficiency of the truss; the greatest efficiency occurs in the truss that resembles the lattice pattern and which extends laterally beyond its supports. The last truss is a Michell configuration.

Figure 17.37 A proposed high-rise building design by engineer Wacław Zalewski and architect Wojciech Zablocki that features Michell truss wind bracing as a feature of the exterior expression of the building. This would use substantially less material than conventional patterns of wind bracing.

Exercises

1. Draw a floor plan for a child's playhouse, 8 ft by 10 ft in plan. The house is supported by concrete piers at the four corners. The floor is made of 3/4-in. OSB on wood joists spaced at 16 in. Draw a framing plan for the floor and find the required sizes of all members of the frame. Assume design values of stress that are 20 percent lower than those of southern pine that were used in the example in this chapter. Show all calculations.

2. What size southern pine beam is required for a beam that supports a factory crane that weighs a maximum of 2,500 lb in the middle of a 24-ft span? The beam is laterally supported to prevent buckling. Include the self-weight of the beam. Show all calculations.

3. A wood vertical window mullion is 13 ft high and is spaced 7 ft from similar mullions on either side. It is made of Douglas fir, which has design stress values similar to those of southern pine. It supports glass that is subjected to maximum wind pressure of 17 psf. Find a member size for this mullion such that it is sufficiently strong in bending and does not exceed a deflection of $L/240$. (Hint: A mullion is a beam turned on its end. It acts against horizontal wind forces. The self-weight of the mullion does not enter into this determination.)

4. How would the deck example be different if the deck met the house not on one side but on two sides that are at right angles to one another? On three sides? Explain the similarities and differences in design approaches for these constraints and opportunities.

5. Find an example of a deck attached to another main structure and make a measured drawing of its components if they are visible. How are issues of watertightness and other weather-resisting measures evident in its actual construction? Can you find out what kinds of loading it has experienced or is used for currently? What deflections are noticeable?

Key Terms and Concepts

bending moment, M

$$M_R = f_b^{max} \frac{bd^2}{6} \quad [17\text{-}1]$$

$$M = f_b^{max} S \quad [17\text{-}2]$$

$$f_b^{max} = \frac{M_{max}}{S} \quad [17\text{-}3]$$

$$f_b^{max} = \frac{6M_{max}}{bd^2} \quad [17\text{-}4]$$

resisting moment

depth-to-span ratio

longitudinal stress

bending stress, f_b

web stress, f_v

truss model

K-truss

modified K-truss

principle of least work

neutral axis, neutral plane

stress block

$$f_v^{max} = \frac{3V_{ext}}{2bd} \quad [17\text{-}5]$$

$$f_v^{max} = 1.5\frac{V_{ext}}{A} \quad [17\text{-}6]$$

$$f_{c\perp} = \frac{R}{bl_B} \quad [17\text{-}7]$$

total longitudinal bending force, TF_t and TF_c

depth of beam, d

width of beam, b

arm of internal forces

arm of resisting moment

section modulus, S

$$\Delta_{max} = \frac{5}{384}\frac{WL^3}{EI} \quad [17\text{-}8]$$

$$\Delta_{max} = \frac{5}{384}\frac{wL^4}{EI} \quad [17\text{-}9]$$

self-weight

bearing stress

stress perpendicular to grain, parallel to grain

moment of inertia, I

"shear" stress in beams

Gerber beams

Michell beams

Further Resources

Claus Mattheck (translated by W. Linnard). *Design in Nature: Learning from Trees.* Dresden: Springer, 2004. Analyses of trees, bones, and other examples from nature are used to illustrate how stress and bending actions influence growth and strength. These lessons are extended toward models for structures with efficient material configurations.

CHAPTER 18

Bending Resistance in Beams of Any Shape

- *Properties of complex cross-sectional shapes*
- *Moment of inertia*
- *Composite action*
- *Designing bays of steel framing*

We're designing an 11-story office building that will be framed with structural steel (Figure 18.1). We have reached the stage of preliminary design where we must lay out the frame and determine the sizes of the beams and girders (Figure 18.2). We need to consider the placement of columns in the structural bays, as we discussed in Chapter 15, and we will need to expand our knowledge of the bending resistance of beams from Chapters 16 and 17 to understand how to assign sizes to beams with complex cross-sectional shapes.

STEEL

The *steel* used in structural framing is composed of iron that has been refined so that it contains about three-tenths of 1 percent carbon. This reduction in carbon content produces a metal that is ductile and strong. Today, most steel in the United States is manufactured from recycled steel scrap in electric furnaces. The quality is carefully monitored throughout manufacture to assure that it is very high. Various grades of steel are available in varying strengths, but all structural steels, even those with very high strengths, have the same modulus of elasticity, about 29,000,000 psi. Structural steel is usually designed with an allowable stress in bending of 24,000 psi.

Production of Shapes

Steel is *hot-rolled* into structural elements, referred to as *shapes*, in a steel mill by passing hot steel blanks through a series of specially formed rollers that squeeze the steel into the desired form (Figure 18.3). The hot-rolled shape most commonly used in framing is the *wide-flange*, a more efficient variation of the now-obsolete American Standard shape often referred to as an I-beam. We learned in the previous chapters that bending stress in a beam increases linearly from zero at the neutral axis to maximum values at the very top and bottom faces of the beam (the material in the top and bottom faces is often called the *extreme fibers*). Only the material in the extreme fibers is working to its full allowable stress when the beam is subjected to its maximum safe bending moment. This means that we could use material more efficiently by shaping the cross section of a beam so as to place as much material as possible near the top and bottom faces. This is the rationale for the wide-flange shape. The top and bottom *flanges* contain most of the metal. They are connected by a vertical *web* that is usually thinner than the flanges. The role of the web is to transfer the lattice-pattern flows (see Chapter 17) from one flange to the other.

Wide-flange shapes are produced in nominal sizes that range from 4 to 18 in. in increments of 2 in., and from 21 to 36 in. in 3-in. increments; 40-in.-deep shapes are available from some mills. By adjusting the spacing of the rollers, a mill produces shapes

Figure 18.1 An ironworker guides a wide-flange steel beam toward its position in a building frame.
Photo courtesy of Bethlehem Steel Corporation.

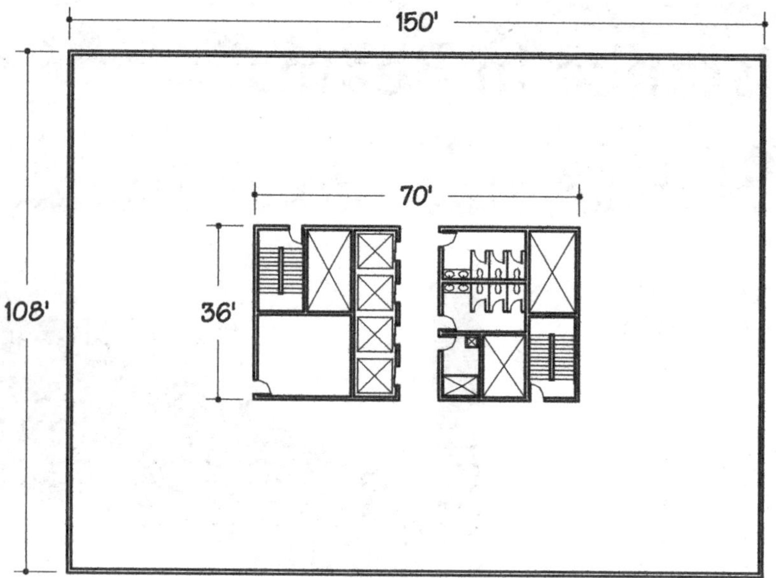

Figure 18.2 A preliminary floor plan for a small office building.

of each nominal size designation in a wide range of actual thicknesses of flange metal, giving the structural designer a large array of choices of members.

Wide-flange shapes are produced in two basic proportions: ones that are much deeper than they are wide, which are intended for use as beams; and ones that are more or less square in cross section, which are intended as columns (Figure 18.4).

Many other hot-rolled shapes are produced for structural use, including *angles, channels, tees, plates,* and *bars* both rectangular and round (Figure 18.3). Angles are particularly useful in connecting steel members to create a frame, and as members of light trusses, where they are sometimes used singly and other times in pairs that are fastened symmetrically to either side of connector plates. Channels are often used as very small beams and as truss members. Tees, which are made by cutting wide-flange shapes longitudinally along the center of the web, are useful chiefly in connections. Steel *pipes* and *tubes,* round, square, and rectangular, are made by bending steel plate into the desired form and welding the longitudinal seam (Figure 18.5).

Steel is also rolled into thin sheets that may be passed through shaped rollers to produce sheets of *corrugated decking* for floors and roofs. The corrugation adds bending resistance. Decking is available in many depths and corrugation patterns, to accommodate different spans and uses (Figure 18.6).

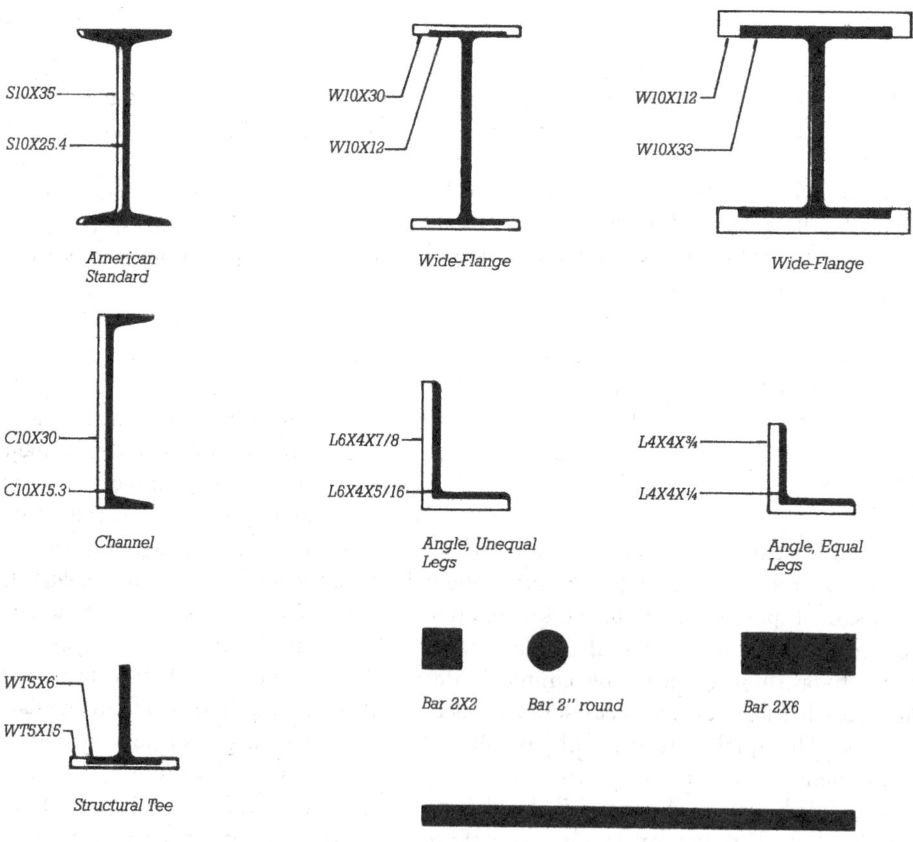

Figure 18.3 Hot-rolled steel shapes.

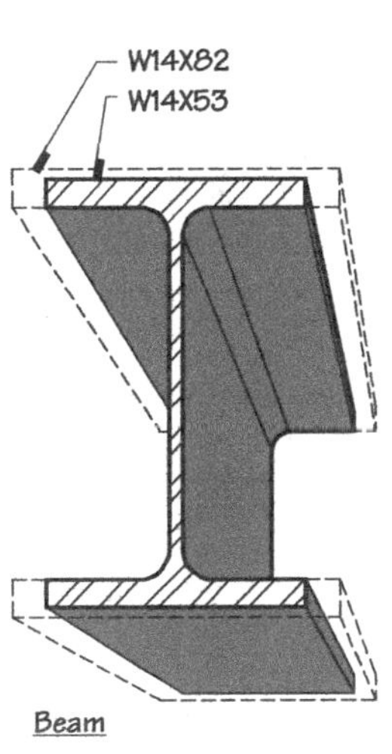

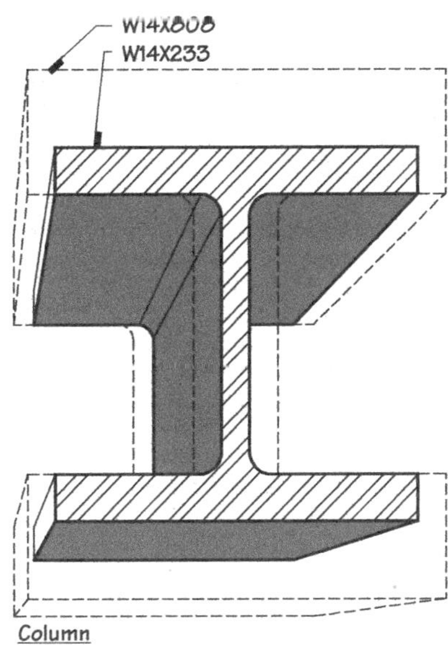

Figure 18.4 Wide-flange shapes come in two different proportions: beams (left) and columns (right). By changing the spacing of the rollers in the rolling mill, steelworkers produce a number of different weights of each nominal size. The broken lines indicate the maximum size in each of these series of nominal 14-in. beams.

Figure 18.6 Corrugated steel decking is manufactured in many depths and corrugation styles.

Courtesy of Wheeling Corrugating Company Division, Wheeling-Pittsburgh Steel Corp.

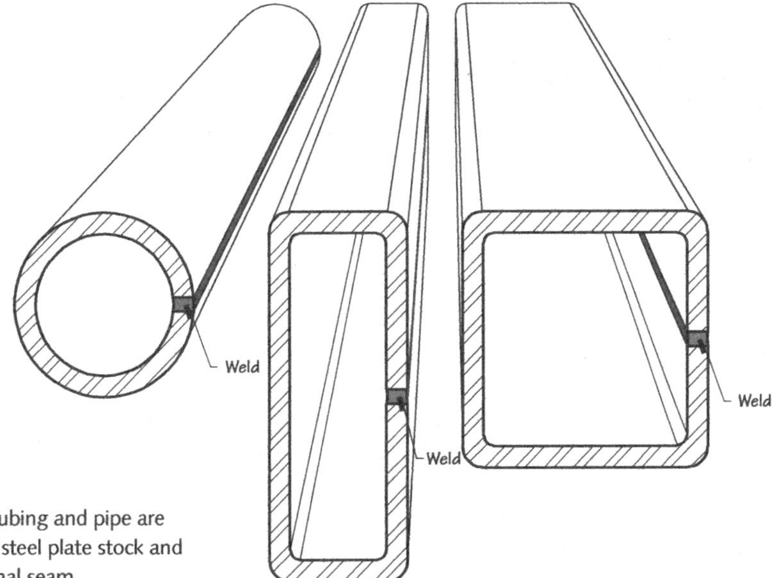

Figure 18.5 Steel tubing and pipe are produced by bending steel plate stock and welding the longitudinal seam.

Other types of steel framing members are produced from rolled steel: *open-web steel joists*, often called *bar joists*, are standardized trusses that are welded together from angles, bars, and/or rods. Standard depths range from 8 to 72 in. These are used in parallel arrays spaced typically 2 to 10 ft apart, supported by wide-flange shapes or heavier trusses called *joist girders*. They can span up to 144 ft for roofs and 96 ft for floors (Figure 18.7). *Castellated beams* are manufactured by cutting a zigzag path along the web of a wide-flange shape (Figure 18.8), realigning the halves of the beam, and welding them together to form a deeper beam with voids in the web (Figure 18.9). A considerably greater depth is achieved with the same weight of steel as the original beam, making castellated beams less expensive overall.

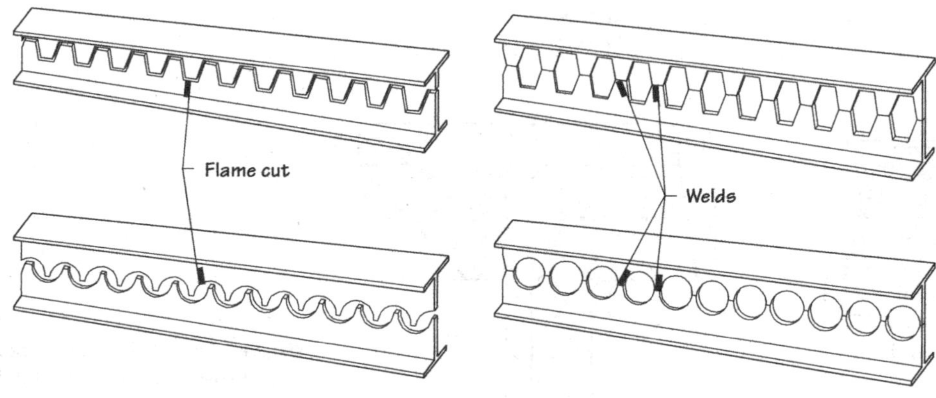

Figure 18.8 Castellated beams are available in two basic styles.

Figure 18.7 The roof of this single-story industrial building is framed with open-web steel joists supported by joist girders. The girders rest on square tube columns.

Figure 18.9 A detail of castellated beams framing into a column; decking is visible above.

Courtesy of Castelite Steel Products, Midlothian, Texas

Thin sheet steel is bent at room temperature into C-shapes and channels that are used to frame partitions and light load-bearing walls, floors, and roofs. These are cut to length on the construction site and assembled with screws or by crimping the pieces together with a special tool (Figure 18.10). Sheathing and finish materials are fastened to the metal frame with special screws that drill their own holes and make their own threads. This *light-gauge steel framing* is used in place of wood light framing in situations where the code requires noncombustible construction.

The Team

Structural steel frames are produced cooperatively by a design and construction team composed of several players. Architects prepare dimensioned drawings of a frame. Structural engineers determine the required sizes of the beams, girders, columns, and braces, and enter them on structural plan drawings. These are passed on to a *fabricator*. The fabricator first prepares detailed *shop drawings* of all the pieces of steel in the frame, indicating the types of connections to be used. The shop drawings are checked for conformance with the original drawings by the engineer and/or architect. Then they are used by the fabricator's shop personnel to cut, drill, punch, shear, bolt, and weld the steel components, ready to erect. Some special components are built out of steel plate stock that is cut to shape and welded together.

The *erector* is the player who assembles the steel components on the building site, using workers who (by tradition) continue to be known as *ironworkers*. Various types of cranes are used to lift the components. Ironworkers guide each component into position and

Figure 18.10 Assembling a tilt-up wall frame made of light-gauge steel cee studs (so called because their section resembles the letter "C") and steel strap diagonal braces.

Courtesy of United States Gypsum Company

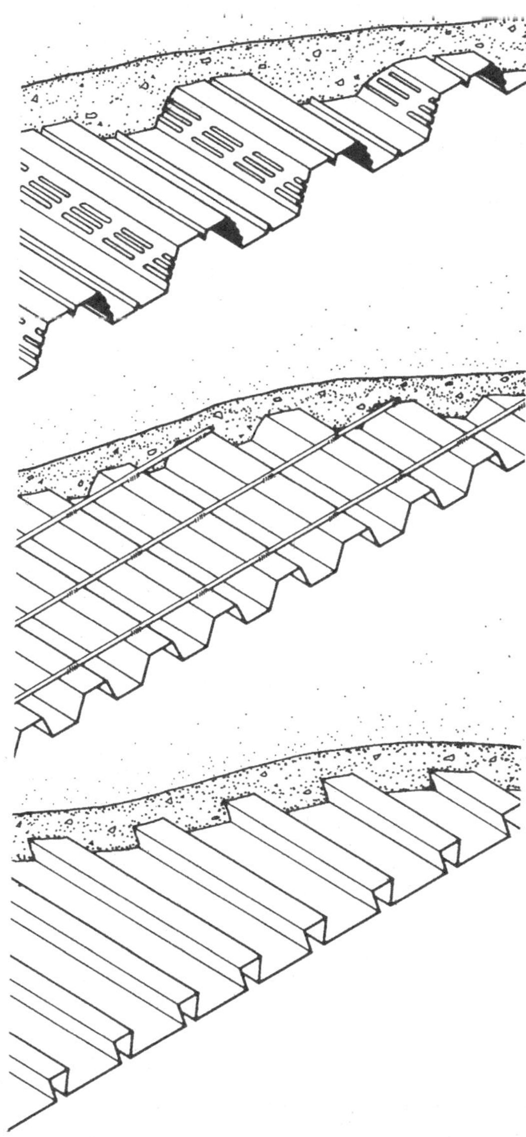

Figure 18.11 Composite decking acts as steel reinforcing for the concrete topping installed over it. The top example bonds to the concrete with deformed ribs, and the middle example with welded steel rods. The bottom type furnishes dovetail channels for the insertion of special fasteners to hang ductwork, piping, electrical conduits, and machinery from the ceiling.

bolt it loosely to adjoining components. Columns are usually furnished in two-story-high pieces; the two stories framed with each set of column pieces are referred to as a *tier*. After each tier of the building has been assembled, it is *plumbed up*, which means that it is pulled into alignment, vertical and square, with diagonal cables and turnbuckles. Then the permanent bracing elements are added and the bolts are tightened to fix the tier in its final position. Welds are made as specified. No steel is cut or drilled on the building site—all of it is prepared in the fabricator's shop, ready to assemble.

Corrugated steel decking is laid over the beams and fastened to them with welds, screws, or other fastening devices. Finally, a mesh of steel reinforcing wires is laid over the decking, and several inches of concrete are cast and leveled over the decking to produce the floor surface. Roofs are often decked with systems that use lightweight insulating boards rather than a concrete fill.

Some types of decking are produced with deformations that interlock with the concrete floor fill so as to allow the steel deck to act as reinforcing for the concrete (Figure 18.11). This *composite construction* can also be extended to the beams and girders by welding steel *shear studs* to the tops of the beams (Figure 18.12). This is done with specialized equipment that is capable of accomplishing a satisfactory weld to the beam, even through the corrugated steel decking. The studs cause the concrete to act together with the steel framing element to resist bending, with the steel beam furnishing the tensile flange and web, and a strip of the concrete acting as part of the compression flange. The end result is that a smaller, less expensive steel shape can be used for the beam.

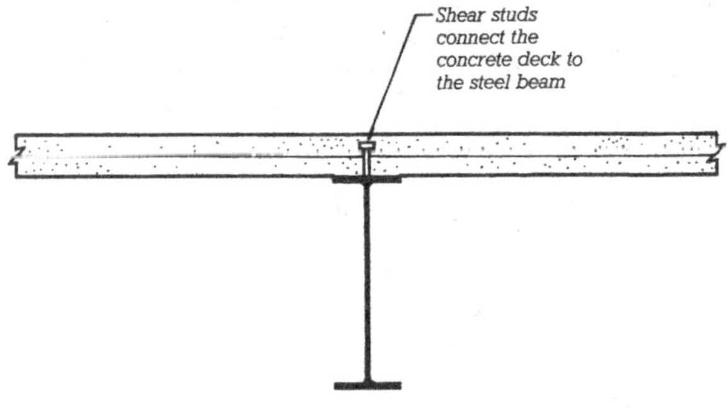

Figure 18.12 Casting a concrete fill over steel decking, using a concrete pump on the street below to deliver the concrete. Vertical shear studs are visible over the lines of beams. Welded wire reinforcing fabric protects the slab against cracking.

Courtesy of Schwing America, Inc.

Fireproofing

Steel melts only at a very elevated temperature, but it loses most of its strength at much lower temperatures that are often reached in building fires. Because of this, except in low, small buildings and voluminous industrial spaces, structural steel must be insulated with *fireproofing* material to prevent it from failing structurally in a fire. This may be done by encasing the steel members in concrete or masonry, by mechanically attaching insulating panels over the members, by enclosing the members with lath and plaster or gypsum wallboard, or by spraying on a thick layer of noncombustible insulation. If the steel members are to be exposed to view as features of the architecture, it is possible to fireproof them with a thin coating of *intumescent paint*, which expands when heated to form a stable insulating layer.

THE VOCABULARY OF STRUCTURAL STEEL FRAMING

Figure 18.13 shows what an ordinary structural steel frame looks like. Various of its connections are identified by letters that key them to the connection details in Figure 18.14. It's important that we become conversant with these details, because we will use them again and again over a lifetime of practice.

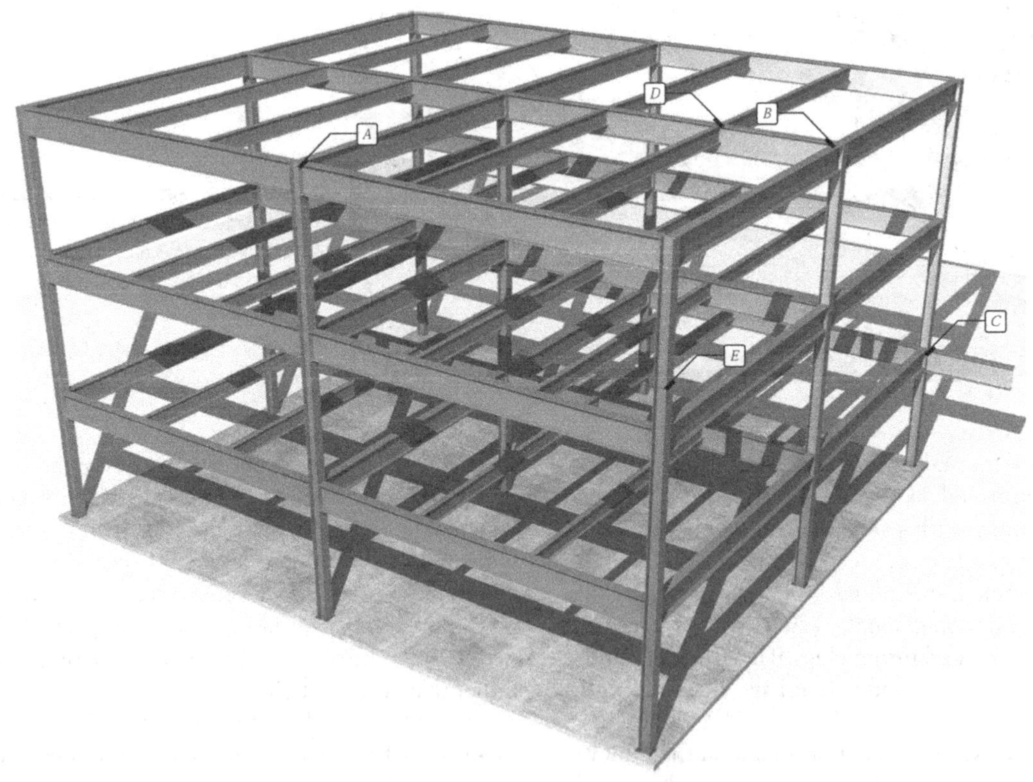

Figure 18.13 A typical steel frame for a small building. The letters are keyed to the detailed illustrations of connections that follow.

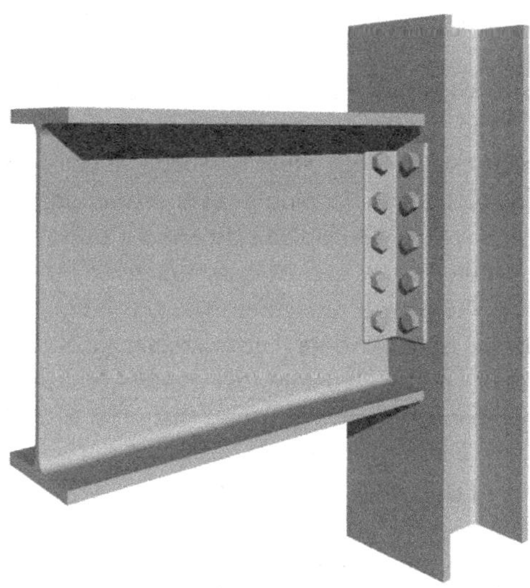

Figure 18.14a A typical framed connection of a beam or girder to the flange of a column, using a steel angle on each side of the beam web. Despite all the bolts, this is considered to be a pinned or hinged connection, because the flanges of the beam, where most of the stiffness of the beam resides, are not connected to the column.

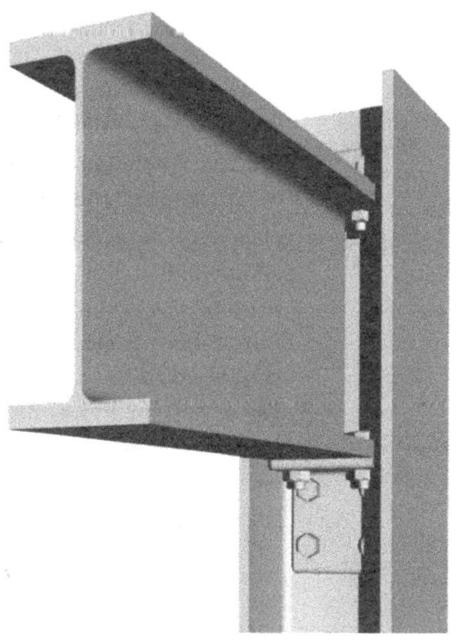

Figure 18.14b This seated connection is used to connect a beam to a column web because there is usually insufficient space between the column flanges to insert a power wrench to tighten the bolts in a framed connection. Although the flanges are bolted to the column, this is considered to be a pinned connection because the bolts are not nearly numerous enough to transfer the entire force from the flanges to the column.

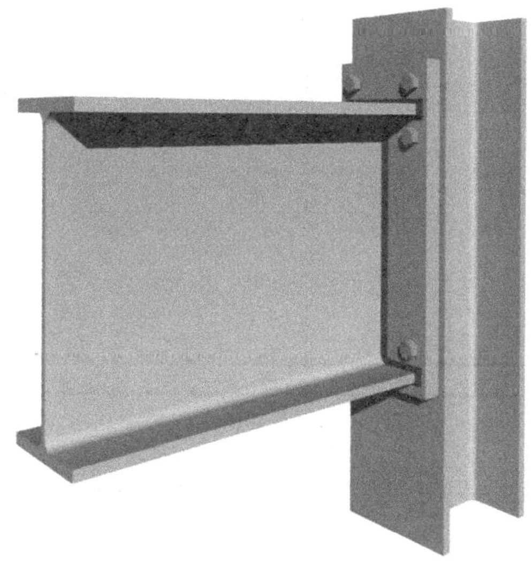

Figure 18.14c This end plate connection is shop-welded to the beam and field-bolted. It can be used for a moment (rigid) connection with a relatively limited capacity.

Figure 18.14d Where beams connect to a girder, the top flange of each beam is coped so that the top of the beam and the top of the girder lie in the same plane. This simplifies decking installation.

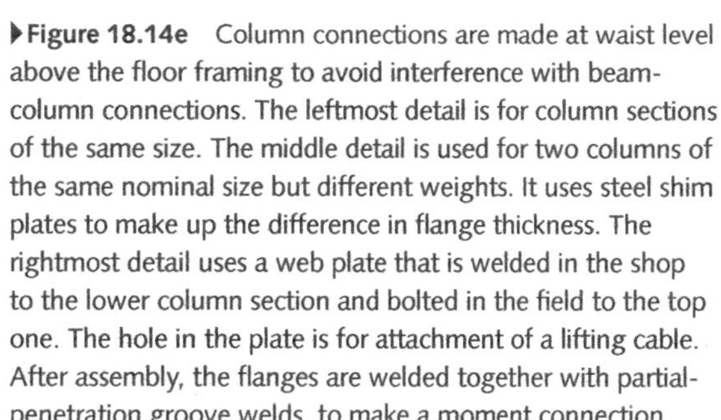

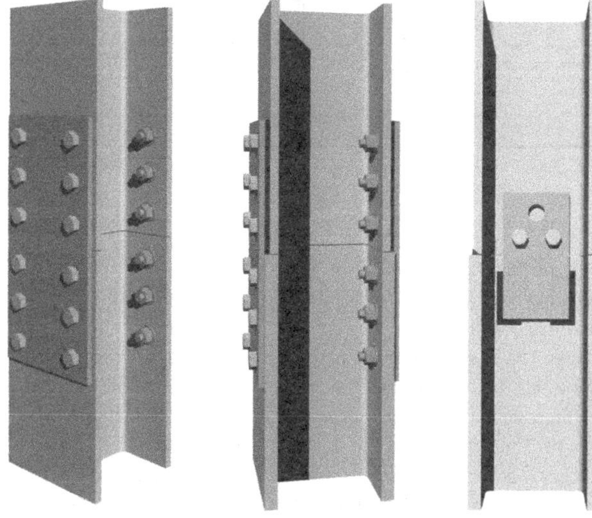

▶**Figure 18.14e** Column connections are made at waist level above the floor framing to avoid interference with beam-column connections. The leftmost detail is for column sections of the same size. The middle detail is used for two columns of the same nominal size but different weights. It uses steel shim plates to make up the difference in flange thickness. The rightmost detail uses a web plate that is welded in the shop to the lower column section and bolted in the field to the top one. The hole in the plate is for attachment of a lifting cable. After assembly, the flanges are welded together with partial-penetration groove welds, to make a moment connection.

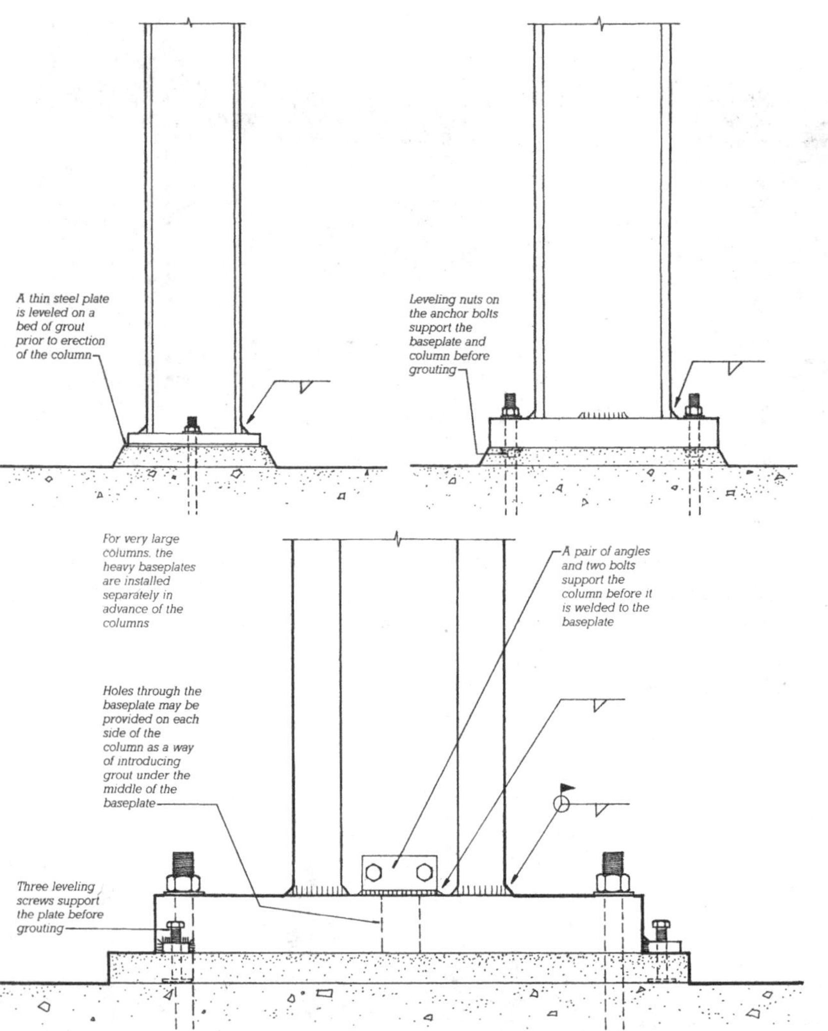
A thin steel plate is leveled on a bed of grout prior to erection of the column
Leveling nuts on the anchor bolts support the baseplate and column before grouting
For very large columns, the heavy baseplates are installed separately in advance of the columns
A pair of angles and two bolts support the column before it is welded to the baseplate
Holes through the baseplate may be provided on each side of the column as a way of introducing grout under the middle of the baseplate
Three leveling screws support the plate before grouting

◀**Figure 18.14f** Steel baseplates spread the force from a column, which is highly stressed, to the larger area of relatively weak concrete where the column joins the foundation. The grout bed enables the baseplate to be leveled and aligned accurately, and to make full contact with the foundation. Anchor bolts embedded in the concrete hold the column down. The small bent arrows with attached triangles are standard symbols for a fillet weld, which is a weld placed in the right angle where the pieces join.

▶**Figure 18.14g** The flanges in this connection are fully welded to the column, allowing the transfer of full bending moments between the two members. The bolts support the beam while the weld is made, and stay in place to transfer vertical forces. The beam flanges are narrowed to create a weak spot that is distant from the welds. This assures that the welds will not become overstressed during an earthquake and that any permanent deformation of the frame will occur in the beams. The stretching of the steel in the narrowed flanges also absorbs earthquake energy that might otherwise cause the collapse of the building. The stiffener plates between the column flanges are not always required.

LAYING OUT A STRUCTURAL STEEL FRAME

The suburban office building mentioned at the beginning of the chapter requires 11 floors with gross areas of 16,200 sq ft each. Steel has been selected as the framing material for its rapidity of construction, its suitability to various open-plan office space uses, its noncombustible nature, and its capability to be fireproofed to any level of fire resistance that the building code requires. A tentative floor plan is a rectangle 108 by 150 ft (Figure 18.2) with a core for elevators, stairs, toilets, and mechanical/electrical spaces that is 36 by 70 ft.

Gravity Forces

Experience has shown that the most economical steel frames are those made up of bays of about 1,000 sq ft each. The ratio of bay width to bay length should lie in the range of 1.25 to 1.5. Beams should span in the longer direction of the bay and frame into the girders at the third points of the girder span (Figure 18.15). Bay sizes and proportions that fall outside these guidelines may be somewhat less economical, but they are usually feasible and often necessary.

The owner of this building wants a column-free width of 35 ft between the core and the long walls of the building for open-plan offices so that no occupied portion of tenants' offices is too far from the daylighting provided by windows in the exterior façade. A bay of 1,000 sq ft, with one side 35 ft long, will have a second side of about 28.6 ft. Its ratio of length to width is 35/28.6, which is 1.22, a value that lies just outside the most economical range but still very acceptable.

The proposed length of the building is 150 ft. Dividing this by the tentative bay width of 28.6 ft, we find that the building would have a length of 5.24 bays, which is awkward. If we divide the building length into 5 bays, each will be 30 ft wide, and the ratio of bay length to width will be 1.17, which lies even farther outside the most economical range but is still reasonable. We might also try to divide the length of the building into 6 bays of 25 ft each. The ratio of length to width for these bays would be 1.44, which falls within the economical range.

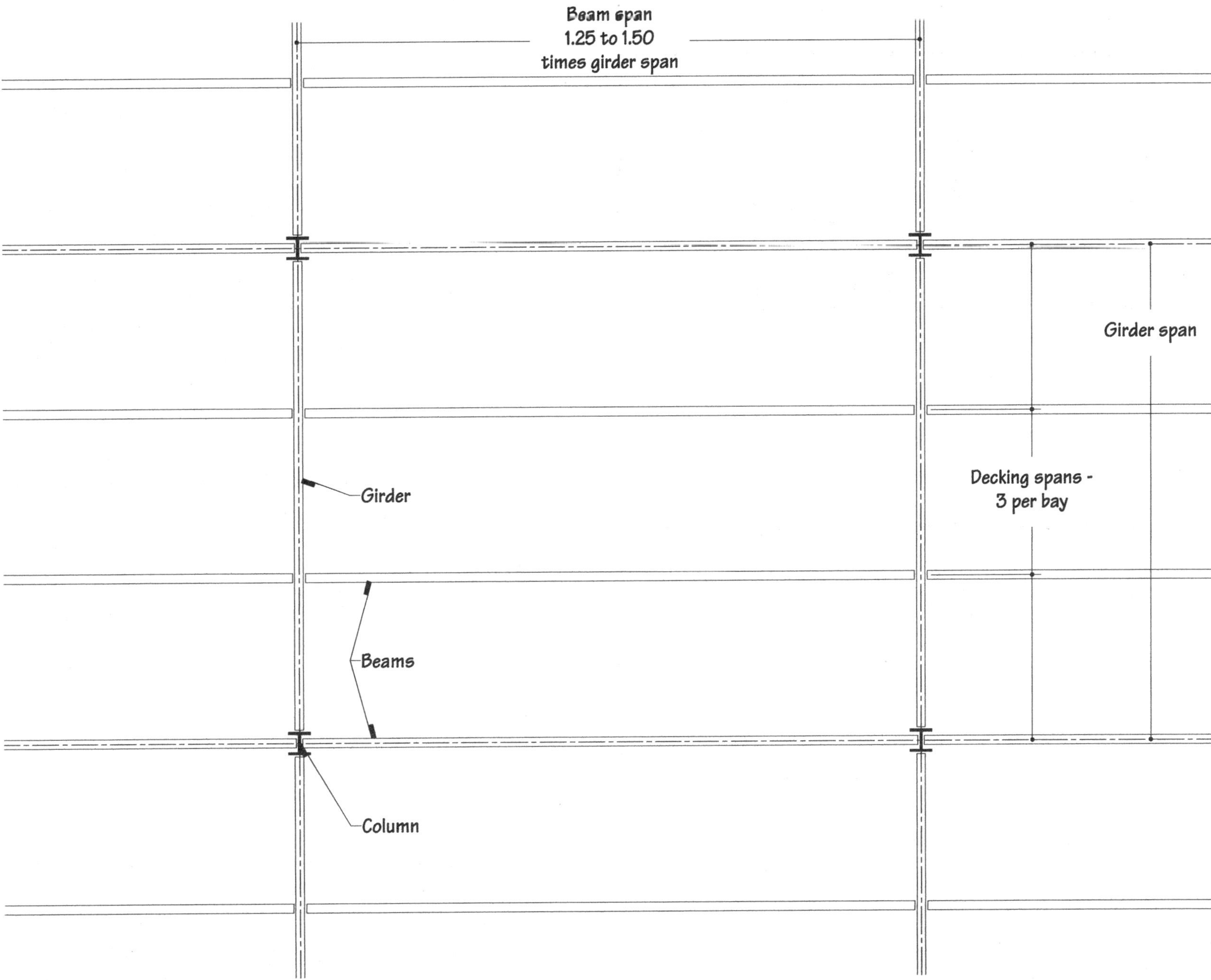

Figure 18.15 A plan of a bay of framing in the building we are designing.

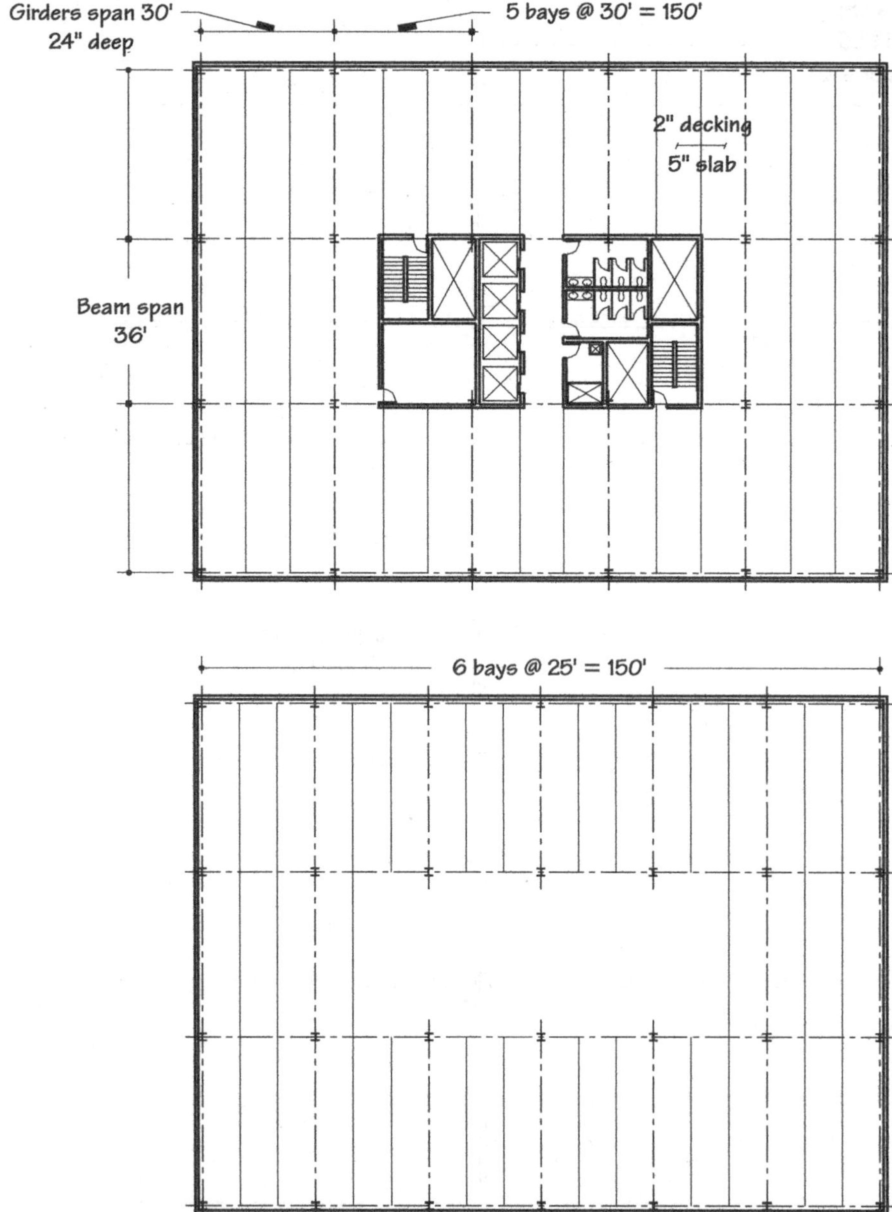

Figure 18.16 Two alternative framing plans for the building.

We try both these spacings on the floor plan of the building (Figure 18.16). The five-bay layout is a good fit. It leaves four interior columns exposed between the core area and the ends of the building. If the owner feels that these will interfere with use patterns of the offices and their workers, it may be feasible to replace them with columns within the core by either of two means (Figure 18.17).

The six-bay layout is also reasonable. It has the same problem with exposed columns at the ends of the cores, and similar solutions are possible. It requires two more footings and columns than the five-bay layout, which will be costly. The final decision between the two layouts will be made largely on the basis of how well they suit the anticipated office partition arrangements and furnishings.

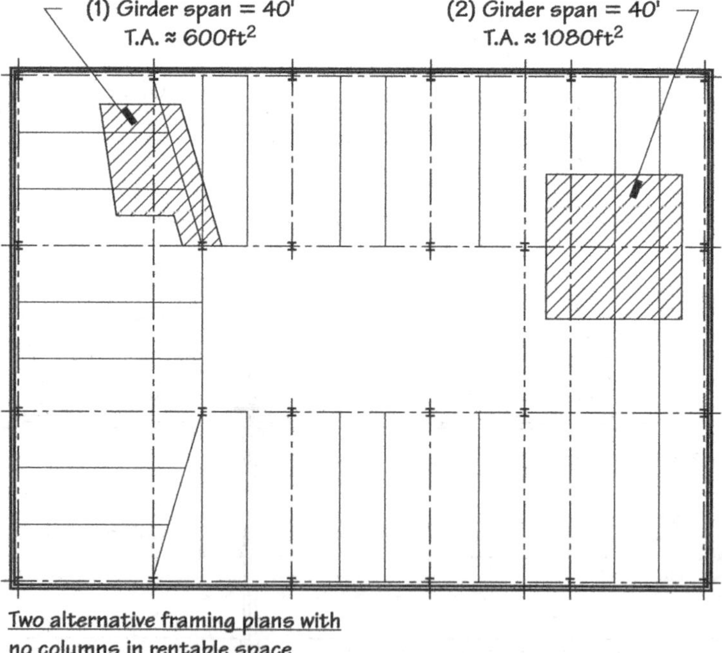

Figure 18.17 Two ways of framing the building without interior columns except in the core; one uses an angled girder (left) while another uses a longer girder span (right).

Lateral Forces

With regard to resisting lateral forces, there are several possibilities to be considered: shear walls, braced frames, rigid joints, and combinations of the three. Shear walls or braces could be installed in both the principal directions of the core (see Chapter 15). Given the central location of the core and its generous dimensions, this would provide sufficient bracing for the entire frame. The floors and roof would act as horizontal diaphragms to transmit forces between the perimeter walls and the rigid core.

Another possibility would be to use rigid joints for lateral stability. The deepest beams, namely the girders, are the best candidates for rigid joints because they provide a maximum moment arm at each connection. In the framing layout that we are considering, the girders run in the long direction of the building, which is the easiest to stabilize because it has the longest moment arm in the plane of the ground. If a sufficient number of the girder-column joints were made rigid, the relatively deep girders would impart stability in the longitudinal direction. Stability in the short direction of the building would be somewhat harder to provide with rigid joints because of the relative narrowness of the building, as well as the lesser depth of the beams compared to the girders. However, it could be achieved easily by bracing in the central core of the building, by exposed bracing in the end façades, or by shear walls in the core.

Diagonal bracing is usually less costly than rigid joints, and we select it for this building. Unless we want to expose it for architectural reasons, the bracing typically will run between columns in the outside planes of the building core. *Inverted V-bracing*, also known as *chevron bracing*, is usually the most economical. It is easy to connect to the beams and columns (Figure 18.18). It allows doors and corridors to pass through the middle of a bay, as in the access to the hall at the center of the core. And together with the columns that they join, inverted V-braces form vertical, cantilevered K-trusses, which

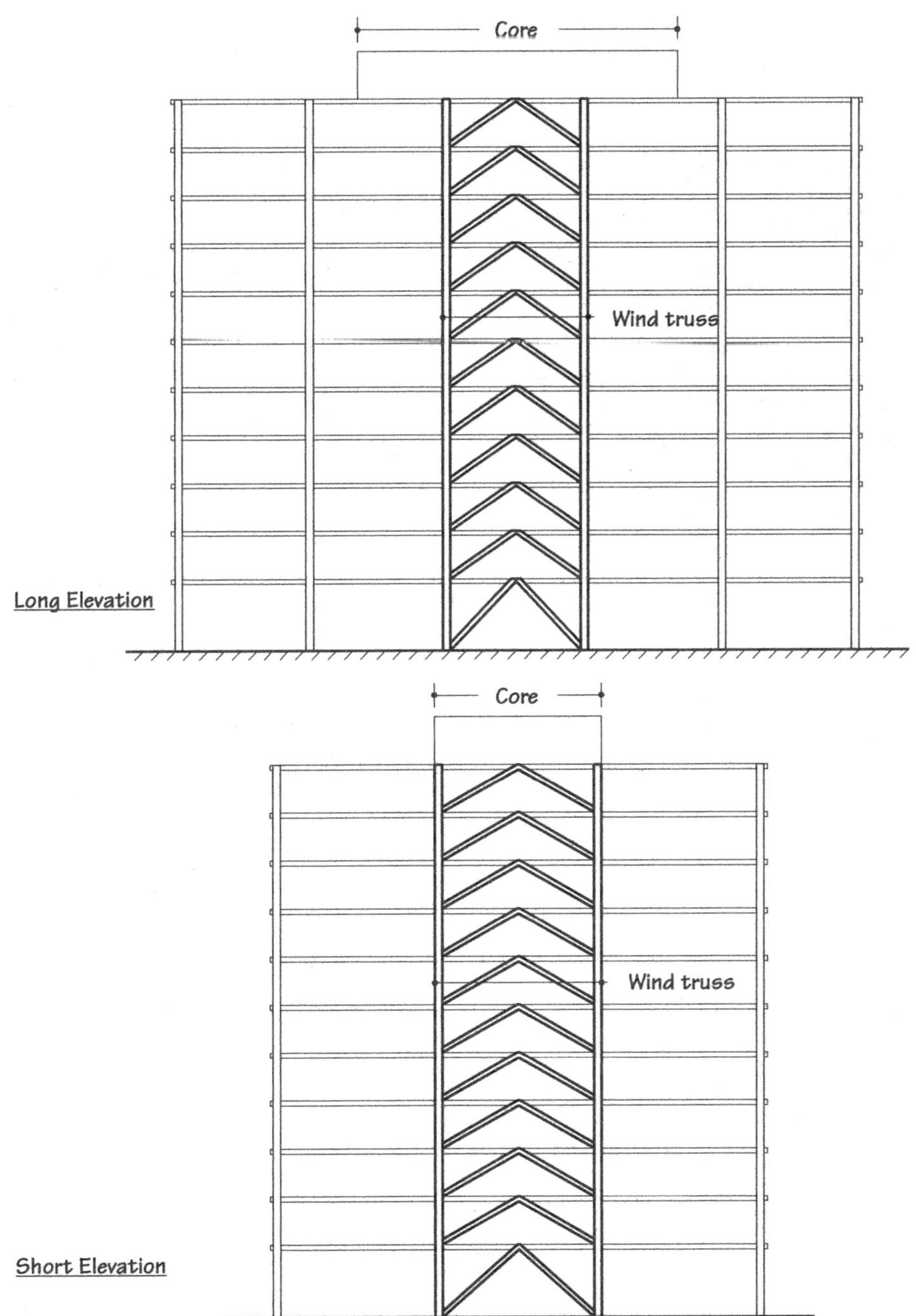

Figure 18.18 Partial sections through the building showing wind trusses in the walls of the core.

Figure 18.19 This 10-story steel-framed building is approximately the same size as the one we are designing. In the image, we can see it uses open-web steel joists and wide-flange steel girders. The first six floors have already been decked at this point in construction, while the upper floors and roof have not.

Image courtesy of Vulcraft Division of Nucor.

For Preliminary Design of a Steel Structure

- Estimate the depth of **corrugated steel roof decking** at 1/40 of its span. Standard depths are 1, 1½, 2, and 4 inches (25, 38, 50, and 100 mm).
- Estimate the overall depth of corrugated steel floor decking plus concrete topping at 1/24 of its span. Typical overall depths range from 2½ to 7 inches (65–180 mm).
- Estimate the depth of **steel open-web joists** at 1/20 of their span for heavily loaded floors or widely spaced joists, and 1/24 of their span for roofs, lightly loaded floors, or closely spaced joists. The spacing of joists depends on the spanning capability of the decking material. Typical joist spacings range from 2 to 10 ft (0.6–3.0 m). Standard joist depths are given earlier in this chapter.
- Estimate the depth of **steel beams** at 1/20 of their span, and the depth of **steel girders** at 1/15 of their span. The width of a beam or girder is usually 1/3 to 1/2 of its depth. For composite beams and girders, use the same ratios but apply them to the overall depth of the beam or girder, including the floor deck and concrete topping. Standard depths of steel wide-flange shapes are given earlier in this chapter.
- Estimate the depth of **triangular steel roof** trusses at 1/4 to 1/5 of their span. For rectangular trusses, the depth is typically 1/8 to 1/12 of their span.
- To estimate the size of a **steel column**, add up the total roof and floor area supported by the column. A W8 column can support up to about 3,000 square feet (280 m^2), and a W14 25,000 square feet (2300 m^2). Very heavy W14 shapes, which are substantially larger than 14 in. in dimension, can support up to 50,000 square feet (4600 m^2). Steel column shapes are usually square or nearly square in proportion.

These approximations are valid only for purposes of preliminary building layout, and must not be used to select final member sizes. They apply to the normal range of building occupancies such as residential, office, commercial, and institutional buildings and parking garages. For manufacturing and storage buildings, use somewhat larger members.

For more comprehensive information on preliminary selection and layout of a structural system and sizing of structural members, see Allen, Edward, and Joseph Iano, *The Architect's Studio Companion* (4th ed.), Hoboken, NJ: John Wiley & Sons, Inc., 2007, from which these approximations were derived.

are very efficient configurations for parallel-chord trusses, as we showed in Chapter 6, and as we applied to bay framing in Chapters 15 and 17. The chevrons in these *wind trusses* open toward the direction of increasing bending moment, which is the most efficient layout. As we configure this bracing, we see that we need to relocate the door at the lower-left hand corner of the mechanical room, shown in the core of Figure 18.2, to the other end of the wall so the door passes under the high point of the chevron.

The braces at the top floor have only light work to do, but the braces in each successive floor below experience larger and larger forces when the building is subjected to wind or seismic loads. The most heavily loaded braces are those just above the foundations. The columns on either side of the braces also experience increasing forces from top to bottom of the building, both from accumulation of gravity loads and from the higher forces in the columns that serve as chords of the cantilevered wind truss. Were we to choose alternative lateral force strategies, we would place the shear walls in the same locations as the wind trusses. If we were to use rigid joints, they would be distributed symmetrically around the perimeter of the building.

ASSIGNING APPROXIMATE SIZES TO MEMBERS OF THE FRAME

To arrive at a first approximation of member sizes, we use rules of thumb that are based on average calculated values from actual practice (see sidebar). Working from the top down, we estimate the depth of the corrugated steel floor decking and concrete fill at 1/24 of its span. Its span is equal to the girder span divided by 3, which is 10 ft. The approximate depth of the steel decking plus its concrete fill is 1/24 of 10 ft, which is 5 in.

We estimate the depth of the floor beams to be 1/20th of their span, which is 21 in. The depth of the girders will be about 1/15th of their span, which works out to 24 in.

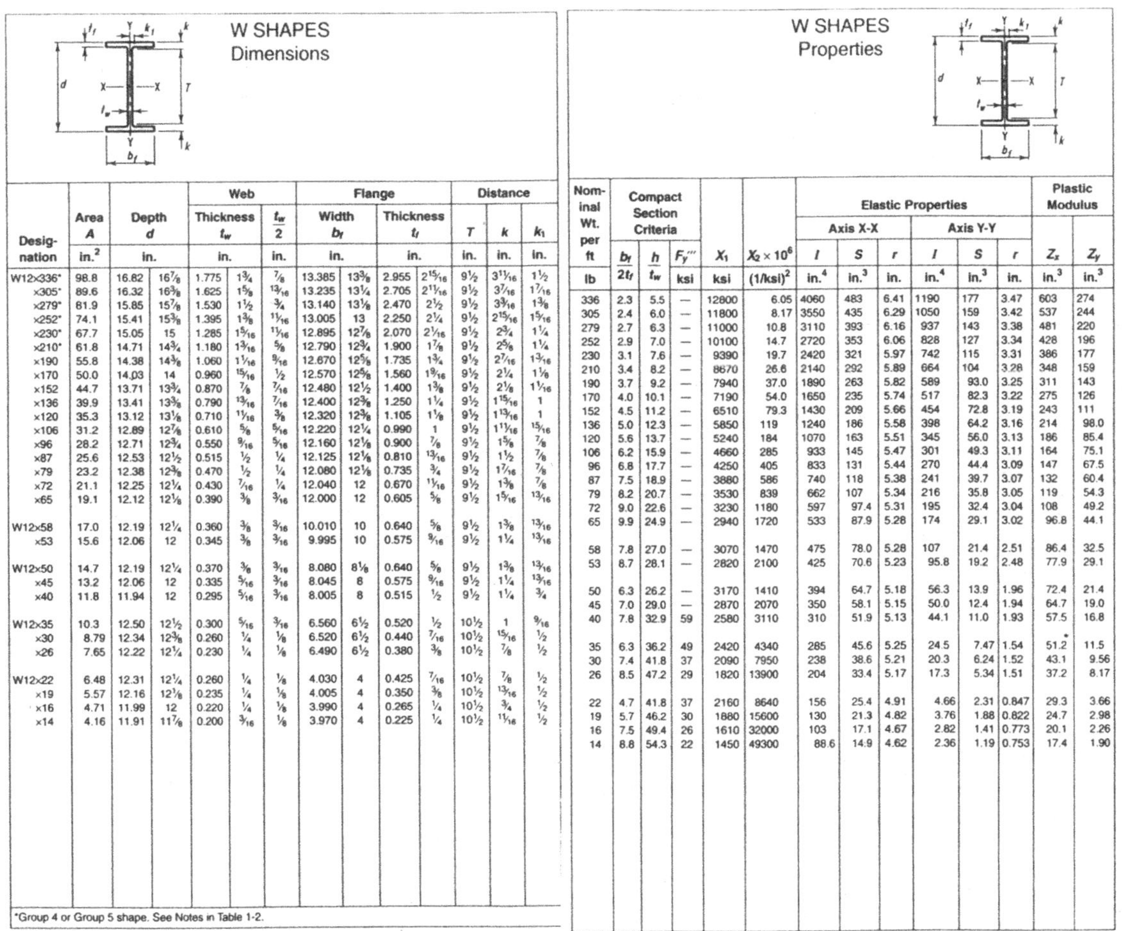

W SHAPES
Dimensions

Designation	Area A (in.²)	Depth d (in.)		Web Thickness t_w (in.)		$t_w/2$ (in.)	Flange Width b_f (in.)		Flange Thickness t_f (in.)		Distance T (in.)	k (in.)	k_1 (in.)
W12×336*	98.8	16.82	16 7/8	1.775	1 3/4	7/8	13.385	13 3/8	2.955	2 15/16	9 1/2	3 11/16	1 1/2
×305*	89.6	16.32	16 3/8	1.625	1 5/8	13/16	13.235	13 1/4	2.705	2 11/16	9 1/2	3 7/16	1 7/16
×279*	81.9	15.85	15 7/8	1.530	1 1/2	3/4	13.140	13 1/8	2.470	2 1/2	9 1/2	3 3/8	1 3/8
×252*	74.1	15.41	15 3/8	1.395	1 3/8	11/16	13.005	13	2.250	2 1/4	9 1/2	2 15/16	1 5/16
×230*	67.7	15.05	15	1.285	1 5/16	11/16	12.895	12 7/8	2.070	2 1/16	9 1/2	2 3/4	1 1/4
×210*	61.8	14.71	14 3/4	1.180	1 3/16	5/8	12.790	12 3/4	1.900	1 7/8	9 1/2	2 5/8	1 1/4
×190	55.8	14.38	14 3/8	1.060	1 1/16	9/16	12.670	12 5/8	1.735	1 3/4	9 1/2	2 7/16	1 3/16
×170	50.0	14.03	14	0.960	15/16	1/2	12.570	12 5/8	1.560	1 9/16	9 1/2	2 1/4	1 1/8
×152	44.7	13.71	13 3/4	0.870	7/8	7/16	12.480	12 1/2	1.400	1 3/8	9 1/2	2 1/8	1 1/16
×136	39.9	13.41	13 3/8	0.790	13/16	7/16	12.400	12 3/8	1.250	1 1/4	9 1/2	1 15/16	1
×120	35.3	13.12	13 1/8	0.710	11/16	3/8	12.320	12 3/8	1.105	1 1/8	9 1/2	1 13/16	1
×106	31.2	12.89	12 7/8	0.610	5/8	5/16	12.220	12 1/4	0.990	1	9 1/2	1 11/16	15/16
×96	28.2	12.71	12 3/4	0.550	9/16	5/16	12.160	12 1/8	0.900	7/8	9 1/2	1 5/8	7/8
×87	25.6	12.53	12 1/2	0.515	1/2	1/4	12.125	12 1/8	0.810	13/16	9 1/2	1 1/2	7/8
×79	23.2	12.38	12 3/8	0.470	1/2	1/4	12.080	12 1/8	0.735	3/4	9 1/2	1 7/16	7/8
×72	21.1	12.25	12 1/4	0.430	7/16	1/4	12.040	12	0.670	11/16	9 1/2	1 3/8	7/8
×65	19.1	12.12	12 1/8	0.390	3/8	3/16	12.000	12	0.605	5/8	9 1/2	1 5/16	13/16
W12×58	17.0	12.19	12 1/4	0.360	3/8	3/16	10.010	10	0.640	5/8	9 1/2	1 3/8	13/16
×53	15.6	12.06	12	0.345	3/8	3/16	9.995	10	0.575	9/16	9 1/2	1 1/4	13/16
W12×50	14.7	12.19	12 1/4	0.370	3/8	3/16	8.080	8 1/8	0.640	5/8	9 1/2	1 3/8	13/16
×45	13.2	12.06	12	0.335	5/16	3/16	8.045	8	0.575	9/16	9 1/2	1 1/4	13/16
×40	11.8	11.94	12	0.295	5/16	3/16	8.005	8	0.515	1/2	9 1/2	1 1/4	3/4
W12×35	10.3	12.50	12 1/2	0.300	5/16	3/16	6.560	6 1/2	0.520	1/2	10 1/2	1	9/16
×30	8.79	12.34	12 3/8	0.260	1/4	1/8	6.520	6 1/2	0.440	7/16	10 1/2	15/16	1/2
×26	7.65	12.22	12 1/4	0.230	1/4	1/8	6.490	6 1/2	0.380	3/8	10 1/2	7/8	1/2
W12×22	6.48	12.31	12 1/4	0.260	1/4	1/8	4.030	4	0.425	7/16	10 1/2	7/8	1/2
×19	5.57	12.16	12 1/8	0.235	1/4	1/8	4.005	4	0.350	3/8	10 1/2	13/16	1/2
×16	4.71	11.99	12	0.220	1/4	1/8	3.990	4	0.265	1/4	10 1/2	3/4	1/2
×14	4.16	11.91	11 7/8	0.200	3/16	1/8	3.970	4	0.225	1/4	10 1/2	11/16	1/2

*Group 4 or Group 5 shape. See Notes in Table 1-2.

W SHAPES
Properties

Nominal Wt. per ft (lb)	Compact Section Criteria $b_f/2t_f$	h/t_w	F_y''' (ksi)	X_1 (ksi)	$X_2 \times 10^6$ (1/ksi)²	Elastic Properties Axis X-X I (in.⁴)	S (in.³)	r (in.)	Axis Y-Y I (in.⁴)	S (in.³)	r (in.)	Plastic Modulus Z_x (in.³)	Z_y (in.³)
336	2.3	5.5	—	12800	6.05	4060	483	6.41	1190	177	3.47	603	274
305	2.4	6.0	—	11800	8.17	3550	435	6.29	1050	159	3.42	537	244
279	2.7	6.3	—	11000	10.8	3110	393	6.16	937	143	3.38	481	220
252	2.9	7.0	—	10100	14.7	2720	353	6.06	828	127	3.34	428	196
230	3.1	7.6	—	9390	19.7	2420	321	5.97	742	115	3.31	386	177
210	3.4	8.2	—	8670	26.6	2140	292	5.89	664	104	3.28	348	159
190	3.7	9.2	—	7940	37.0	1890	263	5.82	589	93.0	3.25	311	143
170	4.0	10.1	—	7190	54.0	1650	235	5.74	517	82.3	3.22	275	126
152	4.5	11.2	—	6510	79.3	1430	209	5.66	454	72.8	3.19	243	111
136	5.0	12.3	—	5850	119	1240	186	5.58	398	64.2	3.16	214	98.0
120	5.6	13.7	—	5240	184	1070	163	5.51	345	56.0	3.13	186	85.4
106	6.2	15.9	—	4660	285	933	145	5.47	301	49.3	3.11	164	75.1
96	6.8	17.7	—	4250	405	833	131	5.44	270	44.4	3.09	147	67.5
87	7.5	18.9	—	3880	586	740	118	5.38	241	39.7	3.07	132	60.4
79	8.2	20.7	—	3530	839	662	107	5.34	216	35.8	3.05	119	54.3
72	9.0	22.6	—	3230	1180	597	97.4	5.31	195	32.4	3.04	108	49.2
65	9.9	24.9	—	2940	1720	533	87.9	5.28	174	29.1	3.02	96.8	44.1
58	7.8	27.0	—	3070	1470	475	78.0	5.28	107	21.4	2.51	86.4	32.5
53	8.7	28.1	—	2820	2100	425	70.6	5.23	95.8	19.2	2.48	77.9	29.1
50	6.3	26.2	—	3170	1410	394	64.7	5.18	56.3	13.9	1.96	72.4	21.4
45	7.0	29.0	—	2870	2070	350	58.1	5.15	50.0	12.4	1.94	64.7	19.0
40	7.8	32.9	59	2580	3110	310	51.9	5.13	44.1	11.0	1.93	57.5	16.8
35	6.3	36.2	49	2420	4340	285	45.6	5.25	24.5	7.47	1.54	51.2	11.5
30	7.4	41.8	37	2090	7950	238	38.6	5.21	20.3	6.24	1.52	43.1	9.56
26	8.5	47.2	29	1820	13900	204	33.4	5.17	17.3	5.34	1.51	37.2	8.17
22	4.7	41.8	37	2160	8640	156	25.4	4.91	4.66	2.31	0.847	29.3	3.66
19	5.7	46.2	30	1880	15600	130	21.3	4.82	3.76	1.88	0.822	24.7	2.98
16	7.5	49.4	26	1610	32000	103	17.1	4.67	2.82	1.41	0.773	20.1	2.26
14	8.8	54.3	22	1450	49300	88.6	14.9	4.62	2.36	1.19	0.753	17.4	1.90

Figure 18.20 Properties of some steel wide-flange shapes. This is a portion of a much larger table in the *Manual of Steel Construction*. Courtesy of the American Institute of Steel Construction.

At the perimeter of the building, each column supports a half-bay of tributary area, 525 sq ft. At ground level, the total area of floors and roof that are tributary to any one column is 11 floors times 525 sq ft per floor, which comes to 5,775 sq ft. A simple calculation based on Figure 18.20 tells us that this requires a W12 column at the base of the building. An interior column will carry twice the tributary area and twice the load. It can probably be a heavier member of the W12 family of columns. Due to the effort required to design many variations in dimensions of column enclosures, it may be most economical to simplify details of the connections by using nominal 12-in. shapes throughout the height of the building, reducing their weight per foot in the higher stories, rather than stepping down to 10 and 8 in. A glance at the table of dimensions of wide-flange shapes in the *Manual of Steel Construction* tells us that W12 column shapes (those with more or less square proportions) are available in 17 different weights, from 65 to 336 lb per foot (Figure 18.20). The dimensions of column shapes often bear little relationship to their nominal depth: Overall depths of nominal 12-in. columns vary from about 12 to 16 in., with flanges up to 3 in. thick. The top-floor columns would lie at or near the 65-lb weight, whereas those at the foundations would be heavier.

These approximate member sizes play important roles in determining the feasibility of the framing scheme, working out such critical dimensions as floor-to-floor heights, and estimating the self-weights of the members during detailed calculations of member sizes.

SIZING NONRECTANGULAR BEAMS

In Chapters 16 and 17, we learned to find sizes for wood framing members, which are rectangular in cross section. Steel beams are more complex in shape and require a slightly different approach.

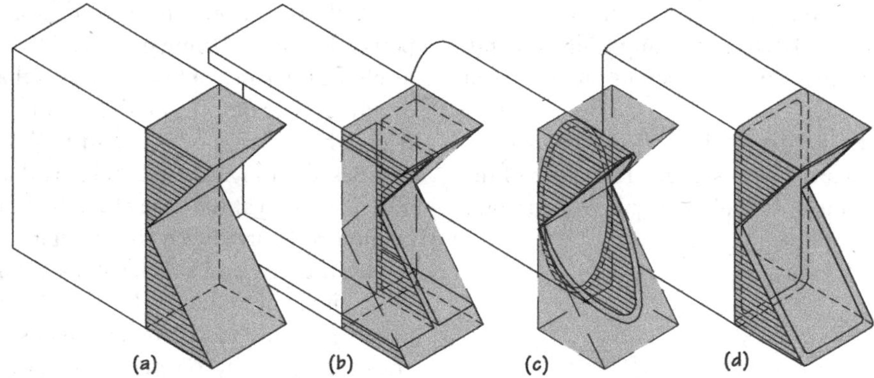

Figure 18.21 Wedge-shaped stress blocks occur in beams of every shape, but each shape utilizes only a part of the wedges.

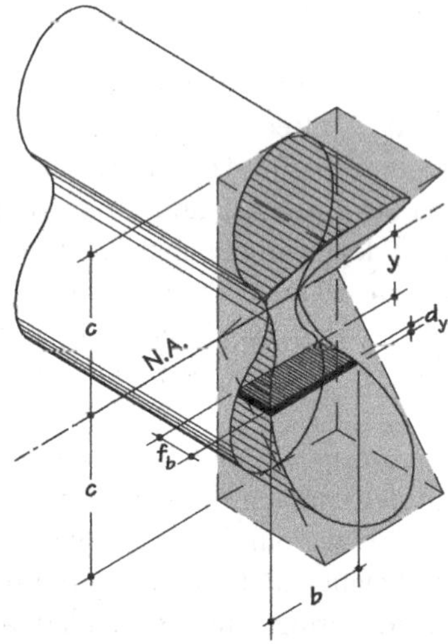

Figure 18.22 The derivation of the resisting moment of any arbitrary shape.

Distribution of Longitudinal Stresses in Nonrectangular Beams

All beams, regardless of shape, experience a linear distribution of bending stresses, in which their bending stresses diminish to zero at the neutral axis (Figure 18.21). If we divide the cross section of any beam into very small elements, each element is capable of exerting a partial resisting moment that is equal to the total force in the element multiplied by the moment arm of the element about the neutral axis. The total force in the very small element is equal to the area of the element, dA, multiplied by the stress in its material, f_y. Referring to the example illustrated in Figure 18.22, the partial resisting moment of any very small element that lies at distance y from the neutral axis of a beam is given by the expression:

$$M^{\text{partial}}_{\text{resist}} = yf_y \, dA$$

The bending stress in the element, f_y, is equal to the maximum bending stress in the beam, $f_b^{\max}$, multiplied by the ratio of y to the distance of the extreme fiber from the neutral axis, c, in that portion of the beam section. The area of dA is equal to its height, dy, multiplied by its width, b (Figure 18.22). Thus the partial resisting moment of any small element in a beam of any shape can be expressed:

$$M^{\text{partial}}_{\text{resist}} = f_b^{\max}\left(\frac{y}{c}\right)by\,dy = f_b^{\max}\left(\frac{b}{c}\right)y^2\,dy$$

To find the resisting moment for the entire beam section, we add together the partial resisting moments exerted by all the small elements of area. We do this for values of y that range from $-c$, the distance from the neutral axis to the extreme bottom fiber, to c, the extreme top fiber.

$$M^{l}_{\text{resist}} = f_b^{\max}\left(\frac{b}{c}\right)\sum_{y=-c'}^{y=c} y^2\,dy$$

The summation of the areas of all the small differential elements, each multiplied by the square of its distance from the neutral axis, is a constant that is readily calculated for any particular section. It is defined as the *moment of inertia, I*, of that section.

$$I = b\sum_{y=-c'}^{y=c} y^2\,dy$$

Substituting this latter equation into the one previous:

$$M_{\text{resist}} = \frac{f_b^{\max} I}{c}$$

Up to the limit of its safe load-carrying capacity, the resisting moment of a beam is equal to the applied external bending moment, M. Substituting M for M_{resist} and rearranging terms, we arrive at the fundamental equation for bending stress that is applicable to beams of any cross-sectional shape:

$$f_b^{\max} = \frac{Mc}{I} \qquad \textbf{[18-1]}$$

where:

$f_b^{\max}$ is the maximum bending stress in the beam,
M is the bending moment,
c is the perpendicular distance from the neutral axis to the extreme fiber, and
I is the moment of inertia.

I, the moment of inertia of a beam cross section, represents in a single, miraculously powerful constant all the geometric characteristics and dimensions that affect the elastic behavior of a beam. Its units are in.^{4} or mm^4.

For any given beam shape, *c* and *I* are constants. If *I*/*c* is defined as the *section modulus, S*, then:

$$f_b = \frac{M}{S} \qquad [18\text{-}2]$$

To find the bending stress at any distance *y* from the neutral axis, we use another form of equation [18-1]:

$$f_b^y = \frac{My}{I} \qquad [18\text{-}3]$$

Finding the Moment of Inertia of Any Shape

To use these expressions, we need to be able to find a numerical value for the moment of inertia, *I*, of any shape. We have defined moment of inertia as the sum for all the thin layers of material in the beam of the cross-sectional area of each layer times the square of its distance from the neutral axis (Figure 18.22).

For a rectangular section, *y* is equal to half the height of the beam, *d*/2, and *b,* the width of the beam, is constant. Using calculus-based notation, each thin layer has a thickness of *dy*. The area of each thin layer is therefore *b dy*, and its distance from the neutral axis is *y*. We can find the moment of inertia for a rectangular section by integration:

$$I_{rect} = b\int_{y=-d/2}^{y=d/2} y^2\,dy = b\left[\frac{y^3}{3}\right]_{-d/2}^{d/2} = \frac{bd^3}{(3)(8)} - \frac{b(-d)^3}{(3)(8)} = \frac{bd^3}{12}$$

This verifies an identical expression that we derived by a different path in Chapter 17. It also typifies a method for finding the moment of inertia of any regular geometric shape.

FINDING MOMENTS OF INERTIA OF COMPOSITE SHAPES

A *composite* shape is one that is made up of two or more *component* shapes. When these shapes share the same neutral axis, the moment of inertia of the composite shape is the sum of the moments of inertia of the component shapes. This is illustrated in Figure 18.23.

Joining of Shapes in Composite Beams

For component shapes that do not share a common neutral axis to work together and act structurally as a

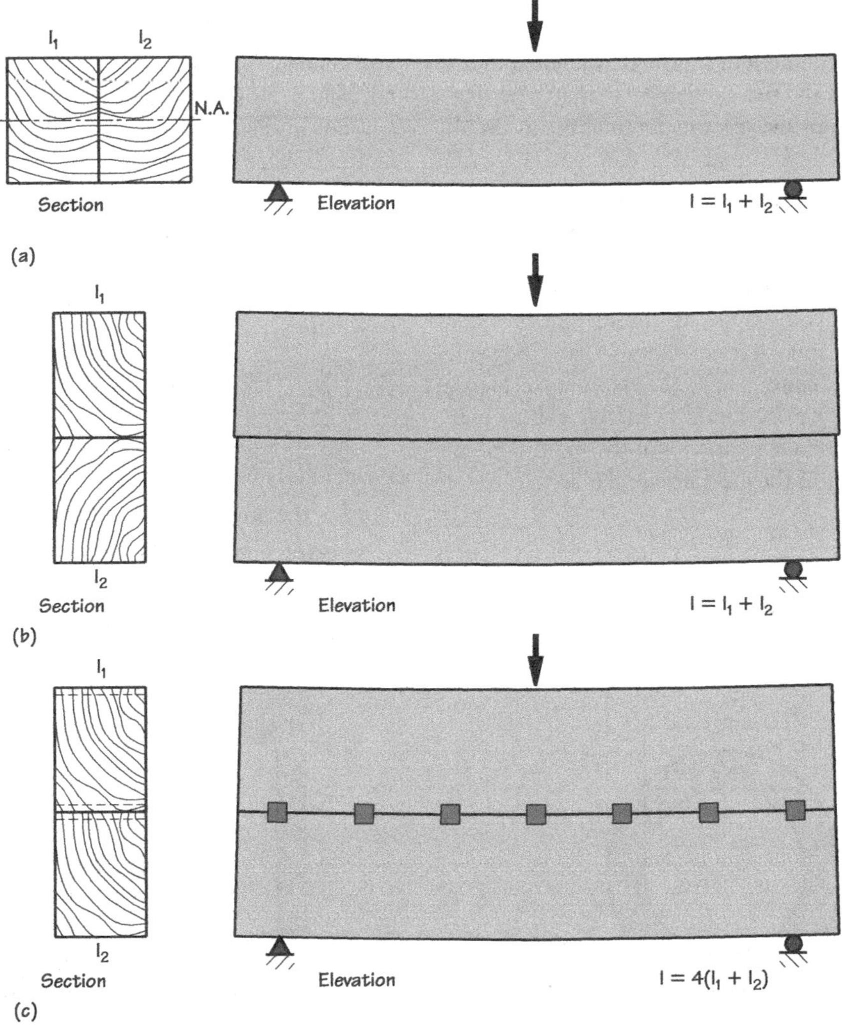

Figure 18.23 It is only by preventing horizontal slipping between beam components that we can achieve maximum strength and stiffness in a beam.

single composite beam, they must be joined securely together. Consider the two wood beams in Figure 18.23: If they are situated side by side (a), they share a common neutral axis and will work together even if they are not fastened to one another. The moment of inertia of their composite area in this case is equal to the sum of their individual moments of inertia. If the beams are placed one on top of the other without being joined (b), the two beams still work independently and their composite moment of inertia is still equal to the same sum. But if the two are joined so that their mating surfaces cannot slip (c), the depth of the assembly is effectively doubled, creating a moment of inertia that is eight times as great as that of one of the beams and four times as great as the moment of inertia of the unjoined combination.

It is easy to find the moment of inertia of a hollow member, such as a tube or box, by subtraction, provided that the interior and exterior sections share the same neutral axis. In Figure 18.24, the moment of inertia of a round tube may be found by simple subtraction, deducting the moment of inertia of the interior circular area from that of the exterior circular area:

$$I_X^{net} = I_X^{ext} - I_X^{int}$$

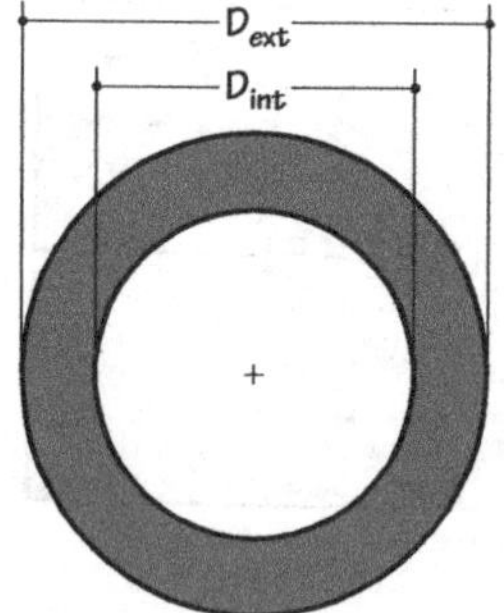

Figure 18.24 The moment of inertia, *I*, of a steel tube or pipe may be found by deducting the moment of inertia of the smaller circle from that of the larger one.

In Figure 18.25, the moment of inertia of either the box section or the C-section can be found in a similar manner. This method is not applicable directly to the determination of a section modulus; we must first find the moment of inertia, then divide it by the half-height of the beam, to arrive at the section modulus.

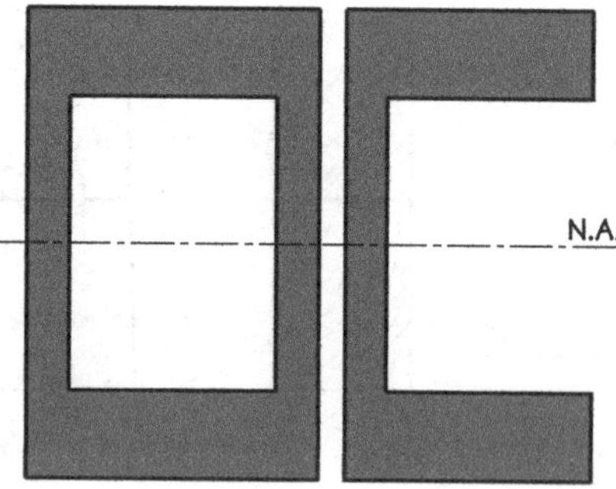

Figure 18.25 Values of *I* for these two shapes can be found in each case by deducting the *I* of the inner shape from that of the outer.

Transfer Formula for Moments of Inertia

For shapes that are made of components that do not share the same neutral axis, we utilize a *transfer formula* to change the reference axis of moments of inertia (Figure 18.26):

$$I_x = \bar{I}_x + Ad^2 \qquad [18\text{-}4]$$

In which:

I_x is the moment of inertia of any shape about a desired axis,

$\bar{I}_x$ is the moment of inertia of the shape about a parallel axis,

A is the area of the shape, and

d is the perpendicular distance between the axes.

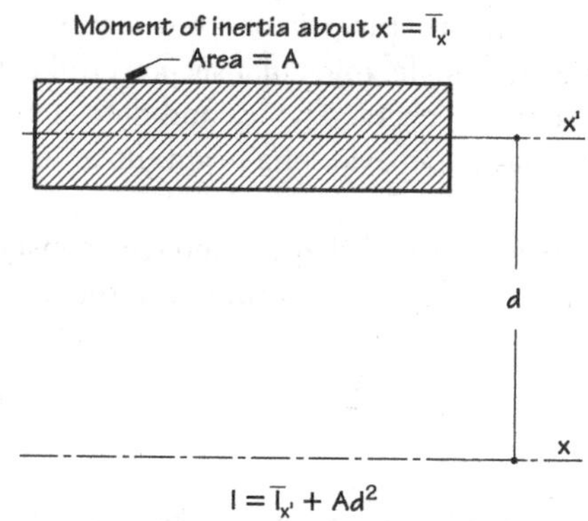

Figure 18.26 The transfer formula allows us to find easily the moment of inertia of an area about any axis that is parallel to its own axis.

Given the moments of inertia of simple geometric shapes that are given in Figure 18.27, this expression makes it possible to find the moment of inertia of almost any cross-sectional shape.

Suppose that we wish to make a large steel girder by welding three plates together, as shown in Figure 18.28. To find the bending stress in the girder, we must know its moment of inertia. The girder shape is a composite of three rectangular areas that represent two flange plates and a web plate. The neutral axis of the web plate coincides with the neutral axis of the composite section, so we can find its contribution to the moment of inertia of the composite shape directly:

$$I_{web} = \frac{bh^3}{12} = \frac{(1\text{ in.})(55\text{ in.})^3}{12} = 13{,}865\text{ in.}^4$$

To avoid confusion, we represent the height of a rectangle with h, and the transfer distance with d. For the two identical flanges, we must employ the transfer formula.

$$\bar{I}_{flange} = \frac{bh^3}{12} = \frac{(15\text{ in.})(2.5\text{ in.})^3}{12} = 19.53\text{ in.}^4$$

$$A_{flange} = bh = (15\text{ in.})(2.5\text{ in.}) = 37.5\text{ in.}^2$$

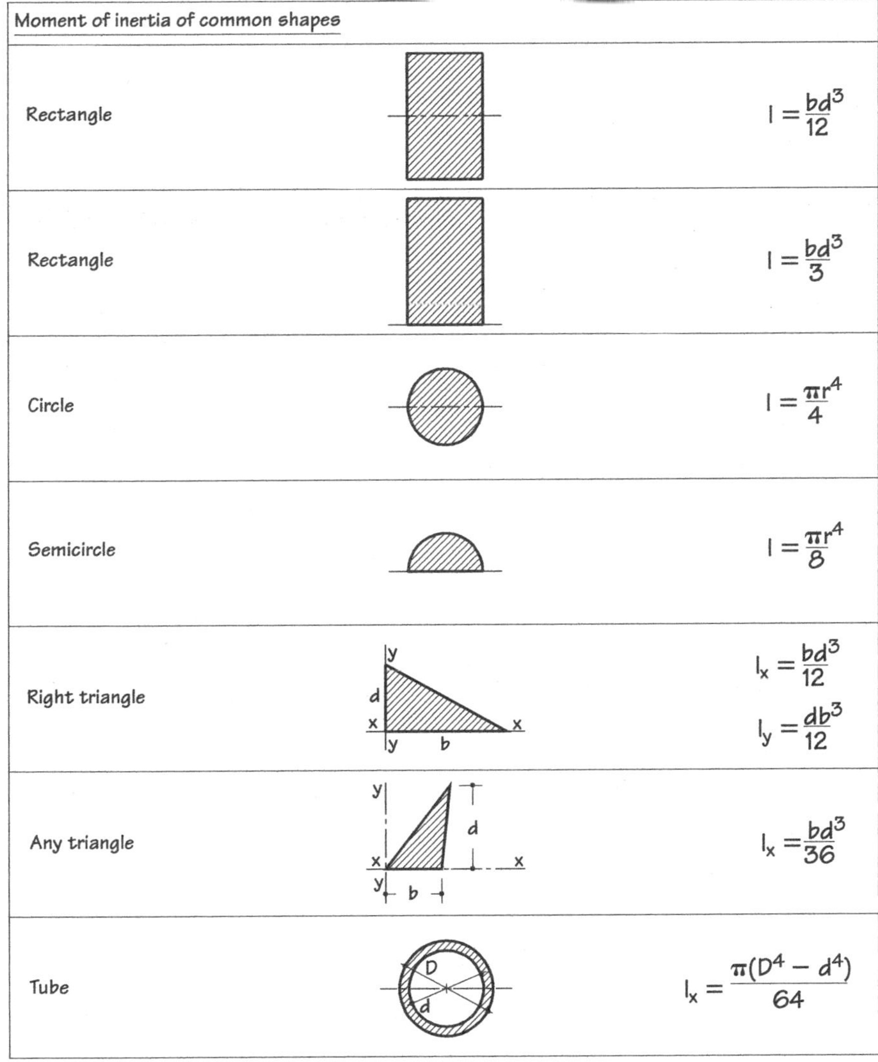

Moment of inertia of common shapes
Rectangle
$I = \frac{bd^3}{12}$
Rectangle
$I = \frac{bd^3}{3}$
Circle
$I = \frac{\pi r^4}{4}$
Semicircle
$I = \frac{\pi r^4}{8}$
Right triangle
$I_x = \frac{bd^3}{12}$
$I_y = \frac{db^3}{12}$
Any triangle
$I_x = \frac{bd^3}{36}$
Tube
$I_x = \frac{\pi(D^4 - d^4)}{64}$

Figure 18.27 Moments of inertia for some elementary shapes.

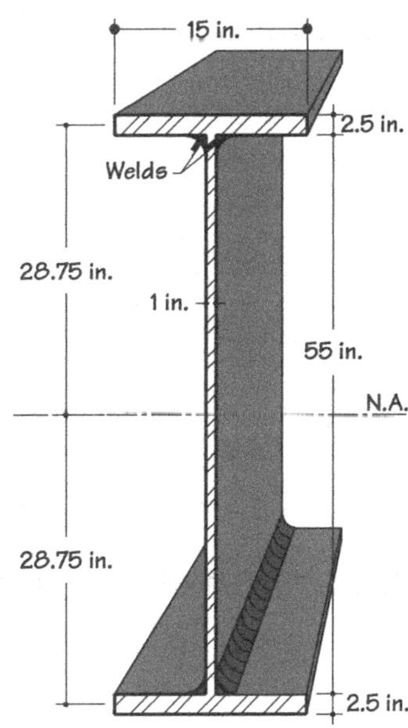

Figure 18.28 A diagram for finding the moment of inertia of a beam made of three plates.

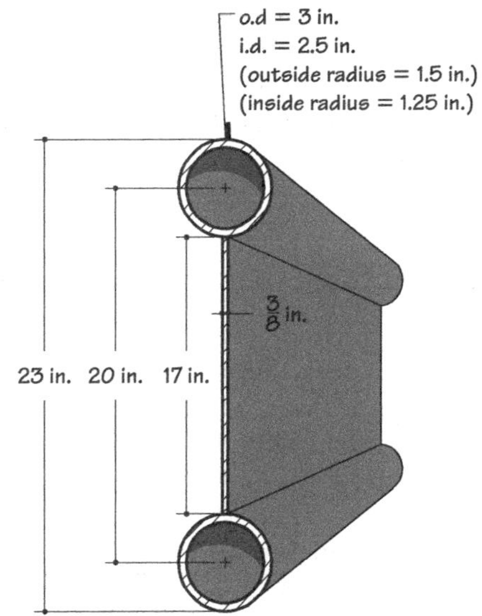

Figure 18.29 Finding the moment of inertia of a custom-made beam. We will explore this configuration of beam further in Chapter 22.

$$I_X^{\text{flange}} = \overline{I}_{\text{flange}} + Ad^2 = 19.53 \text{ in.}^4 + (37.5 \text{ in.}^2)(28.75 \text{ in.})^2$$
$$= 31{,}016 \text{ in.}^4$$

$$I_{\text{total}} = I_{\text{web}} + 2I_{\text{flange}} = 13{,}865 \text{ in.}^4 + 2(31{,}016 \text{ in.}^4)$$
$$= 75{,}897 \text{ in.}^4$$

A factor of 2 is applied to the moment of inertia of a flange in the next-to-last line of this computation because there are two identical flanges.

Another girder is made up of two round steel tubes welded to a web plate (Figure 18.29). To find its moment of inertia, we first find the moment of inertia of one of the tubes by subtracting the moment of inertia of the inside circle from that of the outside circle:

$$I_{circle} = \frac{\pi r^4}{4}$$

$$I_{tube} = \left(\frac{\pi(1.5\text{ in.})^4}{4}\right) - \left(\frac{\pi(1.25\text{ in.})^4}{4}\right) = 2.06\text{ in.}^4$$

$$A_{tube} = \pi[(1.5\text{ in.})^2 - (1.25\text{ in.})^2] = 2.16\text{ in.}^2$$

$$I_{flange} = \overline{I}_X + Ad^2 = 2.06\text{ in.}^4 + (2.16\text{ in.}^2)(10\text{ in.})^2 = 218.06\text{ in.}^4$$

$$I_{web} = \frac{bh^3}{12} = \frac{(0.375\text{ in.})(17\text{ in.})^3}{12} = 153.53\text{ in.}^4$$

$$I_{total} = 2I_{flange} + I_{web} = 2(218.06\text{ in.}^4) + (153.53\text{ in.}^4) = 589.7\text{ in.}^4$$

Suppose that this beam spans 37 ft and supports a load of 20,000 lb distributed uniformly over its span. What is the maximum bending stress? First we find the maximum bending moment:

$$M = \frac{WL}{8} = \frac{(20,000\text{ lb})(37\text{ ft})(12\text{ in./ft})}{8} = 1,110,000\text{ lb-in.}$$

Then we insert the moment of inertia into equation [18-2]. We see that y, the distance from the neutral axis to the extreme fiber, is 11.5 in., which is half the 23-in. depth of the beam:

$$f_b^{max} = \frac{My}{I} = \frac{(1,110,000\text{ lb-in.})(11.5\text{ in.})}{589.7\text{ in.}^4} = 21,648\text{ psi}$$

Worksheet 18A will extend these concepts of moments of inertia to other structural forms.

FINDING BENDING STRESSES IN STANDARD NONRECTANGULAR BEAMS

When we use standard structural shapes, we don't need to calculate moments of inertia. Structural handbooks tabulate I and S with respect to both vertical and horizontal neutral axes for all standard shapes and sizes of steel, aluminum, and wood structural members; that is, for all standard beams made of homogeneous structural materials (Figures 18.30, 17.25). Steel-reinforced concrete beams, because they are made of two materials of very different properties, are analyzed by analogous but slightly different methods that are beyond the scope of this text, so as to consider the concrete acting in compression and the steel acting in tension.

Tabulated values of S and I make it very easy for us to find bending stress in standard manufactured beams of any material. If, for example, a W18×50 steel wide-flange beam is subjected to a bending moment of 1.9 million lb-in., what is the maximum bending stress in the beam? What is the bending stress at a distance of 2 in. below the neutral axis?

We can find the S and I values for this section in Figure 18.30: They are 88.9 in.^{3} and 800 in.^{4}, respectively. (Notice that there are two sets of values in this table for S and I. The first set of values are with respect to the *strong axis* of the beam, with flanges top and bottom. The second set relates to the *weak axis*, with flanges on edge.) We substitute these values into equations [18-2] and [18-3]:

$$f_b^{max} = \frac{M}{S} = \frac{1,900,000\text{ lb-in.}}{88.9\text{ in.}^3} = 21,370\text{ psi}$$

$$f_b^{-2"} = \frac{My}{I} = \frac{1,900,000\text{ lb-in.}(2\text{ in.})}{800\text{ in.}^4} = 4,750\text{ psi (tension)}$$

The allowable bending stress in ordinary structural steel is 24,000 psi. These calculations show that the extreme fibers of this beam at the point of maximum moment are stressed nearly to this value, while the steel near the neutral axis at that point is working at only a fraction of its capacity.

WEB STRESSES IN NONRECTANGULAR BEAMS

The general formula for web stress at any point in a beam of any cross-sectional shape is:

$$f_v = \frac{VQ}{Ib} \qquad [18\text{-}5]$$

where:

V is the vertical force at the shape that is being examined; this may be taken from the V diagram for the beam loading (Chapter 16),

Q is the statical moment, with respect to the neutral axis of the shape, of the portion of the cross section of the beam that lies above the plane that is being examined,

I is the moment of inertia of the shape, and

b is the width of the shape at the plane in the cross section that is being examined.

These terms are illustrated in Figure 18.31. This equation is somewhat laborious to use, but for the more usual types of beam sections there are special-case expressions that are much more convenient. One of these, for the maximum web stress in a rectangular section, we have already learned:

$$f_v^{max} = \frac{3V}{2bd} \qquad [18\text{-}6]$$

The other special-case expression for web stress that is most commonly used is for steel wide-flange beams. Because so much of the steel is concentrated in the flanges and so little in the web, the flow of

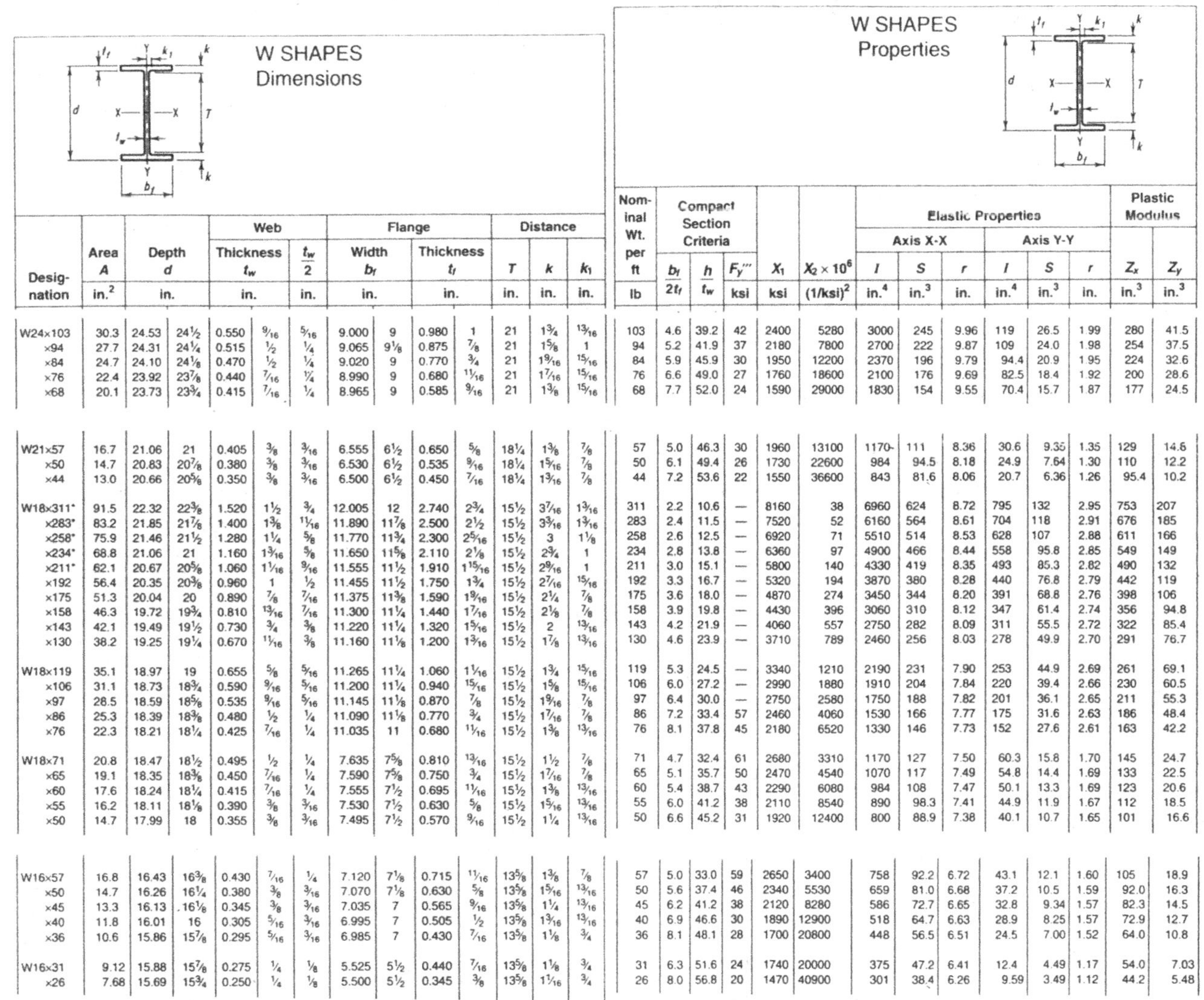

W SHAPES
Dimensions

Designation	Area A	Depth d		Web Thickness t_w		Web $\frac{t_w}{2}$	Flange Width b_f		Flange Thickness t_f		Distance T	Distance k	Distance k_1
	in.^{2}	in.		in.		in.	in.		in.		in.	in.	in.
W24×103	30.3	24.53	24 1/2	0.550	9/16	5/16	9.000	9	0.980	1	21	1 3/4	13/16
×94	27.7	24.31	24 1/4	0.515	1/2	1/4	9.065	9 1/8	0.875	7/8	21	1 5/8	1
×84	24.7	24.10	24 1/8	0.470	1/2	1/4	9.020	9	0.770	3/4	21	1 9/16	15/16
×76	22.4	23.92	23 7/8	0.440	7/16	1/4	8.990	9	0.680	11/16	21	1 7/16	15/16
×68	20.1	23.73	23 3/4	0.415	7/16	1/4	8.965	9	0.585	9/16	21	1 3/8	15/16
W21×57	16.7	21.06	21	0.405	3/8	3/16	6.555	6 1/2	0.650	5/8	18 1/4	1 3/8	7/8
×50	14.7	20.83	20 7/8	0.380	3/8	3/16	6.530	6 1/2	0.535	9/16	18 1/4	1 5/16	7/8
×44	13.0	20.66	20 5/8	0.350	3/8	3/16	6.500	6 1/2	0.450	7/16	18 1/4	1 3/16	7/8
W18×311*	91.5	22.32	22 3/8	1.520	1 1/2	3/4	12.005	12	2.740	2 3/4	15 1/2	3 7/16	1 3/16
×283*	83.2	21.85	21 7/8	1.400	1 3/8	11/16	11.890	11 7/8	2.500	2 1/2	15 1/2	3 3/16	1 3/16
×258*	75.9	21.46	21 1/2	1.280	1 1/4	5/8	11.770	11 3/4	2.300	2 5/16	15 1/2	3	1 1/8
×234*	68.8	21.06	21	1.160	1 3/16	5/8	11.650	11 5/8	2.110	2 1/8	15 1/2	2 3/4	1
×211*	62.1	20.67	20 5/8	1.060	1 1/16	9/16	11.555	11 1/2	1.910	1 15/16	15 1/2	2 9/16	1
×192	56.4	20.35	20 3/8	0.960	1	1/2	11.455	11 1/2	1.750	1 3/4	15 1/2	2 7/16	15/16
×175	51.3	20.04	20	0.890	7/8	7/16	11.375	11 3/8	1.590	1 9/16	15 1/2	2 1/4	7/8
×158	46.3	19.72	19 3/4	0.810	13/16	7/16	11.300	11 1/4	1.440	1 7/16	15 1/2	2 1/8	7/8
×143	42.1	19.49	19 1/2	0.730	3/4	3/8	11.220	11 1/4	1.320	1 5/16	15 1/2	2	13/16
×130	38.2	19.25	19 1/4	0.670	11/16	3/8	11.160	11 1/8	1.200	1 3/16	15 1/2	1 7/8	13/16
W18×119	35.1	18.97	19	0.655	5/8	5/16	11.265	11 1/4	1.060	1 1/16	15 1/2	1 3/4	15/16
×106	31.1	18.73	18 3/4	0.590	9/16	5/16	11.200	11 1/4	0.940	15/16	15 1/2	1 5/8	15/16
×97	28.5	18.59	18 5/8	0.535	9/16	5/16	11.145	11 1/8	0.870	7/8	15 1/2	1 9/16	7/8
×86	25.3	18.39	18 3/8	0.480	1/2	1/4	11.090	11 1/8	0.770	3/4	15 1/2	1 7/16	7/8
×76	22.3	18.21	18 1/4	0.425	7/16	1/4	11.035	11	0.680	11/16	15 1/2	1 3/8	13/16
W18×71	20.8	18.47	18 1/2	0.495	1/2	1/4	7.635	7 5/8	0.810	13/16	15 1/2	1 1/2	7/8
×65	19.1	18.35	18 3/8	0.450	7/16	1/4	7.590	7 5/8	0.750	3/4	15 1/2	1 7/16	7/8
×60	17.6	18.24	18 1/4	0.415	7/16	1/4	7.555	7 1/2	0.695	11/16	15 1/2	1 3/8	13/16
×55	16.2	18.11	18 1/8	0.390	3/8	3/16	7.530	7 1/2	0.630	5/8	15 1/2	1 5/16	13/16
×50	14.7	17.99	18	0.355	3/8	3/16	7.495	7 1/2	0.570	9/16	15 1/2	1 1/4	13/16
W16×57	16.8	16.43	16 3/8	0.430	7/16	1/4	7.120	7 1/8	0.715	11/16	13 5/8	1 3/8	7/8
×50	14.7	16.26	16 1/4	0.380	3/8	3/16	7.070	7 1/8	0.630	5/8	13 5/8	1 5/16	13/16
×45	13.3	16.13	16 1/8	0.345	3/8	3/16	7.035	7	0.565	9/16	13 5/8	1 1/4	13/16
×40	11.8	16.01	16	0.305	5/16	3/16	6.995	7	0.505	1/2	13 5/8	1 3/16	13/16
×36	10.6	15.86	15 7/8	0.295	5/16	3/16	6.985	7	0.430	7/16	13 5/8	1 1/8	3/4
W16×31	9.12	15.88	15 7/8	0.275	1/4	1/8	5.525	5 1/2	0.440	7/16	13 5/8	1 1/8	3/4
×26	7.68	15.69	15 3/4	0.250	1/4	1/8	5.500	5 1/2	0.345	3/8	13 5/8	1 1/16	3/4

W SHAPES
Properties

Nominal Wt. per ft	Compact Section Criteria $\frac{b_f}{2t_f}$	$\frac{h}{t_w}$	F_y'''	X_1	$X_2 \times 10^6$	Elastic Properties Axis X-X I	S	r	Axis Y-Y I	S	r	Plastic Modulus Z_x	Z_y
lb			ksi	ksi	(1/ksi)^2	in.^{4}	in.^{3}	in.	in.^{4}	in.^{3}	in.	in.^{3}	in.^{3}
103	4.6	39.2	42	2400	5280	3000	245	9.96	119	26.5	1.99	280	41.5
94	5.2	41.9	37	2180	7800	2700	222	9.87	109	24.0	1.98	254	37.5
84	5.9	45.9	30	1950	12200	2370	196	9.79	94.4	20.9	1.95	224	32.6
76	6.6	49.0	27	1760	18600	2100	176	9.69	82.5	18.4	1.92	200	28.6
68	7.7	52.0	24	1590	29000	1830	154	9.55	70.4	15.7	1.87	177	24.5
57	5.0	46.3	30	1960	13100	1170	111	8.36	30.6	9.35	1.35	129	14.6
50	6.1	49.4	26	1730	22600	984	94.5	8.18	24.9	7.64	1.30	110	12.2
44	7.2	53.6	22	1550	36600	843	81.6	8.06	20.7	6.36	1.26	95.4	10.2
311	2.2	10.6	—	8160	38	6960	624	8.72	795	132	2.95	753	207
283	2.4	11.5	—	7520	52	6160	564	8.61	704	118	2.91	676	185
258	2.6	12.5	—	6920	71	5510	514	8.53	628	107	2.88	611	166
234	2.8	13.8	—	6360	97	4900	466	8.44	558	95.8	2.85	549	149
211	3.0	15.1	—	5800	140	4330	419	8.35	493	85.3	2.82	490	132
192	3.3	16.7	—	5320	194	3870	380	8.28	440	76.8	2.79	442	119
175	3.6	18.0	—	4870	274	3450	344	8.20	391	68.8	2.76	398	106
158	3.9	19.8	—	4430	396	3060	310	8.12	347	61.4	2.74	356	94.8
143	4.2	21.9	—	4060	557	2750	282	8.09	311	55.5	2.72	322	85.4
130	4.6	23.9	—	3710	789	2460	256	8.03	278	49.9	2.70	291	76.7
119	5.3	24.5	—	3340	1210	2190	231	7.90	253	44.9	2.69	261	69.1
106	6.0	27.2	—	2990	1880	1910	204	7.84	220	39.4	2.66	230	60.5
97	6.4	30.0	—	2750	2580	1750	188	7.82	201	36.1	2.65	211	55.3
86	7.2	33.4	57	2460	4060	1530	166	7.77	175	31.6	2.63	186	48.4
76	8.1	37.8	45	2180	6520	1330	146	7.73	152	27.6	2.61	163	42.2
71	4.7	32.4	61	2680	3310	1170	127	7.50	60.3	15.8	1.70	145	24.7
65	5.1	35.7	50	2470	4540	1070	117	7.49	54.8	14.4	1.69	133	22.5
60	5.4	38.7	43	2290	6080	984	108	7.47	50.1	13.3	1.69	123	20.6
55	6.0	41.2	38	2110	8540	890	98.3	7.41	44.9	11.9	1.67	112	18.5
50	6.6	45.2	31	1920	12400	800	88.9	7.38	40.1	10.7	1.65	101	16.6
57	5.0	33.0	59	2650	3400	758	92.2	6.72	43.1	12.1	1.60	105	18.9
50	5.6	37.4	46	2340	5530	659	81.0	6.68	37.2	10.5	1.59	92.0	16.3
45	6.2	41.2	38	2120	8280	586	72.7	6.65	32.8	9.34	1.57	82.3	14.5
40	6.9	46.6	30	1890	12900	518	64.7	6.63	28.9	8.25	1.57	72.9	12.7
36	8.1	48.1	28	1700	20800	448	56.5	6.51	24.5	7.00	1.52	64.0	10.8
31	6.3	51.6	24	1740	20000	375	47.2	6.41	12.4	4.49	1.17	54.0	7.03
26	8.0	56.8	20	1470	40900	301	38.4	6.26	9.59	3.49	1.12	44.2	5.48

Figure 18.30 Properties of more steel wide-flange shapes from the *Manual of Steel Construction.*

Courtesy of the American Institute of Steel Construction.

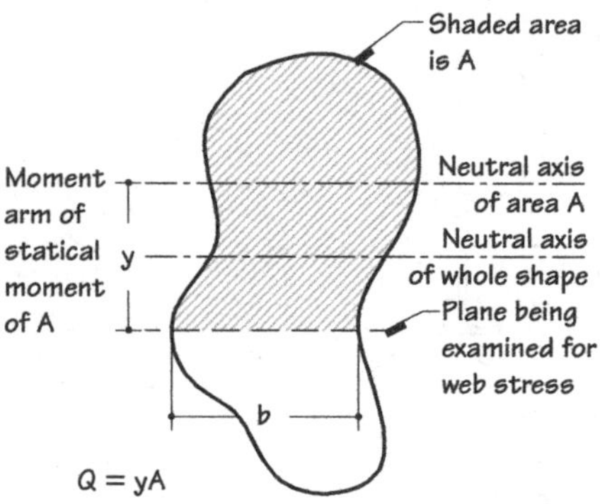

Figure 18.31 Finding web stress at any location in a beam of any shape.

forces in the web is almost purely diagonal (Figure 18.32). The resulting distribution of web stresses over the height of the section (Figure 18.33) is so nearly constant that we employ an expression for it that assumes a constant distribution:

$$f_v^{max} = \frac{V}{A_w} \qquad [18\text{-}7]$$

where:

V is the maximum vertical force on the beam, taken from the V diagram, and

A_w is the cross-sectional area of the web of the beam, which is the product of the depth of the beam and the thickness of the web.

Consider for our office building a W16×26 beam that carries a uniformly distributed load, including its own weight, of 92,000 lb. What is the maximum web stress?

A W16×26 is a wide-flange shape that is nominally 16 in. deep and weighs 26 lb/ft. In the *Manual of Steel Construction,* (Figure 18.30), we find that the actual depth of this beam is 15.69 in., and the thickness of the web is 0.25 in. The maximum value of V for this beam occurs at the reactions, each of which

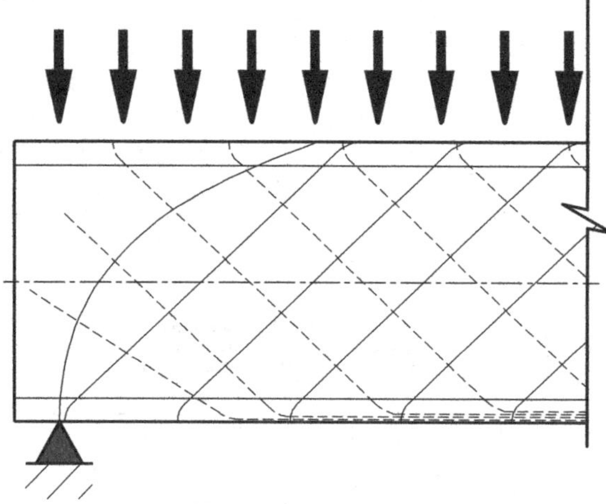

Figure 18.32 The flow of forces in a wide-flange beam. Web stress is almost constant across the height of the web.

is half the total load, or 46,000 lb. The maximum web stress may be approximated as:

$$f_v^{max} = \frac{V}{A_w} = \frac{46{,}000 \text{ lb.}}{(15.69 \text{ in.})(0.25 \text{ in.})} = 11{,}700 \text{ psi}$$

The allowable web stress in A36 structural steel is 14,500 psi, so this is a satisfactory result.

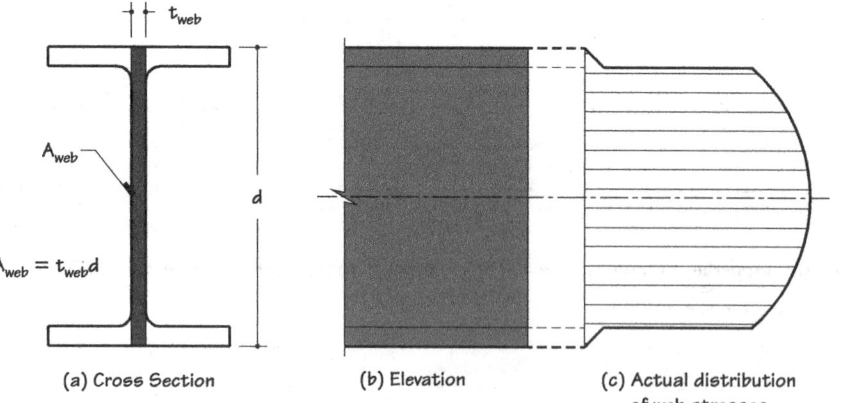

Figure 18.33 (a) The shaded area is considered to be the area of the web of a wide-flange beam. (b) A side view of the beam. (c) The distribution of web stresses, which we approximate as a rectangle.

NONRECTANGULAR BEAMS IN MATERIALS OTHER THAN STEEL

The expressions and methods developed in this chapter are essential tools in our structural design toolbox. They apply not only to steel shapes but to any beam shape in any homogeneous material (Figure 18.34). A common example is the use of tree trunks for beams in rustic buildings; these are treated as beams with circular cross sections. Another is plywood or steel box girders. We may wish to develop corrugated materials for decking, sandwich panels, stressed-skin panels, or (at larger scale) folded plate structures. With the formulas in this chapter, we will find the values of I and S for known material configurations, as well as new ones of our own design, and confront these situations with confidence.

SELECTING BEAM AND GIRDER SECTIONS FOR A STEEL-FRAMED OFFICE BUILDING

We now return to the task of finding the required sizes of typical steel beams and girders for the office building we are designing. Figure 18.35 is a portion of a framing plan. We have settled on

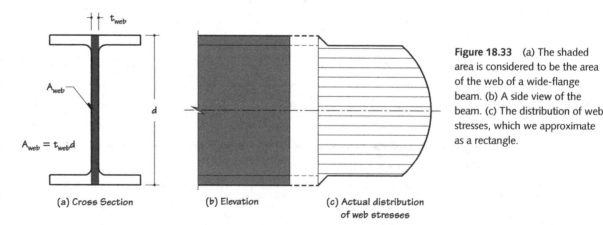

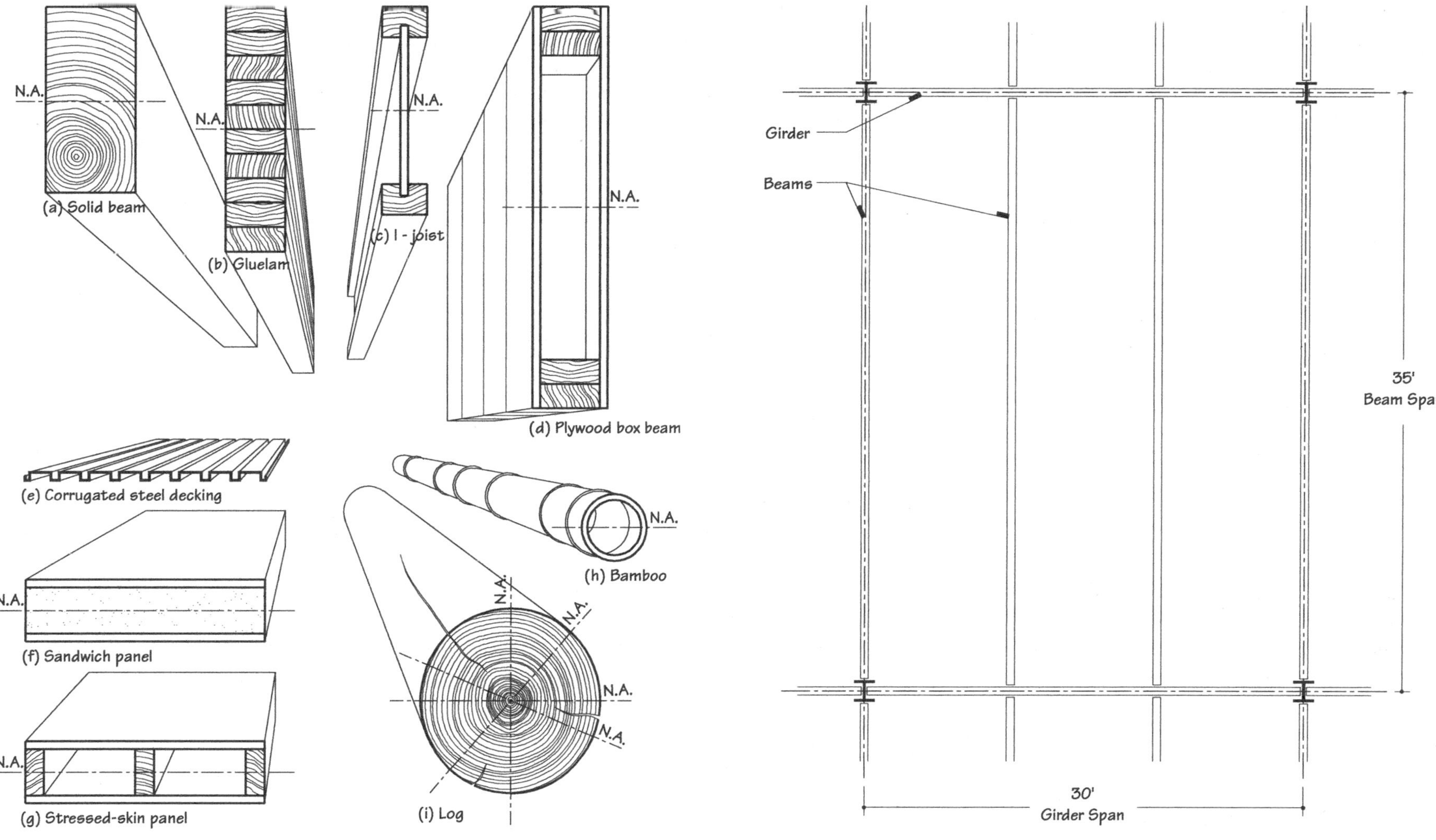

Figure 18.34 Other shapes and other materials used as beams.

Figure 18.35 A bay of framing in the building we are designing.

a bay size of 30 ft by 35 ft. (The span has been shortened by a foot in order to accommodate the exterior wall system that is being used.) The floor is supported by corrugated steel decking sheets that span across wide-flange beams spaced 10 ft apart. The beams span 35 ft between wide-flange girders that span 30 ft. The live load, in this case the minimum specified by the building code, is 50 lb per square foot, and the dead load of the floor structure is estimated at 65 lb per square foot. The allowable stresses in the steel are 24,000 psi for bending stresses and 14,500 psi for web stresses. What sizes of steel wide-flange shapes are required for typical beams and girders?

Selecting the Beam

Each beam supports a tributary area that is 10 ft wide and 35 ft long, a total of 350 sq ft. A steel beam generally has a depth of about 1/20th of its span:

$$\text{Approximate depth of beam} = \frac{L}{20} = \frac{(35 \text{ ft})(12 \text{ in./ft})}{20}$$
$$= 21 \text{ in.}$$

As stated, wide-flange shapes are furnished in nominal sizes that are even numbers of inches up to 18 in., after which they increase in 3-in. increments. Thus we will assume a 21-in. nominal depth. By picking a weight from the middle of the range of 21-in. shapes in the *Manual of Steel Construction*, we estimate the self-weight of the beam at 60 lb per foot of length. Now we are ready to estimate the total load on the beam and determine its size. We include the estimated self-weight of the beam:

$$\text{Total load} = W = (65 \text{ psf } DL + 50 \text{ psf } LL)(350 \text{ ft}^2) + (35 \text{ ft})(60 \text{ lb/ft}) = 42{,}350 \text{ lb}$$

$$M_{max} = \frac{WL}{8} = \frac{(42{,}350 \text{ lb})(35 \text{ ft})(12 \text{ in./ft})}{8} = 2{,}223{,}000 \text{ lb-in.}$$

$$S_{req} = \frac{M_{max}}{f_b} = \frac{2{,}223{,}000 \text{ lb-in.}}{24{,}000 \text{ lb/in.}^3} = 92.6 \text{ in.}^3$$

Consulting the design tables in the *Manual of Steel Construction*, we find that a W21×50, with a section modulus of 94.5, is the smallest beam of this depth that will suffice. The beam is about 350 lb lighter than our estimate, a difference of less than 1 percent of the total load, which is inconsequential.

We must also check web stress, using detailed dimensions from the *Manual of Steel Construction*. V_{max} is half the total load on the beam, 21,175 lb:

$$f_v^{max} = \frac{V_{max}}{A_w} = \frac{21{,}175 \text{ lb}}{(20.83 \text{ in.})(0.380 \text{ in.})} = 2{,}675 \text{ psi} < 14{,}500 \quad \text{okay}$$

The deflection of this beam under full load should not exceed $L/360$. We reduce the total load by 350 lb to reflect the difference between the estimated and actual weights of the beam:

$$\Delta_{max} = \frac{5}{384}\frac{WL^3}{EI} = \frac{5}{384}\frac{(42{,}000 \text{ lb})(420 \text{ in.})^3}{(29{,}000{,}000 \text{ psi})(984 \text{ in.}^4)} = 1.42 \text{ in.}$$

This is $L/296$, which is excessive. We try the next larger size beam, W21×57, which has a moment of inertia of 1,170. Ignoring the trivial effect of the additional weight of the beam, we can get a quick idea of its deflection by multiplying the previously calculated deflection, 1.42 in., by the ratio of the two moments of inertia:

$$\Delta_{max} = \frac{984}{1170}(1.42 \text{ in.}) = 1.19 \text{ in.}$$

This is $L/352$, slightly below $L/360$. We could adopt a W21×62 instead, or stay with the W21×57, on the basis that the majority of the total load on the beam is dead load and that, consequently, the live-load deflection will be satisfactory.

Selecting the Girder

An interior girder supports beams from both sides, so its loads will be double that of the girders in the exterior walls. The beams will be attached to the girder with standard *coped connections*, in which the top flange of the beam is cut back (*coped*) to provide level support for the steel decking (Figure 18.14d). Because the bending moment in the last few inches of a span approaches zero, the web is able to resist all the stress in this region, and the beam is not affected by the cope. In order to have sufficient space for the end of the beam to nest inside the flanges of the girder, the girder must be at least one standard size deeper than the beam. This suggests a preliminary selection of a 24-in.-wide flange for the girder. The rule-of-thumb depth for a girder is 1/15 of the span:

$$d = \frac{L}{15} = \frac{360 \text{ in.}}{15} = 24 \text{ in.}$$

We adopt a 24-in. depth as a preliminary size for the girder.

The primary loads on the girder are two concentrated loads at its third points of 42,350 lb each, the sum of the reactions of the two beams that it supports at that point. There is also a self-weight for the girder, a distributed load that we estimate to be 100 lb/ft, for a total of 3,000 lb. We derive the expression for the maximum moment for the third-point loadings by drawing V and M diagrams (Figure 18.36), and find the maximum total bending moment by adding the moments attributable to the two loadings:

$$M_{max} = \frac{PL}{3} + \frac{wL^2}{8}$$

$$M_{max} = \frac{(42{,}350 \text{ lb})(30 \text{ ft})(12 \text{ in./ft})}{3} + \frac{(3{,}000 \text{ lb})(30 \text{ ft})(12 \text{ in./ft})}{8} = 5{,}217{,}000 \text{ lb-in.}$$

$$S_{req} = \frac{M_{max}}{f_b} = \frac{5{,}217{,}000 \text{ lb-in.}}{24{,}000 \text{ lb/in.}^2} = 217 \text{ in.}^3$$

A W24×94, with $S = 222$ in.³, is selected from the *Manual of Steel Construction*.

We check the maximum web stress. The maximum value of vertical force is equal to the reaction:

$$R = \frac{2(42{,}350 \text{ lb}) + (94 \text{ lb/ft})(30 \text{ ft})}{2} = 43{,}760 \text{ lb}$$

We check deflection for the two concentrated loads with a formula from the *Manual of Steel Construction* that is general for two loads in any symmetrical pair of locations. We simplify the formula by substituting values for the locations of the two loads of $L/3$ from the ends of the span:

$$\Delta_{max} = 0.0355\frac{PL^3}{EI} = 0.0355\frac{(43{,}760 \text{ lb})(360 \text{ in.})^3}{(29{,}000{,}000 \text{ psi})(2{,}700 \text{ in.}^4)} = 0.93 \text{ in.}$$

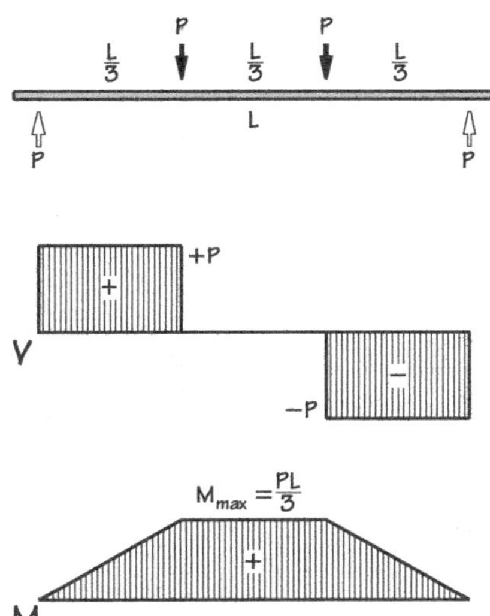

Figure 18.36 Finding the maximum bending moment in a beam loaded at its third points.

To this we add the deflection attributable to the beam's self-weight:

$$\Delta_{max} = \frac{5}{384}\frac{WL^3}{EI} = \frac{5}{384}\frac{(2{,}820 \text{ lb})(360 \text{ in.}^3)}{(29{,}000{,}000 \text{ psi})(2{,}700 \text{ in.}^4)} = 0.02 \text{ in.}$$

$$f_v^{max} = \frac{V_{max}}{A_w} = \frac{43{,}760 \text{ lb}}{(24.31 \text{ in.})(0.515 \text{ in.})} = 3{,}495 \text{ psi} < 14{,}500 \quad \text{okay}$$

The total deflection of the girder at midspan is 0.95 in. This is $L/379$, which is good.

OTHER FACTORS IN SELECTING AND SIZING STRUCTURAL STEEL BEAMS

Buckling of the Compression Edge

Like any other compression member, the compression edge of a beam (the top edge in a simply supported beam) may buckle. Beams that support floor or roof decks are generally fastened very securely to the decking along their top edges. The compression flange of each beam and girder in the floor structure that we are considering is laterally supported by being welded or screwed to the corrugated steel decking. The compression edge of a wood floor joist is nailed or screwed to the plywood subfloor above, and often glued as well. In neither case is buckling likely. However, a beam that is not attached to a deck or otherwise restrained may be in danger of buckling. Empirical formulas are used to reduce the allowable bending stresses in such beams to levels low enough that buckling is not likely.

Web Crippling

Webs of deep steel beams, especially plate girders, may crush or *cripple* under the concentrated vertical forces that occur at the supports of the beam or at points where loads are applied. In actuality, what happens is essentially a buckling of the thin web where it is loaded like a tall, thin wall. Vertical stiffener plates or angles on either side of the web are the usual response to this problem (Figure 18.37).

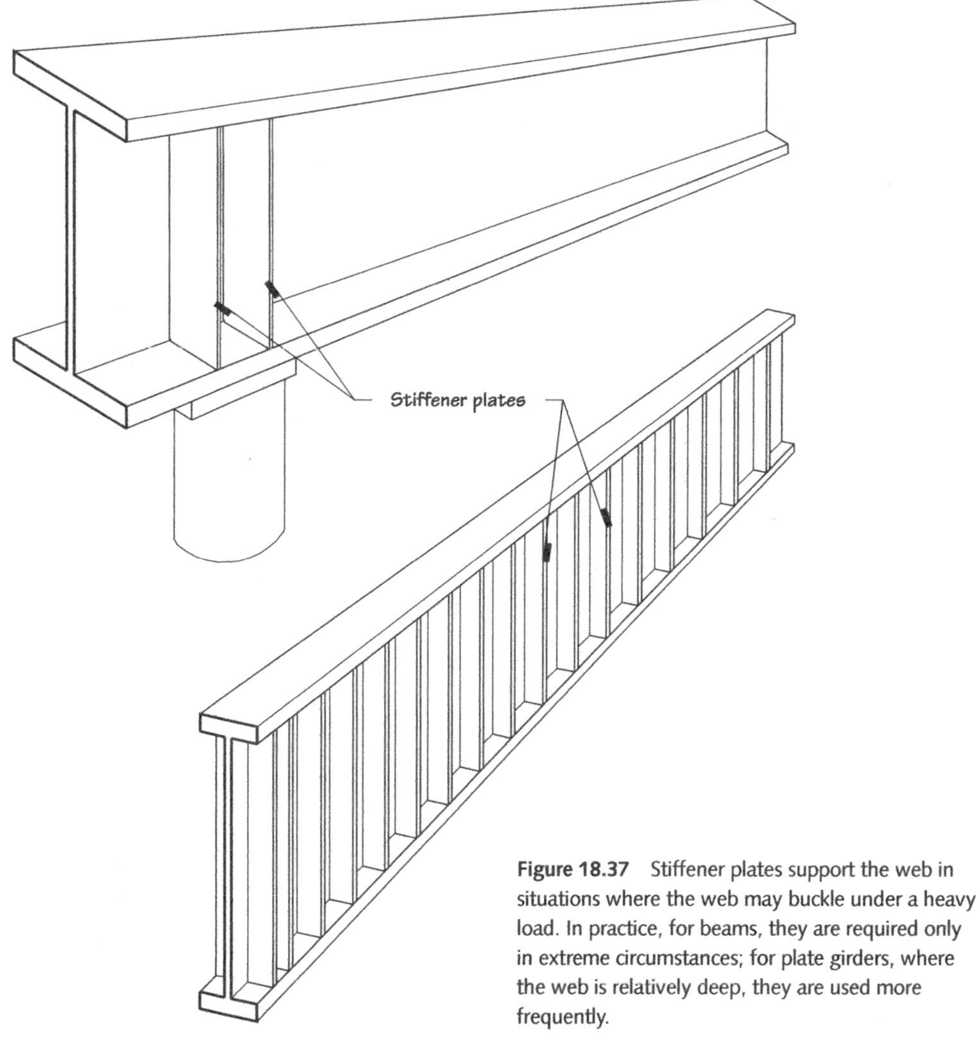

Figure 18.37 Stiffener plates support the web in situations where the web may buckle under a heavy load. In practice, for beams, they are required only in extreme circumstances; for plate girders, where the web is relatively deep, they are used more frequently.

THE IMPORTANCE OF FINDING GOOD SHAPES FOR BEAM SECTIONS

Figure 18.38 summarizes the most valuable lesson of this chapter: **The manner in which the material of a beam is arranged is vitally important.** The seven beam shapes in this illustration each contain 100 in.^{2} of material, but the stiffest of the seven, as measured by its moment of inertia, is about 360 times as stiff as the weakest. Even with readily available shapes, we can develop a repertoire of design strategies to both reduce material and to use it more effectively, to reduce and rationalize joints and connections where necessary and practical, and to combine materials and components in creative and useful ways.

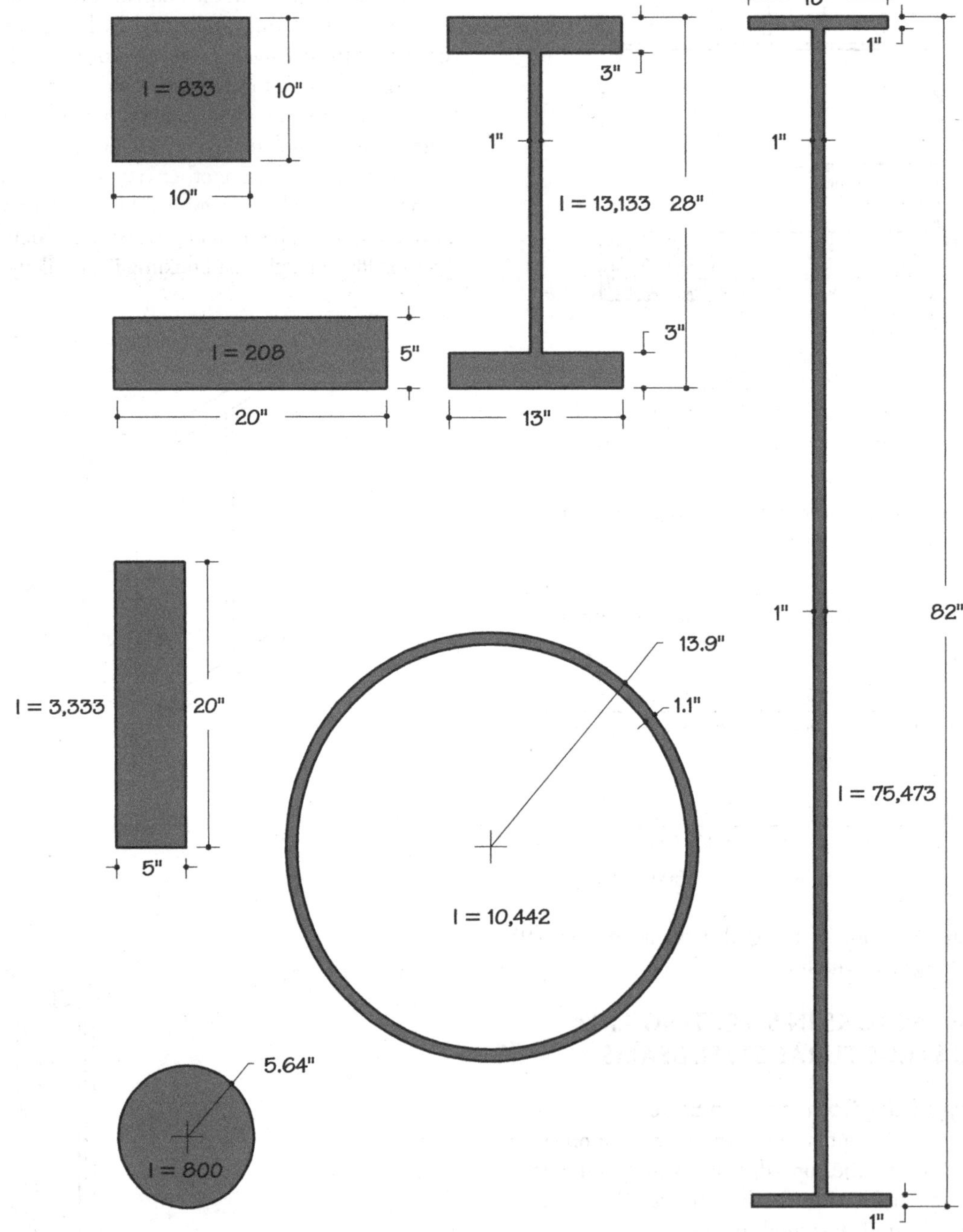

Figure 18.38 Each of these shapes contains exactly 100 sq in. of steel, yet the moments of inertia vary from 208 to more than 75,000.

Exercises

1. Select a shape for an interior girder in the building we have been working on, assuming that the building is 6 bays long at 25 ft each.

2. The building we have designed has a two-story lobby space at the entry. The balcony guardrail has a railing 4 ft high that is supported by vertical steel members spaced 9 ft apart. The space between the railing and the floor is filled with large sheets of tempered glass. The building code requires that the guardrail be capable of resisting a uniform horizontal load on the railing of 50 lb per linear foot. It must also be capable of resisting a single horizontal load of 200 lb applied to the railing at any point. Figure 18.39 shows a tentative detail of a typical vertical. The angles that attach it to the beam will be welded to both members. Find the required depth of a steel plate vertical member that is 1 in. thick. The 1-in. dimension is measured parallel to the railing at the top. Develop a detail for the entire guardrail that will give it an appropriate character for the building.

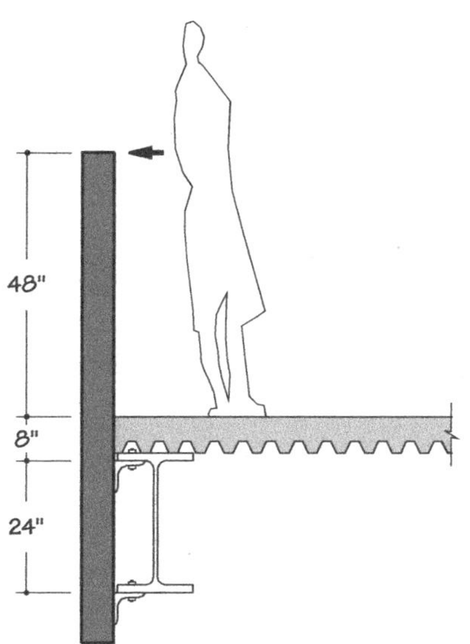

Figure 18.39 A diagram of the proposed guardrail for the office building.

Figure 18.40 Italian engineer Pier Luigi Nervi framed each roof bay in his Palazzo del Lavoro in Turin, Italy, with custom-designed steel plate girders radiating from a central concrete column. The tapering profile of each girder reflects the decrease in bending moments that takes place with increasing distance from the supports. Why do you think he did not make the profile of the girder match more closely the curve of the moment diagram? For that matter, what would be the ideal profile for a girder in this situation, where the tributary area and load increase with increasing distance from the support? Notice the visual interest added by the orderly pattern of stiffeners.

Source: Pier Luigi Nervi, *Aesthetics and Technology in Building*. Cambridge, MA: Harvard University Press, 1965.

3. A beam spans 28 ft and carries a load of 675 lb per foot. Find sizes for two alternate choices: a steel beam and a glulam wood beam. Which is deeper? Which is heavier?

4. How large a beam would be required if we decided to substitute a steel beam for the wood one under the deck in Chapter 17?

5. One end of a steel wide-flange beam is embedded in a masonry wall. At the other end, 13 ft 5 in. from the face of the wall, it supports a pulley that may become loaded by as much as 12,000 lb. Ignoring for this exercise the risk of buckling or twisting of the beam, how large does it need to be?

6. Is there a shape that would be more resistant than a wide-flange to buckling and twisting (torsion) in question 5? Why?

Key Terms and Concepts

steel
shapes
wide-flange shapes
extreme fibers
flanges
web
angles
channels
tees
plates
bars
pipes
tubes
corrugated steel decking
light-gauge steel framing
open-web steel joist
joist girders
castellated beams
fabricator
shop drawings
ironworker
erector
plumbed-up
composite construction
shear studs
fireproofing
intumescent paint
inverted V-bracing
wind trusses
plate girder
I-joist
box beam
sandwich panel
stressed-skin panel
composite shape
component shapes
moment of inertia, I
section modulus, S
transfer formula

$$f_b^{max} = \frac{Mc}{I} \quad [18\text{-}1]$$

$$f_b = \frac{M}{S} \quad [18\text{-}2]$$

$$f_b^y = \frac{My}{I} \quad [18\text{-}3]$$

$$I_x = \bar{I}_x + Ad^2 \quad [18\text{-}4]$$

$$f_v = \frac{VQ}{Ib} \quad [18\text{-}5]$$

$$f_v^{max} = \frac{3V}{2bd} \quad [18\text{-}6]$$

$$f_v^{max} = \frac{V}{A_w} \quad [18\text{-}7]$$

coped connection
web crippling
web stiffener

Further Resources

American Institute of Steel Construction. *Manual of Steel Construction.* Chicago: AISC; updated frequently. See also www.aisc.org. This is the standard reference of the American steel industry, with comprehensive data on available structural shapes and alloys, allowable strengths, connections, details, and much more.

Eggen, Arne Petter, and Bjorn Norman Sandeker. *Steel Structure and Architecture.* New York: Whitney Library of Design, 1995. The authors have crafted a beautiful, heavily illustrated introduction to the visual aspects of steel construction.

www.greatbuildings.com/types/construction/steel.html

CHAPTER 19

Designing Columns, Frames, and Load-Bearing Walls

- *Types of columns: short, intermediate, long; buckling and deflection*
- *Designing column restraints; designing optimum forms for columns*
- *Load-bearing walls*
- *Portal frames; hinges*
- *Architectural and historical expressions of columns*

In this chapter we will learn about columns and load-bearing walls, the vertical elements of building frames that carry primarily axial loads. We will also explore rigid frames, in which columns and beams work together in bending to resist gravity and lateral loads.

Although we will discuss some of the factors that are involved in assigning sizes to columns and walls, we will not derive all of the specialized mathematical expressions for this purpose. Preliminary sizing may be done using the charts in *The Architect's Studio Companion*. More refined estimates of column sizes can be found rapidly by using tables of precalculated columns in the *Manual of Steel Construction*, the *Concrete Reinforcing Steel Institute Handbook*, *Concrete Masonry Design Tables*, and *Wood Structural Design Data*, which are listed under Further Resources at the end of the chapter.

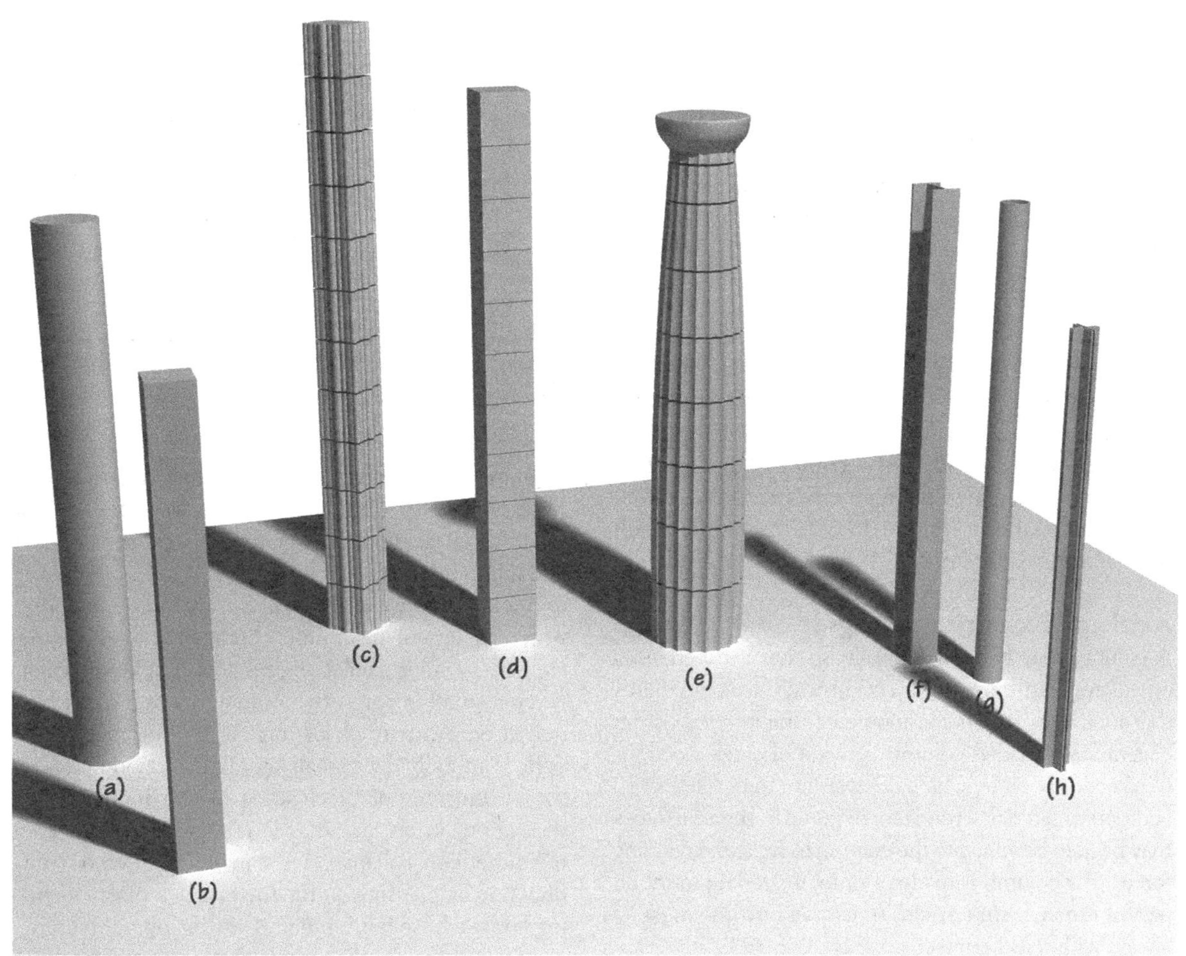

Figure 19.1 A sampling of column styles: (a, b) concrete or wood columns, cylindrical and rectangular; (c) gothic limestone; (d) square stone; (e) Doric marble; (f) steel wide-flange; (g) steel pipe; (h) four steel angles joined in an X-configuration.

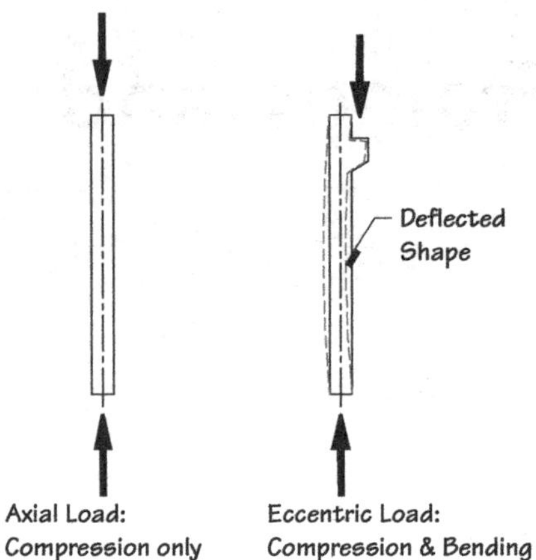

Figure 19.2 An axial load on a column creates uniform compressive stress. An eccentric load creates bending and a linear distribution of stress, some of which may be tensile.

COLUMNS

The physical function of columns is to receive the loads from the floor and roof framing of a building and pass them safely via the foundations into the earth beneath a building. Over the course of history, columns have often been given an expressive role as well as a functional one (Figure 19.1), a theme to which we will return a bit later.

Axial and Eccentric Loadings

A column may be loaded axially, so that it experiences only compressive forces, or eccentrically, which requires that it also resist bending moments (Figure 19.2). If an eccentrically loaded column is made of steel, wood, or reinforced concrete, which are resistant to tensile forces, additional material beyond that required by the axial forces may need to be added to the column to resist the bending forces. If a column is made of unreinforced masonry, no part of it may be in tension, so its pressure line must lie always within its kern (see pp. 221, 392, 393).

Buckling

A column can fail because its material is crushed by the load that it carries, or because it buckles, or by a combination of crushing and buckling (Figure 19.3). A *short column* is one that will always fail by the crushing or yielding of its material, because it is thick enough in relation to its length that it has no tendency to buckle. A *long column* will always fail by *buckling*, which is lateral instability characteristic of slender elements under axial compression. Buckling occurs when a small imperfection of material or a small incidental eccentricity of loading causes the member to deflect laterally. This small lateral deflection increases the eccentricity of the loading, which increases the deflection, in an instantaneous repetition that leads to immediate collapse. We can readily demonstrate buckling by pressing on the top end of a plastic drinking straw whose bottom end is resting on a tabletop.

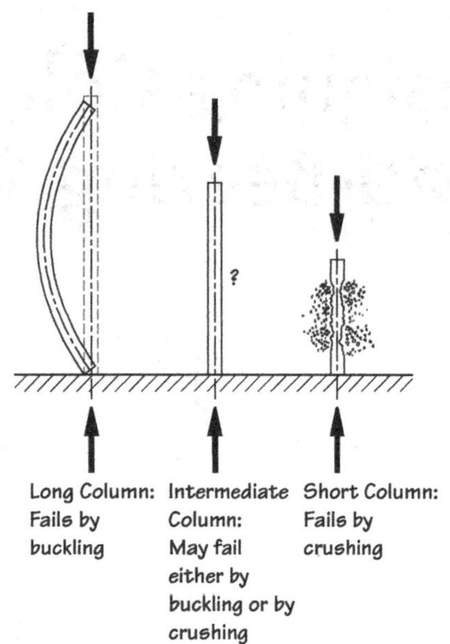

Figure 19.3 Long columns fail by buckling, and short columns by crushing or yielding. Intermediate columns may fail by either mechanism.

Some columns that are neither as long as long columns nor as short as short columns may fail by either buckling or crushing. These are classified as *intermediate columns*. We have reasonably reliable mathematical tools for predicting the load-bearing capacity of short and long columns. There is no satisfactory theoretical expression for the corresponding capacity of intermediate columns. Consequently, the mathematics of intermediate columns is based largely on empirical tests of actual columns, as well as interpolation between expressions relating to short and long columns.

The classification of a column as short, medium, or long is based on its *slenderness ratio*. For a wooden column, the slenderness ratio is L/s, the length of the column divided by the cross-sectional dimension of its shorter side. For example, the slenderness ratio of a wood 4 × 6 column 9 ft high (whose actual cross-sectional dimensions are 3.5 and 5.5 in.) is its height in inches, 108, divided by the lesser dimension of the cross section, 3.5 in. This comes to 30.9. If this column is supported laterally at midheight so that it cannot buckle in the 3.5-in. direction, its slenderness ratio becomes its length divided by its larger dimension, 5.5 in., which is 19.6.

The greatest slenderness ratio permitted by code for a wood column is 50. The length of the longest column that we can make from a wood 6 × 6, which actually measures 5.5 in. on each side, is thus:

$$L/s = 50$$

$$L/5.5 \text{ in.} = 50$$

$$L = 275 \text{ in.} = 22 \text{ ft-11 in.}$$

For a wood 4 × 4, actually 3.5 in. square, the maximum length works out to 14 ft–7 in., and for a wood 2-in. member, it is 6 ft–3 in. Columns may be longer than these dimensions if they are restrained laterally against buckling at appropriate interior points.

Because of the much greater diversity of shapes used for steel columns than for wood ones, their slenderness ratio is based on a property of the section called its *radius of gyration*, abbreviated r. The value of r is equal to the square root of the moment of inertia of the section divided by its area:

$$r = \sqrt{\frac{I}{A}}$$

Values of r for structural steel shapes are presented in the tables of section properties in the *Manual of Steel Construction*. Slenderness ratios in steel columns may not exceed 200.

End Conditions and Effective Lengths of Columns

Figure 19.4 shows that the same column can have several different load-bearing capacities, depending on its end conditions. The base condition is a column that is pinned (hinged) at both ends (a), which is arbitrarily assigned a coefficient k, of 1.0. If both ends of the column are fixed so they cannot rotate (b), the column has a coefficient of 0.5, meaning that its buckling potential is calculated on the basis of an *effective length* that is half of its actual length. If one end is pinned and the other fixed, k is 0.7. If one end is fixed and the other free of restraint or support, like a flagpole, k is 2.0: This column acts like a column twice as long that is pinned at both ends. In other words, the load-bearing capacity of a column is greatly increased by fixing one or both of its ends so they cannot rotate. It is greatly decreased if one end is fixed and the other is free of any support.

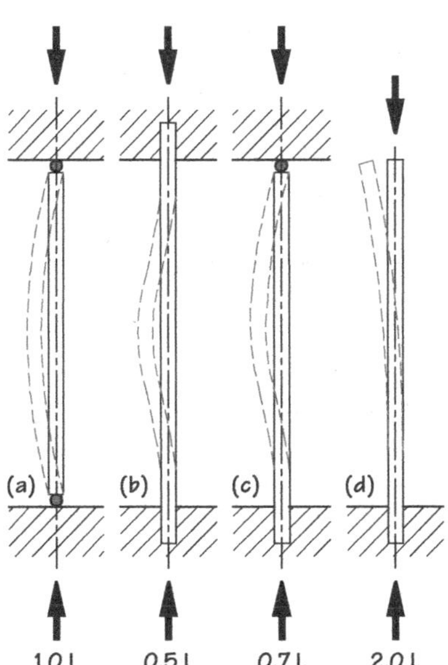

Figure 19.4 The effective length of a column depends on its end conditions.

Predicting the Buckling Load on a Column

The Swiss mathematician Leonhard Euler (pronounced OY-lur;1707–1783) published in 1757 the expression that is still the basis for sizing of long columns. It establishes the theoretical load at which a column will buckle:

$$P_{cr} = \frac{\pi^2 EI}{L^2} \qquad [19\text{-}1]$$

where:

P_{cr} is the critical buckling load,

E is the modulus of elasticity of the column material,

I is the moment of inertia of the cross section of the column, and

L is the effective length of the column.

We determined a few paragraphs earlier that the maximum allowable height for an unrestrained wood 6 × 6 column is 275 in. The moment of inertia of a 6 × 6 is 76.26 in.^{3} If the modulus of elasticity of the wood is 1,600,000 psi, what is the buckling load for a 6 × 6 column of maximum height?

$$P_{cr} = \frac{(3.14)^2(1{,}600{,}000 \text{ psi})(76.26 \text{ in.}^4)}{(275 \text{ in.})^2} = 15{,}900 \text{ lb}$$

What is the buckling load for a steel W10 × 45 column 30 ft long? We find in the *Manual of Steel Construction* that its moment of inertia is 248 in.^{4}:

$$P_{cr} = \frac{(3.14)^2(29{,}000{,}000 \text{ psi})(248 \text{ in.}^4)}{[(30 \text{ ft})(12 \text{ in./ft})]^2} = 547 \text{ kips}$$

We don't want to put this much load on either column, however. Euler's formula gives the load at which the column is likely to buckle, and includes no factor of safety.

For short columns, buckling is not an issue. The column can be predicted to fail at the ultimate compressive strength of the material. If a 6 × 6 wood column is 4 ft long and the ultimate compressive strength of the wood is 3,250 psi, we can predict that it will fail by crushing at an applied load of approximately:

$$F_u = \frac{P_{cr}}{A}$$

$$P_{cr} = F_{cr}A = (3{,}250 \text{ psi})(5.5 \text{ in.})^2 = 98{,}300 \text{ lb}$$

Again, this is the predicted load at failure. A factor of safety must be applied to determine a safe load.

Restrained Columns

Figure 19.5 depicts three columns. Two of them are restrained laterally by wheels, one at its midpoint and the other at its third points. Because each column

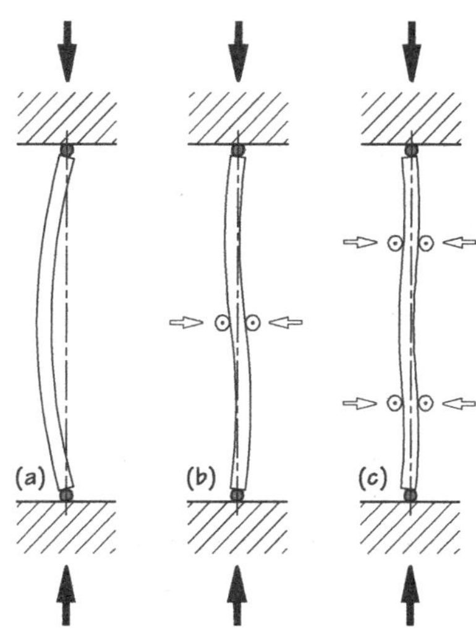

Figure 19.5 Lateral support affects both the potential buckling pattern of a column and its load-bearing capacity. Column (b) can support four times the load of (a); if the lateral restraints on column (c) were at its third points, it would support nine times as much load as (a).

is continuous between the pairs of wheels, buckling occurs in the patterns shown, and the effective length of the column is greatly reduced. The buckling loads on columns (b) and (c) are four times and nine times that of (a), respectively. The force that the restraining wheels must exert on the column is difficult to determine, but a value of about 2 percent of the maximum axial load is widely used.

We tend to think of columns as having hinged or pinned ends. This simplifies the assumptions that we make concerning their behavior, but fixing one or both ends, as we saw in Figure 19.4, saves material. It is relatively easy to achieve fixity by embedding the bottom end of a steel column at ground level in a concrete foundation to create a rigid joint. The top end may be embedded in concrete or welded to the beams and/or girders of the next level of framing, if fixity is desired.

Fixity is much more difficult to create in wood joints, which cannot be embedded in concrete in most circumstances without risking decay of the wood, and which can't be welded.

Sitecast concrete columns are just the opposite: It is much more difficult to make pinned joints than fixed ones. Nearly all concrete buildings have very rigid joints and take advantage of them to reduce member sizes for both columns and beams.

In longer-span structures such as arches and cables, we generally use hinged connections. This assures that the structures will experience axial forces rather than bending. But in shorter-span structures that act in bending, fixity of joints is often desirable.

Strong and Weak Axes of Columns

Figure 19.6 shows a column that is restrained at mid-height in one direction but not the other. This will behave as two different columns, one twice as long as the other, and must be checked for buckling in both directions. In situations like this, we often use a column that is stiffer with respect to one axis than the other, such as a wood 4 × 8 that is restrained in the 4-in. direction only.

Columns in Multistory Buildings

In a multistory building, the columns on the top floor support only the roof. Those on the next floor down support the roof plus one floor. At each floor, the columns must support the entire weight of the building above that floor. Floor by floor, the loads on the columns accumulate from top to bottom, so that the lowest columns support the maximum load. This is often expressed in columns that grow visibly in size from the top of the building to the bottom (Figure 19.7). This strategy conserves material, but for concrete columns it may result in increased expense for labor and formwork. Frequently, the columns in a multistory concrete building are all made the same size regardless of the level on which they occur. The amount of reinforcing steel in the columns may grow from top to bottom without altering the economy of using the same external column dimensions throughout the building.

Steel shapes with the same nominal dimensions are manufactured in a variety of metal thicknesses. For example, 8-in. round steel tubes are available in wall thicknesses of 0.322 in., 0.500 in., and 0.875 in., with cross-sectional areas of 8.4, 12.8, and 21.3 sq in., respectively. Nominal 10-in.-wide flange column shapes have cross-sectional areas that vary from 14.4 to 32.9 sq in. These ranges of sizes allow all the columns in a building to look much the same while their allowable loads vary considerably. On the other hand, many designers prefer the expressiveness of columns that change size visibly in proportion to the loads they carry.

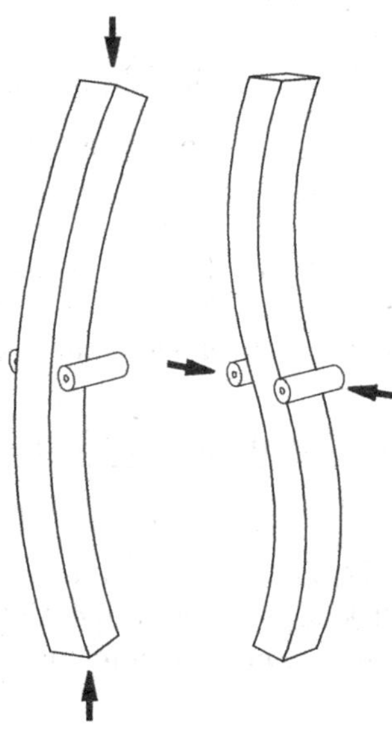

Figure 19.6 A rectangular column is more resistant to buckling in the direction of its larger dimension, but if restraint is provided in the smaller dimension, the column may buckle in its larger dimension first.

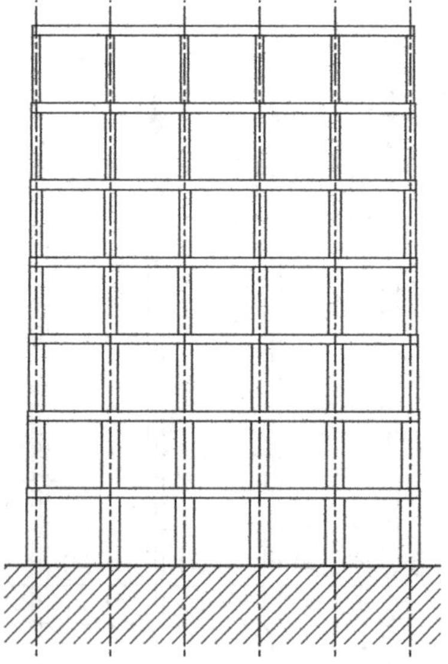

Figure 19.7 Column loads accumulate from the top of the building to the bottom. If columns in a tall building are sized purely on the basis of the loads they carry, they will be larger at the bottom than at the top.

COMBINING BEAMS AND COLUMNS: RIGID FRAMES

If beams are joined to columns with rigid connections that are capable of transmitting full bending moments from one member to the other, a *rigid frame* is created. A simple, single-story version of the rigid frame is widely used in prefabricated steel buildings (Figure 19.8). There are two common configurations for single-story frames, two-hinged and three-hinged.

The bending moments in single-story, three-hinged rigid frames may be diagrammed approximately by superimposing a parabola that passes through the three hinges. The bending moment is proportional to the distance between the parabola and the centerline of the frame, measured perpendicular to the parabola.

The bending moments in a two-hinged frame may be measured in the same way, except that the parabola is constructed so that it passes through both hinges and has an area equal to the area under the centerline of the frame. (The area under a frame is generally easy to calculate, since the frame itself usually encloses a rectangle or a rectangle plus a triangle. The area under a parabola is two-thirds of the product of its base and altitude.)

The large bending moments at the connections in single-story frames are usually accommodated by deepening the frame in these areas. Because they utilize the bending resistance of the columns and joints as well as that of the beams, single-story rigid frames can span much longer distances than beams of the same cross-sectional dimensions that are hinged at their supports.

Figure 19.9 illustrates the process of determining gravity-load bending moments in a three-hinged single-story rigid frame with a uniformly distributed roof load. In part (a), we isolate half of the frame as a free body. This half is subject to three forces: the gravity load, a horizontal thrust at the top joint, and a reaction of unknown intensity and direction at the foundation.

In part (b), we begin to find the direction and magnitude of the reaction by substituting a concentrated load for the distributed load. Then we find the point of intersection of the lines of action of the load and the horizontal force that passes through the hinge at the peak. The line of action of the only other force on this body, the reaction, must pass through this intersection. A simple force polygon gives us the values of the three forces.

If this were the actual loading, the bending moment diagram would be bounded by the axis of the frame members and the lines of action of the reaction and the horizontal force, as diagrammed in part (c). Moments would be proportional to the distance between these lines, measured perpendicular to the reaction line.

Of course, the actual loading is uniform, not concentrated. In part (d) of Figure 19.9, we construct the funicular line for a uniform load, a parabola. This is done in the same way as we found the parabolic curve for a hanging cable or arch early in this book: We mark a point at double the height of the frame on its centerline and draw the first segment at the base of the parabola along a line that passes from this point to the base hinge. We know that the center segment of the parabola will be horizontal at the ridge of the frame. These two pieces of information allow us to construct a force polygon and complete the curve of the parabola. Bending moments are proportional to the distance between the parabola and the centerline of the frame, measured perpendicular to the parabola. (As with our earlier construction of a parabola, each segment of the load is represented by a vector at its center, which results in half-spaces at the two ends of the parabola.) The more common way of depicting these bending moments is to show them plotted perpendicular to the centerlines of the frame, as in part (e). The shape of the moment diagram is reflected in the tapered members and deep *haunch* of the frame, where the bending moment is maximum. These concepts are explored for other load patterns in the frame and are shown in Worksheet 19A on the supplemental site.

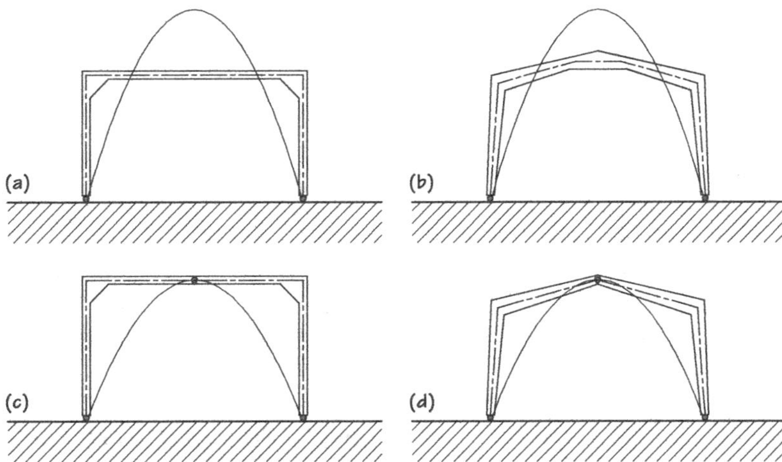

Figure 19.8 Generating bending moment diagrams for uniformly loaded single-story rigid frames. (a, b) For two-hinged frames, the parabolic bending moment diagram is equal in area to the area beneath the frame. (c, d) For three-hinged frames, the parabolic bending moment diagram passes through all three hinges.

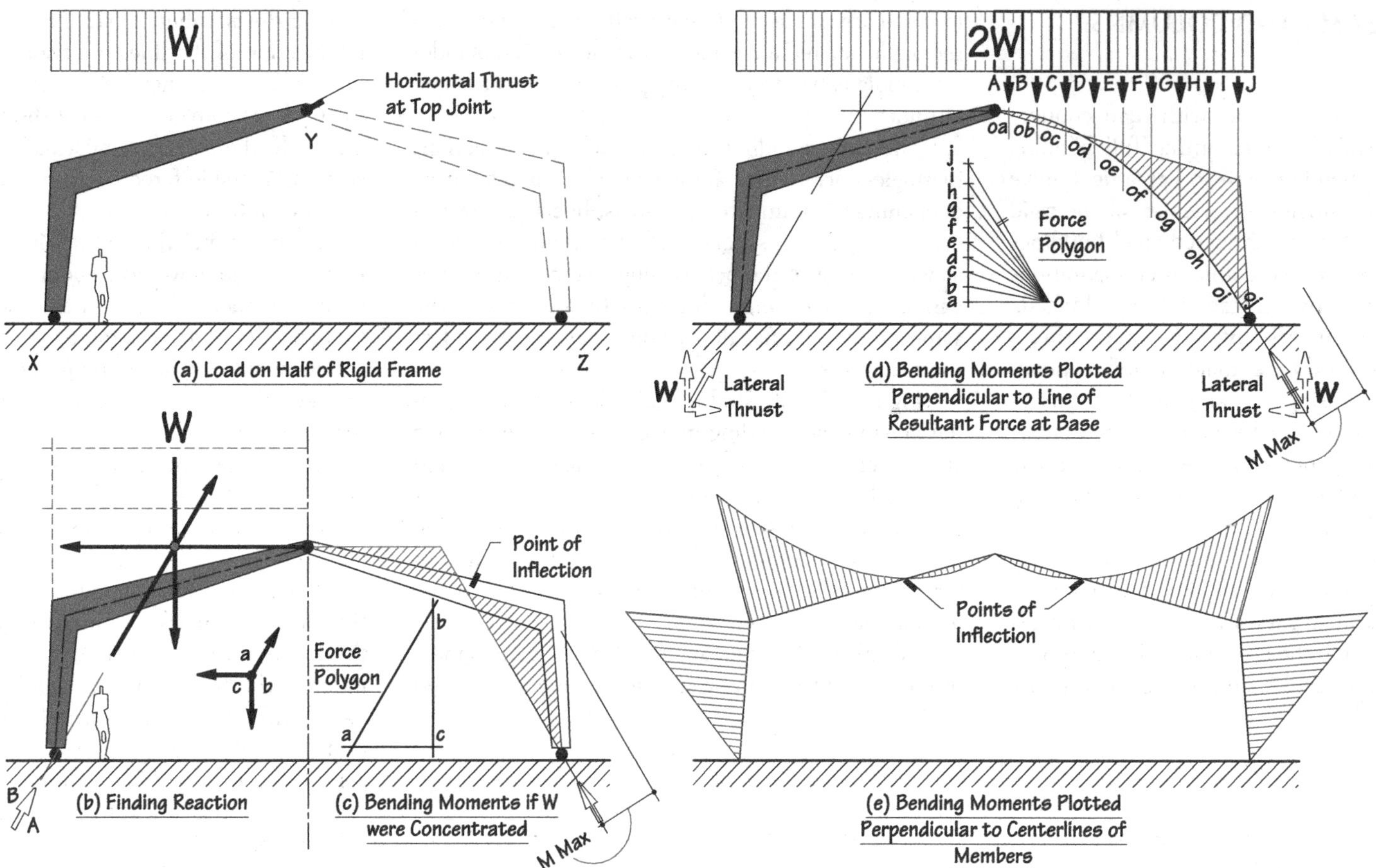

Figure 19.9 Evaluating bending moments on a three-hinged rigid frame. (a, b) Finding the base reaction: The line of action of the force through the base hinge must pass through the intersection of the resultant of the load on half the frame with the line of action of the top thrust. This determines the angle of the base reaction. If *W* were a concentrated load, the bending moment diagram would be as shown in part (c). In part (d), the actual bending moment curve is a parabola through the three hinges of the frame. The distance at any point between the parabola and the centerline of the frame, measured perpendicular to the parabola, is proportional to the bending moment at that point. In part (e), the bending moments for the components of the frame are separated from one another for clarity. The moments at the top of the column and the base of the beam must be equal.

The more closely the frame resembles a parabola, the lower its internal forces will be and the greater the distance it can span. A single-story frame is essentially a distorted arch, and like an arch, it exerts a lateral thrust. This is resisted by a steel tie rod across the bottom that is embedded in the floor slab.

In prefabricated steel industrial buildings, the rigid frames are spaced according to the allowable spans of the purlins that support the roof deck (Figure 19.10). The walls are supported on purlinlike beams known as *girts*. Steel Z-shapes are commonly used for purlins and girts because they allow full access to the inside ends of the bolts that hold them to these rigid frames. The girts are usually oriented with their strong axes horizontal, to resist wind loads, which leaves them likely to deflect excessively around their weak axes under the load of the walls, so they are usually provided with *sag rods*, threaded steel tension rods that transmit loads from the girts up to the purlin at the top of the wall.

MULTISTORY RIGID FRAMES

Rigid frame action is often employed as the primary means of resisting lateral wind and seismic loads in multistory buildings up to about 20 stories

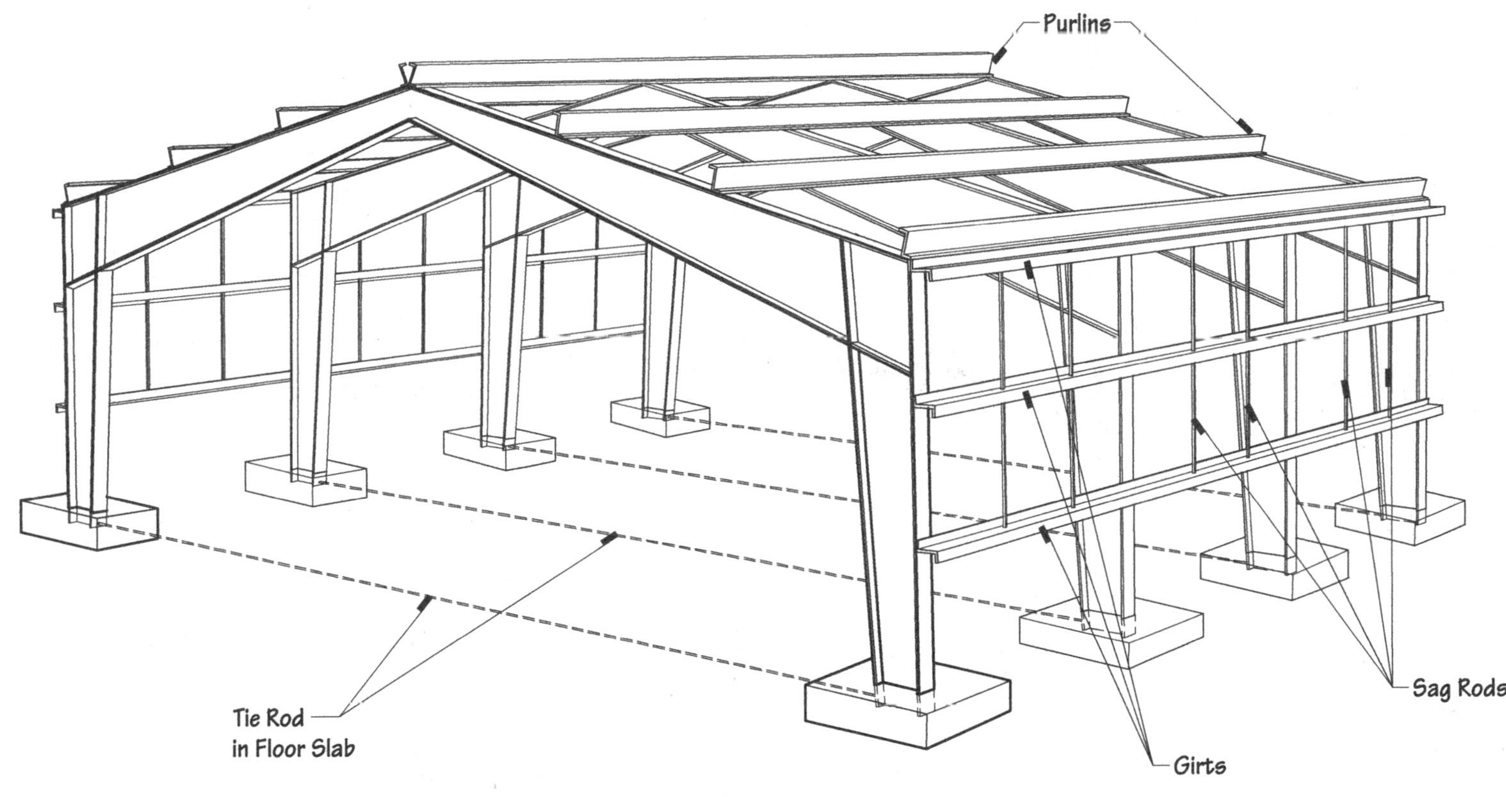

Figure 19.10 Steel single-story rigid frames provide an economical structure for so-called packaged buildings that are widely used for institutional, retail, and governmental buildings. The Z-shapes were selected for purlins and girts because they give generous space for power tools to be used for tightening fasteners. Packaged buildings are predesigned and often prefabricated in advance of any order to purchase. This makes them ideal for purchasers who need enclosed space quickly and for a low price.

in height. Not all the joints in the frame need be rigid in most cases; a common practice is to place the rigid joints around the perimeter of the building and use ordinary hinged connections at interior columns. The same general principle may be applied to buildings in the 50-story range by using much closer column spacings in the exterior walls, and joining the columns to deep spandrel beams to form *tube* structures (Figure 19.11), so named because the rigid exterior wall acts much like a huge, monolithic rectangular tube in resisting lateral loads. Both steel and concrete are appropriate materials for rigid and tube frames.

Using a model, Figure 19.12 demonstrates in exaggerated form how a multistory rigid frame behaves under load. The beams and columns are strips of thin card stock joined rigidly by being glued to wood blocks. This produces a rigid-jointed frame with very flexible beams and columns. We can observe bending actions by the deformations of the members of the model. In part (a), a gravity load on a beam is resisted not only by the beam, but also by the adjacent columns. The rigid joints do not allow the ends of the beam to rotate under load unless the columns also rotate. In this way, the columns contribute to the resistance of the beam. In part (b) of Figure 19.12, the model is pulled laterally, and every joint and member in the frame has gone to work to resist the pull.

Because of the high degree of interdependence of the members of multistory rigid frames, analytical determination of the moments and forces in individual members is arduous. Manual methods formerly used for this task have been replaced by computer programs.

Rigidly jointed frames do not necessarily have to have their fixed joints at floor level. The cross-shaped, pin-jointed members in Figure 19.13 act together with the spandrel beams of the floors to create rigidity. The tapering of the arms of the crosses reflects the variation in bending moments.

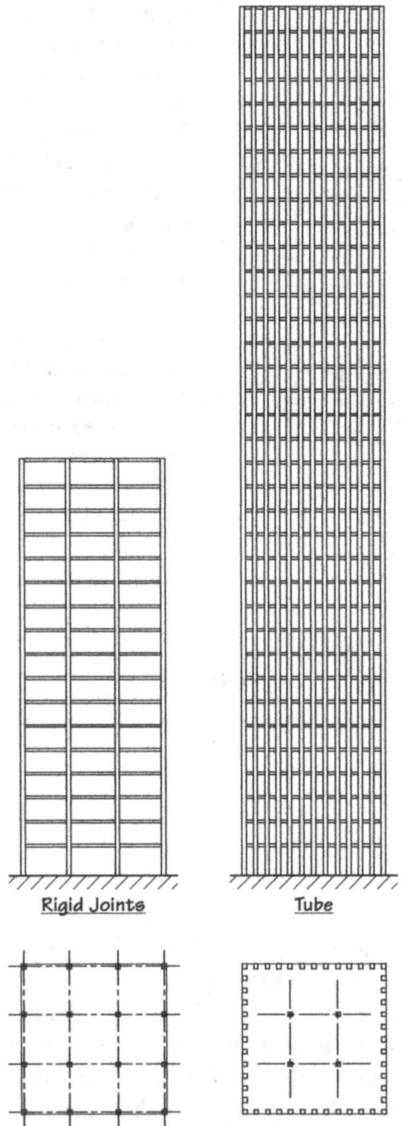

Figure 19.11 Rigid joints are used to stabilize buildings in two different height ranges. (a) Up to about 20 stories, rigid joints in selected locations in the frame are sufficient for stability. (b) A large number of rigid connections closely spaced in the outside framing members create a "tube" that can stabilize buildings up to about 50 stories.

(a)

(b)

Figure 19.12 (a) In a multistory rigid frame building, the bending resistance of floor beams is enhanced by bending of the adjacent columns. (b) Lateral loads on a rigid frame are resisted by bending in every member of the frame.

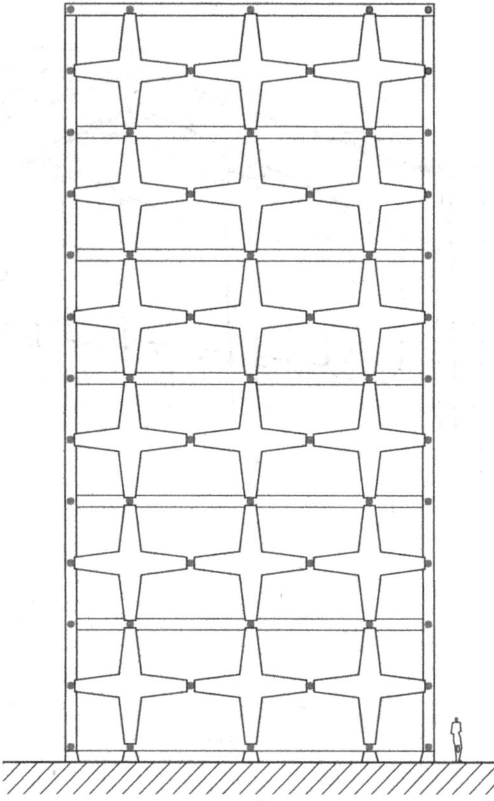

Figure 19.13 Cross-shaped elements brace one another laterally by acting as a mesh of three-hinged frames. The crosses are tapered to be strongest and stiffest at their hubs, where bending moments are maximum.

GOOD SHAPES FOR COLUMNS

Cross Sections

It is evident in the Euler equation that for maximum economy we should seek to maximize the moment of inertia of a column section. Expressions for the moments of inertia of various shapes all multiply each small area of material in the cross section by the square of its distance from the centroid of the

FAZLUR KHAN

Bangladeshi–American engineer Fazlur Khan (1929–1983) first came from his home near Dhaka to the United States to study for a PhD in engineering as a Fulbright Scholar at the University of Illinois. Khan's daughter, Yasmin Sabina Khan (also a civil engineer), has written about how her father's education and approach drew upon optimization techniques and graphical methods for analysis and design with complex load combinations. After his studies and brief periods working for the architecture-engineering firm Skidmore Owings, and Merrill (SOM) on projects such as the U.S. Air Force Academy in Colorado (1955–1959), Khan returned home in 1957. He returned permanently to Chicago and SOM in 1960. An effective and imaginative collaborator with teams of engineers and architects, his focus on innovating within high-rise typologies led him to develop the "trussed-tube" strategy for the John Hancock Center, in 1965, and then the "bundled-tube" strategy for the Sears Tower, in 1974. Even though the initial focus of his graduate study involved particular applications in precast concrete, he adapted the same goals of using material effectively in his professional work from steel skyscrapers to the fabric-covered Hajj Terminal in Jeddah, Saudi Arabia. Always searching for structural solutions that would contribute to broader human concerns, he strove to make his work creative and visionary, not just an "arithmetic solution to a problem rather than a social or a socioeconomic solution." He began work on the Hajj lightweight tent structure in 1977 and designed many other large-scale projects before dying unexpectedly of a heart attack at the age of 53.

shape. Thus, an ideal cross section is one that places as much material as possible as far as possible from the centroid. If a steel column is symmetrically loaded and not restrained in either direction by lateral supports, the ideal cross section is a cylindrical tube (Figure 19.14a). If the column is restrained at midheight in one direction but not the other, the ideal is an ellipse whose major axis is oriented perpendicular to the plane of restraint (Figure 19.14b). Square and rectangular steel tubes (c) make excellent columns.

The steel wide-flange shapes that are intended for use as columns have very broad flanges so that they are approximately square in proportion (Figure 19.14d). These shapes are fairly efficient because of the concentration of metal distant from the centroid in the flanges, but they have very different stiffnesses in their two principal directions, and their flanges, with their free outer edges, are prone to buckling.

A number of other relatively efficient cross-sectional shapes are used for columns in wood, steel, and concrete. The common patterns of reinforcement in concrete columns all place the vertical bars as far from the centroid as possible, with just enough concrete cover outside the bars to resist fire and corrosion of the bars. The force in a concrete column is shared by the concrete and vertical steel bars acting together. The bars act as long, slender columns. They are prevented from buckling inward by the mass of concrete to the inside of them. To prevent outward buckling, *ties* made of small-diameter steel reinforcing bars are wrapped around the vertical bars. The ties may be either discrete pieces of bent bar or a continuous spiral that wraps around a circular array of vertical bars.

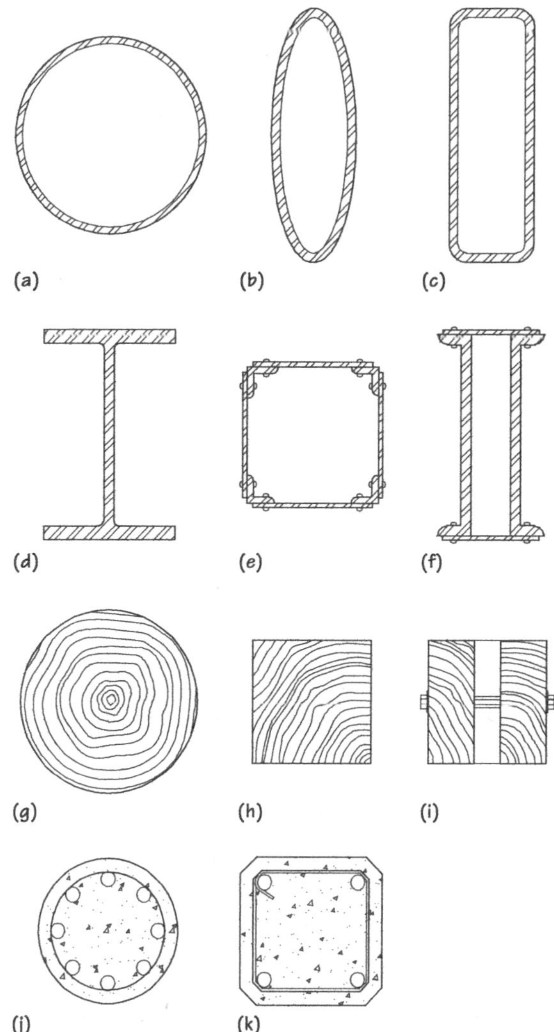

Figure 19.14 Some cross sections of typical columns in several materials; parts (a) through (f) are steel: (a) round tube; (b) elliptical tube; (c) rectangular or square tube; (d) wide-flange; (e) four vertical steel angles laced together with diagonal steel straps; (f) back-to-back steel channels laced together. Columns (g) through (i) are wood: (g) a tree trunk; (h) a square timber; (i) spaced columns bolted together. Columns (j) and (k) are concrete: (j) round column with spiral confinement; (k) rectangular column with separate steel ties.

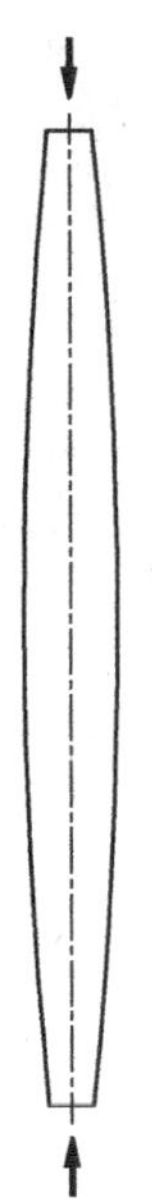

Figure 19.15 A good shape for a column with pinned ends (albeit one that can be difficult to construct in some materials) is a double-tapered configuration, which has maximum bending resistance at midheight, where buckling is likely to occur.

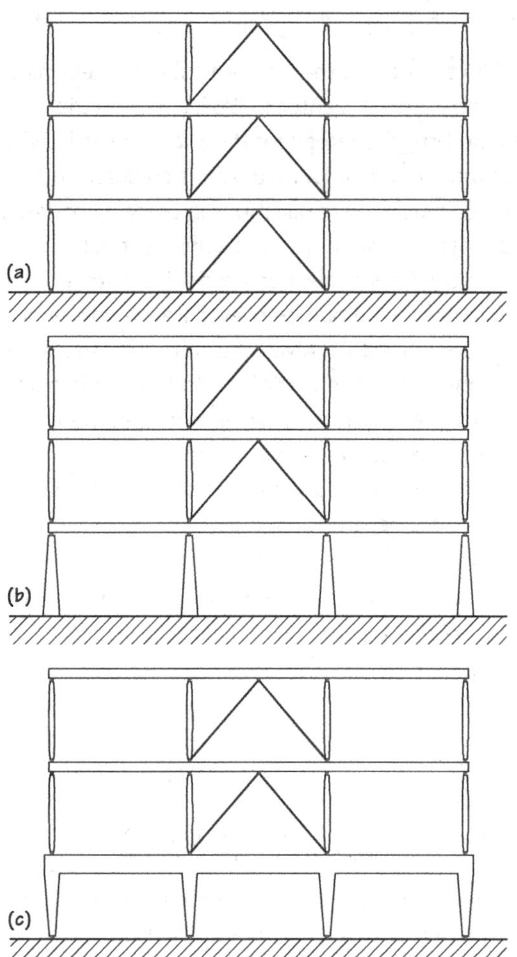

Figure 19.16 Single-tapered columns are a logical choice in situations where each column is pinned at one end and rigidly attached at the other.

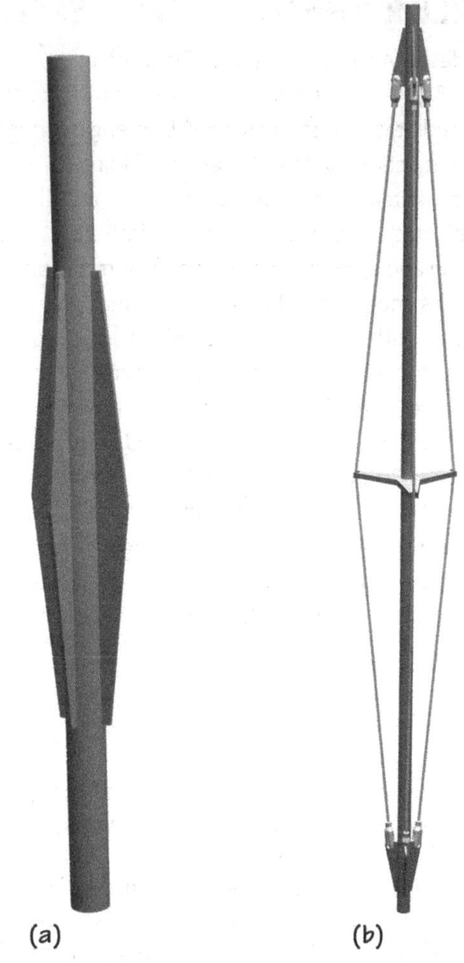

Figure 19.17 The resistance of slender columns, in this case steel, can be augmented by stiffening the central region of the shaft with tight guy rods or welded, finlike stiffener plates.

Good Longitudinal Shapes

All other factors being equal, buckling in a column that is pinned at both ends occurs at midheight. This suggests that a column that is pinned at both ends should have maximum bending resistance at midheight, and can have less in the vicinity of the ends. A doubly tapered shape (Figures 19.15 and 19.16a) is excellent in this regard. If a column is rigidly fixed to its foundation and pinned to the beam or slab that it supports, its ideal shape tapers from a broad base to a narrow top (Figure 19.16b). If it is rigidly fixed to the frame above and pinned where it joins the foundation (Figure 19.16c), it should taper from a narrow base to a thick top.

Tubular columns of constant diameter may be made more material-efficient by adding stiffness to their midsections (Figure 19.17a) in the form of welded fins, or rings with steel rod stays. Very long, slender columns can be made more resistant to buckling by the addition of funicular rods and perpendicular struts in three or four vertical planes spaced equally around the perimeter (Figure 19.17b). In large assemblies of this type, provision should be made for regulating the tensions in the stay rods so that each assembly can be "tuned" for symmetrical performance.

STRUTS AND TIES

Struts are designed as columns. Their orientation makes little difference in their function unless they are made of materials that are dense enough to cause significant sagging of the strut that encourages buckling in a particular direction. The *Manual of Steel Construction* contains tables of precalculated capacities of columns made of pipes, rectangular and square tubes, structural tees, doubled channels, and doubled angles. These tables may be used to assign approximate sizes to steel struts and truss members. Similar tables are available in wood and concrete construction manuals. Tie members cannot buckle, so they are sized on the basis of allowable stress.

COMBINED MEMBERS

A common roof rafter bears two types of loads simultaneously: It is bent by the snow and wind loads on its tributary area, and it experiences axial compression as part of the top chord of a simple triangular truss that resists gravity loads (Figure 19.18). This makes it a *combined member*, one that must resist bending and axial stress at the same time. The sizing of a combined member is a trial-and-error process that involves trying different sizes of members until one is found that satisfies the following expression:

$$\frac{f_b}{F_b} + \frac{f_{axial}}{F_{axial}} \leq 1.0 \qquad [19\text{-}2]$$

where:

f_b is the calculated stress in bending,
F_b is the allowable stress in bending,
f_{axial} is the calculated axial stress, and
F_{axial} is the allowable axial stress.

This expression works for an axial force that is either tensile or compressive. It says, in essence, that the percentage of bending capacity utilized in the member, plus the percentage of axial capacity, should add up to 100 percent or less.

The rafter problem is particularly interesting because a rafter is generally 1.5 in. thick and 12 ft or more in length, which gives it a slenderness ratio about its weak axis of approximately twice the allowable maximum for a wood column. However, the roof sheathing is nailed to the compression edge of the

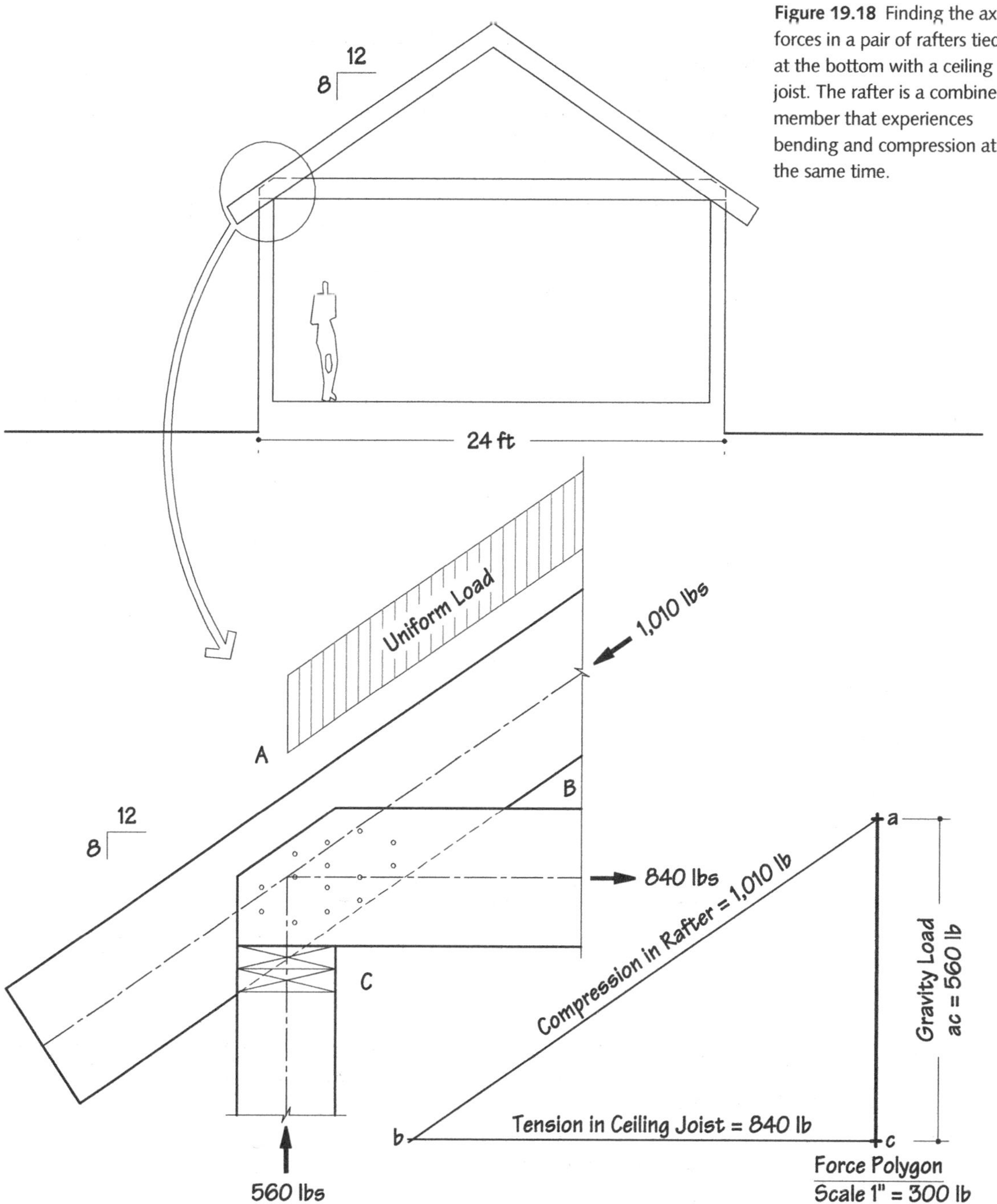

Figure 19.18 Finding the axial forces in a pair of rafters tied at the bottom with a ceiling joist. The rafter is a combined member that experiences bending and compression at the same time.

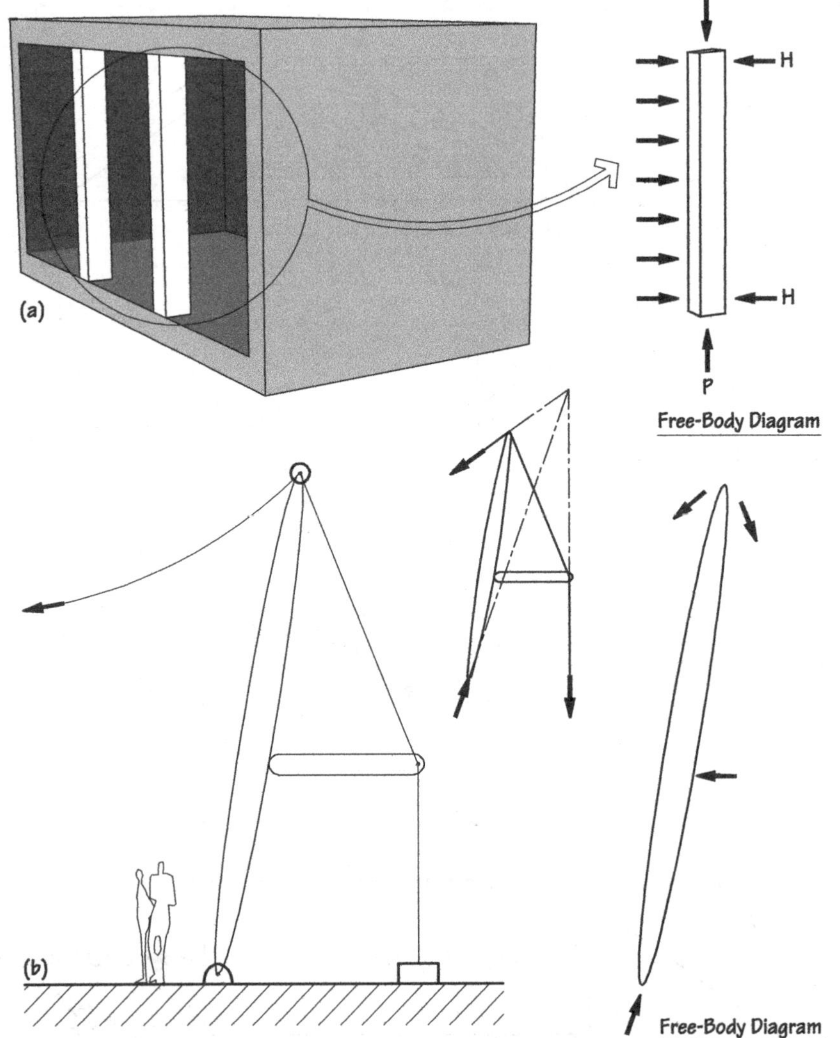

Figure 19.19 Two situations in which a column is a combined member: (a) a column that bears a roof load plus a lateral wind load transmitted to it by a glass wall, and (b) a mast for a cable structure that has a side strut to deflect the backstay toward the ground as close to the structure as possible.

rafter every few inches, effectively restraining it from buckling about its weak axis. The strong axis of the rafter is at least 5.5 in. deep, giving it a very acceptable slenderness ratio of less than 30. The bending moments from the uniform loading are resisted by beam action in the rafter. It is evident that when sizing a combined member, the designer should find a size such that the sum of the capacities is as close as practical to 1.0 in order to use material as efficiently as possible.

ECCENTRICALLY LOADED COLUMNS

A column that is loaded eccentrically is stressed both by compressive forces and bending forces, and is evaluated as a combined member. The column in Figure 19.20 is made of laminated wood and is 12 in. square. A floor and roof above bring to it an axial load of 40 kips. A beam load of 20 kips is applied to a corbel with an eccentricity of 10 in. The allowable bending stress is 1,600 psi, and the allowable compressive stress 975 psi. Is the column adequate?

To find the maximum stresses, we must first determine the resultant of the two gravity loads, which is a vertical force of 60 kips with an eccentricity that we must determine. The eccentricity of the resultant is found by applying Bow's notation to the two loads, constructing a load line, adopting an arbitrary pole location, drawing rays, and drawing a funicular polygon on the lines of action of the loads. The extensions of the first and last rays intersect on the line of action of the resultant force. The eccentricity of this line of action is measured as 4 in. The bending moment is 60 kips multiplied by 4 in. Now the axial stress and maximum bending stress are computed by the normal means.

$$f_c = \frac{P}{A} = \frac{60{,}000 \text{ lb}}{144 \text{ in.}^2} = 416 \text{ psi}$$

$$f_b = \frac{M}{S} = \frac{240{,}000 \text{ lb-in.}}{288 \text{ in.}^3} = 833 \text{ psi}$$

Are these stresses satisfactory? We apply equation [19-2]:

$$\frac{f_b}{F_b} + \frac{f_{\text{axial}}}{F_{\text{axial}}} \leq 1.0$$

$$\frac{833 \text{ psi}}{1{,}600 \text{ psi}} + \frac{416 \text{ psi}}{975 \text{ psi}} = 0.95 < 1.0 \quad \text{okay}$$

This is a good solution because we are using the member to approximately 95 percent of its capacity.

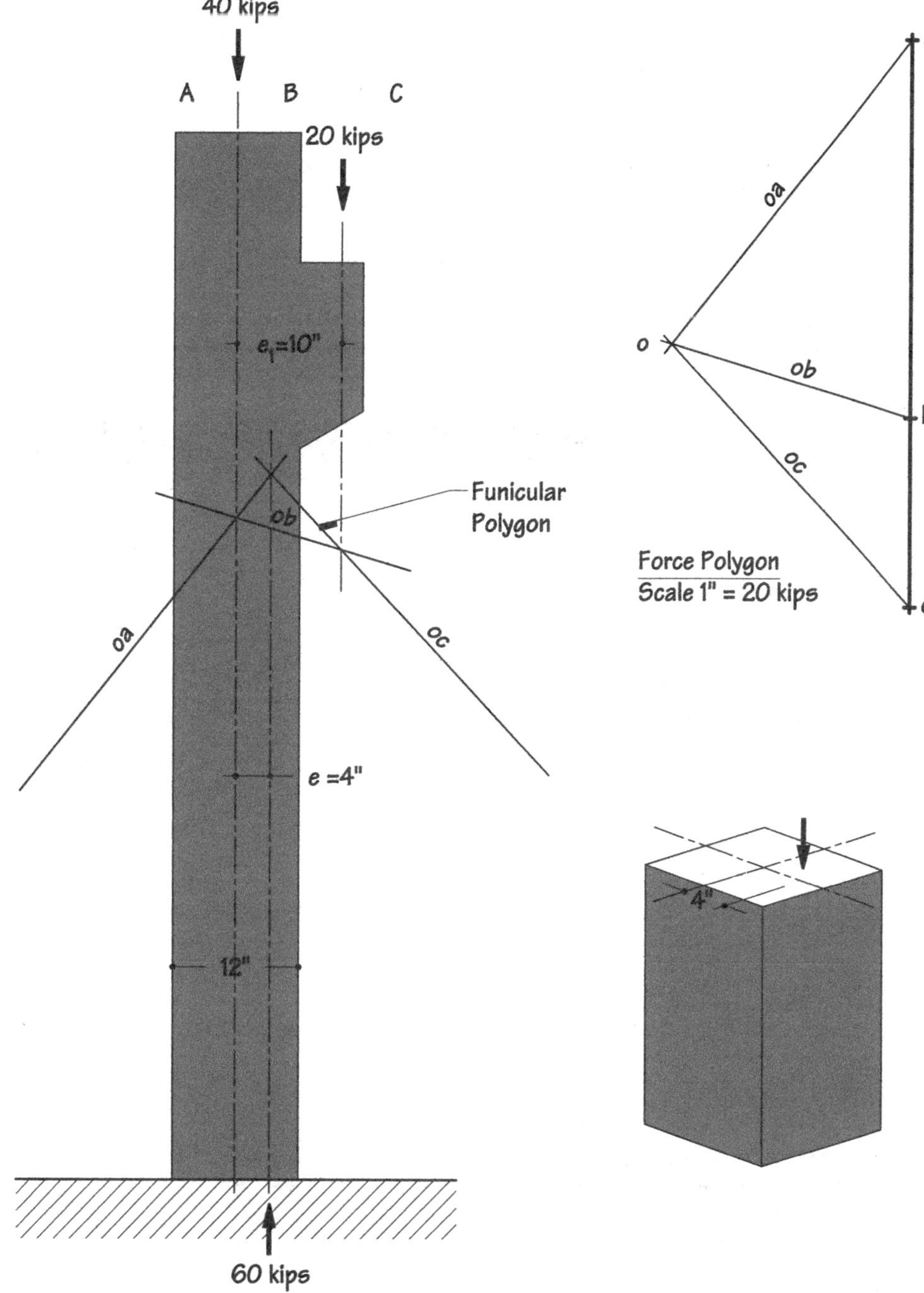

COLUMNS IN ARCHITECTURE

Because they stand parallel to our upright bodies and are threaded through the inhabited spaces of buildings, columns bring themselves to our attention more insistently than beams, girders, and slabs. Thus, it's no accident that columns have been important components of every architectural style from the very first human constructions.

One architectural role of columns is to carry the outer trappings of an endless parade of architectural styles, as exemplified in Figure 19.1. A more powerful role is that of helping to define, divide, and regulate architectural space. Figure 19.21 shows a number of possible ways in which a dozen columns can act spatially. These are only a sampling. You are encouraged to sketch other possibilities. Coordinating such patterns of columns with necessary structural column locations in a building can be a difficult if not impossible task, unless the designer has formed a comprehensive concept that involves both the structural and spatial needs, which is a desirable goal.

Figures 19.22 to 19.28 show inspired architectural use of columns by a number of designers.

◀**Figure 19.20** Finding the stress in an eccentrically loaded column. The resultant of the two vertical forces is found first. This is done by drawing a load line that is made up of the two forces, adopting an arbitrary pole, and drawing rays. The first and last segments of the funicular polygon are extended to determine a point on the line of action of the resultant. The magnitude of the resultant is the length of the load line. The formula for beam bending is used to find the maximum stress in the column caused by bending, and the overall load is divided by the cross-sectional area to find the stress caused by axial action. The sum of the two stresses is the maximum stress in the column.

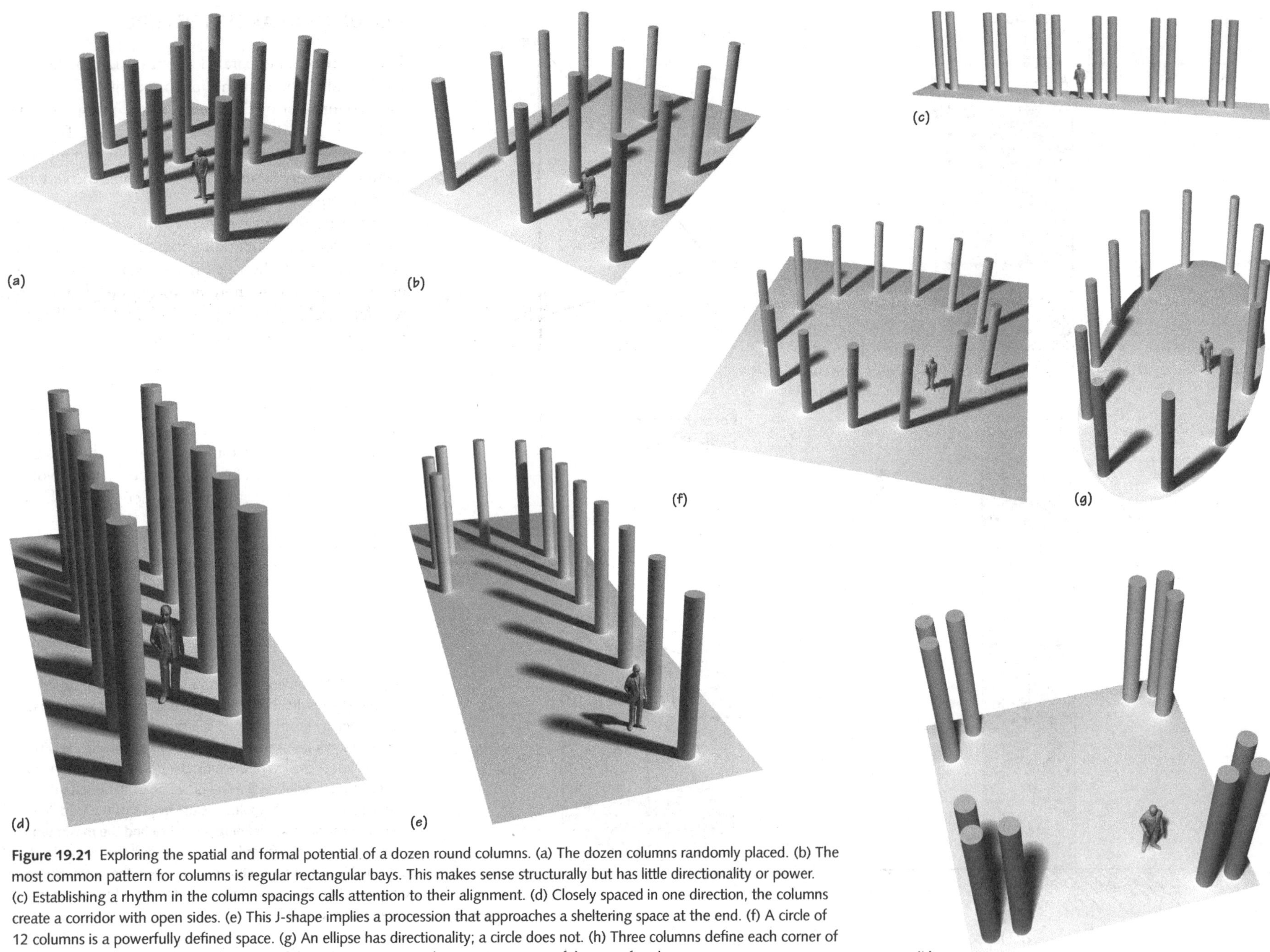

Figure 19.21 Exploring the spatial and formal potential of a dozen round columns. (a) The dozen columns randomly placed. (b) The most common pattern for columns is regular rectangular bays. This makes sense structurally but has little directionality or power. (c) Establishing a rhythm in the column spacings calls attention to their alignment. (d) Closely spaced in one direction, the columns create a corridor with open sides. (e) This J-shape implies a procession that approaches a sheltering space at the end. (f) A circle of 12 columns is a powerfully defined space. (g) An ellipse has directionality; a circle does not. (h) Three columns define each corner of an important space. The relative spacings of the columns are crucial in creating a powerful sense of enclosure.

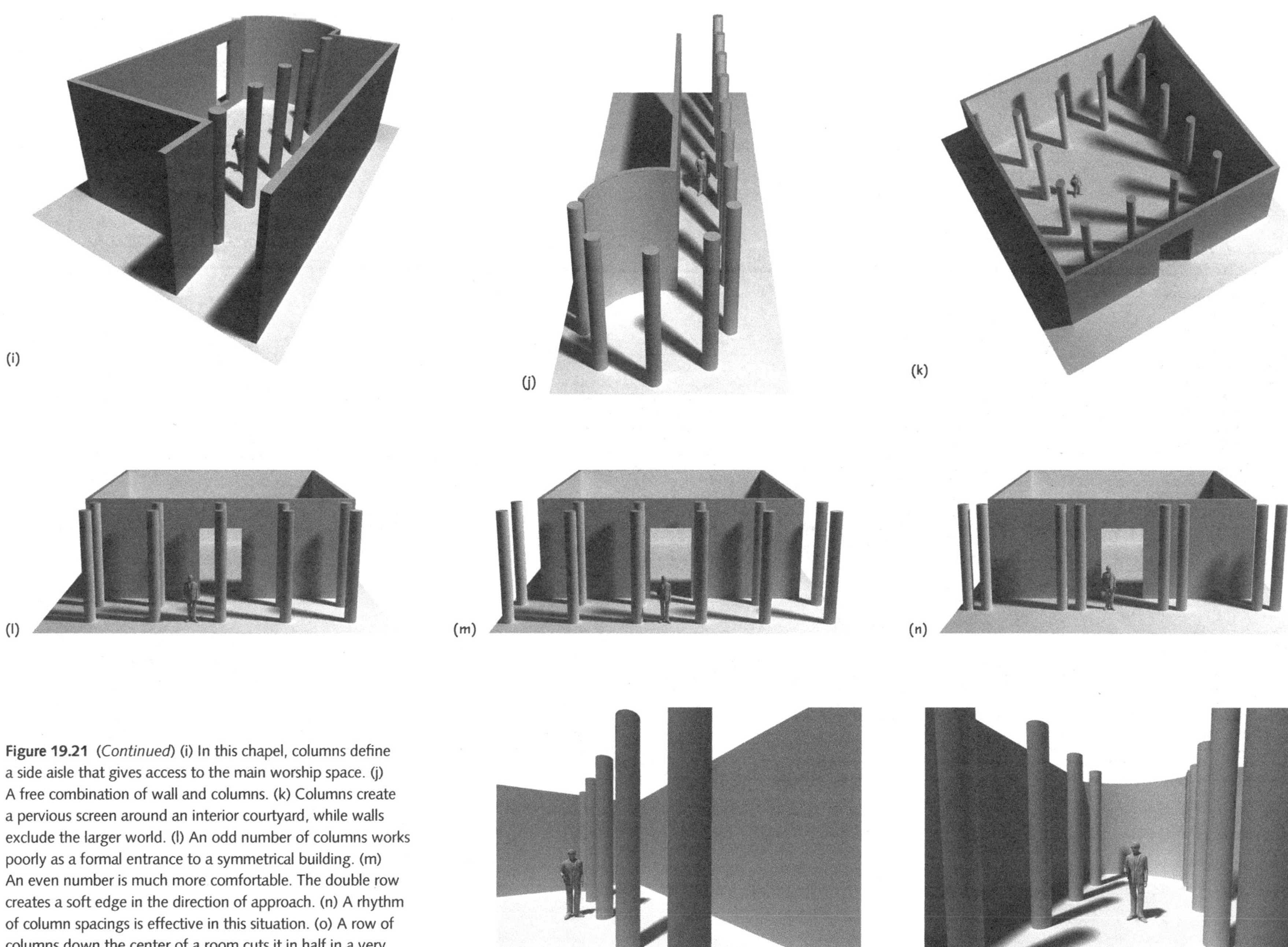

Figure 19.21 (*Continued*) (i) In this chapel, columns define a side aisle that gives access to the main worship space. (j) A free combination of wall and columns. (k) Columns create a pervious screen around an interior courtyard, while walls exclude the larger world. (l) An odd number of columns works poorly as a formal entrance to a symmetrical building. (m) An even number is much more comfortable. The double row creates a soft edge in the direction of approach. (n) A rhythm of column spacings is effective in this situation. (o) A row of columns down the center of a room cuts it in half in a very disturbing way. (p) Two rows of columns work much better in this situation, defining a major space in the middle of the room.

▲**Figure 19.22** The Parthenon atop the Acropolis in Athens, Greece, is an ancient example of columns executed with a great degree of care in their details and in their proportional relationships of slenderness and spacing.

Photo: Edward Allen.

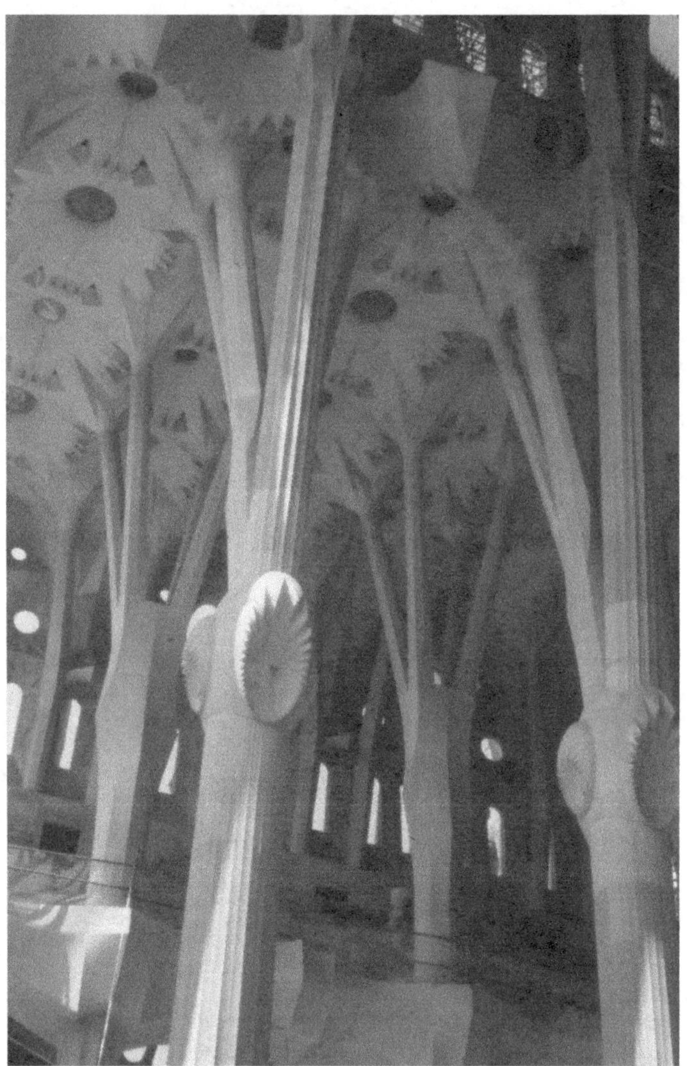

▲**Figure 19.23** Antoni Gaudi inclined the branches of columns in his Sagrada Familia Temple in Barcelona in such a way that the forces flow along their axes, eliminating bending moments.

Photo: Edward Allen.

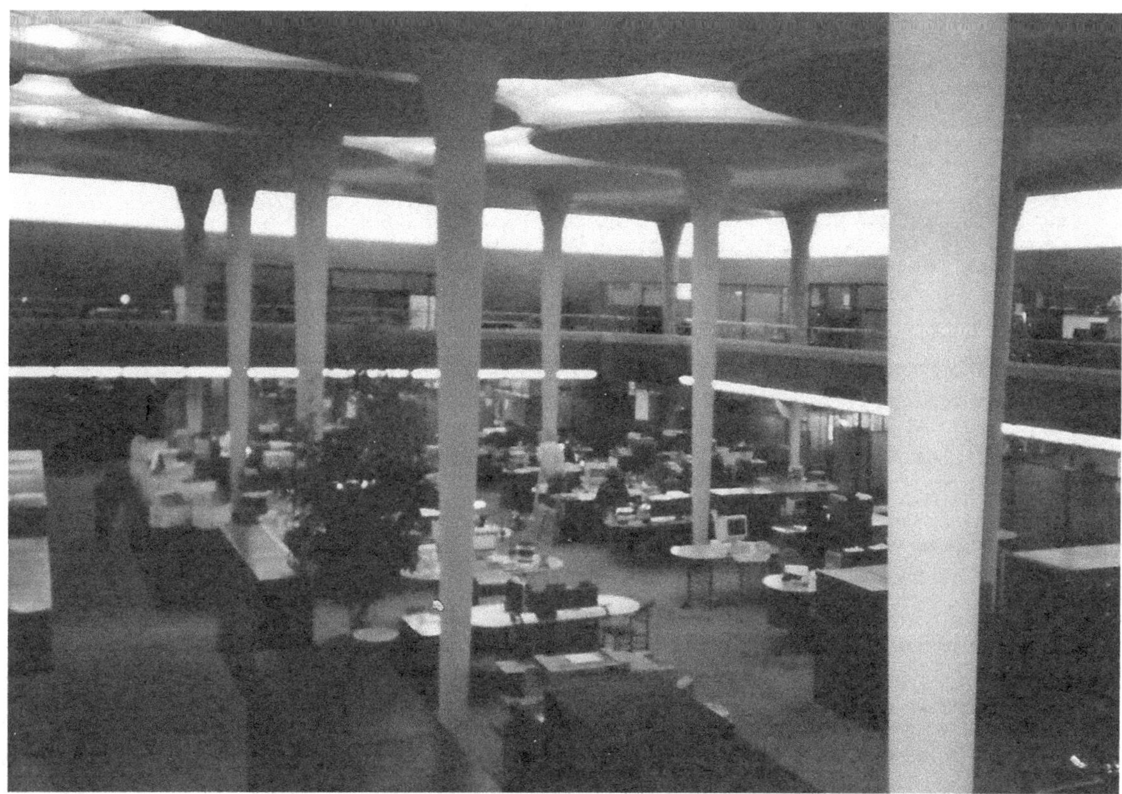

▶**Figure 19.24** The columns in Frank Lloyd Wright's Johnson Wax building in Racine, Wisconsin, are smallest in diameter at the floor, then taper out gradually before exploding into large disks at the top.

Photo: David M. Foxe.

◀**Figure 19.25** The columns in the Passerelle Simone de Beauvoir bridge across the Seine in Paris are made visually lighter (perhaps *too* light) by using several smaller tubular steel sections to connect the lower and upper pedestrian decks of this lenticular span, designed by Dietmar Feichtinger Architects with RFR (Rice Francis Ritchie) Architects and Engineers, 2006.

Photo: David M. Foxe.

◀ **Figure 19.26** The Scholastic Building, designed by Aldo Rossi, constructed alongside historic cast-iron structures in the SoHo area of Manhattan, uses a bold contemporary expression of rigid portal frames in its rear façade.

Photo: David M. Foxe.

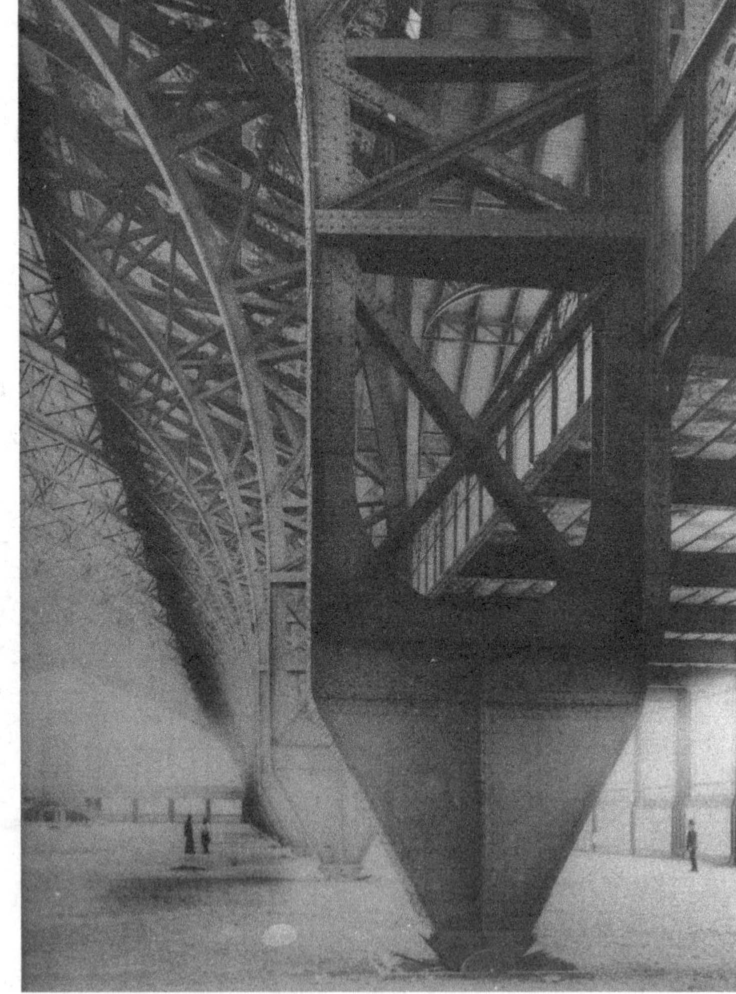

▶ **Figure 19.27** The Palais de Machines, designed by architect Ferdinand Dutert and engineer Victor Contamin, stood opposite the Eiffel Tower on the Champs de Mars in Paris from 1889 to 1909. Erected for the same world exposition as the tower, its main hall included a trussed arch spanning 111 m, over 50 percent greater than had been previously constructed. This image showing the hinge at the base of the three-hinged trussed arch was published in the journal *Engineering* on May 3, 1889; the base hinges are expressed in the narrowing of the frames to a huge cylindrical pin. What kind of flow pattern do the forces follow in this portion of the frame?

Figure 19.28 Columns in the United Airlines Terminal at O'Hare Airport in Chicago are each made of several steel tubes joined by perforated splice plates. The transparency and lightness that this implies is more suitable to the soaring glass roof canopy than a solid column would be. Some columns are made up of as many as five tubes. Children play in and out of the columns; grownups occupy the columns with their eyes. Architect: Murphy Jahn.

Photo: Edward Allen.

(a) Perimeter Load-bearing Wall with Interior Columns

(b) Perimeter and Interior Load-bearing Walls

Figure 19.29 Two ways of using load-bearing walls, seen in plan view.

LOAD-BEARING WALLS

Walls are often used as both exterior and interior load-bearing elements of buildings. Such buildings may be classified in two general configurations (Figure 19.29):

- Buildings in which a perimeter load-bearing wall is combined with interior columns;
- Buildings in which all vertical supports are walls.

Both configurations are constructed quickly and economically, because the walls often serve a multiplicity of functions simultaneously: enclosure, partitions, gravity-load framing, and shear walls for lateral load resistance. This reduces the number of trades on the job and speeds construction.

The interior spaces of buildings with configuration (a) are interrupted only by columns, and may be partitioned and developed in an endless variety of ways. Buildings of configuration (b), with interior load-bearing walls, are much less flexible. They are suited primarily for hotels, motels, dormitories, apartments,

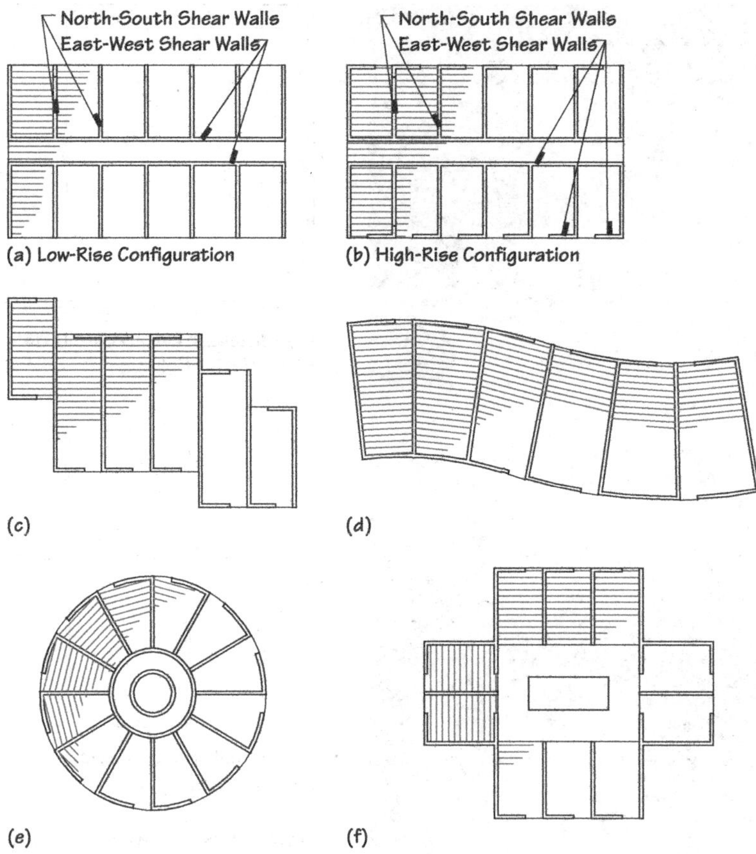

Figure 19.30 Some variations on the theme of perimeter and interior bearing walls.

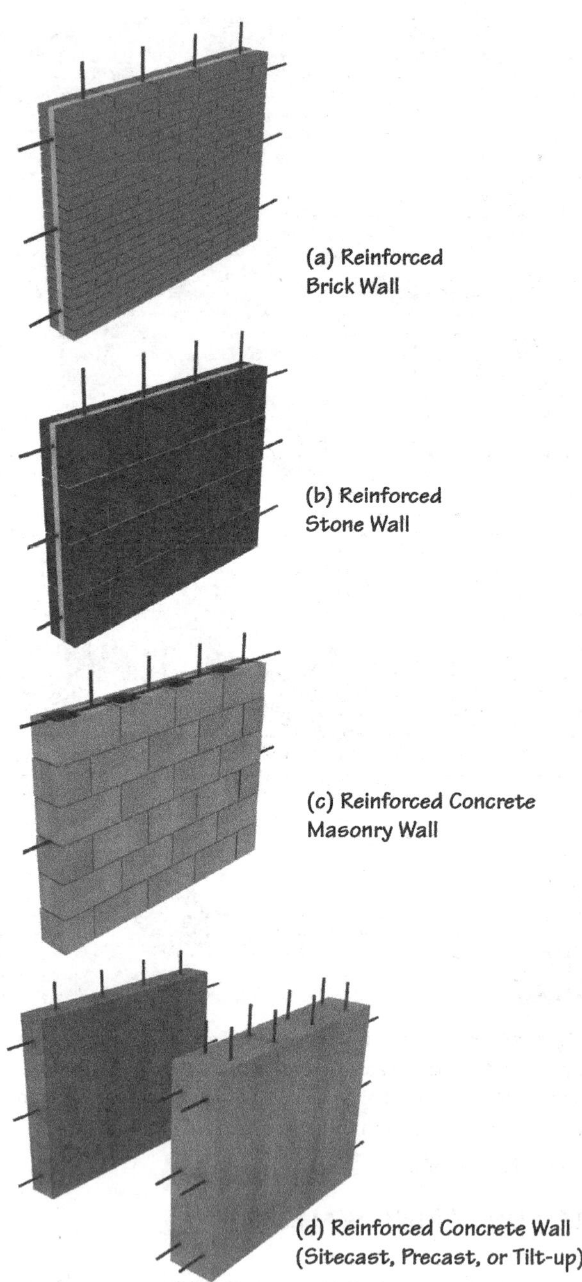

Figure 19.31 Masonry and concrete load-bearing wall construction.

and classrooms, all of which utilize relatively small cells of space that do not change significantly over time. Some typical plans are shown in Figure 19.30. Shopping malls, warehouses, and factories are invariably type (a) configuration buildings with masonry or concrete walls.

Wall construction for both building configurations is typically of concrete masonry, brick masonry, stone masonry, sitecast concrete, precast concrete, or concrete tilt-up panels (Figure 19.31). But wood frame bearing walls are common in houses, small apartment buildings, and small commercial and institutional buildings. If noncombustible construction is required, these same building types can be built with light-gauge steel wall framing.

Load-bearing walls may be used to support roof and floor constructions of every kind. The height and floor area of a building is regulated by building code according to the use of the building and the fire resistance of its construction. With noncombustible exterior load-bearing walls, if wood light framing is used for floors and roof, the building may generally be no taller than three to four stories, and floor area is limited. With heavy timber floors and roof, five to six stories are possible. The greater story height in each case is permitted when an automatic sprinkler system is installed for fire suppression.

Proportions of Load-bearing Walls

The International Building Code restricts masonry bearing walls to a maximum length between lateral supports of 20 times its thickness if the wall is solid, or 18 times its thickness for a wall made of hollow masonry units. Lateral support may be provided by cross walls, pilasters, structural frame members, or floor and roof diaphragms. Minimum wall thicknesses are 6 in. for a single-story building or 8 in. for a multistory building (Figure 19.32). With 8-in.-thick hollow concrete block walls, the maximum distance between pilasters is 18 times 8 in., which works out to 12 ft.

With load-bearing masonry or concrete walls and concrete or steel floor and roof construction of suitable fire resistance, the International Building Code does not restrict building height. The maximum height of the building is governed only by the structural capacity of the walls. A typical maximum height for a building with reinforced masonry or concrete walls is about 20 stories, but with walls as thick as 24 in. at ground level, heights of 60 stories are physically possible. A load-bearing wall can change horizontal location from one floor to the next only by adding large, expensive transfer girders. The economic reality is that it must remain in the same plane throughout the height of a building.

Small openings in load-bearing walls for doors and windows are typically spanned with lintels made of steel, concrete, or reinforced masonry (Figure 19.33). Arches and corbels are also suitable. Lintels in masonry walls carry light loads because of the corbeling action of the masonry units. Only a small triangle of masonry above the opening is considered to rest on the lintel (Figure 19.34).

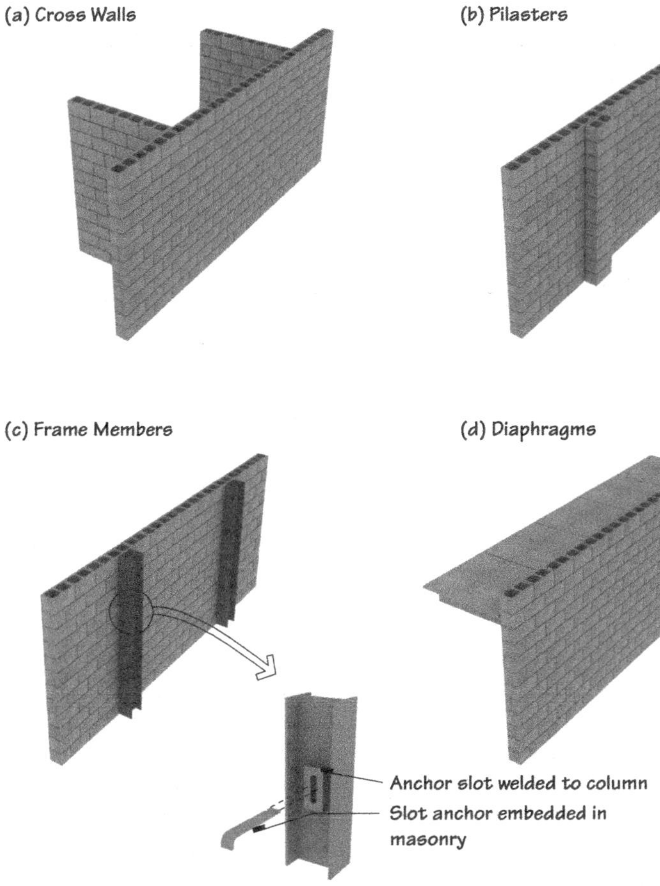

(a) Cross Walls

(b) Pilasters

(c) Frame Members

(d) Diaphragms

Anchor slot welded to column

Slot anchor embedded in masonry

Figure 19.32 Ways of stabilizing walls against lateral buckling.

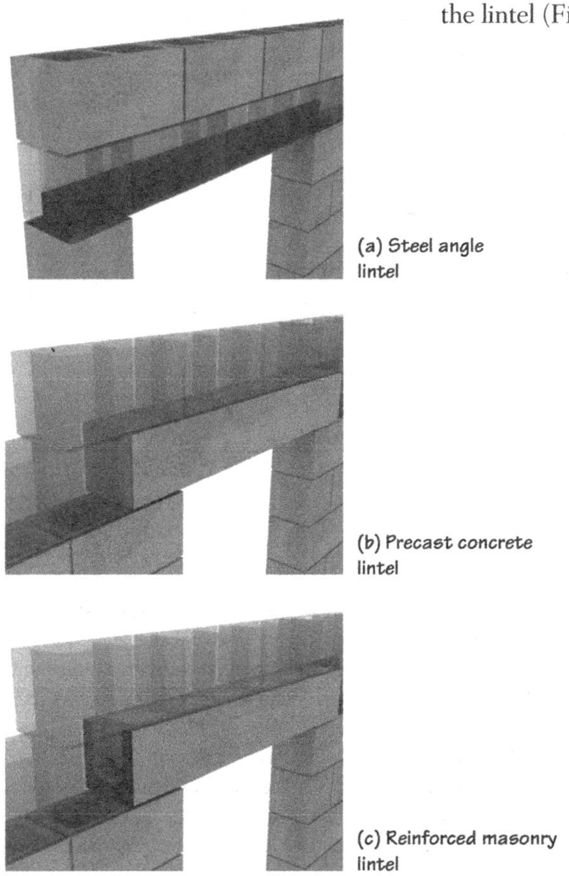

(a) Steel angle lintel

(b) Precast concrete lintel

(c) Reinforced masonry lintel

Figure 19.33 Lintels are used to span openings in masonry walls.

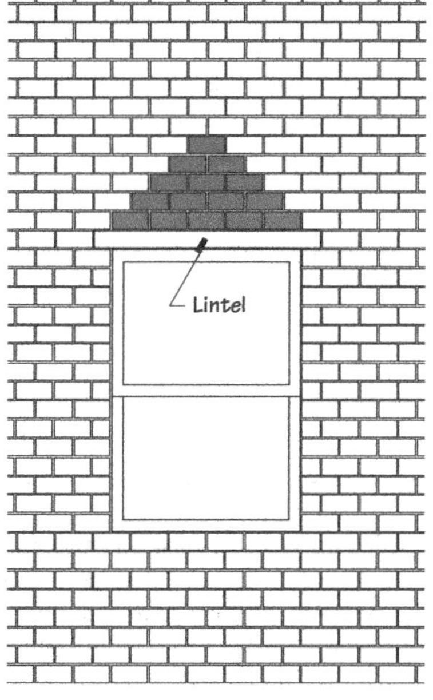

Figure 19.34 Because of corbelling action in the masonry, a lintel supports only a triangular area of a masonry wall above.

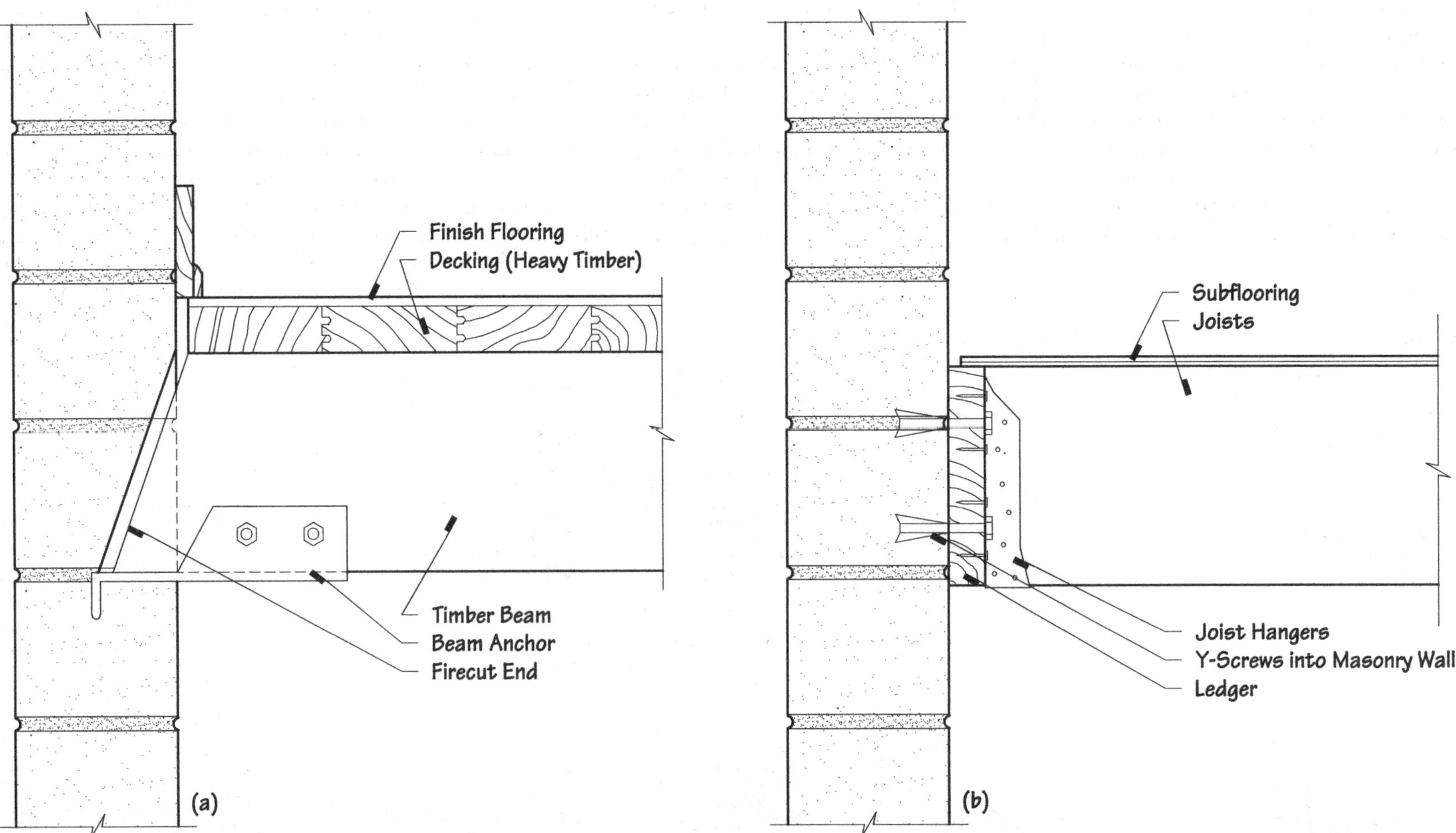

Figure 19.35 (a) Where a heavy timber beam joins a masonry wall, it is tied to the wall with a steel beam anchor embedded in the masonry. If the beam should burn through in a fire, the inclined firecut end allows it to rotate downward, bending the anchor, without causing the wall to topple. (b) Wood joists are often attached to masonry walls through ledger boards that are tied to the masonry with screws driven into expansion anchors in the wall. The joists are joined to the ledger by means of joist hangers and nails. (c) Hollow-core precast concrete planks are laid on hard rubber bearing pads that transfer their loads to the masonry without stress concentrations. Reinforcing bars cast into the concrete topping layer bend down into the grout-filled cores of the masonry units to tie everything securely together. (d) Steel open-web joists are generally welded to steel bearing plates that are anchored into the cores of the masonry units with steel studs and grout. The masons chip away a bit of the block to fit it around the joist end. Corrugated steel decking and concrete fill complete the floor or roof.

Load-bearing walls that support floor and roof construction (Figure 19.35) can also act simultaneously as shear walls to resist lateral loads. The gravity loads on such a wall act to resist overturning of the wall itself under strong lateral loadings.

The inherent simplicity of load-bearing walls and columns make them well suited to designing buildings that are unique and innovative as well as straightforward and utilitarian (Figures 19.36–19.38).

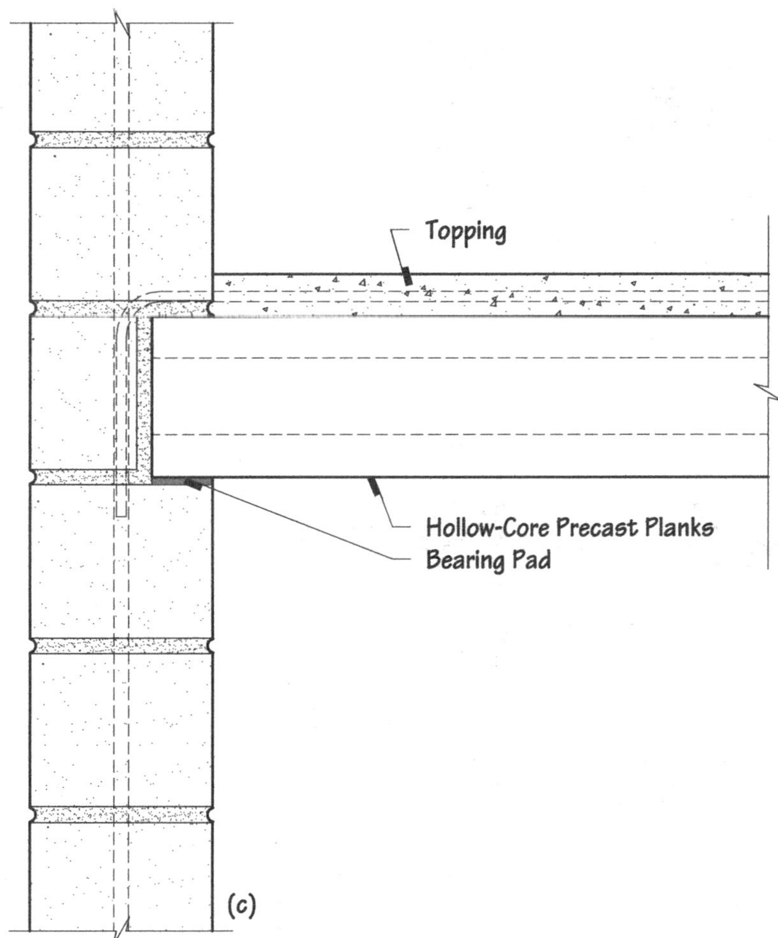

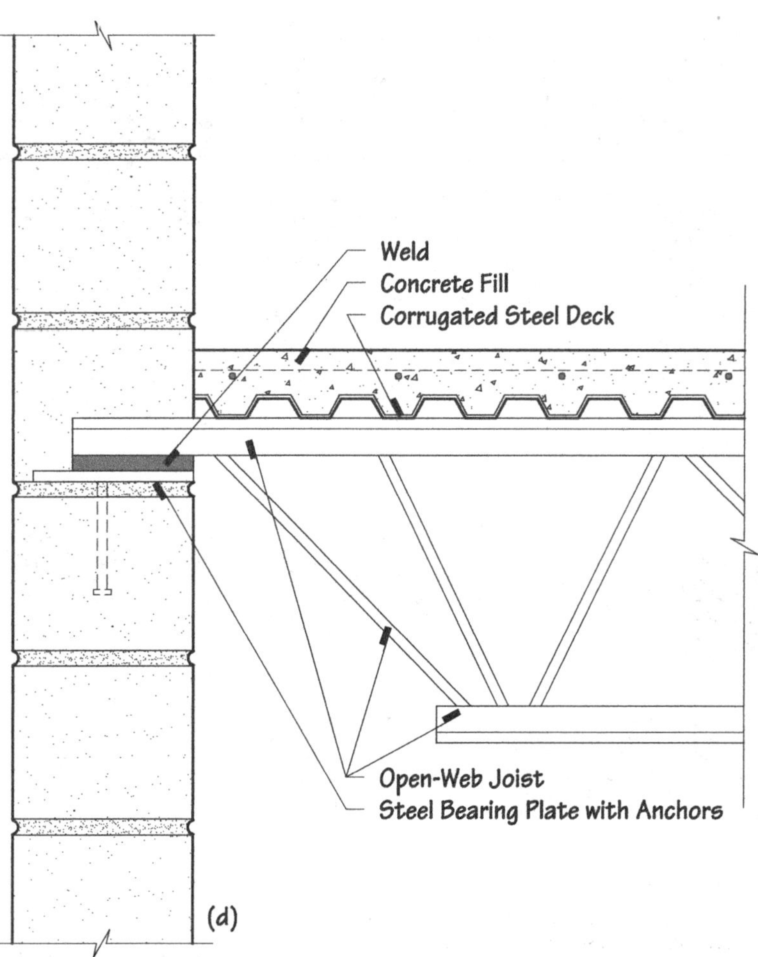

Figure 19.35 *(Continued)*

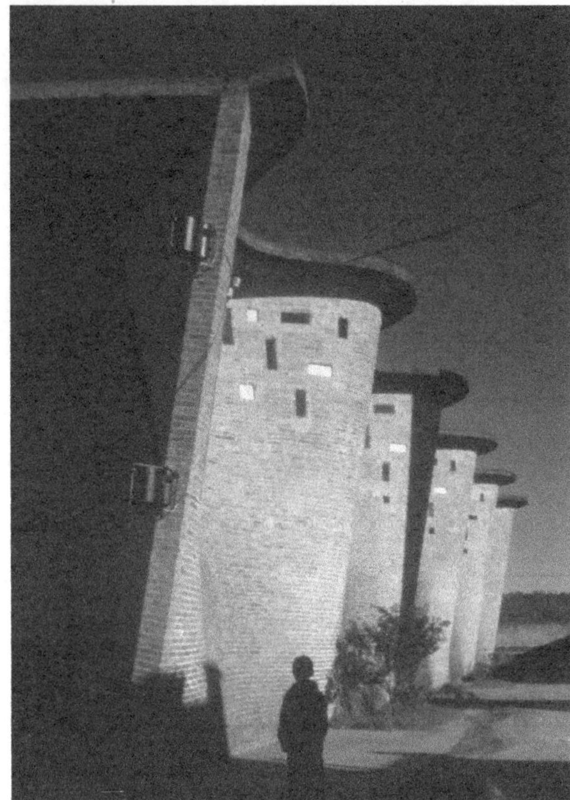

Figure 19.36 Uruguayan engineer Eladio Dieste constructed the brick walls of the Atlantida Church of Christ the Worker as ruled surfaces that start as straight lines at the foundation and become sinusoidal at the top. This facilitates the creation of a very strong joint between the walls and the billowing brick shells of the roof.

Photo: Edward Allen.

Figure 19.37 Architect Mark West proposes treelike columns of concrete cast in fabric tubes to support the barrel vaults of this roof.

Photo courtesy of Mark West.

Figure 19.38 This observation tower in Killesburg, Germany, by engineers Schlaich Bergermann and Partner is supported by a single steel tube 0.5 m (20 in.) in diameter and 41 m (135 ft) tall. The tube is restrained against buckling at four points by radiating beams holding the platforms. The cable net supports the outer edges of the platforms and stabilizes the tube. Why was the cable net designed to be hyperbolic rather than cylindrical?

Photo courtesy of Schlaich Bergermann and Partner.

Exercises

1. Imagine that you are provided with a dozen concrete columns. Each is a rectangle in plan that measures 1 ft thick, 3 ft long, and 9 ft high. Sketch a number of ways in which these columns can be used for architectural effect, much like the dozen round columns shown earlier in this chapter. What are the most important spatial and formal qualities of these columns that the round columns do not have? What architectural and structural opportunities do these qualities create?

2. In a 2 × 10 rafter of a gabled building 24 ft wide with a roof pitch of 4/12 and an unsupported ridge, find the maximum stress in the rafter if the total live and dead load is 40 lb per linear foot of rafter in horizontal projection. If the nails that connect the rafter to the ceiling joist can safely transfer 100 lb each, how many nails are required at this connection? (Note: The span of the rafter is half of 24 ft, which is 12 ft. Because of the slope of the rafter, it is substantially longer than 12 ft. However, we do not have to take this greater length into account when calculating the bending stress. We will get the correct answer by using 12 ft as the span.)

3. A square wood column is 14 ft high and supports a total load of 16 kips. The wood for the column has an allowable compressive stress of 1,050 psi and a modulus of elasticity of 1.4 million psi. Assuming that this is a long column and can be sized by using the Euler equation, what size column is required to maintain a factor of safety of 2?

Key Terms and Concepts

$$P_{cr} = \frac{\pi^2 EI}{L^2} \quad [19\text{-}1]$$

$$\frac{f_b}{F_b} + \frac{f_{axial}}{F_{axial}} \leq 1.0 \quad [19\text{-}2]$$

buckling

short column

intermediate column

long column

slenderness ratio

radius of gyration, r

$$r = \sqrt{\frac{I}{A}}$$

effective length

k

strong axis/weak axis

column tie

rigid frame

haunch

girt

sag rod

tube structure

combined member

$$\frac{f_b}{F_b} + \frac{f_{axial}}{F_{axial}} \leq 1.0$$

eccentrically loaded column

load-bearing wall

bearing wall

Further Resources

Note: Tables for column sizing are found in the following publications:

American Institute of Steel Construction. *Manual of Steel Construction*. Chicago: AISC, updated frequently.

American Wood Council. *Wood Structure Design Data*. Washington, DC: American Wood Council, 2004. Also available as PDF files from awcpubs@afandpa.org.

Concrete Reinforcing Steel Institute. *CRSI Handbook*. Schaumburg, IL: CRSI, updated frequently.

National Concrete Masonry Association. *TR-121 Concrete Masonry Design Tables*. Herndon, VA: NCMA, 2000.

CHAPTER 20

Designing a Sitecast Concrete Building

- *Composite action of steel and concrete in concrete beams, slabs, and columns*
- *Selection and design criteria for reinforced concrete framing*
- *Opportunities and constraints for slab openings*
- *Relationship of structural system to program*
- *Designing bays of reinforced concrete framing*

We are preparing a preliminary design for an apartment building that will be 12 stories tall with approximately 24,000 sq ft per floor. It will contain a total of 154 apartments of various sizes as well as retail spaces on the ground floor. The site is very irregular in shape. Our initial scheme is characterized by floor plans with a freely shaped outline (Figure 20.1). Based on our experience and the preliminary configuration of the building, the bay size that seems to fit best with the floor plans is 21 ft by 22 ft.

The apartment market in this region is very competitive, so we must keep construction costs as low as possible. One way of economizing is to keep the floor-to-floor height as low as possible to save on the cost of the columns, wind bracing, and exterior walls. Minimal floor heights are easier to achieve in apartment construction than in office buildings or laboratories, because each apartment can have its own heating and cooling system with short, local runs of ductwork; there is no need for lengthy ducts to run horizontally above the ceilings of the building as a whole. The reduced area of exterior walls also lowers fuel costs for heating and cooling over the life of the building. Another way of saving money is to select a structural system that can be left exposed or painted on the underside as the finish ceiling, eliminating the need for application of a finish ceiling. The owner concurs with all these ideas.

BUILDING CODE REQUIREMENTS FOR THE STRUCTURE

The International Building Code designates the *Occupancy Group* for multifamily housing as R-2. We look next at the code's table of height and area limitations for buildings (Figure 20.2). The columns of this

Figure 20.1 An early sketch of a design for a 12-story apartment building shows the irregular massing of the exterior and a partial plan of the ninth floor.

TABLE 503
ALLOWABLE HEIGHT AND BUILDING AREAS[a]
Height limitations shown as stories and feet above grade plane.
Area limitations as determined by the definition of "Area, building," per story

		TYPE OF CONSTRUCTION								
		TYPE I		TYPE II		TYPE III		TYPE IV	TYPE V	
		A	B	A	B	A	B	HT	A	B
	HGT(feet)									
GROUP	HGT(S)	UL	160	65	55	65	55	65	50	40
A-1	S	UL	5	3	2	3	2	3	2	1
	A	UL	UL	15,500	8,500	14,000	8,500	15,000	11,500	5,500
A-2	S	UL	11	3	2	3	2	3	2	1
	A	UL	UL	15,500	9,500	14,000	9,500	15,000	11,500	6,000
A-3	S	UL	11	3	2	3	2	3	2	1
	A	UL	UL	15,500	9,500	14,000	9,500	15,000	11,500	6,000
A-4	S	UL	11	3	2	3	2	3	2	1
	A	UL	UL	15,500	9,500	14,000	9,500	15,000	11,500	6,000
A-5	S	UL	UL	UL	UL	UL	UL	UL	UL	UL
	A	UL	UL	UL	UL	UL	UL	UL	UL	UL
B	S	UL	11	5	4	5	4	5	3	2
	A	UL	UL	37,500	23,000	28,500	19,000	36,000	18,000	9,000
E	S	UL	5	3	2	3	2	3	1	1
	A	UL	UL	26,500	14,500	23,500	14,500	25,500	18,500	9,500
F-1	S	UL	11	4	2	3	2	4	2	1
	A	UL	UL	25,000	15,500	19,000	12,000	33,500	14,000	8,500
F-2	S	UL	11	5	3	4	3	5	3	2
	A	UL	UL	37,500	23,000	28,500	18,000	50,500	21,000	13,000
H-1	S	1	1	1	1	1	1	1	1	NP
	A	21,000	16,500	11,000	7,000	9,500	7,000	10,500	7,500	NP
H-2[d]	S	UL	3	2	1	2	1	2	1	1
	A	21,000	16,500	11,000	7,000	9,500	7,000	10,500	7,500	3,000
H-3[d]	S	UL	6	4	2	4	2	4	2	1
	A	UL	60,000	26,500	14,000	17,500	13,000	25,500	10,000	5,000
H-4	S	UL	7	5	3	5	3	5	3	2
	A	UL	UL	37,500	17,500	28,500	17,500	36,000	18,000	6,500
H-5	S	4	4	3	3	3	3	3	3	2
	A	UL	UL	37,500	23,000	28,500	19,000	36,000	18,000	9,000
I-1	S	UL	9	4	3	4	3	4	3	2
	A	UL	55,000	19,000	10,000	16,500	10,000	18,000	10,500	4,500
I-2	S	UL	4	2	1	1	NP	1	1	NP
	A	UL	UL	15,000	11,000	12,000	NP	12,000	9,500	NP
I-3	S	UL	4	2	1	2	1	2	2	1
	A	UL	UL	15,000	10,000	10,500	7,500	12,000	7,500	5,000
I-4	S	UL	5	3	2	3	2	3	1	1
	A	UL	60,500	26,500	13,000	23,500	13,000	25,500	18,500	9,000
M	S	UL	11	4	4	4	4	4	3	1
	A	UL	UL	21,500	12,500	18,500	12,500	20,500	14,000	9,000
R-1	S	UL	11	4	4	4	4	4	3	2
	A	UL	UL	24,000	16,000	24,000	16,000	20,500	12,000	7,000
R-2	S	UL	11	4	4	4	4	4	3	2
	A	UL	UL	24,000	16,000	24,000	16,000	20,500	12,000	7,000
R-3	S	UL	11	4	4	4	4	4	3	3
	A	UL	UL	UL	UL	UL	UL	UL	UL	UL
R-4	S	UL	11	4	4	4	4	4	3	2
	A	UL	UL	24,000	16,000	24,000	16,000	20,500	12,000	7,000
S-1	S	UL	11	4	3	3	3	4	3	1
	A	UL	48,000	26,000	17,500	26,000	17,500	25,500	14,000	9,000
S-2[b, c]	S	UL	11	5	4	4	4	5	4	2
	A	UL	79,000	39,000	26,000	39,000	26,000	38,500	21,000	13,500
U[c]	S	UL	5	4	2	3	2	4	2	1
	A	UL	35,500	19,000	8,500	14,000	8,500	18,000	9,000	5,500

For SI: 1 foot = 304.8 mm, 1 square foot = 0.0929 m^2.
UL = Unlimited, NP = Not permitted.
a. See the following sections for general exceptions to Table 503:
1. Section 504.2, Allowable height increase due to automatic sprinkler system installation.
2. Section 506.2, Allowable area increase due to street frontage.
3. Section 506.3, Allowable area increase due to automatic sprinkler system installation.
4. Section 507, Unlimited area buildings.
b. For open parking structures, see Section 406.3.
c. For private garages, see Section 406.1.
d. See Section 415.5 for limitations.

table start on the left with the most fire-resistant *Construction Type*, and finish on the right with the least fire-resistant. For Occupancy Group R-2, we see that for our building, which is 12 stories tall with an area of 24,000 sq ft per floor, the most fire-resistant type of construction, Type I-A, is required. If we were to use the next most resistant, Type I-B, we could build unlimited floor area, but not more than 11 stories tall. However, a paragraph of the code that is found near this table allows one additional floor of height for any building built with automatic fire suppression sprinklers throughout. For life safety, we intended to install sprinklers anyway, and it is virtually impossible to purchase insurance on a building of this size and type that does not have sprinklers.

The structural material and system for this construction type are not specified directly by the code, except that the structure must be noncombustible, which means that it must be made of steel, concrete, or masonry. On another table in the International Building Code (reproduced here as Figure 20.3), the required fire-resistant characteristics of all the construction types are given. We learn that for Type I-B, the entire load-bearing structure must have two hours of fire resistance, except for the roof, for which only a one-hour rating is required. Type I-A construction requires three-hour ratings rather than two, which would add considerably to the cost of the building, so we are happy to settle for Type I-B with automatic sprinklers.

What does a two-hour rating mean? The *fire-resistance ratings* of structural elements of buildings are determined by laboratory testing in accordance with Procedure E-119 of the American Society for Testing and Materials (ASTM). A full-scale specimen of the slab, beam, or column is constructed in a large

◀**Figure 20.2** A table of allowable heights and floor areas for various types of constructions, reproduced from the *2006 International Building Code*.

Source: *2006 International Building Code*, Copyright © 2006, Washington, DC: International Code Council. Reproduced with permission. All rights reserved. www.iccsafe.org.

TABLE 601
FIRE-RESISTANCE RATING REQUIREMENTS FOR BUILDING ELEMENTS (hours)

BUILDING ELEMENT	TYPE I		TYPE II		TYPE III		TYPE IV	TYPE V	
	A	B	A[e]	B	A[e]	B	HT	A[e]	B
Structural frame[a]	3[b]	2[b]	1	0	1	0	HT	1	0
Bearing walls Exterior[g] Interior	3 3[b]	2 2[b]	1 1	0 0	2 1	2 0	2 1/HT	1 1	0 0
Nonbearing walls and partitions Exterior	See Table 602								
Nonbearing walls and partitions Interior[f]	0	0	0	0	0	0	See Section 602.4.6	0	0
Floor construction Including supporting beams and joists	2	2	1	0	1	0	HT	1	0
Roof construction Including supporting beams and joists	$1\frac{1}{2}$[c]	1[c, d]	1[c, d]	0[d]	1[c, d]	0[d]	HT	1[c, d]	0

For SI: 1 foot = 304.8 mm.

a. The structural frame shall be considered to be the columns and the girders, beams, trusses and spandrels having direct connections to the columns and bracing members designed to carry gravity loads. The members of floor or roof panels which have no connection to the columns shall be considered secondary members and not a part of the structural frame.

b. Roof supports: Fire-resistance ratings of structural frame and bearing walls are permitted to be reduced by 1 hour where supporting a roof only.

c. Except in Group F-1, H, M and S-1 occupancies, fire protection of structural members shall not be required, including protection of roof framing and decking where every part of the roof construction is 20 feet or more above any floor immediately below. Fire-retardant-treated wood members shall be allowed to be used for such unprotected members.

d. In all occupancies, heavy timber shall be allowed where a 1-hour or less fire-resistance rating is required.

e. An approved automatic sprinkler system in accordance with Section 903.3.1.1 shall be allowed to be substituted for 1-hour fire-resistance-rated construction, provided such system is not otherwise required by other provisions of the code or used for an allowable area increase in accordance with Section 506.3 or an allowable height increase in accordance with Section 504.2. The 1-hour substitution for the fire resistance of exterior walls shall not be permitted.

f. Not less than the fire-resistance rating required by other sections of this code.

g. Not less than the fire-resistance rating based on fire separation distance (see Table 602).

Figure 20.3 Fire-resistance rating requirements for building elements in the various types of construction, reproduced from the *2006 International Building Code*.

test furnace. The full structural load for which the element is designed is applied to it. A fire is started in the furnace, raising the temperature gradually to 2000°F after four hours. The fire endurance of a beam or column, which is measured in hours from the beginning of the test, is established when it fails to support the load for which it is designed, or the temperature of any of its reinforcing steel reaches 1100°F, whichever occurs first. For a floor, wall, or roof assembly, it may also be established when the surface that is not exposed to the fire reaches an average temperature of 250°F, or 325°F in any location, or when cotton waste placed on the side of the assembly away from the fire ignites, or when the assembly disintegrates when subjected to a stream of water from a fire hose. Such tests are usually sponsored by trade associations or manufacturers that promote various materials or systems. The results are published and become the bases on which we design.

For steel construction, fire-resistance ratings depend on the amount and type of fireproofing material that is applied to the columns, girders, and beams to insulate them from the heat of a fire.

The fire resistance of concrete framing systems is mainly dependent on the massiveness of the concrete. Thicker slabs and beams can absorb more heat than thinner ones. Additionally, the thickness of the concrete cover over the reinforcing bars is crucial because the cover protects the steel from excessive temperatures. Generally speaking, two-hour fire resistance ratings are achieved by concrete elements with the following minimum dimensions:

Slabs	5 in.
Columns	10 in.
Reinforcing cover	1 in.

We also consult the code for one additional piece of information that is important with regard to the load-bearing structure of our building: The design live load for an apartment building is specified as 40 pounds per square foot.

SELECTING A STRUCTURAL SYSTEM

Summarizing the criteria that we will use to select a structural material and system for this building:

- The building code requires that the structural system have at least a two-hour fire-resistance rating.
- Residential live loads are established by the same code as 40 lb/ft², which is relatively light.
- We need a structural system for this building that will minimize building height.
- We would like the structural system to provide a smooth underside that, when painted, will work well as a finished ceiling in an apartment.
- Given the irregular outline of the building we want to construct, we would also like to use a system that is tolerant of occasional irregularity in column spacings.

With these criteria in mind, we evaluate our options:

- Steel-framed floors are generally rather deep, which may increase floor-to-floor heights.
- The underside of a steel-framed floor or roof looks cluttered, with at least two different sizes of members (girder and beam) in each bay, and fuzzy, fragile fireproofing material on the major members. A suspended finish ceiling is almost always required for a good appearance.

- Precast concrete framing does not have the formal freedom to follow readily a curving plan outline. And because the slabs and stems of precast members are so thin, an application to the underside of fireproofing material like that used on steel framing members may be required. Precast hollow-core planks are minimal in thickness and can be painted on their undersides as finish ceilings, but they span in only one direction and must have beams or loadbearing walls to support them.
- There are framing systems in sitecast concrete that have smooth undersurfaces, allow some offsetting of selected columns from their positions on the structural grid, and achieve floor-to-floor heights that are the least of any material or system. These appear to be the most promising for further exploration.

Based on this knowledge, we must learn more about sitecast concrete framing systems and their various attributes in order to proceed with our design.

SITECAST CONCRETE FRAMING SYSTEMS

Concrete

Concrete is essentially manmade stone. It consists of *coarse aggregate* (usually crushed stone), *fine aggregate* (sand), *portland cement* (a very fine, gray powder), and water. *Structural lightweight concrete* is sometimes used to reduce the self-weight of a structure. It is produced by replacing the crushed stone in the mixture with expanded shale. It is about 20 percent less dense than normal concrete, yet nearly as strong, but more costly. We can formulate concrete in a wide range of strengths and other properties by controlling the amounts of its ingredients, including special admixtures, and supervising its manufacture, placement, and curing very carefully.

When the ingredients of concrete are mixed together, they form an unstable slurry that is deposited in *formwork* that supports it, gives it the shape that we desire, and helps retain its moisture until it has cured. The *curing* of concrete is a process in which water combines chemically with the constituents of the portland cement to form a strong binding substance that transforms the slurry into a stonelike solid. Concrete takes several weeks of curing to reach its intended strength. Because the hardening of concrete is due to hydration and not to drying, concrete cannot be allowed to dry out during the curing process or its strength will be seriously compromised.

Reinforcing

Concrete has no useful resistance to tensile forces, but it is an economical material for resisting compressive forces. A beam experiences both tension and compression. By adding steel rods called *reinforcing bars* (or *rebars* for short) to the regions of a concrete beam where tension occurs, we create a composite member in which the portion of the beam cross section on the compressive side resists the compression, and the embedded steel bars resist tension. Less than half the concrete in a beam, the portion above the neutral plane, has a compressive role. The rest serves mainly to protect the reinforcing steel, to embed it solidly in the beam, and to transfer diagonal web forces from one edge of the beam to the other.

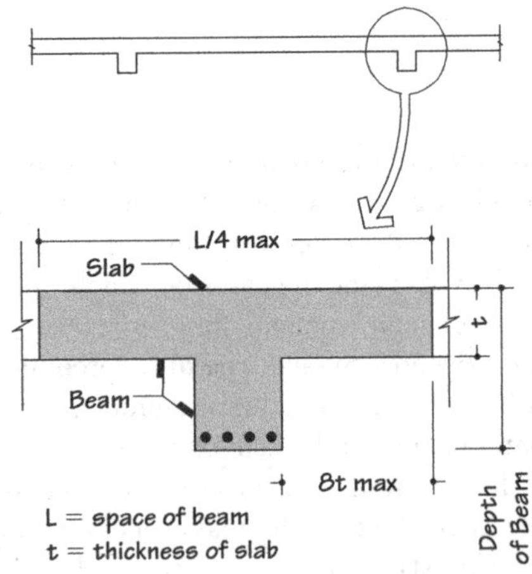

Figure 20.4 In concrete one-way solid slab structures, a portion of the floor slab up to a maximum of one-fourth of the span, *L*, may be considered as being part of the beam.

The slab, beams, and girders of a sitecast concrete building frame are all cast in a single step as a continuous mass of concrete. A useful consequence of this is that the beams and girders utilize a portion of the slab to resist compression, which allows the depth of those members to be somewhat smaller than would otherwise be the case (Figure 20.4).

Reinforcing steel is also used in columns, to share compressive loads and impart resistance to buckling and bending. Large vertical bars do the major work. Small-diameter steel *ties* or *spirals* that are wrapped around the vertical bars to prevent them from buckling and to confine the concrete core of the column so as to increase its load-bearing capacity (Figure 20.5).

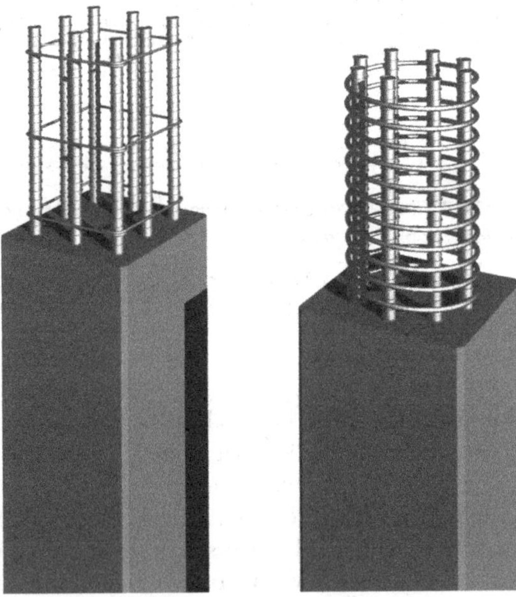

Figure 20.5 Concrete columns are reinforced with large vertical reinforcing bars that share the compressive force with the concrete. The vertical bars are wrapped with either column ties (left), or a column spiral (right), in either case made of small-diameter bars. Inward buckling is impossible because of the core of concrete inside the vertical bars. Outward buckling is prevented by the ties acting in tension. The ties also confine the concrete in the core of the column to increase its strength.

Reinforcing bars are manufactured in a range of standard diameters (Figure 20.6). They are usually cut to length and bent as required in fabrication shops, then brought to the construction site ready for installation in the formwork. *Welded wire fabric*, a mesh of steel wires or rods, is supplied in rolls or sheets that save time and effort when reinforcing slabs.

Ideally, we would place the reinforcing bars in a concrete beam along the lines of tension in the lattice pattern (Figure 20.7). This would be costly and difficult, however, because it would require a large inventory of differently bent bars on the construction site and a similarly large inventory of devices to support the different bent shapes in the formwork. Instead, we place horizontal bars in the main regions of tensile flow, and add vertical loops of reinforcing called *stirrups* in the end regions of a beam (Figure 20.8). These stirrups intercept the diagonal lines of tensile web force and control cracking in these regions near the ends of the beam. The original open-top *U-stirrup* has largely been replaced by the closed *stirrup-tie* (Figure 20.9), which imparts to the beam an increased resistance to the torsional forces that can occur in concrete frames that are subjected to large lateral loads by winds or earthquakes.

Concrete *slabs* are simply shallow, broadened beams that serve as decking in concrete framing systems. They work the same as concrete beams do, but because of the greater volume of concrete that they contain relative to their depth, they generally do not require stirrups.

ASTM Standard Reinforcing Bars

Bar Size		Nominal Dimensions					
		Diameter		Cross-Sectional Area		Weight (mass)	
American	Metric	in.	mm	in.^{2}	mm^2	lb/ft	kg/m
#3	#10	0.375	9.5	0.11	71	0.376	0.560
#4	#13	0.500	12.7	0.20	129	0.668	0.944
#5	#16	0.625	15.9	0.31	199	1.043	1.552
#6	#19	0.750	19.1	0.44	284	1.502	2.235
#7	#22	0.875	22.2	0.60	387	2.044	3.042
#8	#25	1.000	25.4	0.79	510	2.670	3.973
#9	#29	1.128	28.7	1.00	645	3.400	5.060
#10	#32	1.270	32.3	1.27	819	4.303	6.404
#11	#36	1.410	35.8	1.56	1006	5.313	7.907
#14	#43	1.693	43.0	2.25	1452	7.65	11.38
#18	#57	2.257	57.3	4.00	2581	13.6	20.24

(a)

Metric Reinforcing Bars

Size Designation	Nominal Mass, kg/m	Nominal Dimensions	
		Diameter, mm	Cross-Sectional Area, mm^2
10M	0.785	11.3	100
15M	1.570	16.0	200
20M	2.355	19.5	300
25M	3.925	25.2	500
30M	5.495	29.9	700
35M	7.850	35.7	1000
45M	11.775	43.7	1500
55M	19.625	56.4	2500

(b)

Figure 20.6 Dimensions of standard reinforcing bars for concrete in American standard sizes (a) and "hard metric" sizes (b).

FORMWORK FOR CONCRETE

Formwork for concrete must have high-quality faces against which the concrete is cast, because the concrete will mirror faithfully even the smallest flaw. Wet concrete is very dense and requires extremely strong, rigid structures to support the formwork that holds it. Structural failure of concrete formwork is a disaster that must be avoided at any cost because it wastes money, delays the construction schedule, and can cause injury or death to workers. Thus, formwork is one of the costliest aspects of sitecast concrete construction. It is imperative that we seek ways of reducing its cost without compromising its quality or safety.

The largest economies stem from standardization and repetition. Formwork for a frame that is identical in every bay reduces the inventory of parts and offers a construction process that can be learned quickly by the construction crew and then repeated again and again with increasing speed and greater accuracy. A single beam that is special, a corner that has an unusual angle, or a bay that contains a unique feature, are all expensive and mistake-prone. This is not to say that they cannot be done, but rather that they should be done only in instances where there is money in the budget to make them possible and where they contribute strongly to the quality of the design.

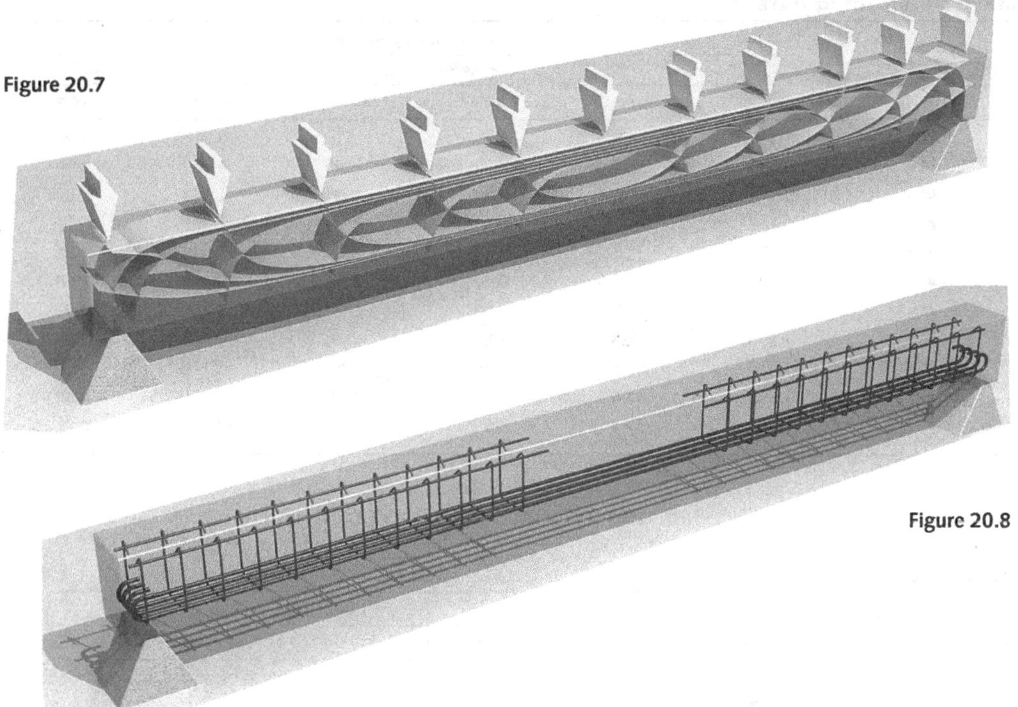

Figure 20.7 For maximum efficiency of material, the steel reinforcing bars in a beam would follow the paths of the cable-like tensile trajectories, represented as ribbons in this transparent drawing. In reality, this reinforcing pattern would be difficult and costly because of the large number of different bending patterns that would be required for the bars, and because of the difficulty of supporting the curving bars in the formwork.

Figure 20.8 The standard way of reinforcing a simply-supported concrete beam places straight longitudinal steel bars near the bottom of the beam. The ends of these bars are bent into hooks that transfer any remaining forces at the ends of the bars into the concrete. The vertical stirrups act in tension much like the vertical members in a Howe truss, and the concrete acts like the compression diagonals. Because the beam is not continuous, there is no need for longitudinal top bars. The top bars shown here are minimal in diameter and serve only to support the top ends of the stirrups.

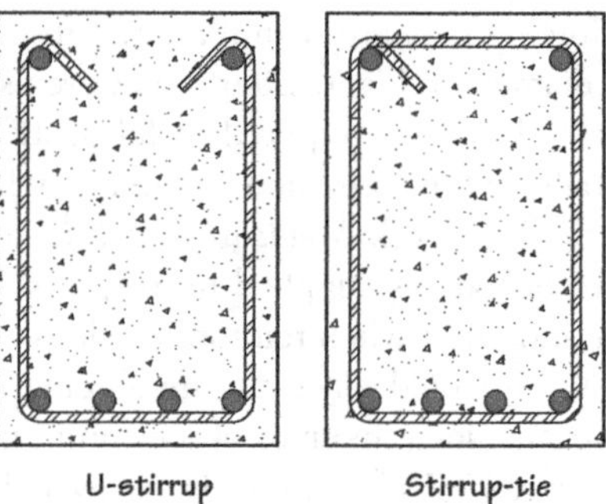

Figure 20.9 Stirrup-ties provide more torsional resistance to a beam than the older U-stirrup design.

SITECAST CONCRETE ONE-WAY FRAMING SYSTEMS

Concrete frames for buildings were first used in the mid to late nineteenth century. Early concrete frames generally imitated the forms of timber or steel frames, employing girders and beams to support slabs that acted in one direction only, much as steel and wood members do. Such systems are called *one-way solid slab-and-beam* systems (Figure 20.10a). Because of their versatility, formal flexibility, and capability to carry heavy loads, they are still valid today, especially for highly customized buildings, buildings with heavy floor loads, and buildings with columns that are spaced farther apart in one direction than in the other.

Slab Bands

One-way solid slabs are often supported on integral concrete beams that are very broad and shallow (Figure 20.10b). These flattened beams are called *slab bands*. They reduce the thickness of the floor structure substantially. They also reduce the spans of the slabs and therefore their thicknesses, with consequent savings of concrete and reinforcing steel. Taken together, these reductions in thickness translate into a reduced story-to-story height that saves money on columns and exterior walls.

Concrete Joists

When solid slabs are used for relatively long spans, they become so thick that their self-weight is an excessive burden. This difficulty may be overcome by eliminating much of the nonworking concrete in the lower part of the slab with a *one-way concrete joist system*, also called a *rib slab* (Figure 20.10c). The system is formed on a flat plywood surface by adding standardized steel pans that form the voids between the joists. The ends of the pans are tapered to thicken the joists where they join their supporting beams so that the concrete in them can resist the higher web forces in this region.

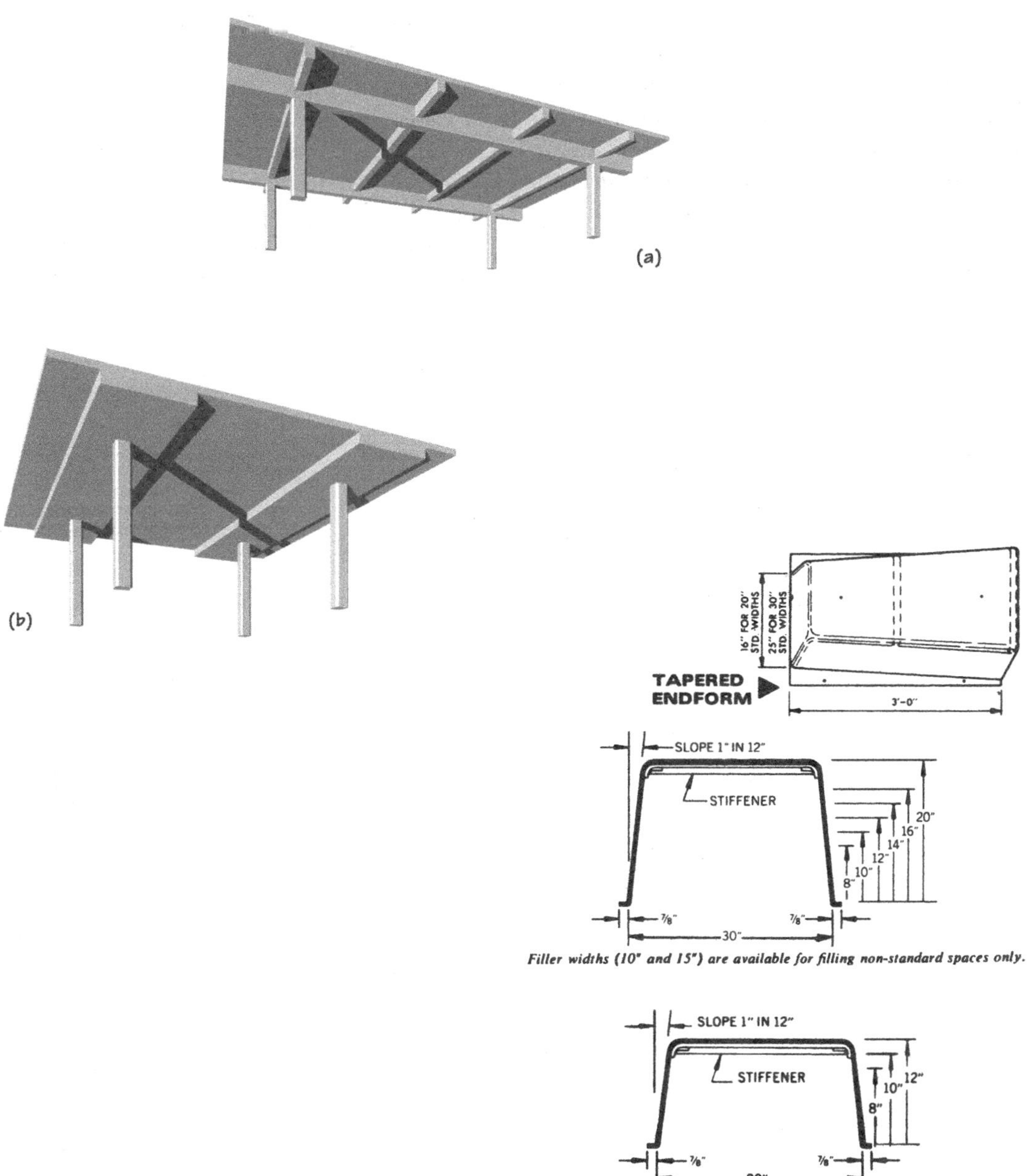

Figure 20.10 One-way concrete framing systems: (a) one-way solid slab and beam system, (b) one-way solid slab with slab bands, (c) one-way concrete joist system (rib slab), (d) wide module concrete joist system. Standard formwork pan sizes for rib slabs are shown at the lower right.

Joist Bands

Usually it is most economical to make a concrete beam at least twice as deep as it is wide. In the overall context of a floor slab, however, the formwork for beams of this proportion would need to extend below the plywood platform on which the pans are placed, which would make it rather costly to build. It is less expensive to make the beams the same depth as the concrete joists, even though this makes them broad and heavy, because a single horizontal plane of plywood serves to form the bottoms of both the joists and the beams. Such broad, shallow beams are called *joist bands*, and can be seen in (c) and (d) of Figure 20.10. Their advantages and disadvantages are similar to those of slab bands. The bottom-line cost for a system of joists and joist bands is usually lower than for a system that uses beams whose proportions have been optimized.

Wide-Module Concrete Joist Systems

With their close spacings, concrete joists are spanned by a concrete slab deck (cast at the same time as the joists in a seamless process) that needs to be no more than 3 to 4.5 in. deep. This is less than the 5-in. minimum slab thickness for two-hour floor construction. When the thickness of the slab is increased to 5 in. to achieve a two-hour rating, it is capable of spanning much farther than the 2-ft spacing of traditional concrete joists. This has led to the introduction of *wide-module* concrete joist systems, in which the joists are produced by special formwork pans that double the spacing of the joists, as compared to ordinary joist pans (Figure 20.10d). The wider spacing doubles the load on the joists, which causes excessive diagonal tension stress near the ends of the joists. This is overcome by the insertion of stirrups into the ends of the forms. Because the joists are narrow, these may be ordinary U-stirrups installed on an angle so they fit into the forms, or single-leg stirrups.

SITECAST CONCRETE TWO-WAY FRAMING SYSTEMS

Two-Way Plates and Slabs

Slab systems that span simultaneously in two directions at once without using beams (Figures 20.11, 20.12) were developed early in the twentieth century when innovative structural engineers realized that concrete was uniquely capable of being utilized in this highly efficient way. Bays for two-way systems should be square or nearly square, so that the bending moments may be shared equally by the two mutually perpendicular directions of the slabs. Reinforcing bars for two-way systems are placed in half-bay-wide strips in both directions of the slab. The *column strip* is centered on the line of columns. Because it experiences higher bending moments, its reinforcing bars are heavier than those in the *middle strip* (Figure 20.13).

Column Heads for Two-Way Concrete Systems

An ideal two-way slab system would incorporate a smoothly curving transition from the slab to the column, to accommodate a smooth flow of forces and reduce stress concentrations at this critical junction. Some early projects are graceful examples of this possibility (Figure 20.14). As usual, however, economic factors dictate shapes that are easier and

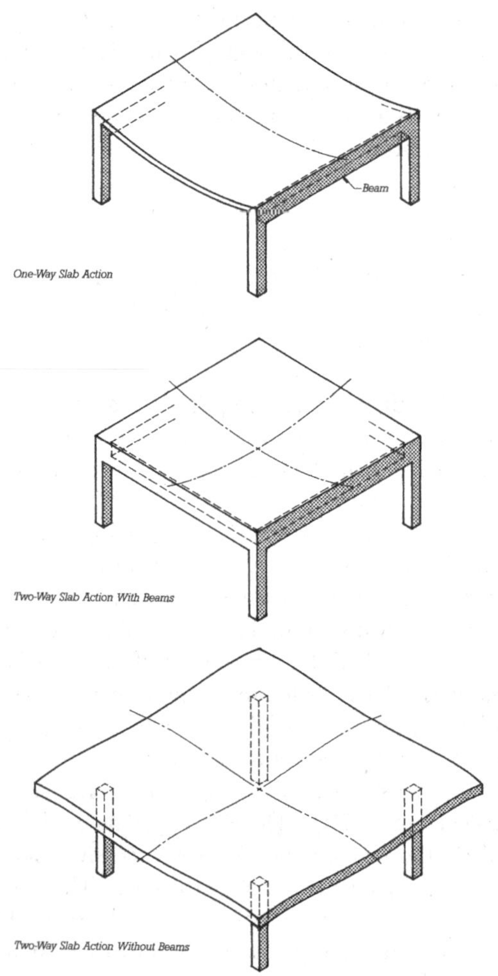

Figure 20.11 A comparison of one-way and two-way action.

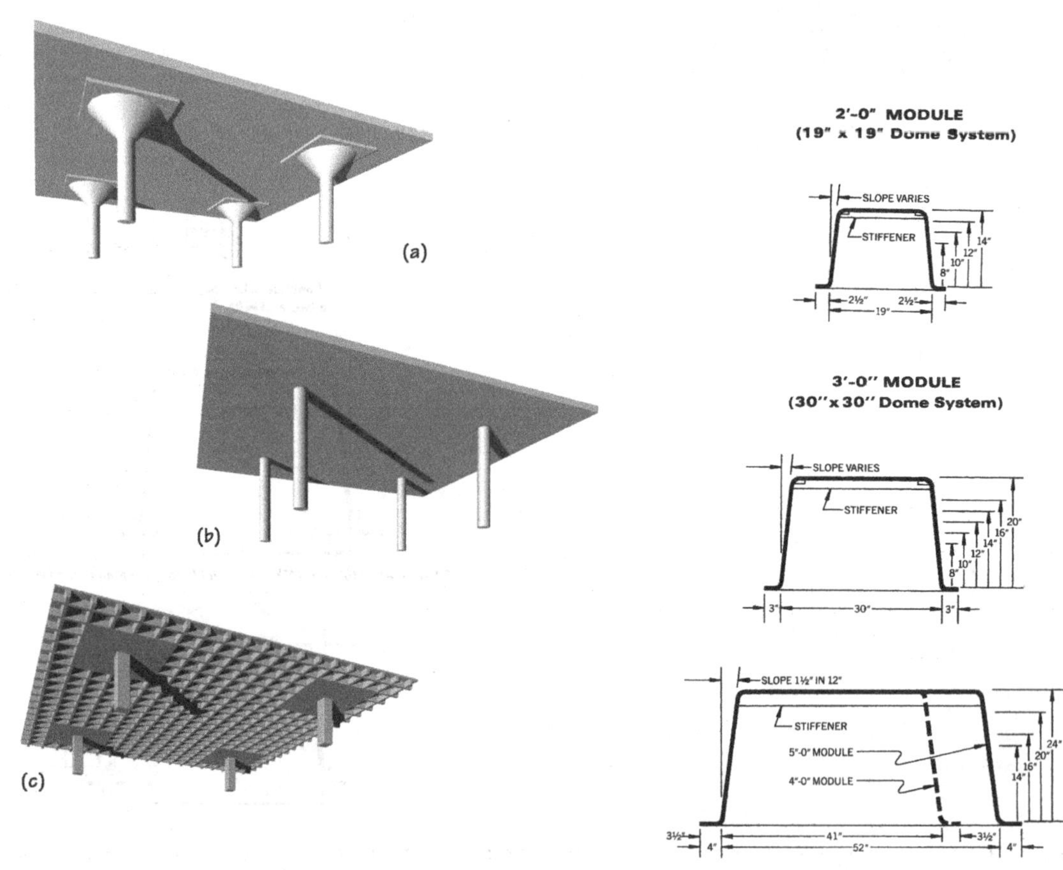

Figure 20.12 Two-way concrete framing systems: (a) two-way concrete flat slab with mushroom capitals and drop panel, (b) two-way flat plate, (c) two-way concrete joist system (waffle slab), with standard pan sizes to the right.

Column Strip
Middle Strip
Column Strip
Middle Strip
Column Strip

Column Strip | Middle Strip | Column Strip | Middle Strip | Column Strip

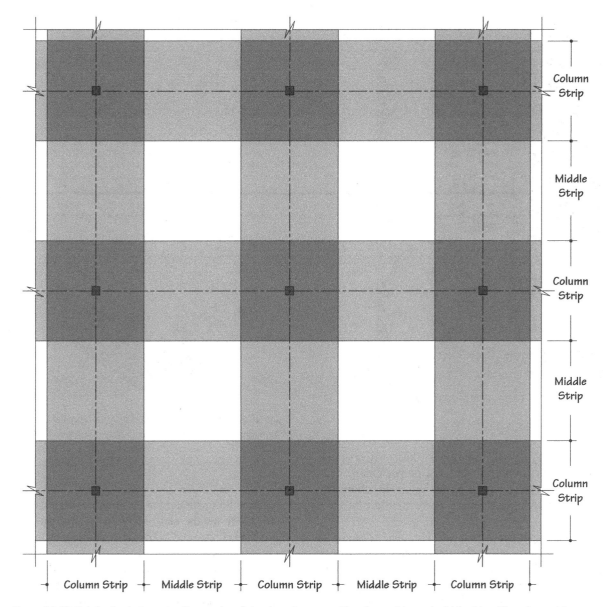

Figure 20.13 Reinforcing in two-way floor and roof structures is arranged in column strips and middle strips. The column strips are more heavily reinforced because they carry larger bending moments.

Figure 20.14 The column heads in this Zurich warehouse, constructed in 1910 by Robert Maillart, are shaped to encourage a smooth flow of forces from the slabs into the columns.

Figure 20.15 The standard U.S. column head design for two-way flat slabs includes a drop panel and a mushroom capital.

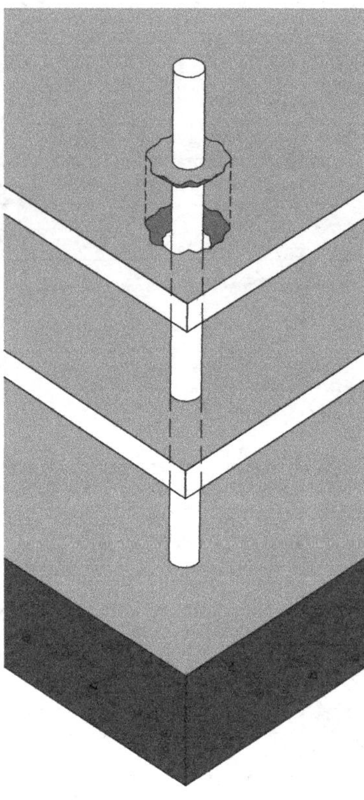

Figure 20.16 Punching shear occurs in a two-way flat plate when diagonal tensile forces in the vicinity of a column are too high.

less expensive to form. For heavily loaded industrial floors, a *drop panel and mushroom capital* are formed with standardized, reusable components to create a *two-way flat slab system* (Figure 20.15). These approximate the shape of the earlier, smooth transitions. Many buildings today are built without the mushroom capitals and use only the drop panels. For lightly loaded floors, even the drop panels are eliminated, replaced by an internal grid of reinforcing bars at each column intersection, to form the ubiquitous *two-way flat plate system* (Figure 20.12b). Because this system uses only a simple platform of formwork, it is the least expensive of all sitecast concrete framing systems. It is used for an ever-widening set of purposes, including bays that are as much as twice as long as they are wide and floors that carry relatively heavy loads. In nonsquare bays, proportionally more reinforcing steel is used in the longer direction than in the shorter so as to allow both directions to share the load.

When designing two-way flat plate systems, it is important to design the slab connections to resist *punching shear*, which is analogous to the punching of holes in paper but is actually a diagonal tension failure in the concrete (Figure 20.16). This involves specifying a column size that has sufficient perimeter to distribute the tensile force over enough concrete to keep stresses within acceptable limits. As a first approximation, the side of a square column should be no less than 2.0 times the thickness of the slab. A round column should have a minimum diameter of about 2.6 times the slab thickness. Additional steel reinforcing is provided in the slab/column junction to resist tensile forces.

For special areas of a building, particularly when there is a more generous construction budget, there is scope for more imaginative ways of creating additional column perimeter, some of which are sketched in Figure 20.17. The best would be forms similar to those designed by Robert Maillart (Figure 20.14), since they provide easy, gently curving paths for the forces to flow from the slab into the column.

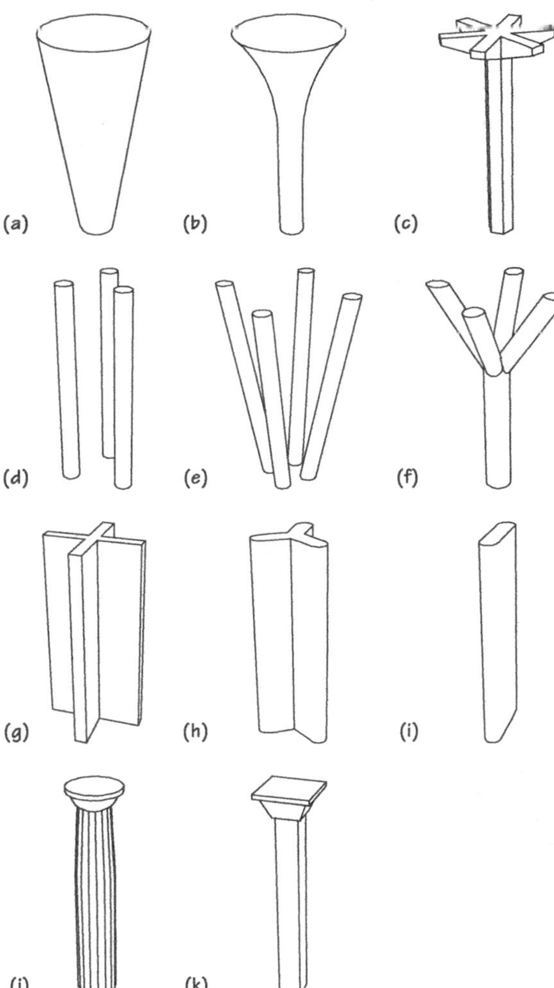

Figure 20.17 Several ideas for providing more column perimeter to resist punching shear.

ROBERT MAILLART

Swiss engineer Robert Maillart (pronounced "ma-YAR") was born in 1872. He studied at the ETH in Zurich from 1890–1894 with Wilhelm Ritter, Karl Culmann's successor. After earning his diploma and working in structural engineering offices, he designed and executed a three-hinged arch bridge in Zuoz in 1901. Over the next four decades he produced one innovation after another in bridge and building designs. He completed his first deck-stiffened arch bridge in Waggital in 1924. Shortly before his death in 1940 he was nominated as the sole honorary member of the special department for bridge builders of the Swiss Union for Engineers and Architects.

Maillart understood that the monolithic nature of reinforced concrete demands a uniquely holistic approach to its conception. He wrote in a 1938 article in the *Schweizerische Bauzeitung*, "It is not only the feeling for beauty which makes desirable the conception of the whole. . . . Seeing the structure as a whole nearly always brings economical advantages as well." Rather than follow precise calculations that don't account for possible real-world variability, Maillart advocated giving more freedom and responsibility to the on-site constructing engineer rather than to laws or codes, since calculations to satisfy "legal prescriptions should never be taught to students, because they can only be injurious to the freedom of their field of vision" (Maillart, *Schweizerische Bauzeitung*, 1931).

Maillart's sequence of dramatic bridges in the early 1900s demonstrates a gradual removal of unnecessary elements in three-hinged arched bridges: first a simplification of the profile, next a removal of the wedge of material between the deck and the lower arch at the sides at the Tavanasa bridge (1905), then a removal of intermediary wedges between the arch and the deck at Aare (1912). The widest-spanning arch Maillart constructed leaps 90 m (300 ft) across a crevasse at Salginatobel (1929, pp. 317–319). While most of his well-known designs were for vehicular bridges, he also completed curved and segmented-arch bridges for aqueducts, pedestrians, and railroad lines, as well as dozens of buildings with his beamless floor construction known for its smooth column-slab transitions and two-way patterns of steel reinforcement. In fact, these building projects constituted the majority of the work in his office during many of his years of practice. Maillart, like Nervi, Dieste, and countless other structural innovators, had won these many chances to design and build by proposing designs that were lowest in cost due to their careful deployment of materials. As news and images of these visually stunning designs reached outside of Switzerland, Maillart was acclaimed for the aesthetics of his structures. His work was profiled in a 1947 monograph by Max Bill and, more recently, in David Billington's writings, which reaffirm Maillart's beliefs that the designer earns freedom from ordinary solutions by gaining understanding from real-world tests and observations.

Waffle Slabs

As with one-way systems, two-way plates and slabs become ponderous at longer spans because of their own dead weight. The *two-way concrete joist system*, known universally as a *waffle slab*, extends the span range by omitting much of the nonworking concrete from the slab (Figure 20.12c). This is done by placing formed steel or plastic pans over the formwork platform. Pans are omitted in the vicinity of columns to form column heads that facilitate the transitional flow of forces from horizontal to vertical. Waffle slabs exhibit an attractive geometric pattern that is often left exposed as a finish ceiling.

LATERAL LOAD RESISTANCE OF CONCRETE BUILDING FRAMES

Joints in concrete building frames are inherently rigid because reinforcing bars run through them and the concrete around the bars is monolithic. Concrete framing systems that have sufficient depth of connection between horizontal and vertical elements are usually designed as moment-resisting frames that are capable of resisting wind and seismic loads without additional bracing or shear walls. Two-way concrete flat plate structures, lacking deep connections between their shallow slabs and thick columns, have relatively little resistance to moments and are inadequate to brace a building that is more than a few stories high. Our 12-story building will need diagonal bracing or shear walls to serve as the main agents of lateral resistance. Shear walls are usually easier, especially if they can be concentrated around elevator shafts, stairways, and vertical utility cores. The building code requires us to provide two different egress paths from the door of each apartment. This has the effect of forcing us to locate enclosed stairways near the ends of the building. The elevators, which are not considered to be emergency egress devices, may be concentrated in the middle. The walls of the stairways and elevator shafts may serve as shear walls and are located appropriately for this purpose. But 12 stories may still be too tall for these relatively small walls to provide all the resistance required, in which case, we will design selected corridor walls, and *party walls* between adjacent apartments as shear walls.

SELECTING A FRAMING SYSTEM FOR THE APARTMENT BUILDING

Figure 20.18 presents a decision tree for selecting an appropriate sitecast concrete framing system for any building. The bays of our building are nearly square, 21 ft by 22 ft, and the floors are lightly loaded. The spans are less than 30 ft. These characteristics lead us rapidly through the tree toward the conclusion that a sitecast concrete two-way flat plate system is the best one for our apartment project.

A check of the preliminary design approximations for a two-way flat plate structure (Figure 20.19) tells us that the thickness of the slab, if it is conventionally reinforced, will be in the neighborhood of 1/30th of the span, which works out to about 9 in. If we posttension the slabs, this thickness can be reduced to about 1/45th of the span, or 6 in. The difference between these two thicknesses is 3 in., and 3 in. per floor multiplied by 12 floors is 36 in. This is not a very significant height reduction for the building, but the thinner posttensioned slab does save about a third of the concrete required by a conventionally reinforced slab, and deserves further consideration as the design of the building progresses.

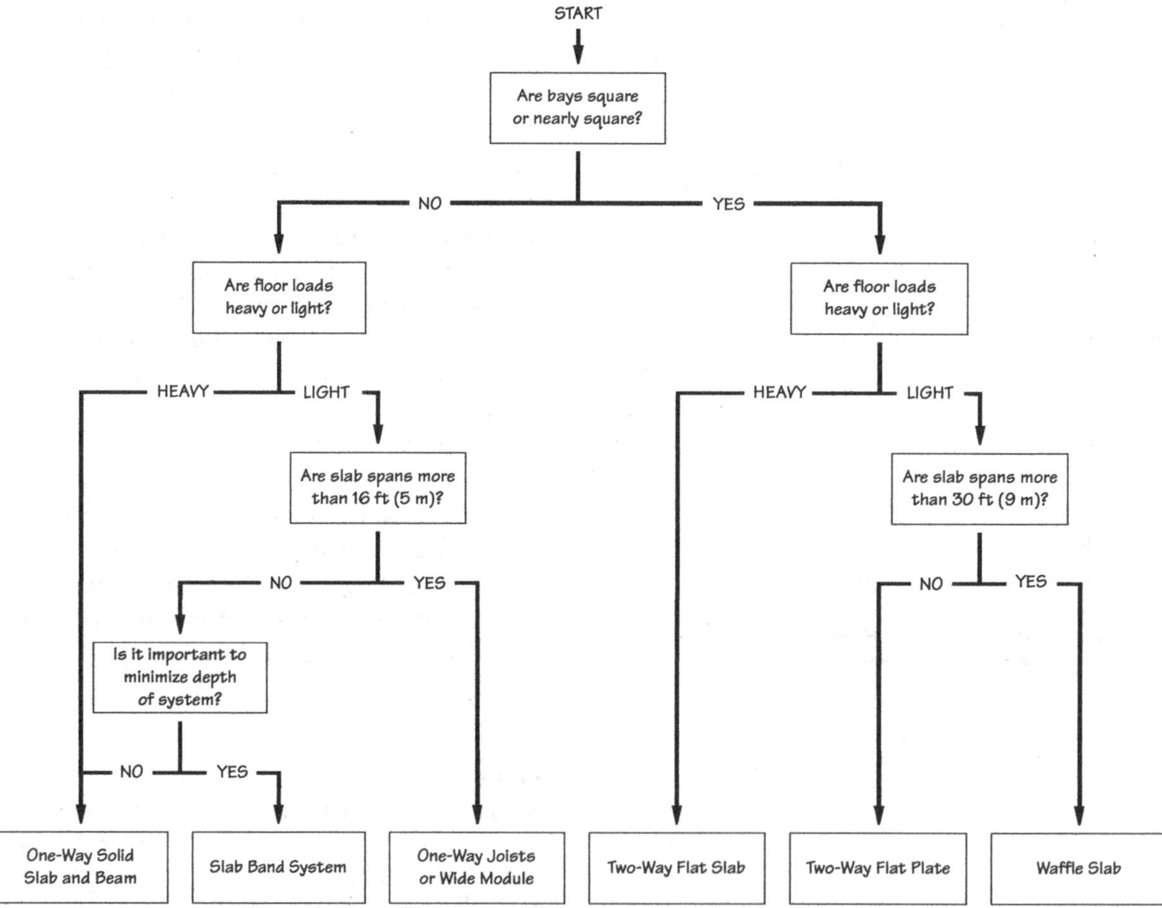

Figure 20.18 Structural criteria for selecting a concrete construction system.

FOR PRELIMINARY DESIGN OF A SITECAST CONCRETE STRUCTURE

- Estimate the depth of a **one-way solid slab** at 1/22 of its span if it is conventionally reinforced, or 1/40 of its span if it is posttensioned. Depths range typically from 4 to 10 in. (100–250 mm).
- Estimate the total depth of a **one-way concrete joist system or wide-module system** at 1/18 of its span if it is conventionally reinforced, or 1/24 of its span if it is posttensioned. For standard sizes of the pans used to form these systems, see Figure 20.10. To arrive at the total depth, a slab thickness of 3 to 4½ in. (75–115 mm) must be added to the depth of the pan that is selected.
- Estimate the depth of **concrete beams** at 1/16 of their span if they are conventionally reinforced, or 1/21 of their span if they are posttensioned. For concrete girders, use ratios of 1/12 and 1/20, respectively.
- Estimate the depth of **two-way flat plates** and **flat slabs** at 1/30 of their span if they are conventionally reinforced, or 1/45 of their span if they are posttensioned. Typical depths are 5 to 12 in. (125–305 mm). The minimum column size for a flat plate is approximately 2.6 times the depth of the slab. The width of a drop panel for a flat slab is usually ⅓ of the span, and the projection of the drop panel below the slab is about ½ the thickness of the slab.
- Estimate the depth of a **waffle slab** at 1/24 of its span if it is conventionally reinforced, or 1/35 of its span if it is posttensioned. For standard sizes of the domes used to form waffle slabs, see Figure 20.12. To arrive at the total depth, a slab thickness of 3 to 4½ in. (75–115 mm) must be added to the depth of the dome that is selected.
- To estimate the size of a **concrete column**, add up the total roof and floor area supported by the column. A 12-in. (300-mm) column can support up to about 2000 square feet (185 m²) of area, a 16-in. (400-mm) column 3000 square feet (280 m²), a 20-in. (500-mm) column 4000 square feet (370 m²), a 24-in. (600-mm) column 6000 square feet (560 m²), and a 28-in. (700-mm column 8000 square feet (740 m²). These sizes are greatly influenced by the strength of the concrete used and the ratio of reinforcing steel to concrete. Columns are usually round or square.
- To estimate the thickness of a **concrete load-bearing wall**, add up the total width of a floor and roof slabs that contribute load to a 1-ft length of wall. An 8-in. (200-mm) wall can support approximately 400 ft (120 m) of slab, a 10-in. (250-mm) wall 550 ft (170 m), a 12-in. (300-mm) wall 700 ft (210 m), and a 16-in. (100-mm) wall 1000 ft (300 m). These thicknesses are greatly influenced by the strength of the concrete used and the ratio of reinforcing steel to concrete.

These approximations are valid only for purposes of preliminary building layout, and must not be used to select final member sizes. They apply to the normal range of building occupancies such as residential, office, commercial, and institutional buildings, and parking garages. For manufacturing and storage buildings, use somewhat larger members.

For more comprehensive information on preliminary selection and layout of a structural system and sizing of structural members, see Allen, Edward, and Joseph Iano. *The Architect's Studio Companion* (4th ed.), Hoboken, NJ: John Wiley & Sons, Inc., 2007.

Figure 20.19 Approximations for preliminary sizing of concrete members.

These values are based on information given in Allen, Edward, and Joseph Iano, *The Architect's Studio Companion* (4th ed.). Hoboken, NJ: John Wiley & Sons, Inc., 2007.

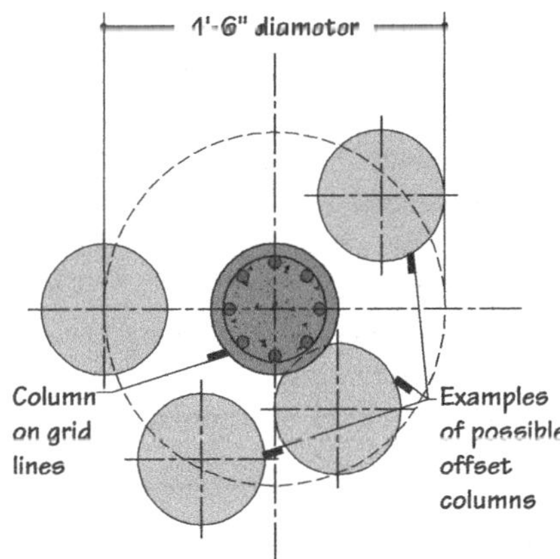

Figure 20.20 Column offset limits for the building that we are designing. If a column is offset on one floor, it must be offset in the same position on all floors so that it is continuous from foundation to roof.

Offsetting Columns

To facilitate the irregularities of plan shape that we contemplate, we will want to offset some columns from the 21 ft by 22 ft grid. The maximum offset should be no more than 10 percent of the span, which in our case is about 2 ft–3 in. This means that the centers of offset columns should fall within a circle centered on the regular column location with a diameter of 4 ft–6 in. (Figure 20.20). We will keep this in mind as we develop the floor plans for the building in greater detail. We are mindful of the need for column axes to align with one another from one floor to the next: If a column is offset from the grid on one floor, it must be offset to the same position on all floors both above and below, so that vertical forces will flow unimpeded to the foundations.

Punching Shear

The minimum column size to prevent punching shear is approximately 2.6 times the slab thickness of 9 in. In round figures, this is about 24 in. Figure 20.19 tells us that a 24-in. column can support a total slab area on all floors of about 6,000 sq ft. Our 21 ft by 22 ft bay contains 462 sq ft. Therefore, a 24-in. column will support about 13 stories of these bays, which is one story more than the height of our building. We should consider standardizing the column diameter at 24 in., which will be more than sufficient for the entire building. This would simplify the formwork inventory for the project, which would reduce costs slightly. The amount of reinforcing steel in the columns will vary from minimal at the top story to heavier reinforcing at ground level, in accordance with the accumulation of loads from top to bottom.

Slab Edges

At the perimeter of the building, slabs should project beyond the column line by about 20 percent of the main span in order to take maximum advantage of their continuity. For our 22 ft by 21 ft bays, this will be 4 to 4.5 ft (Figure 20.21). This overhang ends the slab at a line of zero bending moment, whereas a slab that does not project beyond the perimeter columns ends at a line of maximum moment, and thus requires a perimeter beam to resist it. The exterior walls are likely to bear on the slab at the perimeter. If they are heavy, then the overhang of the slab may need to be diminished somewhat.

Some of our apartments feature two-story open spaces with balconies. This will involve omitting areas of the floor slabs. Such penetrations can best occur at dividing lines between reinforcing strips, which are areas with decreased bending moment. Figure 20.22 shows some examples of how this may be done. If the cutouts in the floor are curvilinear, they should approximate the indicated openings as closely as possible, or else perimeter beams will be required. This same diagram shows a shaded circle around each column within which the centers of offset columns may be located. This diagram is useful as an underlay for tracing paper investigations of cutouts, offset columns, and slab perimeters with respect to proposed floor plans of this particular building. The curving lines of exterior walls can be accomplished by cutting the slab in areas of low bending moment as much as possible and by utilizing column offsets. Occasional perimeter beams and extra

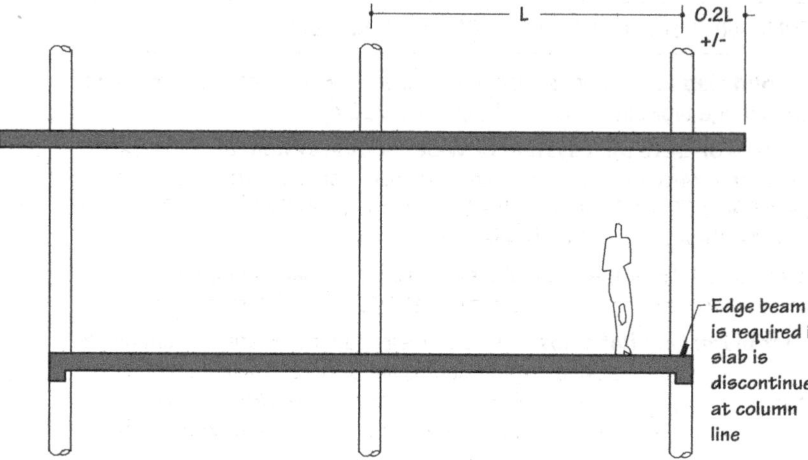

Figure 20.21 For maximum economy, two-way concrete slabs and plates should overhang the line of the last columns by about 20 percent of the main span. If this is not done, an edge beam must be introduced.

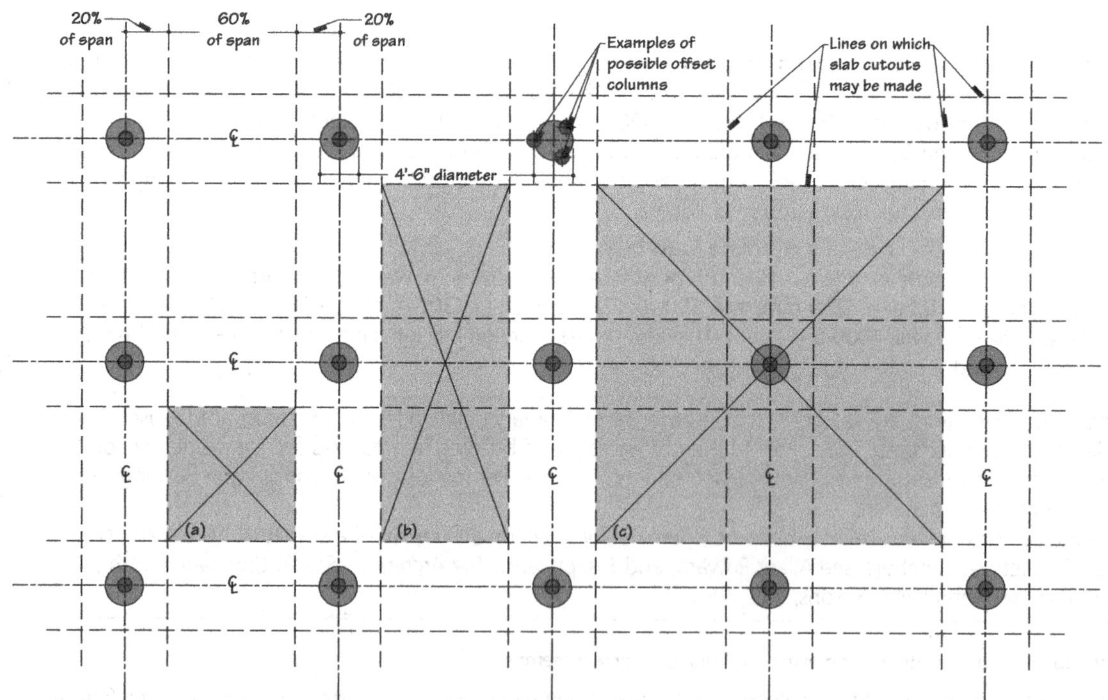

Figure 20.22 Two-way structures may be cut and discontinued at lines of zero bending moment. The large, square cutout will leave a two-story-high column in the middle of the space that must be designed for its increased effective length.

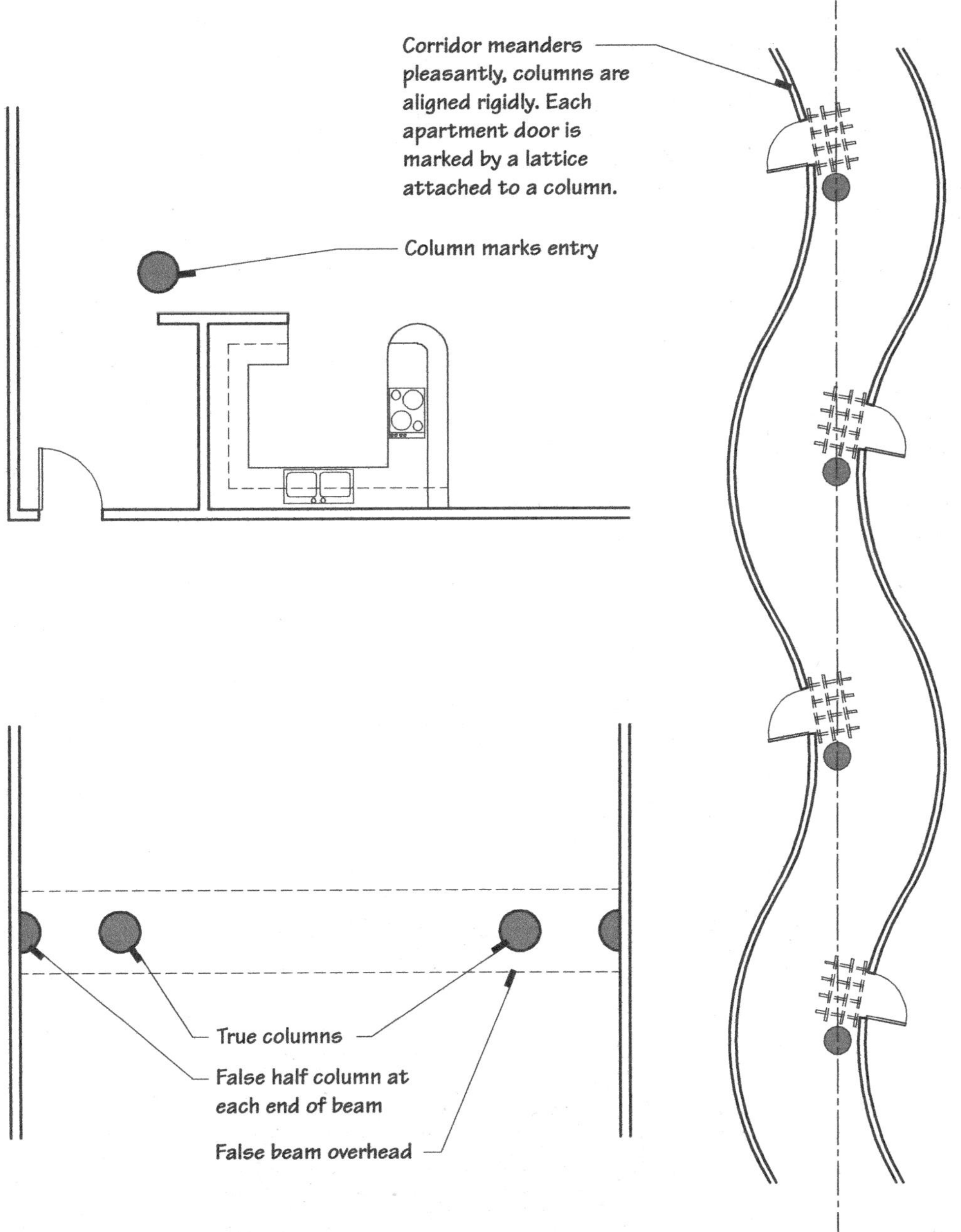

Figure 20.23 Columns may be utilized as architectural features of various kinds, instead of concealing them within partitions. These are several of the many possibilities.

columns may be required to get everything to work out. Depending on the frequency of such interventions and their location relative to shear walls, we may need to give special attention to avoiding compromise of the rigidity of the larger structure.

Columns

When doing detailed design of individual apartments, many designers will try to bury all the columns in partitions or closets. This may be done, but one should consider the potential of freestanding columns to work with the partitions to create architectural ways of composing and articulating spaces (Figure 20.23).

When choosing whether to use square or round columns, keep in mind that a round column is often the better choice in areas such as lobbies and corridors where people are constantly moving past it. Round columns do not have edges to harass the users of the building by snagging their skin or clothing. Remember also that a square column presents differing apparent widths to the eye, depending on the angle from which it is viewed. These vary from 1.0 to more than 1.4 times the actual face dimension of the column.

Worksheet 20A offers further experience with laying out framing plans in sitecast concrete.

Acoustics

A characteristic of concrete slabs that we must consider is that they readily transmit the noise of footsteps downward to the rooms below. This can be a major source of tenant complaints in an apartment building. We will specify soft carpets with thick pads to cushion the impact of footsteps and avoid this problem. In areas such as kitchens and bathrooms where hard flooring materials such as tile, stone, or hardwood are used, we will specify the installation of soft sound-deadening panels between the finish floor material and the structural slab.

Posttensioning

We may wish to *posttension* the steel in the slabs of this building in order to save concrete and reduce the

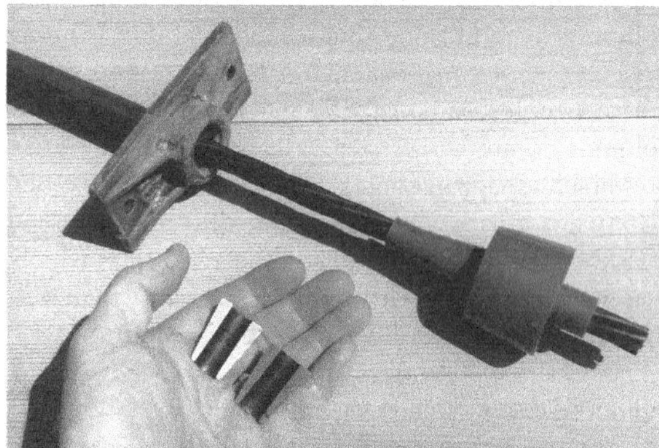

◀**Figure 20.24** The end anchorage for posttensioning tendons is ingeniously simple: A steel anchor plate and a plastic pocket former are nailed to the inside of the concrete formwork, with the larger circular face of the pocket former placed against the vertical face of the formwork. The end of the tendon extends through a hole drilled in the formwork. As indicated in the center image, after the concrete has cured, the formwork is stripped and the pocket former is pulled away, leaving a neat pocket in the edge of the slab for access to the anchor plate, which lies recessed below the surface of the concrete. Two conical wedges with sharp ridges inside are inserted around the tendon and into the conical hole in the anchor plate. The hydraulic jack presses against the wedges and draws the tendon through them until the gauge on the pump indicates that the proper tension has been achieved. When the jack is withdrawn, the wedges are drawn into the conical hole in the plate, grip the tendon, and maintain the tension permanently. After all the tendons have been tensioned, the excess length of tendon is cut off and the pocket is grouted flush with the edge of the slab.

depth of the structure. Special steel strands called *tendons*, twisted together from very high-strength steel wires, are used for this purpose (Figure 20.24). The steel strand stock from which tendons are made comes from the factory encased in a plastic tube that will keep it from bonding to concrete. With its tube, the tendon is installed in the formwork and anchored at one end to a steel plate embedded near one end of a beam or one edge of a slab. The other end of the tendon, at the opposite end or side of the beam or slab, passes through another special steel plate as shown and then out through a hole in the formwork.

The tendon is not tensioned until after the concrete has cured to a specified strength. At that time, a worker cuts away the plastic tube on the projecting end and installs around the end of the tendon and into a tapered pocket in the steel plate two conical wedges with ridges inside that are capable of gripping the tendon with tremendous force. The end of the tendon is inserted into a small hydraulic jack that grips it firmly, pulls on it, and pushes on the concrete and wedges with equal force until the specified tension has been reached. As the jack is removed, the tendon pulls the wedges into the pocket and thus anchors itself firmly and permanently to the edge or end of the concrete member (Figure 20.25). The tendon remains unbonded to either the tube or the concrete.

Figure 20.25 The hydraulic pump and jack for posttensioning are small and portable, yet can exert tremendous force.

Photo courtesy of Constructive Services, Inc., Dedham, Massachusetts.

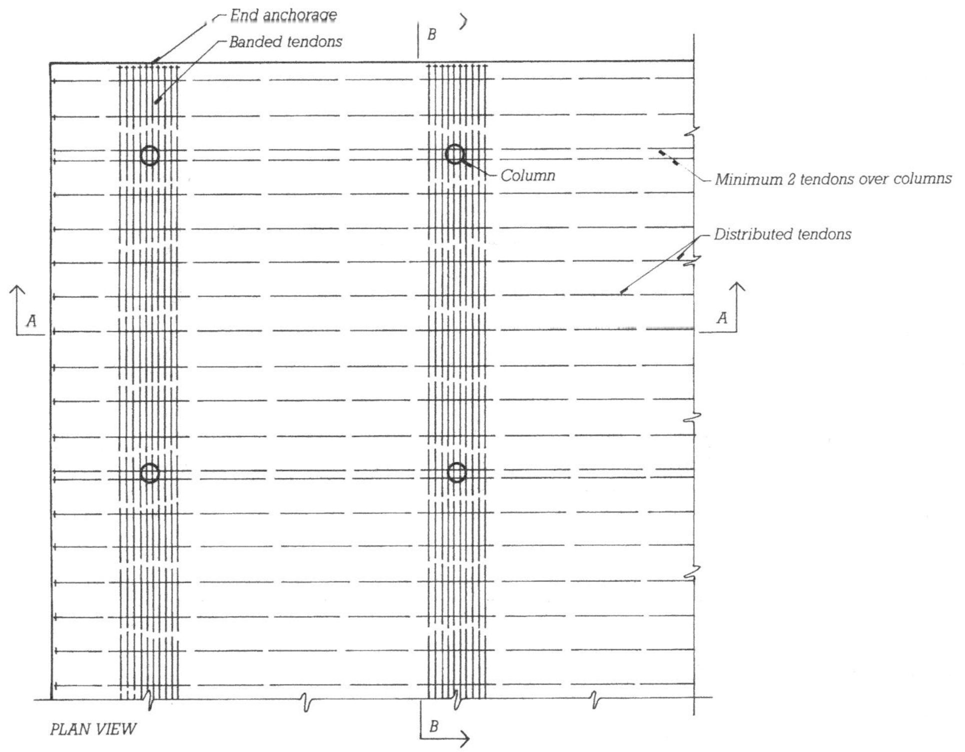

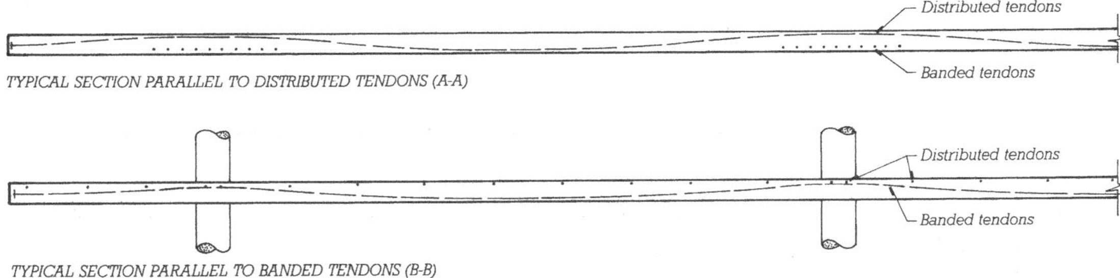

Figure 20.26 A plan and two larger-scale sections of the tendon layout in a two-way flat plate floor with banded posttensioning. The same number of tendons run in each direction, but those in one direction are concentrated into bands that run through the columns. The draping of the tendons is evident in the section drawings. In addition to the tendons, conventional reinforcing is used around the columns and in midspan, but this has been omitted from these drawings for the sake of clarity.

Tendons are usually *draped* within the slab or beam to follow lines of maximum tension in the member. In two-way flat plate structures, the tendon patterns are different in the two directions of the slab (Figure 20.26). The numbers of tendons in each direction are identical, but those in one direction are *banded* (concentrated into a narrow band through a line of columns). This greatly facilitates the placement of the tendons, as compared to a scheme in which draped tendons would be distributed evenly in both directions. The force from the banded tendons flares out from their end plates in a half-plane fan and fills the entire width of the slab within a short distance. At columns, conventional reinforcing bars are used to strengthen against punching shear (Figure 20.27).

HOW STEEL-REINFORCED CONCRETE BEAMS RESIST BENDING

In each of these one-way and two-way configurations, we predict stresses in concrete beams and slabs based on the assumption that concrete in the tensile region of a beam has cracked and has no resistance to tensile forces. This means that all the tensile forces in these lower regions are transferred to the steel reinforcing bars in that portion, while the concrete in the compressive region of the beam furnishes all the resistance to compression.

In actuality, when we look up at a concrete beam that is carrying a load near its capacity, we can see cracks that extend through the tensile region and end at the neutral axis. This is normal. The concrete in the tensile region is still performing its function, which is to hold the longitudinal steel bars in place and to exert diagonal compressive force in the same manner as the diagonals in a Howe truss (Figure 20.28).

Figure 20.29 illustrates another aspect of the recent evolution in our understanding of how a concrete beam works. Drawing (a) represents the earliest interpretation of concrete beam function: The steel bars in the tensile zone furnish all the tensile

Figure 20.27 Banded tendons run directly through the concrete column of this flat plate floor. A substantial amount of conventional reinforcing is used for resistance to the diagonal tension forces of punching shear. Notice the end anchorage plates nailed to the vertical surface of the formwork at the upper right.

Photo courtesy of the Post-Tensioning Institute.

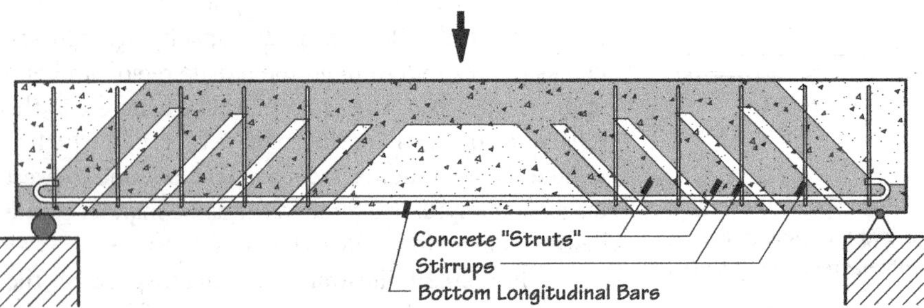

Figure 20.28 Strut-and-tie model of the interior behavior of a concrete beam. The struts shown are representative of an infinite number of internal diagonal actions.

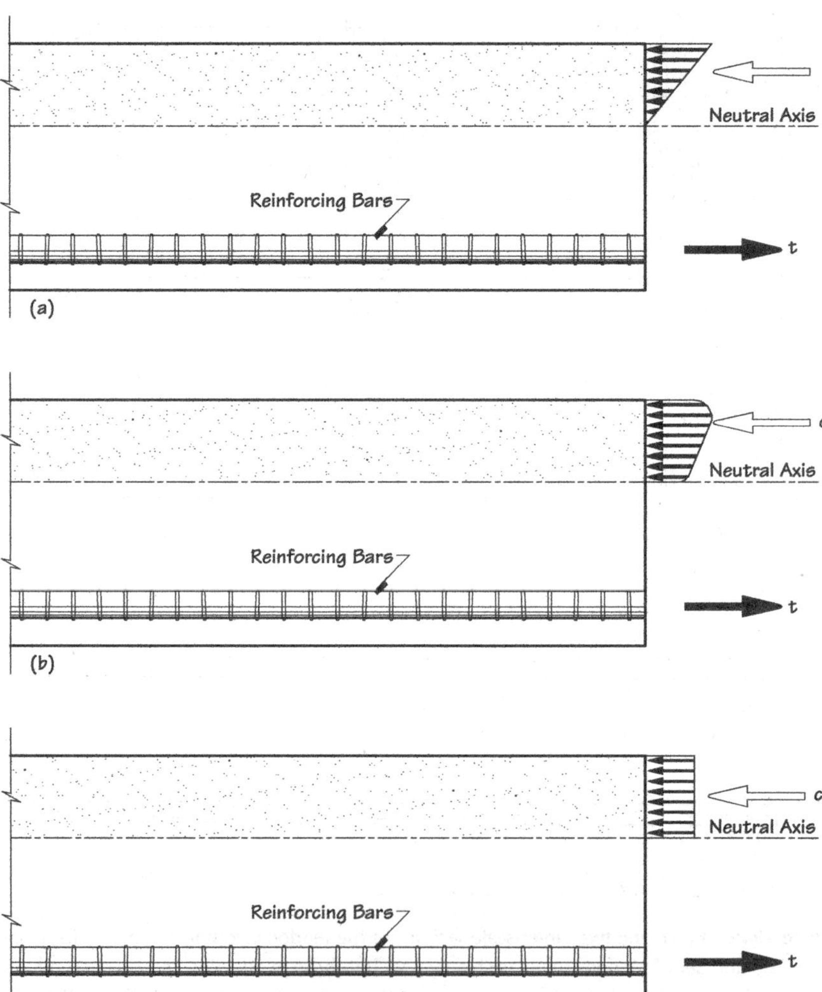

Figure 20.29 The gradual evolution of our assumptions about the distribution of compressive stress in a reinforced concrete beam.

resistance. Because steel is so much stronger and stiffer than concrete, a relatively small cross-sectional area of steel can balance a much larger area of compression in the concrete at the top of the beam. The resisting moment of the beam is equal to one of these horizontal forces multiplied by the distance between them.

Laboratory testing subsequently showed that the unique characteristics of concrete and steel lead to the formation of a compressive stress block in the concrete that is not a pure triangular wedge, as it is in steel and wood beams, but a rounded, trapezoidal wedge (b). It was decided by researchers and practitioners that for purposes of stress calculations this stress block could be represented with a uniform distribution of force, (c). This has led to a simplification of concrete beam calculations. Simplification is a relative quality, however: Concrete beams are generally continuous over several spans, so that tensile regions lie at the bottom of the beam in the center of the spans and at the top of the beam in the vicinity of the columns. Beams are connected rigidly to their columns, which also bend to some extent as the beams bend.

As was represented in Figure 20.4, in a one-way solid slab structure, a portion of the slab may be considered to act as part of the beam (Figure 20.30). This portion of the slab does double duty, resisting beam bending in one direction and slab bending in the other. This has little effect on the slab, but it gives a considerable boost to the beam by giving it a much larger compression area.

It is important that if a beam should fail, it fail gradually and give warning of its incipient failure. If we put too much reinforcing steel in a beam, the concrete will fail by crushing before the steel fails, and the beam will collapse suddenly and without warning. If we put too little steel in a beam, the ductile steel will fail first. As it does so, it will stretch and allow widening cracks to appear in the region below the neutral axis of the beam, giving advance notice of its distress. For this reason, we always *underreinforce* concrete beams, using slightly less steel than the optimum amount.

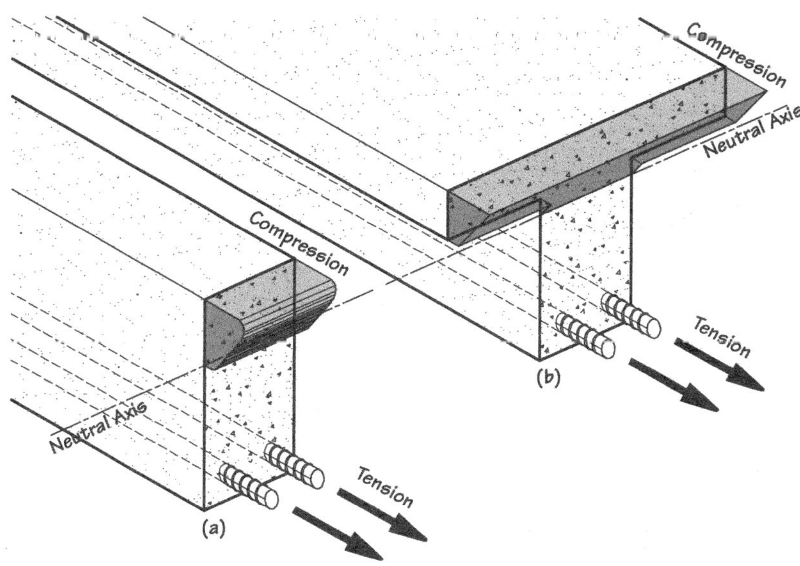

Figure 20.30 A portion of a one-way solid slab can be considered to act in compression as part of a beam.

Figure 20.31 shows a typical situation for a concrete beam in the frame of a building. The beam is continuous with adjacent spans and with the columns that support it. This causes it to bend in both positive and negative directions, in accordance with the distribution of bending moments, which is shown above the beam in (a). The beam deflects as shown in (b). A handy way to know where to put the longitudinal reinforcing bars in any beam is to sketch an exaggerated drawing of the deflected shape. Then put the bars on the convex side, which is where tension will occur. We can see in this three-span example that the heaviest longitudinal reinforcing bars are placed in the top of the beam in the vicinity of each column, where bending moments are highest. These bars extend a short distance into the zone of positive bending moment.

Bottom steel bars are heaviest in the middle of each span. Some bottom steel is continued through the columns. This gives the frame the capability to adjust to seismic and wind loads that can cause reversal of moments. Stirrups are necessary in the portions of the beams that are near supports to accept the tensile components of the web forces in the beam.

Reinforcing bars are sometimes added to the compressive regions of concrete beams, as well as the tensile regions, in order to reduce beam depths.

INNOVATIVE SITECAST CONCRETE FRAMING SYSTEMS

Because concrete structures are in effect "manufactured" on the construction site, they lend themselves to being shaped in nonstandard ways. Such opportunities for creative forms are often chosen to

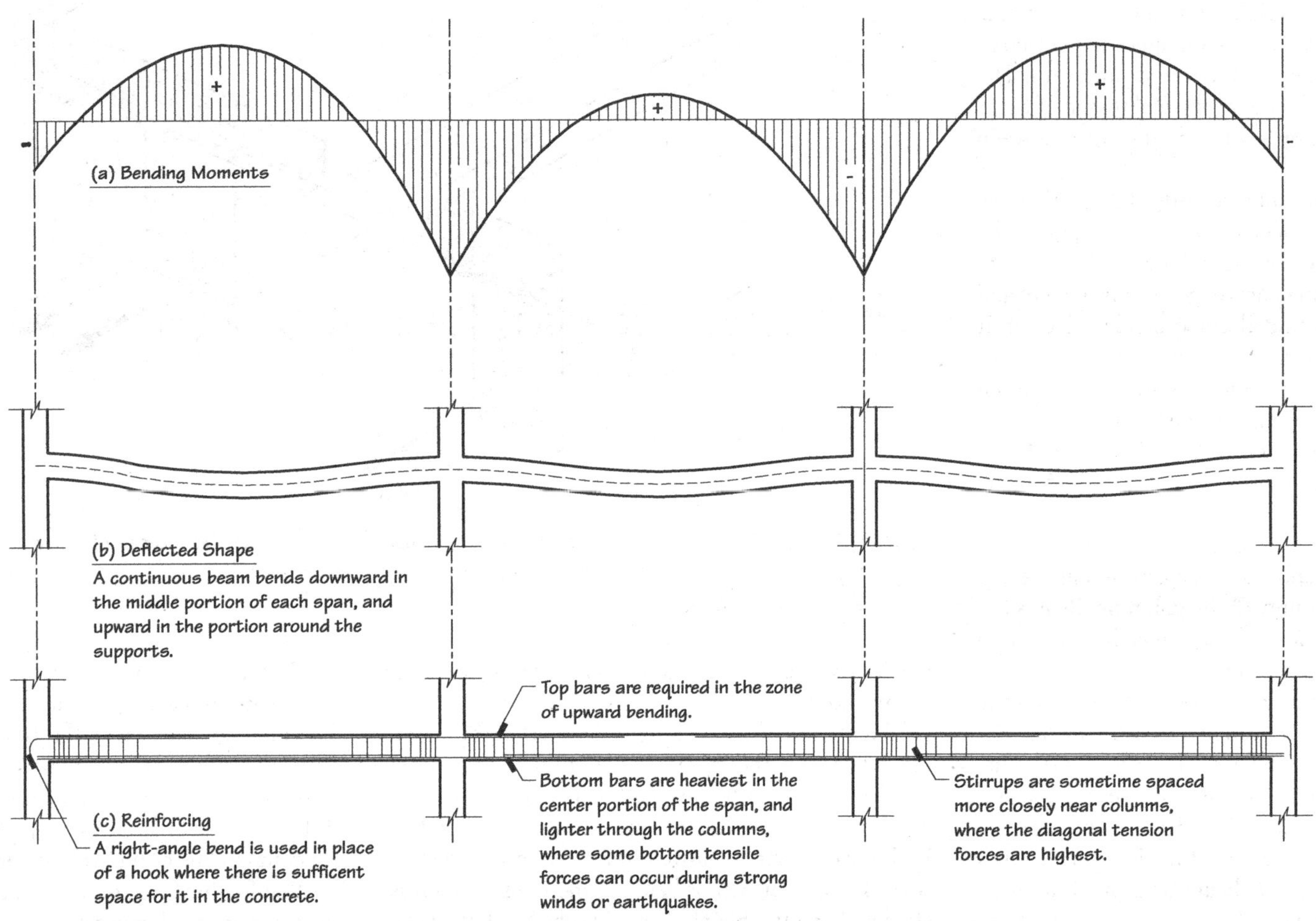

(a) Bending Moments
(b) Deflected Shape
A continuous beam bends downward in the middle portion of each span, and upward in the portion around the supports.
Top bars are required in the zone of upward bending.
(c) Reinforcing
A right-angle bend is used in place of a hook where there is sufficent space for it in the concrete.
Bottom bars are heaviest in the center portion of the span, and lighter through the columns, where some bottom tensile forces can occur during strong winds or earthquakes.
Stirrups are sometime spaced more closely near colunms, where the diagonal tension forces are highest.

Figure 20.31 (a) Bending moment distribution in continuous beams. (b) Exaggerated deflections. (c) The standard pattern of reinforcing bars.

increase some aspect of their efficiency and/or to reduce construction costs. A concrete highway bridge designed by Jörg Schlaich epitomizes this approach (Figures 20.32–20.34). We can see that the bridge is shaped so that its depth is proportional to its bending moments: deep in midspan and shallow at points of zero moment. The vigorous inward slope of the supporting legs applies a powerful compressive stress to the main span, reducing the need for tensile reinforcing. In fact, the bridge functions as something halfway between an arch and a rigid-jointed frame.

As one experiment in his ongoing development of textile fabric formwork for concrete, architect Mark West produced a reinforced concrete beam with two overhangs that is sculpted to reflect the flow of forces in a continuous beam (Figures 20.35–20.37). Because its form resembles its bending moment diagram, web forces are minimal. West produced this structure, like all his structures, using very low-cost formwork made primarily of inexpensive geotechnical fabric that is produced for other construction purposes.

◀**Figure 20.32** A concrete vehicular bridge over the autobahn between Kirchheim and Teck in Germany is shaped to resemble its bending moment diagram.

Photo courtesy of Gert Elsner.

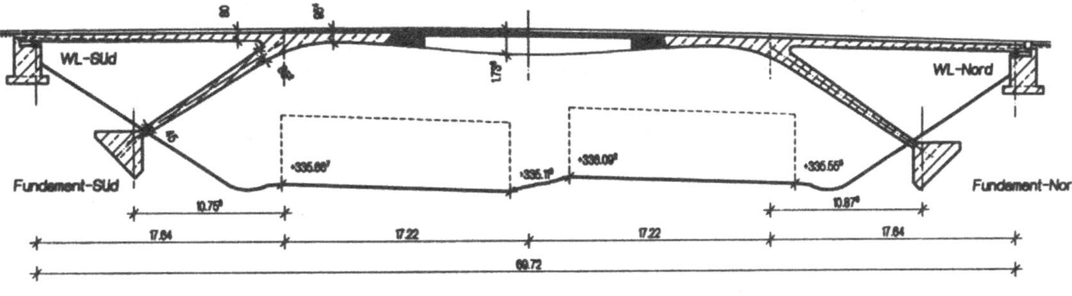

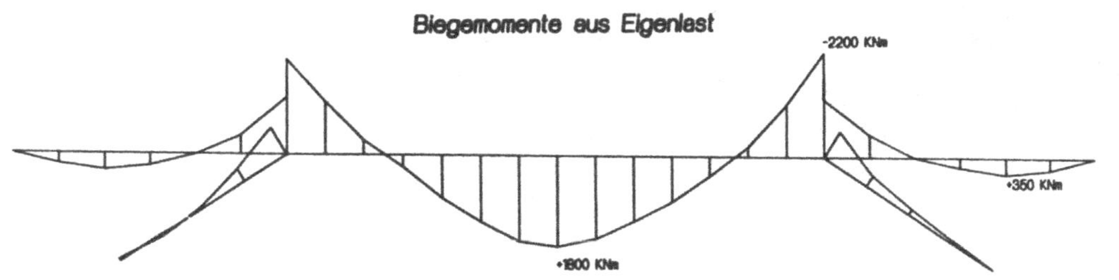

▲**Figure 20.33** Structural engineer Jörg Schlaich used a one-way ribbed construction to eliminate much of the self-weight of the concrete.

Photo courtesy of Schlaich Bergermann and Partner.

◀**Figure 20.34** The profile of the bridge (above), and its bending moment diagram (below).

Image courtesy of Schlaich Bergermann and Partner.

Figure 20.35 A reinforced concrete beam with two overhanging ends, shaped with fabric formwork to match its bending moment diagram by architect Mark West. The lifting loops used to hoist this beam in the precasting yard where it was manufactured are located on the axes of the future columns that will support the beam.

Photo courtesy of Mark West.

Figure 20.37 The ghosted volume applied to this photograph may be used to compare the amount of concrete in a rectangular beam with that in the beam by Mark West. West's beam uses about 20 percent of the concrete of the normal beam.

Photo courtesy of Mark West.

Figure 20.36 A profile view of the beam by Mark West.

Photo courtesy of Mark West.

Engineer Pier Luigi Nervi designed a two-way concrete slab system for a factory in which curving, intersecting ribs follow the flow of forces from mid-bay to column heads (Figure 20.38). This design is both visually elegant and economical of material. It is relatively labor-intensive, however, and its formwork would have to be manufactured specifically to match the bay size and proportions of each project, so it has seldom been copied.

Engineer Wacław Zalewski has designed and built many buildings in Poland that utilize what is in effect a precast concrete two-way system (Figures 20.39 20.42). The four concrete arms of each column head reach out diagonally to support a square two-way panel in the center of each bay. Hexagonal panels are laid on the arms to provide a floor or roof surface between the columns. A concrete topping layer with steel mesh reinforcing is poured over the entire assembly to unite it into a continuous structure. Although the structural components of these buildings were all cast on site (on the ground, not in place), they could equally well have been manufactured in a central plant and trucked to the site if their dimensions did not exceed highway clearances.

These innovations are only a few of the many ways that concrete construction can be shaped and formed in expressive and creative ways. While concrete is widely used in many standard and nonstandard shapes and configurations around the world, it is essential to work with local building authorities and building code officials from early on in the design process to maximize the effective communication about how these innovations can be built safely and efficiently.

Figure 20.38 Ribs in a two-way industrial slab for the Gatti Wool Mill by Pier Luigi Nervi (1951) follow the lines of principal stresses in the floor.

Source: Pier Luigi Nervi, *Structures*. New York: F. W. Dodge, 1956.

Figure 20.39 The "Capital" precast system designed by Wacław Zalewski, showing a bay of components in place before the topping layer was added.

Photo: Wacław Zalewski.

Figure 20.40 The precast "Capital" elements were cast at the building site on the ground in preparation for the erection of an industrial storage facility.

Photo: Wacław Zalewski.

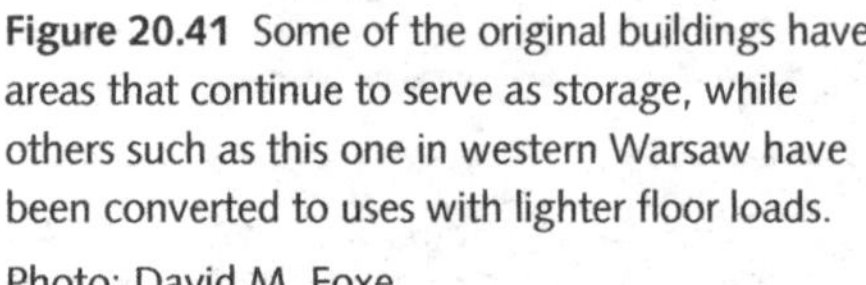

Figure 20.41 Some of the original buildings have areas that continue to serve as storage, while others such as this one in western Warsaw have been converted to uses with lighter floor loads.

Photo: David M. Foxe.

Figure 20.42 Part of the original design concept was to take advantage of the capacity to omit certain portions of floor areas to create vertical shafts and multistory open spaces. This potential is visualized in a computer rendering of various configurations.

Image courtesy of Jeff Anderson.

Exercises

1. Select sitecast concrete floor framing systems for the following buildings. List the reasons for your choice in each case. Assign approximate sizes to the components of each system:

a. A university laboratory building, moderate floor loads, bays 18 by 36 ft

b. A paper products warehouse, heavy floor loads, bays 20 by 26 ft

c. An elementary school, light floor loads, bays 16 by 30 ft

d. An office building, moderate floor loads, bays 32 ft square

2. Choose one of the buildings in Exercise 1 and develop it to the point that you can work on both its exterior and interior appearance. How will you express the framing system inside and out? Does the system lend itself to any special details? Could concrete load-bearing walls play a major role in this building? What would they look like?

3. Develop a plan of a typical two-bedroom apartment for the building that is the theme of this chapter. Does the proposed bay size work well? If not, what size would you propose? What architectural role(s) do the columns play in your design? How do you create a usable balcony?

4. Consider the column configurations that increase perimeter, as shown in Figure 20.17. What might a twelfth option be that would achieve this goal?

Key Terms and Concepts

Occupancy Group
Construction Type
fire-resistance rating
concrete
portland cement
coarse aggregate
fine aggregate
structural lightweight concrete
formwork
curing
reinforcing bars/rebars
ties
spirals
welded wire fabric
stirrups
U-stirrups
stirrup-ties
slab
one-way solid slab-and-beam system
slab band
one-way concrete joist system
rib slab
joist band
wide-module concrete joist system
column strip
middle strip
drop panel and mushroom capital
two-way flat slab system
two-way flat plate system
punching shear
two-way concrete joist system
waffle slab
shear walls
party walls
posttensioning
tendon
draped tendons
banded tendons

Further References

Allen, Edward, and Joseph Iano. *Fundamentals of Building Construction, Materials, and Methods* (5th ed.). Hoboken, NJ: John Wiley & Sons, Inc. 2009. One hundred forty pages of this book introduce and explain every aspect of concrete construction, both sitecast and precast.

Concrete Reinforcing Steel Institute. *Manual of Standard Practice*. Schaumburg, IL: CRSI (updated frequently). Everything having to do with reinforcing steel is in this volume, including tables that can be used for preliminary selection and design of columns and spanning systems.

Portland Cement Association. *Design and Control of Concrete Mixtures*. Skokie, IL: PCA (updated frequently). Everything you want to know about making, placing, finishing, and curing concrete is in this authoritative book.

CHAPTER 21

Master Lesson: Designing In Precast Concrete

- *Multidisciplinary project design teams*
- *Medium-rise building planning and choice of framing systems*
- *Integration with life safety and egress planning*
- *Integration with mechanical and electrical services*
- *Designing with precast concrete framing elements*

"Let me introduce my design team to you, Curtis," said Bruce. "You already know Diane, my structural engineer, of course. You and she have worked directly together on a number of projects. This is Avram, our mechanical engineer; and Tricia, to my right, is our electrical engineer and lighting designer. These are the primary professionals who will be working on your building. I've also invited Franklin, your general contractor. He's coming, but he said he's going to be a few minutes late.

"Curtis, this meeting is the beginning of the process of designing your building (21.1). To get underway, each of us will report today on the major aspects of his or her specialization that are relevant to the overall design of this project. But we should hear from you first—what are your goals for your new building?"

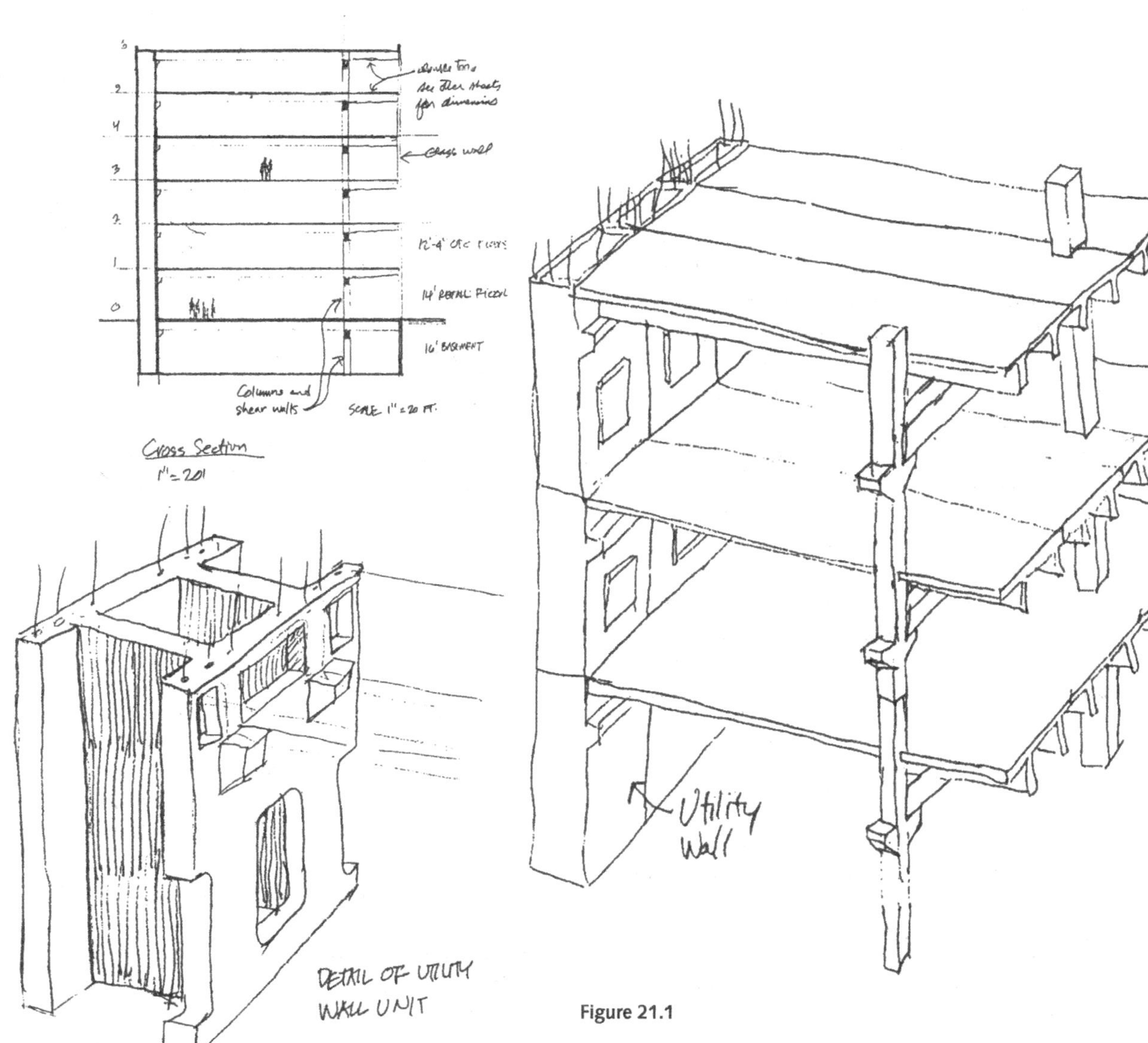

Figure 21.1

THE OWNER'S GOALS

Curtis Wilkerton pulled a site survey drawing from his briefcase and laid it on the table (21.2).

"My company, Keystone Precast Concrete Products, needs new administrative offices. We've grown a lot in recent years, and we're bulging at the seams of our present building. We've bought this empty site in downtown, along with a parking garage on an adjacent parcel that will give us more than the parking we need for a building of the size that I want to build. The building site is on a corner, with the long side facing northeast to the street.

"The original building on the site was destroyed by fire two years ago. It was five stories tall plus a basement, and it sat on concrete spread footings. The dimensions of the parcel are 78 ft by 176.4 ft, for an area of 13,760 sq ft. There's a seven-story building against the longer lot line. The rear of the site faces a service alley. I assume that we'll build right out to the lot lines and fill our entire site. I've made up this small booklet that lists our needs in detail. We'll rent out the ground floor for retail shops, keeping a small part of it for the entrance and reception area for our offices. At this time, we will occupy only about a third of the total office space, and rent out the rest. Including the retail space, we need a net floor area for the entire building of about 60,000 sq ft. I don't know what this translates into for gross floor area."

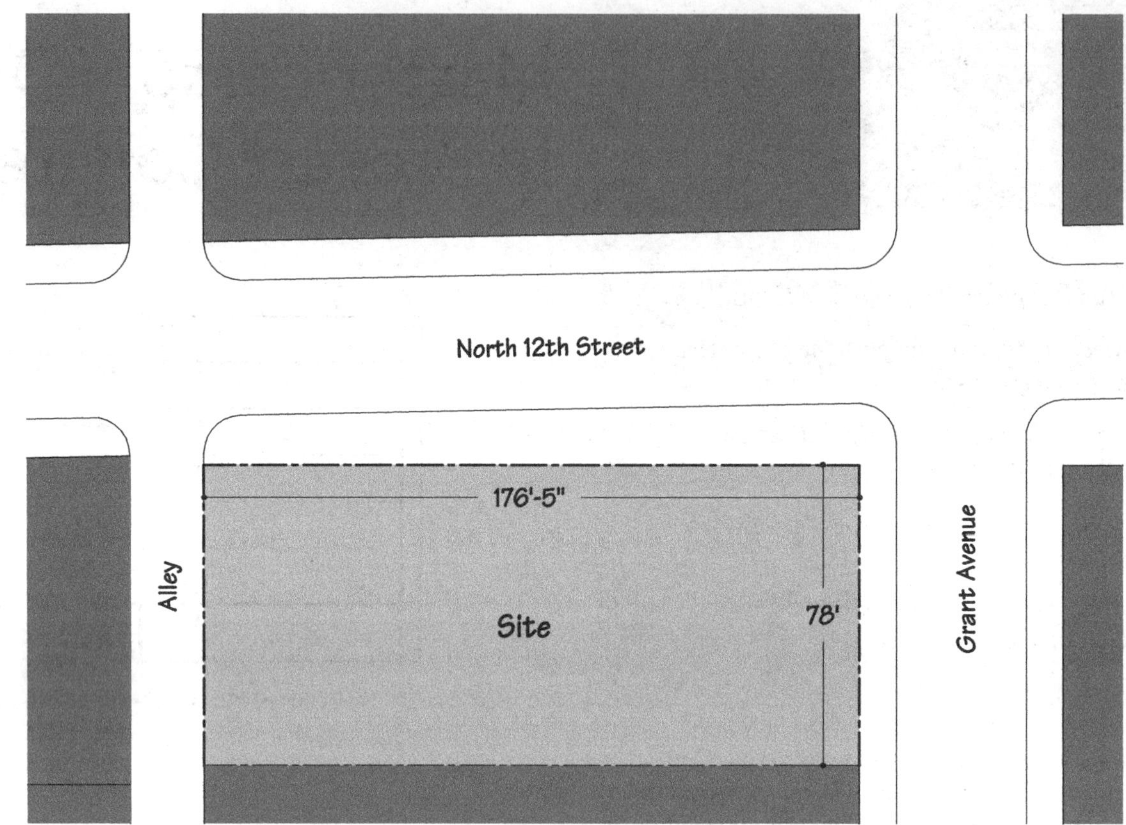

Figure 21.2

Bruce did a quick calculation on his scratch pad.

"Allowing for stairs, elevators, HVAC shafts, structure, and all that, which I figure will occupy about 25 percent of the gross building area, this means that we'll have to build a gross area of about 75,000 sq ft. On a 14,000-sq–ft site, we'll have to go six stories high to do it."

"Thanks, Bruce," said Curtis. "Well, folks, those are the bare figures and facts. Here are my aspirations for the project: I want this building to be exemplary in every way. First of all, I want it to be a great place for my people to work—sunny, airy, open, bright, and cheerful. I want some spatial variety so that the whole interior doesn't look the same. I don't want any long, dark corridors or cramped cubicles.

"Second, I want this building to be an example of environmental consciousness: economical of energy, nonpolluting, efficient in its use of materials, and fully accessible to everyone in the population. I want it to earn the highest LEED rating there is. I want this to be a building that my children can enjoy and be proud of.

"And third, I want it to be a sparkling, innovative example of what can be done with precast concrete construction, which of course is the business I'm in. Most office buildings this size are built with steel frames, but I believe that precast concrete offers unique advantages of its own. I want this building to demonstrate those advantages and create a distinctive image for my company and its products. That's it. You're my design team. I look forward to seeing what you can do."

Bruce stood and glanced at several sheets of notes that he held in his hand.

"Thank you, Curtis. You've given us a challenge, and you can be sure that we're going to respond with an exciting building. Now each of us will report on the aspects of his or her area of expertise that will exert major influences on the form and space of the building. This will give all of us the boundary conditions within which we work and an idea of how our work will interlock. I'll lead off by taking you through the major legal requirements that will have an effect on the form of this project."

BUILDING CODE REQUIREMENTS

"Under the International Building Code, IBC, which has been adopted by our state, an office building is Use Group B, Business," explained Bruce. "We want to build a six-story building with a total gross floor area of 75,000 sq ft. If we fill the site completely to a six-story height, the actual gross area will be 82,560 sq ft. Curtis, I know that both you and your insurance company want automatic fire suppression sprinklers throughout the building. With sprinklers, the least restrictive type of construction that we can use is Type II–A, which is one-hour construction. The precast concrete components that we are likely to use all satisfy the requirements of this construction type, assuming that we use a 2-in. concrete topping over the slab elements. If we were to build floors without the topping, they would not have enough resistance to the passage of fire to qualify as Type II–A, and we would not be able to build as large a building.

"Under the IBC, the occupancy load for this building is figured on the basis of 100 sq ft per person. That's 138 people per story. The code requires a minimum of two exits from a floor this size. The maximum permitted exit travel distance is 300 ft from any point on a floor to the nearest enclosed stairway. We comply with this requirement automatically, given the dimensions of the site. We'll put one exit stairway at or near each end of the building.

"For our occupant load of 138 people per story, the IBC specifies that the minimum egress door width is 32 in., and the minimum width for corridors and stairways is 44 in. Diane, what floor-to-floor dimension do you figure that we need?"

Diane began to sketch as she answered.

"That depends on what kind of slab components we use and the ceiling height that we want. If we assume a clear ceiling height of 9 ft-6 in., with 10-in. hollow core slabs and a 2-in. concrete topping cast over them, the minimum floor-to-floor height will be 10 ft-6 in. If we use double tees, they'll probably be 24 in. to 26 in. deep. Add a 2-in. topping, and the floor-to-floor height will be more like 11-1/2 to 12 ft" (21.3).

Avram broke in, "But look what's going to happen when I run my ductwork under the slab (21.4). If we use hollow-core planks for the floor structure, we would need to add at least 10 in. to that for ductwork at the ceiling. We might need to add more for light fixtures and a suspended ceiling. If we use double tees instead of planks, on the other hand, the ducts can run between the stems of the tees."

Avram added a duct to each of Diane's sketches.

Bruce went on, "Let's assume for now that the floor-to-floor height will be 12 to 12-1/2 ft. Let's also

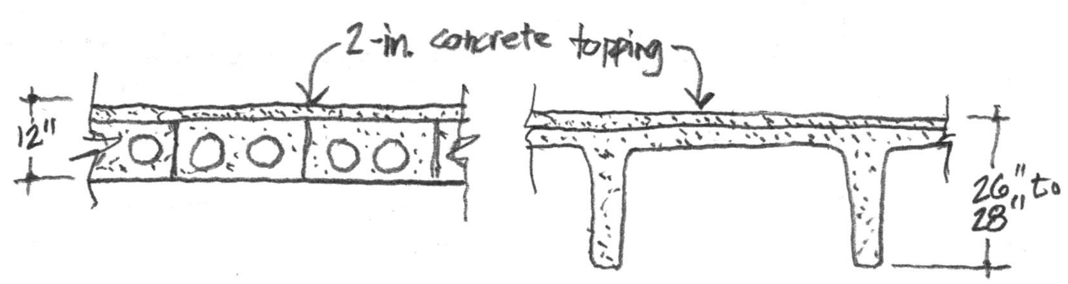

Figure 21.3

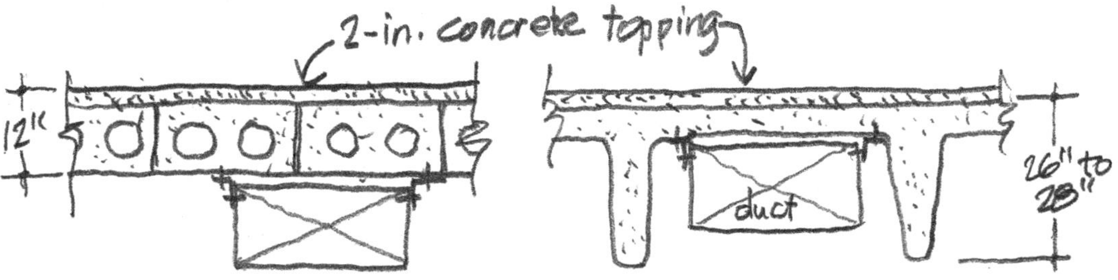

Figure 21.4

assume that we're not going to cover up Curtis's products with a suspended ceiling. Instead, we'll specify a higher grade of work by the various trades so that the visual quality of the ducts and conduits will be of sufficient architectural quality.

"To climb 12 ft, we will need 21 risers in the stairways. We'll probably double each stair back on itself, with a 44-in. landing at each end. If we use 8-in. masonry to build the walls . . .

Curtis broke in quickly:

"Forget about masonry in my buildings. We'll precast the stair enclosures and stairs as single-piece, story-high units, and the walls will be only 4 to 6 in. thick."

He found a drawing in his briefcase and laid it on the table (21.5).

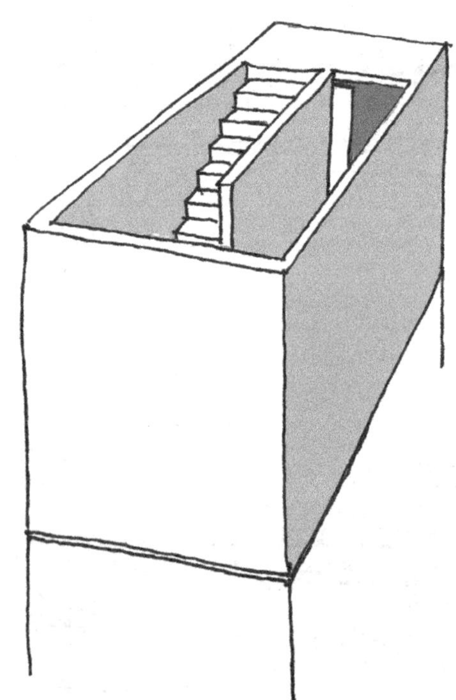

Figure 21.5

An embarrassed Bruce was equally quick to respond.

"Precast concrete stairs, of course. The stairway dimensions will have to increase a bit to include provisions for fire emergencies. These include a vertical duct to pressurize the stair enclosure so as to keep smoke out of it, and an enlarged landing at each floor level to provide an area of refuge where disabled people can wait for assistance. This will add about 5 ft to the length of the stair enclosure, to bring us up to 10 by 23 ft (21.6).

"Just a couple of things more: We'll need two passenger elevators of 3,000-lb capacity each, plus a small freight elevator. If we put the passenger elevators side by side in one shaft . . . "—he stole a sideways look at Curtis— " . . . and enclose the shaft with precast concrete walls, its outside dimensions will be about 18 by 9 ft (21.7). And the last item on my list is that we'll need two toilet rooms per floor, each of which will occupy a space approximately 8 by 16 ft in plan. We'll do these as precast concrete units, of course."

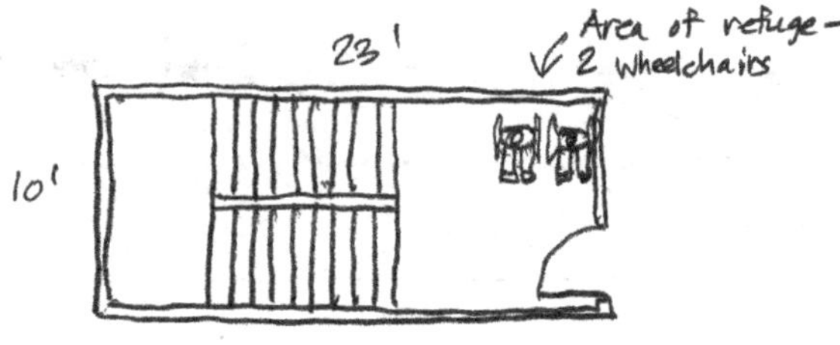

Figure 21.6

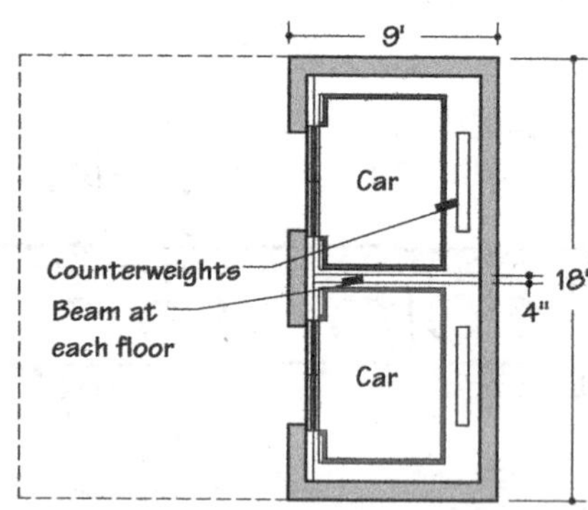

Figure 21.7

"Don't," said Curtis. "Lousy idea. We've found it's cheaper and easier to build toilet rooms out of light-gauge steel studs and gypsum board."

A perplexed Bruce was growing redder each second.

"Does that size of toilet room allow for wheelchair accessibility?" asked Curtis.

"Yes, it does. In fact, the code requires that we make the whole building accessible."

"Good," replied Curtis. "I learned all about inaccessible buildings last March when I got a bad ankle sprain skiing."

"Many of us have had similar experiences," said Bruce. "I've been taking care of my 70-year-old parents for nearly a year, and it's been a crash course in planning for accessibility.

"Here's a copy for each of you of my notes and sketches of all the requirements that I've spoken of. Any other questions?"

Silence.

"Okay, Avram, you've been scribbling busily while I've been talking. What can you tell us about the heating and cooling strategies for this building?"

MECHANICAL SYSTEMS

Avram adjusted his glasses and rearranged his notes, then began:

"Well, I recommend a variable air volume (VAV) system for both heating and cooling, using natural gas as fuel. I've worked up some preliminary facts and figures for you."

"Wait a minute," Curtis interjected. "What's a variable air volume system?"

"It's a relatively simple, economical way to heat and cool a building of this size (21.8). Central fans and a single set of ducts distribute conditioned air throughout the building at a single temperature, warm in winter and cool in summer. The building is divided into zones. Each zone has its own thermostat that is connected to a VAV terminal—a sheet-metal box with a motorized damper in it that hangs overhead at the ceiling (21.9). It receives air through the duct from the central fan and controls the amount of it that is released into the space. If the zone thermostat calls for heat in winter, the damper opens and allows more heated air into the space. In summer, the VAV terminal controls the volume of cooled air. It's like opening and closing a register to control the temperature in your house, except that it's all done automatically.

"This system, like any HVAC system, requires a lot of space. I'll need most of the basement for a boiler to produce heat, a chiller to produce coolness, and fans to circulate the air. I'll need a chimney about 4-ft square that goes up through all the floors and the roof for the boiler exhaust. For my vertical duct risers, Tricia's electrical and communications risers, and the risers for the sprinkler system, I'll need continuous shaft space from the basement up through all the floors that is equal to 2 to 3 percent of the area of one floor. This comes to about 350 sq ft. These shafts need to connect easily at each story to horizontal spaces for ducts and conduits that can reach all parts of the building. Every portion of every floor needs to be served by a supply duct and a return duct for heating and cooling. The VAV terminal for each zone will hang from the ceiling near the duct risers for that zone, and we'll run horizontal ducts from the VAV boxes overhead to air diffusers at the workstations.

"I'll need a cooling tower or two on the roof. These are big rectangular devices in which water that has absorbed heat from the chiller in the basement of the building is pumped to the top and splashes down through an open matrix against a strong current of fan-forced air, so that it gives off as much water vapor as possible (21.10). This results in loss of a portion of the water. The latent

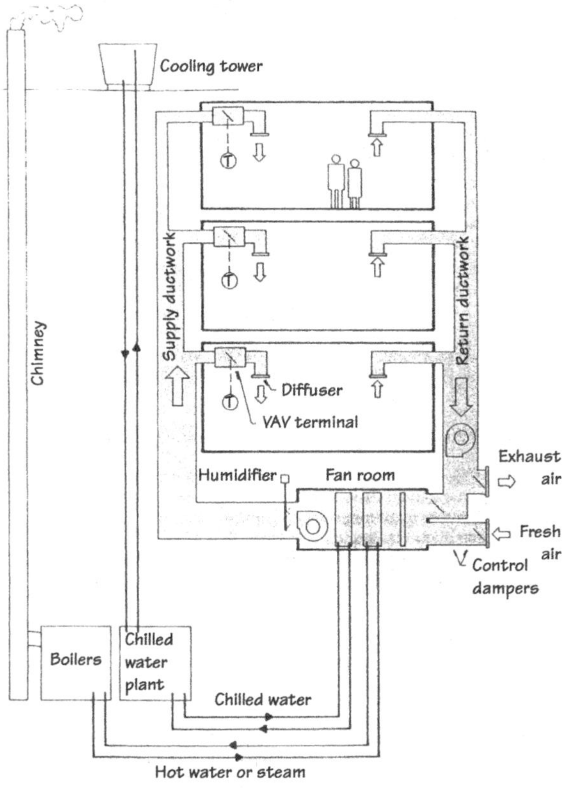

SINGLE DUCT, VARIABLE AIR VOLUME (VAV)

Figure 21.8

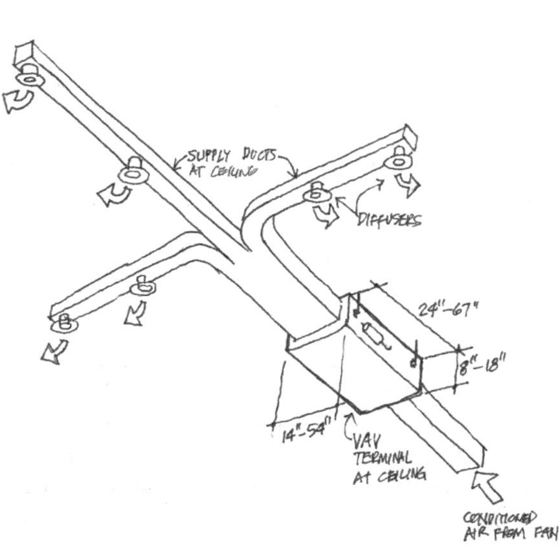

Figure 21.9

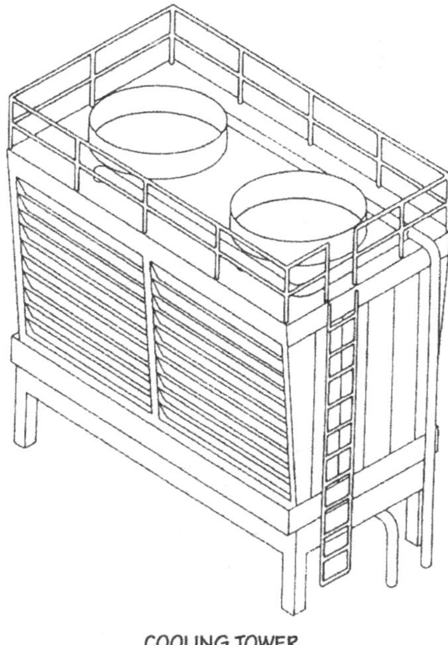

COOLING TOWER

Figure 21.10

heat of vaporization cools the remaining water, which then returns to the chiller in the basement to absorb more heat. In other words, the cooling tower is where the heat from an air-conditioned building is given off to the atmosphere. We shouldn't put any windows or air intakes near the cooling towers, because they sometimes become breeding places for bacteria and viruses.

"The last thing on my list is that I need two outdoor air louvers, one to exhaust stale air from the building and one to bring in fresh, clean air (21.11). To minimize the expense and inefficiency of ductwork, these should be located not too far from the basement fans—although if we have to, we can put them on the roof. Wherever they go, they have to be far enough apart that the stale outgoing air won't get sucked back into the system. You'll notice on my handout that these louvers are fairly large—between 100 and 200 sq ft each."

Figure 21.11

Bruce was whistling nervously.

"Large indeed! Where can we hide them? I guess they'll have to go back in the alley, or on the roof, as you say."

"There's always a way," was Avram's smiling response. "Curtis, your emphasis on energy conservation in your presentation today has started me thinking about possibly installing radiant floor heating as a supplement to the VAV system. To create the system, we would put plastic tubes in the topping over the floor slab elements. In the wintertime, these would be fed with warm water from a boiler in the basement to heat all the floors in the building. The warm floors would be the primary source of heat, supplemented by the VAV system only when outdoor temperatures are very low."

Curtis was visibly baffled.

"Why would I want a second heating system if the VAV system can do the job alone?"

"Radiant floor heat has a couple of major advantages," explained Avram. "Number one, it's very comfortable; it makes people feel good to have warm surfaces around them. Number two, when people are warmed by direct radiation from warm surfaces, they don't need such warm air temperatures to remain comfortable. A lower thermostat setting can be used for the VAV system, which results in lower heat losses from the building and lower heating fuel costs. The only problem is, the radiant heating system can't cool the building or circulate fresh air. We'd still need the VAV system for that. Overall, a radiant floor heating system will increase the cost of the equipment for heating and cooling but it will cost less to operate and will pay for itself in just a few years.

"I'll be doing some life-cycle cost analyses to determine if this is a good way to go. I'll also look into some options that would increase the efficiency of the HVAC system, such as a heat-recovery system that recovers heat or coolness from the exhaust air and adds it to the incoming air; and possibly operational options such as running nighttime air flushes to cool the spaces naturally. This night flush option may be particularly useful in a building with high mass such as this one constructed of precast concrete."

"That does it for me. Tricia?"

ELECTRICAL AND COMMUNICATIONS SERVICES

Now Tricia took the floor.

"Like Avram, I need substantial floor and shaft areas for electrical and communication services, though nothing like the quantity that he needs. And it's a sure bet that the future will bring increased sizes for these areas as new technologies develop. My largest and most basic need is an electrical transformer room that is about 400 sq ft in area and 11 ft high. This is usually put in the basement. It needs good ventilation, hopefully natural, to get rid of the heat that the equipment gives off. Next to it, I need a room of 600 sq ft for electric switchgear. Both rooms should be about 20 ft wide."

"Why do we need a transformer inside the building?" asked Bruce.

"It will save Curtis a lot of money over the life of the building. It allows him to buy electricity at a wholesale rate. The building will be served by an underground line at 13,800 volts, at a relatively low cost per kilowatt hour. The primary transformers in the vault—that's the 400-sq-ft room—will step this down to 480 and 277 volts. The primary lighting system will work at 277 volts. The 480-volt current will be distributed to small transformers in electrical closets on each floor, which will take it down to 120/240 volt lines for the receptacles."

"Why all the different voltages?" asked Diane.

"When you transmit electricity through a long wire, some of it is lost as heat along the way. The higher the voltage, the lower those losses. So we distribute the electricity over long distances at very high voltages that are reduced progressively inside the building to the lower, safer voltages that we use.

"Transformers eventually wear out and need to be replaced. The same goes for Avram's boilers, chillers, and fans. All of these are big pieces of equipment. So we need to work together to provide for such replacement work with something like a wide service corridor in the basement that extends below large access panels in the sidewalk, where a portable crane can lift out the old machine and drop in the new one."

"What about the electrical closets you mentioned? Bruce asked. "How big are they, and where do they go?"

"For each floor, we need at least one closet for electrical and telecommunications that has the riser shaft running through it (21.12). The closet needs to be about 7 ft by 12 ft in dimension, with the shaft across the far end so that we can connect to vertical runs of wires and cables. At the bottom of this shaft will be a telecommunications room of 200 sq ft, and maybe more to provide for future expansion."

"What about fiber optics?" It was Curtis asking the question. "We're starting to use fiber-optic services more and more for data communication. Will this system handle that?"

"With the cooperation of your architect and structural engineer, I will provide space for fiber optics and generous expansion space for future systems that we can only imagine," replied Tricia.

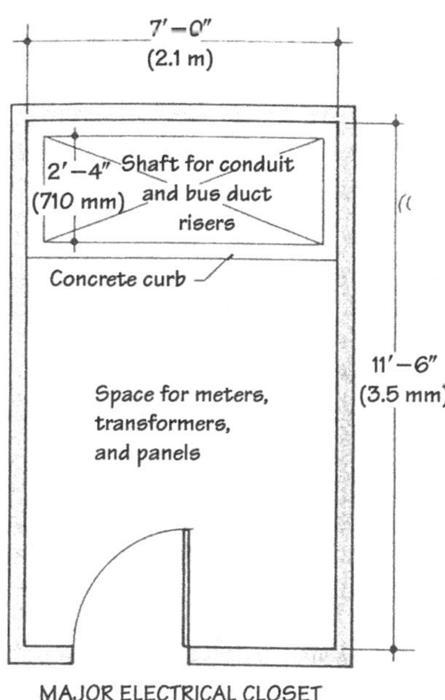

Figure 21.12

"This leaves lighting as my last topic. To meet Curtis's goals, I'd like to daylight the offices as much as possible. It's easy to get daylight to desks within about 30 ft of a window wall, but the main room on each floor of this building is going to be nearly 70 ft deep, measuring perpendicular to the long north wall. I think it will be worthwhile to try to find feasible ways of daylighting the offices, nevertheless. Certainly we can use skylights for this purpose on the top floor, so this will be a problem to solve on floors 2 through 5."

Tricia laid down the last of her notes and Bruce looked up from his notebook.

"Does that end your presentation, Tricia? If so, we'll finish with Diane's, the last one of the day."

Tricia nodded her assent, and Diane stepped forward.

THE STRUCTURAL SYSTEM

"Because this is Curtis's building, it's given that the structure will be made of precast concrete components. He and I have already talked about it, and have reached some preliminary conclusions. For decking, we have two options. The first is to use hollow-core precast concrete planks (21.13). With a 2-in. topping of poured concrete, 10-in.-deep planks can span up to about 30 ft, with the 100 psf loading of an office, and 12-in. planks 36 to 38 ft. These would produce a deck that is a foot to 14 in. thick. He also manufactures a 16-in. plank that can span up to 50 ft.

"The planks would rest on precast concrete rectangular beams. The depth of these beams would be about equal to the span divided by 14. For example, a 28-ft span would require a beam 2 ft deep and about a foot wide. We would have to decide which way to run the beams, crossways of the site or longitudinally.

"The beams would be supported by precast concrete columns. The easiest kind of connection of beams to columns is probably to use corbels, but there are other ways of doing it, too.

"The other option for the floor decks is precast concrete double tees (21.14). These come in a variety of depths. We would use a depth of 22 to 26 in. to span 65 to 80 ft. The actual depth, including topping, would be 2 in. more than this. These depths are much greater than those of hollow-core planks, but the VAV ducts can be tucked up between the stems of the double tees, which will make up most of the difference. Tricia, we can also coordinate ways of introducing lighting in these areas between the stems as well.

"For lateral load resistance, we will probably use a combination of things. The long utility wall that abuts the neighboring building can serve as a shear wall. We can also utilize the precast concrete

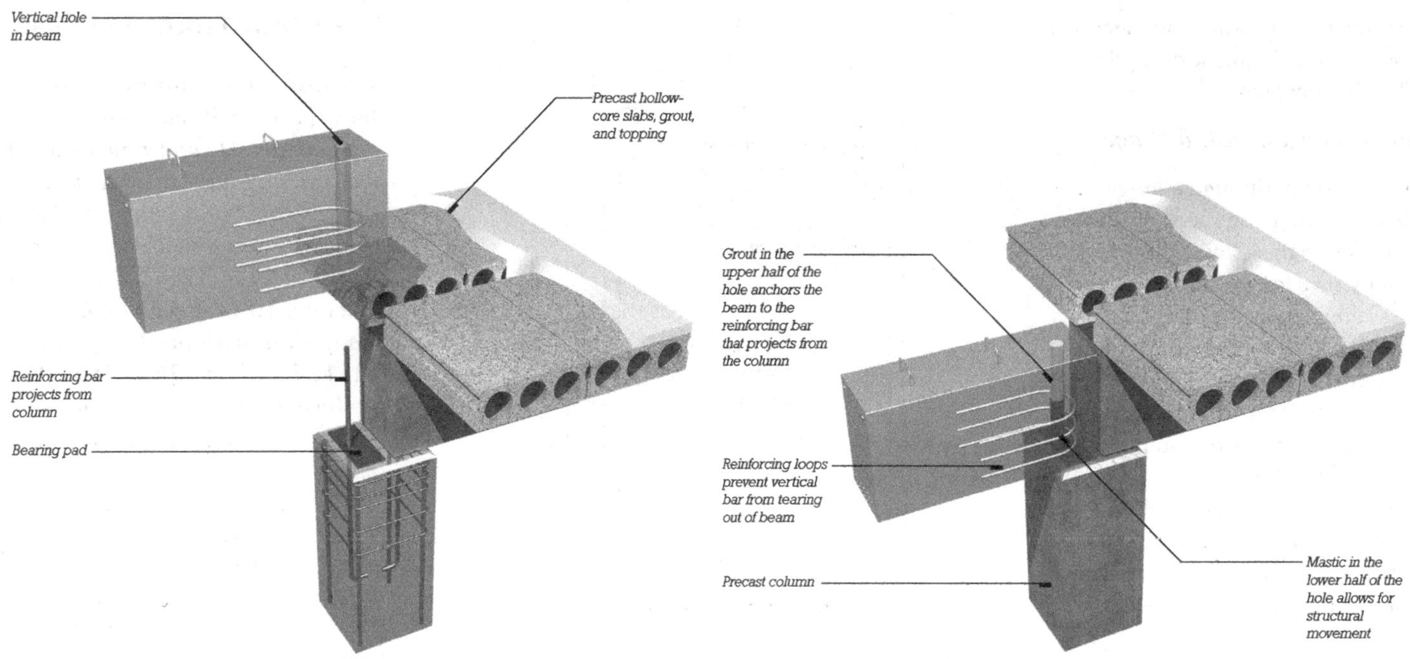

Figure 21.13

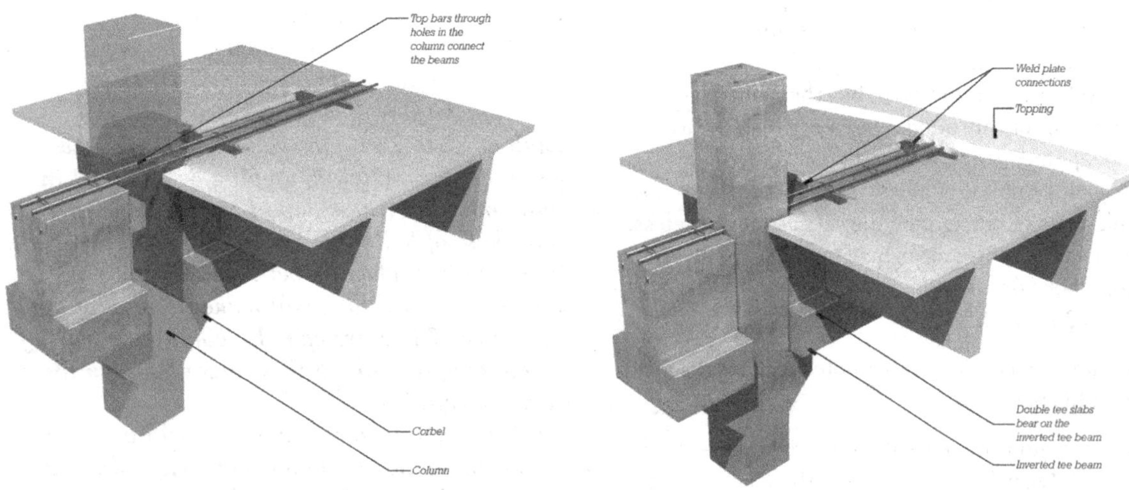

Figure 21.14

stair wells and elevator shafts as shear walls. That may still leave us with a need for further planes of bracing, perhaps rigid beam-to-column joints or precast shear walls. That's about all I can say until we have preliminary floor plans."

THE CONTRACTOR'S PERSPECTIVE

Franklin Dempsey had let himself into the room quietly toward the end of Diane's presentation.

"Sorry I'm late," he murmured. "We had a crisis on the warehouse project I'm building out by the rail yards. An apprentice formwork carpenter failed to brace a form properly and it split out and created a river of fresh concrete."

Curtis slapped him on the back with a big chuckle.

"Lucky you! What a nightmare! That would never have happened if you'd used precast concrete!"

"Not true," protested Franklin. "They were pouring a topping over some hollow-core planks that we got from you."

Curtis stammered for a moment, then attempted to move the meeting ahead.

"Frank, if you can get your mind off your concrete river for a couple of minutes, we're talking about a six-story precast concrete office building for Keystone Precast on my site downtown. Do you have any advice for my team as they begin to design it?"

"Yes. First off, keep the structure as simple and repetitive as you can. If there are a lot of special, individually atypical precast units, or curves, or complicated geometries, it will take a lot longer for my crew to put it together, and it can get to be expensive. Then be careful about the lengths of the components. It's a fairly tight site. We'll have to block off a portion of the street for my crane and for unloading trucks. If the components are too long or too heavy, they can be hard to maneuver in this situation. And keep the number of trades to a minimum by avoiding too many different materials and components. I'll be happy to work with you during the design process to help keep the building as economical as possible; and the more we consult early in the process, the more I can help to give you ballpark information on what this implies for construction cost."

"Certainly, that would be welcome," replied Bruce. "Does anyone have anything to add?"

"Yes," said Curtis with a grin, "several things. With regard to Franklin's point about the tight site, one thing that we often do in similar situations is to erect the frame starting from one end of the site and moving to the other, building each bay to its full height before moving laterally. This leaves much of the site open for use as a staging and stockpiling area until the frame is nearly finished.

"And some comments concerning sustainability. While portland cement is inherently an energy-intensive product, the process of precasting makes very economical use of aggregate, water, and cement, and saves considerable energy. By manufacturing the components in a plant, we're able to keep waste of materials to a minimum. Our forms are made of steel and are used hundreds of times before they need replacement, whereas forms for sitecast concrete are made of wood and have to be discarded after only a few uses. Because of trucking costs, precast concrete tends to be locally produced, as ours is, which results in fuel savings. And our main materials, crushed stone and sand, come from a quarry right at the plant.

"We use fly ash and silica fume to replace a significant fraction of the portland cement, further improving the efficiency. Fly ash and silica fume are waste products of other industries, namely electric power generation and semiconductor manufacture, that would end up in landfills if we didn't make use of them. The net result is a huge saving in embodied energy in our product.

"Another aspect of sustainability is that most of our products have excellent surface characteristics and can be left without further finishing operations, except maybe for a coat of paint. This saves a lot of material and labor.

"And finally, precast concrete, like all concrete, holds a lot of heat. In desert climates, it can act like adobe walls in storing nighttime coolness for the day and releasing daytime heat to the outdoors at night. We can also produce concrete panels with integral thermal insulation. So we can save heating and cooling energy, too. That about covers it. Any questions?"

Avram raised his hand.

"What's our deadline?"

"I'm in a hurry," answered Curtis. "We're busting the seams of our old building. I need this new building yesterday."

"Yesterday takes longer," replied Bruce. "But we'll get right on it."

"Designing engages more than a lone engineer at a drafting board or workstation. The design . . . engages a wide variety of people. . . . All can and do influence the design, and all must come to agreement in order to realizing the design. The process is thus social."

—Louis L. Bucciarelli

A DESIGN IS BORN

That night, dinner dishes having been cleared away, Bruce, Diane, Tricia, and Avram remained at Avram's dining table, which was now laden with rolls of thin tracing paper, soft pencils, and mugs of coffee. Avram was sketching on a piece of tracing paper laid over the site plan.

"It would be ideal from my standpoint," he said, "if we could have a vertical slot—let's call it a utility wall—running from basement to roof along the entire blank side of the building, to use for risers for ductwork, wiring, and pipes. I could bring horizontal runs of supply and return ductwork off of this slot at the ceiling of each floor (21.15)."

"If we did that," replied Bruce, "we could also place the stairwells, elevators, electrical closets, and toilets next to it, so as to keep the floors clear for unbroken, flexible office space."

"Yes, as long as we remember that a horizontal run of ductwork can't pass through an elevator shaft or stairwell," Avram cautioned.

"Hmm, yes, of course," agreed Bruce. "Ducts could pass over the toilet rooms, however, if they're not too deep."

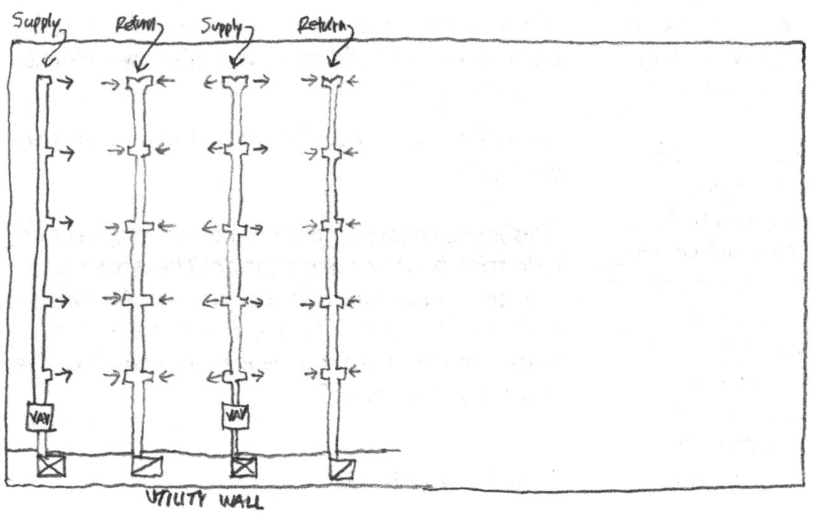

Figure 21.15

Figure 21.16

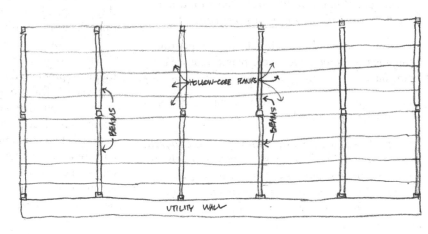

"Sure," said Avram, "but look out for the plumbing risers!"

"We've just started using three-dimensional modeling of our engineering components," offered Tricia, "and it can check for interference between systems like that."

Bruce said, "I like the idea of the utility wall along the south side of the building. As Diane pointed out this afternoon, it can serve as a shear wall, and it can also bear gravity loads."

"Let's try a couple of structural layouts," suggested Diane. "One based on hollow-core planks and one on double tees. Avram, this utility wall that you're talking about, how thick would it have to be?"

"I'd say 5 or 6 ft, depending on the thicknesses of its walls."

"That would leave a clear floor width of about 72 ft. Either we use 12-in. planks over two spans or 10-in. planks over three spans, if we run them perpendicular to the hollow wall. The 16-in. planks don't really have any advantage here because they would still require a beam, since they can't span the whole distance. Tricia, can we use the hollow cores of the planks to bring wiring out to the office area?"

"Yes, it's possible, but if you're adding a 2-inch sitecast concrete topping to the slabs, we could embed conduits or raceways in the topping, which would be easier and give us more flexibility in locating fixtures."

Diane furrowed her brow.

"That would mean that the planks could span in either direction of the site, because their cores wouldn't have to run perpendicular to the utility wall in order to distribute wires. In fact, it would work better to run the cores parallel to the utility wall, because that would orient the beams perpendicular to the wall so that ductwork wouldn't have to cross under them. Let's try the 12-in. planks over spans of 36 ft, to cut down on the number of columns in the space."

She sketched a tracing paper overlay to illustrate this arrangement (21.16).

"This scheme is simple and presumably economical," Bruce noted, "although I'm worried about the cost of all those beams and columns and column footings."

Diane again rolled out tracing paper over the site plan.

"Just to be able to make comparisons, let's consider a double-tee design at the same time. It could be fairly dramatic because of the long distances double tees are able to span: One end of the tees could rest on the utility wall, and they would extend from there all the way to the other edge of the site, to the north. A single line of beams and columns, running at or near the end of the tees, could support the north end (21.17)."

Bruce was clearly interested in Diane's proposal.

"That's astonishingly simple and visually very strong, with the long span of the double tees and only the single plane of beams and columns. And it could create a bold asymmetry. How far could the double tees overhang the beam at the north end?"

"Normally, we'd like to support all precast slab elements at their ends, given that their prestressing strands are usually located and pretensioned for this condition. But it's possible to add plain steel reinforcing in the top of the tee in the vicinity of the beam and out into the overhang, so as to make an overhang possible. Often it's possible to put the top reinforcing for the negatively bent portion of the tees into the poured topping. We may also be able to stretch some prestressing strands in the top of each double tee before it's cast, and put plastic sleeves on the part of the strand length that is in the main part of the span—the part with positive bending. The sleeves prevent this portion of the strands from bonding to the concrete, leaving bonded only the portion where negative bending occurs. I haven't worked out yet the maximum length of an overhang, but it will be on the order of 10 to 12 . . . perhaps, 15 ft."

"I like the idea of the double tees," Avram offered. "Ductwork would run straight out of the utility wall between the stems of the tees. Once outside the vertical shafts, the ducts wouldn't need any bends at all. The duct layouts would be very simple and economical, not to mention efficient."

"It also cuts the number of footings and columns in half, compared to the framing plan that's based on the hollow-core planks," noted Diane.

"The beam that supports the north end of the double tees: How large does it need to be?" Avram asked.

"The span is almost 30 ft," answered Diane. "The depth will have to be about a fifteenth of that, 2 ft.

"If the bottoms of the stems of the double tees are 9 ft-6 in. above the floor below, then the clearance under the beam will be only about 7 ft-6 in. (21.18)."

"That's awfully low," Bruce said. "It will really block the space and the flow of daylight from the windows."

"But keep in mind that the stems of the double tees are very narrow, so that there will be a lot of space and daylight over the beam as well as under," Diane observed.

Bruce was involved in some elaborate doodling that he soon concluded by showing the sheet of paper to the group (21.19).

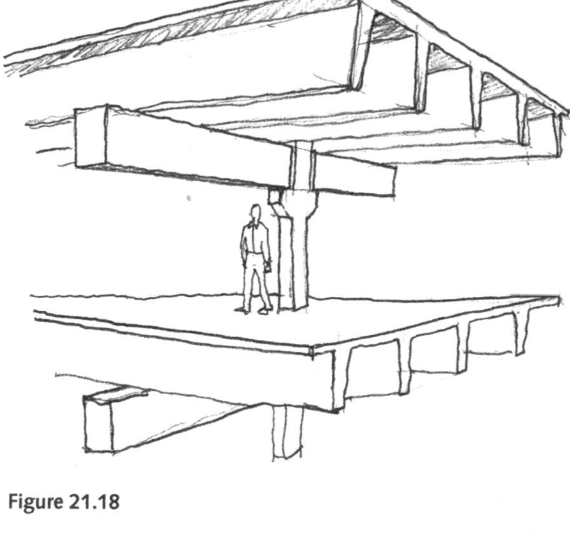

Figure 21.18

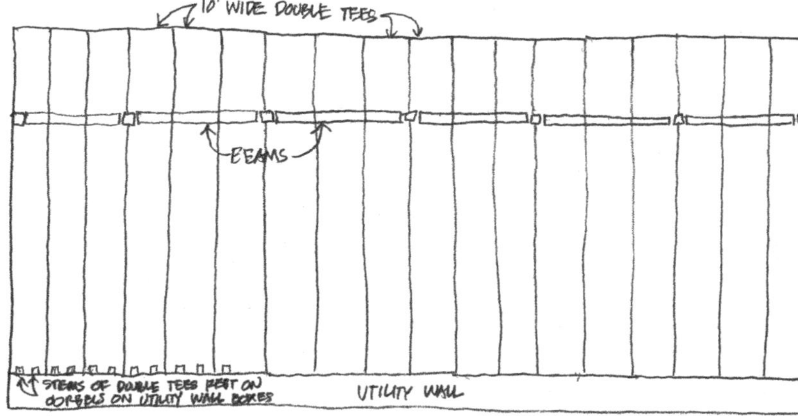

Figure 21.17

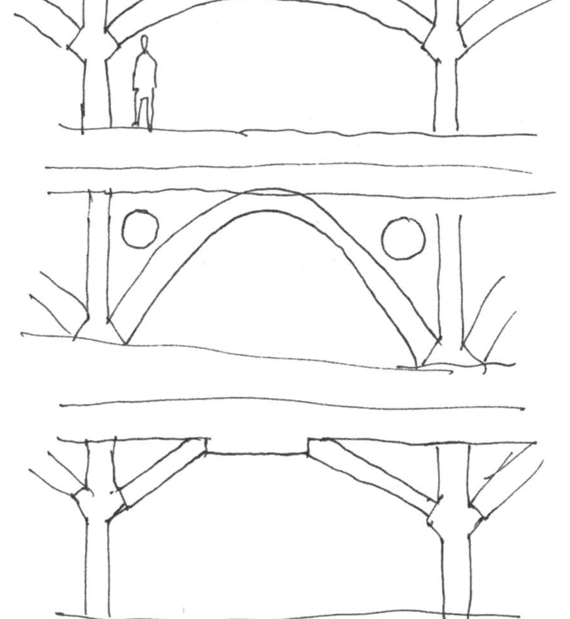

Figure 21.19

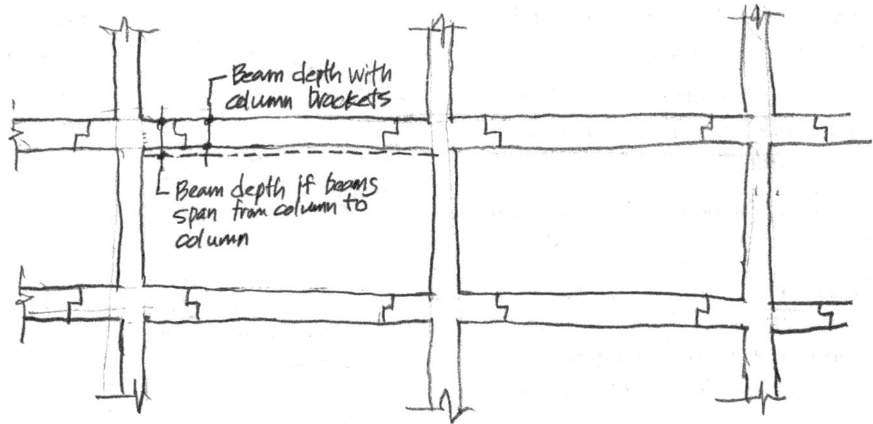

Figure 21.20

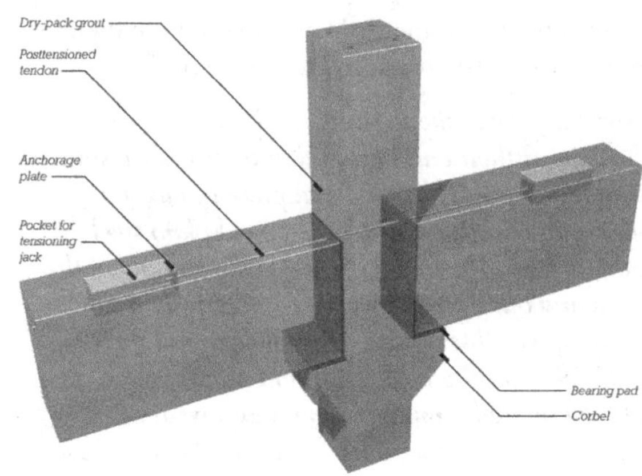

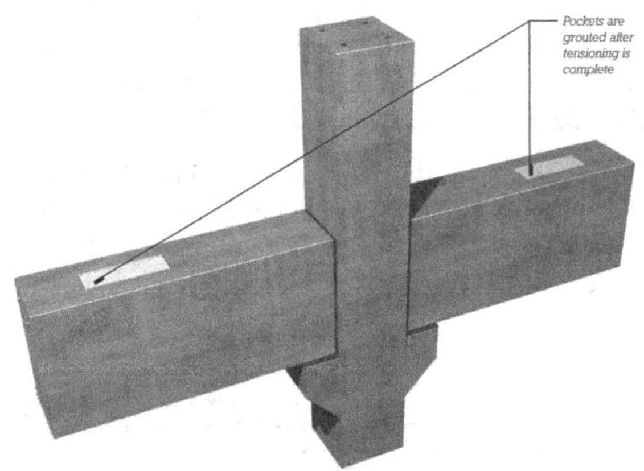

Figure 21.21

"I was trying some alternatives to the precast concrete beam. The arches are the most appealing option, but they actually block the open space under the beam more than the beam does. The sloping struts might work, if we could find a way to tie or buttress the thrusts at the east and west ends of the building. But all in all, I imagine that our best option might be to reduce the span of the beam by joining beams at points of inflection rather than on the columns. The depth of the beam can then be reduced proportionally (21.20). These are called Gerber beams."

"We can achieve the same reduction in beam depth by supporting the beams directly at the column faces and making the beams continuous over the columns," offered Diane.

"How do we do that?" asked Bruce. "Don't the columns have to be continuous from top to bottom? We can't interrupt them with beams at every floor."

"We don't have to. There's a very simple way to posttension the beam by running tendons through holes in the column."

Diane pulled a book out of her portfolio, searched its pages for a few seconds, and showed a picture of the connection (21.21).

"There's a rectangular pocket cast into the top of the beam near each end, big enough to hold a prestressing jack. A longitudinal duct for a tendon is also cast into the beam, running from the pocket to the end. This duct lines up with one through the column, and on to the duct in the next beam. After the beams are in place, a short piece of tendon is threaded through the three ducts and posttensioned. Finally, the pockets are grouted."

"That's ingenious!" exclaimed Bruce. "How much beam depth can it save?"

"Probably only a couple of inches, but every bit helps. A side benefit may be that the plane of beams and columns could be a rigid frame to brace the building laterally, but I'll need to look at that more closely."

IS IT BEAUTIFUL?

"What is the outside going to look like?" queried Tricia.

Bruce replied, "I've been thinking that we should wrap the concrete structure in a high-performance all-glass curtain wall system that's supported by stainless steel rods and hardware. The effect would be like putting the precast components, Curtis's pride and joy, into a huge jewelry display case."

"But a glass box is not always very energy efficient," cautioned Avram, "especially when its major surfaces have northern exposure and can't collect wintertime solar heat."

"True," replied Bruce, "but if we make substantial areas of the wall out of insulated panels, and if the window areas are all double-glazed with a low-conductivity gas fill and a low-emissivity coating on one interior surface, we should be able to come up with a pretty good thermal performance for the building. Especially when you consider that the walls won't experience much solar heat gain during the cooling season. We can do solar studies as we develop the exterior, based on sun angles and the massing of surrounding buildings, to guide how we configure the curtain-wall units on each elevation with glazing."

"While we're talking about solar heat, we should consider putting solar collection panels on the roof," Avram noted. "These could heat domestic water, or they could put heat into the radiant floors, maybe even both."

"There could also be PV panels that would generate electricity, since the roof is the only major opportunity to collect solar energy on the site year-round," Tricia contributed. "But the overall design doesn't hinge on these things. We can worry about solar heat and electricity a little later, when the basic scheme of the building has been settled. We just have to remember in the meantime not to mess up too much of the roof surface with penthouses and exhaust fans and such. We need to leave room for solar panels."

"I think we should proceed on the basis of this double-tee framing scheme," Bruce declared. "It's simple, visually strong, and workable. The only problem I have with it is that the basic structure has the potential to look too much like an ordinary parking garage."

Avram nodded agreement.

"Any ideas on how that can be overcome?"

"I've had a couple of thoughts," said Bruce. "One is that the glass system itself should be more articulated and showy rather than minimal. My other thought is that maybe we could project some of the double tees out several feet beyond the plane of the wall and wrap them in glass enclosures that are extensions of the general glazing scheme. This might break up the huge 'parking garage' look and also create some very special interior spaces; but we will need to know more about the cantilevers before we can know how that can be made feasible."

Diane nodded. Bruce looked at his watch, smiled wearily, and said:

"It's getting late. I'll get some drawings of the double-tee scheme together within the next several days and start modeling them in the computer. After you've seen them and thought about them, let's meet again. And I'll give some thought to the look of the building. If we all still feel good about the scheme after we see these drawings, we can take the design another step forward."

MORE MEETINGS

The next morning, an intern architect in Bruce's office produced a simplified solid model of the building, without its exterior walls (21.22). Bruce knew that the repetitive modularity of the construction could lead to it looking somewhat like a parking garage, but he was determined to keep brainstorming ways

Figure 21.22

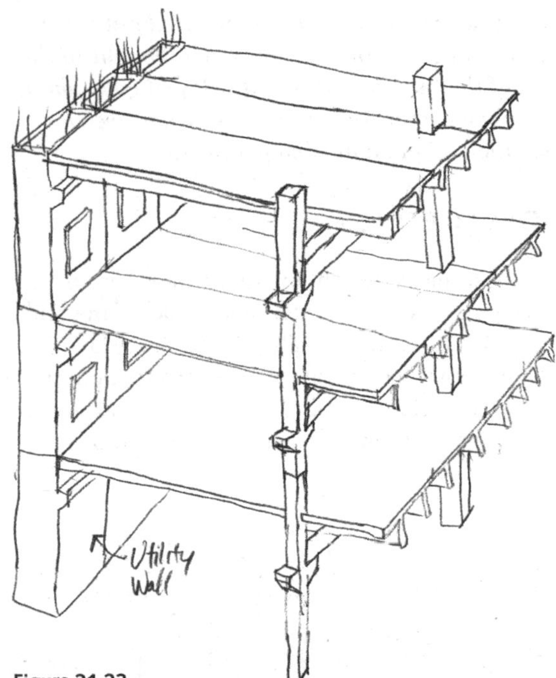

Figure 21.23

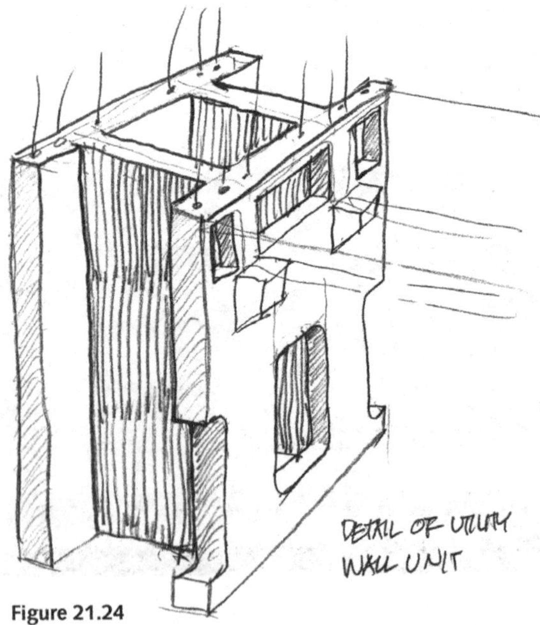

Figure 21.24

to refine the design so it didn't have a heavy, looming appearance. However, for the time being, Bruce scarcely had time to think about this aspect in isolation. In addition to a regular weekly meeting of the entire design team, smaller, informal meetings were constantly occurring between members of the team in various combinations.

In one such meeting, Avram, Bruce, and Diane worked out a preliminary design for the utility wall (21.23, 21.24). It would be made of story-high precast concrete units. These would have projecting lugs on their edges that would mate with depressions in the neighboring units to get the courses of units into perfect alignment. During construction, at several floor levels, stacking of these units would pause while posttensioning tendons were threaded through pipe sleeves cast into their walls. Then the tendons would be tightened with hydraulic jacks to tie the blocks together into a strong unit. Horizontal tendons would keep the wall from spreading apart end to end, and vertical ones would be anchored in the footings and go to the roof to give the wall strength against lateral loads and overturning. The stems of each double tee would rest on concrete corbels on the front of the utility wall, where they would be held in place by welds between matching steel plates embedded in the two elements.

Each block for the utility wall would be reinforced and cast as a complete three-dimensional unit. The front and back faces would be about 5 to 7 in. thick. Two webs would cross the unit from the front to the back. These could be located at the quarter points of its length, so as to align with the corbels that would bring the floor loads from the stems of the double tees into the utility wall. To accomplish this purpose, the webs might need to be a bit thicker than the walls, perhaps as much as 8 in. The gross exterior thickness of the entire wall would be 7 ft. Each block would be 10 ft long to match the width of a precast concrete double-tee floor panel. Its height would be identical to the floor-to-floor height, once that dimension was decided.

On the side of the utility wall that faces the offices, openings would be provided for ductwork and conduits to pass from the vertical shafts into the horizontal spaces between the stems of the double tees. Two options were under consideration: All the openings might be cast without any type of closure. Unused openings could later be closed with steel studs and gypsum board. Or the openings might be cast with thin closure membranes of unreinforced concrete that would be broken out where access to the shafts was required.

Diane was concerned about the heavy loads from the floor panels that would be applied to the wall with an extreme eccentricity by way of the corbels. These actions would cause tension in the side of the wall opposite the corbels, and it would create a tendency for the wall to tip northward, pushing the entire building ahead of it. She sought a consultation with her old structures teacher, Prof. Zalewski, who immediately saw a solution: When provided with a reinforced concrete topping, the floors would act as deep beams lying on their sides to gather the horizontal forces from the eccentrically loaded utility wall at each floor level and transmit them to the stairway walls, which would be constructed as shear walls. He even drew a diagram of the flow of forces in the floor diaphragm (Figure 21.25).

Bruce and Diane convened a small meeting to work on lateral stability of the building. The utility wall constituted a very sturdy shear wall in the long direction at one side of the building. This left the line of columns and beams to be developed as another plane of lateral support, parallel to the utility wall but near the opposite side of the building. The two sketched several precast concrete shear wall designs as alternative possibilities (21.26), including punched openings so the shear walls wouldn't be solid obstructions to light and views within the office spaces. The option of posttensioning the tops of the beams through the columns to create a rigid frame, which was already under consideration as a way of reducing the beam depth through continuous action, was also kept open. It was decided,

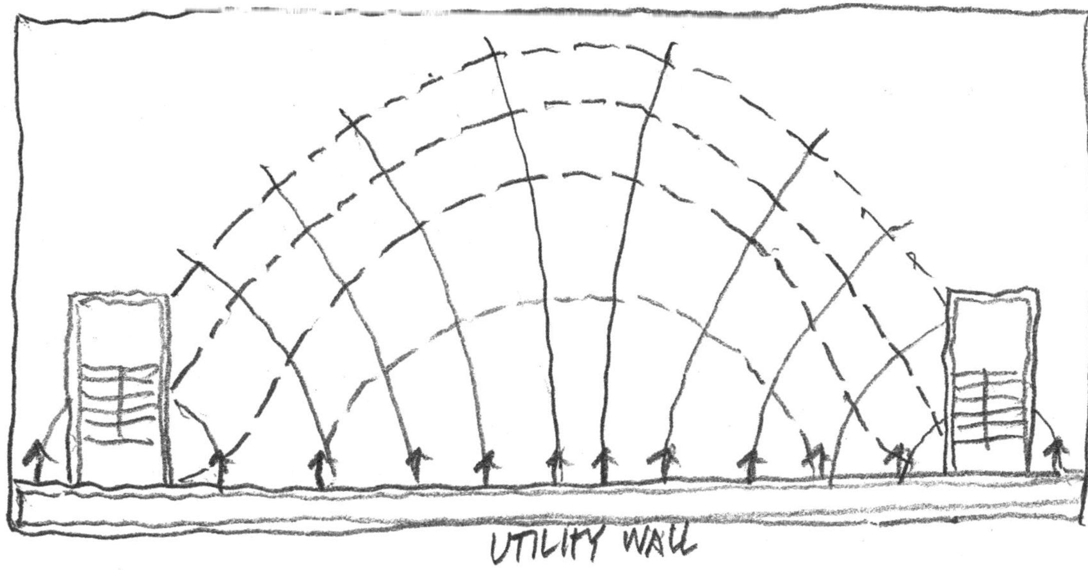

Figure 21.25

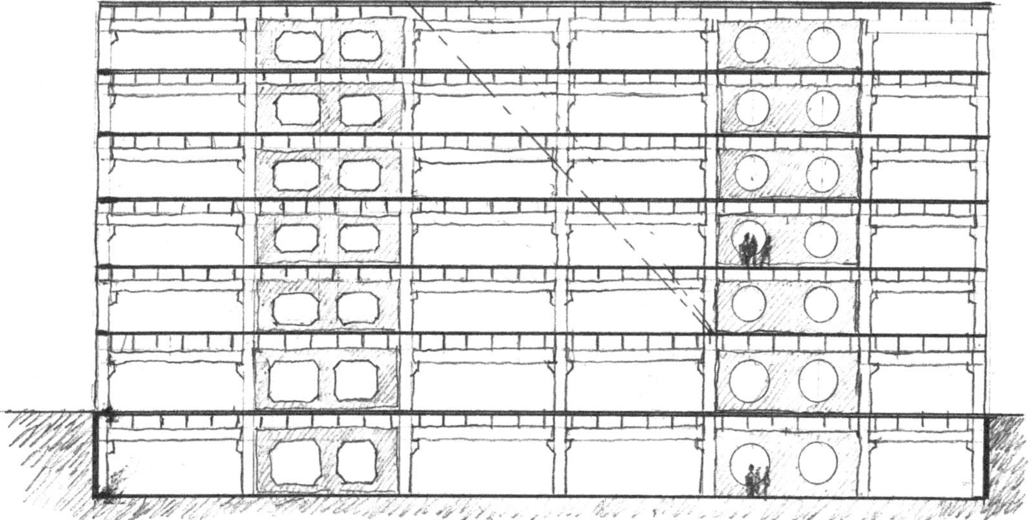

Figure 21.26

pending calculations, that the walls of the precast concrete stairwells probably would provide sufficient shear resistance in the short direction (21.27).

Diane met with Curtis and his engineers to develop an understanding of the complexities caused by the overhanging ends of the double tees. The Keystone Product team took Diane and other members of the team on a tour of the manufacturing facility to demonstrate the process by which the tees are manufactured. They are made on a 24-hour cycle in permanent steel casting beds that are as much as a quarter mile long in many plants (21.28). Each morning, after finished double tees from the previous day's casting have been removed from the casting bed, the bed is cleaned and coated with a release compound that prevents concrete from sticking to it. Then high-strength steel strands are unrolled and placed along the entire length of the bed in the bottoms of the portions of the bed that will form the stems. These strands are anchored at one end of the bed to heavy concrete abutments. At the other end, they are stretched by hydraulic jacks to a high percentage of their breaking strength and anchored to concrete abutments at that end as well. Then separator plates are placed in the bed to divide it into forms of the lengths of tees that are needed. Steel embed plates for welded connections are carefully placed at measured locations; these allow the components to be welded to one another and to the beams that support them. Heavy wire fabric is placed vertically in the stems around support points if it is needed to reinforce against web forces.

When all these arrangements have been completed, everything is checked to be sure it is correct. Then high-early-strength (fast curing) concrete is cast into the bed, except for the short distances between pairs of separator plates that divide the components from one another. Lifting loops (bent pieces of scrap strand) are pushed into the tops of the double-tee components at the proper locations for crane attachments. The entire bed is then covered and steam is introduced under the cover and maintained all night. The heat and

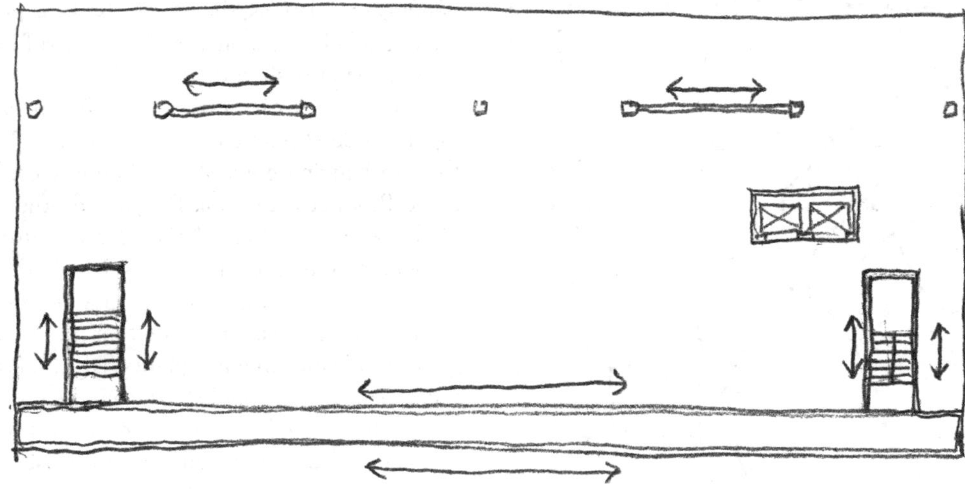

▲ Figure 21.27

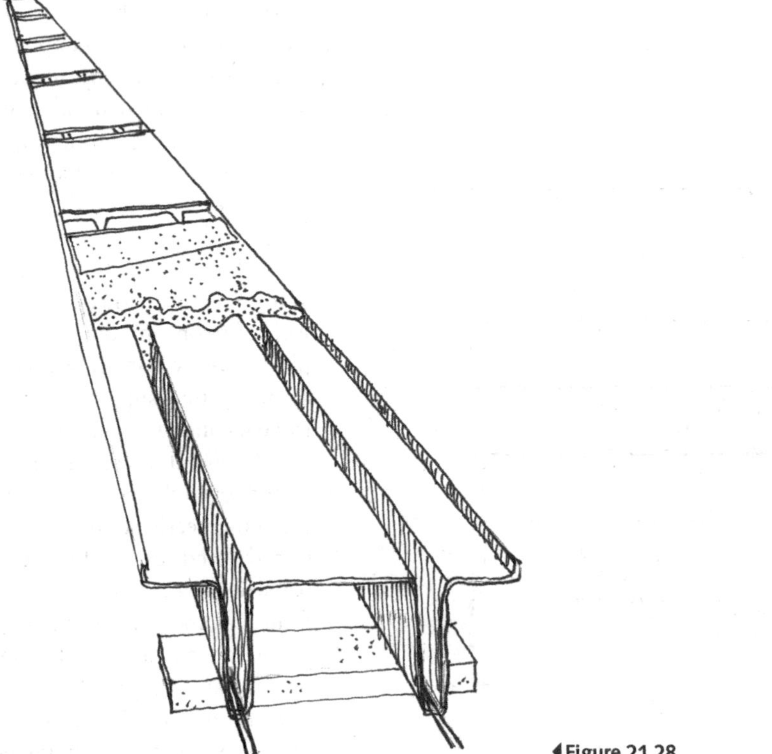

◀ Figure 21.28

moisture of the steam greatly accelerate the curing of the concrete, bringing it to full strength by the start of the next workday. By this time the strands have bonded strongly to the concrete in which they are embedded.

First thing next morning, workers with cutting torches go down the bed, cutting the tightly stretched strands where they are exposed between the separator plates (21.29a). This releases the tension on the strands, but because they have bonded fully to the concrete, a substantial portion of the tension acts to compress the concrete to a fairly high stress. The strands are near the bottoms of the stems of the tees, not at their centroids, so the longitudinal compression induced by the strands is much more intense at the bottoms of the tees than at the top. This causes the cast components to arch upward, creating a decided camber and popping themselves free of the casting bed. They are hoisted out and onto flatbed trucks for stockpiling or delivery to a building site, and the cycle begins anew. (The camber largely disappears when the dead load of the concrete topping is applied).

Overhanging ends create moderate to large negative bending moments in the double tee. If it were a sitecast element, cast into forms on the building site, we would place most of the longitudinal steel reinforcing bars in the top of the overhang to resist the tension in this part of the cross section. But a standard double tee, with its pretensioned strands near the bottom of the stems, is reinforced in exactly the wrong way for this loading. The pull of the strands is working to break off the overhanging portion, not to strengthen it. Thus, in most buildings, double tees are simply supported with no overhangs.

Bruce is determined to have the overhangs because of the economy it generates by eliminating many of the foundations that would otherwise be required, and more importantly, for the way in which it showcases the double tees as a feature of the exterior, visible to passersby on the street. Furthermore, the overhang he wants is of a length that is at the outer limit of what is possible.

Working further with Curtis's structural engineers, Diane has identified and sketched four strategies for creating the necessary tensile strength in the portion

(a)

(b)

Figure 21.29 (a) Workers with cutting torches sever the prestressing strands between double tees in a long casting bed. The members camber upward as the prestressing force is released into them by this process. An overhead crane (b) lifts double tees from the casting bed. The lifting loops are leftover pieces of prestressing strand that were inserted into the concrete before it began to cure.

Photos courtesy of Alvin Ericson.

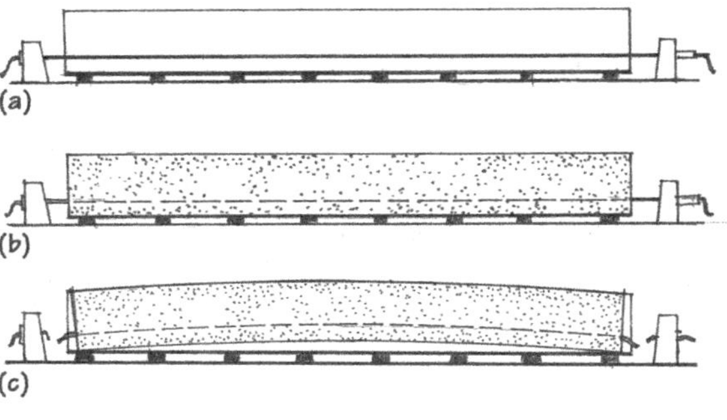

Figure 21.30

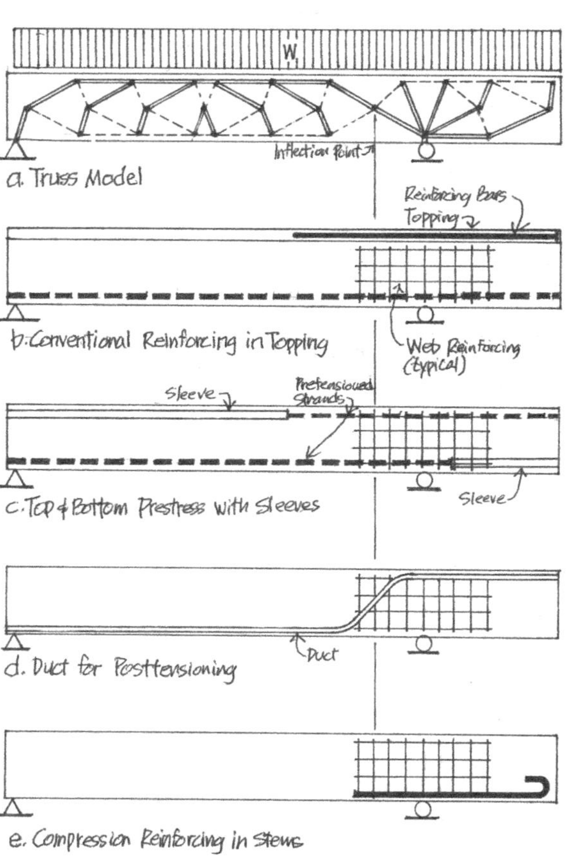

Figure 21.31

of the tees that experiences negative bending (21.31). Part (a) of this drawing is a simplified truss model of the double tee, shown in a diagrammatic profile. The reversal of stress at the inflection point is plainly visible. Part (b) shows a common strategy for providing tensile strength in the top of the double tee: Longitudinal reinforcing bars are embedded in the concrete topping that is poured over the tees. The tees have been manufactured with rough tops so that the topping bonds securely. Grids of web reinforcing are cast into the stems at supports, if needed. The double tee is cast as usual.

Part (c) shows a very different approach to this problem: Strands are stretched near the top of the double tee, as well as the bottom. Thin plastic sleeves are placed over the portions of the strands that would otherwise work against the bending resistance of the component. The concrete can't bond to the sleeve-covered portions, but instead bonds only to the areas where it can do the most good structurally.

Still another possibility is to place a semirigid plastic tube called a *duct* into the casting bed (d), following the line along which tensile strength is most needed. After the concrete has cured, a lubricated length of steel strand is inserted into the duct and tensioned with a hydraulic jack.

A problem common to all of these schemes is that they put most of the compressive forces in the highly stressed portions of the component into the bottoms of the narrow stems, where there is little concrete to resist it. This can result in overstressing of the concrete in these regions. A countermeasure for this is to place steel reinforcing bars in the bottoms of the stems to act as compressive reinforcing (e).

It's probable that the engineers will combine a couple of these strategies to achieve the desired strength and stiffness in the overhanging portions of the double tees. Even so, the possibility remains that the overhangs may have to be shortened or adjusted somewhat as the design develops further. Bruce visited Avram's office to resolve the configuration of the giant air intake and exhaust louvers. In their preliminary plans prepared separately, Bruce had proposed a location for the reception area on the ground floor in the same location that Avram had showed two very large ducts rising from the basement and through the ground floor to the second level, where the ducts turned toward the outdoors. Bruce and Avram considered several different approaches to the louvers, including running the ducts up outside of the building, rising through the sidewalk, where they could be designed as sculptural elements in front of the building. This was initially appealing, but it used up so much site space that it was soon abandoned. The two eventually agreed on a scheme that utilized the last several vertical stacks of blocks in the hollow utility wall at the rear corner of the building. The supply and exhaust ducts would each be routed through two stacks of blocks. These would be unique block types with steel truss webs, rather than the usual concrete ones, to allow large quantities of air to move horizontally between the riser and outdoor louver. The intake duct would be lined with thermal insulation and a warm-side vapor retarder to prevent condensation on the wall surfaces during the winter.

Tricia came to Bruce to discuss concerns about lighting design, acoustics, and electrical distribution. She wanted to coordinate the grid of direct/indirect lighting fixtures with the stems of the double tees for a neat appearance and evenly distributed, low-level ambient illumination. Additionally, each desk or other workstation would have occupant-controlled task lighting for maximum occupant comfort, as well as maximum economy in the building's use of electricity. Based on her initial lighting calculations, she and Bruce agreed to study ways to use sensors on the lighting fixtures at the edge of the building, so that the electric lighting would dim or shut off automatically when there was enough natural light.

Regarding acoustics, the two agreed not to use a suspended sound-absorbing ceiling to quiet the offices, but rather to glue surface-mounted acoustic panels, in a visually rhythmic pattern to be worked out later, between the stems of the tees. Additionally, the floors of most office areas would be covered with a pad and carpet. This combination of ceiling and floor absorption of sound would quiet the offices across a broad spectrum of noise frequencies while leaving the building's structure exposed. The padded carpet would also reduce the downward transmission of impact noise from footsteps to well below accepted levels.

Diane designed a set of typical structural details for review and comments by Curtis and Bruce (21.32). These were uncluttered in appearance and very easy to construct because the embed plates always fitted within the normal double-tee casting bed surfaces rather than requiring fasteners or brackets that would have to penetrate the beds. Diane delayed developing the detail for the exterior edges of the building until she learned how the façade system would be

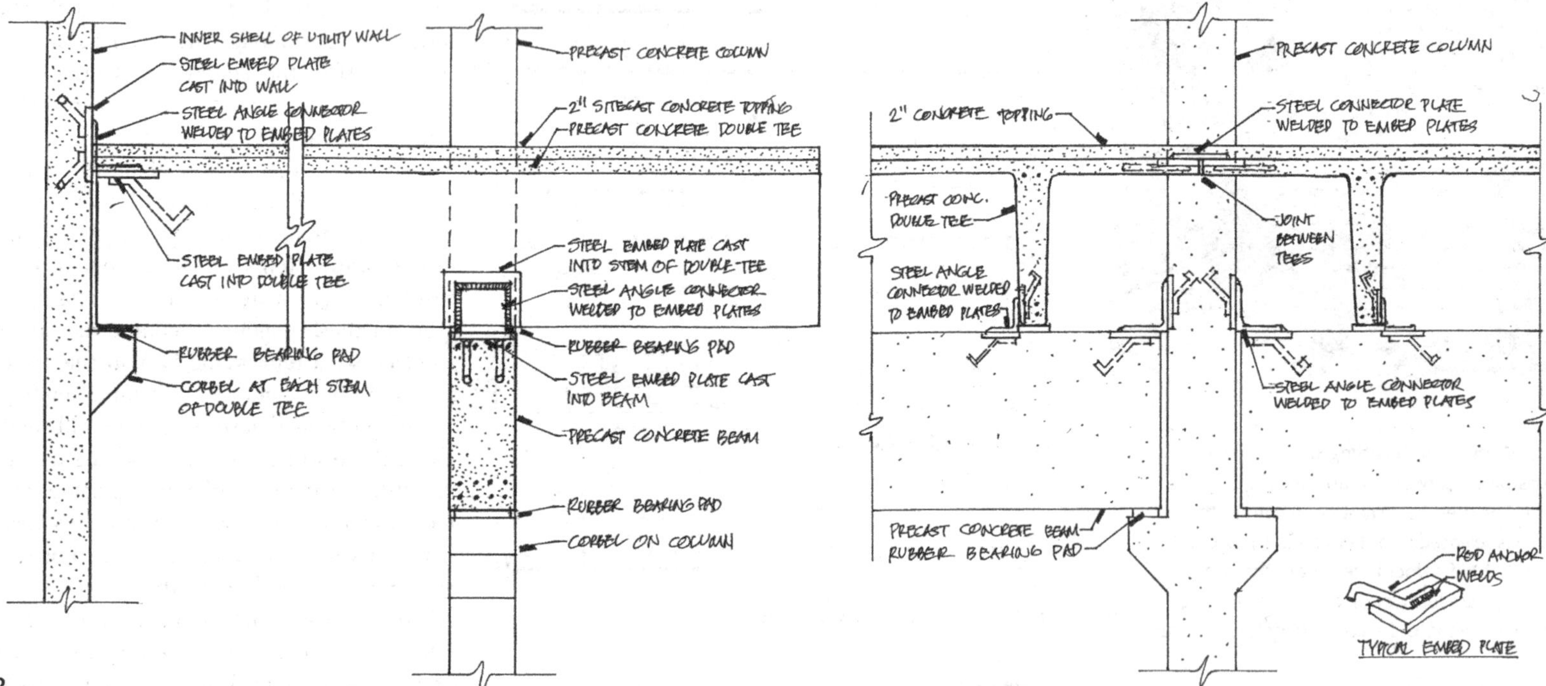

Figure 21.32

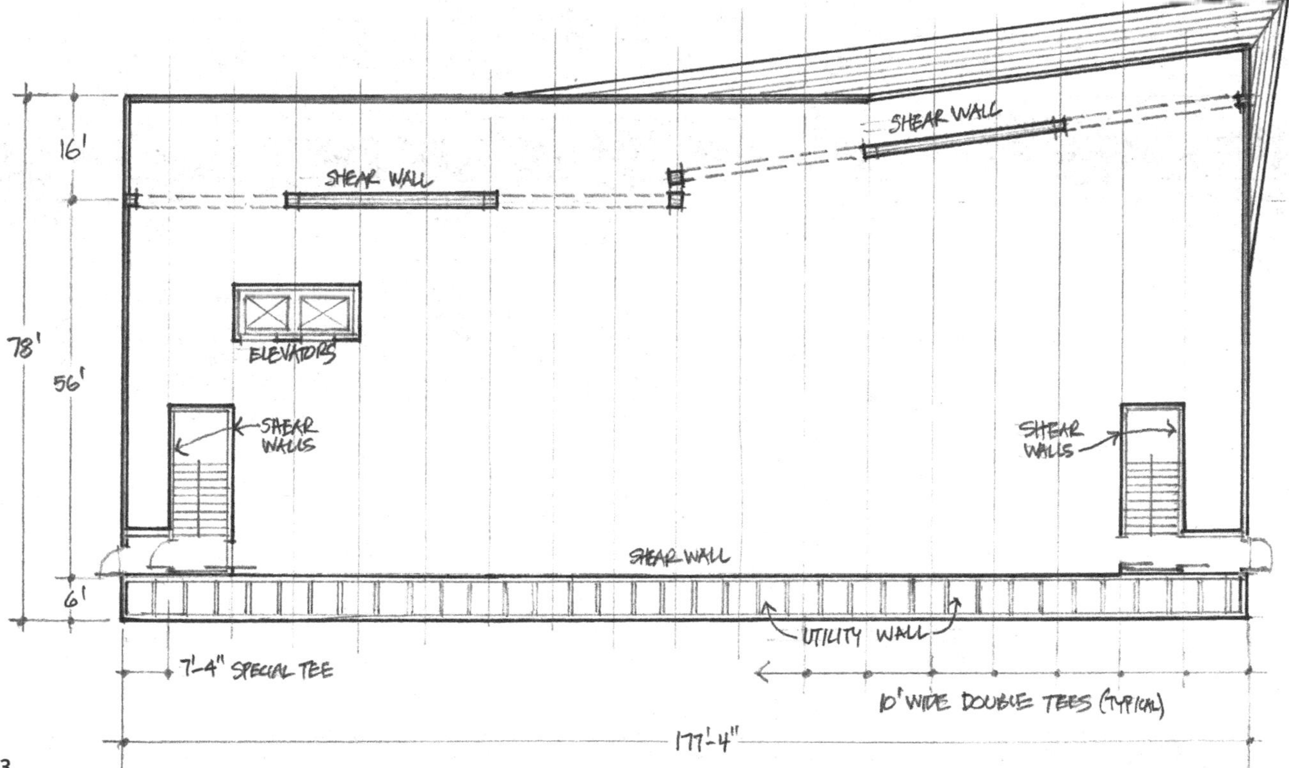

Figure 21.33

connected structurally to the precast, and she kept in touch with Bruce as he weighed different options for the exterior.

Bruce and his staff had been developing alternative cladding systems for the building, when one of them got the idea to adjust the plane of the glass so that it was slightly angled both vertically and horizontally. This would give the prominent corner of the building greater emphasis and pick up on the slight angle to the adjacent street. A portion of the beam would have to be moved and placed on an angle. The ends of the precast tees would all have the same angle as the beam. Since the Keystone manufacturing team had mentioned that they could insert angled separator plates when casting the tees, this would mean that the geometry wouldn't be that complex—even though the tees would be different lengths, they could all use the same separator placed at specific distances. This would need close coordination but it would be an effective way to highlight the properties of precast construction to their advantage, in ways that wouldn't require excessive additional cost. It would also enable the overhang on the tees to be less extreme, and it would create interior spaces that would have more personality without compromising their use as offices (21.33).

Bruce realized with great relief that because of the faceted appearance this slight complexity added to the design, the building no longer resembled a parking garage. Working together, Bruce and his team evolved over several days of effort a design that featured large areas of thermally insulated panels on the end walls of the building, and a long façade that utilized both insulated panels and high-performance glazing units to reduce heat transmission while retaining the appeal of facets of glass (21.34).

At about this time, the results of soil borings on the site that Diane had ordered came in: The soil was indeed relatively well drained, stable, and strong; this meant that the entire building could be supported on spread footings, which are the simplest, most economical type of foundation, as Diane had hoped. Through several weeks more of collaboration their efforts began to bear fruit. The building design emerged bit by bit, taking on a life of its own and an appearance and functionality that were evident in its calm but dramatic exterior appearance. Inwardly, even though he was confident about the quality of the building, Bruce anxiously awaited Curtis's reaction to the preliminary design.

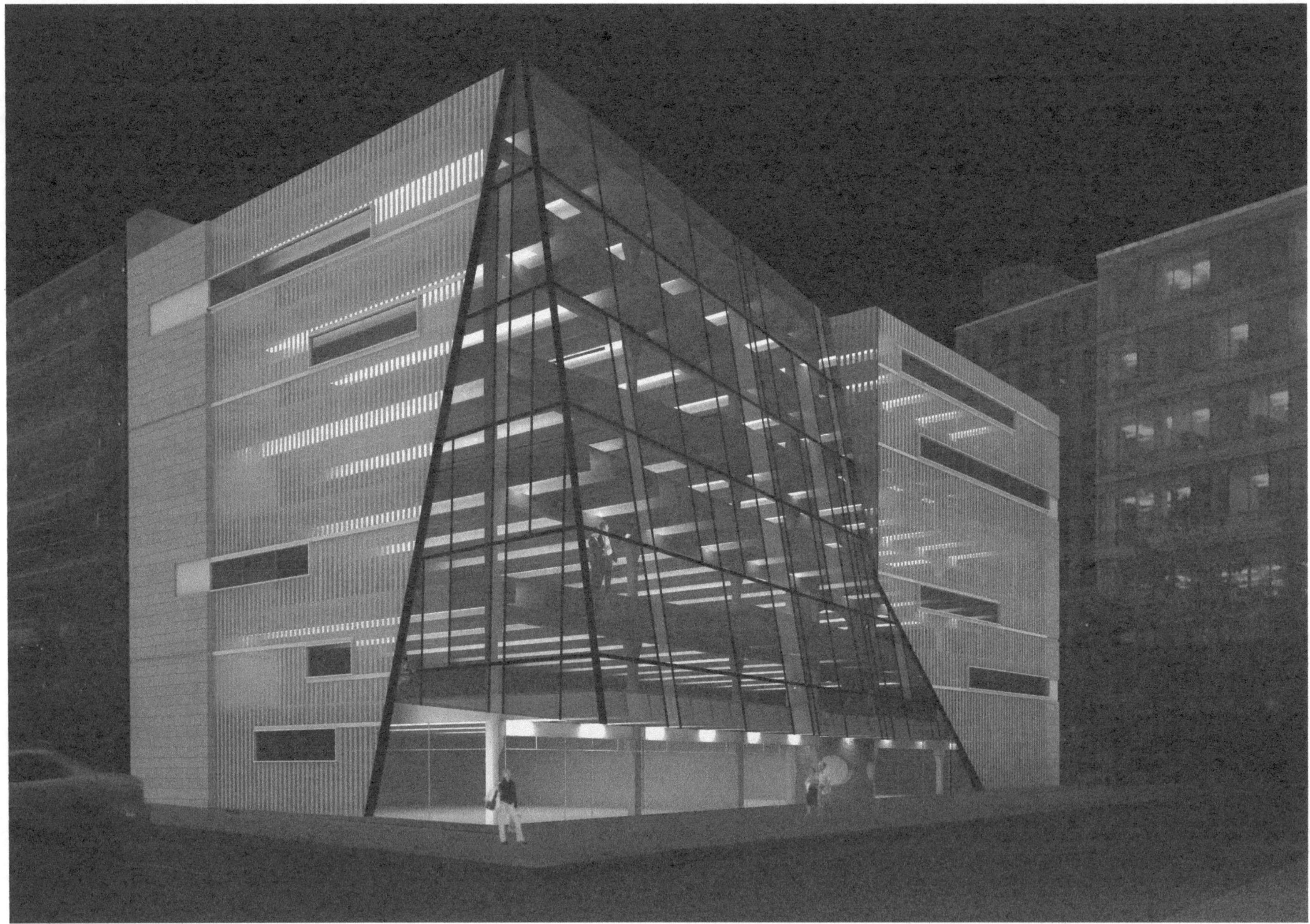

Figure 21.34

For Preliminary Design of a Precast Concrete Structures (Figure 21.35)

Estimate the depth of a precast solid slab (one without hollow cores) at 1/40 of its span. Depths typically range from 3–1/2 to 8 in. (90 to 200 mm).

An 8-in. (200-mm) precast hollow-core slab can span approximately 25 ft (7.6 m); a 10-in. (250-mm) slab, 32 ft (9.8 m); and a 12-in. (300-mm) slab, 40 ft (12 m).

Estimate the depth of precast concrete double tees at 1/28 of their span. The most common depths of double tees are 24, 26, 28, 30, 32, and 34 in. (610, 660, 710, 760, 840, and 860 mm).

A precast concrete single tee 36 in. (915 mm) deep spans approximately 85 ft (25.9 m); and a 48-in. (1,220-mm) tee, 105 feet (32 m).

Estimate the depth of precast concrete beams and girders at 1/15 of their span for light loadings and 1/12 of their span for heavy loadings. These ratios apply to rectangular, inverted tee, and L-shaped beams. The width of a beam or girder is usually about half its depth. The projecting ledgers on inverted tee and L-shaped beams are usually 6 in. (150 mm) wide and 12 in. (300 mm) deep.

To estimate the size of a precast concrete column, add up the total roof and floor area support by the column. A 10-in. (250-mm) column can support up to about 2,000 sq ft (185 m²) of area; a 12-in. (300-mm) column, 2,600 sq ft (240 m²); a 16-in. (400-mm) column, 4,000 sq ft (370 m²); and a 24-in. (600-mm) column, 8,000 sq ft (740 m²). These values may be interpolated to columns in 2-in. (50-mm) increments of size. Columns are usually square.

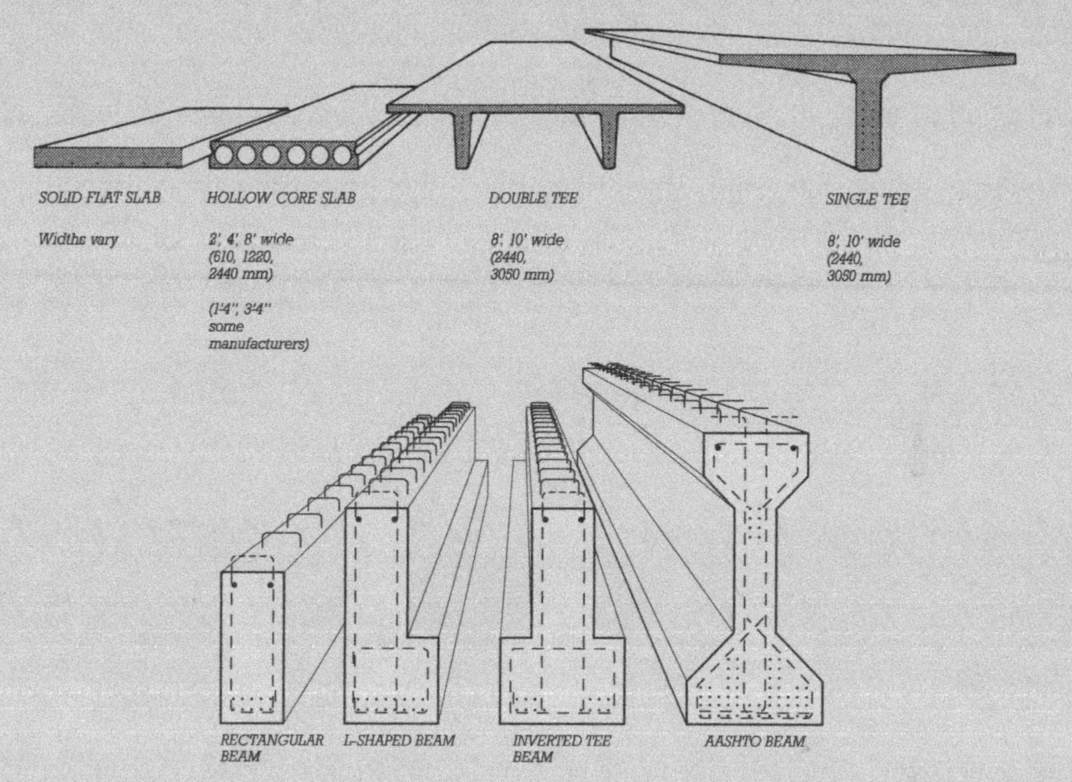

These approximations are valid only for purposes of preliminary building layout, and must not be used to select final member sizes. They apply to the normal range of building occupancies such as residential, office, commercial, and institutional buildings, and parking garages. For manufacturing and storage buildings, use somewhat larger members.

For more comprehensive information on preliminary selection and layout of structural systems and sizings of structural members, see Edward Allen and Joseph Iano, *Fundamentals of Building Construction*, Fifth Edition (Hoboken, NJ: John Wiley & Sons, Inc., 2009), and Edward Allen and Joseph Iano, *The Architect's Studio Companion*, Fourth Edition (Hoboken, NJ: John Wiley & Sons, Inc., 2007). For excellent design advice, see Precast/Prestressed Concrete Institute, *Designing with Precast/Prestressed Concrete* (Chicago, PCI: no date), www.pci.org.

CHAPTER 22 Designing an Entrance Canopy

- *Designing a constant-force beam*
- *Deriving a beam profile from the bending moment diagram*
- *Assuring overall stability of an unusual structure*
- *Combined axial and bending stress in a beam*
- *Guidelines for shaping structures*

The Convention Authority of a large Midwestern city is engaged in remodeling its Convention Center, which hosts trade shows and large professional and political meetings. The goal is to bring the center up to current standards of amenities, safety, and accessibility, and to give it a sparkling new image that will help to attract organizers of major events. The Authority has hired us to design one important aspect of this image: an entrance canopy that will shelter guests as they arrive at the main doors of the center, via buses, parking lot shuttles, and taxis. The Authority has made it clear to us that the canopy must be a spectacular showpiece, which will serve to symbolize the convention center, and a landmark that will help guide people to its doors. They have established a very generous budget for its design and construction.

In our first design session we sketched a number of ideas, but none seemed special enough to meet the Authority's mandate (Figure 22.1). Then one of our group sketched a design proposal in which glass roof panels would be supported by steel beams that cantilever from heavy concrete pylons. The outer

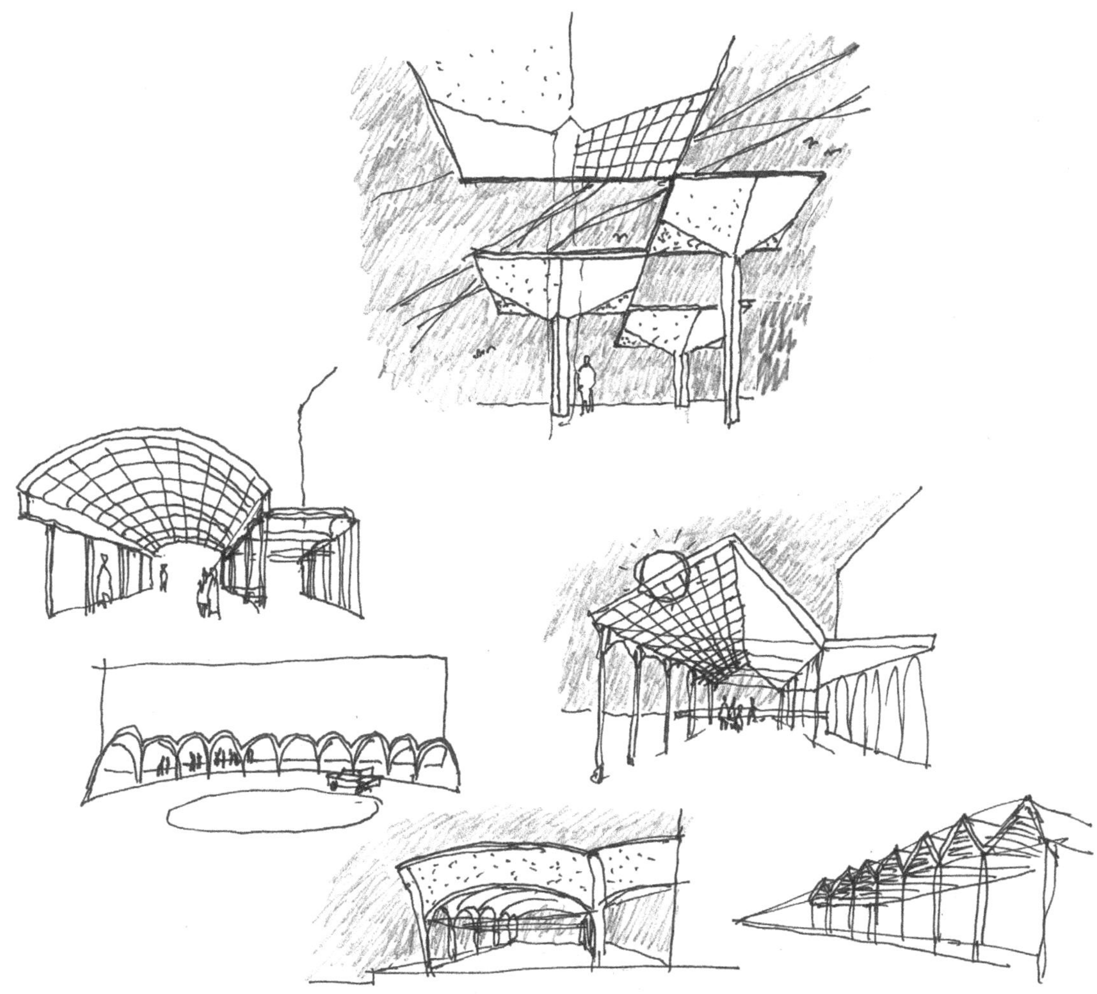

Figure 22.1 An assortment of sketches of early ideas for the entrance canopy.

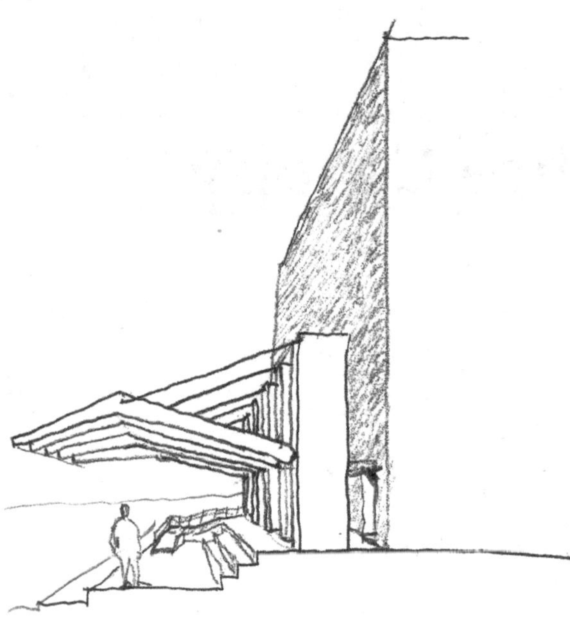

Figure 22.2 An early sketch that shows the scheme to be developed in this chapter.

Figure 22.3 Adding a slight curvature to the line of pylons and beams.

ends of the beams would hang on inclined steel stay rods from the tops of the pylons (Figure 22.2). Everyone on the team is enthused by this idea, and a decision has been reached to develop the design to a stage such that its feasibility can be assessed and its appearance shown in sufficient detail to present it to the client group.

DEVELOPING THE IDEA

We soon realize that a curving line of pylons would be more dramatic than a straight one, and the Authority has agreed to let us rebuild the existing building front with a matching curve (Figure 22.3). After considerable experimentation, we produce a cross section through the canopy and pylons that seems to have the right spatial character (Figure 22.4). With a short downward slope at the outer end of the beams, it shelters the area where people leave their vehicles, then rises to create a major space over the vehicular lanes. The main span of the canopy slopes down to a more intimate scale as one approaches the building. This introduces the visitor to the intentionally squeezed space of the entrance doors and the expansion into the taller spaces in the lobby and halls beyond. We have sculpted the pylons into tapered, backward-leaning concrete volumes that express their function

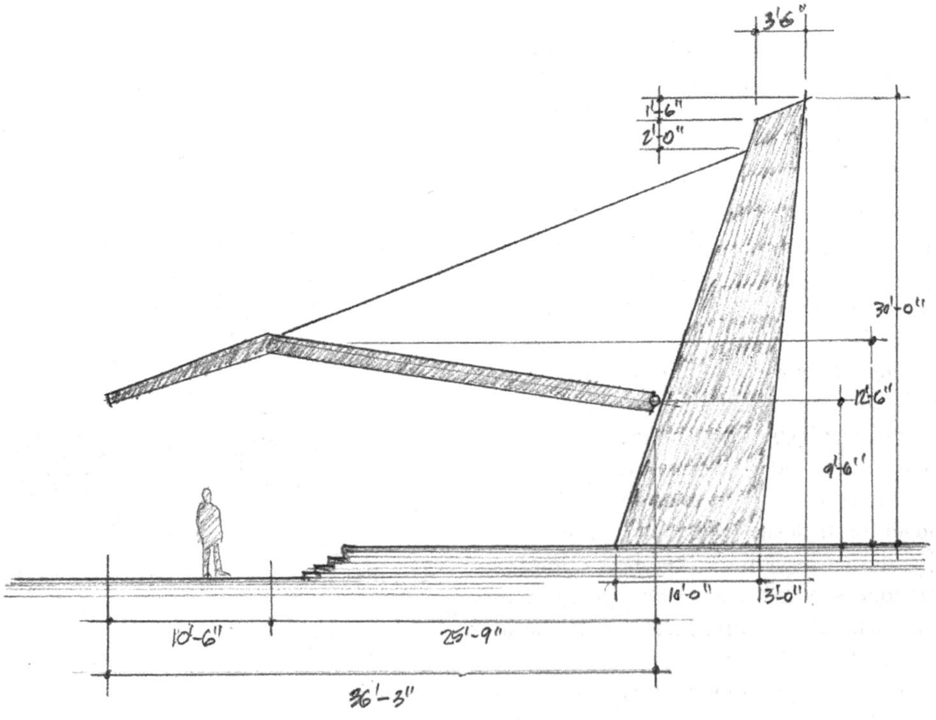

Figure 22.4 Developing the actual dimensions of the canopy structure.

of pulling back against the stay rods that support the outer ends of the beams. A bit farther along in the design process we will check the stability of this pylon shape. For now, however, we turn our attention to the beams themselves.

DESIGNING THE BEAMS

Members of the design team have put forward a number of ideas for the beams: castellated beams made by cutting and welding stock steel beams, delicately scaled steel trusses, and several shapes of more substantial trusses that would cantilever from the concrete pylons without requiring tension rods. Then a young engineer on the project team suggests that the beams be custom-fabricated in a longitudinal profile that resembles the bending moment diagram for the assumed loading and support conditions. He explains that if the beam depth is proportional at every point to the bending moment, the forces in the flanges are parallel and constant throughout the span and there are no web forces of any consequence. Thus, flanges of constant size are fully stressed over the entire length of the beam. He notes that such a beam would be efficient in its use of material and visually expressive of its pattern of bending moments and the way it works internally. This may be contrasted with the lattice pattern of force flow in prismatic beams, in which forces vary considerably, most of the beam material is working well below its capacity, and there is no external expression of the flow pattern of forces within the beam. This idea of *parallel flow* appeals to us and we set to work to discover what sorts of opportunities the bending moment shape offers us. Naturally, our first task is to construct a bending moment diagram.

Because of the curvature of the plan of the canopy, the outer ends of the beams will be slightly closer together than the inner ends. This means that the tributary area of a foot of beam length is less at the outer end than at the inner, and the loading diagram will be a first degree rather than zero-degree curve. We have assumed that the concrete pylons will be spaced at 10 ft center to center. We have also assumed a radius of 300 ft from the face of the pylons nearest the doors to the center of the circular curve. A quick calculation shows that the tips of the beams will be a little less than 9 ft apart with this geometry. We decide that for the sake of speed, it is reasonable to assume for now that the loading is constant throughout the span, and to make corrections as necessary during the detailed design phase.

Earlier, as we were constructing the cross section shown in Figure 22.4, we decided to support the beam in such a way that its maximum positive and negative moments are approximately equal. For a beam with overhanging end such as the one we are considering, this can be accomplished by making the main span 71% of the overall length of the beam, with the overhanging portion comprising 29% of the overall length.

The dead and live loads are estimated; they come to 20 kips for a typical beam. The stay rod will exert both a bending action and an axial action upon the beam by means of the vertical and axial components of its inclined force, respectively. For now, we are interested only in the vertical bending component; we will deal with the axial component later. The reactions on the beam are found by evaluating moments, and the *V* and *M* diagrams are constructed semigraphically (Figure 22.5) The maximum positive and negative bending moments turn out to be almost the same, as we had planned, with only a tiny discrepancy, attributable to rounding of values and slight adjustments in dimensions.

After sketching many alternatives, we decide that we would like the beams to be fabricated with flanges made from steel pipes welded to webs of quarter-inch steel plate (Figure 22.6). A rule-of-thumb beam depth of 1/20 of the main span establishes a tentative depth of 17 in. for the beams. Realizing that the overhang at the outer end of the beam reduces the bending moment in the main span, we reduce this value arbitrarily to 16 in. We can fine-tune this value later if needed.

In the last diagram in Figure 22.5, labeled "$M_{16"}$," we construct the bending moment diagram in both its positive and negative versions; we also reduce its height proportionally so that its maximum height is 16 in. at the scale of the horizontal axis. This establishes the relative proportions of the beam and sets the stage for experimentation with its form.

To arrive at fine-scale fabrication dimensions for the curves of the beam, we could work graphically by hand at very large scale, perhaps 1 in. to the foot or even larger, to construct smooth, accurate curves with the proper depths at each point on the span. Small discrepancies in depth will be of little consequence structurally, but they may make fabrication of the beams difficult, and they could make the finished beams look crude and lumpy. To avoid this possibility, we decide against a graphical approach and instead find numerical values for the depth of the beam at points a foot apart along the horizontal projection of the span. The values are found with the following expression, which applies to parabolas with level closing strings:

$$Y_x = 4s\left[\frac{x}{L} - \frac{x^2}{L^2}\right] \qquad \textbf{[22-1]}$$

where:

Y_x is the height of the curve above the closing string at horizontal location x,

s is the maximum sag or rise of the curve with respect to the closing string,

x is the distance of the point from the left end of the parabola, and

L is the horizontal dimension of the closing string.

For s we substitute 16 in., the desired maximum rise or sag of the curve. For L, we use 254.4 in., the length of the closing string of the full parabola on the *M* diagram.

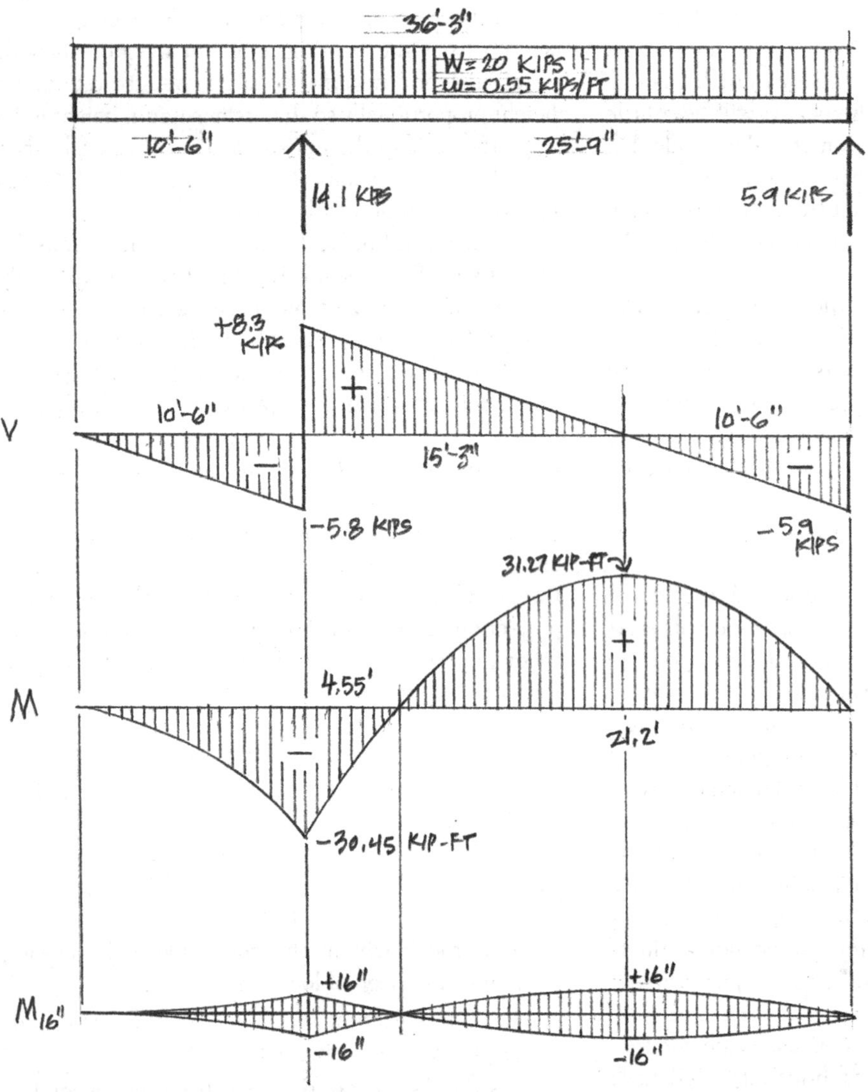

▲ **Figure 22.5** *V* and *M* diagrams for the canopy beams. The last diagram, $M_{16"}$, is made up of two mirror-image bending moment diagrams that have been reduced in height so that their maximum departures from the base line are 16 in. This becomes our basis for exploring alternative beam profiles.

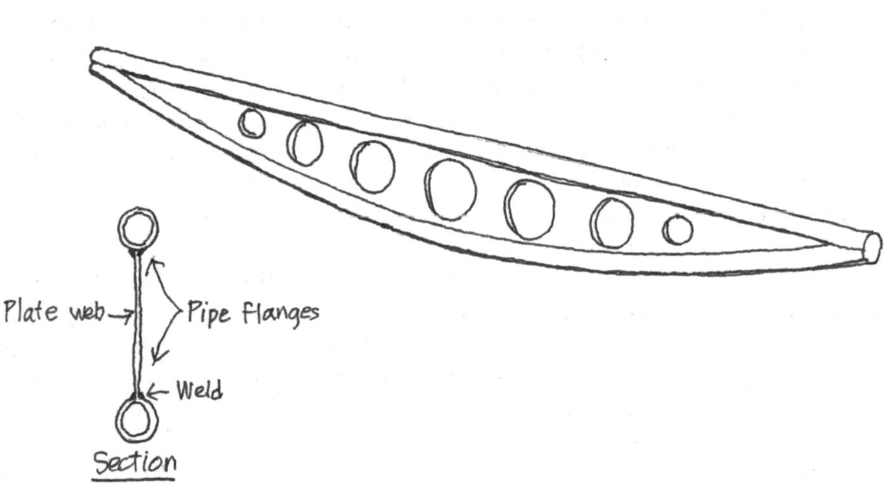

▲ **Figure 22.6** The type of beam construction that we would like to use in the canopy. The beam will not have this profile—the intent of this drawing is merely to establish a formal vocabulary. The pipe flanges will convey a more sculptural quality than the usual flat flanges, and they will be much more resistant to buckling.

$$Y = 4s\left[\frac{x}{L} - \frac{x^2}{L^2}\right], \text{ where } s = 16'', L = 254.4'', L^2 = 64{,}719 \text{ in}^2$$

$$Y_{12} = 4(16'')\left[\frac{12''}{254.4''} - \frac{144 \text{ in}^2}{64{,}719 \text{ in}^2}\right] = 2.88''$$

$$Y_{24} = 64''\left[\frac{24''}{254.4''} - \frac{576 \text{ in}^2}{64{,}719 \text{ in}^2}\right] = 5.47''$$

$$Y_{36} = 64''\left[\frac{36''}{254.4''} - \frac{1{,}296 \text{ in}^2}{64{,}719 \text{ in}^2}\right] = 7.78''$$

$$Y_{48} = 64''\left[\frac{48''}{254.4''} - \frac{2{,}304 \text{ in}^2}{64{,}719 \text{ in}^2}\right] = 9.80''$$

$$Y_{60} = 64''\left[\frac{60''}{254.4''} - \frac{3600 \text{ in}^2}{64{,}719 \text{ in}^2}\right] = 11.53''$$

$$Y_{72} = 64''\left[\frac{72''}{254.4''} - \frac{5{,}184 \text{ in}^2}{64{,}719 \text{ in}^2}\right] = 12.99''$$

$$Y_{84} = 64\left[\frac{84''}{254.4''} - \frac{7{,}056 \text{ in}^2}{64{,}719 \text{ in}^2}\right] = 14.15''$$

$$Y_{96} = 64\left[\frac{96''}{254.4''} - \frac{9{,}216 \text{ in}^2}{64{,}719 \text{ in}^2}\right] = 15.04''$$

$$Y_{108} = 64\left[\frac{108''}{254.4''} - \frac{11{,}664 \text{ in}^2}{64{,}719 \text{ in}^2}\right] = 15.64''$$

$$Y_{120} = 64\left[\frac{120''}{254.4''} - \frac{14{,}400 \text{ in}^2}{64{,}719 \text{ in}^2}\right] = 15.95''$$

$$Y_{127.2} = 64''\left[\frac{127.2''}{254.4''} - \frac{16{,}180 \text{ in}^2}{64{,}719 \text{ in}^2}\right] = 16.00''$$

Figure 22.7 Calculating points on the profile of the beam.

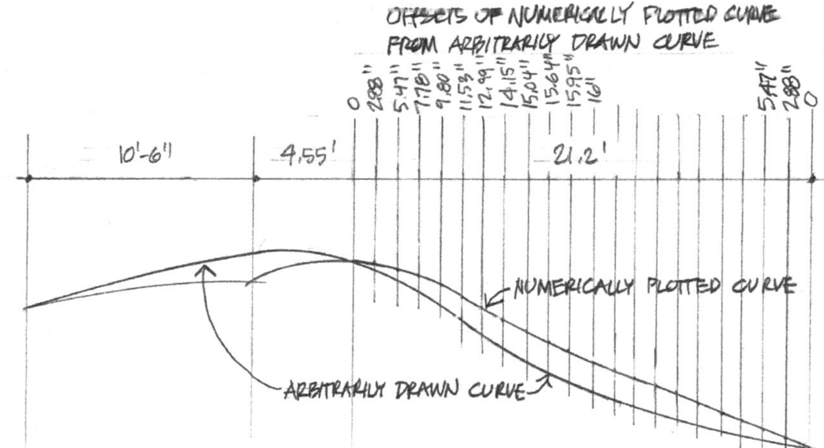

▲**Figure 22.8** An example of how we can use the dimensions from the previous figure (22.7) to construct an efficient beam shape that is based on an arbitrarily curved line.

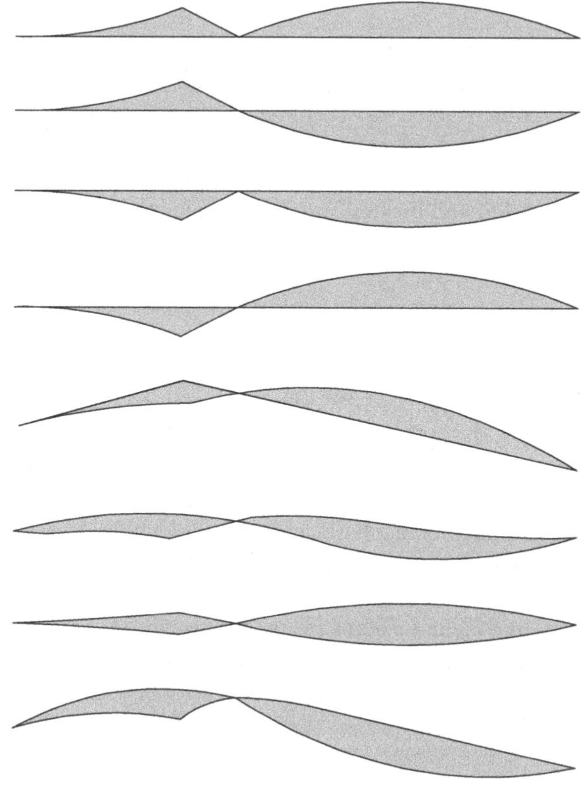

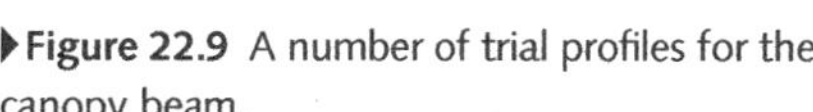

▶**Figure 22.9** A number of trial profiles for the canopy beam.

Figure 22.7 shows the numerical results. These values cover half of the full parabola and are mirrored about the centerline of the string to construct the other half.

To obtain depths for the 4.55-ft-long portion of the beam to the left of the full parabola on the drawing, we can substitute negative values of x into this equation. Depths for the overhanging portion of the beam are found by considering its curve as half of a parabola whose base is 21 ft (twice 10 ft 6 in.) and altitude is −16 in.

Within reason, we can apply the values that we find using this expression to a beam that is arbitrarily curved. In the example shown in Figure 22.8, we first drew arbitrarily a curve that we thought might look good for the bottom edge of the beam. Then we plotted points for the other edge at 1-ft horizontal intervals, using the calculated values from Figure 22.7 as the heights of these points above the arbitrary curve. The result is one possible shape for this portion of the beam that will have parallel flow throughout. Figure 22.9

shows the outcome of a number of similar attempts to arrive at a pleasing longitudinal profile for the beam. The first four are traced quite literally from the preceding moment diagram, using a horizontal baseline. In three of the last four sketches, we have arbitrarily adopted shallow curves as the baselines for the moment diagrams, while continuing to vary the depth with the intensity of the bending moment at each point on the span. You might also wish to try another arbitrary shape for one of the chords of the beam in a further attempt to discover an elegant shape for the member. Many such attempts are often necessary before a satisfactory form is found.

ASSURING THE OVERALL STABILITY OF THE CANOPY IN CROSS SECTION

As our experiments with the profile shape of the beam continue, we examine the overall stability of the structure. In the cross-sectional direction, this may be accomplished for gravity loads by finding the resultant of all the vertical forces that act on the canopy and pylon and making sure that its line of action lies within the kern of the footing that transfers these forces to the soil.

The canopy is made up of two major parts: the beam with its live load and the pylon. We will first find the weight of the pylon and the location of its resultant (Figure 22.10). The irregular quadrilateral shape of the pylon makes it difficult to do this directly, but simply by drawing a diagonal across it, we divide it into two triangles. The area of each triangle is half the product of its base and altitude, remembering that altitude is measured perpendicular to the chosen base. Its volume is found by multiplying this area by 2 ft, the thickness of the pylon. The weight of each triangular volume is calculated by multiplying its volume in cubic feet by 150 lb/ft^3, the density of reinforced concrete.

The line of action of the weight of the pylon is the vector sum of the weights of the two triangular volumes. The first step in finding the line of action of the weight of the pylon is to locate the centroids of the two triangular volumes. Each lies on lines, each of which passes from a vertex to the center of the opposite side, at a distance from the base of one-third of the altitude. We construct a load line that is made up of the weights of the two triangular volumes, adopt an arbitrary pole location, and construct a force polygon. From the force polygon and its rays, we construct a funicular polygon over the drawing of the pylon. The lines of action of the first and last vectors in the funicular polygon, *oa* and *oc*, are extended until they intersect. This point of intersection, labeled x, lies on the line of action of the weight of the pylon.

In a similar operation, we find the location of the line of action of the weight of the entire structure, which is the sum of the weights of the canopy and the pylon (Figure 22.11). We assume conservatively that the canopy weight of 20 kips acts at the midpoint of the beam. The resultant of the total weight of the structure is a vertical line that lies just outside the inner face of the pylon at the point where the pylon enters the ground. We center a concrete spread footing for the pylon and beam on this line, extending the footing symmetrically in both directions until it is sufficiently large to do all of the following:

1. Transfer the load to the soil at a pressure that the earth can sustain.
2. Create a broad enough base to maintain stability under the relatively small fluctuations in loadings that may occur.
3. Avoid tipping rightward before the beam is added.

We add a tapering concrete transition between the front of the pylon and the top of its footing that will be helpful in reducing stress concentrations in the concrete at this point. Later, as we prepare a detailed design for this structure, we will also examine the effects of combined gravity/seismic/wind forces on the pylon structure.

Three external forces act upon the canopy itself (that is, the beams, purlins, and glass, but not the pylons): the sum of its live and dead loads, the pull of the steel rod, and the push of the hinge at the right end. In Figure 22.12, we solve for these forces. The direction, magnitude, and location of the canopy load are known. For the rod, we know the direction and location but not the magnitude. For the hinge, we know neither magnitude nor direction, only the location of a point on its line of action. Despite the seeming insufficiency of this information, we are easily able to solve graphically for all the unknowns. The known lines of action of the rod force and the weight of the canopy intersect at x. In order for this system to be in static equilibrium, the line of action of the hinge force must pass through x and the center of the hinge pin. A force polygon constructed from these three vectors gives us directions and values for all the unknown forces.

We will also need to know the value of the axial compression in the main span of the beam that is caused by the inclined pull of the rod. This is found in Figure 22.13 with a graphical summation of forces at the point where the stay rod joins the beam.

CHECKING THE MAXIMUM STRESS IN THE BEAM

Bending Stress and Axial Stress

Earlier, in order to maintain maximum stresses within acceptable limits, we assigned an approximate depth to the beam of 16 in. Is this sufficient? To find bending stresses, we must find the moment of inertia (I) of the cross-sectional shape of the beam, which will be a composite of moments of inertia of the flanges (the steel pipes at the top and bottom) and the web plate.

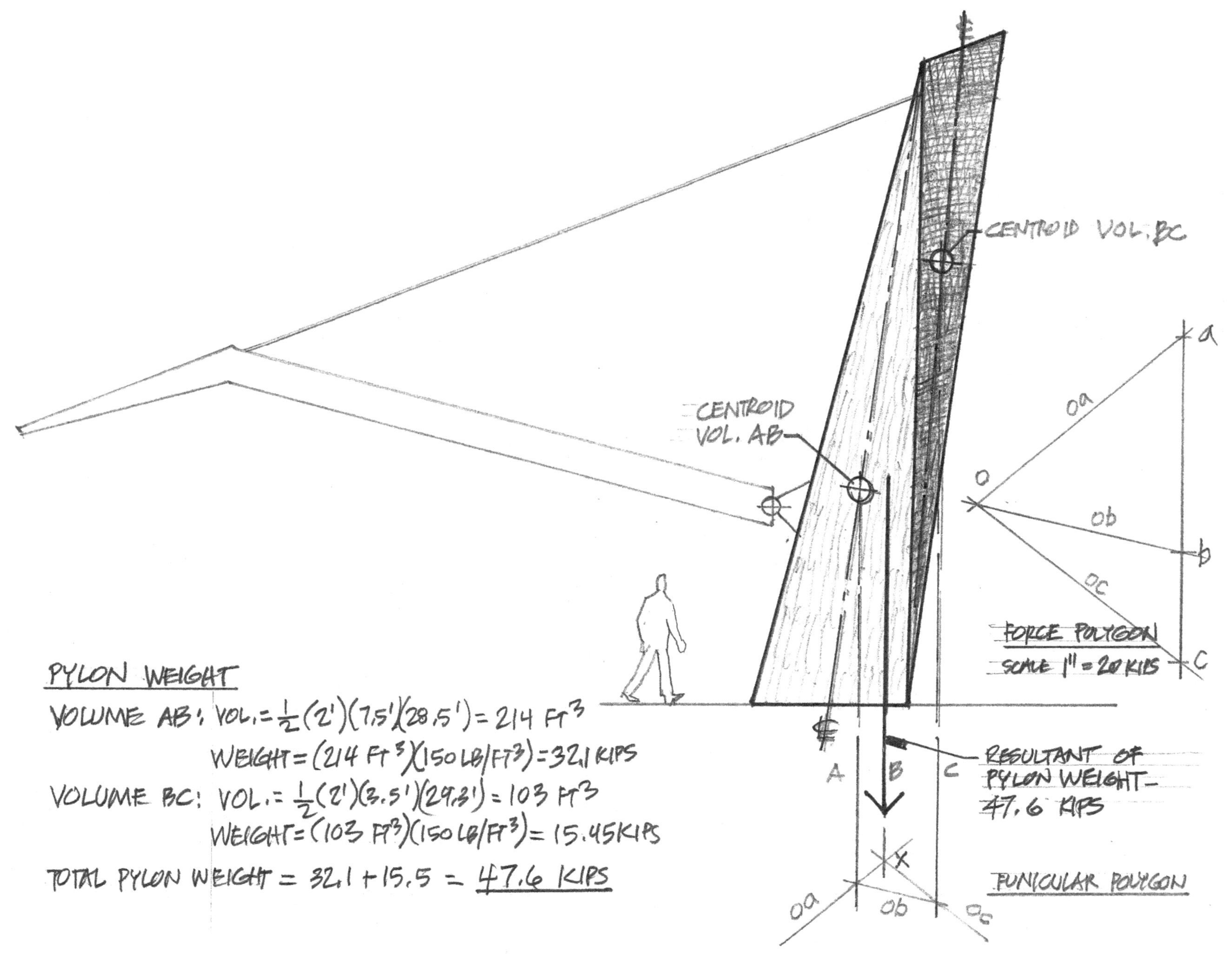

Figure 22.10 Finding the line of action of the weight of the pylon.

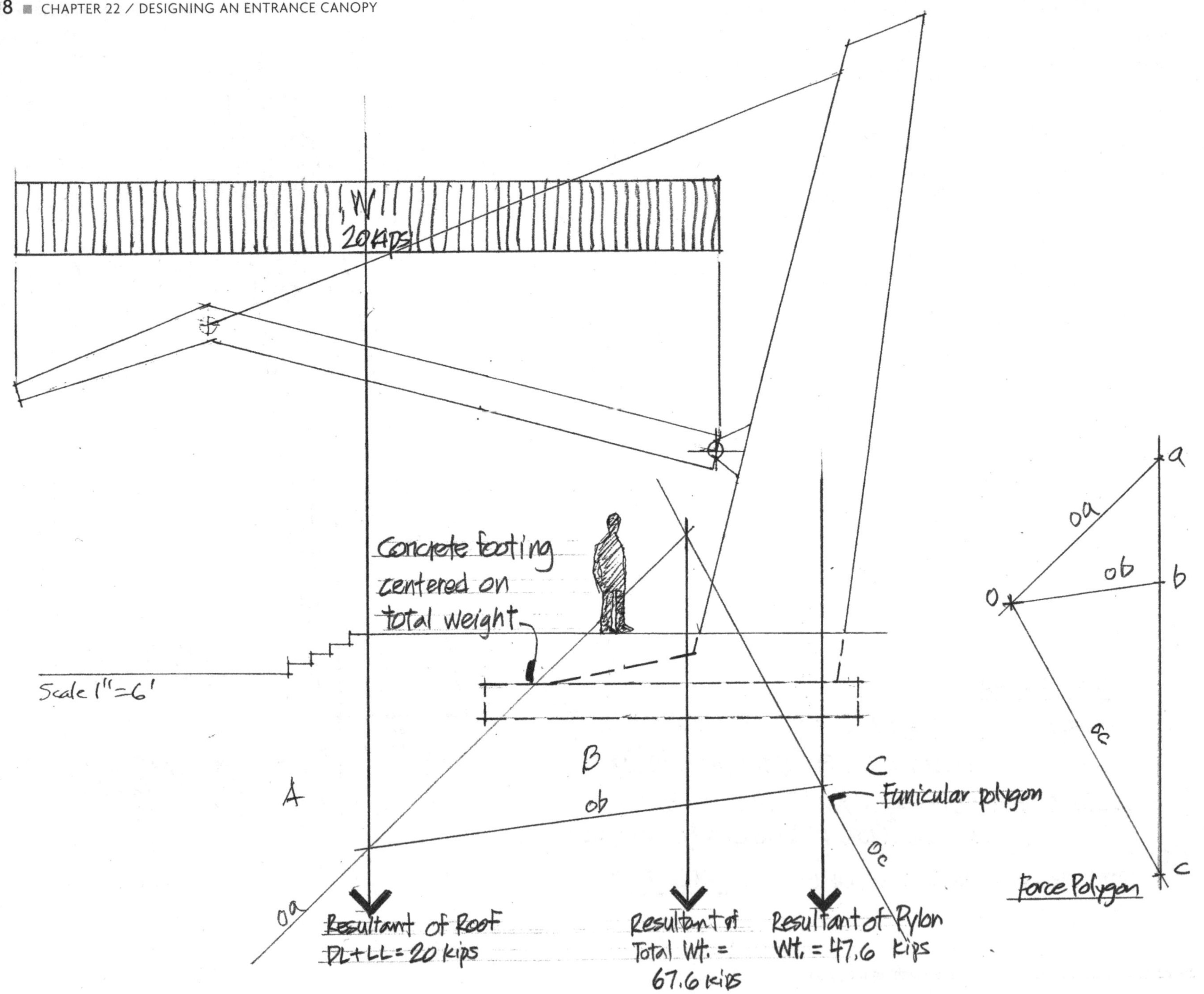

Figure 22.11 Finding the location of the line of action of the total weight of the canopy structure, including both roof and pylons.

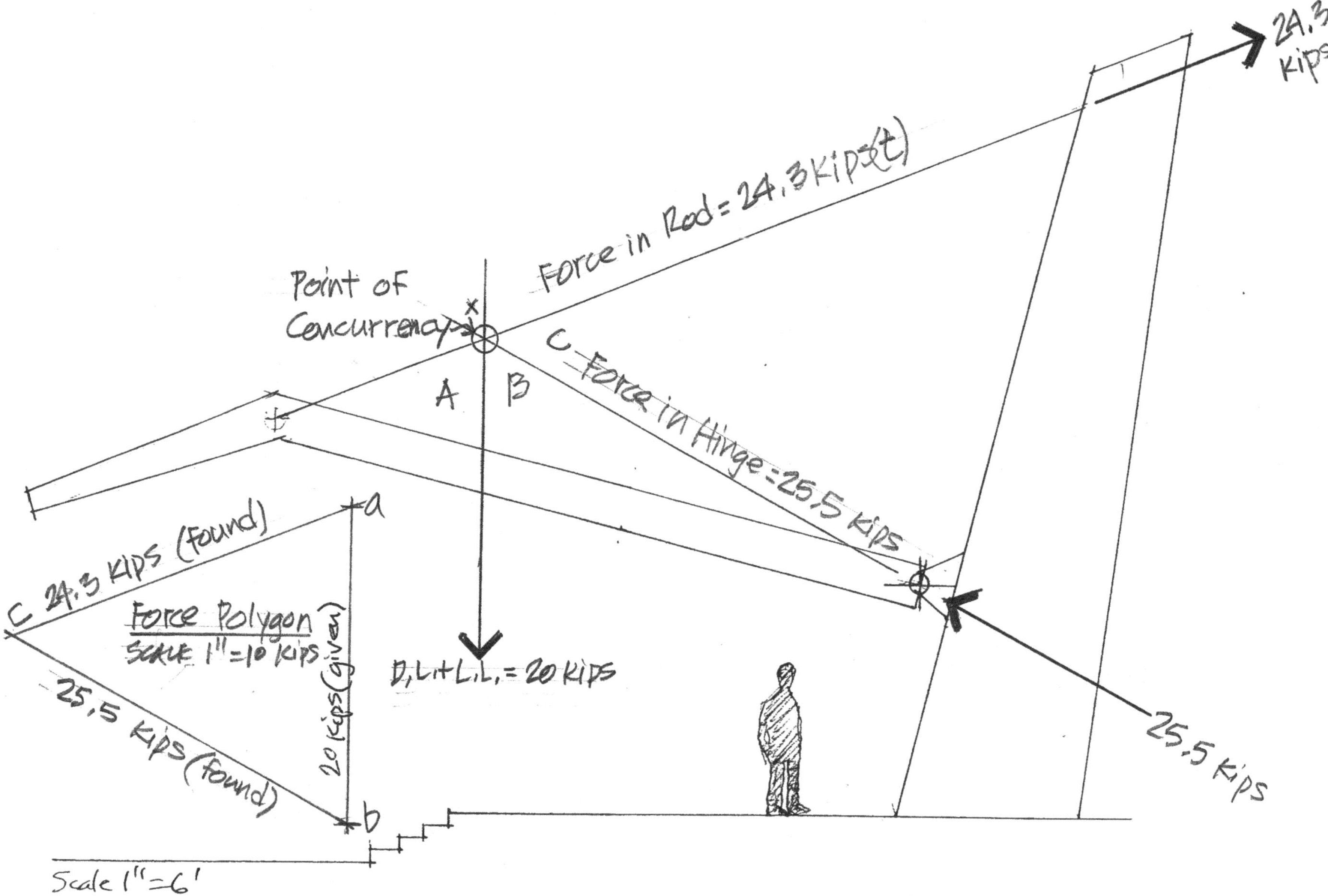

Figure 22.12 Finding the forces in the stay rod and hinge.

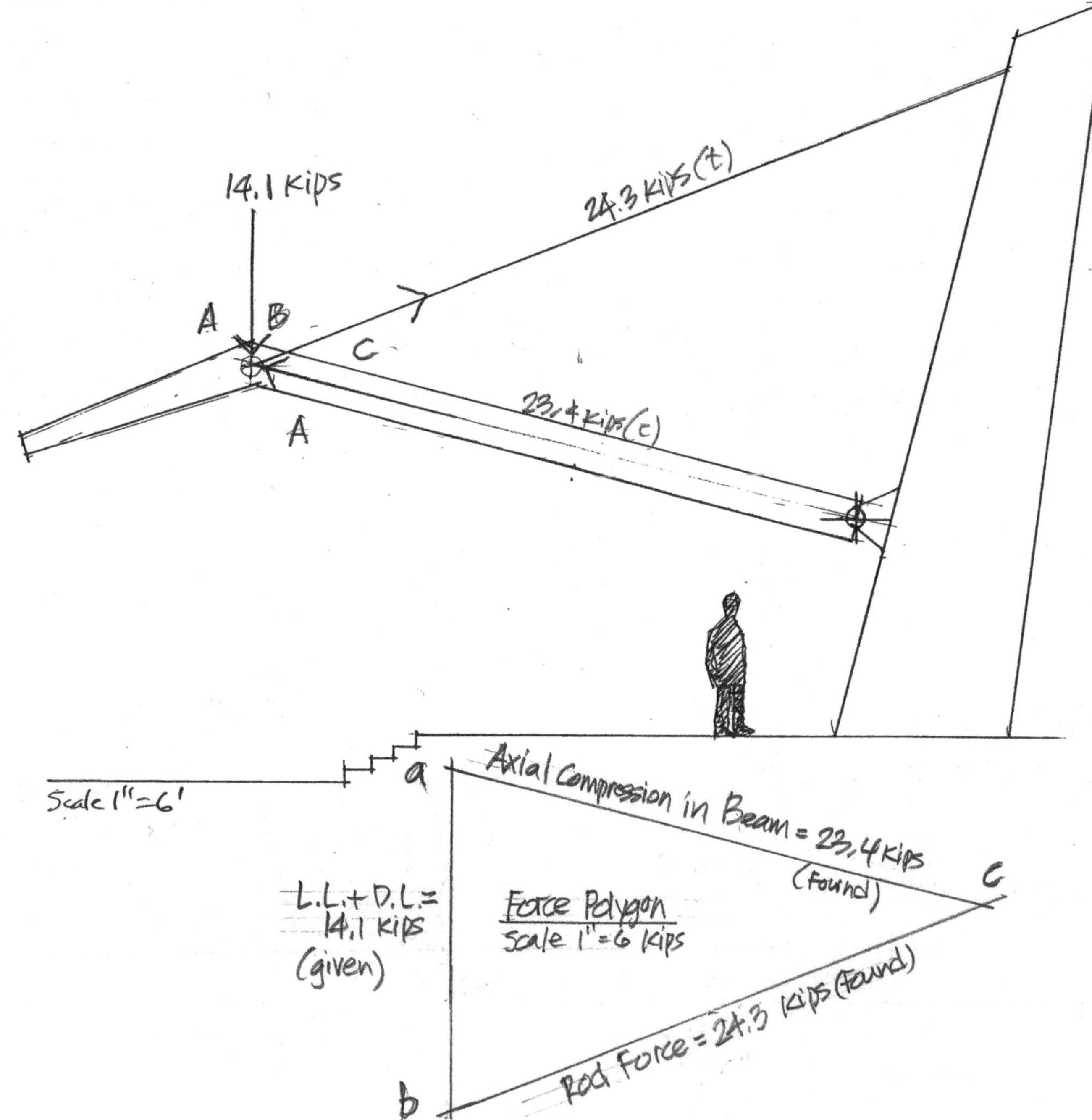

Figure 22.13 Finding the axial compressive force in the main span of the beam.

Guidelines for Shaping Structures

1. SHAPE EACH STRUCTURE IN ACCORDANCE WITH NATURAL LAWS.

Follow the funicular form. A form that is funicular for its typical loading pattern carries that set of loads with minimum material and maximum expressiveness.

Utilize axial forces as much as possible. Funicular and trussed structures experience axial tension or compression under typical loading conditions. Axial forces utilize material far more efficiently than nonaxial forces.

Follow the flow of forces. When designing a structural element that is not funicular, shape the element to follow its internal pattern of force flow. The pattern of flow within tells us what external shape to give a body, where to reinforce or stiffen it, where to cut holes if needed, and how to shape the holes.

Shape to create parallel and fan patterns of flow. Where possible, avoid shapes that require lattice flow, which uses material inefficiently.

Design for constant total force by following the shape of the bending moment diagram. A bending moment diagram is funicular for the given pattern of loads. A truss or beam whose profile is shaped to resemble the moment diagram will contain a total force that is constant along its length. As a consequence, it will experience only parallel and fan patterns of flow, eliminating inefficient lattice flow.

Shape for the full range of possible bending moments. Lay out the centerline of the element along the moment diagram or funicular curve for an average loading condition, then add depth, trussing, or other stiffening measures to accommodate all anticipated combinations of loadings.

2. SHAPE EACH STRUCTURE FOR MAXIMUM ECONOMY OF MATERIAL.

Stress material to its allowable limit. Shape the structure so that its material is fully stressed under maximum anticipated loads.

Eliminate "lazy" material. Cut away material that will experience little or no stress. An excess of material tends to look sloppy. Minimum material solutions tend to be the most expressive and eloquent.

Optimize depth. Find an overall depth for each spanning element that minimizes material use while meeting strength and stiffness criteria.

Utilize continuous action wherever possible. Continuity in bending structures lowers bending moments and reduces total forces.

Shape transitions smoothly. Smooth transitions reduce stresses where one element joins another and around discontinuities in a structure.

Restrain against buckling. Compressive elements can be very slender if they are braced or stiffened to prevent buckling. A slender element with buckling restraint generally uses less material than a thicker element that needs no restraint.

Use local materials. Local materials tend to look more "at home" and appropriate, cost less, and can lead to unique designs. Avoid the temptation to use currently fashionable materials.

3. SHAPE EACH STRUCTURE FOR EASE OF FABRICATION AND CONSTRUCTION.

Make the structure easy to build. Structures that are easy to build are more economical, more conducive to good workmanship, and often more expressive. Design the construction process itself, to be sure that it is easy.

Utilize repetition. Repetition of structural elements establishes rhythms, creates textures and patterns, reduces worker errors, and tends to be economical.

Minimize the number of different parts. The fewer the number of different parts, the fewer the opportunities for errors in assembly. Where possible, design parts so they cannot be installed backward or upside down.

Design forgiving details. Detail the structure with generous dimensional tolerances and plenty of provisions for adjustable fit.

4. SHAPE EACH STRUCTURE EXPRESSIVELY.

Expose the structure in a building. Structure is at its best when it is an integral part of the architecture rather than an invisible system of supports for a stage set. A concealed structure is an opportunity lost.

Express the mode of structural action. People enjoy "reading" a structure that is self-explanatory. Shape the structure and its elements to explain its action. Be forthright in showing hinges, rollers, and other action-related details.

Avoid willfully shaped elements. Stay with forms that are suggested by the action of the structure, which are invariably the most expressive. Avoid introducing elements that are willfully swooped, tapered, or imitative of animal skeletons, which invariably look as false as they are.

Express connections. Connections are the adjectives and adverbs of a structure. If expressed well, they give it life and excitement.

Design each structure to demonstrate how it was built. People enjoy seeing how a structure is put together. Often it is possible to design a structure so that it explains to the viewer how it was built.

Establish structural rhythms. Structural elements can create rhythms that enhance the architectural experience. A row of columns or beams can march to a regular or syncopated beat. Arches waltz in three-quarter time.

Show defiance of forces. A structure is more satisfying when it gives the appearance of carrying its loads with ease. Create soaring shapes that curve upward against the loads that they support. Camber flat elements to avoid the appearance of sagging.

Bring out the patterns and textures of structure. The human eye delights in the patterns and textures of such structural elements as trusses, waffle slabs, rib slabs, open-web steel joists, steel decking, and masonry walls and vaults.

Intensify the primary characteristics of a structure. Celebrate and take delight in the personality of a structure. Enhance its primary elements with chamfers or recessed panels. Elaborate its joints, connections, hinges, and bearings. Use color to bring out unique qualities of the structure.

Design in three dimensions. Structures are spatial, not planar. They should be designed in 3D sketches and models as much as possible.

5. SIMPLIFY!

More often than not, economy, expressiveness, and elegance result from using the most direct, minimal means to accomplish a structural task.

The dimensions, cross-sectional area of steel, and moment of inertia of the pipe that we will use for the beam flanges are found in the *Manual of Steel Construction*. The tabulated values for moments of inertia have been calculated with respect to the central axis of the pipe, but we need to know the values with respect to the neutral axis of the beam, of which the pipes are a part. This is done with the transfer formula (equation [18-4]), which yields a total value for both flanges of 291 in.^{4} (Figure 22.14). To this we add the moment of inertia of the web plate, which is easily calculated as 40.7 in.^{4} at the point of maximum beam depth.

The maximum bending stress in the beam under the assumed load is found by applying equation [18-1], in which c is half the depth of the beam (Figure 22.15). This stress is 11,000 psi. There is also an axial compressive stress in the beam, which is found in Figure 22.16 to be 3,090 psi.

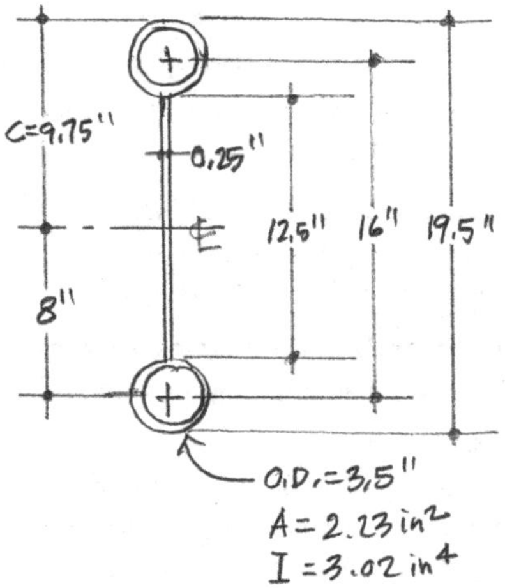

$$I_{flanges} = \bar{I} + Ad^2$$
$$= 2(3.02\ \text{in.}^4 + (2.23\ \text{in.}^2)(8\ \text{in.})^2)$$
$$I_{flanges} = 291\ \text{in.}^4$$
$$I_{web} = \frac{bh^3}{12} = \frac{(0.25\ \text{in.})(12.5\ \text{in.})^3}{12}$$
$$I_{web} = 40.7\ \text{in}^4$$
$$I_{total} = 291\ \text{in.}^4 + 40.7\ \text{in.}^4$$
$$I_{total} = 332\ \text{in.}^4$$

Figure 22.14 Finding the moment of inertia, *I*, of the beam section.

$$f_b = \frac{Mc}{I}$$
$$M = 31.27\ \text{kip-ft.} = (31.27\ \text{kip-ft.})\left(1{,}000\ \frac{\text{lb}}{\text{kip}}\right)\left(12\ \frac{\text{in.}}{\text{ft.}}\right)$$
$$M = 375{,}000\ \text{lb.-in.}$$
$$f_b = \frac{Mc}{I} = \frac{(375{,}000\ \text{lb.-in.})(9.75\ \text{in.})}{332\ \text{in.}^4}$$
$$f_b = 11{,}000\ \text{psi}$$

Figure 22.15 Finding the maximum bending stress in the beam.

$$f_c = \frac{P}{A}$$
$$P = 23{,}400\ \text{lb.}$$
$$A = 2(2.23\ \text{in}^2) + (12.5\ \text{in.})(0.25\ \text{in.}) = 7.59\ \text{in.}^2$$
$$f_c = \frac{23{,}400\ \text{lb.}}{7.59\ \text{in.}^2} = 3{,}090\ \text{psi}$$

Figure 22.16 Finding the axial compressive stress in the beam.

Combined Stress

Normally, we would design a structural steel member for a maximum bending stress of 24,000 psi. Because of the innovative character of our design, especially the slender width of the tubular beam flanges, which could lead to lateral buckling, we have decided to establish the allowable bending stress and axial compressive stress at two-thirds of the usual value, which comes to 16,000 psi.

Frequently a structural member must act to resist both bending and an axial load. The beam that we are designing is this type of member: It acts as a beam in bending, and its main span acts also as a compression strut. To evaluate the adequacy of such a member, we size it with independent consideration of each of its actions, making sure that it is stressed to less than the allowable value for each. Then we calculate the proportion of actual stress to allowable stress for each action and add the two proportions. The sum must be 1 or less:

$$\frac{f_b}{F_b} + \frac{f_c}{F_c} \leq 1 \qquad [22\text{-}2]$$

where:

f_b is the maximum calculated bending stress in the member,

F_b is the allowable bending stress,

f_c is the calculated axial stress, either compression or tension, and

F_c is the allowable axial stress.

This is an expression for evaluating the adequacy of a member, and does not give us the member size directly. Often several trials are necessary to arrive at a size of member that will satisfy this test.

With the aid of equation [22-2], we evaluate the combined stress in the beam that is caused by the combination of bending and axial action. This shows that we are utilizing about 69 percent of the allowable bending stress and 19 percent of the allowable compressive stress, a total of 88 percent of the overall capacity of the member. (Figure 22.17). Ideally, this utilization would be 100 percent, which we could approach by reducing the beam depth a bit, but 88 percent is an acceptable efficiency.

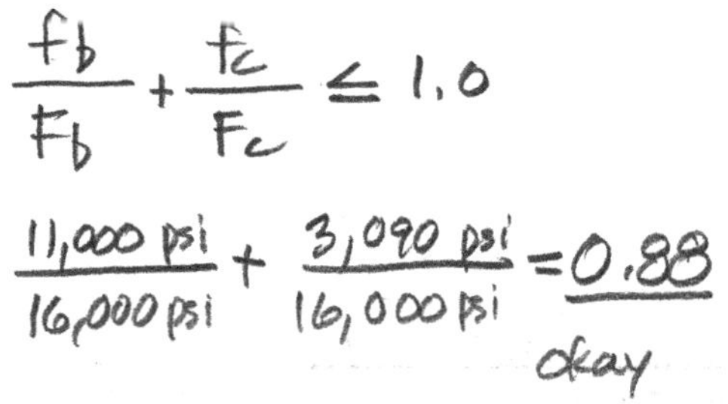

$$\frac{f_b}{F_b} + \frac{f_c}{F_c} \leq 1.0$$

$$\frac{11{,}000 \text{ psi}}{16{,}000 \text{ psi}} + \frac{3{,}090 \text{ psi}}{16{,}000 \text{ psi}} = 0.88$$

okay

Figure 22.17 Evaluating the combination of bending and compression in the beam.

DESIGNING FOR LATERAL AND UPLIFT FORCES

Wind or seismic forces could destroy the entrance canopy in any of several ways. They could fold the beams sideways against the pylons, which we can resist by adding pairs of diagonal rods between the trusses, parallel to plane of the glass and just beneath it. They could topple the line of pylons longitudinally like a string of dominoes, or tip the entire canopy up onto its nose; but the pylons will be thick and strong enough to resist these possibilities. It is possible, however, that wind could lift the roof surface and push it back over the tops of the pylons into the wall of the convention center.

Lifting and blowing back of the roof against the building is a distinct possibility. Figure 22.18 sketches six ways of resisting this action. All six are feasible, but each has drawbacks: Alternative (a) is an ugly, brute-force solution. The pipe in potential solution (b) would appear heavy compared to the rod that it replaces. Alternatives (c) and (d) would also look heavy, and would be statically indeterminate.

Alternative (e) is an excellent way to solve the problem, but its feasibility is questionable unless we create more headroom under the canopy so that the downward-pulling rod can reach far enough out on the span at a steep enough inclination to exert the necessary force.

Alternative (f) does not appeal to us at first. Physically, it is the most efficient and functional of all the potential solutions. Aesthetically, it might be seen as the equivalent of tying down a graceful bird that is trying to fly. From the standpoint of pedestrian safety, the vertical rods would be so thin that people would be unlikely to see them; they might walk into them and injure themselves. If exposed to vehicular traffic, the rods would be likely to be broken off in a matter of hours or days.

A solution is proposed by one of our design team: Have the vertical rods descend into a pool or planting box that is part of the landscape design. In this position, the rods might also be used to guide rainwater runoff from the roof into the pool. Depending on where the pools or planters are located, we might also be able to move these tie-down rods back a few feet from the extreme ends of the trusses.

We need also to design small roofs, probably made of glass, that will pass between the pylons to provide covered passage all the way from the automobiles or buses to the entrance doors of the hall. What we have in mind is a series of curving sheets of glass that are suspended just beneath the lower edge of the larger glass roof on stainless steel rods or supported on small brackets from the pylons (Figure 22.19). We will use these small roofs also to catch rainwater dripping off the low edge of the main canopy and conduct it to drainpipes.

DETAILING THE ROOF

How will we attach the glass to the beams? We want a clean, high-tech appearance, but must choose a way to produce it. One alternative is to bolt tubular purlins across the top flanges of the beams and attach sheets of laminated glass to the purlins. Another might be to dispense with the purlins and use glass thick enough to span the 10 ft from one beam to the next. In either case, we need proper hardware for mounting the glass, which is something we know little about. We will consult with the glass and steel fabricators regarding the best types of devices to connect the glass to the metal frame that we are providing. These must allow for an appropriate amount of movement so that differences in temperature expansion and contraction and structural deflections between the steel frame and the glass won't break the glass (Figure 22.20).

Building codes generally require that *laminated glass* be used in overhead applications. This is made up of one or several inner layers of tough, resilient plastic sandwiched between sheets of glass. Laminated glass was originally developed to prevent sharp chunks from falling if a panel of overhead glass is broken; in this application, its inner layer was relatively soft. More recently, glass laminates have been developed with inner layers of stiff plastic that enables the full depth of the glass to resist bending action. Most glass laminates have sufficient residual strength that even if they should break due to an unexpected load, they remain intact as a unit and do not fall out of their mountings.

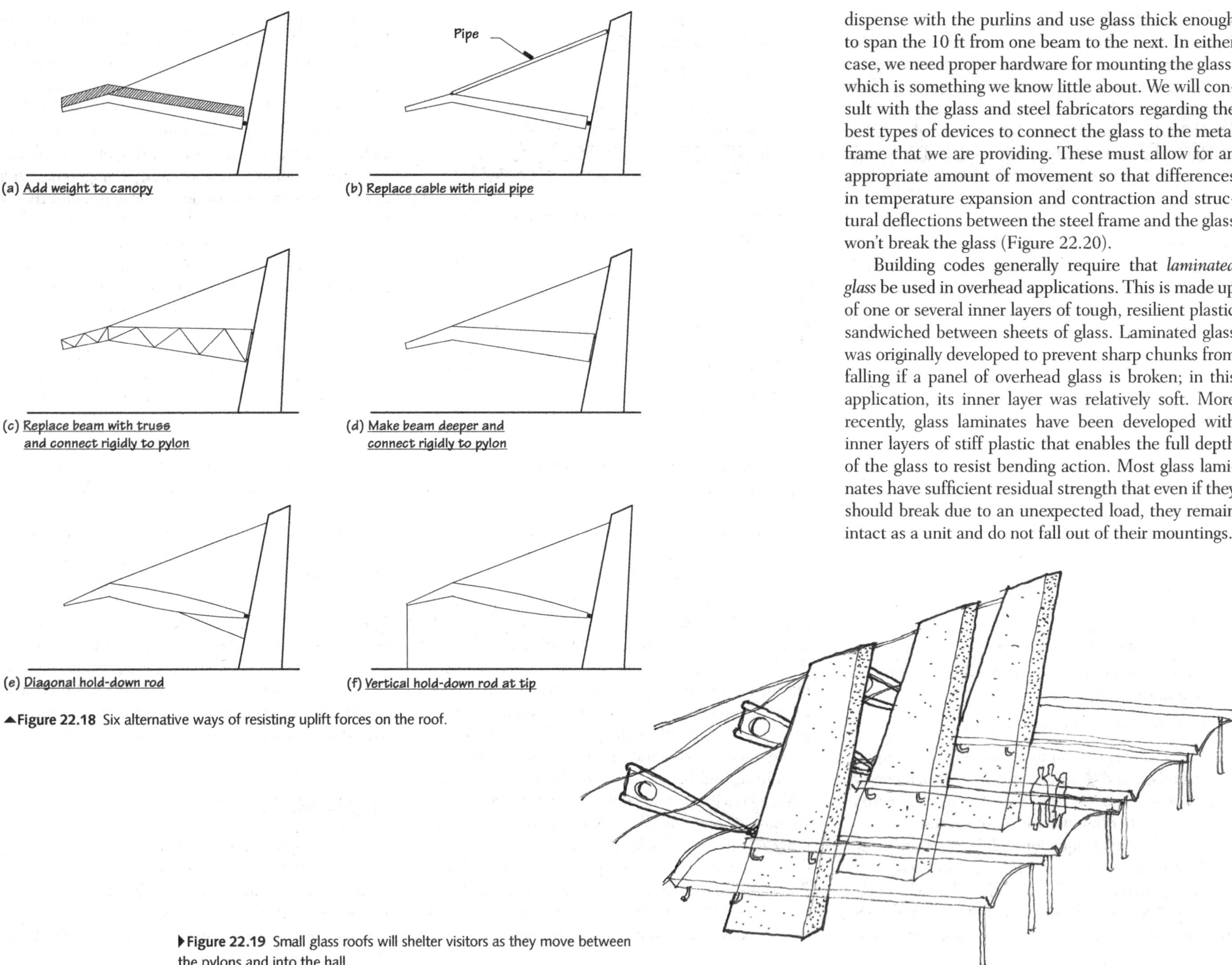

▲**Figure 22.18** Six alternative ways of resisting uplift forces on the roof.

▶**Figure 22.19** Small glass roofs will shelter visitors as they move between the pylons and into the hall.

We return to the beams, which have been shaped for parallel flow, and sketch typical preliminary details (Figures 22.21, 22.22). Wherever the pipes in the chords meet, the junction will need to be mitered, coped, and fully welded, then ground smooth since it will be exposed to view. The chords will carry relatively high but constant stresses. The web stresses, because we have shaped the beam to resemble the bending moment diagram, will be very low. This will allow us to perforate the web in a pattern if we wish.

Examining the results of our details in a view of the assembled canopy (Figure 22.23), we note with satisfaction that we have indeed produced a unique, attention-getting structure that will fulfill the Convention Authority's mandate. As we go on to the next stage of design, we will refer to other designs, small and large, that have used similar strategies (Figures 22.24–22.26).

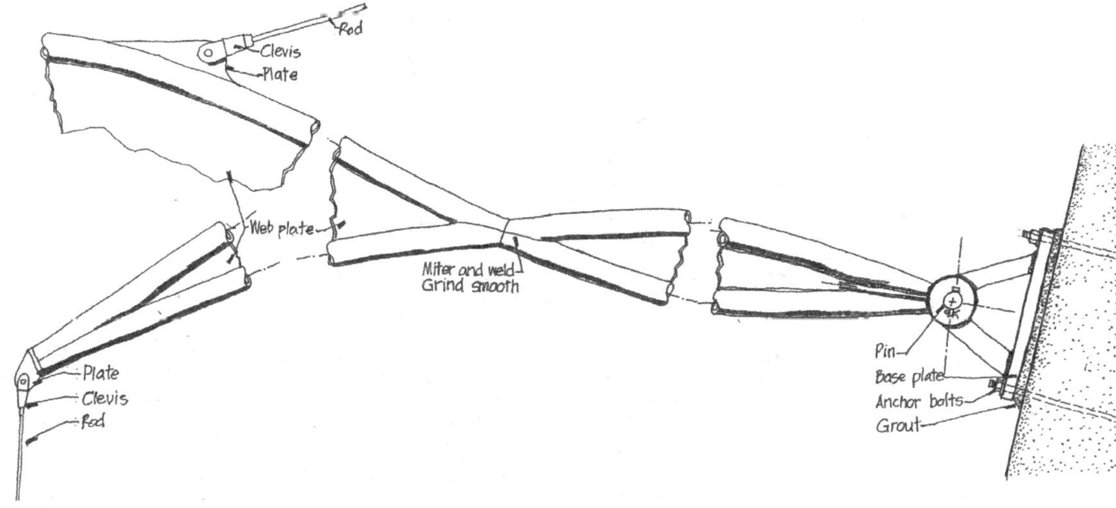

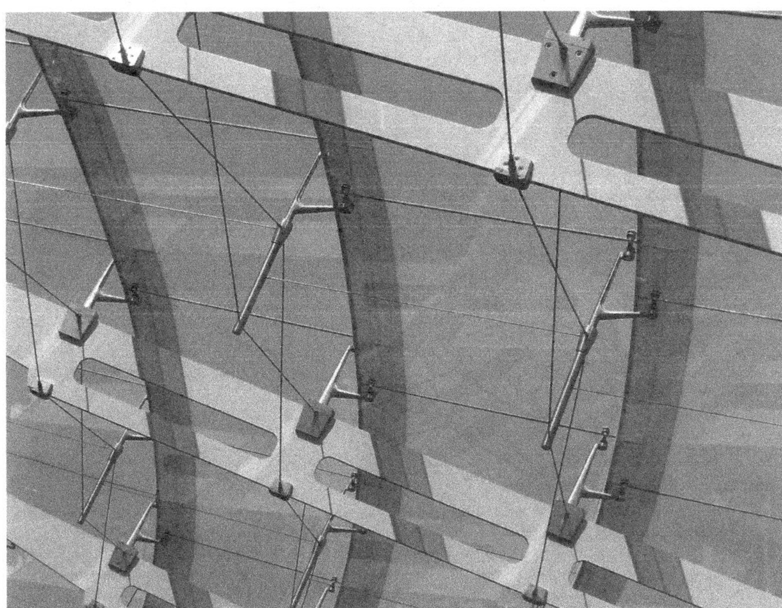

▶**Figure 22.20** An example of a sleek mounting system for structural glass, from the entrance to the Brooklyn Museum designed by Polshek Partnership, with steel and hardware fabricated by TriPyramid Structures.

Photo courtesy of Midge Eliasson.

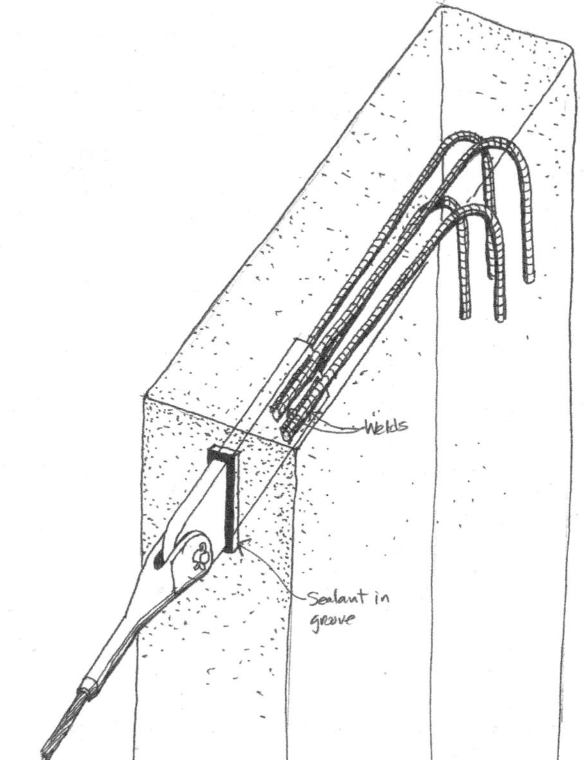

Figures 22.21 and 22.22 Preliminary detail sketches for the steel and concrete components of the canopy.

Figure 22.23 A view of the glass canopy as we have envisioned it.
Design and image by Boston Structures Group.

"Binding as technical demands may be, there always remains [in every project] a margin of freedom sufficient to show the personality if its creator and to become a . . . true work of art."

—Pier Luigi Nervi

FINAL THOUGHTS

This project has led us to bring together many skills and concepts that we have learned in earlier chapters and apply them to the design of an exciting, unconventional structure. The beams that we have designed take their shape from their internal pattern of force flow. This makes them efficient in their use of material and visually expressive of their function. In a lifetime of architectural and engineering practice, there will be a succession of new types of structures to design—ones with unprecedented settings and programs, innovative materials, unfamiliar forms. But even when these new challenges appear unfamiliar and unconventional, we will be able to invent economical, expressive structural forms and understand the forces within them by applying the principles presented in the pages of this book.

▲ **Figure 22.24** A glass entrance canopy for a hospital in Rhode Island. Taylor & Partners, architects.

Photo of Pilkington Planar System courtesy of W&W Glass Systems, Inc.

◀ **Figure 22.25** A large model of a reinforced concrete beam that is shaped for parallel flow. This eliminates most web forces, allowing large openings in the web. This structure is one product of an ongoing investigation of fabric formwork for concrete by architect Mark West of the University of Manitoba.

Photo courtesy of Mark West.

▲**Figure 22.26** The Havel Railway Bridge was designed by Schlaich Bergermann and Partner, with architects von Gerkan Marg and Partner, as a key element in the expansion of high-speed rail lines between Hanover and Berlin. The longitudinal shape of the three continuous spans of the bridge expresses the variation of bending moment in the beam. The steel stiffeners are inclined at varying angles to remain perpendicular to the direction of flow throughout the length of the bridge.

Photo courtesy of Roland Halbe.

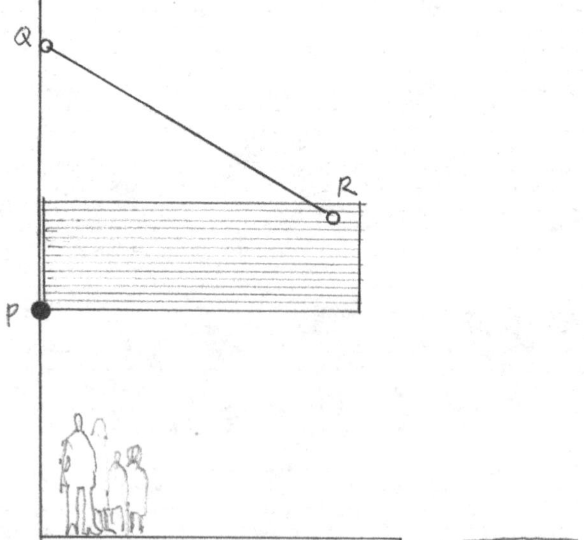

▶**Figure 22.27** A theater marquee.

Exercises

1. The stresses in the beams of this design are low enough that we are utilizing 88 percent of maximum capacity of the structural steel. This indicates that the beam design that we adopted is stronger than it needs to be. Assume another depth for the beam that seems about right. Change the sizes of the pipe flanges if you wish. Then calculate the new moment of inertia of the beam, the maximum bending stress, and the axial compressive stress. Check the combined stress to determine whether it is acceptable.

2. Design another shape for the beams that has a different cross section and a different profile from the one developed in this chapter. Find the maximum stresses in your design.

3. Imagine that the convention center is in Tacoma, Washington, where glue-laminated timbers are especially economical. Design a canopy that is based on this material rather than steel.

4. The theater marquee in Figure 22.27 weighs 9,450 lb. It is supported on each side by hinges at *P* and stay rods *QR*. Find the forces in the hinges and rods. Why are stay rods so widely utilized in this type of structure, rather than just inserting steel columns at the outer corners?

Key Terms and Concepts

$$Y_x = 4s\left[\frac{x}{L} - \frac{x^2}{L^2}\right] \quad [22\text{-}1]$$

$$\frac{f_b}{F_b} + \frac{f_c}{F_c} \leq 1 \quad [22\text{-}2]$$

parallel flow

laminated glass

Further References

www.sbp.de: The Stuttgart-based firm Schlaich Bergermann and Partner has a wide variety of architecture and engineering projects described on its Web site, many of which employ the techniques of shaping structures to resemble their moment diagrams.

www.wwglass.com: W&W Glass Systems, Inc. is a large architectural glass and metal contractor, specializing in curtain wall, storefront glazing, and skylight systems, including Pilkington Planar™ structural glass systems, in the United States.

Afterword: Engineers and Architects

Bruce set his sunglasses down on the wooden table and surveyed the small gathering of friends and associates who were conversing in twos and threes on the patio of his garden.

"Thanks for setting up this event, Diane. It's long overdue."

"Thanks for hosting it, Bruce. It just seemed to me that we should have a time when architects and structural engineers could get together and talk about a whole range of issues. Things like how we interact with one another, how we are educated in our respective professions, and how our educations affect our interactions."

"The educational issues interest me the most," replied Bruce. "I think that a lot of our problems stem from what we were taught in our universities. Like why didn't I know about graphic statics before I started working with you?"

"What puzzles me is, why did your structures teachers only teach you the mathematics of structures? That's the only part of the structural design process that architects almost never get involved with!"

Bruce got up and stretched lazily.

"Yes, and the weird part is, we weren't taught enough of the math to do any structural engineering in the real world."

"And in my engineering education," offered Diane, "I wasn't taught how to draw, or how to design for that matter. I guess they expected us to be merely analysts of structural behavior, and not designers in the true sense of the word."

Bruce added, "Another issue we should be talking about is quality. What constitutes quality in design? Especially as it relates to structures, which is what we have in common. But before we get any more deeply into it, I'm going to light the grill to get it heated up so Jeff can make us some barbecue."

Bill Thoen approached the grill with evident interest in the quality of the ribs that were marinating alongside. Bruce greeted him.

"Bill, you learned graphic statics when you studied engineering at Rensselaer, didn't you?"

"Yes, and 50-some years later I still use graphic statics when I go into the office and work with the younger engineers. They're all so proficient with computers, but most of them don't know how to think with their hands and a pencil. Jeff, you're really expert in turning out drawings with the computer. Do you think students today are too wedded to computers?"

Jeff Anderson began to impale racks of ribs on a long fork and place them carefully on the heated grill as he answered.

"Even though I know how to use a computer to make any kind of drawing I want, I still design with a pencil. It's a more tactile process, and it just works better for me. I think that after years of practice, the pencil becomes part of the thinking process that's associated with designing something. The computer is great, but it's never taken on a role of the same intimacy as a plain old soft pencil."

He adjusted the positions of some of the ribs and closed the lid of the smoking grill.

"That's my feeling, too," Bill added. "When I was an engineering student, we were required to take a number of courses in freehand and mechanical drawing, for which I've been forever grateful. These courses ought to be brought back in all the structural engineering schools. It would really improve the quality of our work if engineers could draw as well as architects do. At the same time, just being able to draw well isn't going to be enough to resolve the tension between architects and engineers. That nonsense has been going on for a couple of centuries, and it's not going to go away quickly."

Diane rejoined the conversation.

"It's like the great engineer Ove Arup said, 'When engineers and quantity surveyors discuss aesthetics, and architects study what construction cranes do, we are on the right road.' Both disciplines have so much to learn from one another."

Bruce continued, "But it seems the real question is not just how we architects and engineers can work well together, but how we can utilize structural considerations to improve the quality of a design, even in projects that are otherwise fairly ordinary. It often seems risky or expensive to try for an inspired design. How do we find the time and money to do things that are, well, not the usual solutions?"

Diane was quick to respond:

"How can we find the time or money not to? Remember, we are always looking at ways to reduce material and increase the economy and sustainability of our designs. An investment in additional design time can often lead to a much less expensive building or bridge. Structural designers like Maillart, Candela, Nervi, and Dieste, who are known for the sculptural qualities of their work, could only get their work built if they were the low bidders. We engineers are proud of our heroes, but they often get recognized for the 'look' of the project without anyone paying any attention to how the 'look' was arrived at."

Diane turned to Wacław Zalewski.

"Did that happen to you, too? Early in your career, you were designing low-cost factory vaults and prefabrication systems for the Polish government, and then the beauty of your constructions got the attention of people besides engineers, especially art critics and art historians. But did these people understand what lay beneath the surface that made your buildings beautiful?"

Wacław paused a moment to think, then responded.

"Most people—and that includes other engineers and architects—didn't understand that such so-called architectural effects of structure are often results of engineering motivations of efficiencies in material or process, combined with opportunities to show how a structure works. This is not always possible; sometimes solutions cannot be shown externally because of other criteria. Sometimes a more simplified solution is more practical."

Bruce asked him, "Do you think beauty is inherently a part of structural design? Is it a measure of quality? I mean, some architects talk about beauty in design, or in natural forms that inspire them, but most engineers seem reluctant or embarrassed to talk about beauty as you do."

"Remember," responded Wacław, "structures are not art. They exist for a purpose, to satisfy a human need. But they may still be elegant or even beautiful. Not because their shape is literally like a form of nature—our criteria for beauty in flowers are not the same as our criteria for structures. We can't make structures beautiful by copying natural forms, by making them look like flowers or trees or bones. All these forms are at scales that are too small to translate directly into structures of the size that we need. Structures must find their own natural forms, the ones that arise from the funicular polygon, the bending moment diagram, the internal flow of forces in structural members."

Wacław continued insistently.

"But what is design? How do architects and engineers think of solutions? Is inventiveness just a number or an equation? Certainly it is not a scientific process. We say we see designs in our 'mind's eye.' How? The subconscious mind often holds the key to unlocking spontaneous understanding. In daydreaming we generate visual imagery. All of us spend time experiencing images in the mind's eye, but few of us have had training in the process of making the images sharper, brighter, and more exact in detail—because our technological culture places little value on it."

Diane was trying valiantly to get a word in and finally succeeded.

"As Michael Dertouzos said at MIT, concentrating too much on calculations in structural design is as if a tennis player were to watch the scoreboard but not the ball. Right, Wacław?"

By sheer effort and repetition, she had learned the correct Polish pronunciation of his name, "VAHTS-waff."

"True. Can you pass me a pencil?"

Wacław sketched on a paper grocery bag the form of an arch, accompanied by a scrawled equation.

"See, even an elementary analysis presupposes that there is a shape or configuration to analyze, even when we use equations. Most of what students have customarily been taught about structures is quantitative. Is there a term 'qualitative structural design' in English? A structural approach that deals with improving the qualities of design?"

Bruce and Diane shrugged at each other, then turned to Bill, who offered:

"I think you might have just coined the term, Wacław. It sounds good, but I think you mean 'qualitative' in more than the usual sense, not just 'approximate,' or somehow less quantitative. Ed, what do you think? You often speak about quality in buildings."

Ed Allen, who sat sketching quietly at the other end of the table, clicked his mechanical pencil and added a few more bold lines to his sketch before speaking.

"Yes, this gets to the heart of what we had talked about as a reason to meet—we aren't just working to get buildings designed and built, we're working to design *good* buildings. That should be the task of the design process, to use forms and materials and details to create an architecture of quality."

Bruce was unconvinced.

"That's not saying very much. We all want quality, but how do we achieve it? Structural considerations are only a small part of what goes into making a good building. But the structure of a building can help to organize and shape it in engaging ways, and sometimes the structure can even amaze us."

"Definitely," Bill agreed, "and quality isn't just about avoiding a wrong answer or checking calculations."

David Foxe, who was Bruce's chief designer, busy cutting more fresh vegetables for the salad, joined the conversation.

"One of the things I've enjoyed in watching how you've worked on these projects, Bruce, is how you and Diane aren't just doing things in strange shapes for their own sake; you're improving the performance of building components by improving their shapes."

"The character of shape determines performance," Wacław confirmed. "Finding good shape for a structure should be a major concern of the architect and of the engineer. Trust in shapes."

David nodded agreement, and added:

"But the way we are discussing shape is very specific. Today's hero architects seem to be concentrating only on creating novel, unprecedented shapes that stand out or make a statement. Few if any of their shapes have merit as load-bearing structures."

Ed picked up where David left off.

"Do their new and different forms for buildings mean better quality? Are buildings that simply look unusual more economical? More efficient? More pleasant to live in and work in? More interesting over the long term, once the novelty has worn off? Do they make their occupants happier? There's no evidence to suggest that they achieve any of these qualities. The main result of our obsession with novelty is that each new building in our cities shouts rudely for attention: It yells, 'Look at me! I'm the latest and greatest! I'm radically different from all the buildings around me. And by the way, isn't my architect a clever person!' And as it is with a group of people in which everyone is shouting and nobody can be understood, so it is that in a neighborhood of shouting buildings no single building can be appreciated. Our urban neighborhoods are confused jumbles of forms rather than cohesive units, and often quite wasteful jumbles at that."

Diane nodded.

"My architecture students still struggle mightily to create shapes that nobody else has done before. And those shapes have become ever more frantic, contorted, and complicated. Their quest for novelty seems to block out every other consideration."

Ed continued.

"Years ago, a critic in the architecture program at the University of California asked one of his students why he had created an odd and not very pleasant shape for his building. The student replied, 'I want to do something different.' To which the critic replied: 'Different? You want to be different? DO SOMETHING GOOD! That'll be different!' But what makes a building good? It's such a simple question, but so hard to answer. How can we develop criteria of quality for our buildings? Where can we turn to learn to design buildings that are truly good? Some answers can be found in using harmonious materials well detailed, some answers can be found in incorporating fantasy as an element of each building, so as to touch our imaginations and stir our emotions in pleasing ways. And some answers can be found in using shapes for structures that are based on their use and their forces, because such structures will tend to resonate with structures from across the broad span of history and geography that all were built to these criteria. They aren't unique to a single style or time."

David tossed a few more tomato slices into the giant salad bowl. Then he dried his hands and reached for an envelope of photographic prints and laid several of them out in the center of the table.

"Have you seen these thin, laminated tile vaults that Michael and John have been building in England and South Africa? They're incredibly elegant. It's too bad these two couldn't join us until later."

"Structures that are efficient tend to have this quality that some call beauty," Wacław stated. "Their tile domes are direct evidence of this."

"It's like that Shaker saying," Bruce offered: "'Beauty rests in utility. All beauty that has not a foundation in use soon grows distasteful and needs continual replacement with something new. That which has in itself the highest use possesses the greatest beauty.' And yet, with regard to this question of quality..."

He paused, struggling to figure out how to phrase his thought.

"Well, we need to talk about function and also about imagination."

Diane responded, "When I learned about structural design in school and early in my career, it was all about physical requirements and accepted solutions. There was no talk of imagination."

Ed nodded, "Yes, that's been too often the pattern in engineering education, which has concentrated almost exclusively on mathematics. What most technologists don't understand is that the goal of building technology is to make dreams come true. To study technology in isolation is to avoid the question, who will dream the dreams? Architects are taught to dream, but only a few very singular engineers ever learn to do it.

"At the same time, a dream without discipline is not worth very much. We have plenty of architects with strong imaginations who grant themselves license to create visual chaos, and plenty of structural engineers who will find ways, no matter how contorted or expensive, to support the unstable piles of geometry created by these architects. In designing a structure, we subject ourselves to the tough discipline imposed by gravity and lateral forces. When a structural designer adds a dream to a design based on the natural flow of forces, the result can be sublime."

Jeff reappeared, bearing aloft a platter laden with fire-browned ribs dripping with a pungent, smoky sauce. Kate Hriczo was just behind with a huge bowl of steaming ears of corn. Avram hurried back and forth with Tricia, setting the places at the table and making room for the food on a side table. Avram started toward the door to the porch.

"I'll let everyone inside know to start gathering."

Bill Thoen looked around as the group assembled around the table on the patio, then said:

"I think, too, that it's important for engineers to know about the history of their own profession, the great engineers and their major works."

Diane agreed.

"And they shouldn't have to learn it from books written for architects. Engineers have often written their own fascinating stories. Some of the greatest engineers have crafted very lucid writings as well as good structures—I'm thinking of Nervi, Torroja, Eiffel, Dieste, Rice, Tony Hunt, Schlaich, Menn.

We can't forget about the voice of the engineer, and we have to look deeper than just the appearances of engineering works."

"Design and construction involve so many people," said David, "they really aren't communicated by a single voice. Design is a process that's like a conversation. It's like you've said, Ed: Learning to design isn't like learning only the grammar and vocabulary of a language, it's like learning to converse. With lots of practice, one becomes fluent. We want to become fluent designers, ones who can draw out the deep truths from a structure and transmute them into art."

Excited voices at the front door announced the arrival of John Ochsendorf, Philippe Block, and Michael Ramage. The reason for their tardy appearance was immediately evident: They had needed two cars to transport some international guests from the airport. John, switching deftly back and forth between Spanish and English, was introducing Eladio Dieste's engineer son, Antonio, and his chief designer, Gonzalo Larrambebere, both newly arrived from Uruguay. Michael was making the rounds with his mentor, Swiss engineer Jurg Conzett. Jörg Schlaich made his own way around the room greeting the attendees one by one in fluent English. Soon the latecomers sat down to join the diners, who were already well into their meals.

As the ribs continued to disappear, the conversation abated to a low murmur, with many continuing the discussion of what had been said and sketched earlier. Then, as often happens, there was a sudden quiet moment, in which Wacław Zalewski could be heard saying to Kate on his left:

"Is structures merely the science of verification, or is it the art of creation?"

Jörg Schlaich responded with enthusiasm..

"Structural design means to combine knowledge with intuition, experience with fantasy, and aims at inventing an efficient structure including a unique form. Architects and engineers can learn a lot from each other: The architects can learn from the engineers about the interrelation of manufacture, form, and load-bearing behavior; about the importance of structural detailing, the aesthetics of a pure, efficient structural form, about how to combine deductive and inductive thinking. The engineers can learn from the architects, first of all about how to see, the view for the visual; about the social and ecological aspects of building; about how to proceed from fragmented detailing to a holistic approach, from analytical to synthetic thinking. A good architect welcomes technical discipline, order through structural intelligence. And a good engineer will take interest in the architect's affairs as well, and follow him or her through the functional, conceptual design of a building."

"I'm pleased that you mention fantasy and intuition alongside synthesis and analysis," responded Gonzalo Larrambebere. "Eladio Dieste wrote, '[I]t is easy to make one of two mistakes: to disdain everything that is not mathematical analysis, or to assume that creation is the child of magical intuition.' Dieste was a poet as well as an engineer, and he valued imagination and fantasy at least as much as he did his equations."

"It shows in the quality of his work," mused Joseph Iano. "Which brings us back to our discussion of quality in structural design. It's apparent to me that both engineers and architects suffer from having been educated only in structural analysis, and not in structural design. It has been only the exceptional individual from either profession who has been able to rise above the stifling influence of the all-mathematics structures curriculum and produce exceptional structures."

"It seems to me," said a grad student from the far end of the table, "that if this group is truly devoted to improving the quality of our buildings and bridges, it ought to dedicate itself to putting together an entirely new approach to teaching structural design, one that stresses the design process, the finding of good forms for structures. Let's be done with the idle chitchat—I hear all the right words, but can you convert the words into a practical curriculum?"

There was a moment of stunned, anticipatory silence, followed by a buzz like the crackle of an accumulating electric charge as pencils and pens were put to barbecue-stained napkins, minds began to work at warp speed, and arguments were joined.

Note

Bruce and Diane speak in their own voices at this fictitious gathering. Wacław Zalewski's words are taken from interviews by David Foxe and Edward Allen. William L. Thoen, David Foxe, Jeff Anderson, and Joseph Iano are quoted from memory and with considerable license by Edward Allen. Edward Allen's words are taken largely from his commencement address at the Boston Architectural College in 2005. Jörg Schlaich is quoted from his paper, "On the Conceptual Design of Structures," in the proceedings of the IABSE/IASS conference Conceptual Design of Structures, Stuttgart, 1996, pp. 15ff. Eladio Dieste's thoughts are taken from the 1997 book *Eladio Dieste 1943–1996*, published by the Junta de Andalucia, p. 41. Diane, Bruce, Tricia, and Avram are wholly fictitious and do not resemble any real people living or dead. All the other characters are real people whose names are given and who play themselves.

Index

D

E

F